A-Z SURREY

CONTENTS

REFERENCE

Motorway	M3
A Road	A246
Under Construction	
Proposed	
B Road	B3430
Dual Carriageway	
One-Way Street	
Traffic flow on A Roads is indicated by a heavy line on the driver's left	
Large Scale Pages Only	
Junction Name	APEX CORNER
Pedestrianized Road	
Restricted Access	
Track and Footpath	
Residential Walkway	
Railway	Tunnel / Level Crossing
Stations: National Rail Network	
Heritage Station	
Underground Station	is the registered trade mark of Transport for London
Croydon Tramlink	Tunnel / Stop
The boarding of Tramlink trams at stops may be limited to a single direction, indicated by the arrow	
Built-Up Area	HIGH STREET
Local Authority Boundary	
Posttown Boundary	
Postcode Boundary (within Posttowns)	

Map Continuation	80 / Large Scale Town Centre 200
Car Park (Selected)	P
Park & Ride	P+
Church or Chapel	†
Fire Station	■
Hospital	H
House Numbers A & B Roads only	51 22 19 48
Information Centre	i
National Grid Reference	535
Police Station	▲
Post Office	★
Toilet	▽
with Facilities for the Disabled	♿
Viewpoint	※ ※
Educational Establishment	
Hospital or Hospice	
Industrial Building	
Leisure or Recreational Facility	
Place of Interest	
Public Building	
Shopping Centre or Market	
Other Selected Buildings	

SCALE

Map Pages 4-199   1:20,267

0	¼	½ Mile

0	250	500	750 Metres

approx. 3 inches (7.94cm) to 1 mile   4.93 cm to 1 km

Map Pages 200-203   1:9051

0	⅛	¼ Mile

0	100	200	300	400 Metres

7 inches (17.78 cm) to 1 mile   11.05 cm to 1 km

Copyright of Geographers' A-Z Map Company Limited

Head Office:
Fairfield Road, Borough Green, Sevenoaks, Kent, TN15 8PP
Telephone 01732 781000 (General Enquiries & Trade Sales)

Showrooms:
44 Gray's Inn Road, London, WC1X 8HX
Telephone 020 7440 9500 (Retail Sales)

www.a-zmaps.co.uk

Ordnance Survey® This product includes mapping data licensed from Ordnance Survey® with the permission of the Controller of Her Majesty's Stationery Office.
© Crown Copyright 2002. Licence number 100017302.

Edition 4 2002

Copyright © Geographers' A-Z Map Co. Ltd. 2002

KEY TO MAP PAGES

				4	5	6	7	8	9
14	15	16	17	18	19	20	21	22	23
30	31	32	33	34	35	36	37	38	39
48	49	50	51	52	53	54	55	56	57
68	69	70	71	72	73	74	75	76	77
88	89	90	91	92	93	94	95	96	97
108	109	110	111	112	113	114	115	116	117
128	129	130	131	132	133	134	135	136	137
148	149	150	151	152	153	154	155	156	157
168	169	170	171	172	173	174	175	176	177
		188	189	190	191	192	193	194	195

LARGE SCALE GUILDFORD 202

MAIDENHEAD
Burnham
Taplow
SLOUGH
Iver Heath
Hillingdon
Hayes
Southall
Bray
Wargrave
Langley
Yiewsley
West Drayton
Eton Wick
Eton
Datchet
Colnbrook
Harmondsworth
Harlington
HESTON
Oakley Green
Caversham
Twyford
Hurst
Shurlock Row
WINDSOR
Old Windsor
Poyle
Wraysbury
Stanwell Moor
London - Heathrow Airport
Cranford
Hatton
Woodley
READING
Winnersh
Dowlesgreen
Binfield
Priestwood
Winkfield
Winkfield Row
Cranbourne
North Ascot
Windsor Great Park
Cheapside
Englefield Green
Hythe End
Egham
STAINES
Stanwell
Ashford
Feltham
Hanworth
Sindlesham
Shinfield
Arborfield Cross
Arborfield Garrison
Wokingham
Eastheath
BRACKNELL
Easthampstead
South Ascot
Ascot
Sunninghill
Sunningdale
Virginia Water
Thorpe
Laleham
Chertsey
Sunbury
Upper Halliford
Shepperton
Walton-on Thames
Wick Hill
Crowthorne
Little Sandhurst
Sandhurst
Yateley
Eversley
Eversley Cross
Bagshot
Camberley
Lightwater
Windlesham
West End
Burrowhill
Chobham
Ottershaw
Addlestone
Row Town
Sheerwater
West Byfleet
Byfleet
Weybridge
Hersham
Frogmore
Hawley
Fox Lane
Hartley Wintney
Frimley
Frimley Green
Bisley
Knaphill
Brookwood
Pyrford
Woking
Ripley
Ockham
Cobham
FLEET
Hook
Farnborough
Pondtail
Fleet
Church Crookham
Crookham Village
Mytchett
Ash Vale
Worplesdon
Fairlands
Send
Send Marsh
West Clandon
East Clandon
Burpham
West Horsley
East Horsley
Little Bookham
Effingham
Odiham
Aldershot
Ewshot
Hale
Weybourne
Ash
Tongham
Flexford
Wood Street Village
GUILDFORD
Onslow Village
Littleton
Puttenham
Shalford
Chilworth
Albury
Shere
Gomshall
Abinger Hammer
Crondall
FARNHAM
Wrecclesham
Bentley
Millbridge
The Sands
Tilford
Elstead
Farncombe
Godalming
Busbridge
Wonersh
Bramley
Shamley Green
Peaslake
Holmbury St. Mary
ALTON
Frensham
Churt
Thursley
Milford
Witley
Hascombe
Thorncombe Street
Rowly
Cranleigh
Ewhurst
Walliswood
Kingsley
Chawton
Headley
Lindford
Arford
Bordon
Headley Down
Grayshott
Beacon Hill
Hindhead
Grayswood
Chiddingfold
Dunsfold
Alfold Crossways
Alfold
Cox Green
Rowhook
Rudgwick
Whitehill
Selborne
Haslemere
Ifold
Loxwood
Plaistow
Slinfold
Northchapel
Greatham
Liphook
Fernhurst
Liss
Rake
Hill Brow
Billingshurst
Wisborough Green
PETERSFIELD

M4 M3 M25 A4 A321 A4155 A404(M) A308 A355 A412 A408 A4020 A312 A329(M) A327 A33 A30 A287 A31 A32 A325 A3 A272 A286 A283 A29

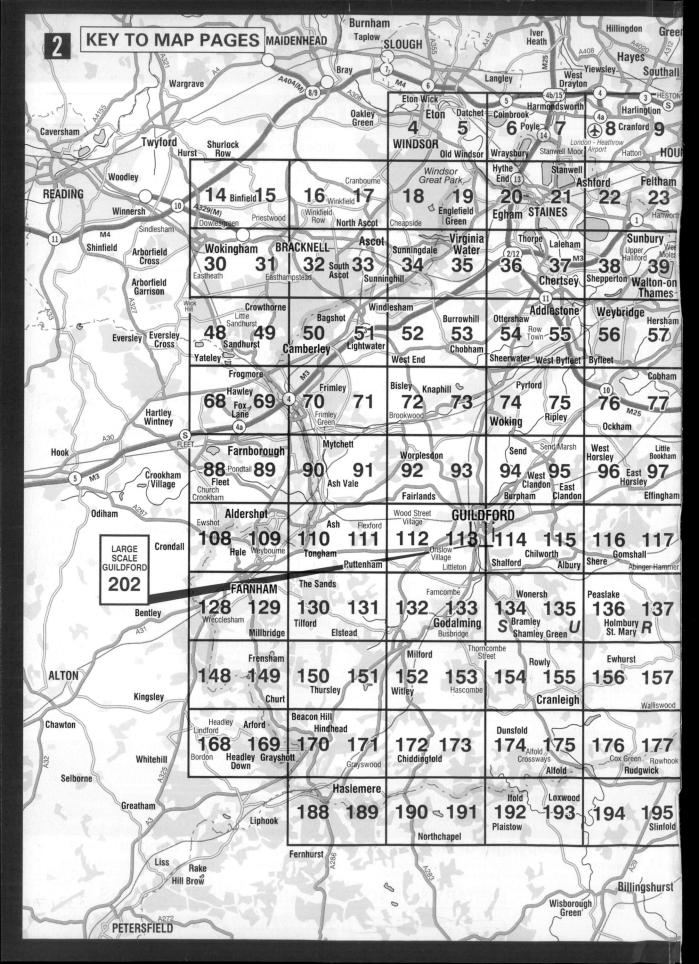

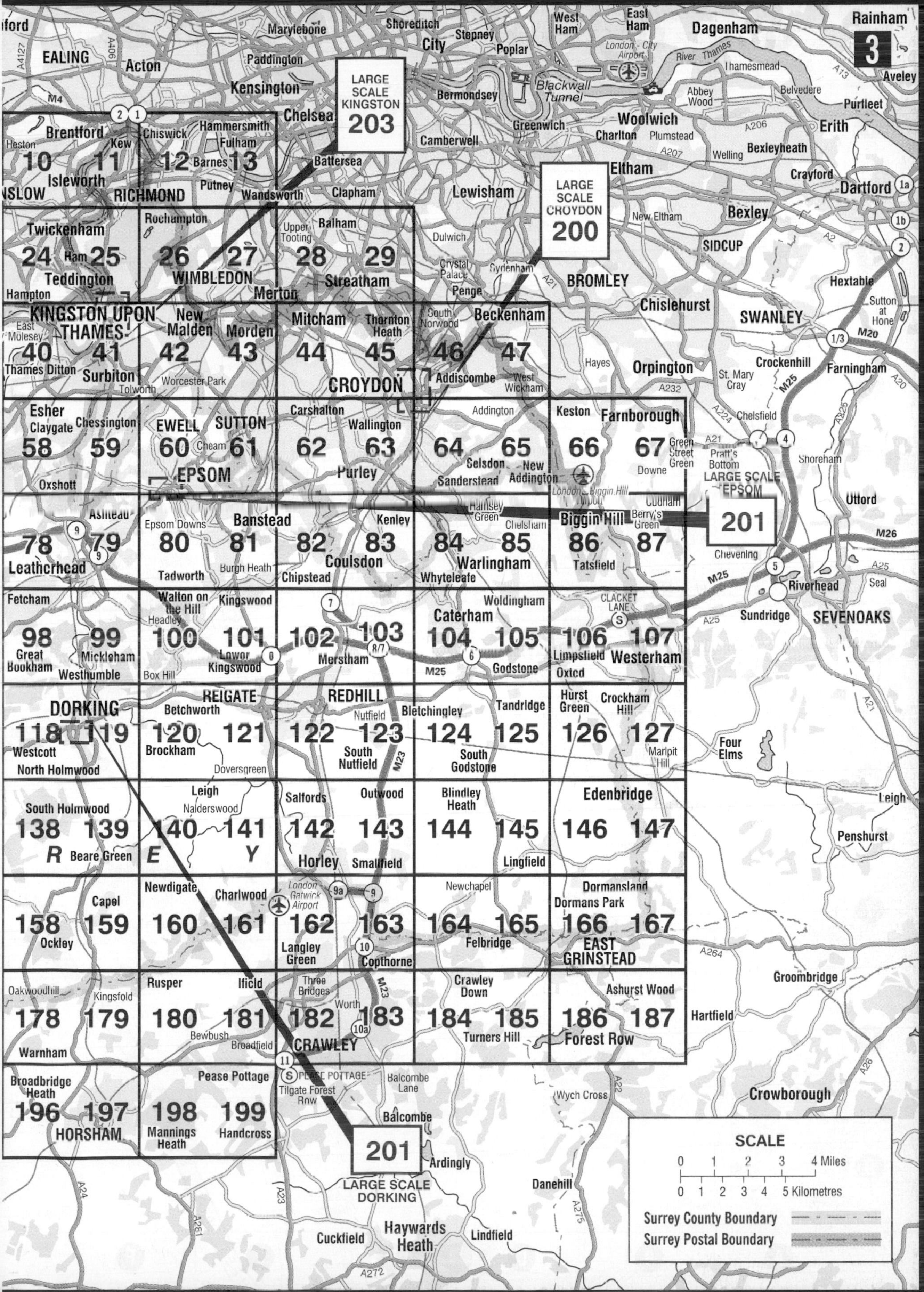
3
Rainham
Ealing
Acton
Marylebone
Shoreditch
City
Stepney
Poplar
West Ham
East Ham
Dagenham
London - City Airport
River Thames
Thamesmead
Aveley
Paddington
Kensington
Bermondsey
Blackwall Tunnel
Abbey Wood
Belvedere
Purfleet
Chelsea
LARGE SCALE KINGSTON
203
Greenwich
Woolwich
Charlton
Plumstead
Erith
Brentford
Kew
Chiswick
Hammersmith
Fulham
Camberwell
Welling
Bexleyheath
Heston
10
11
12
13
Barnes
Battersea
Eltham
Crayford
Isleworth
Putney
Wandsworth
Clapham
Lewisham
LARGE SCALE CROYDON
200
Dartford
RICHMOND
Twickenham
Roehampton
Upper Tooting
Balham
Dulwich
New Eltham
Bexley
24
Ham
25
26
27
28
29
Crystal Palace
Sydenham
SIDCUP
Teddington
WIMBLEDON
Streatham
Hampton
Merton
Penge
BROMLEY
Hextable
KINGSTON UPON THAMES
New Malden
Morden
Mitcham
Thornton Heath
South Norwood
Beckenham
Chislehurst
SWANLEY
Sutton at Hone
East Molesey
40
41
42
43
44
45
46
47
Hayes
Orpington
Crockenhill
Farningham
Thames Ditton
Surbiton
Tolworth
Worcester Park
CROYDON
Addiscombe
West Wickham
St. Mary Cray
Esher
Claygate
Chessington
EWELL
SUTTON
Carshalton
Wallington
Addington
Keston
Farnborough
Chelsfield
58
59
60
Cheam
61
62
63
64
65
66
67
Green Street Green
Pratt's Bottom
Shoreham
EPSOM
Purley
Selsdon
New Addington
Sanderstead
Downe
LARGE SCALE EPSOM
Oxshott
London Biggin Hill Airport
Ashtead
Epsom Downs
Banstead
Kenley
Hamsey Green
Chelsham
Biggin Hill
Berry's Green
201
Otford
78
79
80
81
82
83
84
85
86
87
Chevening
Leatherhead
Tadworth
Burgh Heath
Chipstead
Coulsdon
Whyteleafe
Warlingham
Tatsfield
Riverhead
Seal
Fetcham
Walton on the Hill
Headley
Kingswood
Caterham
Woldingham
CLACKET LANE
Sundridge
SEVENOAKS
98
99
100
101
102
103
104
105
106
107
Great Bookham
Mickleham
Westhumble
Lower Kingswood
Merstham
Limpsfield
Westerham
Box Hill
Godstone
Oxted
DORKING
REIGATE
Betchworth
REDHILL
Nutfield
Bletchingley
Tandridge
Hurst Green
Crockham Hill
118
119
120
121
122
123
124
125
126
127
Westcott
Brockham
South Nutfield
South Godstone
Marlpit Hill
Four Elms
North Holmwood
Doversgreen
Leigh
Nalderswood
Salfords
Outwood
Blindley Heath
Edenbridge
South Holmwood
138
139
140
141
142
143
144
145
146
147
Penshurst
Beare Green
Horley
Smallfield
Lingfield
Newdigate
Capel
Charlwood
London Gatwick Airport
Newchapel
Dormansland
Dormans Park
158
159
160
161
162
163
164
165
166
167
Ockley
Langley Green
Copthorne
Felbridge
EAST GRINSTEAD
Oakwoodhill
Kingsfold
Rusper
Ifield
Three Bridges
Crawley Down
Ashurst Wood
Groombridge
178
179
180
181
182
183
184
185
186
187
Worth
Hartfield
Bewbush
Broadfield
Turners Hill
Forest Row
Warnham
CRAWLEY
Broadbridge Heath
Pease Pottage
Balcombe Lane
Tilgate Forest Row
Wych Cross
Crowborough
196
197
198
199
HORSHAM
Mannings Heath
Handcross
Balcombe
201
Ardingly
LARGE SCALE DORKING
Danehill
Cuckfield
Haywards Heath
Lindfield
SCALE
0 1 2 3 4 Miles
0 1 2 3 4 5 Kilometres
Surrey County Boundary
Surrey Postal Boundary

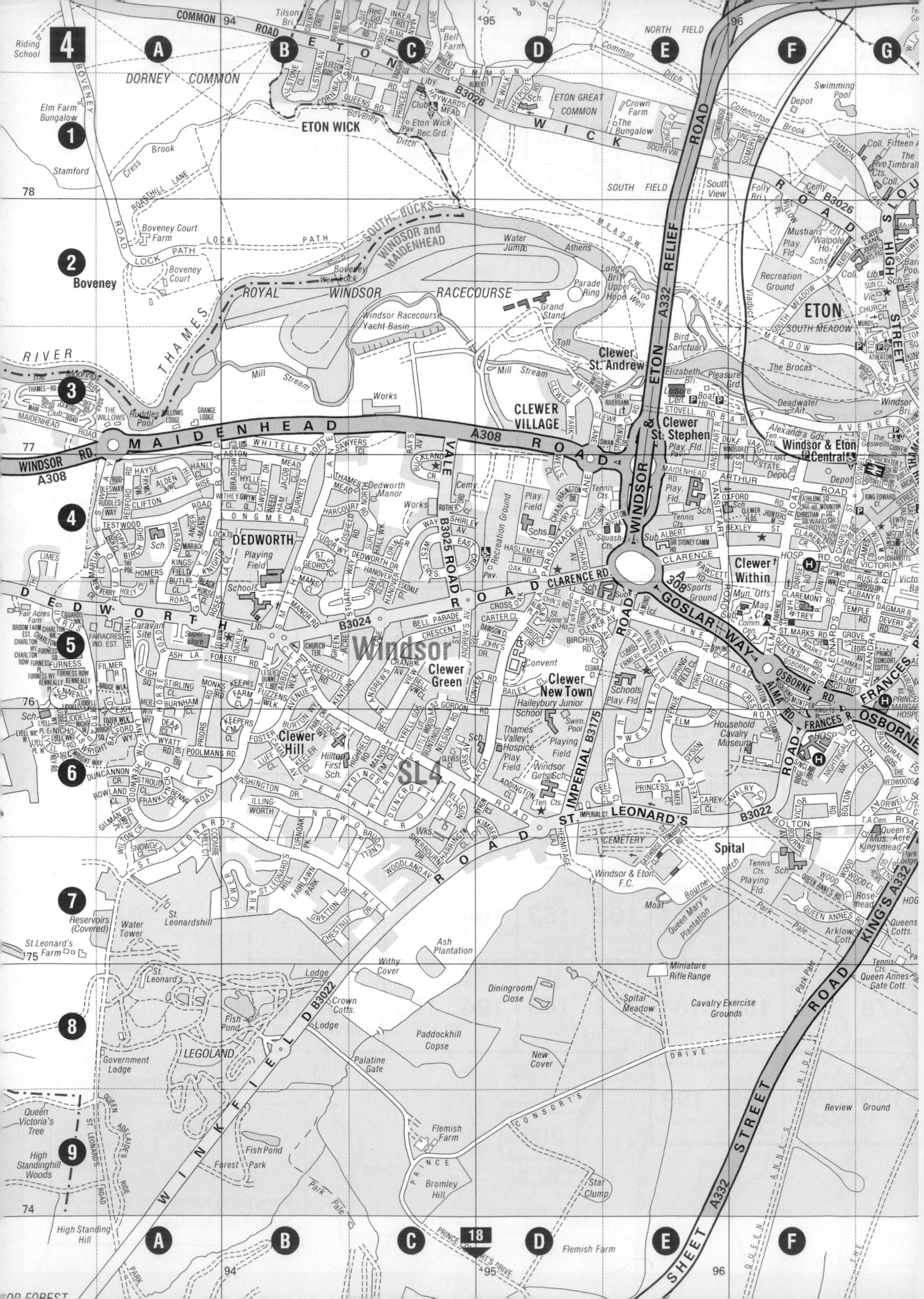

4
A
B
C
D
E
F
G
1
2
3
4
5
6
7
8
9
78
77
76
75
74
94
95
96
18
Riding School
COMMON ROAD
DORNEY COMMON
Elm Farm Bungalow
BOVENEY ROAD
Stamford
Cress Brook
ROASTHILL LANE
Boveney Court Farm
LOCK PATH
Boveney Court
Boveney
RIVER THAMES
The Moorings
THE WILLOWS
Ruddles Pool
WILLOWS LODGE
GRANGE LODGE
MAIDENHEAD ROAD
WINDSOR RD.
A308
ETON
ETON WICK
Boveney Ditch
B3026
ETON WICK ROAD
ETON GREAT COMMON
Crown Farm
The Bungalow
NORTH FIELD
Common Ditch
SOUTH FIELD
South View
Colenorton Brook
RELIEF ROAD
A332
WINDSOR & ETON RELIEF ROAD
SOUTH BUCKS
WINDSOR and MAIDENHEAD
Boveney Lock
Weir
ROYAL WINDSOR RACECOURSE
Windsor Racecourse Yacht Basin
Water Jump
Athens
Parade Ring
Grand Stand
Long Bri.
Upper Hope
Cuckoo Weir
Toll
Bird Sanctuary
Mill Stream
Works
Clewer St. Andrew
CLEWER VILLAGE
Clewer St. Stephen
Elizabeth Bri.
Leisure Cen.
Pleasure Grd.
The Brocas
Deadwater Ait
Windsor Bri.
Windsor & Eton Central
Swimming Pool
Depot
Recreation Ground
Mustians Play. Fld.
Walpole Ho.
Schs.
SOUTH MEADOW
HIGH STREET
Viaduct
Folly Bri.
ETON
DEDWORTH
Playing Field
Schools
Dedworth Manor
Cemy.
Recreation Ground
VALE ROAD
B3025
DEDWORTH ROAD
B3024
CLARENCE RD.
CLARENCE ROAD
Caravan Site
Superstore
FAIRACRES IND. EST.
Windsor
Clewer Green
Clewer Hill
Hilltop First Sch.
SL4
Clewer New Town
Haileybury Junior School
Thames Valley Hospice
Windsor Girls Sch.
Convent
IMPERIAL ROAD
B3175
Schools Play. Fld
GOSLAR WAY
Clewer Within
Sports Ground
Household Cavalry Museum
OSBORNE RD.
FRANCES RD.
KING'S ROAD
A332
ST. LEONARD'S ROAD
B3022
CEMETERY
Spital
Windsor & Eton F.C.
Moat
Queen Mary's Plantation
Bourne Ditch
Park Pale
Arklow Cott.
Queens Cotts.
Queen Annes Gate Cott.
Kingsmead
Park Lodge
Reservoirs (Covered)
Water Tower
St. Leonardshill
St. Leonard's Farm
Ash Plantation
Withy Cover
Lodge
Crown Cotts.
Diningroom Close
Spital Meadow
Miniature Rifle Range
Cavalry Exercise Grounds
Fish Pond
LEGOLAND
Government Lodge
Paddockhill Copse
Palatine Gate
New Cover
DRIVE
CONSORT'S
Review Ground
Queen Victoria's Tree
High Standinghill Woods
Fish Pond
Forest Park
Flemish Farm
PRINCE CONSORT'S DRIVE
Bromley Hill
Star Clump
WINKFIELD ROAD
B3022
SHEET STREET
A332
QUEEN ANNE'S RIDE
High Standing Hill
Flemish Farm
Park Pale

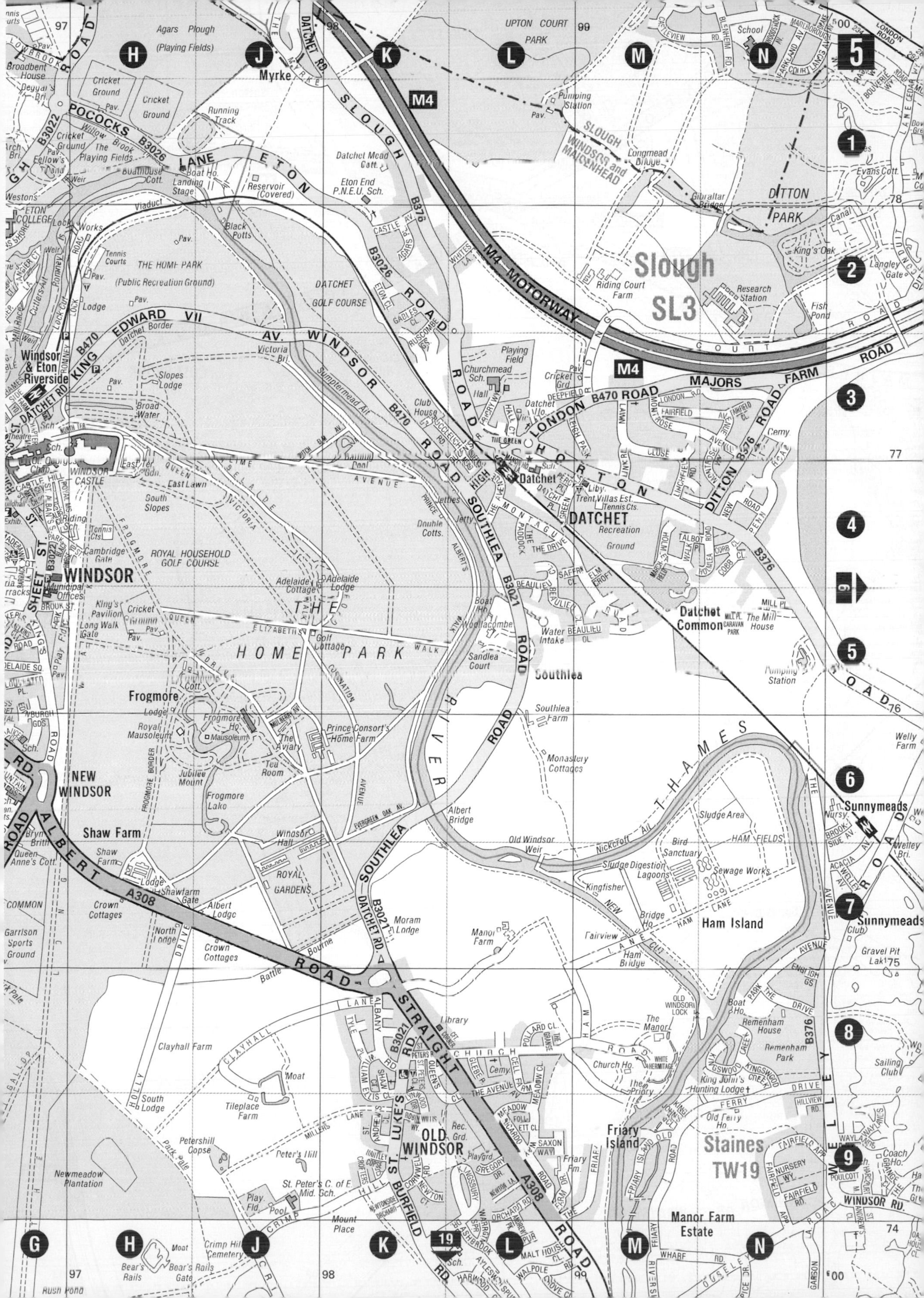

5
WINDSOR
Windsor & Eton Riverside
WINDSOR CASTLE
THE HOME PARK
HOME PARK
DATCHET
Datchet Common
Slough
SL3
DITTON PARK
M4 MOTORWAY
RIVER THAMES
Southlea
Frogmore
NEW WINDSOR
Shaw Farm
Ham Island
OLD WINDSOR
Staines
TW19
Sunnymeads
Manor Farm Estate
Friary Island
Myrke
UPTON COURT PARK
ETON COLLEGE
ROYAL HOUSEHOLD GOLF COURSE
DATCHET GOLF COURSE
KING EDWARD VII AV.
WINDSOR ROAD
LONDON ROAD
HORTON ROAD
MAJORS FARM ROAD
DITTON ROAD
SOUTHLEA ROAD
ALBERT ROAD
STRAIGHT ROAD
SLOUGH ROAD
POCOCKS LANE
ETON ROAD
Albert Bridge
Victoria Bri.
Old Windsor Weir
Old Windsor Lock
Royal Mausoleum
Frogmore Lake
Clayhall Farm
Tileplace Farm
Petershill Copse
Newmeadow Plantation
Crimp Hill Cemetery
Bear's Rails
G H J K L M N
1 2 3 4 5 6 7 8 9
97 98 99 00
74 75 76 77 78
19
6

LANGLEY
Kederminster Park
School
Playing Field
RICHINGS PARK GOLF CLUB
Sutton Court Farm
Home Farm
Home Wood
Club Ho.
Sutton
Mid Sutton
Little Sutton
Oak Plantation
Sutton End Farm
AXIS PARK
Harvey Pk. (Rec. Grd.)
LONDON ROAD A4
HIGH ST. B470
Bowling Green
Lakes
Sports Grd.
Evans Cott.
Mayes Cott.
DITTON PARK
Canal
King's Oak
Research Station
Fish Pond
Langley Gate
Ditton Fm.
Creak Cott.
LANGLEY ROUNDABOUT
Junction 5
M4 MOTORWAY
M4
The Bungalow
King's Ter.
Old Wood
Lake
Colnbrook Covert
Shirley Lodge
COLNBROOK A4
RIDING COURT ROAD
FARM ROAD B470
MAJORS FARM ROAD
Brands Hill
Spital Fm.
Rec. Grd.
COLNBROOK
Brook Farm
Mildridge Farm
Sch.
Anthony Ho. Fm.
Colnbrook Bridge
Tanhouse Farm
Cricket Grd.
WINDSOR and MAIDENHEAD
SLOUGH
Cemy.
B376
HORTON ROAD
THE QUEEN MOTHER RESERVOIR
POYLE
Poyle Manor House
Slough SL3
Horton Lodge
Rectory
The Mill House
Pumping Station
Manor Farm
B376 ROAD
DATCHET ROAD
Horton Cedars
HORTON
Ashgood Farm
Berkin Manor
Welly Farm
Brookfield
STANWELL ROAD
Colne
Weir
Depot
Sunnymeads
Works
Gravel Pit Lake
Welley Bri.
Horton Manor
Manor Farm
Island
Sunnymeads
Club
Gravel Pit Lake
Remenham House
Remenham Park
Sailing Club
Gravel Pit Lake
Works
WRAYSBURY RESERVOIR
Whitehall Nurseries
COPPERMILL ROAD
Rec. Ground
Coach Ho.
Sch.
Ford
Tithe Fm.
Wraysbury
Observation Platform
M25
WELLEY ROAD
WINDSOR RD.
WRAYSBURY
STATION ROAD
GRAVEL PIT
20

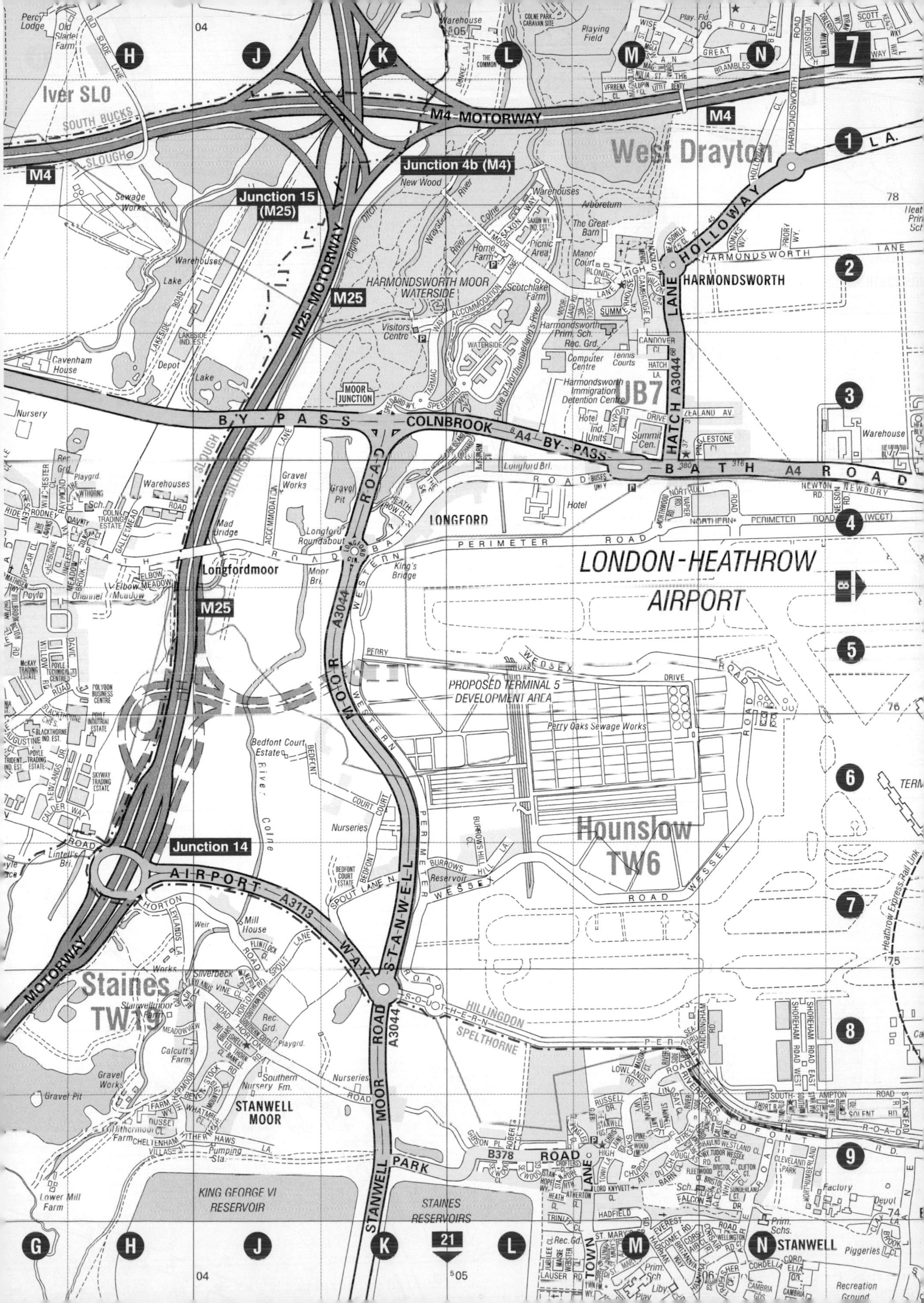

7
West Drayton
Iver SL0
M4-MOTORWAY
M4
Junction 4b (M4)
Junction 15 (M25)
M25-MOTORWAY
M25
HARMONDSWORTH MOOR WATERSIDE
HARMONDSWORTH
UB7
COLNBROOK BY-PASS
A4
BATH ROAD
LONGFORD
Longfordmoor
LONDON-HEATHROW AIRPORT
PROPOSED TERMINAL 5 DEVELOPMENT AREA
Perry Oaks Sewage Works
Hounslow TW6
Junction 14
AIRPORT WAY A3113
STANWELL MOOR ROAD A3044
Staines TW19
STANWELL MOOR
KING GEORGE VI RESERVOIR
STAINES RESERVOIRS
STANWELL
21
8

8
M4
M4-MOTORWAY
Junction 4
Junction 4a
HOLLOWAY A3044
SIPSON LANE
SIPSON
West Drayton UB7
Hayes UB3
HARLINGTON
HIGH STREET A437
A408
BATH ROAD A4
NORTHERN PERIMETER RD.
EASTERN PERIMETER RD.
SOUTH-WEST PERIMETER ROAD
SOUTHERN PERIMETER ROAD
GREAT SOUTH-WEST ROAD A30
TW6
LONDON-HEATHROW AIRPORT
TERMINAL 1
TERMINAL 2
TERMINAL 3
TERMINAL 4
Heathrow Terminals 1,2&3
Heathrow Terminal 4
Heathrow Cen.
Control Tower
Queen's Building
D'Albiac House
Compass Base
Maintenance Area
Cargo Terminal
Vehicle Tunnel
Cargo Tunnel
Heathrow Express Rail Link
Hatton Cross
London Heathrow Hilton Hotel
H.M. Customs & Excise
Heathrow Corporate Cen.
Heathrow Visitors Cen.
The Ramada Hotel
Excelsior Hotel
Marriott Hotel
Skyline Hotel
The Edwardian International Hotel
The Crest Hotel
Ibis Hotel
Garth Hotel
Heathrow Primary School
Sports Ground
Little Harlington Field
Burial Ground
Frogs Ditch Farm
Pinkwell Jun.& Prim. Schs.
Harlington Sch. & Sports Centre
Sam Philp Rec. Grd.
William Byrd Prim. Sch.
Sipson Meadow
Pheasant Nursery
Poultry Farm
The White House
Crane Meadows
Gravel Works
Harlington Bridge
Recreation Ground
Warehouse
Argonaut House
Works
Rec. Grd.
Marjory Kinnon Sch.
Bedfont Jun. Inf. & Nursy. Sch.
The Two Bridges
Longford River
Staines TW19
WEST BEDFONT
STANWELL
Mentone Farm
Factory
Depot
Piggeries
Ashford Football Ground
Playing Field
Warehouses
22
7
A B C D E F G
1 2 3 4 5 6 7 8 9

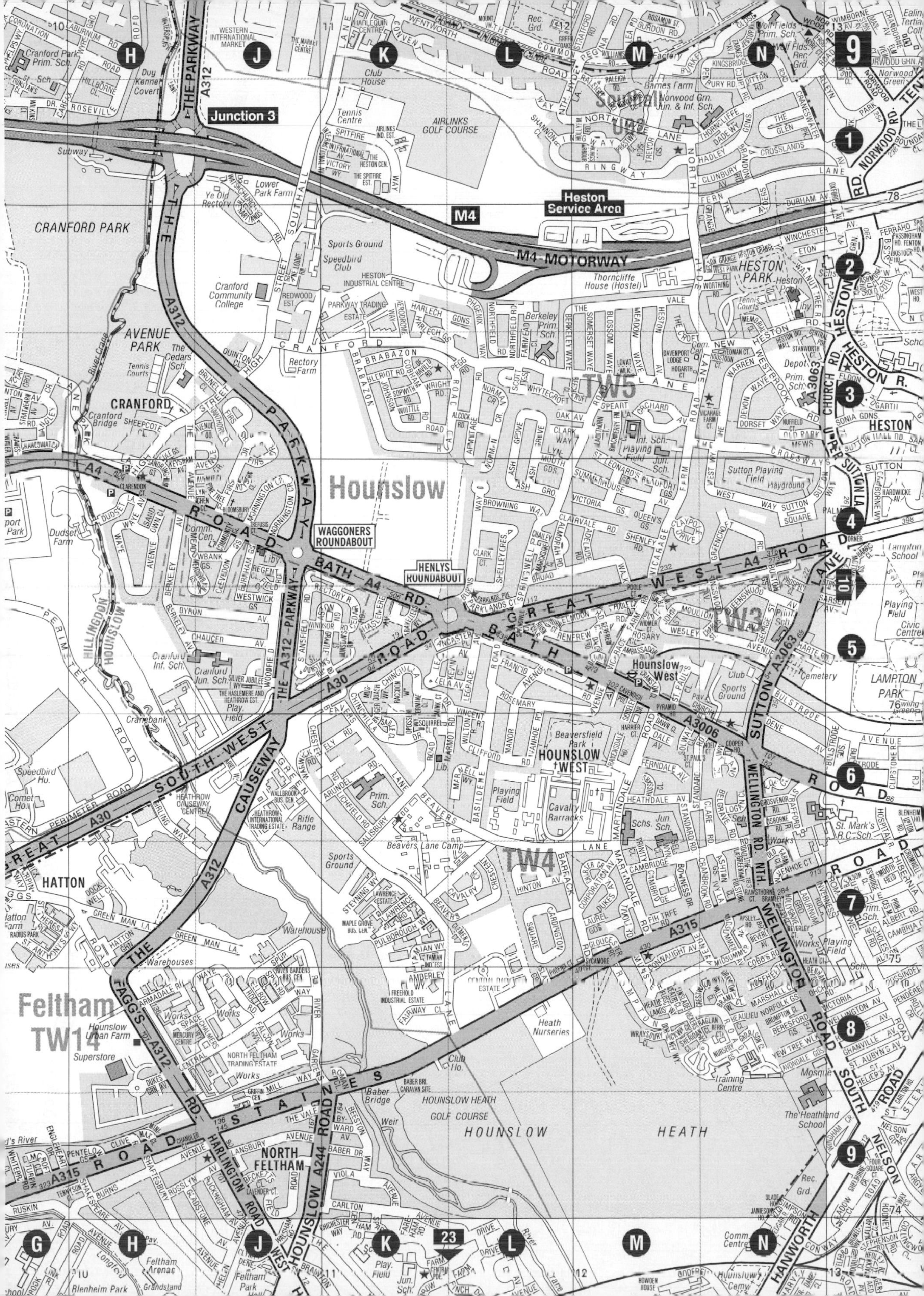

9
Junction 3
M4
Heston Service Area
M4 MOTORWAY
CRANFORD PARK
AVENUE PARK
CRANFORD
Hounslow
TW5
TW4
TW3
TW14
Feltham
WAGGONERS ROUNDABOUT
HENLYS ROUNDABOUT
HESTON PARK
HESTON
LAMPTON PARK
HATTON
NORTH FELTHAM
HOUNSLOW WEST
HOUNSLOW HEATH
HOUNSLOW HEATH GOLF COURSE
AIRLINKS GOLF COURSE
THE PARKWAY
A312
A4
A30
A315
A3006
A3063
A244
GREAT WEST ROAD
BATH ROAD
GREAT SOUTH WEST ROAD
STAINES ROAD
HANWORTH ROAD
WELLINGTON RD. NTH.
HOUNSLOW ROAD
THE CAUSEWAY
HARLINGTON ROAD
FAGG'S RD.
Cranford Community College
Sports Ground
Speedbird Club
Lower Park Farm
Rectory Farm
Beaversfield Park
Cavalry Barracks
Beavers Lane Camp
Rifle Range
Heath Nurseries
Training Centre
The Heathland School
Hounslow Urban Farm
Superstore
Mosque
23
10

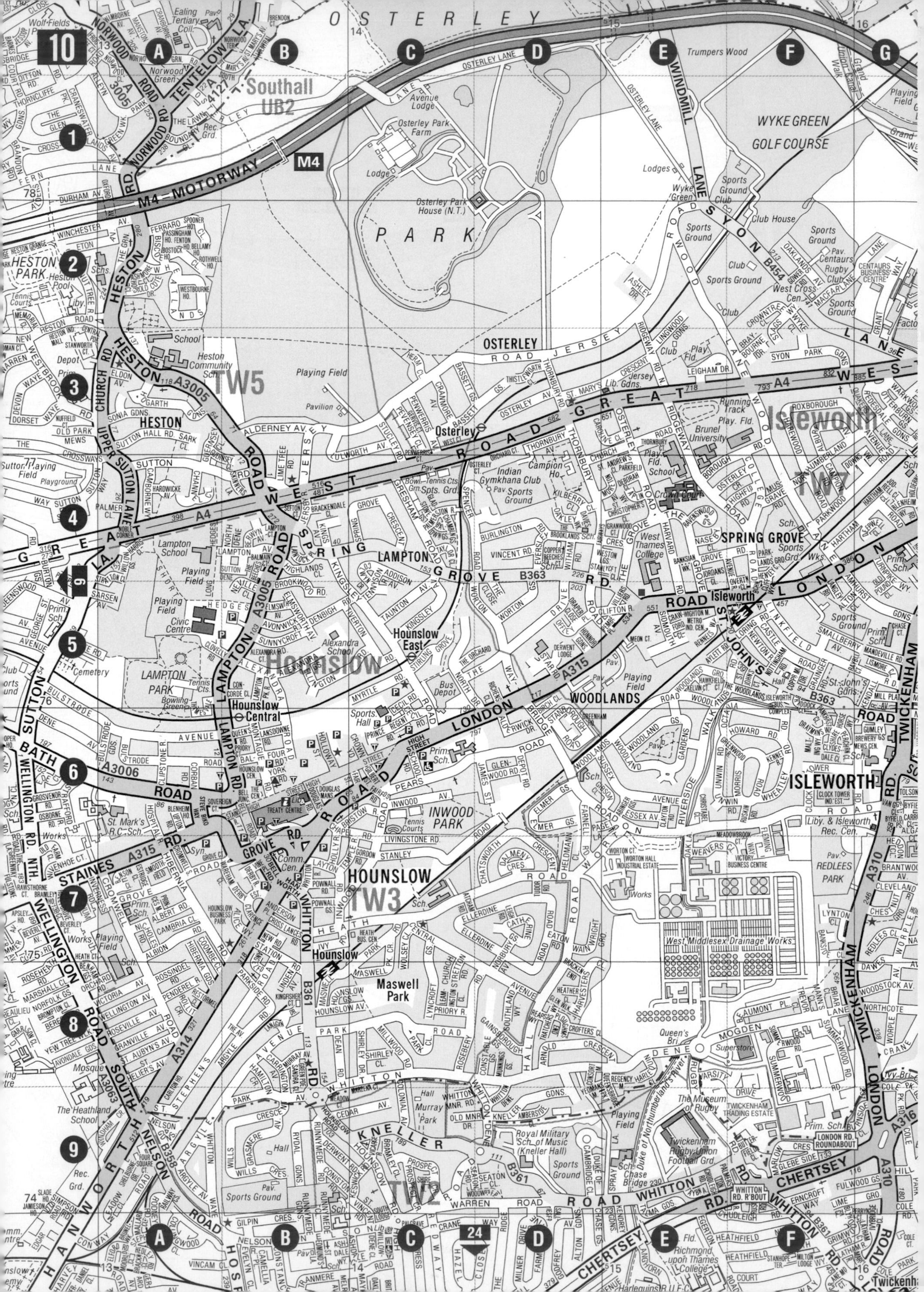

10
OSTERLEY
Southall UB2
M4 MOTORWAY
M4
OSTERLEY LANE
Trumpers Wood
WINDMILL LANE
WYKE GREEN GOLF COURSE
Osterley Park Farm
Osterley Park House (N.T.)
PARK
Avenue Lodge
Lodge
Lodges
Wyke Green
Sports Ground
Club House
Sports Ground
SYON LANE
B454
HESTON PARK
Heston Pool
HESTON
HESTON ROAD
A3005
TW5
Heston Community Sch.
School
Playing Field
Pavilion
OSTERLEY
JERSEY ROAD
GREAT WEST ROAD
A4
Osterley
Isleworth
TW7
Brunel University
Running Track
Indian Gymkhana Club
Sports Ground
Campion Ho.
Crown Court
SPRING GROVE
LAMPTON
SPRING GROVE RD.
B363
West Thames College
Lampton School
Playing Field
Civic Centre
Hounslow
Alexandra School
Hounslow East
LAMPTON PARK
Cemetery
Hounslow Central
Bus Depot
LONDON ROAD
A315
WOODLANDS
Playing Field
ISLEWORTH
BATH ROAD
A3006
STAINES RD.
A315
Treaty Centre
HIGH STREET
INWOOD PARK
HOUNSLOW
TW3
WORTON ROAD
Worton Hall Industrial Estate
Victory Business Centre
West Middlesex Drainage Works
REDLEES PARK
Liby. & Isleworth Rec. Cen.
TWICKENHAM ROAD
A310
Hounslow
Maswell Park
Mogden
Superstore
Queen's Bri.
Duke of Northumberland's River
The Museum of Rugby
Twickenham Trading Estate
Twickenham Rugby Union Football Grd.
LONDON RD. ROUNDABOUT
A316
CHERTSEY RD.
WHITTON ROAD
WHITTON RD. R'BOUT
Royal Military Sch. of Music (Kneller Hall)
Sports Ground
Playing Field
KNELLER
Murray Park
B361
TW2
Sports Ground
The Heathland School
Mosque
HANWORTH RD.
NELSON RD.
B358
A314
Rec. Grd.
Richmond upon Thames College
Harlequins R.U.F.C.
24
Twickenham
A B C D E F G
1 2 3 4 5 6 7 8 9

BRENTFORD
BRENTFORD END
Brentford
Old Brentford
Boston Manor
Boston Manor Park
GUNNERSBURY PARK
Gunnersbury R.C. Sch.
M4 MOTORWAY
Junc. 2
Junc. 1
Kew Bridge
WELLESLEY
Strand on the Green
KEW
Kew Green
Kew Palace
Orangery
Princess of Wales Conservatory
ROYAL BOTANIC GARDENS
KEW GARDENS
Syon Vista
King William's Temple
Temple of Bellona
Pagoda
Temperate House
Marianne North Gallery
Queen Charlotte's Cottage
King's Steps Gate
Isleworth Ferry Gate (Closed)
SYON PARK
Syon House
Syon Garden Centre
Butterfly House
DUKE OF NORTHUMBERLAND ESTATE
RIVER THAMES
HOUNSLOW
RICHMOND upon THAMES
OLD DEER PARK
ROYAL MID-SURREY GOLF COURSE
King's Observatory
Royal Mid-Surrey Golf Club
Richmond Athletic Ground
Old Deer Park Recreation Ground
Obelisk
Old Isleworth
Isleworth Ait
Richmond Lock
Corporation Island
RICHMOND
Richmond Green
Richmond
Twickenham
ST. MARGARETS
St. Margarets
NORTH SHEEN
North Sheen
Kew Gds.
MANOR CIRCUS
RICHMOND CIRCUS
CHALKER'S CORNER
Pesthouse Common
East Sheen Cemetery
EAST SHEEN COMMON
Richmond Cemetery
RICHMOND PARK
Cambrian Gate
Richmond Gate
The Bog
Cole Park
TW8
TW9
TW10
TW1
W5
A4
A315
A3002
A307
A205
A316
A305
A3004
B353
LOWER MORTLAKE RD.
MORTLAKE RD.
SANDYCOMBE RD.
TWICKENHAM RD.
PETERSHAM RD.
QUEEN'S RD.
KINGS ROAD
SHEEN RD.
UPPER RICHMOND RD. W.
CLIFFORD AV.
H J K L M N
G H J K L M N
1 2 3 4 5 6 7 8 9
12
25

GUNNERSBURY
Chiswick Pk.
Turnham Green
Stamford Brook
Ravenscourt Pk.
A B C D E F G
1
2
3
4
5
6
7
8
9
WELLESLEY
Gunnersbury
Strand on the Green
CHISWICK HIGH ROAD
A315
HEATHFIELD TER.
TURNHAM GREEN
W4
GT. WEST RD.
CEDARS RD.
ELLESMERE RD. A4
HOGARTH LA.
HOGARTH RBT.
Junc.1
GREAT WEST RD. A4
Hammersmith
St. Pauls School
CHISWICK
Chiswick House
Chiswick Eyot
Church Wharf
Oliver's Island
Public Record Office
BURLINGTON LA.
A316
Chiswick
GROVE PARK
University of Westminster Sports Ground
Riverside Recreation Ground
Riverside Leisure Centre
Riverside Lands
Playing Fields
DUKE'S MEADOWS
Sports Ground
Driving Range
Barnes Bridge
RIVER THAMES
HOUNSLOW
RICHMOND upon THAMES
Nature Reserve
The Harrodian Sch.
SW13
Peter Scott Visitor Centre
Kew Gds.
Richmond TW9
Main Drainage Works
Mortlake Crematorium
Hammersmith Cemetery
CHISWICK BRI.
GREAT CHERTSEY ROAD
CLIFFORD AV.
MORTLAKE
A3003
MORTLAKE HIGH ST.
Mortlake
CHALKER'S CORNER
NORTH SHEEN
Recreation Ground
BARNES
CHURCH RD. A3003
ROCKS LANE
A306
CASTELNAU
BARNES COMMON
MILL HILL RD.
B349
Barn Elms Playing Fields
Barnes
QUEENS RIDE B306
UPPER RICHMOND RD. WEST A205
(STH. CIRCULAR RD.)
RED ROVER
North Sheen
RICHMOND
SW14
EAST SHEEN
SHEEN LANE B351
ROEHAMPTON PRIORY HOSPITAL
ROEHAMPTON GOLF COURSE
Beverley Brook
Palewell Common
Palewell Fields
Clarence Farm
Froebel College
Digby Stuart College
Roehampton Institute
QUEEN MARY'S UNIVERSITY HOSPITAL
ROEHAMPTON LANE A306
EAST SHEEN COMMON
Sheen Cemetery
Bog Gate
The Bog
Riding Ring
Teck Plantation
Sheen Wood
Adam's Pond
Richmond
TW10
Sheen Cross Wood
Roehampton Gate
Open during daylight hours only
Bog Lodge
SAWYERS HILL
Pen Ponds
Horse Ride
RICHMOND PARK
26
ROEHAMPTON
Maryfield Convent
Club House
College Halls

H
J
K
L
M
N
HAMMERSMITH
Hammersmith
Brook Grn.
WEST KENSINGTON
SOUTH KENSINGTON
EARLS COURT
Earls Court
West Kensington
Barons Court
Hammersmith Cemetery
Earls Court Exhibition Building
HAMMERSMITH FLYOVER
TALGARTH
A4
ROAD
WEST CROMWELL RD.
BROMPTON RD.
W6
W14
SW5
SW10
SW6
SW18
SW 15
West Brompton
WEST BROMPTON
Brompton Cemetery
Riverside Studios
CHARING CROSS HOSP.
FULHAM PALACE ROAD
A219
LILLIE ROAD
A3218
DAWES ROAD
A3219
FULHAM ROAD
A304
Fulham Broadway
Chelsea F.C. (Stamford Bridge)
FULHAM
WALHAM GREEN
KINGS ROAD
A308
WANDSWORTH BRIDGE ROAD
A217
Parsons Grn.
PARSONS GRN.
SANDS END
Gas Works
Castelnau
THE WETLANDS CENTRE
Barn Elms
Barn Elms Schools Sports Centre
Fulham F.C. (Craven Cottage)
Stevenage Wharves
Bishop's Park
Fulham Palace
Moat Garden
The Warren
Putney Bri.
HURLINGHAM PARK
Hurlingham
The Hurlingham Club
SOUTH PARK
RIVER THAMES
HAMMERSMITH and FULHAM
WANDSWORTH
Old Barnes Cemetery
Putney Cemetery
PUTNEY HOSPITAL
LOWER RICHMOND
B349
B306
RICHMOND ROAD
UPPER RICHMOND ROAD
A205
PUTNEY
Putney
PUTNEY HIGH ST.
PUTNEY BRIDGE ROAD
A3209
WANDSWORTH
WANDSWORTH PARK
East Putney
PUTNEY HILL
WEST HILL
A3
WANDSWORTH HIGH ST.
Wandsworth Town
WANDSWORTH GYRATORY
ARMOURY WAY
SWANDON WAY
GARRATT LANE
BUCKHOLD RD.
MERTON ROAD
King George's Park
Solid Waste Transfer Station
PUTNEY HEATH
ROYAL HOSP. FOR NEURO-DISABILITY
TIBBET'S CORNER
Cricket Ground
G
H
J
K
L
M
N
27
1
2
3
4
5
6
7
8
9

14
Hinton Rd.
Haineshill Farm
Haineshill
81
82
83
Wicks La.
Darvills La.
Shurlock Row
The St.
Manor Road
Foxley Prim. Sch.
A
B
C
D
E
F
G
The B3018 Straight Mile
Binfield
74
The Gravelpits
Lodore
Baldasarre Farm
Hurst Lodge
1
Surells Wood
Reading
RG10
M4
Kiln Copse
Broad Common
Charity Wood
Park Farm
Bushy Lees
2
Ferrel Bridge Ockett
Ferrel Bridge
Bonhomie Ct.
Grange Farm
Lane
Nursery
73
Broadcommon Farm
Windsor and Maidenhead
Wokingham
M4 Motorway
Islandstone
Islandstone Pond
Broad Common
Warren Copse
Kayers Bridge
3
Kayersbridge Farm
Pound Lane
Road
Birch Plantation
Billingbear Park Golf Course
Club House
Penn Bushes
Fish Ponds
Billingbear Park
Billingbear Park Farm
The Phoenix
Grange Farm
Nelson's
4
Pound Lane Farm
Twyford Lodge
Billingbear Lane
Billingbear Park Gardens
The Mt. Fm.
Wokingham Road
Oakley Farm
Churchmans Farm
North Ockett Wood
Cross Lane Cottage
Lines Rd
72
Beech Wood
Warren Farm
A321
Mandycot
Misbourne
Carter's Road
5
Pondwood Fm.
Carters Hill Pk.
Billingbear Caravan Park
Cartershill Plantation
Hilcombe
Caswalls
Bracknell Forest
Wokingham
M4
Farley Ho.
Warren Side
Pond Wood
Lane
Billhill
Ashridge Wood
Maidenhead
6
The Lodge
Tippen's Wood
Wiltshire Farm
Monks
Harp Farm
Lanercost
Targetts Farm
Fairview
Tippen's Wood
Green
Marchfield House
71
Forest Road B3034 Forest Road
Long La.
Bill Hill
The Lodge
Pike's Farm
Tiryns
Ashridgewood Place Home Farm
Pike's Farm Cottage
Ashridge Manor
7
Warren
The White Cottage
Foxley Farm
Ashridgewood Farm
Manor Farm
Rushton's Farm
Wokingham
RG40
Depot
A329(M)
A329(M) Motorway
Swain's Copse
8
Long Copse
Twyford Road
Bell Farm
70
Bell Foundry Lane
Filter Beds
Pebblestone Copse
Matthewsgreen Farm
Cantley Recreation Ground
Ashridge Water Reclamation Plant
Keephatch Poultry Farm
Keeper's Cottage
Pebblestone Cottage
Stokes Farm
Top Copse
Matthewsgreen
Ashridge Farm
Warren House Road
Keephatch
Dowles Green Farm
A329(M)
9
Farm Cotts.
Wokingham Theatre
Town Event Field
Cantley
Lodge
Jubilee Av.
Martins
Milton Rd.
Wiltshire Road
Binfield Road
Dowlesgreen
30
Keep Hatch Inf. & Jun. Schs.
Holt Copse
Barnardo High School
Glebelands
Tamarisk Rise
A
B
C
D
E
F
81
82
83
Joel Park
The Holt Cts.

Bracknell
RG42
BINFIELD
Billingbear
POPESWOOD
PRIESTWOOD
BRACKNELL
Jealott's Hill
Moss End
Tickleback Row
West End
Hammond's Wood
Mowbray Dene Farm
Bear Farm
Oak Tree Farm
Elm Lodge
Tennis Court
Binfield Lodge
Allanbay Park
Seven Acres
Fish Pond
Billingbear Farm
Spinneys
Hawland's
Council Houses
Orange Hill
Orange Hill Fm.
Rectory
Paradise House
Binfield Grove
Billingbear House
The White House
Grave Yard
Wicks Green Cottages
Park Lodge
Kennels
Toll House
Manor Nurseries
Pitt's Bridge
Binfield Manor
The Grange
Grange Cottages
BLUE MOUNTAIN GOLF CENTRE
Golf Driving Range
Club House
Binfield Hall (Newbold Sch.)
Whitehouse Farm
Newbold School
Moor Close
Pope's Wood
Popes Meadow
Parkham
Popeswood Lodge
Popes Manor
Murrellhill Farm
Popes Cottage
Blackman's Copse
Farley Wood
Farley Wood Centre
Tennis Courts
Guy's Copse
Benhams Copse
Lynton Cottage
Stratton's Copse
Gardener's Copse
Picketts Point
Point Copse
Picked Point
Felix Farm
Brooklands Farm
Cokely Bridge
Barnicot
Windlesridge
Blossomfield
Hazelwood House
Sewage Works (dis.)
Sewage Works
Ryehurst Farm
White Gables
Westcott Corse
Wilson's Copse
Gough's Barn
Lilac Cottage
Broadview Farm
Sowage Works
Hawthorne Cottage
Nurseries
Hawthorn Lodge
Buckle Lane Farm
Moss End Farm
Hazelwood Wood
Lever's Piece
Hazelwood Copse
Rivermead Plantation
The Grove
The Hooks
Nursery
Home Farm
Westhatch Corner
Scotlands Farm
Scotlands House
Townlow Hall
Sumanga Farm
Westend Farm
Park Farm
Fairclough Farm
Long Copse
Kennel Lane Sch.
Recreation Ground
Frampton's Manor Farm
Tinkers Copse
Jock's Copse
Meadow Vale Primary Sch.
Rounds Hill
Green Acres
Playing Field
Western Ind. Area
ROUNDS HILL INDUSTRIAL ESTATE
ARLINGTON SQUARE
B3018
B3034
B3408
A3095
A329
TWYFORD ROAD
CHURCH HILL
CHURCH ROAD
FOREST ROAD
BINFIELD ROAD
MAIDENHEAD ROAD
WOKINGHAM ROAD
LONDON ROAD
NEWELL GRN.
WARFIELD
BOTTLE LANE
HAZELWOOD LA.
CABBAGE HILL
STUBBS HILL
BUCKLE LA.
BOWYER'S LANE
WEST END LANE
TICKLEBACK ROW
HARVEST RIDE
MURRELL HILL
ST. MARKS ROAD
POPESWOOD ROAD
WICKS GREEN
PENDRY'S LANE
SPINNINGWHEEL LANE
H
J
K
L
M
N
G
1
2
3
4
5
6
7
8
9
31
1E
84
85
86
87
70
71
72
73
74

Bird Hill Golf Course
Cruchfield Manor Farm
Lordland's Farm
Hawthorn Hill
Sewage Works
Hawthorndale Cottages
SL6
West's Copse
Nuptown Orchard
Nuptown Farm
Lower Lodge
Lilac Cottage
Research Station
Reservoir (Covered)
Nuptown Cottages
Steven's Copse
Nuptown Kennels
Chawridge Manor Farm
Broadview Farm
Jealott's Hill
Drown Bay Pond
Nuptown Cottages
Nuptown House
Chillingham Court
Honeywood Farm
Whitelock's Farm
Nuptown
Weller's Covert
Stroud's Copse
Abbey Farm
Hawthorn Lodge
Malt Hill Farm
Maiden's Green Farm
Winkfield Street
Moss End
Buckle Lane Farm
Moss End Farm
Handpost Farm
Fowlers
Maiden's Green
High Pines Caravan Site
Tennis Court
Westhatch Corner
Rectory House
Herbert House
WARFIELD
Brock Hill Cottages
Windmill Hill
Planner's Farm
Brock Hill
Brockhill Farm
Meadowbrook Farm School (Montessori)
Osborne Lane Bridge
RG42
Wane Bridge House
Brockhill Bridge
Brockhill House
Home Farm
Bott Bri.
Scotlands Farm
Darrah Farm
The Moat House
Hayley Green Farm
Scotlands House
Meadowbrook Montessori Pre School (Teacher Training College)
Cricket Ground
Lambrook School
Grove Lodge
Birley House
Nursery
Meml. Grd.
NEWELL GREEN
Warfield House
Brockdale
Box Farm
Row Farm
The Hermitage
Newell Hall
North Farm
Brookfield Farm
Goose Corner
WINKFIELD ROW
Brownlow Hall
West End
Sumanga Farm
Warfield Priory
Rec. Grd.
Prim. Sch.
Tennis Ct.
Fairclough Farm
Forest Farm
Chavey Ho.
Bracknell
Riding Centre
North Lodge Farm
Sports Grd.
Orchard Ho.
Park Farm
Ford
Nursery
WARFIELD PARK
Green Acres
The Elms
Superstore
Lib.
Warfield Park
Warfield Chase
Mushroom Castle
The Larches
Prim. Sch.
Warfield Park Trailer Site
Chaveydownpond
Rec. Grd.
Jun. & Infant Schs.
Double Oak
The Plateau
Chavey Down Farm
Playing Field
Myrong
Hill Copse
BIG WOOD
The Garth Hill School
Pine Ridge Farm
BRACKNELL
RG12
Recreation Ground
Clinton's Hill
Met. Office
Lily Hill House
BULLBROOK
CHAVEY DOWN
Long Hill
Ascot Priory
Jun. & Inf. Schs.
Lily Hill Park
Tennis Courts
Works
A3095
A330
B3022
B3034
B3017
A329
ASCOT ROAD
MAIDENHEAD ROAD
FOREST RD.
NEWELL GRN.
WARFIELD ROAD
WARFIELD STREET
BRACKNELL
NORTH STREET
FOREST ROAD
KINGSCROFT LANE
COCK'S LANE
MAIDEN'S GRN.
CHURCH ROAD
WINKFIELD ROW
CHAVEY DOWN ROAD
PRIORY ROAD
LOCKS RIDE
HARVEST RIDE
COUNTY LA.
PARK ROAD
LONDON ROAD
15
32

Windsor SL4
Ascot SL5
WINDSOR FOREST
CRANBOURNE CHASE
CRANBOURNE
WINKFIELD
NORTH ASCOT
ASCOT HEATH
MILL RIDE GOLF COURSE
ROYAL ASCOT GOLF COURSE
BRACKNELL FOREST
WINDSOR and MAIDENHEAD
Goaters Hill
Burleigh
Brookside
Woodside
Wood End
Radio and Space Research Station
Training Course
Lovel Hill Farm
Plaistowgreen Farm
Winkfield Plain Farm
Old Dairy Farm
Great Oaks Farm
Ranelagh Farm
Circus Headquarters
Cranbourne Hall
Cranbourne Court
Fernhill Park
Forest Farm
Brookside Farm
Hatchetlane Farm
Windsor Forest Farm
Old Huntsman's Ho.
Paddock Wood
Fountainhill Wood
Birch Copse
Platt's Firs
Fireball Hill
Penslade Bottom
A330
A332
B3022
B3034
B383
18
33

Windsor SL4
Ascot SL5
WINDSOR GREAT PARK
CRANBOURNE CHASE
CRANBOURNE PARK
SOUTH FOREST
The Village
Cheapside
Buckhurst Hill
Sunninghill Park
SHEET STREET ROAD A332
WINKFIELD ROAD B3022
SUNNINGHILL ROAD
MOUNTS HILL B383
BRACKNELL FOREST
WINDSOR and MAIDENHEAD
High Standinghill Woods
High Standing Hill
Fish Pond
Forest Park
Bromley Hill
Star Clump
Flemish Farm
Cranbourne Wood
Devil's Gap
Cranbourne Cover
Buck Paddocks
Brook's Corner
Sir Andrew Cope's Clump
Prince of Wales Pond
Ranger's Gate
Beehive Plantation
Sandy Arch
Pickleherring Pond
Ranger's Lodge
Reservoir (Covered)
Cranbourne Tower
Beehive Hill
Seymours Plantation
Fiddle Covert
Russel's Pond
Russel's Plantation
Russell's Field
Marchioness of Hertford Plantation
Equestrian Statue George III
Princess Christian Plantation
Cranbourne Gate
Kingsmead
Forest Gate Cottages
Watchoak Plantation
Prince Consort's Workshops
Richardson's Lawn
The Battery
Quelmans Head
Forest Lodge
Isle of Wight Pond
Forest Gate
Pond
Queen Elizabeth II Coronation Grove
Rec. Grd.
Bowling Green
Timberlodge Hill
Albert Plantation
Deepstrood
Forest Farm
Poets Lawn
Duncum Plantation
Tennis Court
Swim. Pool
Cranbourne
Sandpit Gate
Ox Pond
Fernhill Cottages
Springhill
Dark Wood
Chaplains Lodge
Primrose Hill
Gravel Hill
The Vale
Henhouse Covert
Primrosehill Covert
Prince Christian Plantation
The Vinery
Crispin Cotts.
South Forest Cottage
The Royal Sch.
Queen's Diamond Jubilee Plantation 1897
Woodcock Pen Covert
Hilton's Covert
Mezel Hill
Woodend Cotts.
Hawkshill Wood
Ivy Bridge
Square Covert
Shooting Platforms
Sewage Works
Wood End
Oxshed Covert
Great Meadow Pond
Shooting Platform
Cherry Orchard
Lodge
Home Farm
Slans Hill
Menzies Plantation
Long Wood
Temple Hill
Paddock Wood
Fountainhill Wood
Leiper Hill
Mill Covert
Mill Pond
Nursery
Cork Clump
Prince Consort's Gate
Red Cross Grove of Oaks
Norfolk Plantation
Norfolk Farm
Fountain Hill
Rosy Bottom
Princess Beatrice Plantation
Harewarren Clump
Otley
Round Oak
Norfolk Farm Cottages
The Dawrey
The Garden House
Frank's Plantation
Great Pond
The Rookery
Ascot Gate
Horse Shoe Clump
Pond Head
Manor Hill
Weeden's Field
Ash Covert
Ribblesdale Park
Dark Plantation
Long Plantation
Lower Farm
Lower Farm Cotts.
School
Buckhurst Park
Johnson's Pond
Platt's Firs
Penslade Bottom
Manorhill Cottages
Fireball Hill
Emmet's Wood
Millhill Plantation
American Clump
Silwood Farm
Nash's Copse
The Old Mill
Mill Pond
Boat House
Course
Nursery
HILLTOP CLOSE
WATERSPLASH LANE
DORIAN DR.
PUMP LA.
GREEN LANE
BUCKHURST ROAD
CHEAPSIDE ROAD
LOVEL LA.
WINDSOR ROAD
WOODSIDE LA.
STROOD LANE
HOLLY WALK
LIME AVENUE
TOWER RIDE
QUELMANS HEAD RIDE
FOREST ROAD
PLAIN RIDE
PARK RIDE
PRINCE CONSORT'S DRIVE
QUEEN ANNE'S CL.
DUKES LANE
QUEEN'S LANE
Park Pale
Battle Bourne
THE GALLOP
TAYLOR'S BUSHES
17
4
34

Newmoadow Plantation
Peter's Hill
St. Peter's C. of E. Mid. Sch.
Pool
Mount Place
OLD WINDSOR
Manor Farm Estate
Moat
Crimp Hill Cemetery
Bear's Rails
Bear's Rails Gate
Rush Pond
Bear's Rails Pond
Scout Camp
Woodside Farm
Staines TW19
Old Windsor Wood
Dower House
Woodside
Withy Bed
Liddell Plantation
Old Covert
Duke of York Plantation
Sultan Plantation
Prince Consort's Plantation
Wild Boar Enclosure
The Tilery
Snow Hill
Spring Hill
Queen Victoria's Plantation
Gore Plantation
Prince of Wales Plantation
Cookes Hill
The Dell
Park Place
Main Gate Lodges
Bishopsgate
Chapel Lodge
Royal Lodge
Conservatory Covert
Greenbroom Covert
King George VI Coronation Grove
Cow Pond
Cumberland Lodge
Plainfields
WINDSOR and MAIDENHEAD
RUNNYMEDE
Chapel Wood
Cumberland Gate
Wilderness
THE SAVILL GARDEN
Obelisk Ride
Smith's Lawn
Prince Consort's Statue
Fuzzy Clump
Alder Covet
Cumberland Obelisk
Obelisk Pond
Scarletoak Plantation
Polo Grounds
Pavilion
Flying Barn
Smith's Lawn Cottages
Darkhole Clump
Heather Garden
High Flyer's Hill
Oxshed Clump
CANADIAN MEMORIAL AVENUE
The Punch Bowl
Totem Pole
Wick Pond
Larch Bridge
Eton Bridge
Virginia Water Plantations
Bishopsgate House
Bishops Gate
Bishopsgate Sch.
Round Oak
DELL PARK
Park Close
Egham TW20
Town Green Farm
Parkside House
Parkwood
Forest Estate
Sandylands
Egham Wick
Castlewood House
Egham Wick Plantations
Beach Hill
Ridgemead House
Play. Fld.
Res. (Covered)
Playing Field
Cricket Ground
St. John's Beaumont School
Beaumont R.C. College
Tennis Courts
The Lodge
Home Farm
Runnymede House
Priest Hill House
Runnymede
RUNNYMEDE (National Trust)
South Lodge Farm
John F. Kennedy Memorial
Magna Carta Monument
Priest Hill Farm
Magna Carta Island
Pats Croft Eyot
RIVER THAMES
COOPER'S HILL SLOPES (National Trust)
Oak Lane Cottage
Golf Course
Brunel University (Runnymede Campus)
COOPER'S HILL
Tennis Courts
Air Forces Memorial
Langham's Pond
Englefield Green
Castle Hill
Castlehill Farm
Sports Ground
Kingswood
Bulkeley House
ENGLEFIELD GREEN
Englefield Lodge
Inf. School
QUEEN ELIZABETH HOSP.
Sutherland Ho.
Ripley Springs
Royal Holloway Coll.
Athlone Hall
Cameron Hall
Royal Holloway Univ. of London
CEMETERY
Lubbock House
Park House
Bakeham Ho.
Queenswood
Ulverscroft
Alderhurst
The American Community School (Woodlee)
Glenwood
Huntersdale
Callow Hill
Great Wood
STRAIGHT ROAD A308
WINDSOR ROAD A308
PRIEST HILL A328
ST. JUDES ROAD
EGHAM HILL A30
LONDON ROAD A30
BURFIELD B3021
CRIMP HILL
BISHOPSGATE ROAD
WICK LANE
KINGS LANE
PRUNE HILL
BAKEHAM LANE
HIGH STREET
BOND STREET
VICTORIA ST.
WICK ROAD

20
WRAYSBURY
WRAYSBURY RESERVOIR
GRAVEL PIT
TW19
Junction 13
M25 MOTORWAY
HYTHE END
COOPER'S HILL SLOPES
COOPER'S HILL
RUNNYMEDE
RUNNYMEDE PARK
EGHAM
Egham TW20
Pooley Green
Glanty
EGHAM HYTHE
THORPE LEA
Ripley Springs
Royal Holloway Coll.
Great Fosters
Church Lammas
The Moor

21
STANWELL
KING GEORGE VI
RESERVOIR
STAINES
RESERVOIRS
(BIRD SANCTUARY)
STAINES MOOR
NATURE RESERVE
Bone Head
Lower Mill Farm
Staines
STAINES
Ashford
TW15
ASHFORD
Ashford Park
Hengrove Farm
Birch Green
KNOWLE GREEN
Shortwood Common
Shortwood Farm
CROOKED BILLET ROUNDABOUT
FORDBRIDGE ROUNDABOUT
TW18
RUNNYMEDE
QUEEN MARY RESERVOIR
Penton Hook Lock
Penton Hook Farm
Sweep's Bridge
Sports Ground
Gravel Pits
Works
Intake Channel
Pumping Station
The Matthew Arnold Sch.
Buckland Jun. & Inf. Schs.
The Ashford High Sch.
Ashford Cemetery
The Holloway Unit
Superstore
STANWELL MOOR ROAD
A3044
A30
LONDON ROAD
STAINES BYPASS
A308
KINGSTON ROAD
STAINES ROAD
LALEHAM ROAD
THAMES
A320
B376
B377
B378
ASHFORD ROAD
CHERTSEY LANE
FORD BRIDGE RD.
CHURCH ROAD
STANWELL ROAD
H
J
K
L
M
N
G
1
2
3
4
5
6
7
8
9
7
37

WEST BEDFONT
STANWELL
Staines
TW19
EAST BEDFONT
TW14
CLOCKHOUSE ROUNDABOUT
GREAT SOUTH-WEST RD.
A30
LONDON ROAD
STAINES ROAD
BEDFONT LAKES COUNTRY PARK
Feltham
H.M. Young Offenders Institution Feltham
LOWER FELTHAM
ASHFORD
Ashford
TW15
CHATTERN HILL
ASHFORD ROAD
B377
B3003
CLOCKHOUSE LANE
ASHFORD MANOR GOLF COURSE
KINGSTON ROAD
A308
Staines Reservoirs Aqueduct
SCHOOL ROAD JUNCTION
Littleton Common
ASHFORD COMMON
CHERTSEY ROAD
A244
Sports Ground
Shepperton
QUEEN MARY RESERVOIR
TW17
Filter Beds
Water Works
M3 MOTORWAY
Junc.1
Upper Halliford
Ford Bridge
Manor House (Club House)
Spelthorne College
St. David's School
The Ashford High Sch.
Echelford Prim. Sch.
Spelthorne Jun. & Inf. Schs.
Edward Pauling Prim. Sch.
Feltham Hill Inf. Sch.
Bedfont Cemetery
Ashford Cemetery
Playing Field
Recreation Ground
Warehouses
Works
Nursery
Piggeries
Laboratories
Pumping Station
Club Ho.
8
21
38
07
08
09
70
71
72
73
74
A
B
C
D
E
F
G
1
2
3
4
5
6
7
8
9

NORTH FELTHAM
Hounslow TW4
Feltham Arenas
Blenheim Park
Feltham Park Hall
Playing Field
South West Middlesex Crematorium
Twickenham TW2
Feltham
HANWORTH RD. EAST
HANWORTH RD. WEST
UXBRIDGE ROAD A312
HARLINGTON RD. EAST
HARLINGTON RD. W.
HOUNSLOW ROAD A314
HIGH STREET A244
Grosvenor Park
FELTHAM
Feltham Community College
Ordnance Depot
Sports Ground
Feltham Airparc Leisure Centre
Hanworth Park House
HANWORTH PARK
Nature Reserve
School
Playing Field
APEX CORNER
GREAT CHERTSEY RD.
TWICKENHAM RD.
TW13
Hounslow College
HANWORTH
Garden Centre
Rugby Football Ground
FELTHAMHILL
Kenyngton Manor Prim. Sch.
SUNBURY COMMON
Hampton Community College
Reservoir
Hampton
TW12
Staines Reservoirs Aqueduct
Half Moon Covert
Hatherop Park
Sunbury-on-Thames
KEMPTON PARK
RACECOURSE
TW16
SUNBURY CROSS
STAINES ROAD A308
Football Ground
Hydes Field
Portlane Bridge
UPPER A308 SUNBURY ROAD
St. Paul's Catholic Coll.
SUNBURY
Kenton Court Meadow
Stain Hill East Reservoir
Grand Junction Reservoir
Water Works
Filter Beds
H J K L M N
1 2 3 4 5 6 7 8 9
G H J K L M N
9
24
39

A
B
C
D
E
F
G
1
2
3
4
5
6
7
8
9
10
23
40
Twickenham
TW1
TW2
TW4
TW12
WHITTON
Whitton
HANWORTH RD.
NELSON RD.
HOSPITAL BRIDGE ROAD
CHERTSEY ROAD
A316
GREAT CHERTSEY RD.
STAINES ROAD
A305
TWICKENHAM RD.
APEX CORNER
UXBRIDGE ROAD
A312
PARK ROAD
A313
HAMPTON ROAD
WELLINGTON ROAD
WELLINGTON STREET
HIGH STREET
A311
SIXTH CROSS ROAD
B358
STANLEY ROAD
FULWELL RD.
THE GREEN
HEATH ROAD
WALDEGRAVE ROAD
A309
STRAWBERRY VALE
CROSS DEEP
A310
LONDON RD.
KNELLER ROAD
WHITTON ROAD
UPPER SUNBURY ROAD
A308
THAMES ST.
HAMPTON CT. RD.
BROAD ST.
CHURCH ROAD
B360
QUEEN'S ROAD
PARK RD.
Twickenham Cemetery
Twickenham Rugby Union Football Grd.
Harlequins R.U.F.C. (Stoop Meml. Grd.)
Richmond upon Thames College
Kneller Gdns.
Whitton R'BOUT
Twickenham Green
Strawberry Hill
STRAWBERRY HILL
STRAWBERRY HILL GOLF COURSE
St. Mary's Strawberry Hill
Radnor Gardens
Swan Island
Fulwell Park
TWICKENHAM GOLF COURSE
FULWELL GOLF COURSE
Fulwell
Hospital Bridge
HOSPITAL BRIDGE ROUNDABOUT
Waldegrave Sch. for Girls
St. James' R.C. Prim. Sch.
Stanley Jun. & Inf. Schs.
Cemetery
Heathfield Jun. & Inf. Schs.
Bridge Farm Nursery
Recreation Grd.
Nature Reserve
Feltham
Hampton Community College
Hampton School
Lady Eleanor Holles Sch.
HAMPTON HILL
Hampton
HAMPTON
Carlisle Park
Pantile Bridge
Canal Plantation
National Physical Laboratory
Bushy House
Bartons Cottage
Round Plantation
BUSHY P
Longford River
Willow Plantation
River Lodge
Waterhouse Woodland Garden
Waterhouse Pond
Fisher's Pond
Broom Clumps
CHESTNUT AVENUE
Hampton & Richmond Borough F.C.
Grand Junction Reservoir
Water Works
Filter Beds
Garrick's Ait
Hurst Park Open Space
St. Alban's Lodge
Deer Pen
TEDDINGTON
Teddington
Teddington Lodge
Sports Ground
Clarendon Sch.
Superstore
Oldfield Works
St. Mary's Lodge

25
The Bog
Riding Ring
St. Margarets
Cole Park
TWICKENHAM
RICHMOND ROAD
A305
MARBLE HILL PARK
Marble Hill House
Orleans Ho. Gallery
RIVER THAMES
Glover's Island
Petersham Meadows
Petersham Farm
PETERSHAM ROAD
A307
Richmond Hill
Royal Star & Garter Home
Richmond Gate
Cambrian Gate
Bog Lodge
Bishop's Pond
Conduit Wood
SAWYER'S HILL
(Open during daylight hours only)
Saw Pit Plantation
Jubilee Plantation
Kidney Wood
RICHMOND
SIDMOUTH WOOD
King Henry VIII Mound
PARK
Leg of Mutton Pond
Queen Elizabeth's Plantation
Oak Lodge
Pembroke Lodge (Cafeteria)
Whiteash Lodge
Pond Plantation
Pond Slade
Ham Cross Plantation
Ham Cross
Ham Bottom
Ham Gate
High Wood
Deer Fold
Coronation Plantation
The Flat
Gallows Pond
King's Clump
PETERSHAM
PETERSHAM PARK
Ham House
Polo Ground
The German Sch., London
The Russell Prim. Sch.
Strathmore Sch.
The Copse
Richmond
Grey Court School
TW10
SUDBROOK PARK
Sudbrook Park (Club Ho.)
The Wilderness
RICHMOND GOLF COURSE
HAM GATE AVENUE
B352
HAM COMMON
HAM
Ham Fields
Thames Young Mariners Base
Nature Reserve
Miniature Rifle Range
Playing Field
UPPER HAM RD.
The Cassel Hosp.
RICHMOND ROAD
St. George's Industrial Estate
Teddington Lock
Teddington Weir
Teddington Studios
Lensbury Club
Trowlock Island
The Tiffin Girls' Sch.
Fernhill Prim. Sch.
KT2
Teddington
TW11
Teddington Sch. & Sports Cen.
Recreation Ground
KINGSTON ROAD
A310
NORMANSFIELD HOSP.
Steven's Eyot
Canbury Gardens
Kingston upon Thames
KINGSTON UPON THAMES
Kingston Gate
QUEENS RD.
B351
KINGSTON HILL
A308
KINGSTON HOSP.
COOMBE RD.
A238
Norbiton
NORBITON
LONDON RD.
CAMBRIDGE RD.
CROMWELL R.
Warren Plantation
East Molesey
KT1
Half Moon Plantation
Leg-of-Mutton Pond
Hampton Wick
HAMPTON WICK
Hampton Wick Royal Cricket Ground
The King's Field
HIGH ST.
KINGSTON BRI.
203
41
11
26

RICHMOND PARK
Richmond
TW10
ROEHAMPTON
PUTNEY VALE
KINGSTON VALE
WIMBLEDON COMMON
KT2
Kingston upon Thames
COOMBE
KT1
KT3
New Malden
NORBITON
SW20
COPSE HILL
The Bog
Riding Ring
Bog Lodge
Sheen Cross Wood
Roehampton Gate
Polo Field
Playing Field
Barn Wood Pond
Saw Pit Plantation
Jubilee Plantation
Queen's Ride
Deer Pen
White Lodge Plantation
Duchess' Wood
White Lodge (The Royal Ballet School)
Pen Ponds
Leg of Mutton Pond
Queen Elizabeth's Plantation
Lawn Plantation
SPANKERS HILL WOOD
Treebox Wood
DEER PARK
King George V Jubilee Plantation
Pond Plantation
Whiteash Lodge
Tercentenary Plantation
Horse Ride
Robin Hood Gate
Prince Charles's Spinney
Ham Cross Plantation
Ham Cross
Peg's Pond
Thomson's Pond
ISABELLA PLANTATION
Gibbet Wood
Broomfield Hill
Broomfield Hill Wood
High Wood
Still Pond
Deer Fold
Coronation Plantation
Dann's Pond
Ladderstile Gate
Gallows Pond
King's Clump
Killcat Corner
RICHMOND PARK GOLF COURSE
Kingsfarm Plantation
Victory Plantation
Beverley Brook
Beverley Bridge
Hyde Park Nursery
Chohole Gate
Silver Hill
STAG LANE
Putney Vale Crematorium
PUTNEY VALE CEMETERY
Kingston University (Roehampton Vale Centre)
Memorial Gardens
War Memorial
Hall School Wimbledon
WANDSWORTH
MERTON
Silent Pools
Stag Bog
ROBIN HOOD
Robin Hood Prim. Sch.
KINGSTON UNIVERSITY
Horse Exercise Area
Horse Exercise Ring
Gravelly Hill
WIMBLEDON COMMON & LONDON SCOTTISH GOLF COURSE
White Cottage
Farm Bog
Farm Ravine
Caesar's Camp
Warren Farm
Fishpond Wood
Mill Corner
ROYAL WIMBLEDON GOLF COURSE
Shadwell Wood
The Warren
COOMBE HILL GOLF COURSE
Warren House
COOMBE WOOD GOLF COURSE
Kingston Gate
Holy Cross Preparatory R.C. Sch.
Rockeby Sch.
Marymount International School
Coombe Hill Jun. & Inf. Schools
KINGSTON HOSPITAL
NEW VICTORIA HOSPITAL
COOMBE LANE
COOMBE FLYOVER
Wimbledon College Playing Fields
St. Matthew's C. of E. First Sch.
The Wolfson Rehabilitation Cen.
Rowans Sch.
MALDEN GOLF COURSE
Coombe Brook
Civil Service Sports Ground
Coombe Girls' Sch.
Norbiton
QUEEN MARY'S UNIVERSITY HOSPITAL
Maryfield Convent
College Halls
Club House
A3
A306
A308
A238
B283
KINGSTON BY-PASS
ROBIN HOOD WAY
KINGSTON VALE
KINGSTON HILL
COOMBE LANE WEST
TRAPS LANE
COOMBE ROAD
GEORGE ROAD
KINGSTON ROAD
QUEENS ROAD
BEVERLEY WAY
ROEHAMPTON VALE
SAWYER'S HILL
12
25
42

27
PUTNEY HEATH
WEST HILL
SOUTHFIELDS
EARLSFIELD
SW18
WIMBLEDON PARK
SUMMERSTOWN
SW19
WIMBLEDON
SOUTH WIMBLEDON
MERTON
COTTENHAM PARK
TIBBET'S CORNER
ROEHAMPTON LANE
Wimbledon All England Lawn Tennis & Croquet Club
Wimbledon Park Golf Course
Wimbledon Cemetery
Cannizaro Park
King George's Park
Wimbledon Chase
Raynes
Haydons Road
Merton Park
Dundonald Rd.
WIMBLEDON PARK SIDE
DURNSFORD ROAD
PLOUGH LANE
HAYDONS ROAD
THE BROADWAY
MERTON HIGH ST.
KINGSTON ROAD
WORPLE ROAD
HIGH ST.
WIMBLEDON HILL RD.
ALEXANDRA RD.
MORDEN RD.
HARTFIELD ROAD
MERANTUN WY.
GAP ROAD

EARLSFIELD
WANDSWORTH COMMON
Wandsworth Common
H.M.P. Wandsworth
SW18
SW11
SW12
BALHAM
Balham
SW17
Tooting Bec
UPPER TOOTING
TOOTING
Tooting Broadway
TOOTING GRAVENEY
FURZEDOWN
SUMMERSTOWN
Wimbledon Stadium (Greyhound)
Haydons Road
SOUTH WIMBLEDON
SW19
Colliers Wood
COLLIER'S WOOD
Tooting
Mitcham
CR4
MERTON
STREATHAM VALE
Lonesome
Clapham Sth.
Wandsworth Cemetery
Lambeth Cemetery
Streatham Cemetery
Springfield University Hospital
St. George's Hospital
The Central London Golf Centre
Tooting Graveney Common
Garratt Green
Wandle Meadow Nature Park
Tamworth Rec. Grd.
27
44

H
J
K
L
M
N
SE24
BROCKWELL
PARK
H.M.P. Brixton
Open Air Theatre
The Mansion
New Lodge
Playground
Bowling Green
Herne Hill Stadium
Sports Ground
Tennis Courts
Belair
1
2
3
4
5
6
7
8
9
POYNDERS RD
A205
ATKINS RD
STREATHAM PL
CHRISTCHURCH
ROAD
BRIXTON HILL
A23
KINGS AVENUE
B221
SW2
SE21
TULSE HILL
Tulse Hill
A204
NORWOOD ROAD
A215
Knight's Hill
THURLOW PARK
West Dulwich
WEST DULWICH
CROXTED ROAD
A2199
STREATHAM HILL
Streatham Hill
THORNTON AV.
STERNHOLD AV.
Football Pitch
COMMON
Carriage Shed
Bus Depot
Hillside
Tennis Courts
Hitherfield Prim. Sch.
West Norwood Cemetery and Crematorium
Catacombs
Library
West Norwood
WEST NORWOOD
Tonge Ho.
SE27
KNIGHTS HILL
NORWOOD HIGH ST
ELDER ROAD
GIPSY ROAD
Kingswood Prim. Sch.
NORWOOD WOOD
Playground
Playing Field
WANDSWORTH
GARRAD'S RD
Swimming Pool
A214 ROAD
TOOTING BEC
AMBLESIDE AV.
STREATHAM PARK
STREATHAM HIGH ROAD
STREATHAM
Streatham
Baths
Ice Rink
SW16
School
Convent
Fish Pond
STREATHAM COMMON NORTH
CROWN LA.
CROWN DALE
CENTRAL HILL
STREATHAM COMMON
Streatham Common
Horse Ride
The Rookery
Tennis Courts
Bowling Green
Norwood Grove Recreation Ground
St. Joseph's College
SE19
BEULAH HILL
A215
St. Joseph's R.C. Jun. & Inf. Schs.
Virgo Fidelis Convent Sch.
NORWOOD NEW TOWN
Rockmount Prim. Sch.
Recreation Ground
GREYHOUND LA.
Superstore
Streatham Common
STREATHAM VALE
B272
LAMBETH
A216
Biggin Wood
Downsview Prim. Sch.
Playing Field
Westwood High Sch.
UPPER NORWOOD
GREEN LA.
B273
Pavilion
NORBURY PARK
Hermitage Bridge
NORBURY
Norbury
Norbury Manor Girls High Sch.
Thornton Heath
CR7
Kensington Avenue Jun. & Inf. Schs.
David Livingstone Prim. Sch.
School Playing Fields
Sports Ground
Stanford Middle Sch.
Works
LONDON RD.
A23
NORBURY TRADING ESTATE
Sports Ground
G
H
J
K
45
L
M
N
ROWAN RD.

WOKINGHAM
Wokingham
RG41
RG40
Dowlesgreen
Chapel Green
Holme Green
Eastheath
Gardeners Green
Gorrick
GORRICK PLANTATION
WOKINGHAM WITHOUT
Wick Hill
A329(M)
A329(M) MOTORWAY
LONDON ROAD
A329
A321
B3430
NINE MILE RIDE
SANDHURST ROAD
FINCHAMPSTEAD ROAD
Wokingham Hospital
Sports Cen.
Superstore
Ludgrove School
Holme Grange School
Luckley-Oakfield School
Waterloo Crossing
Starlane Crossing
King George V Playing Field
Recreation Ground
Queen's Mere
Heath Lake
Hewlett Packard
Ravenswood Village Settlement Special Boarding Sch.

14
48

31
15
32
49
H
J
K
L
M
N
G
1
2
3
4
5
6
7
8
9
84
85
86
87
65
66
67
68
69
BRACKNELL
Bracknell RG12
Crowthorne RG45
WILDRIDINGS
EASTHAMPSTEAD
GREAT HOLLANDS
HANWORTH
Birch Hill
Amen Corner
Farley Wood
Rounds Hill
Western Ind Area
Southern Industrial Area
Skimped Hill
WOKINGHAM ROAD
BERKSHIRE WAY
A329
A3095
A322
B3408
B3430
B3348
NINE MILE RIDE
DOWNSHIRE WAY
BAGSHOT ROAD
CHURCH RD.
MILL LANE
CROWTHORNE ROAD
FORESTERS WAY
SOUTH HILL ROAD
RINGMEAD
LONDON ROAD
OLD BRACKNELL LANE
EASTHAMPSTEAD PARK
DOWNSHIRE (PUBLIC) GOLF COURSE
Easthampstead Park School
Bracknell Crematorium & Cemetery
Meteorological Office Experimental Site
Water Pollution Control Centre
Transport and Road Research Laboratory
Caesar's Camp (Fort)
Tarman's Copse
Jennett's Hill
Riggs Copse
Buckhurst Moors
Peacock Farm
The Lodge
West Garden
Yew Tree Corner
Foresters Cottage
Hut Hill
Redoubt
Wagbullock Hill
Gorrick Well (Disused)
Windyridge
Round Hill
Nursery
The Point Leisure Centre
Mill Pond
Mill Park
Wildridings Prim. Sch.
Fox Hill Primary Sch.
The Brakenhale School
Great Hollands Inf. & Jun. Schools
Wooden Hill Primary Sch.
The Pines Inf. & Jun. Schools
Gormoor Pond (Fish Pond)
Pinewood Leisure Cen.
Club House
Playing Field
Sandpits
Northerams Woods Nature Reserve
Amen Corner Business Park
Popes Manor
Murrellhill Farm
Blackman's Copse
Ski Slope
Rose Farm
Manor Farm
Crowthorne
Earthworks

32
A
B
C
D
E
F
G
16
31
50
BRACKNELL
Bracknell
RG12
Crowthorne
RG45
BULLBROOK
HARMANSWATER
EASTHAMPSTEAD
CHAVEY DOWN
Eastern Industrial Area
Martin's Heron
The Warren
SWINLEY PARK
BERKSHIRE GOLF COURSE
LAVENDER PARK GOLF CENTRE
Crown Wood
Birch Hill
Forest Park
Lily Hill Park
Heathfield School
Ascot Priory
Ranelagh School
Fox Hill Primary Sch.
Bracknell Sports & Leisure Cen.
The Point Leisure Centre
Coral Reef Leisure Pool
South Hill Park
The Look out (Discovery Outpost)
Kervinic
Gormoor Farm
Gormoor Pond (Fish Pond)
Penny Hill
Gravel Hill
Pudding Hill
Mill Pond
Nut Covert
Red Cottage
Broom Covert
White Cottage
Rapley Farm
Dene Copse
New England Hill
Kiln Covert
Thornhill
Allotment
Blane's Allotment
Bright's Allotment
Blane's Farm
The Rough
Worlds End
Worldsend Hill
Icehouse Hill
Blacksmith's Hill
Swinley Lodge
Whitmoor Bog
Sewage Works
Filter Beds
Land Treatment Area
Gas Pressure Reducing Sta.
Pinewood Lodge
Westwood
Hereford
Forester's Hill
Starch Copse
Scott's Hill
Dennis Pilcher House
Brookham House
Savernake Pond
Worldsend Bridge
Sandpits
A329
A322
B3430
B3017
B3022
LONDON ROAD
BAGSHOT ROAD
NEW FOREST RIDE
NINE MILE RIDE
SWINLEY ROAD
CHURCH RD
DOWNSHIRE WY.
PRIORY
87
88
89
90
65
66
67
68
69
1
2
3
4
5
6
7
8
9

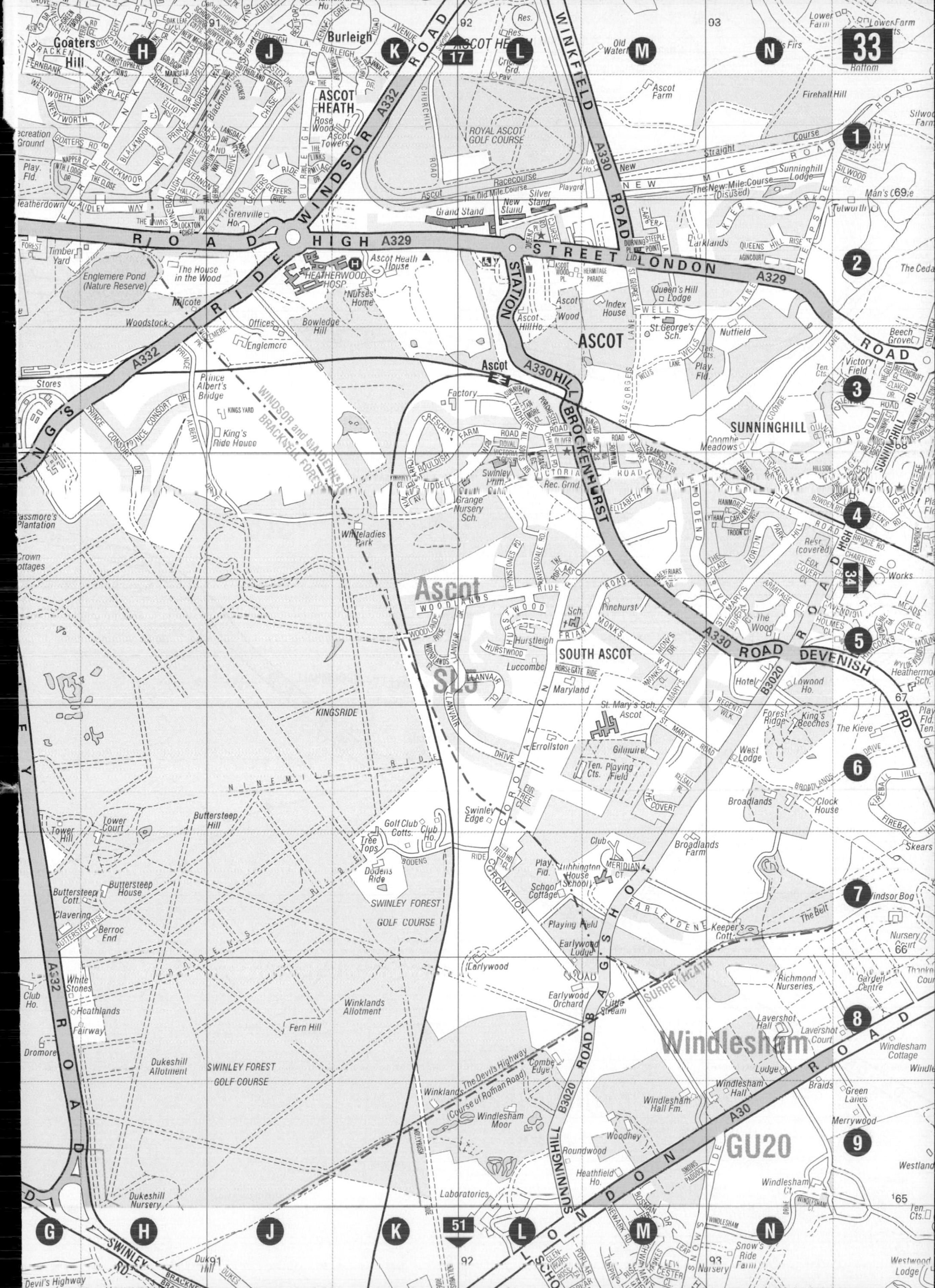

33
Goaters Hill
Burleigh
ASCOT HEATH
Royal Ascot Golf Course
Grand Stand
Heatherwood Hosp.
Englemere Pond (Nature Reserve)
ASCOT
SUNNINGHILL
SOUTH ASCOT
Ascot
SL5
Swinley Forest Golf Course
Windlesham
GU20
Kingsride
Buttersteep Hill
Dukeshill Allotment
Winklands Allotment
Fern Hill
The Devil's Highway
(Course of Roman Road)
Windlesham Moor
Windlesham Hall Fm.
Broadlands Farm
St. Mary's Sch. Ascot
Whiteladies Park
Fireball Hill

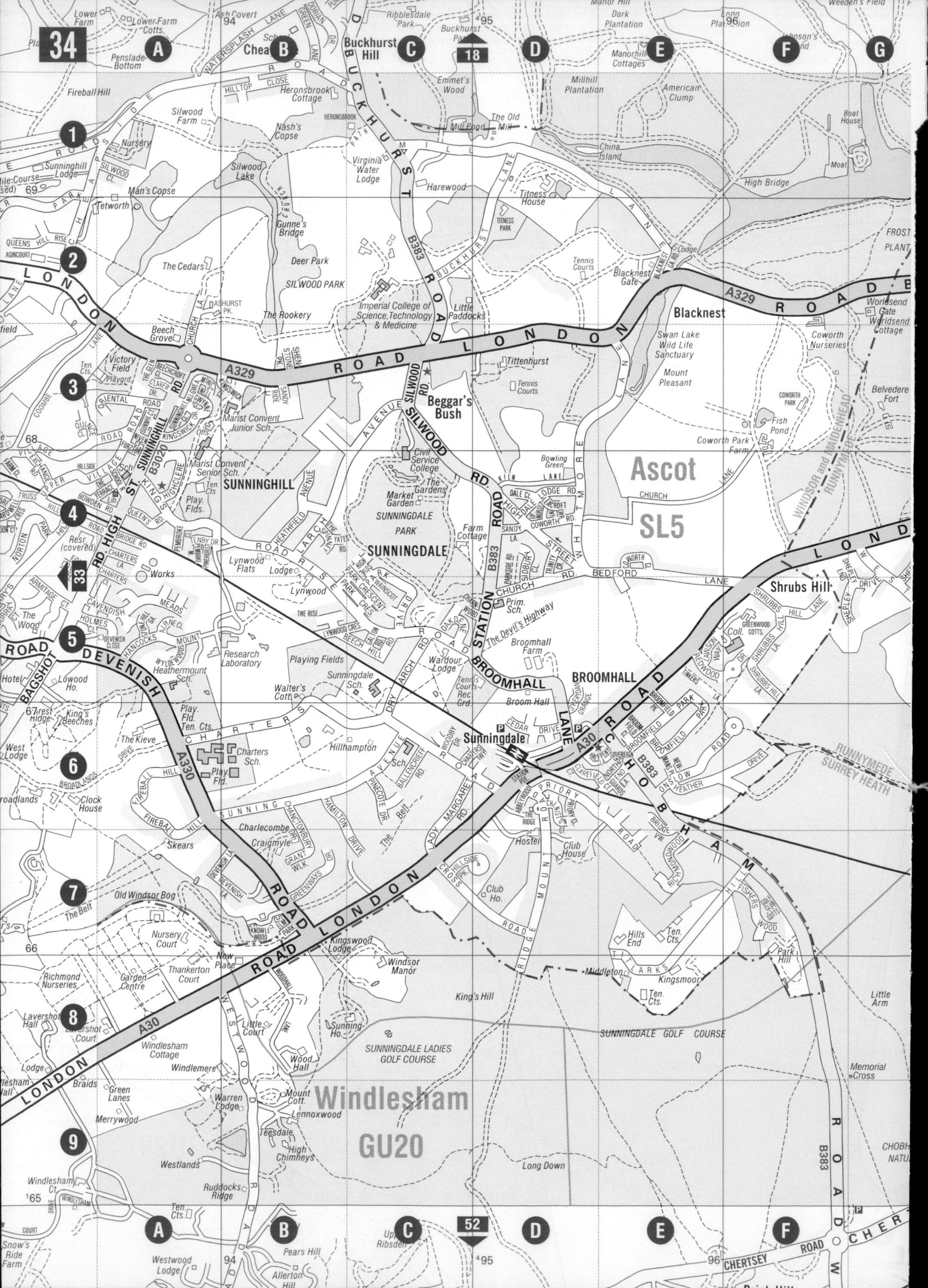
Buckhurst Hill
18
Cheapside
Silwood Park
Imperial College of Science, Technology & Medicine
Blacknest
Swan Lake Wild Life Sanctuary
Mount Pleasant
Beggar's Bush
Ascot
SL5
SUNNINGHILL
SUNNINGDALE
Sunningdale Park
Civil Service College
Shrubs Hill
BROOMHALL
Sunningdale
33
Marist Convent Junior Sch.
Marist Convent Senior Sch.
Heathermount Sch.
Charters Sch.
Research Laboratory
Sunningdale Sch.
SUNNINGDALE LADIES GOLF COURSE
SUNNINGDALE GOLF COURSE
Windlesham
GU20
52
A329
A30
A330
B383
B3020
LONDON ROAD
DEVENISH ROAD
CHOBHAM ROAD
CHERTSEY ROAD
WINDSOR and MAIDENHEAD
RUNNYMEDE
SURREY HEATH
Virginia Water Lodge
China Island
High Bridge
Coworth Park Farm
Old Windsor Bog
Kingswood Lodge
Windsor Manor
King's Hill
Long Down
Memorial Cross
Little Arm
Westlands
Ruddocks Ridge
Pears Hill
Allerton Hill
Snow's Ride Farm
Westwood Lodge

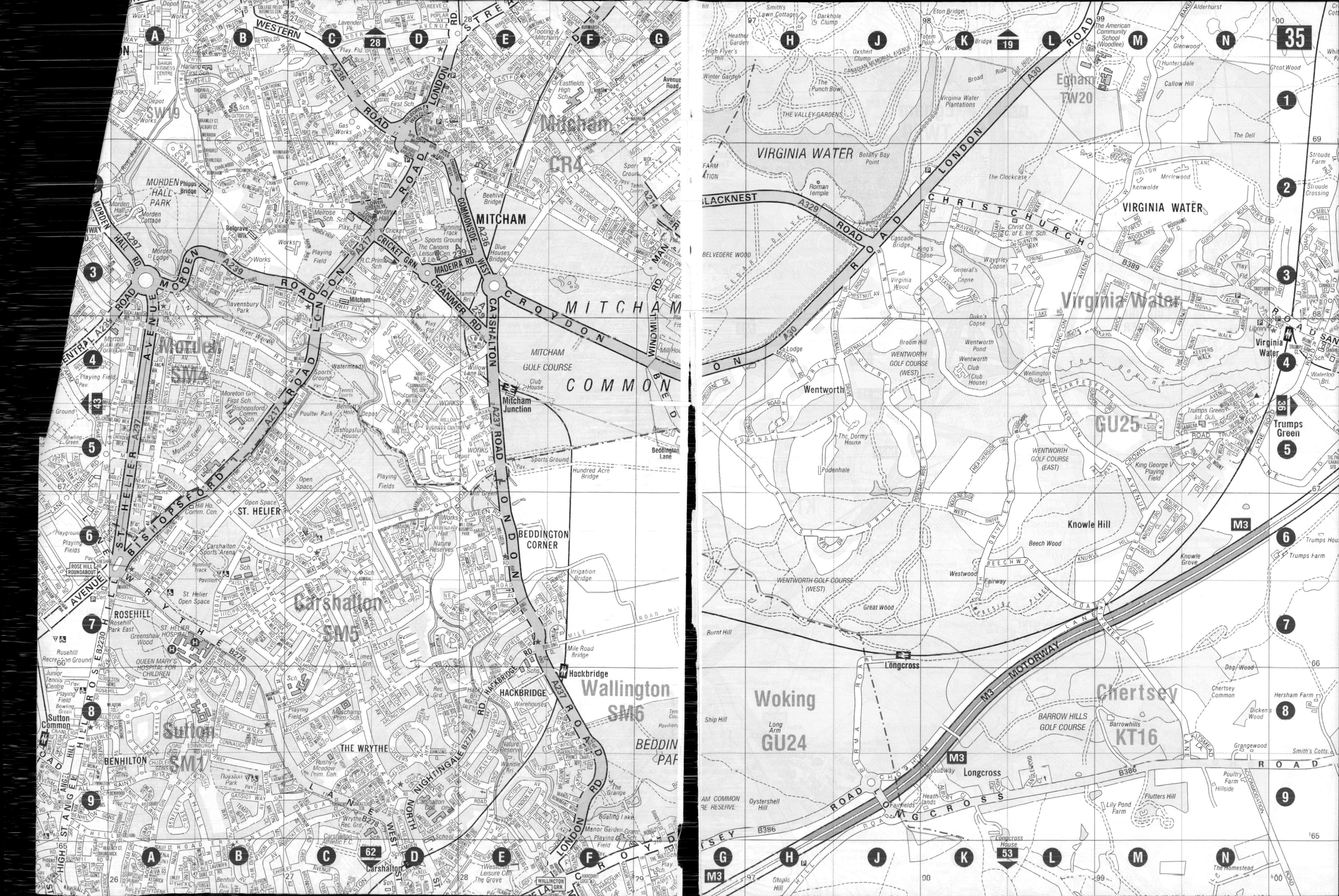

Mitcham
CR4
MITCHAM
MITCHAM COMMON
MITCHAM GOLF COURSE
Mitcham Junction
MORDEN HALL PARK
Morden SM4
ST. HELIER
Carshalton SM5
ROSEHILL
Sutton SM1
Sutton Common
BENHILTON
THE WRYTHE
HACKBRIDGE
BEDDINGTON CORNER
Wallington SM6
Carshalton
SW19
WESTERN ROAD
LONDON ROAD
CROYDON ROAD
BISHOPSFORD ROAD
ST. HELIER AVENUE
WRYTHE LANE
VIRGINIA WATER
Virginia Water
GU25
Egham TW20
Wentworth
WENTWORTH GOLF COURSE (WEST)
WENTWORTH GOLF COURSE (EAST)
Knowle Hill
Trumps Green
Longcross
Woking GU24
Chertsey KT16
BARROW HILLS GOLF COURSE
M3 MOTORWAY
LONGCROSS ROAD
CHRISTCHURCH ROAD
LONDON ROAD
BLACKNEST ROAD
THE VALLEY GARDENS

38
QUEEN MARY RESERVOIR
M3
CHARLTON
LITTLETON
SHEPPERTON FILM STUDIOS
SHEPPERTON GREEN
Shepperton TW17
M3 MOTORWAY
SUNBURY GOLF COURSE
UPPER HALLIFORD
Upper Halliford
UPPER HALLIFORD BY-PASS
Shepperton
Pool End
SHEPPERTON
Lower Halliford
WALTON BRIDGE
GASTON BRIDGE
CHERTSEY ROAD
RENFREE WAY
RUSSELL RD
WALTON LANE
RIVER THAMES
DESBOROUGH ISLAND
Sailing Club
Shepperton Lock
Hamhaugh Island
Dockett Point
RUNNYMEDE
Thames Meadow
Cowey Sale
Weybridge KT13
WEYBRIDGE
OATLANDS PARK
OATLANDS DRIVE
Ham Moor
Sunbury-on-Thames
SUNBURY TW16
Sunbury Locks
Elmbridge Leisure Centre
HURST ROAD
WALTON ROAD
KNIGHTS RESERVOIR
QUEEN ELIZABETH II RESERVOIR
WEST MOLESEY
Fieldcommon
Walton-on-Thames KT12
WALTON-ON-THAMES
CHURCH STREET
TERRACE
HERSHAM ROAD
Rydens
Hersham
HERSHAM VILLAGE GOLF CLUB
Ashley Park
Walton-on-Thames
40
44
TOLWORTH JUNCTION
22
23
37
39
56
57

NORBURY
Norbury
29
SW16
Thornton Heath
CR7
THORNTON HEATH
Thornton Heath Pond
BROAD GREEN
46
CROYDON
West Croydon
East Croydon
200
Croydon
CR0
WADDON
Waddon
BEDDINGTON
Beddington Sewage Treatment Works
Croydon Cemetery
Croydon Crematorium
Mayday University Hosp.
Wandle Park
Lombard Roundabout
Therapia Lane
Ampere Way
Waddon Marsh
Croydon Tramlink
Queen's Road Cemetery
63
LONDON ROAD
MITCHAM ROAD
PURLEY WAY
A23
A236
A235
A232
A222
A213
B272
B273
B266
BRIGSTOCK ROAD
WINDMILL RD.
ST. JAMES'S RD.
WELLESLEY RD.
ROMAN WAY
OLD TOWN
DUPPAS HILL RD.
FLYOVER
THORNTON ROAD
PARCHMORE
GREEN LANE
NORTHBOROUGH ROAD
BEDDINGTON LANE
J
K
L
M
N
G
H
1
2
3
4
5
6
7
8
9
30
31
32

46
A
B
C
D
E
F
1
2
3
4
5
6
7
8
9
UPPER NORWOOD
Beaulieu Heights
T.V. Station
Cypress Inf. Sch.
Cypress Jun. Sch.
Playing Field
SE19
Bowling Green
Tennis Courts
South Norwood Lake
Athletic Grounds
Orchard School Sports Centre
Nursing Home
Anerley Prim. Sch.
Games Court
ANERLEY
Betts Park
SE20
Birkbeck
Beckenham Crematorium
BROMLEY
CROYDON
Harrington Rd.
Elmers End
Thornton Heath
CR7
Spurgeon's College
Grangewood Recreation Ground
SOUTH NORWOOD
High Sch.
Stanley Hall
Bromley Junction
PENGE
SE25
Crystal Palace F.C. & Wimbledon F.C. (Selhurst Park)
Norwood Junc.
Priory Sch.
Recreation Ground
Pitch & Putt Course
SOUTH NORWOOD COUNTRY PARK
Croydon Tramlink
Playground
Croydon Sports Arena
Ryelands Prim. Sch.
Arena
Croydon Golf Driving Range
St. Chad's R.C. Prim. Sch.
Heavers Farm Prim. Sch.
Adult Training Centre
Selhurst
SELHURST
Depot
Wks.
Norbury Brook
45
Ecclesbourne Jun. & Inf. Schs.
WOODSIDE
Woodside
Blackhorse La.
Ashburton Park
Library
Davidson Jun. & Inf. Schs.
Ashburton High Sch.
Ashburton Playing Fields
SHIRLEY OAKS HOSPITAL
Playing Fields
Shirley Oaks
CROYDON
Council Offices
West Croydon
200
East Croydon
Wellesley Rd.
George St.
Addiscombe
ADDISCOMBE
Recreation Ground
Croydon CR0
Lebanon Rd.
Sandilands
Club House
Trinity Sch.
Playing Field
SHIRLEY
Trinity School Playing Field
SHIRLEY PARK GOLF COURSE
Bowling Green
Sports Ground
Oaks Farm
Shirley Towermill (disused)
Coloma Convent R.C. Sch.
Hall Grange
Coombe Cliff (Educ. Cen.)
Cambridge Tutors Coll.
64
Coombe Park
LLOYD PARK
Winwood
WHITEHORSE ROAD
LOWER ADDISCOMBE RD.
ADDISCOMBE ROAD A232
LONG LANE A222
SHIRLEY ROAD
WICKHAM RD.
PORTLAND RD.
SPRING LA.
SELHURST RD.
NORWOOD
SOUTH NORWOOD HILL
CROYDON RD. A213
ELMERS END

47
BECKENHAM
Beckenham
BR3
BR2
BR4
Clock House
BECKENHAM HOSPITAL
Recreation Ground
Bandstand
Beau Lodge
Kelsey Park
Elgood Playing Field
Kelsey Park Sch.
Crease Park
Putting Green
SHORTLANDS
Shortlands
Bromley
SLOANE HOSP.
SHORTLANDS GOLF COURSE
PARK LANGLEY
ELMERS END
EDEN PARK
Eden Park
Langley Court (Research Labs)
Langley Park Schools
Sports Ground
LANGLEY PARK GOLF COURSE
LANGLEY PARK
The Rookery
UPPER ELMERS END
Crouch Oak Wood
MONKS ORCHARD
Cold Shaw
High Broom Wood
THE BETHLEM ROYAL HOSPITAL
Park Farm
Nurses' Home
Caravan Park
Edenham High Sch.
Parkfields Recreation Ground
West Wickham
West Wickham Pools
WEST WICKHAM
Hawes Down Jun & Int. Schs.
Glebe Sch.
Blake Recreation Ground
Oak Lodge Prim. Sch.
SPRING PARK
Spring Park Wood
Primary School
Spring Park
Millers Pond
Benson Prim. Sch.
Shirley High Sch.
Foxes Wood
Pinewoods
Cheyne Site
Sparrow's Den Playing Fields
Bowling Green Recreation Ground
Coney Hall Rec. Grd.
ADDINGTON GOLF COURSE
SPRING PARK
Kennel Wood
ADDINGTON
HIGH STREET
BECKENHAM ROAD A234
MANOR RD.
BROMLEY A222
HAYES ROAD
ELMERS END A214 ROAD
SOUTH EDEN PARK RD B230
UPPER ELMERS END
WICKHAM A232 ROAD
GLEBE WAY A232
CROYDON RD A2022
65

NINE MILE RIDE B3430
Wick Hill
Wokingham RG40
Kingsmere House
King's Bridge
Pineridge Farm
30
King's Mere
Club House
Queen's Bri.
Jack's Bri.
LOWER WOKINGHAM ROAD A321
Ravenswood Village Settlement (Special Boarding Sch.)
The Green
Oaklands Inf.& Jun. Schools
EAST BERKSHIRE GOLF COURSE
Club House
Roman Road (course of)
THE DEVIL'S HIGHWAY
ROMAN RIDE
The Devil's Highway
Heath Pond
Simons Wood (N.T.)
Blencathra
Armholes
Rhododendron Corner
WELLINGTONIA AVENUE
B3348
The Ridges
FINCHAMPSTEAD RIDGES (National Trust)
DUKE'S RIDE B3348
WATERLOO
Talbot House
Swim Pool
Gardens Cottage
WELLINGTON BUSINESS PK.
WELLINGTONIA ROUNDABOUT
Crowthorne
Wellington Sports Cen.
Cricket Ground
Chaucer Woods
WELLINGTON COLLEGE
Picton House
Stanley House
Ckt. Grd.
Derby Field
Playing Field
Benson House
Pollock Bridge
Tennis Courts
Edgbarrowhill Star
WOKINGHAM BRACKNELL FOREST
Spout Pond
Fisher's Copse
Sandhurst Lodge
BACK DRIVE
Beech Hill
Ambarrow Hill
Smallbrook Bottom
Edgbarrow Hill
Rosina Cottage
LOWER SANDHURST ROAD
Hawthorns
Moor Green Farm
Foxglade
Hall Farm
Hilton Cottage
Grove Farm House
Coalpit Copse
Ambarrow Wood
Ambarrow Farm
Yonder Riding Stables
Grove Farm
New Scotland Hill Prim. Sch.
Eagle House School
LITTLE SANDHURST
Play. Fld.
Perry Bridge Farm
Perry's Bridge
Watersports Centre
Long Down
HIGH STREET
YORKTOWN ROAD
Hurts Hill
Basingstoke RG27
BLACKWATER VALLEY GOLF CLUB
Club House
Mill Farm
Mill Bridge
Church Farm
Scotland Hill
Trilakes Country Park
Yateley Bridge
Sandhurst
SANDHURST
LAKESIDE BUSINESS PARK
Works
Yateley
Yateley Green
READING ROAD
VICARAGE
Depot
Yateley Industries
THE YATELEY LAKES
Playground
Village Hall
Yateley Manor Prep. Sch.
Play. Flds.
YATELEY
St. Peter's Jun. Sch.
B3272
Works
GU46
Play. Fld.
Yateley School
Yateley Inf. Sch.
DARBY GREEN
Pond Farm
Clark's Farm
Yateley Comm.
Lib.
Comm. Centre
Jun. & Inf. Schs.
Playing Fields
68
Potley Hill Sch.
Two Oaks Farm
Cricket

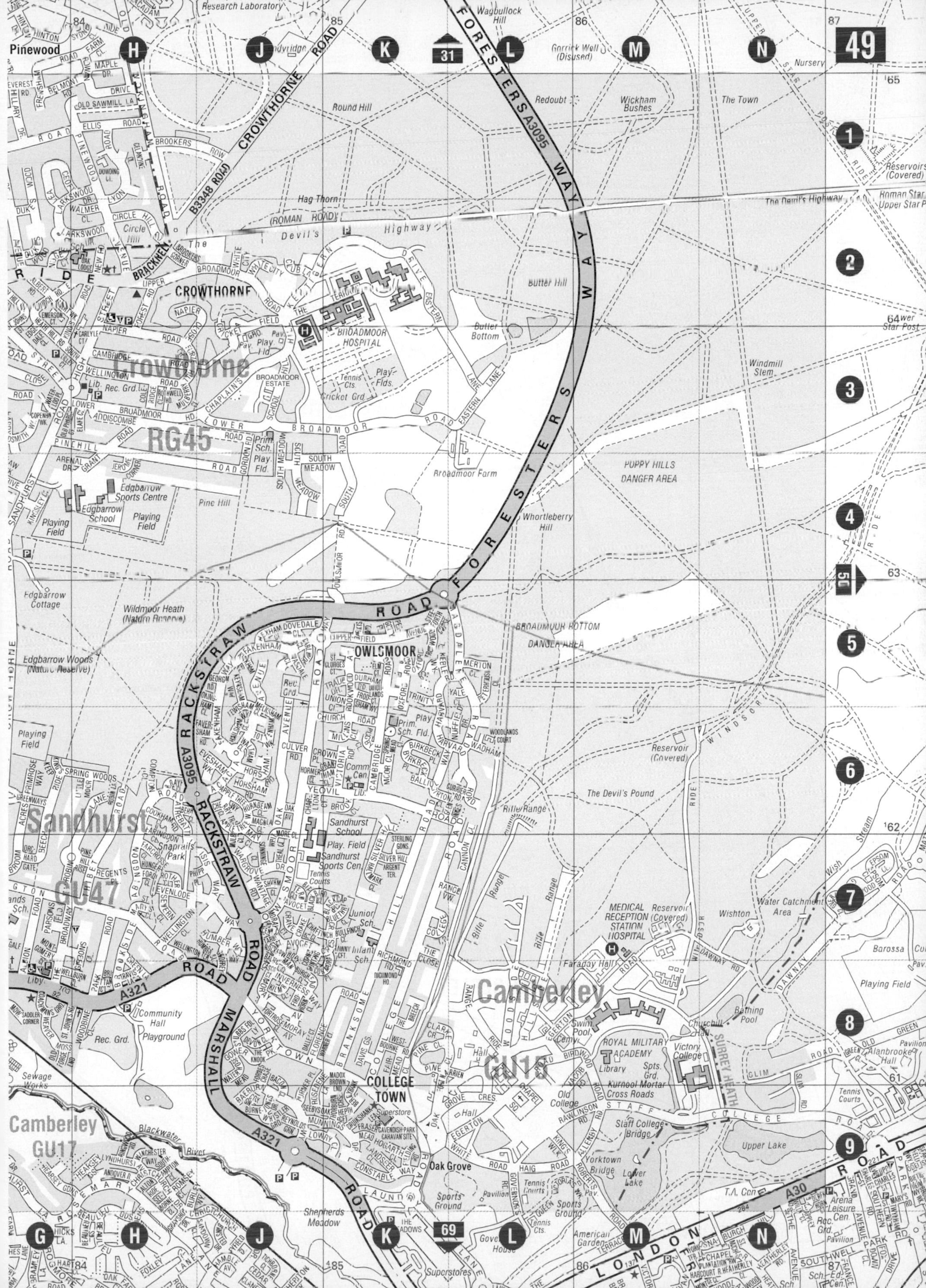
49
Research Laboratory
Wagbullock Hill
Pinewood
Gorrick Well (Disused)
Nursery
Round Hill
Redoubt
Wickham Bushes
The Town
CROWTHORNE ROAD
FORESTERS WAY A3095
B3348 ROAD
Reservoirs (Covered)
Hag Thorn
(ROMAN ROAD)
Devil's Highway
The Devil's Highway
Roman Star
Upper Star Post
Butter Hill
CROWTHORNE
BROADMOOR HOSPITAL
Butter Bottom
Lower Star Post
Crowthorne
BROADMOOR ESTATE
Windmill Stem
Tennis Cts.
Play. Flds.
Cricket Grd.
LOWER BROADMOOR ROAD
RG45
Broadmoor Farm
POPPY HILLS DANGER AREA
Edgbarrow Sports Centre
Edgbarrow School
Pine Hill
Playing Field
Whortleberry Hill
Edgbarrow Cottage
Wildmoor Heath (Nature Reserve)
RACKSTRAW ROAD
BROADMOOR BOTTOM DANGER AREA
OWLSMOOR
Edgbarrow Woods (Nature Reserve)
Reservoir (Covered)
WINDSOR RIDE
The Devil's Pound
Rifle Range
Sandhurst
Sandhurst School
Play. Field
Sandhurst Sports Cen.
Snaprails Park
GU47
Junior Sch.
Infant Sch.
Wish Stream
MEDICAL RECEPTION STATION HOSPITAL
Reservoir (Covered)
Wishton
Water Catchment Area
Barossa
Playing Field
Faraday Hall
Camberley
A321 ROAD
MARSHALL ROAD
Community Hall
Playground
Rec. Grd.
Bathing Pool
Churchill Hall
SURREY HEATH
ROYAL MILITARY ACADEMY
Victory College
Library
Spts. Grd.
Kurnool Mortar Cross Roads
Alanbrooke Hall
Sewage Works
COLLEGE TOWN
GU15
Superstore
Old College
STAFF COLLEGE ROAD
Staff College Bridge
Upper Lake
Tennis Courts
Camberley GU17
Blackwater River
Oak Grove
Yorktown Bridge
Lower Lake
T.A. Cen.
A30
Arena Leisure Cen.
Sports Ground
Tennis Courts
Pavilion
Shepherds Meadow
American Garden
LONDON ROAD
Superstores
31
50
69
84
85
86
87
65
64
63
62
61

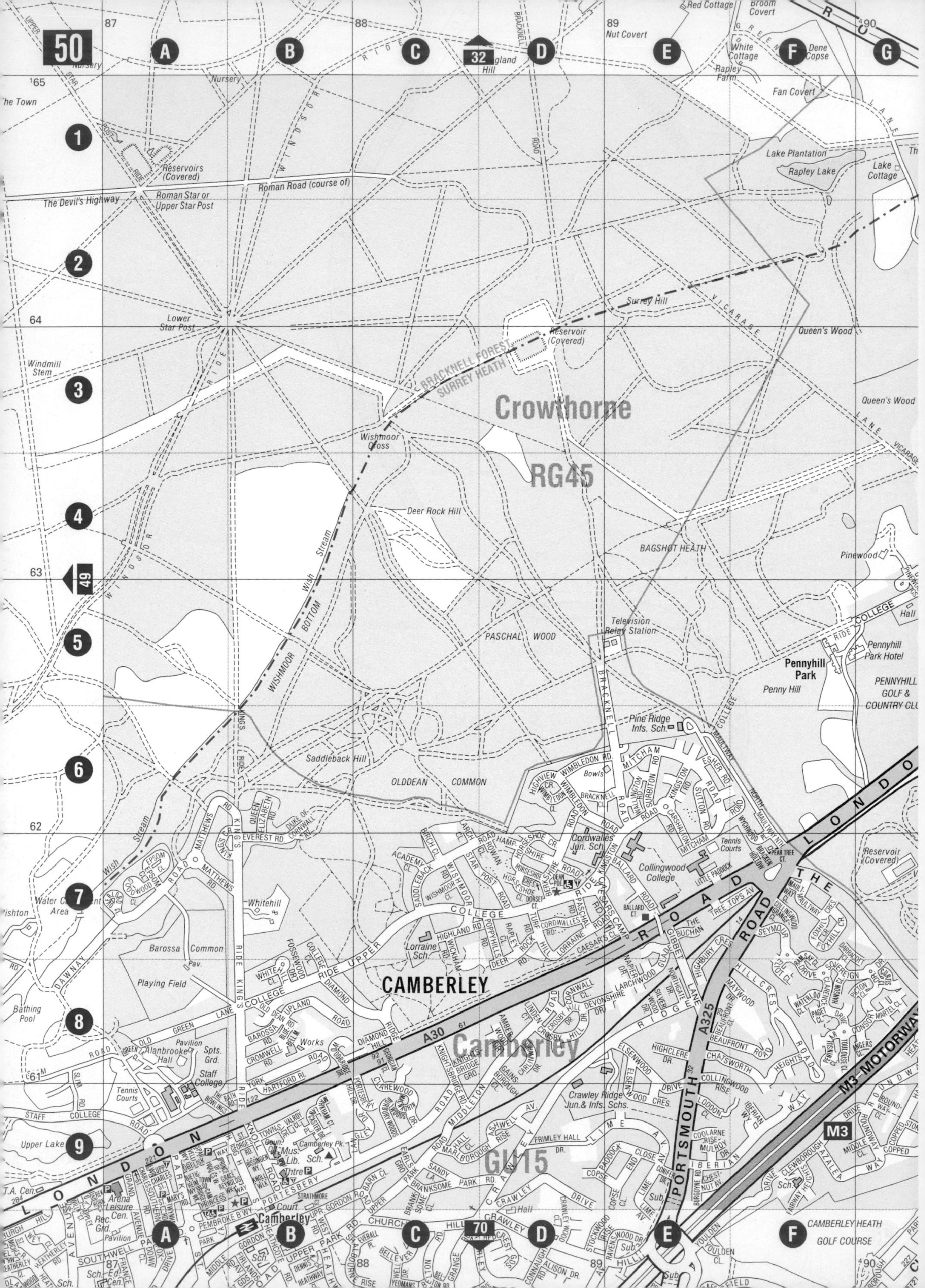
32
49
70
Red Cottage
Broom Covert
Nut Covert
White Cottage
Dene Copse
Rapley Farm
Fan Covert
Nursery
The Town
Reservoirs (Covered)
Roman Road (course of)
The Devil's Highway
Roman Star or Upper Star Post
Lake Plantation
Rapley Lake
Lake Cottage
Surrey Hill
Lower Star Post
Reservoir (Covered)
Queen's Wood
Windmill Stem
BRACKNELL FOREST
SURREY HEATH
Crowthorne
RG45
Wishmoor Cross
Deer Rock Hill
BAGSHOT HEATH
Pinewood
Television Relay Station
PASCHAL WOOD
Pennyhill Park Hotel
Pennyhill Park
Penny Hill
PENNYHILL GOLF & COUNTRY CLU
Pine Ridge Infs. Sch.
Saddleback Hill
OLDDEAN COMMON
Wish Stream
WISHMOOR BOTTOM
Cordwalles Jun. Sch.
Collingwood College
Tennis Courts
Reservoir (Covered)
Whitehill
Water Catchment Area
Wishton
Barossa Common
Playing Field
Lorraine Sch.
CAMBERLEY
Bathing Pool
Alanbrooke Hall
Pavilion
Spts. Grd.
Staff College
Works
Camberley
Crawley Ridge Jun.& Infs. Schs.
M3-MOTORWAY
M3
Upper Lake
Tennis Courts
T.A. Cen.
Arena Leisure Cen.
Rec. Grd.
Pavilion
Camberley Pk. Sch.
Court
Camberley
GU15
Hall
CAMBERLEY HEATH GOLF COURSE
A30
A325
LONDON ROAD
PORTSMOUTH ROAD
COLLEGE RIDE
KINGS RIDE
UPPER COLLEGE RIDE
VICARAGE LANE
BRACKNELL ROAD
FRIMLEY HALL DR.
CRAWLEY HILL
CHURCH HILL
STAFF COLLEGE ROAD
OLD GREEN LANE
DAWNAY RD
MATTHEWS RD
EVEREST RD.
HIGHVIEW
WIMBLEDON RD.
MITCHAM
ESHER RD
KINGSTON RD
SURBITON RD
SUTTON RD
CARSHALTON RD
MAULTWAY
HIGHLAND RD
WISHMOOR CL.
DIAMOND RIDGE
UPLAND RD.
CROMWELL RD.
HARTFORD RI.
YORK
KNIGHTSBRIDGE RD
MIDDLETON RD
ASHWELL AV.
MARLBOROUGH RISE
SANDY LA
BRANKSOME PARK RD.
CRAWLEY DRIVE
LIME AV.
IBERIAN WAY
COLLINGWOOD RISE
CHATSWORTH
BEAUFRONT RD
HEIGHTS RD.
HILLCREST
SEYMOUR
HIGHCLERE DR.
ELSENWOOD DR
LARCHWOOD GLADE
GIBBET LANE
RIDGE
DEVONSHIRE DR.
CROSBY HILL DR.
PORTESBERY
PEMBROKE B'WY.
SOUTHWELL PARK
GORDON
UPPER PARK RD.
YOULDEN DR.
A

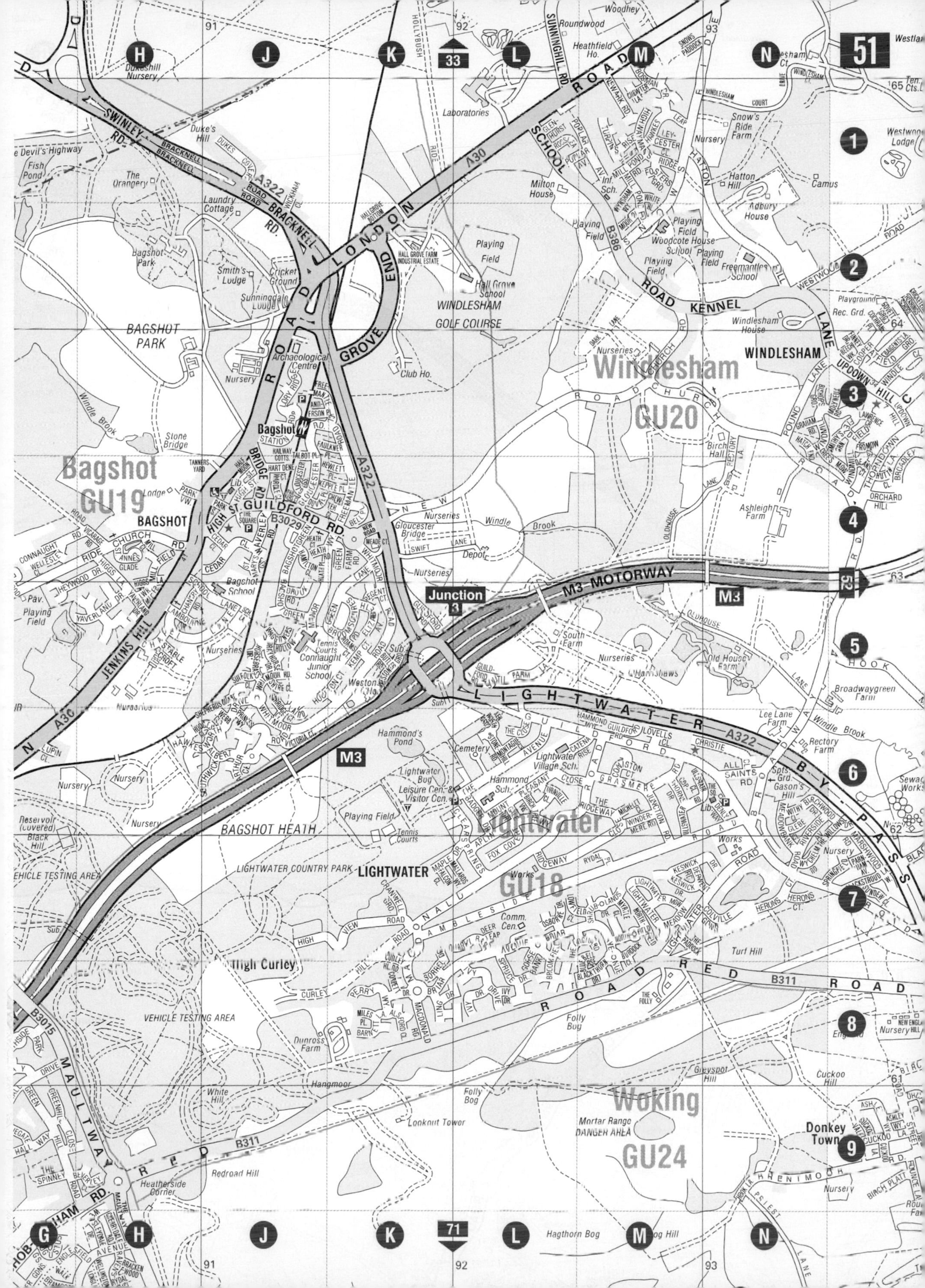
H
J
K
L
M
N
33
71
G
91
92
93
1
2
3
4
5
6
7
8
9
Woodhey
Roundwood
Heathfield Ho.
SUNNINGHILL RD
LONDON ROAD
A30
Dukeshill Nursery
SWINLEY RD.
BRACKNELL ROAD
A322
The Devil's Highway
Fish Pond
Duke's Hill
The Orangery
Laundry Cottage
Bagshot Park
Smith's Lodge
Cricket Ground
Sunningdale Lodge
BAGSHOT PARK
Laboratories
Playing Field
Hall Grove School
WINDLESHAM GOLF COURSE
GROVE END
Archaeological Centre
Club Ho.
Nursery
Windle Brook
Stone Bridge
Bagshot
Bagshot GU19
BAGSHOT
HIGH ST.
BRIDGE RD.
GUILDFORD RD.
B3029
Lodge
CHURCH RD.
CONNAUGHT RD.
HEYWOOD DR.
Playing Field
Pav.
JENKINS HILL
A30
Bagshot School
Nurseries
Connaught Junior School
Weston
Tennis Courts
Junction 3
M3 MOTORWAY
M3
Gloucester Bridge
SWIFT LANE
Depot
Windle Brook
Nurseries
SCHOOL ROAD
B386
Milton House
Inf. Sch.
Playing Field
Woodcote House School
Freemantles School
KENNEL ROAD
Snow's Ride Farm
Nursery
Hatton Hill
Camus
Adbury House
Windlesham House
WINDLESHAM
Windlesham
GU20
CHURCH ROAD
Birch Hall
Nurseries
Playground
Rec. Grd.
UPDOWN HILL
Ashleigh Farm
ORCHARD HILL
South Farm
Old House Farm
Lighthaws
Broadwaygreen Farm
Lee Lane Farm
Windle Brook
Rectory Farm
LIGHTWATER BY-PASS
A322
Hammond's Pond
Cemetery
Lightwater Village Sch.
Hammond Sch.
Lightwater Bog
Leisure Cen. & Visitor Cen.
Playing Field
Tennis Courts
Lightwater
BAGSHOT HEATH
LIGHTWATER COUNTRY PARK
LIGHTWATER
GU18
Works
Nursery
VEHICLE TESTING AREA
Comm. Cen.
Turf Hill
High Curley
HIGH VIEW ROAD
RED ROAD
B311
Folly Bog
Dunross Farm
Hangmoor
Greyspot Hill
Cuckoo Hill
White Hill
Folly Bog
Lookout Tower
Woking
Mortar Range DANGER AREA
GU24
Donkey Town
Redroad Hill
Heatherside Corner
B3015
MAULTWAY
Nursery
BIRCH PLATT
Hagthorn Bog

52
34
72
51
A
B
C
D
E
F
G
1
2
3
4
5
6
7
8
9
94
95
96
65
64
63
62
61
Windlesham
WINDLESHAM
GU20
GU24
GU18
Lightwater
Valley End
Brick Hill
Sparrow Row
WEST END
Penny Pot
Donkey Town
M3 MOTORWAY
M3
A322
A319
B386
B383
B311
LIGHTWATER BY-PASS
GUILDFORD ROAD
BAGSHOT ROAD
RED ROAD
CHERTSEY ROAD
WINDSOR ROAD
KENNEL LANE
WESTWOOD ROAD
UPDOWN HILL
CHURCH ROAD
WOODLANDS LANE
HEATHPARK DRIVE
HIGHAMS LANE
WINDLESHAM ROAD
HALEBOURNE LANE
STEEP LANE
WOODCOCK LANE
SPARROW ROW
CHESTNUT LANE
VALLEY END ROAD
HOOK MILL LANE
GROVE END
RYE GROVE
BLIND LANE
BLACKSTROUD LANE
HOOKSTONE LANE
BRENTMOOR ROAD
BIRCH ROAD
BELDAM BRIDGE RD.
PENNYPOT LANE
SCOTTS GROVE ROAD
CLAPPERS LANE
BENNER LANE
STREETS HEATH
FENNS LANE
Teesdale
High Chimneys
Westlands
Ruddocks Ridge
Ten. Cts.
Long Down
Snow's Ride Farm
Upper Ribsden
Pears Hill
Westwood Lodge
Allerton Hill
Camus
Adbury House
Westwoods
Ribsden Holt
Updown Hill House
Valley End Farm
Coworth Park School
Birch Hill
Offices
Leech Pond
Walk End
Chobham Place Wood
Updown Court
Tennis Courts
Swim. Pool
Playground
Rec. Grd.
Heathpark Wood
Westley Green Fm.
The Old Vicarage
Shergolds Stud Fm.
Valley Wood Place
Highams Fm.
Valley End C. of E. Infants Sch.
Pembroke House
Russell Hill
Nursery
Chobham Place
Oak Wood
Cricket Grnd.
Pavilion
Home Farm House
Ashleigh Farm
Orchard Hill
Windlesham Park
Park Wood
White Bridge
Westcroft Park
Westcroft Farm
Woodlands Farm
Twelve Oaks
Steep Acre Farm
Biddle Farm
Manx Farm
Clappers Brook
Nursy.
Poultry Farm
Buckstone Farm
Broadwaygreen Farm
Halebourne Copse
Lee Lane Farm
Windle Brook
Manor Farm Wood
Shrubb's Farm
Rectory Farm
Manor Farm Cottages
Halebourne House
Higher Park Farm
Sewage Works
Brooklands Farm
Hale Bourne
WINDLEMERE GOLF COURSE
Club Ho.
Hookstone Farm
Hookstone Green
Pankhurst Farm
Brook Place
Turf Hill
Playing Field
Holly Farm
Gordon's School
Streets Heath
The Laurels
New England
Sandpit Hill
Holy Trinity C. of E. Prim. School
Little Barn
Cuckoo Hill
The Oaks
Hatchgate Farm
Ford
Lovelands Farm
Nurseries
Beldam Bridge Farm
Beldam Bri.
Rounce Farm
Fenns Fm.
Rosedene Farm
Scott's Farm
Grove Farm
Trulley Brook
Lucas Green Manor
Trulleys
The Bourne
New Bridge

53
Chertsey
KT16
Woking
GU21
CHOBHAM
Burrowhill
Stonehill
Stanners Hill
MIMBRIDGE
CASTLE GREEN
CHOBHAM COMMON
M3
35
73
54
LONGCROSS ROAD
Longcross House
Fairfields
Lily Pond Farm
Flutters Hill
The Homestead
The Lodge
Upper Childown
Childown
North Lodge
Fish Pond
Pipers Green Stud
Staple Hill
Albury Bottom
The Bee Garden
Gracious Pond
Old Slade
Bee Garden (Earthwork)
RUNNYMEDE
Childown Lodge
Little Fir Clump
Clearmount
Butts Hill
Livery Stables
Gracious Pond Farm
GRACIOUS POND ROAD
Childown Farm Cottage
Langshot Bog
Fish Pond
Ram Bridge
Mossat Farm
Stannershill Farm
Westways Farm
Little Manor Farm
Paradise Farm
Works
Burrow Hill Farm
Woods Farm
WINDSOR ROAD
RED LION ROAD
Little Heath
Chobham Park House
Partridge Farm
Chobham Park Farm
Dunstall Green
Stanyards
Greenacres
Stanners Hill
Stanyards Cottage
Stanyards Farm
Henage Corner
Nursery
Nurseries
Playing Field
B383
Wishmore Cross Sch.
OAKDENE
MINCING LANE
PARK DRIVE
Larkenshaw
Larkenshaw Farm
Records Office
Fishpool Bridge
Sowmoor Plantation
OLD CHERTSEY ROAD
CHERTSEY ROAD
A319
Copyhold
Sow Moor
KALIMA CARAVAN SITE
Millbourne Bridge
Bourne
Mill Bourne
Riverside Nursery
Emmetts Mill
Brooklands Farm
Burnside Nursery
Sunfield Farm
Little Goldbridge Farm
HIGH ST.
(VICARAGE RD.)
School
Cricket Field
Grave Yards
Recreation Ground
Grant's Bridge
Broadford
Broadford Farm
Flexlands School
Piggery
STATION ROAD
A3046
SANDPIT HALL ROAD
Highfield
Milford Green
Nurseries
Warehouse
Sewage Works
SURREY HEATH
WOKING
Cox Hill
Milford House
Milford Farm
Coxhill Green
Border Farm
White Lodge Farm
PHILPOT LANE
Wapshott Farm
Heather Farm
Mim Br.
Shaw's Farm
Scotchers Farm Cotts.
Millbrook Animal Centre
Castle Gn.
Nursery
Drop Pool Farm
CHOBHAM ROAD
Knaphill Manor Farm
Beetle Cottage
Knaphill
Graylands
CARTHOUSE LANE
HORSELL COMMON ROAD
H J K L M N
G H J K L M N
1 2 3 4 5 6 7 8 9
97 98 99 500
65 64 63 62 61

54
A
B
C
D
E
F
G
1
2
3
4
5
6
7
8
9
36
53
74
FOXHILLS GOLF COURSE
HOMEWOOD RESOURCE CENTRE
Chertsey South
The Homestead
The Lodge
Club House
Foxhills Country Club
Garden Cottage
Fox Hills
Foxhills Lodge
Dower House
Upper Childown
Childown
Fish Pond
Budds Cottage
North Lodge
Kitchenride Corner
Kitchenride Cotts.
Penny Farthing Cottage
Homewood Park Open Space
Home Wood
Church Farm
LITTLE GREEN LANE FARM ESTATE
Oracle Pk.
ST. PETER'S
GUILDFORD RD.
A320
HILLSWOOD
Playground
Ether Hill
Great Grove Farm
Stonehill Cottage
Stone Hill
Childown Lodge
Merlewood
STONE HILL ROAD
ACCOMMODATION ROAD
FOXHILLS
Rec. Grd.
Bowling Green
Pav.
Ten Acres
Tennis Courts
OTTERSHAW
MURRAY
B3121
ROAD
Coach House
The Paddock
Queenwood House
Queenwood Farm
Stonehill
A319
CHOBHAM ROAD
Fern Hill
Stanners Hill
South Lodge
Otterbourne Fm.
Tulk House
OTTERSHAW PARK
Timber Hill
The Common
Meath School
Chertsey KT16
Bousley Farm
Otterhill Nursery
Sch.
Brox
Caravan Site
Hawks Hill
Hawks Hill Cottage
Timber Hill
Playing Field
Pav.
Hill Crest
Stanyards
Timber Hill Cotts.
Greenacres
GU24
Tennis Courts
Play. Fld.
Miniature Rifle Range
Brox Copse
Bourne Rise Farm
Brox Wood
Holly Farm
ROSE PARK CARAVAN SITE
Beyond
Stanyards Farm
Stanyards Cottage
Long Copse
Play. Fld.
Little Blackmole Pond
Bramshill
Sandpit Plantation
Gable Cottage
Great Wood
ANNINGSLEY PARK
Samson's Wood
OTTERSHAW PARK
Berwin Park
Beech Hill Clump
Records Office
RUNNYMEDE
SURREY HEATH
South Plantation
The Wey Farm
Great Blackmole Pond
Summerhill
The Warren
Halls
Birch Wood
Grovers Farm
Copyhold
FAIROAKS AIRPORT
CHERTSEY ROAD
Bridge House
Thatch Cottage
Ware Copse
Anningsley Park
Tennis Court
Decoy Plantation
Old Farm
Dunford Ho.
Dunford Bridge
Riverside Nursery
Woking
Bonsey's Bridge
PARAGON TECHNOLOGY CENTRE (UNDER CONSTRUCTION EST. COMP. 2003)
Brooklands Farm
Burnside Nursery
Sunfield Farm
The Bourne
Durnford
The Cottage
Hoyt Wood
The Hoyte
Hoyte Lodge
Club House
Tennis Courts
Durnford Farm
Timber Yard
GU21
Young Stroat Farm
Scotchers Farm
Scotchers Farm Cotts.
Bonseys Cotts.
Bonseys Cotts.
Pinewood Cotts.
Anthonys
MARTYRS
NEW ZEALAND GOLF COURSE
Shaw's Farm
New Houses
A245
LANE
Danewell
Gutter
Danewell Hill
Danewell House
Tennis Courts
The Bishop David Brown Sch.
Play. Fld.
SHEERWATER
Sheerwater Recreation Ground
Running Track
Broadmere Prim. Sch.
Playgrd.
Comm. Cen.
Basingstoke Canal
WOODHAM
HORSELL COMMON
CHERTSEY
WOODHAM HALL ESTATE
Youth
SHORES ROAD
ROAD

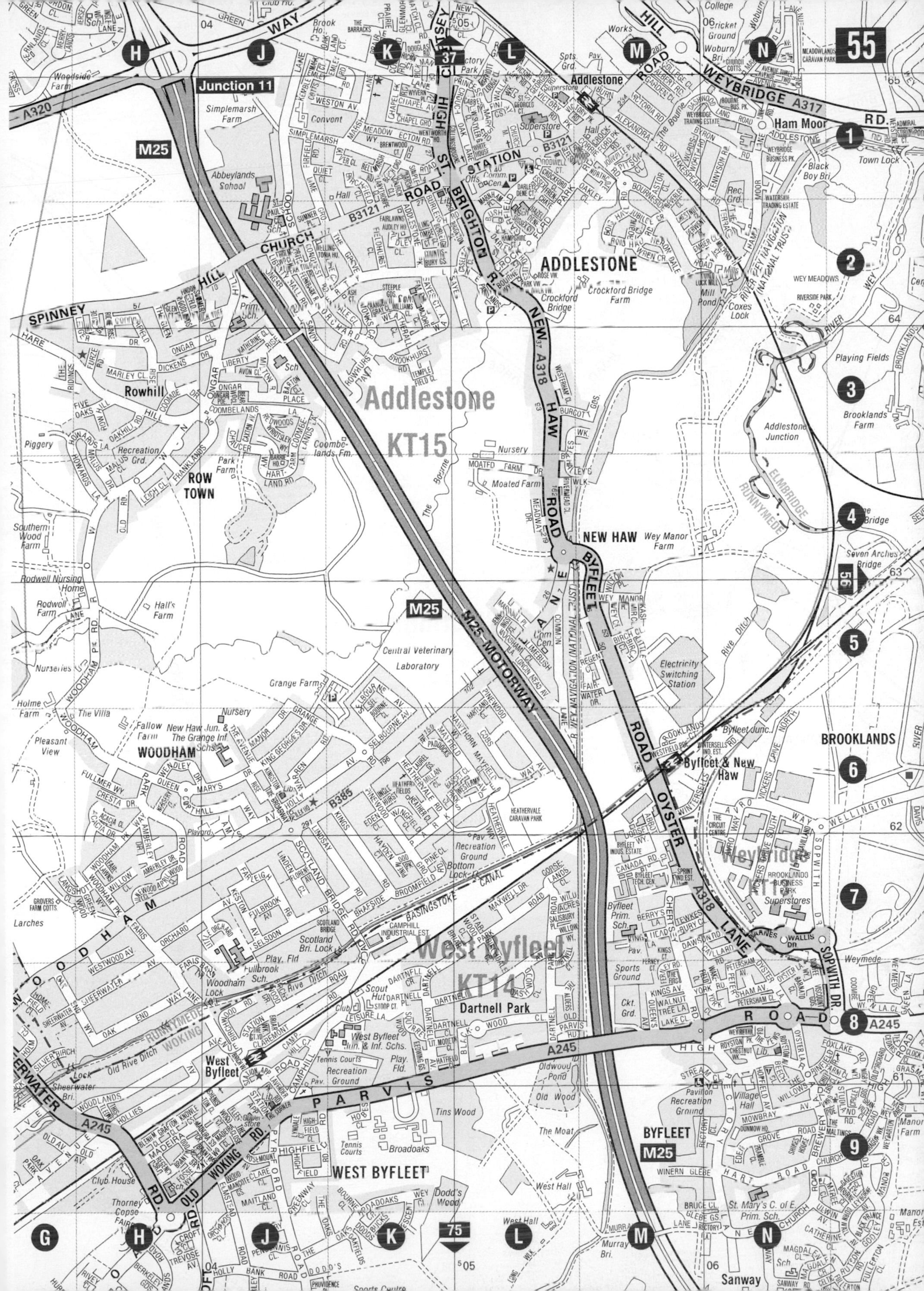

Junction 11
M25
A320
WEYBRIDGE A317
Ham Moor
Addlestone
Simplemarsh Farm
Abbeylands School
Convent
CHURCH ROAD
B3121
STATION ROAD
BRIGHTON RD.
HIGH ST.
CHERTSEY
ADDLESTONE
Crockford Bridge
Crockford Bridge Farm
Mill Pond
Coxes Lock
RIVER WEY NAVIGATION (NATIONAL TRUST)
WEY MEADOWS
RIVERSIDE PARK
Town Lock
Black Boy Bri
Playing Fields
Brooklands Farm
Addlestone Junction
SPINNEY
HILL
Rowhill
Piggery
Recreation Grd.
Park Farm
ROW TOWN
Addlestone
KT15
Coombelands Fm.
Nursery
Moated Farm
NEW HAW ROAD
A318
NEW HAW
Wey Manor Farm
Seven Arches Bridge
56
ELMBRIDGE
RUNNYMEDE
Southern Wood Farm
Rodwell Nursing Home
Rodwell Farm
Hall's Farm
Central Veterinary Laboratory
M25 MOTORWAY
Electricity Switching Station
Grange Farm
Nurseries
Holme Farm
The Villa
Pleasant View
Fallow Farm
New Haw Jun. & The Grange Inf. Schs.
WOODHAM
BYFLEET ROAD
Byfleet Junc.
Byfleet & New Haw
BROOKLANDS
OYSTER LANE
Weybridge
KT13
Superstores
B385
HEATHERVALE CARAVAN PARK
Recreation Ground
BASINGSTOKE CANAL
Larches
Scotland Bri. Lock
Fullbrook Sch.
Woodham Lock
CAMPHILL INDUSTRIAL EST.
West Byfleet
KT14
Dartnell Park
West Byfleet Jun. & Inf. Schs.
Tennis Courts
Recreation Ground
Play. Fld.
A245
PARVIS ROAD
Oldwood Pond
Old Wood
Tins Wood
The Moat
West Hall
Broadoaks
WEST BYFLEET
Dodd's Wood
Sheerwater Bri.
Club House
Thorney Copse
BYFLEET
Pavilion Recreation Ground
Village Hall
St. Mary's C. of E. Prim. Sch.
Byfleet Prim. Sch.
Sports Ground
Ckt. Grd.
Weymede
Manor Farm
Murray Bri.
Sanway
75
G H J K L M N
1 2 3 4 5 6 7 8 9

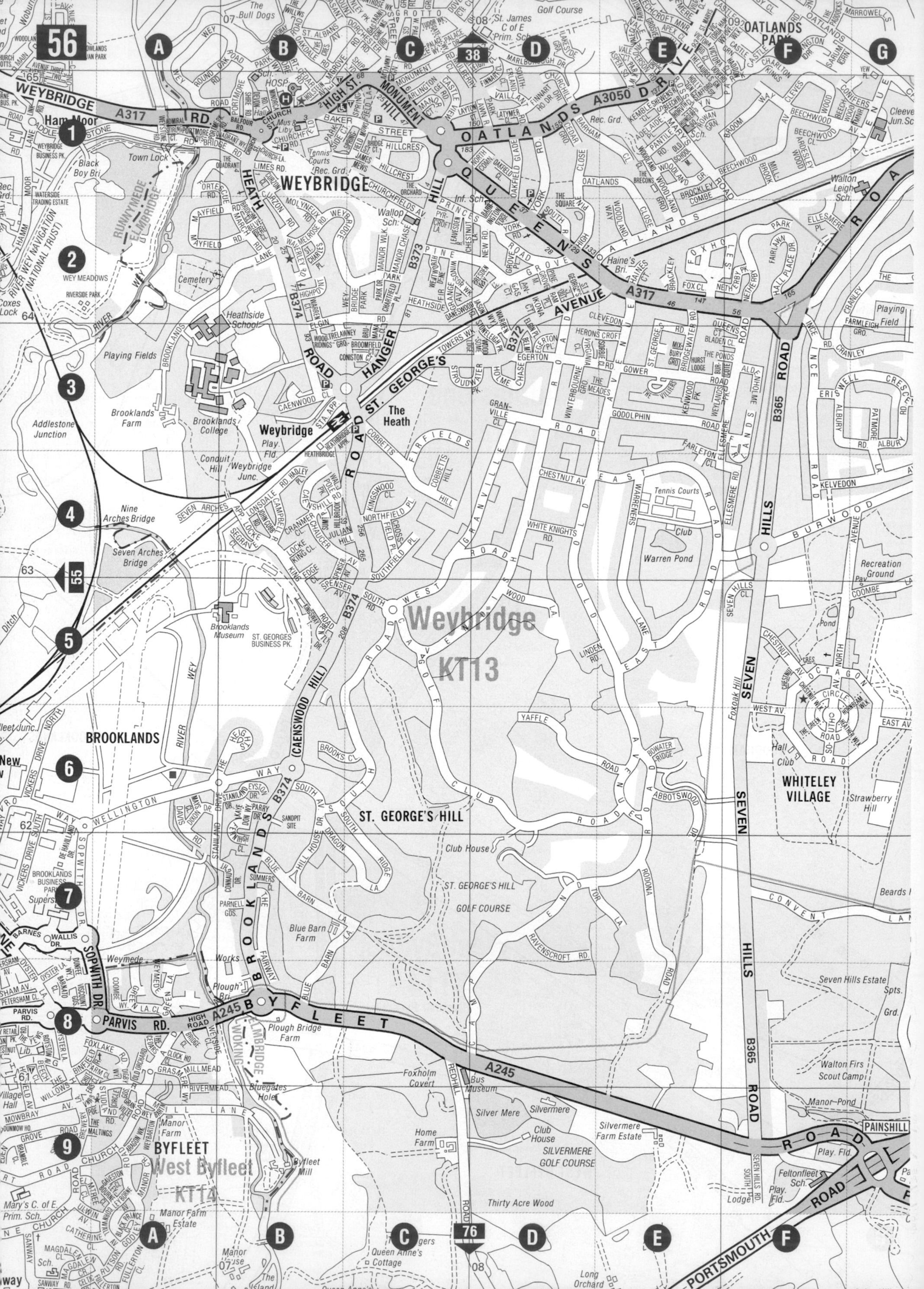
56
38
55
76
A
B
C
D
E
F
G
1
2
3
4
5
6
7
8
9
WEYBRIDGE
Ham Moor
Town Lock
Black Boy Bri.
WATERSIDE TRADING ESTATE
RIVER WEY NAVIGATION (NATIONAL TRUST)
WEY MEADOWS
RIVERSIDE PARK
Coxes Lock
RUNNYMEDE
ELMBRIDGE
Cemetery
Heathside School
Playing Fields
Brooklands Farm
Brooklands College
Addlestone Junction
Weybridge
The Heath
Play Fld.
Conduit Hill
Weybridge Junc.
Nine Arches Bridge
Seven Arches Bridge
Brooklands Museum
ST. GEORGES BUSINESS PK.
Weybridge
KT13
BROOKLANDS
ST. GEORGE'S HILL
Club House
ST. GEORGE'S HILL GOLF COURSE
Blue Barn Farm
Sandpit Site
Works
Plough Bri.
Plough Bridge Farm
Weymede
BROOKLANDS BUSINESS PARK
BYFLEET
West Byfleet
KT14
Manor Farm
Manor Farm Estate
Byfleet Mill
Bluegates Hole
Foxholm Covert
Bus Museum
Silver Mere
Silvermere
Club House
SILVERMERE GOLF COURSE
Silvermere Farm Estate
Home Farm
Thirty Acre Wood
Queen Anne's Cottage
Long Orchard
Warren Pond
Tennis Courts
Club
WHITELEY VILLAGE
Strawberry Hill
Hall
Club
Recreation Ground
Pond
Seven Hills Estate
Walton Firs Scout Camp
Manor Pond
Feltonfleet Sch.
Play. Fld.
Lodge
PAINSHILL
OATLANDS PARK
Golf Course
St. James C of E Prim. Sch.
The Bull Dogs
Rec. Grd.
Tennis Courts
Walton Leigh Sch.
Playing Field
Haine's Bri.
Wallop Sch.
Inf. Sch.
A317
A3050
A245
B374
B373
B372
B365
WEYBRIDGE RD.
HIGH ST.
BAKER STREET
MONUMENT HILL
OATLANDS DRIVE
QUEENS ROAD
HEATH ROAD
HANGER HILL
ST. GEORGE'S AVENUE
BROOKLANDS ROAD
CAENSWOOD HILL
SEVEN HILLS ROAD
BYFLEET ROAD
PORTSMOUTH ROAD
SOPWITH DR.
PARVIS RD.
WELLINGTON WAY
CHURCH RD.
BURWOOD ROAD
CONVENT LANE
ST. GEORGE'S HILL
Mary's C. of E. Prim. Sch.
Magdalen Sch.

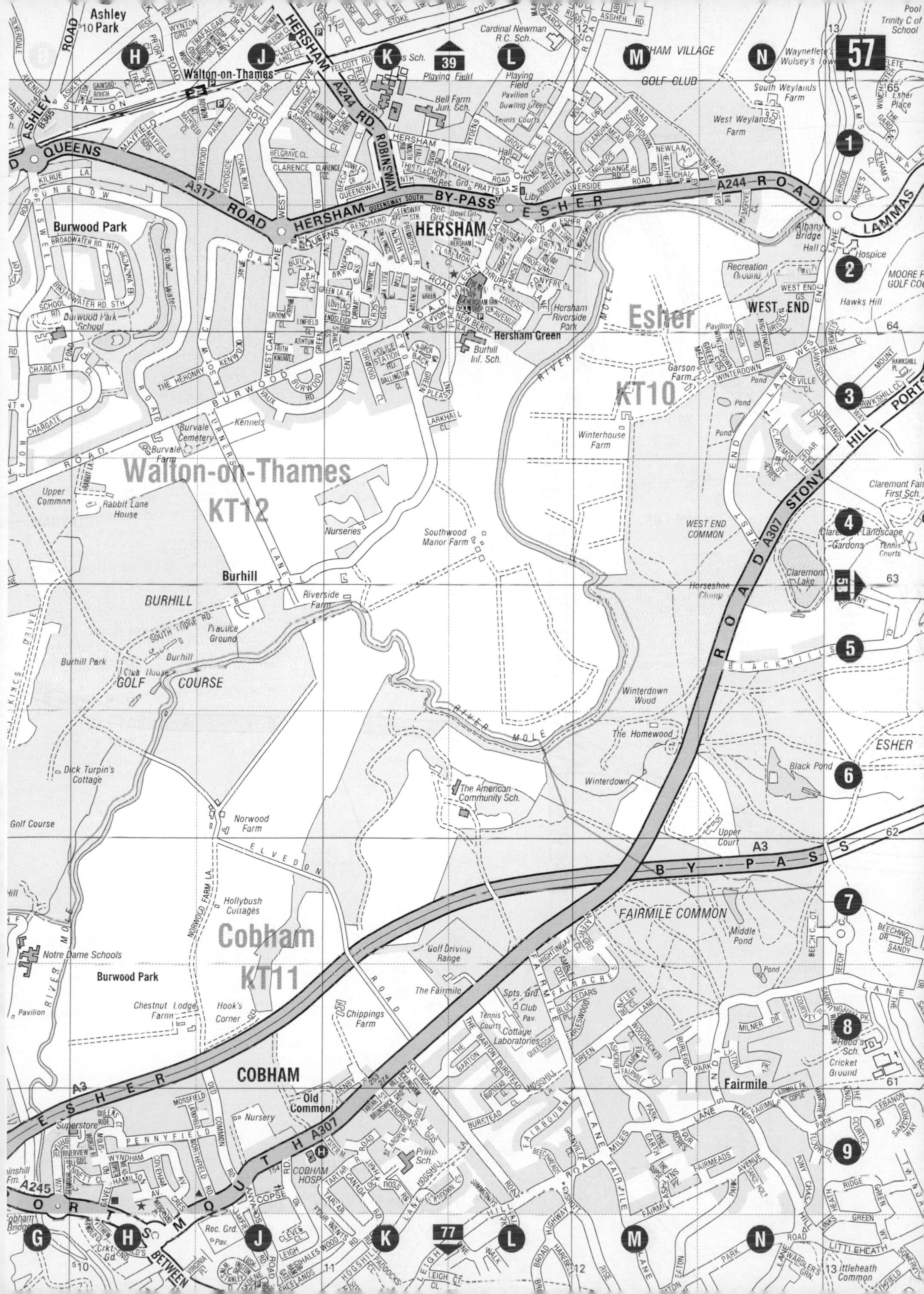

57
Ashley Park
Walton-on-Thames
Cardinal Newman R.C. Sch.
Playing Field
39
Bell Farm Jun. Sch.
Golf Club
South Weylands Farm
West Weylands Farm
Esher Place
Queens Road
A317
Hersham By-Pass
Esher Road
A244
Burwood Park
Burwood Park School
Hersham
Hersham Green
Hersham Riverside Park
Burhill Inf. Sch.
Esher
West End
KT10
Hospice
Hawks Hill
Moore Place Golf Course
Garson Farm
Winterhouse Farm
Burvale Cemetery
Burvale Farm
Kennels
Upper Common
Rabbit Lane House
Walton-on-Thames
KT12
Nurseries
Southwood Manor Farm
West End Common
Claremont Fan First Sch.
Claremont Landscape Gardens
Claremont Lake
Horseshoe Clump
58
Burhill
Riverside Farm
Practice Ground
Burhill Park
Golf Course
Club House
River Mole
Winterdown Wood
The Homewood
Black Pond
Esher
Winterdown
Dick Turpin's Cottage
The American Community Sch.
Norwood Farm
Upper Court
A3
Esher By-Pass
Stony Hill Road
A307
Fairmile Common
Middle Pond
Hollybush Cottages
Cobham
KT11
Golf Driving Range
Notre Dame Schools
Burwood Park
The Fairmile
Spts. Grd.
Club Pav.
Tennis Courts
Cottage Laboratories
Chestnut Lodge Farm
Hook's Corner
Chippings Farm
Reed's Sch.
Cricket Ground
Fairmile
Cobham
Old Common
Nursery
Superstore
Cobham Hosp
Prim. Sch.
Portsmouth Road
A245
Rec. Grd.
Pav.
Crkt. Gd.
77
Littleheath Common

58
A
B
C
D
E
F
G
1
2
3
4
5
6
7
8
9
13
14
15
16
65
64
63
62
61
40
57
78
Pool
Trinity C of E School
Grand Stand
Littleworth Common
Ski Slope
The Warren
Esher Place
Weylands Farm
ESHER
Civic Centre
Sandown
HINCHLEY WOOD
Hinchley Wood
Pavilion
Sports Grd.
Tennis Courts
Littlemead
Cricket Ground
Nursery
Albany Bridge
Hall
Hospice
Club Ho.
Recreation Ground
MOORE PLACE GOLF COURSE
Hawks Hill
WEST END
Claygate Ho.
Bowling Green
Harelane Grn.
Wingham Lodge
Slough Farm
Prim. Sch.
School
Play. Fld.
The Lake
CLARE HILL GOLF COURSE
Loseberry
Claygate
Loseberry Farm
Milbourne Lodge Sch.
Claremont Fan Ct. Middle Sch.
Claremont Fan Ct. First Sch.
Claremont Park
Stable Pond
Esher
KT10
Claygate Prim. Sch.
Recreation Ground
CLAYGATE
Rowan Prep. Sch.
Claremont Landscape Gardens
Tennis Courts
Claremont Lake
Arbrook Common
CLAYGATE COMMON
Oak Cottage
Vale Farm
Horridon Farm
Arbrook Farm
Round Hill
ESHER COMMON
ESHER COMMON
Holroyd's Plantation
Birch Wood
Great Oaks
Milbournehold
Plantation
Leatherhead
Limekiln Wood
Old Carpenter Plantation
Stokesheath Farm Cottages
KT22
Middle Pond
Pond
The Milbournehold Wood
Heckets
Brickyard Plantation
NEW WOOD
Cobham
Fairmile
Reed's Sch.
Cricket Ground
OXSHOTT
HEATH
Oxshott
Pinewoods Ho.
OXSHOTT
Stoke Wood
Jessop's Well
PRINCE'S COVERTS
KT11
Sch.
Adecroft Furze Field
Tennis Courts
Rec. Grd
Sch.
Littleheath Common
D'Abernon Cottage
PORTSMOUTH ROAD
STONY HILL
LAMMAS LA.
HIGH ST.
A244
A307
A3
ESHER BY-PASS
COPSEM LANE
WARREN LANE
FAIROAK LANE
SANDY LANE
BLACKHILLS
MEADWAY
LITTLEWORTH ROAD
OAKEN LANE
HARE LANE
CHURCH RD.
B280
NEW ROAD
BIRCHWOOD
STOKESHEATH
HIGH ST. LEATHERHEAD

59
HOOK
SURBITON GOLF COURSE
A3
BY-PASS
CLAYTON
Playing Field
Lovelace Prim. Sch.
Manor Farm House
Lower Wood
Manor Farm
Elm Farm
EMBRIDGE
KINGSTON upon THAMES
Chessington North
Four Oaks Centre
Buckland Inf. Sch.
Moor Lane Jun. Sch.
CHESSINGTON
Church Fields Recreation Ground
Chessington South
GARRISON
CHESSINGTON GOLF CENTRE
Chessington
KT9
Barwell Court
Barwell Farm
Recreation Ground
Sports Ground
Winey Hill
BARWELL BUSINESS PARK
Chessington & Hook United F.C.
CHALKY LA.
Main Entrance
Zoo
CHESSINGTON WORLD OF ADVENTURES
South Entrance
Park Farm
Sixty Acre Wood
Castle Hill
Butcher's Grove
HORTON COUNTRY PARK
Four Acre Wood
KT19
Horton Park Children's Farm
Pond Wood
Aeronautical Radio Station
KINGSTON upon THAMES
EPSOM and EWELL
Electricity Sub-Station
Jubilee Wood
Chessington Wood
Acre Hill Farmhouse
THE NEW EPSOM & EWELL COTTAGE HOSPITAL
West Park Farm
Epsom
West Park Hospital, Parklands Day Hospital
MALDEN RUSHETT
RUSHETT B280
LANE
CHRIST CHURCH B280
SILVERGLADE BUSINESS PARK
Byhurst Farm
Glanmire Farm
Hollywood Lodge
Stamford Green Prim. Sch.
Stamford Green
Bunkers Hill
Rushett Farm
Stew Pond
KT18
LEATHERHEAD
A243
Telegraph Hill
Reservoir (Covered)
Newton Wood
79
EPSOM COMMON
G H J K L M N
17 18 19
1 2 3 4 5 6 7 8 9
65 64 63 62 61

A
B
C
D
E
F
G
1
2
3
4
5
6
7
8
9
20
21
22
165
64
63
62
61
42
59
201
80
Chessington
KT9
KT19
KT17
STONELEIGH
WEST EWELL
EWELL
Epsom
EPSOM
Horton
Stamford Green
Stoneleigh
Ewell West
Ewell East
BEGGAR'S HILL
ORGAN CROSSROADS
KINGSTON upon THAMES
EPSOM and EWELL
KINGSTON ROAD
A240
A24
B284
B2200
B280
A2022
B288
B290
RUXLEY LANE
CHESSINGTON ROAD
HOOK ROAD
LONG GROVE
LONGMEAD ROAD
EWELL BY-PASS
LONDON ROAD
REIGATE ROAD
CHEAM ROAD
EAST ST.
EPSOM RD.
HIGH ST.
SPRING ST.
ALEXANDRA ROAD
CHRIST CHURCH ROAD
WEST HILL
COLLEGE
King George's Field Playing Field
Tolworth Court Farm
Tolworth Court Bridge
Wandgas Athletic Ground
Cuddington Prim. Sch.
Cuddington Recreation Ground
Auriol Park
Riverview C.of E. Prim. Sch.
Sports Ground
Epsom & Ewell High Sch.
West Ewell Inf. Sch.
Playing Field
Hogsmill River
Chamber Mead
HORTON PARK GOLF & COUNTRY CLUB
HORTON COUNTRY PARK
Butcher's Grove
Hook Arena
St. Ebba's Farm Cottage
Cemetery
Bourne Hall Museum
Highway House
Gibraltar Rec.Grd.
Sewage Wks.
Glyn Tech. Sch.
Hatch Furlong
Cherry Orchard Farm
Ewell Castle Sch.
Priest Hill Cotts.
NESCOT Epsom's College of Further & Higher Education
Horton Park Children's Farm
West Park Farm
Longmead Business Cen.
Rainbow Leisure Centre
Court Recreation Grd.
Stamford Green Prim. Sch.
Kingswood Ho. Sch.
Ashley Centre
Wallace Fields Jun. Sch.
The Downs Farm

61
NORTH CHEAM
Worcester Park
KT4
SM3
QUEEN VICTORIA
A24 ROAD
MALDEN ROAD
A2043
43
ST. DUNSTAN'S HILL
A217
Westbourne Prim. Sch.
Collingwood Road Recreation Ground
Sutton United F.C.
West Sutton
SM1
SUTTON
Water Works
CHEAM ROAD A232
Sutton Cricket Ground
Sutton
HIGH ST.
ST. NICHOLAS
THROWLEY
CARSHALTON ROAD
Cheam Recreation Ground
Bowling Green
Oak Plantation
London Road Plantation
EPSOM and EWELL
SUTTON
NONSUCH PARK
Mansion House
Nonsuch Park
CHEAM PARK
CHEAM
ST. DUNSTAN'S
CHEAM VILLAGE
EWELL RD.
Cheam
Nonsuch High Sch. for Girls
Harefield Playing Field
Warren Fm.
BURDON LANE
BELMONT RISE
Sutton
BELMONT
Overton Grange High Sch.
Sports Ground
SUTTON GENERAL HOSPITAL
THE ROYAL MARSDEN HOSP. (SUTTON)
Rugby Football Grd.
SM2
The Avenue Prim. Sch.
Belmont
EAST EWELL
A232
Sports Ground
Priest Hill
Sports Centre
Greenacres
CUDDINGTON GOLF COURSE
REIGATE and BANSTEAD
BANSTEAD DOWNS
BANSTEAD DOWNS GOLF COURSE
BRIGHTON ROAD A217
H.M.P. HIGHDOWN
Resr. (Covered)
Reservoir (covered)
North Looe
North Looe Farm
The Looe
Banstead
Golf Course
SM7
Gally Hills Tumuli
COTSWOLD RD.
B2218
B2230
Banstead
81
WINKWORTH ROAD
Littlecroft
DRIFT BRIDGE
G
H
J
K
L
M
N
1
2
3
4
5
6
7
8
9
62
63
64
65
23
24
25
26

62
44
82
61
CARSHALTON
SUTTON
Sutton
SM1
SM2
Carshalton SM5
Banstead SM7
Coulsdon CR5
Carshalton
Wallington
Carshalton Beeches
CARSHALTON BEECHES
CARSHALTON ON THE HILL
WOODCOTE GREEN
LITTLE WOODCOTE
THE OAKS PARK
OAKS SPORTS CENTRE GOLF COURSE
WOODCOTE PARK GOLF COURSE
H.M.P. HIGHDOWN
H.M.P. DOWNVIEW
SUTTON GENERAL HOSPITAL
THE ROYAL MARSDEN HOSP. (SUTTON)
CARSHALTON WAR MEMORIAL HOSP.
Merton & Sutton Comm. N.H.S. Trust H.Q.
Biological Research Labs.
Diamond Riding Centre
Carshalton Athletic F.C.
Westcroft Leisure Cen.
The Grove
CARSHALTON PARK
The Frying Pan
Hogpit Pond
Manor Park
Benhill Rec. Grd.
St. Philomenas Convent
Stowford College
Seaton Ho. Prep. Sch.
White Lodge
Little Holland Ho.
Orchard Hill
Banstead Mobility Cen.
Woodland Craft Centre
South Lodge
Hunters Field Farm
Fairlawn Farm
The Oaks Farm
Little Woodcote Estate
Little Woodcote Farm
Old Lodge Farm
Lower Pillory Downs
Woodcote Grove House
Orford House
Hylands Nurseries
Ruffet Wood
Caravan Park
Sports Ground
High Sch. for Girls
Playing Fields
CARSHALTON ROAD
CROYDON LANE
CROYDON ROAD
WOODMANSTERNE LANE
WOODMANSTERNE LA.
LITTLE WOODCOTE
BANSTEAD ROAD
BEECHES AV.
PARK HILL
RUSKIN ROAD
GROSVENOR AVENUE
GROSVENOR RD.
STANLEY PARK ROAD
BOUNDARY RD.
WOODCOTE ROAD
MANOR ROAD
LONDON RD.
HIGH ST.
BRIGHTON ROAD
SUTTON LANE
COTSWOLD RD.
CHILTERN ROAD
THROWLEY WAY
WEST ST.
NORTH ST.
POUND ST.
ACRE LA.
A232
A237
A2022
B278
B271
B2218
B2230
A
B
C
D
E
F
G
1
2
3
4
5
6
7
8
9
26
27
28
29
61
62
63
64
65

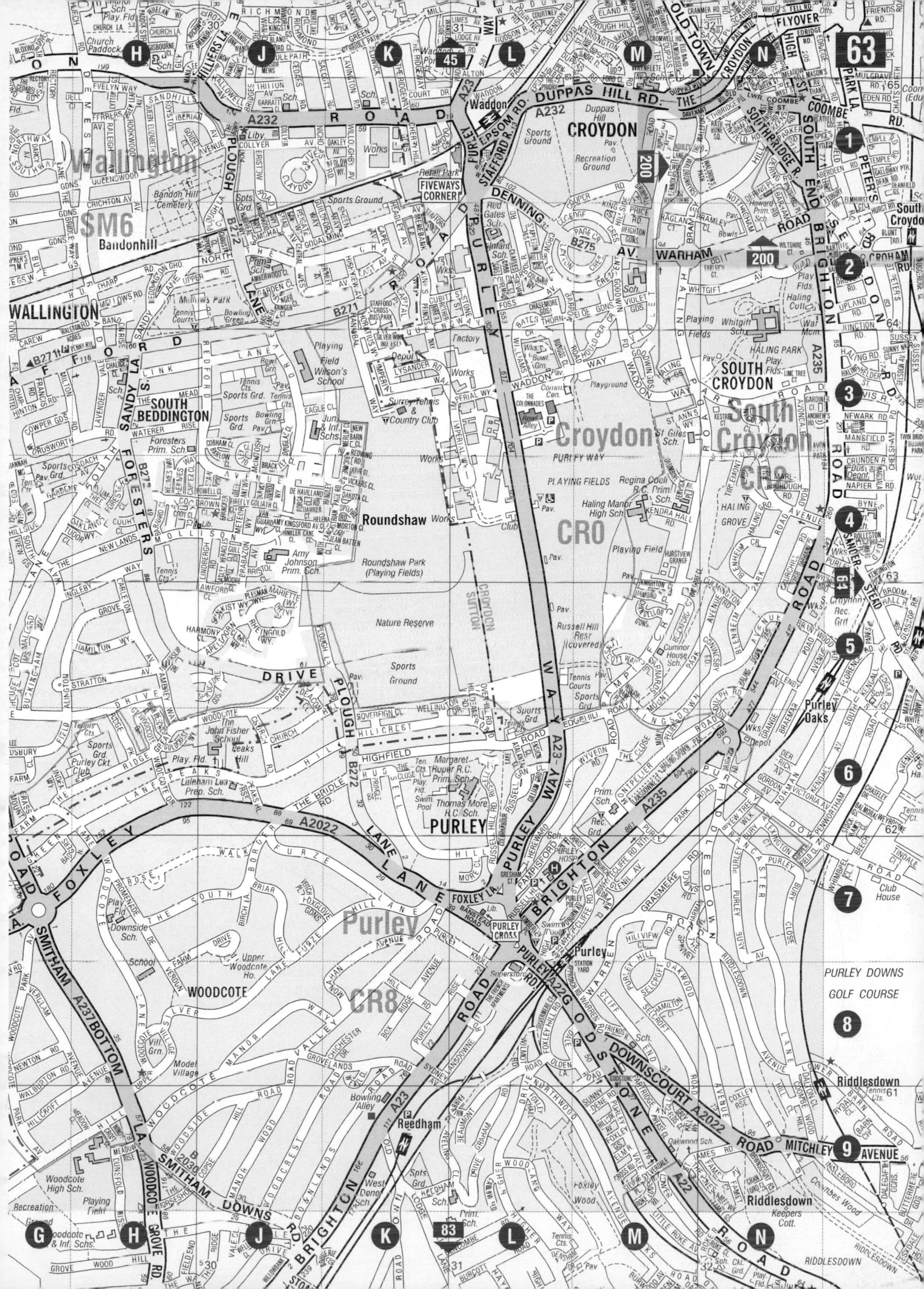

45
200
61
83
H
J
K
L
M
N
G
1
2
3
4
5
6
7
8
9
Wallington
WALLINGTON
SM6
Bandonhill
Bandon Hill Cemetery
SOUTH BEDDINGTON
Roundshaw
Roundshaw Park (Playing Fields)
Nature Reserve
Sports Ground
CROYDON
SUTTON
Waddon
FIVEWAYS CORNER
Retail Park
Duppas Hill
Recreation Ground
Sports Ground
CROYDON
OLD TOWN
FLYOVER
Croydon
CR0
PURLEY WAY PLAYING FIELDS
Haling Manor High Sch.
Regina Coeli R.C. Prim. Sch.
SOUTH CROYDON
South Croydon
HALING PARK Play. Flds.
Whitgift Sch.
HALING GROVE
Russell Hill Resr (covered)
Purley Oaks
PURLEY
Purley
PURLEY CROSS
Purley
CR8
WOODCOTE
Upper Woodcote Ho.
Model Village
Downside Sch.
Woodcote High Sch.
Reedham
Foxley Wood
Riddlesdown
RIDDLESDOWN
PURLEY DOWNS GOLF COURSE
Club House
The John Fisher School
Peaks Hill
Laleham Lea Prep. Sch.
Amy Johnson Prim. Sch.
Wilson's School
Surrey Tennis & Country Club
Foresters Prim. Sch.
Thomas More R.C. Sch.
Margaret Roper R.C. Prim. Sch.
Purley Ckt. Club
A232
A23
A235
A2022
A237
A22
B271
B272
B275
B278
ROAD
DUPPAS HILL RD.
DENNING AV.
WARHAM
PURLEY WAY
BRIGHTON ROAD
FOXLEY LANE
PLOUGH LANE
STAFFORD RD.
SANDY LA.
FORESTERS DRIVE
MOLLISON DRIVE
HIGHFIELD RD.
SOUTHRIDGE R.
SOUTH END
SANDERSTEAD RD.
MITCHLEY AVENUE
DOWNSCOURT ROAD
GODSTONE ROAD
SMITHAM BOTTOM LA.
SMITHAM DOWNS RD.
WOODCOTE GROVE RD.
WOODCOTE VALLEY ROAD
PARK LA.
COOMBE RD.
CROHAM RD.

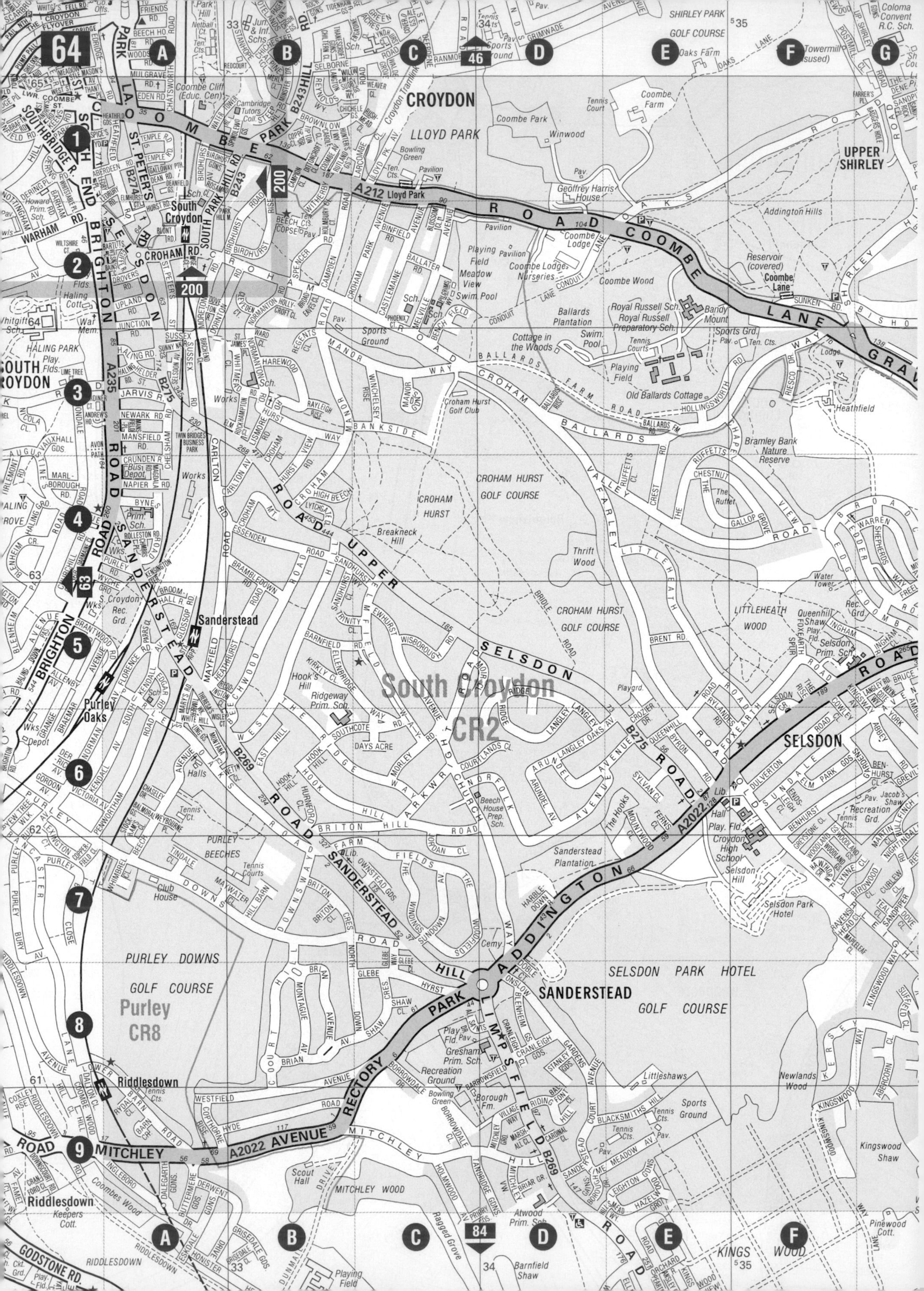

CROYDON
LLOYD PARK
Lloyd Park
SOUTH CROYDON
South Croydon
UPPER SHIRLEY
SHIRLEY PARK GOLF COURSE
Coombe Farm
Coombe Park
Coombe Wood
Addington Hills
Royal Russell Sch.
Royal Russell Preparatory Sch.
Ballards Plantation
Cottage in the Woods
Old Ballards Cottage
Croham Hurst Golf Club
CROHAM HURST GOLF COURSE
CROHAM HURST
Breakneck Hill
Thrift Wood
Bramley Bank Nature Reserve
LITTLEHEATH WOOD
South Croydon CR2
SELSDON
Selsdon Park Hotel
SELSDON PARK HOTEL GOLF COURSE
SANDERSTEAD
Sanderstead
Sanderstead Plantation
PURLEY BEECHES
PURLEY DOWNS GOLF COURSE
Purley CR8
Purley Oaks
Riddlesdown
MITCHLEY WOOD
Kingswood Shaw
Newlands Wood
KINGS WOOD
A212
A235
A2022
B269
B275
COOMBE ROAD
UPPER SELSDON ROAD
ADDINGTON ROAD
BRIGHTON ROAD
SANDERSTEAD ROAD
MITCHLEY AVENUE

46
200
63
84

65
ADDINGTON GOLF COURSE
ADDINGTON PALACE GOLF COURSE
Addington Palace
ADDINGTON
ADDINGTON PARK
Addington Village
SPRING PARK
ADDINGTON VILLAGE RD.
ADDINGTON WAY A2022
KENT GATE
GRAVEL HILL A212
SELSDON PARK ROAD A2022
West Wickham
BR4
Croydon
CR0
NEW ADDINGTON
ADDINGTON COURT NEW GOLF COURSE
ADDINGTON COURT OLD GOLF COURSE
FORESTDALE
SELSDON WOOD
(Nature Reserve)
FARLEIGH COURT GOLF COURSE
Warlingham CR6
CROYDON
TANDRIDGE
BROMLEY
Wickham Court
Emmaus Conference Centre
St. John Rigby R.C. College
Coney Hall Rec. Grd.
Applegarth Jun. & Inf. Schs.
Gilbert Scott Jun. & Inf. Schs.
Monks Hill Sports Centre
John Ruskin College
Forestdale Prim. Sch.
Courtwood Prim. Sch.
Greenvale Prim. Sch.
Rowdown Primary School
Fairchildes Prim. Sch.
Wolsey Junr. & Inf. Schs.
Fieldway
King Henry's Dr.
New Addington
FRITH WOOD
PUPLET WOOD
FRYLANDS WOOD
(Scout Camp)
Bears Wood
(Scout Camp)
Birchen Shaw
Dumpsy Derry
Crab Wood
Limekiln Shaw
Coldblow Shaw
Bograms Wood
Chapel Hill
Hutchinson's Bank Nature Reserve
Threecorner Grove
Gushyfank Shaw
FICKLESHOLE
Fickleshole Farm
Farleigh
Little Farleigh Green Farm
47
85
99

CONEY HALL
West Wickham
BR4
West Wickham Common
HAYES COMMON
CROYDON ROAD
A232
Bromley BR2
KESTON
HEATHFIELD
Keston C.of E. Prim. Sch.
Forest Lodge
FISHPONDS ROAD
KESTON COMMON
Wickham Court
Emmaus Conference Centre
St. John Rigby R.C. College
Wickham Court Farm
The Cottages
The Bungalows
Well Wood
Rouse Farm
Arlington Orchard
Keston Court Riding School
Hast Hill
Baston Manor
Elm Farm
NASH
Nash Farm
North Pole Farm
Cooper's Wood
Long Shaw
Waytes
Fuller's Wood
James's Wood
Baldwin Shaw
Bradmanshill Wood
Fox Hill Nursery
Jackass Shaw
Foxhill Fm.
Leafy Grove
Knightons
War Bank
WESTERHAM ROAD
Wilberforce Oak
The Temple (Roman Mausoleum)
Keston Court Farm
Milchden
CHURCH LANE
Glebe Farm
Westerham Lodge
DOWNE ROAD
Keston BR2
Rushfield Shaw
Metropolitan Police Dog Training Establishment
Broomfieldbank Shaw
NEW ADDINGTON
Pitch and Putt Golf Course
Electricity Sub Station
Layham's Farm
Longlands Nurseries
Kimberley Poultry Farm
A233
Furze Bottom
Vale Farm
Works
Factory
Warehouses
Sports Ground
Greyhound Training Kennels
Croydon CR0
West Wickham Res. (Covered)
Hoppershatch Shaw
Highams Hill
Higham's Hill
Warlingham
CR6
Jewels Wood
SHEEPBARN LANE
Fairchildes Prim. Sch.
Addington High Sch.
Fairchildes Cotts.
Playing Field
Colinette Farm
High House Farm
Bradmoor
Greenacres Riding Sch.
LEAVES GREEN
The Green
Milking Lane Farm
Passenger Terminal
LONDON - BIGGIN HILL AIRPORT
Babington Place
Gasholder Station
Westerham TN16
MAIN ROAD
SALTBOX HILL
North Lodge
South Lodge
Fairchildes Farm
Blackmans Cotts.
Coxs Cottage
FICKLESHOLE
Fickleshole Farm
South London
65
86

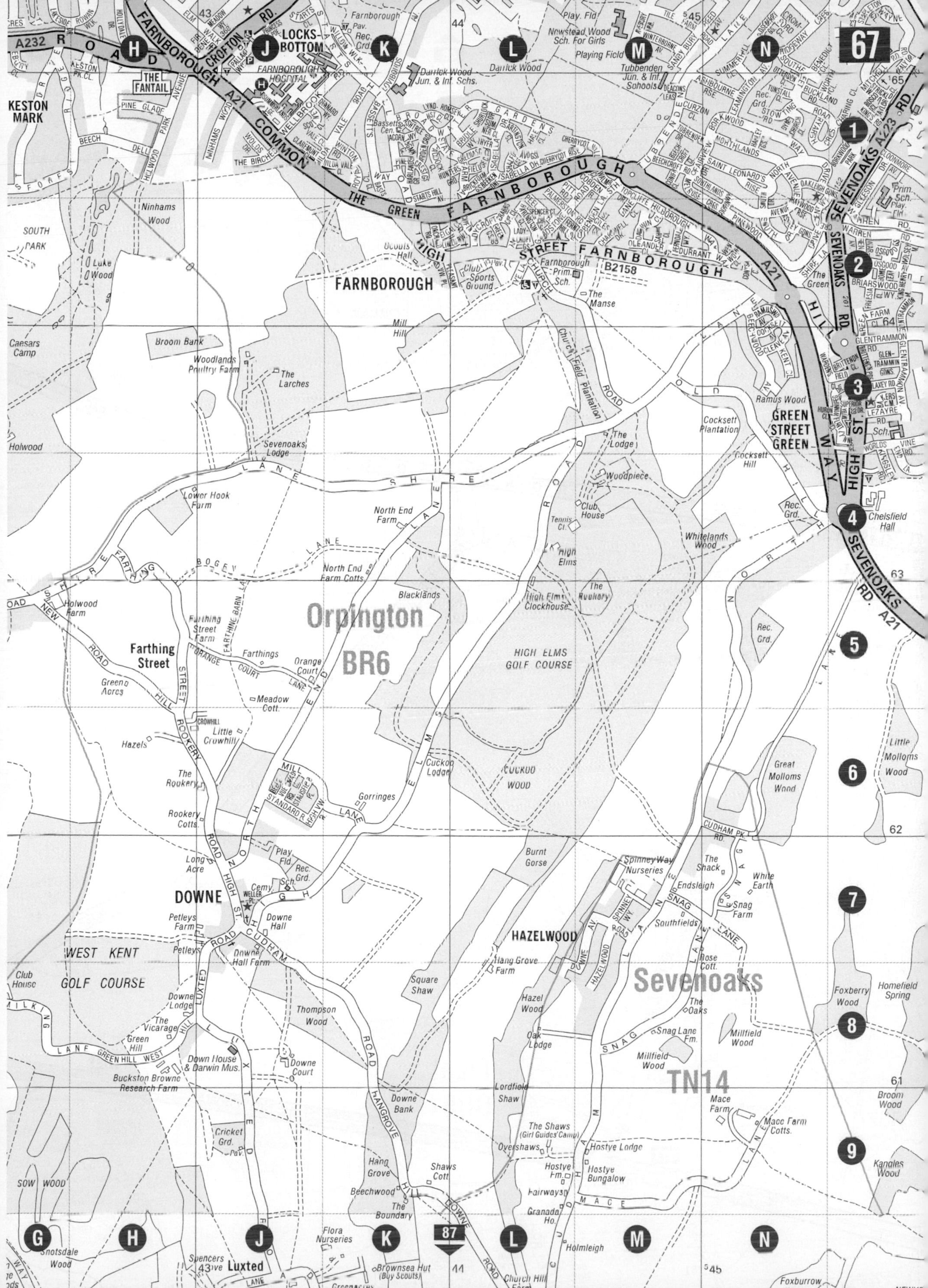
FARNBOROUGH
A21 COMMON
THE GREEN
FARNBOROUGH
HIGH STREET FARNBOROUGH
B2158
A232
KESTON MARK
LOCKS-BOTTOM
FARNBOROUGH HOSPITAL
THE FANTAIL
Darrick Wood
Darrick Wood Jun. & Inf. Schs.
Newstead Wood Sch. For Girls
Playing Field
Tubbenden Jun. & Inf. Schools
Ninhams Wood
SOUTH PARK
Luke Wood
Caesars Camp
Broom Bank
Woodlands Poultry Farm
The Larches
Mill Hill
Church Field Plantation
The Manse
Holwood
Sevenoaks Lodge
SHIRE LANE
Lower Hook Farm
North End Farm
BOGEY LANE
North End Farm Cotts
Holwood Farm
Farthing Street
Farthing Street Farm
Farthings
Orange Court
Blacklands
Orpington
BR6
HIGH ELMS GOLF COURSE
High Elms Clockhouse
The Rookery
High Elms
Club House
Woodpiece
The Lodge
Cocksett Plantation
Cocksett Hill
Ramus Wood
GREEN STREET GREEN
Whitelands Wood
Rec. Grd.
Chelsfield Hall
SEVENOAKS RD. A21
SEVENOAKS WAY
Greeno Acres
Meadow Cott.
Hazels
Little Crowhill
The Rookery
Rookery Cotts.
Cuckoo Lodge
CUCKOO WOOD
Gorringes
Great Molloms Wood
Little Molloms Wood
Burnt Gorse
Spinney Way Nurseries
The Shack
White Earth
Endsleigh
Snag Farm
Southfields
DOWNE
Long Acre
Petleys Farm
Downe Hall
Downe Hall Farm
WEST KENT GOLF COURSE
Club House
HAZELWOOD
Hang Grove Farm
Square Shaw
Hazel Wood
Rose Cott.
Sevenoaks
The Oaks
Foxberry Wood
Homefield Spring
Thompson Wood
Oak Lodge
Snag Lane Fm.
Millfield Wood
Downe Lodge
The Vicarage
Green Hill
Down House & Darwin Mus.
Downe Court
Buckston Browne Research Farm
Lordfield Shaw
TN14
Mace Farm
Mace Farm Cotts.
Broom Wood
Downe Bank
The Shaws (Girl Guides' Camp)
Overshaws
Hostye Lodge
Hostye Fm.
Hostye Bungalow
Kangles Wood
Cricket Grd.
SOW WOOD
Hang Grove
Shaws Cott
Beechwood
The Boundary
Fairways
Granada Ho.
Holmleigh
Snotsdale Wood
Flora Nurseries
Brownsea Hut (Boy Scouts)
Spencers Grove
Luxted
Greenacres
Church Hill Farm
Foxburrow Wood
87
G H J K L M N
1 2 3 4 5 6 7 8 9

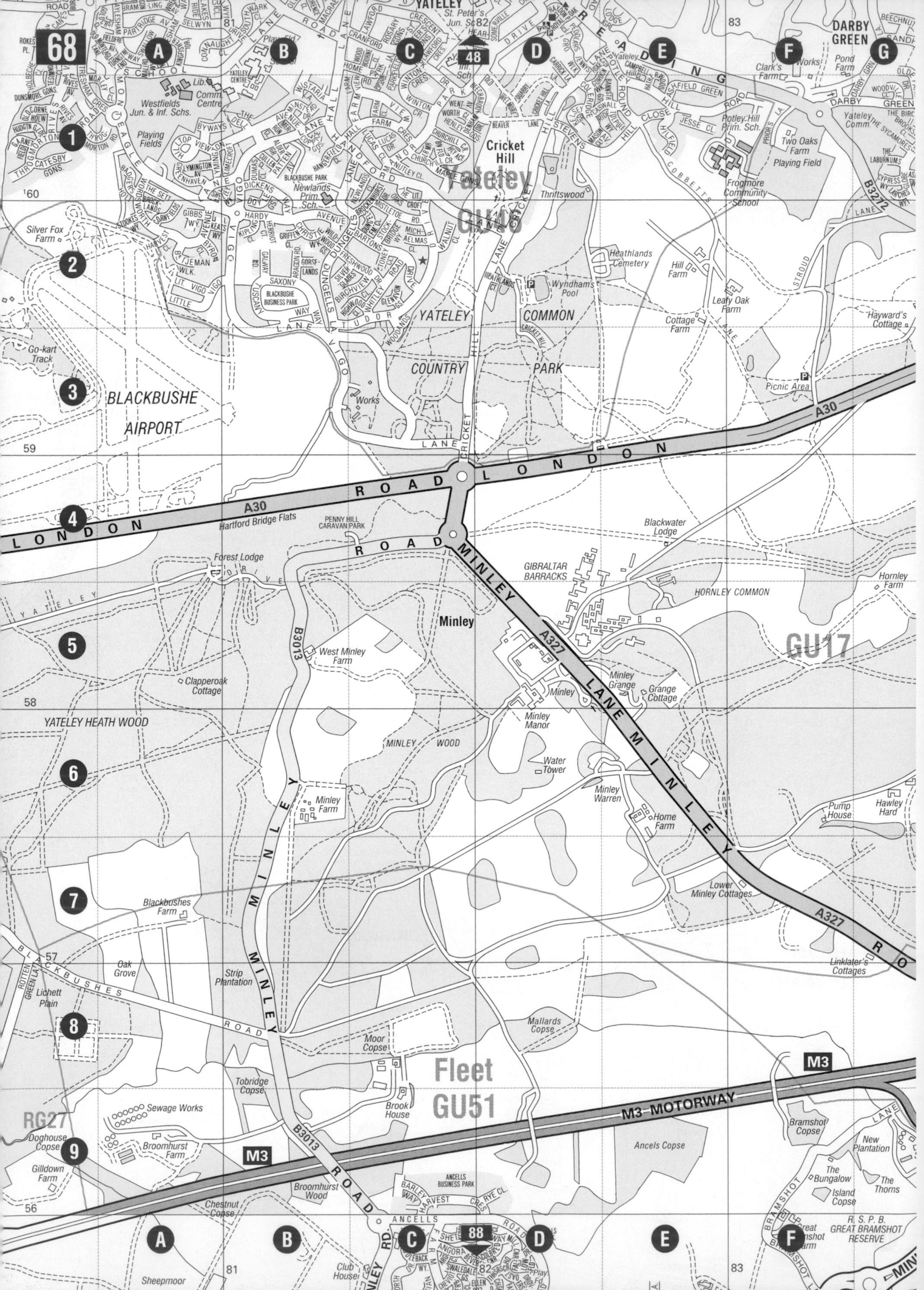
YATELEY
St. Peter's Jun. Sch.
48
DARBY GREEN
Westfields Jun. & Inf. Schs.
Playing Fields
Lib.
Comm. Centre
Cricket Hill
Yateley GU46
Newlands Prim. Sch.
Frogmore Community School
Potley Hill Prim. Sch.
Two Oaks Farm
Playing Field
Clark's Farm
Pond Farm
Thriftswood
Silver Fox Farm
Heathlands Cemetery
Hill Farm
Leafy Oak Farm
Wyndham's Pool
YATELEY COMMON COUNTRY PARK
Cottage Farm
Hayward's Cottage
Go-kart Track
BLACKBUSHE AIRPORT
BLACKBUSHE BUSINESS PARK
Works
Picnic Area
A30
LONDON ROAD
Hartford Bridge Flats
PENNY HILL CARAVAN PARK
Forest Lodge
Blackwater Lodge
GIBRALTAR BARRACKS
Hornley Farm
HORNLEY COMMON
Minley
A327
MINLEY LANE
GU17
West Minley Farm
Clapperoak Cottage
Minley Grange
Grange Cottage
Minley Manor
YATELEY HEATH WOOD
MINLEY WOOD
Water Tower
Minley Warren
Minley Farm
Home Farm
Pump House
Hawley Hard
B3013
Lower Minley Cottages
Blackbushes Farm
Linklater's Cottages
Oak Grove
Strip Plantation
Lichett Plain
BLACKBUSHES ROAD
Mallards Copse
Moor Copse
M3
Fleet GU51
Tobridge Copse
Sewage Works
Brook House
M3 MOTORWAY
Bramshot Copse
RG27
Doghouse Copse
Broomhurst Farm
Ancels Copse
New Plantation
Gilldown Farm
Broomhurst Wood
ANCELLS BUSINESS PARK
The Bungalow
Island Copse
The Thorns
Chestnut Copse
R. S. P. B. GREAT BRAMSHOT RESERVE
88
Sheepmoor
Club House
A B C D E F G
1 2 3 4 5 6 7 8 9
81 82 83
56 57 58 59 60

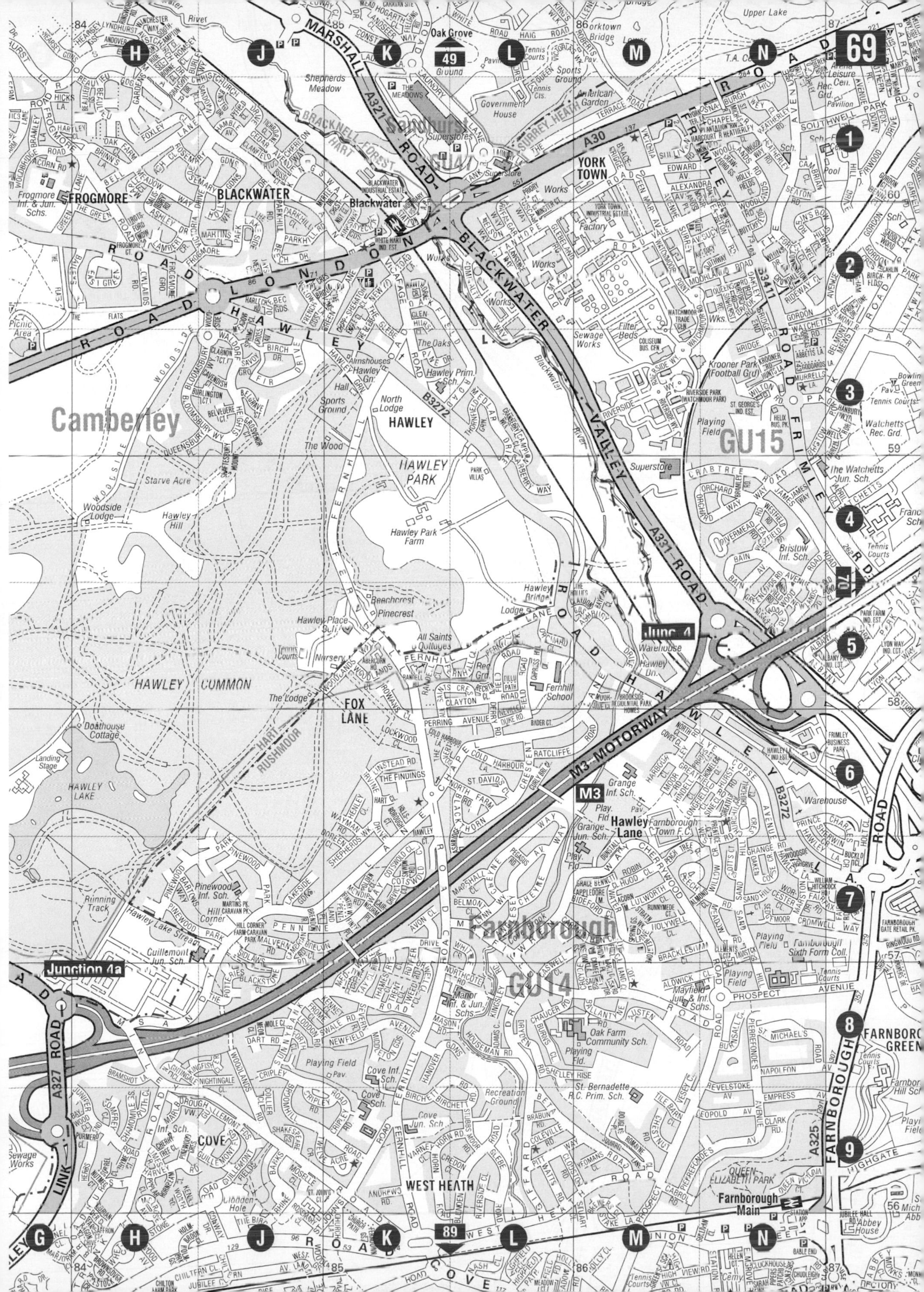

69
Oak Grove
49
Shepherds Meadow
Sandhurst
Government House
American Garden
Sports Ground
Upper Lake
Arena Leisure Cen.
YORK TOWN
FROGMORE
BLACKWATER
Blackwater
Frogmore Inf. & Jun. Schs.
Camberley
HAWLEY
HAWLEY PARK
Hawley Park Farm
North Lodge
Hawley Prim. Sch.
Sports Ground
The Wood
Starve Acre
Woodside Lodge
Hawley Hill
Sewage Works
Filter Beds
Krooner Park (Football Grd)
Playing Field
GU15
Superstore
The Watchetts Jun. Sch.
Bristow Inf. Sch.
Watchetts Rec. Grd.
Junc 4
Warehouse
Hawley Bridge
Beechcrest
Pinecrest
Hawley Place
All Saints Cottages
HAWLEY COMMON
The Lodge
FOX LANE
Fernhill School
Boathouse Cottage
Landing Stage
HAWLEY LAKE
M3 MOTORWAY
M3
Grange Inf. Sch.
Grange Jun. Sch.
Hawley Lane
Farnborough Town F.C.
Frimley Business Park
Pinewood Inf. Sch.
Hill Corner
Running Track
Hawley Lake Stream
Guillemont Jun. Sch.
Junction 4a
Farnborough
GU14
Farnborough Sixth Form Coll.
Mayfield Jun. & Inf. Schs.
Manor Inf. & Jun. Schs.
Oak Farm Community Sch.
Playing Fld.
St. Bernadette R.C. Prim. Sch.
Recreation Ground
Cove Inf. Sch.
Cove Sch.
Cove Jun. Sch.
Playing Field
COVE
WEST HEATH
Lodden Hole
Sewage Works
FARNBOROUGH GREEN
QUEEN ELIZABETH PARK
Farnborough Main
89
Abbey House
A30
A321
A331
A325
A327
B3272
B3411
LONDON ROAD
HAWLEY ROAD
BLACKWATER VALLEY ROAD
FRIMLEY ROAD
FARNBOROUGH ROAD
PROSPECT AVENUE
LINK ROAD
G
H
J
K
L
M
N
1
2
3
4
5
6
7
8
9
84
85
86
87

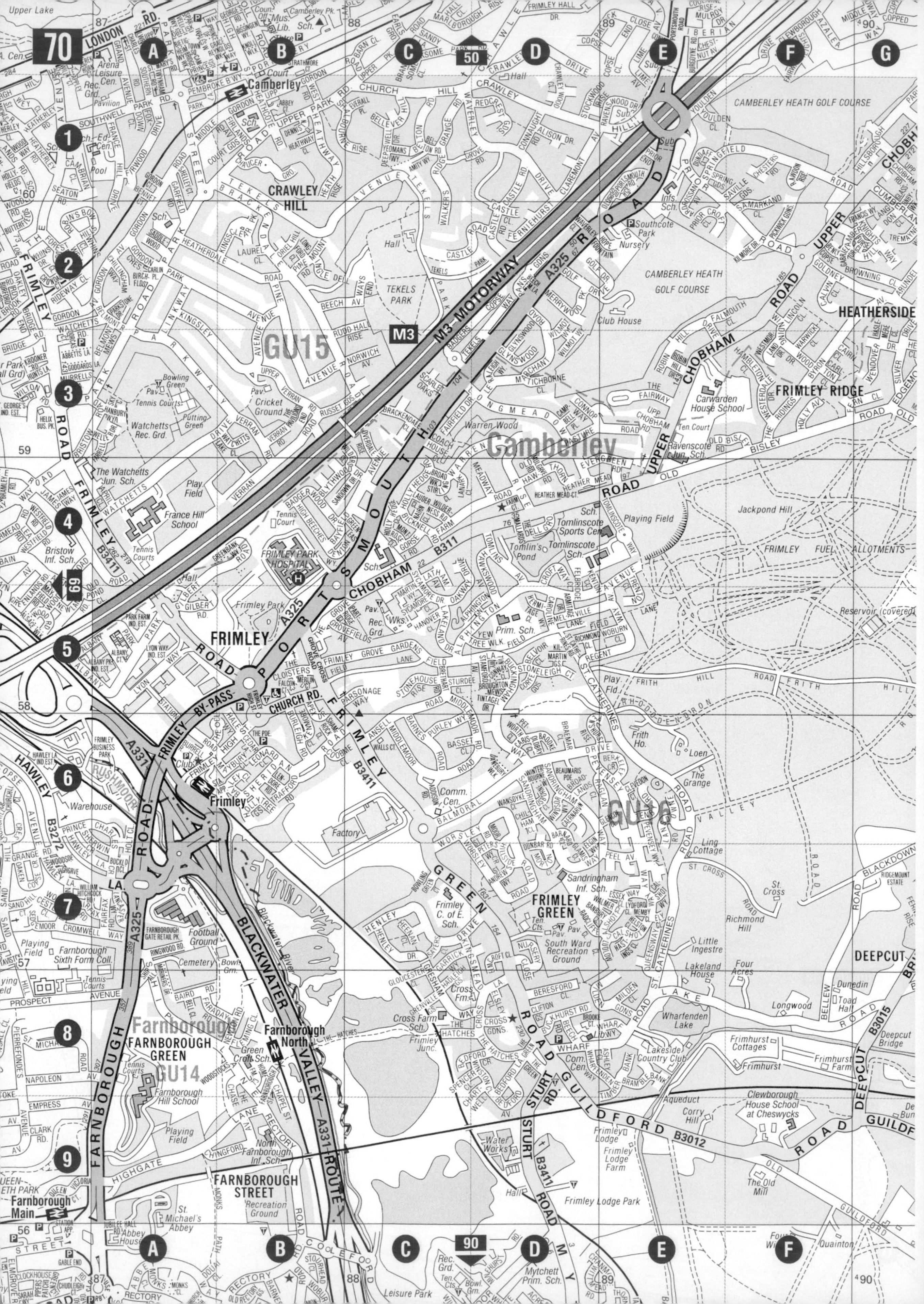
70
LONDON RD.
Camberley
CRAWLEY HILL
GU15
M3
M3 MOTORWAY
CAMBERLEY HEATH GOLF COURSE
Camberley Heath Golf Course
Club House
Southcote Park
HEATHERSIDE
FRIMLEY RIDGE
Carwarden House School
Camberley
Tekels Park
Watchetts Rec. Grd.
France Hill School
The Watchetts Jun. Sch.
Frimley Park Hospital
FRIMLEY
Frimley Park
Tomlinscote Sports Cen.
Tomlinscote Sch.
Jackpond Hill
FRIMLEY FUEL ALLOTMENTS
Reservoir (covered)
CHOBHAM ROAD
PORTSMOUTH ROAD
A325
B311
B3411
FRIMLEY BY-PASS
Frimley
Factory
FRIMLEY GREEN
GU16
Frimley C. of E. Sch.
South Ward Recreation Ground
Sandringham Inf. Sch.
Wharfenden Lake
Lakeside Country Club
Clewborough House School at Cheswycks
Frimley Lodge
Frimley Lodge Farm
Frimley Lodge Park
The Old Mill
DEEPCUT
Deepcut Bridge
Frimhurst Farm
Frimhurst Cottages
Four Acres
Lakeland House
Little Ingestre
Richmond Hill
St. Cross
Ling Cottage
The Grange
Frith Ho.
BLACKWATER VALLEY A331 ROUTE
Blackwater River
Farnborough
FARNBOROUGH GREEN
GU14
Farnborough North
Farnborough Hill School
Farnborough Sixth Form Coll.
Football Ground
Cemetery
FARNBOROUGH STREET
North Farnborough Inf. Sch.
Recreation Ground
Farnborough Main
St. Michael's Abbey
FARNBOROUGH ROAD
GUILDFORD ROAD
B3012
Water Works
Mytchett Prim. Sch.
Leisure Park
Cross Farm Sch.
Frimley Junc.
RUSHMOOR
Warehouse
B3272
HAWLEY
69
50
90
A B C D E F G
1 2 3 4 5 6 7 8 9
87 88 89 90
56 57 58 59 60

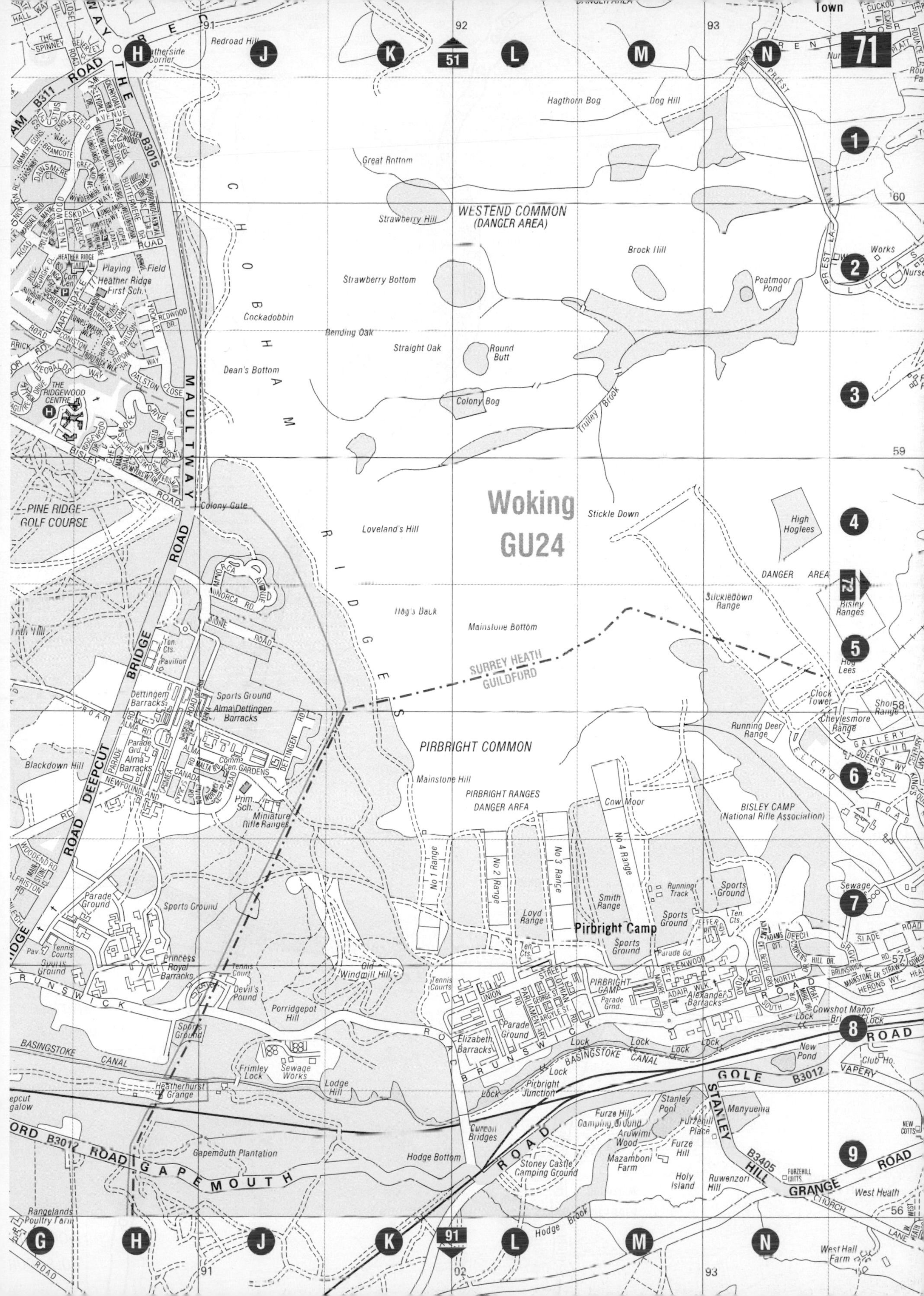
WESTEND COMMON
(DANGER AREA)
Woking
GU24
PIRBRIGHT COMMON
Hagthorn Bog
Dog Hill
Great Bottom
Strawberry Hill
Strawberry Bottom
Brock Hill
Peatmoor Pond
Cockadobbin
Bending Oak
Straight Oak
Round Butt
Dean's Bottom
Colony Bog
Trulley Brook
Stickle Down
High Hoglees
DANGER AREA
Loveland's Hill
Hog's Back
Mainstone Bottom
Stickledown Range
Bisley Ranges
Hog Lees
SURREY HEATH
GUILDFORD
Clock Tower
Running Deer Range
Cheylesmore Range
Mainstone Hill
PIRBRIGHT RANGES
DANGER AREA
Cow Moor
BISLEY CAMP
(National Rifle Association)
No 1 Range
No 2 Range
No 3 Range
No 4 Range
Smith Range
Loyd Range
Pirbright Camp
Sports Ground
Dettingen Barracks
Alma Dettingen Barracks
Alma Barracks
Miniature Rifle Ranges
PINE RIDGE GOLF COURSE
Colony Gate
MAULTWAY
DEEPCUT BRIDGE ROAD
Blackdown Hill
Princess Royal Barracks
Devil's Pound
Porridgepot Hill
Old Windmill Hill
Elizabeth Barracks
Alexander Barracks
BASINGSTOKE CANAL
Frimley Lock
Sewage Works
Lodge Hill
Heatherhurst Grange
Pirbright Junction
Curzon Bridges
Gapemouth Plantation
Hodge Bottom
GAPEMOUTH ROAD
Stoney Castle Camping Ground
Furze Hill Camping Ground
Aruwimi Wood
Mazamboni Farm
Stanley Pool
Furzehill Place
Manyuema
Holy Island
Ruwenzori Hill
STANLEY HILL
GOLE ROAD
GRANGE ROAD
West Heath
Cowshot Manor
Rangelands Poultry Farm
Hodge Brook
West Hall Farm
THE RIDGEWOOD CENTRE
Heather Ridge First Sch.
Playing Field
Redroad Hill
Featherside Corner
G H J K L M N
1 2 3 4 5 6 7 8 9
91 92 93
56 57 58 59 60
51 72 91

72
52
71
92
GU24
BISLEY
KNAPHILL
Woking
BROOKWOOD
PIRBRIGHT
Staffordlake
BISLEY COMMON
CHOBHAM GOLF COURSE
WEST HILL GOLF COURSE
BISLEY CAMP (National Rifle Association)
Bisley Camp
Cowshot Common
Brookwood
BROOKWOOD CEMETERY
Military Cemetery
H.M.P. COLDINGLEY
Princess Christian Homes & Training Centre
Grindstone Handle Corner
Bisley Ranges
Century Range
Short Siberia Range
Long Siberia Range
GOAL FARM GOLF COURSE
Peatmoor Pond
Lucas Green Manor
Hangmoor Copse
Shrubb's Copse
Sheet's Heath
Burrow Hill
The Green
Pirbright Prim. Sch.
SURREY HEATH
WOKING
GUILDFORD
GUILDFORD ROAD A322
BAGSHOT ROAD A322
CONNAUGHT ROAD A324
BROOKWOOD LYE RD.
DAWNEY HILL A324
SCHOOL LANE
B3405
B3012

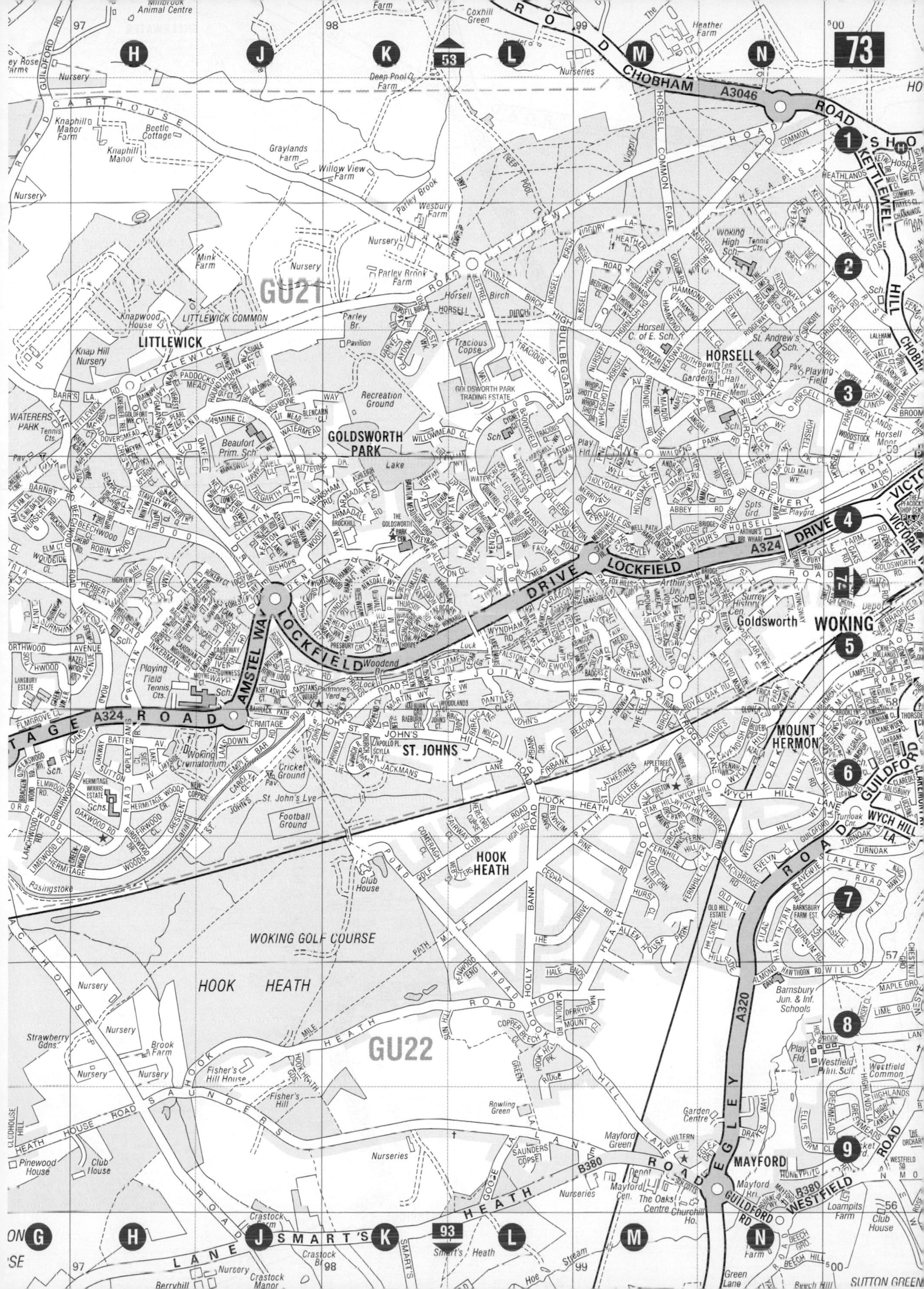
GU21
LITTLEWICK
GOLDSWORTH PARK
HORSELL
WOKING
ST. JOHNS
MOUNT HERMON
HOOK HEATH
WOKING GOLF COURSE
GU22
MAYFORD
LOCKFIELD DRIVE
A324
A3046
CHOBHAM ROAD
A320
B380
53
93
74

74
A
B
C
D
E
F
G
54
HORSELL COMMON
CHOBHAM RD.
SHORES ROAD
A245
WOODHAM LANE
SHEERWATER
Basingstoke Canal
Woodham Hall Estate
Youth Club
GU21
KETTLEWELL HILL
A3046
CHOBHAM RD.
CHERTSEY ROAD
A320
MONUMENT RD.
WEST BYFLEET GOLF COURSE
Monument Bri.
Woking Business Park
Genesis Business Park
Monument Hill Prim. Sch.
Playing Field
Canal
Ditch
Chertsey Rd. Bri.
Basingstoke
Rec. Grd.
Horsell Moor
St. Andrew's Sch.
Playing Field
Lion Retail Park
Mosque
Maybury Estate
Pyrford Common
Tennis Courts
VICTORIA WAY
A324
LOCKFIELD DR.
Civic Cen.
Peacocks Shop. Cen.
Wolsey Pl. Shop. Cen.
THE BROADWAY
R.C. Prim. Sch.
MAYBURY
St. Peter's Conv.
THE ROUGH
B382
Woking
Piggery
73
Goldsworth
WOKING
Surrey History Cen.
HEATHSIDE
Shey Copse
HOEBRIDGE GOLF COURSE
Fox Hill
Hockering Estate
Ashwood
Club Ho.
MOUNT HERMON
Swimming Pool
Leisure Centre
WOKING PARK
Sports Ground
Playing Field
St. John the Baptist Catholic Comp. Sch. Woking
Elm Bridge Estate
Monument Hill
The Trees School
Roundbridge Farm
Hoebridge Farm
Hoebridge Sch.
Sewage Works
GUILDFORD ROAD
WYCH HILL
KINGFIELD
A247
KINGFIELD
Woking College
GU22
Woking F.C. Ground
Kingfield Green
LOOP RD.
B381
OLD WOKING
CARTERS LANE
The Pollenarium
Woking Park Farm
Moat
Oldhall Copse
EGLEY ROAD
A320
HIGH STREET
VICARAGE RD.
Barnsbury Jun. & Inf. Schools
Westfield Common
Westfield Prim. Sch.
B380
WESTFIELD
Mill Moor
Hipley Bri.
Riverdale Farm
River Wey
Sports Ground
Works
Weir
Cartbridge House
BROADMEAD ROAD
A247
Broad Mead
Broadmead Cut
River Wey Navigation
Mill
MAYFORD
Cricket Grd.
Nurseries
Nursery
Moorlane Farm
Loampits Farm
Club Ho.
Mayford Bri.
WESTFIELD
SEND ROAD
Cart Bri.
Lodge
CARTBRIDGE
94
Works
Nursery
Elm Trees Farm
Westfield Common
Burton House
SUTTON GREEN
Beech Hill
Runtley Wood
500
01
02
03
56
57
58
59
60
1
2
3
4
5
6
7
8
9

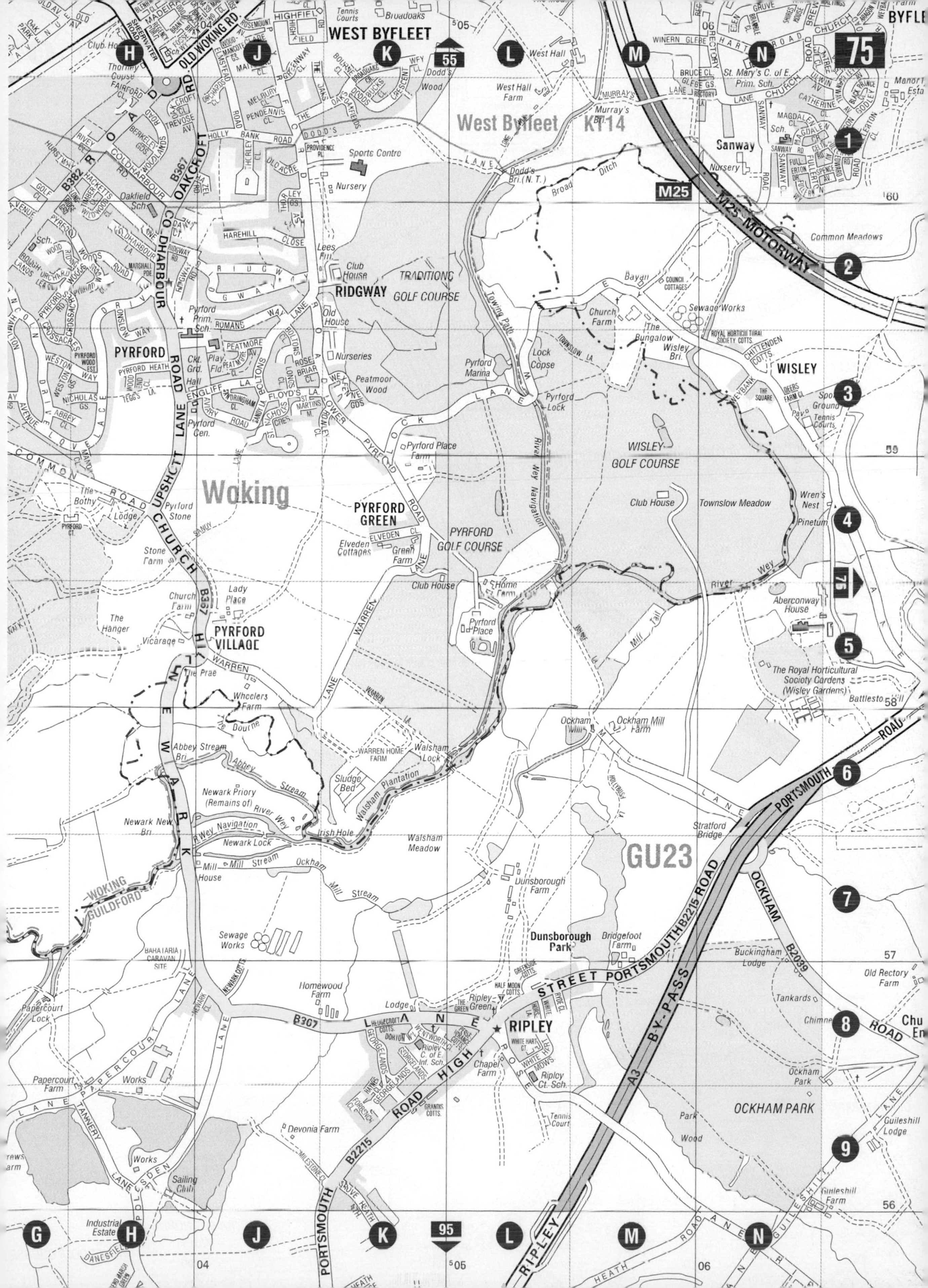

75
WEST BYFLEET
West Byfleet KT14
55
H
J
K
L
M
N
1
2
3
4
5
6
7
8
9
RIDGWAY
PYRFORD
Woking
PYRFORD GREEN
PYRFORD VILLAGE
WISLEY
Sanway
M25
M25 MOTORWAY
TRADITIONAL GOLF COURSE
WISLEY GOLF COURSE
PYRFORD GOLF COURSE
The Royal Horticultural Society Gardens (Wisley Gardens)
River Wey Navigation
Newark Priory (Remains of)
Newark Lock
Walsham Lock
Walsham Meadow
Ockham Mill
Ockham Mill Farm
GU23
Dunsborough Park
RIPLEY
OCKHAM PARK
A3 BY-PASS
PORTSMOUTH ROAD
B2215
B367
B2039
RIPLEY
Sewage Works
Papercourt Lock
Papercourt Farm
Devonia Farm
Sailing Club
Industrial Estate
Guileshill Farm
Guileshill Lodge
Buckingham Lodge
Old Rectory Farm
Tankards
Park Wood
WOKING
GUILDFORD
G
95
04
05
06
56
57
58
59
60

BYFLEET
Byfleet Mill
West Byfleet
KT14
WOKING
Park Barn Farm
Queen Anne's Hills
The Hangers
Queen Anne's Cottage
Nursery
Foxwarren Park
Red Hill
SILVERMERE GOLF COURSE
Thirty Acre Wood
Long Orchard Farm
Highlands Farm
Belt Wood
A3 ROAD
PAINSHILL
Feltonfleet Sch.
Play. Fld.
Heyswood-Girl Guide Camp
The Broom
Pains Hill House Farm
Chinese Bridge
Grotto
Gothic Temple
The Lake
Waterwheel
Wheel Island
Tower Hill
Gothic Tower
Common Meadows
Buxton Wood
Clearmount
M25 MOTORWAY
M25
WISLEY INTERCHANGE
Junction 10
Oak Pollard
Red Hill
Redhill Bottom
Chatley Wood
WISLEY
Sports Ground
Tennis Courts
Wisley Common
Woolger's Wood
Pond Farm
Cockcrow Hill
Sandpit Hill
Chatley Farm
RIVER MOLE
Chatley Cott.
The Bogs
WISLEY COMMON
Hut Hill Cottage
Hut Hill
Currie's Clump
OCKHAM COMMON
Chatley Heath
Breach Hill Wood
Telegraph Hill
Chatley Heath Semaphore Tower
Lodge Copse
Wren's Nest
Aberconway House
Bolder Mere
ELMBRIDGE
GUILDFORD
Hatchford Wood
Woodside Cottage
The Royal Horticultural Society Gardens (Wisley Gardens)
Battleston Hill
Oakham Village Green
Fellside Cottages
ELM LA
ELM CORNER
Wilderness Farm
Hunt's Copse
THE GARDENS
Hatchford End
Elm Cottage
Nurseries
Hatchford Park
Hatchford
Highfield Farm
Cold Norton Farm
Orchard Farm
Hazeldene Farm
Woking
GU23
Wisley Airfield (disused)
El. Sub. Sta.
Bridge End Farm
Little Upton Cottages
MARTYR'S GREEN
Pound Farm
May's Green
Tanner's Copse
The Lodge
Upton Farm
OCKHAM
Old Rectory Farm
Bridge End
Trulliber Copse
Chaffers Copse
Hook Wood
Tankards
Chestnut Farm
Appstree Farm
Pavilion Recreation Ground
Church End
ROAD B2039
OCKHAM
Alms Heath
SCHOOL LA
Ockham Park
OCKHAM PARK
Guileshill Lodge
Tennis Court
Stumps Grove
Stumpsgrove Cottages
Blackmoor Farm
Guileshill Farm
Slade Farm
Slade Cottage
BARNSTHORNS WOOD
DRIFT GOLF COURSE
Ridings Copse
LONG REACH
NORTH
56
75
96
A B C D E F G
1 2 3 4 5 6 7 8 9
07 08 09
56 57 58 59 60

77
57
97
PORTSMOUTH ROAD
A307
BETWEEN STREETS
A245
HIGH ST.
MILL RD.
STOKE ROAD
COBHAM
Cobham Mill
Rec. Grd.
Wood Hill
Lodge Cottages
Nursery
Pyports
Rose Lodge Wood
Lower Cobham Till
Cobham Court Farm
Downside Bri.
DOWNSIDE ROAD
Cobham Park Nursery
Cobham Park
COBHAM PARK
Big Roundabout
Little Roundabout
Park Wood
RIVER MOLE
Elm Farm
Upper Cobham Tilt
Cemetery
Ash Ford
Cobham Stud
Tennis Court
Curtain Pond Cottages
Cossins
Cossins Farm
Cobham Lodge
Cobham
KT11
Halfpenny Cross
Wrens Nest Cottage
Chilbrook Farm
Bramble Wood
Bramble Cottages
CHILBROOK
Pointers Green
Poynters Farm
Forge Cottages
Brickfield Copse
Pondtail Farm
Downside Nursery Sch.
Downside Common
Downside
Downside Farm Cottage
Downside Saw Mill
Downside Farm
DOWNSIDE COMMON RD
MIDDLETON RD
Rye Salters
Nurseries
NORTON LA
GOOSE GRN
Highway Farm
Norton Wood
New Barn Farm
BOOKHAM
Braemar Little Orchard
Bull Riding Farm
Oakdene Farm
Old Oak Common
The New Preserve
Peaked Rough
Roundabout
Hurst Hill
Withy Bed
Down Wood
Chasemore Wood
Chasemore Farm
MOLE VALLEY
Spring Meadow Wood
Thornets Wood
Wrens Hill Wood
Muggeridge Wood
M25
M25-MOTORWAY
Sports Ground
Athletic Ground
Tennis Courts
Sports Grd.
Cobham & Stoke D' Abernon
STOKE D' ABERNON
Lower Farm
Farm
Nursery
Parkside Sch.
South Lodge
Old Parks Copse
Recreation Ground
Knowle Hill
Little Heath
Polyapes Scout Camp
LITTLEHEATH
Pond
FAIRMILE
Bookham Lodge Stud
Bookham Lodge
Yehudi Menuhin School
Gardeners Cottage
Gate Lodge
The Birches
Hundred Pound Bridge Wood
Hill Farm
Hundred Pound Bridge
New Barn Wood
Newmarsh Farm
North Surrey Gun Club
Oakdene Nurseries
Brick Kiln Copse
Clamp Rough
Bushy Thicket
Thicket Copse
Bank's Common
Bank's Farm
Little Bookham Common
KT23
GREAT BOOKHAM COMMON
The Common
Merfitt's Cottage
Manor Cottage
Oak Tree Cottage
The White House
Leatherhead
Little Mornshill Wood
Banks Way House
Mornshill Farm
KT24
GREAT MORNSHILL WOOD
Effingham Junction
Gallows Grove
Barns Thorns
HORSLEY ROAD
Effingham Junction
Sewage Works
Beehive Farm

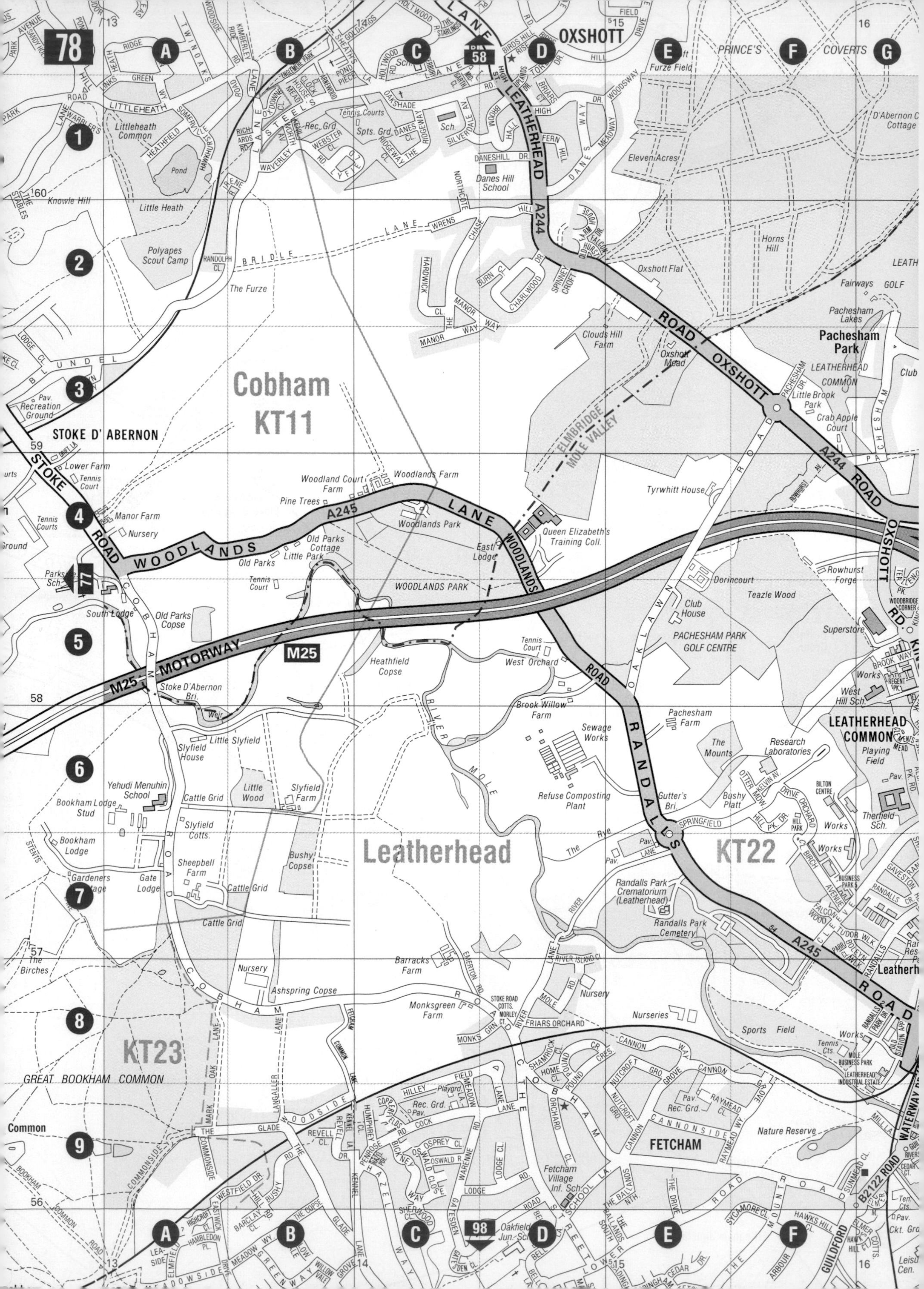
78
OXSHOTT
PRINCE'S COVERTS
Furze Field
Littleheath Common
Little Heath
Polyapes Scout Camp
Knowle Hill
The Furze
Danes Hill School
Eleven Acres
Horns Hill
Oxshott Flat
Fairways GOLF
Pachesham Lakes
Pachesham Park
LEATHERHEAD COMMON
Clouds Hill Farm
Oxshott Mead
Little Brook Park
Crab Apple Court
ELMBRIDGE MOLE VALLEY
Cobham KT11
STOKE D' ABERNON
Recreation Ground
Lower Farm
Manor Farm
Nursery
Woodland Court Farm
Woodlands Farm
Pine Trees
Woodlands Park
Queen Elizabeth's Training Coll.
Tyrwhitt House
East Lodge
Old Parks Cottage
Old Parks
Little Park
WOODLANDS PARK
Dorincourt
Teazle Wood
Rowhurst Forge
Club House
PACHESHAM PARK GOLF CENTRE
Superstore
South Lodge
Old Parks Copse
M25 MOTORWAY
M25
Heathfield Copse
West Orchard
Stoke D'Abernon Bri.
Weir
Brook Willow Farm
Pachesham Farm
Sewage Works
The Mounts
Research Laboratories
West Hill Sch.
LEATHERHEAD COMMON
Playing Field
Little Slyfield
Slyfield House
Yehudi Menuhin School
Bookham Lodge Stud
Cattle Grid
Little Wood
Slyfield Farm
Refuse Composting Plant
Gutter's Bri.
Bushy Platt
Therfield Sch.
Slyfield Cotts.
Bookham Lodge
Sheepbell Farm
Bushy Copse
Leatherhead
KT22
Gate Lodge
Randalls Park Crematorium (Leatherhead)
Randalls Park Cemetery
The Birches
Nursery
Barracks Farm
Ashspring Copse
Monksgreen Farm
Nurseries
Sports Field
KT23
GREAT BOOKHAM COMMON
LEATHERHEAD INDUSTRIAL ESTATE
MOLE BUSINESS PARK
Nature Reserve
FETCHAM
Fetcham Village Inf. Sch.
Oakfield Jun. Sch.
Common
A244
A245
B2122
OXSHOTT ROAD
LEATHERHEAD ROAD
WOODLANDS LANE
STOKE ROAD
COBHAM ROAD
RANDALLS ROAD
GUILDFORD ROAD
77
58
98
A B C D E F G
1 2 3 4 5 6 7 8 9
13 14 15 16
56 57 58 59 60

79
59
99
80
H
J
K
L
M
N
G
1
2
3
4
5
6
7
8
9
17
18
19
60
59
58
57
56
Rushett Farm
Telegraph Hill
Reservoir (Covered)
Chessington
KT9
KINGSTON upon THAMES
MOLE VALLEY
THE FOREST
Newton Wood
EPSOM COMMON
Epsom
KT18
EPSOM and EWELL
The Wells
ASHTEAD COMMON
D'Abernon Ho.
LEATHERHEAD ROAD
KINGSTON ROAD
A243
Caen Wood
The Oaks
Ashley Court
Hillthorpe
Paddock Lodge Stables
Wood Field
The Rye
Trevona
Ashtead
Ashtead
KT21
Newton Wood
DORKING RD.
Woodcote Stud Farm
Woodcote Park
The Cottage in the Park
ASHTEAD PARK
Island Pond
Ashtead House
Nursery
Playing Field
ASHTEAD PARK
City of London Freeman's School
Playing Field
William III Gate
Larch Field
Tudor Croft
Ermyn Lodge
Thirty Acres Barn
Junction 9
M25 MOTORWAY
M25
ASHTEAD
LOWER ASHTEAD
Barnett Wood
Rec. Grd.
Ckt. Grd.
Parsons Mead Sch.
ASHTEAD HOSP.
Prim Sch.
Convent
Play. Field
St. Peters R. C. Prim Sch
St. Andrew's R. C. Sec. Sch.
Downsend School
Swim Pool
Junc. 9
BY-PASS RD.
THE STREET
EPSOM ROAD
LEATHERHEAD ROAD
A24
Frederick Milner House
Playing Field
Offices
Warren Farm
Epsom
KT18
M25-MOTORWAY
M25
Stane Street Roman Road (course of)
Addlestead Wood
Highdale
Highlands Farm
Reservoir (covered)
Hambleton
HEADLEY ROAD
LEATHERHEAD
Football Ground
Fairfield
The Woodville School
LEATHERHEAD HOSP.
Woodlands Sch.
St.Mary's C.of E. Inf. Sch.
HIGHLANDS RD.
B2033
REIGATE RD.
BY-PASS
A243
KNOLL ROUNDABOUT
PLOUGH INDUSTRIAL ESTATE
KINGSTON ROAD
A245
BULL HILL
STATION R.
Factory
Club
KINGSTON

80
EPSOM
WOODCOTE
Woodcote Park
R. A. C. COUNTRY CLUB
GOLF COURSE
EPSOM DOWNS
WALTON DOWNS
EPSOM DOWNS
Langley Vale
Langley Bottom
ASHTEAD PARK
Ashtead KT21
Epsom
KT18
KT17
Tattenham Corner
M25 MOTORWAY
DORKING ROAD
EPSOM RD.
COLLEGE RD.
BURGH HEATH ROAD
DOWNS RD.
LANGLEY VALE
HEADLEY ROAD
WALTON ROAD
ASHLEY RD.
TATTENHAM CORNER
Epsom General Hospital
Epsom College
City of London Freeman's School
The Durdans
Halfmoon Clump
Crockingham Wood
Langley Bottom Wood
Langley Bottom Farm
Nohome Farm
Downs View Wood
Round Wood
Addlestead Wood
Addlestead Farm
Walton Hurst Farm
Little Hurst Wood
Wingfield Farm Cottages
Gilletts Cottages
Thirty Acres Barn
Tudor Croft
Ermyn Lodge
The Warren
Grand Stand
The Derby Day Experience
EPSOM and EWELL
MOLE VALLEY
REIGATE and BANSTEAD
201
60
79
100
A
B
C
D
E
F
G
1
2
3
4
5
6
7
8
9

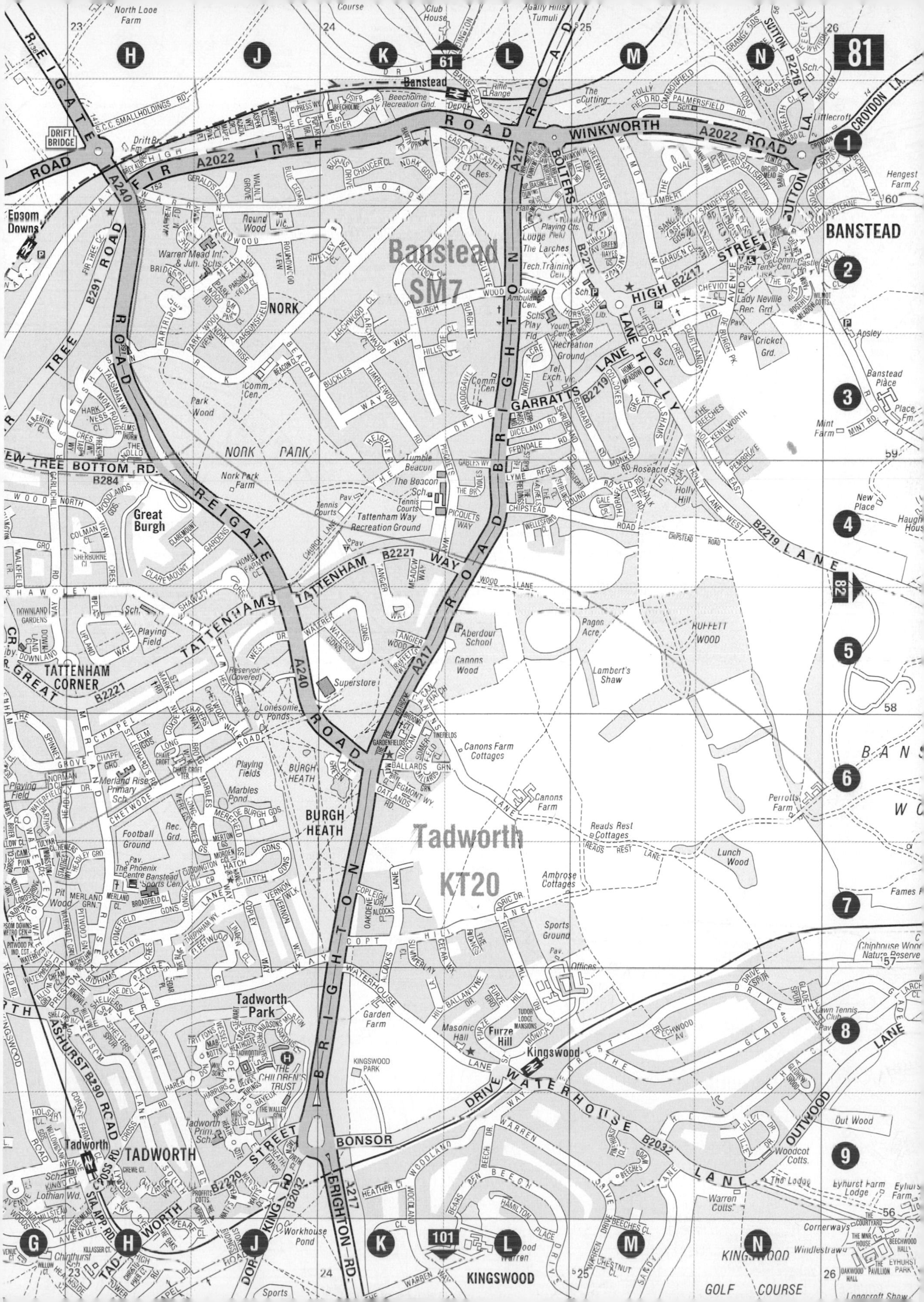

81
H
J
K
L
M
N
G
1
2
3
4
5
6
7
8
9
61
101
82
23
24
25
26
56
57
58
59
60
North Looe Farm
Course
Club House
Gally Hills Tumuli
Banstead
Beecholme Recreation Gnd.
Rifle Range
Depot
The Cutting
Littlecroft
CROYDON LA.
Hengest Farm
REIGATE ROAD
DRIFT BRIDGE
S.C.C. SMALLHOLDINGS RD.
FIR A2022 TREE ROAD
WINKWORTH A2022 ROAD
BRIGHTON ROAD
A217
A240
A2022
Epsom Downs
Warren Mead Inf. & Jun. Schs.
Round Wood
Banstead
SM7
NORK
Bolters
Playing Cts. Field
Lodge
The Larches
Tech.Training Cen.
County Ambulance Cen.
Youth Centre
Recreation Ground
Tel. Exch.
HIGH B2217 STREET
BANSTEAD
Lady Neville Rec. Grd.
Cricket Grd.
Apsley
Banstead Place
Place Fm.
Mint Farm
MINT RD.
Park Wood
Comm. Cen.
NORK PARK
Nork Park Farm
TREE BOTTOM RD.
B284
Great Burgh
Tumble Beacon
The Beacon Sch.
Tennis Courts
Tattenham Way Recreation Ground
GARRATTS LANE
B2219
HOLLY LANE
Roseacre
Holly Hill
CHIPSTEAD ROAD
B2219 LANE
New Place
TATTENHAM B2221 WAY
TATTENHAMS
Playing Field
TATTENHAM CORNER
GREAT B2221
Aberdour School
Canons Wood
Pagoa Acre
HUFFETT WOOD
Lambert's Shaw
Reservoir (Covered)
Superstore
Lonesome Ponds
Canons Farm Cottages
Canons Farm
Playing Fields
Marbles Pond
BURGH HEATH
Merland Rise Primary Sch.
Football Ground
Rec. Grd.
The Phoenix Centre
Banstead Sports Cen.
Tadworth
KT20
Reads Rest Cottages
READS REST LANE
Lunch Wood
Perrotts Farm
Ambrose Cottages
Sports Ground
Offices
Chiphouse Wood Nature Reserve
Pit Wood
Tadworth Park
Garden Farm
Masonic Hall
Furze Hill
Tudor Lodge Mansions
Kingswood
Lawn Tennis Club
KINGSWOOD PARK
THE CHILDREN'S TRUST
Tadworth Prim. Sch.
WATERHOUSE LANE
B2032
OUTWOOD LANE
Out Wood
Woodcot Cotts.
The Lodge
Eyhurst Farm Lodge
Warren Cotts.
BONSOR DRIVE
Tadworth
TADWORTH
ASHURST B290 ROAD
Lothian Wd.
Workhouse Pond
KINGSWOOD
Cornerways
Windlestraw
KINGSWOOD GOLF COURSE
Chinthurst Sch.
Sports
Longcroft Shaw

82
A
B
C
D
E
F
G
62
1
2
3
4
5
6
7
8
9
26
27
28
29
60
59
58
57
56
81
102
CROYDON LANE
A2022
SUTTON LANE
WINKWORTH ROAD
Littlecroft
Hengest Farm
Boundary Farm
Weston Acres
Nicola Farm
Lodge
Barn Grove
Hylands Nurseries
Hillside Cotts.
Sports Ground
Ruffett Wood
Woodcote Grove House
Orme House
Club Ho.
MEADOW WALK
CARSHALTON ROAD
B278
Woodmansterne Primary Sch.
CEDARS
MERRYMEET
Village Hall
Recreation Ground
Tennis Cts.
Rectory
Manor Court Farm
Big Wood
Playground
Sports Grd.
LONGLANDS
RICHLAND AV
LLOYD AV
DOWNLANDS CL.
AVENUE
MOUNT
FRYSTON AV
Woodcote Grove Farm
CLOCK HOUSE
WOODCOTE PARK GOLF COURSE
REIGATE and BANSTEAD
SUTTON
CORRIGAN AV
WHITETHORN AV
REDFORD AV
BEECHWOOD AV
RICHMOND
LYNWOOD AV.
CLIFTON RD
WOODMANSTERNE LANE
BANSTEAD
CHALMERS RD
CUNNINGHAM RD
KENNETH RD
BARRY CL.
STAG LEYS CL.
KINGSCROFT RD
BECKENSHAW GDS
FIELDHOUSE VILLAS
Beckens Shaw
Cricket Grnd.
Pav.
RECTORY LANE
The Manor Ho.
The Old School
MANOR HILL
HATCH LANE
WOODMANSTERNE
Tennis Cts.
Prospect Plantation
Woodmansterne
Sch.
WINIFRED
NUTFIELD RD
BRIGSTOCK RD
ALEXANDER RD
MELROSE RD
ST. ANDREW'S RD
LYNDHURST RD
LINDEN AV
VALLEY
VINCENT RD
SHERWOOD
Lady Neville Rec. Grd.
Cricket Grd.
Apsley
The Shrubbery
Banstead
Puckstead Shaw
LAKERS RISE
THE READENS
PRESTBURY CRES
HEMPSHAW AV
Banstead Place
Place Fm.
Piggery
Scratch Wood
SM7
Mint Farm
MINT RD
Courtlands Farm
Farmside
Tall Trees
MANOR WAY
CHIPSTEAD WAY
PINES
UPPER PINE
WALK
Works
B278 LANE
CHIPSTEAD VALLEY
B2032
Chipstead Valley Prim. Sch.
Playing Fld.
GIDD HILL
WESTLEIGH
CHIPSTEAD CL.
GROVE
PORTNALLS RISE
PORTNALLS CL.
Lodge
Twin Sha
Great Solom's Wood
COURT
Little Solom's Wood
New Place
Haughdell House
Woodend
SOLOMS
Walwood
Solom's Court
HIGHFIELD ROAD
HILL
WAY ROAD
LANE
WOODLANDS
RIDGEMOUNT AV
PARKSIDE GDS.
Postern Wood
Page Hill
White Hill
Tennis Courts
Recreation Ground
The Postern
Play. Fld.
CANE HILL MENTAL HO
HOLLY
WEST
PARK DOWNS
ROAD
B2219
LANE
LWR. PK. RD
Park Farm
HOW HILLS
CHIPSTEAD GOLF COURSE
LACKFORD
STATION APP.
Chipstead
HIGHWOLD
THE PINES
RICKMAN HILL RD
BOUVERIE RD
LISSOMS RD
Club House
Nature Reserve
STAGBURY AV
HAZELWOOD
BOURKE HILL
West Ridge
HOLLYMEAD
How Green
HOLLYMEAD ROAD
Marlfield Shaw
WOODFIELD
STARROCK
B2032
STAGBURY HO.
OLD OAK AV
STAGBURY CL.
HAZEL WAY
WALPOLE AV
CHIPSTEAD
BANSTEAD
WOOD
YEW TREE CL.
CROYDON
REIGATE and BANSTEAD
DENE CL.
CLEAVE PRIOR
BRIDGE WY
Perrotts Farm
Dene Farm
COULSDON
DOGHURST AV
FARM CL.
VINCENT GRN.
VINCENT CL.
Starrock Court Cottage
Starrock Wood
GRASSFIELD CL.
Star Shaw
Fames Rough
OUTWOOD LANE
BOTTOM
CHIPSTEAD
CASTLE
Longshaw
STARROCK LANE
Chipstead Meads (Recreation Ground)
Rec. Grd.
Chiphouse Wood Nature Reserve
Well Copse
Old School House
Little Manor
LARCH CL.
GLADE
SPUR
DRIVE
Chipstead Bottom
Elmore
Club
Elmore Pond
Club
Lawn Tennis Club
Pav.
B2032
Outwood Shaw
Poorfield Wood
ROAD
ELMORE
The Rectory
Ley Cottage
HOOLEY
Hooley Lodge
Community Centre
Star Bridge
ROWAN WAY
CLOVER HILL
MAPLE GRO
ST. MARGARET'S RD
Court Lodge
STAR
LA.
FORGE BRIDGE LA.
Forge Bridge
Lower Lodge
Embers Shaw
OUTWOOD
Tadworth
Out Wood
KT20
Church Green
Church Shaw
CHURCH LANE
CHURCH LANE DR.
BRIGHTON ROAD
A23
NETHERNE
Club
Porters Wood
The Lodge
Eyhurst Farm Lodge
Eyhurst Farm
HIGH
The Grove
HOGSCROSS
Noke Farm
BROAD WLK.
GARDEN WLK.
South Lodge
The Belt
The Long Plantation
Cornerways
Eyhurst Farm House
THE COURTYARD
Windlestraw
KINGSWOOD
THE PAVILION
EYHURST PARK
OAKWOOD HALL
Tennis Courts
Four Acre
WHITE HILL
Ruffett
Round Wood
Northdean Shaw
Longcroft Shaw
COURSE

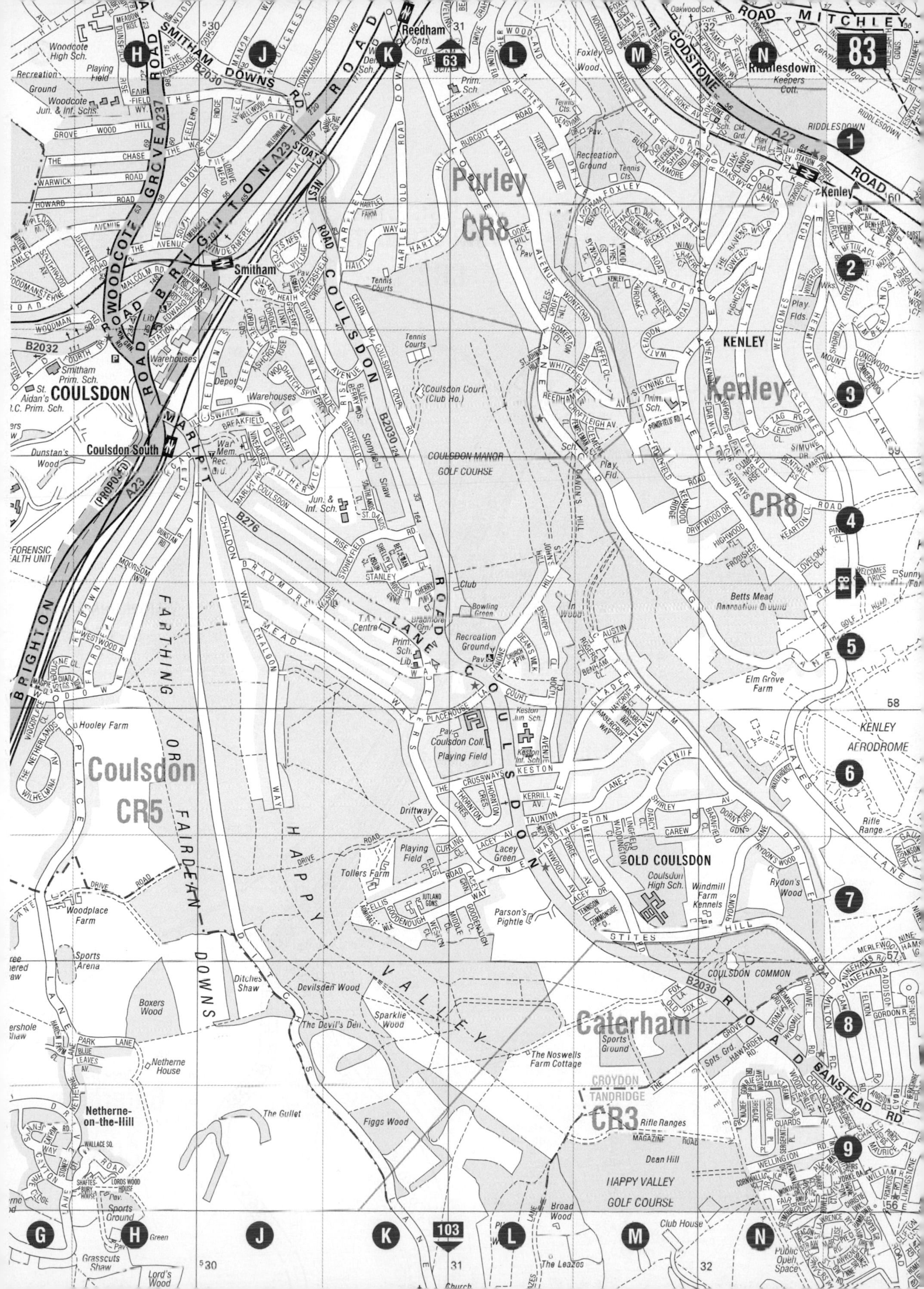

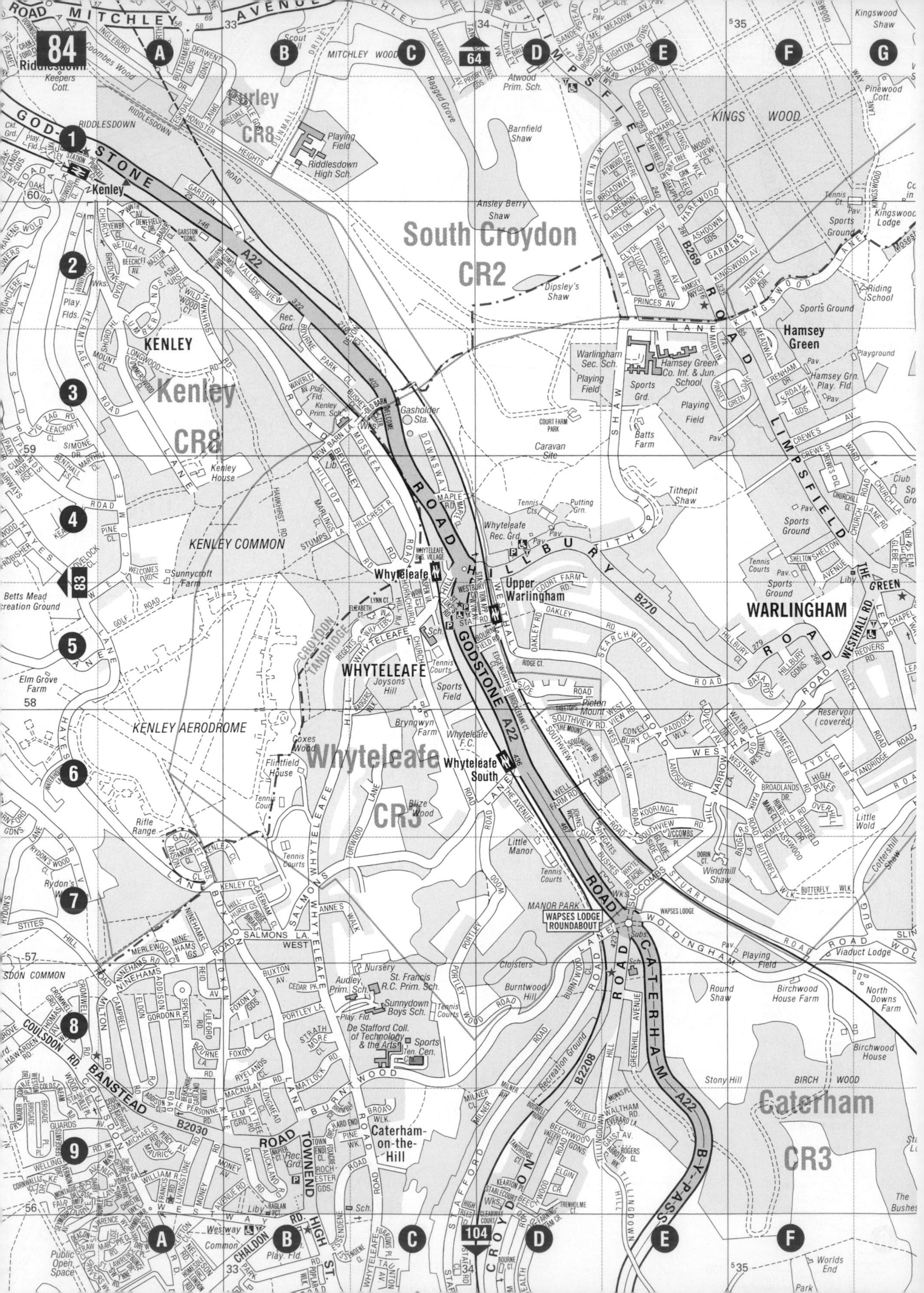
84
A
B
C
D
E
F
G
64
83
104
1
2
3
4
5
6
7
8
9
Riddlesdown
Purley
CR8
South Croydon
CR2
Kenley
KENLEY
KENLEY COMMON
KENLEY AERODROME
WHYTELEAFE
Whyteleafe
CR3
Upper Warlingham
WARLINGHAM
Hamsey Green
KINGS WOOD
Caterham
Caterham-on-the-Hill
MITCHLEY AVENUE
GODSTONE ROAD
A22
B269
B270
B2208
B2030
CATERHAM BY-PASS
LIMPSFIELD ROAD
WAPSES LODGE ROUNDABOUT
Whyteleafe South
Riddlesdown High Sch.
Warlingham Sec. Sch.
Hamsey Green Co. Inf. & Jun. School
Kenley Prim. Sch.
Atwood Prim. Sch.
St. Francis R.C. Prim. Sch.
Sunnydown Boys Sch.
De Stafford Coll. of Technology & the Arts
Audley Prim. Sch.
CROYDON
TANDRIDGE
Kingswood Shaw
Pinewood Cott.
Kingswood Lodge
Riding School
Birchwood House Farm
North Downs Farm
Birchwood House
BIRCH WOOD
Viaduct Lodge
Round Shaw
Stony Hill
Worlds End
Public Open Space
Coulsdon Common
Elm Grove Farm
Sunnycroft Farm
Kenley House
Betts Mead Recreation Ground
Rifle Range
Flintfield House
Coxes Wood
Blize Wood
Little Manor
Manor Park
Cloisters
Burntwood Hill
Tithepit Shaw
Batts Farm
Caravan Site
Gasholder Sta.
Barnfield Shaw
Ansley Berry Shaw
Dipsley's Shaw
Ragged Grove
MITCHLEY WOOD
Windmill Shaw
Little Wold
Cottershill Shaw
Reservoir (covered)
Bryngwyn Farm
Joysons Hill
Whyteleafe F.C.
Whyteleafe Rec. Grd.
Keepers Cott.
33
34
35
56
57
58
59
60

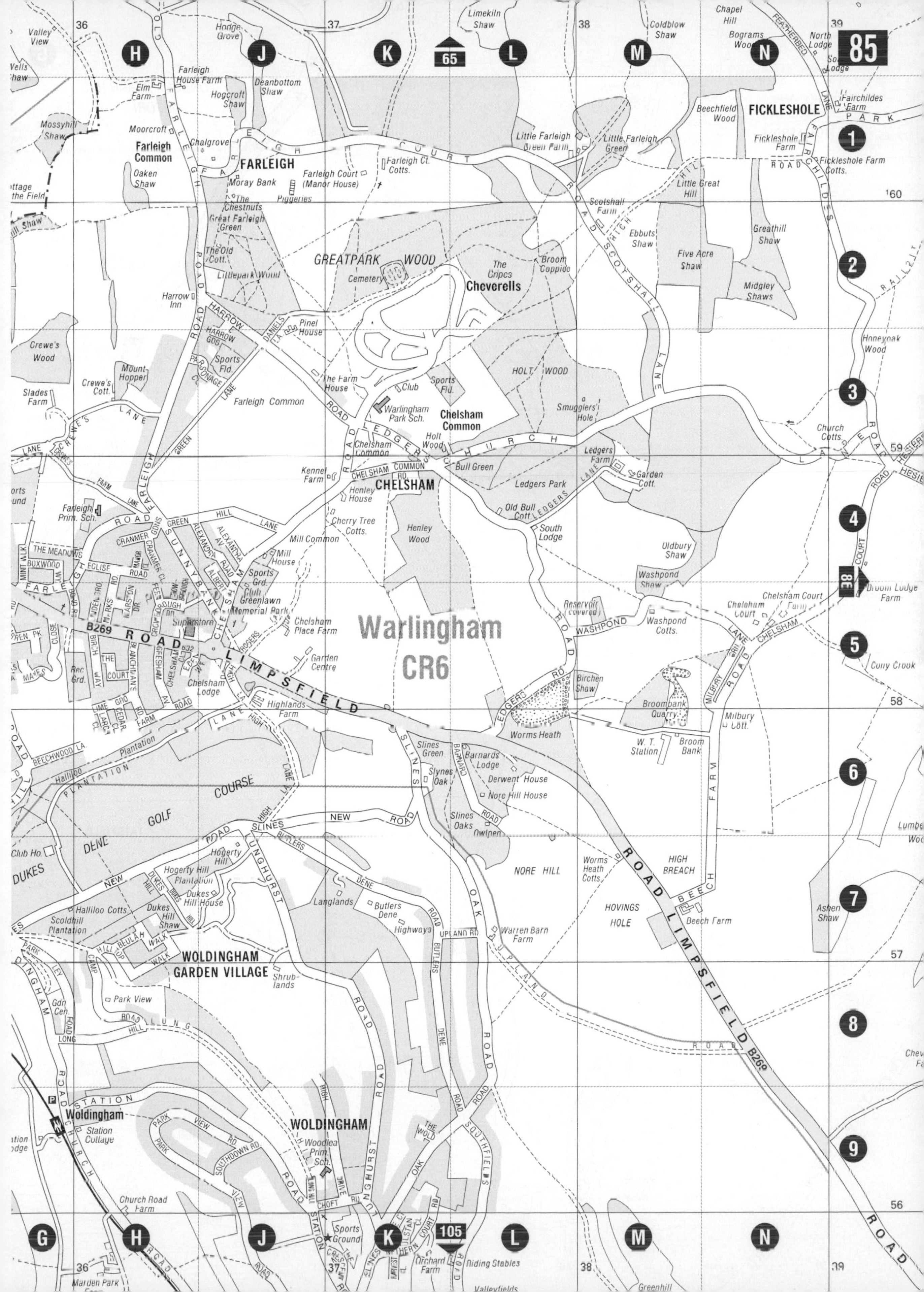
65
FARLEIGH
Farleigh Common
FICKLESHOLE
GREATPARK WOOD
Cheverells
Chelsham Common
CHELSHAM
Warlingham
CR6
Farleigh Common
HOLT WOOD
Henley Wood
Worms Heath
NORE HILL
HIGH BREACH
HOVINGS HOLE
GOLF COURSE
DUKES
WOLDINGHAM GARDEN VILLAGE
WOLDINGHAM
Woldingham
B269
LIMPSFIELD ROAD
38
105

86
66
85
106
A
B
C
D
E
F
G
1
2
3
4
5
6
7
8
9
39
540
41
42
60
59
58
57
56
Saltbox
Gasholder Station
Fairchildes Farm
Park
Road
Fickleshole
Fickleshole Farm
Fickleshole Farm Cotts.
Fairchildes
South Lodge
Skid Hill
Blackman's La.
Blackmans Cotts.
Coxs Cottage
Lane
Greathill Shaw
Midgley Shaws
Railpit
Honeyoak Wood
Skid Hill House
Skid Hill Farm
Ash
Crown
Road
Church
Church Cotts.
Lane
Hesiers
Hesiers Hill
Court Road
Mollards Wood
Jerry Reddins Shaw
Broom Lodge Farm
Chelsham Court Farm
Chelsham Court
Chelsham Road
Beddlestead
Owls Wood
Warlingham
CR6
Cony Crook
White Bank
Cowyard Shaw
Beddlestead House
Forge Cott.
Beddlestead Farm
Culver Keys
Beddlestead Farm Cotts.
Norheads
Lane
Round Wood
Cherry Tree Shaw
Shepherds Shaw
Lumberdine Wood
Ashen Shaw
Longlands Shaw
Kitchen Grove
Cheverells Farm
Limpsfield
B269
Pitchers Wood
Works
Pitchers Copse Farm
Wireless Station
Glengarry
Sports Field
Furze Corner
Waylands
Approach
Beacon Shaw
Park
Wood
Clarkslane Shaw
Clarks Lane Farm
Clarks Lane
B2024
Paygate Cott.
London - Biggin Hill Airport
South London Aero Club
Main Road
A233
Oaklands
Crown Ash
Hill
Victor
Sunningvale
Christy
Arthur
Oaklands Jun.Sch.
Oaklands Inf.Sch.
Norheads Farm
Norheads Farm Cotts.
Long Coppice
Biggin Hill
Recreation Ground
Cemetery
Library
Magnolia
Acer
Drive
Church
Allenby
Haig Rd.
Tudor Ct.
Long Coppice
Parsons Shaw
Farley Kennels
Kingscote
Isle Shaw
Lusted Hall Farm
Cedar Lodge
Home Wood
Paynesfield Coppice
Tatsfield
Gorsey Down Farm
Ricketts Hill
Hillingdale
Beech
Alexandra
Richmond
Melody
Westmore
Goatsfield
Greenway
Crossways
Whitewood Cotts.
Limehouse
Bottom
Ninehams
Maesmaur
Edgar
Borough Rd.
Colegates
Tatsfield Green
Rag Hill
Old Lane
Manor
Tatsfield Prim. Sch.
Playing Field
Golf
Church Farm
Clubhouse
Chestnut
Church Hill
Lusted Hall
Bromley
Tandridge
Rectory

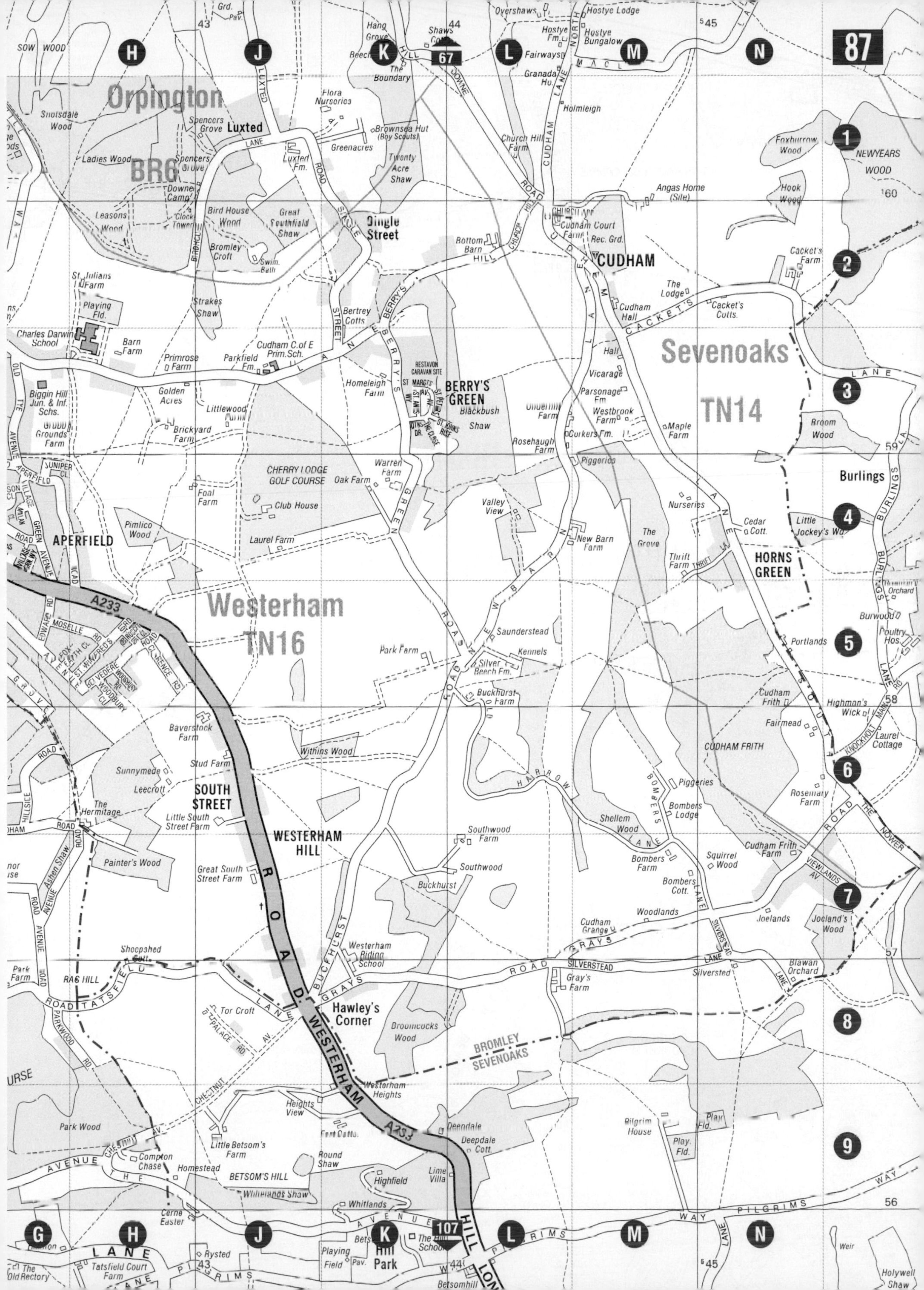

Orpington
BR6
Luxted
Single Street
CUDHAM
Sevenoaks
TN14
BERRY'S GREEN
Westerham
TN16
APERFIELD
HORNS GREEN
Burlings
SOUTH STREET
WESTERHAM HILL
Hawley's Corner
BROMLEY
SEVENOAKS
Biggin Hill Jun. & Inf. Schs.
Charles Darwin School
CHERRY LODGE GOLF COURSE
CUDHAM FRITH
WESTERHAM ROAD
A233
PILGRIMS WAY
67
107
Hill Park

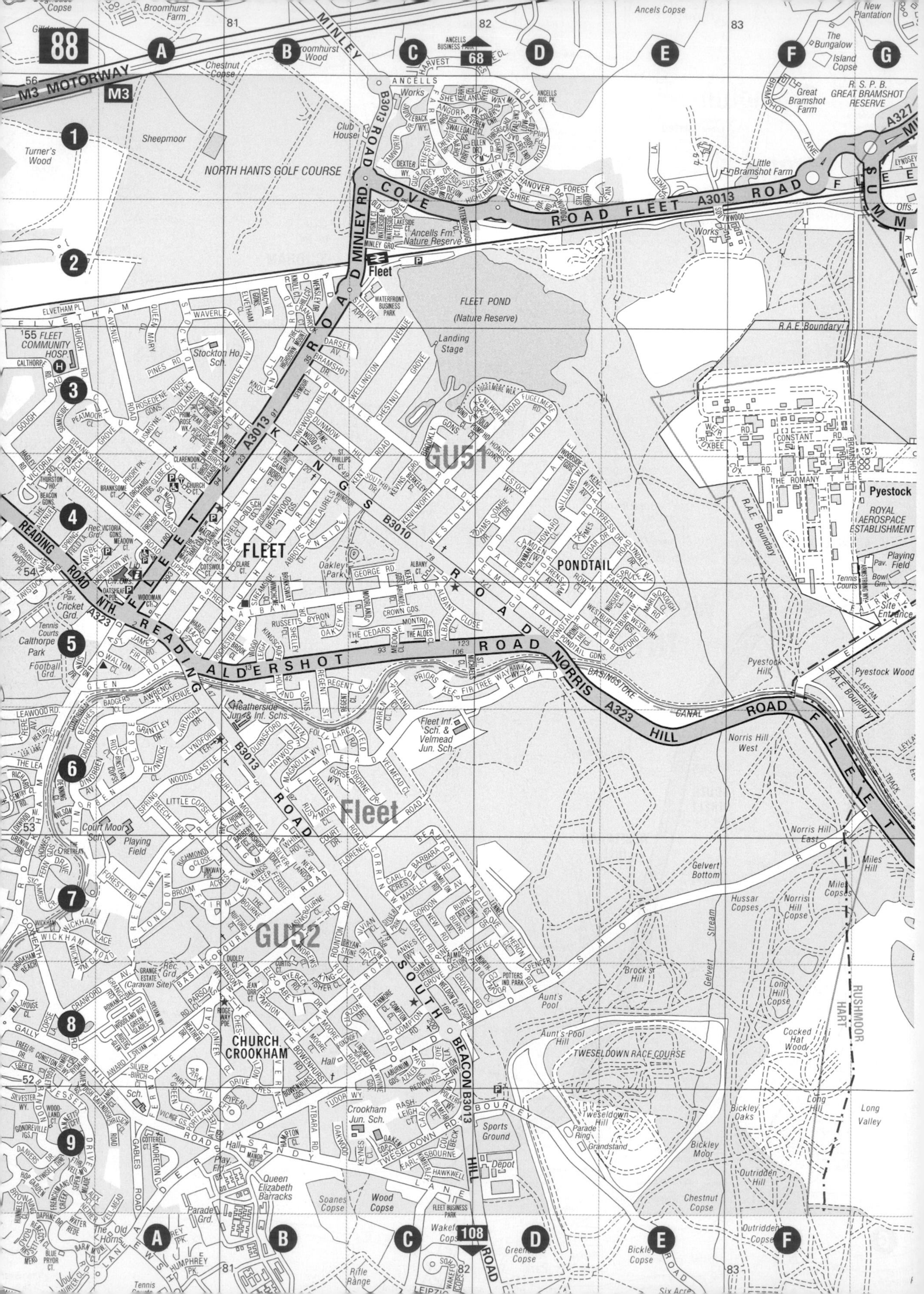

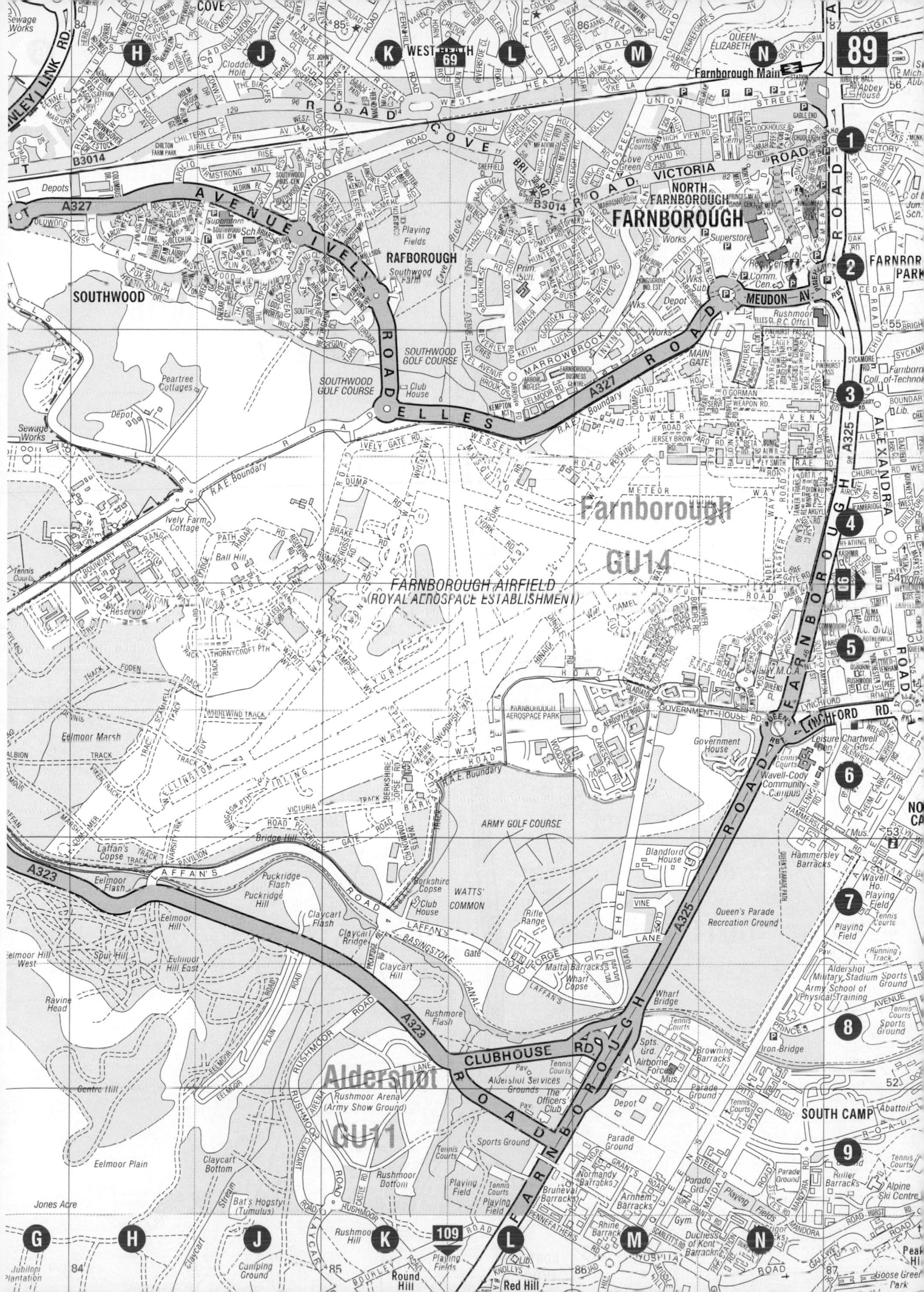

89
COVE
WEST HEATH
69
Farnborough Main
FARNBOROUGH
NORTH FARNBOROUGH
RAFBOROUGH
SOUTHWOOD
Farnborough
GU14
FARNBOROUGH AIRFIELD
(ROYAL AEROSPACE ESTABLISHMENT)
SOUTHWOOD GOLF COURSE
ARMY GOLF COURSE
Government House
Queen's Parade Recreation Ground
Aldershot
GU11
Rushmoor Arena (Army Show Ground)
SOUTH CAMP
Eelmoor Marsh
Eelmoor Plain
Jones Acre
Rushmoor Bottom
Red Hill
Round Hill
109
A327
A325
A323
B3014
CLUBHOUSE RD.
LYNCHFORD RD.
FARNBOROUGH ROAD
ELLES ROAD
IVELY ROAD
VICTORIA ROAD
MEUDON AV.
ALEXANDRA ROAD
H
J
K
L
M
N
G
1
2
3
4
5
6
7
8
9
84
85
86
87
56
55
54
53
52

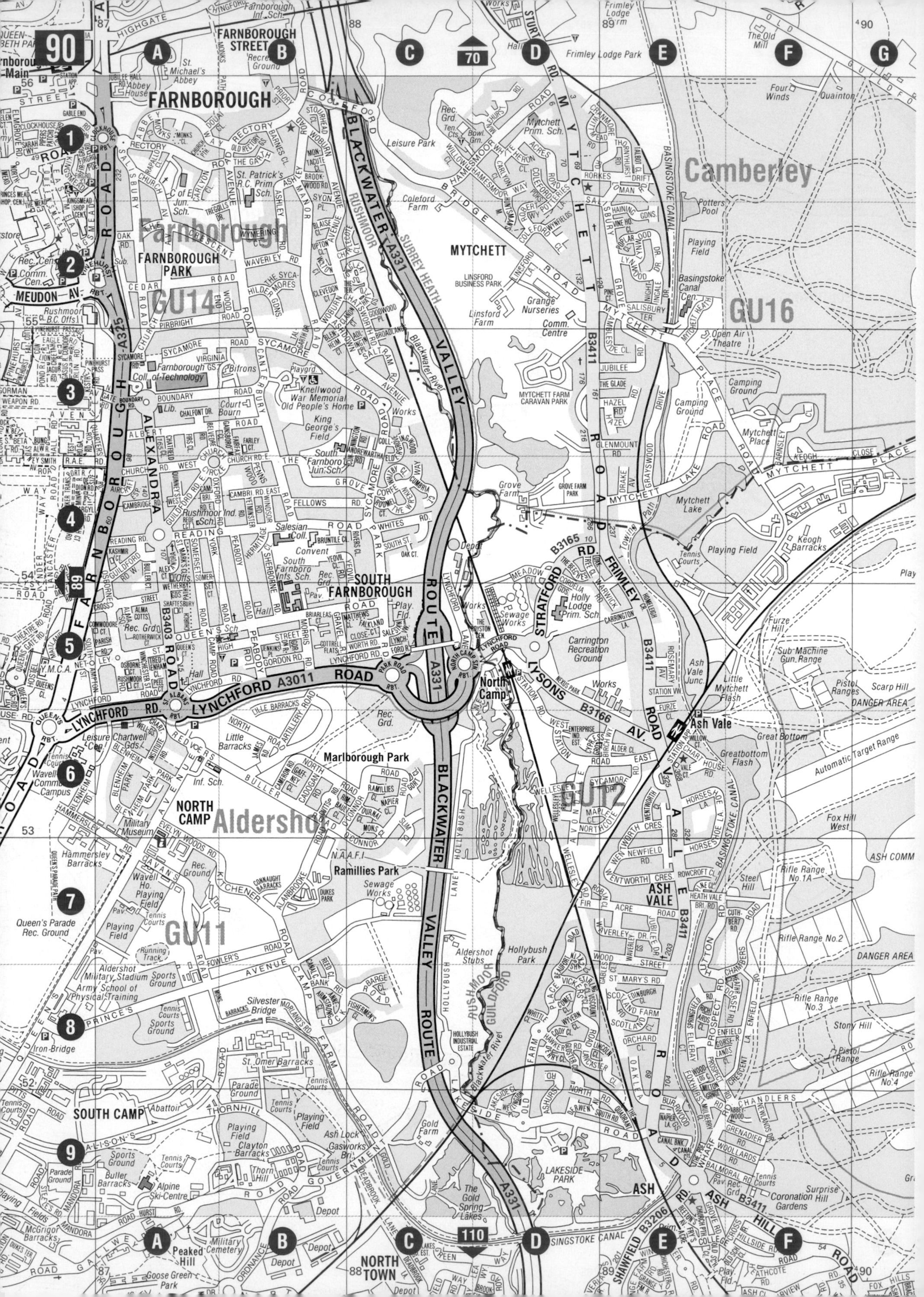

90
A
B
C
D
E
F
G
70
110
1
2
3
4
5
6
7
8
9
FARNBOROUGH
Farnborough
FARNBOROUGH PARK
FARNBOROUGH STREET
GU14
MYTCHETT
Camberley
GU16
SOUTH FARNBOROUGH
NORTH CAMP
Aldershot
GU11
GU12
ASH VALE
ASH
SOUTH CAMP
NORTH TOWN
Frimley Lodge Park
Leisure Park
Coleford Farm
Linsford Farm
LINSFORD BUSINESS PARK
Grange Nurseries
Comm. Centre
MYTCHETT FARM CARAVAN PARK
Mytchett Lake
Mytchett Place
Keogh Barracks
Playing Field
Basingstoke Canal Cen.
Open Air Theatre
Camping Ground
Potters Pool
Four Winds
Quainton
The Old Mill
Grove Farm
GROVE FARM PARK
Carrington Recreation Ground
Holly Lodge Prim. Sch.
Sewage Works
Little Mytchett Flash
Ash Vale Junc.
Ash Vale
Greatbottom Flash
Great Bottom
Automatic Target Range
Sub Machine Gun Range
Pistol Ranges
Scarp Hill
DANGER AREA
Furze Hill
Fox Hill West
Rifle Range No.1A
Steel Hill
Rifle Range No.2
Rifle Range No.3
Stony Hill
Pistol Range
Rifle Range No.4
Coronation Hill Gardens
Surprise Hill
Hollybush Park
Aldershot Stubs
HOLLYBUSH INDUSTRIAL ESTATE
LAKESIDE PARK
The Gold Spring Lakes
Gold Farm
Blackwater River
Marlborough Park
Ramillies Park
N.A.A.F.I.
Military Museum
Hammersley Barracks
Queen's Parade Rec. Ground
Aldershot Military Stadium
Army School of Physical Training
Sports Ground
Running Track
Silvester Bridge
St. Omer Barracks
Parade Ground
Abattoir
Clayton Barracks
Ash Lock
Gasworks Bri.
Thorn Hill
Buller Barracks
Alpine Ski-Centre
McGrigor Barracks
Peaked Hill
Military Cemetery
Goose Green Park
Depot
Iron Bridge
Wavell Comm. Campus
Leisure Cen.
Salesian Coll.
Convent
South Farnboro Infs. Sch.
South Farnboro Jun. Sch.
King George's Field
Knellwood War Memorial Old People's Home
Farnborough Coll. of Technology
Bifrons
Court Bourn
Rushmoor Ind. Est.
St. Patrick's R.C. Prim. Sch.
St. Michael's Abbey
Abbey House
Rushmoor B.C. Offs.
BLACKWATER VALLEY ROUTE
A331
A3011
A325
B3411
B3165
B3166
B3403
B3206
LYNCHFORD ROAD
FARNBOROUGH ROAD
ALEXANDRA ROAD
MYTCHETT ROAD
FRIMLEY ROAD
LYSONS AV.
VALE ROAD
ASH HILL ROAD
BASINGSTOKE CANAL
RUSHMOOR
SURREY HEATH
GUILDFORD
Mytchett Prim. Sch.
Rec. Grd.

Woking
GU24
Guildford
GU3
PIRBRIGHT COMMON
CLEYGATE COMMON
FOX HILLS
Gapemouth Plantation
Hodge Bottom
Stoney Castle Camping Ground
Mazamboni Farm
Furze Hill
Holy Island
Ruwenzori Hill
Rangelands Poultry Farm
West Hall Farm
Hodge Brook
No. 1 Range
Vines Farm
Hazelacre Hill
Reservoir (Covered)
Longdown Hill
DANGER AREA
Stoney Castle Ranges
Mortar Range
No. 2 Range
Tunnel Hill
Emperor's Hill
Bowling Hill
SURREY HEATH
GUILDFORD
Chair Hill
Track End
Mytchett Gate
Hangman's Hill
Bush Bottom
Double Clump
Kiln Hill
Bridge Hill
Frimley Ridges
The Bungalow
Rails Farm
Spur Hill
CLEYGATE COMMON
Scragley Hill
Oldfield Wood
Crown Prince Hill
Sheep Hill
Peat Moor
Romping Downs
Westwind
Ash Ranges
Foxholes Bottom
Long Hill
Peatmoor Pond
Henleypark Lake
Henley Park Ranges
Lookout Hill
Longhill Bottom
Standinghill Wood
Peatmoor Hill
Pit Hill
Bastion Hill
Slyfield Wood
Whitepatch Hill
The Glen
Engineering Works
Henley Park Farm
Dukes Hill
Whitepatch Bottom
Vine Farm
Henleypark Farm
Ricochet Hill
WYKE COMMON
Kiln Copse
Dolleyshill
DOLLEYSHILL CARAVAN PARK
Hunts Hill
Normandy Hill
Normandy Lodge Farm
Hunts Hill Farm
Anchor Copse
Woodlands
Elm Hill
Cricket Grd.
Football Field
Orchard Dene
Roughs Farm
Normandy Common
Normandy Pond
Rand's Plantation
Sandpit Farm
Fair View Farm
Slade Cottage
Wyke Prim. Sch.
NORMANDY
Wyke Heath Farm
ELM HILL
WYKE CROSS
WYKE
Manor Fruit Farm
A324
A323
PIRBRIGHT ROAD
GUILDFORD ROAD
71
111
92
Stanford
55
54
53
52

PIRBRIGHT
Burrow Hill
The Green
72
Woking
GU24
Bullswater Common
BULLSWATER COMMON
PIRBRIGHT COMMON
Worplesdon Golf Course
Fox Corner
STANFORD COMMON
Stanford Common
The Animal Virus Research Institute
Sewage Disposal Works
91
COBBETTHILL COMMON
COBBETT HILL
MERRIST WOOD
Merrist Wood College (Agricultural)
MERRIST WOOD GOLF CLUB
Littlefield Common
FAIRLANDS
GU3
Wireless Station (Disused)
A324
A323
A322
B3032
B380
ALDERSHOT ROAD
GUILDFORD ROAD
WILLEY GREEN
Broad Street Common
112

H
J
K
L
M
N
73
MAYFORD
Woking
GU22
SMART'S HEATH LANE
B380
Crastock Farm
Crastock Manor
Berryhill Nursery
Smart's Heath
Kemishford Bridge
PREY HEATH ROAD
Prey Heath or Pray Heath
Worplesdon
PREY HEATH CL.
Hoe Stream
Bridley Manor Farm
Bridley Manor
Bridley Copse
Bonnieshott Wood Farm
Burdenshott Hill
BURDENSHOTT ROAD
Havering Farm
Blanketmill Farm
Rye Farm
White Lodge
Hockley Lands
WOKING
GUILDFORD
Nursery
Whitmoor Pond
PYLE HILL
Wingstone
GU4
Frog Lane Farm
SUTTON GREEN GOLF COURSE
Loampits Farm
Club House
Elm Trees Farm
Green Lane Farm
Beech Hill
MAYBOURNE RISE
WOODPECKER WAY
Gooserye
Upper Jordan
Gooserye Cottage
Whitmoor Hatch
Woodcorner Farm
Heather Court
JORDAN HILL
GOOSE RYE ROAD
Rickford Common
Perryhill Cottage
CHURCH LANE
WORPLESDON
Perry Hill
Vine House
Perry Hill Farm
Maryland
WHITMOOR COMMON
Mount Pleasant
Hurst View
Willow Grange
Poor Jack's Wood
The Old Cottage
Whitmoor House
Whitmoor Wood
Whitmoor Farm
Sunridge House
Elm Nursery
94
Cox's Farm
A320 WOKING ROAD
GUILDFORD ROAD
WHITMOOR LANE
SUTTON LANE
CLAY LANE
Britten's Pond
Rectory
Greenacre
Sudpre
A322
WORPLESDON ROAD
Nursery
Guildford
SALT BOX ROAD
Field Research Station
Rifle & Pistol Range
PITCH PLACE
Tangley Place Farm
Queen Elizabeth Barracks
Playing Field
Queen Elizabeth Park
Parade Grd.
Stringer's Common
Stringers Common
Gunners Farm
Bullens Hill Farm
Stringer's Farm
Stoke Hill
JACOBS WELL
DENNIS WAY
SLYFIELD INDUSTRIAL ESTATE
Abattoir
Cattle Mkt.
MOORFIELD ROAD
GU1
BELLFIELDS
SLYFIELD GREEN
KEENS LANE
Works
Smallholding
Chittys Common
Liddington Hall Farm
GU2
Depot
Play. Fld.
Northmead Jun. Sch.
Stoke Hill Prim. Sch.
Bishop Reindorp C of E Sch.
Stoke New Cemetery
Weyfield Prim. Sch.
Sewage Works
Stoke Lock
Holly Farm
Liddington Lodge
Rydeshill Lodge
Ryde's Hill
A323
STOUGHTON
BELMONT AVENUE
BYREFIELD ROAD
Rydeshill
G
H
J
K
L
M
N
113
Recreation Ground
Shepherd's Hill
1
2
3
4
5
6
7
8
9

MAYFORD
CARTBRIDGE
SEND
SUTTON GREEN GOLF COURSE
GU22
PYLE HILL
Crickets Hill
SUTTON GREEN
Sutton Park
SUTTON PARK
Sutton Place
JACOBS WELL
Guildford
BURPHAM
SLYFIELD GREEN
GU1
ABBOTSWOOD
Merrow Common
74
93
114

75
115
96
Woking
SEND MARSH
BURNTCOMMON
GU23
GU4
Grove Heath
WEST CLANDON
Clandon
EAST CLANDON
Hatchlands
CLANDON PARK
CLANDON REGIS GOLF COURSE
FRITHYS WOOD
RIPLEY BY-PASS
A3
A247
A246
B368
B2215
PORTSMOUTH ROAD
CLANDON ROAD
THE STREET
EPSOM ROAD
RIPLEY ROAD
HUNGRY HILL
GAMBLES LANE
TITHEBARNS LANE
GREEN LANE
GRANGE
LIME GROVE
Send Marsh Green
Loveland's Copse
Ryde Farm
Roborow Wood
Sheppardsgrove Copse
Brambleride Copse
Holride Farm
August Hill
Sussex Farm
Humphreys Copse
Fish Pond
Buttinham Copse
Martin Furze
Gason Wood
Cammocks Wood
Withybed Plantation
Norcote Wood
Home Farm
Fullers Hill
Fullers Farm
H.M.P. SEND
Dedswell Manor Farm House
Dedswell Manor Farm
Garlick's Arch Copse
Oldlands Copse
Tithe Barns
Tythebarns Farm
Cedarwood
Oak Ride Farm
Hazelhurst Cottage
Highcotts Wood
Southernwood
Royal Surrey Regiment Museum
Clandon House
Temple Court
Club House
Summers
Tanfield Place
Blake's Lane Farm

A
B
C
D
E
F
G
76
95
116
Guileshill Farm
Blackmoor Farm
Slade Farm
Bramble Cottage
Slade Cottage
Ridings Copse
BARNSTHORNS WOOD
Cobham
DRIFT GOLF COURSE
Woking
Romer Cottage
The Old Cottage
Rydings Farm
Roborow
Roborow Wood
Bachelor's Copse
Russets
KT11
Blue Ride
Club House
The Drift
The Forest
North Forest Lodge
Even Wood
Works
Old Brickyard
GU23
Camping Site
Waterloo Farm
B2039
OCKHAM ROAD NORTH
OCKHAM DR.
NIGHTINGALE AVENUE
NIGHTINGALE CRESCENT
NORTHCOTE CRES.
The Raleigh Sch.
Broom House
Football Ground
Pav.
Tennis Courts
Gas Pumping Station
Brambleride Copse
Jury Farm
Depot
Manor Farm
Horsley
Lollesworth Wood
Brambleride
Roundtree Farm
WEST HORSLEY
Furze Copse
Parkrow Copse
Cricket Ground
Lower-Hammond's Farm
Frenchlands Copse
Roam Wells
Martin Furze
Gason Wood
Barcombe Farm
Dene Place
Pincott Farm
West Horsley Place
Place Farm
Guildford
GU4
Hammonds Farm
Cammocks Wood
Britains Farm
Nursery
Cranmore Sch.
Little Wix Wood
Great Wix Wood
Tennis Courts
EPSOM ROAD
A246
Wix Farm
Poultry Farm
Lodge
Hatchlands Park (National Trust)
Fullers Hill
Fullers Farm
Hatchlands
Wix Hill House
Woolgars Farm
Wix Hill Stud Farm
Weston Wood
SHEEP LEAS
Angel Clump
Training Course
Wood's Plantation
Blake's Lane Farm
Daws Dene
Tyrellswood
Green Plantation
ROAD GUILDFORD

Effingham Junction
Bookham
Little Bookham
Leatherhead
EFFINGHAM COMMON
THORNET WOOD
EFFINGHAM
KT23
KT24
EAST HORSLEY
EFFINGHAM GOLF COURSE
Dorking
RH5
GUILDFORD ROAD
A246
MOLE VALLEY
GUILDFORD
Howard of Effingham School
Manor House Sch.
St. Teresa's Prep. Sch.
Preston Cross
The Grange (Training Centre)
Effingham Hill
Horsley Towers
Oakdene Rd.
Church Rd.
Lower Farm
Indian Farm
Upper Leewood Farm
Great Ridings Plantation
Orestan Plantation
Warren Farm
High Barn
Stonyrock Copse

Bookham
FETCHAM
GREAT BOOKHAM
Leatherhead
KT22
KT23
Fetcham Downs
Polesden Lacey
NORBURY PARK
Polesden Lacey (National Trust)
Tanner's Hatch (Youth Hostel)
GUILDFORD ROAD
LEATHERHEAD RD.
YOUNG
A246
B2122 (HAWK'S HILL)
78
97
118

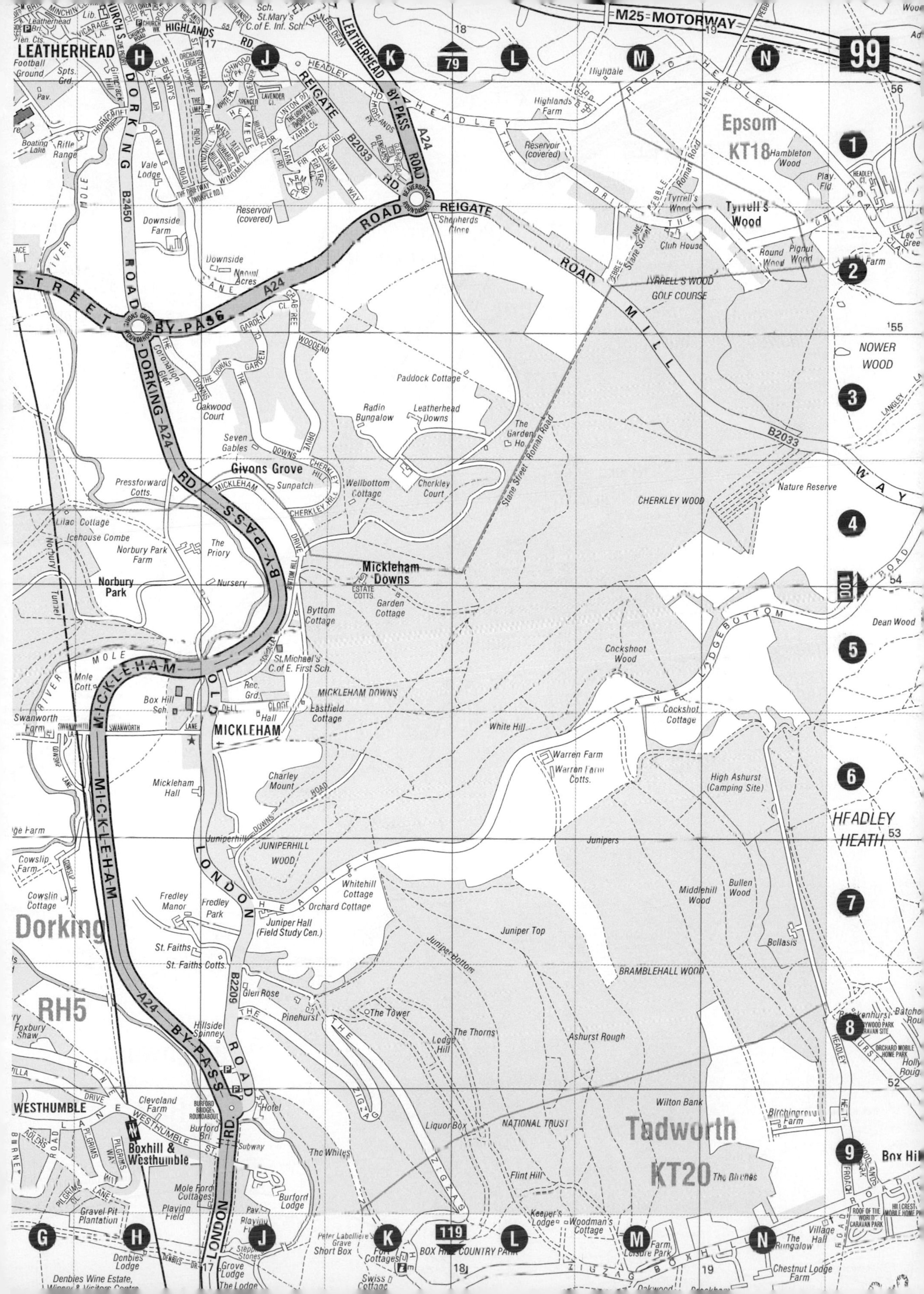

99
79
100
119
LEATHERHEAD
M25 MOTORWAY
Epsom
KT18
Givons Grove
Mickleham Downs
MICKLEHAM
Dorking
RH5
WESTHUMBLE
Boxhill & Westhumble
Tadworth
KT20
HEADLEY HEATH
NOWER WOOD
CHERKLEY WOOD
Tyrrell's Wood
TYRRELL'S WOOD GOLF COURSE
Norbury Park
Juniper Hall (Field Study Cen.)
NATIONAL TRUST
BOX HILL COUNTRY PARK
BRAMBLEHALL WOOD
Juniper Top
Cockshoot Wood
High Ashurst (Camping Site)
Stane Street Roman Road

100
A
B
C
D
E
F
G
80
99
120
20
21
22
56
55
54
53
52
M25
M25 MOTORWAY
Epsom
KT18
Dorking
RH5
Tadworth
KT20
Betchworth
RH3
WALTON ON THE HILL
HEADLEY
Tot Hill
Box Hill
Walton Heath
NOWER WOOD
GREAT HURST WOOD
WALTON PARK WOOD
SANDHILL WOOD
HEADLEY HEATH
HEADLEY COMMON
HEADLEY ROAD
DORKING ROAD
PEBBLE HILL ROAD
PEBBLE HILL RD.
CHEQUERS LANE
HURST ROAD
CHURCH LANE
LEECH LA.
MILL WAY
LODGEBOTTOM ROAD
BOXHILL ROAD
STATION RD.
BUCKLAND ROAD
RECTORY LANE
LAWRENCE LANE
TYE LANE
B2033
B2032
B220
REIGATE and BANSTEAD
MOLE VALLEY
Addlestead Farm
North Lodge
Loretta Lodge
Walton Hurst Farm
The Hurst
Hurst Wood
Round Wood
Wingfield Farm Cottages
Wildwoods
Police Training School
Twistwood
Edes Barn Cottages
Headley Park Farm
Headley Park
Hook Wood
Hambledon Wood
Play Fld.
Round Wood
Pignut Wood
Court Farm
Oyster Hill
Great Hurst Wood
Costal Wood
Tumber House
Rectory
Tunbarr
Hayes Cotts.
Kingsbarns
Nature Reserve
Manor House
Heath Farm
Goodman's Furze
Cricket Ground
Pav.
Great Hayes
Dean Wood
White Lodge
Frith Park
Frith Park Farm
Hedgecroft
Ebbisham Farm
Walton Manor
Walton Manor Farm
Bramley Sch.
Recreation Ground
Lovelands
Club House
Mere Pond
Prim. Sch.
Comm. Cen.
Sturt House
Herring Grove
Queen's Wood
LITTLE HEATH
Walton Oaks
The Hermitage
Experimental Farm
Headley Grove Farm
Headley Grove
Little Heath Cottages
Pebble Coombe
Headley Reservoir
Fraser Heath
Headley Plantation
Boidier Hurst Scout Camping Site
Swimming Pool (Covered)
Mus.
Heath Plantation
White's Wood
Dawcombe Wood
Dewriding Plantation
Lady Hill
Round Wood
Pilgrims' Way
Harebeating Brow
Prestige Farm
Brackenhurst
Batchelor's Rough
Bellasis
Holly Rough
Betchworth Hills Wood
Betchworth Hills
Poor's Field
Kemp's Farm
Kemp's Farm Cottages
Wildecroft
Birchingrove Farm
Boxhill Nurseries
Betchworth Clump
Quarry
Dorking Lime Works
Village Hall
The Bungalow
Chestnut Lodge Farm
Fort (dismantled)
Brockham Hills
Betchworth
The Sloughs
Birches

101
TADWORTH
KINGSWOOD
KINGSWOOD GOLF COURSE
BANSTEAD HEATH
WALTON HEATH
WALTON HEATH GOLF COURSE
LOWER KINGSWOOD
MUGSWELL
Coulsdon CR5
MOGADOR
MARGERY
REIGATE HILL INTERCHANGE
Junction 8
M25 MOTORWAY
BRIGHTON ROAD
A217
Reigate RH2
Tadworth Postmill
Kingswood Warren
Club House
Business Park
Recreation Ground
Kingswood Prim. Sch.
Natural Gas Pressure Reducing Station
Colley Hill
The Saddle Knob
Juniper Hill
Queen's Park
Reigate Hill
Fort (dismantled)
Pilgrims' Way
81
102
121

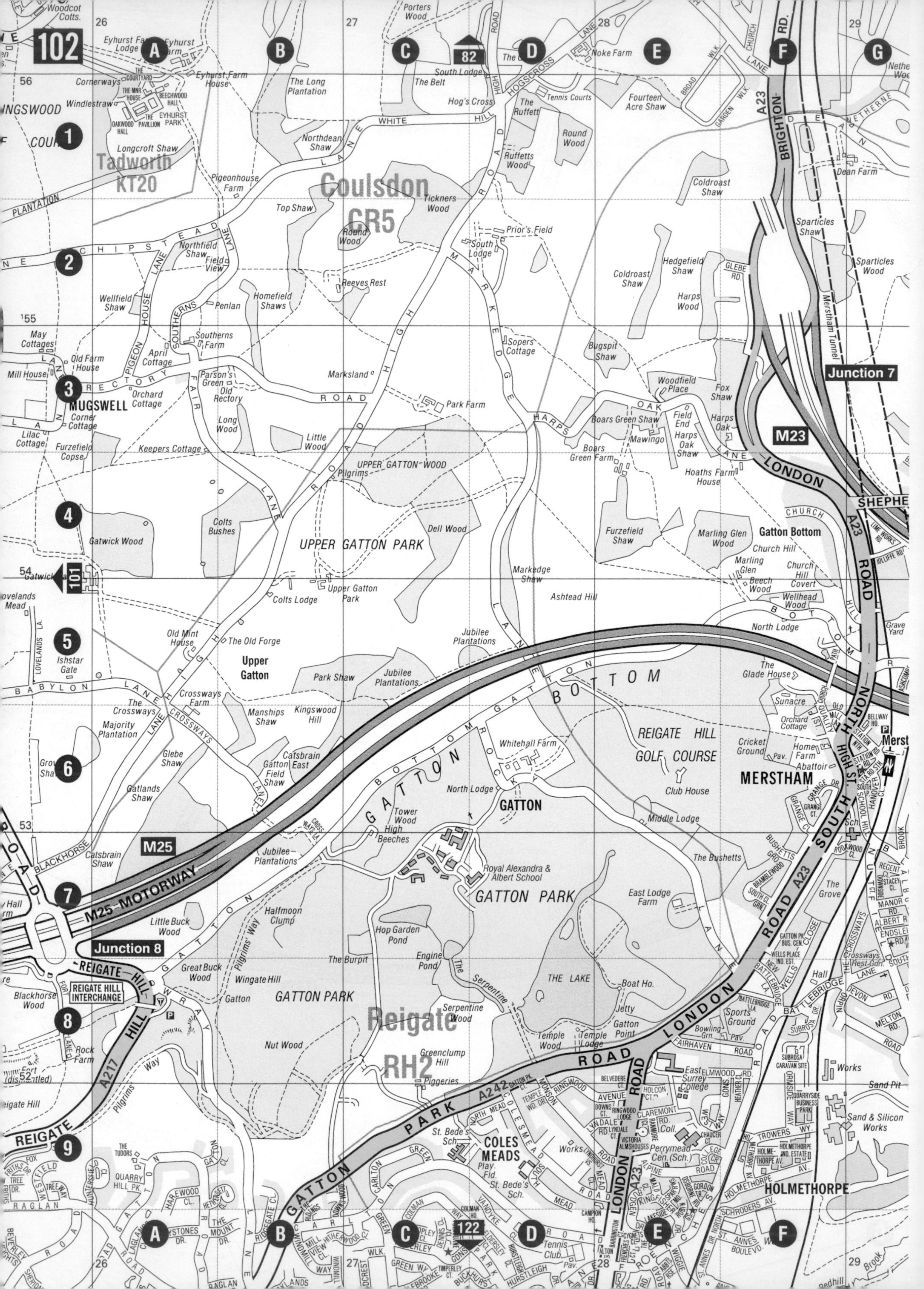

82
101
122
Junction 7
Junction 8
M23
M25
M25 MOTORWAY
A23
A217
A242
Coulsdon
CR5
Tadworth
KT20
Reigate
RH2
MUGSWELL
MERSTHAM
GATTON
HOLMETHORPE
COLES MEADS
UPPER GATTON PARK
GATTON PARK
REIGATE HILL GOLF COURSE
REIGATE HILL INTERCHANGE
Upper Gatton
Gatton Bottom
Woodcot Cotts.
Eyhurst Farm Lodge
Eyhurst Farm
Eyhurst Farm House
Cornerways
Windlestraw
Longcroft Shaw
Porters Wood
The Long Plantation
The Belt
South Lodge
Hog's Cross
Northdean Shaw
Pigeonhouse Farm
Top Shaw
Round Wood
Tickners Wood
Prior's Field
Noke Farm
Fourteen Acre Shaw
The Ruffett
Tennis Courts
Round Wood
Ruffetts Wood
Coldroast Shaw
Sparticles Shaw
Sparticles Wood
Dean Farm
Mersham Tunnel
Northfield Shaw
Field View
Reeves Rest
Homefield Shaws
Wellfield Shaw
Penlan
Hedgefield Shaw
Harps Wood
May Cottages
Southerns Farm
April Cottage
Old Farm House
Mill House
Parson's Green
Old Rectory
Orchard Cottage
Corner Cottage
Lilac Cottage
Marksland
Sopers Cottage
Bugspit Shaw
Woodfield Place
Fox Shaw
Park Farm
Long Wood
Little Wood
Boars Green Shaw
Field End
Harps Oak
Mawingo
Harps Oak Shaw
Boars Green Farm
Hoaths Farm House
Furzefield Copse
Keepers Cottage
Upper Gatton Wood
Pilgrims
Colts Bushes
Dell Wood
Furzefield Shaw
Marling Glen Wood
Church Hill
Marling Glen
Beech Wood
Church Hill Covert
Gatwick Wood
Markedge Shaw
Ashtead Hill
Wellhead Wood
Upper Gatton Park
Colts Lodge
Lovelands Mead
North Lodge
Grave Yard
Old Mint House
The Old Forge
Jubilee Plantations
Ishstar Gate
Park Shaw
The Glade House
The Crossways
Crossways Farm
Manships Shaw
Kingswood Hill
Sunacre
Majority Plantation
Orchard Cottage
Whitehall Farm
Cricket Ground
Home Farm
Abattoir
Glebe Shaw
Catsbrain East
Gatton Field Shaw
Club House
Gatlands Shaw
North Lodge
Tower Wood
High Beeches
Middle Lodge
Catsbrain Shaw
Jubilee Plantations
Royal Alexandra & Albert School
The Bushetts
East Lodge Farm
The Grove
Little Buck Wood
Halfmoon Clump
Hop Garden Pond
Engine Pond
The Burpit
The Serpentine
THE LAKE
Boat Ho.
Great Buck Wood
Wingate Hill
Gatton
Blackhorse Wood
Rock Farm
Serpentine Wood
Jetty
Gatton Point
Temple Wood
Temple Lodge
Sports Ground
Bowling Grn.
Pav.
Nut Wood
Greenclump Hill
Piggeries
East Surrey College
Works
Sand Pit
Sand & Silicon Works
St. Bede's Sch.
Victoria Almshouses
Perrymead Cen. (Sch.)
Play. Fld.
Tennis Club
Subrosa Caravan Site
Holmethorpe Ind. Estate
Gatton Pk Bus. Cen.
Wells Place Ind. Est.
Crossways Rest Gdn.
Reigate Hill
Fort (dismantled)
The Tudors
Quarry Hill Pk.
CHIPSTEAD LANE
WHITE HILL LANE
HOGSCROSS LANE
HIGH ROAD
MARKEDGE LANE
RECTORY ROAD
PIGEON HOUSE LANE
SOUTHERNS LANE
FAIR LANE
HARPS OAK LANE
LONDON ROAD
BRIGHTON RD.
CHURCH LANE
SHEPHERDS HILL
NORTH STATION RD.
BOTTOM LANE
BABYLON LANE
CROSSWAYS LANE
BLACKHORSE LANE
GATTON BOTTOM
ROCKY LANE
REIGATE HILL
WRAY LANE
GATTON PARK ROAD
NORTH HIGH ST.
SOUTH HIGH ST.
BATTLEBRIDGE LANE
FAIRHAVEN ROAD
FRENCHES ROAD
NUTLEY LANE
RAGLAN RD.
A
B
C
D
E
F
G
1
2
3
4
5
6
7
8
9
26
27
28
29
56
55
54
53
52

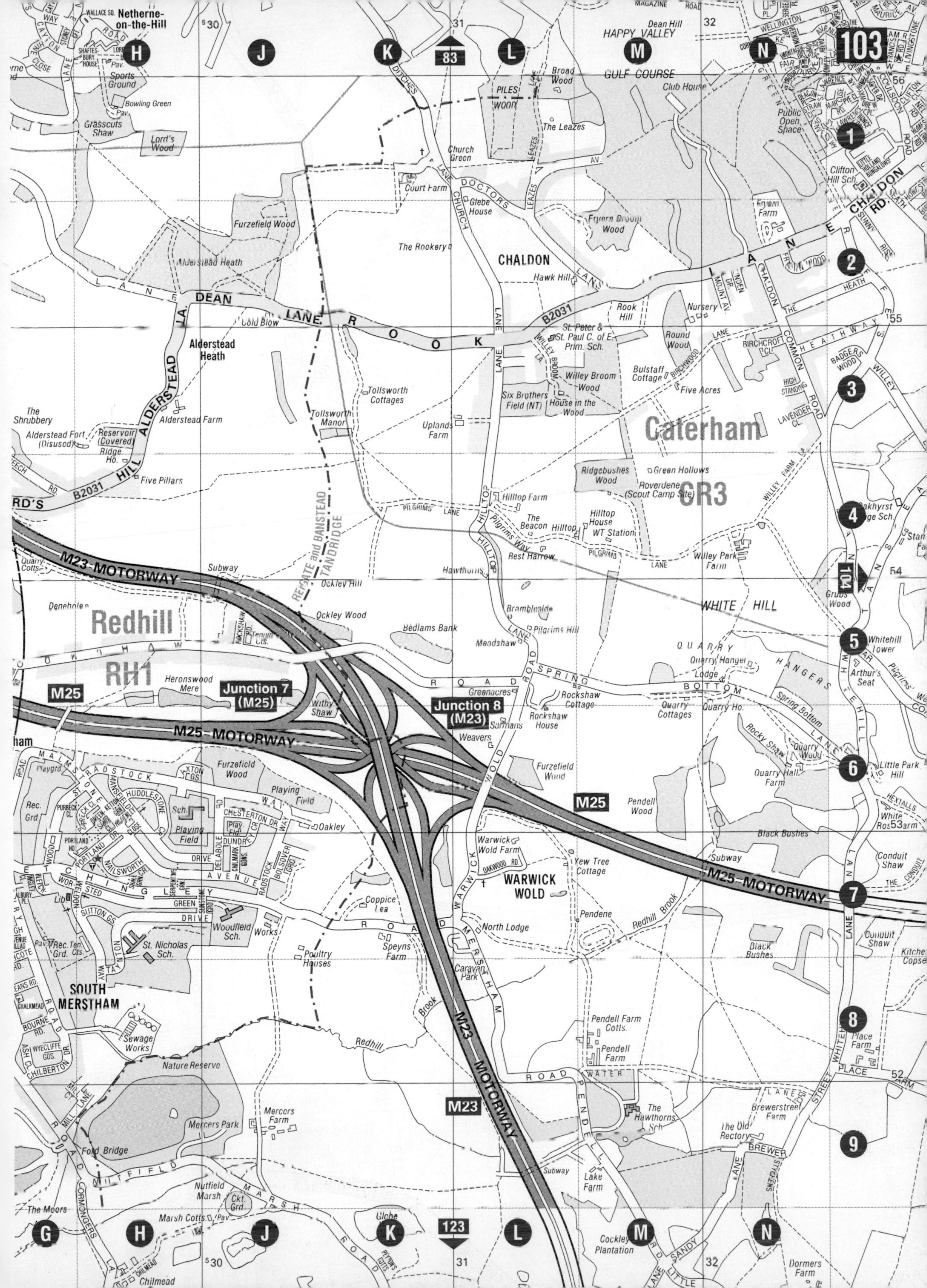
Netherne-on-the-Hill
Sports Ground
Bowling Green
Grasscuts Shaw
Lord's Wood
HAPPY VALLEY
Dean Hill
GOLF COURSE
Club House
Broad Wood
PILES WOOD
The Leazes
Church Green
Court Farm
Glebe House
DOCTORS
Furzefield Wood
Alderstead Heath
The Rookery
CHALDON
Hawk Hill
Fryern Broom Wood
DEAN LANE
ROOK LANE
B2031
Cold Blow
Alderstead Heath
Rook Hill
St. Peter & St. Paul C. of E. Prim. Sch.
Round Wood
Nursery
Bulstaff Cottage
Five Acres
Willey Broom Wood
Six Brothers Field (NT)
House in the Wood
Tollsworth Cottages
Tollsworth Manor
Uplands Farm
Caterham
CR3
The Shrubbery
Alderstead Farm
Alderstead Fort (Disused)
Reservoir (Covered)
Ridge Ho.
Five Pillars
ALDERSTEAD HILL
Ridgebushes Wood
Green Hollows
Roverdene (Scout Camp Site)
Hilltop Farm
The Beacon
Hilltop
Hilltop House
WT Station
Rest Harrow
Willey Park Farm
PILGRIMS LANE
REIGATE and BANSTEAD
TANDRIDGE
M23 MOTORWAY
Subway
Ockley Hill
Hawthorns
Redhill
Ockley Wood
Bedlams Bank
Brambleside
Pilgrims Hill
WHITE HILL
Meadshaw
RH1
Heronswood Mere
Junction 7 (M25)
Withy Shaw
Junction 8 (M23)
M25
SPRING BOTTOM ROAD
QUARRY HANGERS
Quarry Hanger Lodge
Quarry Cottages
Quarry Ho.
Rockshaw Cottage
Rockshaw House
Greenacres
M25 MOTORWAY
Weavers
Furzefield Wood
Furzefield Wood
Playing Field
Pendell Wood
Quarry Hall Farm
Little Park Hill
Whitehill Tower
Arthur's Seat
Oakley
Black Bushes
Warwick Wold Farm
Yew Tree Cottage
WARWICK WOLD
Conduit Shaw
Coppice Lea
Works
Pendene
North Lodge
Redhill Brook
Speyns Farm
Poultry Houses
Caravan Park
Woodfield Sch.
St. Nicholas Sch.
SOUTH MERSTHAM
Sewage Works
Nature Reserve
Pendell Farm Cotts.
Pendell Farm
Place Farm
Brewerstreet Farm
The Old Rectory
The Hawthorns Sch.
M23 MOTORWAY
Mercers Farm
Mercers Park
Fold Bridge
Nutfield Marsh
Ckt. Grd.
Marsh Cotts.
Lake Farm
Subway
The Moors
Glebe
Cockley Plantation
Dormers Farm
Chilmead
83
123
104
30
31
32
1
2
3
4
5
6
7
8
9
55
54
53
52
56

Caterham-on-the-Hill
CATERHAM
Caterham CR3
Godstone RH9
Redhill RH1
GODSTONE
Church Town
A B C D E F G
1 2 3 4 5 6 7 8 9
84
103
124
CATERHAM-BY-PASS A22
GODSTONE ROAD
GODSTONE HILL A22
M25 MOTORWAY
M25
Junction 6
GODSTONE INTERCHANGE
OXTED A25
BLETCHINGLEY RD. A25
CHALDON ROAD B2031
ROOK LA.
CROYDON ROAD B2208
HIGH ST.
CHURCH HILL B2030
GODSTONE ROAD B2030
HARESTONE VALLEY ROAD
GRAVELLY HILL
WEALD WAY
STANSTEAD ROAD
WHITE HILL LANE
WAR COPPICE ROAD
Pilgrims' Way
ROUGHETS LANE
PLACE FARM ROAD
NORTH PARK LANE
CHURCH LANE
Caterham School
Caterham Preparatory School
Marie Curie Cen. Caterham
NORTH DOWNS HOSP.
Oldpark Wood
Queens Park
Tillingdown Farm
Paddock Wood
Ockley Wood
Fosterdown Wood
Pilgrim Fort
Godstone Vineyards
Quarry Farm
Winders Hill
Tyler's Green
East Reservoir
West Reservoir
Nature Reserve
Godstone Green
Bay Pond Nature Reserve
Bletchingley Golf Course
Ivy Mill Farm
Stangrave Hall
Windsor Farm Nursery
North Park Farm
Big Pickle
Little Pickle
Earthwork
Hopgarden Shaw
Place Farm
Brewerstreet Farm
Kitchen Copse
Conduit Shaw
White Hill House
The Roughets
Surrey Crest
Whitehill Tower
Arthur's Seat
Little Park Hill
The Mound
War Coppice House
White Rose Farm
Black Bushes
Stanstead Farm
Oakhyrst Grange Sch.
Grubs Wood
Fryern Farm
Worlds End
Park Shaw
Beechwood Riding School
Marden Hillboxes Farm
Carr's Croft
Paddock Barn
The Chalet Farm
Eight Acre Wood
Upwood Gorse
Ten Acre Shaw
Valley Sports Ground
St. John's C. of E. Inf. & Jun. Sch.
Freer Mink Farm
Castle View
Old Garston Farmhouse
Little Place Fm.
Flower Farm

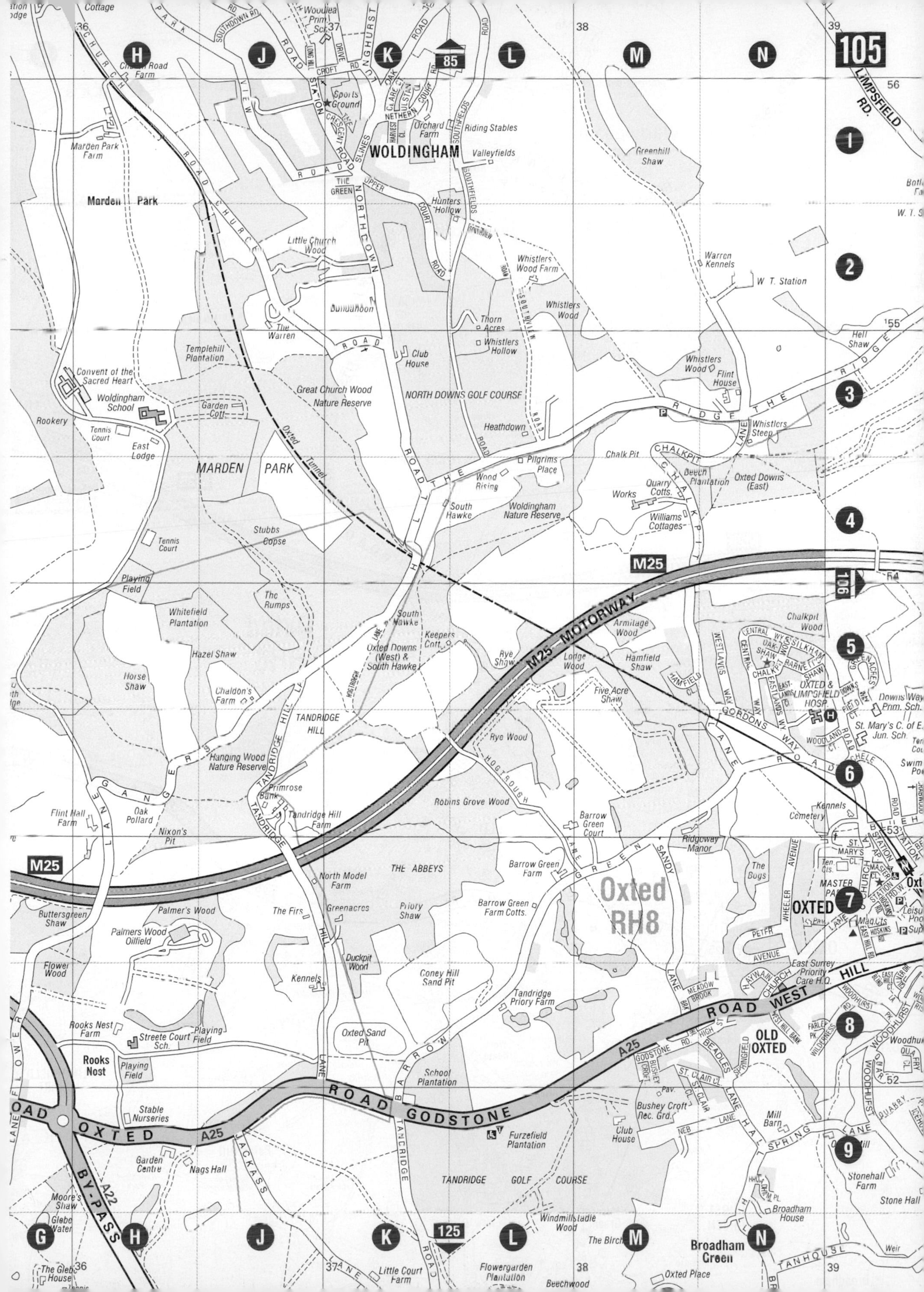

Cottage
Woodlea Prim. Sch.
Church Road Farm
85
Sports Ground
Orchard Farm
Riding Stables
Marden Park Farm
WOLDINGHAM
Valleyfields
Greenhill Shaw
Marden Park
Hunters Hollow
Little Church Wood
Whistlers Wood Farm
Warren Kennels
W. T. Station
The Warren
Thorn Acres
Whistlers Wood
Templehill Plantation
Club House
Whistlers Hollow
Hell Shaw
Convent of the Sacred Heart
Great Church Wood Nature Reserve
NORTH DOWNS GOLF COURSE
Whistlers Wood
Flint House
Woldingham School
Garden Cott.
Rookery
Tennis Court
East Lodge
Heathdown
Whistlers Steep
MARDEN PARK
Oxted Tunnel
Pilgrims Place
Chalk Pit
Wood Rising
Beech Plantation
Oxted Downs (East)
Quarry Cotts.
Works
South Hawke
Woldingham Nature Reserve
Williams Cottages
Stubbs Copse
Tennis Court
M25
Playing Field
The Rumps
Whitefield Plantation
South Hawke
Armitage Wood
Chalkpit Wood
Keepers Cott.
Oxted Downs (West) & South Hawke
Hazel Shaw
Rye Shaw
Lodge Wood
Hamfield Shaw
M25 MOTORWAY
Horse Shaw
Chaldon's Farm
Five Acre Shaw
OXTED & LIMPSFIELD HOSP.
Downs Way Prim. Sch.
TANDRIDGE HILL
St. Mary's C. of E. Jun. Sch.
Rye Wood
Hanging Wood Nature Reserve
Primrose Bank
Robins Grove Wood
Flint Hall Farm
Oak Pollard
Tandridge Hill Farm
Barrow Green Court
Kennels
Cemetery
Nixon's Pit
Ridgeway Manor
M25
North Model Farm
THE ABBEYS
Barrow Green Farm
The Bogs
Oxted RH8
OXTED
Buttersgreen Shaw
Palmer's Wood
The Firs
Greenacres
Priory Shaw
Barrow Green Farm Cotts.
Palmers Wood Oilfield
Duckpit Wood
Flower Wood
Coney Hill Sand Pit
Kennels
East Surrey Priority Care H.Q.
Tandridge Priory Farm
Rooks Nest Farm
Streete Court Sch.
Playing Field
Oxted Sand Pit
OLD OXTED
Rooks Nest
Playing Field
School Plantation
Bushey Croft Rec. Grd.
Stable Nurseries
Club House
Mill Barn
Furzefield Plantation
Garden Centre
Nags Hall
TANDRIDGE GOLF COURSE
Stonehall Farm
Moore's Shaw
Glebe Water
Stone Hall
Broadham House
Windmillstadle Wood
125
The Birch
Broadham Green
The Glebe House
Little Court Farm
Flowergarden Plantation
Oxted Place
Beechwood
A25
A22
OXTED BY-PASS
GODSTONE ROAD
ROAD WEST HILL
THE RIDGE
LIMPSFIELD RD.
106

86
105
126
Warlingham
CR6
Caterham
CR3
Oxted
RH8
PITCHERS WOOD
Pitchers Copse Farm
Works
Beacon Shaw
41 PARK
Clarkslane
Church Farm
Clubhouse
CHESTNUT
CLARKS LANE
Clarks Lane Farm
B2024
BEDDLESTEAD LANE
APPROACH RD
LIMPSFIELD ROAD
B269
Paygate Cott.
BOTLEY HILL
Botley Hill Farm
W. T. Station
Park Lane Cotts.
Botley Hill Cotts.
RIDGE ROAD
CLARKS TITSEY
High Trees
Coldharbour Beeches
WHITE LANE
RECTORY LANE
PILGRIMS LANE
Pilgrims' Farm
Pilgrims Cotts
TITSEY PLANTATION
Hell Shaw
THE RIDGE
Whistlers Steep
Oxted Downs (East)
Titsey Place
TITSEY
Lodge
Titsey Court
Rectory
EVELYN AVENUE
PILGRIMS
TITSEY HILL
TITSEY ROAD
River Eden
Church Wood
Roughfield Shaw
Square Wood
The Rookery
Barton Shaw
Pitchfont Farm
PITCHFONT LANE
Limpsfield Lodge Fm.
TITSEY PARK
M25
Clacket Lane Service Area
Park Farm
WATER LANE
South Green
BROOMLANDS LANE
TITSEY WOOD
M25 MOTORWAY
Chalkpit Wood
Broomlands Farm
Ashen Coppice
Moorhouse Sand Pits
Streatfield's Copse
Limpsfield Grange Sch.
SANDY LANE
Playing Field
OXTED & LIMPSFIELD HOSP.
Downs Way Prim. Sch.
St. Mary's C. of E. Jun. Sch.
Tennis Courts
Swimming Pool
Oxted Co. Sch.
Laverock Sch.
BLUEHOUSE LANE
Hookwood Park
Hookwood
Playing Fields
Wymondley
Kentish Border
Hookwood Bungalows
Grubstreet Shaw
Grubstreet Copse
Grubbe Street Wood
Sunridge
The Rips
Kennels
Cemetery
LIMPSFIELD
HIGH STREET
De Tillens
DETILLENS LANE
B2025
GRESHAM ROAD
GRANVILLE ROAD
STATION ROAD
Liby.
Tandridge D.C. Offs.
Oxted
The Bogs
MASTER PARK
Leisure Pool
Superstore
Mag.Cts
WESTERHAM ROAD
WESTERHAM HILL
A25
Court Langley
Pebble Hill
Pebble Hill Ho.
Scout Hall
Ckt. Gd.
Sch.
The Gate House
Club Ho.
LIMPSFIELD CHART GOLF COURSE
Ballards Shaw
KENT HILL
OXTED
PETER AVENUE
East Surrey Priority Care H.Q.
EAST HILL
WEST HILL
OLD OXTED
ROCKFIELD ROAD
BRASSEY ROAD
Play. Fld.
Andrew's Wood
Oakshaw Cott
LIMPSFIELD COMMON
Ridlands Fm.
Woodhurst Bridge
Wildshaw
West Heath
Limpsfield Tunnel
Pollards Wood
Greenflags
Broadway
The Red House
Briars Cross
RIDLANDS LANE
LIMPSFIELD CHART
CHAPEL ROAD
Court Hayes
Hazelwood Sch.
Mill Barn
SPRING LANE
Oxted Mill
Lunch Wood
Viewlands
Pains Hill
PASTENS ROAD
Little Heath
Chartfield Ho.
Reservoir (covered)
Tenchleys Park
Stonehall Farm
Stone Hall
Broadham House
HURST GREEN
Hurst Green
The Alders
Boulthurst Fm.
Tenchleys Wood
TANHOUSE ROAD
Tanhouse Fm.
Broadham
Hall
Comm. Cen.
Hurst Green School
Loampit Wood

Westerham
TN16
WESTERHAM
Edenbridge
TN8
Force Green
M25
M25 MOTORWAY
A25
A233
B2024
B2026
B269
MOORHOUSE
Moorhouse Bank
Hill Park
Goodley Stock
Kent Hatch
Hosey Hill
French Street
WESTERHAM WOOD
SQUERRYES PARK
TOWER WOOD
HOSEY COMMON
CROCKHAMHILL COMMON
Squerryes Court
Hartley Wood
Rowtye Wood
Wet Wood
Dunsdale Wood
Chartwell (NT)
SEVENOAKS
TANDRIDGE
87
127

108
A
B
C
D
E
F
G
88
128
Fleet
GU52
GU10
Farnham
Queen Elizabeth Barracks
Parade Grd.
Soanes Copse
Wood Copse
Wakefords Copse
Depot
Grandstand
Bickley Moor
Outridden Hill
Chestnut Copse
Outridden Copse
Greendane Copse
Bickley Copse
Six Acre Copse
Chandler's Copse
Bourley Camping Ground
Ewshot Camping Grd.
Rifle Range
Playing Field
Tennis Court
Leipzig Barracks
Tennis Courts
Redfields Racing Stables
Decks Lodge
Blackmore Copse
Wychwood
Stillers Farm
Beacon Hill Cottages
Beaconhill Copse
Parkhurst Hill
Water Works
Firs Hill
Burn's Plain
Reservoir (covered)
Riding's Copse
Reservoir
Bourley Bottom
Bourley Hill
Beacon Hill Farm
Beacon Hill
Dare's Corner
Seymour Farm
Pilridden Copse
Rec. Grd
Hall
Woodlands
Homecroft Farm
Abury Hill
Hebrew Cottage
Midtrees
Skains Copse
Turner's Copse
Combe Wood
EWSHOT
Reservoir No.5
Caesar's Camp
DANGER
Bushylease Farm
Bushylease Farm House
Ewshot Wood
Bricksbury Hill
DANGER AREA
Heath House
Redlands
Orchard Farm
Redlands Farm
Warren Corner
Heath Corner
Hale Prim. Sch.
OAK PARK GOLFING COMPLEX
Club House
Ewshot Hall
Ewshot Farm
Reservoir (covered)
Lands Copse
The Tileries
The Warren
Heath Hill
Lawn Copse
Dora's Green Farm
Dora's Green
Upper Old Park
The Mount
Knowle Farm
Claypit Wood
Middle Old Park
CLARE PARK BUPA HOSPITAL
Clare Park Farm
Pond Copse
Lower Old Park
Old Park Farm
Upper Clare Farm
Lower Old Park Farm
Hilyour's Copse
Meads
The Surrey Institute of Art & Design
Powderham Castle
Motte
Stocks Copse
Works
Overdeans Court
FARNHAM ROAD
A287
ODIHAM ROAD
UPPER FOLLY HILL
BEACON HILL ROAD
B3013
EWSHOT LANE
TADPOLE LANE
CHURCH LANE
REDLANDS LANE
HEATH LANE
DORA'S GREEN LANE
GREEN LANE
CRONDALL LANE
MIDDLE OLD PARK
UPPER OLD PARK LA
OLD PARK LANE
HEATHYFIELDS RD
BOURLEY ROAD
HART
RUSHMOOR
WAVERLEY
BEAVERS HILL
81
82
83
51
50
49
48
47
1
2
3
4
5
6
7
8
9

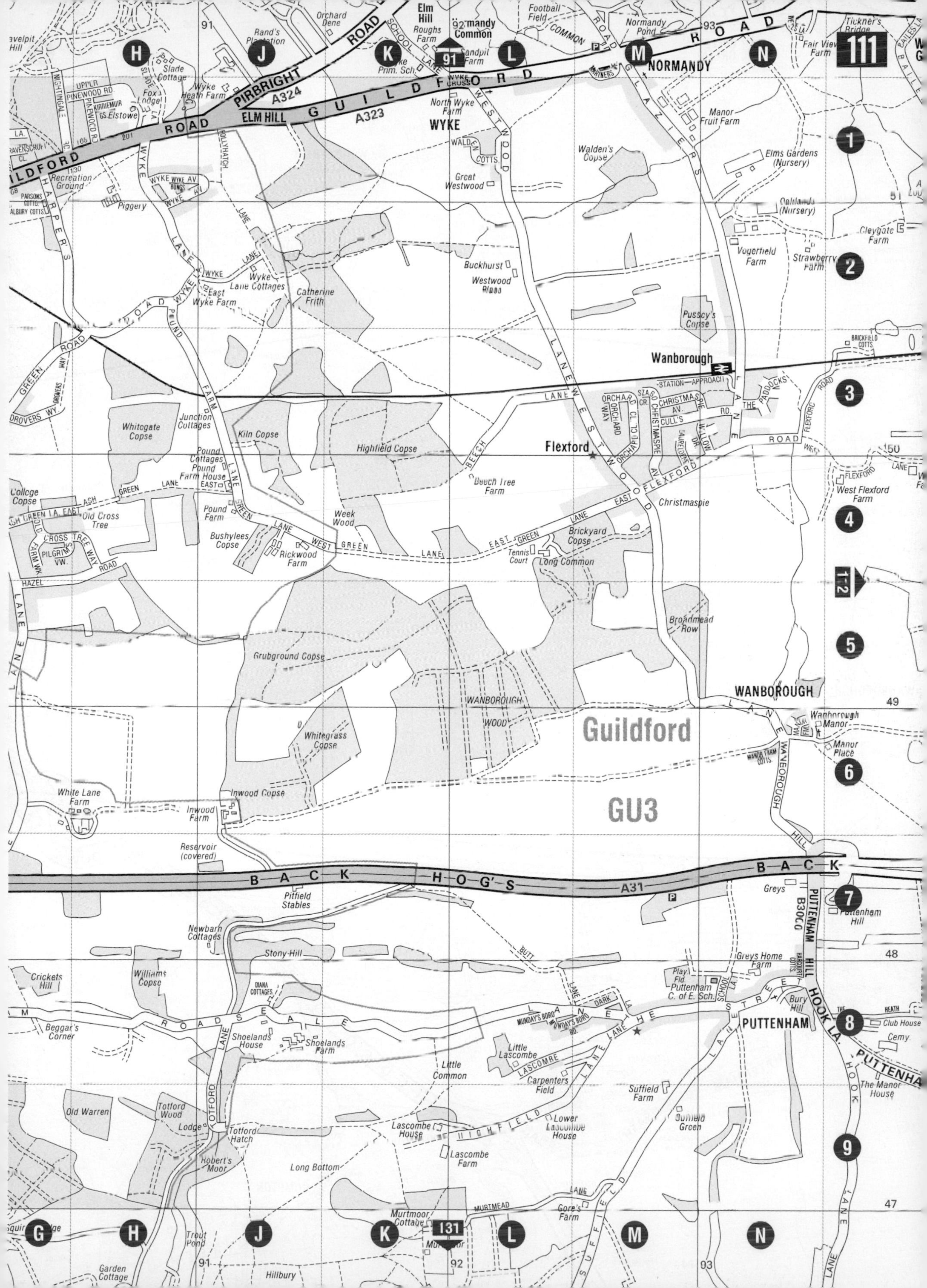
111
Normandy
Wyke
Wanborough
Flexford
Christmaspie
Guildford
GU3
Puttenham
Elm Hill
Normandy Common
Normandy Pond
Football Field
Orchard Dene
Rand's Plantation
Roughs Farm
Sandpit Farm
Slade Cottage
Fox Lodge
Elstowe
Wyke Heath Farm
North Wyke Farm
Manor Fruit Farm
Fair View Farm
Tickner's Bridge
Walden's Copse
Elms Gardens (Nursery)
Great Westwood
Recreation Ground
Piggery
Wyke Lane Cottages
East Wyke Farm
Catherine Frith
Buckhurst
Westwood Place
Vogerfield Farm
Strawberry Farm
Cleygate Farm
Pussey's Copse
Whitegate Copse
Junction Cottages
Kiln Copse
Highfield Copse
Pound Cottages
Pound Farm House
Pound Farm
Beech Tree Farm
West Flexford Farm
College Copse
Old Cross Tree
Bushylees Copse
Week Wood
Rickwood Farm
Brickyard Copse
Tennis Court
Long Common
Broadmead Row
Grubground Copse
Wanborough Wood
Whitegrass Copse
Wanborough Manor
Manor Place
White Lane Farm
Inwood Copse
Inwood Farm
Reservoir (covered)
Pitfield Stables
Greys
Puttenham Hill
Newbarn Cottages
Stony Hill
Crickets Hill
Williams Copse
Greys Home Farm
Play Fld.
Puttenham C. of E. Sch.
Bury Hill
Beggar's Corner
Shoelands House
Shoelands Farm
Little Lascombe
Carpenters Field
Little Common
Club House
Cemy.
Suffield Farm
The Manor House
Old Warren
Totford Wood
Lodge
Totford Hatch
Lascombe House
Lower Lascombe House
Robert's Moor
Lascombe Farm
Long Bottom
Gore's Farm
Murtmoor Cottage
Trout Pond
Garden Cottage
Hillbury
A324
A323
A31
B3000
PIRBRIGHT ROAD
GUILDFORD ROAD
ELM HILL
BACK HOG'S BACK
SEALE ROAD
THE STREET
HOOK LANE
PUTTENHAM HILL
WANBOROUGH HILL
WESTWOOD LANE
GLAZIERS LANE
FLEXFORD ROAD
EAST FLEXFORD LANE
WEST GREEN LANE
EAST GREEN LANE
POUND FARM LANE
BEECH LANE
HARPER'S ROAD
WYKE LANE
GREEN ROAD
DROVERS WAY
HIGHFIELD LANE
SUFFIELD LANE
TOTFORD LANE
MURTMEAD LANE
WANBOROUGH LANE
H J K L M N
G H J K L M N
1 2 3 4 5 6 7 8 9
91 92 93
51 50 49 48 47
131

112
WILLEY GREEN
Tickner's Bridge
Bales Farm
HOMESTEAD & MIDDLE VIEW MOBILE HOME PARK
92
Nursery
Works
WOOD STREET VILLAGE
Graylands Farm
Hillplace Farm
Hook Farm
Springflower Cotts.
Dunmore Farm
Broad Street Common
Elms Gardens (Nursery)
Oaklands (Nursery)
Ashfield Lodge Farm
Russellplace Farm
Wood Street Inf. Sch.
Pinks Hill
Vogerfield Farm
Strawberry Farm
Cleygate Farm
Passenger's Farm
Football Ground
Elm'field Cottages
Pink's Hill
Caravan Site
Cleygate Copse
Hook Farm
Woodlands Farm
Backside Common
Chapelhouse Farm
BROADSTREET
Brickfield Cotts.
Bushy Hill
Nursery
Wildfields Farm
Bushy Farm
The Folleys
The Surrey Research Park
Youth Hostel
Wildfield Copse
Homestead Farm
West Flexford Farm
West Flexford Farm Cottages
Pond Hill
Strawberry Grove
Blackwell Farm
111
Greencut Copse
Misley Copse
Manor Copse
Dean Bottom
Manor Farm Cotts
Down Place
WANBOROUGH
Wanborough Manor
Manor Place
Manor Farm Cotts.
Lodge
East Flexford Holding
Rathfarnham Ho.
GU3
Chalkpit Wood
Flexford House
A31
HOG'S BACK
Greys
Upper Lodge
Puttenham Hill
Greyfriars Farm
Gardeners Cott.
Monkshatch Cottage
Monkshatch Bungalow
Greyhome Farm
PUTTENHAM
GUILDFORD & GODALMING
DOWN LANE
Monkgrove Copse
Garden Cottage
The Watts Gallery
Pilgrims' Way
North Downs Way
Bury Hill
Club House
Cemy.
Frowsbury Hill
Monk Grove
Hurt Hills
Perton Rough
Perton Hill
Coneycroft Farm
Rowbury Hill
Compton Heath
PUTTENHAM GOLF COURSE
Wanborough Common
Sandy Knowe
Polsted Manor
The Manor House
PUTTENHAM HEATH ROAD
B3000
Puttenham Heath
Wanborough Common
Summer Wood
Budburrow Hill
Watts Memorial Chapel
Rectory
Cypress Farm
Hurlands
A3
Berthorpe
Berthorpe Farm
Westbury Copse
Eastbury Manor
COMPTON
Compton St. Nicholas Church
Bummoor Copse
Sewage Works
Pipkin Copse
Playing Fld.
Westbury Barn
132
Nightingales
Compton Wood
Compton Common
STREET
POLSTED LANE
PRIORSFIELD ROAD
HOOK LANE

H
J
K
L
M
N
93
97
98
99
1
2
3
4
5
6
7
8
9
51
50
49
48
47
Rydeshill
Rydeshill Lodge
Holly Farm
Liddington Lodge
Ryde's Hill
STOUGHTON
Stoke New Cemetery
Stoke Cemy.
Stoke Lock
Depot
Stoke Mill Ho.
GU1
WOODBRIDGE HILL
Recreation Ground
Shepherd's Hill Nursery Sch.
St. Joseph's R.C. Prim. Sch.
Barnwood Community Prim. Sch.
Youth Cen.
Westborough
Pond Meadow Sch.
PARK BARN
King's Manor Sch.
Westwood Park Prim. Sch.
GUILDFORD
UNIVERSITY OF SURREY
Play. Fld.
Cathedral
Stag Hill
GUILDFORD PARK
Superstore
THE GUILDFORD NUFFIELD HOSP.
THE ROYAL SURREY COUNTY HOSP
Biological Research Cen. (Univ. of Surrey)
Tennis Courts
Pavilion
The Priestley Centre
The Philip Henman Sports Grd.
Hotel
Dennisville
Jun. Sch.
Guildford
GU2
FARNHAM RD. HOSP.
Manor Farm
Manor Farm Cotts
ONSLOW VILLAGE
Onslow Inf. Sch.
Rec. Grd.
Henley Grove
Henley Fort School Camp
Reservoirs (Covered)
Sunnydown Plantation
Play. Fld.
Conduit Farm
Piccard's Farm
Sheepwalk
Piccard's Rough
St. Catherine's Hill
Brabboeuf Manor (College of Law)
Mount Browne (Police H.Q.)
ARTINGTON
East Warren
West Warren
Littleton Cross
Pilgrim Gardens
Sports Grd.
Ridge Farm
Artington Manor Farm
Shalford Junction
St. Catherine's Lock
GU4
Rushy Platts Farm
LITTLETON
Polstead Lodge
Lake
LOSELEY PARK
Loseley Park Farm
Loseley House
Moat Cottages
The Grove
Loseley Park
Orange Court Farm
Rush Croft
Works
Rushcroft Farm House
Lodge
Ashen Copse
Puddock Copse
Grove Cottage
Brickfields Farm Cott.
133
Old Claypits
Broadford Bridge
BROADFORD RD.
SHALFORD
Shalford
St. Catherine's Lockhouse
Shalford Park
Water Works
Shalford Mill (dis.)
DAGLEY FARM CARAVAN PARK
Guildford Coll. of Further & Higher Education
STOKE PARK
Bowling Green
Lido
London Road
High Sch. for Girls
Home Farm
Civ. Hall
Pewley Down Inf. Sch.
Teachers Cen.
Guildford R.C. Offs.
Guildford Cricket Club Grd.
Dapdune Wharf
Depot
Woodbridge Business Pk.
Cinema
202
114
Cemy.
A3
A25
A31
A320
A322
A323
A246
A281
A3100
ALDERSHOT ROAD
WORPLESDON ROAD
WOKING ROAD
LADYMEAD
PARKWAY
WOODBRIDGE ROAD
MIDLETON RD.
STOKE ROAD
YORK ROAD
HIGH ST.
GUILDFORD BY-PASS
FARNHAM ROAD
PORTSMOUTH ROAD
OLD PORTSMOUTH ROAD
MILLBROOK
QUARRY ST.
SHALFORD ROAD
THE STREET
HOG'S BACK
HIGH VIEW ROAD
GUILDOWN
WOODCOTE
SANDY LANE
LITTLETON LANE
PILGRIMS WAY
NORTH DOWNS WAY
EGERTON ROAD
GILL AVENUE
SOUTHWAY
RIDGEMOUNT
THE CHASE
THE OVAL
MADRID RD.
ELEANOR'S
WESTON ROAD
CHANTRY VIEW ROAD
WARWICK'S BENCH

ABBOTSWOOD
George Abbot School
Playing Fld.
Sports Stadium
Thorneycrofts
STOKE PARK
Spectrum Leisure Complex
Stoke Mill Ho.
Sewage Works
Depot
RIVER WEY
A3
A3100
LONDON ROAD
PARKWAY
A25
Burchatt's Farm Cotts.
Lido
Bowling Green
Guildford Coll. of Further & Higher Education
GUILDFORD
STOKE PARK
Playing Field
Putting Grn.
Nursery
Home Farm
High Sch. for Girls
London Road
YORK ROAD
WATERDEN RD.
HIGH ST
EPSOM ROAD
A246
Civic Hall
Allen Gds.
Tormead Sch.
Prep. Sch.
BOXGROVE ROAD
Boxgrove Prim. Sch.
Infant Sch.
MERROW
BUSHY HILL
Bushy Hill School
Play. Fld.
St. Peter's Catholic Comp. Sch.
Play Fld.
Hall
Sch.
Club Ho.
Offices
Merrow Common
MERROW WOODS
PARK LANE
B2234
Cricket Grd.
Pavilion
GUILDFORD GOLF
MERROW DOWNS
Merrow Downs
Harewarren
WALNUT
Tennis Courts
Urn Field
Pav.
Playing Field
DOWNSIDE ROAD
WARREN ROAD
LITTLE WARREN CL.
ONE TREE HILL
Burwood Farm
The Warren
GU1
Warren Farm
Play. Field.
Holy Trinity School, Guildford
Hosp.
Pewley Down Inf. Sch.
Charlotteville
Pewley Hill
Pewley Point
Pewley Down
FORT ROAD
WHITE LANE
LONGDOWN ROAD
Whiteways
The Shieling
TYTING COTTS.
Guildford
HALFPENNY LANE
Fairywood
WARWICK'S BENCH
CHANTRY VIEW ROAD
PIT ROAD
Tyting Farm
Pilgrims' Way
South Warren Farm
Whinney Hill
Farthing Copse
PILGRIMS WAY
North Downs Way
St. Martha's Priory Lodge
ST. MARTHA'S HILL
Reservoir (covered)
Shalford Park
Chantries
Halfpenny Copse
Great Halfpenny Farm
Old Great Halfpenny
Marigold Cottage
Chilworth Manor
DOWNS LINK
Water Works
Tillingbourne
Little Halfpenny Farm
Longmead
St. Catherine's Lock
Tilehouse Farm
Shalford Mill (dis.)
The Lodge
Manor Farm
Manor Cottage
SHALFORD ROAD
GU4
Lodge
East Shalford
Kingfishers
Mud Wood
CHILWORTH
Chilworth C. of E. Sch.
Chilworth
St. Catherine's Lockhouse
Brickfield Cottage
Old Manor Farm
OLD MANOR LA.
Fish Pond
ROAD
A281
THE STREET
Shalford
Cemy.
DAGLEY FARM
CARAVAN PARK
Hall
Old Croft
NEW ROAD
A248
Playing Field
Tangley Mere
Wood Cottage
Tillingbourne Jun. Sch.
KINGS RD.
CHRISTMAS HILL
Shalford Common
Bradstone Brook
BROADFIELD RD.
HORSHAM ROAD
SHALFORD
Lodge
94
202
113
134

115
95
116
135
WEST CLANDON
EAST CLANDON
Clandon Park
High Clandon
CLANDON DOWNS
NETHERLANDS
Newlands Corner
Newlands Corner Countryside Centre
ALBURY DOWNS
ALBURY
Lockner Holt
Albury Heath
ALBURY PARK
GU5
EPSOM ROAD
SHERE ROAD
THE STREET
CHILWORTH ROAD
SHERBOURNE
Silent Pool
Hatchlands
Clandon Regis
CLANDON REGIS GOLF COURSE
Royal Surrey Regiment Museum
Clandon House (N.T.)
The Wilderness
Henchley Gate
Bamptylde Cotts.
Chalk Pit
The Wild Wood
Long Acre Farm
Sunray Farm
Reservoir (covered)
Dean Bottom
Sun Valley Farm
Harrowhill Copse
Amberwell
Harrowhill
Stables
Upper Lodge
Plovers Field
Harrow Hill Farm
Netherlands
Old Scotland Farm
Tickners Copse
New Scotland Farm
Chantry Wood
Albury West Hanger
The Buxwood
Mother Webb's Corner
Pilgrims' Way
Sherbourne Farm
Sherbourne Pond
Timbercroft
Weston Wood
Home Farm
Farm Hill Wood
Silver Wood
Cook's Place
White Lane Farm
Newbarn
Water Lane Cottages
Water Lane Farm
Colyers Hanger
Lidwell Copse
Dalton Hill
Waterloo Pond
Postford Pond
Old Rectory
Weston Farm
Waterloo
Cuckoo Copse
Belmount Copse
Albury Ho.
Weston House
Rectory
Dimmingham Farm
Birget Hill
Albury Warren
Res. (covered)
Oak Pollard
Chantry Bridge
Lockner Farm
Lockner Lodge
Lockner Holt
LOCKNER HOLT
Aston House
Lockner Brake
Ford Crossing
Kiln Rough
Football & Cricket Ground
Shere Heath Crossing
Little
THE BOTTOM
The Roughs
COURSE
Training Course
Blake's Lane Farm
High Clandon Farm
H J K L M N G
1 2 3 4 5 6 7 8 9
04 05 06
51 50 49 48 47
A25 A246 A247 A248

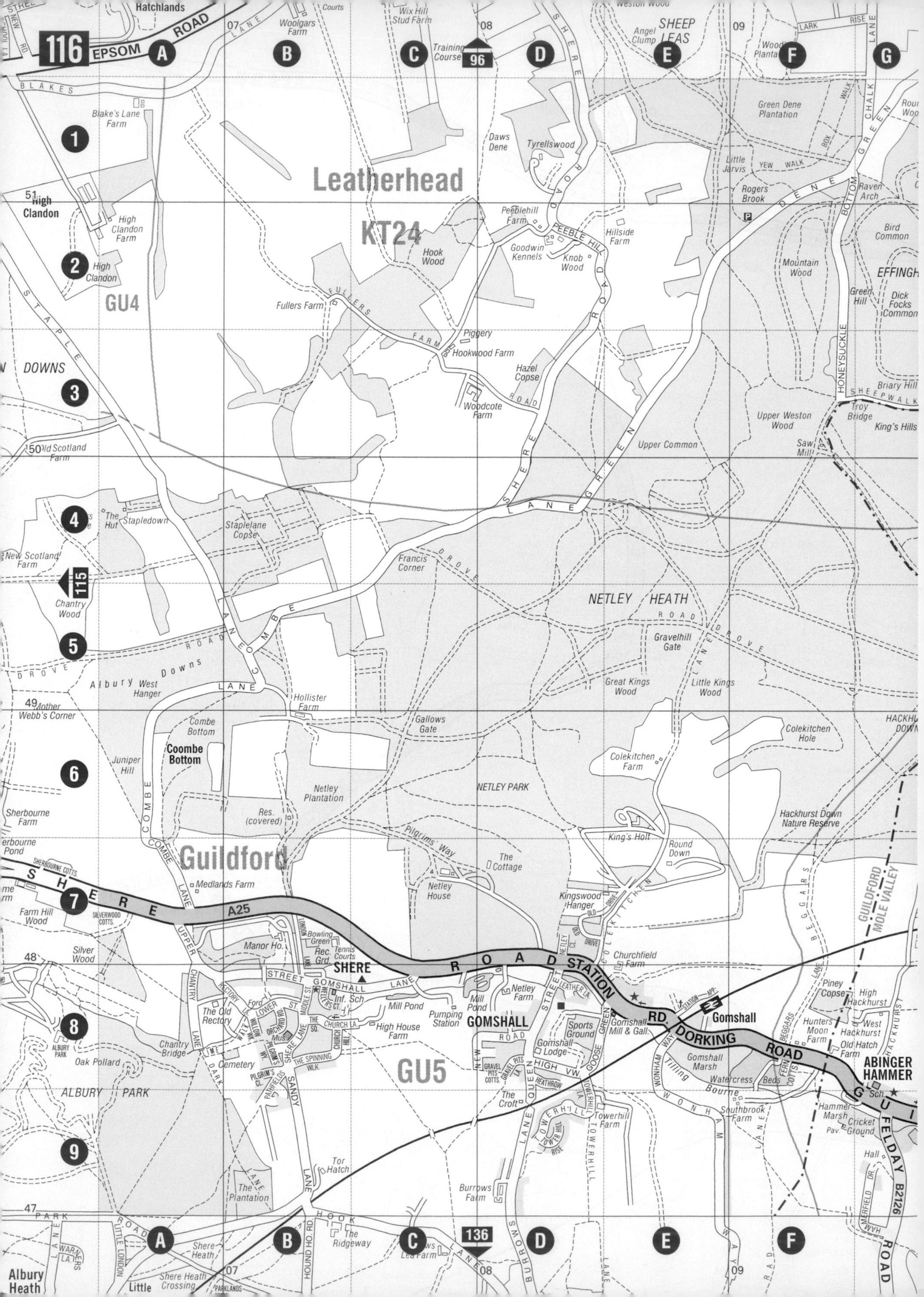
116
EPSOM ROAD
Hatchlands
Woolgars Farm
Courts
Wix Hill Stud Farm
Training Course
96
Angel Clump
SHEEP LEAS
LARK RISE
BLAKES
Blake's Lane Farm
Green Dene Plantation
Daws Dene
Tyrellswood
Little Jarvis
YEW WALK
Leatherhead
High Clandon
High Clandon Farm
Rogers Brook
Raven Arch
KT24
Peeblehill Farm
PEEBLE HILL
Hillside Farm
Bird Common
Hook Wood
Goodwin Kennels
Knob Wood
Mountain Wood
EFFINGH
GU4
Fullers Farm
FULLERS FARM
Green Hill
Dick Focks Common
STAPLE
Piggery
Hookwood Farm
Hazel Copse
DOWNS
HONEYSUCKLE
Briary Hill
Woodcote Farm
SHEEPWALK
Troy Bridge
Upper Weston Wood
King's Hills
Old Scotland Farm
Upper Common
Saw Mill
SHERE LANE
GREEN
The Hut
Stapledown
Staplelane Copse
New Scotland Farm
Francis Corner
DROVE
115
Chantry Wood
NETLEY HEATH
COMBE
Gravelhill Gate
Albury West Hanger
Downs
Great Kings Wood
Little Kings Wood
Mother Webb's Corner
Hollister Farm
Combe Bottom
Coombe Bottom
Gallows Gate
Colekitchen Hole
HACKHURST DOWN
Juniper Hill
Colekitchen Farm
Netley Plantation
NETLEY PARK
Sherbourne Farm
Res. (covered)
Hackhurst Down Nature Reserve
Sherbourne Pond
King's Holt
Round Down
Guildford
Pilgrims' Way
The Cottage
SHERBOURNE COTTS
Medlands Farm
Netley House
Kingswood Hanger
GUILDFORD MOLE VALLEY
Farm Hill Wood
SILVERWOOD COTTS.
A25
Manor Ho.
Bowling Green
Rec. Grd.
Tennis Courts
Churchfield Farm
Silver Wood
SHERE
STATION ROAD
GOMSHALL LANE
Netley Farm
Piney Copse
High Hackhurst
The Old Rectory
Inf. Sch.
Mill Pond
Gomshall
Pumping Station
GOMSHALL
Sports Ground
Gomshall Mill & Gall.
Hunters Moon Farm
West Hackhurst
Old Hatch Farm
Chantry Bridge
Mus.
High House Farm
DORKING ROAD
Oak Pollard
Cemetery
Gomshall Lodge
Gomshall Marsh
ABINGER HAMMER
ALBURY PARK
GU5
HIGH VW.
Watercress Beds
Tilling Bourne
The Croft
Towerhill Farm
Southbrook Farm
Hammer Marsh
Cricket Ground
Pav.
Tor Hatch
Hall
The Plantation
Burrows Farm
B2126
FELDAY
136
HOOK LANE
The Ridgeway
Shere Heath
Shere Heath Crossing
Albury Heath
Little London
PARKLANDS

97
118
137
H
J
K
L
M
N
G
1
2
3
4
5
6
7
8
9
51
50
49
48
47
Effingham Hill
St. Teresa's School
DOGKENNEL GREEN
Dorking
RH5
RH4
WHITE DOWNS
OAKEN GROVE
Wotton
Effingham Upper Common
White Down Lane
High Barn Road
Crocknorth Road
Ranmore Common Road
Hogden Lane
Sheepwalk Lane
Coast Hill Lane
A25
Guildford Road
Coast Road
Abinger Lane
Raikes Lane
Hollow Lane
West Lane
Wotton Drive
St. Johns Church Road
Brickyard
Sheephouse Lane
Pilgrims' Way
Hermitage Wood
The Hermitage
Crabtree Plantation
Birchetts
Crocknorth Farm
Crocknorth Cottage
Birchetts Plantation
Dick Focks Pond
Fieldhouse
Cherry Tree Rew
Briary Hill Bridge
Dorking Arch
Coles Copse
Oak Field Plantation
Hangers Wood
Horsecloise Copse
Kiln Field Coppice
Stony Dene Plantation
Stony Dene Bridge
Oldlands
Buckles Plantation
Six Acre Copse
Hazel Bucket
The Glaziers
Chippens Copse
Pump Pond Wood
Long Wood
Burrows Wood
West Lodge
Garden Copse
Robinsgrove Wood
The Long Barn
Effingham Hill Farm
Stonyrock Copse
Stonyrock
Ranmore Farm
Hogden Copse
Long Shaw
Yewtree Farm
Yewtree Shaw
Lonesome Cottage
Garlic Cottages
Bakehouse Cottages
Gatehouse
Hogden Cottages
Haileys
Friars Elm
White Lodge
Grassy Shaw
Courtlands
Meadow Plat
Meadow Plat Bridge
Osborne Plantation
Old Malthouse Cottage
Octagon Lodge
The Coppice
Primrose Rew
Dunley Hill Farm
Sun Haven
Club
Works
Red Gables
Ranmore Lodge
High Beeches
Great Copse
Nature Trail
Lillies Copse
The Roundabouts
Burnetts Leaf
Pickett's Hole
Coomb Farm
Coombe Farmhouse
Coombe Cottages
Old Simm's Copse
Dunley Wood
Reservoir (covered)
Park Farm House
Park Farm
Vale Farm
Swimming Pool
Rookery Wood
Icehouse Wood
The Rookery
New Barn Farm
Hackhurst Farm
Leasers Barn
Deerleap Wood
Firtree Copse
The Rough
Broomy Downs
Abinger Roughs
The Plantation
The Paddock
Laisure Copse
Birchin Copse
Westlane Barn
Fir Plantation
Coast Hill Farm
Furze Field
The Rectory
Sheephouse Green
Horsley Copse
Sewage Works
Green Broom
The Roundabout
Manor Farm
Homefield
Firtree Plat
Lodge
The Crossways
Crossways Farm
Bourne
Tilling
Watercress Beds
Paddington Farm
Abinger Mill
The Dene
Coldings Copse
Brickyard Cotts
Sewage Works
Wotton House
Damphurst Wood
Damphurst Hollow
Townhurst Wood
Whitings
510
11
12
13

118
A
B
C
D
E
F
G
98
117
201
138
1
2
3
4
5
6
7
8
9
RANMORE COMMON
Dorking
Dorking West
WESTCOTT
Ranmore Common
DENBIES HILLSIDE
RH5
RH4
A25
GUILDFORD ROAD
HILL
COAST HILL
WESTCOTT ROAD
RANMORE COMMON ROAD
Pilgrims' Way
Pipp Brook
Hole Hill
Westcott Common
Old Bury Hill
Bagden Wood
Dorking Wood
Long Bottom
Belcham's Copse
Prospect Lodge
Yewtree Farm
Yewtree Shaw
Tanner's Hatch Youth Hostel
Round Copse
Old Dean Cottage
Ashleigh Grange
Ashcombe
Ashcombe Wood
Ashcombe Cottage
The Forts
Long Shaw
Hogden Copse
Lonesome Cottage
Keswick Plantation
Denbies Farm
Green Terrace
Lodge
Rectory
Denbies
Ranmore Roundabout
Timber Yard
The Spains
Lillies Copse
Nature Trail
The Roundabouts
Landbarn Farm
Horley's Copse
Clay Copse
Pipp Brook
Warehouse
Washway Bri.
Springfield
Bushy Plat
Bushy Plot
Holehill Copse
Hurst Copse
The Dene
Garden Cottage
Rokefield
Miltoncourt Farm
Works
Milton Heath House
Sondes Field
Sondes Place
Coombe Farmhouse
Coombe Cottages
Coombe Copse
Hacklebarney
Westcott House
Milton Bridge
Cricket Ground
The Priory C.of E. Sch.
Powell-Corderoy Prim. Sch.
Milton Heath
Milton Farm
Westcott C of E First Sch.
The Observatory
The Temple
The Nower
Nower Lodge Sch.
Osier Plantation
Swimming Pool
Rookery Hill Farm
Westcott Heath
Hill Farm
Grave Yard
Holcombe Copse
Boat House
The Lake
Home Farm
Sandy Cross
Bushy Plat
Rookery Wood
Icehouse Wood
Hanger Wood
Furzefield Copse
Durrants Wood
Claypit Copse
The Hazels
Longmoor Wood
Furzefield Plantation
Applegarth Farm
Lower Durrants Copse
Upper Durrants Copse
Mad Horse Copse
Fir Plantation
Coast Hill Farm
The Tolt
Logmore Place
Milton Brook
The Grove
Milehouse
Sylvanus Wood
Britt's Wood
Brook Farm
Westlees Farm
Harelands Wood
Horsley Copse
Sewage Works
Damphurst Wood
Damphurst Hollow
Oldpark Hill
Logmore Copse
Logmore Green
Alder Copse
Three Cornered Copse
Square Copse
Chadhurst Farm
Chadhurst Cottages
Colchester
COLDHARBOUR LANE
WOLVENS LANE
LOGMORE LANE
MILTON STREET
STATION RD
VINCENT LANE

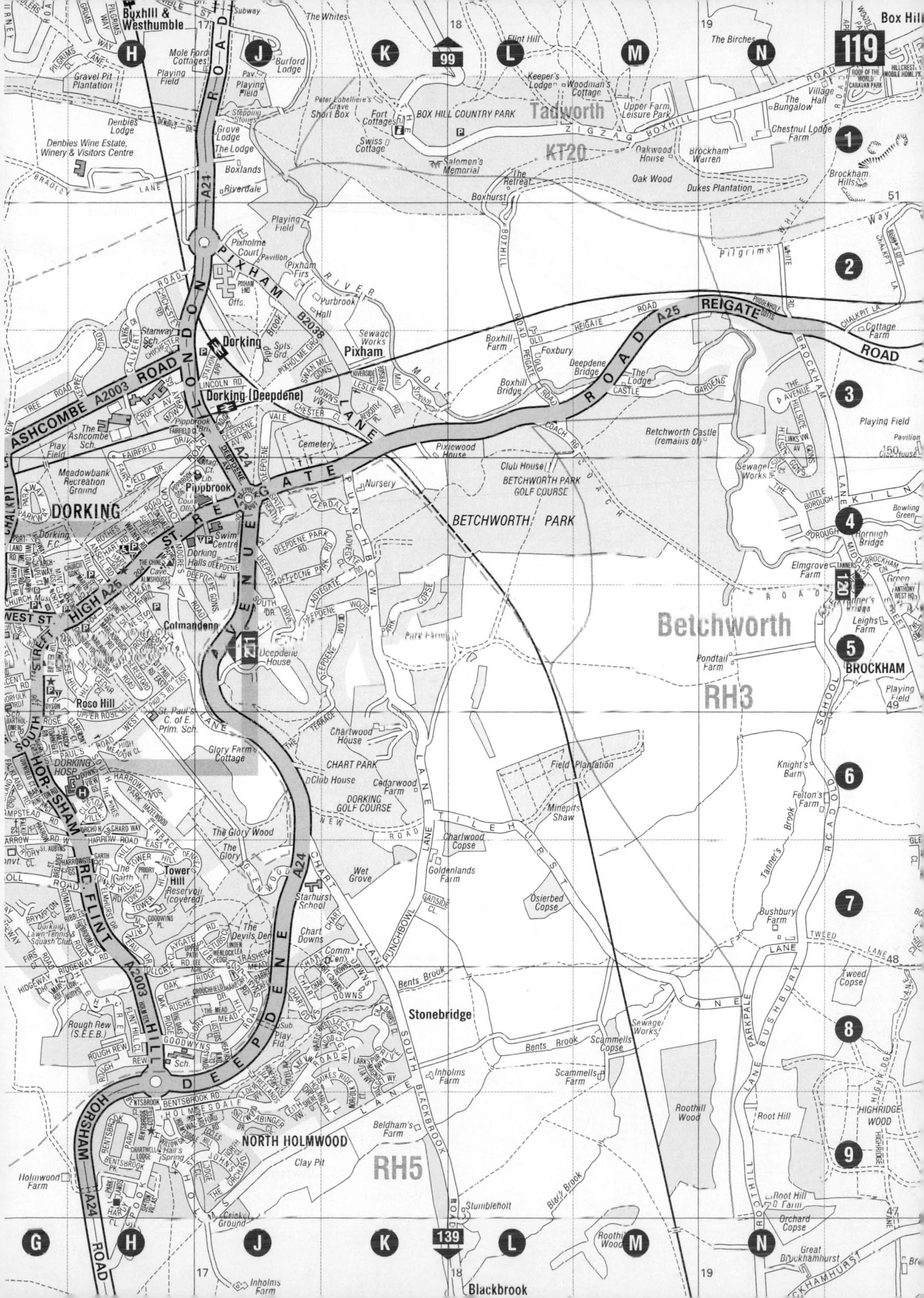

119
Box Hill
Boxhill & Westhumble
The Whites
Mole Ford Cottages
Burford Lodge
Playing Field
Gravel Pit Plantation
Denbies Lodge
Denbies Wine Estate, Winery & Visitors Centre
Flint Hill
Keeper's Lodge
Woodman's Cottage
Peter Labelliere's Grave
Short Box
Fort Cottages
BOX HILL COUNTRY PARK
Tadworth
KT20
Swiss Cottage
Salomon's Memorial
Upper Farm Leisure Park
The Birches
Village Hall
The Bungalow
Chestnut Lodge Farm
Oakwood House
Brockham Warren
Oak Wood
Dukes Plantation
Brockham Hills
The Retreat
Boxhurst
Stepping Stones
Grove Lodge
The Lodge
Boxlands
Riverdale
Pixholme Court
Pavilion
Pixham Firs
Purbrook Hall
Sewage Works
Pixham
PIXHAM LANE
LONDON ROAD
A24
B2038
Dorking
Dorking (Deepdene)
Stanway Sch.
ASHCOMBE ROAD
A2003
The Ashcombe Sch.
Play. Field
Meadowbank Recreation Ground
DORKING
Dorking F.C.
Pippbrook
Cemetery
Nursery
REIGATE ROAD
A25
Boxhill Farm
Foxbury
Deepdene Bridge
Boxhill Bridge
The Lodge
CASTLE GARDENS
Pixiewood House
Betchworth Castle (remains of)
Club House
BETCHWORTH PARK GOLF COURSE
BETCHWORTH PARK
Playing Field
Pavilion
Bowling Green
Borough Bridge
Elmgrove Farm
Leighs Farm
Betchworth
BROCKHAM
Pondtail Farm
RH3
HIGH ST.
A25
WEST ST.
Dorking Halls
Swim Centre
Cotmandene
DEEPDENE AVENUE
Deepdene House
Park Farm
Rose Hill
St. Paul's C. of E. Prim. Sch.
Glory Farm Cottage
Chartwood House
CHART PARK
Club House
Cedarwood Farm
DORKING GOLF COURSE
DORKING HOSP.
Field Plantation
Minepits Shaw
Knight's Barn
Felton's Farm
Tanner's Brook
The Glory Wood
The Glory
Tower Hill Reservoir (covered)
Charlwood Copse
Goldenlands Farm
Wet Grove
Starhurst School
TILEHURST LANE
Osierbed Copse
Dorking Lawn Tennis & Squash Club
FLINT HILL
The Devils Den
Chart Downs
Bushbury Farm
TWEED LANE
Tweed Copse
Bents Brook
Stonebridge
Rough Rew (S.E.E.B.)
DEEPDENE
Sewage Works
Scammells Copse
Scammells Farm
Inholms Farm
Roothill Wood
Root Hill
HIGHRIDGE WOOD
BUSHBURY LANE
PARKPALE LANE
ROOTHILL LANE
NORTH HOLMWOOD
Beldham's Farm
Clay Pit
RH5
HORSHAM ROAD
A24
Holmwood Farm
Cricket Ground
Stumbleholt
Black Brook
Root Hill Farm
Orchard Copse
Great Brockhamhurst
Blackbrook
Inholms Farm
99
139
120
121
G H J K L M N
1 2 3 4 5 6 7 8 9
17 18 19
51 50 49 48 47

120
Box Hill
Tadworth
KT20
Brockham Hills
Betchworth
BETCHWORTH
REIGATE ROAD
A25
B2032
Buckland
Betchworth
RH3
BROCKHAM
Strood Green
Dawesgreen
LEIGH
Borough Bridge
River Mole
Betchworth Bridge
Wonham Manor
Wonham Mill
Brockham School
Highridge Wood
Gad Brook
Mark Mead Plantation
Wilderness Wood
Oldpark Wood
100
119
140

121
101
141
122
H
J
K
L
M
N
G
1
2
3
4
5
6
7
8
9
23
24
25
26
Reigate
RH2
REIGATE
REIGATE HEATH GOLF COURSE
Reigate Heath
Reigate Heath Postmill
Club House
BUCKLAND ROAD
ROAD WEST
A25
STREET
HIGH ST.
CHURCH
STREET
REIGATE
ROAD
CROYDON
A242
LONDON RD.
BELL ST.
A217
BELL STREET
COCKSHOT
HILL
DOVERS
GREEN
A217
RJAD
REIGATE RD
REIGATE HILL
Buckland Corner
Shagbrook
Shag Brook
Round Alders
Tap Wood
Colley Pit
Playing Field
Works
Dowde's Farm
Bushy Shaw
Clifton's Shaw
Colleyland Shaw
Bushfield Coppice
Claypit Shaw
Warehouses
Northland Shaw
Broadleas
Colley Copse
Colley Wood
Sports Ground
Fairhall
Nurseries
Cricket Ground
MOLE VALLEY
REIGATE and BANSTEAD
Ivy Cottage
Garthlands
Heathfield Farm
Dungate Manor
Heathfield
The Lithe
Trumpet Hill
Trumpetshill Copse
June Farm
Stepstile Meadow
Littleton
Littleton Manor Farm
Wallace Brook
Gilbert's Farm
Santon House
FLANCHFORD
Clayhall Farm
Greenlane Cottages
Flanchford Farm
Little Flanchford Farm
Flanchford Bridge
Mill Pond
The Lodge
Little Flanchford Cottages
Oakshade
Denshot Farm
Skeets Farm
Burys Court School
Butler's Shaw
Hilly Furze Field
Round Island
Birchett Copse
Bures Manor
Magpie Shaw
Alder Copse
No Man's Land
River Field Plantation
CLAYHALL
SLIPSHATCH
ROAD
Slipshatch Cotts.
Withy Wood
Slipshatch Wood
Hartswood Farm Cotts.
Hartswood Farm
Pond Field Plantation
Old Sawpit Orchard
Stable Plantation
Ninetythree Plantation
Upper Kiln Field Plantation
Broad Ten Plantation
Park Plantation
Kiln Field Plantation
Gravelpit Plantation
Twelve Acre Plantation
Sidlow Bridge
Sidlow Bridge Sch.
Sidlow
Church Meadow Farm
Riverside Meadows
RIVER MOLE
Dovers Farm
Turner's Shaw
DOVERSGREEN
Dovers Green
Dovers Green Infs. Sch.
Recreation Ground
Rushetts Farm
WOODHATCH
WOOD HATCH RD.
Woodhatch
SOUTH PARK
King George's Field
Playing Field
Community Centre
WHITEHALL
PARK LANE
Reservoir (covered)
Park Hill
Monument
REIGATE PARK
Reigate Priory Playing Fields
Priory Pond
Priory Museum
School
Tennis Courts
Playing Fields
Cricket Gnd.
GREEN LANE
Superstore
Reigate Coll.
Town Hall
Castle
LESBOURNE RD.
B2034
BLACKBOROUGH RD
Reigate Gram. Sch.
Cemetery
Brooklands Sch.
Fire Brigade East Division H.Q.
DOODS
Hosebank Cotts.
SOMERS
WRAY PARK
PILGRIMS WAY
Hotel

122
102
121
142
A B C D E F G
1 2 3 4 5 6 7 8 9
REDHILL
Reigate
RH2
EARLSWOOD
WOODHATCH
DOVERSGREEN
MEAD VALE
HOLMETHORPE
COLES MEADS
Wray Common
REDHILL COMMON
EARLSWOOD COMMON
REDHILL & REIGATE GOLF COURSE
REDHILL GOLF CENTRE
EAST SURREY HOSPITAL
Petridge Wood Common
Earlswood Lakes
Boating Lake
Redstone Hill
Kennedys Wood
Sidlow Bridge
Sidlow
Salfords
White Bushes
The Plantation
Felland Copse
Recreation Ground
Rushetts Farm
Home Grove
Petridge Wood
Brookside Farm
Maple Manor
Burnt Oak Farm
New Pond Farm
Dovers Farm
Turner's Shaw
Hollow Shaw
Lonesome
Dean Farm
Mason's Bridge
Robin Cooks Farm
Hazelhurst Farm
Old Garston's House
Garston's Wood
Byes Wood
Hillsbrow
Sandpit
Earlswood
Redhill
A23
A25
A242
A2044
B2034
LONDON ROAD
BRIGHTON ROAD
STATION RD.
NUTFIELD HILL
REIGATE ROAD
CROYDON ROAD
GATTON PARK ROAD
BLACKBOROUGH ROAD
WOODHATCH ROAD
DOVERS GREEN ROAD
HORLEY ROAD
THE CUTTING
HATCHLANDS RD.
REDSTONE HILL
HIGH ST.
MARKETFIELD WY.
PRINCESS WY.
26 27 28 29
51 50 49 48 47

Ford Bridge
NUTFIELD MARSH
Nutfield Marsh
Ckt. Grd.
The Moors
Marsh Cotts.
Pav
CORMONGERS
Glebe Lake
103
Subway
PENDELL
Lake Farm
The Old Rectory
BREWER
STYCHENS
Chilmead Farm
CHILMEAD
PEYTON'S COTTS.
Cockley Plantation
SANDY
LANE
Dormers Farm
COMMON
LITTLE
COMMON
M23
NUTFIELD CT.
BLETCHINGLEY
Little Comn.
Play. Fld.
BACK
Adult Education Cen.
CHURCH HILL
ROAD
NUTFIELD
Park Wood
Works
Spls. Grd.
Doods Brow Sch.
PARKWOOD RD.
PARK WORKS RD.
ST. BLETCHINGLEY RD. CASTLE A25 STREET HIGH ST.
Castle Place
Castle Hill
Bletchingley Castle
CASTLE SQ.
CASTLE CL.
Pimlico Hill
Works
Cemy.
ROAD HIGH
A25
Robert Denholm House
Capenor Nursery
Coombes Coppice
Stanley's Wood
Patteson Court
Adlington Cotts.
Fox Hole
HOLMESDALE PARK
North Park
COOPERS
M23 MOTORWAY
Castlehill Farm
Poor
Ten. Cts.
The Priory
Playing Field
Furze Hill
Priory Farm
Nutfield Lodge
Nutfield Priory
Stoners Hill
Stockers Hill
WOOD LANE
Subway
Sandhills
Oakbarn Cotts.
50
Little Cormongers Farm
Nutfield Priory Lake
Bowerhill Wood
HOGTROUGH LANE
SANDCROSS
Bower Hill
BOWER
Redhill
BRAES MEAD
KENTWYNS
R.C.
Pav.
Play. Fld.
High Beech
Lyttel Hall
Sandhills Farm
124
Bray's Farm
Nutfield Church Prim. Sch.
Rec. Grd.
Ckt. Grd.
Colgate's Barn
Bower Hill Farm
RH1
HOLMESDALE RD
Hall
Nutfield
SOUTH NUTFIELD
Brook
Nutfield
ld Gladstone's House
KINGSMEAD
THE COPSE
Cricket Grnd.
Maple Farm
King's Mill
KINGS
BOWER HILL CL.
NETHERLEIGH PK.
MORRIS RD.
THE AVENUE
CRICKET HILL
49
Thepps Shaw
LANE
Nutfield Brook
CROSS
THEPPS CL.
KINGS ACRE
Nutfield Park
Ketwin's Wood
Crab Hill House
Works
The Park
Ridge Green
Tennis Cts.
Theppswood Hse.
Henhaw Farm
Kenne
Redhill
Depot
Depot
Warehouse
Crab Hill Farm
Bransland Wood
Staplehurst Farm
Hale Farm
Crab Hill
Nutfield Nurseries
CRAB HILL
Brook
MILL
Temple Wood
The Rookery
Ten. Ct.
Helicopter Landing Square
Indoor Tennis Centre
48
M23
MOTORWAY
REDHILL AERODROME AND HELIPORT
Perimeter Cotts.
REIGATE and BANSTEAD
TANDRIDGE
Helicopter Landing Square
Helicopter Landing Square
Stream
Salfords
Hope Farm
Lawn Hill
Burstow Park Farm
Lodge
LANE
ROAD
South Hale Farm
MOATS
PRINCE OF WALES ROAD
Spring Field Wood
47
143
Ruffet
HATCH
Browns Shaw
G
H
J
K
L
M
N
1
2
3
4
5
6
7
8
9
30
31
32

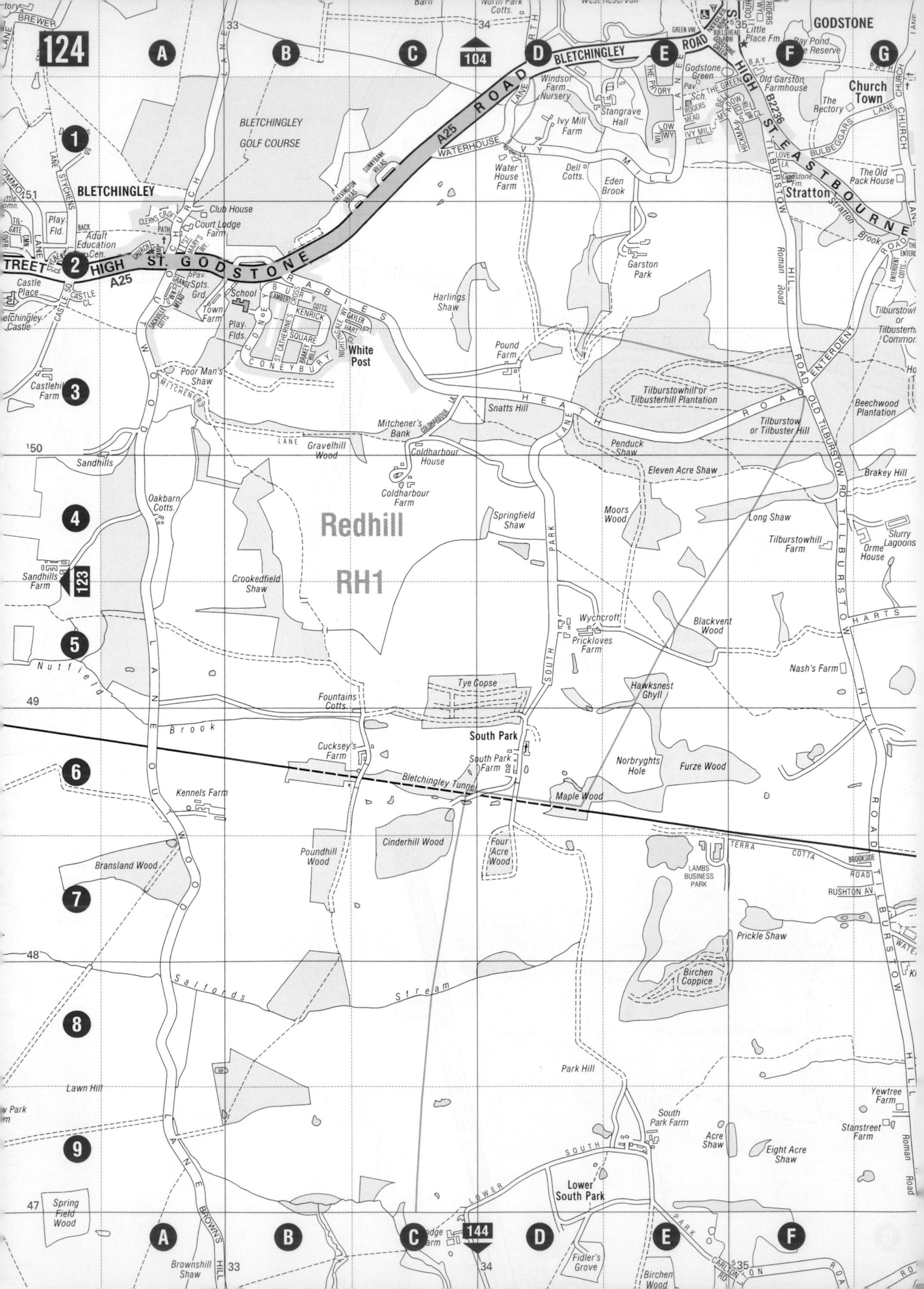

124
A
B
C
D
E
F
G
104
123
144
1
2
3
4
5
6
7
8
9
33
34
35
51
150
49
48
47
BLETCHINGLEY
GODSTONE
Church Town
Stratton
BLETCHINGLEY GOLF COURSE
A25
BLETCHINGLEY ROAD
HIGH ST.
GODSTONE ROAD
A25 ROAD
B2236
HIGH ST.
EASTBOURNE ROAD
Redhill
RH1
Club House
Court Lodge Farm
Adult Education Cen.
Play. Fld.
Castle Place
Bletchingley Castle
Castlehill Farm
School
Town Farm
Play. Flds.
Pav. Spts. Grd.
White Post
Poor Man's Shaw
CONEYBURY
RABIES HEATH ROAD
Windsor Farm Nursery
Ivy Mill Farm
Stangrave Hall
Water House Farm
Dell Cotts.
Eden Brook
Godstone Green
Old Garston Farmhouse
The Rectory
Little Place Fm.
Bay Pond Nature Reserve
The Old Pack House
Garston Park
Harlings Shaw
Pound Farm
Snatts Hill
Mitchener's Bank
Gravelhill Wood
Coldharbour House
Coldharbour Farm
Tilburstowhill or Tilbusterhill Plantation
Tilburstow or Tilbuster Hill
Penduck Shaw
Eleven Acre Shaw
Beechwood Plantation
Brakey Hill
Tilburstowhill or Tilbusterhill Common
Sandhills
Sandhills Farm
Oakbarn Cotts.
Springfield Shaw
Moors Wood
Long Shaw
Tilburstowhill Farm
Orme House
Slurry Lagoons
Crookedfield Shaw
Wychcroft
Prickloves Farm
Blackvent Wood
Nash's Farm
Nutfield Brook
Fountains Cotts.
Tye Copse
Hawksnest Ghyll
South Park
South Park Farm
Cucksey's Farm
Norbryghts Hole
Furze Wood
Kennels Farm
Bletchingley Tunnel
Maple Wood
Bransland Wood
Poundhill Wood
Cinderhill Wood
Four Acre Wood
LAMBS BUSINESS PARK
TERRA COTTA ROAD
BROOKSIDE
RUSHTON AV.
Prickle Shaw
Birchen Coppice
Salfords Stream
OUTWOOD LANE
SOUTH PARK LANE
TILBURSTOW HILL ROAD
Roman Road
Park Hill
Lawn Hill
South Park Farm
Acre Shaw
Eight Acre Shaw
Yewtree Farm
Stanstreet Farm
LOWER SOUTH PARK
Lower South Park
Spring Field Wood
Brownshill Shaw
BROWN'S HILL
Lodge Farm
Fidler's Grove
Birchen Wood
CARLTON ROAD

Garden Centre
Nags Hall
Plantation
Oxted Mill
TANDRIDGE GOLF COURSE
105
Moory's Shaw
Glebe Water
Broadham House
Stone Hall
Windmillstadle Wood
The Birches
TANHOUSE ROAD
Weir
The Glebe House
Tennis Court
Little Court Farm
Flowergarden Plantation
Beechwood Hill
Oxted Place
Broadham Green
Castlehill Wood
Leigh Place
The Lodge
Tandridge Court
New Bustons Wood
Bustons Wood
The Mount
Leigh Place Pond
Oldpark Wood
Tandridge Court Fm.
Round Wood
Stonepit Shaw
Castlehill Wood
Maizenhill Shaw
Taylors Hill Depot
Leigh Mill House
Southlands
Perrysfield Fm.
Refuse Tips
TANDRIDGE
Maizenhill Shaw
TANDRIDGE PARK
Smokey Hollow
Dean Shaw Cottages
Dean Shaw
Roddings Wood
St. Peter's C.of E. Inf. Sch.
Merelend Wood
Sewage Works
Gibbs Brook
Tandridge Hall
Southlands Shaws
Stocket Manor
GODSTONE BY-PASS
A22
B2236 ROAD
Southlands Lodge
Caperway Cottages
SOUTHLANDS
Southlands Wood
Rose Farm
Godstone
EASTBOURNE
Stow Coppice
Oxted
RH9
RH8
NEW ROAD
Newhouse Farm
Holly Bush Farm
126
MILES LANE
Brook Farm
Piper's Wood
Steadmanshill Wood
Paygate Wood
TANDRIDGE LANE
New Zealand Cottages
Bushey Croft
Barnfield Shaw
Postern Gate Farm
GIBBS BROOK LANE
Foyle Tolt
Gibbs Brook
Lagham Wood
St. Stephen's C.of E. Prim.Sch.
SOUTH GODSTONE
Chathill
Foyle Tolt
LAGHAM PARK
WOODLANDS DR.
HUNTERS CHASE
EASTER WAY
Chathill Park Farm
STATION ROAD
Playing Field
Old Hall Farm
Pound Wood
Godstone
LAGHAM
Works
ST. JOHNS CT.
Lagham Park Farm
Dodds Coppice
Oakhurst Court
Depot
CROWHURST LANE
Crowhurst Lane End
Lagham Manor
Drewsherne Farm
RSPCA Animal Cen.
Brickmakers' Wood
Playing Field
Moat
Hall
Works
St. George's Cottages
Pound
Lagham Lodge Farm
Ashen Plantations
Church Farm
The Mount
Lingfield
Crowhurst
Bradford Wood
Hobbs Farm
Ashen Shaw
Mansionhouse Farm
FAYGATE LANE
RH7
Altar Cottages
TANDRIDGE LANE
Godstone Place
Stocks and Kingswood Farms
Anglefield Corner
Gaysland Cottages
145
Oak Tree Farm
Comforts Farm
Blackgrove Farm
DANEMORE LANE
VILLAGE ROAD
G
H
J
K
L
M
N
1
2
3
4
5
6
7
8
9
36
37
38
39
47
48
49
50
51

126
Oxted
RH8
Lingfield
RH7
Hurst Green
HURST GREEN
HOLLAND
Merle Common
Crowhurst
Broadham Green
Pains Hill
Oxted Mill
Viewlands
Stonehall Farm
Stone Hall
Broadham House
Tanhouse Fm.
Weir
Moor House Sch.
Ten Cts.
Pav.
Mill Lane Playing Field
Mill Pond
Coltsford House
Perrysfield Fm.
Stockett's Manor
Stockett's Manor Farm
Rose Farm
Sewage Treatment Works
Depot
Dunks Pond
King George's Field
FAIRVIEW INDUSTRIAL ESTATE
Holland Junior Sch.
Red Lane Farm
Redlane Cottages
Hurst Green School
Comm. Cen.
Hall
The Alders
Boulthurst Fm.
Reservoir (covered)
Chartfield Ho.
Tenchleys Wood
Loampit Wood
Whitegates Farm
Grants Cottage
Grants Paddock
Doghurst
Crabbett Wood
Crabbett Wood Farm
Tenchleys Manor
ITCHINGWOOD COMMON
Parishcroft Wood
Parishcroft Wood Farm
Crooked River
Connerton Farm
Stockenden Fm.
Collesters Wood
Honesland Wood
Mollstones Wood
Gincox Farm
Finch's Cross
Playing Field
Gincox Tolt
Eden
River
Couldens Farm
Brills Farm
Bushey Croft
Kitchengarden Shaw
Tennis Court
High Ridge Farm
Little Earls Wood
Foyle Fm.
Foyle Tolt
Sunt Wood
Comforts Cottage
Monks Fm.
Staffhurst Wood Nature Reserve
Great Earls Wood
Caper's Farm
Five Acre Wood
Sunt Farm
Kiln Coppice
White House Farm
Grubbs Farm
Butcherswood Bank
Black Robin's Farm
Partridge Fm.
Hall
St. George's Cotts.
Pound Farm
Caterfield Bridge
Whitehouse Wood
Bombers Farm
Kennels
Galley's Wood
Church Farm
Mansionhouse Farm
Oldhouse Farm
Wintersell Wood
Altar Cottages
Shingle Barn Farm
Wintersell Farm
Shinglebarn Wood
Oak Pollard
106
125
146
TANHOUSE ROAD
BROADHAM GREEN
HURST GREEN ROAD
HOLLAND LANE
HOLLAND ROAD
RED LANE
WARREN LANE
POPES LANE
MERLE COMMON ROAD
STAFFHURST WOOD ROAD
GRANTS LANE
PAINS HILL
ITCHINGWOOD COMMON ROAD
SHORT LANE
MONKS LANE
HONEYPOT LANE
CATERFIELD LANE
CROWHURST LANE
GIBBS BROOK LANE
CROWHURST VILLAGE ROAD
PARK ROAD
CHURCH WAY
WOLFS WOOD
OAK ROAD
POLLARDS WOOD ROAD
MEADOWLANDS
ROSEACRE
COLDSHOTT
A B C D E F G
1 2 3 4 5 6 7 8 9
39 540 41 42
51 150 49 48 47

127
KENT HATCH
Kent Hatch
107
CROCKHAMHILL COMMON
Champion's Farm
Champions Place
Marie Curie Research Institute
Chart Edge
Chartlands
Chartlands Farm
Scearn Bank
The Old House
Kent Hatch House
The Cearne
Roundmead Shaw
Troverawe
The Moat Farm
Swaynesland
SWAYNESLAND
DAIRY LANE
Hurst Farm
Old Dairy Farm
TANDRIDGE
SEVENOAKS
Kent Brook
Crockham Hill Farm
Rusholme
Newlands
Stubblefield
OAKDALE LA
SMITHS LANE
West House
Youth Hostel
DEANERY RD
Crockham Hill First School
CROCKHAM HILL
The Red House
Froghole Farm
Froghole
HOSEY COMMON ROAD
B2026
B269
Chartwell (NT)
The Grove (NT)
Chartwell Farm
Chartwell Cott.
Mariners Hill
Mariners
Ruddle's Wood
Eastfield
Little Mariners
Little Court
Gudge Meadow
Longmeadow Bulls.
Chandler's Wood
Chandlers
Coachmans
Lewins
SPOUT LANE
POOTINGS
DENNETTSLAND RD
Ten Ct
Playing Field
Grange Farm
Crockham Grange
Longcroft Wood
Haftcroft Wood
Roman Road (course of)
Redland Farm
Edenbridge
TN8
GUILDABLES LANE
Guildables Park Farm
Guildables Wood
Langhurst
Sports Field
Model Fm.
Roselands
Oakfield Farm
Coakham Farm
Coakham Lodge Farm
Coakham Wood
Pootings
ROAD
Rushett
Birds Wood
HOLE LANE
Scamperdale Cottages
Appledore
Broxham Wood
MAIN ROAD
Batchelor's Farm
Gaywood Farm
Moat
Broxham Manor
Broxham Farm
HOMESTEAD RD
FAIRMEAD RD.
HIGHFIELDS RD
Swan Lane Farm
Troy Town
Yew Tree Farm
Batchelor's Wood
Hilders
OAKFIELD RD.
HILLCREST RD
BROWNINGS
MARLPIT HILL
SWAN LANE
HILDERS LANE
TROY LANE
LITTLE BROWNS LANE
Little Browns Farm
Little Browns Wood
Crouch House Wood
CROUCH HOUSE ROAD
Breezehurst Farm
Holdings Fm.
Hamsell Mead Fm.
ST. BRELADE'S COURT RESIDENTIAL PARK
MEADOW LA
Works
Edenbridge
STATION ROAD
MARLPIT CL
RIDGE LANE
SWAN RIDGE
CROWN RD
ELMS ROAD
B2027
Mowshurst
Little Broxham
Alfriston
Sewage Works
FIRCROFT WAY
ENTERPRISE WAY
Industrial Estate
SUNNYSIDE
COMMERCE WY.
Spitals Cross
Spitals Cross Estate
FOUR ELMS RD
EDENBRIDGE GOLF & COUNTRY CLUB
EDENBRIDGE
SKINNERS LANE
Crouch House Farm
GRESHAMS WAY
147
Eden Valley Sch.
Playing Fields
Works
Cauk Wood
A B C D E F G H J K L M N
1 2 3 4 5 6 7 8 9
43 44 45 47 48 49 50 51

Wimble Hill
Dippenhall
Wrecclesham
Shortheath
Boundstone
Holt Pound
Rowledge
Frensham Heights
GU10
Farnham Road
Alton Road
Wrecclesham Road
Holt Pound Inclosure
Glenbervie Inclosure
Alice Holt Forest
Birdworld & Underwater World
The Surrey Institute of Art & Design

129
109
130
149
GU9
FARNHAM
Farnham
COMPTON
MOOR PARK
MIDDLE BOURNE
LOWER BOURNE
THE BOURNE
MILLBRIDGE
SHORTFIELD
BY-PASS
FIRGROVE HILL
FRENSHAM ROAD
WAVERLEY LANE
B3001
B3384
A287
A31
FARNHAM
GONG HILL
RIVER WEY
Farnham College
St. Polycarp's R.C. Prim. Sch.
Hospice
South Farnham Sch.
The Abbey Sch.
Compton Rec. Grd.
Culverlands
Compton Hill
Delarden House
The Thatched House
Reservoir (Covered)
Priory Farm
Waverley Abbey House
Long Barn
Waverley Abbey (Remains)
Ancora Farm House
Redhill House
Red Hill
Monk's Walk Farm
Lodge Farm
Woodlarks Camp Site
The Bourne School
Lodge Hill House
Lobswood Manor
Black Lake
Bournelands
Alice Holt Forest
Bourne Wood
Sheephatch Copse
Sheephatch Farm
Tilfordmill Bridge
Nightingale Farm
Tilford House Farm
Tilford Green
Gong Hill
Old Kiln Museum & Rural Life Centre
The Reeds
Tilford Reeds
Birchen Hey
Play Fld.
Edgeborough School
Kennel Farm
More House School
Burtleys Copse
Keepers Field
TANKERSFORD COMMON
Meadow End Farm
Stonehills
Shortfield House
Hollow Dene
Pierrepont
Chutor's
Farnham Maltings
New Ashgate Gall.

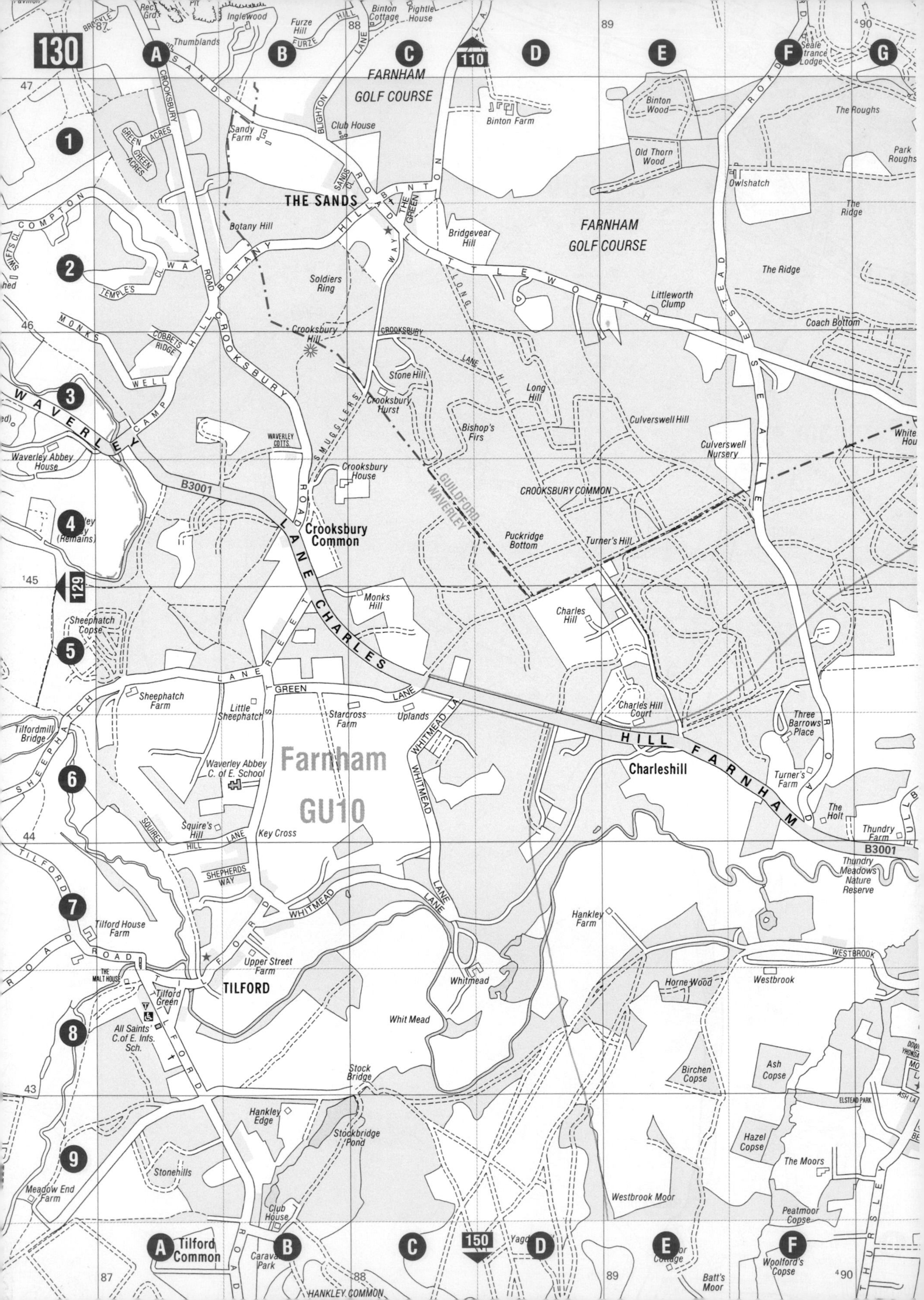
THE SANDS
FARNHAM GOLF COURSE
Crooksbury Hill
Crooksbury Common
CROOKSBURY COMMON
Farnham
GU10
Charleshill
TILFORD
Tilford Common
Waverley Abbey House
Sheephatch Farm
Little Sheephatch
Waverley Abbey C. of E. School
Tilford House Farm
Upper Street Farm
Hankley Farm
Westbrook
Whitmead
Whit Mead
Stock Bridge
Stockbridge Pond
Hankley Edge
Westbrook Moor
Thundry Meadows Nature Reserve
Littleworth Clump
Culverswell Hill
Culverswell Nursery
Puckridge Bottom
Turner's Hill
Charles Hill
Charles Hill Court
Three Barrows Place
Turner's Farm
The Holt
Thundry Farm
Binton Farm
Binton Wood
Old Thorn Wood
Owlshatch
The Roughs
Park Roughs
The Ridge
Coach Bottom
Bridgevear Hill
Soldiers Ring
Botany Hill
Sandy Farm
Club House
Inglewood
Thumblands
Stone Hill
Crooksbury Hurst
Crooksbury House
Long Hill
Bishop's Firs
Monks Hill
Starcross Farm
Uplands
Squire's Hill
Key Cross
Tilford Green
All Saints' C.of E. Infs. Sch.
Stonehills
Meadow End Farm
Sheephatch Copse
Tilfordmill Bridge
Horne Wood
Birchen Copse
Ash Copse
Hazel Copse
The Moors
Peatmoor Copse
Woolford's Copse
Batt's Moor
Caravan Park
HANKLEY COMMON
B3001
GUILDFORD
WAVERLEY
110
129
150

Guildford
GU3
PUTTENHAM COMMON
HAMPTON PARK
Godalming
GU8
ELSTEAD
SHACKLEFORD
Peper Harow
PEPER HAROW PARK
Gatwick
Pot Common
ROYAL COMMON
Bagmoor Common Nature Reserve
B3001
Long Bottom
Murtmoor Cottage
Murtmoor
Gore's Farm
Church Croft
Hillbury
Garden Cottage
Hampton
Trout Pond
Long Pond
General's Pond
Warren Pond
Dairy Cottage
The Warren
Warren Lodge
Warren Cottage
The Tarn
Cuttmill Pond
Cutt Mill House
Overponds
Cuttmill Rise
Cutt Corner
Little Rodsall
Rodsall Manor
Top Rodsall Cottages
Long Cutts Wood
Lydling Farm
Barfield Copse
New Barn
Puckstool Wood
Whirl Hill
Lower Pyramid
The Marsh
Broad Firs
New Six Acres
The Breaches
Mitchen Hall Plantation
Archfield Cottages
Aldro Sch.
Redhill Plantation
Prospect House
Mitchen Hall
Mulberry House
Glebe
Britty Wood
Britty Hill Cottage
Britty Hill
Water Works
Britty Copse
Halesmoor Wood
Heath Cottage
Cutmill Cottage
Cutmill Platts
Broomfields
Sugarbaker Hill
Broomfield Wood
Broomfield Cottage
Sugarbaker Hill Farm
Gatwick Alder Bed
New Pond
Attleford
Jackass Moor
Warren Lodge Farm
Headland Plantation
Headlands
Warren Clump
Warren Hill
Warren Hill Farm
Hazel Copse
Jackman's Hill
Farnham Lodge
Twotree Hill
Mount Sion
Home Farm
Norney Grange
Fullbrook Farm Cottage
Fullbrook House
Brookfield
Polshot Manor
Sewage Works
Woodside Farm
Home Covert
Square Copse
Elstead Bridge
The Mill House
Cemetery
The Alders
Engineering Works
Somerset Farm
Somerset Bridge
Kennels
Deer Bridge
Blacklands Rue
Deer Bridge Plantation
Playing Field
Burford Lodge
Blacklands Farm
Blacklands House
Oxenford Bridge
Brook Walk
Oxenford Grange
Hazel Copse
Lower Helves
Upper Helves
Poultry Farm
Lex Farm
Royal Farm House
Oxenford Farm Cottages
St. James C. of E Prim. Sch.
Great Hookley Poultry Farm
Guinea Common
Guinea Copse
Ashen Copse
Thurnets Copse
Bagmoor Wood
Bagmoor Cottage
Red House Farm
RIVER WEY
SUFFIELD LANE
RODSALL LANE
PUTTENHAM LANE
THE STREET
ELSTEAD ROAD
PEPERHAROW LANE
ATTLEFORD LANE
SHACKLEFORD ROAD
MILFORD ROAD
LOWER HAM LA.
HAZELWOOD
BACK LA.
HOOKLEY LANE
SILVER BIRCHES WAY
WEST HILL
THE GREEN
BROOMFIELD
SPRINGFIELD
BURFORD LEA
PARK AVENUE
THE BOTHY
SHACKLEFORD
COMMON VIEW RD.
MURTMEAD LANE
GREVILLE
BROOKERS LA.
H J K L M N G
1 2 3 4 5 6 7 8 9
111
132
151
91 92 93
47 46 45 44 43

132
A
B
C
D
E
F
G
1
2
3
4
5
6
7
8
9
47
46
45
44
43
94
95
96
112
131
152
Hurlands
Berthorpe
Berthorpe Farm
Westbury Copse
Eastbury Manor
Compton St. Nicholas Church
Cypress Farm
Bummoor Copse
Sewage Works
Pipkin Copse
Nightingales
Westbury Barn
Round Hill
GU3
COMPTON
B3000
STREET
Playing Fld.
Compton Wood
Compton Common
Burl's Rew
Lone Barn
New Barn
Kiln Copse
The Common
Island Cottage
Field Place
Eastbury Park
Eastbury Copse
Eastbury Barn
Two Stacks
Prior's Wood
Barfield Copse
PUTTENHAM
Abbot's Wood
Prior's Field School
Swim. Pool
PRIORS HATCH LANE
Fox Hanger
Meadow Barn
Fox Hanger Farm
BINSCOMBE
CHALK LANE
Home Farm
HURTMORE GOLF COURSE
MARK WAY
CORNER BUNGALOWS
Broom & Lees
Charterhouse
SHACKLEFORD
Aldro Sch.
HURTMORE
Club House
ROKERS LA.
GRENVILLE ROAD
Hurtmore Holt
Granton Ho.
Dormy Lodge
NORTHWAY
North Lodge
Under Green (Ckt. Grd.)
Charterhouse School
Glebe Farm
Mulberry House
Mushroom Farm Lodge
Grenville
Rec. Grd.
Playing Field
Wildernesse
Ben Travers Theatre
Norney Grange
St. Mary's C. of E. Inf. Sch.
By-Pass Cott.
Hurtmore Bottom
Fir Walk
Fives Courts
FRITH HILL
Tennis Courts
Headlands
Shackleford Heath
Norney Wood
NORNEY
Withy Bed
Milton Wood
Racquets & Squash Cts.
Swimming Bath
PEPERHAROW ROAD
The Rough
Norney Farm
Eashing Copse
Hell Ditch
GU7
Works
Farnham Lodge
Twotree Hill
GU8
Slowley Copse
Westbrook
Mount Sion
Peper Harow
Godalming
GUILDFORD WAVERLEY
Westhanger Cott.
Meath Home
WESTBROOK
EASHING
Eashing Farm
Halfway House
Westaway
RIVER
Lower Eashing
Upper Eashing
Eng. Wks.
Nursery
PEPER HARROW PARK
Eashing Lodge
THE HOLLOW
Aaron's Hill
Ockford Wood
Pond
Oxenford Bridge
Eashing Bri.
Eashing Moor Copse
St. Mark's C.of E. Prim. Sch.
Oxenford Grange
Brook Walk
Bonville Hanger
Eashing Cemetery
Club
OCKFORD RIDGE
St. Hilary's Sch.
OCKFORD RD.
MILFORD
B3001
ROAD
Oxenford Farm Cottages
A3 BY-PASS
A283
GUILDFORD & GODALMING BY-PASS ROAD
PRIMROSE
A3100
Thurnets Copse
Play-ground
Active Workings
Ladywell Farm
Playing Field
Amberley Farm
PORTSMOUTH
LOWER
Garden Centre
Weir
Wood Farm
Lake
Kennel

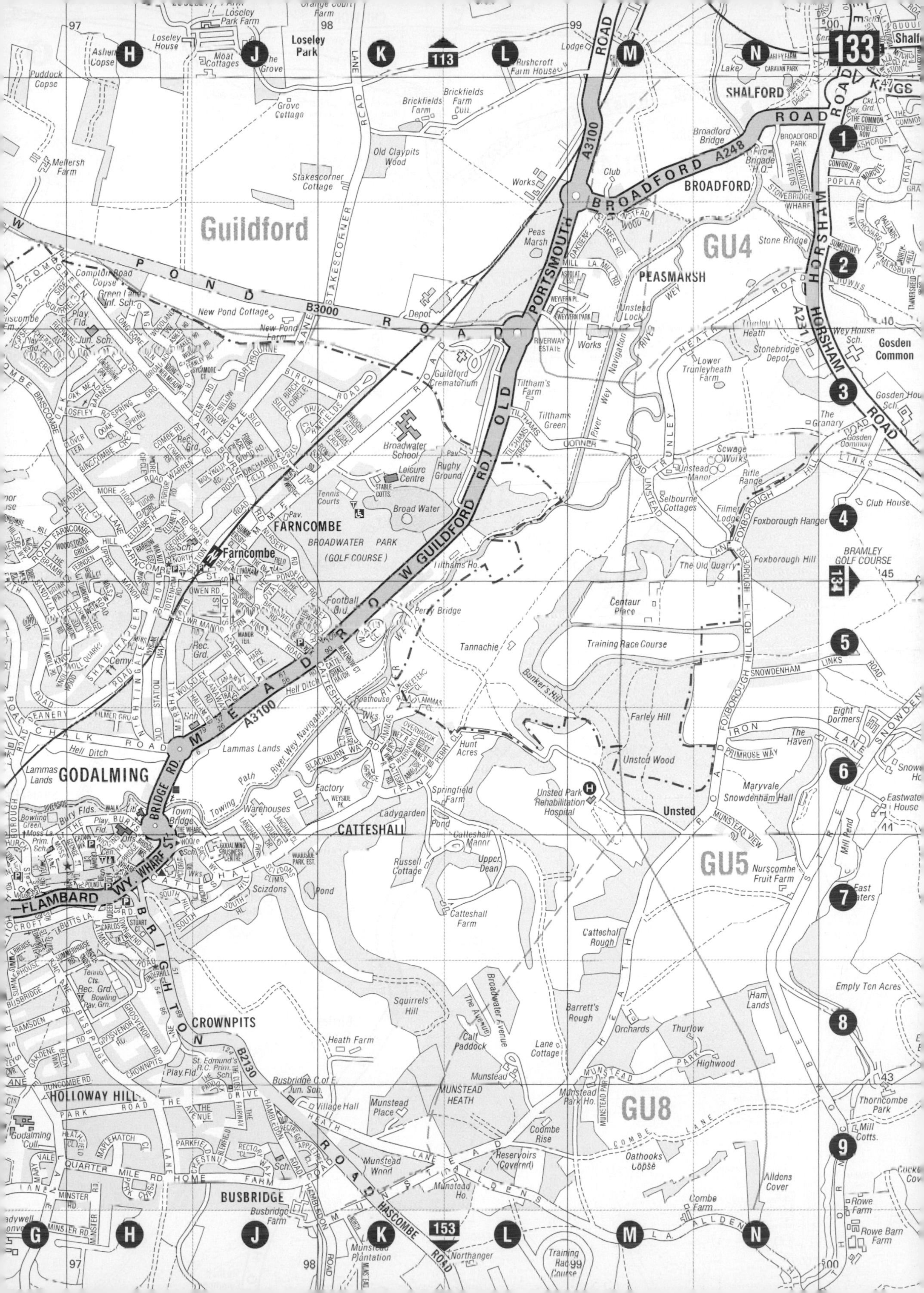

134
CHILWORTH
Shalford
SHALFORD
GU4
KINGS ROAD
CHRISTMAS HILL
A248
A281
HORSHAM ROAD
BROADFORD ROAD
Brickfield Cottage
Old Manor Farm
114
Bradstone Brook
Playing Field
Tillingbourne Jun. Sch.
Brooks Wood
Tangley Mere
Wood Cottage
Great Tangley Manor House
Great Tangley Manor Farm
Hornhatch Farm
Wonersh Common
Lower Chinthurst Farm
Tangley Hill
Monastery
Tangley Way
Fire Brigade H.Q.
Stonebridge Wharf
Stone Bridge
Stonebridge Depot
Gosden Common
Wey House Sch.
Gosden House Sch.
Chinthurst Farm
Chinthurst Hill Tower
Chinthurst Hill
Chinthurst Hill Farm
Works
The Granary
Sewage Works
Rifle Range
Filmer Lodge
Club House
Foxborough Hill
Foxborough Hanger
BRAMLEY GOLF COURSE
133
Oak Cottage
Hotel
St. Catherine's Sch.
STATION ROAD
B2129
HIGH STREET
BIRTLEY
BRAMLEY
Bramley Manor
Bramley Park Farm
WONERSH
Guildford
B2128
CRANLEIGH ROAD
WONERSH COMMON
BLACKHEATH LANE
Nursery
Chestnut Corner Hall
Derry's Hill
The Lodge
Barnett Hill Red Cross House
Museum
Cemetery
Lynes Farm
Derry's Wood
Derrysfold
Woodyers Farm
Wonersh Court
Wonersh Ho.
Sports Field
St. John's Seminary
Upper Lostiford Ho.
Lostiford Ho.
Northcote Farm
Pound Land
Northcote Hill
Mill Pond
Wonersh Mill
Heron's Wood
Norley Common
Norley Ho.
Norley Farm
Wonersh & Shamley Green C.of E. Infs. Sch.
SHAMLEY GREEN
Barnett Farm
Yieldhurst
Sewage Works
Westland Farm
Thanescroft
Lordshill Common
Longacre Sch.
Hullbrook Ho.
Hullhatch
Jersey Cotts.
Hullbrook Farm
Long Common Ho.
Plonks Hill
Eight Dormers
The Haven
Snowdenham House
Eastwater House
Maryvale
Snowdenham Hall
Mill Pond
Nurscombe Fruit Farm
East Waters
Hurst Hill
Hurst Hill Farm
Woodrough
Foresters Farm
Emply Ten Acres
Ham Lands
Emply Barn
Wisdom's Hanger
Furze Field
Thorncombe Park
Mill Cotts.
Alldens Cover
Cockedhat Cover
Rowe Farm
Tennis Courts
Birtley Farm
Birtley House
Birtley Green
Cattle Manger
Birtley Brook
Wey & Arun Junction Canal (Disused)
Fanesbridge Cott.
Rooks Hill Farm
ROOKS HILL
Rooks Hill Cotts.
Brookwell
Upper Bonhurst
Leagate Ho.
154
Ridings Brook
Rushett Common
Long Common

Chilworth
Blackheath
BLACKHEATH (N. T.)
Albury Heath
Little London
Brook
FARLEY GREEN
Farley Heath
FARLEY HEATH
GU5
Stroud Common
Winterfold Heath
WINTERFOLD HEATH
Albury Warren
Ford Crossing
Kiln Rough
Little Ford Farm
Watercress Beds
Woodside
Hare Dene
Brook Crossing
Brook Lodge
Brook Farm
Fir Croft
Ponds Farm
Broomfields
Mustard Copse
Foxholes Wood
Foxholes
Lipcombe Cotts
Home Villas
Jugs Copse
Heathfields
Piners Landing
Hallams Court
The Hallams
Northbrook Hill
Northbrook
Hallam's Farm
Darbyn's Brook
Watercress Beds
Haldish Farm
Nursery
Blackmoor Paddock
Holmcroft
Blackmoor Lodge
Greenlane Farm
Jelley's Copse
Greenglade
Rompin Downs
Far Plantation
New Field
Skemp Pond
Mayorhouse Holt
Sheepwalk
Edgeley Caravan Park
Club
Farley Green Hall Farm
Kingsfield
East Hills
Mardons
Caravan Site
Dick's Hill
Lee Farm
Reelhall Hill
Shamley Wood Ho
Sandhurst Hill
Sandhurst Copse
Tanyard Farm
Works
Kiln Hanger
Kilnhanger
Upper Woodhill Farm
Woodcock Hill
Mayor House
Mayorhouse Farm
The Burrows
Swimming Pool
Tree Tops Caravan Park
Winterfold Cottages
Tumblers Court
Woodlands
Friars Oak
Reelhall Farm
Woodhill Manor
Reelhall
Plonks Farm
Pasturewood
Pithouse Copse
Helmet Copse
The Ball
Stroud Farm
Nail Copse
Madgehole Copse
Madgehole
Madgehole Farm
Keepers Cottage
Franklin's Farm
Crist Hill Farm
Winterfold Cottage
Great Copse
Risney Cott.
Long Copse
Warren Cottage
Willinghurst Farm
Spring Wood
Rock Copse
Winterfold Hill
Barn Plaits
Willinghurst House
Spanish House
Garden Cottage
Stroud Lodge
Knob Copse
Kill Copse
Lapscombe Copse
South Copse
The Shaws
Alderbrook Garage
Alderbrook Copse
Hurtwood House
Run Farm
Run Common
Lockhurst Hatch Farm
BLACKHEATH LANE
SANDY LANE
NEW ROAD
PARK LANE
LONDON ROAD
BROOK LANE
PONDS LANE
AUGUST LA.
SHOPHOUSE LA.
LOCKHURST HATCH LANE
FARLEY HEATH ROAD
MADGEHOLE LANE
GREEN LANE
LITTLEFORD LANE
WOODHILL LANE
STROUD LANE
UPPER HOME LANE
HILL STROUD COMMON
B2128
GUILDFORD RD.
WAVERLEY
GUILDFORD
115
155
136
04
05
06
45
46
43
44
47

Albury Heath
Little London
Shere Heath
Shere Heath Crossing
The Plantation
Tor Hatch
The Ridgeway
Burrows Lea Farm
116
Parklands Farm
Parklands House
Fir Croft
Ponds Farm
Drydown Farm
Burrows Cross
Engine Wood
Burrows Lea
BURROWS CROSS
Hazelhatch
Fourways
Hazel Brow
Fulvenden Farm
Kennels
Burrows Cross House
Lawbrook
Cotterell's Farm
Leigh Cottages
Horseshoes Farm
Burgesses
Pursers Hollow
Furzefield
Hoe
Dilton Farm
Club
Guildford
Lane End Farm
Pursers Farm
Timbers Ridge
Hoe Farm
Caravan Site
Playing Field
Silton
Dilton Copse
Smoky Hole
Hazel Hall
GU5
135
Lockhurst Hatch Farm
Hound House Farm
Colman's Hill
Riding Bottom
Knowle Grange
Hazel Hall Hollow
Quakers Orchard
Hound House
PEASLAKE
Blackstone
Kiln Platt Cottage
Spurfold Copse
Rosewood Cottage
Wickham's Copse
Ridgmount
Ridge Hill
Riding Copse
Dick's Hill
Hurtwood House
Grave Yard
Churt Halewell
Wepens Copse
Camping Site
Bentley Copse
Swimming Pool
Tree Tops Caravan Park
High Banks
Burnt House
Dewdney
Dewdney Cottage
Bentlys
Winterfold Cottages
Gasson Farm
Reservoir (covered)
Winterfold Forest
Dewdney's Well
Hurt Wood
Helmet Copse
Gasson Copse
Coverwood Lakes
Coverwood Farm
Coverwood
Playing Field
Nursery
Guildford
Waverley
Winterfold Cottage
Heath
Playing Field
Cranleigh
Playing Field
GU6
Mill Bottom
Quarry
Duke of Kent School
Lake House
Mill Plain
Holt Copse
Winterfold Hill
Ewhurst Towermill
Magalee
Woolpit Wood
Reynards Hill
Mill Hollow
Pitch Hill
156
Highland Cottage
Woolpit Farm
The Warren
Hurtwood House
Alderbrook Copse
Pitch Hill
Isemongers Farm

137
117
138
157
Dorking
RH5
SUTTON ABINGER
ABINGER COMMON
Friday Street
HOLMBURY ST. MARY
Abinger Bottom
Abinger Mill
Tilling Bourne
Wotton House
Damphurst Wood
Dampshurst Hollow
Oldpark Hill
Townhurst Wood
Ellix Wood
Ellix Plantation
Chandlers Wood
Whitings Wood
The Grove
The Wilderness
High Copse
Park Row
Rectory Copse
Mundies Plantation
Bushy Wood
Raikes Farm
Paddington Tolt
Oxmoor Copse Nature Reserve
MOLE VALLEY
GUILDFORD
B2126
Ellix Wood Cottages
The Rectory
Abinger Common School
Abinger Castle
Abinger Manor
Football Ground
Mark Ash
Kempslade Farm
Millpond Copse
Noons Copse
Noons Corner
Broadmoor
Mill Pond
Sutton Abinger
Frolbury Manor
The Old Farm
Cony Copse
Deers Hill
Woodhouse Farm
Woodhouse Copse
Woodhouse Pond
High Top Lawns
Tenningshook Wood
Fairhaven
Hurtwood Chase
Felday Houses
Felbury House
PASTURE WOOD
ABINGER COMMON
Severells Copse (N.T.)
Goddards
Parkhurst Wood
Park House Farm
Park House
King George's Hill
Leylands
Kingsfield Cottage
Sewer's Farm
Lemon's Fm.
Leylands Farm
Foldemore
Feldemore Corner
Felday
Belmont School
Belmont Lodge
Playing Field
The Old Barn
Beatrice Webb House
The Gables
Cottage Copse
Riding School
The Coppers
Sewer's Copse
High Toby
Foxholt
Deers Wood
Surrey Cottage
Pitland Street
Playing Field
Bulmer Farm
Pitland Street House
Cricket Ground
Pond Copse
Pasture Wood
Holmdale
Upper Foxmoor Wood
Somerset Hill
Pump House
High Ashes Farm
Highashes Hill
Furzefield Plantation
Highashes Wood
Hopedene Farm
Rosiers Wood
GREAT FOXMOOR WOOD
Stonymoor Wood
Moxley
Holmbury Hill
Pipers Lea
The Aldermoor
Burnthouse Copse
Starveall Corner
Smith's Wood
Buildings Copse
Uptolds Farm
Reservoir (covered)
The Coach House
Moseley Copse
Whitefield Wood
Highfield Copse
Joldwynds
Tanhurst
Piny Coppice
Bushy Copse
The Wilderness
Ockham Farm House
Georges Plot
Hurtwood House College
Holmbury House
Pollard Corner
Tanhurst Wood
Shiffolds
Sherborne
Radnor House
Great Aldermoor Copse
Pratsham Farm
LEITH HILL PLACE (WEST)
Leith Hill Place
Little Birketts
Round Copse
HORSHAM ROAD
HOLMBURY LA.
THREE MILE RD.
SHEEPHOUSE LANE
LEITH HILL LANE
FRIDAY STREET
ABINGER COMMON ROAD
ABINGER LANE
RAIKES HOLLOW
WATER LANE
SUTTON LANE
DONKEY LANE
PASTURE WOOD ROAD
NOONS CORNER RD
H
J
K
L
M
N
G
1
2
3
4
5
6
7
8
9
10
11
12
13
43
44
45
46
47

138
A
B
C
D
E
F
G
118
137
158
RH4
Friday Street
Broadmoor
King George's Hill
ABINGER FOREST
COLDHARBOUR
WOTTON COMMON
LEITH HILL
Redlands
Dampfhurst Wood
Dampfhurst Hollow
Oldpark Hill
The Wilderness
Bushy Wood
Kempslade Farm
Noons Copse
Noons Corner
Home Farm
Severells Copse (N.T.)
Leylands
Kingsfield Cottage
Leylands Farm
Lemon's Farm
Sewer's Farm
Abinger Bottom
Sewer's Copse
Deers Wood
Surrey Cottage
Highashes Hill
Starveall Corner
Reservoir (covered)
Tanhurst
Tanhurst Wood
Shiffolds
Georges Plot
Piny Coppice
Campfield Place
Farmhouse Copse
Leith Hill Farm
Leith Hill Place Farm
Leith Hill Place
LEITH HILL PLACE (WEST)
LEITH HILL PLACE (EAST)
Hooks Copse
Brambly Copse
Smither's Copse
Nine Acre Copse
Sherlocks Row
Broome Hall Farm
Broome Hall
Nutfold
Round Copse
Logmore Copse
Logmore Green
Britt's Wood
Brook Farm
Alder Copse
Stonepit Copse
Bridlegate Copse
Garston's Lower Wood
Squire's Farm
Squire's Great Wood
Stable Copse
The Garden Cottage
Waterfall Copse
Simons Copse
Westcott Gore
Tower Copse
Wotton Common
Pond Cottage
Tankards Pond
Mag's Well
Brookwick Copse
Upper Merriden Farm
Shootlands
Tilling Springs
Warren Farm
Broadmoor Bottom
Whiteberry Hill
The Duke's Warren
Whiteberry Gate
Snakes Hill
Leith Hill Tower
Cockshot Hollow
Cockshot Farm
Hangers Field
Windy Gap
Slittens Copse
MOSSES WOOD
Round Wood
Highland Copse
Snarals Copse
Reservoir (covered)
Bushy Copse
Three Cornered Copse
Square Copse
Chadhurst Farm
Colchesters
Chadhurst Moor
The Roundabouts
Chadhurst Cottages
Rifle Range
Butts
Redlands Farm
Reservoir (covered)
Robbing Gate
Hambridge Brow
Res. (covered)
High Field
Collickmoor Farm
Pondfield Copse
Ham Copse
Lower Merriden Farm
Milton Gore
Waterden Wood
Coldharbour Common (N.T.)
Crockers Farm
Reservoir (covered)
Anstiebury Farm
Anstiebury
Nursery
Anstie Grange
Ryefield Copse
Spring Copse
Moor Wood
Cricket Pitch
Pav.
Hog Orchard Copse
Kitlands Farm
Kitlands
East Lodge
Bonets Wood
The Landslip
Springate Copse
Gill Wood
Lower Gill Wood
Minnick
Harelands Wood
DAMPHURST LANE
SHEEPHOUSE LANE
NOONS CORNER ROAD
WOLVENS LANE
WHITEBERRY LANE
JACOBS WALK
WHITEBERRY ROAD
LOGMORE LANE
COLDHARBOUR LANE
ANSTIE ROAD
ABINGER ROAD
BROOMEHALL ROAD
LEITH HILL LANE
LEITH HILL RD.
TANHURST LANE
MOOR LANE
HENHURST LANE
SEWERS FARM RD.
LEMON'S FARM RD.
Tilling Bourne
Pipp Brook
13
14
515
16
47
46
45
44
43

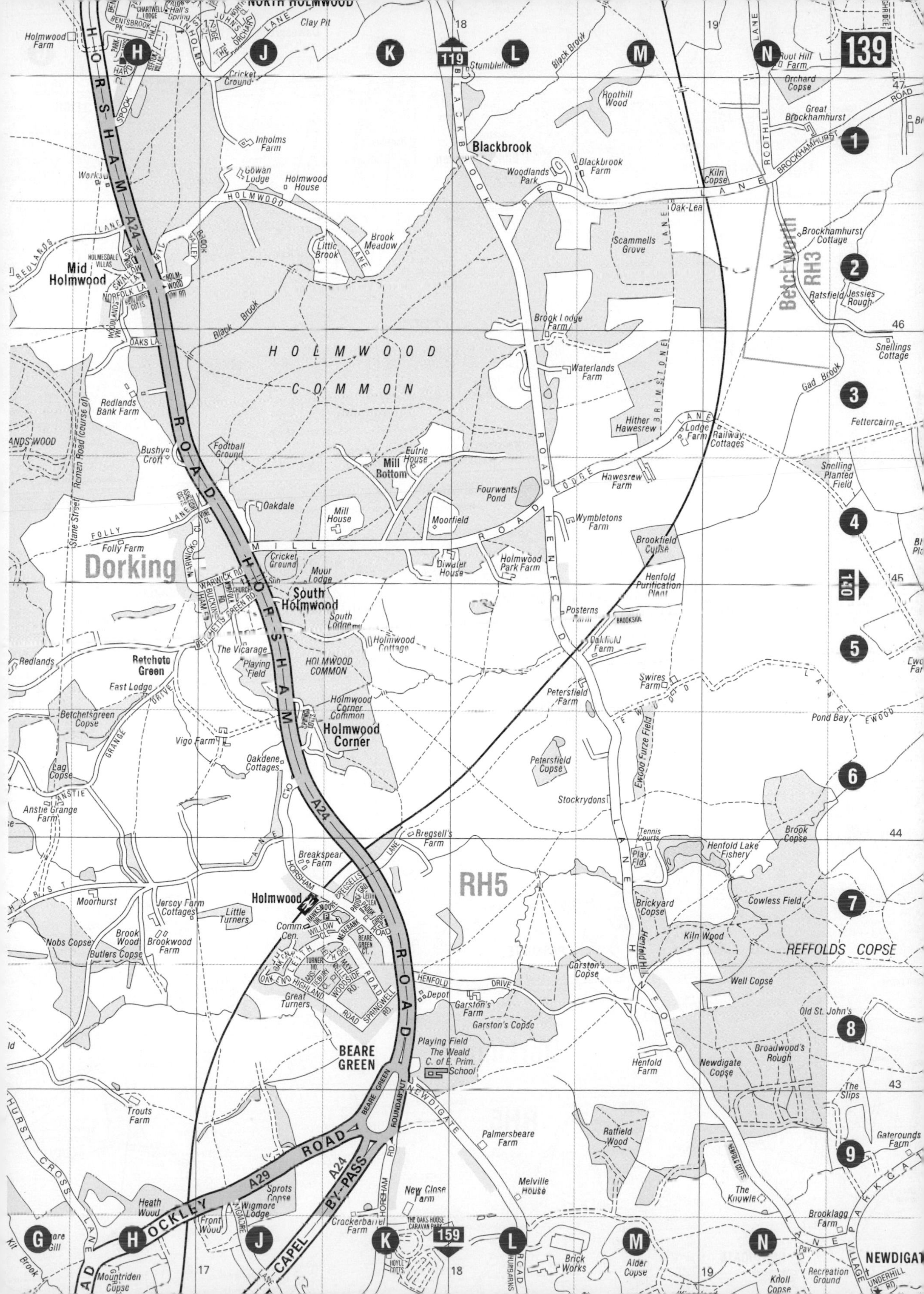

139
NORTH HOLMWOOD
Holmwood Farm
Clay Pit
Cricket Ground
Inholms Farm
Gowan Lodge
Holmwood House
Blackbrook
Stumbleholm
Blackbrook Farm
Woodlands Park
Roothill Wood
Root Hill Farm
Orchard Copse
Great Brockhamhurst
Brockhamhurst
Kiln Copse
Oak-Lea
Scammells Grove
Brockhamhurst Cottage
Betchworth
RH3
Ratsfield
Jessies Rough
Mid Holmwood
Little Brook
Brook Meadow
Black Brook
HOLMWOOD COMMON
Brook Lodge Farm
Waterlands Farm
Snellings Cottage
Gad Brook
Redlands Bank Farm
Hither Hawesrew
Lodge Farm
Railway Cottages
Fettercairn
Bushy Croft
Football Ground
Eutrie House
Mill Bottom
Hawesrew Farm
Snelling Planted Field
Fourwents Pond
Oakdale
Mill House
Moorfield
Wymbletons Farm
Folly Farm
Brookfield Copse
Dorking
Cricket Ground
Moor Lodge
Diwaler House
Holmwood Park Farm
Henfold Purification Plant
140
South Holmwood
South Lodge
Posterns Farm
Oakfield Farm
Holmwood Cottage
The Vicarage
Redlands
Betchets Green
Playing Field
HOLMWOOD COMMON
East Lodge
Swires Farm
Petersfield Farm
Holmwood Corner Common
Holmwood Corner
Pond Bay
Betchetsgreen Copse
Vigo Farm
Oakdene Cottages
Petersfield Copse
Lag Copse
Anstie Grange Farm
Stockrydons
Bregsell's Farm
Breakspear Farm
Tennis Courts
Play. Fld.
Henfold Lake Fishery
Brook Copse
RH5
Moorhurst
Jersey Farm Cottages
Little Turners
Holmwood
Comm. Cen.
Brickyard Copse
Cowless Field
Nobs Copse
Brook Wood
Brookwood Farm
Butlers Copse
Kiln Wood
REFFOLDS COPSE
Carston's Copse
Well Copse
Great Turners
Depot
Garston's Farm
Garston's Copse
Old St. John's
Playing Field
The Weald C. of E. Prim. School
BEARE GREEN
Henfold Farm
Newdigate Copse
Broadwood's Rough
Trouts Farm
The Slips
Palmersbeare Farm
Ratfield Wood
Gaterounds Farm
Heath Wood
Sprots Copse
Wigmore Lodge
New Close Farm
Melville House
The Knowle
Brooklagg Farm
Front Wood
Crackerbarrel Farm
The Oaks House Caravan Park
159
Brick Works
Alder Copse
Knoll Copse
Recreation Ground
NEWDIGATE
Mountriden Copse
Kit Brook
HORSHAM ROAD
A24
A29
HOCKLEY ROAD
CAPEL BY-PASS

Betchworth
Bunce Common
Dawesgreen
LEIGH
Shellwood Cross
PARKGATE
Dorking
RH3
RH5
NEWDIGATE
Orchard Copse
Great Brockhamhurst
Great Brockhamhurst Farm
Brockhamhurst Cottage
Ratsfield
Jessies Rough
Snellings Cottage
Gad Brook
Fettercairn
Snelling Planted Field
New Barn Shaw
Birch Platts
Westwood Farm
Bunts Place Farm
Bunts Place
Bunts End
Oakleigh Grange
Orchard Cottage
Oaklands
Twenty Acre Shaw
Bunce Common Shaw
Hook Copse
Hook Copse Arm
Shellwood Pond
Abbots Pass Hall
Dawes Green House
The Acorns First School (Leigh Base)
Rec. Grd.
Charman's Farm
Brown's Copse
Coomber's Rough
Oak Farm
Clayhill Farm
Lowbridge Farm
Lowbridge Cottage
Hammer Bridge
Willow Cottage
Brook Cottage
Leigh Bridge
Vancouver House
Leigh Place
Profits Farm
Shellwood Manor
Shellwood Farm Cottages
Shellwood Manor Cottages
Little Shellwood
Kiln Copse
Wheelgates
Rye Barn
Shellwood Cross Shaw
Brook Farm
Rigden Rough
Mynthurst Old Farm
Rigden Farm
Mynthurst Nursery
Hilly Copse
Fortune Farm
Herons Head Farm
Puckles Wood
Orchard Four Acre Plantation
Six Acre Copse
Furzefield Copse
Broadlane Rough
Ewood Cottages
Ewood Farm
Hammond's Farm
Parkhouse Copse
Rookery Wood
Cowroom Copse
Ewood House
Pond Bay
Ram Field
Parkgate Copse
HAMMOND'S COPSE NATURE RESERVE
Parkhouse Farm
Dowces Farm
Brook Copse
Cowless Farm
REFFOLDS COPSE
Ewood Copse
Parkgate Place
KILN COTTS.
Collaroy Farm
Nursery
Batts Farm
Hales Bridge
Halesbridge Farm
Springfield Farm
Curls Copse
Cherry Hurst
Blank's Farm
Well Copse
Old St. John's
Broadwood's Rough
The Slips
Westcoats Wood
Wellpools
Westcoats Farm
Coombers Farm
Mulberry Farm
Hound House Farm
The Clock House
The Red House
Gaterounds Farm
Lumber Wood
Alder Gill
Sturtwood Farm
The Knowle
Oak Lane Farm
Lakes
Hatchett's Shaw
Brooklagg Farm
Pockmires Wood
Beam Brook
Beggars Gill
Greenfield Gill
Recreation Ground
Knoll Copse
Toogoolawah
Square Copse
BROCKHAMHURST ROAD
BUNCE COMMON ROAD
SHELLWOOD ROAD
CLAYHILL ROAD
NEWDIGATE ROAD
TAPNERS ROAD
LEIGH PLACE
SMALLS HILL
GREEN LANE
EWOOD LANE
BROAD LANE
MILL LANE
BECKET WOOD
PARTRIDGE LANE
BLANKS LANE
STANS LANE
PARKGATE ROAD
NEW BARN LANE
WOODPECKER LA.
VILLAGE LANE
UNDERHILL RD
A B C D E F G
1 2 3 4 5 6 7 8 9
47 46 45 44 43
20 21 22
120
139
160

Reigate
RH2
Horley
RH6
Sidlow
Irons Bottom
Nalderswood
Mynthurst
Wrays
Norwood Hill
Bures Manor
Bures Manor Cottages
Alder Copse
Firwood
Magpie Shaw
River Field Plantation
No Man's Land
Sidlow Bridge Sch
Sidlow Farm
Sidlow Bridge
Church Meadow Farm
Riverside Meadows
Broad Ten Plantation
Gravelpit Plantation
Stable Plantation
Ninetythree Plantation
Twelve Acre Plantation
Birchett Copse
Butler's Shaw
School
Bell Copse
Lower Swains Farm
Old Swains Farm
Swains Farm
Dene Farm
Tamworth
Little Stumblehole
Stumblehole Farm
Stumblehole Common
Deanoak Bridge
Dean Oak Farm
Nalderswood House
Dabdon Bridge
New Cotts
Magpie Wood
Slab Castle
Fontigarry Farm
Kinnersley Manor
New Rivernook
Dulands Copse
Swains Copse
Ashurst Farm
Mynthurst Barn
Small's Hill Nurseries
Grove Cottage
Grove Farm
Little Mynthurst
Tennis Courts
Wolvers
Wolvers Home Farm
Ridgewood Stud
Bush House Copse
Orchard Cotts
Duxhurst
Duxhurst Farm
Lower Duxhurst Farm
Horseshoe Farm
Collendean Copse
Crutchfield Copse
Little Orchard Farm
Nursery
Deanoak Brook
Little Mynthurst Farm
Nutley Dean Farm
Norwood Place Farm
Chantersluer Plantation
Cherry Tree Farm
Rose Cottage Farm
Little Chantersluer
Chantersluer Farm
Horsehills Farm
Wrays Wood
Crutchfield Farm
Collendean Farm
Phoenix Lodge
Rowgardens Wood
Rowgardenswood
Playing Field
Woodlands
Oak Lodge
Ferriers Grange
Wrays Farm
Ferriers Forge
Rushmeads
Chantersluer Wood
Rickettswood Farm
Norwood Hill Orchard
Brittleware Farm
Brittleware Cotts
Ricketts Wood
Pond
REIGATE and BANSTEAD
MOLE VALLEY
Spencer's Gill
Rainbow Wood
Highworth Farm
Edolphs Copse Nature Reserve
Spourmead Shaw
Stanhill Court
Edolphs Farm
Depot
Westland Farm
REIGATE ROAD
A217
DOVERS GRN. RD.
RIVER MOLE
BOTTOM ROAD
IRONS BOTTOM
DEANOAK LANE
DEANOAK
MYNTHURST ROAD
SMALLS HILL ROAD
COLLENDEAN LANE
CROTCHFIELD LANE
DUXHURST LANE
HORSE HILL
NORWOOD HILL
NORWOOD ROAD
NORWOOD HILL ROAD
FOAD CRES
SPENCERS LANE
121
142
161
23
24
25
26
47
46
45
44
43

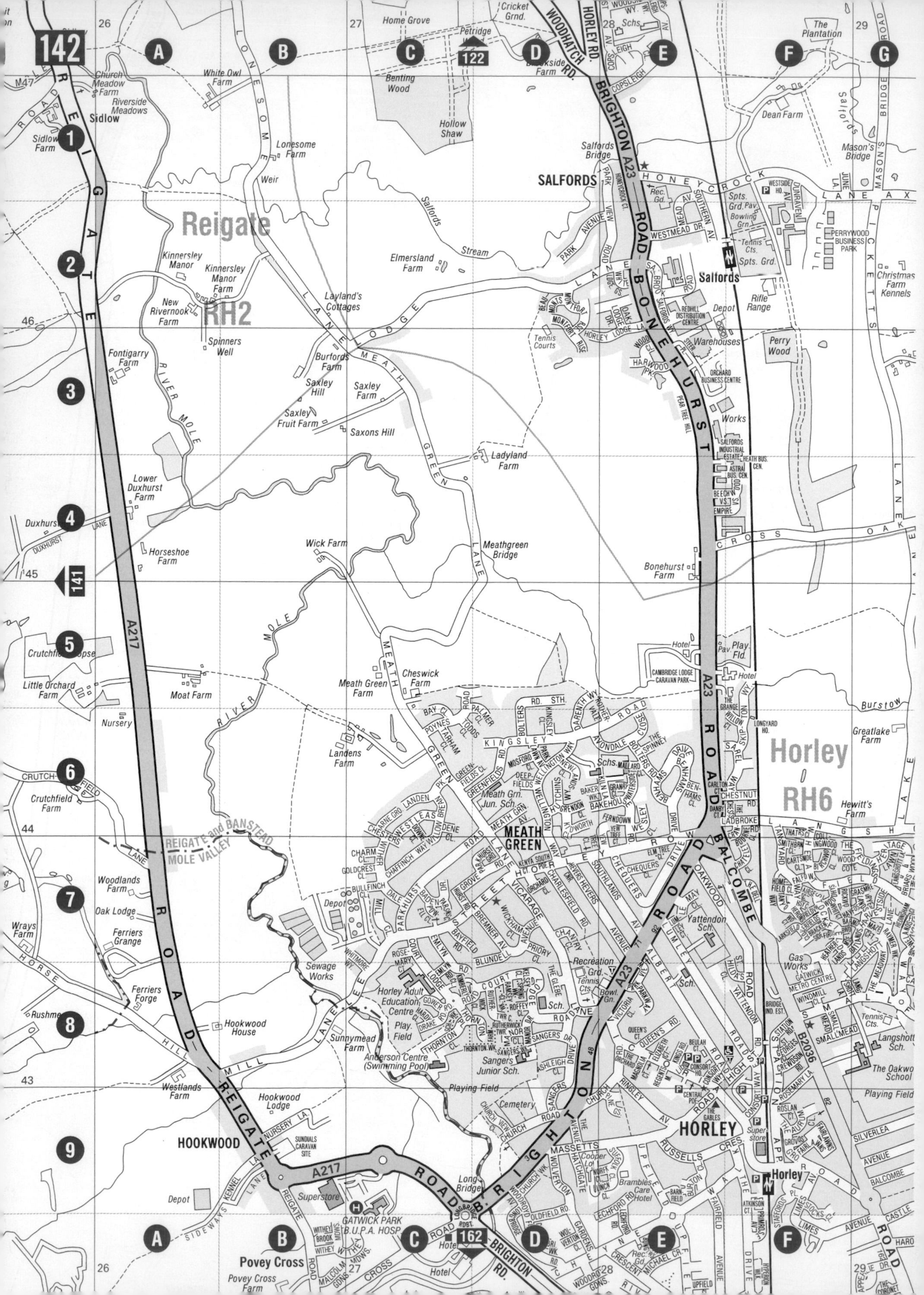

143
Redhill
RH1
OUTWOOD
Outwood Common
Langshott
Weatherhill
SMALLFIELD
Broadbridge
M23 MOTORWAY
123
163
144
South Hale Farm
Spring Field Wood
Ruffet
The Rookery
Thornfield Cott
Dairy House Farm
Cyprus Farm
Axes Farm
Meesons Farm
Furzefield Wood
Shepherd's Hurst
Stone House Farm
Cocks Copse
West View Farm
Timber Yard
Lamberts Place
Cobbler's Corner
Woolborough Hatch Farm
Torvcross Shaw
Orchard Park Caravan Site
War Memorial
Wadlands Shaw
Hookhouse Farm
Picketts Farm
Job's Farm
Woolborough Hol. Fm.
Woolborough Farm
Greenmeads Farm
Orchard Farm
Wasp Green Farm
Wasp Green
Marl House
Reservoir (covered)
Marl Pond
Hunters Moon Farm
Batchelor's Farm
Brightleigh Farm
Tennis Cts.
Rookery Hill
Coldland Wood
Rookery Farm
Littlelake Farm
Westfield Cotts.
Hathersham Farm
Drivers Green
Old Hall Farm
Tandridge
Reigate and Banstead
Stream
The Rookery
Longyards Shaw
Courtoak Green
Burstow Manor
Little Firs
Burstow Lodge Farm
Burstow Lodge Business Centre
Lodge
Hollesley Farm
Tanyard Farm
Langshott Manor
Brook Wood
Sewage Works
Depot
Langshott Wood
Lost Sevens
Oak Bed
Weatherhill Common
Cherry Farm
Long Pond
Harrowsley Green Farm
Dowlands Bungalows
Playground
Playing Field
Green Farm
Wilgers Farm
Farney View Farm
Perrylands
Haroldslea Poultry Farm
Bridgeham Wood
Bridgeham Farm
Bridgeham Grange
Cricket Ground
Moat
Thunderfield Castle (site of)
Newstead Hall
Haroldslea House
Lower Broadbridge Farm
Redehall Preparatory School
Sacconex Farm
Broadmead Farm
Broadbridge Farm
Vanderel Farm
Homestead
The Acorns
Sch.
Hall
Works
Green Lane
Lane
Brickfield
Prince of Wales Road
St. George's Road
St. George's Hill
New House Lane
Hathersham Lane
Rookery Hill
Miller's Lane
Courtoak Lane
Norman's Road
Cogmans Lane
Weatherhill Road
Plough Lane
Chapel Road
Redehall Road
Haroldslea
Haroldslea Drive
Dowlands Lane
Wood Lane
Hathersham Cl.
Charlotte Gro.
The Cravens
Haydn Wk.
Carey's Wood
Raleigh Dr.
Tudor Cl.
Grangeway
Crescent Way
Grange End
Woodside
Wheeler Way
Church Hill
Orchard
Meadow View
Bridgeham Way
Kings Mead
New Rd.
Caravan Park
Langshott
Furze Cl.
Acorn Cl.
Copse La.
Jennings Wy.
Clifton Cl.
Castle Drive
Harrowsley
Burstow Stream
Weatherhill Cl.
Toronto Dr.
Ontario Cl.
Wilmots Way
Daysey's Hill
Wasp Green Lane
Radland Rd.
Gayhouse Lane
H
J
K
L
M
N
G
1
2
3
4
5
6
7
8
9
30
31
32
43
44
45
46
47

144
124
164
143
Spring Field Wood
Brownshill Shaw
Browns Hill
North Lodge
Harewood House
South Lodge
Harewood Home Farm
Lodge Farm
Lower South Park
South Park
Lwr.
Fidler's Grove
Birchen Wood
Carlton Rd.
Carlton Road
Brooklands
The Lake
Hookstile Gully
Eight Acre Shaw
Roman Road
Redhill
RH1
Cobbler's Corner
Putney Gill
Hangdog Wood
Marl Farm
Byers Wood
Hookhouse Farm
Outwood Common
The Pheasantry
Nine Corner Wood
Tile Barn
Gayhouse Furzes
Hookstile Gully
Wadlands Shaw
Outwood Common
Outwood
Hall
Ckt. Gd.
Miller's Lane
Wasp Green
Outwood Postmill
Outwood Lane
Gay House
Gayhouse Lane
Bannister Shaw
Tedham Lane
Osney Lodge Farm
Blue Anchor Wood
Corn Mill
Godstone
Lightleigh Farm
Marl House
Reservoir (covered)
Marl Pond
Wilmots
Copsley Court
Hornecourt Wood
Axeland Croft Shaw
Rowe Tye
Tedham Farm
Jarves Farm
Beggars Roost
Upper Barn Farm
Byers Lane
Hays Bridge Houses
Whitewood
Hays Bridge Business Centre
RH9
Hornecourt Manor Farm
Hornecourt Manor Farm Cotts.
Horne Court Hill
Playing Field
Old Hall Farm
Wilmot's Farm
Wilmots Lane
Scotts Hill
Church Road
Ermyn Cotts.
Byers La.
Whitewood
Whitewood House Farm
Brickhouse Lane
Lane
Road
Courtoak Green
Horne
Yew Tree Nursery School
Church Farm
Playground
Homefield Cottages
Farm Approach
Hays Bridge Farm
Long Meadows Farm
Cogmans Lane
Hollesley Farm
Horne House Farm
Eulyn Farm
Hay's Bridge
Southlands Nurseries
Barn Lane
Cherrydown Farm
Green Patch
Little Abbots Farm
Redroof
Croydon Road
Short Acre Farm
Long Acre Farm
Goulds Farm
Branford Farm
Acre Cr.
Cattle Grid
Croydonbarn Wood
White House
Whitehouse Farm
Barncote
Hadesmead Wood
Horley
RH6
Mole End
Smallfield Place
Long Pond
Smallfield Road
Plough Road
Chithurst Lane
Dowlands Lane
Highfield Farm
Pav.
Playground
Playing Field
Dowlands Bungalows
Moat
Bysshe Court Farm
Rough Beech Farm
Green Farm
Triddles Farm
Horne Park
Glen Farm
Timber Yard
Horne Park Farm
Clay Lane
Bones Lane
Stock Cottage
Homelea
The Plantation
Bones Wood
Lower Dowlands Wood
East Park Lane
Little Brook
Laburnum Court (Caravan Park)
Verel Farm Homestead
Roughbeech Wood
Dowlands Wood
The Bungalow
A
B
C
D
E
F
G
1
2
3
4
5
6
7
8
9
33
34
35
43
44
45
46
47

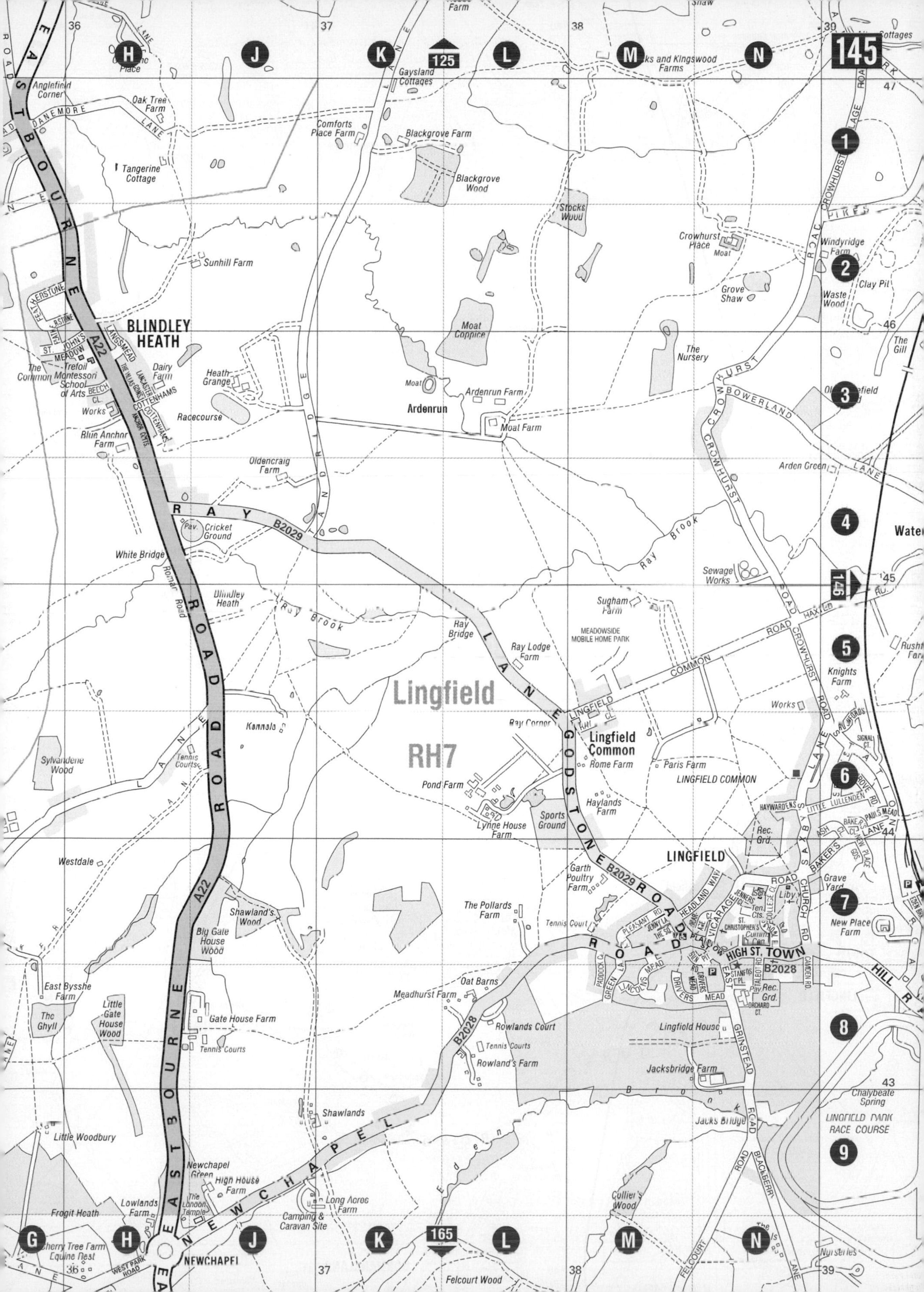

H
J
K
125
L
M
N
Gaysland Cottages
Kingswood Farms
Anglefield Corner
Oak Tree Farm
DANEMORE LANE
Comforts Place Farm
Blackgrove Farm
Tangerine Cottage
Blackgrove Wood
Stocks Wood
Crowhurst Place
Moat
Windyridge Farm
Sunhill Farm
Grove Shaw
Clay Pit
Waste Wood
BLINDLEY HEATH
Moat Coppice
The Gill
The Common
ST. JOHN'S MEADOW
Trefoil Montessori School of Arts
BEECH CL.
Dairy Farm
Heath Grange
COTTENHAMS
The Nursery
Ardenrun Farm
Ardenrun
Moat Farm
BOWERLAND
Works
Racecourse
Blue Anchor Farm
Oldencraig Farm
Arden Green
LANE
CROWHURST ROAD
CROWHURST LANE
RAY LANE
B2029
Pav.
Cricket Ground
White Bridge
Ray Brook
Sewage Works
146
Blindley Heath
Sugham Farm
Ray Bridge
MEADOWSIDE MOBILE HOME PARK
Ray Lodge Farm
COMMON ROAD
HAXTED RD.
Knights Farm
Lingfield
RH7
Works
Kennels
Ray Corner
LINGFIELD
Lingfield Common
Rome Farm
Paris Farm
LINGFIELD COMMON
Sylvandene Wood
Tennis Courts
Pond Farm
Lynne House Farm
Sports Ground
Haylands Farm
HAYWARDENS
LITTLE LULLENDEN
SAXBYS LANE
Rec. Grd.
LINGFIELD
Westdale
GODSTONE ROAD
Garth Poultry Farm
HEADLAND WAY
VICARAGE
CHURCH RD.
Liby.
Grave Yard
New Place Farm
The Pollards Farm
Tennis Court
Shawland's Wood
Big Gate House Wood
EASTBOURNE ROAD
A22
HIGH ST. TOWN
B2028
HILL
East Bysshe Farm
The Ghyll
Little Gate House Wood
Oat Barns
Meadhurst Farm
DRIVERS MEAD
Rec. Grd.
Gate House Farm
Rowlands Court
Lingfield House
Tennis Courts
Rowland's Farm
Tennis Courts
Jacksbridge Farm
GRINSTEAD ROAD
EAST
Chalybeate Spring
Shawlands
Jacks Bridge
LINGFIELD PARK RACE COURSE
Little Woodbury
Eden Brook
NEWCHAPEL ROAD
Newchapel Green
High House Farm
Long Acres Farm
Collier's Wood
BLACKBERRY LANE
FELCOURT ROAD
Frogit Heath
Lowlands Farm
The London Temple
Camping & Caravan Site
G
H
J
K
165
L
M
N
Cherry Tree Farm Equine Rest
WEST PARK ROAD
NEWCHAPEL
Nurseries
Felcourt Wood
36
37
38
39
1
2
3
4
5
6
7
8
9
47
46
45
44
43

Altar Cottages
Crowhurst Village Road
Park Road
Caterfield Lane
Chellows Lane
Pikes Road
Pikes Fm.
Crowhurst Brickworks
Chellows Farm
Windyridge Farm
Clay Pit
Waste Wood
Grove Shaw
The Gill
Bowerland Farm
Chellows Park
Old Furzefield Wood
Bowerland Lane
Arden Green
Waterside
Haxted Road
Oak Pollard
River Eden
Shingle Barn Farm
Wintersell Farm
Shinglebarn Wood
Waterham Pit
Dwelly Farm
Dwelly Lane
Virgintree Wood
The Eden Kennels
Haxted Hill
Haxted Mill & Museum
Rose Cottages
Puttenden Manor
Barrow Green Farm
Haxted Mead Cottages
Haxted Mead Farm
Mill Stream
Water Lane
Eden Brook
Lingfield
RH7
Rushford Farm
Knights Farm
Works
Crowhurst Rd.
Station Road
Signal Ct.
Rushfords
Selbys
Grove Rd.
Little Lullenden
Haywardens
Saxbys Lane
Pauls Mead
Bakers Lane
Park Farm
Billeshurst Wood
Dencher Wood
St. Pier's Farm
Longwalk Shaw
Starborough Farm
Starborough Road
St. Piers Lane
Common
Rec. Grd.
Grave Yard
Lingfield
Margaret's Hill
Gratwick's Wood
St. Piers School
Play Field
Furze Wood
Playground
Playing Field
Tennis Courts
Margaret's Wood
Bottoms Wood
New Place Farm
High St.
Town Hill
B2028
Camden Rd.
Talbot Rd.
East Grinstead Road
Pav. Rec. Grd.
Orchard Ct.
Lingfield
Racecourse Road
Notre Dame School (Junior Sch.)
Notre Dame School
Reservoir
Carewell Farm
Carewell Wood
Windermere
Moor Farm
Moor Lane
Cedar Lodge
Oxenlees Wood
Winns
Poultons
Drill Hall
Chalybeate Spring
Club House
Bridge
Woodgate
Lodge
Ford Manor Rd.
Ford House
Lingfield Park Racecourse
Dormans Road
Parklands Poultry Farm
West Street
Plough Road
Filter Beds
Black Road
Lingfield Park Golf Course
Club
Dormans Cross
Icehouse
Cattle Grid
The Laurels
Nurseries
Dormansland
Home Birches
Greathed Manor
Ford Manor
Home Farm
Depots
Locks Mdw.
126
145
166

147
H
J
K
L
M
N
1
2
3
4
5
6
7
8
9
G
127
167
EDENBRIDGE GOLF
& COUNTRY CLUB
Club House
Ten. Cts.
Crouch House
Farm
Crouch
House Green
Moat
ST. BRELADE'S COURT
RESIDENTIAL PARK
Industrial
Estate
Spitals Cross
Estate
Sewage Works
Cauk
Wood
EDENBRIDGE
WESTWAYS
FOUR ELMS
B2027
Eden Valley
Sch.
Playing
Fields
Works
Skinners
Farm
Skinners
Edenbridge
Town
Leisure Cen.
Stangrove
Park
STATION APP.
GRANGE
Edenbridge
Prim. Sch.
FORGE
CHURCH
Cemy.
THE PLAT
STREET
RIVERSIDE
River Eden
Superstore
Rec. Grd.
Pav.
Playing Fields
KATHERINE
RD.
VICTORIA
Depot
EDENBRIDGE
TRADING CENTRE
WARSOP
TRADING ESTATE
Delaware
Cotts.
EDENBRIDGE
& DISTRICT
WAR MEMORIAL
HOSPITAL
MEAD RD.
Cricket
Ground
Mill Race
Moat
Devils'
Den
STATION
ROAD
HIGH
B2026
STREET
MILL
HILL
Skeynes
Farm
Skeynes
West Haxted
Cottages
LINGFIELD
ROAD
Skeynes Farm
Cottages
Haxted
West
Haxted
Farm
East Haxted
Farm
SEVENOAKS
TANDRIDGE
RIVER
EDEN
Brook
Edenbridge
TN8
Cernes Farm
Gabriel's
Farm
Gabriel's
Manor
Den Cross
HARTFIELD
ROAD
New Farm
Lydens
Farm
Dencross
Farm
B2028
Booms
Farm
Stanford's
End Farm
White
Lodge
Leydens
Farm
Redpath Poultry
Farm
Broomsmead
MARSH GREEN
B2026
Lingfield Lodge Farm
Moat
Chiswell Hall
Leydens
House
Manor Farm
Chiswell
Farm
Brook
Street
Farm
ROAD
GREEN
Hillands
Marsh
Green
Wood
Christmas
Place
Christmas Mill
Little
Brookstreet
Bildie
Lane
Farm
SHERNDEN
SHERNDEN LANE
Shernden Farm
Marsh Green
Wood
Smoaky
Cottage
Prinkham
House
Prinkham
Shaw
Howlets
Farm
Old Forge
MARSH
Prinkham Cottages
Gilridge
Wood
Skitts Farm
Ockhams
New Barns
Farm
Clatfields
Pierce's Plats
Cobhambury
Farm
Birches
Wood
Potter's
Wood
Shernden Wood
Kiln
Wood
Coalhearth
Wood
Hoopers Farm
Middleroom
Wood
Greybury Farm
Codhambury
Wood
Round
House
Farm
Nann's
Common
Clump
Greybury
Furzes
GREYBURY LANE
Spring
Wood
Spode
Gilridge
Lodge
SPODE LA.
Greybury
Wood
Old Plantation
Reynolds Wood
Ash
Plantation
43
44
45
46
47
145

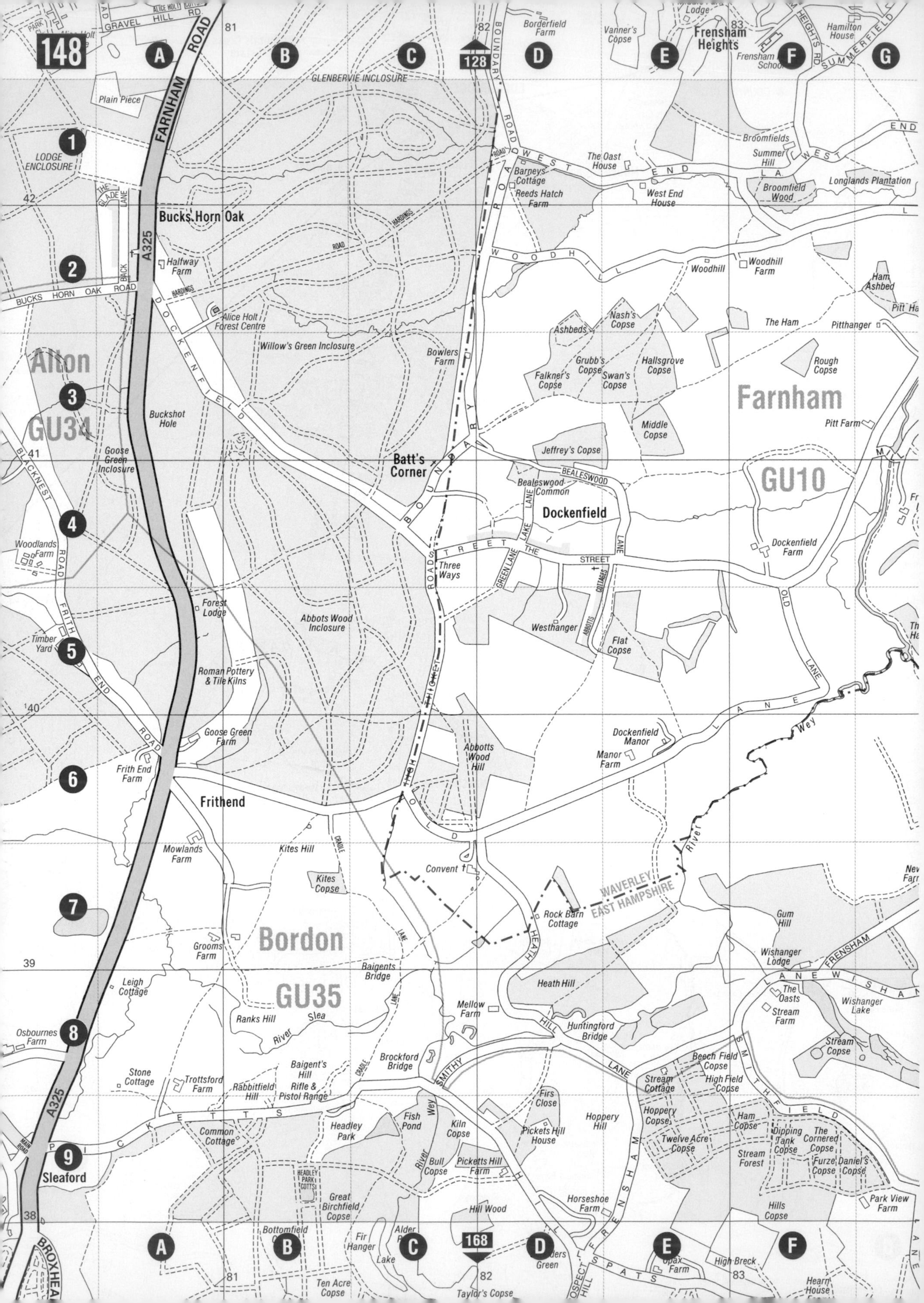
148
A
B
C
D
E
F
G
128
168
81
82
83
42
41
140
39
38
1
2
3
4
5
6
7
8
9
Alton
GU34
Farnham
GU10
Bordon
GU35
Frensham Heights
Frensham School
Hamilton House
Borderfield Farm
Vanner's Copse
GLENBERVIE INCLOSURE
Plain Piece
LODGE ENCLOSURE
Bucks Horn Oak
Halfway Farm
Alice Holt Forest Centre
Willow's Green Inclosure
Bowlers Farm
Barneys Cottage
Reeds Hatch Farm
The Oast House
West End House
Broomfields
Summer Hill
Broomfield Wood
Longlands Plantation
Woodhill
Woodhill Farm
Ham Ashbed
The Ham
Pitthanger
Ashbeds
Nash's Copse
Grubb's Copse
Swan's Copse
Hallsgrove Copse
Falkner's Copse
Rough Copse
Middle Copse
Pitt Farm
Jeffrey's Copse
Buckshot Hole
Goose Green Inclosure
Batt's Corner
Bealeswood Common
Dockenfield
Dockenfield Farm
Woodlands Farm
Three Ways
Westhanger
Flat Copse
Forest Lodge
Abbots Wood Inclosure
Timber Yard
Roman Pottery & Tile Kilns
Goose Green Farm
Frith End Farm
Dockenfield Manor
Manor Farm
Abbotts Wood Hill
Frithend
Mowlands Farm
Kites Hill
Kites Copse
Convent
Rock Barn Cottage
WAVERLEY
EAST HAMPSHIRE
Gum Hill
Wishanger Lodge
Grooms Farm
Baigents Bridge
Heath Hill
Leigh Cottage
Ranks Hill
River Slea
Mellow Farm
Huntingford Bridge
The Oasts
Stream Farm
Wishanger Lake
Stream Copse
Osbournes Farm
Stone Cottage
Trottsford Farm
Rabbitfield Hill
Baigent's Hill Rifle & Pistol Range
Brockford Bridge
Beech Field Copse
High Field Copse
Stream Cottage
Firs Close
Hoppery Hill
Hoppery Copse
Ham Copse
Twelve Acre Copse
Dipping Tank Copse
The Cornered Copse
Stream Forest
Furze Copse
Daniel's Copse
Common Cottage
Headley Park
Fish Pond
Kiln Copse
Pickets Hill House
Sleaford
River Wey
Bull Copse
Picketts Hill Farm
HEADLEY PARK COTTS
Great Birchfield Copse
Hill Wood
Horseshoe Farm
Park View Farm
Hills Copse
Bottomfield
Fir Hanger
Alder
Lake
Green
Upax Farm
High Breck
Ten Acre Copse
Taylor's Copse
Hearn House
A325
FARNHAM ROAD
GRAVEL HILL RD.
ALICE HOLT COTTS
BUCKS HORN OAK ROAD
BACK LANE
THE GLADE
HARDINGS
HARDINGS ROAD
DOCKENFIELD
BOUNDARY ROAD
WEST END LA.
WOODHILL
HEIGHTS RD
SUMMERFIELD
BEALESWOOD
LAKE LANE
THE STREET
GREEN LANE
ABBOTTS COTTAGES
OLD LANE
BLACKNEST
FRITH END ROAD
HIGH THICKET ROAD
OLD LANE
CRADLE LANE
HEATH HILL
SMITHY LANE
PICKETTS
MAIN ROAD
FRENSHAM LANE
WISHANGER LANE
SMITHFIELD
FRENSHAM
SPATS
BROXHEAD

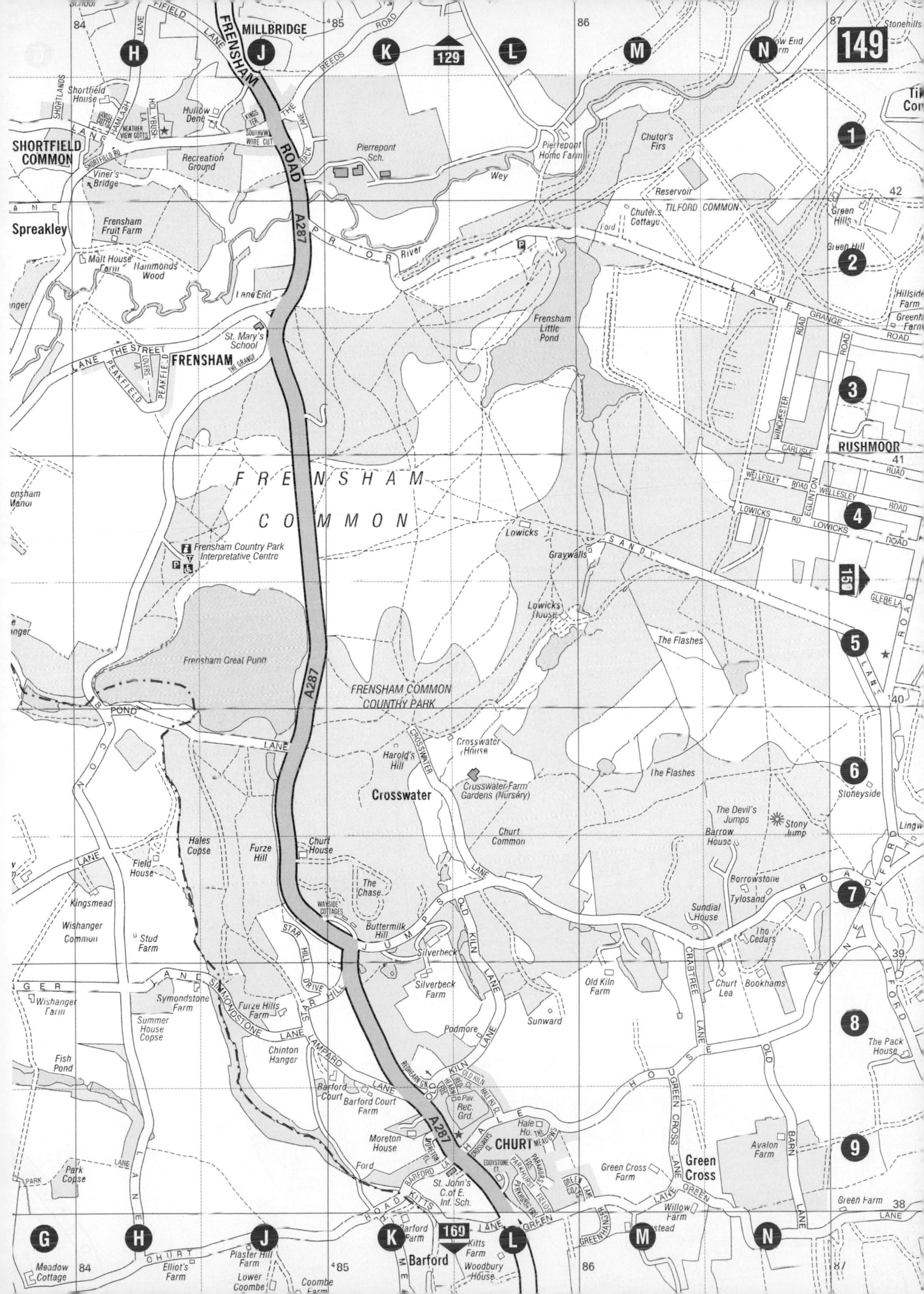
MILLBRIDGE
FRENSHAM ROAD
A287
SHORTFIELD COMMON
Spreakley
Shortfield House
Hollow Dene
Recreation Ground
Pierrepont Sch.
Pierrepont Home Farm
Chutor's Firs
Reservoir
TILFORD COMMON
Chuter's Cottage
Green Hills
Green Hill
Frensham Fruit Farm
Malt House Farm
Hammonds Wood
River Wey
PRIOR LANE
GRANGE ROAD
Lane End
St. Mary's School
THE STREET
FRENSHAM
Frensham Little Pond
RUSHMOOR
WINCHESTER ROAD
CARLISLE ROAD
WELLESLEY ROAD
EGLINTON ROAD
LOWICKS RD.
LOWICKS ROAD
FRENSHAM COMMON
Frensham Country Park Interpretative Centre
Lowicks
Graywalls
SANDY LANE
Lowicks House
The Flashes
Frensham Great Pond
FRENSHAM COMMON COUNTRY PARK
POND LANE
Harold's Hill
Crosswater House
Crosswater Farm Gardens (Nursery)
Crosswater
Hales Copse
Furze Hill
Churt House
Churt Common
The Devil's Jumps
Stony Jump
Barrow House
Stoneyside
Field House
Kingsmead
The Chase
Borrowstone
Tylosand
Sundial House
The Cedars
Wishanger Common
Stud Farm
Wayside Cottages
Buttermilk Hill
JUMPS ROAD
Silverbeck
Silverbeck Farm
OLD KILN LANE
Old Kiln Farm
CRABTREE LANE
Churt Lea
Bookhams
Wishanger Farm
Symondstone Farm
Furze Hills Farm
SYMONDSTONE LANE
STAR HILL
Podmore
Sunward
Summer House Copse
Chinton Hanger
LAMPARD LANE
Fish Pond
Barford Court
Barford Court Farm
Rec. Grd.
Hale Ho.
THE MEADOWS
CHURT
HALE HOUSE LANE
GREEN CROSS LANE
Green Cross
Avalon Farm
BARN LANE
The Pack House
Moreton House
Ford
St. John's C.of E. Inf. Sch.
Green Cross Farm
Willow Farm
Green Farm
Park Copse
Barford Farm
Kitts Farm
Barford
Woodbury House
Meadow Cottage
Elliot's Farm
Plaster Hill Farm
Lower Coombe
Coombe Farm
CHURT ROAD
TILFORD ROAD
129
151
169
84
85
86
87
42
41
40
39
38
H
J
K
L
M
N
G
1
2
3
4
5
6
7
8
9

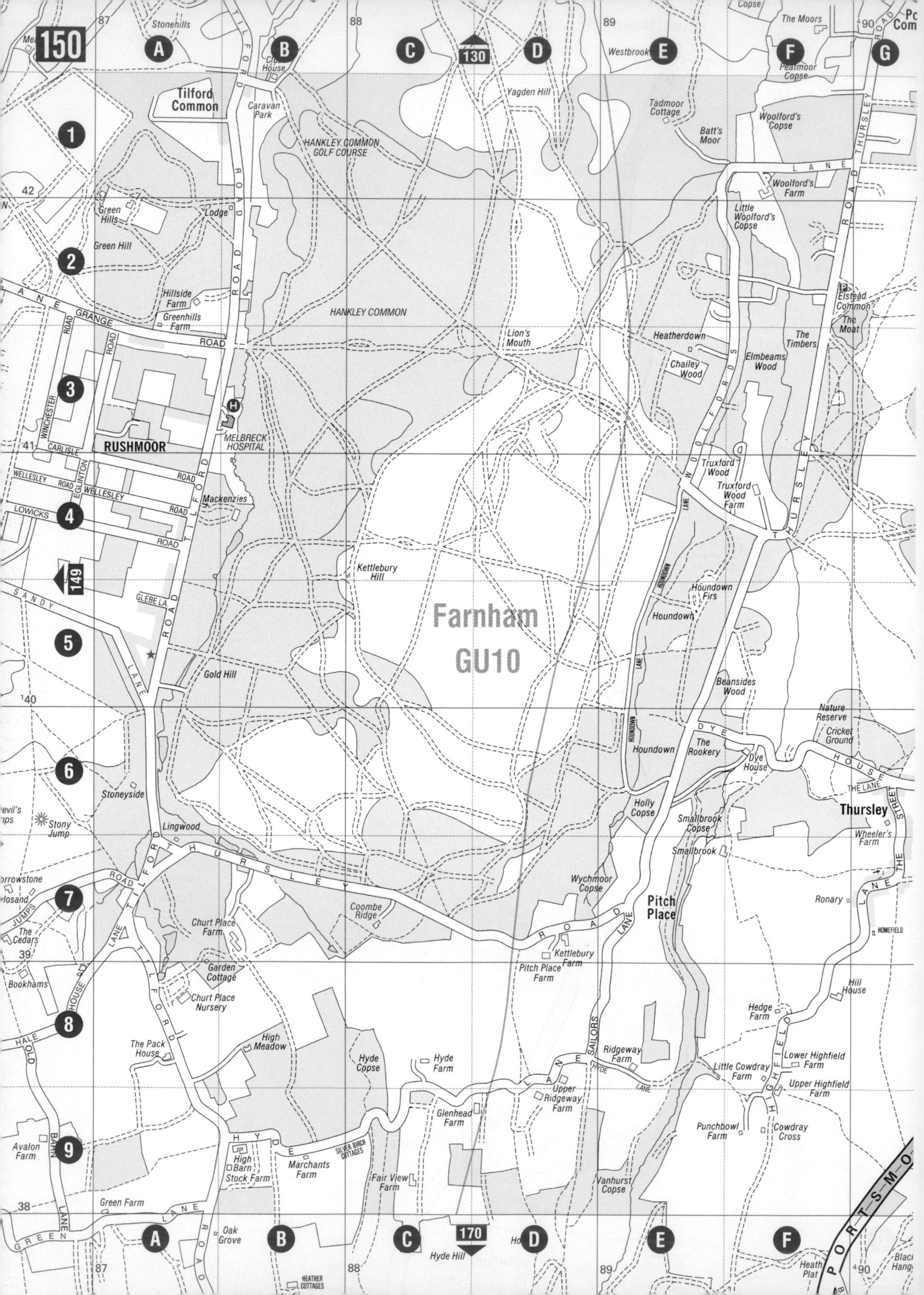

Tilford Common
RUSHMOOR
MELBRECK HOSPITAL
HANKLEY COMMON GOLF COURSE
HANKLEY COMMON
Farnham
GU10
Kettlebury Hill
Lion's Mouth
Yagden Hill
Thursley
Pitch Place
Elstead Common
Tadmoor Cottage
Batt's Moor
Woolford's Copse
Woolford's Farm
Little Woolford's Copse
Heatherdown
Chailey Wood
Elmbeams Wood
The Timbers
The Moat
Truxford Wood
Truxford Wood Farm
Houndown Firs
Houndown
Beansides Wood
The Rookery
Dye House
Nature Reserve
Cricket Ground
Holly Copse
Smallbrook Copse
Smallbrook
Wheeler's Farm
Wychmoor Copse
Ronary
Kettlebury Farm
Pitch Place Farm
Hill House
Hedge Farm
Ridgeway Farm
Upper Ridgeway Farm
Little Cowdray Farm
Lower Highfield Farm
Upper Highfield Farm
Punchbowl Farm
Cowdray Cross
Vanhurst Copse
Stonehills
Club House
Caravan Park
Westbrook
The Moors
Peatmoor Copse
Green Hills
Green Hill
Lodge
Hillside Farm
Greenhills Farm
Mackenzies
Gold Hill
Stoneyside
Stony Jump
Lingwood
Churt Place Farm
Coombe Ridge
Garden Cottage
Churt Place Nursery
Bookhams
The Cedars
The Pack House
High Meadow
Hyde Copse
Hyde Farm
Glenhead Farm
High Barn
Stock Farm
Marchants Farm
Fair View Farm
Avalon Farm
Green Farm
Oak Grove
Hyde Hill
Heath Plat
HEATHER COTTAGES
SILVER BIRCH COTTAGES
HOMEFIELD
GRANGE ROAD
WINCHESTER ROAD
CARLISLE ROAD
WELLESLEY ROAD
EGLINTON ROAD
LOWICKS ROAD
SANDY LANE
GLEBE LA
TILFORD ROAD
THURSLEY ROAD
WOOLFORDS LANE
HOUNDOWN LANE
DYE HOUSE ROAD
THE LANE
THE STREET
SAILORS LANE
HYDE LANE
HIGHFIELD LANE
HALE HOUSE LANE
OLD BARN LANE
GREEN LANE
JUMPS ROAD
PORTSMOUTH ROAD
130
149
170

Godalming
GU8
Elstead Common
Fir Plantation
Red House Farm
Guinea Copse
ROYAL COMMON
Bagmoor Wood
Ashen Copse
Thurnets Copse
Bagmoor Cottage
Bagmoor Common Nature Reserve
Kennel Moor
Mousehill Down
Mistlebrooks Wood
Burchetts Copse
Burchetts
Mousehill Corner
Temple Hill
Borough Farm
Borough Copse
Lower Level
Upper Level
UCKLEY COMMON
Pudmore Pond
Rodborough Hill
RODBOROUGH HILL COTTAGES
Roundabouts
Forked Pond
Home Pond
Warren Mere
WITLEY COMMON NATURE RESERVE
THURSLEY COMMON
Nature Reserve
Will Reeds
HAMMER POND COTTAGES
Silkmill Pond
Birch Copse
Coldharbour Wood
Caravan Park
WARREN PARK
Witley Common Nature Centre
Depot
Hammer Pond
Penmead Copse
Tumuli
Tumulus
Sewage Works
PORTSMOUTH ROAD
A3
HASLEMERE ROAD
A286
WEBB ROAD
COACH ROAD
ROKE LANE
Heath House
Milford Lodge
Foldsdown
PORTSMOUTH ROAD
OLD
Milhanger
COSFORD
French Hill
Lake Cottages
The Shrubbery
Stable Lake
Thursley Lake
The Grove
Witley Park
The Hanger
Upper Lake
West Firs
Witley Park House
Reservoir (covered)
Parsonage House
Parsonage Farm
Heath Hall
Cosford House
Cosford Farm
Bedford Farm
Kiln Close
Long Copse
The Rocks
Rockwoods
Banacle Common
Heath Hall Farm
LOWER HOUSE ROAD
Mount Pleasant
Bowlhead Green
King's Firs
Daws Copse
Chocolates
Furzefield Wood
Longbeer Copse
Reservoir (covered)
Heath Hills
The Hill House
Blackhanger Farm
BOWLHEAD GREEN
Hanger Copse
Brook
Recreation Ground
Pav.
Banacle Firs
Fintry
Sandh
Bedford and Hole Farm
Bowlhead Green Farm
BEECH
Stables
Birch Copse
Brook Farm
Ox Heart Copse
Emley Copse
Emley Farm
Rutton Hill
RUTTON HILL ROAD
Beech Hanger
Southern's Hanger
Kingwood
Tylands Copse
BROOK ROAD
H J K L M N
G H J K L M N
1 2 3 4 5 6 7 8 9
131
171
152
91 92 93
42 41 40 39 38

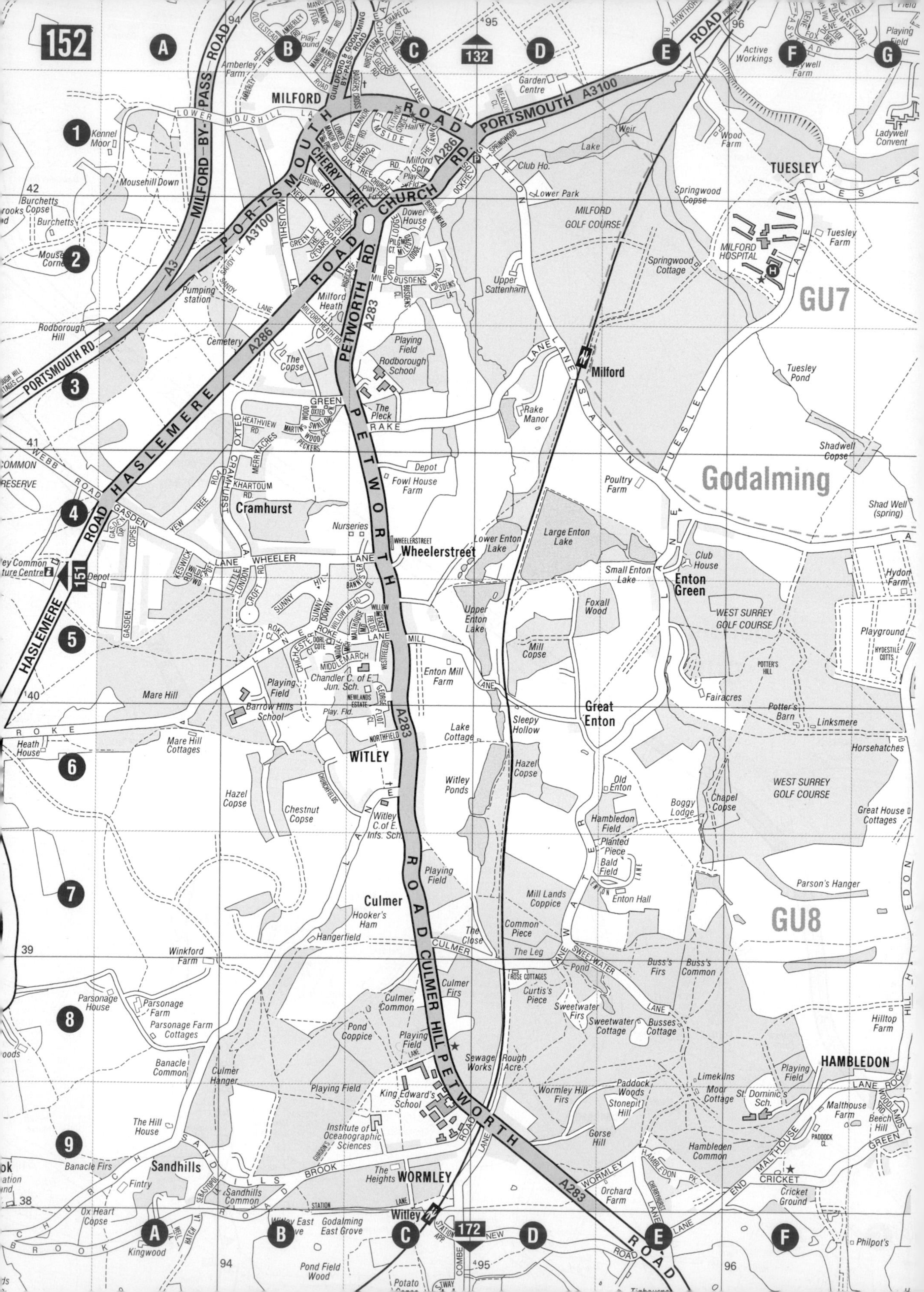
A
B
C
D
E
F
G
1
2
3
4
5
6
7
8
9
132
151
172
94
95
96
42
41
140
39
38
MILFORD
MILFORD-BY-PASS-ROAD
PORTSMOUTH ROAD A3100
PORTSMOUTH RD.
HASLEMERE ROAD A286
PETWORTH RD. A283
PETWORTH ROAD
CHURCH RD.
CULMER HILL
GUILDFORD & GODALMING BY-PASS ROAD
Amberley Farm
Kennel Moor
Mousehill Down
Burchetts Copse
Burchetts
Mouse Corner
Pumping station
Rodborough Hill
Cemetery
The Copse
Milford Heath
Playing Field
Rodborough School
The Pleck
Garden Centre
Club Ho.
Lower Park
Weir
Lake
MILFORD GOLF COURSE
Springwood Copse
Springwood Cottage
Upper Sattenham
Wood Farm
Active Workings
Ladywell Farm
Ladywell Convent
Playing Field
TUESLEY
Tuesley Farm
MILFORD HOSPITAL
GU7
Milford
Rake Manor
Tuesley Pond
Shadwell Copse
Godalming
Shad Well (spring)
Poultry Farm
Depot
Fowl House Farm
Cramhurst
Nurseries
Wheelerstreet
Lower Enton Lake
Large Enton Lake
Small Enton Lake
Club House
Enton Green
Foxall Wood
WEST SURREY GOLF COURSE
Hydon Farm
Playground
Upper Enton Lake
Mill Copse
Enton Mill Farm
Great Enton
Sleepy Hollow
Fairacres
Potter's Barn
Linksmere
Horsehatches
Mare Hill
Playing Field
Barrow Hills School
Chandler C. of E. Jun. Sch.
Heath House
Mare Hill Cottages
WITLEY
Lake Cottage
Hazel Copse
Witley Ponds
Old Enton
Hazel Copse
Chestnut Copse
Witley C.of E. Infs. Sch.
Boggy Lodge
Chapel Copse
Great House Cottages
Hambledon Field
Planted Piece
Bald Field
Playing Field
Culmer
Hooker's Ham
Mill Lands Coppice
Enton Hall
Parson's Hanger
GU8
Hangerfield
The Close
Common Piece
The Leg
Winkford Farm
Culmer Firs
Buss's Firs
Buss's Common
Parsonage House
Parsonage Farm
Parsonage Farm Cottages
Culmer, Common
Curtis's Piece
Sweetwater Firs
Sweetwater Cottage
Busses Cottage
Hilltop Farm
Pond Coppice
Playing Field
Sewage Works
Rough Acre
Banacle Common
Culmer Hanger
HAMBLEDON
Playing Field
Limekilns
Moor Cottage
Paddock Woods
Stonepit Hill
Wormley Hill Firs
St. Dominic's Sch.
Malthouse Farm
Beech Hill
Playing Field
King Edward's School
The Hill House
Institute of Oceanographic Sciences
Gorse Hill
Hambleden Common
Banacle Firs
Sandhills
Fintry
The Heights
WORMLEY
Orchard Farm
Cricket Ground
Sandhills Common
Ox Heart Copse
Witley East Grove
Godalming East Grove
Witley
Kingwood
Philpot's
Pond Field Wood
Potato Copse

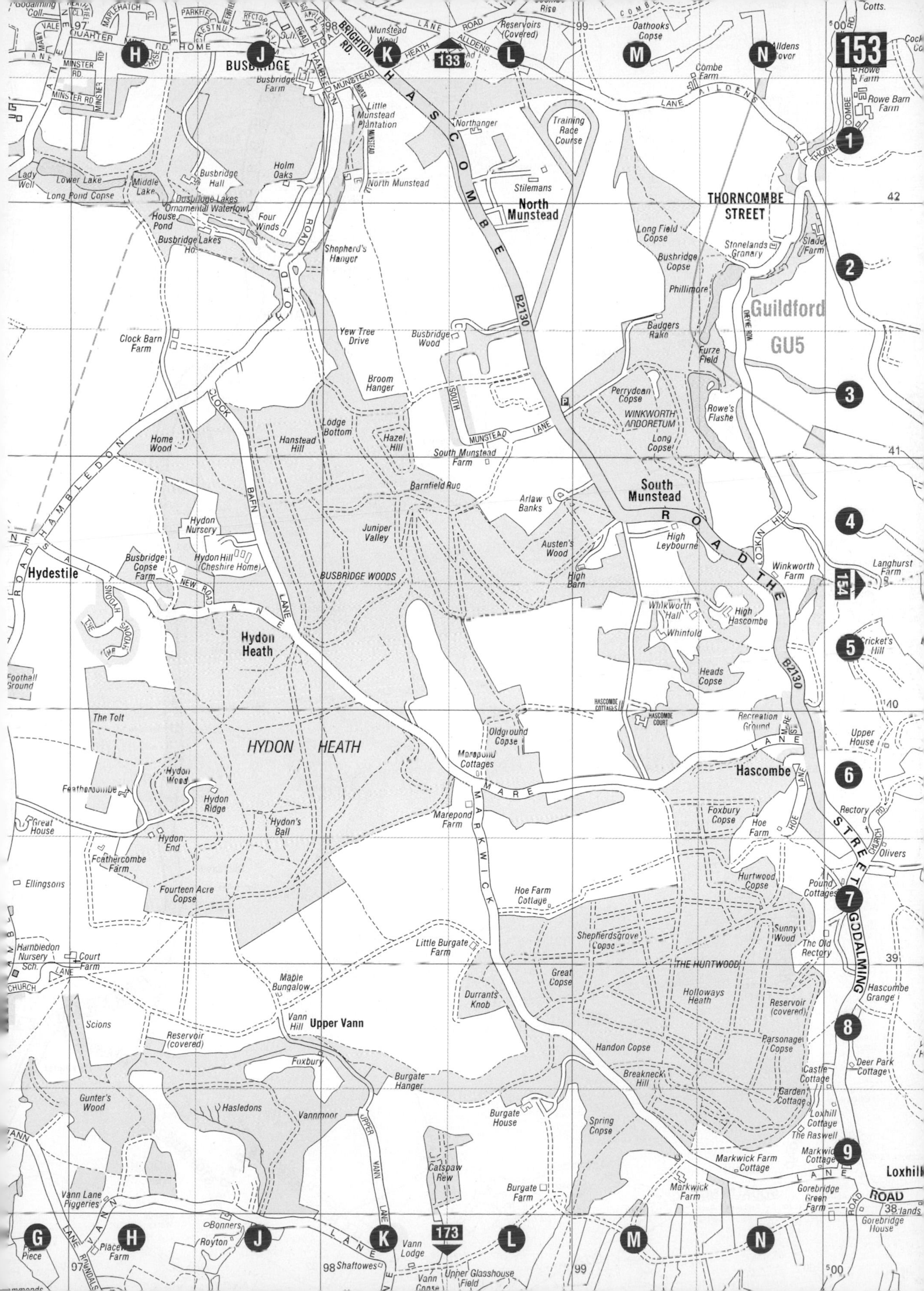
BUSBRIDGE
Busbridge Farm
Little Munstead Plantation
Northanger
Training Race Course
Munstead Wood
Reservoirs (Covered)
Oathooks Copse
Alldens Cover
Combe Farm
Rowe Farm
Rowe Barn Farm
Lady Well
Lower Lake
Middle Lake
Long Pond Copse
Busbridge Hall
Holm Oaks
North Munstead
Stilemans
North Munstead
THORNCOMBE STREET
Busbridge Lakes Ornamental Waterfowl
House Pond
Four Winds
Busbridge Lakes Ho
Shepherd's Hanger
Long Field Copse
Stonelands Granary
Slade Farm
Bushridge Copse
Phillimore
Guildford
GU5
Clock Barn Farm
Yew Tree Drive
Busbridge Wood
Badgers Rake
Furze Field
Broom Hanger
Perrydean Copse
WINKWORTH ARBORETUM
Rowe's Flashe
Home Wood
Lodge Bottom
Hanstead Hill
Hazel Hill
South Munstead Farm
Long Copse
Barnfield Rue
Arlaw Banks
South Munstead
Hydon Nursery
Juniper Valley
Austen's Wood
High Leybourne
Winkworth Farm
Langhurst Farm
Hydestile
Busbridge Copse Farm
Hydon Hill (Cheshire Home)
BUSBRIDGE WOODS
High Barn
Winkworth Hall
Whinfold
High Hascombe
Hydon Heath
Cricket's Hill
Football Ground
Heads Copse
HASCOMBE COTTAGES
HASCOMBE COURT
The Tolt
Oldground Copse
Recreation Ground
Upper House
HYDON HEATH
Marepond Cottages
Hascombe
Hydon Wood
Feathercombe
Hydon Ridge
Great House
Hydon's Ball
Marepond Farm
Foxbury Copse
Hoe Farm
Rectory
Hydon End
Feathercombe Farm
Olivers
Ellingsons
Hurtwood Copse
Fourteen Acre Copse
Hoe Farm Cottage
Pound Cottages
Shepherdsgrove Copse
Sunny Wood
Hambledon Nursery Sch.
Court Farm
Little Burgate Farm
The Old Rectory
Maple Bungalow
Great Copse
THE HURTWOOD
Durrants Knob
Holloways Heath
Reservoir (covered)
Hascombe Grange
Scions
Vann Hill
Upper Vann
Reservoir (covered)
Handon Copse
Parsonage Copse
Foxbury
Burgate Hanger
Breakneck Hill
Castle Cottage
Deer Park Cottage
Gunter's Wood
Hasledons
Vannmoor
Burgate House
Garden Cottage
Spring Copse
Loxhill Cottage
The Raswell
Markwick Farm Cottage
Markwick Cottage
Loxhill
Catspaw Rew
Vann Lane Piggeries
Burgate Farm
Markwick Farm
Gorebridge Green Farm
Gorebridge House
Bonners
Royton
Placen Farm
Vann Lodge
Shaftowes
Upper Glasshouse Field
Vann Copse
HAMBLEDON ROAD
CLOCK BARN LANE
HASCOMBE ROAD
B2130
THE STREET
GODALMING ROAD
MARKWICK LANE
MARE LANE
UPPER VANN LANE
VANN LANE
SALT LANE
NEW ROAD
SOUTH MUNSTEAD LANE
ALLDENS LANE
THORNCOMBE STREET
LOCKIN HILL
HOE LANE
CHURCH RD
BRIGHTON RD.
HOME RD.
MINSTER RD.
CHURCH LANE
133
154
173
H J K L M N
G H J K L M N
1 2 3 4 5 6 7 8 9
97 98 99 00
42 41 40 39 38

Thorncombe Street
Rooks Hill
Rushett Common
Grafham
Guildford
GU5
Selhurst Common
Palmers Cross
Godalming
GU8
Hascombe
Smithbrook
Loxhill
Barrihurst
Horsham Road
A281
B2130 Road
Dunsfold Road
Godalming Road
Hall Place

134
153
174

155
H
J
K
L
M
N
135
175
G
1
2
3
4
5
6
7
8
9
156
04
05
06
41
40
39
38
Stroud Common
Run Common
Run Farm
Slaughter's Cott.
Upper House Farm
Ridgebridge Hill
Hatchways
Gaston Farm
Nurseries
East Whipley Farm
Raasay
Pump House
Nursery
Bridgeham Farm
Mushroom Farm
Rowly Farm
Norther Farm
Rydinghurst Farm
Rydinghurst
Rye Farm
Sewage Works
Lodge
The Wayside
Elm Bridge
Elmbridge Farm
Nanhurst Farm
Nursery Park Farm
Nanhurst
Forres
Ruffold Farm
Hollyhocks
Understaw Farm
Knowle Wood
West Cranleigh Nurseries
Depot
Utworth Manor
Utworth Cottages
Little Sparrow Wood
Little Sparrow Copse
Keepers Mount
Mill Farm
Barn Plaits
Stroud Lodge
Kill Copse
Knob Copse
South Copse
Willinghurst Farm
Spring Wood
Warren Cottage
Rock Copse
Spanish House
Garden Cottage
Lapscombe Copse
The Shaws
Willingshurst Lake
Lapscombe Farm
Pittance Wood
Pittance Farm
Field House
Smith's Cottage
Smithwood Farm
Manor Cottage
SMITHWOOD COMMON
Brackenbrook
Nells Platt
Winterfold Heath
Winterfold Hill
Highland Cottage
Alderbrook Garage
Alderbrook Copse
Hurtwood House
Sandy Hill
Jelleys Hollow
Alderbrook
Gardeners Cottage
The Bothy
Alderbrook Park
Fowls Copse
Alderbrook Farm
ALDERBROOK FARM COTTAGES
HIGHLAND VW.
Lowerhouse Farm
Cranleigh Nurseries
ROWLY
Nursery
Garden Cottage
Thorn Cott.
Mossy Copse
WHITETHORN COTTAGES
Thorn's Flush
High Upfold Farm
Spring Cottage
Mannings Hill
Field Cottage
Golf Course
Playing Field
Cranleigh School
Packhurst Lag
Wyphurst Home Farm
Playing Field
St. Joseph's School
Loreta Lodge
Hillard's House
Hilliards Barn Cottage
Francis Field
Cranleigh Prep. School
Cranleigh
GU6
Playing Field
Normanhurst
Playing Field
Glebelands School
Works
Cricket Grd.
Factory
CRANLEIGH
St. Nicholas Sch.
Cemetery
Cranleigh First School
R.C. Prim. Sch.
Lib.
Recreation Centre
Tennis Courts
Osier Bed
Rec. Grd.
Knowle
Coldharbour Farm
Bushy Copse
GUILDFORD ROAD
STROUD COMMON
B2128
B2130
B2127
SMITHWOOD COMMON ROAD
ALDERBROOK ROAD
HIGH STREET
EWHURST ROAD
HORSHAM ROAD
KNOWLE LANE
ALFOLD ROAD
ELMBRIDGE ROAD
AMLETS LANE
MANNINGS HILL
ROWLY DRIVE
DOWNS LINK
Wey & Arun Junction Canal

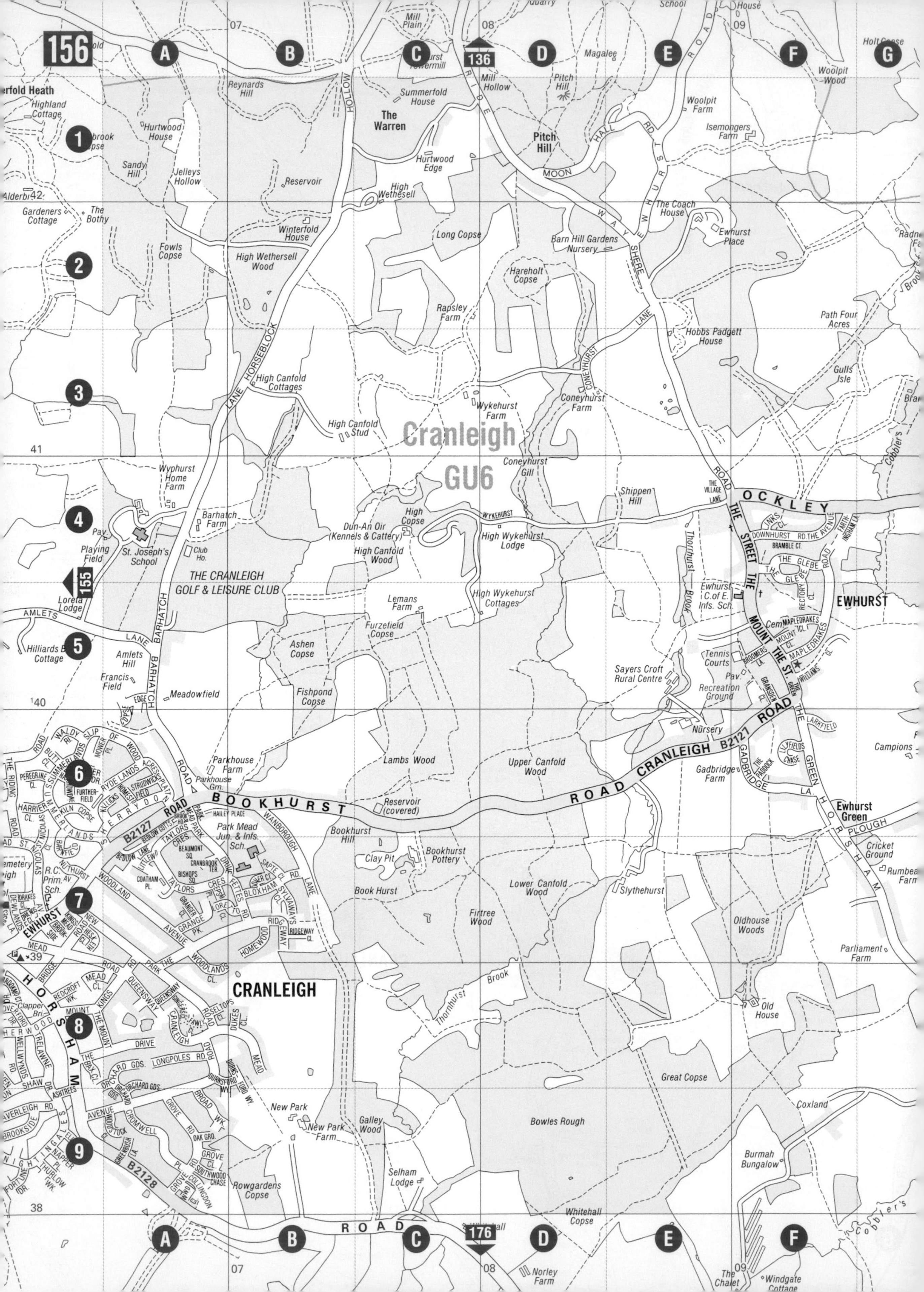
Cranleigh
GU6
CRANLEIGH
EWHURST
OCKLEY
The Warren
Pitch Hill
Ewhurst Green
THE CRANLEIGH GOLF & LEISURE CLUB
BOOKHURST ROAD
CRANLEIGH ROAD B2127
HORSHAM ROAD
B2128
HORSEBLOOK LANE
BARHATCH ROAD
MOON HALL RD
SHERE ROAD
Reynards Hill
Summerfold House
Hurtwood House
Sandy Hill
Jelleys Hollow
Reservoir
Hurtwood Edge
High Wethesell
Winterfold House
High Wethersell Wood
Fowls Copse
Long Copse
Barn Hill Gardens Nursery
Hareholt Copse
Rapsley Farm
The Coach House
Ewhurst Place
Hobbs Padgett House
Path Four Acres
Gulls Isle
Woolpit Farm
Isemongers Farm
Woolpit Wood
Magalee
Mill Plain
Mill Hollow
Pitch Hill
Highland Cottage
Gardeners Cottage
The Bothy
High Canfold Cottages
High Canfold Stud
Wykehurst Farm
Coneyhurst Farm
Coneyhurst Gill
Shippen Hill
Wyphurst Home Farm
Barhatch Farm
St. Joseph's School
Playing Field
Loreta Lodge
Dun-An Oir (Kennels & Cattery)
High Copse
High Canfold Wood
High Wykehurst Lodge
High Wykehurst Cottages
Lemans Farm
Furzefield Copse
Ashen Copse
Fishpond Copse
Amlets Hill
Francis Field
Meadowfield
Hilliards Cottage
Sayers Croft Rural Centre
Tennis Courts
Recreation Ground
Ewhurst C.of E. Infs. Sch.
Nursery
Parkhouse Farm
Lambs Wood
Upper Canfold Wood
Gadbridge Farm
Reservoir (covered)
Bookhurst Hill
Clay Pit
Bookhurst Pottery
Book Hurst
Lower Canfold Wood
Slythehurst
Fintree Wood
Oldhouse Woods
Parliament Farm
Cricket Ground
Rumbeam Farm
Campions
Park Mead Jun. & Infs. Sch.
Thornhurst Brook
Old House
Great Copse
Bowles Rough
Coxland
New Park
New Park Farm
Galley Wood
Selham Lodge
Rowgardens Copse
Burmah Bungalow
Whitehall Copse
Norley Farm
The Chalet
Windgate Cottage
136
155
176
A B C D E F G
1 2 3 4 5 6 7 8 9
07 08 09
41 40 38

157
137
153
177
Guildford
GU5
Dorking
RH5
Little Birketts
FOREST GREEN
Mayes Green
WALLISWOOD
SOMERSBURY
BUILDINGS WOOD
STONEHOUSE WOOD
GATTON MANOR GOLF COURSE
HOLMBURY LANE
OCKLEY ROAD
B2126
B2127
HORSHAM ROAD
LYEFIELD LANE
LOWER BREACHE ROAD
MOLE VALLEY
WAVERLEY

158
138
157
178
A
B
C
D
E
F
G
1
2
3
4
5
6
7
8
9
13
14
515
16
42
41
140
39
38
Georges Plot
Abinger Road
Leith Hill Place (West)
Leith Hill Place (East)
Leith Hill Place
Leith Hill Farm
Leith Hill Place Farm
Farmhouse Copse
Hooks Copse
Shiffolds
Dingwall Wood
Orchard Copse
Brambly Copse
Smither's Copse
Nine Acre Copse
Broome Hall Farm
Broome Hall
Broomehall Road
Reservoir (covered)
Round Copse
Sherlocks Row
Hartshurst Farm
Fatting Hovel Copse
Nutfold Copse
Stane Street Roman Road (course of)
Great Copse
Buckinghill Farm
Beggarsbrook Gill
Lodgeland Copse
Knowlfield Copse
Lodgelands Farm
Church Wood
Meares Copse
Mearshurst
Radlin Row
New Barn
Etherley Farm
Etherley Copse
Etherley Hill
Ockley Road
Beare Green
Burywood Hill
Highfield Wood
Pennsylvania Copse
Aviary Barn
Aviary Copse
Goster Wood
Bushy Copse
Rishet's Copse
Cox Corner
B2126
High Woods
Sheep Green
Forest Green Road
Stane Street
Square Copse
Holms Gill
Holmswood Park
Wellspring Pond
Home Farm
Jayes Park
Hatch Park
Gosterwood Manor Farm
Kissing Copse
Jayes Park
Coles Lane
Ockley Court Farm
Ockley Court
Nursery
Heathfield Copse
Woodstock House
Volvens Farm
Mole Street
Winks Cottage
Boat Pond
Courtbottom Wood
Stubbits Wood
Castle Copse
Castle Cottage
Hall
Ockley
The Green
Church Copse
The Plantation
Grimston Copse
Weavers Pond
Weaver's Wood
Copse Cottage
Grub Pond
Elderslie
Vann Farm
Wickney Holt
Kiln Wood
Pisley Farm
Applegate
Parklands
Grave Yard
Scott-Broadwood C.E.Inf. Sch.
Cricket Grd.
Friday Street
Fishfold Farm
Pisley Lane
Quagmire Copse
Sewage Works
Love La.
Cricketers Cl.
Elderslie Farm
Council Cotts.
Vann Farm Rd.
Vann House
Draysey Wood
Vann Lake
Drayseywood
Pisley Copse
Sandpit Gill
Parkland Farmhouse
RH5
Brickyard Copse
Fridays
Vann Lake Nature Reserve
Vann Water
Draysey Wood
Gatton Manor Golf Course
Brook
Garrett's Gill
Four Oaks
New House Farm
Rectory Cl.
Elmers Farm
Caravan Park
Cherry Orchard
New Barn Lane
Oak House
Cathill Lane
Stane House
Mill Copse
Vann Lake Rd.
Weirs
Lake House
New Barn
Fulwood
Threeways
Palace Wood
Vann Bri.
Weir
Holdenbrook
New Barn Row
Cathill Wood
Tiphams
Leith Vale Cotts.
Standon Cotts.
Gatton Manor (Club House)
Standon Homestead
Sewage Works
A29
Stane Street (Roman Road)
Birches Wood
Leith Vale
Gatton Manor Golf Course
The Lodge
Holbrook Wood
Street Gill
Hannah Peschar Gallery Gdn.
Standon
Copse Lodge
Hutchings Copse
Fir Copse
Eversheds Farm
Standon Lane
Sunny Ridge
Middle Lodge
Mill Cottage
Waleys Lane
Oakwood Mill Farm
Radio Beacon
Puttocks Wood
Hopgardens Rue
Yew Tree Cottage
Holbrook Farm
Pollingfold
Church Lane
Walls Gill
Waleys
Weare Street
Hale House
Stane St.
Chapel Copse
Oakwood Hill
Timber Gill
Moat
Weare Street Gill

159
139
179
1E0
Dorking
NEWDIGATE
Kingsland
CAPEL
Ockley
Clark's Green
A24 CAPEL BY-PASS
A24 HORSHAM ROAD
A29 OCKLEY ROAD
(Proposed)
Brick Works
Alder Copse
Clay Pit
Kingsland Copse
Knoll Copse
The Whewes
Little Jackmans Wood
Broomells
The Plantation
Green's Copse
Broomell's Farm
Misbrooks Green
Birchy Copse
Misbrook Farm
Green's Farm
Grass Copse
Lodge Copse
Tanhouse Farm
Aldhurst Farm
Lodge Farm
Hatchland Copse
Capel House Farm
Sewage Works
Playground Recreation Ground
The Vicarage
Parsonage Farm
Scott-Broadwood C. of E. Infants Sch.
Rugge Farm
Hillhouse Copse
Hillhouse Farm
Seaman's Green
Bottom Copse
Ewekene's Farm
Ewekene's Copse
Ryersh Farm
Hoyle Farm
Crackerbarrel Farm
New Close Farm
Wigmore Lodge
Heath Wood
Beare Gill
Mountriden Copse
Garden Copse
Park Copse
Alder Copse
Park Farm
Fishing Lake
Heathcrockham Copse
Wickney Holt
Bennett's Wood
Old Kiln Farm
Clarks Green Farm
Kiln Copse
Peter's Wood
Cole's Wood Works
Playing Fld
Strood Copse
Oxpasture Copse
Temple Elfande
Stylehurst Farm
Stylehurst
Spring Copse
Grenehurst
Grenehurst Park
Nightless Copse
Pleystowe
Pleystowe Farm
Pleystowe House
Old Mead
Red Roofs
Grenehurst Copse
Knoll Wood
Auclaye Brickworks
Knoll Farm
Sawmill
Clock House
Osbrooks Lodge
Clock House Works
Taylors
Taylor's Gill
Temple Wood
North Barn
East Wood
Alder Gill
Brookwell
Oshrooks
Farneyfield Copse
Sewells Copse
Clay Pit
Fylls Brook Cott.
Fylls Brook
Lyne House
Lyne Farm
Mosshouse Walk
Cowix Gills
Cowix Furzefield
Cowix Farm
Osbrook's Gill
Alder Hew
Lodge Copse
Upper Gages Farm
Gages Gill
Mosshouse Gill
Greatwood
Lower Gages Farm
Bonnetts
Rome Wood
CLARKS GREEN ROAD
TEMPLE LANE
VICARAGE LANE
RUSPER ROAD
KINGSLAND
STREET
RYERSH LANE
COLES LANE
Misbrooks
Melville House
The Knowle
Brooklagg Farm
Recreation Ground
Newdigate C. of E.
17
18
19
38
39
40
41

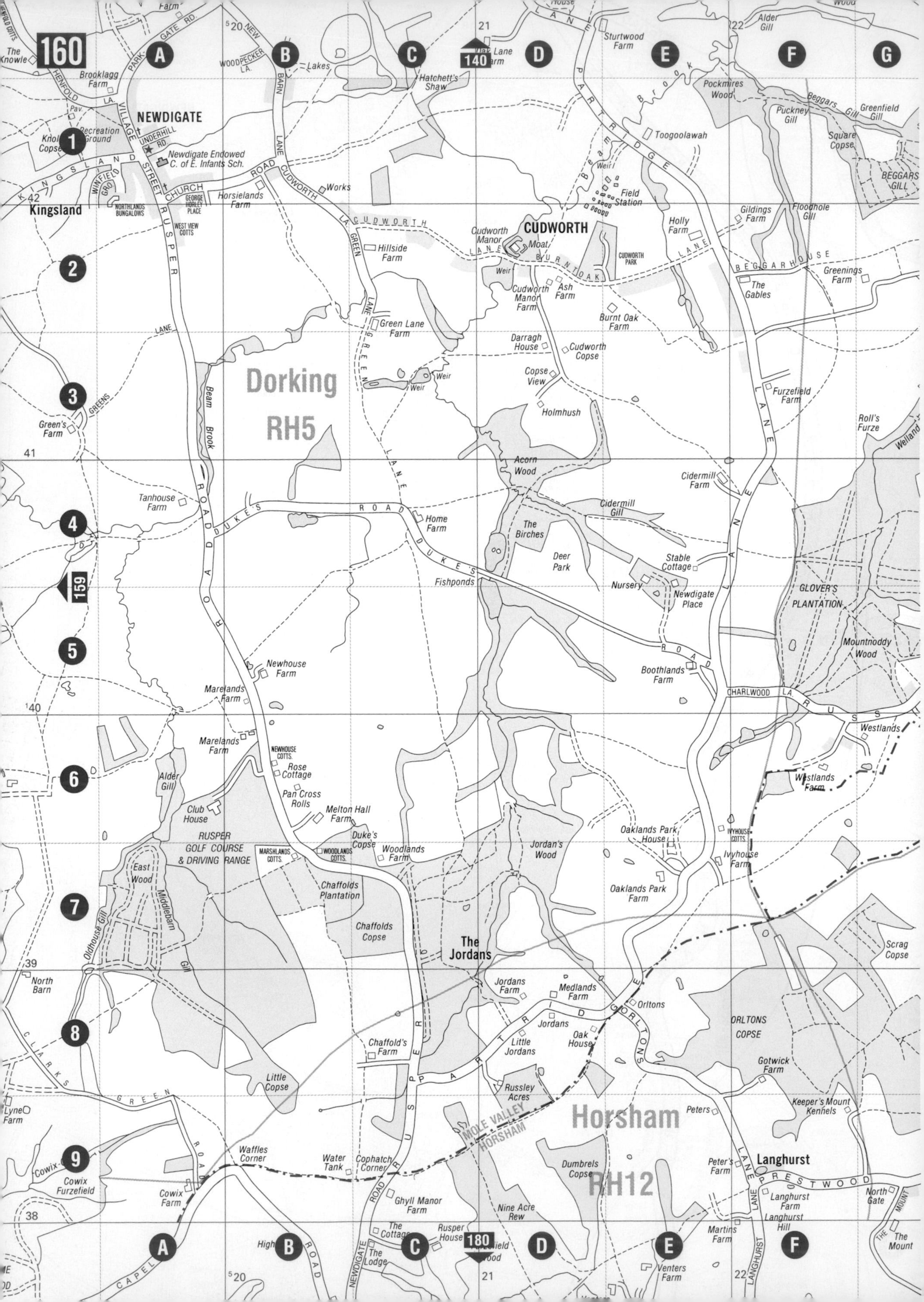

160
A
B
C
D
E
F
G
140
NEWDIGATE
Kingsland
CUDWORTH
Dorking
RH5
Horsham
RH12
The Knowle
Brooklagg Farm
Recreation Ground
Knoll Copse
Newdigate Endowed C. of E. Infants Sch.
Horsielands Farm
Works
Lakes
Hatchett's Shaw
Sturtwood Farm
Alder Gill
Pockmires Wood
Toogoolawah
Puckney Gill
Greenfield Gill
Square Copse
BEGGARS GILL
Field Station
Gildings Farm
Floodhole Gill
Holly Farm
Cudworth Manor
Moat
Hillside Farm
CUDWORTH PARK
Cudworth Manor Farm
Ash Farm
Burnt Oak Farm
The Gables
Greenings Farm
Green Lane Farm
Darragh House
Cudworth Copse
Copse View
Holmhush
Furzefield Farm
Roll's Furze
Green's Farm
Beam Brook
Acorn Wood
Cidermill Farm
Cidermill Gill
Tanhouse Farm
Home Farm
The Birches
Deer Park
Stable Cottage
Fishponds
Nursery
Newdigate Place
GLOVER'S PLANTATION
Mountnoddy Wood
159
Newhouse Farm
Marelands Farm
Boothlands Farm
Westlands
Westlands Farm
NEWHOUSE COTTS.
Rose Cottage
Pan Cross Rolls
Melton Hall Farm
Alder Gill
Club House
RUSPER GOLF COURSE & DRIVING RANGE
Duke's Copse
Woodlands Farm
MARSHLANDS COTTS.
WOODLANDS COTTS.
Jordan's Wood
Oaklands Park House
IVYHOUSE COTTS.
Ivyhouse Farm
Oaklands Park Farm
East Wood
Chaffolds Plantation
Chaffolds Copse
The Jordans
Scrag Copse
North Barn
Oldhouse Gill
Middlebarn Gill
Jordans Farm
Medlands Farm
Orltons
ORLTONS COPSE
Jordans
Oak House
Little Jordans
Chaffold's Farm
Little Copse
Gotwick Farm
Russley Acres
Keeper's Mount Kennels
Lyne Farm
Peters
MOLE VALLEY
HORSHAM
Waffles Corner
Water Tank
Cophatch Corner
Dumbrels Copse
Peter's Farm
Langhurst
Cowix Furzefield
Cowix Farm
Ghyll Manor Farm
Nine Acre Rew
Langhurst Farm
Langhurst Hill
North Gate
The Cottage
Rusper House
180
Martins Farm
The Mount
The Lodge
Venters Farm
High
KINGSLAND
VILLAGE STREET
RUSPER ROAD
CHURCH ROAD
CUDWORTH LANE
GREEN LANE
DUKE'S ROAD
PARTRIDGE LANE
CHARLWOOD LA.
BEGGARHOUSE LANE
BURNTOAK LANE
CLARKS GREEN ROAD
ORLTONS LANE
PETER'S LANE
PRESTWOOD
LANGHURST LANE
NEWDIGATE ROAD
CAPEL ROAD

161
141
162
181
Horley
RH6
CHARLWOOD
Gatwick
RH6
LONDON - GATWICK
AIRPORT
Crawley
RH11
Russ Hill
Pagewood
Ifieldwood
Ifield Green
LANGLEY
GREEN
Johnson's
Common
Highworth
Farm
Sourmead
Shaw
Stanhill
Court
Edolphs Copse
Nature
Reserve
Spencer's Gill
Rainbow
Wood
Edolphs
Farm
Telvet
Copse
Brackenwood
Farm
Greysouthern
Country Club
Charlwood
Place
Barfield
Farm
Greening's
Wood
Dolby
Brook
Spottles
Farm
Charlwood
Village
School
Glovers Meadow
Dairy Farm
GLOVER'S WOOD
NATURE RESERVE
Little
Glovers
Farm
Gatwick Zoo
& Aviaries
Lowfield
Heath
Postmill
Welling
Barn
Farm
Spicers
Farm
Charlwood Place
Farm
Orchard
Farm
Spicers
Bridge
Titters
Farm
Mans Brook
CRAWLEY
MOLE VALLEY
NORTH WEST ZONE
River Mole
Windacre
Farm
Works
Fire Training Ground
Russ Hill
Farm
Gatwick
Wena Hotel
Waggoners
Farm
Birchfield
House
Staff Car Park
Charlwood
House
West
Point
Kemtheutic
House
Amberley
Mayfield
Ho.
Upper
Prestwood
Farm
St. Annes
CRAWLEY
HORSHAM
Great Burlands
Little Park
Farm
Spikemead
Farm
Caravan
Park
Hyder's
Farm House
Brooklyn
Farm
Prestwood
Copse
Prestwood
House
Water
Hall
Red
Gables
Naldretts
Farm
Furze Field
The
Grove
Manor
Ho.
Amberley
Farm
Hyder's Farm
Burlands
Copse
Naldretts
Farmhouse
Kilmarnock
Farm
Ifield
Hall
Brooklyn
Oak Tree
Farm
Cophall
Wood
Playing Fie
Lower
Prestwood
Farm
Ifield Court
Farm
Crawley
Rugby
Club
Willoughby
Fields
Stafford
Ho.
Bowling
Green
TILGATE
Glenhervie
Moat
Ifield
Court
Stafford
Bridge
The Gables
Nursing
Home
The
Druids
Wildacres
Hilly Barn
Farmhouse
The Mount
Farm
Pockney's
Farm
Kirk
Farm
Riding
Stables
Bonwycks
Place
Ifield Barn
Middle
Sch.
Depot
Deerswood
LANE
HILL
ROAD
PUDDING LANE
RECTORY
RUSS HILL RD
STREET
LOWFIELD HEATH
CHARLWOOD ROAD
PRESTWOOD LANE
IFIELD WOOD
BONNETTS LANE
HILLYBARN
RECTORY LA
LANGLEY
FARMFIELD DRIVE
G
H
J
K
L
M
N
1
2
3
4
5
6
7
8
9
23
24
25
26
42
41
40
39
38

HOOKWOOD
Povey Cross
HORLEY
Gatwick
LONDON-
GATWICK AIRPORT
RH6
NORTH TERMINAL
SOUTH TERMINAL
Gatwick Airport
Junction 9a
LOWFIELD HEATH
TINSLEY GREEN
Crawley
RH11
County Oak
LANGLEY GREEN
MANOR ROYAL INDUSTRIAL ESTATE
GATWICK MANOR GOLF COURSE
Horleyland Wood
Rowley Wood
Huntsgreen Wood
Hydehurst Furze
Spikemead Farm
Charlwood House
Mayfield Ho.
Amberley Farm
NORTH WEST ZONE
North Terminal Long Term Car Park
South Terminal Long Term Car Park
Fuel Farm
Cargo Area
Control Tower
Northern Ancillary Zone
Maintenance Area 1
Maintenance Area 2
Fire Station
Pier 1
Pier 2
Pier 3
Pier 4
Pier 5
SATELLITE
Spectator Gallery
The Beehive
GATWICK BUSINESS PARK
Hawthorne Farm
Rowley Farm
Oldlands Farm
Tinsley Bridge
Old Rolls Farm
Sports Ground
Summersvere Wood
Grattons Park
Gasholder Station
The Larches
The Birches
Hazelwick School
Milton Mount First & Middle School
Playing Field
Magpie Wood
Laboratories
MEADOW BROOK INDUSTRIAL CENTRE
SUSSEX MANOR BUSINESS PARK
FLEMING WAY INDUSTRIAL CENTRE
GATWICK INTERNATIONAL DISTRIBUTION CENTRE
P.O. Sorting Office
Riverside Gdn. Pk.
Lake
GATWICK PARK B.U.P.A. HOSP.
Superstore
Depot
Caravan Park
Catherington Sch.
Langley Grn. First Sch.
Prim. Sch.
A23
A2011
BRIGHTON ROAD
AIRPORT WAY
LONDON ROAD
CRAWLEY AVENUE
FLEMING WAY
CHARLWOOD ROAD
PERIMETER ROAD
142
161
182

Farney View Farm
Haroldslea Poultry Farm
HAROLDSLEA
Cricket Ground
Newstead Hall
Thunderfield Castle (site of)
Haroldslea House
Bridgeham Farm
Bridgeham Grange
Lower Broadbridge Farm
Depot
Redehall Preparatory School
Sacconex Farm
Triddles Farm
143
M23 MOTORWAY
Broadbridge
Broadmead Farm
Broadbridge Farm
BROADBRIDGE COTTS
LABURNUM COURT (CARAVAN PARK)
Vanderel Farm
Homestead Farm
The Roughs
The Plantation
THE CLOSE
Tanners Farm
Peeks Rough Farm
REIGATE and BANSTEAD
TANDRIDGE
Horley
RH6
Broadbridge Stables
Poultry Houses
Gunyah Farm
Bellhatch Wood
Collins Wood
Junction 9
Bridges Wood
CHURCH LANE
Dalrana
Rede Hall
Redeham Hall
Redeham Hall Farm
Masefield Ho.
Broadfield Farm
Fern Court Farm
FERNHILL ROAD
Fernhill
Gatwick House
Mushroom Farm
Moat
BURSTOW
Eastland Shaw
Westlands Farm
Burstow Stream
Pullcotts Farm
Greenwood Flats
Park House
Keeper's Corner
EFFINGHAM ROAD
Rivington Farm
Teizers Farm
Burstow Hall
Shipley Bridge
B2037
ANTLANDS LANE
ANTLANDS LA. EAST
Brook Farm
Lodge Kiln Heath
164
The Hollies
Greyhound Training Track
Shipley Bridge
BURSTOW PARK GOLF COURSE
Newhouse Farm
COPTHORNE BANK
Allingham Farm
Allen's Wood
Courtlands
The Grange
Club Ho.
Burstow Park Farm
Burstow Park
Black Corner
Thornbridge Farm
Nyahlands Farm
CLAY HALL LANE
B2036
The Rabbitry
Blackcorner Wood
Playing Field
Stonelands Farm
Roundabouts Farm
Rec. Grd.
Wellfield Copse
Forge Farm
Toovies Farm
CRAWLEY
MID SUSSEX
C. of E. Sch.
WESTWAY
BROOKSIDE
COPTHORNE
Golf Course
Club House
Copthorne Common
Rickmans Green
RH10
Heathy Ground Farm
Crematorium
Heathy Ground
Copthorne Fairway Inf. Sch.
COPTHORNE GOLF COURSE
Courthouse Farm
Haynes Farm
Forge Wood
AVENUE
COPTHORNE WAY
A264
COPTHORNE COMMON
COPTHORNE ROAD
Copthorne Common
Woodmans Farm
Bashfords Wood
Squash Club
Hotel
Heathyground Wood
Junction 10
Refuse Tip
Coombers Wood Farm
A2220
Pot Common
COOMBERS WOOD
COPTHORNE WOOD
M23
Garden Centre
Driver's Wood
Rowfant Piggeries
King's Wood
Birchen Wood
The Station
183
Rowfant
Old Rowfant
Fish Pond
G H J K L M N
1 2 3 4 5 6 7 8 9
30 31 32
38 39 40 41 42

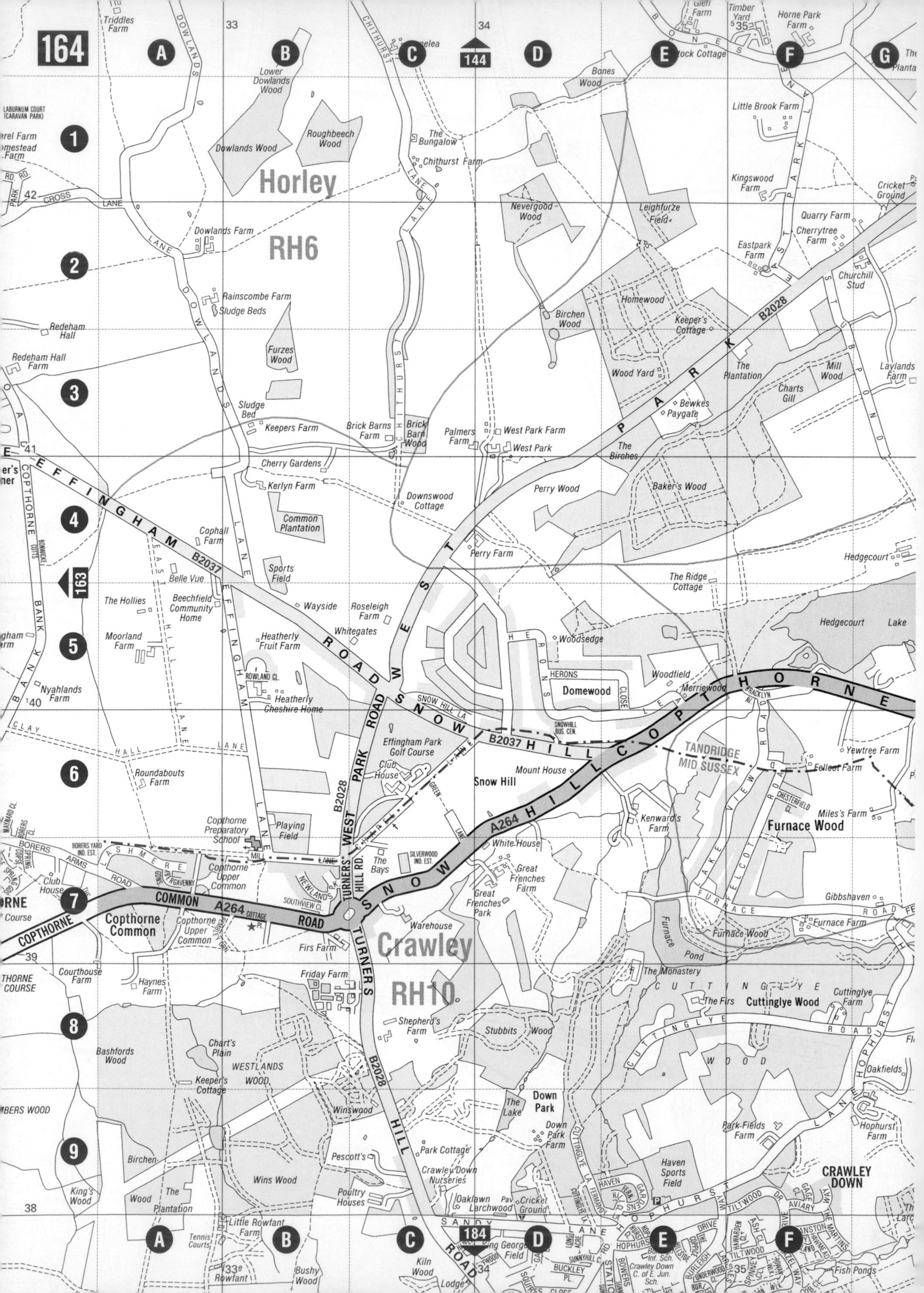
Horley
RH6
Crawley
RH10
Copthorne Common
Snow Hill
Furnace Wood
Domewood
CRAWLEY DOWN
Effingham Park Golf Course
Copthorne Preparatory School
Dowlands Wood
Roughbeech Wood
Hedgecourt Lake
Cuttinglye Wood
Furnace Pond
TANDRIDGE
MID SUSSEX
B2037
B2028
A264
144
163
184

165
Lingfield
RH7
East Grinstead
RH19
EAST GRINSTEAD
FELBRIDGE
Felcourt
NEWCHAPEL
North End
BALDWINS HILL
LINGFIELD PARK RACE COURSE
CHARTHAM PARK GOLF COURSE
EASTBOURNE ROAD
WOODCOCK HILL
LONDON ROAD
NEWCHAPEL ROAD
FELCOURT ROAD
BLACKBERRY ROAD
Felcourt Wood
Green Wood
High Wood
Wire Mill Lake
Wire Mill Nurseries
Woodcock Bridge
Sewage Works
HOBBS INDUSTRIAL ESTATE
Cooper's Moors
Moat Wood
Park Farm
Green Meadows Farm
Park Wood
Whittington College (Almshouses)
The Kennels
Garthfields Farm
Ward's Farm
Chartham Manor
Chartham Park Farm
Chartham Wood
The Alders
The Mount
Frith Manor
Baldwyns
Lowerbarn Farm
Adeline Genée Theatre
Lodge Field Shaw
Cromwell Hall Farm
The Grange
Chalybeate Spring
Kingsley Farm
Southernleigh
The Laurels
Nurseries
Felcourt Dairy Farm
Felcourt Farm
Fishpond Shaw
Kennels
Frogit Heath
Lowlands Farm
Cherry Tree Farm Equine Rest
The London Temple (Mormon Temple)
Newchapel Green
Long Acres Farm
Camping & Caravan Site
Eden Brook
Gunshot Shaw
Stockriding Wood
Upper Stockriding Wood
Six Gates Wood
Five Gates Wood
Gunner's Wood
The Belt
Yew Lodge
The Shrubbery
Club House
Ranworth Farm
Tennis Courts
Lyndhurst Poultry Farm
Nursery
Felbridge Prim. Sch.
Bowling Green
Oak Farm
Rec. Grd.
Nurseries
Avenue Wood
Moat
Waldenor
The Birches
Imberhorne School
Imberhorne Farm
Gullege
Greenfield Shaw
Railway Shaw
Gullege Pit
Gullege Wood
Fish Pond
Coles Wood
GREAT WOOD
Depot
Weir
Halsford Park Prim. Sch.
St. Peter's Catholic Prim. Sch.
Baldwin's Hill Prim. Sch.
Sports Grd.
Adult Educ. Cen. & Imber Sports Cen.
Swim. Pool
Rec. Grd.
Chetnole Sch.
Superstore
East Grinstead
Pleasure Ground
King's Cen. (Spts. Cen.)
Moat Pond
Convent
Swim. Bath
Brooklands Park
Cemy.
Lib.
Cricket Ground
Fel Bridge
THE FELBRIDGE CEN.
BIRCHES INDUSTRIAL ESTATE
THE INDEPENDENT BUSINESS PARK
IMBERHORNE BUSINESS CENTRE
CHARLWOODS BUSINESS PARK
145
166
185

Lingfield
East Grinstead
DORMANSLAND
DORMANS PARK
Stonequarry
Blackwell
EAST GRINSTEAD
RH7
RH19
Dormans
Lingfield Park Race Course
Lingfield Park Golf Course
Queen Victoria Hospital
East Grinstead Town Museum
Adeline Genee Theatre
Old Surrey Hall
A264
A22
B2110
146
165
186

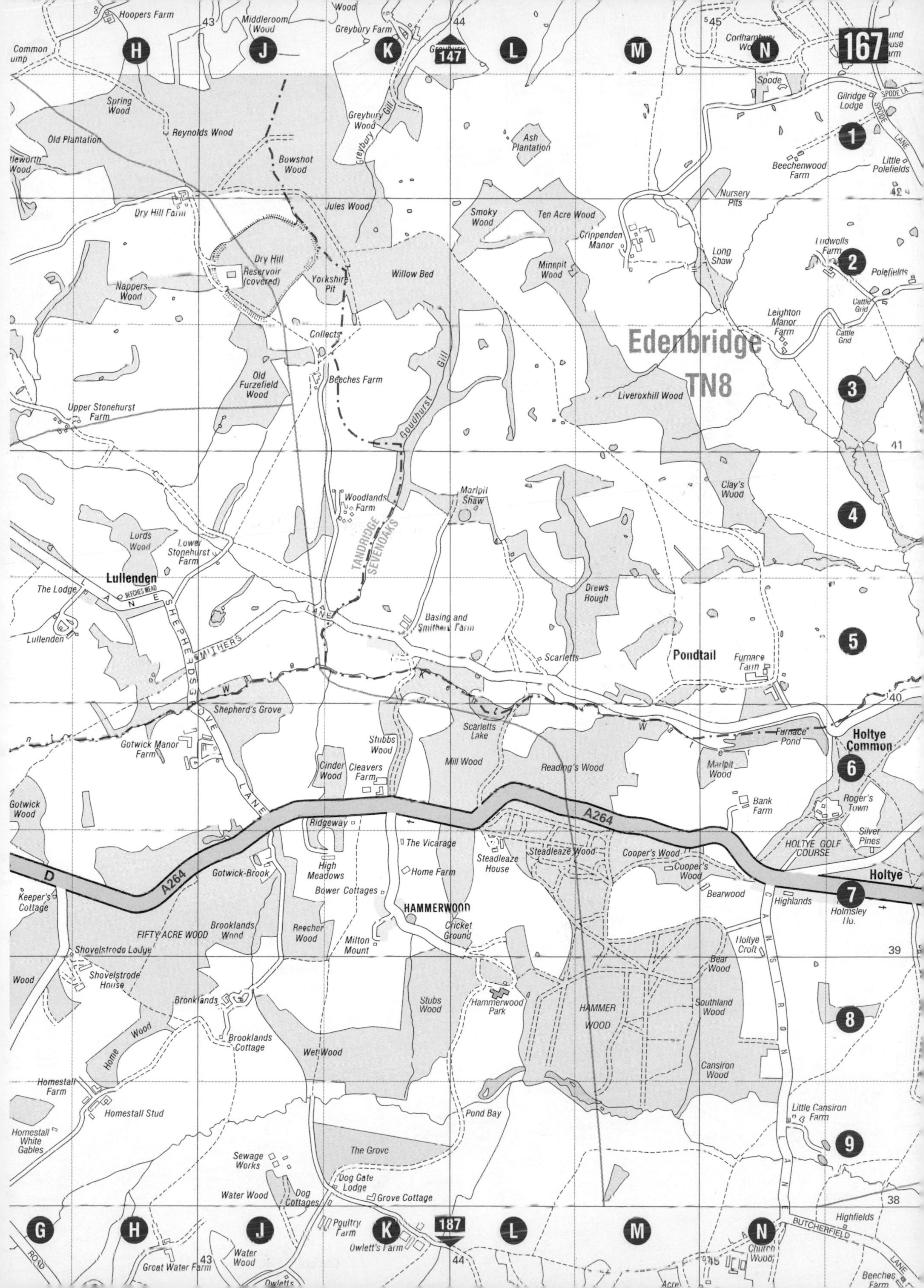
Hoopers Farm
Middleleroom Wood
Greybury Farm
Codhambury Wood
Spode
Gilridge Lodge
SPODE LA
SPODE LANE
Common
147
H
J
K
L
M
N
43
44
45
Spring Wood
Reynolds Wood
Old Plantation
Greybury Wood
Greybury Gill
Ash Plantation
Bowshot Wood
Beechenwood Farm
Little Polefields
Nursery Pits
Jules Wood
Dry Hill Farm
Smoky Wood
Ten Acre Wood
Crippenden Manor
Long Shaw
Ludwells Farm
Polefields
Dry Hill Reservoir (covered)
Yorkshire Pit
Willow Bed
Minepit Wood
Nappers Wood
Leighton Manor Farm
Cattle Grid
Collects
Edenbridge
TN8
Old Furzefield Wood
Beeches Farm
Gouthurst Gill
Liveroxhill Wood
Upper Stonehurst Farm
41
Marlpit Shaw
Clay's Wood
Woodlands Farm
TANDRIDGE
SEVENOAKS
Lords Wood
Lower Stonehurst Farm
Lullenden
The Lodge
BEECHES MEAD
LANE
Drews Rough
Basing and Smithers Farm
Lullenden
SMITHERS
SHEPHERDS GROVE
Scarletts
Pondtail
Furnace Farm
40
Shepherd's Grove
Scarletts Lake
Furnace Pond
Holtye Common
Gotwick Manor Farm
Stubbs Wood
Mill Wood
Reading's Wood
Marlpit Wood
Cinder Wood
Cleavers Farm
Bank Farm
Roger's Town
Gotwick Wood
Ridgeway
A264
Silver Pines
HOLTYE GOLF COURSE
The Vicarage
Steadleaze Wood
Cooper's Wood
Steadleaze House
Cooper's Wood
Holtye
Gotwick-Brook
High Meadows
Home Farm
Bearwood
Keeper's Cottage
Bower Cottages
Highlands
HAMMERWOOD
Holmsley Ho.
Cricket Ground
FIFTY ACRE WOOD
Brooklands Wood
Beecher Wood
Milton Mount
Holtye Croft
Shovelstrode Lodge
39
Shovelstrode House
Bear Wood
Wood
Bronklands
Stubs Wood
Hammerwood Park
HAMMER WOOD
Southland Wood
CANSIRON LANE
Home Wood
Brooklands Cottage
Wet Wood
Cansiron Wood
Homestall Farm
Homestall Stud
Pond Bay
Little Cansiron Farm
Homestall White Gables
The Grove
Sewage Works
Dog Gate Lodge
Water Wood
Dog Cottages
Grove Cottage
38
Poultry Farm
187
Highfields
BUTCHERFIELD LANE
G
ROAD
Owlett's Farm
Church Wood
Water Wood
Great Water Farm
Owletts
Beeches Farm
1
2
3
4
5
6
7
8
9

148
Bordon
GU35
HEADLEY
LINDFORD
Deadwater
Standford
BORDON
Hollywater
Passfield
Liphook
GU30
ARFORD
Beech Hill
Hearn
Conford
BROXHEAD COMMON (Nature Reserve)
PASSFIELD COMMON
LINDFORD ROAD
FRENSHAM LANE
HEADLEY ROAD
MILL LANE
CRABTREE LA
FULLERS VALE
BEECH HILL
STANDFORD LANE
LIPHOOK ROAD
HOLLYWATER ROAD
WHITEHILL ROAD
BRAMSHOTT ROAD
TUNBRIDGE LANE
GENTLES LANE
HURLAND LANE
LONG CROSS HILL
SPATS LANE
PROSPECT HILL
CURTIS LANE
B3002
B3004

Farnham
GU10
CHURT
Barford
Green Cross
Moreton House
Ford
Park Copse
Meadow Cottage
Plaster Hill Farm
Elliott's Farm
Lower Coombe Farm
Coombe Farm
Barford Farm
Kitts Farm
Woodbury House
Willow Farm
Chipstead
Avalon Farm
Green Cross Farm
Hungry Coombe
Road Farm
Chiltens Copse
Land of Nod Wood
Dalen Copse
Fully Plantation
Cain Farm
Land of Nod
Assisi
Hatch Hill House
HINDHEAD GOLF COURSE
Linkside
Club House
Windy Gap
Grey Cottage
Flat Wood
Gunsgreen
Whitmoor Vale
Beacon Hill
Southlands
Woodcock Bottom & Whitmore Vale
House-in-the-Wood
Stream Farm
Purchase Farm
Whitmoor Bottom
Whitmoor Hanger
Grayshott Hall Farm
Hindhead
GU26
HEADLEY DOWN
Dunehelm
Grayshott Hall
GRAYSHOTT
B3002
HEADLEY ROAD
CHURT ROAD
A287
The Dower House
Grayshott Playing Field
Philips Ho.
Pinewood
Convent
Marylands
Ludshott House
Ladygate
LUDSHOTT COMMON
Gentle's Copse
Stoney Bottom
Hunters Moon
Kingswood Firs
Kingswood Chase
Mount Alvernia
Chasemoor
Dog Kennel Firs
Chestnuts
Firtree Cottage
North Lodge
The Loampits
Woolmer Farm
Garden Clump
Ludshott Manor
Croaker's Patch
Summerden
Wakeners or Waggoners Wells
Bramshott Chase
Chase Farm
Kent's Hill
The Hanger
Long Plantation
Coach House Copse
Spring Pond Lodge
Spring Pond
Spring Pond Hanger
Downlands Farm
Black Bungalow
Downlands
BRAMSHOTT CHASE
BRAMSHOTT COMMON
PORTSMOUTH ROAD
A3
The Peppercorn
Glebe Ho. Farm
Downlands Lodge
Bramshott
RECTORY LA.
149
170

170
150
169
188
Farnham GU10
BEACON HILL
Linkside
HINDHEAD
DEVIL'S PUNCH BOWL
HINDHEAD COMMON (N.T.)
GRAYSHOTT
Hindhead
GU26
NUTCOMBE
Polecat
BRAMSHOTT CHASE
Inval
Avalon Farm
High Barn Stock Farm
Marchants Farm
Silver Birch Cottages
Fair View Farm
Vanhurst Copse
Green Farm
Oak Grove
Howlings
Hyde Hill
Heather Cottages
Heath Plat
Hill Lodge
Marchants Hill
Churt Wynde Reservoir (covered)
Gravel Hanger
Kiln Copse
Hindhead Playing Field
Highcomb Copse
Begley Farm
Gnome Cottage
The Central Deaconess House
Highcombe Farm
Youth Hostel
Twizzletwig
Broome Acres
Boundless Copse
Club House
Rec. Grd.
Beacon Sch.
Manormead (Nursing Home)
Woodcock Green
Southlands
Stoneycrest
The Beacon
Woodcock Bottom & Whitmore
House-in-the-Wood
Highcombe Edge
Thirlestane Court
Golden Valley
Gibbet Hill
Huntingdon House (Nursing Home)
Holmwood Heath
Whitmore Vale Farm
Hind Head
Tyndalls Wood
Longdown Chase
Combswell
Abbey Ho.
Bryanston
Playing Field
St. Edmund's School
Nutcombe Down
Nutcombe Valley
Stoney Bottom
Kingswood Firs
Hunters Moon
The Royal Sch.
The Royal Naval Sch. for Girls
Coombe Head
Kingswood Chase
Crossways
Hindhead Court
High Rough
The Barn Cottage
Kilmoray
Mount Alvernia
Chasemoor Corner
Chasemoor
The Grove Sch.
Craig's Wood
The Croft Ho.
Amesbury School
Stoatley Green (N.T.)
Muirfield
Coombswell Copse
Chase Farm
Chase Cottages
Mole End
New Place
High Pitfold Farm
Honeyhanger
Thursley
The Moat
Little Stoatley Farm
Ravensdale Cottages
Polecat Copse
Thursley Hall
Sports Ground
Fish Ponds
Branksome Hilders
Woolmer Hill School
Tennis Courts
Reynards Wood
Woolmer Hill
Frensham Hall Farm
St. Mary's Abbey
Holy Cross
St. Bartholomew C.of E. Prim. Sch.
CHURT ROAD
A287
TILFORD ROAD
HEADLEY ROAD
B3002
LONDON RD.
PORTSMOUTH ROAD
A3
HINDHEAD ROAD
HIGHCOMB BOTTOM
BOUNDLESS ROAD
WAVERLEY
EAST HAMPSHIRE

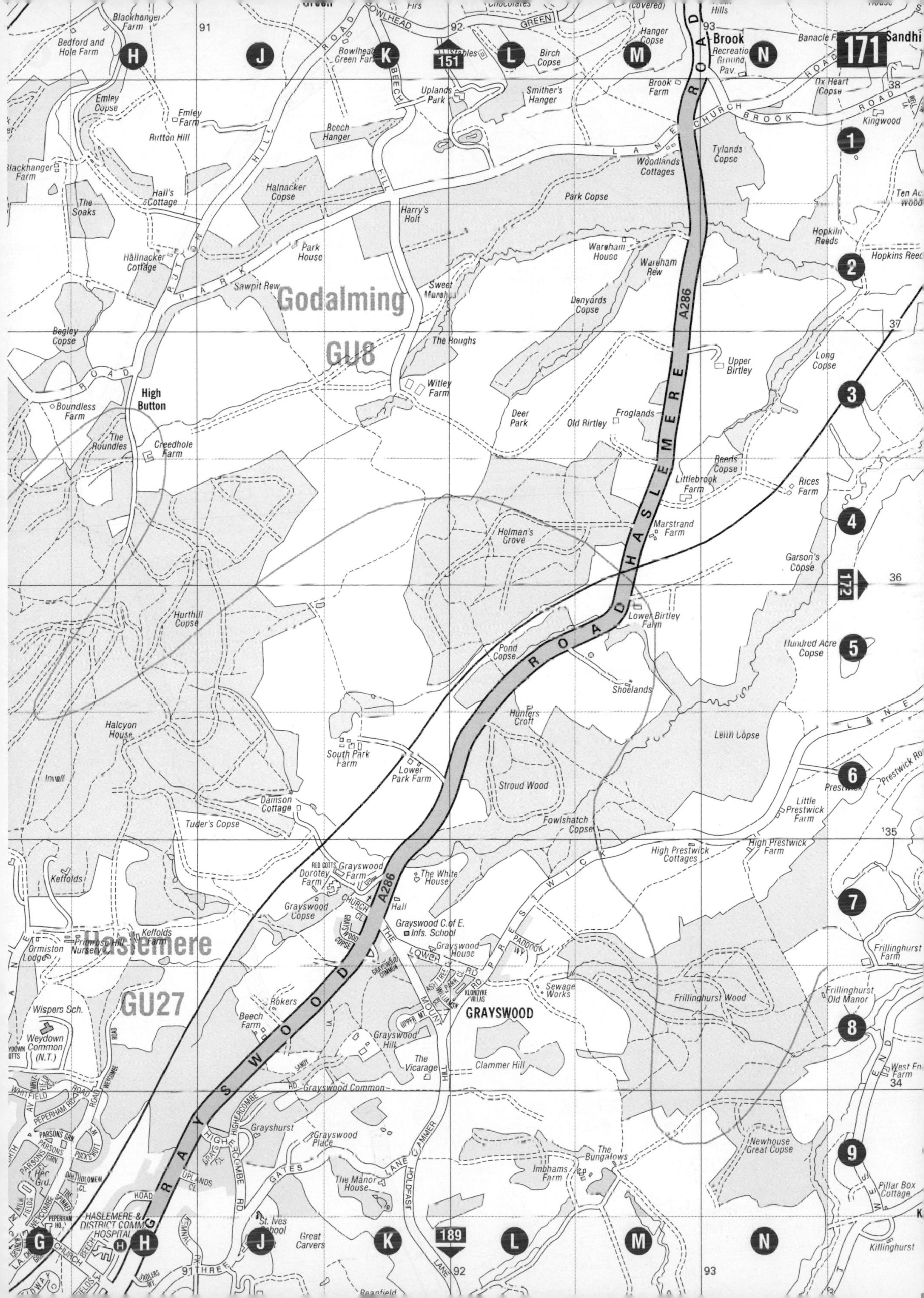

171
151
172
189
Godalming
GU8
Haslemere
GU27
GRAYSWOOD
Brook
High Button
HASLEMERE ROAD
GRAYSWOOD ROAD
A286
Blackhanger Farm
Bedford and Hole Farm
Bowlhead Green Farm
Stables
Birch Copse
Hanger Copse
Brook Recreation Ground
Pav.
Banacle Farm
Sandhi
Uplands Park
Smither's Hanger
Brook Farm
Ox Heart Copse
Kingwood
Emley Copse
Emley Farm
Button Hill
Beech Hanger
Tylands Copse
Woodlands Cottages
Blackhanger Farm
The Soaks
Hall's Cottage
Halnacker Copse
Harry's Holt
Park Copse
Ten Acre Wood
Hopkiln Reeds
Hopkins Reed
Hallnacker Cottage
Park House
Wareham House
Wareham Rew
Sawpit Rew
Sweet Marshes
Denyards Copse
Begley Copse
The Roughs
Upper Birtley
Long Copse
Witley Farm
Boundless Farm
Deer Park
Froglands
Old Birtley
The Roundles
Creedhole Farm
Reeds Copse
Littlebrook Farm
Rices Farm
Holman's Grove
Marstrand Farm
Garson's Copse
Hurthill Copse
Lower Birtley Farm
Pond Copse
Hundred Acre Copse
Shoelands
Hunters Croft
Halcyon House
Leith Copse
South Park Farm
Lower Park Farm
Stroud Wood
Prestwick
Prestwick Rd
Little Prestwick Farm
Damson Cottage
Tuder's Copse
Fowlshatch Copse
High Prestwick Cottages
High Prestwick Farm
Keffolds
Grayswood Farm
Dorotey Farm
The White House
Hall
Grayswood Copse
Keffolds Farm
Primrose Hill Nursery
Ormiston Lodge
Grayswood C.of E. Infs. School
Grayswood House
Frillinghurst Farm
Sewage Works
Frillinghurst Wood
Frillinghurst Old Manor
Wispers Sch.
Rokers
Beech Farm
Weydown Common (N.T.)
Grayswood Hill
The Vicarage
Clammer Hill
West End Farm
Grayswood Common
Grayshurst
Grayswood Place
The Bungalows
Newhouse Great Copse
Imbhams Farm
The Manor House
Pillar Box Cottage
HASLEMERE & DISTRICT COMM. HOSPITAL
St. Ives School
Great Carvers
Killinghurst
Reanfield
BROOK ROAD
CHURCH LANE
PARK LANE
BOWLHEAD GREEN
BEECH HILL
ROAD
PUTTOCK HILL
PRESTWICK LANE
LOWER ROAD
MOUNT HILL
CLAMMER HILL
HOLDFAST LANE
GATES LANE
HIGHERCOMBE RD
THREE GATES LANE
WEYCOMBE ROAD
WHITFIELD ROAD
PEPERHAM RD
PARSONS GRN
UPLANDS CL
SANDY LA
PADDOCK WY
KLONDYKE VILLAS
RED COTTS
WEST END LANE
H
J
K
L
M
N
G
1
2
3
4
5
6
7
8
9
91
92
93
38
37
36
35
34

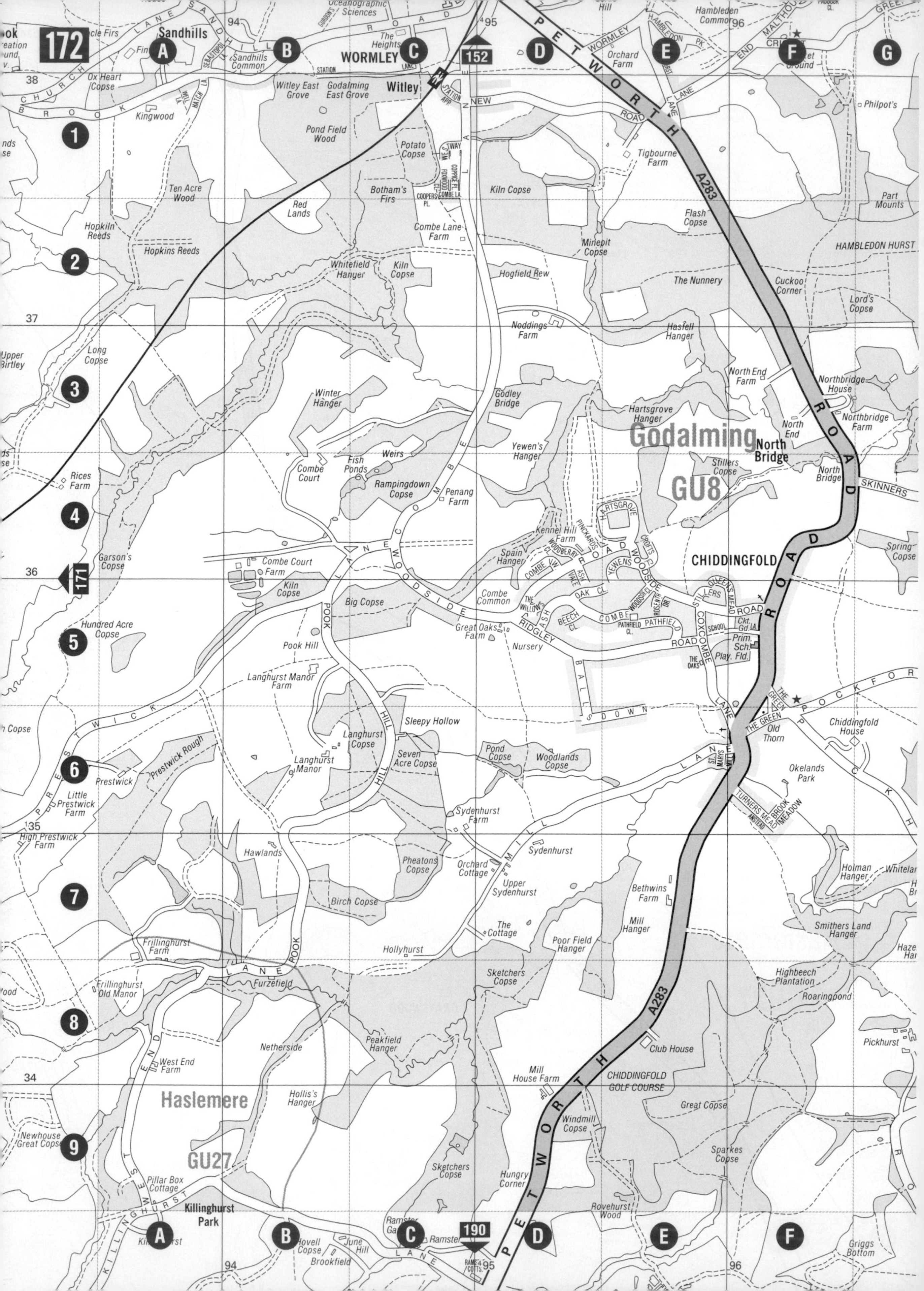

172
Sandhills
A
B
C
D
E
F
G
WORMLEY
Witley
152
Hambleden Common
Orchard Farm
Sandhills Common
Ox Heart Copse
Witley East Grove
Godalming East Grove
Kingwood
Pond Field Wood
Potato Copse
Philpot's
Ten Acre Wood
Red Lands
Botham's Firs
Kiln Copse
Tigbourne Farm
Hopkiln Reeds
Hopkins Reeds
Combe Lane Farm
Minepit Copse
Flash Copse
Part Mounts
HAMBLEDON HURST
Whitefield Hanger
Kiln Copse
Hogfield Rew
The Nunnery
Cuckoo Corner
Lord's Copse
Noddings Farm
Hasfell Hanger
Long Copse
Upper Birtley
North End Farm
Northbridge House
Winter Hanger
Godley Bridge
Hartsgrove Hanger
Northbridge Farm
North End
Godalming
North Bridge
Yewen's Hanger
Weirs
Fish Ponds
Combe Court
Rampingdown Copse
Stillers Copse
North Bridge
GU8
Rices Farm
Penang Farm
Kennel Hill Farm
Spain Hanger
CHIDDINGFOLD
Garson's Copse
Combe Court Farm
Spring Copse
171
Kiln Copse
Big Copse
Combe Common
Hundred Acre Copse
Great Oaks Farm
Nursery
Pook Hill
Langhurst Manor Farm
Sleepy Hollow
Chiddingfold House
Old Thorn
Langhurst Copse
Seven Acre Copse
Pond Copse
Woodlands Copse
Prestwick Rough
Langhurst Manor
Okelands Park
Prestwick
Little Prestwick Farm
Sydenhurst Farm
High Prestwick Farm
Hawlands
Sydenhurst
Pheatons Copse
Orchard Cottage
Upper Sydenhurst
Holman Hanger
Bethwins Farm
Birch Copse
Mill Hanger
Smithers Land Hanger
The Cottage
Frillinghurst Farm
Poor Field Hanger
Hollyhurst
Sketchers Copse
Highbeech Plantation
Furzefield
Frillinghurst Old Manor
Roaringpond
Netherside
Peakfield Hanger
Club House
Pickhurst
West End Farm
Mill House Farm
CHIDDINGFOLD GOLF COURSE
Haslemere
Hollis's Hanger
Great Copse
Newhouse Great Copse
Windmill Copse
Sparkes Copse
GU27
Pillar Box Cottage
Sketchers Copse
Hungry Corner
Killinghurst Park
Rovehurst Wood
190
Hovell Copse
June Hill
Brookfield
Griggs Bottom
A283
PETWORTH ROAD
WOODSIDE ROAD
POOK LANE
POOK HILL
MILL LANE
PRESTWICK LANE
WEST END LANE
KILLINGHURST LANE
RIDGLEY ROAD
COMBE LANE
BALLS DOWN
PICKHURST ROAD
1
2
3
4
5
6
7
8
9
38
37
36
35
34
94
95
96

97
98
99
00
H
J
K
L
M
N
153
173
Loxhill
Catspaw
Markwick Cottage
Markwick Farm Cottage
Markwick Farm
MARKWICK LANE
Gorebridge Green Farm
Farlands
Gorebridge House
38
Vann Lane Piggeries
Donners
Royton
VANN LANE
UPPER VANN LANE
Vann Lodge
Shaftowes
Park Piece
Placewood Farm
ROUNDALS LANE
Hammonds Piece
Nutcombe
Clay Pit
Vann Copse
Upper Glasshouse Field
Glasshouse Copse
Great Godalming Copse
Enticknaps Copse
Woodside Farm
HOOKHOUSE
Vann Cottages
Sawpit Piece
Works
NUTBOURNE COTTAGES
Vann
Prest Wood
Standages
Hook House Farm
Blunden's Wood
VANN COPSE
Stella Cottage
Walnut Tree Cottages
Woodcock Rew
Hookhouse Hanger
Shernalls Pond
Little Pond Field
PEARTREE GN
Six Acre Pond
Coleman's Copse
Halfpenny Copse
Little Pockford Cottage
Dunsc Copse
Farm Bottom
Crabtree Cottage
37
Brookside
Stone Cottage
Pockford Farm Cottages
Dunns
Davids Copse
Field Place
DUNSFOLD
Stonehurst Hanger
Lower Wood
Pockford Lodge
Pockford House
Duns Farm
Field Place Farm Cottages
Grattons
Sewage Works
The Grove
Pockford Brook
Pockford Farm
HOUSE LANE
Cowpasture Hanger
Stonehurst
Kiln Copse
Birchen Copse
Skinners Land Farm
Church Close Farm
CHURCH GREEN
CHURCH
SHOPPE ROAD
Canterbury Rew
Church Closes
Pockford Harbour
Barns Meadow
Alderlands Copse
ROAD
Eves Copse
WHITE BEECH LANE
White Beech Cott.
White Beech
Whitebeech Copse
Mill Hanger
Millhanger Cott.
Fairwood
The Mill House
174
36
White Beech Farm
Bulls Back
Duns Copse
Duns
Snarham Land
Millhanger
Willards
Old Furze Field
Burton Fld
Ryestreet Common
Pembridge
Snarham Land
Wetwood Rough
Prestwick Manor Farm
CHIDDINGFOLD ROAD
STREET
Standing Wood
Wetwood
Blacknest Farm (Dunsfold Hatchery)
WHOTHAM
Floodgate Hanger
Servetree Copse
Brookland Copse
BIRCHEN COPSE
Loxley Bridge
Prestwick Copse
Lion's Copse
Copse Cottage
Barbins
Barbins Copse
Fowlhurst Copse
Hazelbridge House
Cat's Copse
35
Frome Copse
Twelve Acre Copse
Dunsfold Ryse Farm
Highstreet Green
Frome Hanger
Eight Acre Copse
PLAISTOW
Hazel Bridge Court
Furze Field
Watlands Ghyll
Lower Lagfold Copse
Gales Farm
Timbers Chase
BOTANY BAY
Dunsfold Ryse
LAGFOLD COPSE
HIGH STREET
Burningfold Manor Stud
Old Pickhurst
Round Copse
Corner Farm
Peartree Piece
34
Tugley Farm
OAKEN WOOD
Canterbury Copse
OLD LAND'S
Burntwood Kennels
Peartree Hanger
TIDY'S COPSE
Fisherland Hanger
The Hatchetts
G
191
TUGLEY WOOD
Durfold Hatch
Birch Copse
1
2
3
4
5
6
7
8
9

174
Markwick Farm Cottage
Markwick Cotts
00
01
02
03
Loxhill
A
B
C
D
E
F
G
154
Grubbins Farm
GODALMING
ROAD
B2130
DUNSFOLD
STOVOLDS
Bayhurst Copse
Sewage Works
Gorebridge Green Farm
Farlands
Rose Cottages
Gorebridge House
Sussex Lodges
The Coach House
Pound House
Park Hatch
38
1
Enticknaps Copse
Woodside Farm
Majorland Rew
Lay Field
Lime Kiln Cottage
Gate House
The Lodge
Pratts Corner
Painshill Copse
Thatchedhouse Farm
Thatchedhouse Planted Piece
HOOKHOUSE
Hook House Farm
Ten Acre Pond
Park Farm
COMMON
HIGH
The Moor
The Burchetts
Hawkin's Farm
Hall Place Farm
2
Hookhouse Hanger
Six Acre Pond
GRIGGS MEADOW
WINDWAYS
High Loxley
LOXLEY
High Loxley Furze
Stovoldshill Farm
PEARTREE GN.
Crabtree Cottage
37
King George's Field
Coombebury Cottage
Godalming
High Billinghurst
HILL
Field Place
Field Place Cottage
3
HOOK HOUSE LANE
THE GREEN
Dunsfold Green
Grattons
Gratton Corner
Chenells Copse
Sayers Land
Benbow Rew
Furtherfits
Aircraft Works
NUGENT CL.
CHURCH GREEN
Church Close Farm
CHURCH
SHOPPE HILL
St. Mary's C.of E. Prim. Sch.
THE MEWS
BINHAMS LEA
Jewings Hurst
Benbow Rew
GU8
Barns Meadow
Long House
New Pound Farm
Honey Mead
DUNSFOLD AERODROME
4
Mill Hanger
DUNSFOLD
Pound Farm
36
173
SUN INN RD
Nursery
Springfield Rew
Chalcrofts Rough
Millhanger
Willards
Ckt. Grd.
The Common
ALFOLD
5
Dunsford Common
The Garden Cottage
Old Rickhurst
Reservoir (covered)
BENBOW LANE
Shiftland Copse
Standing Wood
Eng. Works
Furze Croft Farm
Barnfield
KNIGHTONS
Burnwood Copse
Blacknest Farm (Dunsford Hatchery)
CHAPEL
Whitehall
Rickhurst Rews
Piddles Copse
Bottom
Roundles Copse
Tickners Heath Farm
Lower Seven Acre Copse
CHIDDINGFOLD ROAD
WROTHAM HILL
Loxley Bridge
Merton Cottage
Baker's
Ticknersheath Bridge
6
Merton Place
Three Limes
Little Rickhurst Copse
Fir Tree Copse Nature Reserve
Cobdens Farm
Tickners Heath
Tickner's Heath
Saffron Gate
SACHEL COURT RD
Copse Cottage
Barbins Copse
Fry's Cross Farm
Sethern
35
Wrotham Great Copse
Fry's Cross
RAMS
LANE
Sachel Ct.
SPRINGBOK COTTS.
SACHEL CT. MEWS
SPRINGBOK ESTATE
7
Firfield Rough
Sedgehurst (Kennels)
Sedgehurst Wood
Warren Copse
Sprunks
PLAISTOW
HURLANDS
Hurlands
Velhurst Copse
SACHEL
Burningfold Manor Stud
Hurst Hill
Howicks
SIDNEY WOOD
Park Copse
8
Furnace Bridge
Knightons
Woodlands
34
Velhurst Farm
Hurlands Copse
Lodge
Old Knightons
Crossway Field Copse
Canterbury Copse
Ireland
Glasshouse Copse
Old Lock House
Priorswood Farm
ROSEMARY
9
Lodge
High Bridge
TIDY'S COPSE
The Hatchetts
Upper Ifold
Inside Copse
Upper Ifold Fm
Sidney Wood
Sydney Wood Cott
Westland Copse
192
Upper Ifold House
The White House
Merrow Farm
Upper Oakhurst

Cranleigh
GU6
Horsham
RH12
Alfold Crossways
ALFOLD
Alfold Bars
Laker's Green
Hall Place
GUILDFORD ROAD
HORSHAM ROAD
A281
B2133
WILDWOOD LANE
KNOWLE LANE
LOXWOOD ROAD
WAVERLEY
HORSHAM
Wey & Arun Junction Canal
WILDWOOD GOLF COURSE
Rikkyo School in England
155
176
193

Cranleigh
GU6
HORSHAM ROAD
B2128
Whitehall
Whitehall Copse
Norley Farm
Owlbarn Copse
Longhurst Hill
Furzefield Copse
Rowgardens Copse
Selham Lodge
Burmah Bungalow
The Chalet
Windgate Cottage
Cobbler's
The Wind Break
Tothill Wood
Eastgate Wood
Vachery Pond
Vachery House
Thornhurst Brook
Home Wood
Kiln Copse
Nightingales
Baynards
Brooklands Farm
Baynards Park
Song Hurst
Horsham Lodge
Baynard's Park
New Cottages
Home Farm
Vachery Farm
Moat
Sharpe's Copse
Newhouse Farm
Pond
Collins Copse
Collins Farm
White Cottage
BAYNARD'S PARK
Tillhouse Farm
Pollingfold House
Lodge Copse
Massers Wood
New Barn
Grub Copse
Chemical Works
DOWNS LINK
LAWNS ROAD
Lawn Cottages
North Wood
STATION ROAD
LINACRE DRIVE
Nob Copse
Ruet
Maybanks Manor
Tolt Garth
KNOWLE LANE
Shrubs Copse
Baynards Lodge
Ivelle Farm
Fair View
Broomhall Cottage
COX GREEN ROAD
Tithe Cottage
Woodthorpe
Cox Green
HERMONGER
Withy Copse
Starveall Copse
Firtree Copse
Furzefield Wood
South Wood
BAYNARDS ROAD
Little Hawks Hill
Great Inholms
Little Inholms
Broomhall Copse
WAVERLEY
HORSHAM
Hazel Copse
Hobbs Copse
Clay Pit
Little Birchett
HILLHOUSE LANE
Brick Works
Woodsomes Farm
Aliblastairs
GUILDFORD ROAD
A281
The Knob
Four Winds
Dukes Farm
Greathouse Hanger
Greathouse Farm
Lynwick Hanger
Canfields Farm
RUDGWICK
CHURCH STREET
Hemstocks
Hornshill Wood
Well Grove
Tip Pond
Hatches
Gravatt's Farm
Gravatt's Hanger
Hornshill Farm
COOKS HILL LANE
LYNWICK STREET
Old Cottage
Field Cottage
156
175
194
Pennthorpe Sch.
Rudgwick

177
157
178
195
WALLISWOOD
SOMERSBURY WOOD
Nags Wood
Dorking
RH5
OAKWOODHILL
Horsham
RH12
Ellen's Green
Millfield
Rowhook
Hormongers
ROMAN WOODS
WAVERLEY
MOLE VALLEY
MOLE VALLEY
HORSHAM
B2128
HORSHAM ROAD
HONEYWOOD LANE
FURZEN LANE
GUILDFORD ROAD
BOGNOR RD.
ROWHOOK ROAD
Stane Street
Roman Road (course of)
Smokejack Brickworks
Exfold Wood
Oakwood Hill
Pollingfold Copse
Reservoirs
Rowhook Farm

Dorking RH5
OAKWOODHILL
WARNHAM
STANE STREET
BOGNOR ROAD
A29
MOLE VALLEY
HORSHAM
158
177
196

Horsham
RH12
KINGSFOLD
Lipscomb's Corner
Langhurst
Hulbrook
Warnham
HORSHAM ROAD
A24
(Proposed)
DORKING ROAD
DURFOLD HILL
A264
NORTHERN BY-PASS
HOLBROOK
PARK
ROME WOOD
HORSEGILLS WOOD
Horsham Business Park
Graylands
Clay Pit
Brookhurst Wood
Holbrook Park House
Moated House Farm
Kingsfold
159
197
180

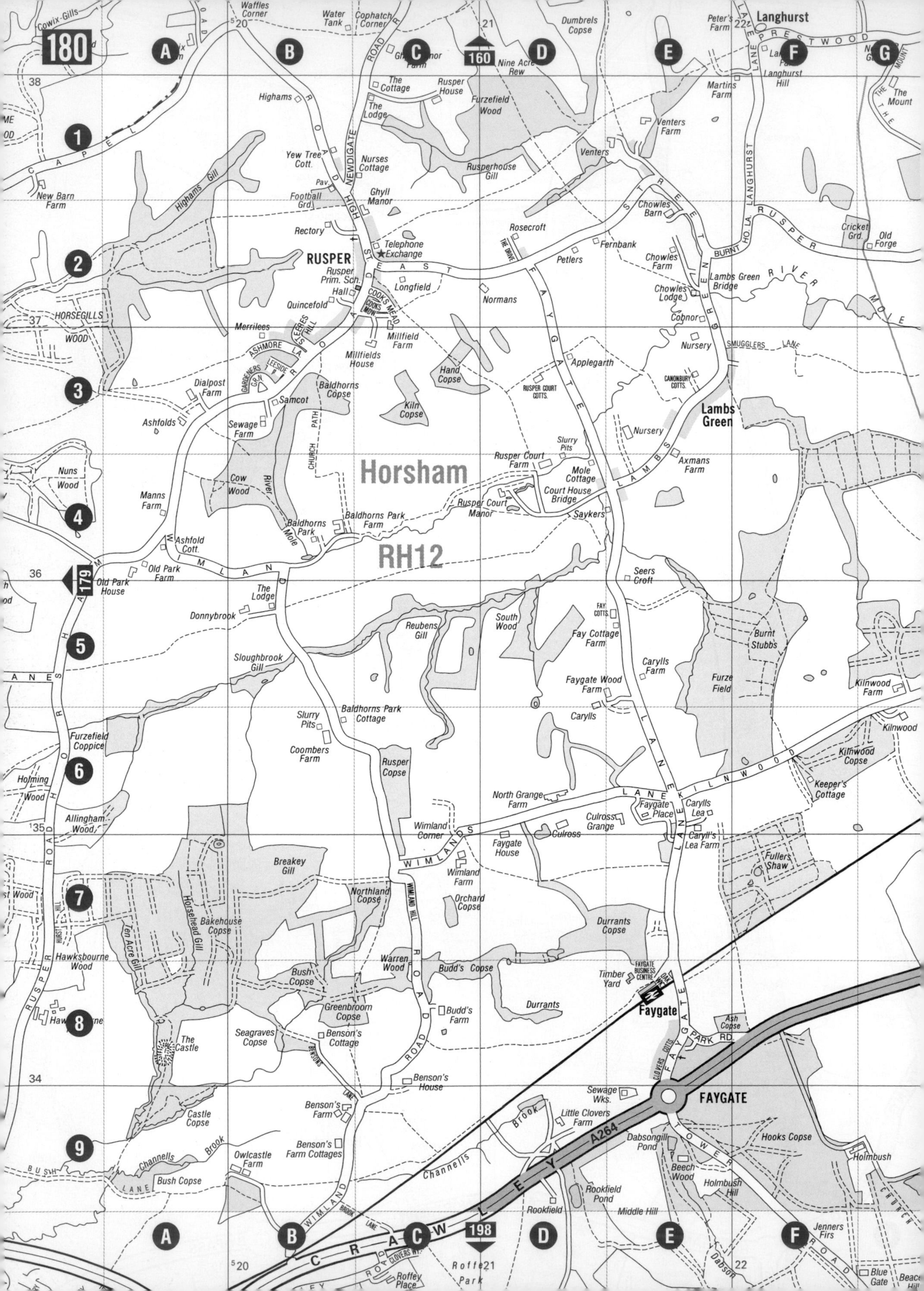
Waffles Corner
Water Tank
Cophatch Corner
Dumbrels Copse
Peter's Farm
Langhurst
Prestwood
160
Nine Acre Rew
Cowix-Gills
The Cottage
Rusper House
Furzefield Wood
Highams
The Lodge
Langhurst Hill
Martins Farm
The Mount
Venters Farm
Venters
Yew Tree Cott.
Nurses Cottage
Rusperhouse Gill
Newdigate
High Road
Capel
New Barn Farm
Highams Gill
Pav.
Football Grd.
Ghyll Manor
Chowles Barn
Rosecroft
Rectory
Telephone Exchange
Fernbank
Cricket Grd.
Old Forge
RUSPER
Rusper Prim. Sch.
Hall
East Street
Petlers
Chowles Farm
Burnt Ho. La.
Rusper
Lambs Green Bridge
River Mole
Longfield
Normans
Chowles Lodge
Quincefold
Cooks Mead
Horsegills Wood
Merrilees
Millfield Farm
Cobnor
Ashmore La
Leeside
Gardeners Grn
Millfields House
Faygate
Applegarth
Nursery
Smugglers Lane
Hand Copse
Canonbury Cotts.
Dialpost Farm
Baldhorns Copse
Rusper Court Cotts.
Samcot
Kiln Copse
Lambs Green
Ashfolds
Sewage Farm
Church Path
Nursery
Slurry Pits
Horsham
Rusper Court Farm
Axmans Farm
Nuns Wood
Cow Wood
River Mole
Mole Cottage
Court House Bridge
Manns Farm
Rusper Court Manor
Saykers
Baldhorns Park
Baldhorns Park Farm
Ashfold Cott.
RH12
Wimland
Old Park Farm
Seers Croft
179
Old Park House
The Lodge
Donnybrook
Fay Cotts.
South Wood
Reubens Gill
Fay Cottage Farm
Burnt Stubbs
Sloughbrook Gill
Carylls Farm
Furze Field
Faygate Wood Farm
Kilnwood Farm
Carylls
Slurry Pits
Baldhorns Park Cottage
Kilnwood
Furzefield Coppice
Coombers Farm
Rusper Copse
Kilnwood Copse
Holming Wood
North Grange Farm
Faygate Place
Carylls Lea
Keeper's Cottage
Allingham Wood
Wimland Corner
Culross Grange
Culross
Caryll's Lea Farm
Faygate House
Fullers Shaw
Breakey Gill
Wimland Farm
Northland Copse
Wimland Hill
Orchard Copse
Horsehead Gill
Bakehouse Copse
Durrants Copse
Ten Acre Gill
Hawksbourne Wood
Rusper Road
Hurst Hill
Warren Wood
Bush Copse
Budd's Copse
Faygate Business Centre
Timber Yard
Oak Way
Greenbroom Copse
Budd's Farm
Durrants
Faygate
Ash Copse
The Castle
Seagraves Copse
Benson's Cottage
Park Rd.
Clovers Cotts.
Benson's House
Sewage Wks.
FAYGATE
Castle Copse
Benson's Farm
Little Clovers Farm
Brook
Dabsongill Pond
Hooks Copse
Benson's Lane
Benson's Farm Cottages
Owlcastle Farm
Channells Brook
A264
Tower Road
Holmbush
Bush Lane
Bush Copse
Beech Wood
Channells
Holmbush Hill
Rookfield Pond
Rookfield
Middle Hill
Church
Wimland
Brook Lane
Crawley
198
Jenners Firs
Clovers Wy.
Roffey Place
Roffey Park
Dabson
Blue Gate
Beach Hill

181
Ifieldwood
The Druids
Wildacres
The Gables Nursing Home
161
The Mount Farm
Hillybarn Farm
Pockney's Farm
Kirk Farm
Ifield Green
Riding Stables
Bonwycks Place
The Court House
Ifield Barn Theatre
Rectory Farm
The Grove
Broomhill House
Works
Granthams Bridge
Lower Barn
Crawley
IFIELD
Ifield Community College
Playing Field
Sandalwood
Furlong Farm
Stumbleholm Farm
RH11
HORSHAM
CRAWLEY
Ifield Mid. Sch.
Burial Ground
IFIELD GOLF & COUNTRY CLUB
Club House
Hyde Hill
Ifield
CRAWLEY
GOFFS PARK
Model Railway
Ifield Mill
GOSSOPS GREEN
St. Wilfrid's RC School
Ifield Pond
Waterfield First Sch.
Upper Bewbush
House Copse
Woldhurstlea Wood
The Holy Trinity C. of E. Sch.
Bewbush Brook
Capon Grove
BEWBUSH
Pondtail Shaw
Hopper's Brook
Bewbush Leisure Centre
BROADFIELD
A264 ROAD HORSHAM
A2220
A23
CRAWLEY AVENUE
BUCHAN COUNTRY PARK
Information Centre
CRAWLEY SOUTH WEST BY PASS
HOLMBUSH POTTERIES INDUSTRIAL ESTATE
Holmbush Farm
Hopper Farm
Spruce Hill Brook
Spruce Hill
Creasy's Forest
Broadfield Kennels
Target Hill
Douster Pond
Silver Hill
Island Pond
Middle Covert
BUCHAN HILL FOREST
Buchan Hill
Creasy's Brook
Ckt. Grd
Foxhole Pond
Shepherdsfield
COTTESMORE GOLF COURSE
Fish Pond
Cottesmore School
PEASEPOTTAGE FOREST
House Pond
Playing Field
Shepherdsfield Farm
199
Club House
Buchan House
HOLMBUSH FOREST
G H J K L M N
1 2 3 4 5 6 7 8 9
23 24 25 26
182
CRAWLEY HOSPITAL

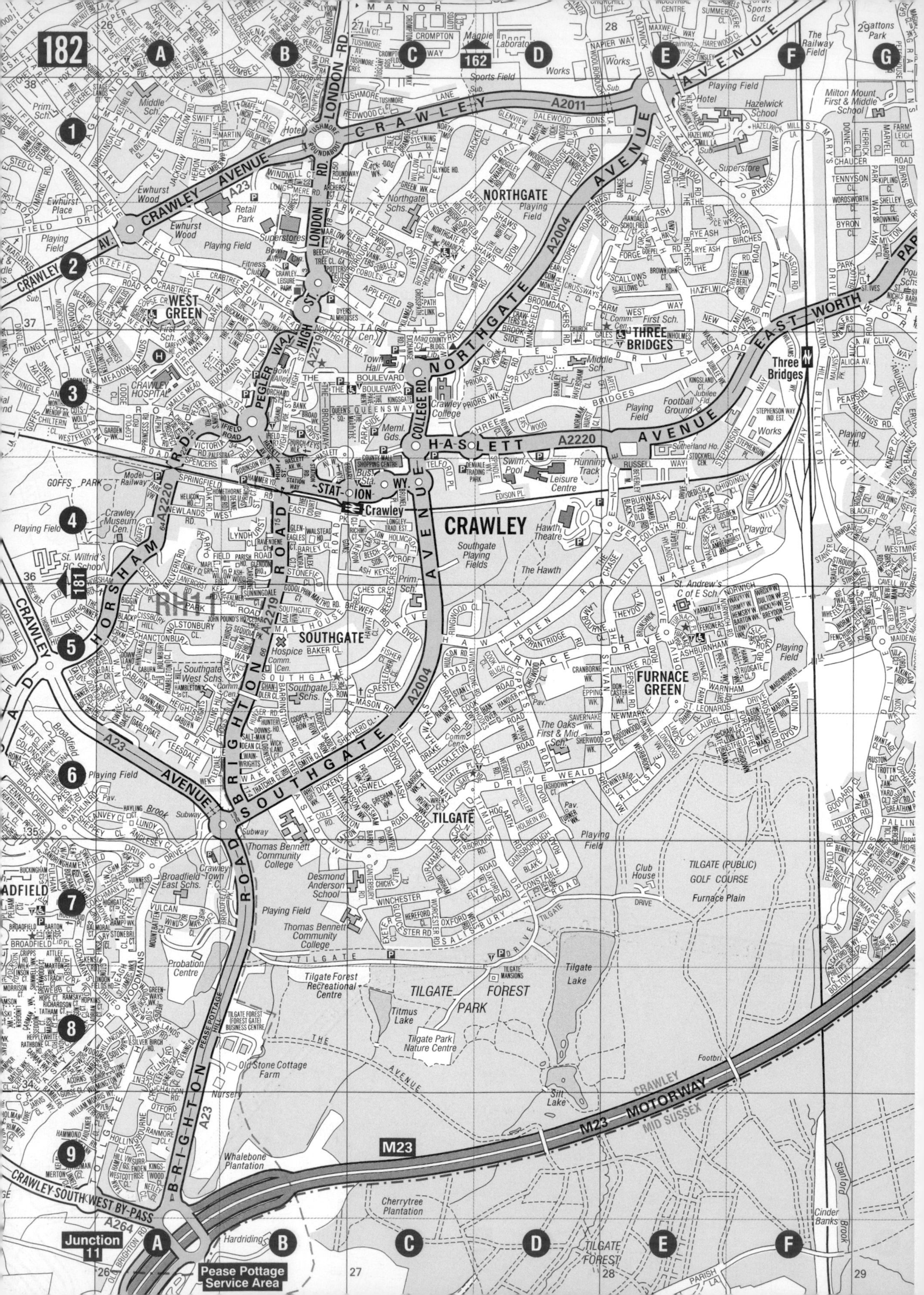

182
CRAWLEY
NORTHGATE
WEST GREEN
THREE BRIDGES
SOUTHGATE
FURNACE GREEN
TILGATE
TILGATE FOREST PARK
TILGATE FOREST
CRAWLEY AVENUE
A2011
A23
A2219
A2004
A2220
A264
M23 MOTORWAY
CRAWLEY-SOUTH WEST BY-PASS
HORSHAM RD.
BRIGHTON ROAD
SOUTHGATE AVENUE
NORTHGATE AVENUE
HASLETT AVENUE
EAST WORTH AVENUE
LONDON RD.
HIGH ST.
PEGLER WAY
COLLEGE RD.
STATION WY.
Crawley
Three Bridges
Crawley Hospital
Crawley College
Town Hall
Hawth Theatre
Leisure Centre
Southgate Playing Fields
The Hawth
Tilgate Lake
Titmus Lake
Silt Lake
Tilgate Park Nature Centre
Tilgate Forest Recreational Centre
TILGATE (PUBLIC) GOLF COURSE
Furnace Plain
Thomas Bennett Community College
Probation Centre
Whalebone Plantation
Cherrytree Plantation
Old Stone Cottage Farm
Junction 11
Pease Pottage Service Area
Goffs Park
RH11
162
181
CRAWLEY
MID SUSSEX

183
163
184
Crawley
RH10
WORTH FOREST
WORTHLODGE FOREST
OLDHOUSE WARREN
COWDRAY FOREST
Haywards Heath
RH17
POUND HILL
WORTH
MAIDENBOWER
WORTH ABBEY
Rowfant
Old Rowfant
Copthorne Wood
Driver's Wood
King's Wood
Birchen
The Plantation
Home Farm
Fish Pond
Crabbet Park
Crabbet Park House
Crabbet Park Equitation Centre
Brewhouse Wood
Wentworth Lodge
Leyhouse Farm
Ley House
Lake House
Blackpond Shaw
Mill Pond
Rowfant House
Lodge
Hayheath
Layhouse Wood
Horsepasture Wood
West Lodge
Depot
Works
Woodlands
Compasses Corner
Compasses Wood
High Cott.
Worth Lodge Farm
Fourteen Acre Rough
Oaken Wood
The Burches
Worth Hall
Worth Hall Farm
The Gill
Stony Plats
Lodge Wood
Standinghall Farm
High Lines
Junction 10a
Hotel
Maidenbower Schools
Maidenbower Park
Flax Field
Rats Wood
Coldharbour Farm
Hough Wood
Long Shaw
Brickkiln Wood
Playing Field
Swimming Baths & Squash Club
South Hill Wood
Mount Noddy
Halfsmock Bottom
Brick Field South
Worth Abbey & School
Bulls Copse
Rugs Corner
Whitely Hill
Woodside
Spring Wood
Harrowdean Wood
The Park
Downside Wood
Bennetts Rough
Bushy Wood
Sports Ground
Pav
Oldhouse Warren
Denches Copse
Beechfield Cottage
Burnt Place
Kiln Wood
Paddockhurst Park
M23
A2220
B2036
B2110
COPTHORNE RD.
COPTHORNE AVENUE
BALCOMBE ROAD
TURNERS HILL ROAD
WORTH WAY
PADDOCKHURST ROAD
MAJOR'S HILL ROAD
WALLAGE LANE
BACK LANE
STANDINGHALL LANE
WHITELY HILL
BALCOMBE LA.

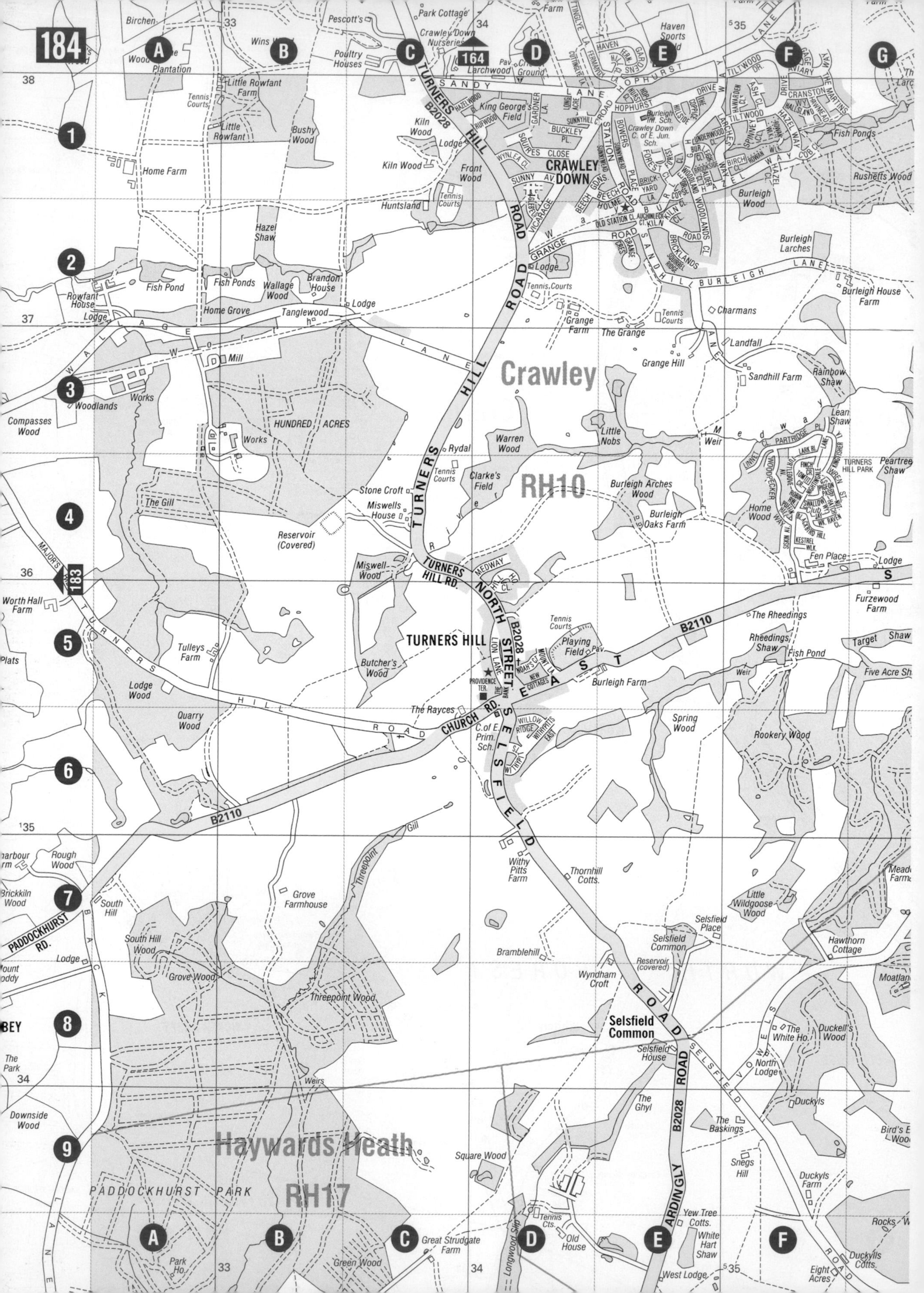
184
164
183
A
B
C
D
E
F
G
1
2
3
4
5
6
7
8
9
38
37
36
35
34
33
Crawley
RH10
Haywards Heath
RH17
CRAWLEY DOWN
TURNERS HILL
Selsfield Common
Birchen
Plantation
Wins Wood
Pescott's
Park Cottage
Crawley Down Nurseries
Poultry Houses
Larchwood
Cricket Ground
Haven Sports Field
Little Rowfant Farm
Little Rowfant
Tennis Courts
Bushy Wood
Kiln Wood
Home Farm
Front Wood
Huntsland
Hazel Shaw
Fish Pond
Fish Ponds
Wallage Wood
Brandon House
Rowfant House
Lodge
Home Grove
Tanglewood
Mill
Works
Woodlands
Compasses Wood
HUNDRED ACRES
The Gill
Reservoir (Covered)
Stone Croft
Miswells House
Miswell Wood
Rydal
Warren Wood
Clarke's Field
Little Nobs
Grange Farm
The Grange
Grange Hill
Charmans
Landfall
Sandhill Farm
Rainbow Shaw
Burleigh House Farm
Burleigh Larches
Burleigh Wood
Rushetts Wood
Fish Ponds
Burleigh Arches Wood
Burleigh Oaks Farm
Home Wood
Fen Place
Furzewood Farm
The Rheedings
Rheedings Shaw
Target Shaw
Five Acre Shaw
Peartree Shaw
TURNERS HILL PARK
Lean Shaw
Medway
Weir
Worth Hall Farm
Tulleys Farm
Lodge Wood
Quarry Wood
Butcher's Wood
The Rayces
Playing Field
Burleigh Farm
Spring Wood
Rookery Wood
C.of E. Prim. Sch.
PROVIDENCE TER.
Withy Pitts Farm
Thornhill Cotts.
Grove Farmhouse
Gill
Threepoint
Rough Wood
Brickkiln Wood
South Hill
South Hill Wood
Grove Wood
Threepoint Wood
Little Wildgoose Wood
Selsfield Place
Selsfield Common
Reservoir (covered)
Hawthorn Cottage
Bramblehill
Wyndham Croft
Moatlands
The White Ho.
Duckell's Wood
North Lodge
Selsfield House
The Ghyl
The Baskings
Duckyls
Bird's Eye Wood
Snegs Hill
Duckyls Farm
Square Wood
Weirs
Downside Wood
The Park
PADDOCKHURST PARK
Park Ho.
Green Wood
Great Strudgate Farm
Longwood Gill
Tennis Cts.
Old House
Yew Tree Cotts.
White Hart Shaw
West Lodge
Rocks Wood
Duckylls Cotts.
Eight Acres
TURNERS HILL ROAD
B2028
B2110
SANDY LANE
HOPHURST LANE
WALLAGE LANE
TURNERS HILL RD.
NORTH STREET
EAST STREET
CHURCH RD.
SELSFIELD ROAD
ARDINGLY ROAD
PADDOCKHURST RD.
BACK LANE
VOWELS LANE
GRANGE ROAD
SANDHILL LANE
BURLEIGH LANE
STATION ROAD
MAJOR'S HILL
LION LANE
TILTWOOD DR.
HAZEL WAY
WOODLANDS ROAD
BRICKLANDS
Burleigh Inf. Sch.
Crawley Down C. of E. Jun. Sch.
Kiln Wood
Fish Pond

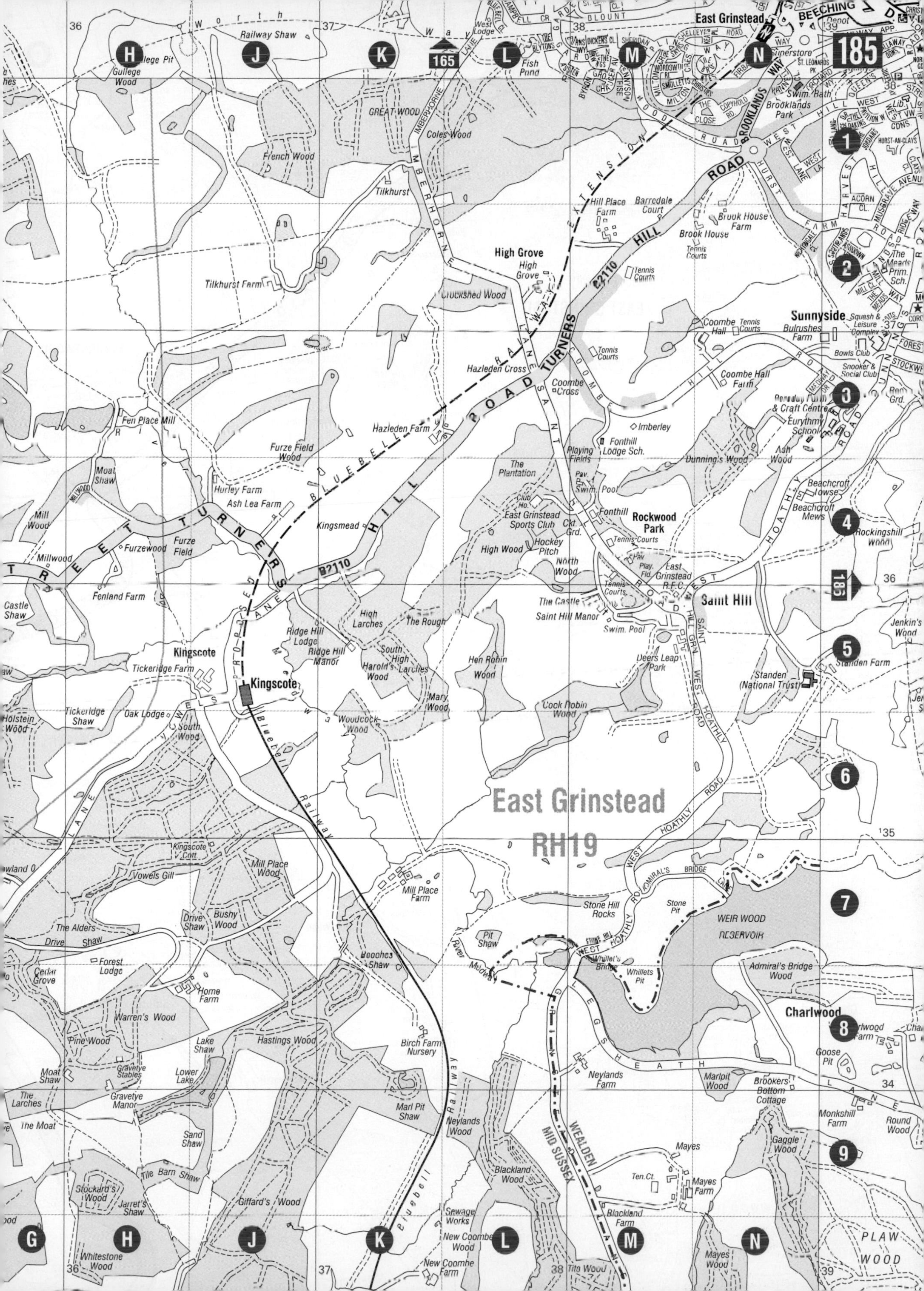

185
165
East Grinstead
RH19
Kingscote
Sunnyside
Saint Hill
Charlwood
High Grove
Rockwood Park
TURNERS HILL ROAD
B2110
WEIR WOOD RESERVOIR
Standen (National Trust)
Bluebell Railway
MID SUSSEX
WEALDEN
Worth Way
Railway Shaw
Gullege Wood
Great Wood
French Wood
Coles Wood
Tilkhurst
Tilkhurst Farm
Crockshed Wood
Hazleden Cross
Hazleden Farm
Furze Field Wood
Fen Place Mill
Moat Shaw
Mill Wood
Millwood
Hurley Farm
Ash Lea Farm
Furzewood
Furze Field
Fenland Farm
Castle Shaw
Kingsmead
Hill Place Farm
Barredale Court
Brook House Farm
Brook House
Coombe Hall
Coombe Hall Farm
Coombe Cross
Imberley
Fonthill Lodge Sch.
The Plantation
East Grinstead Sports Club
High Wood
North Wood
Fonthill
East Grinstead R.F.C.
The Castle
Saint Hill Manor
Deers Leap Park
Dunning's Wood
Ash Wood
Beachcroft House
Beachcroft Mews
Rockingshill Wood
Jenkin's Wood
Standen Farm
High Larches
The Rough
Ridge Hill Lodge
Ridge Hill Manor
South High Larches
Harold's Wood
Mary Wood
Hen Robin Wood
Cock Robin Wood
Tickeridge Farm
Tickeridge Shaw
Oak Lodge
South Wood
Woodcock Wood
Holstein Wood
Kingscote Cott.
Mill Place Wood
Vowels Gill
Mill Place Farm
The Alders
Drive Shaw
Bushy Wood
Pit Shaw
Stone Hill Rocks
Stone Pit
Whillet's Bridge
Whillets Pit
Admiral's Bridge Wood
Forest Lodge
Cedar Grove
Home Farm
Warren's Wood
Pine Wood
Hastings Wood
Birch Farm Nursery
Lake Shaw
Lower Lake
Moat Shaw
Gravetye Stables
Gravetye Manor
The Larches
The Moat
Sand Shaw
Marl Pit Shaw
Neylands Wood
Neylands Farm
Marlpit Wood
Brookers Bottom Cottage
Goose Pit
Monkshill Farm
Round Wood
Gaggle Wood
Mayes
Mayes Farm
Blackland Wood
Blackland Farm
Tile Barn Shaw
Stockard's Wood
Jarret's Shaw
Giffard's Wood
Sewage Works
New Coombe Wood
New Coombe Farm
Tits Wood
Mayes Wood
Whitestone Wood
PLAW WOOD
Brooklands Park
Bulrushes Farm
Bowls Club
Snooker & Social Club
Eurythmy School

A · B · C · D · E · F · G

166

EAST GRINSTEAD

Sunnyside

East Grinstead
RH19

ASHURSTWOOD

Wall Hill

WEIR WOOD
RESERVOIR

Weir Wood

MID SUSSEX
WEALDEN

Charlwood

Kidbrooke Park

KIDBROOKE
PARK

KIDBROOKE WOOD

PLAW WOOD

Edenbridge
TN8
Forest Row
RH18
Hartfield
TN7
FOREST ROW
Highgate
Tompset's Bank
Pixton Hill
Quabrook
Little Parrock
Upper Parrock
Coleman's Hatch
167
H
J
K
L
M
N
G
1
2
3
4
5
6
7
8
9
43
44
45
38
37
36
35
34
B2110
A22
Homestall
White Gables
Sewage Works
Water Wood
The Grove
Dog Gate Lodge
Dog Cottages
Grove Cottage
Poultry Farm
Owlett's Farm
Water Wood
Great Water Farm
Little Water Farm
Owletts House
Harelands Kennels
Barton House
Tennis Courts
New Cottages
Crockers Bank
Salmon Wood
Culver Farm
Thornhill
Songhurst Shaw
Goring Wood
Great Surries
Surries Wood
Great Surries Farm
Rest Harrow
Thornhill Cottage
Box Farm
Tanner's Hill Pett
Thornhill Farm
Little Surries
Little Surries Wood
Little Surries Farm
Mount Pleasant Nursery
Grove Farm
Ashurstwood Abbey
Play. Field
Leg of Mutton Shaw
Bushy Shaw
Owletts Cottage
Pollard Wood
Woodcock Shaw
Shipyard Pett
Orchard Cotts
Black Windmill Cottages
Home Wood
Hazel Wood
Highams Wood
Holden Wood
Acre Wood
Church Wood
Poultry Farm
Highfields
Beeches Farm
Roughfield Wood
Tugmore Shaw
Paupersdale Wood
North Clays
Collingsbush Wood
Wick Wood
Clay Wood
Spanden Wood
Wallhill Farm
Spanden
Minepits Wood
Gill Wood
Pixton Hill Farm
Ashdown Farm Cottages
Ashdown Farm
Ashdown House School
Oatland Shaw
Heasmans
Playing Field
Lower Parrock
Cedar Cotts
Pumping Station
Tablehurst Farm
Cobbers
Emerson College
River Medway
Forest Way
Sewage Works
Furzefield Wood
Penfield Shaw
Shepherdsfield Wood
Parrock Meadow
Gassensfield Wood
Blacklands Farm
Brookside
Upper Parrock Farm
Lines Farm
Lines Bungalow
Felis Ho.
Rystwood Lodge
Rystwood Ho
Parrock Place
Ashenplat Shaw
Ave Maria Wood
Wychcote
Andrews Bank
Little Parrock Farm
Paternoster Wood
Rystwood Farm
Hotel
Play. Fld.
Prim. Sch.
Lib.
Pav.
Rec. Grd.
Ten Ct.
Shalesbrook
Club Ho.
Vale Cott.
Popular Farm
Greenhall Cott.
Old White's Farm
Gorseycop Farm
Gatehouse Farm
Upper Quabrook
Hall
Paradise Wood
Bank Cott.
Forest View
Yew Tree Hall Cotts.
Hollycroft
Yew Tree Hall
ROYAL ASHDOWN FOREST GOLF COURSE
Wych Warren
Water Farm
Little Shepherd's Farm
Forest View
Shepherd's Gate Cotts.
Shepherd's Gate
Holly Hill
Little Broadstone Farm
Foxbury Wood
The Birches
Yew Tree Cottage
The Lodge
Vangsard Way
CANSIRON LANE
BUTCHERFIELD LANE
HOMESTALL ROAD
DIRTY LANE
HARTFIELD ROAD
SHEPHERD'S HILL
CAT STREET
PARROCK LANE
FOREST ROAD
WOOD ROAD
PARK ROAD
DALE RD.
SHALESBROOK LANE
UPPER CLOSE
ASHDOWN RD.
CHAPEL LANE
PRIMROSE LA
TITS LANE
HIGHGATE WORKS
FOREST ROW BUS. PK.
STATION RD.
LOWER SQ.
UPPER SQ.
RIVERSIDE
MEDWAY CL.
BLACKLANDS CRES
PARK CRES.
STONEPARK DR.
STONE DENE CL.
HATCH END
WOOD COTE RD.
SCHOOL LA
COLEMANS HATCH RD.

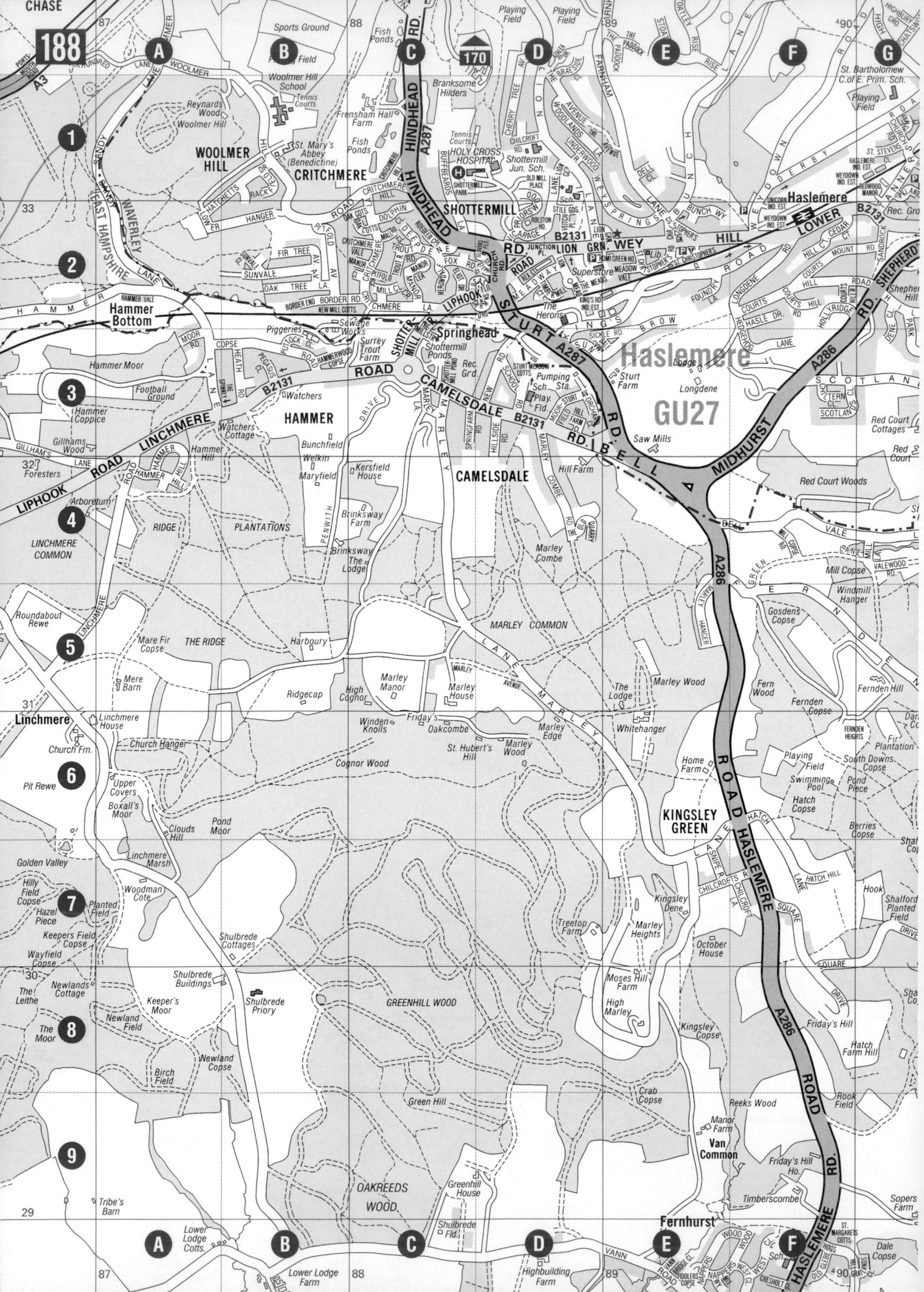

188
CHASE
A3
Sports Ground
Playing Field
Fish Ponds
170
HINDHEAD RD.
A287
Woolmer Hill School
Tennis Courts
Reynards Wood
Woolmer Hill
WOOLMER HILL
St. Mary's Abbey (Benedictine)
Frensham Hall Farm
Fish Ponds
CRITCHMERE
Branksome Hilders
HOLY CROSS HOSPITAL
Shottermill Jun. Sch.
SHOTTERMILL
St. Bartholomew C.of E. Prim. Sch.
Haslemere
B2131
LOWER
HILL
Rec. Grd.
WOOLMER LANE
SANDY LANE
EAST HAMPSHIRE
WAVERLEY
HATCHETTS
HANGER
FIR TREE AV.
SUNVALE
OAK TREE LA.
BORDER RD.
CRITCHMERE LA.
LIPHOOK RD.
JUNCTION PL.
LION GRN.
WEY
Superstore
FOUNDRY LA.
LONGDENE
COURTS HILL RD.
HASLE DR.
HOLLYRIDGE
SHEPHERDS
HAMMER VALE
Hammer Bottom
MOOR RD.
COPSE
Hammer Moor
Football Ground
Piggeries
Sewage Works
Surrey Trout Farm
Springhead
Shottermill Ponds
Rec. Grd.
The Herons
KING'S BROW
STURT RD.
Haslemere
Lodge
Sturt Farm
Longdene
GU27
Pumping Sta.
Sch.
Play. Fld.
Watchers
HAMMER
CAMELSDALE
Hammer Coppice
Watchers Cottage
Gillhams Wood
Hammer Hill
Foresters
LINCHMERE ROAD
LIPHOOK ROAD
Bunchfield
Welkin
Maryfield
Kersfield House
Saw Mills
Hill Farm
Red Court Cottages
Red Court
Red Court Woods
MIDHURST
A286
Arboretum
RIDGE
PLANTATIONS
LINCHMERE COMMON
Brinksway Farm
Brinksway
The Lodge
Marley Combe
VALE
Mill Copse
Windmill Hanger
Roundabout Rewe
Mare Fir Copse
THE RIDGE
Harbourry
MARLEY COMMON
Gosdens Copse
Mere Barn
Ridgecap
High Cognor
Marley Manor
Marley House
The Lodge
Marley Wood
Fern Wood
Fernden Hill
Linchmere
Linchmere House
Church Fm.
Church Hanger
Winden Knolls
Friday's
Oakcombe
St. Hubert's Hill
Marley Wood
Marley Edge
Whitehanger
Fernden Copse
Fir Plantation
Cognor Wood
Home Farm
Playing Field
South Downs Copse
Pit Rewe
Upper Covers
Boxall's Moor
Swimming Pool
Pond Piece
Hatch Copse
KINGSLEY GREEN
Clouds Hill
Pond Moor
Berries Copse
Golden Valley
Linchmere Marsh
Hilly Field Copse
Hazel Piece
Planted Field
Woodman Cote
Kingsley Dene
Treetop Farm
Marley Heights
Hook
Shalford Planted Field
Keepers Field Copse
Wayfield Copse
Shulbrede Cottages
October House
The Leithe
Newlands Cottage
Shulbrede Buildings
Shulbrede Priory
Keeper's Moor
GREENHILL WOOD
Moses Hill Farm
High Marley
The Moor
Newland Field
Kingsley Copse
Friday's Hill
Hatch Farm Hill
Newland Copse
Birch Field
Green Hill
Crab Copse
Reeks Wood
Rook Field
Manor Farm
Van Common
Friday's Hill Ho.
Tribe's Barn
OAKREEDS WOOD
Greenhill House
Timberscombe
Sopers Farm
Lower Lodge Cotts.
Shulbrede Fld.
Fernhurst
Lower Lodge Farm
Highbuilding Farm
VANN RD.
HASLEMERE RD.
Dale Copse
HASLEMERE ROAD

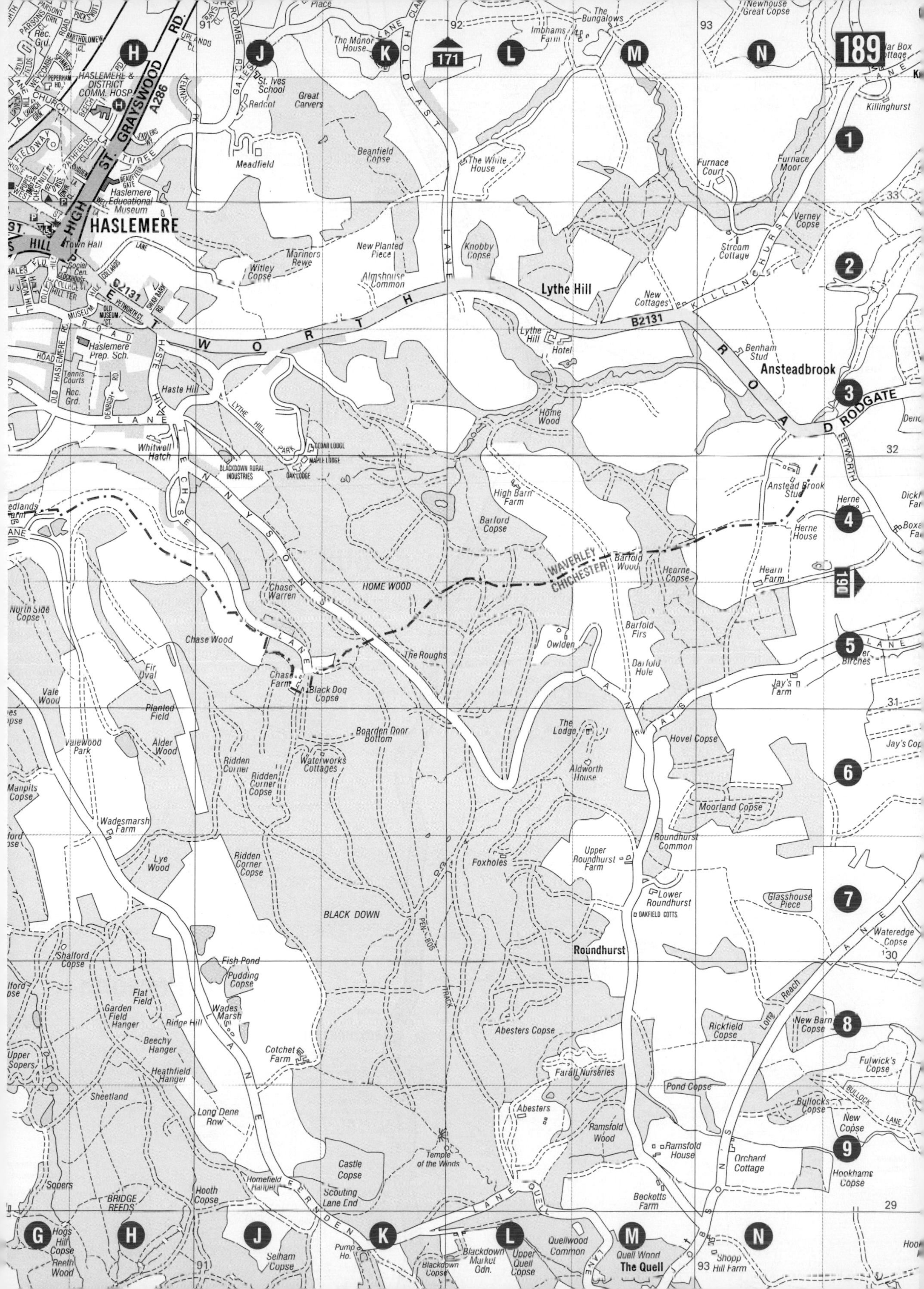

HASLEMERE
Lythe Hill
Ansteadbrook
Roundhurst
The Quell
BLACK DOWN
HOME WOOD
Haslemere & District Comm. Hosp.
Haslemere Educational Museum
Town Hall
Haslemere Prep. Sch.
St. Ives School
Redcot
Great Carvers
Meadfield
Beanfield Copse
The Manor House
The White House
Imbhams Farm
The Bungalows
Newhouse Great Copse
Killinghurst
Furnace Court
Furnace Moor
Verney Copse
Stream Cottage
New Cottages
Benham Stud
Knobby Copse
New Planted Piece
Almshouse Common
Marinors Rewe
Witley Copse
Lythe Hill Hotel
Home Wood
Haste Hill
Whitwell Hatch
Blackdown Rural Industries
Cedar Lodge
Maple Lodge
Oak Lodge
High Barn Farm
Barford Copse
Anstead Brook Stud
Herne House
Hearn Farm
Hearne Copse
Barfold Wood
Barfold Firs
Barfold Hole
Owlden
Jay's Farm
Hovel Copse
Jay's Copse
The Roughs
Chase Warren
Chase Wood
Chase Farm
Black Dog Copse
North Side Copse
Vale Wood
Fir Oval
Planted Field
Valewood Park
Alder Wood
Boarden Door Bottom
Waterworks Cottages
Ridden Corner
Ridden Corner Copse
The Lodge
Aldworth House
Moorland Copse
Manpits Copse
Wadesmarsh Farm
Lye Wood
Foxholes
Upper Roundhurst Farm
Roundhurst Common
Lower Roundhurst
Oakfield Cotts.
Glasshouse Piece
Wateredge Copse
Shalford Copse
Fish Pond
Pudding Copse
Flat Field
Garden Field Hanger
Wades Marsh
Ridge Hill
Beechy Hanger
Abesters Copse
Rickfield Copse
New Barn Copse
Long Reach
Fulwick's Copse
Upper Sopers
Heathfield Hanger
Cotchet Farm
Farall Nurseries
Pond Copse
Bullocks Copse
New Copse
Sheetland
Long Dene Row
Abesters
Ramsfold Wood
Ramsfold House
Orchard Cottage
Hookhams Copse
Castle Copse
Temple of the Winds
Sopers
Bridge Reeds
Hooth Copse
Homefield Hanger
Scouting Lane End
Beckotts Farm
Hogs Hill Copse
Reeth Wood
Selham Copse
Pump Ho.
Blackdown Market Gdn.
Blackdown Copse
Upper Quell Copse
Quellwood Common
Quell Wood
Shopp Hill Farm
WAVERLEY
CHICHESTER
B2131
A286
WORTHING ROAD
PETWORTH
RODGATE
KILLINGHURST LANE
HOLDFAST LANE
TENNYSON'S LANE
CHASE LANE
LYTHE HILL PARK
FERNDEN LANE
QUELL LANE
JAYS LANE
BULLOCK LANE
HASTE HILL
ST. GRAYSWOOD RD.
HIGH ST.
PEN-Y-BOS TRACK
171
190

190
172
189
Killinghurst Park
Killinghurst
Furnace Moor
Verney Copse
Hovell Copse
June Hill
Brookfield
Ramster Gardens
Ramster
Sketchers Copse
Hungry Corner
Chaleshurst Copse
Killinghurst Great Copse
RAMSNEST COMMON
Ramsnest Common
The Weigh House
Chaleshurst
Bushman's Copse
Redlands Farm
Rovehurst Wood
Gostrode Farm
Griggs Bottom
Glasshouse Rew
Sparkes Copse
White's Hill
WAVERLEY
CHICHESTER
Furze Field
Alder Bed Copse
Lambels Copse
Big Copse
Quennel's Pond Copse
Potlane Farm
Brickyard Cottages
Upper North Pond
Walk Copse
Shillinglee
Rodgates
Benham Stud
Ansteadbrook
PETWORTH ROAD
RODGATE LANE
B2131
Dickhurst House
Dencher Copse
CRIPPLECRUTCH HILL
FISHER STREET
PETWORTH ROAD
A283
Godalming
Stilland Cottages
Stilland Farm
Fairhurst
Parkgate
Bulls End
Lower Rough
Lower North Pond
Shillinglee Home Farm
East Broadlands
Anstead Brook Stud
Dickhurst Great Copse
Dickhurst Farm
Herne Lodge
Boxalland Farm
Gaston's Farm
Sawhouse Thicket
Turnour's Wood
Gospelgreen Copse
GU8
Deer Tower
Hearn Farm
New Copse
Gospel Green
Fisherstreet
Boxalland Copse
JAYS LANE
Eastland Farm
Silver Birches
Jay's Farm
Redlands Farm
Breachhurst Copse
The Creek
China Bridge
Fisherstreet Farm
Blanshotts Copse
Jay's Copse
Frith Lodge
Haslemere
Deer Barn Rew
FRITH WOOD
The Plantation
Frith Lodge
Frith Hill
Fisherstreet Copse
GU27
Greenland Copse
Copygrove Copse
Wateredge Copse
Greenland Farm
JOBSONS
Long Reach
Little Rewe
Petworth
GU28
SANDROCK COTTS.
VALENTINES LEA
NORTHCHAPEL
MITCHELL PARK FARM COTTS.
Barn Copse
Upper Diddlesford Farm
Shonks Farm
HONEYDOWN COTTS
Fulwick's Copse
VINE COTTS.
THE GRN.
Hall
Chapel Copse
PEPERS LANE
Bullocks Copse
BULLOCK LANE
New Copse
Round Copse
Northchapel Comm. Prim. School
Peacock's Farm
Diddlesfold Manor Farm
LUFFS MEADOW
Hortons Farm
Garlands
Orchard Cottage
Hookhams Copse
Air Navigational Radio Beacon
Sewage Treatment Works
Little Wood Meadow
Little Wood
Hookhams Farm
Hillgrove
WET WOOD

191
173
192
Billingshurst
RH14
DURFOLD WOOD
ASHPARK WOOD
KINGSPARK WOOD
BIRCHFOLD COPSE
ROUNDWYCK COPSE
TUGLEY WOOD
PLAISTOW
SHILLINGLEE ROAD
PLAISTOW ROAD
DUNSFOLD ROAD
FISHER LANE
PIPERS LANE
SHILLINGLEE PARK GOLF COURSE (PUBLIC)
Old Land's
Fisherland Hanger
Peartree Hanger
Burntwood Kennels
The Hatchetts
Oak Wood
Durfold Hatch Cott.
Birch Copse
Durfold Hall Farm
Fisher Lane Nursery
Robins Farm
Surrey Copse
Little Tugley
The Holmes
Works
Oakhurst Farm
Dungate Farm
Surrey Belt
Surrey Cottage
Surrey Rough
Fisherlane Wood
Club House
Shillinglee Park
Icehouse Copse
Downlands
Weald Barkfold Copse
Shortland Copse
Downlands Wood
Newhouse Furze
Manorhill Copse
Pound Cottage
Paddock Copse
Old Furze Field
Newhouse Farm
East End Farm
Winkins Wood
Weald Barkfold
Cockhat Piece
Catfield Rew
Clay Pit
Brick Works
Short's Farm
Highbridge House
Nine Acre Rew
Beanfield Copse
Black Copse
Little Haymans Farm
Landing Stage
Twenty Four Acres
Haymans Farm
The Lake
Lake Cottage
Park Mill Farm
Mill Copse
Nell Ball
Ifold Copse
Alder Platt
Hazel Toll
Seven Acre
Rumbolds Cottage
Dale's Farm Hanger
Dale's Farm Copse
Sparrwood Hangar
Dale's Farm
Chilsford Farm
Rumbolds Farm
Mitchell Park Farm
Sparrwood Farm
Red Copse
Hammer Cottages
Hammer Bridge
Swear Farm
Piper's Cottages
Upper Frithfold Farm
Piper's Copse
Sixteen Acre Rew
Roundwyck House
Freehold Copse
Frithfold Farm
Kiln Copse
97
98
99
00
33
32
31
30
29
1
2
3
4
5
6
7
8
9
G
H
J
K
L
M
N

Godalming
GU8
Cranleigh
GU6
Upper Ifold
Sidney Wood
TIDY'S COPSE
The Hatchetts
Upper Ifold Inside Copse
Upper Ifold House
The White House
Upper Ifold Fm.
Merrow Farm
Sydney Wood Cott.
Lodge
Westland Copse
Upper Oakhurst
Upper Ifold Wood
Weald Barkfold Copse
WAVERLEY
CHICHESTER
Lee House Farm
Thirds Copse
Sydney Cotts.
Sydney Farm
Old Manor House
Gennets Wood
Bonfire Hanger
Oakhurst Farm
HOG WOOD
Barberry Furze
Barberry Bridge
Gennets Bridge
Gennets Furze
Watermoor Copse
Gennets Farm
Oxoncroft Copse
Lakeside
Forest View
Furzen Wood
Shortland Copse
Barkfold Hanger
Weald Barkfold
Hog Copse
The Ranch
Camperdown
Southlands
Dale Farm
Four Pines
Hogwood Farm
Cherry Blossom Fm.
Sweetbriar
Three Oaks
Barn Wood
Wey and Arun Junction
Short's Farm
Lyons Farm
Plaistow Place
Poundfield Wood
Loxwoodhills Pond
Plaistow Inf. Sch.
Hall
IFOLD
Nell Ball
PLAISTOW
Quennells
Quennells Farm
Pittsgate
Spring Copse
Charleshurst
Strudgwick Farm
Charleshurst Hill
Beggars Copse
Ifold Copse
Alder Platt
Corner Copse
Hazel Tolt
Seven Acre Furze
Rumbolds Cottage
Rumbold Wood
Flitchings Farm
Little Springfield Fm.
Foxbridge Hanger
Little Headfoldswood Copse
Rumbolds Farm
Foxbridge Farm
Club House
Red Copse
FOXBRIDGE GOLF COURSE
Wephurst Wood
Orchard Cottage
Limekiln Wood
Hardnip's Barn
Hardnip's Copse
The Mount
Streeter's Farm
The Bungalow
Swear Farm
Redlands Farmhouse
Old Furze Field
Kiln Platt
Pond Field Plantation
Wellhurst Copse
Crouchland
Furze Field
Costrong Copse
Broad Field
Ravensnest Copse
Nursery
Irrigational Resr.
Glasshouse Copse
Walthurst Copse
Blackwell Wood
Middleground Copse
Middleground Hanger
Laneland
Irrigational Resr.
Costrong Farm
Wephurst Park
Spitwick Barn
Laneland Farm Cotts.
Ainsworth Copse
Wephurst Park Farm
Wephurst Furze
DUNSFOLD ROAD
VALENTINES
NELL BALL
THE STREET
LOXWOOD ROAD
RICKMANS LANE
PLAISTOW LANE
FOXBRIDGE LANE
PLAISTOW ROAD
THE DRIVE
IFOLDHURST
CHALK
THE RIDE
FOREST ROAD
THE LANE
HOGWOOD RD.
174
191

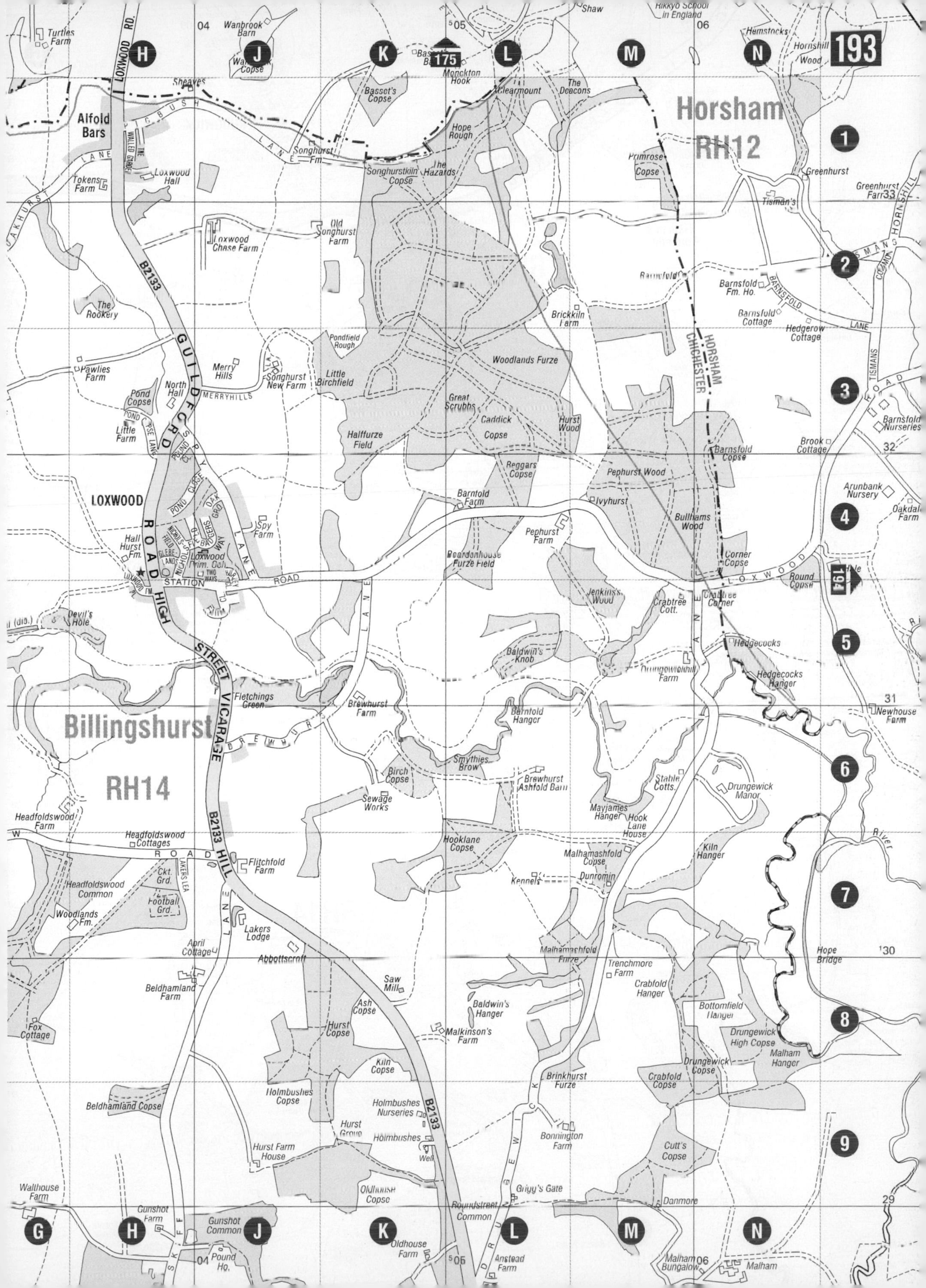
175
194
Horsham
RH12
Alfold
Bars
LOXWOOD
Billingshurst
RH14
Turtles Farm
Wanbrook Barn
Wanbrook Copse
Sheaves
Basset's Copse
Monckton Hook
Clearmount
The Deacons
Shaw
Rikkyo School in England
Hemstocks
Hornshill Wood
Hope Rough
Songhurst Fm.
Songhurstkiln Copse
The Hazards
Loxwood Hall
Tokens Farm
Primrose Copse
Greenhurst
Greenhurst Farm
Tisman's
Old Songhurst Farm
Loxwood Chase Farm
Barnsfold Fm. Ho.
Barnsfold Cottage
Hedgerow Cottage
Brickkiln Farm
The Rookery
Pondfield Rough
Woodlands Furze
Merry Hills
Songhurst New Farm
Little Birchfield
Pawlies Farm
North Hall
Pond Copse
Little Farm
Great Scrubbs
Caddick Copse
Hurst Wood
Halffurze Field
Barnsfold Copse
Brook Cottage
Barnsfold Nurseries
Reggars Copse
Pephurst Wood
Arunbank Nursery
Oakdale Farm
Barnfold Farm
Ivyhurst
Bullhams Wood
Spy Farm
Hall Hurst Fm.
Loxwood Prim. Sch.
Pephurst Farm
Boardenhouse Furze Field
Corner Copse
Round Copse
Jenkins's Wood
Crabtree Cott.
Crabtree Corner
Devil's Hole
Baldwin's Knob
Hedgecocks
Drungewick Farm
Hedgecocks Hanger
Fletchings Green
Brewhurst Farm
Barnfold Hanger
Newhouse Farm
Smythies Brow
Birch Copse
Brewhurst Ashfold Barn
Stable Cotts.
Drungewick Manor
Sewage Works
Mayjames Hanger
Hook Lane House
Headfoldswood Farm
Headfoldswood Cottages
Flitchfold Farm
Hooklane Copse
Malhamashfold Copse
Kiln Hanger
Ckt. Grd.
Headfoldswood Common
Football Grd.
Kennels
Dunromin
Woodlands Fm.
Lakers Lodge
April Cottage
Abbottscroft
Malhamashfold Furze
Trenchmore Farm
Hope Bridge
Saw Mill
Crabfold Hanger
Beldhamland Farm
Ash Copse
Baldwin's Hanger
Bottomfield Hanger
Fox Cottage
Hurst Copse
Malkinson's Farm
Drungewick High Copse
Malham Hanger
Kiln Copse
Brinkhurst Furze
Drungewick Copse
Crabfold Copse
Beldhamland Copse
Holmbushes Copse
Holmbushes Nurseries
Hurst Group
Holmbushes
Well
Bonnington Farm
Cutt's Copse
Hurst Farm House
Walhouse Farm
Oldhouse Copse
Grigg's Gate
Danmore
Roundstreet Common
Gunshot Farm
Gunshot Common
Oldhouse Farm
Pound Ho.
Anstead Farm
Malham Bungalow
Malham
LOXWOOD RD.
GUILDFORD ROAD
HIGH STREET
VICARAGE HILL
B2133
PIGBUSH LANE
LANE
MERRYHILLS
POND COPSE LANE
SPY LANE
POND CLOSE
STATION ROAD
LOXWOOD ROAD
BARNSFOLD LANE
TISMANS COMMON
HORNSHILL LANE
BREWHURST
LAKERS LEA
LAKERS LANE
DRUNGEWICK
HORSHAM
CHICHESTER
River
H J K L M N G
1 2 3 4 5 6 7 8 9
04 05 06 01
33 32 31 30 29

194
A
B
C
D
E
F
G
1
2
3
4
5
6
7
8
9
176
193
GUILDFORD ROAD
A281
B2128
RUDGWICK
Bucks Green
RH12
RH14
Billingshurst
The Haven
Tisman's Common
Morgan's Green
River Arun
Lynwick Hanger
Canfields
Hatches
Well Grove
Hornshill Farm
Old Cottage
Field Cottage
Tip Pond
Gravatt's Farm
Gravatt's Hanger
Pennthorpe Sch.
Rudgwick Prim. Sch.
Playing Field
Watts Corner
Up. Smithers Copse
Swaynes Farm
Smithers Rough
Greenhurst
Greenhurst Farm
Weyhurst Copse
Bucks Cottage
Weyhurst Farm
Tisman's
Hall
Fairlee
Wagonford
Woodfalls
Barnsfold Fm. Ho.
Barnsfold Cottage
Hedgerow Cottage
Exfold Farm
Wanford Bridges
Wanford Mill
Rudgwick Two Tiered Bridge
Axel Cottage
Lodge
Roundabout Cotts.
Mill Cottages
Chephurst Farm
Upper Barn
Warhams
Barnsfold Nurseries
Rolls Farm
Naldretts Farm
Morelands
Brook Cottage
Sewage Works
Arunbank Nursery
Oakdale Farm
Rudgwick Grange
Chephurst Copse
Hurstlands
Rudgwick Fruit Fm.
Howick Farm
The Rookery
Colin's Cross
Corner Copse
Hale
Smithwood Copse
Pensfold Plantation
Mill Farm Hanger
Howick Copse
Keepers Cottage
Hedgecocks
Hedgecocks Hanger
Tittlesfold Copse
Couzens Hanger
Garlands
Birch Copse
Tittlesfold Farm
Newhouse Farm
Mill House
Gibbons
Havenhurst Farm
Gibbons Mill
Mill Fm. Ho.
Hawks Rewe
Havenhurst
Drungewick Manor
Mill Lodge
Gibbons Mill Farm
Lower Lodge Farm
Lugmore
Marshall's Farm
Heathers Furze Field
Smerricks Copse
Horse Ride
Kings Hanger
Cousins Farm
Heathers Copse
Wayside Cottage
Heathers Farm
Hope Bridge
Hope Farm
Long Copse
Lannard's Copse
Furze Field
Drungewick High Copse
Malham Hanger
Hope Rough
CHICHESTER
HORSHAM
Marshall's Hanger
Shortloes Farm
Leverance Copse
Muttons Farm
Shortloes Hanger
Muttons Hanger
Muttons Copse
Hoglands Cottages
Hogland Rough
Leverance Farm
Planted Field
Holman's Copse
Sewage Works
Bignor Farm
Bignor Wood
Great Wood
Hadhurst Copse
Inglefield Manor School
Square Copse
Malham
CHURCH ST.
HAVEN ROAD
NALDRETTS LANE
PENSFOLD LANE
MARLES LANE
HORNSHILL LANE
TISMANS COMMON
BARNSFOLD LANE
COMMON ROAD
WOODS HILL
LYNWICK STREET
DOWNS LINK
OKEHURST LANE
07
08
09
29
30
31
32
33

195
Hyes Hanger
Great Copse
Windover
Upper Furzefields
Colts Bushes
Long Copse
Hyes
Waterland Farm
H
J
K
L
M
N
ROMAN WOODS
177
Chaldens
Davies Wood
Furnacehouse Copse
Kiln Copse
Plattershill Copse
Townhouse Copse
WOOD LEA COTTAGES
RD.
Woodland Cott.
A281
Poor Man's Croft
Clemsfold Farm
ROAD
GUILDFORD
1
Southfields Bungalow
Lower Townhouse Copse
Roman Gate
Roman Gate Cottage
Furnacehouse Farm
Hyes Lodge
Weir
Alfoldean Bridge
Brookhurst Farm
Southfields
Roman Station (site of)
33
Moat
Dedisham
Dedisham Farm
Dedisham School
2
Violets Farm
Townhouse Farmhouse
A29
STREET
Depot
Iris Copse
Pondtail Copse
(ROMAN ROAD)
Whales Copse
Claypits Row
Nowhurst Farm
NOWHURST
3
Pensfold Farm
Fladgates
Nowhurst
Hill House
Rogerspool Copse
Sewage Works
CLAPGATE
Farm Copse
32
Hapkyns
Rowfold Farm
Timehill Copse
Cook's Copse
Birch Copse
RIVER
Horsham
Clapgate Cottage
Theale Copse
4
Mercy in the Bottom
Rowadams Copse
Bob Inn Farm
The Rectory Sch.
South Lodge
Newbuildings
ARUN
Huntingrove Farm
Furze Field
Stone Cottage
The Birches
Theale Farm
196
PARKSTREET LANE
PARK STREET
Old Stables
TANNERY CL.
Sports Grd.
FORGE
Park Street
Oaklands
LYONS
Merle
Lime Kiln Cottage
Little Birches
Kilsyth
LINK
STANE
Park House
Amber Field
Slinfold
WEST WY.
GREENFIELD RD.
THE GRATTONS
Theale Croft
5
Park Farm
Driving Range
DOWNS
Caravan Site
SPRING
PARK RD.
STREETFIELD
Ashlands Farm
SLINFOLD PARK GOLF & COUNTRY CLUB
Club House
SPRING COPSE BUSINESS PARK
Mead Farm
CLOVER FIELD
ROAD
31
Gaskyns
MAYDWELL AVENUE
Slinfold Lodge
The Lodge
Hayeshill Copse
Works
RH13
Lackham
Meadowhurst
6
Oldhouse Copse
PINKHURST
Piggeries
Woodstock
Hall Land Rough
LINK
Rosemary
Rudocts
HAYES
Wild Harry's
Holmbush Manor Farm
Black Barn Gill
Whitebreads
7
Bottlehouse Gills
Oak Leigh
Lucerne
Hayes Grange
Highlands
Hill Croft
LANE
Holmbush Upper Rough
ROAD
30
Riddens Farm
Black Barn Farm
Bramble Hill Farm
Farthings Barn
Toat Hill Farm
TOAT HILL
Bottlehouse Copse
A264
Toat Hill House
Toat Hill
8
Lydwicke Farm
Ranfold
Furze Copse Farm
HILL
BASHURST
Cousin's Copse
Toat Copse
Chafers Copse
Fulford Farm
Lydwicke
Holmbush Lwr. Rough
OAKS
Bashurst Copse
Lydwicke Hanger
Eastedfield Wood
LANE
COPSE
Slinfold Manor
A264
9
Weir
Rookerywood
Rookery Wood
Lowertoat Farm
CHILTINGTON
FIVE
Hayes Oak
Elmhurst Farm
WEST
Chuch Farm
29
Holman's Barn
G
Buckman Corner
HORSHAM RD
ELMHURST
North Gill
Itchingfield
ITCHINGFIELD ROAD
STANE
Gleniffer Farm
LANE
12
South Gill
Itchingfield Prim. Sch.
510
11
13

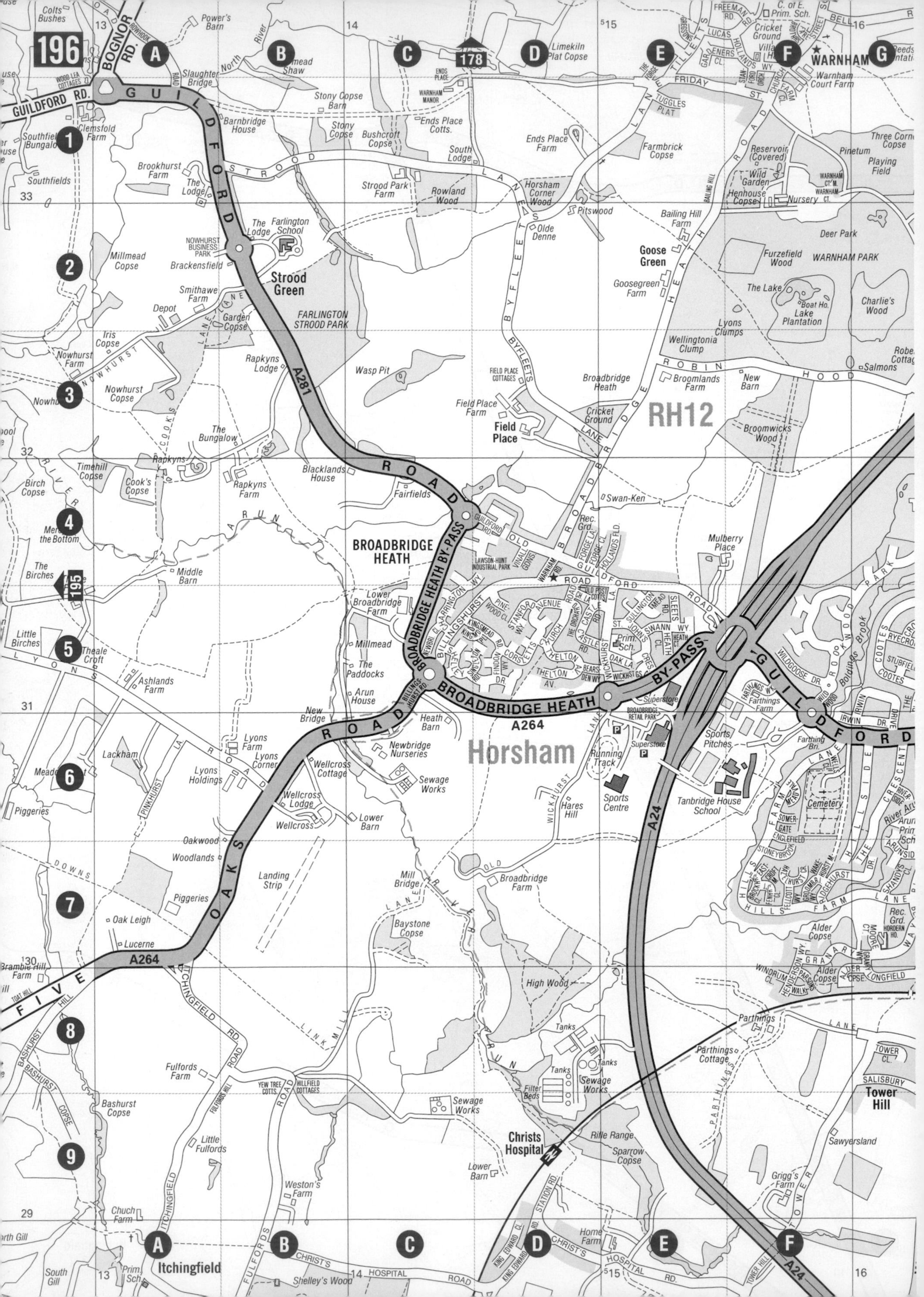

196
178
195
GUILDFORD RD.
BOGNOR RD.
GUILDFORD ROAD
A281
BROADBRIDGE HEATH BY-PASS
A264
OAKS ROAD
FIVE OAKS
A24
Strood Green
BROADBRIDGE HEATH
Horsham
RH12
WARNHAM
WARNHAM PARK
Goose Green
Field Place
Christs Hospital
Tower Hill
Itchingfield
Warnham Court Farm
Farlington School
FARLINGTON STROOD PARK
Broadbridge Heath
Tanbridge House School
Sports Centre
Running Track
Superstore
Lower Broadbridge Farm
Broadbridge Farm
Wasp Pit
Landing Strip
Sewage Works
Rifle Range
Sparrow Copse
High Wood
Lyons Farm
Lyons Corner
Wellcross
Fulfords Farm
Bashurst Copse
Chuch Farm
South Gill
Shelley's Wood
CHRIST'S HOSPITAL ROAD

HORSHAM
RH13
Holbrook
HOLBROOK PARK
Littlehaven
Little Haven
Roffey
Oakhill
New Town
Denne Park
Doomsday Green
Coolhurst
The Common
HORSHAM PARK
HORSHAM GOLF PARK
ROOKWOOD GOLF COURSE
Warnham Nature Reserve
Warnham Mill Pond
Warnham Mill
Warnham Place
Warnhamplace Farm
Great Daux Roundabout
Millpond Plantation
Walnutree Plantation
Tommy's Clump
Coachroad Clump
Limits Copse
Cricket Ground Clump
Westons Farm
Pondtail Farm
Pondtail House
Home Farm
North Heath Copse
Pondtail Bri.
Chesworth Farm
Chesworth House
Denne Meadows Farm
Hill Top Cottage
Hill View
Cup & Saucer Ponds
Amiesmill House
Amiesmill Bridge
Amiesmill Farm
White's Bridge
Whitesbridge Farm
Hornbrook Farm
Hilliers Garden Centre & Huxleys Experience
Garden House
Park House
Corner Wood
Pavilion Wood
Birchen Bri.
Birchenbridge House
Highland Copse
Townhouse Copse
Leechpool Wood
Horsham R.U.F.C.
Horsham Cricket Club Ground
Barrackfield Crossing
Horsham F.C.
Football Ground
Bennett's Hold (Rec. Grd.)
The Forest Sch.
Smiths Barn Playing Field
Millais Sch.
Sports Cen.
Heron Way Prim. Sch.
Horsham
Swimming Pool
The College of Richard Collyer
HORSHAM HOSPITAL
Superstore
DORKING ROAD
A24
A264
NORTHERN BY-PASS
HORSHAM ROAD
WARNHAM ROAD B2237
RUSPER ROAD
CRAWLEY ROAD
HARWOOD ROAD
B2195
BRIGHTON ROAD
A281
BISHOPRIC
ALBION ROAD
NORTH PARADE
B2237
WORTHING ROAD
HURST ROAD
NORTH STREET
B2180
179
193
17
18
19
29
30
31
32
33
G
H
J
K
L
M
N
1
2
3
4
5
6
7
8
9

198
A
B
C
D
E
F
G
1
2
3
4
5
6
7
8
9
180
197
20
21
22
33
32
31
30
29
Channells
Brook
Copse
Benson's
Farm Cottages
Dabson
Hooks Copse
Holmbush
Rookfield Pond
Rookfield
Middle Hill
Beech Wood
Holmbush Hill
Jenners Firs
Blue Gate Lodge
Beacon Hill
HORSHAM
NORTHERN
BY-PASS
A264
CRAWLEY
ROAD
WIMLAND
CLOVERS WY.
Roffey Place
Roffey Park
Roffey F.C.
Newhouse Farm
NEWHOUSE BUSINESS CENTRE
Moorhead Farm
Woodlands Farm
Faygate Forest
Dabson Gill
Reservoir
Sand Plat
Rookfield Farm
Beacon Hill Cross
Road Farm
Roffey Park
FOREST
ROAD
BEEDINGWOOD DR.
Beedingwood
Roffey Park Management Institute
Pine Ridge Farm
Beedingwood Farm
Brickyard Copse
Stonelodge Hanger
EARLES
MEADOW
OLD
High Wood
The Birches
RH12
R.C. Prim. Sch.
B2195
Spursorchard Wood
Woodside Farm
Roffey Hurst
Seymours Vineyard
Spursorchard Cottages
Stonelodge Plain
The Minepits
Combe Bottom Wood
Forest Heights Farm
Knights Strength
Highbirch Hill
Playing Field
Rec. Grd.
Roffey
Cricket Grd.
Jun. Sch.
Cemy.
Roffey Corner
PINETOPS
St. Leonards Forest
GRANGE
St. Leonards Forest House
Whitevane Beech
Forest Grange Manor
Garage Cottages
Owlbeech Wood
Severals Bottom
Alder Gill
Playing Fields
Whitevane Pond
Whitevane Hill
RACE
MILL'S
MICK
Combe Bottom
LANE
The Knott
ST. LEONARD'S FOREST
Springfield Farm
SPRINGFIELD
Race Hill
Old Springfield Stud
HARWOOD
Leechpool Wood
Park Wood
Sewage Wks.
Whitevane Plain
Home Farm
Paddocks Farm
Townhouse Copse
ST. LEONARDS PARK
St. Leonard's Park
Horsham
Greenbroom Hill
HAMPER'S
Reservoir (Covered)
Sandpit Clump
Stew Pond
Dry Pond
SUNOAK
Turf Plain
Lily Beds
Gill
Grouselands
Grouselands Farm
Barnsnap
WOODLANDS
Golden Folly
Sheepwash Wood
Scragged Oak Hill
Scragged Oak
Sheepwash
Mick's Cross
Heron Way Prim. Sch.
GREBE
WAY
CRESCENT
Highland Copse
Horn Brook
Sunoak Plantation
Inholms
Greenslade Wood
Frenchbridge
Tattleton Farm
The Glen
Playing Field
Sun Oak Farm
St. Leonard's Forest Nature Reserve
Horsham R.U.F.C.
Coolhurst
RH13
HAMMERPOND
ROAD
ROOSTHOLE HILL
Doomsday Green
Park House
Roosthole Pond
Mill Farm
Tennis Courts
Coolhurst Wood
Pond Bay
Alder Copse
Roost-hole
Golding's House
Hawkins Pond
Old Copse
Millfield Copse
BRIGHTON
Corner Wood
Fullers
Lower Golding's Farm
GROUSE
Birchen Bri.
Pavilion Wood
Sheephovel Wood
Northland Wood
Gaggle Wood
Golding's
Cinderbank Copse
Boat Ho.
Hammer Pond
Lodge
Birchenbridge House
Sewage Works
Club House
Saddler's Farm
Rec. Grd.
MANNINGS HEATH GOLF COURSE
A281
Mannings Heath
Paulshill Copse
Stream
The Russells
CHURCH LA.
BUCKLEY LANE
MASONS FIELD
GOLDING

199
181
Junction 11
Pease Pottage Service Area
Foxhole Pond
Shepherdsfield Farm
Fish Pond
House Pond
Cottesmore School
Playing Field
PEASEPOTTAGE FOREST
CRAWLEY WEST SOUTH BY PASS
A264
HOLMBUSH FOREST
COTTESMORE GOLF COURSE
Club House
Buchan House
Horsham Corner
PEASE POTTAGE GOLF COURSE & DRIVING RANGE
Reservoir (Covered)
Meteorological Station
South Lodge
Club Ho
Black Hill Stud
FOREST ROAD
HORSHAM ROAD
COLGATE
Colgate House
Colgate Prim. Sch.
Black Hill Wood
Crawley
PEASE POTTAGE
Finches
Cherry Tree Fm.
BLACKHOUSE ROAD
Colgate Farm
Colgate Lodge
Shelley Cottages
Finches Shaw
Hotel
Nursery
RH11
HORSHAM
MID SUSSEX
A23
BRIGHTON ROAD
OLD BRIGHTON ROAD
SPRINGFIELD
Blackhouse Farm
Southover Farm
Poultry House
Pearl Cottage
Shelley Farm Cottages
Shelley Farm
Tilgate Forest Row
Woodhurst Farm
The Home Farm
New Barn Cott.
New Barn House
New Barn Farm
Newstead
Furze Field
Shelley Middle Gill
Shelley Plain Farm
Hungry Down
Blindman's Wood
Home Wood
Gill
Greenbroom
Pyefall
LANE
Spring Farm
Barnsnap
Newstead Ghyll
Woodhurst Plantation
Horse Bridge
Desmond's Castle
The Pheasantry
The Larches
Peewit Ghyll
Stone Edge Nursery
Hyde
Cooper's Wood
Stedman's Wood
Lythmere
Hydehill Wood
GROUSE ROAD
Elenge Plat Farm
Nashland Wood
Nashlands Farm
B2114
Newstead Farm
Buttock Corner
Old Copse
Sandpits
Tower Grouse Farm
Holkham's Corner
POUND WALK
Handcross Prim. Sch.
Hoggy Hole
Forest Lodge
Bunnyland
Rough Park
Darkalley Gill
Hoadlands Farm
Mount Noddy
Buckwheat Plantation
The Hyde
Haywards Heath
Home Beat
The Square
Sports Ground
Duckhouse
Beechey Toll
Hoadlands Wood
Swigg Cott.
Carter's Lodge
American Walk
Darkalley Pond
Upper Pond
Truckershatch Wood
HIGH ST.
HANDCROSS
Carterslodge Pond
Chestnut Hill
Fourteen Acre Wood
RH17
STAPLEFIELD RD.
CARTERSLODGE
Dropstone
Trucker's Hatch
Badgers Plantation
Truckers Ghyll
B2110
Ashfold Cotts.
Sewage Works
HORSHAM ROAD
Hammerhill Wood
WARREN WOOD
Ashfold Farm
Matcham's Grove
The Warren
Scotchbank Wood
West Park Farm
Homestead Wood
Marchant's Gill
Orange Gill
High Beech Farm
Jackson's Farm
Willis Farm
Cross Trees
The Roughground
PARK ROAD
ROAD

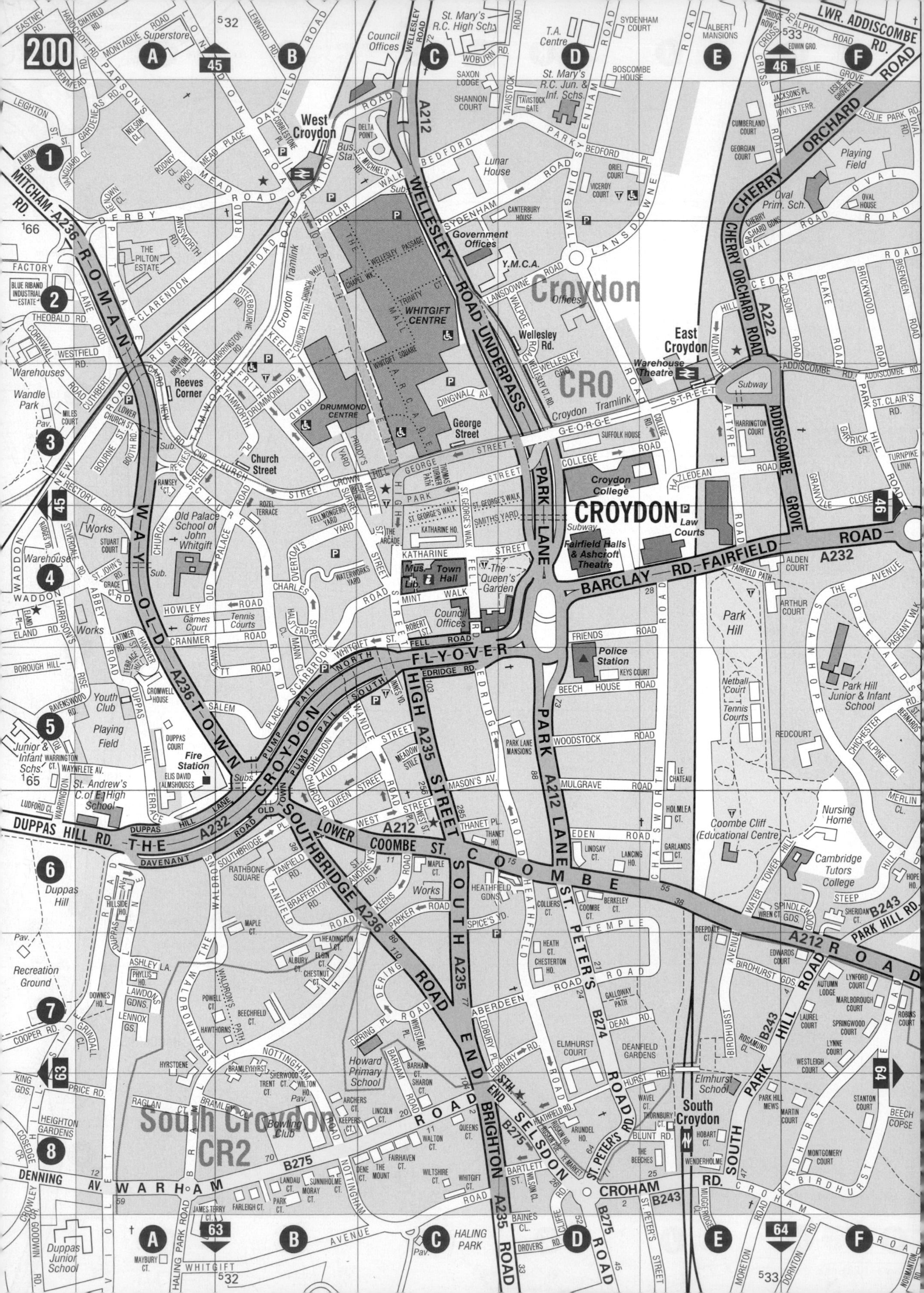

A
B
C
D
E
F
1
2
3
4
5
6
7
8
45
46
63
64
532
533
166
165
West Croydon
East Croydon
South Croydon
Croydon
CROYDON
CR0
South Croydon
CR2
Council Offices
St. Mary's R.C. High Sch.
T.A. Centre
St. Mary's R.C. Jun. & Inf. Schs.
Superstore
Lunar House
Government Offices
Y.M.C.A.
Offices
WHITGIFT CENTRE
DRUMMOND CENTRE
George Street
Church Street
Reeves Corner
Warehouse Theatre
Croydon College
Law Courts
Fairfield Halls & Ashcroft Theatre
Mus. Lib.
Town Hall
The Queen's Garden
Police Station
Old Palace School of John Whitgift
Games Court
Tennis Courts
Works
Youth Club
Playing Field
Fire Station
Junior & Infant Schs.
St. Andrew's C. of E. High School
Duppas Hill
Recreation Ground
Howard Primary School
Bowling Club
Elmhurst School
Park Hill
Netball Court
Tennis Courts
Coombe Cliff (Educational Centre)
Nursing Home
Cambridge Tutors College
Park Hill Junior & Infant School
Oval Prim. Sch.
Playing Field
Wandle Park
Warehouses
Warehouse
Duppas Junior School
HALING PARK
Croydon Tramlink
Bus Sta.
Subway
WELLESLEY ROAD UNDERPASS
A212
A236
A232
A235
A222
B243
B274
B275
ROMAN WAY
OLD TOWN
CROYDON FLYOVER
PARK LANE
HIGH STREET
SOUTH END
BRIGHTON ROAD
SOUTHBRIDGE ROAD
COOMBE ROAD
LOWER COOMBE ST.
BARCLAY RD.
FAIRFIELD ROAD
CHERRY ORCHARD ROAD
ADDISCOMBE GROVE
ADDISCOMBE RD.
LWR. ADDISCOMBE RD.
MITCHAM RD.
DUPPAS HILL RD.
THE WARHAM
DENNING AV.
CROHAM RD.
SELSDON ROAD
ST. PETER'S ROAD
PARK HILL ROAD
SOUTH PARK HILL ROAD
NOTTINGHAM ROAD

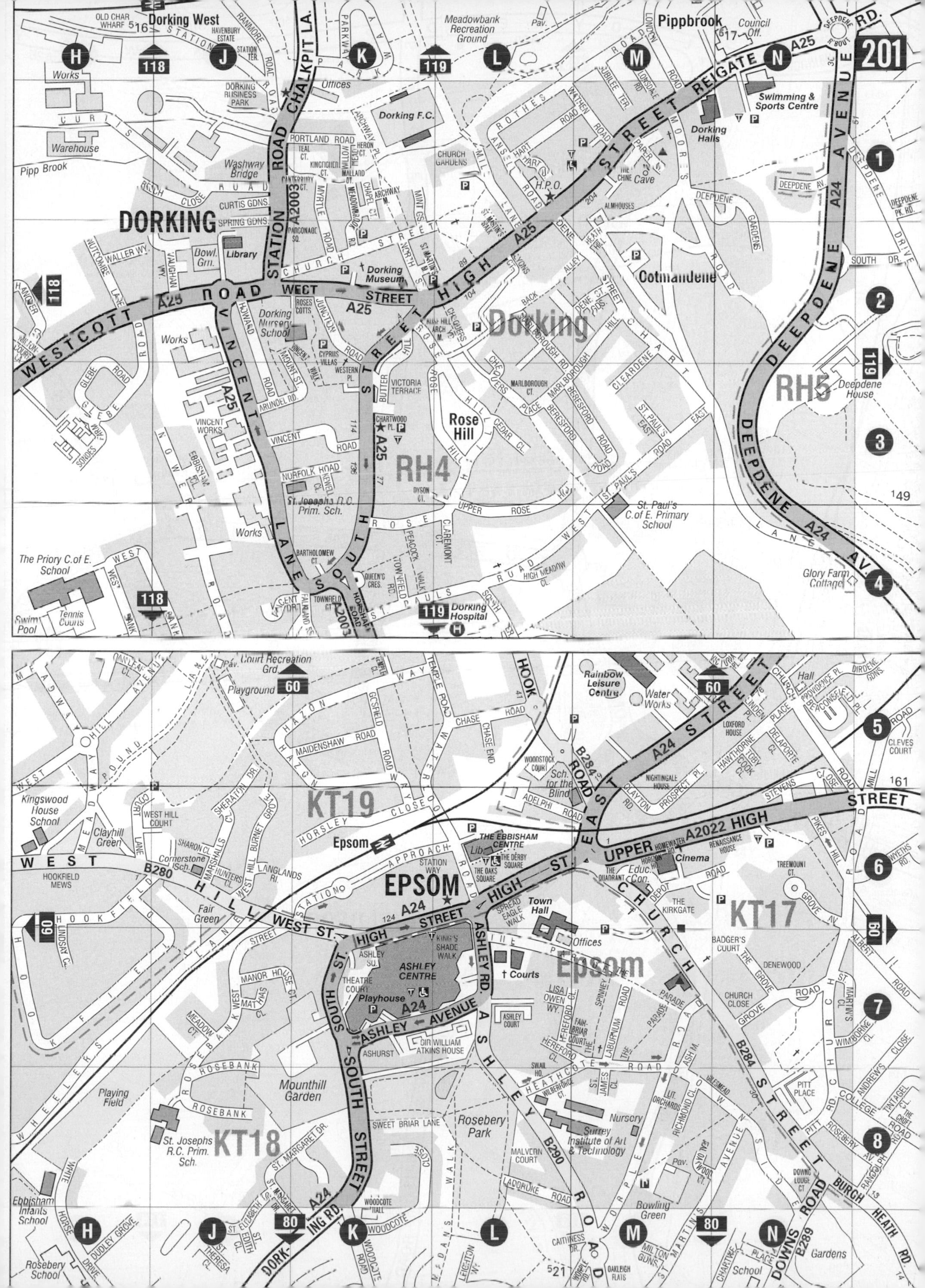
Dorking West
OLD CHAR WHARF
HAVENBURY ESTATE
STATION TER.
118
119
CHALKPIT LA.
Meadowbank Recreation Ground
Pav.
Pippbrook
Council Off.
DEEPDENE R'BOUT
DEEPDENE AVENUE
A24
A25
Works
Warehouse
Pipp Brook
Offices
DORKING BUSINESS PARK
Dorking F.C.
PORTLAND ROAD
Swimming & Sports Centre
Dorking Halls
Washway Bridge
CURTIS GDNS.
SPRING GDNS.
DORKING
Library
Bowl. Grn.
CHURCH GARDENS
H.P.O.
Cave
THE CHINE
ALMSHOUSES
DEEPDENE AV.
DEEPDENE PK. RD.
DEEPDENE GARDENS
SOUTH DR.
Dorking Museum
CHURCH STREET
STATION ROAD
A2003
WESTCOTT ROAD
WEST STREET
HIGH STREET
REIGATE ROAD
Cotmandene
Dorking Nursery School
Dorking
Works
VICTORIA TERRACE
Rose Hill
RH5
Deepdene House
RH4
VINCENT WORKS
VINCENT LANE
VINCENT ROAD
NORFOLK ROAD
St. Josephs R.C. Prim. Sch.
Works
The Priory C.of E. School
Tennis Courts
Swim. Pool
St. Paul's C.of E. Primary School
ST. PAUL'S ROAD
UPPER ROSE HILL
SOUTH STREET
Glory Farm Cottage
Dorking Hospital
DEEPDENE AV.
Court Recreation Grd.
Playground
60
HOOK ROAD
Rainbow Leisure Centre
Water Works
EAST STREET
Kingswood House School
Clayhill Green
WEST HILL COURT
KT19
HORSLEY CLOSE
Epsom
Sch. for the Blind
NIGHTINGALE HOUSE
LOXFORD HOUSE
STREET
A2022 HIGH
UPPER HIGH ST.
THE EBBISHAM CENTRE
Cinema
RENAISSANCE HOUSE
TREEMOUNT CT.
WEST HILL
B280
HOOKFIELD MEWS
Cornerstone Sch.
EPSOM
STATION APPROACH
Fair Green
Town Hall
THE KIRKGATE
KT17
WEST ST.
HIGH STREET
Offices
BADGER'S COURT
DENEWOOD
ASHLEY CENTRE
Playhouse
Courts
Epsom
CHURCH STREET
ASHLEY AVENUE
ASHLEY RD.
SOUTH ST.
ASHLEY COURT
SIR WILLIAM ATKINS HOUSE
ASHURST
CHURCH CLOSE
HEATHCOTE ROAD
B284
ROSEBANK
Mounthill Garden
Playing Field
Rosebery Park
Surrey Institute of Art & Technology
Nursery
St. Josephs R.C. Prim. Sch.
KT18
SOUTH STREET
SWEET BRIAR LANE
MALVERN COURT
B290
Pav.
Bowling Green
Ebbisham Infants School
80
WOODCOTE HALL
DORKING RD.
DOWNS ROAD
B289
BURGH HEATH RD.
Gardens
Rosebery School
School

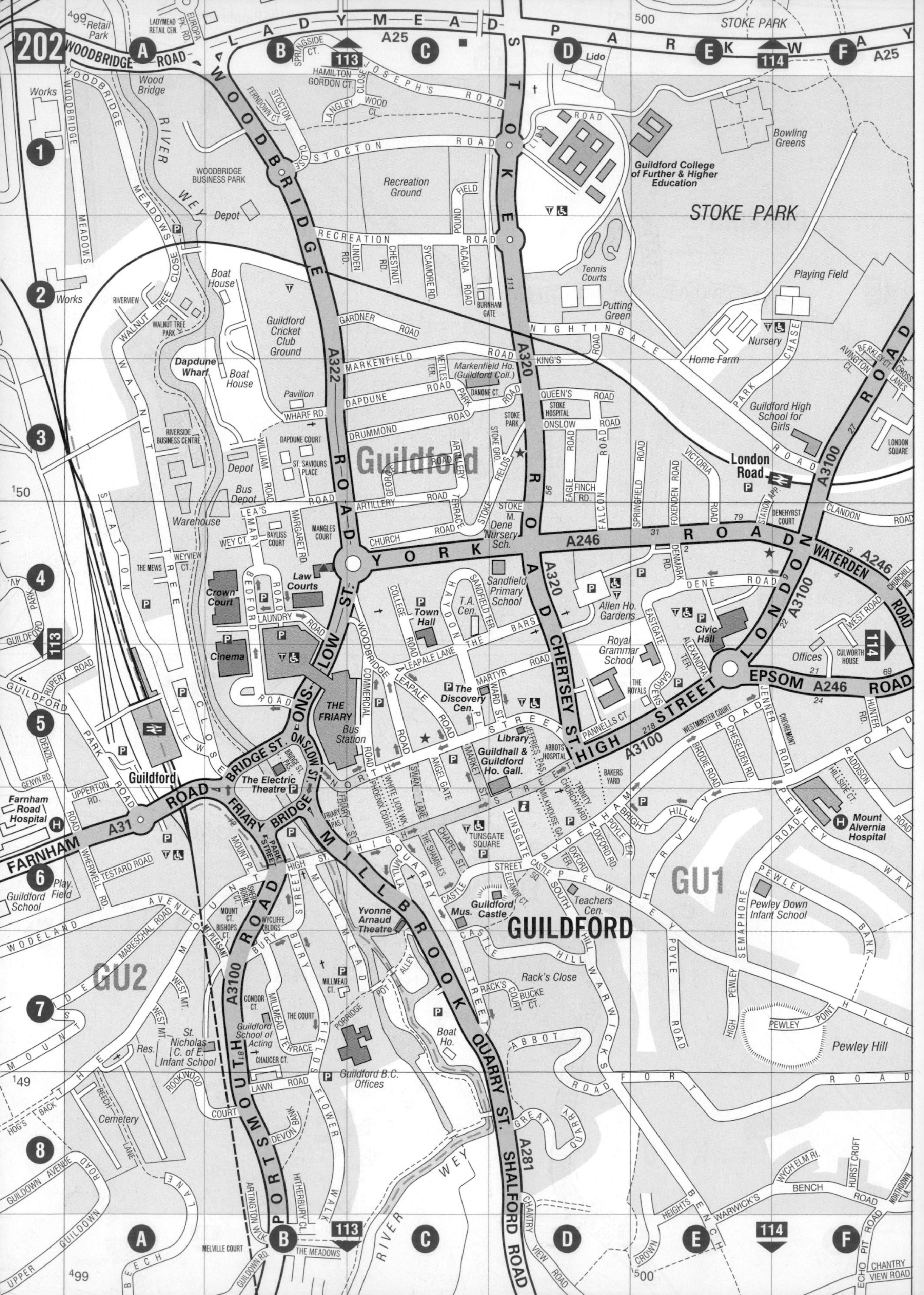

WOODBRIDGE ROAD
LADYMEAD
PARKWAY
A25
STOKE PARK
Lido
113
114
Retail Park
LADYMEAD RETAIL CEN.
EUROPA PK. RD.
SPRINGSIDE CT.
HAMILTON GORDON CT.
JOSEPH'S ROAD
Works
Wood Bridge
RIVER WEY
WOODBRIDGE BUSINESS PARK
Depot
STOCTON ROAD
Recreation Ground
RECREATION ROAD
Guildford College of Further & Higher Education
Bowling Greens
STOKE PARK
Tennis Courts
Putting Green
Playing Field
NIGHTINGALE ROAD
Nursery
Home Farm
PARK CHASE
Guildford High School for Girls
London Road
Boat House
Guildford Cricket Club Ground
GARDNER ROAD
MARKENFIELD ROAD
Markenfield Ho. (Guildford Coll.)
Dapdune Wharf
Pavilion
DAPDUNE ROAD
QUEEN'S ROAD
STOKE HOSPITAL
ONSLOW ROAD
DRUMMOND ROAD
RIVERSIDE BUSINESS CENTRE
Guildford
Depot
Bus Depot
Warehouse
ARTILLERY ROAD
CHURCH ROAD
Stoke Dene Nursery Sch.
YORK ROAD
A246
A322
A320
A3100
WATERDEN ROAD
CLANDON ROAD
Crown Court
Law Courts
Sandfield Primary School
Allen Ho. Gardens
DENE ROAD
Cinema
Town Hall
T.A. Cen.
Royal Grammar School
Civic Hall
Offices
CULWORTH HOUSE
EPSOM ROAD
THE FRIARY
Bus Station
The Discovery Cen.
HIGH STREET
NORTH STREET
Library
Guildhall & Guildford Ho. Gall.
ABBOTS HOSPITAL
Guildford
Farnham Road Hospital
FARNHAM ROAD
A31
BRIDGE ST.
FRIARY BRIDGE
The Electric Theatre
ONSLOW ST.
MILLBROOK
TUNSGATE SQUARE
SYDENHAM ROAD
HARVEY ROAD
Mount Alvernia Hospital
GU1
GU2
Guildford School
Play. Field
Mus.
Guildford Castle
Teachers Cen.
GUILDFORD
Yvonne Arnaud Theatre
Pewley Down Infant School
PEWLEY HILL
Rack's Close
Guildford School of Acting
St. Nicholas C. of E. Infant School
Res.
Guildford B.C. Offices
Boat Ho.
Pewley Hill
FORT ROAD
Cemetery
PORTSMOUTH ROAD
QUARRY ST.
SHALFORD ROAD
A281
A3100
WARWICK'S BENCH
BENCH ROAD
CHANTRY VIEW ROAD
GUILDOWN AVENUE
UPPER GUILDOWN
THE MEADOWS
MELVILLE COURT
A B C D E F
1 2 3 4 5 6 7 8
499
500
150
149

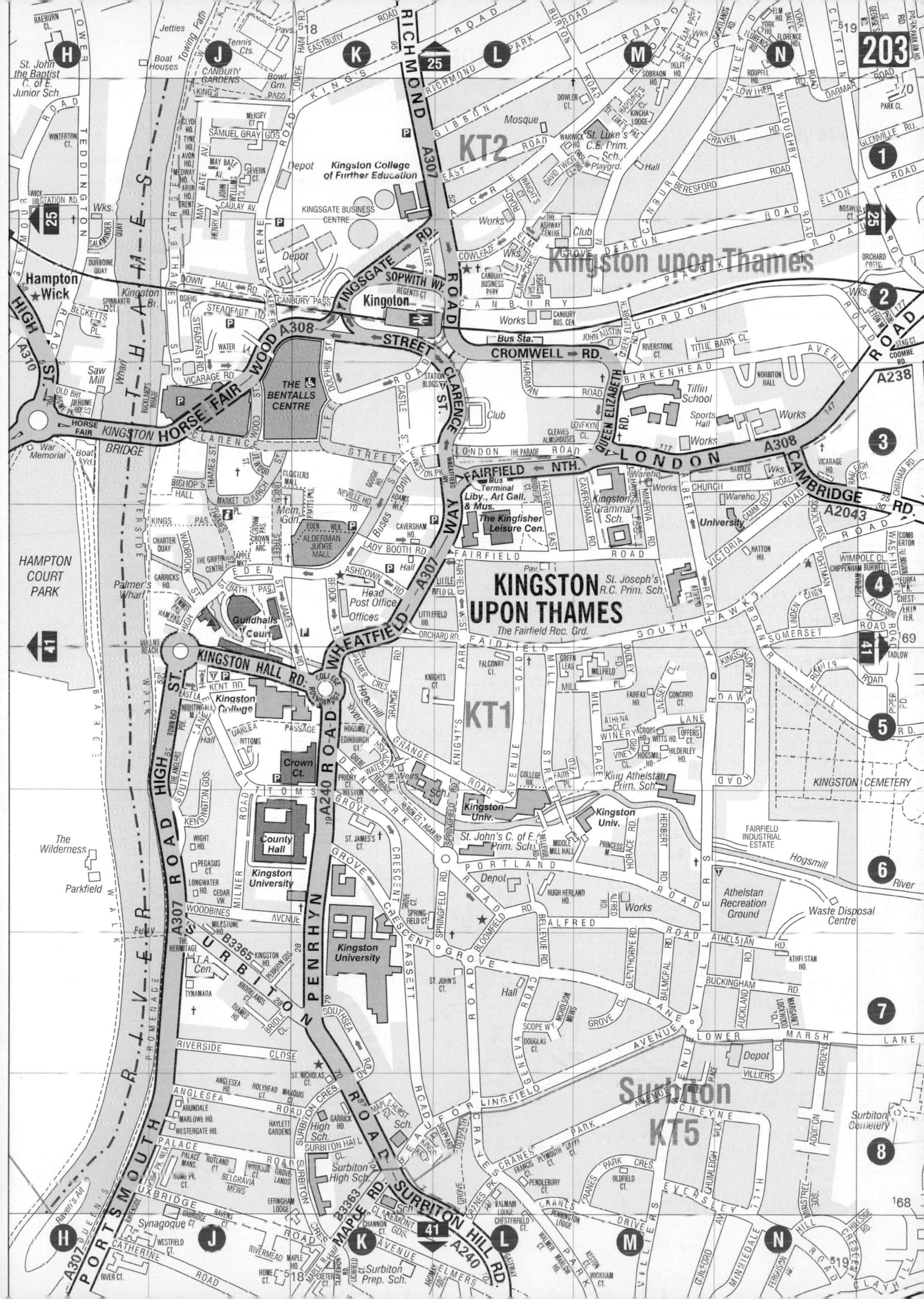
KINGSTON UPON THAMES
Kingston upon Thames
KT2
KT1
KT5
Surbiton
Kingston College of Further Education
THE BENTALLS CENTRE
Kingston
HAMPTON COURT PARK
Hampton Wick
KINGSTON CEMETERY
Tiffin School
Kingston Grammar Sch.
The Kingfisher Leisure Cen.
County Hall
Kingston University
Crown Ct.
Guildhalls Court
Head Post Office Offices
The Fairfield Rec. Grd.
Athelstan Recreation Ground
FAIRFIELD INDUSTRIAL ESTATE
Surbiton High Sch.
RICHMOND ROAD
CLARENCE ST.
WHEATFIELD WAY
PENRHYN ROAD
PORTSMOUTH ROAD
SURBITON HILL RD.
LONDON ROAD
CAMBRIDGE RD.
CROMWELL RD.
HORSE FAIR
KINGSTON HALL RD.
HIGH ST.
A307
A308
A240
A238
A2043
A310
B3365
B3363
25
41
H
J
K
L
M
N
1
2
3
4
5
6
7
8

INDEX

Including Streets, Places & Areas, Industrial Estates, Selected Subsidiary Addresses,
Junction Names and Selected Places of Interest.

HOW TO USE THIS INDEX

1. Each street name is followed by its Posttown or Postal Locality and then by its map reference; e.g. Aaron's Hill. *G'ming* —7E **132** is in the Godalming Posttown and is to be found in square 7E on page **132**. The page number being shown in bold type.
   A strict alphabetical order is followed in which Av., Rd., St., etc. (though abbreviated) are read in full and as part of the street name; e.g. Abbeyfield Clo. appears after Abbey Dri. but before Abbey Gdns.

2. Streets and a selection of Subsidiary names not shown on the Maps, appear in the index in *Italics* with the thoroughfare to which it is connected shown in brackets;
   e.g. *Abbey Pde. SW19 —8A **28** (off Merton High St.)*

3. Places and areas are shown in the index in **bold type**, the map reference to the actual map square in which the Town or Area is located and not to the place name; e.g. **Abbotswood. —1B 114**

4. An example of a selected place of interest is **Abinger Roughs. —8J 117**

5. Map references shown in brackets; e.g. Abbey Rd. *Croy* —9M **45** (4A **200**) refer to entries that also appear on the large scale pages **200-203**

GENERAL ABBREVIATIONS

All : Alley	Cir : Circus	Gt : Great	M : Mews	Sq : Square
App : Approach	Clo : Close	Grn : Green	Mt : Mount	Sta : Station
Arc : Arcade	Comn : Common	Gro : Grove	Mus : Museum	St : Street
Av : Avenue	Cotts : Cottages	Ho : House	N : North	Ter : Terrace
Bk : Back	Ct : Court	Ind : Industrial	Pal : Palace	Trad : Trading
Boulevd : Boulevard	Cres : Crescent	Info : Information	Pde : Parade	Up : Upper
Bri : Bridge	Cft : Croft	Junct : Junction	Pk : Park	Va : Vale
B'way : Broadway	Dri : Drive	La : Lane	Pas : Passage	Vw : View
Bldgs : Buildings	E : East	Lit : Little	Pl : Place	Vs : Villas
Bus : Business	Embkmt : Embankment	Lwr : Lower	Quad : Quadrant	Vis : Visitors
Cvn : Caravan	Est : Estate	Mc : Mac	Res : Residential	Wlk : Walk
Cen : Centre	Fld : Field	Mnr : Manor	Ri : Rise	W : West
Chu : Church	Gdns : Gardens	Mans : Mansions	Rd : Road	Yd : Yard
Chyd : Churchyard	Gth : Garth	Mkt : Market	Shop : Shopping	
Circ : Circle	Ga : Gate	Mdw : Meadow	S : South	

POSTTOWN AND POSTAL LOCALITY ABBREVIATIONS

Ab C : Abinger Common	*Cheam* : Cheam	*Eve* : Eversley	Hyde : Hydestile	*Old Win* : Old Windsor
Ab H : Abinger Hammer	*Chels* : Chelsfield	*Ewe* : Ewell	*If'd* : Ifield	*Old Wok* : Old Woking
Add : Addlestone	*Chel* : Chelsham	*Ewh* : Ewhurst	*Iswth* : Isleworth	*Onsl* : Onslow Village
Alb : Albury	*Cher* : Chertsey	*Ews* : Ewshot	*Itch* : Itchingfield	*Orp* : Orpington
Alder : Aldershot	*Chess* : Chessington	*F'boro* : Farnborough (Kent)	*Iver* : Iver	*Ott* : Ottershaw
Alf : Alfold	*C'fold* : Chiddingfold	*Farn* : Farnborough (Hampshire)	*Jac* : Jacob's Well	*Out* : Outwood
Adgly : Ardingly	*Chil* : Chilworth	*Farnc* : Farncombe	*Kenl* : Kenley	*Owl* : Owlsmoor
Art : Artington	*Chip* : Chipstead	*Farnh* : Farnham	*Kes* : Keston	*Oxs* : Oxshott
Asc : Ascot	*Chob* : Chobham	*Fay* : Faygate	*Kew* : Kew	*Oxt* : Oxted
As : Ash	*C Hosp* : Christs Hospital	*Felb* : Felbridge	*Kingf* : Kingfield	*Pass* : Passfield
Afrd : Ashford	*C Crook* : Church Crookham	*Felc* : Felcourt	*K'fold* : Kingsfold	*Peas P* : Pease Pottage
Ash G : Ash Green	*Churt* : Churt	*Felt* : Feltham	*K'ley* : Kingsley	*Peasl* : Peaslake
Asht : Ashtead	*Clar P* : Claremont Park	*Fern* : Fernhurst	*K Grn* : Kingsley Green	*P'mrsh* : Peasmarsh
Ash W : Ashurst Wood	*Clay* : Claygate	*Fet* : Fetcham	*King T* : Kingston Upon Thames	*Pep H* : Peper Harow
Ash V : Ash Vale	*Cobh* : Cobham	*Finch* : Finchampstead	*Kgswd* : Kingswood	*Pirb* : Pirbright
Bad L : Badshot Lea	*Cold* : Coldharbour	*Fleet* : Fleet	*Kird* : Kirdford	*Plais* : Plaistow
Bag : Bagshot	*Cole H* : Colemans Hatch	*F Grn* : Forest Green	*Knap* : Knaphill	*Prat B* : Pratts Bottom
Bans : Banstead	*Colg* : Colgate	*F Row* : Forest Row	*Knock* : Knockholt	*Purl* : Purley
Bear G : Beare Green	*Coll T* : College Town	*Four E* : Four Elms	*Lale* : Laleham	*P'ham* : Puttenham
Beck : Beckenham	*Coln* : Colnbrook	*Fren* : Frensham	*Langl* : Langley	*Pyr* : Pyrford
Bedd : Beddington	*Comp* : Compton	*Frim* : Frimley	*Lea* : Leatherhead	*Ran C* : Ranmore Common
Bedf : Bedfont	*Copt* : Copthorne	*Frim G* : Frimley Green	*Leigh* : Leigh	*Red* : Redhill
Belm : Belmont	*Coul* : Coulsdon	*Frog* : Frogmore	*Lei H* : Leith Hill	*Reig* : Reigate
B'ley : Bentley	*Cowd* : Cowden	*Gat A* : London Gatwick Airport	*Light* : Lightwater	*Rich* : Richmond
Berr G : Berrys Green	*Cowf* : Cowfold	*G'ming* : Godalming	*Limp* : Limpsfield	*Rip* : Ripley
Bet : Betchworth	*Cran* : Cranford	*God* : Godstone	*Limp C* : Limpsfield Chart	*Rowf* : Rowfant
Bew : Bewbush	*Cranl* : Cranleigh	*Gom* : Gomshall	*Lind* : Lindford	*Rowh* : Rowhook
Big H : Biggin Hill	*Craw* : Crawley	*Gray* : Grayshott	*Ling* : Lingfield	*Rowl* : Rowledge
B'bear : Billingbear	*Craw D* : Crawley Down	*G'wood* : Grayswood	*Lip* : Liphook	*Rud* : Rudgwick
Bil : Billingshurst	*Crock H* : Crockham Hill	*G Str* : Green Street Green	*L Sand* : Little Sandhurst	*Runf* : Runfold
Binf : Binfield	*Cron* : Crondall	*Guild* : Guildford	*Longc* : Longcross	*Rusp* : Rusper
Bisl : Bisley	*Crow* : Crowhurst	*Hack* : Hackbridge	*Lwr Bo* : Lower Bourne	*St G* : St Georges Hill
B'hth : Blackheath	*Crowt* : Crowthorne	*Ham* : Ham	*Lwr E* : Lower Eashing	*St J* : St Johns
Black : Blacknest	*Croy* : Croydon	*Hamb* : Hambledon	*Lwr K* : Lower Kingswood	*Salf* : Salfords
B'water : Blackwater	*Cud* : Cudham	*Hamm* : Hammerwood	*Low H* : Lowfield Heath	*Sand* : Sandhurst
Blet : Bletchingley	*Dat* : Datchet	*Hamp* : Hampton	*Loxh* : Loxhill	*Seale* : Seale
Blind H : Blindley Heath	*Deep* : Deepcut	*Hamp H* : Hampton Hill	*Loxw* : Loxwood	*Send* : Send
Bookh : Bookham	*Dipp* : Dippenhall	*Hamp W* : Hampton Wick	*Lyne* : Lyne	*Shack* : Shackleford
Bord : Bordon	*Dit H* : Ditton Hill	*Hand* : Handcross	*M'bowr* : Maidenbower	*Shalf* : Shalford
Brack : Bracknell	*Dock* : Dockenfield	*Hanw* : Hanworth	*M'head* : Maidenhead	*Sham G* : Shamley Green
Brmly : Bramley	*Dork* : Dorking	*Harm* : Harmondsworth	*Maid G* : Maidens Green	*Sheer* : Sheerwater
Bram : Bramshott	*D'land* : Dormansland	*Hartf* : Hartfield	*Man H* : Mannings Heath	*Shep* : Shepperton
Bram C : Bramshott Chase	*Dor P* : Dormans Park	*Hasc* : Hascombe	*M Grn* : Marsh Green	*Shere* : Shere
Bras : Brasted	*Dor* : Dorney	*Hasl* : Haslemere	*Mayf* : Mayford	*Ship B* : Shipley Bridge
Bren : Brentford	*Dow* : Downe	*Hayes* : Hayes	*Mers* : Merstham	*Short* : Shortlands
Broad H : Broadbridge Heath	*D'side* : Downside	*Head* : Headley (Bordon)	*Mick* : Mickleham	*Shot* : Shottermill
Broadf : Broadfield	*Duns* : Dunsfold	*H'ley* : Headley (Epsom)	*Mid H* : Mid Holmwood	*Shur R* : Shurlock Row
Brock : Brockham	*Earl* : Earlswood	*H'row* : Heathrow	*Milf* : Milford	*Slea* : Sleaford
Brom : Bromley	*E Clan* : East Clandon	*H'row A* : London Heathrow Airport	*Mitc* : Mitcham	*Slin* : Slinfold
Brook : Brook	*E Grin* : East Grinstead	*Head D* : Headley Down	*Mit J* : Mitcham Junction	*Slou* : Slough
Bro I : Brooklands Ind. Est.	*E Hor* : East Horsley	*Hever* : Hever	*Mord* : Morden	*Sly I* : Slyfield Ind. Est.
Bro P : Brooklands Ind. Pk.	*E Mol* : East Molesey	*Hin W* : Hinchley Wood	*Myt* : Mytchett	*Small* : Smallfield
Brkwd : Brookwood	*Eden* : Edenbridge	*Hind* : Hindhead	*New Ad* : New Addington	*S'hall* : Southall
Buck : Buckland	*Eff* : Effingham	*Holm M* : Holmbury St Mary	*Newc* : Newchapel	*S Asc* : South Ascot
Bucks H : Bucks Horn Oak	*Eff J* : Effingham Junction	*Holmw* : Holmwood	*Newd* : Newdigate	*S Croy* : South Croydon
Burp : Burpham	*Egh* : Egham	*Holt P* : Holt Pound	*New H* : New Haw	*S God* : South Godstone
Burs : Burstow	*Elst* : Elstead	*Hkwd* : Hookwood	*N Mald* : New Malden	*S Nut* : South Nutfield
Busb : Busbridge	*Elv* : Elvetham	*Horl* : Horley	*Norm* : Normandy	*S Pk* : South Park
Byfl : Byfleet	*Eng G* : Englefield Green	*Horne* : Horne	*N Asc* : North Ascot	*Swd D* : Southwood Bus. Pk.
Camb : Camberley	*Ent* : Enton	*Hors* : Horsell	*N'chap* : Northchapel	*Stai* : Staines
Capel : Capel	*Eps* : Epsom	*H'ham* : Horsham	*N Holm* : North Holmwood	*Stand* : Standford
Cars : Carshalton	*Esh* : Esher	*Hort* : Horton	*Nutf* : Nutfield	*Stanw* : Stanwell
Cat : Caterham	*Eton* : Eton	*Houn* : Hounslow	*Ock* : Ockham	*Stoke D* : Stoke D'Abernon
Charl : Charlwood	*Eton C* : Eton College	*Hurst* : Hurst	*Ockl* : Ockley	*S'leigh* : Stoneleigh
Chav D : Chavey Down	*Eton W* : Eton Wick	*Hurt* : Hurtmore	*Oke H* : Okewood Hill	*Str G* : Strood Green

Sun : Sunbury-on-Thames
S'dale : Sunningdale
S'hill : Sunninghill
Surb : Surbiton
Sur R : Surrey Research Park
Sutt : Sutton
Sut G : Sutton Green
Tad : Tadworth
Tand : Tandridge
Tap : Taplow
Tats : Tatsfield
Tedd : Teddington
Th Dit : Thames Ditton
T Hth : Thornton Heath
Thorpe : Thorpe
Thor I : Thorpe Ind. Est.
Thur : Thursley
Tilf : Tilford
Tin G : Tinsley Green
T'sey : Titsey
Tong : Tongham
Turn H : Turners Hill
Twic : Twickenham
Up Har : Upper Hartfield
Vir W : Virginia Water
Wall : Wallington
Wal W : Wallis Wood
W on T : Walton-on-Thames
Wanb : Wanborough
Warf : Warfield
Warf P : Warfield Park
Warl : Warlingham
Warn : Warnham
Wel C : Wellington College
W Byf : West Byfleet
W Cla : West Clandon
Westc : Westcott
W Dray : West Drayton
W End : West End
W'ham : Westerham
W Ewe : West Ewell
W Hoa : West Hoathly
W Hor : West Horsley
Westh : Westhumble
W Mol : West Molesey
W Wick : West Wickham
Wey : Weybridge
W'hill : Whitehill
W Vil : Whiteley Village
Whit : Whitton
Whyt : Whyteleafe
W'sham : Windlesham
Wind : Windsor
Wind C : Windsor Castle
Wink : Winkfield
Wink R : Winkfield Row
Wis G : Wisborough Green
Wis : Wisley
Witl : Witley
Wok : Woking
Wokgm : Wokingham
Wold : Woldingham
Won : Wonersh
Wdhm : Woodham
Wood S : Wood Street Village
Wor Pk : Worcester Park
Wmly : Wormley
Worp : Worplesdon
Worp H : Worplesdon Hill
Worth : Worth
Wott : Wotton
Wray : Wraysbury
Wrec : Wrecclesham
Yat : Yateley

INDEX

Aaron's Hill. —7E 132
Aaron's Hill. G'ming —7E 132
Abbess Clo. SW2 —2M 29
Abbetts La. Camb —3N 69
Abbey Chase. Cher —6K 37
Abbey Clo. Brack —4B 32
Abbey Clo. Cranl —8H 155
Abbey Clo. Wok —3G 75
Abbey Clo. Wokgm —1B 30
Abbey Ct. Camb —1B 70
Abbey Ct. Cher —6K 37
Abbey Ct. Farnh —1H 129
Abbey Ct. Hamp —8A 24
Abbey Ct. Stai —3L 37
Abbey Dri. SW17 —6E 28
Abbey Dri. Stai —3L 37
Abbeyfield Clo. Mitc —1C 44
Abbey Gdns. W6 —2K 13
Abbey Gdns. Cher —5J 37
Abbey Grn. Cher —5J 37
Abbey Ind. Est. Mitc —4D 44
Abbey M. Ash W —3H 187
Abbey M. Stai —3L 37
Abbey Pde. SW19 —8A 28
(off Merton High St.)
Abbey Pl. Cher —2J 37
Abbey Rd. SW19 —8A 28
Abbey Rd. Cher —6K 37
Abbey Rd. Croy —9M 45 (4A 200)
Abbey Rd. Shep —7B 38
Abbey Rd. S Croy —6G 64
Abbey Rd. Vir W —4N 35
Abbey Rd. Wok —4M 73
Abbey St. Farnh —1H 129
Abbey Wlk. W Mol —2B 40
Abbey Way. Farn —1A 90
Abbeywood. Ash V —9F 90
Abbeywood. S'dale —6D 34
Abbot Clo. Byfl —9M 55
Abbot Clo. Stai —8M 21
Abbot Rd. Guild —5N 113 (7D 202)
Abbots Av. Eps —7N 59
Abbotsbury. Brack —4L 31
Abbotsbury Ct. H'ham —5L 197
Abbotsbury Rd. Mord —4N 43
Abbots Clo. Fleet —4B 88
Abbot's Clo. Guild —6H 113
Abbots Dri. Vir W —4L 35
Abbotsfield Rd. If'd —4J 181
Abbotsford Clo. Wok —4C 74
Abbots Grn. Croy —3G 65
Abbots Hospital. —5D 202
Abbots Hospital. Guild —5D 202
Abbots La. Kenl —3N 83
Abbotsleigh Clo. Sutt —4N 61
Abbotsleigh Rd. SW16 —5G 28
Abbots Mead. Rich —5K 25
Abbotsmede Clo. Twic —3F 24
Abbots Pk. SW2 —2L 29
Abbot's Ride. Farnh —3K 129
Abbots Ri. Red —1E 122
Abbotstone Rd. SW15 —6H 13
Abbots Wlk. Wind —5B 4
Abbots Way. Cher —6H 37
Abbots Way. Guild —2F 114
Abbotswood. —1B 114
Abbotswood. Guild —1B 114
Abbotswood Clo. Guild —9B 94
Abbotswood Dri. Wey —6E 56
Abbotswood Rd. SW16 —4H 29
Abbott Av. SW20 —9J 27
Abbott Clo. Hamp —7M 23
Abbotts Cotts. Dock —5D 148
Abbotts Rd. Mitc —3G 45
(in two parts)
Abbotts Rd. Sutt —1K 61
Abbott's Tilt. W on T —9M 39
Abbotts Wlk. Cat —9E 84
Abelia Clo. W End —9B 52
Abercairn Rd. SW16 —8G 28
Aberconway Rd. Mord —3N 43
Abercorn Clo. S Croy —9G 64
Abercorn Ho. B'water —5K 69
Abercorn M. Rich —7M 11
Abercorn Way. Wok —5K 73
Aberdare Clo. W Wick —8M 47
Aberdeen Rd. Croy
—1N 63 (7C 200)
Aberdeen Ter. Gray —5B 170
Aberfoyle Rd. SW16 —7H 29
(in two parts)
Abergavenny Gdns. Copt —7A 164
Abingdon. W14 —1L 13
(off Kensington Village)
Abingdon Clo. SW19 —7A 28
Abingdon Clo. Brack —4C 32
Abingdon Clo. Wok —5M 73
Abingdon Rd. SW16 —1J 45
Abingdon Rd. Sand —7H 49
Abinger Av. Sutt —5H 61
Abinger Bottom. —5N 137
Abinger Castle. —2K 137 (5D 202)
Abinger Clo. New Ad —3M 65
Abinger Clo. N Holm —9J 119
Abinger Clo. Wall —2J 63
Abinger Common. —3L 137
Abinger Comn. Rd. Ab C —4M 137
Abinger Ct. Wall —2J 63
Abinger Dri. Red —5C 122
Abinger Gdns. Iswth —6E 10
Abinger Hammer. —8G 116
Abinger Keep. Horl —7G 142
(off Langshott La.)
Abinger La. Ab H —9J 117
Abinger Rd. Lei H —9A 138
Abinger Roughs. —8J 117
Abinger Way. Guild —7D 94
Aboyne Dri. SW20 —1F 42
Aboyne Rd. SW17 —4B 28
Abrahams Rd. Craw —8M 181
Abury La. Brack —5D 32
Acacia Av. Bren —3H 11
Acacia Av. Owl —6J 49
Acacia Av. Shep —4B 38
Acacia Av. Wok —7N 73
Acacia Av. Wray —7A 6
Acacia Clo. SE20 —1D 46
Acacia Clo. Wdhm —6H 55
Acacia Ct. Brack —3N 31
Acacia Dri. Bans —1J 81
Acacia Dri. Sutt —7M 43
Acacia Dri. Wdhm —6H 55
Acacia Gdns. W Wick —8M 47
Acacia Gro. SE21 —3N 29
Acacia Gro. N Mald —2C 42
Acacia M. W Dray —2M 7
Acacia Rd. SW16 —9J 29
Acacia Rd. Beck —2J 47
Acacia Rd. Guild —3N 113 (2C 202)
Acacia Rd. Hamp —7A 24
Acacia Rd. Mitc —1E 44
Acacia Rd. Stai —6K 21
Academy Clo. Camb —7C 50
Academy Gdns. Croy —7C 46
Accommodation La. W Dray —2L 7
(Moor La.)
Accommodation La. W Dray —4J 7
(Old Bath Rd.)
Accommodation Rd. Eps —2F 60
Accommodation Rd. Longc
—9N 35
A.C. Court. Th Dit —5G 40
Ace Pde. Chess —9L 41
Acer Dri. W End —9C 52
Acer Rd. Big H —3F 86
Acfold Rd. SW6 —4N 13
Acheulian Clo. Farnh —4H 129
Achilles Pl. Wok —4M 73
Ackmar Rd. SW6 —4M 13
Ackrells Mead. Sand —6E 48
Acorn Clo. E Grin —1A 186
Acorn Clo. Hamp —7B 24
Acorn Clo. Horl —7G 143
Acorn Dri. Wokgm —1B 30
Acorn Gdns. SE19 —1C 46
Acorn Gro. Hayes —3G 9
Acorn Gro. Tad —2L 101
Acorn Gro. Wok —8A 74
Acorn Keep. Farnh —4J 109
Acorn M. Farn —7M 69
Acorn Rd. B'water —1G 69
Acorns. H'ham —4N 197
Acorns, The. Craw —8N 181
Acorns, The. Small —8M 143
Acorns Way. Esh —2C 58
Acorn Way. Beck —4M 47
Acorn Way. Orp —1K 67
Acre La. Cars & Wall —1E 62
Acre Pas. Wind —4G 4
Acre Rd. SW19 —7B 28
Acre Rd. King T —9L 25 (1L 203)
Acres Gdns. Tad —6J 81
Acres Platt. Cranl —6A 156
Acris St. SW18 —8N 13
Acropolis Ho. King T —5M 203
Acton La. W3 & W4 —1B 12
(in three parts)
Acuba Rd. SW18 —3N 27
Adair Clo. SE25 —2E 46
Adair Wlk. Brkwd —8M 71
Adams Clo. Surb —5M 41
Adams Cft. Brkwd —7N 71
Adams Dri. Fleet —4D 88
Adamson Ct. Craw —8N 181
Adams Pk. Rd. Farnh —8J 109
Adams Rd. Beck —4H 47
Adams Wlk. King T —1L 41 (3K 203)
Adams Way. Croy —5C 46
Adam Wlk. SW6 —3H 13
(off Crabtree La.)
Adare Wlk. SW16 —4K 29
Addington. —2K 65
Addington Clo. Wind —6D 4
Addington Ct. SW14 —6C 12
Addington Heights. New Ad —7M 65
Addington Rd. Croy —7L 45
Addington Rd. S Croy —8D 64
Addington Rd. W Wick —1M 65
Addington Village Rd. Croy —3J 65
(in two parts)
Addiscombe. —7D 46
Addiscombe Av. Croy —7D 46
Addiscombe Ct. Rd. Croy —7B 46
Addiscombe Gro. Croy
—8B 46 (3E 200)
Addiscombe Rd. Crowt —3H 49
Addiscombe Rd. Croy
—8D 46 (3F 200)
Addison Av. Houn —4C 10
Addison Clo. Cat —9A 84
Addison Ct. Guild —5B 114
Addison Gdns. Surb
—3M 41 (8N 203)
Addison Pl. SE25 —3D 46
Addison Rd. SE25 —3D 46
Addison Rd. Cat —8A 84
Addison Rd. Frim —6C 70
Addison Rd. Guild —5A 114 (5F 202)
Addison Rd. Tedd —7H 25
Addison Rd. Wok —4B 74
Addisons Clo. Croy —8J 47
Addison Ter. W4 —1B 12
(off Chiswick Rd.)
Addlestone. —1K 55
Addlestone Moor. —9J 37
Addlestone Moor. Add —8L 37
Addlestone Pk. Add —2K 55
Addlestone Rd. Add & Wey —1N 55
Adecroft Way. W Mol —2C 40
Adela Av. N Mald —4G 42
Adela Ho. W6 —1H 13
(off Queen Caroline St.)
Adelaide Clo. Craw —9B 162
Adelaide Clo. H'ham —4M 197
Adelaide Pl. Wey —1E 56
Adelaide Rd. SW18 —8M 13
Adelaide Rd. Afrd —6M 21
Adelaide Rd. Houn —4M 9
Adelaide Rd. Rich —7M 11
Adelaide Rd. Surb —4L 41
Adelaide Rd. Tedd —7F 24
Adelaide Rd. W on T —9H 39
Adelaide Rd. Wind —4J 5
Adelaide Sq. Wind —5G 4
Adelaide Ter. Bren —1K 11
Adelina M. SW12 —2H 29
Adelphi Clo. M'bowr —5H 183
Adelphi Ct. W4 —2C 12
Adelph Rd. Eps —9C 60 (6L 201)
Adeney Clo. W6 —2J 13
Adlers La. Westh —9G 99
Adlington Pl. Farn —3C 90
Admark Ho. Eps —2A 80
Admiral Ct. Cars —7C 44
Admiral Ho. Tedd —5G 25
Admiral Kepple Ct. Asc —8J 17
Admiral Rd. Craw —6M 181
Admiral's Bri. La. E Grin —7M 185
Admirals Ct. Guild —2D 114
Admirals Rd. Bookh & Fet —6C 98
Admiral's Rd. Pirb —4K 91
Admiral Stirling Ct. Wey —1A 56
Admirals Wlk. Coul —7K 83
Admiral's Wlk. Dork —8B 98
Admiralty Rd. Tedd —7F 24
Admiralty Way. Camb —2L 69
Admiralty Way. Tedd —7F 24
Adrian Ct. Craw —8N 181
Adrian M. SW10 —2N 13
Advance Rd. SE27 —5N 29
Aerodrome Way. Houn —2K 9
Aerospace Boulevd. Farn —6M 89
Agar Clo. Surb —8M 41
Agar Cres. Brack —8N 15
Agar Ho. King T —6K 203
Agars Pl. Dat —2K 5
Agate La. H'ham —3L 197
Agates La. Asht —5K 79
Agincourt. Asc —2N 33
Agnes Scott Ct. Wey —9C 38
(off Palace Dri.)
Agraria Rd. Guild —4L 113
Ailsa Av. Twic —8G 11
Ailsa Clo. Craw —6N 181
Ailsa Rd. Twic —8H 11
Ainger Clo. Alder —1B 110
Ainsdale Way. Wok —5K 73
Ainslie Wlk. SW12 —1F 28
Ainsworth Rd. Croy
—7M 45 (2A 200)
Aintree Clo. Coln —4G 6
Aintree Est. SW6 —3K 13
(off Aintree St.)
Aintree Rd. Craw —5E 182
Aintree St. SW6 —3K 13
Airborne Forces Mus. —8M 89
Airbourne Ho. Wall —1G 62
(off Maldon Rd.)
Aircraft Esplanade. Farn —4A 90
Airedale Av. W4 —1E 12
Airedale Av. S. W4 —1E 12
Airedale Rd. SW12 —1D 28
Air Forces Memorial. —5N 19
Airlinks Ind. Est. Houn —1K 9
Air Pk. Way. Felt —3J 23
Airport Ind. Est. Big H —2F 86
Airport Way. Gat A —2E 162
Airport Way. Stai —7J 7
Aisgill Av. W14 —1L 13
(in two parts)
Aisne Rd. Deep —5J 71
Aitken Clo. Mitc —6D 44
Akabusi Clo. Croy —5D 46
Akehurst Clo. Copt —7L 163
Akehurst St. SW15 —9F 12
Akerman Rd. Surb —5J 41
Alamein Rd. Alder —2N 109
Alanbrooke Clo. Knap —5F 72
Alanbrooke Rd. Alder —7B 90
Alan Hilton Ct. Ott —3F 54
(off Cheshire Clo.)
Alan Rd. SW19 —6K 27
Alan Turing Rd. Sur R —3G 113
Albain Cres. Afrd —3N 21
Albany Clo. SW14 —7A 12
Albany Clo. Esh —5A 58
Albany Clo. Fleet —5C 88
Albany Clo. Reig —9M 101
Albany Ct. Camb —5A 70
Albany Ct. Fleet —4C 88
Albany Cres. Clay —3E 58
Albany M. King T —7K 25
Albany M. Sutt —2N 61
Albany Pde. Bren —2L 11
Albany Pk. Camb —5N 69
Albany Pk. Coln —4F 6
Albany Pk. Ind. Est. Camb —5A 70
Albany Pk. Rd. King T —7K 25
Albany Pk. Rd. Lea —6G 78
Albany Pas. Rich —8L 11
Albany Pl. Egh —5D 20
Albany Reach. Th Dit —4F 40
Albany Rd. SW19 —6N 27
Albany Rd. Bren —2K 11
Albany Rd. Craw —3N 181
Albany Rd. Fleet —5B 88
Albany Rd. N Mald —3C 42
Albany Rd. Old Win —8K 5
Albany Rd. Rich —8M 11
Albany Rd. W on T —1L 57
Albany Rd. Wind —5F 4
Albany Ter. Rich —8M 11
(off Albany Pas.)
Albatross Gdns. S Croy —7G 65
Albemarle. SW19 —3J 27
Albemarle Av. Twic —2N 23
Albemarle Gdns. N Mald —3C 42
Albemarle Pk. Beck —1L 47
Albemarle Rd. Beck —1L 47
Alben Rd. Binf —6H 15
Alberta Av. Sutt —1K 61
Alberta Dri. Small —8L 143
Albert Av. Cher —2J 37
Albert Carr Gdns. SW16 —6J 29
Albert Crane Ct. Craw —1M 181
Albert Dri. SW19 —3K 27
Albert Dri. Stai —6J 21
Albert Dri. Wok —2E 74
Albert Gro. SW20 —9J 27
Albertine Clo. Eps —3G 81
Albert Mans. Croy —1E 200
Albert M. Red —6E 122
Albert Pl. Eton W —1D 4
Albert Rd. SE25 —3D 46
Albert Rd. Add —1M 55
Albert Rd. Alder —2N 109
Albert Rd. Afrd —6A 22
Albert Rd. Asht —5M 79
Albert Rd. Bag —6J 51
Albert Rd. Brack —9N 15
Albert Rd. Crowt —2G 49
Albert Rd. Eng G —7N 19
Albert Rd. Eps —9E 60 (7N 201)
Albert Rd. Farn —3A 90
Albert Rd. Hamp H —6C 24
Albert Rd. Horl —7F 142
Albert Rd. Houn —7A 10
Albert Rd. King T —1M 41 (3M 203)
Albert Rd. Mitc —2D 44
Albert Rd. N Mald —3E 42
Albert Rd. Red —7G 102
Albert Rd. Rich —8L 11
Albert Rd. Sutt —2B 62
Albert Rd. Tedd —7F 24
Albert Rd. Twic —2F 24
Albert Rd. Warl —4J 85
Albert Rd. Wind & Old Win —6G 5
Albert Rd. Wokgm —3A 30
Albert Rd. N. Reig —2L 121
Albert Rd. S. Reig —2L 121
Albert St. Fleet —5A 88
Albert St. Wind —4E 4
Albert Wlk. Crowt —2G 49
Albery Clo. H'ham —4H 197
Albion Clo. Craw —4H 183
Albion Cotts. Holm M —5K 137
Albion Ct. W6 —1G 13
(off Albion Pl.)
Albion Ho. Slou —1D 6
Albion Ho. Wok —4B 74
Albion M. W6 —1G 13
Albion Pl. SE25 —2D 46
Albion Pl. W6 —1G 13
Albion Pl. Wind —5D 4
Albion Rd. Houn —7A 10
Albion Rd. King T —9B 26
Albion Rd. Reig —4A 122
Albion Rd. Sand —8G 49
Albion Rd. Sutt —3B 62
Albion Rd. Twic —2E 24
Albion St. Croy —7M 45 (1A 200)
Albion Way. Eden —9K 127
Albion Way. H'ham —7H 197
Albury. —8K 115
Albury Av. Iswth —3F 10
Albury Av. Sutt —5H 61
Albury Clo. Eps —5A 60
Albury Clo. Hamp —7B 24
Albury Clo. Longc —9K 35
Albury Cotts. As —2G 111
Albury Ct. Mitc —1B 44
Albury Ct. S Croy —7B 200
Albury Ct. Sutt —1A 62
Albury Heath. —1M 135
Albury Ho. Guild —5B 114

Ansteadbrook—Ash St.

Ansteadbrook. —3N 189
Anstice Clo. W4 —3D 12
Anstiebury Clo. Bear G —8J 139
Anstie Grange Dri. Holmw —6G 139
Anstie La. Cold —6E 138
Anston Ct. Guild —3H 113
Anthony Rd. SE25 —5D 46
Anthonys. —8C 54
Anthony Wall. Warf —9D 16
Anthony W. Ho. Brock —5A 120
Antlands La. Ship B —4J 163
Antlands La. E. Ship B —4K 163
Antlands La. W. Ship B —4J 163
Anton Cres. Sutt —9M 43
Antrobus Clo. Sutt —2L 61
Anvil Clo. SW16 —8G 28
Anvil La. Cobh —1H 77
Anvil Rd. Sun —2H 39
Anyards Rd. Cobh —9J 57
Anzio Clo. Alder —2M 109
Apeldoorn Dri. Wall —5J 63
Aperdele Rd. Lea —5G 79
Aperfield. —4G 87
Aperfield Rd. Big H —4G 87
Aperfields. Big H —4G 86
Apers Av. Wok —8B 74
Apex Clo. Wey —9E 38
Apex Corner. (Junct.) —4N 23
Apex Dri. Frim —5B 70
Apex Retail Pk. Felt —4N 23
Apley Rd. Reig —6M 121
Aplin Way. Iswth —4E 10
Aplin Way. Light —7L 51
Apollo Dri. Bord —7A 168
Apollo Pl. St J —6K 73
Apollo Ri. Swd B —1H 89
Apostle Way. T Hth —1M 45
Apperlie Dri. Horl —1G 162
Appleby Clo. Twic —3D 24
Appleby Gdns. Felt —2G 22
Appleby Ho. Eps —7C 60
Appledore. Brack —5L 31
Appledore Clo. SW17 —3D 28
Appledore M. Farn —7M 69
Appledown Ri. Coul —2G 83
Applefield. Craw —2C 182
Apple Gth. Bren —1K 11
Applegarth. Clay —2F 58
Applegarth. G'ming —4G 132
Applegarth. New Ad —4L 65
(in two parts)
Applegarth Av. Guild —3G 112
Apple Gro. Chess —1L 59
Applelands Clo. Wrec —7F 128
Apple Mkt. King T —1K 41 (1J 203)
Appleton Gdns. N Mald —5F 42
Appleton Sq. Mitc —9C 28
Apple Tree Clo. Fet —2C 98
Appletree Clo. G'ming —9J 133
Appletree Ct. Guild —9E 94
Appletree Pl. Brack —9M 15
Appletrees Pl. Wok —6M 73
Apple Tree Way. Owl —6J 49
Appley Ct. Camb —1N 69
Appley Dri. Camb —9N 49
Approach Rd. SW20 —1H 43
Approach Rd. Afrd —7D 22
Approach Rd. Farnh —2H 129
Approach Rd. Purl —8L 63
Approach Rd. Tats —1D 106
Approach Rd. W Mol —4A 40
Approach, The. Bookh —1M 97
Approach, The. Dor P —4B 166
April Clo. Asht —5M 79
April Clo. Camb —4A 70
April Clo. Felt —4H 23
April Clo. H'ham —4J 197
Aprilwood Clo. Wdhm —7H 55
Apsey Ct. Binf —8K 15
Apsley Ct. Craw —5L 181
Apsley Ho. Houn —7N 9
Apsley Rd. SE25 —3E 46
Apsley Rd. N Mald —2B 42
Aquarius. Twic —2H 25
Aquarius Ct. Craw —5K 181
Aquila Clo. Lea —8L 79
Arabella Dri. SW15 —7D 12
Aragon Av. Eps —6G 60
Aragon Av. Th Dit —4F 40
Aragon Clo. New Ad —6A 66
Aragon Clo. Sun —7G 22
Aragon Ct. Brack —3A 32
Aragon Ct. E Mol —3C 40
Aragon Rd. King T —6L 25
Aragon Rd. Mord —5J 43
Aragon Rd. Yat —2B 68
Aragon Wlk. Byfl —9A 56
Aram Ct. Wok —2E 74
Aran Ct. Wey —8E 38
Arbor Clo. Beck —1L 47
Arborfield Clo. SW2 —2K 29
Arbour Clo. Fet —1F 98
Arbour, The. Hurt —2C 132
Arbrook Chase. Esh —3C 58
Arbrook La. Esh —3C 58
Arbury Ct. SE20 —1F 46
Arbutus Clo. Red —5A 122
Arbutus Rd. Red —6A 122
Arcade. Croy —8N 45 (3C 200)
Arcade Pde. Chess —2K 59
Arcade, The. Alder —2M 109
Arcade, The. Croy —4C 200
Arcade, The. Wokgm —2B 30
Arcadia Clo. Cars —1E 62
Archaeological Con. —3J 51
Archbishop's Pl. SW2 —1K 29
Archdale Pl. King T —2A 42
Archel Rd. W14 —2L 13
Archer Clo. King T —8L 25
Archer M. Hamp H —7C 24
Archer Rd. SE25 —3F 46
Archers Ct. Craw —1B 182
Archers Ct. S Croy —8B 200
Arches, The. Wind —4F 4
(off Goswell Rd.)
Arch Rd. W on T —9L 39
Archway Clo. SW19 —4N 27
Archway Clo. Wall —9H 45
Archway M. Dork —4G 119 (1K 201)
Archway Pl. Dork —4G 119 (1K 201)
Archway St. SW13 —6D 12
Arcturus Rd. Craw —6K 181
Arden Clo. Brack —1D 32
Arden Clo. Reig —7N 121
Arden Gro. Orp —1K 67
Arden Rd. Craw —5D 182
Ardenrun. —3L 145
Ardent Clo. SE25 —2B 46
Ardesley Wood. Wey —1F 56
Ardfern Av. SW16 —2L 45
Ardingly. Brack —5M 31
Ardingly Clo. Craw —1N 181
Ardingly Clo. Croy —9G 47
Ardingly Rd. W Hoa —9E 184
Ardleigh Gdns. Sutt —6M 43
Ardlui Rd. SE27 —3N 29
Ardmay Gdns. Surb —4L 41 (8K 203)
Ardmore Av. Guild —1L 113
Ardmore Ho. Guild —1L 113
Ardmore Way. Guild —1L 113
Ardrossan Av. Camb —2E 70
Ardrossan Gdns. Wor Pk —9F 42
Ardshiel Clo. SW15 —6J 13
Ardshiel Dri. Red —5C 122
Ardwell Clo. Crowt —2D 48
Ardwell Rd. SW2 —3J 29
Arena La. Alder —9J 89
Arenal Dri. Crowt —4G 49
Arethusa Way. Bisl —3C 72
Arford. —3E 168
Arford Comn. Head —3E 168
Arford Rd. Head —4F 168
Argent Clo. Egh —7E 20
Argent Ct. Chess —9N 41
Argente Clo. Fleet —1C 88
Argent Ter. Coll T —7K 49
Argon M. SW6 —3M 13
Argosy Gdns. Stai —7H 21
Argosy La. Stanw —1M 21
Argus Wlk. Craw —6M 181
Argyle Av. Houn —9A 10
(in two parts)
Argyle Pl. W6 —1G 13
Argyle Rd. Houn —8B 10
Argyle St. Brkwd —8L 71
Ariel Way. Houn —6J 9
Arkell Gro. SE19 —8M 29
Arkendale. Felb —6K 165
Arklow M. Surb —8L 41
Ark, The. W6 —1J 13
(off Talgarth Rd.)
Arkwright Dri. Brack —1J 31
Arkwright Ho. SW2 —1J 29
(off Streatham Pl.)
Arkwright Rd. Coln —5G 6
Arkwright Rd. S Croy —6C 64
Arlesey Clo. SW15 —8K 13
Arlington Bus. Pk. Brack —1M 31
Arlington Clo. Brack —9M 15
Arlington Clo. Sutt —8M 43
Arlington Clo. Twic —9J 11
Arlington Ct. Hayes —1F 8
Arlington Ct. Reig —1N 121
Arlington Dri. Cars —8D 44
Arlington Gdns. W4 —1B 12
Arlington Lodge. Wey —1C 56
Arlington M. Twic —9H 11
Arlington Pk. Mans. W4 —1B 12
(off Sutton La. N.)
Arlington Pas. Tedd —5F 24
Arlington Rd. Afrd —6A 22
Arlington Rd. Rich —3K 25
Arlington Rd. Surb —5K 41
Arlington Rd. Tedd —5F 24
Arlington Rd. Twic —9J 11
Arlington Sq. Brack —1M 31
Arlington Ter. Alder —2L 109
Armadale Rd. SW6 —3M 13
Armadale Rd. Felt —8H 9
Armadale Rd. Wok —4K 73
Armfield Clo. W Mol —4N 39
Armfield Cres. Mitc —1D 44
Armistice Gdns. SE25 —2D 46
Armitage Ct. Asc —5N 33
Armitage Dri. Frim —5D 70
Armoury Way. SW18 —8M 13
Armstrong Clo. W on T —5H 39
Armstrong Mall. Swd B —1J 89
Armstrong Rd. Eng G —7M 19
Armstrong Rd. Felt —6M 23
Armstrong Way. Farn —4G 88
Army Physical Training Corps Mus.
(off Queen's Av.) —8N 89
Armytage Rd. Houn —3L 9
Arnal Cres. SW18 —1K 27
Arncliffe. Brack —4M 31
Arndale Wlk. SW18 —8N 13
Arndale Way. Egh —6C 20
Arne Clo. Craw —6L 181
Arne Gro. Horl —6C 142
Arnewood Clo. SW15 —2F 26
Arnewood Clo. Oxs —1B 78
Arneys La. Mitc —6E 44
Arnfield Clo. If'd —4K 181
Arnhem Barracks. Alder —9M 89
Arnhem Clo. Alder —2N 109
Arnhem Dri. New Ad —7N 65
Arnison Rd. E Mol —3D 40
Arnold Cres. Iswth —8D 10
Arnold Dri. Chess —3K 59
Arnold Mans. W14 —2L 13
(off Queen's Club Gdns.)
Arnold Rd. SW17 —8D 28
Arnold Rd. Stai —8L 21
Arnold Rd. Wok —2D 74
Arnott Clo. W4 —1C 12
Arnulls Rd. SW16 —7M 29
Arodene Rd. SW2 —1K 29
Arosa Rd. Twic —9K 11
(in two parts)
Arragon Gdns. SW16 —8J 29
Arragon Gdns. W Wick —9L 47
Arragon Rd. SW18 —2M 27
Arragon Rd. Twic —1G 24
Arran Clo. Craw —6N 181
Arran Clo. Wall —1F 62
Arran Ct. H'ham —6G 197
Arran Way. Esh —8B 40
Arras Av. Mord —4A 44
Arreton Mead. Hors —1B 74
Arrivals Rd. Gat A —2D 162
(off Gatwick Way)
Arrol Rd. Beck —2F 46
Arrow Ct. SW5 —1M 13
(off W. Cromwell Rd.)
Arrow Ind. Est. Farn —3L 89
Arrow Rd. Farn —3L 89
Artel Cft. Craw —3E 182
Arterberry Rd. SW20 —8H 27
Arthur Clo. Bag —6J 51
Arthur Clo. Farnh —2G 129
Arthur Ct. Croy —4F 200
Arthur Henderson Ho. SW6 —5L 13
(off Fulham Rd.)
Arthur Rd. SW19 —6L 27
Arthur Rd. Big H —2E 86
Arthur Rd. Farnh —2G 129
(in two parts)
Arthur Rd. H'ham —7K 197
Arthur Rd. If'd —3K 181
Arthur Rd. King T —8N 25
Arthur Rd. N Mald —4G 43
Arthur Rd. Wind —4E 4
Arthur's Bri. Rd. Wok —4M 73
Arthur's Bri. Wharf. Wok —4N 73
Arthurstone Birches. Binf —6J 15
Arthur St. Alder —2N 109
Artillery Rd. Alder —2N 109
(High St.)
Artillery Rd. Alder —6B 90
(North Rd.)
Artillery Rd. Guild —4N 113 (4C 202)
Artillery Ter. Guild —3N 113 (3C 202)
Artington. —8M 113
Artington Clo. Orp —1L 67
Artington Wlk. Guild
—6M 113 (8B 202)
Artslink Theatre. —9B 48
(off Reading Rd.)
Arun Ct. SE25 —4D 46
Arundale. King T —8J 203
Arundel Av. Eps —6G 60
Arundel Av. Mord —3L 43
Arundel Av. S Croy —6D 64
Arundel Clo. Craw —3G 182
Arundel Clo. Croy —9M 45
Arundel Clo. Fleet —5C 88
Arundel Clo. Hamp H —6B 24
Arundel Clo. Pass —9C 168
Arundel Ct. Brom —1N 47
Arundel Ho. Croy —8D 200
Arundel Mans. SW6 —4L 13
(off Kelvedon Rd.)
Arundel Pl. Farnh —1G 128
Arundel Rd. Camb —2G 70
Arundel Rd. Croy —5A 46
Arundel Rd. Dork —5G 118 (3J 201)
Arundel Rd. Houn —6K 9
Arundel Rd. King T —1A 42
Arundel Rd. Sutt —4L 61
Arundel Ter. SW13 —2G 13
Arun Ho. King T —9K 25 (1J 203)
Arunside. H'ham —7G 196
Arun Way. H'ham —7L 197
Aschurch Rd. Croy —6C 46
Ascot. —3L 33
Ascot Ct. Alder —3M 109
Ascot Heath. —1K 33
Ascot M. Wall —5G 63
Ascot Pk. Asc —2H 33
Ascot Rd. SW17 —7E 28
Ascot Rd. Felt —2B 22
Ascot Rd. M'head & Warf —1B 16
Ascot Wood Pl. Asc —2L 33
Ash. —9E 90
Ashbourne. Brack —5L 31
Ashbourne Clo. As —1G 110
Ashbourne Clo. Coul —5G 83
Ashbourne Ct. As —1G 110
Ashbourne Gro. W4 —1D 12
Ashbourne Ri. Orp —1M 67
Ashbourne Rd. Mitc —8E 28
Ashbourne Ter. SW19 —8L 27
Ash Bri. Cvn. Pk. As —4C 110
Ashbrook Rd. Old Win —1L 19
Ashburnham Ct. Beck —1M 47
Ashburnham Pk. Esh —1C 58
Ashburnham Rd. SW10 —3N 13
Ashburnham Rd. Craw —5E 182
Ashburnham Rd. Rich —4H 25
Ashburn Pl. SW7 —1N 13
Ashburton Av. Croy —7E 46
Ashburton Clo. Croy —7D 46
Ashburton Enterprise Cen. SW15
—9H 13
Ashburton Gdns. Croy —8D 46
Ashburton Memorial Homes. Croy
—6E 46
Ashburton Rd. Croy —8D 46
Ashbury Cres. Guild —1E 114
Ashbury Dri. B'water —5M 69
Ashbury Pl. SW19 —7A 28
Ashby Av. Chess —3N 59
Ashby Ct. H'ham —6L 197
Ashby Wlk. Croy —5N 45
Ashby Way. W Dray —3B 8
Ash Chu. Rd. As —2F 110
Ash Clo. SE20 —1F 46
Ash Clo. As —1F 110
Ash Clo. B'water —1H 69
Ash Clo. Cars —8D 44
Ash Clo. Craw D —1F 184
Ash Clo. Eden —2K 147
Ash Clo. Ling —6A 146
Ash Clo. N Mald —1C 42
Ash Clo. Pyr —2J 75
Ash Clo. Red —8G 103
Ash Clo. Tad —9B 100
Ash Clo. Wok —7A 74
Ash Combe. C'fold —5D 172
Ashcombe Av. Surb —6K 41
Ashcombe Dri. Eden —8K 127
Ashcombe Rd. SW19 —6M 27
Ashcombe Rd. Cars —3E 62
Ashcombe Rd. Dork —3G 118
Ashcombe Rd. Red —5G 102
Ashcombe Sq. N Mald —2B 42
Ashcombe St. SW6 —5N 13
Ashcombe Ter. Tad —7G 80
Ash Ct. SW19 —8K 27
Ash Ct. Add —2K 55
Ash Ct. Eps —1B 60
Ash Ct. Wokgm —2B 30
Ashcroft. Shalf —1A 134
Ashcroft Pk. Cobh —8M 57
Ashcroft Ri. Coul —3J 83
Ashcroft Rd. Chess —9M 41
Ashcroft Sq. W6 —1H 13
Ashdale. Bookh —4C 98
Ashdale Clo. Stai —3N 21
Ashdale Clo. Twic —1C 24
Ashdale Pk. Finch —1B 48
Ashdale Way. Twic —1B 24
Ashdene Clo. Afrd —8D 22
Ashdene Cres. As —1E 110
Ashdene Rd. As —1E 110
Ashdown Av. Farn —2B 90
Ashdown Clo. Beck —1L 47
Ashdown Clo. Brack —1E 32
Ashdown Clo. F Row —7J 187
Ashdown Clo. Reig —7N 121
Ashdown Ct. Craw —6D 182
Ashdown Ct. Sutt —3A 62
Ashdown Dri. Craw —6D 182
Ashdown Gdns. S Croy —2E 84
Ashdown Ga. E Grin —8M 165
Ashdown Pl. F Row —9G 186
Ashdown Pl. Th Dit —6G 40
Ashdown Rd. Eps —9E 60
Ashdown Rd. F Row —7H 187
Ashdown Rd. King T —1L 41 (4K 203)
Ashdown Rd. Reig —7N 121
Ashdown Vw. E Grin —2A 186
Ashdown Way. SW17 —3E 28
Ash Dri. Red —5E 122
Ashe Ho. Twic —9K 11
Ashenden Rd. Guild —3J 113
Ashen Gro. SW19 —4M 27
Ashen Va. S Croy —5G 65
Asher Dri. Asc —9G 17
Ashfield Av. Felt —2J 23
Ashfield Clo. Rich —2L 25
Ashfield Grn. Yat —1E 68
Ashfield Ho. W14 —1L 13
Ashfields Ct. Reig —1N 121
Ashford. —5A 22
Ashford Av. Afrd —7C 22
Ashford Bus. Complex. Afrd —6D 22
(Sandell's Av.)
Ashford Bus. Complex. Afrd —5D 22
(Shield Rd.)
Ashford Clo. Afrd —5N 21
Ashford Common. —8E 22
Ashford Cres. Afrd —4N 21
Ashford Gdns. Cobh —3L 77
Ashford Park. —5M 21
Ashford Rd. Afrd —8D 22
Ashford Rd. Felt —5E 22
Ashford Rd. Stai —1L 37
Ash Green. —4G 111
Ash Grn. La. E. Ash G —4G 111
(in two parts)
Ash Grn. La. W. Tong & Ash
(in two parts) —4D 110
Ash Grn. Rd. Ash G —3G 110
Ash Gro. SE20 —1F 46
Ash Gro. Felt —2F 22
Ash Gro. Guild —3K 113
Ash Gro. Houn —4L 9
Ash Gro. Stai —7L 21
Ash Gro. W Wick —8M 47
Ashgrove Rd. Afrd —6D 22
Ash Hill Rd. As —9E 90
Ashington Rd. SW6 —5L 13
Ash Keys. Craw —4C 182
Ashlake Rd. SW16 —5J 29
Ash La. Elst —9G 130
Ash La. Wind —5A 4
Ashleigh Av. Egh —8E 20
Ashleigh Clo. Horl —8D 142
Ashleigh Cotts. Holmw —4H 139
Ashleigh Gdns. Sutt —8N 43
Ashleigh Rd. SE20 —2E 46
Ashleigh Rd. SW14 —6D 12
Ashleigh Rd. H'ham —3J 197
Ashley Av. Eps —9C 60 (7K 201)
Ashley Av. Mord —4M 43
Ashley Cen. Eps —9C 60 (7K 201)
Ashley Clo. Bookh —3N 97
Ashley Clo. Frim G —8E 70
Ashley Clo. W on T —7G 38
Ashley Ct. Eps —9C 60 (7L 201)
Ashley Ct. Wok —5J 73
Ashley Dri. Bans —1M 81
Ashley Dri. B'water —2H 69
Ashley Dri. Iswth —2F 10
Ashley Dri. Twic —2B 24
Ashley Dri. W on T —9H 39
Ashley Gdns. Orp —2N 67
Ashley Gdns. Rich —3K 25
Ashley Gdns. Shalf —1B 134
Ashley Ho. G'ming —3H 133
Ashley La. Croy —1M 63 (7A 200)
Ashley Park. —9H 39
Ashley Pk. Av. W on T —8G 39
Ashley Pk. Cres. W on T —7H 39
Ashley Pk. Rd. W on T —8H 39
Ashley Ri. W on T —1G 57
Ashley Rd. SW19 —7N 27
Ashley Rd. Eps —9C 60 (7L 201)
Ashley Rd. Farn —1B 90
Ashley Rd. Hamp —9A 24
Ashley Rd. Rich —6L 11
Ashley Rd. Th Dit —5F 40
Ashley Rd. T Hth —3K 45
Ashley Rd. W on T —1G 57
Ashley Rd. Westc —6C 118
Ashley Rd. Wok —5J 73
Ashley Sq. Eps —7K 201
Ashley Way. W End —9A 52
Ashling Rd. Croy —7D 46
Ash Lodge Clo. As —3E 110
Ash Lodge Dri. As —3E 110
(in two parts)
Ashlone Rd. SW15 —6H 13
Ashlyns Pk. Cobh —9M 57
Ashlyns Way. Chess —3K 59
Ashmead Rd. Felt —2H 23
Ashmere Av. Beck —1N 47
Ashmere Clo. Sutt —2J 61
Ash M. Eps —9D 60 (7M 201)
Ashmore Ct. Houn —2A 10
Ashmore Ho. Craw —9B 162
Ashmore La. Kes —7E 66
Ashmore La. Rusp —3B 180
Ashmore La. Wind —1D 16
Ashridge. Farn —7L 69
Ashridge Grn. Brack —9N 15
Ashridge Rd. Wokgm —9C 14
Ashridge Way. Mord —2L 43
Ashridge Way. Sun —7H 23
Ash Rd. Alder —3A 110
Ash Rd. Craw —2E 182
Ash Rd. Croy —8K 47
Ash Rd. Pirb —4C 92
Ash Rd. Shep —3B 38
Ash Rd. Sutt —6K 43
Ash Rd. W'ham —3M 107
Ash Rd. Wok —7N 73
Ash St. As —3D 110

Ashtead—Balgowan Clo.

Ashtead. —5M 79
Ashtead Gap. Lea —3H 79
Ashtead La. G'ming —9F 132
Ashtead Park. —5N 79
Ashtead Woods Rd. Asht —4J 79
Ashton Clo. Sutt —1M 61
Ashton Clo. W on T —3J 57
Ashton Gdns. Houn —7N 9
Ashton Rd. Wok —4J 73
Ashtree Av. Mitc —1B 44
Ash Tree Clo. Croy —5H 47
Ash Tree Clo. Farn —2H 89
Ash Tree Clo. G'wood —8K 171
Ashtree Clo. Orp —1K 67
Ash Tree Clo. Surb —8L 41
Ashtrees. Cranl —9N 155
Ash Tree Way. Croy —4G 47
Ashurst. Eps —1C 80 (7K 201)
Ashurst Clo. SE20 —1E 46
Ashurst Clo. H'ham —3N 197
Ashurst Clo. Kenl —2A 84
Ashurst Dri. Craw —3H 183
Ashurst Dri. Shep —4N 37
Ashurst Dri. Tad —8A 100
Ashurst Gdns. SW2 —2L 29
Ashurst Pk. Asc —2A 34
Ashurst Rd. Ash V —9D 90
Ashurst Rd. Tad —8G 81
Ashurst Wlk. Croy —8E 46
Ashurstwood. —3F 186
Ash Vale. —6E 90
Ash Va. C'fold —4D 172
Ashvale Rd. SW17 —6D 28
Ash Vw. Clo. Afrd —7N 21
Ash Vw. Gdns. Afrd —6N 21
Ashville Way. Wokgm —3A 30
Ashway Cen., The. King T —9L 25 (2L 203)
Ashwell Av. Camb —9D 50
Ashwick Clo. Cat —2D 104
Ashwindham Ct. Wok —5J 73
Ashwood. Craw —4B 182
Ashwood. Warl —7F 84
Ashwood Gdns. New Ad —3L 65
Ashwood Pk. Fet —1C 98
Ashwood Pk. Wok —5C 74
Ashwood Rd. Eng G —7L 19
Ashwood Rd. Wok —5B 74
Ashworth Est. Croy —7J 45
Ashworth Pl. Guild —3J 113
Askill Dri. SW15 —8K 13
Aslett St. SW18 —1N 27
Asmar Clo. Coul —2J 83
Aspen Clo. Guild —9F 94
Aspen Clo. Stai —4H 21
Aspen Clo. Stoke D —3M 77
Aspen Ct. Vir W —3A 36
Aspen Gdns. W6 —1G 13
Aspen Gdns. Afrd —6D 22
Aspen Gdns. Mitc —4E 44
Aspenlea Rd. W6 —2J 13
Aspen Sq. Wey —9E 38
Aspen Va. Whyt —5C 84
Aspen Way. Bans —1J 81
Aspen Way. Felt —4J 23
Aspen Way. H'ham —4L 197
Aspin Way. B'water —1G 68
Aspley Rd. SW18 —8N 13
Asprey Gro. Cat —2E 104
Assembly Wlk. Cars —6C 44
Assher Rd. W on T —9M 39
Astede Pl. Asht —5M 79
Astleham Rd. Shep —2N 37
Astolat Est. P'mrsh —2M 133
Aston Clo. Asht —5J 79
Aston Ct. Craw —8N 181
Aston Grn. Houn —5K 9
Aston Mead. Wind —4B 4
Aston Pl. SW16 —7M 29
Aston Rd. SW20 —1H 43
Aston Rd. Clay —2E 58
Aston Ter. SW12 —1F 28
Astonville St. SW18 —2M 27
Aston Way. Eps —2E 80
Astor Clo. Add —1M 55
Astor Clo. King T —7A 26
Astor Ct. SW6 —3N 13
(off Maynard Clo.)
Astoria Mans. SW16 —4J 29
Astra Bus. Cen. Red —4F 142
Astra Mead. Wink R —7F 16
Astrid Ho. Felt —3K 23
Asylum Arch Rd. Red —6D 122
Atalanta Clo. Purl —6L 63
Atalanta St. SW6 —3J 13
Atbara Rd. C Crook —9B 88
Atbara Rd. Tedd —7H 25
Atcham Rd. Houn —7C 10
Atfield Gro. W'sham —3A 52
Atheldene Rd. SW18 —2N 27
Athelstan Clo. Worth —3J 183
Athelstan Ho. King T —7N 203
Athelstan Rd. King T —3M 41 (7N 203)
Athelstan Way. H'ham —8L 197
Athena Clo. King T —2M 41 (5M 203)
Atherfield Rd. Reig —6A 122
Atherley Way. Houn —1N 23
Atherton Clo. Shalf —9A 114
Atherton Clo. Stanw —9M 7
Atherton Ct. Eton —3G 4
Atherton Dri. SW19 —5J 27
Atherton Rd. SW13 —3F 12
Athlone. Clay —3E 58
Athlone Rd. SW2 —1K 29
Athlone Sq. Wind —4F 4
Atkins Clo. Wok —5K 73
Atkins Dri. W Wick —8N 47
Atkinson Ct. Horl —9F 142
Atkinson Rd. M'bowr —5G 182
Atkins Rd. SW12 —1G 28
Atney Rd. SW15 —7K 13
Atrebatti Rd. Sand —6H 49
Attebrouche Ct. Brack —6B 32
Atte La. Warf —7A 16
Attenborough Clo. Fleet —2C 88
Atterbury Clo. W'ham —4M 107
Attfield Clo. As —3D 110
Attfield Ct. King T —4M 203
Attlee Clo. T Hth —4N 45
Attlee Gdns. C Crook —9A 88
Attlee Ho. Craw —7N 181
Attleford La. Shack —5K 131
Attwood Clo. S Croy —1E 84
Atwater Clo. SW2 —2L 29
Atwell Pl. Th Dit —7F 40
Atwood. Bookh —2M 97
Atwood Av. Rich —5N 11
Atwoods All. Rich —4N 11
Aubyn Hill. SE27 —5N 29
Aubyn Sq. SW15 —8F 12
Auchinleck Ct. Craw D —2E 184
Auchinleck Way. Alder —2K 109
Auckland Clo. SE19 —1C 46
Auckland Clo. Craw —9B 162
Auckland Gdns. SE19 —1B 46
Auckland Hill. SE27 —5N 29
Auckland Rd. SE19 —1C 46
Auckland Rd. Cat —9B 84
Auckland Rd. King T —3M 41 (7N 203)
Auden Pl. Cheam —1H 61
Audley Clo. Add —2K 55
Audley Ct. Twic —4D 24
Audley Dri. Warl —2F 84
Audley Firs. W on T —1K 57
Audley Ho. Add —2K 55
Audley Pl. Sutt —4N 61
Audley Rd. Rich —8M 11
Audley Way. Asc —2H 33
Audrey Clo. Beck —5L 47
Audric Clo. King T —9N 25
Augur Clo. Stai —6H 21
Augusta Clo. W Mol —3N 39
Augusta Rd. Twic —3C 24
Augustine Clo. Coln —6G 7
Augustine Wlk. Warf —8C 16
August La. Alb —4M 135
Augustus Clo. Bren —3J 11
Augustus Ct. SW16 —3H 29
Augustus Ct. Felt —5N 23
Augustus Gdns. Camb —1G 71
Augustus Rd. SW19 —2J 27
Aultone Way. Cars —9D 44
Aultone Way. Sutt —8N 43
Aurelia Gdns. Croy —4K 45
Aurelia Rd. Croy —5J 45
Auriol Clo. Wor Pk —9D 42
Auriol Pk. Rd. Wor Pk —9D 42
Auriol Rd. W14 —1K 13
Aurum Clo. Horl —9F 142
Austen Clo. E Grin —9L 165
Austen Rd. Farn —8M 69
Austen Rd. Guild —4B 114
Austin Clo. Coul —5M 83
Austin Clo. Twic —8J 11
Austins Cotts. Farnh —1G 128
Australia Ter. Deep —6H 71
(off Cyprus Rd.)
Austyn Gdns. Surb —7A 42
Autumn Clo. SW19 —7A 28
Autumn Dri. Sutt —5N 61
Autumn Lodge. S Croy —7F 200
Avalon Clo. SW20 —1K 43
Avalon Rd. SW6 —4N 13
Avard Gdns. Orp —1L 67
Avarn Rd. SW17 —7D 28
Avebury. Brack —5M 31
Avebury Clo. H'ham —1N 197
Avebury Pk. Surb —6K 41
Avebury Rd. SW19 —9L 27
Avebury Rd. Orp —1M 67
Aveley Clo. Farnh —4H 129
Aveley La. Farnh —5G 129
Aveling Clo. M'bowr —5G 182
Aveling Clo. Purl —9K 63
Aven Clo. Cranl —8N 155
Avening Rd. SW18 —1M 27
Avening Ter. SW18 —1M 27
Avenue C. Add —9N 37
Avenue Clo. Houn —4J 9
Avenue Clo. Tad —9G 81
Avenue Ct. Tad —1G 101
Avenue Cres. Houn —4J 9
Avenue de Cagny. Pirb —9C 72
Avenue Elmers. Surb —4L 41 (8K 203)
Avenue Gdns. SE25 —1D 46
Avenue Gdns. SW14 —6D 12
Avenue Gdns. Horl —9G 142
Avenue Gdns. Houn —3J 9
Avenue Gdns. Tedd —8F 24
Avenue One. Add —1N 55
Avenue Pde. Sun —2J 39
Avenue Pk. Rd. SE27 —3M 29
Avenue Rd. SE20 & Beck —1F 46
Avenue Rd. SE25 —1C 46
Avenue Rd. SW16 —1H 45
Avenue Rd. SW20 —1G 42
Avenue Rd. Bans —2N 81
Avenue Rd. Bren —1J 11
Avenue Rd. Cat —9A 84
Avenue Rd. Cobh —3L 77
Avenue Rd. Cranl —9N 155
Avenue Rd. Eps —1C 80
Avenue Rd. Farn —1B 90
Avenue Rd. Felt —4G 23
Avenue Rd. Fleet —3A 88
Avenue Rd. Gray —6A 170
Avenue Rd. Hamp —9B 24
Avenue Rd. Iswth —4F 10
Avenue Rd. King T —2L 41 (5L 203)
Avenue Rd. N Mald —3D 42
Avenue Rd. Stai —6F 20
Avenue Rd. Sutt —6M 61
Avenue Rd. Tats —7G 87
Avenue Rd. Tedd —8G 24
Avenue Rd. Wall —4G 62
Avenue S. Surb —6N 41
Avenue Sucy. Camb —2M 69
Avenue Ter. N Mald —2B 42
Avenue, The. SW18 —1C 28
Avenue, The. Alder —5A 110
Avenue, The. Asc —8K 17
Avenue, The. Brock —3N 119
Avenue, The. Camb —2N 69
Avenue, The. Cars —4E 62
Avenue, The. Chob —5J 53
Avenue, The. Clay —3E 58
Avenue, The. Comp & G'ming —1F 132
Avenue, The. Coul —2H 83
Avenue, The. Cran —4H 9
Avenue, The. Craw —8B 182
Avenue, The. Crowt —1F 48
Avenue, The. Croy —9B 46 (4F 200)
Avenue, The. Dat —4L 5
Avenue, The. E Grin —4C 166
Avenue, The. Egh —5D 20
Avenue, The. Eps & Sutt —4G 60
Avenue, The. Ewh —4F 156
Avenue, The. Fleet —4A 88
Avenue, The. G'ming —9H 133
Avenue, The. Gray —6B 170
Avenue, The. Hamp —7N 23
Avenue, The. Hand —8L 199
Avenue, The. Hasl —1D 188
Avenue, The. Horl —9D 142
Avenue, The. Houn —8B 10
Avenue, The. Kes —1F 66
Avenue, The. Light —6L 51
Avenue, The. New H —6J 55
Avenue, The. Old Win —8L 5
Avenue, The. Oxs —7F 58
Avenue, The. Rich —5M 11
Avenue, The. Rowl —8D 128
(in two parts)
Avenue, The. S Nut —6J 123
Avenue, The. Stai —9K 21
Avenue, The. Sun —9J 23
Avenue, The. Surb —5M 41
Avenue, The. Sutt —6L 61
Avenue, The. Tad —9G 80
Avenue, The. Twic —8H 11
Avenue, The. W'ham —9H 87
Avenue, The. W Wick —6M 47
Avenue, The. Whyt —6D 84
Avenue, The. Wokgm —7K 31
Avenue, The. Wor Pk —8E 42
Avenue, The. Worp —5H 93
Avenue, The. Wray —6N 5
Avenue Three. Add —9N 37
Avenue Two. Add —1N 55
Avenue Vs. Red —7G 103
Averil Gro. SW16 —7M 29
Averill St. W6 —2J 13
Avern Gdns. W Mol —3B 40
Avern Rd. W Mol —3B 40
Avery Ct. Alder —2N 109
(off Alice Rd.)
Avia Pk. Felt —2C 22
Aviary Rd. Wok —3J 75
Aviary Way. Craw D —9F 164
Aviemore Clo. Beck —4J 47
Aviemore Way. Beck —4H 47
Avington Clo. Guild —3A 114 (2F 202)
Avoca Rd. SW17 —5E 28
Avocet Cres. Coll T —7J 49
Avon Clo. Add —3J 55
Avon Clo. As —3D 110
Avon Clo. Farn —7K 69
Avon Clo. Sutt —1A 62
Avon Clo. Wor Pk —8F 42
Avon Ct. Binf —7H 15
Avon Ct. Farnh —2H 129
Avondale. Ash V —6D 90
Avondale Av. Esh —9G 40
Avondale Av. Stai —8H 21
Avondale Av. Wor Pk —7E 42
Avondale Clo. Horl —6D 142
Avondale Clo. W on T —2K 57
Avondale Gdns. Houn —8N 9
Avondale Rd. SW14 —6D 12
Avondale Rd. SW19 —6N 27
Avondale Rd. Alder —4N 109
Avondale Rd. Afrd —4M 21
Avondale Rd. Fleet —3B 88
Avondale Rd. S Croy —3N 63
Avon Gro. Brack —8A 16
Avon Ho. W14 —1L 13
(off Avonmore Rd.)
Avon Ho. King T —9K 25 (1J 203)
Avonmead. Wok —5M 73
Avonmore Av. Guild —2B 114
Avonmore Gdns. W14 —1L 13
Avonmore Rd. W14 —1L 13
Avon Path. S Croy —3N 63
Avon Rd. Farnh —2H 129
Avon Rd. Sun —8G 22
Avon Wlk. Craw —4L 181
Avonwick Rd. Houn —5B 10
Avro Way. Bro I —6N 55
Avro Way. Wall —4J 63
Award Rd. C Crook —8A 88
(in two parts)
Axbridge. Brack —4C 32
Axes La. Red —1G 142
Axis Pk. Slou —1D 6
Axwood. Eps —2B 80
Ayebridges Av. Egh —8E 20
Ayesgarth. C Crook —8C 88
Ayjay Clo. Alder —5N 109
Aylesbury Ct. Sutt —9A 44
Aylesford Av. Beck —4H 47
Aylesham Way. Yat —9A 48
Aylesworth Spur. Old Win —1L 19
Aylett Rd. SE25 —3E 46
Aylett Rd. Iswth —5E 10
Ayliffe Clo. King T —1N 41
Ayling Ct. Farnh —5L 109
Ayling Hill. Alder —3L 109
Ayling La. Alder —4L 109
Aylward Rd. SW20 —1L 43
Aymer Clo. Stai —9G 21
Aymer Dri. Stai —9G 20
Aynscombe Path. SW14 —5B 12
Ayrshire Gdns. Fleet —1C 88
Aysgarth. Brack —5L 31
Aysgarth Ct. Sutt —9N 43
Ayshe Ct. Dri. H'ham —5L 197
Azalea Av. Lind —4B 168
Azalea Ct. Wok —6N 73
Azalea Dri. Hasl —9D 170
Azalea Gdns. C Crook —8C 88
Azalea Way. Camb —9F 50

Babbacombe Clo. Chess —2K 59
Babbage Way. Brack —5M 31
Babbs Mead. Farnh —2F 128
Baber Bri. Cvn. Site. Felt —8K 9
Baber Dri. Felt —9K 9
Babington Rd. SW16 —6H 29
Babylon La. Lwr K —5M 101
Bachelors La. Ock —2N 95
Back All. Dork —5H 119 (2L 201)
Back Dri. Crowt —5D 48
Back Grn. W on T —3K 57
Back La. Bren —2K 11
Back La. Bucks H —2A 148
Back La. E Clan —9M 95
Back La. Elst —7H 131
Back La. Fren —1J 149
Back La. Plais —6A 192
Back La. Rich —3J 25
(in two parts)
Back La. Turn H & Adgly —7N 183
Backley Gdns. SE25 —5D 46
Bk. of High St. Chob —7H 53
Back Path. Blet —2N 123
Back Rd. Tedd —8E 24
Bacon Clo. Coll T —8J 49
Bacon La. Churt —6H 149
Badajos Rd. Alder —1L 109
Baden Clo. Stai —8K 21
Baden Dri. Horl —7C 142
Baden Powell Clo. Surb —8M 41
Baden Rd. Guild —1K 113
Bader Clo. Kenl —2A 84
Bader Ct. Farn —6L 69
Badger Clo. Felt —4J 23
Badger Clo. Guild —9L 93
Badger Clo. Houn —6K 9
Badger Dri. Light —6L 51
Badgersbridge Ride. Wind —1M 17
Badgers Clo. Afrd —6A 22
Badgers Clo. Fleet —5A 88
Badgers Clo. G'ming —3G 133
Badgers Clo. H'ham —2M 197
Badgers Clo. Wok —5M 73
Badgers Copse. Camb —3C 70
Badgers Copse. Wor Pk —8E 42
Badger's Ct. Eps —9D 60 (7N 201)
Badgers Cross. Milf —1C 152
Badgers Hill. Vir W —4M 35
Badgers Hole. Croy —1G 64
Badgers Hollow. G'ming —5G 132
Badgers Holt. Yat —1A 68
Badgers La. Warl —7F 84
Badgers Sett. Crowt —2E 48
Badgers Wlk. N Mald —1D 42
Badgers Wlk. Purl —7G 63
Badgers Wlk. Whyt —5C 84
Badgers Way. Brack —9D 16
Badger's Way. E Grin —8B 166
Badgers Way. Loxw —4J 193
Badgers Wood. Cat —3A 104
Badgers Wood. Ott —3F 54
Badger Wlk. Norm —6N 91
Badger Way. Ews —4C 108
Badgerwood Dri. Frim —4B 70
Badingham Dri. Fet —1E 98
Badminton Rd. SW12 —1E 28
Badshot Farm La. Bad L —7M 109
Badshot Lea. —7M 109
Badshot Lea Rd. Bad L —8L 109
Badshot Pk. Bad L —6M 109
Bagden Hill. Westh —8D 98
Bagley's La. SW6 —4N 13
Bagot Clo. Asht —3M 79
Bagshot. —4J 51
Bagshot Grn. Bag —4J 51
Bagshot Rd. Asc —8M 33
Bagshot Rd. Brack & Crowt —2N 31
Bagshot Rd. Crowt & Bag —7C 32
Bagshot Rd. Eng G —8M 19
Bagshot Rd. Knap & Brkwd —5E 72
Bagshot Rd. W End & Chob —8B 52
Bagshot Rd. Worp H & Worp —8F 72
Bahram Rd. Eps —6C 60
Baigents La. W'sham —3A 52
Bailes La. Norm —9A 92
Bailey Clo. Frim —6B 70
Bailey Clo. H'ham —1M 197
Bailey Clo. Wind —5D 4
Bailey M. W4 —2A 12
(off Hervert Gdns.)
Bailey Rd. Westc —6C 118
Baileys Clo. B'water —2H 69
Bailing Hill. Warn —1E 196
Baillie Rd. Guild —4B 114
Bain Av. Camb —4N 69
Bainbridge Clo. Ham —6L 25
Baines Clo. S Croy —2A 64 (8D 200)
Bainton Mead. Wok —4K 73
Baird Clo. Craw —9E 162
Baird Dri. Wood S —2E 112
Baird Rd. Farn —8A 70
Bakeham La. Eng G —8M 19
Bakehouse Barn Clo. H'ham —1L 197
Bakehouse M. Alder —2M 109
Bakehouse Rd. Horl —6E 142
Baker Boy La. Croy —9H 65
Baker Clo. Craw —5B 182
Baker Ct. Wind —6E 4
Baker La. Mitc —1E 44
Baker's Clo. Ling —6A 146
Bakers Ct. SE25 —2B 46
Bakers End. SW20 —1K 43
Bakers Gdns. Cars —8C 44
Bakers La. Ling —7N 145
Bakers Mead. God —8F 104
Bakers M. Orp —3N 67
Baker St. Wey —1B 56
Bakers Way. Capel —5J 159
Baker's Yd. Guild —4N 113 (5D 202)
Bakery M. Surb —7N 41
Bakewell Way. N Mald —1D 42
Balaam Ho. Sutt —1M 61
Balaclava Rd. Surb —6J 41
Balchins La. Westc —7A 118
Balcombe Ct. Craw —2H 183
Balcombe Gdns. Horl —9G 142
Balcombe La. Adgly —9K 183
Balcombe Rd. Craw & Worth —2H 183
Balcombe Rd. Horl —7F 142
Baldreys. Farnh —3F 128
Baldry Gdns. SW16 —7J 29
Baldwin Clo. M'bowr —6G 183
Baldwin Cres. Guild —1E 114
Baldwin Gdns. Houn —4C 10
Baldwin Ho. SW2 —2L 29
Baldwins Fld. E Grin —6N 165
Baldwins Hill. —7N 165
Baldwins Shore. Eton —2G 4
Balfern Gro. W4 —1D 12
Balfont Clo. S Croy —9D 64
Balfour Av. Wok —9A 74
Balfour Cres. Brack —4N 31
Balfour Gdns. F Row —9G 187
Balfour Pl. SW15 —7G 12
Balfour Rd. SE25 —4D 46
Balfour Rd. SW19 —8N 27
Balfour Rd. Cars —4D 62
Balfour Rd. Houn —6B 10
Balfour Rd. Wey —1B 56
Balgowan Clo. N Mald —4D 42

Balgowan Rd.—Beauclerc Ct.

Balgowan Rd. *Beck* —2H **47**
Balham. —2F 28
Balham Continental Mkt. SW12 (off Shipka Rd.) —2F **28**
Balham Gro. *SW12* —1E **28**
Balham High Rd. *SW17 & SW12* —4E **28**
Balham Hill. *SW12* —1F **28**
Balham New Rd. *SW12* —1F **28**
Balham Pk. Rd. *SW12* —2D **28**
Balham Sta. Rd. *SW12* —2F **28**
Balintore Ct. *Coll T* —7J **49**
Ballands N., The. *Fet* —9E **78**
Ballands S., The. *Fet* —1E **98**
Ball & Wicket La. *Farnh* —5H **109**
Ballantine St. *SW18* —7N **13**
Ballantyne Dri. *Kgswd* —8L **81**
Ballantyne Rd. *Farn* —8M **69**
Ballard Clo. *King T* —8C **26**
Ballard Ct. *Camb* —7E **50**
Ballard Grn. *Wind* —3B **4**
Ballard Rd. *Camb* —7E **50**
Ballards Farm Rd. *S Croy & Croy* (in two parts) —3D **64**
Ballards Grn. *Tad* —6K **81**
Ballards La. *Oxt* —7E **106**
Ballards Ri. *S Croy* —3D **64**
Ballards Way. *S Croy & Croy* —3D **64**
Ballater Rd. *S Croy* —2C **64**
Ballencrieff Rd. *Asc* —6C **34**
Ballfield Rd. *G'ming* —5G **133**
Balliol Clo. *Craw* —9G **163**
Balliol Way. *Owl* —6K **49**
Ballsdown. *C'fold* —5D **172**
Balmain Ct. *Houn* —4B **10**
Balmain Lodge. *Surb* —8L **203**
Balmoral. *E Grin* —1C **186**
Balmoral Av. *Beck* —3H **47**
Balmoral Clo. *SW15* —9J **13**
Balmoral Ct. *SE27* —5N **29**
Balmoral Ct. *Craw* —7N **181**
Balmoral Ct. *Sutt* —4M **61**
Balmoral Ct. *Wor Pk* —8G **42**
Balmoral Cres. *Farnh* —6G **108**
Balmoral Cres. *W Mol* —2A **40**
Balmoral Dri. *Frim* —6C **70**
Balmoral Dri. *Wok* —3E **74**
Balmoral Gdns. *S Croy* —6A **64**
Balmoral Gdns. *Wind* —6G **4**
Balmoral Rd. *Ash V* —9E **90**
Balmoral Rd. *King T* —3M **41** (7M **203**)
Balmoral Rd. *Wor Pk* —9G **42**
Balmoral Way. *Sutt* —6M **61**
Balmuir Gdns. *SW15* —7H **13**
Balquhain Clo. *Asht* —4K **79**
Baltic Cen., The. *Bren* —1K **11**
Baltic Clo. *SW19* —8B **28**
Balvernie Gro. *SW18* —1L **27**
Balvernie M. *SW18* —1M **27**
Bampfylde Clo. *Wall* —9G **44**
Bampton Way. *Wok* —5K **73**
Banbury. *Brack* —6C **32**
Banbury Clo. *Frim* —7D **70**
Banbury Clo. *Wokgm* —2A **30**
Banbury Ct. *Sutt* —4M **61**
Bancroft Clo. *Afrd* —6B **22**
Bancroft Ct. *Reig* —3N **121**
Bancroft Rd. *M'bowr* —4H **183**
Bancroft Rd. *Reig* —3M **121**
Banders Ri. *Guild* —2E **114**
Band La. *Egh* —6B **20**
Bandonhill. —2H 63
Bandon Ri. *Wall* —2H **63**
Bangalore St. *SW15* —6H **13**
Bank Av. *Mitc* —1B **44**
Bank Bldgs. Rd. *Cranl* —7M **155**
Bank La. *SW15* —8D **12**
Bank La. *Craw* —3B **182**
Bank La. *King T* —8L **25**
Bank M. *Sutt* —3A **62**
Bank Rd. *Alder* —8B **90**
Banksian Wlk. *Iswth* —4E **10**
Bankside. *Farnh* —5L **109**
Bankside. *S Croy* —3C **64**
Bankside. *Wok* —5L **73** (in three parts)
Bankside Clo. *Big H* —5E **86**
Bankside Clo. *Cars* —3C **62**
Bankside Clo. *Elst* —8H **131**
Bankside Clo. *Iswth* —7F **10**
Bankside Dri. *Th Dit* —7H **41**
Bank's La. *Eff* —1H **97**
Banks Rd. *Craw* —3G **182**
Banks Way. *Guild* —9B **94**
Bank Ter. Shere —8B **116** *(off Gomshall La.)*
Bank, The. *Turn H* —5D **184**
Bannister Clo. *SW2* —2L **29**
Bannister Clo. *Witl* —5C **152**
Bannister Gdns. *Yat* —1E **68**
Bannister's Rd. *Guild* —5J **113**
Banstead. —2M 81
Banstead Rd. *Cars* —5B **62**
Banstead Rd. *Cat* —8A **84**
Banstead Rd. *Eps & Bans* —6G **61**
Banstead Rd. *Purl* —7L **63**
Banstead Rd. S. *Sutt* —7A **62**
Banstead Way. *Wall* —2J **63**
Barataria Cvn. Site. *Rip* —7H **75**
Barbara Clo. *C Crook* —7C **88**
Barbara Clo. *Shep* —4C **38**
Barber Clo. *M'bowr* —7G **182**
Barber Dri. *Cranl* —6N **155**
Barberry Clo. *Fleet* —6B **88**
Barberry Way. *B'water* —4L **69**
Barbon Clo. *Camb* —3H **71**
Barchard St. *SW18* —8N **13**
Barclay Clo. *SW6* —3M **13**
Barclay Clo. *Fet* —1B **98**
Barclay Rd. *SW6* —3M **13**
Barclay Rd. *Croy* —9A **46** (4D **200**)
Barcombe Av. *SW2* —3J **29**
Bardney Rd. *Mord* —3N **43**
Bardolph Av. *Croy* —5H **65**
Bardolph Rd. *Rich* —6M **11**
Bardon Wlk. *Wok* —4L **73**
Bardsley Clo. *Croy* —9C **46**
Bardsley Dri. *Farnh* —3F **128**
Barfield Ct. *Red* —1E **122**
Barfields. *Blet* —2M **123**
Barford. —1K 169
Barford Clo. *Fleet* —5E **88**
Barford Copse. —4L 189
Barford La. *Churt* —9K **149**
Bargate Clo. *N Mald* —6F **42**
Bargate Ct. *Guild* —3H **113**
Bargate Ri. *G'ming* —7F **132**
Barge Clo. *Alder* —8C **90**
Barge Wlk. *E Mol* —2D **40**
Barge Wlk. *Hamp W* —9K **25** (2J **203**)
Barge Wlk. *King T* —2K **41** (5H **203**)
Barham Clo. *Wey* —1D **56**
Barham Ct. *S Croy* —7C **200**
Barham Rd. *SW20* —8F **26**
Barham Rd. *S Croy* —1N **63** (7C **200**)
Barhatch La. *Cranl* —5A **156**
Barhatch Rd. *Cranl* —5A **156**
Baring Rd. *Croy* —7D **46**
Barker Clo. *N Mald* —3A **42**
Barker Grn. *Brack* —4N **31**
Barker Rd. *Cher* —6G **37**
Barker St. *SW10* —2N **13**
Barker Wlk. *SW16* —4H **29**
Barkham Rd. *Wokgm* —3A **30**
Barkhart Dri. *Wokgm* —1B **30**
Barkhart Gdns. *Wokgm* —1B **30**
Barkis Mead. *Owl* —5K **49**
Barkston Gdns. *SW5* —1N **13**
Barley Clo. *Craw* —4B **182**
Barleymead. *Horl* —7F **142**
Barley Mead. *Warf* —8C **16**
Barley Mow Clo. *Knap* —4G **72**
Barleymow Ct. *Bet* —3B **120**
Barley Mow Hill. *Head* —3E **168**
Barley Mow La. *Knap* —3F **72**
Barley Mow Pas. *W4* —1C **12**
Barley Mow Rd. *Eng G* —6M **19**
Barleymow Way. *Shep* —3B **38**
Barley Way. *Fleet* —9C **68**
Barlow Clo. *Wall* —3J **63**
Barlow Rd. *Craw* —6K **181**
Barlow Rd. *Hamp* —8A **24**
Barmouth Rd. *SW18* —9N **13** & 1A **28**
Barmouth Rd. *Croy* —8G **47**
Barnard Clo. *Frim* —6D **70**
Barnard Clo. *Sun* —8J **23**
Barnard Clo. *Wall* —4H **63**
Barnard Ct. *Wok* —5H **73**
Barnard Gdns. *N Mald* —3F **42**
Barnard Rd. *Mitc* —2E **44**
Barnard Rd. *Warl* —6L **85**
Barnards Pl. *S Croy* —5M **63**
Barnard Way. *Alder* —1L **109**
Barnato Clo. *W Byf* —8N **55**
Barnby Rd. *Knap* —4G **73**
Barn Clo. *Afrd* —8C **22**
Barn Clo. *Bans* —2B **82**
Barn Clo. *Brack* —1B **32**
Barn Clo. *Camb* —9C **50**
Barn Clo. *Eps* —2B **80**
Barn Clo. *Peas P* —1N **199**
Barn Cres. *Purl* —9A **64**
Barncroft. *Farnh* —2H **129** (in two parts)
Barn Elms Pk. *SW15* —6H **13**
Barnes. —5E 12
Barnes All. *Hamp* —1C **40**
Barnes Av. *SW13* —3F **12**
Barnes Av. *S'hall* —1N **9**
Barnes Clo. *Farn* —1B **90**
Barnes End. *N Mald* —4F **42**
Barnes High St. *SW13* —5E **12**
Barnes Rd. *Frim* —6C **70**
Barnes Rd. *G'ming* —3H **133**
Barnes Wallis Dri. *Wey* —7N **55**
Barnett Clo. *Lea* —6H **79**
Barnett Clo. *Won* —3E **134**
Barnett Ct. *Brack* —1B **32**
Barnett Grn. *Brack* —5N **31**
Barnett La. *Light* —8K **51**
Barnett La. *Won* —4D **134**
Barnett Row. *Guild* —7N **93**
Barnett's Shaw. *Oxt* —5N **105**
Barnett Wood La. *Lea & Asht* —7H **79**
Barnfield. *Bans* —1N **81**
Barnfield. *Cranl* —7N **155**
Barnfield. *Horl* —9E **142**
Barnfield. *N Mald* —5D **42**
Barn Fld. *Yat* —1C **68**
Barnfield Av. *Croy* —8F **46**
Barnfield Av. *King T* —5K **25**
Barnfield Av. *Mitc* —3F **44**
Barnfield Clo. *SW17* —4B **28**
Barnfield Clo. *Coul* —6N **83**
Barnfield Cotts. *D'land* —1C **166**
Barnfield Gdns. *King T* —5L **25**
Barnfield Rd. *Craw* —2B **182**
Barnfield Rd. *S Croy* —5B **64**
Barnfield Rd. *Tats* —7F **86**
Barnfield Way. *Oxt* —2C **126**
Barnfield Wood Clo. *Beck* —5N **47**
Barnfield Wood Rd. *Beck* —5N **47**
Barn Hawe. *Eden* —9L **147**
Barnlea Clo. *Felt* —3M **23**
Barnmead. *Chob* —6J **53**
Barn Mdw. Clo. *C Crook* —1A **108**
Barn Mdw. La. *Bookh* —2N **97**
Barnmead Rd. *Beck* —1H **47**
Barnsbury Clo. *N Mald* —3B **42**
Barnsbury Cres. *Surb* —7B **42**
Barnsbury Farm Est. *Wok* —7N **73**
Barnsbury La. *Surb* —8A **42**
Barnscroft. *SW20* —2G **43**
Barnsfold La. *Rud* —2N **193**
Barnsford Cres. *W End* —9D **52**
Barnsley Clo. *Ash V* —3F **90**
Barnsnap. —5G 199
Barnsnap Clo. *H'ham* —2K **197**
Barns, The. *Shack* —3N **131**
Barnway. *Eng G* —6M **19**
Barnwood. *Craw* —2G **183**
Barnwood Clo. *Guild* —1H **113**
Barnwood Rd. *Guild* —2H **113**
Barnyard, The. *Tad* —2F **100**
Baron Clo. *Sutt* —6N **61**
Baron Gro. *Mitc* —3C **44**
Barons Court. —1K 13
Barons Ct. *Wall* —9H **45**
Baron's Ct. Rd. *W14* —1K **13**
Barons Court Theatre. —1K 13 ***(off Comeragh Rd.)***
Baronsfield Rd. *Twic* —9H **11**
Baron's Hurst. *Eps* —3B **80**
Barons Keep. *W14* —1K **13**
Baronsmead Rd. *SW13* —4F **12**
Barons, The. *Twic* —9H **11**
Baron's Wlk. *Croy* —5H **47**
Barons Way. *Egh* —7F **20**
Baron's Way. *Reig* —7M **121**
Baron Wlk. *Mitc* —3C **44**
Barossa Rd. *Camb* —8B **50**
Barracane Dri. *Crowt* —2F **48**
Barrackfield Wlk. *H'ham* —8H **197**
Barrack La. *Wind* —4G **5**
Barrack Path. *Wok* —6J **73**
Barrack Rd. *Alder* —2M **109**
Barrack Rd. *Guild* —1K **113**
Barrack Rd. *Houn* —7L **9**
Barracks, The. *Add* —9K **37**
Barrens Brae. *Wok* —5C **74**
Barrens Clo. *Wok* —6C **74**
Barrens Pk. *Wok* —5C **74**
Barrett Cres. *Wokgm* —2C **30**
Barrett Rd. *Fet* —2D **98**
Barrhill Rd. *SW2* —3J **29**
Barricane. *Wok* —6L **73**
Barrie Clo. *Coul* —3G **82**
Barrie Ho. *Add* —4J **55**
Barrie Rd. *Farnh* —5F **108**
Barrihurst. —8F 154
Barrihurst La. *Cranl* —8F **154**
Barringer Sq. *SW17* —5E **28**
Barrington Ct. *Dork* —6G **119**
Barrington Ct. *Red* —1E **122**
Barrington Lodge. *Wey* —2D **56**
Barrington Rd. *Craw* —5B **182**
Barrington Rd. *Dork* —6G **119**
Barrington Rd. *H'ham* —6L **197**
Barrington Rd. *Purl* —8G **62**
Barrington Rd. *Sutt* —8M **43**
Barrosa Dri. *Hamp* —9A **24**
Barrow Av. *Cars* —4D **62**
Barrowgate Rd. *W4* —1B **12**
Barrow Grn. Rd. *Oxt* —8K **105**
Barrow Hedges Clo. *Cars* —4C **62**
Barrow Hedges Way. *Cars* —4C **62**
Barrowhill. *Wor Pk* —8D **42**
Barrowhill Clo. *Wor Pk* —8D **42**
Barrow Rd. *SW16* —7H **29**
Barrow Rd. *Croy* —2L **63**
Barrowsfield. *S Croy* —8C **64**
Barrow Wlk. *Bren* —2J **11**
Barr's La. *Knap* —3G **72** (in two parts)
Barry Av. *Wind* —3F **4**
Barry Clo. *Craw* —6C **182**
Barry Sq. *Brack* —6B **32**
Bars, The. *Guild* —4N **113** (4C **202**)
Barston Rd. *SE27* —4N **29**
Barstow Cres. *SW2* —2K **29**
Bartholomew Clo. *Hasl* —9H **171**
Bartholomew Ct. *Dork* —6G **119** (4K **201**)
Bartholomew Pl. *Warf* —8C **16**
Bartholomew Way. *H'ham* —2N **197**
Bartlett Rd. *W'ham* —4L **107**
Bartlett St. *S Croy* —2A **64** (8D **200**)
Barton Clo. *Add* —3J **55**
Barton Clo. *Alder* —3K **109**
Barton Clo. *Shep* —5C **38**
Barton Ct. W14 —1K **13** *(off Baron's Ct. Rd.)*
Barton Cres. *E Grin* —1C **186**
Barton Grn. *N Mald* —1C **42**
Barton Ho. SW6 —6N **13** *(off Wandsworth Bri. Rd.)*
Barton Pl. *Guild* —9D **94**
Barton Rd. *W14* —1K **13**
Barton Rd. *Brmly* —5C **134**
Bartons Dri. *Yat* —2C **68**
Bartons Way. *Farn* —7H **69**
Barton, The. *Cobh* —8L **57**
Barton Wlk. *Craw* —5F **182**
Barts Clo. *Beck* —4K **47**
Barttelot Rd. *H'ham* —7K **197**
Barwell Bus Pk. *Chess* —4K **59**
Barwell Clo. *Crowt* —2E **48**
Barwood Av. *W Wick* —7L **47**
Basden Gro. *Felt* —3A **24**
Basden Ho. *Felt* —3A **24**
Basemoors. *Brack* —1C **32**
Basford Way. *Wind* —6A **4**
Bashford Way. *Worth* —1H **183**
Bashurst Copse. *Itch* —8N **195**
Bashurst Hill. *Itch* —8N **195**
Basildene Rd. *Houn* —6L **9**
Basildon Clo. *Sutt* —5N **61**
Basildon Way. *Bew* —6K **181**
Basil Gdns. *SE27* —6N **29**
Basil Gdns. *Croy* —7G **46**
Basingbourne Clo. *Fleet* —7B **88**
Basingbourne Rd. *Fleet* —8A **88**
Basing Clo. *Th Dit* —6F **40**
Basing Dri. *Alder* —5N **109**
Basingfield Rd. *Th Dit* —6F **40**
Basinghall Gdns. *Sutt* —5N **61**
Basing Rd. *Bans* —1L **81**
Basingstoke Canal Cen. —2E 90
Basing Way. *Th Dit* —6F **40**
Baskerville Rd. *SW18* —1C **28**
Basset Clo. *Frim* —8C **70**
Basset Clo. *New H* —6K **55**
Bassett Clo. *Sutt* —5N **61**
Bassett Dri. *Reig* —2M **121**
Bassett Gdns. *Iswth* —3C **10**
Bassett Rd. *M'bowr* —6H **183**
Bassett Rd. *Wok* —3E **74**
Bassett's Clo. *Orp* —1K **67**
Bassetts Hill. *D'land* —1C **166**
Bassett's Way. *Orp* —1K **67**
Bassingham Rd. *SW18* —1A **28**
Baston Mnr. Rd. *Brom* —1D **66**
Baston Rd. *Brom* —1E **66**
Basuto Rd. *SW6* —4M **13**
Bat & Ball La. *Wrec* —5F **128** (in two parts)
Batavia Clo. *Sun* —9J **23**
Batavia Rd. *Sun* —9J **23**
Batchelors Acre. *Wind* —4G **4**
Batcombe Mead. *Brack* —6C **32**
Bateman Ct. *Craw* —6E **182**
Bateman Gro. *As* —4D **110**
Bates Cres. *SW16* —8G **28**
Bates Cres. *Croy* —2L **63**
Bateson Way. *Wok* —1E **74**
Bates Wlk. *Add* —3L **55**
Bathgate Rd. *SW19* —4J **27**
Bath Ho. Rd. *Croy* —7J **45**
Bath Pas. *King T* —1K **41** (4J **203**)
Bath Pl. W6 —1H **13** *(off Fulham Pal. Rd.)*
Bath Rd. *Camb* —9B **50**
Bath Rd. *Coln* —3F **6**
Bath Rd. *Houn* —4K **9**
Bath Rd. *W Dray & H'row* —4K **7** (in two parts)
Baths App. *SW6* —3L **13**
Bathurst Av. *SW19* —9N **27**
Batley Clo. *Mitc* —6D **44**
Batsworth Rd. *Mitc* —2B **44**
Batten Av. *Wok* —6H **73**
Battersea Ct. *Guild* —3K **113**
Battlebridge La. *Red* —8F **102**
Battle Clo. *SW19* —7A **28**
Batt's Corner. —4C 148
Batts Hill. *Red* —1C **122**
Batts Hill. *Reig* —1D **122**
Batty's Barn Clo. *Wokgm* —3C **30**
Baulk, The. *SW18* —1M **27**
Bavant Rd. *SW16* —1J **45**
Bawtree Clo. *Sutt* —6A **62**
Bax Clo. *Cranl* —9N **155**
Baxter Av. *Red* —3D **122**
Baxter Clo. *M'bowr* —5F **182**
Bayards. *Warl* —5F **84**
Bay Clo. *Horl* —6C **142**
Bay Dri. *Brack* —1C **32**
Bayeux. *Tad* —9J **81**
Bayfield Av. *Frim* —4B **70**
Bayfield Rd. *Horl* —7C **142**
Bayford Clo. *B'water* —5M **69**
Baygrove M. *Hamp W* —9J **25**
Bayham Rd. *Mord* —3N **43**
Bayhorne La. *Horl* —1G **162**
Bay Ho. *Brack* —1C **32**
Bayleaf Clo. *Hamp H* —6D **24**
Bayliss Ct. *Guild* —4M **113** (4B **202**)
Baylis Wlk. *Craw* —8N **181**
Baynards. —2E 176
Baynards Park. —3D 176
Baynards Rd. *Rud* —7A **176**
Bayonne Rd. *W6* —2K **13**
Bay Path. *God* —9F **104**
Bay Rd. *Brack* —9C **16**
Bays Farm Ct. *W Dray* —4L **7**
Bay Tree Av. *Lea* —7G **79**
Baywood Clo. *Farn* —9H **69**
Bazalgette Clo. *N Mald* —4C **42**
Bazalgette Gdns. *N Mald* —4C **42**
Beach Gro. *Felt* —3A **24**
Beach Ho. SW5 —1M **13** *(off Philbeach Gdns.)*
Beach Ho. *Felt* —3A **24**
Beachy Rd. *Craw* —8M **181**
Beacon Clo. *Bans* —3J **81**
Beacon Clo. *Wrec* —6F **128**
Beacon Ct. *H'ham* —4N **197**
Beacon Gdns. *Fleet* —4A **88**
Beacon Gro. *Cars* —1E **62**
Beacon Hill. —3A 170
Beacon Hill. *D'land* —2D **166**
Beacon Hill. *Wok* —6M **73**
Beacon Hill Ct. *Hind* —3B **170**
Beacon Hill Pk. *Hind* —3N **169**
Beacon Hill Rd. *C Crook & Ews* —8C **88**
Beacon Hill Rd. *Hind* —3A **170**
Beacon Pl. *Croy* —9J **45**
Beacon Rd. *H'row A* —9B **8**
Beaconsfield Clo. *W4* —1B **12**
Beaconsfield Pl. *Eps* —8D **60** (5N **201**)
Beaconsfield Rd. *Clay* —4E **58**
Beaconsfield Rd. *Croy* —5A **46**
Beaconsfield Rd. *Eps* —6C **80**
Beaconsfield Rd. *N Mald* —1C **42**
Beaconsfield Rd. *Surb* —6M **41**
Beaconsfield Rd. *Twic* —9H **11**
Beaconsfield Rd. *Wok* —7D **74**
Beaconsfield Wlk. *SW6* —4L **13**
Beacon Vw. Rd. *Elst* —9G **130**
Beacon Way. *Bans* —3J **81**
Beadles La. *Oxt* —8N **105**
Beadlow Clo. *Cars* —5B **44**
Beadman St. *SE27* —5M **29**
Beadon Rd. *W6* —1H **13**
Beaford Gro. *SW20* —2K **43**
Beagle Clo. *Felt* —5J **23**
Beale Clo. *Wokgm* —1A **30**
Beale Ct. *Craw* —6M **181**
Beales La. *Wey* —9C **38**
Beales La. *Wrec* —4E **128**
Beales Rd. *Bookh* —5B **98**
Bealeswood La. *Dock* —4D **148**
Beam Hollow. *Farnh* —5H **109**
Bean Oak Rd. *Wokgm* —2D **30**
Beard Rd. *King T* —6M **25**
Beard's Hill. *Hamp* —9A **24**
Beard's Hill Clo. *Hamp* —9A **24**
Beard's Rd. *Afrd* —7F **22**
Beare Green. —8K 139
Beare Grn. Ct. *Bear G* —7K **139**
Beare Grn. Rd. *Bear G* —2E **158**
Beare Grn. Roundabout. *Bear G* —9K **139**
Bearfield Rd. *King T* —8L **25**
Bear La. *Farnh* —9G **109**
Bear Rd. *Felt* —5L **23**
Bears Den. *Kgswd* —9L **81**
Bearsden Way. *Broad H* —5D **196**
Bears Rail Pk. *Old Win* —1J **19**
Bearwood Clo. *Add* —3J **55**
Bearwood Cotts. Wrec —4E **128** *(off Street, The)*
Bearwood Gdns. *Fleet* —4B **88**
Beasley's Ait. *Sun* —5G **39**
Beasley's Ait La. *Sun* —5G **39**
Beatrice Av. *SW16* —2K **45**
Beatrice Ho. W6 —1H **13** *(off Queen Caroline St.)*
Beatrice Rd. *Oxt* —7A **106**
Beatrice Rd. *Rich* —8M **11**
Beatrix Ho. SW5 —1N **13** *(off Old Brompton Rd.)*
Beattie Clo. *Bookh* —2N **97**
Beattie Clo. *Felt* —1G **22**
Beatty Av. *Guild* —2C **114**
Beauchamp Rd. *SE19* —9N **29**
Beauchamp Rd. *Sutt* —1M **61**
Beauchamp Rd. *Twic* —1G **25**
Beauchamp Rd. *W Mol & E Mol* —4B **40**
Beauchamp Ter. *SW15* —6G **13**
Beauclare Clo. *Lea* —7K **79**
Beauclerc Ct. *Sun* —1K **39**

Beauclerk Clo. Felt —2J 23
Beauclerk Ho. SW16 —4J 29
Beaufield Ga. Hasl —1H 189
Beaufort Clo. SW15 —1G 27
Beaufort Clo. Reig —2L 121
Beaufort Clo. Wok —3E 74
Beaufort Ct. Rich —5J 25
Beaufort Gdns. SW16 —8K 29
Beaufort Gdns. Asc —9J 17
Beaufort Gdns. Houn —4M 9
Beaufort M. SW6 —2L 13
Beaufort Rd. Ash V —8D 90
Beaufort Rd. C Crook —6C 88
Beaufort Rd. Farnh —9H 109
Beaufort Rd. King T —3L 41 (8K 203)
Beaufort Rd. Reig —2L 121
Beaufort Rd. Rich —5J 25
Beaufort Rd. Twic —1J 25
Beaufort Rd. Wok —3E 74
Beauforts. Eng G —6M 19
Beaufort Way. Eps —4F 60
Beaufoy Ho. SE27 —4M 29
Beaufront Clo. Camb —8E 50
Beaufront Rd. Camb —8E 50
Beaulieu Clo. Brack —2D 32
Beaulieu Clo. Dat —4L 5
Beaulieu Clo. Houn —8N 9
Beaulieu Clo. Mitc —9E 28
Beaulieu Clo. Twic —9K 11
Beaulieu Gdns. B'water —1H 69
Beaulieu Ho. Binf —7H 15
Beaumaris Pde. Frim —6D 70
Beaumont. W14 —1L 13
(off Avonmore Rd.)
Beaumont Av. W14 —1L 13
Beaumont Av. Rich —6M 11
Beaumont Clo. If'd —4K 181
Beaumont Clo. King T —8N 25
Beaumont Ct. W4 —1B 12
Beaumont Cres. W14 —1L 13
Beaumont Dri. Afrd —6E 22
Beaumont Gdns. Brack —4C 32
Beaumont Gro. Alder —2K 109
Beaumont Pl. Iswth —8F 10
Beaumont Rd. SE19 —7N 29
Beaumont Rd. SW19 —1K 27
Beaumont Rd. Purl —9L 63
Beaumont Rd. Wind —5F 4
Beaumonts. Red —2D 142
Beaumont Sq. Cranl —7A 156
Beaverbrook Roundabout. Lea —1K 99
Beaver Clo. Hamp —9B 24
Beaver Clo. H'ham —2L 197
Beaver Clo. Wokgm —5A 30
Beaver La. Yat —1D 68
Beavers Clo. Farnh —1F 128
Beavers Clo. Guild —2H 113
Beavers Cres. Houn —7K 9
Beavers Hill. Farnh —1E 128
Beavers La. Houn —5K 9
Beavers M. Bord —5A 168
Beavers Rd. Farnh —1F 128
Beavor Gro. W6 —1F 12
(off Beavor La.)
Beavor La. W6 —1F 12
Bechtel Ho. W6 —1J 13
(off Hammersmith Rd.)
Beck Ct. Beck —2G 46
Beckenham. —1K 47
Beckenham Crematorium. Beck —2F 46
Beckenham Gro. Brom —1N 47
Beckenham Rd. Beck —1H 47
Beckenham Rd. W Wick —6L 47
Beckenshaw Gdns. Bans —2C 82
Becket Clo. SE25 —5D 46
Becket Clo. SW19 —8N 27
(off High Path)
Beckett Av. Kenl —2M 83
Beckett Clo. SW16 —3H 29
Beckett Clo. Wokgm —2D 30
Beckett La. Craw —9B 162
Becketts Clo. Felt —9J 9
Becketts Pl. Hamp W —9K 25 (2H 203)
Beckett Way. E Grin —1B 186
Becket Wood. Newd —6B 140
Beckford Av. Brack —5N 31
Beckford Rd. Croy —5C 46
Beckford Way. M'bowr —7F 182
Beck Gdns. Farnh —6G 108
Beckingham Rd. Guild —1K 113
Beck La. Beck —2G 46
Beck River Pk. Beck —1K 47
Beck Way. Beck —2J 47
Beckway Rd. SW16 —1H 45
Beclands Rd. SW17 —7E 28
Becmead Av. SW16 —5H 29
Bective Pl. SW15 —7L 13
Bective Rd. SW15 —7L 13
Bedale Clo. Craw —5A 182
Beddington. —9J 45
Beddington Corner. —6E 44
Beddington Farm Rd. Croy —6J 45
Beddington Gdns. Cars & Wall
(in two parts) —3E 62
Beddington Gro. Wall —2H 63
Beddington La. Croy —4G 44
Beddington Pk. Cotts. Wall —9H 45
Beddington Ter. Croy —6K 45
Beddington Trad. Est. Croy —7J 45
Beddlestead La. Warl —4B 86
Bedfont Clo. Felt —9D 8
Bedfont Clo. Mitc —1E 44
Bedfont Ct. Stai —6J 7
Bedfont Ct. Est. Stai —7K 7
Bedfont Grn. Clo. Felt —2D 22
Bedfont Ind. Pk. Ashf —4D 22
Bedfont Lakes Country Pk. —3D 22
Bedfont La. Felt —1G 22
Bedfont Pk. Ind. Est. Afrd —4D 22
Bedfont Rd. Felt —2D 22
Bedfont Rd. Stanw —9N 7
Bedford Av. Frim G —9D 70
Bedford Clo. W4 —2D 12
Bedford Clo. Wok —2M 73
Bedford Ct. Croy —7N 45
(off Tavistock Rd.)
Bedford Cres. Frim G —8C 70
Bedford Hill. SW12 & SW16 —2F 28
Bedford La. Asc —4E 34
Bedford La. Frim G —8D 70
Bedford Pk. Croy —7N 45 (1C 200)
Bedford Pas. SW6 —3K 13
(off Dawes Rd.)
Bedford Pl. Croy —7A 46 (1D 200)
Bedford Rd. Guild —4M 113 (4B 202)
Bedford Rd. H'ham —7K 197
Bedford Rd. Twic —4D 24
Bedford Rd. Wor Pk —8H 43
Bedfordshire Down. Warf —7D 16
Bedgebury Gdns. SW19 —3K 27
Bedlow Cotts. Cranl —7A 156
Bedlow La. Cranl —7A 156
Bedlow Way. Croy —1K 63
Bedser Clo. T Hth —2N 45
Bedser Clo. Wok —3C 74
Bedster Gdns. W Mol —1B 40
Bedwell Gdns. Hayes —1F 8
(in two parts)
Beech Av. Bren —3H 11
Beech Av. Camb —2B 70
Beech Av. Eff —6L 97
Beech Av. Lwr Bo —6H 129
Beech Av. S Croy —7A 64
Beech Av. Tats —6F 86
Beechbrook Av. Yat —1D 68
Beech Clo. SW15 —1F 26
Beech Clo. SW19 —7H 27
Beech Clo. Afrd —6E 22
Beech Clo. Blind H —3H 145
Beech Clo. Byfl —8N 55
Beech Clo. Cars —8D 44
Beech Clo. C'fold —5D 172
Beech Clo. Cobh —8A 58
Beech Clo. Dork —4F 118 (1H 201)
Beech Clo. E Grin —8N 165
Beech Clo. Eff —6L 97
Beech Clo. Stanw —1M 21
Beech Clo. Sun —1L 39
Beech Clo. W on T —1K 57
Beech Clo. Ct. Cobh —7N 57
Beech Copse. S Croy —2B 64 (8F 200)
Beech Ct. Farnh —1A 128
Beech Ct. Surb —6K 41
Beech Cres. Tad —8B 100
Beechcroft. Asht —6M 79
Beechcroft Av. Kenl —2A 84
Beechcroft Av. N Mald —9B 26
Beechcroft Clo. SW16 —6K 29
Beechcroft Clo. Asc —3A 34
Beechcroft Clo. Houn —3M 9
Beechcroft Clo. Orp —1M 67
Beechcroft Ct. Brack —2N 31
Beechcroft Ct. Sutt —4A 62
Beechcroft Dri. Guild —6G 113
Beechcroft Mnr. Wey —9E 38
Beechcroft Rd. SW14 —6B 12
Beechcroft Rd. SW17 —3C 28
Beechcroft Rd. Chess —9M 41
Beechcroft Rd. Orp —1M 67
Beechdale Rd. SW2 —1K 29
Beech Dell. Kes —1H 67
Beechdene. Tad —9G 80
Beech Dri. B'water —2J 69
Beech Dri. Kgswd —9L 81
Beech Dri. Reig —3B 122
Beech Dri. Rip —2J 95
Beechen Cliff Way. Iswth —5F 10
Beechen La. Tad —3L 101
Beeches Av. Cars —4C 62
Beeches Clo. SE20 —1F 46
Beeches Clo. Kgswd —1M 101
Beeches Cres. Craw —5C 182
Beeches La. Ash W —3F 186
Beeches Mead. E Grin —5H 167
Beeches Rd. SW17 —4C 28
Beeches Rd. Sutt —7K 43
Beeches, The. Ash V —4D 90
Beeches, The. Bans —3N 81
Beeches, The. Brmly —5B 134
Beeches, The. Fet —2E 98
Beeches, The. Houn —4B 10
Beeches, The. S Croy —8D 200
Beeches, The. Stai —6J 21
Beeches Wlk. Cars —5B 62
Beeches Wood. Tad —9M 81
Beechey Clo. Copt —7M 163
Beechey Way. Copt —7M 163
Beech Farm La. Camb —2D 70
Beech Farm Rd. Warl —7M 85
Beechfield. Bans —9N 61
Beechfield Ct. S Croy —7B 200
Beech Fields. E Grin —7B 166
Beech Gdns. Craw D —2D 184
Beech Gdns. Wok —2A 74
Beech Glen. Brack —3N 31
Beech Gro. Add —1K 55
Beech Gro. Bookh —5A 98
Beech Gro. Brkwd —7N 71
(in two parts)
Beech Gro. Cat —4B 104
Beech Gro. Eps —4G 80
Beech Gro. Guild —3J 113
Beech Gro. Mayf —1N 93
Beech Gro. Mitc —4H 45
(in two parts)
Beech Gro. N Mald —2C 42
Beech Hall. Ott —4E 54
Beech Hanger End. Gray —6N 169
Beech Hanger Rd. Gray —6N 169
Beech Hill. —3F 168
Beech Hill. Brook —9K 151
Beech Hill. Head D —5F 168
Beech Hill. Wok —1N 93
Beech Hill Rd. Asc —5C 34
Beech Hill Rd. Head —3E 168
Beech Holme. Craw D —1E 184
Beech Holt. Lea —9J 79
Beech Ho. Rd. Croy —9A 46 (5D 200)
Beeching Clo. As —1F 110
Beeching Way. E Grin —9N 165
Beech La. Gray —5N 169
Beech La. Guild —6M 113 (8A 202)
(in two parts)
Beech La. Norm —4L 111
Beechlawn. Guild —4B 114
Beechlee. Wall —6G 62
Beech Lodge. Stai —6G 21
Beechmeads. Cobh —9L 57
Beechmont Av. Vir W —4N 35
Beechmore Gdns. Sutt —8J 43
Beechnut Dri. B'water —9G 48
Beechnut Ind. Est. Alder —3N 109
Beechnut Rd. Alder —3N 109
Beecholme. Bans —1K 81
Beecholme Av. Mitc —9F 28
Beech Ride. Fleet —6A 88
Beech Ride. Sand —7G 49
Beech Rd. SW16 —1J 45
Beech Rd. Big H —6D 86
Beech Rd. Eps —2E 80
Beech Rd. Farn —7M 69
Beech Rd. Felt —1F 22
Beech Rd. Frim G —8D 70
Beech Rd. Hasl —1H 189
Beech Rd. H'ham —3A 198
Beech Rd. Red —4G 103
Beech Rd. Reig —1M 121
Beech Rd. Wey —1E 56
Beechrow. Ham —5L 25
Beechside. Craw —4C 182
Beechtree Av. Eng G —7L 19
Beech Tree Clo. Craw —2B 182
Beech Tree Dri. Bad L —7M 109
Beech Tree La. Stai —1K 37
Beech Tree Pl. Sutt —2N 61
Beechvale. Wok —5B 74
(off Fairview Av.)
Beech Wlk. Eps —7F 60
Beech Wlk. W'sham —3A 52
Beech Way. Eps —2E 80
Beech Way. G'ming —8G 133
Beechway. Guild —2D 114
Beech Way. S Croy —9G 65
Beech Way. Twic —4A 24
Beechwood Av. Coul —2F 82
Beechwood Av. Kgswd —8M 81
Beechwood Av. Orp —2N 67
Beechwood Av. Rich —4N 11
Beechwood Av. Stai —7K 21
Beechwood Av. Sun —7H 23
Beechwood Av. T Hth —3M 45
Beechwood Av. Wey —1F 56
Beechwood Clo. Asc —8J 17
Beechwood Clo. Knap —4H 73
Beechwood Clo. Surb —6J 41
Beechwood Clo. Wey —1F 56
Beechwood Ct. W4 —2C 12
Beechwood Ct. Cars —1D 62
Beechwood Ct. Sun —7H 23
Beechwood Dri. Cobh —7A 58
Beechwood Dri. Kes —1F 66
Beechwood Gdns. Cat —9D 84
Beechwood Gro. Surb —6J 41
Beechwood Hall. Kgswd —1A 102
Beechwood La. Warl —6G 85
Beechwood Mnr. Wey —1F 56
Beechwood Pk. Lea —9J 79
Beechwood Pk. Tad —9A 100
Beechwood Rd. Cat —9D 84
Beechwood Rd. Knap —4H 73
Beechwood Rd. S Croy —6B 64
Beechwood Rd. Vir W —6K 35
Beechwood Vs. Red —4E 142
Beecot La. W on T —8K 39
Beeding Clo. H'ham —3N 197
Beedingwood Dri. Colg —2D 198
Beedon Dri. Brack —5J 31
Beehive La. Binf —1H 31
Beehive Ring Rd. Gat A —5F 162
Beehive Rd. Binf —9J 15
Beehive Rd. Stai —6H 21
Beehive Way. Reig —7N 121
Beeken Dene. Orp —1L 67
Beeleigh Rd. Mord —3N 43
Beemans Row. SW18 —3A 28
Beeston Way. Felt —9K 9
Beeton's Av. As —9E 90
Beggarhouse La. Newd & Charl —2F 160
Beggar's Bush. —3C 34
Beggar's Hill. (Junct.) —3E 60
Beggar's Hill. Eps —4E 60
Beggars La. Ab H —8F 116
Beggars La. Chob —7F 52
Beggars La. W'ham —3M 107
Beggars Roost La. Sutt —3M 61
Begonia Pl. Hamp —7A 24
Behenna Clo. Bew —4K 181
Beira St. SW12 —1F 28
Beldam Bri. Rd. W End & Chob —9D 52
Beldham Gdns. W Mol —1B 40
Beldham Rd. Farnh —4E 128
Belfast Rd. SE25 —3E 46
Belfield Rd. Eps —5C 60
Belfry M. Sand —7E 48
Belfry Shop. Cen., The. Red —2D 122
Belgrade Rd. Hamp —9B 24
Belgrave Clo. W on T —1J 57
Belgrave Ct. W4 —1B 12
Belgrave Ct. B'water —3J 69
Belgrave Cres. Sun —9J 23
Belgrave Mnr. Wok —6A 74
Belgrave Rd. SE25 —3C 46
Belgrave Rd. SW13 —3E 12
Belgrave Rd. Houn —6N 9
Belgrave Rd. Mitc —2B 44
Belgrave Rd. Sun —9J 23
Belgrave Wlk. Mitc —2B 44
Belgravia Ct. Horl —8F 142
(off St Georges Clo.)
Belgravia M. King T —3K 41 (8J 203)
Bellamy Clo. W14 —1L 13
Bellamy Ho. Houn —2A 10
Bellamy Rd. M'bowr —7G 182
Bellamy St. SW12 —1F 28
Belland Dri. Alder —3K 109
Bellasis Av. SW2 —3J 29
Bell Bri. Rd. Cher —7H 37
Bell Cen., The. Craw —8D 162
Bell Clo. Farn —8A 70
Bell Corner. Cher —6H 37
Bell Cres. Coul —8F 82
Bell Dri. SW18 —1K 27
Bellever Hill. Camb —1C 70
Belle Vue Clo. Alder —2B 110
Belle Vue Clo. Stai —9J 21
Belle Vue Enterprise Cen. Alder —2C 110
Bellevue Pk. T Hth —2N 45
Bellevue Rd. SW13 —5F 12
Bellevue Rd. SW17 —2C 28
Belle Vue Rd. Alder —2B 110
Bellevue Rd. King T —2L 41 (6L 203)
(in two parts)
Belle Vue Rd. Orp —6J 67
Bellew Rd. Deep —8F 70
Bellew St. SW17 —4A 28
Bellfield. Croy —5H 65
Bellfields. —8M 93
Bellfields Ct. Guild —8M 93
Bellfields Rd. Guild —1N 113
Bell Foundry La. Wokgm —8A 14
Bell Hammer. E Grin —1A 186
Bell Hill. Croy —8N 45 (3B 200)
Bell Ho. Gdns. Wokgm —2A 30
(in two parts)
Bellingham Clo. Camb —2G 71
Bell Junct. Houn —6B 10
Bell La. B'water —1H 69
Bell La. Eton W —1C 4
Bell La. Fet —1D 98
Bell La. Rowl —8D 128
Bell La. Twic —2G 25
Bell La. Clo. Fet —1D 98
Bellmarsh Rd. Add —1K 55
Bell Mdw. God —1E 124
Belloc Clo. Craw —2F 182
Belloc Ct. H'ham —5N 197
Bello Clo. SE24 —1M 29
Bell Pde. Wind —5C 4
Bell Pl. Bag —4K 51
Bell Rd. E Mol —4D 40
Bell Rd. Hasl —4E 188
Bell Rd. Houn —6B 10
Bell Rd. Warn —9F 178
Bells All. SW6 —5M 13
Bells La. Hort —6D 6
Bell St. Reig —3M 121
Belltrees Gro. SW16 —6K 29
Bell Va. La. Hasl —4E 188
Bell Vw. Wind —6C 4
Bell Vw. Clo. Wind —5C 4
Bellway Ho. Mers —6G 102
Bellweir Clo. Stai —3D 20
Bellwether La. Out —3M 143
Belmont. —6M 61
Belmont. Wey —3D 56
Belmont Av. Guild —9J 93
Belmont Av. N Mald —3F 42
Belmont Clo. Farn —7L 69
Belmont Gro. W4 —1C 12
Belmont M. SW19 —3J 27
Belmont M. Camb —3A 70
Belmont M. Head —4D 168
Belmont Ri. Sutt —3L 61
Belmont Rd. SE25 —4E 46
Belmont Rd. W4 —1C 12
Belmont Rd. Beck —1H 47
Belmont Rd. Camb —2A 70
Belmont Rd. Crowt —1G 49
Belmont Rd. Lea —9G 79
Belmont Rd. Reig —4A 122
Belmont Rd. Sutt —6M 61
Belmont Rd. Twic —3D 24
Belmont Rd. Wall —2F 62
Belmont Ter. W4 —1C 12
Belmore Av. Wok —3F 74
Beloe Clo. SW15 —7F 12
Belsize Gdns. Sutt —1N 61
Belstone M. Farn —7M 69
Beltane Dri. SW19 —4J 27
Belthorn Cres. SW12 —1G 29
Belton Rd. Camb —1C 70
Beltran Rd. SW6 —5N 13
Belvedere Av. SW19 —6K 27
Belvedere Clo. Esh —2B 58
Belvedere Clo. Guild —1L 113
Belvedere Clo. Tedd —6E 24
Belvedere Clo. Wey —2B 56
Belvedere Ct. SW15 —7H 13
Belvedere Ct. B'water —3J 69
Belvedere Ct. Craw —2F 182
Belvedere Ct. Red —8E 102
Belvedere Dri. SW19 —6K 27
Belvedere Gdns. W Mol —4N 39
Belvedere Gro. SW19 —6K 27
Belvedere Rd. Big H —5H 87
Belvedere Rd. Farn —3A 90
Belvedere Sq. SW19 —6K 27
Belvoir Clo. Frim —5D 70
Bembridge Ct. Crowt —3D 48
Bemish Rd. SW15 —6J 13
Benbow La. Loxh —5E 174
Benbricke Grn. Brack —8M 15
Benbrick Rd. Guild —4K 113
Bence, The. Egh —2D 36
Bench Fld. S Croy —3C 64
Benchfield Clo. E Grin —1D 186
Bench, The. Rich —4J 25
Bencombe Rd. Purl —1L 83
Bencroft Rd. SW16 —8G 29
Bencurtis Pk. W Wick —9N 47
Bendemeer Rd. SW15 —6J 13
Bendon Valley. SW18 —1N 27
Benedict Clo. Orp —1N 67
Benedict Dri. Felt —1E 22
Benedict Grn. Warf —8C 16
Benedict Rd. Mitc —2B 44
Benedict Wharf. Mitc —2B 44
Benen-Stock Rd. Stai —8J 7
Benetfeld Rd. Binf —7G 15
Benett Gdns. SW16 —1J 45
Benfleet Clo. Cobh —8M 57
Benfleet Clo. Sutt —9A 44
Benham Clo. Chess —3J 59
Benham Clo. Coul —5M 83
Benham Gdns. Houn —8N 9
Benhams Clo. Horl —6E 142
Benhams Dri. Horl —6E 142
Benhill Av. Sutt —1N 61
Benhill Rd. Sutt —9A 44
Benhill Wood Rd. Sutt —9A 44
Benhilton. —9A 44
Benhilton Gdns. Sutt —9N 43
Benhurst Clo. S Croy —6G 64
Benhurst Ct. SW16 —6L 29
Benhurst Gdns. S Croy —6F 64
Benhurst La. SW16 —6L 29
Benjamin Rd. M'bowr —5H 183
Benland Cotts. Warn —7D 178
Benner La. W End —8C 52
Bennet Ct. Camb —1A 70
Bennett Clo. Cobh —9H 57
Bennett Clo. Hamp W —9J 25
Bennett Clo. M'bowr —7F 182
Bennetts Av. Croy —8H 47
Bennetts Clo. Mitc —9F 28
Bennetts Farm Pl. Bookh —3N 97
Bennetts Rd. H'ham —7L 197
Bennett St. W4 —2D 12
Bennetts Way. Croy —8H 47
Bennetts Wood. Capel —5J 159
Bennett Way. W Cla —7J 95
Benning Clo. Wind —6A 4

Bennings Clo.—Blackhorse La.

Bennings Clo. Brack —8M 15
Benning Way. Wokgm —9B 14
Benn's All. Hamp —1B 40
Benns Wlk. Rich —7L 11
(off Michelsdale Dri.)
Bens Acre. H'ham —6N 197
Bensbury Clo. SW15 —1G 27
Bencham Clo. T Hth —3N 45
Bensham Gro. T Hth —1N 45
Bensham La. T Hth & Croy —3M 45
Bensham Mnr. Rd. T Hth —3N 45
Benson Clo. Houn —7A 10
Benson Rd. Crowt —2E 48
Benson Rd. Croy —9L 45
Bensons La. Fay —8B 180
Bentalls Cen., The. King T
—1K 41 (3J 203)
Benthall Gdns. Kenl —4N 83
Bentham Av. Wok —2E 74
Bentley Copse. Camb —2F 70
Bentley Dri. Wey —5B 56
Bentons La. SE27 —5N 29
Benton's Ri. SE27 —6N 29
Bentsbrook Clo. N Holm —9H 119
Bentsbrook Cotts. N Holm —9H 119
Bentsbrook Pk. N Holm —9H 119
Bentsbrook Rd. N Holm —9H 119
Benwell Ct. Sun —9H 23
Benwell Rd. Brkwd —6C 72
Benwood Ct. Sutt —9A 44
Beomonds Row. Cher —6J 37
Berberis Clo. Guild —1M 113
(in two parts)
Bere Rd. Brack —5C 32
Beresford Av. Surb —7A 42
Beresford Av. Twic —9J 11
Beresford Clo. Frim G —8D 70
Beresford Gdns. Houn —8N 9
Beresford Rd. Dork
—5H 119 (3M 201)
Beresford Rd. King T
—9M 25 (1M 203)
Beresford Rd. N Mald —3B 42
Beresford Rd. Sutt —4L 61
Berestede Rd. W4 —1E 12
Bergenia Ct. W End —9B 52
Berisford M. SW18 —9N 13
Berkeley Av. Houn —4H 9
Berkeley Clo. Bren —2G 11
Berkeley Clo. Craw —7J 181
Berkeley Clo. Fleet —4C 88
Berkeley Clo. King T —8L 25
Berkeley Clo. Stai —3F 20
Berkeley Clo. Twic —4E 24
(off Wellesley Rd.)
Berkeley Ct. Asht —5M 79
Berkeley Ct. Croy —6D 200
Berkeley Ct. Surb —6K 41
Berkeley Ct. Wall —9G 44
Berkeley Ct. Wey —8E 00
Berkeley Cres. Frim —6E 70
Berkeley Dri. W Mol —2N 39
Berkeley Dri. Wink —2M 17
Berkeley Gdns. Clay —3G 59
Berkeley Gdns. W on T —6G 39
Berkeley Gdns. W Byf —1H 75
Berkeley Ho. Bren —2K 11
(off Albany Rd.)
Berkeley Pl. SW19 —7J 27
Berkeley Pl. Eps —3C 80
Berkeley Rd. SW13 —4F 12
Berkeleys, The. Fet —2E 98
Berkeley Waye. Houn —2L 9
Berkely Clo. Sun —2K 39
Berkley Ct. Guild —3A 114 (2F 202)
Berkshire Clo. Cat —9A 84
Berkshire Ct. Brack —1L 31
Berkshire Rd. Camb —7D 50
Berkshire Sq. Mitc —3J 45
Berkshire Way. Mitc —3J 45
Berkshire Way. Wokgm & Brack
—2H 31
Bermuda Ter. Deep —6H 71
(off Crimea Rd.)
Bernadine Clo. Warf —0D 10
Bernard Ct. Camb —2N 69
Bernard Gdns. SW19 —6L 27
Bernard Rd. Wall —1F 62
Bernel Dri. Croy —9J 47
Berne Rd. T Hth —4N 45
Bernersh Clo. Sand —6H 49
Berney Ho. Beck —4H 47
Berney Rd. Croy —6A 46
Berrington Dri. E Hor —2G 97
Berrybank. Coll T —9K 49
Berry Ct. Houn —8N 9
Berrycroft. Brack —9B 16
Berrylands. —5N 41
Berrylands. SW20 —2H 43
Berrylands. Surb —5M 41
Berrylands Rd. Surb —6M 41
Berry La. W on T —2L 57
Berry La. Warf —1D 16
Berry La. Worp & Wok —3F 92
(in two parts)
Berry Meade. Asht —4M 79
Berrymeade Wlk. If'd —4K 181
Berryscroft Ct. Stai —8L 21
Berryscroft Rd. Stai —8L 21
Berry's Green. —3K 87
Berry's Grn. Rd. Berr G —3K 87
Berry's Hill. Berr G —2K 87
Berry's La. Byfl —7M 55
Berry Wlk. Asht —6M 79
Berstead Wlk. Craw —6L 181
Bertal Rd. SW17 —6C 28
Bertram Cotts. SW19 —8M 27
Bertram Rd. King T —8N 25
Bertrand Ho. SW16 —4J 29
(off Leigham Av.)
Bert Rd. T Hth —4N 45
Berwyn Av. Houn —4B 10
Berwyn Rd. SE24 —2M 29
Berwyn Rd. Rich —7A 12
Beryl Rd. W6 —1J 13
Berystede. King T —8A 26
Besley St. SW16 —7G 29
Bessant Dri. Rich —4N 11
Bessborough Rd. SW15 —2F 26
Beswick Gdns. Brack —9D 16
Beta Rd. Chob —6J 53
Beta Rd. Farn —9L 69
Beta Rd. Wok —3D 74
Beta Way. Egh —9E 20
Betchets Green. —3J 139
Betchetts Grn. Rd. Holmw —5J 139
Betchley Clo. E Grin —7A 166
Betchworth. —3D 120
Betchworth Clo. Sutt —2B 62
Betchworth Way. New Ad —5M 65
Betchworth Works. Charl —4J 161
Bethany Pl. Wok —5N 73
Bethany Waye. Felt —1F 22
Bethel Clo. Farnh —6J 109
Bethel La. Farnh —5H 109
Bethune Clo. Worth —4H 183
Bethune Rd. H'ham —7L 197
Betjeman Clo. Coul —4K 83
Betjeman Wlk. Yat —2A 68
Betley Ct. W on T —9J 39
Betony Clo. Croy —7G 47
Bettridge Rd. SW6 —5L 13
Betts Clo. Beck —1H 47
Betts Way. SE20 —1E 46
Betts Way. Craw —8B 162
Betts Way. Surb —7H 41
Betula Clo. Kenl —2A 84
Between Streets. Cobh —1H 77
Beulah Av. T Hth —1N 45
Beulah Ct. Horl —8F 142
Beulah Cres. T Hth —1N 45
Beulah Gro. Croy —6N 45
Beulah Hill. SE19 —7M 29
Beulah Rd. SW19 —8L 27
Beulah Rd. Sutt —1M 61
Beulah Rd. T Hth —2N 45
Beulah Wlk. Wold —7H 85
Bevan Ct. Craw —8N 181
Bevan Ct. Croy —2L 63
Bevan Ho. Twic —9K 11
Bevan Pk. Eps —6E 60
Beveren Clo. Fleet —1C 88
Beverley Av. SW20 —9E 26
Beverley Av. Houn —7N 9
Beverley Clo. SW13 —5E 12
Beverley Clo. Add —2M 55
Beverley Clo. As —3D 110
Beverley Clo. Camb —9H 51
Beverley Clo. Chess —1J 59
Beverley Clo. Eps —7H 61
Beverley Clo. Wey —8F 38
Beverley Cotts. SW15 —4D 26
Beverley Ct. W4 —1B 12
Beverley Ct. Houn —7N 9
Beverley Cres. Farn —3L 89
Beverley Gdns. SW13 —6E 12
Beverley Gdns. Wor Pk —7F 42
Beverley Heights. Reig —1N 121
Beverley La. SW15 —4E 26
Beverley La. King T —8D 26
Beverley M. Craw —4E 182
Beverley Path. SW13 —5E 12
Beverley Rd. SE20 —1E 46
Beverley Rd. SW13 —6E 12
Beverley Rd. W4 —1E 12
Beverley Rd. King T —9J 25
Beverley Rd. Mitc —3H 45
Beverley Rd. N Mald —3F 42
Beverley Rd. Sun —9G 22
Beverley Rd. Whyt —3B 84
Beverley Rd. Wor Pk —8H 43
Beverley Trad. Est. Mord —6J 43
Beverley Way. SW20 & N Mald
—9E 26
Beverstone Rd. T Hth —3L 45
Bevill Allen Clo. SW17 —6D 28
Bevill Clo. SE25 —2D 46
Bevington Rd. Beck —1L 47
Bevin Sq. SW17 —4D 28
Bewbush. —6L 181
Bewbush Dri. Craw —6K 181
Bewbush Pl. Craw —6L 181
Bewlys Rd. SE27 —6M 29
Bexhill Clo. Felt —3M 23
Bexhill Rd. SW14 —6B 12
Bexley St. Wind —4F 4
Beynon Rd. Cars —2D 62
Bicester Rd. Rich —6N 11
Bickersteth Rd. SW17 —7D 28
Bickley Ct. Craw —6M 181
Bickley St. SW17 —6C 28
Bicknell Rd. Frim —4C 70
Bickney Way. Fet —9C 78
Bicknoller Clo. Sutt —6N 61
Biddulph Rd. S Croy —6N 63
Bideford Clo. Farn —7M 69
Bideford Clo. Felt —4N 23
Bidhams Cres. Tad —8H 81
Bield, The. Reig —5M 121
Bietigheim Way. Camb —9A 50
Big All. M Grn —6K 147
Big Barn Gro. Warf —8B 16
Big Comn. La. Blet —2M 123
Biggin Av. Mitc —9D 28
Biggin Clo. Craw —5A 182
Biggin Hill. —4F 86
Biggin Hill. SE19 —9M 29
Biggin Hill Bus. Pk. Big H —2F 86
Biggin Hill Clo. King T —6J 25
Biggin Way. SE19 —8M 29
Bigginwood Rd. SW16 —8M 29
Biggs Row. SW15 —6J 13
Bignor Clo. H'ham —2N 197
Bilberry Clo. Craw —6N 181
Bilbets. H'ham —5J 197
(off Rushams Rd.)
Billet Rd. Stai —4J 21
Bill Hill. —6A 14
Billingbear. —4G 15
Billingbear Cvn. Pk. Wokgm —5E 14
Billingbear La. Binf —4D 14
Billingbear La. Binf —4G 15
Billing Pl. SW10 —3N 13
Billing Rd. SW10 —3N 13
Billingshurst Rd. Broad H —5C 196
Billing St. SW6 —3N 13
Billinton Dri. M'bowr —3F 182
Billinton Hill. Croy —8A 46 (2E 200)
Billockby Clo. Chess —3M 59
Bilton Cen. Lea —6F 78
Bilton Clo. Coln —5G 7
Bilton Ind. Est. Brack —3K 31
Bina Gdns. SW5 —1N 13
Bindon Grn. Mord —3N 43
Binfield. —7H 15
Binfield Rd. Binf & Brack —7L 15
Binfield Rd. Byfl —8N 55
Binfield Rd. Shur R & Binf —1F 14
Binfield Rd. S Croy —2C 64
Binfield Rd. Wokgm —7F 14
Bingham Dri. Stai —8M 21
Bingham Dri. Wok —5J 73
Bingham Rd. Croy —7D 46
Bingley Rd. Sun —8H 23
Binhams Lea. Duns —4B 174
Binhams Mdw. Duns —4B 174
Binley Ho. SW15 —9E 12
Binney Ct. Craw —9J 163
Binns Rd. W4 —1D 12
Binns Ter. W4 —1D 12
Binscombe. —3G 133
Binscombe. G'ming —2G 132
Binscombe Cres. G'ming —4H 133
Binscombe La. G'ming —3G 133
Binstead Clo. Craw —1N 181
Binstead Copse. Fleet —6A 88
Binsted Dri. B'water —1J 69
Binton La. Seale —1C 130
Birchanger. G'ming —7H 133
Birchanger Rd. SE25 —4D 46
Birch Av. Cat —2A 104
Birch Av. Fleet —4A 88
Birch Av. Lea —7F 78
Birch Circ. G'ming —3J 133
Birch Clo. Bren —3H 11
Birch Clo. Camb —7C 50
Birch Clo. Craw D —1F 184
Birch Clo. Houn —5D 10
Birch Clo. New H —6M 55
Birch Clo. Send —3H 95
Birch Clo. Shep —1F 38
Birch Clo. Tedd —6G 25
Birch Clo. Wok —6M 73
Birch Clo. Wrec —7F 128
Birch Ct. Crowt —2F 48
Birch Ct. Wall —1F 62
Birchcroft Clo. Cat —3N 103
Birchdale Clo. W Byf —7L 55
Birch Dri. B'water —3J 69
Birchend Clo. S Croy —3A 64
Birches Clo. Eps —2D 80
Birches Clo. Mitc —2D 44
Birches Ind. Est. E Grin —7K 165
Birches Rd. H'ham —3A 198
Birches, The. B'water —1G 69
Birches, The. Craw —1E 182
Birches, The. E Hor —4F 96
Birches, The. Farn —1J 89
Birches, The. Houn —1N 23
Birches, The. Man H —9D 198
Birches, The. Orp —1J 67
Birches, The. Wok —5B 74
Birchett Rd. Alder —2M 109
Birchett Rd. Farn —9K 69
Birchetts Clo. Brack —9N 15
Birchfield Clo. Add —1K 55
Birchfield Clo. Coul —3K 83
Birchfield Gro. Eps —6H 61
Birchfield Pk. Ind. Units. Charl
—6J 161
Birchfields. Camb —2A 70
Birch Green. —5J 21
Birch Grn. Stai —5H 21
Birch Gro. Brack —3A 32
Birch Gro. Cobh —1K 77
Birch Gro. Guild —9M 93
Birch Gro. Shep —1F 38
Birch Gro. Tad —2K 101
Birch Gro. Wind —4A 4
Birch Gro. Wok —2F 74
Birch Hill. —6N 31
Birch Hill. Croy —2G 65
Birch Hill Rd. Brack —6N 31
Birch Ho. SW2 —1L 29
(off Tulse Hill)
Birchington Rd. Surb —6M 41
Birchington Rd. Wind —5D 4
Birchlands Av. SW12 —1D 28
Birchlands Ct. Sand —5K 49
Birch La. Asc —9E 16
Birch La. Purl —7J 63
Birch La. W End —8A 52
Birch Lea. Craw —9E 162
Birch Pde. Fleet —4A 88
Birch Platt. W End —9A 52
Birch Rd. Felt —6L 23
Birch Rd. G'ming —3J 133
Birch Rd. Head D —3F 168
Birch Rd. W'sham —3B 52
Birch Side. Crowt —1E 48
Birch Tree Av. W Wick —2B 66
Birch Tree Vw. Light —6L 51
Birch Tree Way. Croy —8E 46
Birch Va. Cobh —8A 58
Birchview Clo. Yat —2B 68
Birch Wlk. Mitc —9F 28
Birch Wlk. W Byf —8J 55
Birch Way. Ash V —6E 90
Birchway. Red —5F 122
Birch Way. Warl —5H 85
Birchwood Av. Beck —3J 47
Birchwood Av. Wall —9E 44
Birchwood Clo. Horl —7F 142
Birchwood Clo. M'bowr —6G 183
Birchwood Clo. Mord —3N 43
Birchwood Dri. Light —6N 51
Birchwood Dri. W Byf —8J 55
Birchwood Gro. Hamp —7A 24
Birchwood La. Cat —3M 103
Birchwood La. Esh & Oxs —6D 50
Birchwood Rd. SW17 —6F 28
Birchwood Rd. W Byf —8J 55
Birdham Clo. Craw —1N 181
Birdhaven. Wrec —5F 128
Birdhouse La. Orp —2H 87
Birdhurst Av. S Croy
—1A 64 (7E 200)
Birdhurst Gdns. S Croy
—1A 64 (7E 200)
Birdhurst Ri. S Croy —2B 64 (8F 200)
Birdhurst Rd. SW18 —8N 13
Birdhurst Rd. SW19 —7C 28
Birdhurst Rd. S Croy
—2B 64 (8F 200)
Bird M. Wokgm —2A 30
Birdsgrove. Knap —5E 72
Birds Hill Dri. Oxs —9D 58
Birds Hill Ri. Oxs —9D 58
Birds Hill Rd. Oxs —8D 58
Birdswood Dri. Wok —6H 73
Bird Wlk. Twic —2N 23
Birdwood Clo. S Croy —7F 64
Birdwood Clo. Tedd —5E 24
Birdwood Rd. Coll T —8L 49
Bird World & Underwater World.
—8B 128
Birkbeck Hill. SE21 —2M 29
Birkbeck Pl. SE21 —3N 29
Birkbeck Pl. Owl —6K 49
Birkbeck Rd. SW19 —6N 27
Birkbeck Rd. Beck —1F 46
Birkdale. Brack —6K 31
Birkdale Dri. If'd —4J 181
Birkdale Gdns. Croy —1G 65
Birkenhead Av. King T
—1M 41 (3M 203)
Birkenholme Clo. Head D —5H 169
Birkheads Rd. Reig —2M 121
Birkwood Clo. SW12 —1H 29
Birnam Clo. Rip —2J 95
Birtley Green. —8D 134
Birtley Ri. Brmly —6C 134
Birtley Rd. Brmly —6C 134
Biscay Rd. W6 —1J 13
Biscoe Clo. Houn —2A 10
Bisenden Rd. Croy —8B 46 (2F 200)
Bisham Clo. Cars —7D 44
Bisham Clo. M'bowr —6H 183
Bishop Ct. Rich —6L 11
Bishopdale. Brack —3M 31
Bishop Duppas Pk. Shep —6F 38
Bishop Fox Way. W Mol —3N 39
Bishopric. H'ham —6H 197
Bishopric Ct. H'ham —6H 197
Bishop's Av. SW6 —5J 13
Bishops Clo. W4 —1B 12
Bishop's Clo. Coul —5L 83
Bishops Clo. Fleet —7B 88
Bishops Clo. Rich —4K 25
Bishop's Clo. Sutt —9M 43
Bishop's Cotts. Bet —2A 120
Bishops Ct. Asc —7K 17
Bishops Ct. Guild —6B 202
Bishops Ct. H'ham —7J 197
Bishop's Dri. Felt —9F 8
Bishop's Dri. Wokgm —1B 30
Bishopsford Rd. Mord —6A 44
Bishops Gate. —4K 19
Bishopsgate Rd. Eng G —4K 19
Bishop's Gro. Hamp —5N 23
Bishops Gro. W'sham —3N 51
Bishops Gro. Cvn. Site. Hamp
—5A 24
Bishop's Hall. King T
—1K 41 (3J 203)
Bishops Hill. W on T —6H 39
Bishop's La. Warf —1E 16
Bishop's Mans. SW6 —5J 13
(in two parts)
Bishops Mead. Farnh —1G 128
Bishops Mead Clo. E Hor —6F 96
Bishopsmead Clo. Eps —6C 60
Bishopsmead Dri. E Hor —7G 96
Bishopsmead Pde. E Hor —7F 96
Bishop's Pk. Rd. SW6 —5J 13
Bishops Pk. Rd. SW16 —9J 29
Bishops Rd. SW6 —4K 13
Bishop's Rd. Croy —6M 45
Bishops Rd. Farnh —9G 108
Bishops Sq. Cranl —7A 156
Bishopstone Wlk. Craw —8A 182
Bishop Sumner Dri. Farnh —6H 109
Bishops Wlk. Croy —2G 64
Bishops Way. Egh —7F 20
Bishops Wood. Wok —4J 73
Bisley. —2C 72
Bisley Camp. —6A 72
Bisley Clo. Wor Pk —7H 43
Bisley Grn. Bisl —3C 72
Bison Ct. Felt —1J 23
Bissingen Way. Camb —9B 50
Bitmead Clo. If'd —4K 181
Bittams La. Cher —1F 54
Bittern Clo. Coll T —7J 49
Bittern Clo. If'd —4J 181
Bitterne Dri. Wok —4J 73
Bittoms Ct. King T —2K 41 (5J 203)
Bittoms, The. King T
(in two parts) —2K 41 (5J 203)
Blackberry Clo. Guild —9L 93
Blackberry Clo. Shep —3F 38
Blackberry Farm Clo. Houn —3M 9
Blackberry La. Ling —9N 145
Blackberry Rd. Felc & Ling —2M 165
Blackbird Clo. Coll T —7J 49
Blackbird Hill. Turn H —4F 184
Blackborough Clo. Reig —3A 122
Blackborough Rd. Reig —4A 122
Blackbridge Ct. H'ham —6H 197
Blackbridge La. H'ham —7G 197
Blackbridge Rd. Wok —6N 73
Blackbrook. —1L 139
Blackbrook Rd. Dork —9K 119
Blackburn, The. Bookh —2N 97
Blackburn Way. G'ming —6J 133
Blackbush Clo. Sutt —4N 61
Blackbushe Airport. B'water —3A 68
Blackbushe Bus. Pk. Yat —2B 68
Blackbushe Pk. Yat —1B 68
Blackbushes Rd. Eve & Fleet —7A 68
Blackcap Clo. Craw —5A 182
Blackcap Pl. Coll T —7K 49
Black Corner. —5H 160
Black Dog Wlk. Craw —1C 182
Black Down. —7K 189
Blackdown Av. Wok —2G 74
Blackdown Clo. Wok —3E 74
Blackdown Rd. Deep —7G 70
Blackdown Rural Industries. Hasl
—4J 189
Black Eagle Clo. W'ham —5L 107
Black Eagle Sq. W'ham —5L 107
Blackett Clo. Stai —1G 37
Blackett Rd. M'bowr —4G 182
Blackett St. SW15 —6J 13
Blackfold Rd. Craw —4E 182
Blackford Clo. S Croy —5M 63
Blackford's Path. SW15 —1F 26
Blackheath. —2G 136
Blackheath. —2H 135
Blackheath. Craw —1H 183
Blackheath Gro. Won —3D 134
Blackheath La. Alb —2K 135
Blackheath La. Won & D'side
—3D 134
Blackheath Rd. Farnh —5F 108
Blackhills. Esh —5N 57
Black Horse Clo. Wind —5A 4
Black Horse La. Croy —6D 46
Blackhorse La. Tad —7N 101

Blackhorse Rd.—Bow La.

Blackhorse Rd. Wok —7G 72
Blackhorse Way. H'ham —6H 197
Black Horse Yd. Wind —4G 5
Blackhouse Rd. Colg —2H 199
Black Lake Clo. Egh —9C 20
Blacklands Cres. F Row —7H 187
Blacklands Mdw. Nutf —2J 123
Black Lion La. W6 —1F 12
Black Lion M. W6 —1F 12
Blackman Gdns. Alder —4N 109
Blackman's La. Warl —1A 86
Blackmeadows. Brack —5A 32
Blackmoor Clo. Asc —1H 33
Blackmoor Wood. Asc —1H 33
Blackmore Cres. Wok —2E 74
Blackmore's Gro. Tedd —7G 24
Blackness La. Kes —5F 66
Blackness La. Wok —6A 74
Blacknest. —2E 34
Blacknest Ga. Rd. Asc —2E 34
Blacknest Rd. Asc & Vir W —2G 35
Blacknest Rd. Black —3A 148
Black Pond La. Lwr Bo —5H 129
Black Prince Clo. Byfl —1A 76
Blackshaw Rd. SW17 —5A 28
Blacksmith Clo. Asht —6M 79
Blacksmith La. Chil —8E 114
Blacksmith Row. Slou —1C 6
Blacksmiths Hill. S Croy —9D 64
Blacksmiths La. Cher —6J 37
Blacksmiths La. Stai —2K 37
Blacks Rd. W6 —1H 13
Blackstone Clo. Farn —8J 69
Blackstone Clo. Red —4C 122
Blackstone Hill. Red —4B 122
Blackstroud La. E. Light —7A 52
Blackstroud La. W. Light —7A 52
Black Swan Clo. Peas P —1N 199
Blackthorn Clo. Craw —1A 182
Blackthorn Clo. H'ham —6N 197
Blackthorn Clo. Reig —5A 122
Blackthorn Ct. Houn —3M 9
Blackthorn Cres. Farn —6L 69
Blackthorn Dri. Light —8M 51
Blackthorne Av. Croy —7F 46
Blackthorne Cres. Coln —5G 7
Blackthorne Ind. Est. Coln —6G 7
Blackthorne Rd. Bookh —4C 98
Blackthorne Rd. Coln —6G 6
Blackthorn Pl. Guild —9M 93
Blackthorn Rd. Big H —3F 86
Blackthorn Rd. Reig —5A 122
Blackwater. —2K 69
Blackwater Clo. As —3E 110
Blackwater Ind. Est. B'water —1K 69
Blackwater La. Craw —4G 183
Blackwater Pk. Alder —3C 110
Blackwater Trad. Est. Alder —4C 110
Blackwater Valley Rd. Camb —2L 69
Blackwater Valley Route. Alder —6C 90
Blackwater Valley Route. Farn —7B 70
Blackwater Vw. Finch —5A 48
Blackwater Way. Alder —4B 110
Blackwell. —8A 166
Blackwell Av. Guild —3G 112
Blackwell Farm Rd. E Grin —7B 166
Blackwell Hollow. E Grin —8B 166
Blackwell Ho. SW4 —1H 29
Blackwell Rd. E Grin —8B 166
Blackwood Clo. W Byf —8L 55
Blade M. SW15 —7L 13
Bladen Clo. Wey —3E 56
Blades Clo. Lea —7K 79
Blades Ct. SW15 —7L 13
Blades Ct. W6 —1G 13
(off Lower Mall)
Bladon Clo. Guild —2C 114
Bladon Ct. SW16 —7J 29
Blagdon Rd. N Mald —3E 42
Blagdon Wlk. Tedd —7J 25
Blair Av. Esh —8C 40
Blair Ct. Beck —1L 47
Blairderry Rd. SW2 —3J 29
Blaire Pk. Yat —7A 48
Blaise Clo. Farn —2B 90
Blake Clo. Cars —7C 44
Blake Clo. Craw —7D 182
Blake Clo. Crowt —3H 49
Blake Clo. Wokgm —9D 14
Blakeden Dri. Clay —3F 58
Blake Gdns. SW6 —4N 13
Blakehall Rd. Cars —3D 62
Blakemore Rd. SW16 —4J 29
Blakemore Rd. T Hth —4K 45
Blakeney Clo. Eps —7C 60
Blakenham Rd. SW17 —5D 28
Blake Rd. Croy —8B 46 (2F 200)
Blake Rd. Mitc —2C 44
Blakes Av. N Mald —4E 42
Blakes Ct. Cher —7J 37
Blake's Grn. W Wick —7M 47
Blakes La. E Clan & W Hor —1N 115
Blakes La. N Mald —4E 42
Blakesley Wlk. SW20 —1L 43
Blakes Ride. Yat —9A 48
Blakes Ter. N Mald —4F 42
Blakewood Clo. Felt —5K 23
Blamire Dri. Binf —7K 15
Blanchard Ho. Twic —9K 11
(off Clevedon Rd.)
Blanchards Hill. Guild —6A 94
Blanchland Rd. Mord —4N 43
Blanchman's Rd. Warl —5H 85
Blandfield Rd. SW12 —1E 28
Blandford Av. Beck —1H 47
Blandford Av. Twic —2B 24
Blandford Clo. Croy —9J 45
Blandford Clo. Wok —4D 74
Blandford Rd. Beck —2F 46
Blandford Rd. Tedd —6D 24
Blane's La. Brack —7D 32
Blanford Rd. Reig —4A 122
Blanks La. Newd —8D 140
Blatchford Clo. H'ham —5M 197
Blatchford Rd. H'ham —5M 197
Blays Clo. Eng G —7M 19
Blay's La. Eng G —8L 19
Blear Ho. Eps —7E 60
Blegborough Rd. SW16 —7G 29
Blencarn Clo. Wok —3J 73
Blenheim Clo. SW20 —2H 43
Blenheim Clo. Craw —9H 163
Blenheim Clo. E Grin —7C 166
Blenheim Clo. Tong —5C 110
Blenheim Clo. Wall —4G 63
Blenheim Clo. W Byf —9H 55
Blenheim Ct. Farn —3B 90
Blenheim Ct. Sutt —3A 62
Blenheim Cres. Farnh —7F 108
Blenheim Cres. S Croy —4N 63
Blenheim Fields. F Row —6G 187
Blenheim Gdns. King T —8A 26
Blenheim Gdns. S Croy —8D 64
Blenheim Gdns. Wall —3G 62
Blenheim Gdns. Wok —6L 73
Blenheim Ho. Houn —6A 10
Blenheim Pk. Alder —6A 90
Blenheim Pk. Rd. S Croy —5N 63
Blenheim Rd. SW20 —2H 43
Blenheim Rd. Alder —6N 89
Blenheim Rd. Eps —7C 60
Blenheim Rd. H'ham —3K 197
Blenheim Rd. Slou —1N 5
Blenheim Rd. Sutt —9M 43
Blenheim Way. Iswth —4G 10
Blenkarne Rd. SW11 —1D 28
Bleriot Rd. Houn —3K 9
Bletchingley. —2A 124
Bletchingley Castle. —2N 123
Bletchingley Clo. Red —7G 103
Bletchingley Clo. T Hth —3M 45
Bletchingley Rd. God —9D 104
Bletchingley Rd. Mers —7G 102
Bletchingley Rd. Nutf —2L 123
Bletchmore Clo. Hayes —1E 8
Blewburton Wlk. Brack —3C 32
Blewfield. G'ming —9J 133
Bligh Clo. Craw —5D 182
Blighton La. Farnh —8B 110
Blincoe Clo. SW19 —3J 27
Blind La. Bans —2C 82
Blind La. Brock —6B 120
Blind La. Oxt —8A 106
Blind La. W End —6C 52
Blindley Heath. —3H 145
Blindley Rd. Craw —9H 163
Bloggs Way. Cranl —7M 155
Blomfield Dale. Brack —1J 31
Blondell Clo. W Dray —2M 7
Bloomfield Clo. Knap —4H 73
Bloomfield Dri. Brack —8B 16
Bloomfield Rd. King T —3L 41 (7L 203)
Bloomfield Ter. W'ham —3M 107
Bloom Gro. SE27 —4M 29
Bloomhall Rd. SE19 —6N 29
Bloom Pk. Rd. SW6 —3L 13
Bloomsbury Clo. Eps —6C 60
Bloomsbury Ct. Guild —5B 114
(off St Lukes Sq.)
Bloomsbury Ct. Houn —4J 9
Bloomsbury Pl. SW18 —8N 13
Bloomsbury Way. B'water —3H 69
Bloor Clo. H'ham —1K 197
Blossom Clo. S Croy —2C 64
Blossom Way. W Dray —1B 8
Blossom Waye. Houn —2M 9
Blount Av. E Grin —9M 165
Blount Cres. Binf —8K 15
Bloxham Cres. Hamp —8N 23
Bloxham Rd. Cranl —7B 156
Bloxworth Clo. Brack —3D 32
Bloxworth Clo. Wall —9G 45
Blue Anchor All. Rich —7L 11
Blue Ball La. Egh —6B 20
Blue Barn La. Wey —7B 56
Bluebell Clo. Craw —6N 181
Bluebell Clo. E Grin —9L 165
Bluebell Clo. H'ham —3L 197
Bluebell Clo. Wall —7F 44
Bluebell Cottage. Comp —2C 132
Bluebell Ct. Wok —6N 73
Bluebell Hill. Brack —9C 16
Bluebell La. E Hor —7F 96
Bluebell M. Camb —8B 50
Bluebell Railway. —6J 185
Bluebell Ri. Light —8M 51
Bluebell Rd. Lind —4B 168
Bluebell Wlk. Fleet —3A 88
Blueberry Gdns. Coul —3K 83
Blue Cedars. Bans —1J 81
Blue Cedars Pl. Cobh —8L 57
Blue Coat Wlk. Brack —4B 32
Bluefield Clo. Hamp —6A 24
Bluegates. Ewe —4F 60
Bluehouse Gdns. Oxt —6C 106
Bluehouse La. Oxt —6A 106
Blue Leaves Av. Coul —8H 83
Blue Pryor Ct. C Crook —1A 108
Blue Riband Ind. Est. Croy —8M 45 (2A 200)
Bluethroat Clo. Coll T —7K 49
Blue Water. SW18 —7N 13
Bluff Cove. Alder —1A 110
Blundel La. Stoke D —3N 77
Blundell Av. Horl —7D 142
Blunden Ct. Brmly —5C 134
Blunden Dri. Slou —1E 6
Blunden Rd. Farn —1L 89
Blunt Rd. S Croy —2A 64 (8D 200)
Blunts Av. W Dray —3B 8
Blunts Way. H'ham —5J 197
Blyth Clo. Twic —9F 10
Blythewood La. Asc —2J 33
Blythwood Dri. Frim —4B 70
Blytons, The. E Grin —9L 165
Board School Rd. Wok —3B 74
Boars Head Yd. Bren —3K 11
Bocketts Farm Pk. —3F 98
Bocketts La. Fet —2F 98
Bockhampton Rd. King T —8M 25
Boddicott Clo. SW19 —3K 27
Boden's Ride. Asc —8H 33
(in two parts)
Bodiam Clo. Craw —3G 183
Bodiam Rd. SW16 —8H 29
Bodley Clo. N Mald —4D 42
Bodley Mnr. Way. SW2 —1L 29
Bodley Rd. N Mald —5C 42
Bodmin Gro. Mord —4N 43
Bodmin Pl. SE27 —5M 29
Bodmin St. SW18 —2M 27
Bodnant Gdns. SW20 —2F 42
Bogey La. Orp —4J 67
Bog La. Brack —4D 32
Bognor Rd. Broad H & Warn —3C 178
Boileau Rd. SW13 —3F 12
Bois Hall Rd. Add —2M 55
Bolderwood Way. W Wick —8L 47
Bolding Ho. La. W End —9C 52
Boleyn Av. Eps —6G 60
Boleyn Clo. M'bowr —6H 183
Boleyn Clo. Stai —6G 20
Boleyn Ct. Red —2E 122
(off St Anne's Ri.)
Boleyn Dri. W Mol —2N 39
Boleyn Gdns. W Wick —8L 47
Boleyn Gro. W Wick —8M 47
Boleyn Wlk. Lea —7F 78
Bolingbroke Gro. SW11 —1D 28
Bollo La. W3 & W4 —1B 12
Bolney Ct. Craw —6L 181
Bolney Way. Felt —4M 23
Bolsover Gro. Red —7J 103
Bolstead Rd. Mitc —9F 28
Bolters La. Bans —1L 81
Bolters Rd. Horl —6E 142
Bolters Rd. S. Horl —6D 142
Bolton Av. Wind —6F 4
Bolton Clo. SE20 —1D 46
Bolton Clo. Chess —3K 59
Bolton Cres. Wind —6F 4
Bolton Gdns. SW5 —1N 13
Bolton Gdns. Tedd —7G 24
Bolton Gdns. M. SW10 —1N 13
Bolton Rd. W4 —3B 12
Bolton Rd. Chess —3K 59
Bolton Rd. M'bowr —8F 182
Bolton Rd. Wind —6F 4
Boltons Clo. Wok —3J 75
Boltons Ct. SW5 —1N 13
(off Old Brompton Rd.)
Boltons La. Binf —7K 15
Bolton's La. Hayes —3C 8
Boltons La. Wok —3J 75
Boltons Pl. SW5 —1N 13
Boltons, The. SW10 —1N 13
Bombers La. W'ham —6M 87
Bomer Clo. W Dray —3B 8
Bonchurch Clo. Sutt —4N 61
Bond Gdns. Wall —1G 63
Bond Rd. Mitc —1C 44
Bond Rd. Surb —8M 41
Bond Rd. Warl —5G 85
Bond's La. Mid H —2H 139
Bond St. W4 —1C 12
Bond St. Eng G —6L 19
Bond Way. Brack —9N 15
Bonehurst Rd. Salf & Horl —2E 142
Bone Mill La. God —3H 125
Bones La. Horne & Newc —7D 144
Bonner Hill Rd. King T
(in two parts) —1M 41 (4N 203)
Bonners Clo. Wok —9B 74
Bonnetts La. If'd —8M 161
Bonneville Gdns. SW4 —1G 28
Bonnys Rd. Reig —4J 121
Bonser Rd. Twic —3F 24
Bonsey Clo. Wok —8A 74
Bonsey La. Wok —8A 74
Bonseys La. Chob —5B 54
Bonsor Dri. Tad —9K 81
Bonwicke Cotts. Copt —4N 163
Bookham Comn. Rd. Bookh —8M 77
Bookham Ct. SW19 —2B 44
Bookham Ct. Bookh —1N 97
Bookham Gro. Bookh —4B 98
Bookham Ind. Est. Bookh —1N 97
Bookham Rd. D'side —6K 77
Bookhurst Rd. Cranl —6B 156
Boole Heights. Brack —4M 31
Booth Dri. Stai —7M 21
Booth Rd. Craw —6K 181
Booth Rd. Croy —8M 45 (3A 200)
Booth Way. H'ham —5L 197
Borage Clo. Craw —6M 181
Border Chase. Copt —8L 163
Border Ct. E Grin —6B 166
Border End. Hasl —2B 188
Border Gdns. Croy —1L 65
Bordergate. Mitc —9C 28
Border Rd. Hasl —2B 188
Borderside. Yat —9A 48
Bordesley Rd. Mord —4N 43
Bordeston Ct. Bren —3J 11
(off Augustus Clo.)
Bordon. —7A 168
Bordon Wlk. SW15 —1F 26
Boreen, The. Head —4G 169
Borelli M. Farnh —1H 129
Borelli Yd. Farnh —1H 129
Borers Arms Rd. Copt —6M 163
Borers Clo. Copt —6N 163
Borers Yd. Ind. Est. Copt —7N 163
Borkwood Pk. Orp —1N 67
Borkwood Way. Orp —1N 67
Borland Rd. Tedd —8H 25
Borneo St. SW15 —6H 13
Borough Hill. Croy —9M 45 (5A 200)
Borough Rd. G'ming —6G 133
Borough Rd. Iswth —4E 10
Borough Rd. King T —9N 25
Borough Rd. Mitc —1C 44
Borough Rd. Tats —8F 86
Borough, The. Brock —4N 119
Borough, The. Farnh —1G 129
Borrodaile Rd. SW18 —9N 13
Borrowdale Clo. Craw —5N 181
Borrowdale Clo. Egh —8D 20
Borrowdale Clo. S Croy —9C 64
Borrowdale Dri. S Croy —8C 64
Borrowdale Gdns. Camb —1H 71
Bosco Clo. Orp —1N 67
Boscombe Clo. Egh —9E 20
Boscombe Gdns. SW16 —7J 29
Boscombe Ho. Croy —1D 200
Boscombe Rd. SW17 —7E 28
Boscombe Rd. SW19 —9N 27
Boscombe Rd. Wor Pk —7H 43
Bosham Rd. M'bowr —6G 183
Bosher Gdns. Egh —7B 20
Bosman Dri. W'sham —9M 33
Bostock Av. H'ham —3N 197
Bostock Ho. Houn —2A 10
Boston Gdns. W4 —2D 12
Boston Gdns. Bren —1G 11
Boston Manor. —1G 11
Boston Manor House. —1H 11
Boston Mnr. Rd. Bren —1H 11
Boston Pk. Rd. Bren —1J 11
Boston Rd. Croy —5K 45
Boswell Ct. King T —1N 203
Boswell Path. Hayes —1G 8
Boswell Rd. Craw —6C 182
Boswell Rd. T Hth —3N 45
Boswell Row. Cat —9D 84
Botany Hill. Farnh & Seale —2B 130
Botery's Cross. Blet —2M 123
Bothwell Rd. New Ad —6M 65
Bothwell St. SW6 —2J 13
Bothy, The. Pep H —6A 132
Botsford Rd. SW20 —1K 43
Bottle La. Binf & Warf —1K 15
Boucher Clo. Tedd —6F 24
Boughton Hall Av. Send —2H 95
Bouldish Farm Rd. Asc —4K 33
Boulevard, The. SW17 —3E 28
Boulevard, The. SW18 —7N 13
Boulevard, The. Craw —3B 182
(in two parts)
Boulogne Rd. Croy —5N 45
Boulters Ho. Brack —3C 32
Boulter's Rd. Alder —2N 109
Boulthurst Way. Oxt —1D 126
Boulton Ho. Bren —1L 11
Boundaries Rd. SW12 —3D 28
Boundaries Rd. Felt —2K 23
Boundary Bus. Cen., The. Wok —2C 74
Boundary Bus. Ct. Mitc —2B 44
Boundary Clo. SE25 —1D 46
Boundary Clo. Craw —2C 182
Boundary Clo. King T —2A 42
Boundary Clo. S'hall —1A 10
Boundary Cotts. Chil —8J 115
Boundary Rd. SW19 —7B 28
Boundary Rd. Afrd —6L 21
Boundary Rd. Cars & Wall —3F 62
Boundary Rd. Craw —2C 182
Boundary Rd. Dock & Rowl —4C 148
Boundary Rd. Farn —3A 90
Boundary Rd. Gray —6B 170
Boundary Rd. Wok —3C 74
Boundary Vs. B'water —2K 69
Boundary Way. Croy —2K 65
Boundary Way. Wok —2C 74
Boundless Rd. Brook —1F 170
Boundstone. —6F 128
Boundstone Clo. Wrec —6G 128
Boundstone Rd. Rowl & Wrec —7E 128
Bourdon Rd. SE20 —1F 46
Bourg-de-Peage Av. E Grin —9C 166
Bourke Clo. SW4 —1J 29
Bourke Hill. Coul —5D 82
Bourley La. Ews —2E 108
Bourley Rd. Alder —2G 108
Bourley Rd. C Crook & Ews —9D 88
Bourne Av. Cher —2J 37
Bourne Av. Wind —6F 4
Bourne Bus. Pk. Add —1N 55
Bourne Clo. Chil —9D 114
Bourne Clo. Th Dit —8F 40
Bourne Clo. W Byf —9K 55
Bourne Ct. W4 —2B 12
Bourne Ct. Alder —4M 109
Bourne Ct. Cat —1D 104
Bourne Ct. H'ham —5L 197
Bourne Dene. Wrec —6F 128
Bourne Dri. Mitc —1B 44
Bournefield Rd. Whyt —5D 84
Bourne Firs. Lwr Bo —6J 129
Bourne Gro. Asht —6K 79
Bourne Gro. Lwr Bo —4K 129
Bourne Gro. Clo. Lwr Bo —4K 129
Bourne Gro. Dri. Lwr Bo —4K 129
Bourne Hall Mus. —5E 60
Bourne Heights. Farnh —3H 129
Bourne La. Cat —8A 84
Bourne Mdw. Egh —3D 36
Bourne Mill Ind. Est. Farnh —9K 109
Bournemouth Rd. SW19 —9M 27
Bourne Pk. Clo. Kenl —3B 84
Bourne Pl. W4 —1C 12
Bourne Rd. G'ming —3J 133
Bourne Rd. Red —8G 103
Bourne Rd. Vir W —4N 35
Bourneside. Vir W —6K 35
Bourneside Rd. Add —1M 55
Bourne St. Croy —8M 45 (3A 200)
Bourne, The. —5J 129
Bourne, The. Fleet —7B 88
Bournevale Rd. SW16 —5J 29
Bourne Vw. Kenl —2A 84
Bourne Way. Add —2L 55
Bourne Way. Eps —1B 60
Bourne Way. Sutt —2L 61
Bourne Way. Wok —9N 73
Bousley Ri. Ott —3F 54
Bouverie Gdns. Purl —1K 83
Bouverie Rd. Coul —5E 82
Bouverie Way. Slou —1A 6
Boveney. —2A 4
Boveney New Rd. Eton W —1B 4
Boveney Rd. Dor —1A 4
Bovingdon Rd. SW6 —4N 13
Bovingdon Sq. Mitc —3J 45
Bowater Gdns. Sun —1K 39
Bowater Ridge. St G —6E 56
Bowater Rd. M'bowr —6G 183
Bowcott Hill. Head —4E 168
Bowcroft La. Rud —1F 194
Bowden Clo. Felt —2F 22
Bowden Rd. Asc —4N 33
Bowenhurst Gdns. C Crook —9B 88
Bowenhurst Rd. C Crook —8B 88
Bowens Wood. Croy —5J 65
Bower Ct. Wok —3D 74
Bowerdean St. SW6 —4N 13
Bower Hill Clo. S Nut —6J 123
Bower Hill La. S Nut —4H 123
Bowerland La. Ling —3N 145
Bower Rd. Wrec —6F 128
Bowers Clo. Guild —8C 94
Bowers Farm Dri. Guild —8C 94
Bowers La. Guild —7C 94
Bowers Pl. Craw D —1E 184
Bower, The. Craw —4G 182
Bowes Clo. H'ham —5L 197
Bowes Lyon Clo. Wind —4F 4
(off Alma Rd.)
Bowes Rd. Stai —6G 20
Bowes Rd. W on T —8J 39
Bowfell Rd. W6 —2H 13
Bowie Clo. SW4 —1H 29
Bowland Dri. Brack —6C 32
Bow La. Mord —5K 43

Bowlhead Green—Bridle Rd.

Bowlhead Green. —9K 151
Bowlhead Grn. Rd. Brook —9K 151
Bowling Grn. Clo. SW15 —1G 27
Bowling Grn. Cl. Frim G —7C 70
Bowling Grn. La. H'ham —5K 197
Bowling Grn. Rd. Chob —5H 53
Bowlings, The. Camb —9A 50
Bowman Ct. Craw —2D 182
(off London Rd.)
Bowman Ct. Wel C —3E 48
Bowman M. SW18 —2L 27
Bowmans Mdw. Wall —9F 44
Bowness Clo. If'd —4J 181
Bowness Cres. SW15 —6D 26
Bowness Dri. Houn —7M 9
Bowry Dri. Wray —9B 6
Bowsley Ct. Felt —3H 23
Bowsprit, The. Cobh —2K 77
Bowyer Cres. Wokgm —9B 14
Bowyers Clo. Asht —5M 79
Bowyer's La. Warf —3N 15
Bowyer Wlk. Asc —9J 17
Boxall's Gro. Alder —5M 109
Boxall's La. Alder —5M 109
Boxall Wlk. H'ham —7K 197
Box Clo. Craw —8A 182
Boxford Clo. S Croy —8G 65
Boxford Ridge. Brack —2N 31
Boxgrove Av. Guild —1C 114
Boxgrove La. Guild —2C 114
Boxgrove Rd. Guild —2C 114
Box Hill. —9B 100
Boxhill Country Park & Info. Cen. —1K 119
Boxhill Rd. Dork —2L 119
Boxhill Rd. Tad —1M 119
Boxhill Way. Str G —7A 120
Box La. Ash W —3G 186
Boxley Rd. Mord —3A 44
Box Ridge Av. Purl —8K 63
Box Tree Wlk. Red —6A 122
Box Wlk. E Hor —1F 116
Boxwood Way. Warl —4G 85
Boyd Clo. King T —8N 25
Boyd Ct. Brack —9M 15
Boyd Rd. SW19 —7B 28
Boyle Farm Rd. Th Dit —5G 40
Brabazon Av. Wall —4J 63
Brabazon Rd. Houn —3K 9
Brabon Rd. Farn —9L 69
Brabourne Ri. Beck —4M 47
Brabrook Ct. Wall —1F 62
Bracebridge. Camb —1M 69
Bracewood Gdns. Croy —9C 46
Bracken Av. SW12 —1E 28
Bracken Av. Croy —9K 47
Bracken Bank. Asc —9G 17
Bracken Clo. Bookh —2N 97
Bracken Clo. Copt —7M 163
Bracken Clo. Craw —1C 182
Bracken Clo. Sun —7G 22
Bracken Clo. Twic —1A 24
Bracken Clo. Wok —5B 74
Bracken Clo. Won —5C 134
Brackendale Clo. Camb —3C 70
Brackendale Clo. Houn —4B 10
Brackendale Rd. Camb —1B 70
Brackendene. As —1G 110
Brackendene Clo. Wok —2C 74
Bracken End. Iswth —8D 10
Bracken Gdns. SW13 —5F 12
Bracken Gro. H'ham —3A 198
Brackenhill. Cobh —8B 58
Bracken Hollow. Camb —7F 50
Bracken La. Yat —9A 48
Brackenlea. G'ming —4G 132
Bracken Path. Eps —9A 60
Brackenside. Horl —7F 142
Brackens, The. Asc —2F 32
Brackens, The. Crowt —9F 30
Bracken Way. Chob —6J 53
Bracken Way. Guild —1H 113
Brackenwood. Camb —1H 71
Brackenwood. Sun —9H 23
Brackenwood Rd. Wok —6G 73
Bracklesham Clo. Farn —7M 69
Brackley. Wey —2E 56
Brackley Clo. Wall —4J 63
Brackley Rd. W4 —1D 12
Brackley Ter. W4 —1D 12
Bracklyn Av. Dor P —5B 166
Bracklyn Av. Felb —5F 164
Bracknell. —1A 32
Bracknell Beeches. Brack —2N 31
Bracknell Clo. Camb —6D 50
Bracknell Enterprise Cen. Brack —1M 31
Bracknell Rd. Bag —1H 51
Bracknell Rd. Camb —5D 50
Bracknell Rd. Crowt —7D 32
(Bagshot Rd.)
Bracknell Rd. Crowt —2H 49
(Duke's Ride)
Bracknell Rd. Warf —6C 16
Bracknell Wlk. Craw —7K 181
Bracondale. Esh —2C 58
Bradbourne St. SW6 —5M 13
Bradbury Rd. M'bowr —6G 182
Braddock Clo. Iswth —5F 10
Braddon Rd. Rich —6M 11
Bradenhurst Clo. Cat —4C 104
Bradfield Clo. Guild —9C 94
Bradfield Clo. Wok —5A 74
Bradfields. Brack —4B 32
Bradford Dri. Eps —3E 60
Brading Rd. SW2 —1K 29
Brading Rd. Croy —5K 45
Bradley Clo. Belm —6N 61
Bradley Dri. Wokgm —6A 30
Bradley La. Dork —1G 119
Bradley M. SW17 —2D 28
Bradley Rd. SE19 —7N 29
Bradmore Way. Coul —4J 83
Bradshaw Clo. SW19 —7M 27
Bradshaw Clo. Wind —4B 4
Bradshawe Clo. SE25 —2D 46
Bradstock Rd. Eps —2F 60
Braemar Av. SW19 —3M 27
Braemar Av. S Croy —6N 63
Braemar Av. T Hth —2L 45
Braemar Clo. Frim —6D 70
Braemar Clo. G'ming —8G 132
Braemar Gdns. W Wick —7M 47
Braemar Rd. Bren —2K 11
Braemar Rd. Wor Pk —9G 42
Braeside. Brack —1H 31
Braeside. New H —7K 55
Braeside Av. SW19 —9K 27
Braeside Clo. Hasl —9D 170
Braeside Rd. SW16 —8G 29
Braes Mead. S Nut —4J 123
Brafferton Rd. Croy —1N 63 (6B 200)
Bragg Rd. Tedd —7E 24
Braid Clo. Felt —3N 23
Brailsford Clo. SW19 —8C 28
Brainton Av. Felt —1J 23
Brakey Hill. Blet —3B 124
Bramber Clo. Craw —1C 182
Bramber Clo. H'ham —3A 198
Bramber Ct. W5 —1L 11
Bramber Rd. W14 —2L 13
Brambleacres Clo. Sutt —4M 61
Bramblebank. Frim G —8E 70
Bramble Banks. Cars —5E 62
Bramble Clo. Beck —4M 47
Bramble Clo. Copt —7M 163
Bramble Clo. Croy —1K 65
Bramble Clo. Guild —1H 113
Bramble Clo. Red —5E 122
Bramble Clo. Shep —3F 38
Bramble Ct. Ewh —4F 156
Brambledene Clo. Wok —6M 73
Bramble Down. Stai —9K 21
Brambledown Rd. Cars & Wall —4E 62
Brambledown Rd. S Croy —4B 64
Bramblegate. Crowt —1F 48
Bramble La. Hamp —7N 23
Bramble Ri. Cobh —2K 77
Brambles Clo. As —3F 110
Brambles Clo. Cat —9B 84
Brambles Clo. Iswth —3H 11
Brambles Pk. Brmly —5B 134
Brambles, The. SW19 —6L 27
(off Woodside)
Brambles, The. Crowt —1C 48
Brambles, The. G'ming —4G 133
Brambles, The. W Dray —1M 7
Brambleton Av. Farnh —3G 128
Bramble Twitten. E Grin —9C 166
Brambletye La. F Row —5F 186
Brambletye Pk. Rd. Red —5D 122
Brambletye Rd. Craw —4E 182
Bramble Wlk. Eps —1A 80
Bramble Wlk. Red —5E 122
Bramble Way. Rip —2H 95
Bramblewood. Red —7F 102
Bramblewood Clo. Cars —7C 44
Bramblewood Pl. Fleet —4A 88
Brambling Clo. H'ham —7N 197
Brambling Rd. H'ham —7N 197
Bramcote. Camb —1G 71
Bramcote Av. Mitc —3D 44
Bramcote Rd. SW15 —7G 13
Bramerton Rd. Beck —2J 47
Bramford Rd. SW18 —7N 13
Bramham Gdns. SW5 —1N 13
Bramham Gdns. Chess —1K 59
Bramley. —5B 134
Bramley Av. Coul —2G 82
Bramley Av. Shep —2F 38
Bramley Bus. Cen. Brmly —4B 134
(off Station Rd.)
Bramley Clo. Cher —7K 37
Bramley Clo. Craw —3D 182
Bramley Clo. Red —5C 122
Bramley Clo. S Croy —2N 63 (8A 200)
Bramley Clo. Stai —7L 21
Bramley Clo. Twic —9C 10
Bramley Ct. Crowt —3D 48
Bramley Ct. Mitc —1B 44
Bramley Gro. Crowt —2C 48
Bramley Hill. S Croy —2M 63 (8A 200)
Bramley Ho. SW15 —9E 12
(off Tunworth Cres.)
Bramley Ho. Houn —7N 9
Bramley Ho. Red —4E 122
Bramleyhyrst. S Croy —7B 200
Bramley La. B'water —1G 69
Bramley Rd. Camb —4N 69
Bramley Rd. Cheam —5J 61
Bramley Rd. Sutt —2B 62
Bramley Wlk. Horl —8G 143
Bramley Way. Asht —4M 79
Bramley Way. Houn —8N 9
Bramley Way. W Wick —8L 47
Bramling Av. Yat —9A 48
Brampton Gdns. W on T —2K 57
Brampton Rd. Croy —6C 46
Bramshaw Ri. N Mald —5D 42
Bramshot Dri. Fleet —3B 88
Bramshot La. Farn —8H 69
Bramshot La. Fleet —1F 88
Bramshot Rd. Farn —3F 88
Bramshott. —9H 169
Bramshott Chase. —9N 169
Bramshott Common. —9M 169
Bramshott Rd. Pass —8E 168
Bramston Rd. SW17 —4A 28
Bramswell Rd. G'ming —5J 133
Bramwell Clo. Sun —1L 39
Brancaster La. Purl —6N 63
Brancaster Rd. SW16 —4J 29
Brancker Clo. Wall —4J 63
Brandlehow Rd. SW15 —7L 13
Brandon Clo. Camb —2H 71
Brandon Clo. M'bowr —5H 183
Brandon Mans. W14 —2K 13
(off Queen's Club Gdns.)
Brandon Rd. C Crook —9A 88
Brandon Rd. S'hall —1N 9
Brandon Rd. Sutt —1N 61
Brandreth Rd. SW17 —3F 28
Brandries, The. Wall —9H 45
Brands Hill. —2D 6
Brandsland. Reig —7N 121
Brands Rd. Slou —2D 6
Brandy Way. Sutt —4M 61
Brangwyn Cres. SW19 —9A 28
Branksea St. SW6 —3K 13
Branksome Clo. Camb —9C 50
Branksome Clo. Tedd —5D 24
Branksome Clo. W on T —8L 39
Branksome Ct. Fleet —4A 88
Branksome Hill Rd. Coll T & Owl —8K 49
Branksome Pk. Rd. Camb —9C 50
Branksome Rd. SW19 —9M 27
Branksome Way. N Mald —9B 26
Brankscomewood Rd. Fleet —3A 88
Bransby Rd. Chess —3L 59
Branson Rd. Bord —6A 168
Branstone Rd. Rich —4M 11
Brantridge Rd. Craw —5D 182
Brants Bri. Brack —1C 32
Brantwood Av. Iswth —7G 10
Brantwood Clo. W Byf —9J 55
Brantwood Ct. W Byf —9H 55
(off Brantwood Dri.)
Brantwood Dri. W Byf —9H 55
Brantwood Gdns. W Byf —9H 55
Brantwood Rd. S Croy —5N 63
Brasenose Dri. SW13 —2H 13
Brassey Clo. Felt —2H 23
Brassey Clo. Oxt —7C 106
Brassey Hill. Oxt —7C 106
Brassey Rd. Oxt —8B 106
Brasted Clo. Sutt —6M 61
Brasted Rd. W'ham & Bras —4M 107
Brathway Rd. SW18 —1M 27
Bratten Ct. Croy —5A 46
Bravington Clo. Shep —4A 38
Braxted Pk. SW16 —7K 29
Braybourne Dri. Iswth —3F 10
Braybrooke Rd. Brack —8N 15
Bray Clo. M'bowr —6H 183
Bray Ct. SW16 —6J 29
Braycourt Av. W on T —6J 39
Braye Clo. Sand —6H 49
Bray Gdns. Wok —3G 74
Bray Rd. Guild —4L 113
Bray Rd. Stoke D —3M 77
Braywood Av. Egh —7B 20
Braziers La. Wink R —6G 17
Brazil Clo. Bedd —6J 45
Breakfield. Coul —3J 83
Breamore Clo. SW15 —2F 26
Breamwater Gdns. Rich —4H 25
Breasley Clo. SW15 —7G 13
Brecon Clo. Farn —7J 69
Brecon Clo. Mitc —2J 45
Brecon Clo. Wor Pk —8H 43
Brecon Rd. W6 —2K 13
Brecons, The. Wey —1E 56
Bredon Rd. Croy —9C 46
Bredune. Kenl —2A 84
Breech La. Tad —2F 100
Breech, The. Coll T —8K 49
Breer St. SW6 —6N 13
Breezehurst Dri. Craw —6K 181
Bregsells La. Bear G —7K 139
Bremer Rd. Stai —4J 21
Bremner Av. Horl —7D 142
Brenda Rd. SW17 —3D 28
Brende Gdns. W Mol —3B 40
Brendon Clo. Esh —3C 58
Brendon Clo. Hayes —3D 8
Brendon Dri. Esh —3C 58
Brendon Rd. Farn —7J 69
Brenley Clo. Mitc —2E 44
Brentford. —2K 11
Brentford Bus. Cen. Bren —3J 11
Brentford End. —3H 11
Brentford F.C. —2K 11
Brentford Ho. Twic —1H 25
Brentford Musical Mus. —2L 11
Brent Lea. Bren —3J 11
Brentmoor Rd. W End —9N 51
Brent Rd. Bren —2J 11
Brent Rd. S Croy —5E 64
Brent Side. Bren —2J 11
Brentside Executive Cen. Bren —2H 11
Brentwaters Bus. Pk. Bren —3J 11
Brent Way. Bren —3K 11
Brentwick Gdns. Bren —1L 11
Brentwood Ct. Add —1K 55
Brethart Rd. Frim —5C 70
Bretlands Rd. Cher —8G 36
Brettgrave. Eps —6B 60
Brett Ho. Clo. SW15 —1J 27
Brettingham Clo. Craw —6K 181
Brewer Rd. Craw —5C 182
Brewers Clo. Farn —9M 69
Brewers La. Rich —8K 11
Brewer St. Blet —9N 103
Brewery La. Byfl —9N 55
Brewery La. Twic —1F 24
Brewery M. Cen. Iswth —6G 10
Brewery Rd. Wok —4N 73
Brew Ho. Rd. Str G & Brock —7B 120
Brewhouse St. SW15 —6K 13
Brewhurst La. Loxw —6J 193
(in two parts)
Breydon Wlk. Craw —5F 182
Brian Av. S Croy —8B 64
Briane Rd. Eps —6B 60
Briar Av. SW16 —8K 29
Briar Av. Light —8K 51
Briar Banks. Cars —5E 62
Briar Clo. Craw —9A 162
Briar Clo. Eden —9M 127
Briar Clo. Hamp —6N 23
Briar Clo. Iswth —8F 10
Briar Clo. W Byf —7K 55
Briar Ct. SW15 —7G 13
Briar Ct. Sutt —1H 61
Briar Gro. S Croy —9D 64
Briar Hill. Purl —7J 63
Briar La. Cars —5E 62
Briar La. Croy —1L 65
Briarleas Ct. Farn —5B 90
Briar Patch. G'ming —5G 133
Briar Rd. SW16 —2J 45
Briar Rd. Send —2D 94
Briar Rd. Shep —4A 38
Briar Rd. Twic —2E 24
Briars Clo. Farn —2J 89
Briars Ct. Oxs —1D 78
Briars, The. As —3F 110
Briars, The. Slou —1B 6
Briars, The. Stai —8J 7
Briars Wood. Horl —7G 142
Briarswood Clo. Craw —1H 183
Briarswood Way. Orp —2N 67
Briar Wlk. SW15 —7G 13
Briar Wlk. W Byf —8J 55
Briar Way. Guild —8D 94
Briarwood Clo. Felt —5F 22
Briarwood Ct. Wor Pk —7F 42
(off Avenue, The)
Briarwood Rd. Eps —3F 60
Briarwood Rd. Wok —6G 73
Briavels Ct. Eps —2D 80
Brickbarn Clo. SW10 —3N 13
(off King's Barn)
Brickbat All. Lea —8H 79
Brick Farm Clo. Rich —4A 12
Brickfield Clo. Bren —3J 11
Brickfield Cotts. Alder —4J 109
Brickfield Cotts. Crowt —4E 48
Brickfield Cotts. Norm —3A 112
Brickfield Farm Gdns. Orp —1L 67
Brickfield La. Hayes —2E 8
Brickfield Rd. SW19 —5N 27
Brickfield Rd. Out —2L 143
Brickfield Rd. T Hth —9M 29
Brickfields Ind. Pk. Brack —1L 31
Brick Hill. —1F 52
Brickhouse La. S God & Newc —4F 144
Brick Kiln La. Oxt —9E 106
Bricklands. Craw D —2E 184
Brick La. Fleet —3A 88
Bricksbury Hill. Farnh —5H 109
Brickwood Rd. Croy —8B 46 (2F 200)
Brickyard Copse. Ockl —6C 158
Brickyard La. Craw D —1E 184
Brickyard La. Wott —1L 137
Brideake Clo. Craw —6M 181
Bridge Av. W6 —1H 13
Bridge Av. Mans. W6 —1H 13
(off Bridge Av.)
Bridge Barn La. Wok —5N 73
Bridge Clo. Byfl —8A 56
Bridge Clo. Stai —5G 20
Bridge Clo. Tedd —5F 24
Bridge Clo. W on T —6G 38
Bridge Clo. Wok —4M 73
Bridge Ct. Wey —1C 56
Bridge Ct. Wok —4N 73
Bridge End. —7C 76
Bridge End. Camb —2N 69
Bridgefield. Farnh —1J 129
Bridgefield Clo. Bans —2H 81
Bridgefield Rd. Sutt —3M 61
Bridgefoot. Sun —9G 23
Bridge Gdns. Ashf —8D 22
Bridge Gdns. E Mol —3D 40
Bridgeham Clo. Wey —2B 56
Bridgeham Way. Small —9M 143
Bridgehill Clo. Guild —1K 113
Bridge Ho. Sutt —3N 61
(off Bridge Rd.)
Bridge Ind. Est. Horl —8F 142
Bridgelands. Copt —7L 163
Bridge La. Vir W —4A 36
Bridgeman Dri. Wind —5D 4
Bridgeman Rd. Tedd —7G 24
Bridgemead. Frim —6A 70
(off Frimley High St.)
Bridge Mead. Pirb —4C 92
Bridge M. G'ming —7H 133
Bridge M. Tong —5D 110
Bridge M. Wok —4N 73
Bridgend Rd. SW18 —7N 13
Bridgepark. SW18 —8M 13
Bridge Pk. Guild —9E 94
Bridge Pl. Croy —7A 46
Bridge Retail Pk. Wokgm —3A 30
Bridge Rd. Alder —4M 109
Bridge Rd. Asc —4A 34
Bridge Rd. Bag —4J 51
Bridge Rd. Camb —3N 69
Bridge Rd. Cher —6K 37
Bridge Rd. Chess —2L 59
Bridge Rd. Cranl —8N 155
Bridge Rd. E Mol —3D 40
Bridge Rd. Eps —8F 60
Bridge Rd. Farn —1L 89
Bridge Rd. G'ming —6H 133
Bridge Rd. Hasl —1G 189
Bridge Rd. Houn & Iswth —6D 10
Bridge Rd. Rud —1E 194
Bridge Rd. Sutt —3N 61
Bridge Rd. Twic —9H 11
Bridge Rd. Wall —2F 62
Bridge Rd. Wey —1A 56
Bridge Row. Croy —7A 46 (1E 200)
Bridges Clo. Horl —8H 143
Bridges Ct. H'ham —3M 197
Bridges La. Croy —1J 63
Bridges Pl. SW6 —4L 13
Bridges Sq. Farnh —1H 129
Bridges Rd. SW19 —7N 27
Bridges Rd. M. SW19 —7N 27
Bridge St. W4 —1C 12
Bridge St. Coln —3F 6
Bridge St. G'ming —7H 133
Bridge St. Guild —4M 113 (5B 202)
Bridge St. Lea —9G 79
Bridge St. Rich —8K 11
Bridge St. Stai —5G 21
Bridge St. W on T —7F 38
Bridge St. Pas. Guild —5B 202
Bridge Vw. W6 —1H 13
Bridge Vw. Asc —6E 34
Bridge Wlk. Yat —8C 48
Bridgewater Ct. Slou —1C 6
Bridgewater Rd. Wey —3E 56
Bridgewater Ter. Wind —4G 4
Bridgewater Way. Wind —4G 4
Bridge Way. Cobh —9G 57
Bridge Way. Coul —6C 82
Bridge Way. Twic —1C 24
Bridge Wharf. Cher —6L 37
Bridge Wharf Rd. Iswth —6H 11
Bridgewood Rd. SW16 —8H 29
Bridgewood Rd. Wor Pk —1F 60
Bridgford St. SW18 —4N 27
Bridle Clo. Eps —2C 60
Bridle Clo. Gray —6M 169
Bridle Clo. King T —3K 41 (7J 203)
Bridle Clo. Sun —2H 39
Bridle Ct. Alder —2K 109
Bridle End. Eps —9E 60
Bridle La. Stoke D & Oxs —2B 78
Bridle La. Twic —9H 11
Bridle Path. Croy —9J 45
(in two parts)
Bridle Path, The. Eps —6H 61
Bridlepath Way. Felt —2F 22
Bridle Rd. Clay —3H 59
Bridle Rd. Croy —9K 47
(in two parts)

Bridle Rd.—Browngraves Rd.

Bridle Rd. Eps —9E 60
Bridle Rd. S Croy —5D 64
Bridle Rd., The. Purl —6J 63
Bridle Way. Craw —2H 183
Bridle Way. Croy —1K 65
Bridle Way. Orp —1L 67
Bridleway Clo. Eps —6H 61
Bridle Way, The. S Croy —6H 65
Bridleway, The. Wall —2G 63
Bridlington Clo. Big H —6D 86
Bridport Rd. T Hth —2L 45
Brier Lea. Lwr K —4L 101
Brierley. New Ad —3L 65
(in two parts)
Brierley Clo. SE25 —3D 46
Brierley Rd. SW12 —3G 28
Brierly Clo. Guild —1K 113
Brier Rd. Tad —6G 81
Brigade Pl. Cat —9N 83
Briggs Clo. Mitc —9F 28
Bright Hill. Guild —5A 114 (6D 202)
Brightlands Rd. Reig —1A 122
Brightman Rd. SW18 —2B 28
Brighton Clo. Add —2L 55
Brighton Rd. Add —2L 55
Brighton Rd. Alder —4A 110
Brighton Rd. Coul & Purl —5G 83
Brighton Rd. G'ming —7H 133
Brighton Rd. Hand —8N 199
Brighton Rd. Horl —9D 142
Brighton Rd. H'ham —7K 197
Brighton Rd. Kgswd & Lwr K —9K 81
Brighton Rd. Mers & Coul —1F 102
Brighton Rd. Peas P & Hand —5N 199
Brighton Rd. Purl & S Croy —7L 63
Brighton Rd. Red —4D 122
Brighton Rd. Salf —1E 142
Brighton Rd. S Croy —2N 63 (8C 200)
Brighton Rd. Surb —5J 41
Brighton Rd. Sutt —7M 61
Brighton Rd. Tad & Bans —8K 81
Brighton Ter. Red —4D 122
Brightside Av. Stai —8L 21
Brightwell Clo. Croy —7L 45
Brightwell Cres. SW17 —6D 28
Brightwells Rd. Farnh —1H 129
Brigstock Rd. Coul —2F 82
Brigstock Rd. T Hth —4L 45
Brimshot La. Chob —5H 53
Brimstone La. Holmw —3M 139
Brind Cotts. Chob —6J 53
Brindle Clo. Alder —5N 109
Brindles, The. Bans —4L 81
Brinkley Rd. Wor Pk —8G 42
Brinksway. Fleet —4B 88
Brinn's La. B'water —1H 69
Brinsworth Clo. Twic —2D 24
Brinsworth Ho. Twic —3D 24
Brisbane Av. SW19 —9N 27
Brisbane Clo. Craw —9B 162
Briscoe Rd. SW19 —7B 28
Brisson Clo. Esh —2N 57
Bristol Clo. Craw —9H 163
Bristol Clo. Stanw —9N 7
Bristol Clo. Wall —4J 63
Bristol Ct. Stanw —9N 7
Bristol Gdns. SW15 —1H 27
Bristol Rd. Mord —4A 44
Bristow Rd. Camb —3N 69
Bristow Rd. Croy —1J 63
Bristow Rd. Houn —6C 10
Britannia Clo. Bord —6A 168
Britannia Ind. Est. Coln —5G 6
Britannia La. Twic —1C 24
Britannia Rd. SW6 —3N 13
(in two parts)
Britannia Rd. Surb —6M 41
Britannia Way. SW6 —3N 13
(off Britannia Rd.)
Britannia Way. Stanw —1M 21
British Gro. W4 —1E 12
British Gro. Pas. W4 —1E 12
British Gro. S. W4 —1E 12
Briton Clo. S Croy —7B 64
Briton Cres. S Croy —7B 64
Briton Hill Rd. S Croy —6B 64
Brittain Ct. Sand —8H 49
Brittain Rd. W on T —2L 57
Britten Clo. As —2F 110
Britten Clo. Craw —6L 181
Britten Clo. H'ham —4A 198
Brittenden Clo. Orp —3N 67
Brittenden Pde. G Str —3N 67
Brittens Clo. Guild —7K 93
Brittleware Cotts. Charl —8L 141
Brixton Hill. SW2 —1J 29
Brixton Hill Pl. SW2 —1J 29
Broadacre. Stai —6J 21
Broad Acres. G'ming —3H 133
Broadacres. Guild —1H 113
Broadbridge. —1L 163
Broadbridge Cotts. Small —1L 163
Broadbridge Heath. —5D 196
Broadbridge Heath By-Pass. Broad H —5C 196
Broadbridge Heath Rd. Broad H & Warn —4D 196
Broadbridge La. Small —8L 143
Broadbridge Retail Pk. Broad H —5E 196
Broad Clo. W on T —9L 39
Broadcommon Rd. Hurst —1A 14
Broadcoombe. S Croy —4F 64
Broadeaves Clo. S Croy —2B 64
Broadfield. —7N 181
Broadfield Barton. Craw —7N 181
Broadfield Clo. Croy —8K 45
Broadfield Clo. Tad —7H 81
Broadfield Dri. Craw —6N 181
Broadfield Pk. Craw —7B 182
Broadfield Pl. Craw —7N 181
Broadfield Rd. Peasl —2E 136
Broadfields. E Mol —5E 40
Broadford. —1N 133
Broadford La. Chob —8H 53
Broadford Pk. Shalf —1N 133
Broadford Rd. P'mrsh & Shalf —1M 133
Broadgates Rd. SW18 —2B 28
Broad Green. —6M 45
Broad Grn. Av. Croy —6M 45
Broadham Green. —1N 125
Broadham Grn. Rd. Oxt —1N 125
Broadham Pl. Oxt —9N 105
Broad Ha'penny. Wrec —7F 128
Broad Highway. Cobh —1L 77
Broadhurst. Asht —3L 79
Broadhurst. Farn —1H 89
Broadhurst Clo. Rich —8M 11
Broadhurst Gdns. Reig —6N 121
Broadlands. Farn —3C 90
Broadlands. Frim —6D 70
Broadlands. Hanw —4A 24
Broadlands. Horl —7G 142
Broadlands Av. SW16 —3J 29
Broadlands Av. Shep —5D 38
Broadlands Clo. SW16 —3J 29
Broadlands Ct. Brack —9K 15
Broadlands Ct. Rich —3N 11
(off Kew Gdns. Rd.)
Broadlands Dri. S Asc —6N 33
Broadlands Dri. Warl —6F 84
Broadlands Way. N Mald —5E 42
Broad La. Brack —2A 32
Broad La. Hamp —8N 23
Broad La. Newd —7C 140
Broadley Grn. W'sham —4A 52
Broadmead. W14 —1K 13
Broad Mead. Asht —4M 79
Broadmead. Farn —2J 89
Broadmead. Horl —7G 143
Broadmead. Mers —6G 102
(off Station Rd.)
Broadmead Av. Wor Pk —6F 42
Broadmead Clo. Hamp —7A 24
Broadmead Rd. Send & Old Wok —9D 74
Broadmeads. Send —9D 74
Broadmoor. —3A 138
Broadmoor Est. Crowt —3J 49
Broadoak. Sun —7G 23
Broadoaks. Surb —8A 42
Broadoaks Cres. W Byf —9K 55
Broadpool Cotts. Asc —8L 17
Broadrick Heath. Warf —8B 16
Broad St. Guild —1F 112
Broad St. Tedd —7F 24
Broad St. W End —9A 52
Broad St. Wokgm —2B 30
Broad Street Common. —9G 92
Broad St. Wlk. Wokgm —2B 30
Broadview Rd. SW16 —8H 29
Broad Wlk. Cat —9C 84
Broad Wlk. Coul —1E 102
Broad Wlk. Cranl —9A 156
Broad Wlk. Craw —3B 182
Broad Wlk. Eps —6J 81
Broad Wlk. Frim —4C 70
Broad Wlk. Houn —4L 9
Broad Wlk. Rich —3M 11
Broad Wlk., The. E Mol —3F 40
Broadwater Clo. W on T —2H 57
Broadwater Clo. Wok —8F 54
Broadwater Clo. Wray —1A 20
Broadwater Gdns. Orp —1K 67
Broadwater La. G'ming —5J 133
Broadwater Pl. Wey —8F 38
Broadwater Ri. Guild —4C 114
Broadwater Rd. SW17 —5C 28
Broadwater Rd. N. W on T —2G 57
Broadwater Rd. S. W on T —2G 57
Broadway. Brack —1N 31
Broadway. Knap —5E 72
Broadway. Stai —6K 21
Broadway. Surb —7A 42
Broadway. Wink —2M 17
Broadway Arc. W6 —1H 13
(off Hammersmith B'way.)
Broadway Av. Croy —4A 46
Broadway Av. Twic —9H 11
Broadway Cen., The. W6 —1H 13
Broadway Chambers. W6 —1H 13
(off Hammersmith B'way)
Broadway Clo. S Croy —1E 84
Broadway Ct. SW19 —7M 27
Broadway Ct. Beck —2M 47
Broadway Ct. Knap —4F 72
Broadway Gdns. Mitc —3C 44
Broadway Ho. Knap —5F 72
Broadway Mkt. SW17 —5D 28
Broadway Pl. SW19 —7L 27
Broadway Rd. Light —6N 51
Broadway, The. SW14 —5D 12
Broadway, The. SW19 —7L 27
Broadway, The. Cheam —3K 61
Broadway, The. Craw —3B 182
Broadway, The. Croy —1J 63
Broadway, The. Lale —2L 37
Broadway, The. New H —6J 55
Broadway, The. Sand —8G 49
Broadway, The. Sutt —2A 62
Broadway, The. Th Dit —7E 40
Broadway, The. Wok —4B 74
Broadwell Ct. Houn —4L 9
(off Springwell Rd.)
Broadwell Rd. Wrec —5E 128
Broadwood Clo. H'ham —3N 197
Broadwood Cotts. Capel —4L 159
Broadwood Ri. Broadf —8M 181
Brocas St. Eton —3G 4
Brocas Ter. Eton —3G 4
Brockbridge Ho. SW15 —9E 12
Brockdene Dri. Kes —1F 66
Brockenhurst. W Mol —4N 39
Brockenhurst Av. Wor Pk —7D 42
Brockenhurst Clo. Wok —1B 74
Brockenhurst Dri. Yat —2C 68
Brockenhurst Rd. Alder —4N 109
Brockenhurst Rd. Asc —3L 33
Brockenhurst Rd. Brack —2D 32
Brockenhurst Rd. Croy —6E 46
Brockenhurst Way. SW16 —1H 45
Brockham. —5A 120
Brockham Clo. SW19 —6L 27
Brockham Cres. New Ad —4N 65
Brockham Dri. SW2 —1K 29
Brockham Grn. Brock —4A 120
Brockham Hill. Tad —9B 100
(off Boxhill Rd.)
Brockham Hill Pk. Tad —9B 100
Brockham Ho. SW2 —1K 29
(off Brockham Dri.)
Brockhamhurst Rd. Bet —1N 139
Brockham Keep. Horl —7G 142
(off Langshott La.)
Brockham La. Brock —3N 119
Brockham Pk. Bet —8B 120
Brock Hill. —5E 16
Brockhill. Wok —4K 73
Brockhurst Clo. H'ham —7F 196
Brockhurst Cotts. Alf —5H 175
Brocklands. Yat —2A 68
Brocklebank Ct. Whyt —5D 84
Brocklebank Rd. SW18 —1A 28
Brocklesby Rd. SE25 —3E 46
Brockley Combe. Wey —1E 56
Brock Rd. Craw —9N 161
Brocks Clo. G'ming —6K 133
Brocks Dri. Guild —8F 92
Brocks Dri. Sutt —9K 43
Brockshot Clo. Bren —1K 11
Brock Way. Vir W —4M 35
Brockway Clo. Guild —2D 114
Brockway Ho. Slou —1D 6
Brockwell Pk. Gdns. SE24 —1L 29
Broderick Gro. Bookh —4A 98
Brodie Rd. Guild —4A 114 (5E 202)
Brodrick Rd. SW17 —3C 28
Brograve Gdns. Beck —1L 47
Broke Ct. Guild —9E 94
Broken Furlong. Eton —1E 4
Brokes Cres. Reig —1M 121
Brokes Rd. Reig —1M 121
Bromford Clo. Oxt —2C 126
Bromley Gro. Brom —1N 47
Bromley Rd. Beck & Short —1L 47
Brompton Clo. SE20 —1D 46
Brompton Clo. Houn —8N 9
Brompton Pk. Cres. SW6 —2N 13
Bronsart Rd. SW6 —3K 13
Bronson Rd. SW20 —1J 43
Bronte Ct. Red —2E 122
(off St Anne's Ri.)
Bronte Ho. SW4 —1G 29
Brontes, The. E Grin —9N 165
Brook. —9N 151
(Godalming)
Brook. —2N 135
(Guildford)
Brook Av. Farnh —5L 109
Brook Clo. SW17 —3E 28
Brook Clo. SW20 —2G 43
Brook Clo. As —1F 110
Brook Clo. Dork —3J 119
Brook Clo. E Grin —9D 166
Brook Clo. Eps —5D 60
Brook Clo. Fleet —5B 88
Brook Clo. Owl —6K 49
Brook Clo. Stanw —1A 22
Brook Cotts. Yat —9B 48
Brook Ct. Eden —9L 127
Brook Dri. Brack —3C 32
Brooke Ct. Frim G —8D 70
Brooke Forest. Guild —8F 92
Brooke Pl. Binf —6J 15
Brookers Clo. Asht —4J 79
Brookers Corner. Crowt —2H 49
Brookers Row. Crowt —1H 49
Brook Farm Rd. Cobh —2L 77
Brookfield. G'ming —3K 133
Brookfield. Wok —3L 73
Brookfield Av. Sutt —1C 62
Brookfield Clo. Ott —3F 54
Brookfield Clo. Red —9E 122
Brookfield Gdns. Clay —3F 58
Brookfield Rd. Alder —1C 110
Brookfields Av. Mitc —4C 44
Brook Gdns. SW13 —6E 12
Brook Gdns. Farn —3L 89
Brook Gdns. King T —9B 26
Brook Green. —1J 13
Brook Grn. Brack —9L 15
(in two parts)
Brook Grn. Chob —6J 53
(off Chertsey Rd.)
Brook Hill. Alb —3M 135
Brook Hill. Oxt —8M 105
Brookhill Clo. Copt —7L 163
Brookhill Rd. Copt —8L 163
Brook Ho. W6 —1H 13
(off Shepherd's Bush Rd.)
Brook Ho. Cranl —6A 156
(off Park Dri.)
Brook Ho. Farnh —6J 109
(off Fairview Gdns.)
Brookhouse Rd. Farn —2L 89
Brookhurst Fld. Rud —9E 176
Brookhurst Rd. Add —3K 55
Brookland Ct. Reig —1N 121
Brooklands. —6A 56
Brooklands. Alder —3K 109
Brooklands. S God —1E 144
Brooklands Av. SW19 —3N 27
Brooklands Bus. Pk. Wey —7N 55
Brooklands Clo. Cobh —2M 77
Brooklands Clo. Farnh —5J 109
Brooklands Clo. Sun —9F 22
Brooklands Ct. King T —7J 203
Brooklands Ct. Mitc —1B 44
Brooklands Ct. New H —6M 55
Brooklands La. Wey —3A 56
Brooklands Mus. —5B 56
Brooklands Rd. Craw —8A 182
Brooklands Rd. Farnh —5J 109
Brooklands Rd. Th Dit —7F 40
Brooklands Rd. Wey —7B 56
Brooklands, The. Iswth —4D 10
Brooklands Way. E Grin —1N 185
Brooklands Way. Farnh —5K 109
Brooklands Way. Red —1C 122
Brook La. Alb —2N 135
Brook La. Chob —7G 53
Brook La. Fay —9B 180
Brook La. Send —9G 74
Brook La. Bus. Cen. Bren —1K 11
Brook La. N. Bren —1K 11
(in two parts)
Brookley Clo. Farnh —9A 110
Brookleys. Chob —6J 53
Brookly Gdns. Fleet —3C 88
Brooklyn Av. SE25 —3E 46
Brooklyn Clo. Cars —8C 44
Brooklyn Clo. Wok —6A 74
Brooklyn Ct. Wok —6A 74
Brooklyn Gro. SE25 —3E 46
Brooklyn Rd. SE25 —3E 46
Brooklyn Rd. Wok —5A 74
Brook Mead. Eps —3D 60
Brook Mead. Milf —2C 152
Brookmead Ct. Cranl —8N 155
Brookmead Ct. Farnh —2G 128
(off Pengilly Rd.)
Brookmead Ind. Est. Croy —5G 45
Brook Mdw. C'fold —6F 172
Brookmead Rd. Croy —5G 45
Brook Rd. Bag —5J 51
Brook Rd. Camb —2N 69
Brook Rd. Chil —1E 134
Brook Rd. H'ham —2L 197
Brook Rd. Mers —7G 102
Brook Rd. Red —4D 122
Brook Rd. Surb —8L 41
Brook Rd. T Hth —3N 45
Brook Rd. Twic —9G 11
Brook Rd. Wmly —1N 171
Brook Rd. S. Bren —2K 11
Brooksby Clo. B'water —1G 68
Brooks Clo. Wey —6B 56
Brookscroft. Croy —6J 65
Brookside. —7K 17
Brookside. Bear G —5M 139
Brookside. Cars —2E 62
Brookside. Cher —6G 37
Brookside. Coln —3E 6
Brookside. Copt —7L 163
Brookside. Cranl —7N 155
(Ewhurst Rd.)
Brookside. Cranl —9N 155
(Northdowns)
Brookside. Craw —2D 182
Brookside. Craw D —1E 184
Brookside. Farnh —6H 109
Brookside. Guild —7N 93
Brookside. Sand —8H 49
Brookside. S God —7G 124
Brookside Av. Afrd —6L 21
Brookside Av. Wray —6A 6
Brookside Clo. Felt —4H 23
Brookside Cres. Wor Pk —7F 42
Brookside Res. Pk. Homes. Farn —5M 69
Brookside Way. Croy —5G 46
Brooks La. W4 —2N 11
Brooks Rd. W4 —1N 11
Brook St. King T —1L 41 (4K 203)
Brook St. Wind —5G 5
Brook Trad. Est., The. Alder —2C 110
Brook Valley. Mid H —2H 139
Brookview. Copt —7L 163
Brookview Rd. SW16 —6G 28
Brookville Rd. SW6 —3L 13
Brook Way. Lea —5G 78
Brookwell La. Brmly —1C 154
Brookwood. —7D 72
Brookwood. Horl —7F 142
Brookwood Av. SW13 —5E 12
Brookwood Lye Rd. Brkwd —7E 72
Brookwood Rd. SW18 —2L 27
Brookwood Rd. Farn —1B 90
Brookwood Rd. Houn —5B 10
Broom Acres. Fleet —7A 88
Broom Acres. Sand —7G 49
Broom Clo. Esh —2B 58
Broom Clo. Tedd —8K 25
Broomcroft Clo. Wok —3F 74
Broomcroft Dri. Wok —2F 74
Broomdashers Rd. Craw —2D 182
Broome Clo. H'ley —4B 100
Broome Clo. H'ham —3K 197
Broome Clo. Yat —8B 48
Broome Ct. Brack —2N 31
Broome Ct. Tad —6K 81
Broomehall Rd. Cold —9D 138
Broome Rd. Hamp —8N 23
Broomers La. Ewh —5F 156
Broom Farm Est. Wind —5A 4
Broomfield. Elst —7J 131
Broomfield. Guild —2H 113
Broom Fld. Light —8L 51
Broomfield. Stai —7J 21
Broomfield. Sun —9H 23
Broomfield Clo. Asc —6E 34
Broomfield Clo. Guild —1H 113
Broomfield Ct. Wey —3C 56
Broomfield Pk. Asc —6E 34
Broomfield Pk. Westc —6C 118
Broomfield Ride. Oxs —8D 58
Broomfield Rd. Beck —2H 47
Broomfield Rd. New H —7K 55
Broomfield Rd. Rich —4M 11
Broomfield Rd. Surb —7M 41
Broomfield Rd. Tedd —7J 25
Broomfields. Esh —2C 58
Broom Gdns. Croy —9K 47
Broomhall. —5D 34
Broom Hall. Oxs —1D 78
Broomhall End. Wok —3A 74
Broomhall La. Asc —5D 34
Broomhall La. Wok —3A 74
Broomhall Rd. S Croy —5A 64
Broomhall Rd. Wok —3A 74
Broomhill. Ews —4C 108
Broomhill Rd. SW18 —8M 13
Broomhill Rd. Farn —9J 69
Broomhouse La. SW6 —5M 13
Broomhouse Rd. SW6 —5M 13
Broomhurst Ct. Dork —7H 119
Broomlands La. Oxt —4F 106
Broom La. Chob —5H 53
Broomleaf Corner. Farnh —1J 129
Broomleaf Rd. Farnh —1J 129
Broomloan La. Sutt —8M 43
Broom Lock. Tedd —7J 25
Broom Pk. Tedd —8K 25
Broom Rd. Croy —9K 47
Broom Rd. Tedd —6H 25
Broom Squires. Hind —5E 170
Broomsquires Rd. Bag —5K 51
Broom Water. Tedd —7J 25
Broom Water W. Tedd —6J 25
Broom Way. B'water —2J 69
Broom Way. Wey —1F 56
Broomwood Clo. Croy —4G 47
Broomwood Way. Lwr Bo —5H 129
Broster Gdns. SE25 —2C 46
Brougham Pl. Farnh —5G 108
Brough Clo. King T —6K 25
Broughton Av. Rich —4H 25
Broughton M. Frim —5D 70
Broughton Rd. SW6 —5N 13
Broughton Rd. T Hth —5L 45
Browell Ho. Guild —2F 114
(off Merrow St.)
Browells La. Felt —3J 23
Brown Bear Ct. Felt —5L 23
Brown Clo. Wall —4J 63
Browngraves Rd. Hayes —3D 8

Browning Av.—Bute Rd.

Browning Av. *Sutt* —1C **62**
Browning Av. *Wor Pk* —7G **42**
Browning Barracks. *Alder* —8N **89**
Browning Clo. *Camb* —2G **70**
Browning Clo. *Craw* —2G **182**
Browning Clo. *Hamp* —5N **23**
Browning Rd. *C Crook* —9A **88**
Browning Rd. *Fet* —3D **98**
Brownings. *Eden* —8L **127**
Brownings, The. *E Grin* —9M **165**
Browning Way. *Houn* —4L **9**
Brownjohn Ct. *Craw* —2E **182**
Brownlow Dri. *Brack* —8A **16**
Brownlow Rd. *Croy* —1B **64**
Brownlow Rd. *Red* —3C **122**
Brownrigg Cres. *Brack* —9C **16**
Brownrigg Rd. *Afrd* —5B **22**
Brown's Hill. *Out* —1A **144**
Browns La. *Eff* —5L **97**
Brownsover Rd. *Farn* —1H **89**
Brown's Rd. *Surb* —6M **41**
Browns Wlk. *Rowl* —7E **128**
Browns Wood. *E Grin* —6A **166**
Brow, The. *Red* —9E **122**
Brox. —4E 54
Broxhead Farm Rd. *Lind* —1A **168**
Broxhead Trad. Est. *Lind* —3A **168**
Broxholme Ho. SW6 —4N ***13***
(off Harwood Rd.)
Broxholm Rd. *SW16* —4L **29**
Brox La. *Ott* —4E **54**
Brox Rd. *Ott* —3E **54**
Bruce Av. *Shep* —5D **38**
Bruce Clo. *Byfl* —9M **55**
Bruce Dri. *S Croy* —5G **64**
Bruce Hall M. *SW17* —5E **28**
Bruce Rd. *SE25* —3A **46**
Bruce Rd. *Mitc* —8E **28**
Bruce Wlk. *Wind* —5A **4**
Brudenell. *Wind* —6C **4**
Brudenell Rd. *SW17* —4D **28**
Brumana Clo. *Wey* —3C **56**
Brumfield Rd. *Eps* —2B **60**
Brunel Cen., The. *Craw* —8D **162**
Brunel Clo. *Houn* —3J **9**
Brunel Dri. *Crowt* —8H **31**
Brunel Pl. *Craw* —4C **182**
Brunel Wlk. *Twic* —1A **24**
Bruneval Barracks. *Alder* —9L **89**
Brunner Ct. *Ott* —2E **54**
Brunswick. *Brack* —6M **31**
Brunswick Clo. *Craw* —5F **182**
Brunswick Clo. *Th Dit* —7F **40**
Brunswick Clo. *Twic* —4D **24**
Brunswick Clo. *W on T* —8K **39**
Brunswick Ct. Craw —5E ***182***
(off Brunswick Clo.)
Brunswick Ct. *Sutt* —1N **61**
Brunswick Dri. *Brkwd* —7A **72**
Brunswick Gro. *Cobh* —9K **57**
Brunswick M. *SW16* —7H **29**
Brunswick Rd. *Brkwd* —8L **71**
Brunswick Rd. *Deep* —8G **71**
Brunswick Rd. *King T* —9N **25**
Brunswick Rd. *Sutt* —1N **61**
Bruntile Clo. *Farn* —4B **90**
Brushfield Way. *Knap* —6F **72**
Brushwood Rd. *H'ham* —2A **198**
Bruton Rd. *Mord* —3A **44**
Bruton Way. *Brack* —6C **32**
Bryan Clo. *Sun* —8H **23**
Bryan's All. *SW6* —5N **13**
Bryanston Av. *Twic* —2B **24**
Bryanstone Av. *Guild* —8J **93**
Bryanstone Clo. *C Crook* —7B **88**
Bryanstone Clo. *Guild* —9J **93**
Bryanstone Ct. *Sutt* —9A **44**
Bryanstone Gro. *Guild* —8J **93**
Bryce Clo. *H'ham* —3N **197**
Bryce Gdns. *Alder* —5A **110**
Bryer Pl. *Wind* —6A **4**
Brympton Clo. *Dork* —7G **119**
Brynford Clo. *Wok* —2A **74**
Bryn Rd. *Wrec* —4E **128**
Bryony Ho. *Brack* —9K **15**
Bryony Rd. *Guild* —9D **94**
Bryony Way. *Sun* —7H **23**
Buccleuch Rd. *Dat* —3K **5**
Buchan Country Pk. & Info. Cen. —7K 181
Buchan Hill. —9M 181
Buchan Pk. *Craw* —7L **181**
Buchans Lawn. *Craw* —7N **181**
Buchan, The. *Camb* —7E **50**
Bucharest Rd. *SW18* —1A **28**
Buckfast Rd. *Mord* —3N **43**
Buckham Thorns Rd. *W'ham* —4L **107**
Buckhold Rd. *SW18* —9M **13**
Buckhurst Av. *Cars* —7C **44**
Buckhurst Clo. *E Grin* —7M **165**
Buckhurst Clo. *Red* —1C **122**
Buckhurst Gro. *Wokgm* —3F **30**
Buckhurst Hill. —9C 18
Buckhurst Hill. *Brack* —3D **32**
Buckhurst La. *Asc* —2C **34**
Buckhurst Mead. *E Grin* —6M **165**
Buckhurst Rd. *Asc* —9C **18**
Buckhurst Rd. *Frim G* —8D **70**
Buckhurst Rd. *W'ham* —8J **87**
Buckhurst Way. *E Grin* —7M **165**
Buckingham Av. *Felt* —9J **9**
Buckingham Av. *T Hth* —9L **29**
Buckingham Av. *W Mol* —1B **40**
Buckingham Clo. *Guild* —2B **114**
Buckingham Clo. *Hamp* —6N **23**
Buckingham Ct. *Craw* —7N **181**
Buckingham Ct. *Sutt* —5M **61**
Buckingham Dri. *E Grin* —1C **186**
Buckingham Gdns. *T Hth* —1L **45**
Buckingham Gdns. *W Mol* —1B **40**
Buckingham Ga. *Gat A* —3G **162**
Buckingham Rd. *Hamp* —5N **23**
Buckingham Rd. *Holmw* —5J **139**
Buckingham Rd. *King T* —3M **41** (7M **203**)
Buckingham Rd. *Mitc* —3J **45**
Buckingham Rd. *Rich* —3K **25**
Buckingham Way. *Frim* —5D **70**
Buckingham Way. *Wall* —5G **63**
Buckland. —2F 120
Buckland Clo. *Farn* —7A **70**
Buckland Ct. Gdns. *Bet* —2F **120**
Buckland Cres. *Wind* —4C **4**
Buckland La. *Tad* —6F **100**
Buckland Rd. *Chess* —2M **59**
Buckland Rd. *Lwr K* —7L **101**
Buckland Rd. *Orp* —1N **67**
Buckland Rd. *Reig* —2J **121**
Buckland Rd. *Sutt* —6H **61**
Bucklands Rd. *Tedd* —7J **25**
Buckland's Wharf. *King T* —1K **41** (3H **203**)
Buckland Wlk. *Mord* —3A **44**
Buckland Way. *Wor Pk* —7H **43**
Bucklebury. *Brack* —6M **31**
Buckleigh Av. *SW20* —2K **43**
Buckleigh Rd. *SW16* —7H **29**
Buckle La. *Warf* —3M **15**
(in two parts)
Bucklers All. *SW6* —2L **13**
(in two parts)
Buckler's Way. *Cars* —9D **44**
Buckles Way. *Bans* —3K **81**
Buckley La. *H'ham* —9N **197**
Buckley Pl. *Craw D* —1D **184**
Buckmans Rd. *Craw* —2B **182**
Bucknall Way. *Beck* —3L **47**
Bucknills Clo. *Eps* —1B **80**
Bucks Clo. *W Byf* —1K **75**
Bucks Green. —1C 104
Buckshead Hill. *Colg* —9E **198**
Bucks Horn Oak. —2A 148
Bucks Horn Oak Rd. *Bucks H* —2A **148**
Buckswood Dri. *Craw* —5M **181**
Buckthorn Clo. *Wokgm* —1D **30**
Buckthorns. *Brack* —8K **15**
Budd's All. *Twic* —8J **11**
Budebury Rd. *Stai* —6J **21**
Budge La. *Mitc* —6D **44**
Budgen Clo. *Craw* —9H **163**
Budgen Dri. *Red* —9E **102**
Budge's Cotts. *Wokgm* —9D **14**
Budge's Gdns. *Wokgm* —1C **30**
Budge's Rd. *Wokgm* —1C **30**
Budham Way. *Brack* —5N **31**
Buer Rd. *SW6* —5K **13**
Buff Av. *Bans* —1N **81**
Buffbeards La. *Hasl* —1C **188**
Buffers La. *Lea* —6G **79**
Bug Hill. *Wold* —7G **84**
Bulbeggars La. *God* —1F **124**
Bulganak Rd. *T Hth* —3N **45**
Bulkeley Av. *Wind* —6E **4**
Bulkeley Clo. *Eng G* —6M **19**
Bullard Cotts. *W Cla* —1H **115**
Bullard Rd. *Tedd* —7E **24**
Bullbeggars La. *Wok* —3L **73**
Bullbrook. —1C 32
Bullbrook Dri. *Brack* —9C **16**
Bullbrook Row. *Brack* —1C **32**
Buller Barracks. *Alder* —9A **90**
Buller Ct. *Farn* —4A **90**
Buller Rd. *T Hth* —1A **46**
Bullers Rd. *Farnh* —6K **109**
Bullfinch Clo. *Coll T* —7K **49**
Bullfinch Clo. *Horl* —7C **142**
Bullfinch Clo. *H'ham* —1J **197**
Bullfinch Rd. *S Croy* —6G **64**
Bull Hill. *Lea* —8G **79**
Bull La. *Brack* —9N **15**
Bullock La. *Hasl* —9A **190**
Bullrush Clo. *Croy* —5B **46**
Bull's All. *SW14* —5C **12**
Bulls Head Row. *God* —9E **104**
Bullswater Common. —3D 92
Bullswater Comn. Rd. *Pirb* —4D **92**
Bulmer Cotts. *Holm M* —6K **137**
Bulow Est. SW6 —4N ***13***
(off Pearscroft Rd.)
Bulstrode Av. *Houn* —5N **9**
Bulstrode Gdns. *Houn* —6A **10**
Bulstrode Rd. *Houn* —6A **10**
Bunbury Way. *Eps* —3G **80**
Bunce Common. —1C 140
Bunce Comn. Rd. *Leigh* —1C **140**
Bunce Dri. *Cat* —1A **104**
Bunce's Clo. *Eton W* —1E **4**
Bunch La. *Hasl* —1F **188**
Bunch Way. *Hasl* —2E **188**
Bundy's Way. *Stai* —7H **21**
Bungalow Rd. *SE25* —3B **46**
Bungalow Rd. *Ock* —2D **96**
Bungalows, The. *SW16* —8F **28**
Bungalows, The. *Guild* —7J **93**
Bungalows, The. *Wall* —2F **62**
Bunting Clo. *H'ham* —5M **197**
Bunting Clo. *Mitc* —4D **44**
Buntings, The. *Farnh* —3E **128**
Bunyan Clo. *Craw* —6K **181**
Bunyan's La. *Knap* —1F **72**
Bunyard Dri. *Wok* —1E **74**
Burbage Grn. *Brack* —4D **32**
Burbage Rd. *SE24 & SE21* —1N **29**
Burbeach Clo. *Craw* —6N **181**
Burberry Clo. *N Mald* —1D **42**
Burbidge Rd. *Shep* —3B **38**
Burbury Woods. *Camb* —9C **50**
Burchets Hollow. *Peasl* —4E **136**
Burchetts Way. *Shep* —5C **38**
Burcote. *Wey* —3E **56**
Burcote Rd. *SW18* —1B **28**
Burcott Gdns. *Add* —3L **55**
Burcott Rd. *Purl* —1L **83**
Burden Clo. *Bren* —1J **11**
Burdenshott Av. *Rich* —7A **12**
Burdenshott Hill. *Worp* —3K **93**
Burdenshott Rd. *Worp* —3K **93**
Burden Way. *Guild* —7L **93**
Burdett Av. *SW20* —9F **26**
Burdett Clo. *Worth* —4H **183**
Burdett Rd. *Croy* —5A **46**
Burdett Rd. *Rich* —5M **11**
Burdock Clo. *Craw* —7M **181**
Burdock Clo. *Croy* —7G **47**
Burdock Clo. *Light* —7M **51**
Burdon La. *Sutt* —4K **61**
Burdon Pk. *Sutt* —5L **61**
Burfield Clo. *SW17* —5B **28**
Burfield Dri. *Warl* —6F **84**
Burfield Rd. *Old Win* —9K **5**
Burford Bri. Roundabout. *Dork* —9J **99**
Burford Ct. *Wokgm* —3D **30**
Burford Ho. *Bren* —1K **11**
Burford Ho. *Eps* —7H **61**
Burford La. *Eps* —7H **61**
Burford Lea. *Elst* —7J **131**
Burford Rd. *Bren* —1L **11**
Burford Rd. *Camb* —2N **69**
Burford Rd. *H'ham* —6L **197**
Burford Rd. *Sutt* —8M **43**
Burford Rd. *Wor Pk* —6E **42**
Burford Wlk. *SW6* —3N **13**
Burford Way. *New Ad* —3M **65**
Burges Gro. *SW13* —3G **13**
Burgess Clo. *Felt* —5M **23**
Burgess M. *SW19* —7N **27**
Burgess Rd. *Sutt* —1N **61**
Burges Way. *Stai* —6J **21**
Burgh Clo. *Craw* —9H **163**
Burgh Cft. *Eps* —2E **80**
Burghead Clo. *Coll T* —8J **49**
Burghfield. *Eps* —2E **80**
Burgh Heath. —6K 81
Burgh Heath Rd. *Eps* —1E **80** (8N **201**)
Burgh Hill Rd. *Pass* —9E **168**
Burghley Av. *N Mald* —9C **26**
Burghley Hall Clo. *SW19* —2K **27**
Burghley Pl. *Mitc* —4D **44**
Burghley Rd. *SW19* —5J **27**
Burgh Mt. *Bans* —2L **81**
Burgh Wood. *Bans* —2K **81**
Burgoine Quay. *King T* —9K **25** (2H **203**)
Burgos Clo. *Croy* —3L **63**
Burgoyne Rd. *SE25* —3C **46**
Burgoyne Rd. *Camb* —9E **50**
Burgoyne Rd. *Sun* —7G **22**
Burhill. —5H 57
Burhill Rd. *W on T* —5J **57**
Burke Clo. *SW15* —7D **12**
Burket Clo. *S'hall* —1M **9**
Burlands. *Craw* —9M **161**
Burlea Clo. *W on T* —2J **57**
Burleigh. —9J 17
Burleigh Av. *Wall* —9E **44**
Burleigh Clo. *Add* —2K **55**
Burleigh Clo. *Craw D* —1E **184**
Burleigh Gdns. *Afrd* —6D **22**
Burleigh Gdns. *Wok* —4B **74**
Burleigh La. *Asc* —9J **17**
Burleigh La. *Craw D* —2F **184**
Burleigh Pk. *Cobh* —8M **57**
Burleigh Pl. *SW15* —8J **13**
Burleigh Rd. *Add* —2K **55**
Burleigh Rd. *Asc* —1J **33**
Burleigh Rd. *Frim* —6B **70**
Burleigh Rd. *Sutt* —7K **43**
Burleigh Way. *Craw D* —1E **184**
Burley Clo. *SW16* —1H **45**
Burley Clo. *Loxw* —4J **193**
Burley Orchard. *Cher* —5J **37**
Burleys Rd. *Craw* —3G **183**
Burley Way. *B'water* —9H **49**
Burlingham Clo. *Guild* —1F **114**
Burlings. —4N 87
Burlings La. *Knock* —4N **87**
Burlings, The. *Asc* —1J **33**
Burlington Av. *Rich* —4N **11**
Burlington Clo. *Felt* —1E **22**
Burlington Ct. *Alder* —3M **109**
Burlington Ct. *B'water* —3J **69**
Burlington Gdns. *SW6* —5K **13**
Burlington Gdns. *W4* —1B **12**
Burlington La. *W4* —3B **12**
Burlington M. *SW15* —8L **13**
Burlington Pl. *SW6* —5K **13**
Burlington Pl. *Reig* —2M **121**
Burlington Rd. *SW6* —5K **13**
Burlington Rd. *W4* —1B **12**
Burlington Rd. *Iswth* —4D **10**
Burlington Rd. *N Mald* —3E **42**
Burlington Rd. *T Hth* —1N **45**
Burlsdon Way. *Brack* —9C **16**
Burma Rd. *Longc* —9J **35**
Burmarsh Ct. *SE20* —1F **46**
Burmester Rd. *SW17* —4A **28**
Burnaby Cres. *W4* —2B **12**
Burnaby Gdns. *W4* —2A **12**
Burnaby St. *SW10* —3N **13**
Burnbury Rd. *SW12* —2G **29**
Burn Clo. *Add* —1M **55**
Burn Clo. *Oxs* —2D **78**
Burne-Jones Dri. *Coll T* —9J **49**
Burne Jones Ho. W14 —1K ***13***
(off N. End Rd.)
Burnell Av. *Rich* —6J **25**
Burnell Rd. *Sutt* —1N **61**
Burnet Av. *Guild* —9D **94**
Burnet Clo. *W End* —9C **52**
Burnet Gro. *Eps* —9B **60** (6J **201**)
Burnetts Rd. *Wind* —4B **4**
Burney Av. *Surb* —4M **41**
Burney Clo. *Fet* —3C **98**
Burney Ct. *Craw* —6M **181**
Burney Rd. *Westh* —9G **99**
Burnfoot Av. *SW6* —4K **13**
Burnham Clo. *Knap* —5G **73**
Burnham Clo. *Wind* —5A **4**
Burnham Dri. *Reig* —2M **121**
Burnham Dri. *Wor Pk* —8J **43**
Burnham Gdns. *Croy* —6C **46**
Burnham Gdns. *Houn* —4J **9**
Burnham Ga. *Guild* —3N **113** (2C **202**)
Burnham Gro. *Brack* —8A **16**
Burnham Pl. *H'ham* —7K **197**
Burnham Rd. *Knap* —5G **73**
Burnham Rd. *Mord* —3N **43**
Burnhams Rd. *Bookh* —2M **97**
Burnham St. *King T* —9N **25**
Burnhill Rd. *Beck* —1K **47**
Burn Moor Chase. *Brack* —6C **32**
Burnsall Clo. *Farn* —8N **69**
Burns Av. *C Crook* —7C **88**
Burns Av. *Felt* —9H **9**
Burns Clo. *SW19* —7B **28**
Burns Clo. *Cars* —5E **62**
Burns Clo. *Farn* —8L **69**
Burns Clo. *H'ham* —1L **197**
Burns Dri. *Bans* —1K **81**
Burnside. *Asht* —5M **79**
Burnside. *Fleet* —4B **88**
Burnside Clo. *Twic* —9G **10**
Burns Rd. *Craw* —1G **182**
Burns Way. *E Grin* —9M **165**
Burns Way. *Fay* —8H **181**
Burns Way. *Houn* —5L **9**
Burntcommon. —3H 95
Burntcommon Clo. *Rip* —3H **95**
Burnt Comn. La. *Rip* —3J **95**
Burnt Hill Rd. *Wrec & L Bou* —5F **128**
Burnt Hill Way. *Wrec* —6G **128**
Burnt Ho. Gdns. *Warf* —8C **16**
Burnt Ho. La. *Rusp* —2E **180**
Burnthouse Ride. *Brack* —3J **31**
Burnthwaite Rd. *SW6* —3L **13**
Burntoak La. *Newd* —2D **160**
Burnt Pollard La. *Light* —6B **52**
Burntwood Clo. *SW18* —2C **28**
Burntwood Clo. *Cat* —8D **84**
Burntwood Grange Rd. *SW18* —2B **28**
Burntwood La. *SW17* —4A **28**
Burntwood La. *Cat* —9B **84**
Burpham. —9D 94
Burpham Court Farm Pk. —7B 94
Burpham La. *Guild* —7C **94**
Burrell Clo. *Croy* —5H **47**
Burrell Ct. *Craw* —5L **181**
Burrell Rd. *Frim* —6A **70**
Burrell Row. *Beck* —1K **47**
Burrells, The. *Cher* —7K **37**
Burrell, The. *Westc* —6C **118**
Burr Hill La. *Chob* —5J **53**
Burritt Rd. *King T* —1N **41**
Burrow Hill. —5H 53
(Chobham)
Burrow Hill. —9B 72
(Pirbright)
Burrow Hill Grn. *Chob* —5G **53**
Burrows Clo. *Bookh* —2N **97**
Burrows Clo. *Guild* —2J **113**
Burrows Cross. —1D 136
Burrows Cross. *Gom* —1D **136**
Burrows Hill Clo. *H'row A* —6L **7**
Burrows Hill La. *H'row A* —7K **7**
Burrows La. *Gom* —1D **136**
Burrow Wlk. *SE21* —1N **29**
Burr Rd. *SW18* —2M **27**
Burrwood Gdns. *Ash V* —9E **90**
Burstead Clo. *Cobh* —8L **57**
Burstock Rd. *SW15* —7K **13**
Burston Gdns. *E Grin* —6N **165**
Burston Rd. *SW15* —8J **13**
Burstow. —3L 163
Burstow Lodge Bus. Cen. *Horl* —6M **143**
Burstow Rd. *SW20* —9K **27**
Burtenshaw Rd. *Th Dit* —6G **41**
Burton Clo. *Chess* —4K **59**
Burton Clo. *Horl* —9E **142**
Burton Clo. *T Hth* —2A **46**
Burton Clo. *W'sham* —3A **52**
Burton Ct. *SE20* —1F **46**
Burton Dri. *Guild* —7D **92**
Burton Gdns. *Houn* —4N **9**
Burton Rd. *King T* —8L **25** (1L **203**)
Burtons Ct. *H'ham* —6J **197**
Burton's Rd. *Hamp H* —5B **24**
Burton Way. *Wind* —6B **4**
Burtwell La. *SE27* —5N **29**
Burwash Rd. *Craw* —4E **182**
Burway Cres. *Cher* —3J **37**
Burwell. *King T* —4N **203**
Burwood Av. *Kenl* —1M **83**
Burwood Clo. *Guild* —2F **114**
Burwood Clo. *Reig* —3B **122**
Burwood Clo. *Surb* —7N **41**
Burwood Clo. *W on T* —3K **57**
Burwood Pde. Cher —6J ***37***
(off Guildford St.)
Burwood Park. —8H 57
(Cobham)
Burwood Park. —2G 57
(Walton on-Thames)
Burwood Pk. Rd. *W on T* —1J **57**
Burwood Rd. *W on T* —4F **56**
Bury Clo. *Wok* —3N **73**
Bury Fields. *Guild* —5M **113** (7B **202**)
Bury Gro. *Mord* —4N **43**
Bury La. *Wok* —3M **73**
Burys, The. *G'ming* —6H **133**
Bury St. *Guild* —5M **113** (7B **202**)
Burywood Hill. *Dear G* —3E **158**
Busbridge. —9J 133
Busbridge Lakes Ornamental Waterfowl. —1H 153
Busbridge La. *G'ming* —8G **133**
Busch Clo. *Iswth* —4H **11**
Busdens Clo. *Milf* —2C **152**
Busdens La. *Milf* —2C **152**
Busdens Way. *Milf* —2C **152**
Bushbury Rd. *Bet* —8N **119**
Bush Clo. *Add* —2L **55**
Bush Cotts. *SW18* —8M **13**
Bushell Clo. *SW2* —3K **29**
Bushetts Gro. *Red* —7F **102**
Bushey Clo. *Kenl* —3C **84**
Bushey Ct. *SW20* —2G **43**
Bushey Cft. *Oxt* —8M **105**
Bushey Down. *SW12* —3F **28**
Bushey La. *Sutt* —1M **61**
Bushey Mead. —1J 43
Bushey Rd. *SW20* —2G **42**
Bushey Rd. *Croy* —8K **47**
Bushey Rd. *Sutt* —1M **61**
Bushey Shaw. *Asht* —4H **79**
Bushey Way. *Beck* —5N **47**
Bushfield. *Plais* —6B **192**
Bushfield Dri. *Red* —8E **122**
Bush La. *H'ham* —9N **179**
Bush La. *Send* —2F **94**
Bushnell Rd. *SW17* —3F **28**
Bush Rd. *Rich* —2M **11**
Bush Rd. *Shep* —4A **38**
Bush Wlk. *Wokgm* —2B **30**
Bushwood Rd. *Rich* —2N **11**
Bushy Ct. King T —9J ***25***
(off Up. Teddington Rd.)
Bushy Hill. —2F 114
Bushy Hill Dri. *Guild* —1D **114**
Bushy Pk. Gdns. *Tedd* —6D **24**
Bushy Pk. Rd. *Tedd* —8H **25**
(in two parts)
Bushy Rd. *Fet* —9B **78**
Bushy Rd. *Tedd* —7F **24**
Business Cen., The. *Wokgm* —4A **30**
Business Pk. 5. *Lea* —7F **78**
Busk Cres. *Farn* —2L **89**
Butcherfield La. *Hartf* —1N **187**
Bute Av. *Rich* —3L **25**
Bute Ct. *Wall* —2G **62**
Bute Gdns. *W6* —1J **13**
Bute Gdns. *Rich* —2L **25**
Bute Gdns. *Wall* —2G **63**
Bute Gdns. W. *Wall* —2G **62**
Bute Rd. *Croy* —7L **45**

Bute Rd.—Carlton Av.

Bute Rd. *Wall* —1G **62**
Butler Rd. *Bag* —5K **51**
Butler Rd. *Crowt* —1G **48**
Butlers Clo. *Wind* —4A **4**
Butlers Dene Rd. *Wold* —7J **85**
Butlers Hill. *W Hor* —8C **96**
Butlers Rd. *H'ham* —4N **197**
Butt Clo. *Cranl* —6N **155**
Buttercup Clo. *Lind* —4B **168**
Buttercup Clo. *Wokgm* —2F **30**
Buttercup Sq. *Stanw* —2M **21**
Butterfield. *E Grin* —7L **165**
Butterfield Clo. *Twic* —9F **10**
Butterfields. *Camb* —2N **69**
Butterfly Wlk. *Warl* —7F **84**
(in two parts)
Butter Hill. *Cars* —9E **44**
Butter Hill. *Dork* —5G **119** (3K **201**)
Buttermer Clo. *Wrec* —4D **128**
Buttermere Clo. *Farn* —1K **89**
Buttermere Clo. *Felt* —2G **22**
Buttermere Clo. *H'ham* —2A **198**
Buttermere Clo. *Mord* —5J **43**
*Buttermere Ct. Ash V —9D **90***
(off Lakeside Clo.)
Buttermere Dri. *SW15* —8K **13**
Buttermere Dri. *Camb* —1H **71**
Buttermere Gdns. *Brack* —2A **32**
Buttermere Gdns. *Purl* —9A **64**
Buttermere Way. *Egh* —8D **20**
Buttersteep Ri. *Asc* —7G **33**
Butterwick. *W6* —1J **13**
Butt La. *P'ham* —7L **111**
Butts Clo. *Craw* —2N **181**
Butts Cotts. *Felt* —4M **23**
Butts Cres. *Hanw* —4A **24**
Butts La. *G'ming* —7G **133**
(in two parts)
Butts Rd. *Wok* —4A **74**
Butts, The. *Bren* —2J **11**
Butts, The. *Sun* —2K **39**
Buxton Av. *Cat* —8B **84**
Buxton Cres. *Sutt* —1K **61**
Buxton Dri. *N Mald* —1C **42**
Buxton La. *Cat* —7A **84**
Buxton Rd. *SW14* —6D **12**
Buxton Rd. *Afrd* —6M **21**
Buxton Rd. *T Hth* —4M **45**
Byam St. *SW6* —5N **13**
Byards Cft. *SW16* —9H **29**
Byatt Wlk. *Hamp* —7M **23**
Bychurch End. *Tedd* —6F **24**
Bycroft Way. *Craw* —1F **182**
Byegrove Rd. *SW19* —7B **28**
Byerley Way. *Craw* —2H **183**
Byers La. *Horne* —5D **144**
Byers La. *S God* —4F **144**
Byeways. *Twic* —4B **24**
Byeways, The. *Surb* —4N **41**
Byeway, The. *SW14* —6B **12**
Byfeld Gdns. *SW13* —4F **12**
Byfield Pas. *Iswth* —6G **10**
Byfield Rd. *Iswth* —6G **10**
Byfleet. —9A 56
Byfleet Ind. Est. *Byfl* —7M **55**
Byfleet Rd. *Byfl & Cob* —8B **56**
Byfleet Rd. *New H* —4M **55**
Byfleets La. *Warn* —2D **196**
Byfleet Technical Cen. *Byfl* —7M **55**
Bygrove. *New Ad* —3K **65**
Bylands. *Wok* —6C **74**
Byne Rd. *Cars* —8C **44**
Bynes Rd. *S Croy* —4A **64**
By-Pass Rd. *Lea* —7H **79**
Byrd Rd. *Craw* —6L **181**
Byrefield Rd. *Guild* —9J **93**
Byrne Rd. *SW12* —2F **28**
Byron Av. *Camb* —3F **70**
Byron Av. *Coul* —2J **83**
Byron Av. *Houn* —5H **9**
Byron Av. *N Mald* —4F **42**
Byron Av. *Sutt* —1B **62**
Byron Av. E. *Sutt* —1B **62**
Byron Clo. *SE20* —2E **46**
Byron Clo. *SW16* —7J **29**
Byron Clo. *Craw* —2F **182**
Byron Clo. *Fleet* —5B **88**
Byron Clo. *Hamp* —5N **23**
Byron Clo. *H'ham* —2L **197**
Byron Clo. *Knap* —4H **73**
Byron Clo. *W on T* —7M **39**
Byron Clo. *Yat* —2A **68**
Byron Ct. *Wind* —6D **4**
Byron Dri. *Crowt* —4G **48**
Byron Gdns. *Sutt* —1B **62**
Byron Gro. *E Grin* —1M **185**
Byron Ho. *Slou* —1D **6**
Byron Pl. *Lea* —9H **79**
Byron Rd. *Add* —1N **55**
Byron Rd. *S Croy* —6E **64**
Byron Way. *W Dray* —1A **8**
Byton Rd. *SW17* —7D **28**
Byttom Hill. *Mick* —4J **99**
Byward Av. *Felt* —9K **9**
Byways. *Yat* —1A **68**
Byways, The. *Asht* —5K **79**
Byway, The. *Eps* —1E **60**
Byway, The. *Sutt* —5B **62**
Bywood. *Brack* —6M **31**
Bywood Av. *Croy* —5F **46**
Bywood Clo. *Kenl* —2M **83**
Byworth Clo. *Farnh* —1E **128**
Byworth Rd. *Farnh* —1E **128**

Cabbage Hill. *Warf* —6L **15**
Cabbagehill La. *Binf* —5K **15**
Cabbel Pl. *Add* —1L **55**
Cabell Rd. *Guild* —2G **113**
Caberfeigh Pl. *Red* —3B **122**
Cabin Moss. *Brack* —6C **32**
Cabrera Av. *Vir W* —5M **35**
Cabrera Clo. *Vir W* —5N **35**
Cabrol Rd. *Farn* —9M **69**
Caburn Ct. *Craw* —5A **182**
Caburn Heights. *Craw* —5A **182**
*Caci Ho. W14 —1L **13***
(off Avonmore Rd.)
Cacket's La. *Cud* —3M **87**
Cackstones, The. *Worth* —1H **183**
Cadbury Clo. *Iswth* —4G **11**
Cadbury Clo. *Sun* —8F **22**
Cadbury Rd. *Sun* —8F **22**
Caddy Clo. *Egh* —6C **20**
Cader Rd. *SW18* —9N **13** & 1A **28**
Cadet Way. *C Crook* —9C **88**
*Cadman Ct. W4 —1A **12***
(off Chaseley Dri.)
Cadmer Clo. *N Mald* —3D **42**
Cadnam Clo. *Alder* —6A **110**
Cadogan Clo. *Beck* —1N **47**
Cadogan Clo. *Tedd* —6E **24**
Cadogan Ct. *Sutt* —3N **61**
*Cadogan Ho. Guild —4B **114***
(off St Lukes Sq.)
Cadogan Rd. *Alder* —6B **90**
Cadogan Rd. *Surb* —4K **41**
Caenshill Rd. *Wey* —4B **56**
Caenswood Hill. *Wey* —6B **56**
Caenwood Clo. *Wey* —3B **56**
Caen Wood Rd. *Asht* —5J **79**
Caerleon Clo. *Hind* —3A **170**
Caernarvon. *Frim* —6D **70**
Caernarvon Clo. *Mitc* —2J **45**
Caesar Ct. *Alder* —2K **109**
Caesars Camp Rd. *Camb* —7D **50**
Caesar's Clo. *Camb* —7D **50**
Caesars Ct. *Farnh* —6H **109**
Caesars Ga. *Warf* —8C **16**
Caesars Wlk. *Mitc* —4D **44**
Caesars Way. *Shep* —5E **38**
Caffins Clo. *Craw* —1C **182**
Cage Yd. *Reig* —3M **121**
Caillard Rd. *Byfl* —7N **55**
Cain Rd. *Brack* —1J **31**
Cain's La. *Felt* —8F **8**
Cairn Clo. *Camb* —3F **70**
Cairn Ct. *Eps* —6E **60**
Cairngorm Clo. *Tedd* —6G **24**
Cairngorm Pl. *Farn* —7K **69**
Cairo New Rd. *Croy* —8M **45** (3A **200**)
Caistor M. *SW12* —1F **28**
Caistor Rd. *SW12* —1F **28**
Caithness Dri. *Eps* —1C **80** (8L **201**)
Caithness Rd. *Mitc* —8F **28**
Calbourne Rd. *SW12* —1D **28**
Caldbeck Av. *Wor Pk* —8F **42**
*Caldbeck Ho. Craw —6L **181***
(off Salvington Rd.)
Caldecote. *King T* —4N **203**
Calder Ct. *Slou* —1B **6**
Calderdale Clo. *Craw* —5N **181**
Calder Rd. *Mord* —4A **44**
Calder Way. *Coln* —6G **7**
Caldwell Rd. *W'sham* —2A **52**
Caledonian Way. *Gat A* —3F **162**
Caledonia Rd. *Stai* —2N **21**
Caledon Pl. *Guild* —9C **94**
Caledon Rd. *Wall* —1E **62**
Calfridus Way. *Brack* —2C **32**
Calidore Clo. *SW2* —1K **29**
California Rd. *N Mald* —3A **42**
Calley Down Cres. *New Ad* —6N **65**
Callis Farm Clo. *Stanw* —9N **7**
Callisto Clo. *Craw* —6K **181**
Callow Fld. *Purl* —9L **63**
Callow Hill. *Vir W* —2M **35**
Calluna Ct. *Wok* —5B **74**
Calluna Dri. *Copt* —8L **163**
Calonne Rd. *SW19* —5J **27**
Calshot Rd. *H'row A* —5B **8**
(in two parts)
Calshot Way. *Frim* —7E **70**
Calshot Way. *H'row A* —5B **8**
(in two parts)
Calthorpe Gdns. *Sutt* —9A **44**
Calthorpe Rd. *Fleet* —3A **88**
Calton Gdns. *Alder* —5A **110**
Calverley Rd. *Eps* —3F **60**
Calvert Clo. *Alder* —3B **110**
Calvert Cres. *Dork* —3H **119**
Calvert Rd. *Dork* —3H **119**
Calvert Rd. *Eff* —6J **97**
Calvin Clo. *Camb* —2F **70**
Calvin Wlk. *Craw* —6K **181**
Camac Rd. *Twic* —2D **24**
Camargue Pl. *G'ming* —7J **133**
Cambalt Rd. *SW15* —8J **13**
Camber Clo. *Craw* —3G **183**
Camberley. —9B 50
Camberley Av. *SW20* —1G **42**
Camberley Clo. *Sutt* —9J **43**
Camberley Rd. *H'row A* —6B **8**
Camborne Clo. *H'row A* —6B **8**
Camborne Rd. *SW18* —1M **27**
Camborne Rd. *Croy* —6D **46**
Camborne Rd. *Mord* —4J **43**
Camborne Rd. *Sutt* —4M **61**
Camborne Way. *Houn* —4A **10**
Cambourne Rd. *H'row A* —6B **8**
Cambourne Wlk. *Rich* —9K **11**
Cambray Rd. *SW12* —2G **29**
Cambria Clo. *Houn* —7A **10**
Cambria Ct. *Felt* —1J **23**
Cambria Ct. *Stai* —5G **20**
Cambria Gdns. *Stai* —1N **21**
(in two parts)
Cambrian Clo. *SE27* —4M **29**
Cambrian Clo. *Camb* —1N **69**
Cambrian Rd. *Farn* —7J **69**
Cambrian Rd. *Rich* —9M **11**
Cambrian Way. *Finch* —8A **30**
Cambria St. *SW6* —3N **13**
Cambridge Av. *N Mald* —2D **42**
(in two parts)
Cambridge Clo. *SW20* —9G **26**
Cambridge Clo. *Houn* —7M **9**
Cambridge Clo. *W Dray* —2M **7**
Cambridge Clo. *Wok* —5J **73**
Cambridge Cotts. *Kew & Rich* —2N **11**
Cambridge Cres. *Tedd* —6G **24**
Cambridge Gdns. *King T* —1N **41**
Cambridge Gro. *W6* —1G **13**
Cambridge Gro. Rd. *King T* —2N **41**
(in two parts)
Cambridge Ho. *Wind* —4F **4**
Cambridge Lodge Cvn. Pk. *Horl* —5E **142**
Cambridge Meadows. *Farnh* —2E **128**
Cambridge Pk. *Twic* —9J **11**
Cambridge Pk. Ct. *Twic* —1K **25**
Cambridge Pl. *Farnh* —1H **129**
Cambridge Rd. *SE20* —2E **46**
Cambridge Rd. *SW13* —5E **12**
Cambridge Rd. *SW20* —9F **26**
Cambridge Rd. *Alder* —2L **109**
Cambridge Rd. *Afrd* —8D **22**
Cambridge Rd. *Cars* —3C **62**
Cambridge Rd. *Crowt* —3H **49**
Cambridge Rd. *Hamp* —8N **23**
Cambridge Rd. *H'ham* —6K **197**
Cambridge Rd. *Houn* —7M **9**
Cambridge Rd. *King T* —1M **41** (3N **203**)
Cambridge Rd. *Mitc* —2G **44**
Cambridge Rd. *N Mald* —3D **42**
Cambridge Rd. *Owl* —6K **49**
Cambridge Rd. *Rich* —3N **11**
Cambridge Rd. *Tedd* —5F **24**
Cambridge Rd. *Twic* —9K **11**
Cambridge Rd. *W on T* —5J **39**
Cambridge Rd. *W Mol* —3N **39**
Cambridge Rd. E. *Farn* —4A **90**
(in two parts)
Cambridge Rd. N. *W4* —1A **12**
Cambridge Rd. S. *W4* —1A **12**
Cambridge Rd. W. *Farn* —4A **90**
(in two parts)
Cambridgeshire Clo. *Warf* —8D **16**
*Cambridge Sq. Camb —9A **50***
(off Cambridge Wlk.)
Cambridge Wlk. *Camb* —9A **50**
Camden Av. *Felt* —2K **23**
Camden Gdns. *Sutt* —2N **61**
Camden Gdns. *T Hth* —2M **45**
Camden Rd. *Cars* —1D **62**
Camden Rd. *Ling* —7N **145**
Camden Rd. *Sutt* —2N **61**
Camden Wlk. *Fleet* —4D **88**
Camden Way. *T Hth* —2M **45**
Cameford Ct. *SW12* —1J **29**
Camel Gro. *King T* —6K **25**
Camellia Ct. *W End* —9C **52**
Camellia Pl. *Twic* —1B **24**
Camelot Clo. *SW19* —5L **27**
Camelot Clo. *Big H* —3E **86**
Camelot Ct. *If'd* —3K **181**
Camelsdale. —3D 188
Camelsdale Rd. *Hasl* —3C **188**
Cameron Clo. *Cranl* —9N **155**
Cameron Rd. *Alder* —6B **90**
Cameron Rd. *Croy* —5M **45**
Cameron Sq. *Mitc* —9C **28**
Camilla Clo. *Bookh* —3B **98**
Camilla Clo. *Sun* —7G **22**
Camilla Dri. *Westh* —8G **98**
Camille Clo. *SE25* —2D **46**
Camm Av. *Wind* —6B **4**
Camm Gdns. *King T* —1M **41** (4N **203**)
Camm Gdns. *Th Dit* —6F **40**
Camomile Av. *Mitc* —9D **28**
Campana Rd. *SW6* —4M **13**
Campbell Av. *Wok* —8B **74**
Campbell Clo. *SW16* —5H **29**
Campbell Clo. *Alder* —5A **110**
Campbell Clo. *Fleet* —4A **88**
Campbell Clo. *Twic* —3D **24**
Campbell Clo. *Yat* —9E **48**
Campbell Cres. *E Grin* —9L **165**
Campbell Pl. *Frim* —3D **70**
Campbell Rd. *Alder* —1M **109**
Campbell Rd. *Cat* —8A **84**
Campbell Rd. *Croy* —6M **45**
Campbell Rd. *E Mol* —2E **40**
Campbell Rd. *M'bowr* —5G **182**
Campbell Rd. *Twic* —3D **24**
Campbell Rd. *Wey* —4B **56**
Campden Rd. *S Croy* —2B **64**
Campen Clo. *SW19* —3K **27**
Camp End Rd. *Wey* —8D **56**
*Camperdown Ho. Wall —3F **62***
(off Stanley Pk. Rd.)
Camp Farm Rd. *Alder* —8B **90**
Camp Hill. *Farnh* —3A **130**
Camphill Ct. *W Byf* —8J **55**
Camphill Ind. Est. *W Byf* —7K **55**
Camphill Rd. *W Byf* —8J **55**
Campion Clo. *B'water* —3L **69**
Campion Clo. *Lind* —5B **168**
Campion Clo. *S Croy* —1B **64**
Campion Dri. *Tad* —7G **81**
Campion Ho. *Brack* —9K **15**
Campion Ho. *Red* —1D **122**
Campion Rd. *SW15* —7H **13**
Campion Rd. *H'ham* —3L **197**
Campion Rd. *Iswth* —4F **10**
Campion Way. *Wokgm* —9D **14**
Camp Rd. *SW19* —6G **26**
(in two parts)
Camp Rd. *Farn* —5A **90**
Camp Rd. *Wold* —7H **85**
Camp Vw. *SW19* —6G **27**
Camrose Av. *Felt* —5K **23**
Camrose Clo. *Croy* —6H **47**
Camrose Clo. *Mord* —3M **43**
Canada Av. *Red* —7E **122**
Canada Dri. *Red* —7E **122**
Canada Rd. *Byfl* —7M **55**
Canada Rd. *Cobh* —9K **57**
Canada Rd. *Deep* —6H **71**
Canadian Memorial Av. *Asc* —1J **35**
Canal Bank. *Ash V* —9E **90**
Canal Clo. *Alder* —8B **90**
Canal Cotts. *Ash V* —9E **90**
Canal Wlk. *SE25* —5B **46**
Canberra Clo. *Craw* —9B **162**
Canberra Clo. *Yat* —7A **48**
Canberra Pl. *H'ham* —3M **197**
Canberra Rd. *H'row A* —6B **8**
Canbury Av. *King T* —9M **25** (1M **203**)
Canbury Bus. Cen. *King T* —9L **25** (2L **203**)
Canbury Bus. Pk. *King T* —2L **203**
Canbury Pk. Rd. *King T* —9L **25** (2L **203**)
Canbury Pas. *King T* —9K **25** (2J **203**)
Candleford Clo. *Brack* —8A **16**
Candler M. *Twic* —1G **25**
Candlerush Clo. *Wok* —4D **74**
Candover Clo. *W Dray* —3M **7**
Candy Cft. *Bookh* —4B **98**
Cane Clo. *Wall* —4J **63**
(in two parts)
Canes La. *Lind* —4A **168**
Canewden Clo. *Wok* —6A **74**
Canford Dri. *Add* —8K **37**
Canford Gdns. *N Mald* —5D **42**
Canford Pl. *Tedd* —7J **25**
Canham Rd. *SE25* —2B **46**
Can Hatch. *Tad* —5K **81**
Canmore Gdns. *SW16* —8G **29**
Canning Rd. *Alder* —2B **110**
Canning Rd. *Croy* —8C **46**
Cannizaro Rd. *SW19* —7H **27**
Cannon Clo. *Coll T* —7L **49**
Cannon Clo. *SW20* —2H **43**
Cannon Clo. *Hamp* —7B **24**
Cannon Cres. *Chob* —7H **53**
Cannon Gro. *Fet* —9E **78**
Cannon Hill. *Brack* —5A **32**
Cannon Hill La. *SW20* —4J **43**
Cannonside. *Fet* —9E **78**
Cannon Way. *Fet* —8E **78**
Cannon Way. *W Mol* —3A **40**
Canonbury Cotts. *Rusp* —3E **180**
Canons Clo. *Reig* —2L **121**
Canons Hill. *Coul* —5L **83**
(in two parts)
Canons La. *Tad* —5K **81**
Canon's Wlk. *Croy* —9G **46**
Canopus Way. *Stai* —1N **21**
Cansiron La. *Ash W* —3H **187**
(in five parts)
Cansiron La. *Cowd* —7N **167**
(in three parts)
*Cantelupe M. E Grin —9B **166***
(off Cantelupe Rd.)
Cantelupe Rd. *E Grin* —9B **166**
Canterbury Ct. *Dork* —1J **201**
Canterbury Gro. *SE27* —5L **29**
Canterbury Ho. *Croy* —1D **200**
Canterbury M. *Oxs* —9C **58**
Canterbury Rd. *As* —1E **110**
Canterbury Rd. *Craw* —7C **182**
Canterbury Rd. *Croy* —6K **45**
Canterbury Rd. *Farn* —3B **90**
Canterbury Rd. *Felt* —3M **23**
Canterbury Rd. *Guild* —1J **113**
Canterbury Rd. *Mord* —6N **43**
Canter, The. *Craw* —2J **183**
Cantley. —9A 14
Cantley Cres. *Wokgm* —9A **14**
Cantley Gdns. *SE19* —1C **46**
Canvey Clo. *Craw* —6A **182**
Cape Copse. *Rud* —1E **194**
Capel. —4K 159
Capel Av. *Wall* —2K **63**
Capel By-Pass. *Capel* —3H **159**
Capel La. *Craw* —4L **181**
Capel Rd. *Rusp* —2M **179**
Capern Rd. *SW18* —2A **28**
Capital Ind. Est. *Mitc* —4D **44**
Capital Interchange Way. *Bren* —1N **11**
Capital Pk. *Old Wok* —8D **74**
Capital Pl. *Croy* —2K **63**
*Caple Ho. SW10 —3N **13***
(off King's Rd.)
Capricorn Clo. *Craw* —5K **181**
Capri Rd. *Croy* —7C **46**
Capsey Rd. *If'd* —3K **181**
Capstans Wharf. *St J* —5J **73**
Caradon Clo. *Wok* —5L **73**
Caraway Clo. *Craw* —7N **181**
Caraway Pl. *Guild* —7K **93**
Caraway Pl. *Wall* —9F **44**
Carbery La. *Asc* —2M **33**
Cardamom Clo. *Guild* —8K **93**
Card Hill. *F Row* —8H **187**
Cardigan Clo. *Wok* —5H **73**
Cardigan Rd. *SW13* —5F **12**
Cardigan Rd. *SW19* —7A **28**
Cardigan Rd. *Rich* —9L **11**
Cardinal Av. *King T* —6L **25**
Cardinal Av. *Mord* —5K **43**
Cardinal Clo. *Mord* —5K **43**
Cardinal Clo. *S Croy* —9D **64**
Cardinal Clo. *Wor Pk* —1F **60**
Cardinal Cres. *N Mald* —1B **42**
Cardinal Dri. *W on T* —7L **39**
Cardinal Pl. *SW15* —7J **13**
Cardinal Rd. *Felt* —2J **23**
Cardinals, The. —5E 110
Cardinals, The. *Brack* —3N **31**
Cardinals Wlk. *Hamp* —8C **24**
Cardinals Wlk. *Sun* —7F **22**
Cardingham. *Wok* —4K **73**
Cardington Rd. *H'row A* —6C **8**
Cardington Sq. *Houn* —7L **9**
Cardwell Cres. *Asc* —4N **33**
Cardwells Keep. *Guild* —9K **93**
Carew Clo. *Coul* —6M **83**
Carew Ct. *Sutt* —5N **61**
Carew Manor & Dovecote. —9G 45
Carew Mnr. Cotts. *Wall* —9H **45**
Carew Rd. *Afrd* —7D **22**
Carew Rd. *Mitc* —1E **44**
Carew Rd. *T Hth* —3M **45**
Carew Rd. *Wall* —3G **63**
Carey Clo. *Wind* —6E **4**
Carey Ho. *Craw* —3A **182**
Carey Rd. *Wokgm* —3B **30**
Careys Copse. *Small* —8M **143**
Carey's Wood. *Small* —8M **143**
Carfax. *H'ham* —6J **197**
Carfax Av. *Tong* —4D **110**
Carfax Rd. *Hayes* —1G **9**
Cargate Av. *Alder* —3M **109**
Cargate Gro. *Alder* —3M **109**
Cargate Hill. *Alder* —3L **109**
Cargate Ter. *Alder* —3L **109**
Cargill Rd. *SW18* —2N **27**
Cargo Forecourt Rd. *Gat A* —3B **162**
Cargo Rd. *Gat A* —2B **162**
Cargreen Pl. *SE25* —3C **46**
Cargreen Rd. *SE25* —3C **46**
Carina M. *SE27* —5N **29**
Carisbrooke. *Frim* —6D **70**
Carisbrooke Ct. *Cheam* —4L **61**
Carisbrooke Rd. *Mitc* —3H **45**
Carleton Av. *Wall* —5H **63**
Carleton Clo. *Esh* —7D **40**
Carlingford Gdns. *Mitc* —8D **28**
Carlingford Rd. *Mord* —5J **43**
Carlin Pl. *Camb* —2A **70**
Carlinwark Dri. *Camb* —8D **50**
Carlisle Clo. *King T* —9N **25**
Carlisle M. *King T* —9N **25**
Carlisle Rd. *Hamp* —8B **24**
Carlisle Rd. *Sutt* —3L **61**
Carlisle Rd. *Tilf* —3N **149**
Carlisle Way. *SW17* —6E **28**
Carlos St. *G'ming* —7H **133**
Carlton Av. *Felt* —9K **9**
Carlton Av. *Hayes* —1F **8**

Carlton Av.—Chalkpit La.

Carlton Av. S Croy —4B 64
Carlton Clo. Camb —3F 70
Carlton Clo. Chess —3K 59
Carlton Clo. Craw —4C 182
Carlton Clo. Wok —1B 74
Carlton Ct. SE20 —1E 46
Carlton Ct. Horl —6E 142
Carlton Ct. Stai —6J 21
Carlton Cres. C Crook —7C 88
Carlton Cres. Sutt —1K 61
Carlton Dri. SW15 —8J 13
Carlton Grn. Red —9C 102
Carlton Ho. Felt —9G 8
Carlton Pk. Av. SW20 —1J 43
Carlton Rd. SW14 —6B 12
Carlton Rd. Head D —5H 169
Carlton Rd. N Mald —1D 42
Carlton Rd. Reig & Red —1B 122
Carlton Rd. S Croy —3A 64
Carlton Rd. S God —1F 144
Carlton Rd. Sun —8G 22
Carlton Rd. W on T —6J 39
Carlton Rd. Wok —1C 74
Carlton Tye. Horl —8G 142
Carlwell St. SW17 —6C 28
Carlyle Clo. W Mol —1B 40
Carlyle Ct. Crowt —3H 49
Carlyle Pl. SW15 —7J 13
Carlyle Rd. W5 —1J 11
Carlyle Rd. Croy —8D 46
Carlyle Rd. Stai —8J 21
Carlyon Clo. Farn —1A 90
Carlyon Clo. Myt —1D 90
Carlys Clo. Beck —1G 47
Carmalt Gdns. SW15 —7H 13
Carmalt Gdns. W on T —2K 57
Carman Wlk. Craw —8N 181
Carmarthen Clo. Farn —7L 69
Carmel Clo. Wok —5A 74
Carmichael Ct. SW13 —5E 12
(off Grove Rd.)
Carmichael M. SW18 —1B 28
Carmichael Rd. SE25 —4C 46
Carminia Rd. SW17 —3F 28
Carnac St. SE27 —5N 29
Carnation Clo. Crowt —8G 30
Carnation Dri. Wink R —7E 16
Carnegie Clo. Surb —8M 41
Carnegie Pl. SW19 —4J 27
Carnforth Clo. Eps —3A 60
Carnforth Rd. SW16 —8H 29
Carnie Hall. SW17 —4F 28
Carnival Sq. Fleet —4A 88
Carnoustie. Brack —6K 31
Carnwath Rd. SW6 —6M 13
Carolina Rd. T Hth —1M 45
Caroline Clo. SW16 —4K 29
Caroline Clo. Croy —1B 64
Caroline Clo. Iswth —3D 10
Caroline Ct. Afrd —7C 22
Caroline Ct. Craw —4D 182
Caroline Ho. W6 —1H 13
(off Queen Caroline St.)
Caroline Pl. Hayes —3F 8
Caroline Rd. SW19 —8L 27
Caroline Wlk. W6 —2K 13
(off Lillie Rd.)
Caroline Way. Frim —5D 70
Carolyn Clo. Wok —6J 73
Carpenter Clo. Eps —5E 60
Carpenters Ct. Twic —3E 24
Carrara Wharf. SW6 —6K 13
Carrick Clo. Iswth —6G 10
Carrick Ga. Esh —9C 40
Carrick La. Yat —9D 48
Carrington Av. Houn —8B 10
Carrington Clo. Croy —6H 47
Carrington Clo. King T —6B 26
Carrington Clo. Red —2D 122
Carrington La. Ash V —5E 90
Carrington Pl. Esh —2C 58
Carrington Rd. Rich —7N 11
Carroll Av. Guild —3D 114
Carroll Cres. Asc —4K 33
Carrow Rd. W on T —9L 39
Carshalton. —1E 62
Carshalton Athletic F.C. —1C 62
Carshalton Beeches. —5C 62
Carshalton Gro. Sutt —1B 62
Carshalton on the Hill. —4E 62
Carshalton Pk. Rd. Cars —2D 62
Carshalton Pl. Cars —2E 62
Carshalton Rd. Bans —1D 82
Carshalton Rd. Camb —8E 50
Carshalton Rd. Mitc —3E 44
Carshalton Rd. Sutt & Cars —2A 62
Carslake Rd. SW15 —9H 13
Carson Rd. SE21 —3N 29
Cartbridge. —9D 74
Cartbridge Clo. Send —1D 94
Carter Clo. Wall —4H 63
Carter Clo. Wind —5D 4
Carterdale Cotts. Capel —5J 159
Carter Rd. SW19 —7B 28
Carter Rd. M'bowr —6H 183
Carters Clo. Guild —8A 94
Carters Clo. Wor Pk —8J 43
Carter's Cotts. Red —5C 122
Carter's Hill. B'bear & Bint —5F 14
Carters Hill Pk. Wokgm —5E 14
Carters La. Wok —7E 74
Carterslodge La. Hand —9J 199
Cartersmeade Clo. Horl —7F 142
Carters Rd. Eps —2E 80
Carters Wlk. Farnh —4J 109
Carter's Yd. SW18 —8M 13
Carthona Dri. Fleet —6A 88
Carthouse Cotts. Guild —9E 94
Carthouse La. Wok —1H 73
Cartmel Clo. Reig —1C 122
Cartwright Way. SW13 —3G 13
Carville Cres. Bren —1L 11
Cascades. Croy —6J 65
Caselden Clo. Add —2L 55
Casewick Rd. SE27 —6L 29
Casher Rd. M'bowr —6G 183
Cassidy Rd. SW6 —3M 13
(in two parts)
Cassilis Rd. Twic —8H 11
Cassino Clo. Alder —2N 109
Cassiobury Av. Felt —1G 22
Cassland Rd. T Hth —3A 46
Cassocks Sq. Shep —6E 38
Castello Av. SW15 —8H 13
Castelnau. —2G 12
Castelnau. SW13 —4F 12
Castelnau Gdns. SW13 —2G 13
Castelnau Row. SW13 —2G 12
Castle Av. Dat —2K 5
Castle Av. Eps —5F 60
Castle Clo. SW19 —4J 27
Castle Clo. Blet —2N 123
Castle Clo. Brom —2N 47
Castle Clo. Camb —2D 70
Castle Clo. Reig —7N 121
Castle Clo. Sun —8F 22
Castlecombe Dri. SW19 —1J 27
Castle Ct. Farnh —9G 108
Castlecraig Ct. Coll T —8J 49
Castle Dri. Horl —1G 162
Castle Dri. Reig —7M 121
Castle Fld. Farnh —9G 108
Castlefield Ct. Reig —3N 121
Castlefield Rd. Reig —3M 121
Castle Gdns. Dork —3M 119
Castlegate. Rich —6M 11
Castle Green. —9G 53
Castle Grn. Wey —9F 38
Castle Gro. Rd. Chob —9G 53
Castle Hill. Farnh —9G 108
Castle Hill. Guild —5N 113 (7C 202)
Castle Hill. Wind —4G 5
Castle Hill Av. New Ad —5L 65
Castle Hill Rd. Egh —5L 19
Castlemaine Av. Eps —5G 61
Castlemaine Av. S Croy —2C 64
Castle Pde. Eps —4F 60
Castle Pl. W4 —1D 12
Castle Rd. Alder —9K 89
Castle Rd. Broad H —5D 196
Castle Rd. Camb —2C 70
Castle Rd. Coul —7C 82
Castle Rd. Eps —2A 80
Castle Rd. Iswth —5F 10
Castle Rd. Wey —9F 38
Castle Rd. Wok —1B 74
Castle Row. W4 —1C 12
Castle Sq. Blet —2N 123
Castle Sq. Guild —5N 113 (6D 202)
Castle St. Blet —2M 123
Castle St. Farnh —9G 109
Castle St. Fleet —6A 88
Castle St. Guild —5N 113 (6C 202)
Castle St. King T —1L 41 (3K 203)
Castle, The. H'ham —1L 197
Castleton. Cars —7B 62
Castleton Clo. Bans —2M 81
Castleton Clo. Croy —5H 47
Castleton Dri. Bans —2M 81
Castleton Rd. Mitc —3H 45
(in two parts)
Castletown Rd. W14 —1K 13
Castle Vw. Eps —1A 80
Castleview Rd. Slou —1M 5
Castle Vw. Rd. Wey —1C 56
Castle Wlk. Reig —3M 121
Castle Wlk. Sun —2K 39
Castle Way. SW19 —4J 27
Castle Way. Eps —6F 60
Castle Way. Felt —5K 23
Castle Yd. Rich —8K 11
Castor Ct. C Crook —8C 88
Castor Ct. Yat —8A 48
Caswall Clo. Binf —7H 15
Caswall Ride. Yat —1D 68
Caswell Clo. Farn —8L 69
Catalina Rd. H'row A —5C 8
Catalpa Clo. Guild —1M 113
Catena Ri. Light —6L 51
Caterfield La. Crow & Oxt —1B 146
Cater Gdns. Guild —1J 113
Caterham. —2D 104
Caterham By-Pass. Cat —8E 84
Caterham Clo. Cat —7B 84
(in two parts)
Caterham Clo. Pirb —8B 72
Caterham Dri. Coul —5M 83
Caterham-on-the-Hill. —9C 84
Caterways. H'ham —5G 197
Catesby Gdns. Yat —1A 68
Cathcart Rd. SW10 —2N 13
Cathedral Clo. Guild —4L 113
Cathedral Ct. Guild —3K 113
Cathedral Hill Ind. Est. Guild —2K 113
Cathedral Precinct. Guild —4K 113
Cathedral Vw. Guild —3J 113
Catherine Clo. Byfl —1N 75
Catherine Ct. SW19 —6L 27
Catherine Dri. Rich —7L 11
Catherine Dri. Sun —7G 22
Catherine Gdns. Houn —7D 10
Catherine Howard Ct. Wey —9C 38
(off Old Pal. Rd.)
Catherine Rd. Surb —4K 41 (8H 203)
Catherine Wheel Rd. Bren —3K 11
Cat Hill. Ockl —7B 158
Cathill La. Ockl —7B 158
Cathles Rd. SW12 —1F 28
Catlin Cres. Shep —4E 38
Catlin Gdns. God —8E 104
Cator Clo. New Ad —7A 66
Cator Cres. New Ad —7A 66
Cator La. Beck —1J 47
Cator Rd. Cars —2D 62
Cato's Hill. Esh —1B 58
Cat St. Up Har —9N 187
Catteshall. —6K 133
Catteshall Hatch. G'ming —5K 133
Catteshall La. G'ming —7H 133
Catteshall Rd. G'ming —5K 133
(in two parts)
Catteshall Ter. G'ming —6K 133
(off Catteshall Rd.)
Caudwell Ter. SW18 —1B 28
Causeway Ct. Wok —5J 73
Causeway Est. Stai —5D 20
Causewayside. Hasl —1H 189
(off High St.)
Causeway, The. SW18 —8N 13
(in two parts)
Causeway, The. SW19 —6H 27
Causeway, The. Cars —9E 44
Causeway, The. Chess —1L 59
Causeway, The. Clay —4F 58
Causeway, The. Felt & Houn —7H 9
Causeway, The. H'ham —7J 197
Causeway, The. Stai —5E 20
Causeway, The. Sutt —5A 62
Causeway, The. Tedd —7F 24
Cavalier Ct. Surb —5M 41
Cavalier Way. E Grin —2B 186
Cavalry Ct. Alder —2K 109
Cavalry Cres. Houn —7L 9
Cavalry Cres. Wind —6F 4
Cavalry Gdns. SW15 —8L 13
Cavan's Rd. Alder —7A 90
Cavell Ho. Ott —3F 54
Cavell Way. Eps —7N 59
Cavell Way. Knap —6J 72
Cavell Way. M'bowr —4G 182
Cavendish Av. N Mald —4F 42
Cavendish Clo. H'ham —1K 197
Cavendish Clo. Sun —7G 22
Cavendish Ct. B'water —3J 69
Cavendish Ct. Cher —7J 37
(off Victory Rd.)
Cavendish Ct. Coln —4G 6
Cavendish Ct. Sun —7G 22
Cavendish Dri. Clay —2F 58
Cavendish Gdns. SW4 —1G 29
Cavendish Gdns. C Crook —8A 88
Cavendish Gdns. Red —2E 122
Cavendish Meads. Asc —5N 33
Cavendish M. Alder —3M 109
Cavendish Pde. Houn —5M 9
Cavendish Pk. Cvn. Site. Sand —9K 49
Cavendish Rd. SW12 —1G 28
Cavendish Rd. SW19 —8B 28
Cavendish Rd. W4 —4B 12
Cavendish Rd. Alder —3M 109
Cavendish Rd. C Crook —9A 88
Cavendish Rd. Croy —7M 45
Cavendish Rd. N Mald —3E 42
Cavendish Rd. Red —3E 122
Cavendish Rd. Sun —7G 22
Cavendish Rd. Sutt —4A 62
Cavendish Rd. Wey —5C 56
Cavendish Rd. Wok —6N 73
Cavendish Ter. Felt —3H 23
Cavendish Way. W Wick —7L 47
Cavenham Clo. Wok —6A 74
Caverleigh Way. Wor Pk —7F 42
Cave Rd. Rich —5J 25
Caversham Av. Sutt —8K 43
Caversham Ho. King T —4K 203
Caversham Rd. King T —1M 41 (3M 203)
Caves Farm Clo. Sand —7F 48
Cawcott Dri. Wind —4B 4
Cawsey Way. Wok —4A 74
Caxton Av. Add —3J 55
Caxton Clo. Craw —6B 182
Caxton Gdns. Guild —2L 113
Caxton La. Oxt —9G 106
Caxton M. Bren —2K 11
Caxton Ri. Red —2E 122
Caxton Rd. SW19 —6A 28
Cayley Clo. Wall —4J 63
Cayton Rd. Coul —9G 83
Cearn Way. Coul —2K 83
Cecil Clo. Afrd —8D 22
Cecil Clo. Chess —1K 59
Cecil Ct. SW10 —2N 13
(off Hollywood Rd.)
Cecil Pl. Mitc —4D 44
Cecil Rd. SW19 —8N 27
Cecil Rd. Afrd —8D 22
Cecil Rd. Croy —5J 45
Cecil Rd. Houn —5C 10
Cecil Rd. Sutt —3L 61
Cedar Av. B'water —1J 69
Cedar Av. Cobh —2K 77
Cedar Av. Twic —9B 10
Cedar Clo. SE21 —2N 29
Cedar Clo. SW15 —5C 26
Cedar Clo. Alder —4C 110
Cedar Clo. Dag —4J 51
Cedar Clo. Binf —7J 15
Cedar Clo. Cars —3D 62
Cedar Clo. Craw —9A 162
Cedar Clo. Dork —5H 119 (3L 201)
Cedar Clo. E Mol —3E 40
Cedar Clo. Eps —1E 80
Cedar Clo. Esh —3N 57
Cedar Clo. H'ham —5H 197
Cedar Clo. Reig —5A 122
Cedar Clo. Stai —2L 37
Cedar Clo. Warl —6H 85
Cedar Clo. Wokgm —2B 30
Cedar Ct. SW19 —4J 27
Cedar Ct. Bren —2J 11
Cedar Ct. Egh —5C 20
Cedar Ct. Hasl —2F 188
Cedar Ct. Lea —9G 78
Cedar Ct. Sutt —3A 62
Cedar Ct. Wind —5D 4
Cedar Cres. Brom —1G 66
Cedarcroft Rd. Chess —1M 59
Cedar Dri. Asc —3G 35
(Blacknest Rd.)
Cedar Dri. Asc —6D 34
(Broomhall La.)
Cedar Dri. Brack —8A 16
Cedar Dri. Eden —1K 147
Cedar Dri. Fet —1E 98
Cedar Dri. Fleet —4D 88
Cedar Gdns. Sutt —3A 62
Cedar Gdns. Wok —5L 73
Cedar Gro. Bisl —2D 72
Cedar Gro. Wey —1D 56
Cedar Heights. Rich —2L 25
Cedar Hill. Eps —3B 80
Cedar Ho. Guild —1E 114
Cedarland Ter. SW20 —8G 27
Cedar La. Frim —6B 70
Cedar Lodge. Craw —5B 182
Cedar Lodge. Hasl —3J 189
Cedarne Rd. SW6 —3N 13
Cedar Pk. Cat —8B 84
Cedar Rd. Cobh —1J 77
Cedar Rd. Croy —8A 46 (2E 200)
Cedar Rd. E Mol —3E 40
Cedar Rd. Farn —2A 90
Cedar Rd. Felt —2E 22
Cedar Rd. Houn —5K 9
Cedar Rd. Sutt —3A 62
Cedar Rd. Tedd —6G 24
Cedar Rd. Wey —1B 56
Cedar Rd. Wok —7L 73
Cedars. Bans —1D 82
Cedars. Brack —3D 32
Cedars Av. Mitc —3E 44
Cedars Clo. Sand —7E 48
Cedars Ct. Guild —9C 94
Cedars Rd. SW13 —5F 12
Cedars Rd. W4 —2B 12
Cedars Rd. Beck —1H 47
Cedars Rd. Croy —9J 45
Cedars Rd. Hamp W —9J 25
Cedars Rd. Mord —3M 43
Cedars, The. Byfl —8A 56
Cedars, The. Fleet —5C 88
Cedars, The. Guild —9C 94
Cedars, The. Lea —8K 79
Cedars, The. Milf —2B 152
Cedars, The. Pirb —9A 72
Cedars, The. Reig —3D 122
Cedars, The. Tedd —7F 24
Cedars, The. Wall —1G 63
Cedar Ter. Rich —7L 11
Cedar Tree Gro. SE27 —6M 29
Cedar Vw. King T —6J 203
Cedarville Gdns. SW16 —7K 29
Cedar Wlk. Clay —3F 58
Cedar Wlk. Kenl —3N 83
Cedar Wlk. Kgswd —7K 81
Cedar Way. Guild —1M 113
Cedar Way. Slou —1A 6
Cedar Way. Sun —8F 22
Cedarways. Farnh —4G 128
Celandine Clo. Craw —6N 181
Celandine Clo. Crowt —1H 49
Celandine Ct. Yat —8A 48
Celandine Rd. W on T —1M 57
Celery La. Wrec —6G 128
Celia Cres. Afrd —7M 21
Cell Farm Av. Old Win —8L 5
Celtic Av. Brom —2N 47
Celtic Rd. Byfl —1N 75
Cemetery Pales. Brkwd —9D 72
Cemetery Rd. Fleet —6A 88
Centaur Ct. Bren —1L 11
Centaurs Bus. Cen. Iswth —2G 10
Centennial Ct. Brack —1M 31
Central Av. Houn —7C 10
Central Av. Wall —2J 63
Central Av. W Mol —3N 39
Central Gdns. Mord —4N 43
Central Hill. SE19 —6N 29
Central La. Wink —2M 17
Central Pde. Felt —1K 23
Central Pde. Horl —9E 142
Central Pde. Houn —3N 9
Central Pde. New Ad —6M 65
Central Pde. Red —2D 122
Central Pde. Surb —5L 41
Central Pde. W Mol —3N 39
Central Pk. Est. Houn —8L 9
Central Pl. SE25 —4D 46
Central Rd. Mord —5M 43
Central Rd. Wor Pk —7F 42
Central School Path. SW14 —6B 12
Central Ter. Beck —2G 46
Central Wlk. Wokgm —2B 30
Central Way. Cars —4C 62
Central Way. Felt —8H 9
Central Way. Oxt —5N 105
Central Way. Wink —2M 17
Centre Ct. Shop. Cen. SW19 —7L 27
Centre Rd. Wind —3A 4
Centre, The. Felt —3H 23
Centre, The. Houn —6B 10
Centre, The. W on T —7G 39
Centurion Clo. Coll T —7J 49
Centurion Ct. Hack —8F 44
Century Ct. Wok —3B 74
Century Ho. SW15 —7J 13
Century Rd. Stai —6F 20
Century Way. Brkwd —6A 72
Cerne Rd. Mord —5A 44
Cerotus Pl. Cher —6H 37
Ceylon Ter. Deep —6H 71
(off Crimea Rd.)
Chadacre Rd. Eps —3G 60
Chadhurst Clo. N Holm —8K 119
Chadwick Av. SW19 —7M 27
Chadwick Clo. SW15 —1F 26
Chadwick Clo. Craw —8N 181
Chadwick Clo. Tedd —7G 25
Chadwick Pl. Surb —6J 41
Chadworth Way. Clay —2D 58
Chaffers Mead. Asht —3M 79
Chaffinch Av. Croy —5G 46
Chaffinch Bus. Pk. Beck —3G 47
Chaffinch Clo. Coll T —7J 49
Chaffinch Clo. Craw —1B 182
Chaffinch Clo. Croy —4G 46
Chaffinch Clo. H'ham —1K 197
Chaffinch Clo. Surb —9N 41
Chaffinch Rd. Beck —1H 47
Chaffinch Way. Horl —7C 142
Chailey Clo. Craw —6M 181
Chailey Clo. Houn —4L 9
Chailey Pl. W on T —1M 57
Chalcot Clo. Sutt —4M 61
Chalcot M. SW16 —4J 29
Chalcott Gdns. Surb —7J 41
Chaldon. —2L 103
Chaldon Clo. Red —5C 122
Chaldon Comn. Rd. Cat —2N 103
Chaldon Ct. SE19 —9N 29
Chaldon Rd. SW6 —3K 13
Chaldon Rd. Cat —2A 104
Chaldon Rd. Craw —8A 182
Chaldon Way. Coul —4J 83
Chale Rd. SW2 —1J 29
Chalet Hill. Bord —6A 168
Chale Wlk. Sutt —5N 61
Chalfont Dri. Farn —3A 90
Chalfont Rd. SE25 —2C 46
Chalford Clo. W Mol —3A 40
Chalgrove Av. Mord —4M 43
Chalgrove Rd. Sutt —4B 62
Chalice Clo. Wall —3H 63
Chalker's Corner. (Junct.) —6A 12
Chalk Hill Rd. W6 —1J 13
Chalk La. Asht —6M 79
Chalk La. E Hor —1G 116
Chalk La. Eps —2C 80
(in two parts)
Chalk La. Shack —3A 132
Chalkley Clo. Mitc —1D 44
Chalkmead. Red —8G 103
Chalk Paddock. Eps —2C 80
Chalk Pit Cotts. W Hor —8C 96
Chalkpit La. Bet —2A 120
Chalkpit La. Bookh —5N 97

Church La.—Clewer Village

Church La. Brook —1N 171
Church La. Burs —4J 163
Church La. Cat —2L 103
Church La. Chel —3L 85
Church La. Chess —3M 59
Church La. Copt —8L 163
Church La. Coul —9E 82
Church La. Cranl —7N 155
Church La. Craw —2D 182
Church La. E Grin —9B 166
Church La. Eps —4J 81
Church La. Ews —3C 108
Church La. Farn —1K 89
Church La. Gray —6A 170
Church La. Hamb —8G 153
Church La. Hasl —1G 189
Church La. H'ley —2B 100
Church La. Head —3C 168
Church La. Man H —9F 198
Church La. Oke H —9N 157
Church La. Oxt —8N 105
Church La. Pirb —9A 72
Church La. Rich —2L 25
Church La. Rowl —8D 128
Church La. Send —4D 94
Church La. Shere —8B 116
Church La. Tats —9F 86
Church La. Tedd —6F 24
Church La. Th Dit —5F 40
Church La. Twic —2G 25
Church La. Wall —9H 45
Church La. Warf —5B 16
Church La. Warl —4G 84
Church La. Wey —1B 56
Church La. Wind —4G 5
Church La. Wink —3F 16
Church La. Worp —5H 93
Church La. Wrec —4E 128
Church La. Av. Coul —9F 82
Church La. Dri. Coul —9F 82
Church La. E. Alder —3M 109
Church La. W. Alder —3L 109
Church Mdw. Surb —8J 41
Church M. Add —1L 55
Churchmore Rd. SW16 —9G 29
Chu. Paddock Ct. Wall —9H 45
Church Pde. Afrd —5A 22
Church Pas. Farnh —1G 129
Church Pas. Surb —4L 41
Church Pas. Twic —2H 25
Church Path. SW14 —7C 12
(in two parts)
Church Path. SW19 —1L 43
Church Path. As —1F 110
Church Path. Ash V —9E 90
Church Path. Cobh —1J 77
Church Path. Coul —5L 83
Church Path. Croy —8N 45 (2B 200)
(in two parts)
Church Path. Farn —1K 89
(Minley Rd.)
Church Path. Farn —5A 90
(Queen's Rd.)
Church Path. Farn —1A 90
(Rectory Rd.)
Church Path. Mitc —2C 44
(in two parts)
Church Path. Red —5F 102
Church Path. Rusp —4B 180
Church Path. S'hill —2B 34
Church Path. Wok —4B 74
Church Pl. Mitc —2C 44
Church Ri. Chess —3M 59
Church Rd. Ham & Rich —5K 25
Church Rd. SE19 —1B 46
Church Rd. SW13 —5E 12
Church Rd. SW19 —6K 27
Church Rd. SW19 & Mitc —9B 28
Church Rd. Add —2J 55
Church Rd. Alder —5A 110
Church Rd. Asc —3L 33
(Lyndhurst Rd.)
Church Rd. Asc —5D 34
(Station Rd.)
Church Rd. Afrd —4A 22
Church Rd. Asht —5K 79
Church Rd. Bag —4H 51
Church Rd. Big H —4F 86
Church Rd. Bookh —1N 97
Church Rd. Brack —1A 32
Church Rd. Broad H —5D 196
Church Rd. Burs —3L 163
Church Rd. Byfl —1N 75
Church Rd. Cat —1C 104
Church Rd. Chav D —9F 16
Church Rd. Clay —3F 58
Church Rd. Copt —7M 163
Church Rd. Cran —1J 9
Church Rd. Croy —9N 45 (3A 200)
(in two parts)
Church Rd. Duns —4N 173
Church Rd. E Mol —3D 40
Church Rd. Egh —6B 20
Church Rd. Eps —8D 60 (5N 201)
Church Rd. F'boro —2L 67
Church Rd. Felt —6L 23
Church Rd. Fleet —3A 88
Church Rd. Frim —5B 70
Church Rd. Guild —4N 113 (4C 202)
Church Rd. Hasc —7A 154
Church Rd. Hasl —1G 188
(Derby Rd.)
Church Rd. Hasl —2D 188
(Hindhead Rd.)
Church Rd. Horl —9D 142
(in two parts)
Church Rd. Horne —5C 144
Church Rd. Hors —3A 74
Church Rd. H'ham —3A 198
Church Rd. Houn —3A 10
Church Rd. Iswth —4D 10
Church Rd. Kenl —2A 84
Church Rd. Kes —4F 66
Church Rd. King T —1M 41 (3M 203)
Church Rd. Lea —9H 79
Church Rd. Ling —7N 145
Church Rd. Low H —5C 162
Church Rd. Milf —2C 152
Church Rd. Newd —1A 160
Church Rd. Old Win —8L 5
Church Rd. Owl —6K 49
Church Rd. Purl —6J 63
Church Rd. Red —5C 122
Church Rd. Reig —5M 121
Church Rd. Rich —7L 11
Church Rd. St J —6K 73
Church Rd. Sand —6E 48
Church Rd. Shep —6C 38
Church Rd. Short —2N 47
Church Rd. Surb —7J 41
Church Rd. Sutt —3K 61
Church Rd. Tedd —5E 24
Church Rd. Turn H —6C 184
Church Rd. Wall —9G 45
Church Rd. Warl —4G 84
Church Rd. W End —8C 52
Church Rd. W Ewe —4C 60
Church Rd. Whyt —5C 84
Church Rd. W'sham —3M 51
Church Rd. Wold —9G 85
Church Rd. Wor Pk —7D 42
Church Rd. Worth & M'bowr —3J 183
Church Rd. E. Crowt —2G 49
Church Rd. E. Farn —4B 90
Church Rd. Ind. Est. Low H —5D 162
Church Rd. Trad. Est. Low H —5C 162
Church Rd. W. Crowt —3G 48
Church Rd. W. Farn —4A 90
Church Side. Eps —9A 60
Churchside Clo. Big H —4E 86
Church Sq. Shep —6C 38
Church St. W4 —2E 12
Church St. Alder —2L 109
Church St. Bet —4D 120
Church St. Cobh —2J 77
Church St. Craw —3A 182
Church St. Crowt —2G 48
Church St. Croy —9M 45 (4A 200)
Church St. Dork —5G 119 (2K 201)
Church St. Eden —2L 147
Church St. Eff —5L 97
Church St. Eps —5F 60
Church St. Esh —1B 58
Church St. Ewe —9D 60 (6M 201)
Church St. G'ming —7G 132
Church St. Hamp —9C 24
Church St. Iswth —6H 11
Church St. King T —1K 41 (3J 203)
Church St. Lea —9H 79
(in two parts)
Church St. Old Wok —8E 74
Church St. Reig —3M 121
Church St. Rud —1D 194
Church St. Stai —5F 20
Church St. Sun —2J 39
Church St. Sutt —2N 61
Church St. Twic —2G 25
Church St. W on T —7H 39
Church St. Warn —1F 196
Church St. Wey —1B 56
Church St. Wind —4G 5
Church St. E. Wok —4B 74
Church St. W. Wok —4A 74
Church Stretton Rd. Houn —8C 10
Church Ter. Holmw —5J 139
Church Ter. Rich —8K 11
Church Ter. Wind —5B 4
Church Town. —1G 124
Church Vw. As —2E 110
Church Vw. Rich —8L 11
Church Vw. Yat —8C 48
Churchview Clo. Horl —9D 142
Churchview Rd. Twic —2D 24
Church Wlk. SW13 —4F 12
Church Wlk. SW15 —8G 13
Church Wlk. SW16 —1G 45
Church Wlk. SW20 —2H 43
Church Wlk. Blet —2A 124
Church Wlk. Bren —2J 11
(in two parts)
Church Wlk. Cat —2D 104
Church Wlk. Cher —5J 37
Church Wlk. Craw —3B 182
Church Wlk. Fay —9G 180
Church Wlk. G'ming —5J 133
Church Wlk. Horl —9D 142
Church Wlk. Lea —9H 79
Church Wlk. Reig —3N 121
Church Wlk. Rich —8K 11
Church Wlk. Th Dit —5F 40
Church Wlk. W on T —7H 39
Church Wlk. Wey —9B 38
Churchward Ho. W14 —1L 13
(off Ivatt Pl.)
Church Way. Oxt —1B 126
Church Way. S Croy —6C 64
Churston Clo. SW2 —2L 29
Churston Dri. Mord —4J 43
Churt. —9L 149
Churt Rd. Churt & Hind —3M 169
Churt Rd. Head & Churt —3F 168
Churt Wynde. Hind —2B 170
Chuters Clo. Byfl —8N 55
Chuters Gro. Eps —8E 60
Cicada Rd. SW18 —9N 13
Cinder Path. Wok —6M 73
Cinnamon Clo. Croy —6J 45
Cinnamon Gdns. Guild —7K 93
Circle Gdns. SW19 —1M 43
Circle Gdns. Byfl —9A 56
Circle Hill Rd. Crowt —2H 49
Circle Rd. W Vill —5F 56
Circle, The. G'ming —5J 133
Circuit Cen., The. Bro I —6N 55
Circus, The. Lea —7H 79
(off Kingston Rd.)
Cissbury Clo. H'ham —2N 197
Cissbury Hill. Craw —5A 182
City Bus. Cen. H'ham —7K 197
City Bus. Cen., The. Craw —8B 162
City Ho. Wall —7E 44
(off Corbet Clo.)
Clacket La. W'ham —2G 107
Clacy Grn. Brack —8M 15
Claireville Ct. Reig —3B 122
Clairvale Rd. Houn —4L 9
Clairview Rd. SW16 —6F 28
Clammer Hill Rd. G'wood —9K 171
Clancarty Rd. SW6 —5M 13
Clandon Av. Egh —8E 20
Clandon Clo. Eps —3E 60
Clandon Ct. Farn —2B 90
Clandon Ho. Guild —5C 114
Clandon House & Pk. —1J 115
Clandon Park. —1J 115
Clandon Rd. Guild —4A 114 (4F 202)
Clandon Rd. Send & W Cla —3H 95
Clandon Ter. SW20 —1J 43
Clanfield Ride. B'water —1J 69
Clapgate La. Slin —3K 195
Clapham Pk. Est. SW4 —1H 29
Clappers Ga. Craw —2B 182
Clappers La. Chob —7F 52
Clappers Mdw. Alf —6J 175
Clappers Orchard. Alf —6H 175
Clare Av. Wokgm —1B 30
Clare Clo. Craw —9G 162
Clare Clo. W Byf —9J 55
Clare Cotts. Blet —2M 123
Clare Ct. Fleet —4B 88
Clare Ct. Wold —1K 105
Clare Cres. Lea —5G 79
Claredale. Wok —6A 74
Clarefield Ct. Asc —6D 34
Clare Gdns. Egh —6C 20
Clare Hill. Esh —3B 58
Clare Lawn Av. SW14 —8B 12
Clare Mead. Rowl —8E 128
Clare M. SW6 —3N 13
Claremont. Shep —5C 38
Claremont Av. Camb —1D 70
Claremont Av. Esh —3N 57
Claremont Av. N Mald —4F 42
Claremont Av. Sun —9J 23
Claremont Av. W on T —1L 57
Claremont Av. Wok —6A 74
Claremont Clo. SW2 —2J 29
Claremont Clo. Orp —1J 67
Claremont Clo. S Croy —2E 84
Claremont Clo. W on T —2K 57
Claremont Ct. Dork —6H 119 (4L 201)
Claremont Dri. Esh —3B 58
Claremont Dri. Wok —6A 74
Claremont End. Esh —3B 58
Claremont Gdns. Surb —4L 41 (8K 203)
Claremont Gro. W4 —3D 12
Claremont Landscape Garden. —4A 58
Claremont La. Esh —2B 58
Claremont Park. —4A 58
Claremont Pk. Rd. Esh —3B 58
Claremont Rd. Clay —4E 58
Claremont Rd. Croy —7D 46
Claremont Rd. Red —9E 102
Claremont Rd. Stai —6F 20
Claremont Rd. Surb —4L 41 (8K 203)
Claremont Rd. Tedd —6F 24
Claremont Rd. Twic —1J 11
Claremont Rd. W Byf —8J 55
Claremont Rd. Wind —5F 4
Claremont Ter. Th Dit —6H 41
Claremount Clo. Eps —4H 81
Claremount Gdns. Eps —4H 81
Clarence Av. SW4 —1H 29
Clarence Av. N Mald —1B 42
Clarence Clo. Alder —2A 110
Clarence Clo. W on T —1J 57
Clarence Ct. W6 —1G 13
(off Cambridge Gro.)
Clarence Ct. Egh —6B 20
(off Clarence St.)
Clarence Ct. Horl —7H 143
Clarence Cres. SW4 —1H 29
Clarence Cres. Wind —4F 4
Clarence Dri. Camb —8F 50
Clarence Dri. E Grin —2B 186
Clarence Dri. Eng G —5M 19
Clarence La. SW15 —9D 12
Clarence M. SW12 —1F 28
Clarence Rd. SW19 —7N 27
Clarence Rd. W4 —1N 11
Clarence Rd. Big H —5H 87
Clarence Rd. Croy —6A 46
Clarence Rd. Fleet —5A 88
Clarence Rd. H'ham —7K 197
Clarence Rd. Red —6B 122
Clarence Rd. Rich —4M 11
Clarence Rd. Sutt —2N 61
Clarence Rd. Tedd —7F 24
Clarence Rd. Wall —2F 62
Clarence Rd. W on T —1J 57
Clarence Rd. Wind —5D 4
Clarence St. Egh —7B 20
Clarence St. King T —1K 41 (3J 203)
(in three parts)
Clarence St. Rich —7L 11
Clarence St. Stai —5G 21
Clarence Ter. Houn —7B 10
Clarence Wlk. Red —6B 122
Clarence Way. Horl —7H 143
Clarendon Ct. Beck —1L 47
(off Albemarle Rd.)
Clarendon Ct. B'water —3J 69
Clarendon Ct. Fleet —4A 88
Clarendon Ct. Houn —4H 9
Clarendon Ct. Rich —4M 11
Clarendon Cres. Twic —4D 24
Clarendon Dri. SW15 —7H 13
Clarendon Ga. Ott —3F 54
Clarendon Gro. Mitc —2D 44
Clarendon Rd. SW19 —8C 28
Clarendon Rd. Afrd —5A 22
Clarendon Rd. Croy —8M 45 (2A 200)
Clarendon Rd. Red —2D 122
Clarendon Rd. Wall —3G 62
Clare Pl. SW15 —1E 26
Clare Rd. Houn —6N 9
Clare Rd. Stai & Stanw —2M 21
Clares, The. Cat —2D 104
Claret Gdns. SE25 —2B 46
Clareville Rd. Cat —2D 104
Clare Wood. Lea —5H 79
Clarewood Dri. Camb —9C 50
Clarice Way. Wall —5J 63
Claridge Ct. SW6 —5L 13
Claridge Gdns. D'land —9C 146
Claridges Mead. D'land —9C 146
Clarke Cres. Camb —8K 49
Clarkes Av. Wor Pk —7J 43
Clark Pl. Cranl —8H 155
Clark Rd. Craw —8M 181
Clark Rd. Farn —9N 69
Clark's Green. —6J 159
Clarks Grn. Rd. Capel —8N 159
Clarks Hill. Farnh —1B 128
Clarks La. T'sey & Tats —1C 106
Clarks La. W'ham —1F 106
Clark Way. Houn —3L 9
Claudia Pl. SW19 —2K 27
Claverdale Rd. SW2 —1K 29
Claverdon. Brack —6M 31
Claver Dri. Asc —3A 34
Clavering Av. SW13 —2G 13
Clavering Clo. Twic —5G 24
Claverton. Asht —4L 79
Claxton Gro. W6 —1J 13
Clay Av. Mitc —1F 44
Claybrook Rd. W6 —2J 13
Claycart Rd. Alder —9J 89
(in two parts)
Clay Clo. Add —2K 55
(off Monks Cres.)
Clay Corner. Cher —7K 37
Claydon Dri. Croy —1J 63
Claydon Gdns. B'water —5M 69
Claydon Rd. Wok —3K 73
Clayford. D'land —9C 146
Claygate. —3F 58
Claygate Cres. New Ad —3M 65
Claygate La. Esh —8G 40
(in two parts)
Claygate La. Th Dit —7G 40
Claygate Lodge Clo. Clay —4E 58
Claygate Rd. Dork —7H 119
Clay Hall La. Copt —6N 163
Clayhall La. Old Win —8J 5
Clayhall La. Reig —7J 121
Clayhanger. Guild —1E 114
Clayhill. Surb —4N 41 (8N 203)
Clayhill Clo. Brack —2D 32
Clayhill Clo. Leigh —1F 140
Clayhill Rd. Leigh —3D 140
Clay La. Guild —6N 93
Clay La. H'ley —2A 100
Clay La. Newc —9G 144
Clay La. S Nut —4G 123
Clay La. Stanw —1A 22
Clay La. Wokgm —2E 30
Claymore Clo. Mord —6M 43
Claypole Dri. Houn —4M 9
Claypodns Av. W5 & Bren —1L 11
Clayponds Gdns. W5 —1K 11
(in two parts)
Clayponds La. Bren —1L 11
Clays Clo. E Grin —1A 186
Clayton Barracks. Alder —9B 90
Clayton Cres. Bren —1K 11
Clayton Dri. Guild —9J 93
Clayton Gro. Brack —9C 16
Clayton Hill. Craw —5A 182
Clayton Mead. God —8E 104
Clayton Rd. Chess —1J 59
Clayton Rd. Eps —8D 60 (6M 201)
Clayton Rd. Farn —5L 69
Clayton Rd. Iswth —6E 10
Cleardene. Dork —5H 119 (3M 201)
Cleardown. Wok —5D 74
Clears Cotts. Reig —1K 121
Clearsprings. Light —6L 51
Clears, The. Reig —1K 121
Clearwater Pl. Surb —5J 41
Clearway Ct. Cat —9D 84
Cleave Av. Hayes —1F 8
Cleave Av. Orp —3N 67
Cleaveland Rd. Surb —4K 41
Cleave Prior. Coul —6C 82
Cleaverholme Clo. SE25 —5E 46
Cleaves Almshouses. King T —3L 203
Cleeve Ct. Felt —2F 22
Cleeve Rd. Lea —7F 78
Cleeves Ct. Red —2E 122
(off St Anne's Mt.)
Cleeve, The. Guild —3C 114
Cleeve Way. SW15 —1E 26
Clem Attlee Ct. SW6 —2L 13
Clem Attlee Pde. SW6 —2L 13
(off N. End Rd.)
Clement Clo. Purl —3M 83
Clement Gdns. Hayes —1F 8
Clement Rd. SW19 —6K 27
Clement Rd. Beck —1G 47
Clements Ct. Houn —7L 9
Clements Mead. Lea —6G 78
Clements Pl. Bren —1K 11
Clements Rd. W on T —8J 39
Clensham Ct. Sutt —8M 43
Clensham La. Sutt —8M 43
Cleopatra Pl. Warf —8C 16
Clerics Wlk. Shep —6E 38
Clerks Cft. Blet —2A 124
Cleveden Ct. S Croy —2B 64
Clevedon. Wey —2E 56
Clevedon Ct. Farn —2B 90
Clevedon Ct. Frim —6E 70
Clevedon Gdns. Houn —4J 9
Clevedon Rd. SE20 —1G 46
Clevedon Rd. King T —1N 41
Clevedon Rd. Twic —9K 11
(in two parts)
Cleve Ho. Brack —3C 32
Cleveland Av. SW20 —1L 43
Cleveland Av. W4 —1E 12
Cleveland Av. Hamp —8N 23
Cleveland Clo. W on T —9J 39
Cleveland Dri. Stai —1K 37
Cleveland Gdns. SW13 —5E 12
Cleveland Gdns. Wor Pk —8D 42
Cleveland Pk. Stai —9N 7
Cleveland Ri. Mord —6J 43
Cleveland Rd. SW13 —5E 12
Cleveland Rd. Iswth —7G 10
Cleveland Rd. N Mald —3D 42
Cleveland Rd. Wor Pk —8D 42
Cleves Av. Eps —5G 61
Cleves Clo. Cobh —1J 77
Cleves Ct. Eps —8E 60 (5N 201)
Cleves Ct. Wind —6C 4
Cleves Cres. New Ad —7M 65
Cleves Rd. Rich —4J 25
Cleves Way. Hamp —8N 23
Cleves Way. Sun —7G 22
Cleves Wood. Wey —1F 56
Clewborough Dri. Camb —9F 50
Clewer Av. Wind —5D 4
Clewer Ct. Rd. Wind —3E 4
Clewer Fields. Wind —4F 4
Clewer Green. —5C 4
Clewer Hill. —6B 4
Clewer Hill Rd. Wind —5B 4
Clewer New Town. —5E 4
Clewer New Town. Wind —5D 4
Clewer Pk. Wind —3D 4
Clewer St Andrew. —3D 4
Clewer St Stephen. —3E 4
Clewer Village. —4D 4

Clewer Within—Commonfields

Clewer Within. —4F 4
Clew's La. Bisl —3D 72
Clifden Rd. Bren —2K 11
Clifden Rd. Twic —2F 24
Cliff End. Purl —8M 63
Cliffe Ri. G'ming —8F 132
Cliffe Rd. G'ming —9E 132
Cliffe Rd. S Croy —2A 64 (8D 200)
Cliffe Wlk. Sutt —2A 62
(off Greyhound Rd.)
Clifford Av. SW14 —6A 12
(in two parts)
Clifford Av. Wall —1G 62
Clifford Gro. Afrd —5B 22
Clifford Haigh Ho. SW6 —3J 13
Clifford Ho. W14 —1L 13
(off Edith Vs.)
Clifford Mnr. Rd. Guild —7A 114
Clifford Rd. SE25 —3D 46
Clifford Rd. Houn —6L 9
Clifford Rd. Rich —3K 25
Clifton Av. Felt —4K 23
Clifton Av. Sutt —7N 61
Clifton Clo. Add —8K 37
Clifton Clo. Cat —1A 104
Clifton Clo. Horl —8H 143
Clifton Clo. Orp —2L 67
Clifton Clo. Wrec —7F 128
Clifton Ct. Stanw —9N 7
Clifton Gdns. W4 —1C 12
(in two parts)
Clifton Gdns. Frim G —8D 70
Clifton Pde. Felt —5K 23
Clifton Pk. Av. SW20 —1H 43
Clifton Pl. Bans —2M 81
Clifton Ri. Wind —4A 4
Clifton Rd. SE25 —3B 46
Clifton Rd. SW19 —7J 27
Clifton Rd. Coul —2F 82
Clifton Rd. Craw —4G 183
Clifton Rd. Iswth —5E 10
Clifton Rd. King T —8M 25 (1N 203)
Clifton Rd. Tedd —5E 24
Clifton Rd. Wall —2F 62
Clifton Rd. Wokgm —1A 30
Clifton's La. Reig —1J 121
Clifton Ter. Dork —6H 119
(off Cliftonville)
Cliftonville. Dork —6H 119
Clifton Wlk. W6 —1G 13
(off King St.)
Clifton Way. H'row A —6B 8
Clifton Way. Wok —4J 73
Climping Rd. Craw —1N 181
Cline Rd. Guild —5B 114
Clinton Av. E Mol —3C 40
Clinton Clo. Knap —5G 73
Clinton Hill. D'land —1D 100
Clinton Rd. Lea —1J 99
Clintons Grn. Brack —9M 15
Clippesby Clo. Chess —3M 59
Clipstone Rd. Houn —6A 10
Clitherow Ct. Bren —1J 11
Clitherow Gdns. Craw —4C 182
Clitherow Pas. Bren —1J 11
Clitherow Rd. Bren —1H 11
Cliveden Pl. Shep —5D 38
Cliveden Rd. SW19 —9L 27
Clive Grn. Brack —4N 31
(in two parts)
Clive Pas. SE21 —4N 29
Clive Rd. SE21 —4N 29
Clive Rd. SW19 —7C 28
Clive Rd. Alder —3B 110
Clive Rd. Esh —1B 58
Clive Rd. Felt —9H 9
Clive Rd. Twic —5F 24
Clive Way. Craw —3G 182
Clock Barn La. Busb & G'ming —3J 153
Clock House. —1F 82
Clockhouse Clo. SW19 —3H 27
Clock Ho. Clo. Byfl —8A 56
Clock Ho. Cotts. Capel —8J 159
Clockhouse Ct. Beck —1H 47
Clockhouse Ct. Guild —8M 93
Clockhouse Ct. Hasl —2G 189
Clockhouse La. Afrd & Felt —5B 22
Clockhouse La. Brmly —5B 134
Clockhouse La. E. Egh —8D 20
Clockhouse La. W. Egh —8C 20
Clock Ho. Mead. Oxs —1B 78
Clockhouse Pl. SW15 —9K 13
Clock Ho. Rd. Beck —2H 47
Clockhouse Rd. Farn —1N 89
Clockhouse Roundabout. (Junct.) —2D 22
Clockhouse Roundabout. Farn —1N 89
Clock Tower Ind. Est. Iswth —6F 10
Clock Tower Rd. Iswth —6F 10
Clodhouse Hill. Wok —9G 73
Cloister Clo. Tedd —6H 25
Cloister Gdns. SE25 —5F 46
Cloisters Mall. King T —1L 41 (3J 203)
Cloisters, The. Frim —5B 70
Cloisters, The. Wok —8D 74
Cloncurry St. SW6 —5J 13
Clonmel Rd. SW6 —3L 13
Clonmel Rd. Tedd —5D 24
Clonmore St. SW18 —2L 27
Cloonmore Av. Orp —1N 67
Close, The. SE25 —5D 46
Close, The. Asc —1H 33
Close, The. Beck —3H 47
Close, The. Berr G —3K 87
Close, The. Brack —3A 32
Close, The. Cars —5C 62
Close, The. Coll T —7K 49
Close, The. E Grin —1N 185
Close, The. Farnh —2J 129
Close, The. Frim —6A 70
Close, The. G'ming —8J 133
Close, The. Horl —1G 163
Close, The. Iswth —5D 10
Close, The. Light —6L 51
Close, The. Loxw —5F 192
Close, The. Mitc —3D 44
Close, The. N Mald —1B 42
Close, The. Purl —6M 63
(Pampisford Rd.)
Close, The. Purl —6K 63
(Russell Hill)
Close, The. Reig —4N 121
Close, The. Rich —6A 12
Close, The. Str G —7A 120
Close, The. Surb —5L 41
Close, The. Sutt —6L 43
Close, The. Vir W —4N 35
Close, The. W Byf —9J 55
Close, The. Won —4D 134
Closeworth Rd. Farn —5C 90
Cloudesdale Rd. SW17 —3F 28
Clouston Clo. Wall —2J 63
Clouston Rd. Farn —9L 69
Clovelly Av. Warl —6E 84
Clovelly Dri. Hind —2A 170
Clovelly Pk. Hind —2A 170
Clovelly Rd. Hind —3A 170
Clovelly Rd. Houn —5A 10
Clover Clo. Lind —4B 168
Clover Clo. Wokgm —1D 30
Clover Ct. Wok —5N 73
Clover Fld. Slin —6L 195
Cloverfields. Horl —7F 142
Clover Hill. Coul —8F 82
Cloverlands. Craw —1D 182
Clover La. Yat —9A 48
Clover Lea. G'ming —3H 133
Clover Rd. Guild —2H 113
Clovers Cotts. Fay —8E 180
Clovers End. H'ham —3N 197
Clovers Way. Fay —1C 198
Clover Wlk. Eden —9M 127
Clover Way. Small —8N 143
Clover Way. Wall —7E 44
Clowser Clo. Sutt —2A 62
Clubhouse Rd. Alder —8L 89
Club La. Crowt —2J 49
Club Row. Brkwd —8A 72
Clump Av. Tad —9B 100
Clumps Rd. Lwr Bo —7K 129
Clumps, The. Afrd —5E 22
Clunbury Av. S'hall —1N 9
Cluny M. SW5 —1M 13
Clyde Av. S Croy —2E 84
Clyde Clo. Red —2E 122
Clyde Flats. SW6 —3L 13
(off Rhylston Rd.)
Clyde Ho. King T —9K 25 (1J 203)
Clyde Rd. Croy —8C 46
Clyde Rd. Stai & Stanw —2M 21
Clyde Rd. Sutt —2M 61
Clyde Rd. Wall —3G 63
Clydesdale Clo. Iswth —6F 10
Clydesdale Gdns. Rich —7A 12
Clymping Dene. Felt —1J 23
Clyve Way. Stai —9G 21
Coach Ho. Clo. Frim —3C 70
Coach Ho. Gdns. Fleet —2B 88
Coach Ho. La. SW19 —5J 27
Coach Ho. M. Red —4D 122
Coach Ho. Yd. SW18 —7N 13
Coachlads Av. Guild —3J 113
Coachman's Dri. Craw —7N 181
Coachmans Gro. Sand —8G 49
Coach Rd. Asc —8J 17
Coach Rd. Brock —3L 119
(in two parts)
Coach Rd. Gat A —3F 162
(off Ring Rd. S.)
Coach Rd. Ott —3E 54
Coaldale Wlk. SE21 —1N 29
Coalecroft Rd. SW15 —7H 13
Coast Hill. Westc —8N 117
Coast Hill La. Westc —7A 118
Coates Wlk. Bren —2L 11
Coatham Pl. Cranl —7A 156
Cobb Clo. Dat —4N 5
Cobbets Ridge. Farnh —3A 130
Cobbett Clo. Craw —1G 183
Cobbett Hill Rd. Norm —6B 92
Cobbett Rd. Guild —2J 113
Cobbett Rd. Twic —2A 24
Cobbetts Clo. Norm —7C 92
Cobbetts Clo. Wok —4L 73
Cobbetts Hill. Wey —3C 56
Cobbett's La. Yat & B'wtr —1E 68
Cobbetts M. Farnh —1G 128
(off Hart, The)
Cobbetts Wlk. Bisl —2D 72
Cobbetts Way. Farnh —5E 128
Cobblers. Slin —5L 195
Cobblers Wlk. Hamp & Tedd —9C 24
(in two parts)
Cobbles Cres. Craw —2C 182
Cobblestone Pl. Croy —7N 45 (1B 200)
Cobb's Rd. Houn —7N 9
Cob Clo. Craw D —1F 184
Cobden La. Hasl —1H 189
Cobden Rd. SE25 —4D 46
Cobden Rd. Orp —1M 67
Cobham. —1J 77
Cobham Av. N Mald —4F 42
Cobham Bus Mus. —8D 56
Cobham Clo. Wall —3J 63
Cobham Ct. Mitc —1D 44
Cobham Ga. Cobh —1J 77
Cobham Mill. —2K 77
Cobham Pk. Rd. Cobh & D'side —4J 77
Cobham Rd. Houn —3K 9
Cobham Rd. King T —9N 25
Cobham Rd. Stoke D —5A 78
Cobham Way. Craw —6F 162
Cobham Way. E Hor —4F 96
Cobner Clo. Craw —6L 181
Cobs Way. New H —6L 55
Coburg Cres. SW2 —2K 29
Cob Wlk. Craw —3M 181
Cochrane Pl. W'sham —2A 52
Cochrane Rd. SW19 —8K 27
Cock-A-Dobby. Sand —6F 48
Cockcrow Hill. —7K 41
Cock La. Fet —9C 78
Cockpit Path. Wokgm —3B 30
Cocks Cres. N Mald —3E 42
Cocksett Av. Orp —3N 67
Cockshot Hill. Reig —4N 121
Cockshot Rd. Reig —4N 121
Cock's La. Wart —3E 16
Coda Cen., The. SW6 —3K 13
Codrington Ct. Wok —5J 73
Cody Clo. Ash V —8D 90
Cody Clo. Wall —4H 63
Cody Rd. Farn —2L 89
Coe Av. SE25 —5D 46
Coe Clo. Alder —3M 109
Cogman's La. Out —6A 144
Cokenor Wood. Wrec —5E 128
Cokers La. SE21 —2N 29
Colbeck. C Crook —9C 88
Colbeck M. SW5 —1N 13
Colborne Way. Wor Pk —9H 43
Colbred Corner. Fleet —1D 88
Colburn Av. Cat —2C 104
Colburn Cres. Guild —9C 94
Colburn Way. Sutt —9B 44
Colby Rd. W on T —7H 39
Colchester Va. F Row —7G 186
Colcokes Rd. Bans —3M 81
Cold Blows. Mitc —2D 44
Coldharbour. —7D 138
Coldharbour Clo. Egh —2E 36
Coldharbour Common. —6D 138
Coldharbour La. Blet —3C 124
Coldharbour La. Dork & Cold —2E 138
Coldharbour La. Egh —2E 36
Cold Harbour La. Farn —6K 69
(in two parts)
Coldharbour La. Purl —7L 63
Coldharbour La. W End —7C 52
Coldharbour La. Wok —2H 75
Coldharbour Rd. Croy —2L 63
Coldharbour Rd. W Byf —1H 75
Coldharbour Way. Croy —2L 63
Coldshott. Oxt —2C 126
Coldstream Gdns. SW18 —9L 13
Coldstream Rd. Cat —8N 83
Cole Av. Alder —1L 109
Colebrook. Ott —3F 54
Colebrook Clo. SW15 —1J 27
Colebrooke Ri. Brom —1N 47
Colebrooke Rd. Red —1C 122
Colebrook Pl. Ott —4D 54
Colebrook Rd. SW16 —9J 29
Cole Clo. Craw —9N 181
Cole Ct. Twic —1G 24
Coleford Bri. Rd. Myt —1B 90
Coleford Clo. Myt —2D 90
Coleford Paddocks. Myt —1D 90
Coleford Rd. SW18 —8N 13
Cole Gdns. Houn —3H 9
Coleherne Ct. SW5 —1N 13
Coleherne Mans. SW5 —1N 13
(off Old Brompton Rd.)
Coleherne M. SW10 —1N 13
Coleherne Rd. SW10 —1N 13
Colehill Gdns. SW6 —5K 13
Colehill La. SW6 —4K 13
Colekitchen La. Gom —7E 116
Coleman Clo. SE25 —1D 46
Coleman Rd. Alder —3B 110
Colenorton Cres. Eton W —1B 4
Cole Park. —9G 11
Cole Pk. Gdns. Twic —8G 10
Cole Pk. Rd. Twic —9G 10
Cole Pk. Vw. Twic —9G 11
Coleridge Av. Sutt —1C 62
Coleridge Av. Yat —1D 68
Coleridge Clo. Crowt —3H 49
Coleridge Clo. H'ham —2L 197
Coleridge Cres. Coln —4G 6
Coleridge Rd. Afrd —5N 21
Coleridge Rd. Croy —6F 46
Coleridge Way. W Dray —1N 7
Cole Rd. Twic —9G 10
Colesburg Rd. Beck —2J 47
Colescroft Hill. Purl —2L 83
Coleshill Rd. Tedd —7E 24
Cole's La. Capel & Ockl —4L 158
Colesmead Rd. Red —9D 102
Coles Meads. —9D 102
Coleson Hill Rd. Wrec —6E 128
Colet Ct. W6 —1J 13
(off Hammersmith Rd.)
Colet Gdns. W14 —1J 13
Colet Rd. Craw —6B 182
Coleville Rd. Farn —9L 69
Coley Av. Wok —5C 74
Colgate. —2H 199
Colgate Clo. Craw —1N 181
Colin Clo. Croy —9J 47
Colin Clo. W Wick —1B 66
Colinette Rd. SW15 —7H 13
Colin Rd. Cat —1D 104
Coliseum Bus. Cen. Camb —3M 69
Coliston Pas. SW18 —1M 27
Coliston Rd. SW18 —1M 27
Collamore Av. SW18 —2C 28
Collards La. Hasl —2H 189
College Av. Egh —7D 20
College Av. Eps —1E 80
College Clo. Add —9M 37
College Clo. Camb —7B 50
College Clo. E Grin —9B 166
College Clo. Hand —6N 199
College Clo. Ling —7N 145
College Clo. Twic —2D 24
College Ct. W6 —1H 13
(off Queen Caroline St.)
College Cres. Coll T —7K 49
College Cres. Red —9E 102
College Cres. Wind —5E 4
College Fields Bus. Cen. SW19 —9B 28
College Gdns. SW17 —3C 28
(in three parts)
College Gdns. Farnh —1G 128
College Gdns. N Mald —4E 42
College Hill. G'ming —9F 132
College Hill. Hasl —2G 189
College Hill Ter. Hasl —2G 189
College La. E Grin —9B 166
College La. Wok —6M 73
College M. SW18 —8N 13
College Pl. SW10 —3N 13
College Ride. Bag —6E 50
College Ride. Camb —8B 50
College Rd. Coll T —8K 49
College Rd. SW19 —7B 28
College Rd. As —1E 110
College Rd. Brack —3A 32
College Rd. Craw —3C 182
College Rd. Croy —8A 46 (3D 200)
College Rd. Eps —1E 80 (8N 201)
College Rd. Guild —4N 113 (4C 202)
College Rd. Iswth —4F 10
College Rd. Wok —3D 74
College Roundabout. King T —2L 41 (5K 203)
College Town. —9K 49
College Wlk. King T —2L 41 (5L 203)
College Way. Afrd —5A 22
Collendean La. Horl —7K 141
Collens Fld. Pirb —2C 92
Collett's All. H'ham —6J 197
(off Carfax)
Colley La. Reig —2K 121
Colley Mnr. Dri. Reig —2J 121
Colley Way. Reig —9K 101
Collier Clo. Eps —3N 59
Collier Clo. Farn —9J 69
Collier Row. Craw —5B 182
Colliers. Cat —3D 104
Colliers Clo. Wok —4L 73
Colliers Ct. Croy —6D 200
Colliers Shaw. Kes —2F 66
Colliers Water La. T Hth —4L 45
Collier's Wood. —8B 28
Colliers Wood. (Junct.) —8B 28
Collier Way. Guild —1F 114
Collingdon. Cranl —9A 156
Collingham Gdns. SW5 —1N 13
Collingham Pl. SW5 —1N 13
Collingham Rd. SW5 —1N 13
Collingsbourne. Add —1L 55
Collingwood. Farn —3C 90
Collingwood Av. Surb —7B 42
Collingwood Clo. E Grin —2B 186
Collingwood Clo. Horl —7F 142
Collingwood Clo. H'ham —4J 197
Collingwood Clo. Twic —1A 24
Collingwood Cres. Guild —2C 114
Collingwood Grange Clo. Camb —7F 50
Collingwood Pl. W on T —9H 39
Collingwood Ri. Camb —8E 50
Collingwood Rd. Craw —4H 183
Collingwood Rd. H'ham —4J 197
Collingwood Rd. Mitc —2C 44
Collingwood Rd. Sutt —9M 43
Collins Gdns. As —2F 110
Collins Path. Hamp —7N 23
Collins Rd. Bew —5K 181
Collis All. Twic —2E 24
Collyer Av. Croy —1J 63
Collyer Rd. Croy —1J 63
Colman Clo. Eps —4H 81
Colman Ho. Red —1D 122
Colman's Hatch. —9N 187
Colman's Hill. —4F 136
Colman's Hill. Peasl —4F 136
Colman Way. Red —1C 122
Colmer Rd. SW16 —9J 29
Coln Bank. Hort —6E 6
Colnbrook. —3F 6
Colnbrook By-Pass. Coln & Slou —2E 6
Colnbrook Ct. Coln —4H 7
Colndale Rd. Coln —5G 6
Colnebridge Clo. Stai —5G 21
Colne Ct. Eps —1B 60
Colne Dri. W on T —9L 39
Colne Pk. Cvn. Site. W Dray —1L 7
Colne Reach. Stai —8H 7
Colne Rd. Twic —2E 24
Colne Wlk. Craw —5L 181
Colne Way. As —3E 110
Colne Way. Stai —3D 20
Coln Trad. Est. Coln —4H 7
Colonel's La. Cher —5J 37
Colonial Av. Twic —9C 10
Colonial Dri. W4 —1B 12
Colonial Rd. Felt —1F 22
Colonnades, The. Croy —3L 63
Colonsay Rd. Craw —6N 181
Colson Rd. Croy —8B 46 (2F 200)
Colson Way. SW16 —5G 29
Colston Av. Cars —1C 62
Colston Ct. Cars —1D 62
(off West St.)
Colston Rd. SW14 —7B 12
Coltash Rd. Craw —4E 182
Coltsfoot Dri. Guild —9C 94
Coltsfoot Dri. H'ham —3L 197
Coltsfoot La. Oxt —2B 126
Coltsfoot Rd. Lind —4B 168
Columbia Av. Wor Pk —6E 42
Columbia Cen., The. Brack —1N 31
Columbia Sq. SW14 —7B 12
Columbine Av. S Croy —4M 63
Columbus Dri. Swd B —1H 89
Colville Gdns. Light —7N 51
Colvin Rd. T Hth —4L 45
Colwith Rd. W6 —2H 13
Colwood Gdns. SW19 —8B 28
Colworth Rd. Croy —7D 46
Colwyn Clo. SW16 —6G 28
Colwyn Clo. Craw —5L 181
Colwyn Clo. Yat —9B 48
Colwyn Cres. Houn —4C 10
Colyton Clo. Wok —5M 73
Combe La. Brmly & Shere —6A 116
Combe La. C'fold & Wmly —4C 172
Combe La. Farn —8M 69
Combe La. G'ming & Wmly —9M 133
Combe La. Wmly —1C 172
Combemartin Rd. SW18 —1K 27
Combe Ri. Lwr Bo —6J 129
Combermere Clo. Wind —5E 4
Combermere Rd. Mord —5N 43
Combe Rd. G'ming —3H 133
Comberton. King T —4N 203
Comeragh Clo. Wok —7K 73
Comeragh M. W14 —1K 13
Comeragh Rd. W14 —1K 13
Comet Clo. Ash V —8D 90
Comet Rd. Stanw —1M 21
Comford Moor. —9C 168
Comforts Farm Av. Oxt —2B 126
Comfrey Clo. Farn —9H 69
Comfrey Clo. Wokgm —9D 14
Commerce Rd. Bren —2J 11
Commerce Way. Croy —8K 45
Commerce Way. Eden —9L 127
Commercial Rd. Alder —4A 110
Commercial Rd. Guild —4N 113 (5C 202)
Commercial Rd. Stai —7J 21
Commercial Way. Wok —4A 74
Commodore Ct. Farn —5A 90
Common Clo. Wok —1N 73
Commondale. SW15 —6H 13
Commonfield La. SW17 —6C 28
Commonfield Rd. Bans —1M 81
Commonfields. W End —8D 52

Cottenham Pde.—Crocus Clo.

Cottenham Pde. SW20 —1G 43
Cottenham Park. —9G 27
Cottenham Pk. Rd. SW20 —9F 26 (in two parts)
Cottenham Pl. SW20 —8G 26
Cottenhams. Blind H —3H 145
Cotterell Clo. Brack —9N 15
Cotterill Ct. C Crook —9A 88
Cotterill Rd. Surb —8L 41
Cottesbrooke Clo. Coln —4F 6
Cottesloe Clo. Bisl —3C 72
Cottesmore. Brack —6M 31
Cottimore Av. W on T —7J 39
Cottimore Cres. W on T —6J 39
Cottimore La. W on T —6J 39
Cottimore Ter. W on T —6J 39
Cottingham Av. H'ham —1K 197
Cottington Rd. Felt —5L 23
Cotton Clo. Alder —1L 109
Cottongrass Clo. Croy —7G 46
Cotton Ho. SW2 —1J 29
Cotton Row. Holm M —3K 157
Cotton Wlk. Craw —8M 181
Cottrell Flats. Farn —5B 90
Cotts Wood Dri. Guild —7C 94
Couchmore Av. Esh —8E 40
Coulsdon. —3H 83
Coulsdon Ct. Rd. Coul —3K 83
Coulsdon La. Coul —6D 82
Coulsdon Pl. Cat —9A 84
Coulsdon Ri. Coul —4J 83
Coulsdon Rd. Coul & Cat —2K 83
Coulthurst Ct. SW16 —8J 29 (off Heybridge Av.)
Council Cotts. Ockl —6D 158
Council Cotts. W End —8C 52
Council Cotts. Wis —2M 75
Countisbury Gdns. Add —2K 55
Country Way. Hanw —7J 23
Countryways Experience, The. —7G 174
County Bldgs. Craw —3C 182
County La. Warf —7B 16
County Mall Shop. Cen. Craw —3C 182
County Oak. —8B 162
County Oak La. Craw —8B 162
County Oak Retail Pk. Craw —8B 162
County Oak Way. Craw —8B 162
County Pde. Bren —3K 11
County Rd. T Hth —1M 45
Courland Rd. Add —9K 37
Course Rd. Asc —2L 33
Court Av. Coul —5L 83
Court Bushes Rd. Whyt —6D 84
Court Clo. E Grin —9D 166
Court Clo. Twic —4B 24
Court Clo. Wall —4H 63
Court Clo. Av. Twic —4B 24
Court Cres. Chess —2K 59
Court Cres. E Grin —9B 166
Court Downs Rd. Beck —1L 47
Court Dri. Croy —1K 63
Court Dri. Fleet —7B 88
Court Dri. Sutt —1C 62
Courtenay Av. Sutt —5M 61
Courtenay Dri. Beck —1N 47
Courtenay M. Wok —3C 74
Courtenay Rd. Farnh —5K 109
Courtenay Rd. Wok —3C 74
Courtenay Rd. Wor Pk —9H 43
Court Farm Av. Eps —2C 60
Court Farm Gdns. Eps —7B 60
Court Farm Pk. Warl —3D 84
Court Farm Rd. Warl —5D 84
Courtfield M. SW5 —1N 13
Courtfield Ri. W Wick —9N 47
Courtfield Rd. SW7 —1N 13
Courtfield Rd. Afrd —7C 22
Court Gdns. Camb —1A 70
Court Grn. Heights. Wok —7M 73
Court Haw. Bans —2C 82
Court Hill. Coul —5C 82
Court Hill. S Croy —8B 64
Courthope Rd. SW19 —6K 27
Courthope Vs. SW19 —8K 27
Court Ho. Mans. Eps —8C 60
Courtland Av. SW16 —8K 29
Courtlands. Rich —8N 11
Courtlands. W on T —6H 39
Courtlands Av. Esh —3N 57
Courtlands Av. Hamp —7N 23
Courtlands Av. Rich —5A 12
Courtlands Av. Slou —1N 5
Courtlands Clo. S Croy —6C 64
Courtlands Cres. Bans —2M 81
Courtlands Dri. Eps —3D 60
Courtlands Rd. Surb —6N 41
Court La. Eps —9B 60 (6H 201)
Courtleas. Cobh —9A 58
Court Lodge Rd. Horl —7C 142
Courtmead Clo. SE24 —1N 29
Courtmoor Av. Fleet —6B 88
Courtney Cres. Cars —4D 62
Courtney Pl. Cobh —8N 57
Courtney Pl. Croy —9L 45
Courtney Rd. SW19 —8C 28
Courtney Rd. Croy —9L 45
Courtney Rd. H'row A —6B 8
Courtoak La. Out —6M 143
Court Rd. God —9F 104
Court Rd. SE25 —1C 46
Court Rd. Alder —2M 109
Court Rd. Bans —3M 81
Court Rd. Cat —1A 104
Court Rd. S'hall —1N 9
Courts Hill Rd. Hasl —2F 188
Courts Mt. Rd. Hasl —2F 188
Court, The. Guild —5M 113 (7B 202)
Court, The. Warl —5H 85
Court Way. Twic —1F 24
Court Wood La. Croy —7J 65
Courtyard, The. Brack —1B 32
Courtyard, The. Craw —4B 182
Courtyard, The. E Grin —9D 166
Courtyard, The. H'ham —6J 197
Courtyard, The. Kgswd —9A 82
Court Yd., The. W Byf —8J 55
Courtyard, The. W'ham —5M 107
Courtyard, The. Wokgm —3B 30
Coutts Av. Chess —2L 59
Coval Gdns. SW14 —7A 12
Coval La. SW14 —7A 12
Coval Pas. SW14 —7B 12
Coval Rd. SW14 —7A 12
Cove. —9J 69
Coveham Cres. Cobh —9H 57
Coventry Hall. SW16 —6J 29
Coventry Rd. SE25 —3D 46
Coverack Clo. Croy —6H 47
Coverdale Gdns. Croy —9C 46
Cove Rd. Farn —1L 89
Cove Rd. Fleet —1C 88
Covert Clo. Craw —2C 182
Covert Clo. Farnh —8K 109
Covert La. Brack —3A 32
Covert Mead. Hand —9N 199
Coverton Rd. SW17 —6C 28
Coverts Rd. Clay —4F 58
Covert, The. Asc —6M 33
Covert, The. Farn —6K 69
Coves Farm Wood. Brack —1J 31
Covey Clo. SW19 —1N 43
Covey Clo. Farn —6M 69
Covey, The. Worth —1H 183
Covington Gdns. SW16 —8M 29
Covington Way. SW16 —7K 29 (in two parts)
Cowdray Clo. Craw —4C 183
Cowdrey Rd. SW19 —6N 27
Cowfold Clo. Craw —6L 181
Cowick Rd. SW17 —5D 28
Cow La. G'ming —7G 133
Cowleaze Rd. King T —9L 25 (2L 203)
Cowley Av. Cher —6H 37
Cowley Clo. S Croy —5F 64
Cowley Cres. W on T —1K 57
Cowley La. Cher —6H 37
Cowley Lodge. Cher —6H 37
Cowley Rd. SW14 —6D 12
Coworth Clo. Asc —4E 34
Coworth Pk. S'hill —3F 34
Coworth Rd. Asc —4D 34
Cowper Av. Sutt —1B 62
Cowper Clo. Cher —5H 37
Cowper Gdns. Wall —3G 63
Cowper Rd. SW19 —7A 28
Cowper Rd. King T —6M 25
Cowshot Common. —7B 72
Cowshot Cres. Brkwd —7A 72
Cowslip Clo. Lind —5B 168
Cowslip La. Mick —6G 99
Cowslip La. Wok —2L 73
Coxbridge Meadows. Farnh —2E 128
Coxcombe La. C'fold —5E 172
Coxcomb Wlk. Craw —5L 181
Coxdean. Eps —6H 81
Coxes Lock Mill. Add —2N 55
Cox Green. —7F 170
Cox Grn. Coll T —9J 49
Cox Grn. Rd. Rud —7C 176
Coxheath Rd. C Crook —7A 88
Cox Ho. W6 —2K 13 (off Field Rd.)
Cox Ho. H'ham —6H 197
Cox La. Chess —1M 59
Cox La. Eps —2A 60
Coxley Ri. Purl —9N 63
Coxmoor Clo. C Crook —8D 88
Coxs Av. Shep —2F 38
Coxwold Path. Chess —4L 59
Crabbet Park. —2K 183
Crabbet Pk. Worth —2K 183
Crabbet Rd. Craw —2F 182
Crabbs Cft. Clo. Orp —2L 67
Crabhill La. S Nut —7K 123
Crabtree Clo. Bookh —4C 98
Crabtree Dri. Lea —2J 99
Crabtree Gdns. Head —4D 168
Crabtree La. SW6 —3H 13 (in two parts)
Crabtree La. Bookh —4C 98
Crabtree La. Churt —8M 149
Crabtree La. Dork —4B 100
Crabtree La. Head —4D 168
Crabtree La. Westh —8F 98
Crabtree Office Village. Egh —1E 36
Crabtree Rd. Camb —4N 69
Crabtree Rd. Craw —2A 182
Crabtree Rd. Egh & Thorpe —1E 36
Crabtree Wlk. Croy —7D 46
Crabwood. Oxt —6A 106
Craddocks Av. Asht —4L 79
Craddocks Pde. Asht —4L 79 (in two parts)
Cradhurst Clo. Westc —6C 118
Cradle La. Bord —6B 148
Craigans. Craw —3M 181
Craigen Av. Croy —7E 46
Craigmore Tower. Wok —6A 74 (off Guildford Rd.)
Craignair Rd. SW2 —1L 29
Craignish Av. SW16 —1K 45
Craig Rd. Rich —5J 25
Craig's Wood. —8C 170
Craigwell Av. Felt —4H 23
Craigwell Clo. Stai —9G 21
Crail Clo. Wokgm —5A 30
Crakell Rd. Reig —4A 122
Crake Pl. Coll T —7J 49
Cramhurst. —4B 152
Cramhurst La. Witl —4B 152
Crammond Clo. W6 —2K 13
Cramond Ct. Felt —2F 22
Crampshaw La. Asht —6M 79
Cranberry Wlk. B'water —3L 69
Cranborne Av. S'hall —1A 10
Cranborne Av. Surb —9N 41
Cranborne Wlk. Craw —5D 182
Cranbourne. —2M 17
Cranbourne Av. Wind —5C 4
Cranbourne Clo. SW16 —2J 45
Cranbourne Clo. Horl —6F 142
Cranbourne Cotts. Wind —4M 17
Cranbourne Hall Cvn. Site. Wink —2L 17
Cranbourne Hall Cotts. Wink —2M 17
Cranbrook Ct. Bren —2J 11
Cranbrook Ct. Fleet —2B 88
Cranbrook Dri. Esh —7C 40
Cranbrook Dri. Twic —2B 24
Cranbrook Rd. SW19 —8K 27
Cranbrook Rd. W4 —1D 12
Cranbrook Rd. Houn —7N 9
Cranbrook Rd. T Hth —1N 45
Cranbrook Ter. Cranl —7A 156
Cranbury Rd. SW6 —5N 13
Crane Av. Iswth —8G 10
Cranebank M. Twic —7G 11
Cranebrook. Twic —3C 24
Crane Ct. Coll T —7J 49
Crane Ct. Eps —1B 60
Craneford Clo. Twic —1F 24
Craneford Way. Twic —1F 24
Crane Ho. Felt —4A 24
Crane Lodge Rd. Houn —2J 9
Crane Mead Ct. Twic —1F 24
Crane Pk. Rd. Twic —3B 24
Crane Rd. Twic —2E 24
Cranes Dri. Surb —3L 41 (8L 203)
Cranes Pk. Surb —3L 41 (8L 203)
Cranes Pk. Av. Surb —3L 41 (8L 203)
Cranes Pk. Cres. Surb —3M 41 (8M 203)
Craneswater. Hayes —3G 9
Craneswater Pk. S'hall —1N 9
Crane Way. Twic —1C 24
Cranfield Clo. SE27 —4N 29
Cranfield Ct. Wok —5K 73
Cranfield Rd. E. Cars —5E 62
Cranfield Rd. W. Cars —5D 62
Cranford. —4H 9
Cranford Av. C Crook —8A 88
Cranford Av. Stai —1N 21
Cranford Clo. SW20 —8G 26
Cranford Clo. Purl —9N 63
Cranford Clo. Stai —1N 21
Cranford Dri. Hayes —1G 8
Cranford La. Hayes —2E 8
Cranford La. Houn —3J 9
Cranford La. H'row A —4G 8 (in two parts)
Cranford Pk. Dri. Yat —9C 48
Cranford Ri. Esh —2C 58
Cranleigh. —7M 155
Cranleigh Clo. SE20 —1E 46
Cranleigh Clo. S Croy —8D 64
Cranleigh Ct. Farn —1L 89
Cranleigh Ct. Mitc —2B 44
Cranleigh Ct. Rich —6N 11
Cranleigh Gdns. SE25 —2B 46
Cranleigh Gdns. King T —7M 25
Cranleigh Gdns. S Croy —8D 64
Cranleigh Gdns. Sutt —8N 43
Cranleigh Mead. Cranl —8A 156
Cranleigh Rd. SW19 —2M 43
Cranleigh Rd. Esh —7C 40
Cranleigh Rd. Ewh —6F 156
Cranleigh Rd. Felt —5G 22
Cranleigh Rd. Won —4D 134
Cranley Clo. Guild —3C 114
Cranley Gdns. Wall —4G 62
Cranley Pl. Knap —5G 72
Cranley Rd. Guild —3B 114
Cranley Rd. W on T —2G 56
Cranmer Clo. Mord —5J 43
Cranmer Clo. Warl —4H 85
Cranmer Clo. Wey —4B 56
Cranmer Farm Clo. Mitc —3D 44
Cranmer Gdns. Warl —4H 85
Cranmer Rd. Croy —9M 45 (4A 200)
Cranmer Rd. Hamp H —6B 24
Cranmer Rd. King T —6L 25
Cranmer Rd. Mitc —3D 44
Cranmer Ter. SW17 —6B 28
Cranmer Wlk. Craw —4G 183
Cranmore Av. Iswth —3C 10
Cranmore Clo. Alder —3K 109
Cranmore Cotts. W Hor —7C 96
Cranmore Gdns. Alder —3J 109
Cranmore La. Alder —4J 109
Cranmore La. W Hor —7C 96 (in two parts)
Cranmore Rd. Myt —1D 90
Cranston Clo. Houn —5M 9
Cranston Clo. Reig —4N 121
Cranston Rd. E Grin —8A 166
Cranston Way. Craw D —1F 184
Cranstoun Clo. Guild —8J 93
Crantley Pl. Esh —2C 58
Cranwell Gro. Light —7K 51
Cranwell Gro. Shep —3A 38
Cranwell Rd. H'row A —5C 8
Craster Rd. SW2 —1K 29
Cravan Av. Felt —3H 23
Craven Clo. Lwr Bo —5H 129
Craven Gdns. SW19 —6M 27
Craven Rd. Croy —7F 46
Craven Rd. King T —9M 25 (1N 203)
Craven Rd. M'bowr —4F 182
Cravens, The. Small —8L 143
Crawford Clo. Iswth —5E 10
Crawford Gdns. Camb —1N 69
Crawford Gdns. H'ham —4L 197
Crawfurd Way. E Grin —8A 166
Crawley. —3B 182
Crawley Av. Craw —2N 181
Crawley Chase. Wink R —7F 16
Crawley Down. —1F 184
Crawley Down Rd. Felb —7H 165
Crawley Dri. Camb —9D 50
Crawley Hill. —1B 70
Crawley Hill. Camb —1D 70
Crawley La. Craw —2G 182
Crawley Leisure Pk. Craw —2B 182
Crawley Mus. Cen. —4A 182
Crawley Ridge. Camb —9D 50
Crawley Rd. Fay & Craw —3A 198
Crawley Rd. H'ham —4M 197 (in two parts)
Crawley S. W. By-Pass. Peas P —7K 181
Crawley Town Football Club. —7A 182
Crawley Wood Clo. Camb —9D 50
Crawshaw Rd. Ott —3F 54
Crawters Clo. Craw —2D 182
Cray Av. Asht —3L 79
Crayke Hill. Chess —4L 59
Crayonne Clo. Sun —9F 22
Crealock St. SW18 —9N 13
Creasys Dri. Craw —8M 181
Credenhill St. SW16 —7G 28
Crediton Way. Clay —2G 58
Credon Clo. Farn —9L 69
Creek Rd. E Mol —3E 40
Creek, The. Sun —4H 39
Cree's Mdw. W'sham —3N 51
Crefeld Clo. SW6 —2K 13
Cremorne Gdns. Eps —6C 60
Crerar Clo. Farn —2J 89
Crescent Ct. Horl —1E 162
Crescent Ct. Surb —4K 41
Crescent Gdns. SW19 —4M 27
Crescent Gro. Mitc —3C 44
Crescent La. Ash V —8F 90
Crescent Rd. SW20 —9J 27
Crescent Rd. Beck —1L 47
Crescent Rd. Blet —2N 123
Crescent Rd. Cat —2D 104
Crescent Rd. E Grin —9N 165
Crescent Rd. King T —8N 25
Crescent Rd. Reig —5M 121
Crescent Rd. Shep —4D 38
Crescent Rd. Wokgm —3B 30
Crescent Stables. SW15 —8K 13
Crescent, The. SW13 —5E 12
Crescent, The. SW19 —4M 27
Crescent, The. Afrd —6A 22
Crescent, The. Beck —1K 47
Crescent, The. Belm —7M 61
Crescent, The. B'water —2J 69
Crescent, The. Brack —3A 32
Crescent, The. Cher —3J 37
Crescent, The. Croy —5A 46
Crescent, The. Egh —7A 20
Crescent, The. Eps —1N 79 (in two parts)
Crescent, The. Farn —2A 90
Crescent, The. Farnh —5H 109
Crescent, The. Felc —2M 165
Crescent, The. Guild —2K 113
Crescent, The. Hayes —3D 8
Crescent, The. Horl —1E 162 (in two parts)
Crescent, The. H'ham —7G 196
Crescent, The. Lea —9H 79
Crescent, The. N Mald —2B 42
Crescent, The. Red —6B 122
Crescent, The. Reig —3N 121
Crescent, The. Shep —6G 38
Crescent, The. Surb —4L 41
Crescent, The. Sutt —2B 62
Crescent, The. W Mol —3A 40
Crescent, The. W Wick —5N 47
Crescent, The. Wey —9B 38
Crescent, The. Wold —1K 105
Crescent, The. Yat —8C 48
Crescent Way. SW16 —7K 29
Crescent Way. Horl —1E 162
Crescent Way. Orp —2N 67
Cresford Rd. SW6 —4N 13
Cressage Ho. Bren —2L 11 (off Ealing Rd.)
Cressall Clo. Lea —7H 79
Cressall Mead. Lea —7H 79
Cressex Clo. Binf —7H 15
Cressida Chase. Warf —9C 16
Cressingham Gdns. Est. SW2 —1L 29
Cressingham Gro. Sutt —1A 62
Cresswell Gdns. SW5 —1N 13
Cresswell Pl. SW10 —1N 13
Cresswell Rd. SE25 —3D 46
Cresswell Rd. Felt —4M 23
Cresswell Rd. Twic —9K 11
Cresta Dri. Wdhm —6H 55
Crest Hill. Peasl —2E 136
Creston Av. Knap —3H 73
Creston Way. Wor Pk —7J 43
Crest Rd. S Croy —4E 64
Crest, The. Surb —4N 41
Crestway. SW15 —9F 12
Crestwood Way. Houn —8M 9
Creswell Corner. Knap —4G 73
Crewdson Rd. Horl —8F 142
Crewe Ct. Tad —9H 81
Crewe's Av. Warl —3F 84
Crewe's Clo. Warl —4F 84
Crewe's Farm La. Warl —3G 85
Crewe's La. Warl —3F 84 (in two parts)
Crichton Av. Wall —2H 63
Crichton Rd. Cars —3D 62
Cricket Clo. Hind —3B 170
Cricket Ct. E Grin —7A 166
Cricketers Clo. Chess —1K 59
Cricketers Clo. Ockl —6C 158
Cricketers La. Warf —6E 16
Cricketers La. W'sham —2A 52
Cricketers M. SW18 —8N 13
Cricketers Ter. Cars —9C 44
Cricket Fld. Gro. Crowt —3J 49
Cricketfield Rd. H'ham —7H 197
Cricket Grn. Hamb —9F 152
Cricket Grn. Mitc —2D 44
Cricket Hill. —1D 68
Cricket Hill. S Nut —5K 123
Cricket Hill. Yat —3D 68
Cricket Hill La. Yat —3C 68
Cricket La. Lwr Bo —5J 129
Cricket Lea. Lind —4A 168
Crickets Hill. —3D 94
Cricket Way. Wey —8F 38
Cricklade Av. SW2 —3J 29
Crieff Ct. Tedd —8J 25
Crieff Rd. SW18 —1A 28
Criffel Av. SW2 —3H 29
Crimea Rd. Alder —2N 109 (in two parts)
Crimea Rd. Deep —6H 71
Crimp Hill. Old Win & Eng G —1J 19
Cripley Rd. Farn —8J 69
Cripplecrutch Hill. C'fold —3C 190
Cripps Ho. Craw —7N 181
Crispen Rd. Felt —5M 23
Crisp Gdns. Binf —8K 15
Crispin Clo. Asht —5M 79
Crispin Clo. Croy —8J 45
Crispin Cres. Croy —9H 45
Crisp Rd. W6 —1H 13
Cristowe Rd. SW6 —5L 13
Critchmere. —1C 188
Critchmere Hill. Hasl —1C 188
Critchmere La. Hasl —2C 188
Critchmere Va. Hasl —2C 188
Critten La. Ran C —3L 117
Crocker Clo. Asc —9K 17
Crockers La. Ling —7G 144
Crockerton Rd. SW17 —3D 28
Crockery La. E Clan —7M 95
Crockford Clo. Add —1L 55
Crockford Pk. Rd. Add —2L 55
Crockford Pl. Binf —8L 15
Crockham Clo. Craw —5A 182
Crockham Hill. —2L 127
Crocknorth Rd. E Hor —1G 117 (in two parts)
Crocus Clo. Croy —7G 47

Croffets—Dalton Av.

Croffets. Tad —8J 81
Croft Av. Dork —3H 119
Croft Av. W Wick —7M 47
Croft Clo. Hayes —3D 8
Croft Clo. Wokgm —6A 30
Croft Corner. Old Win —8L 5
Croft Ct. Eden —2L 147
Croft End Clo. Chess —9M 41
(off Ashcroft Rd.)
Crofters. Old Win —9K 5
Crofters Clo. Iswth —8D 10
Crofters Clo. Sand —7F 48
Crofters Clo. Stanw —9L 7
Crofters Mead. Croy —5J 65
Croft La. Eden —2L 147
(in two parts)
Croft La. Yat —8B 48
Croftleigh Av. Purl —3L 83
Crofton. Asht —5L 79
Crofton Av. W4 —3C 12
Crofton Av. W on T —9K 39
Crofton Clo. Brack —4C 32
Crofton Clo. Ott —4E 54
Crofton Rd. Orp —1J 67
Crofton Ter. Rich —7M 11
Croft Rd. SW16 —9L 29
Croft Rd. SW19 —8A 28
Croft Rd. Alder —4N 109
Croft Rd. G'ming —7G 133
Croft Rd. Sutt —2C 62
Croft Rd. W'ham —4K 107
Croft Rd. Witl —5B 152
Croft Rd. Wokgm —7A 30
Croft Rd. Wold —9K 85
Crofts Clo. C'fold —4E 172
Croftside, The. SE25 —2D 46
Crofts, The. Shep —3F 38
Croft, The. Brack —8N 15
Croft, The. Craw —3M 181
Croft, The. Eps —1E 80 (8N 201)
Croft, The. Houn —2M 9
Croft, The. Wokgm —3C 30
Croft, The. Yat —8C 48
Croft Way. Frim —4D 70
Croft Way. H'ham —5G 196
Croftway. Rich —4H 25
Croham Clo. S Croy —4B 64
Croham Mnr. Rd. S Croy —4B 64
Croham Mt. S Croy —4B 64
Croham Pk. Av. S Croy —2B 64
Croham Rd. S Croy —2A 64 (8D 200)
Croham Valley Rd. S Croy —3D 64
Croindene Rd. SW16 —9J 29
Cromar Ct. Hors —3M 73
Cromerhyde. Mord —4N 43
Cromer Rd. SE25 —2E 46
Cromer Rd. SW17 —7E 28
Cromer Rd. H'row A —5B 8
Cromer Rd. W. H'row A —6B 8
Cromer Vs. Rd. SW18 —9L 13
Cromford Clo. Orp —1N 67
Cromford Rd. SW18 —8M 13
Cromford Way. N Mald —9C 26
Crompton Fields. Craw —9C 162
Crompton Way. Craw —9C 162
Cromwell Av. W6 —1G 12
Cromwell Av. N Mald —4E 42
Cromwell Clo. W on T —7J 39
Cromwell Cres. W8 —1M 13
Cromwell Gro. Cat —8N 83
Cromwell Ho. Croy —9M 45 (5A 200)
Cromwell Pl. SW14 —6B 12
Cromwell Pl. Cranl —9A 156
Cromwell Pl. E Grin —2B 186
Cromwell Rd. SW19 —6M 27
Cromwell Rd. Asc —3M 33
Cromwell Rd. Beck —1H 47
Cromwell Rd. Camb —8B 50
Cromwell Rd. Cat —8N 83
Cromwell Rd. Croy —6A 46
Cromwell Rd. Felt —2J 23
Cromwell Rd. Houn —7A 10
Cromwell Rd. King T
—9L 25 (2L 203)
Cromwell Rd. Red —3D 122
Cromwell Rd. Tedd —7G 24
Cromwell Rd. W on T —7J 39
Cromwell Rd. Wor Pk —9C 42
Cromwell St. Houn —7A 10
Cromwell Wlk. Red —3D 122
Cromwell Way. Farn —7N 69
Crondace Rd. SW6 —4M 13
Crondall Ct. Camb —2N 69
Crondall End. Yat —8B 48
Crondall La. Dipp & F'ham —1B 128
Crondall Rd. Farnh —4A 128
Cronks Hill. Reig —5A 122
Cronks Hill Clo. Red —5B 122
Cronks Hill Rd. Red —5B 122
Crooked Billet. SW19 —7H 27
Crooked Billet Roundabout.
(Junct.) —5J 21
Crookham Reach. C Crook —8A 88
Crookham Rd. SW6 —4L 13
Crookham Rd. C Crook & Fle —7A 88
Crooksbury Common. —4B 130
Crooksbury La. Seale —2C 130
Crooksbury Rd. Farnh —9N 109
Crosby Clo. Felt —4M 23
Crosby Gdns. Yat —8A 48
Crosby Hill Dri. Camb —8D 50
Crosby Wlk. SW2 —1L 29
Crosby Way. SW2 —1L 29
Crosby Way. Farnh —2F 128
Crossacres. Wok —3G 75
Cross Deep. Twic —3F 24
Cross Deep Gdns. Twic —3F 24
Cross Fell. Brack —3M 31
Crossfield Pl. Wey —4C 56
Cross Gdns. Frim G —8D 70
Cross Gates Clo. Brack —2D 32
Cross Keys. Craw —3B 182
Cross Lances Rd. Houn —7B 10
Crossland Ho. Vir W —3A 36
(off Holloway Dri.)
Crossland Rd. Red —3E 122
Crossland Rd. T Hth —5M 45
Crosslands. Cher —1G 55
Crosslands Av. S'hall —1N 9
Crosslands Rd. Eps —3C 60
Cross La. Frim G —8D 70
Cross La. Ott —3D 54
(in two parts)
Cross La. Small —2N 163
Cross Lanes. Guild —3B 114 (3F 202)
Crossley Clo. Big H —2F 86
Crossman Ct. Craw —8N 181
Cross Oak. Wind —5D 4
Cross Oak La. Red —4K 142
Crosspath. Craw —2C 182
Cross Rd. SW19 —8M 27
Cross Rd. Asc —7C 34
Cross Rd. Ash V —1F 110
Cross Rd. Belm —6M 61
Cross Rd. Croy —7A 46 (1E 200)
Cross Rd. Felt —5M 23
Cross Rd. King T —8M 25
Cross Rd. Purl —9M 63
Cross Rd. Sutt —2B 62
Cross Rd. Tad —9H 81
Cross Rd. Wey —9E 38
Crossroads, The. Eff —6L 97
Cross St. SW13 —5D 12
Cross St. Alder —2M 109
Cross St. Farn —5A 90
Cross St. Hamp H —6C 24
Cross St. Wokgm —2B 30
Crosswater. —6K 149
Crosswater Farm Gardens. —6L 149
Crosswater La. Churt —6K 149
Crossway. SW20 —3H 43
Crossway. Brack —1A 32
Crossway. W on T —8J 39
Crossways. Alder —3A 110
Crossways. Craw —2D 182
Crossways. Eff —5L 97
Crossways. Egh —7F 20
Crossways. S Croy —4H 65
Crossways. Sun —8G 23
Crossways. Sutt —5B 62
Crossways. Tats —7E 86
Crossways Av. E Grin —9M 165
Crossways Clo. Churt —9L 149
Crossways Clo. Craw —2D 182
Crossways La. Reig —6A 102
(in two parts)
Crossways Rd. Beck —3K 47
Crossways Rd. Gray & Hind —6A 170
Crossways Rd. Mitc —2F 44
Crossways, The. Coul —6K 83
Crossways, The. Guild —5J 113
Crossways, The. Houn —3N 9
Crossways, The. Red —7G 102
Crossways, The. Surb —7A 42
Crosswell Clo. Shep —1D 38
Crouchfield. Dork —8J 119
Crouch Ho. Cotts. Eden —1K 147
Crouch House Green. —1J 147
Crouch Ho. Rd. Eden —9J 127
Crouch Ind. Est. Lea —6H 79
Crouch La. Wink —1J 17
Crouch Oak La. Add —1L 55
Crowberry Clo. Craw —7M 181
Crowborough Clo. Warl —5H 85
Crowborough Dri. Warl —5H 85
Crowborough Rd. SW17 —7E 28
Crowhill. Orp —6J 67
Crowhurst. —9A 126
Crowhurst Clo. Worth —3J 183
Crowhurst Keep. Worth —3J 183
Crowhurst La. Crow & Ling —7L 125
Crowhurst Lane End. —7L 125
Crowhurst Mead. God —8F 104
Crowhurst Rd. Crow & Ling —3N 145
Crowhurst Village Rd. Crow —1A 146
Crowland Av. Hayes —1G 8
Crowland Rd. T Hth —3A 46
Crowland Wlk. Mord —5N 43
Crowley Cres. Croy —2L 63 (8A 200)
Crown All. H'ham —6J 197
(off Carfax)
Crown Arc. King T —1K 41 (4J 203)
Crown Ash Hill. Big H —1D 86
Crown Ash La. Warl —3C 86
Crownbourne Ct. Sutt —1N 61
(off St Nicholas Way)
Crown Clo. Coln —3E 6
Crown Clo. W on T —6K 39
Crown Ct. G'ming —7H 133
Crown Dale. SE19 —7M 29
Crown Dri. Bad L —7M 109
Crown Gdns. Fleet —5C 88
Crown Heights. Guild
—6A 114 (8E 202)
Crown Hill. Croy —8N 45 (3B 200)
Crown La. SW16 —6L 29
Crown La. Bad L —7L 109
Crown La. Mord —3M 43
Crown La. Vir W —5N 35
Crown La. Gdns. SW16 —6L 29
Crown Mdw. Coln —3D 6
Crown M. W6 —1F 12
Crown Pde. SE19 —7M 29
Crown Pde. Mord —2M 43
Crown Pas. King T —1K 41 (4J 203)
Crownpits. —8J 133
Crownpits La. G'ming —8H 133
Crown Pl. Owl —6K 49
Crown Ri. Cher —7H 37
Crown Rd. Eden —9M 127
Crown Rd. Mord —3N 43
Crown Rd. N Mald —9B 26
Crown Rd. Sutt —1N 61
Crown Rd. Twic —9H 11
Crown Rd. Vir W —5M 35
Crown Row. Brack —5B 32
Crown Sq. Wok —4B 74
Crown St. Egh —6C 20
Crown Ter. Rich —7M 11
Crown, The. W'ham —4M 107
Crowntree Clo. Iswth —2F 10
Crown Wlk. G'ming —7H 133
Crown Wood. —5B 32
Crown Yd. Houn —6C 10
Crowther Av. Bren —1L 11
Crowther Rd. SE25 —4D 46
Crowthorne. —2H 49
Crowthorne Clo. SW18 —1L 27
Crowthorne Lodge. Brack —3N 31
(off Crowthorne Rd.)
Crowthorne Rd. Brack —4M 31
Crowthorne Rd. Crowt & Brack
—1J 49
Crowthorne Rd. Sand & Crowt
—7F 48
Crowthorne Rd. N. Brack —2N 31
Croxall Ho. W on T —5K 39
Croxden Wlk. Mord —5A 44
Croxted Clo. SE21 —1N 29
Croxted M. SE24 —1N 29
Croxted Rd. SE24 & SE21 —1N 29
Croyde Av. Hayes —1F 8
Croyde Clo. Farn —8M 69
Croydon. —8N 45 (3C 200)
Croydon Barn La. Horne —7C 144
Croydon Clock Tower. —4C 200
Croydon Crematorium. Croy —4K 45
Croydon Flyover, The. Croy
—9N 45 (6A 200)
Croydon Gro. Croy —7M 45
Croydon La. Bans —1N 81
Croydon La. S. Bans —1A 82
Croydon Rd. SE20 —1E 46
Croydon Rd. Beck —4G 46
Croydon Rd. Brom & Kes —1E 66
Croydon Rd. Cat —1D 104
Croydon Rd. H'row A —5C 8
Croydon Rd. Mitc & Croy —3E 44
Croydon Rd. Reig —3N 121
Croydon Rd. Wall & Croy —1F 62
Croydon Rd. W'ham —1H 107
Croydon Rd. W Wick & Brom
—9N 47 & 1C 66
Croydon Rd. Ind. Est. Beck —3G 46
Croylands Dri. Surb —6L 41
Croysdale Av. Sun —2H 39
Crozier Dri. S Croy —6E 64
Cruch La. Tap —1B 16
Cruikshank Lea. Coll T —9K 49
Crunden Rd. S Croy —4A 64
Crundwell Ct. Farnh —9J 109
Crusader Gdns. Croy —9B 46
Crusoe Rd. Mitc —8D 28
Crutchfield La. Hkwd —5M 141
Crutchfield La. W on T —8J 39
Crutchley Rd. Wokgm —1C 30
Crystal Palace F.C. —3B 46
Crystal Ter. SE19 —7N 29
Cubitt Ho. SW4 —1G 28
Cubitt St. Croy —2K 63
Cubitt Way. Knap —5G 72
Cuckfield Clo. Craw —6L 181
Cuckmere Cres. Craw —4L 181
Cuckoo La. W End —9A 52
Cuckoo Pound. Shep —4F 38
Cuckoo Va. W End —9A 52
Cudas Clo. Eps —1E 60
Cuddington Av. Wor Pk —9E 42
Cuddington Clo. Tad —7H 81
Cuddington Ct. Sutt —5J 61
Cuddington Glade. Eps —8N 59
Cuddington Pk. Clo. Bans —9L 61
Cuddington Way. Sutt —8J 61
Cudham. —2M 87
Cudham Clo. Belm —6M 61
Cudham Dri. New Ad —6M 65
Cudham La. N. Cud —1L 87
Cudham La. S. Cud & Knock —2L 87
Cudham Pk. Rd. Cud —6N 67
Cudham Rd. Orp —7J 67
Cudham Rd. Tats —6G 86
Cudworth. —2D 160
Cudworth La. Newd —1B 160
Cudworth Pk. Newd —2E 160
Culham Ho. Brack —3C 32
Cullen Clo. Yat —1B 68
Cullens M. Alder —3M 109
Cullerne Clo. Ewe —6E 60
Cullesden Rd. Kenl —2M 83
Cull's Rd. Norm —3M 111
Culmer. —8C 152
Culmer Hill. Wmly —8C 152
Culmer La. Wmly —7C 152
Culmington Rd. S Croy —5N 63
Culsac Rd. Surb —8L 41
Culvercroft. Binf —8K 15
Culverden Rd. SW12 —3G 28
Culver Dri. Oxt —8A 106
Culverhay. Asht —3L 79
Culverhouse Gdns. SW16 —4K 29
Culverlands Cres. As —1D 110
Culver Rd. Owl —6J 49
Culvers Av. Cars —8D 44
Culvers Retreat. Cars —7D 44
Culvers Way. Cars —8D 44
Culworth Ho. Guild
—4A 114 (5F 202)
Culzean Clo. SE27 —4M 29
Cumberland Av. Guild —7K 93
Cumberland Clo. SW20 —8J 27
Cumberland Clo. Eps —6D 60
Cumberland Clo. Twic —9H 11
Cumberland Ct. Croy
—7A 46 (1E 200)
Cumberland Dri. Brack —9B 16
Cumberland Dri. Chess —9M 41
Cumberland Dri. Esh —8G 40
Cumberland Ho. King T —8A 26
Cumberland Obelisk. —8J 19
Cumberland Pl. Sun —3H 39
Cumberland Rd. SE25 —5E 46
Cumberland Rd. SW13 —4E 12
Cumberland Rd. Afrd —4M 21
Cumberland Rd. Brom —3N 47
Cumberland Rd. Camb —1G 70
Cumberland Rd. Rich —3N 11
Cumberlands. Kenl —2A 84
Cumberland St. Stai —6F 20
Cumberlow Av. SE25 —2C 46
Cumbernauld Gdns. Sun —6G 22
Cumbernauld Wlk. Bew —7K 181
Cumbrae Gdns. Surb —8K 41
Cumbria Ct. Farn —4C 90
Cumnor Gdns. Eps —3F 60
Cumnor Ri. Kenl —4N 83
Cumnor Rd. Sutt —3A 62
Cumnor Way. Brack —3C 32
Cunliffe Clo. H'ley —2A 100
Cunliffe Pde. Eps —1E 60
Cunliffe Rd. Eps —1E 60
Cunliffe St. SW16 —7G 29
Cunningham Av. Guild —2C 114
Cunningham Clo. W Wick —8L 47
Cunningham Rd. Bans —2B 82
Cunnington Rd. Farn —3C 90
Cunworth Ct. Brack —5L 31
Curfew Bell Rd. Cher —6H 37
Curfew Yd. Wind —3G 4
Curlew Clo. S Croy —7G 64
Curlew Ct. Surb —9N 41
Curlew Gdns. Guild —1F 114
Curley Hill Rd. Light —8J 51
Curling Clo. Coul —7K 83
Curling Va. Guild —5K 113
Curl Way. Wokgm —3A 30
Curly Bri. Clo. Farn —6L 69
Curnick's La. SE27 —5N 29
Curran Av. Wall —9E 44
Currie Hill Clo. SW19 —5L 27
Curteys Wlk. Craw —6L 181
Curtis Clo. Camb —8G 50
Curtis Clo. Head —3D 168
Curtis Ct. C Crook —8B 88
Curtis Fld. Rd. SW16 —5K 29
Curtis Gdns. Dork —4G 118 (1J 201)
Curtis La. Head —3C 168
Curtis Rd. Dork —4F 118 (1H 201)
Curtis Rd. Eps —1B 60
Curtis Rd. Houn —1N 23
Curtis's Cotts. H'ham —5M 179
Curvan Clo. Eps —6E 60
Curzon Av. H'ham —5H 197
Curzon Clo. Orp —1M 67
Curzon Clo. Wey —1B 56
Curzon Ct. SW6 —4N 13
(off Maltings Pl.)
Curzon Dri. C Crook —8C 88
Curzon Rd. T Hth —5L 45
Curzon Rd. Wey —2B 56
Cusack Clo. Twic —5F 24
Cuthbert Gdns. SE25 —2B 46
Cuthbert Rd. Ash V —7F 90
Cuthbert Rd. Croy —8M 45 (3A 200)
Cutthroat All. Rich —3J 25
Cuttinglye La. Craw D —9D 164
Cuttinglye Rd. Craw D —8E 164
Cuttinglye Wood. —8E 164
Cutting, The. Red —5D 122
Cutts Rd. Alder —6B 90
Cyclamen Clo. Hamp —7A 24
Cyclamen Way. Eps —2B 60
Cygnet Av. Felt —1K 23
Cygnet Clo. Wok —3L 73
Cygnet Ct. Fleet —2C 88
Cygnets Clo. Red —1E 122
Cygnets, The. Felt —5M 23
Cygnets, The. Stai —6H 21
Cypress Av. Twic —1C 24
Cypress Clo. Finch —8A 30
Cypress Ct. Vir W —3A 36
Cypress Dri. Fleet —4E 88
Cypress Gro. Ash V —6D 90
Cypress Hill Ct. Farn —5L 69
Cypress Ho. Slou —1D 6
Cypress Rd. SE25 —1B 46
Cypress Rd. Guild —1M 113
Cypress Wlk. Eng G —7L 19
Cypress Way. Bans —1J 81
Cypress Way. B'water —1G 68
Cypress Way. Hind —7B 170
Cyprus Rd. Deep —6H 71
Cyprus Vs. Dork —2K 201

D'Abernon Chase. Lea —1G 79
D'Abernon Clo. Esh —1A 58
D'abernon Dri. Stoke D —3M 77
Dacre Rd. Croy —6J 45
Dade Way. S'hall —1N 9
Daffodil Clo. Croy —7G 47
Daffodil Dri. Bisl —3D 72
Daffodil Pl. Hamp —7A 24
Dafforne Rd. SW17 —4E 28
Dagden Rd. Shalf —9A 114
Dagley Farm Cvn. Pk. Shalf —9N 113
Dagley La. Shalf —8N 113
Dagmar Rd. SE25 —4B 46
Dagmar Rd. King T —9M 25 (1N 203)
Dagmar Rd. Wind —5G 4
Dagnall Pk. SE25 —5B 46
Dagnall Rd. SE25 —4B 46
Dagnan Rd. SW12 —1F 28
Dahlia Gdns. Mitc —3H 45
Dahomey Rd. SW16 —7G 28
Daimler Way. Wall —4J 63
Dairy Clo. T Hth —1N 45
Dairyfields. Craw —4M 181
Dairy La. Crock H —3J 127
Dairyman's Wlk. Guild —7D 94
Dairy Wlk. SW19 —5K 27
Daisy Clo. Croy —7G 47
Daisy La. SW6 —6M 13
Dakin Clo. M'bowr —7G 183
Dakins, The. E Grin —1A 186
Dakota Clo. Wall —4K 63
Dalby Rd. SW18 —7N 13
Dalcross. Brack —5C 32
Dalcross Rd. Houn —5M 9
Dale Av. Houn —6M 9
Dalebury Rd. SW17 —3D 28
Dale Clo. Add —2K 55
Dale Clo. Asc —4D 34
Dale Clo. H'ham —3M 197
Dale Clo. Wrec —4E 128
Dale Ct. King T —1N 203
Dale Gdns. Sand —7F 48
Dalegarth Gdns. Purl —9A 64
Daleham Av. Egh —7C 20
Dale Lodge Rd. Asc —4D 34
Dale Pk. Av. Cars —8D 44
Dale Pk. Rd. SE19 —9N 29
Dale Rd. F Row —8H 187
Dale Rd. Purl —8L 63
Dale Rd. Sun —8G 22
Dale Rd. Sutt —1L 61
Dale Rd. W on T —6G 39
Daleside Rd. SW16 —6F 28
Daleside Rd. Eps —3C 60
Dale St. W4 —1D 12
Dale, The. Kes —1F 66
Dale Vw. Hasl —3E 188
Dale Vw. H'ley —1A 100
Dale Vw. Wok —5L 73
Dalewood Gdns. Craw —1D 182
Dalewood Gdns. Wor Pk —8G 43
Dalkeith Rd. SE21 —2N 29
Dallas Rd. Sutt —3K 61
Dallaway Gdns. E Grin —9A 166
Dalley Ct. Sand —8J 49
Dalling Rd. W6 —1G 12
Dallington Clo. W on T —3K 57
Dalmally Rd. Croy —6C 46
Dalmeny Av. SW16 —1L 45
Dalmeny Cres. Houn —7D 10
Dalmeny Rd. Cars —4E 62
Dalmeny Rd. Wor Pk —9G 42
Dalmore Av. Clay —3F 58
Dalmore Rd. SE21 —3N 29
Dalston Clo. Camb —3H 71
Dalton Av. Mitc —1C 44

Dalton Clo.—Derry Rd.

Dalton Clo. *Craw* —8N **181**
Dalton Clo. *Purl* —8N **63**
Dalton St. *SE27* —3M **29**
Damascene Wlk. *SE21* —2N **29**
Damask Clo. *W End* —9B **52**
Damphurst La. *Ab C* —1A **138**
Dampier Wlk. *Craw* —8N **181**
Danbrook Rd. *SW16* —9J **29**
Danbury M. *Wall* —1F **62**
Danby Ct. *Horl* —6E **142**
Dancer Rd. *SW6* —4L **13**
Dancer Rd. *Rich* —6N **11**
Danebury. *New Ad* —3M **65**
Danebury Av. *SW15* —9D **12**
(in two parts)
Danebury Wlk. *Frim* —6D **70**
Dane Clo. *Orp* —2M **67**
Dane Ct. *Wok* —2H **75**
Danecourt Gdns. *Croy* —9C **46**
Danehurst Clo. *Egh* —7A **20**
Danehurst Ct. *Eps* —9E **60**
Danehurst Cres. *H'ham* —6M **197**
Danehurst St. *SW6* —4K **13**
Danemere St. *SW15* —6H **13**
Danemore La. *S God* —1G **145**
Dane Rd. *SW19* —9A **28**
Dane Rd. *Afrd* —7D **22**
Dane Rd. *Warl* —4G **84**
Danesbury Rd. *Felt* —2J **23**
Danes Clo. *Oxs* —1C **78**
Danescourt Cres. *Sutt* —8A **44**
Danesfield. *Rip* —1H **95**
Danesfield Clo. *W on T* —9J **39**
Daneshill. *Red* —2C **122**
Danes Hill. *Wok* —5C **74**
Daneshill Clo. *Red* —2C **122**
Daneshill Dri. *Oxs* —1D **78**
Danesrood. *Guild* —4B **114**
Danes Way. *Oxs* —1D **78**
Daneswood Clo. *Wey* —2C **56**
Danetree Clo. *Eps* —4B **60**
Danetree Rd. *Eps* —4B **60**
Daniel Clo. *SW17* —7C **28**
Daniel Clo. *Houn* —1N **23**
Daniell Way. *Croy* —7J **45**
Daniels La. *Warl* —3J **85**
Daniel Way. *Bans* —1N **81**
Dan Leno Wlk. *SW6* —3N **13**
Danone Ct. *Guild* —3N **113** (3C **202**)
Danses Clo. *Guild* —1F **114**
Danvers Dri. *C Crook* —9A **88**
Danvers Way. *Cat* —1N **103**
Da Palma Ct. SW6 —*2M 13*
(off Anselm Rd.)
Dapdune Ct. *Guild*
—3M **113** (3B **202**)
Dapdune Rd. *Guild*
—3N **113** (3C **202**)
Dapdune Wharf. —3M 113 (3A 202)
Daphne Ct. *Wor Pk* —8D **42**
Daphne Dri. *C Crook* —1A **108**
Daphne St. *SW18* —9N **13** & 1A **28**
Darby Clo. *Cat* —9N **83**
Darby Cres. *Sun* —1K **39**
Darby Gdns. *Sun* —1K **39**
Darby Green. —1F 68
Darby Grn. La. *B'water* —1G **68**
Darby Grn. Rd. *B'water* —1F **68**
Darby Va. *Warf* —7N **15**
Darcy Av. *Wall* —1G **63**
Darcy Clo. *Coul* —6M **83**
D'Arcy Pl. *Asht* —4M **79**
Darcy Rd. *SW16* —1J **45**
D'Arcy Rd. *Asht* —4M **79**
Darcy Rd. *Iswth* —4G **11**
D'Arcy Rd. *Sutt* —1J **61**
Darell Rd. *Rich* —6N **11**
Darenth Gdns. *W'ham* —4M **107**
Darenth Way. *Horl* —6D **142**
Dare's La. *Ews* —3A **108**
Darfield Rd. *Guild* —9C **94**
Darfur St. *SW15* —6J **13**
Dark Dale. *Asc* —4E **32**
Dark La. *P'ham* —8M **111**
Dark La. *Shere* —8A **116**
Dark La. *W'sham* —3M **51**
Darlan Rd. *SW6* —3L **13**
Darlaston Rd. *SW19* —8J **27**
Darley Clo. *Add* —2L **55**
Darley Clo. *Croy* —5H **47**
Darleydale. *Craw* —6A **182**
Darleydale Clo. *Owl* —5J **49**
Darley Dene Ct. *Add* —1L **55**
Darley Dri. *N Mald* —1C **42**
Darley Gdns. *Mord* —5A **44**
Darling Ho. *Twic* —9K **11**
Darlington Rd. *SE27* —6M **29**
Darmaine Clo. *S Croy* —4N **63**
Darnley Pk. *Wey* —9C **38**
Darracott Clo. *Camb* —7F **50**
Darset Av. *Fleet* —3B **88**
Dart Clo. *Slou* —1D **6**
Dart Ct. *E Grin* —7C **166**
Dartmouth Av. *Sheer & Wok* —1E **74**
Dartmouth Clo. *Brack* —2C **32**
Dartmouth Grn. *Wok* —1F **74**
Dartmouth Path. *Wok* —1F **74**
Dartmouth Pl. *W4* —2D **12**
Dartnell Av. *W Byf* —8K **55**
Dartnell Clo. *W Byf* —8K **55**
Dartnell Ct. *W Byf* —8L **55**
Dartnell Cres. *W Byf* —8K **55**
Dartnell Park. —8L 55
Dartnell Pk. Rd. *W Byf* —8K **55**
Dartnell Pl. *W Byf* —8K **55**
Dartnell Rd. *Croy* —6C **46**
Dart Rd. *Farn* —8J **69**
Darvel Clo. *Wok* —3K **73**
Darvills La. *Farnh* —1H **129**
Darvills La. *Shur R* —1E **14**
Darwall Dri. *Asc* —1H **33**
Darwin Clo. *H'ham* —4M **197**
Darwin Clo. *Orp* —2M **67**
Darwin Gro. *Alder* —1A **110**
Darwin Rd. *W5* —1J **11**
Daryngton Dri. *Guild* —3D **114**
Dashwood Clo. *Brack* —9B **16**
Dashwood Clo. *W Byf* —8L **55**
Dashwood Lang Rd. *Add* —1M **55**
Dassett Rd. *SE27* —6M **29**
Datchet. —3L 5
Datchet Common. —4N 5
Datchet Pl. *Dat* —4L **5**
Datchet Rd. *Hort* —6B **6**
Datchet Rd. *Old Win & Wind*
—7K **5**
Datchet Rd. *Slou* —1J **5**
Datchet Rd. *Wind* —3G **5**
Dault Rd. *SW18* —9N **13**
Daux Hill. *Warn* —1H **197**
Davenant Rd. *Croy*
—1M **63** (6A **200**)
Davenport Clo. *Tedd* —7G **24**
Davenport Lodge. *Houn* —3M **9**
Davenport Rd. *Brack* —9C **16**
Daventry Clo. *Coln* —4H **7**
Daventry Ct. *Brack* —9N **15**
David Clo. *Hayes* —3F **8**
David Clo. *Horl* —7F **142**
David Rd. *Coln* —5H **7**
Davidson Rd. *Croy* —7B **46**
David Twigg Clo. *King T*
—9L **25** (1L **203**)
Davies Clo. *Croy* —5C **46**
Davies Clo. *G'ming* —4G **133**
Davies Wlk. *Iswth* —4D **10**
Davis Clo. *Craw* —8M **181**
Davis Gdns. *Coll T* —8K **49**
Davis Rd. *Chess* —1N **59**
Davis Rd. *Wey* —6A **56**
Davmor Ct. *Bren* —1J **11**
Davos Clo. *Wok* —6A **74**
Davy Clo. *Wokgm* —3B **30**
Dawell Dri. *Big H* —4E **86**
Dawes Av. *Iswth* —8G **10**
Dawes Ct. *Esh* —1B **58**
Dawesgreen. —9E 120
Dawes Rd. *SW6* —3K **13**
Dawley Ride. *Coln* —4G **6**
Dawlish Av. *SW18* —3N **27**
Dawnay Clo. *Asc* —9K **17**
Dawnay Gdns. *SW18* —3B **28**
Dawnay Rd. *SW18* —3A **28**
Dawnay Rd. *Bookh* —4B **98**
Dawnay Rd. *Camb* —7N **49**
(in two parts)
Dawn Clo. *Houn* —6M **9**
Dawney Hill. *Pirb* —8B **72**
Dawneys Rd. *Pirb* —9B **72**
Dawn Redwood Clo. *Hort* —6C **6**
Dawn Ri. *Copt* —7L **163**
Dawsmere Clo. *Camb* —1G **71**
Dawson Clo. *Wind* —5D **4**
Dawson Rd. *Byfl* —7M **55**
Dawson Rd. *King T*
—2M **41** (5N **203**)
Daybrook Rd. *SW19* —1N **43**
Day Ct. *Cranl* —8H **155**
Daylesford Av. *SW15* —7F **12**
Daymerslea Ridge. *Lea* —8J **79**
Days Acre. *S Croy* —6C **64**
Daysbrook Rd. *SW2* —2K **29**
Dayseys Hill. *Out* —3L **143**
Dayspring. *Guild* —8L **93**
Deacon Clo. *D'side* —6J **77**
Deacon Clo. *Purl* —5J **63**
Deacon Clo. *Wokgm* —9B **14**
Deacon Fld. *Guild* —2K **113**
Deacon Pl. *Cat* —1N **103**
Deacon Rd. *King T*
—9M **25** (2M **203**)
Deacons Ct. *Twic* —3F **24**
Deacons Leas. *Orp* —1M **67**
Deacons Wlk. *Hamp* —5A **24**
Deadbrook La. *Alder* —1B **110**
(in two parts)
Deadwater. —5A 168
Deal M. *W5* —1K **11**
Deal Rd. *SW17* —7E **28**
Dealtry Rd. *SW15* —7H **13**
Dean Clo. *As* —2G **110**
Dean Clo. *Wind* —6A **4**
Dean Clo. *Wok* —3G **74**
Deanery Pl. G'ming —*7G 133*
(off Church St.)
Deanery Rd. *Crock H* —3L **127**
Deanery Rd. *G'ming* —6G **133**
Deanfield Gdns. *Croy*
—1A **64** (7D **200**)
Dean Gro. *Wokgm* —1B **30**
Deanhill Ct. *SW14* —7A **12**
Deanhill Rd. *SW14* —7A **12**
Dean La. *Red* —1F **102**
Deanoak La. *Leigh* —4H **141**
Dean Pde. *Camb* —7D **50**
Dean Rd. *Croy* —1A **64** (7D **200**)
Dean Rd. *G'ming* —5G **132**
Dean Rd. *Hamp* —6A **24**
Dean Rd. *Houn* —8B **10**
Deans Clo. *W4* —2A **12**
Deans Clo. *Croy* —9C **46**
Deans Clo. *Tad* —2G **100**
Deans Ct. *W'sham* —4A **52**
Deansfield. *Cat* —3C **104**
Deansgate. *Brack* —6N **31**
Deans La. W4 —*2A 12*
(off Deans Clo.)
Deans La. *Nutf* —2L **123**
Deans La. *Tad* —2G **101**
Deans Rd. *Red* —8G **102**
Deans Rd. *Sutt* —9N **43**
Dean's Wlk. *Coul* —5L **83**
Dean Wlk. *Bookh* —4B **98**
Dearn Gdns. *Mitc* —2C **44**
Deauville Ct. *SW4* —1G **29**
Debden Clo. *King T* —6K **25**
Deborah Clo. *Iswth* —4E **10**
De Brome Rd. *Felt* —2K **23**
De Burgh Gdns. *Tad* —6J **81**
De Burgh Pk. *Bans* —2N **81**
De Burgh Rd. *SW19* —8A **28**
Decimus Clo. *T Hth* —3A **46**
Dedisham Clo. *Craw* —4E **182**
Dedswell Dri. *W Cla* —7J **95**
Dedworth. —5B 4
Dedworth Dri. *Wind* —4C **4**
Dedworth Rd. *Wind* —5A **4**
Deedman Clo. *As* —2E **110**
Deepcut. —7G 71
Deepcut Bri. Rd. *Deep* —8G **70**
Deepdale. *SW19* —5J **27**
Deepdale. *Brack* —3M **31**
Deepdale Ct. *S Croy* —6E **200**
Deepdene. *Hasl* —2C **188**
Deepdene. *Lwr Bo* —5J **129**
Deepdene Av. *Croy* —9C **46**
Deepdene Av. *Dork*
—3J **119** (2N **201**)
Deepdene Av. Rd. *Dork* —3J **119**
Deepdene Dri. *Dork*
—4J **119** (1N **201**)
Deepdene Gdns. *SW2* —1K **29**
Deepdene Gdns. *Dork*
—4H **119** (1M **201**)
Deepdene Pk. Rd. *Dork*
—4J **119** (1N **201**)
Deepdene Roundabout. *Dork*
—4J **119** (1N **201**)
Deepdene Va. *Dork* —4J **119**
Deepdene Wood. *Dork* —5J **119**
Deepfield. *Dat* —3L **5**
Deepfield Rd. *Brack* —1B **32**
Deepfields. *Horl* —6D **142**
Deepfield Way. *Coul* —3J **83**
Deep Pool La. *Wok* —1L **73**
Deeprose Clo. *Guild* —8L **93**
Deepwell Clo. *Iswth* —4G **10**
Deep Well Dri. *Camb* —1C **70**
Deerbarn Rd. *Guild* —2L **113**
Deerbrook Rd. *SE24* —2M **29**
Deerhurst Clo. *Felt* —5J **23**
Deerhurst Cres. *Hamp H* —6C **24**
Deerhurst Rd. *SW16* —6K **29**
Deerings Rd. *Reig* —3N **121**
Deer Leap. *Light* —7L **51**
Deerleap Rd. *Westc* —6D **110**
Dee Rd. *Rich* —7M **11**
Dee Rd. *Wind* —3A **4**
Deer Pk. Clo. *King T* —8A **26**
Deer Pk. Gdns. *Mitc* —3B **44**
Deer Pk. Rd. *SW19* —1N **43**
Deer Rock Hill. *Brack* —5A **32**
Deer Rock Rd. *Camb* —8D **50**
Deers Farm Clo. *Wis* —3N **75**
Deers Loop Pk. —6M 185
Deerswood Clo. *Cat* —2D **104**
Deerswood Clo. *Craw* —2N **181**
Deerswood Ct. *Craw* —2M **181**
Deerswood Rd. *Craw* —3N **181**
Deeside Rd. *SW17* —4B **28**
Dee Way. *Eps* —6D **60**
Defiant Way. *Wall* —4J **63**
Defoe Av. *Rich* —3N **11**
Defoe Clo. *SW17* —7C **28**
De Havilland Dri. *Wey* —7N **55**
De Havilland Rd. *Houn* —3K **9**
De Havilland Rd. *Wall* —4J **63**
De Havilland Way. *Stanw* —9M **7**
Delabole Rd. *Red* —7J **103**
Delaford St. *SW6* —3K **13**
Delagarde Rd. *W'ham* —4L **107**
Delamare Cres. *Croy* —5F **46**
Delamere Rd. *SW20* —9J **27**
Delamere Rd. *Reig* —7N **121**
Delancey Ct. H'ham —*4J 197*
(off Wimblehurst Rd.)
Delaporte Clo. *Eps* —8D **60** (5N **201**)
De Lara Way. *Wok* —5N **73**
De La Warr Rd. *E Grin* —9B **166**
Delawyk Cres. *SE24* —1N **29**
Delcombe Av. *Wor Pk* —7H **43**
Delderfield. *Lea* —7K **79**
Delfont Clo. *M'bowr* —5H **183**
Delft Ho. *King T* —1M **203**
Delia St. *SW18* —1N **27**
Delius Gdns. *H'ham* —4A **198**
Dellbow Rd. *Felt* —8J **9**
Dell Clo. *Fet* —1D **98**
Dell Clo. *Hasl* —1E **188**
Dell Clo. *Mick* —5J **99**
Dell Clo. *Wall* —1G **63**
Dell Corner. *Brack* —1J **31**
Deller St. *Bint* —8L **15**
Dell Gro. *Frim* —4D **70**
Dell La. *Eps* —2F **60**
Dell Rd. *Eps* —3F **60**
Dell Rd. *Finch* —4A **48**
Dells Clo. *Tedd* —7F **24**
Dell, The. *Bren* —2J **11**
Dell, The. *E Grin* —9D **166**
Dell, The. *Farnh* —5J **109**
Dell, The. *Felt* —1J **23**
Dell, The. *Horl* —7F **142**
Dell, The. *Reig* —2M **121**
Dell, The. *Tad* —8H **81**
Dell, The. *Wok* —6M **73**
Dell, The. *Yat* —1B **68**
Dell Wlk. *N Mald* —1D **42**
Delmey Clo. *Croy* —9C **46**
Delorme St. *W6* —2J **13**
Delta Bungalows. *Horl* —1E **162**
Delta Clo. *Chob* —6J **53**
Delta Clo. *Wor Pk* —9E **42**
Delta Dri. *Horl* —1E **162**
Delta Ho. Horl —*1E 162*
(off Delta Dri.)
Delta Pk. *SW18* —7N **13**
Delta Point. *Croy* —1C **200**
Delta Rd. *Chob* —6J **53**
Delta Rd. *Wok* —3C **74**
Delta Rd. *Wor Pk* —9D **42**
Delta Way. *Egh* —9E **20**
Delves. *Tad* —8J **81**
Delville Clo. *Farn* —2J **89**
Delvino Rd. *SW6* —4M **13**
De Mel Clo. *Eps* —8A **60**
Demesne Rd. *Wall* —1H **63**
De Montfort Pde. *SW16* —4J **29**
De Montfort Rd. *SW16* —4J **29**
De Morgan Rd. *SW6* —6N **13**
Dempster Clo. *Surb* —7J **41**
Dempster Rd. *SW18* —8N **13**
Denbies Dri. *Dork* —1H **119**
Denbies Hillside. —3C 118
Denbies Wine Estate, Winery & Vis. Cen. —1G 119
Denbigh Clo. *Sutt* —2L **61**
Denbigh Gdns. *Rich* —8M **11**
Denbigh Rd. *Hasl* —3H **189**
Denbigh Rd. *Houn* —5B **10**
Denby Dene. *As* —2F **110**
Denby Rd. *Cobh* —8K **57**
Denchers Plat. *Craw* —9B **162**
Dencliffe. *Afrd* —6B **22**
Den Clo. *Beck* —2N **47**
Dene Av. *Houn* —6N **9**
Dene Clo. *Brack* —4A **16**
Dene Clo. *Coul* —6C **82**
Dene Clo. *Hasl* —3G **188**
Dene Clo. *Horl* —6C **142**
Dene Clo. *Lwr Bo* —5K **129**
Dene Clo. *Wor Pk* —8E **42**
Dene Ct. *S Croy* —8C **200**
Denefield Dri. *Kenl* —2A **84**
Dene Gdns. *Th Dit* —8G **40**
Denehurst Gdns. *Rich* —7N **11**
Denehurst Gdns. *Twic* —1D **24**
Denehyrst Ct. *Guild* —4F **202**
Dene La. *Lwr Bo* —5J **129**
Dene La. W. *Lwr Bo* —6K **129**
Dene Pl. *Wok* —5M **73**
Dene Rd. *Asht* —6M **79**
Dene Rd. *Farn* —2L **89**
Dene Rd. *Guild* —4A **114** (4E **202**)
Dene St. *Dork* —5H **119** (2L **201**)
Dene St. Gdns. *Dork*
—5H **119** (2M **201**)
Dene, The. *Ab H* —9J **117**
Dene, The. *Croy* —1G **64**
Dene, The. *Sutt* —7L **61**
Dene, The. *W Mol* —4N **39**
Dene Tye. *Craw* —2H **183**
Dene Wlk. *Lwr Bo* —5J **129**
Denewood. *Eps* —9D **60** (7N **201**)
Denfield. *Dork* —7H **119**
Denham Cres. *Mitc* —3D **44**
Denham Dri. *Yat* —1C **68**
Denham Gro. *Brack* —5A **32**
Denham Pl. Bear G —*7K 139*
(off Old Horsham Rd.)
Denham Rd. *Egh* —5C **20**
Denham Rd. *Eps* —8E **60**
Denham Rd. *Felt* —1K **23**
Denholm Gdns. *Guild* —9C **94**
Denison Rd. *SW19* —7B **28**
Denison Rd. *Felt* —5G **23**
Denleigh Gdns. *Th Dit* —5E **40**
Denly Way. *Light* —6N **51**
Denman Clo. *Fleet* —4D **88**
Denman Dri. *Afrd* —7C **22**
Denman Dri. *Clay* —2G **58**
Denmans. *Craw* —2H **183**
Denmark Av. *SW19* —8K **27**
Denmark Ct. *Mord* —5M **43**
Denmark Gdns. *Cars* —9D **44**
Denmark Path. *SE25* —4E **46**
Denmark Rd. *SE25* —4D **46**
Denmark Rd. *SW19* —7J **27**
Denmark Rd. *Cars* —9D **44**
Denmark Rd. *Guild*
—4A **114** (4E **202**)
Denmark Rd. *King T*
—2L **41** (5K **203**)
Denmark Rd. *Twic* —4D **24**
Denmark Sq. *Alder* —2B **110**
Denmark St. *Alder* —2B **110**
Denmark St. *Wokgm* —3B **30**
Denmark Wlk. *SE27* —5N **29**
Denmead Ct. *Brack* —5C **32**
Denmead Ho. SW15 —*9E 12*
(off Highcliffe Dri.)
Denmead Rd. *Croy* —7M **45** (1A **200**)
Denmore Ct. *Wall* —2F **62**
Dennan Rd. *Surb* —7M **41**
Dennard Way. *F'boro* —1J **67**
Denne Pde. *H'ham* —7J **197**
Denne Park. —8H 197
Denne Rd. *Craw* —4D **102**
Denne Rd. *H'ham* —7J **197**
Dennett Rd. *Croy* —7L **45**
Dennettsland Rd. *Crock H* —3L **127**
Denning Av. *Croy* —1L **63** (8A **200**)
Denning Clo. *Fleet* —6A **88**
Denning Clo. *Hamp* —6N **23**
Denningtons, The. *Wor Pk* —8D **42**
Dennis Clo. *Afrd* —8E **22**
Dennis Clo. *Red* —1C **122**
Dennis Ho. *Sutt* —1M **61**
Dennison Gro. *SW14* —6C **12**
Dennis Pk. Cres. *SW20* —9K **27**
Dennis Reeve Clo. *Mitc* —9D **28**
Dennis Rd. *E Mol* —3C **40**
Dennistoun Clo. *Camb* —1B **70**
Dennisville. —4K 113
Dennis Way. *Guild & Sly I* —7A **94**
Denny Rd. *Slou* —1B **6**
Den Rd. *Brom* —2N **47**
Densham Dri. *Purl* —1L **83**
Denton Clo. *Red* —8E **122**
Denton Gro. *W on T* —8M **39**
Denton Rd. *Twic* —9K **11**
Denton Rd. *Wokgm* —2B **30**
Denton St. *SW18* —9N **13**
Denton Way. *Frim* —4B **70**
Denton Way. *Wok* —4J **73**
Dents Gro. *Tad* —6L **101**
Dents Rd. *SW11* —1D **28**
Denvale Trad. Pk. *Craw* —4D **182**
Denvale Wlk. *Wok* —5K **73**
Denzil Rd. *Guild* —4L **113** (5A **202**)
Deodar Rd. *SW15* —7K **13**
Departures Rd. Gat A —*2D 162*
(off Gatwick Way)
Depot Rd. *Craw* —9B **162**
Depot Rd. *Eps* —9D **60** (6M **201**)
Depot Rd. *H'ham* —6L **197**
Depot Rd. *Houn* —6D **10**
Derby Arms Rd. *Eps* —4E **80**
Derby Clo. *Eps* —6G **81**
Derby Day Experience, The. —4E 80
Derby Est. *Houn* —7B **10**
Derby Rd. *SW14* —7A **12**
Derby Rd. *SW19* —8M **27**
Derby Rd. *Croy* —7M **45** (1A **200**)
Derby Rd. *Guild* —3J **113**
Derby Rd. *Hasl* —1F **188**
Derby Rd. *Houn* —7B **10**
Derby Rd. *Surb* —7N **41**
Derby Rd. *Sutt* —3L **61**
Derbyshire Grn. *Warf* —8D **16**
Derby Sq., The. *Eps* —6L **201**
Derby Stables Rd. *Eps* —4E **80**
Derek Av. *Eps* —3N **59**
Derek Av. *Wall* —1F **62**
Derek Clo. *Ewe* —2A **60**
Derek Horn Ct. *Camb* —9N **49**
Deridene Clo. *Stanw* —9N **7**
Dering Pl. *S Croy* —1N **63** (7C **200**)
Dering Rd. *Croy* —1N **63** (7C **200**)
Derinton Rd. *SW17* —5D **28**
Deronda Est. *SW2* —2M **29**
Deronda Rd. *SE24* —2M **29**
De Ros Pl. *Egh* —7C **20**
Deroy Clo. *Cars* —3D **62**
Derrick Av. *S Croy* —6N **63**
Derrick Rd. *Beck* —2J **47**
Derry Clo. *Ash V* —8D **90**
Derrydown. *Wok* —8M **73**
Derry Rd. *Croy* —9J **45**
Derry Rd. *Farn* —6L **69**

Derwent Av.—Downsview Gdns.

Derwent Av. SW15 —5D 26
Derwent Av. Ash V —9D 90
Derwent Clo. Add —2M 55
Derwent Clo. Clay —3E 58
Derwent Clo. Craw —4L 181
Derwent Clo. Farn —1K 89
Derwent Clo. Farnh —6F 108
Derwent Clo. Felt —2G 22
Derwent Clo. H'ham —2A 198
Derwent Dri. Purl —9A 64
Derwent Ho. SE20 —1E 46
(off Derwent Rd.)
Derwent Lodge. Iswth —5D 10
Derwent Lodge. Wor Pk —8G 42
Derwent Rd. SE20 —1D 46
Derwent Rd. SW20 —4J 43
Derwent Rd. Egh —8D 20
Derwent Rd. Light —7M 51
Derwent Rd. Twic —9B 10
Derwent Wlk. Wall —4F 62
Desborough Clo. Shep —7B 38
Desborough Ho. W14 —2L 13
(off N. End Rd.)
Desford Ct. Afrd —3B 22
Desford Way. Afrd —3A 22
Detillens La. Oxt —7C 106
Detling Rd. Craw —8A 182
Dettingen Barracks. Deep —5H 71
Dettingen Rd. Deep —6J 71
Devana End. Cars —9D 44
Devas Rd. SW20 —9H 27
Devenish Clo. S'hill —5A 34
Devenish La. Asc —7A 34
Devenish Rd. Asc —5N 33
Devereux La. SW13 —3G 12
Devereux Rd. SW11 —1D 28
Devereux Rd. Wind —5G 4
Devey Clo. King T —8E 26
Devil's Highway, The. Crowt —2D 48
Devil's Jump, The. —6N 149
Devil's La. Egh —7E 20
(in three parts)
Devil's Punchbowl. —4E 170
De Vitre Grn. Wokgm —1E 30
Devitt Clo. Asht —3N 79
Devoil Clo. Guild —8D 94
Devoke Way. W on T —8L 39
Devon Av. Twic —2C 24
Devon Bank. Guild
—6M 113 (8B 202)
Devon Chase. Warf —7C 16
Devon Clo. Coll T —8J 49
Devon Clo. Fleet —1C 88
Devon Clo. Kenl —3C 84
Devon Ct. Hamp —8A 24
Devon Cres. Red —3B 122
Devoncroft Gdns. Twic —1G 25
Devon Ho. Cat —2C 104
Devonhurst Pl. W4 —1C 12
Devon Rd. Red —8G 102
Devon Rd. Sutt —5K 61
Devon Rd. W on T —1K 57
Devonshire Av. Sutt —4A 62
Devonshire Av. Wok —1E 74
Devonshire Dri. Camb —8D 50
Devonshire Dri. Surb —7K 41
Devonshire Gdns. W4 —3B 12
Devonshire Ho. Sutt —4A 62
Devonshire M. W4 —1D 12
Devonshire Pas. W4 —1D 12
Devonshire Pl. Alder —3L 109
Devonshire Rd. SW19 —8C 28
Devonshire Rd. W4 —1D 12
Devonshire Rd. Cars —1E 62
Devonshire Rd. Croy —6A 46
Devonshire Rd. Felt —4M 23
Devonshire Rd. H'ham —6K 197
Devonshire Rd. Sutt —4A 62
Devonshire Rd. Wey —1B 56
Devonshire St. W4 —1D 12
Devonshire Way. Croy —8H 47
Devon Way. Chess —2J 59
Devon Way. Eps —2A 60
Devon Waye. Houn —3N 9
Dewar Clo. If'd —4K 181
Dewey St. SW17 —6D 28
Dewlands. God —9F 104
(in two parts)
Dewlands Clo. Cranl —7N 155
Dewlands La. Cranl —7N 155
Dewlands Rd. God —9F 104
Dewsbury Ct. W4 —1B 12
Dewsbury Gdns. Wor Pk —9F 42
Dexter Dri. E Grin —1A 186
Dexter Way. Fleet —1C 88
Diamedes Av. Stanw —1M 21
Diamond Ct. Red —2E 122
(off St Anne's Mt.)
Diamond Est. SW17 —4C 28
Diamond Hill. Camb —8C 50
Diamond Ridge. Camb —8B 50
Diana Cotts. Seale —8J 111
Diana Gdns. Surb —8M 41
Diana Ho. SW13 —4E 12
Diana Wlk. Horl —8F 142
(off High St.)
Dianthus Clo. Cher —6G 37
Dianthus Ct. Wok —5N 73
Dianthus Pl. Wink R —7F 16
Dibdene La. Sham G —7H 135
Dibdin Clo. Sutt —9M 43
Dibdin Rd. Sutt —9M 43
Diceland Rd. Bans —3L 81
Dickens Clo. E Grin —9M 165
Dickens Clo. Hayes —1F 8
Dickens Clo. Rich —3L 25
Dickens Ct. Wokgm —2A 30
Dickens Dri. Add —3H 55
Dickenson Rd. Felt —6K 23
Dickensons La. SE25 —4D 46
(in two parts)
Dickensons Pl. SE25 —5D 46
Dickens Rd. Craw —6B 182
Dickens Way. Yat —1B 68
Dickenswood Clo. SE19 —8M 29
Dickerage La. N Mald —2B 42
Dickerage Rd. King T —9B 26
Dickins Way. H'ham —8M 197
Dick Turpin Way. Felt —7G 9
Digby Mans. W6 —1G 13
(off Hammersmith Bri. Rd.)
Digby Pl. Croy —9C 46
Digby Way. Byfl —8A 56
Digdens Ri. Eps —2B 80
Dighton Rd. SW18 —8N 13
Dillon Cotts. Guild —7E 94
Dilston Rd. Lea —6G 79
Dilton Gdns. SW15 —2F 26
Dimes Pl. W6 —1G 13
Dingle Rd. Afrd —6C 22
Dingle, The. Craw —3N 181
Dingley La. SW16 —3H 29
Dingwall Av. Croy & New Ad
—8N 45 (3C 200)
Dingwall Rd. SW18 —1A 28
Dingwall Rd. Cars —5D 62
Dingwall Rd. Croy —7A 46 (1D 200)
Dinorben Av. Fleet —6A 88
Dinorben Beeches. Fleet —6A 88
Dinorben Clo. Fleet —6A 88
Dinsdale Clo. Wok —5C 74
Dinsdale Gdns. SE25 —4B 46
Dinsmore Rd. SW12 —1F 28
Dinton Rd. SW19 —7B 28
Dinton Rd. King T —8M 25
Dione Wlk. Bew —6K 181
Dippenhall. —1B 128
Dippenhall Rd. Dipp —1B 128
Dirdene Clo. Eps —8E 60
Dirdene Gdns. Eps —8E 60 (5N 201)
Dirdene Gro. Eps —8D 60
Dirtham La. Eff —6J 97
(in two parts)
Dirty La. Ash W —3G 187
Disbrowe Rd. W6 —2K 13
Discovery Pk. Craw —7E 162
Disraeli Ct. Slou —2D 6
Disraeli Gdns. SW15 —7L 13
Disraeli Rd. SW15 —7K 13
Distillery La. W6 —1H 13
Distillery Rd. W6 —1H 13
Distillery Wlk. Bren —2L 11
Ditches Grn. Cotts. Ockl —8M 157
Ditches La. Coul & Cat —7J 83
Ditchling. Brack —6M 31
Ditchling Hill. Craw —6A 182
Ditton Clo. Th Dit —6G 40
Dittoncroft Clo. Croy —1B 64
Ditton Grange Clo. Surb —7K 41
Ditton Grange Dri. Surb —7K 41
Ditton Hill. Surb —7J 41
Ditton Hill Rd. Surb —7J 41
Ditton Lawn. Th Dit —7G 40
Ditton Pk. Rd. Slou —2A 6
Ditton Reach. Th Dit —5H 41
Ditton Rd. Dat —4N 5
Ditton Rd. Slou —1B 6
Ditton Rd. S'hall —1N 9
Ditton Rd. Surb —8K 41
Divis Way. SW15 —9G 13
(off Dover Pk. Dri.)
Dixon Dri. Wey —6A 56
Dixon Pl. W Wick —7L 47
Dixon Rd. SE25 —2B 46
Dobbins Pl. If'd —4J 181
Doble Ct. S Croy —8D 64
Dobson Rd. Craw —9B 162
Dockenfield. —4D 148
Dockenfield St. Dock —2A 148
Dockett Eddy. Cher —7N 37
Dockett Eddy La. Shep —7A 38
Dock Rd. Bren —3K 11
Dockwell Clo. Felt —7H 9
Doctor Johnson Av. SW17 —4F 28
Doctors La. Cat —1L 103
Dodbrooke Rd. SE27 —4L 29
Dodds Cres. W Byf —1K 75
Dodd's La. Wok —1J 75
(in two parts)
Dodds Pk. Brock —5A 120
Doel Clo. SW19 —8A 28
Dogflud Way. Farnh —9H 109
Doghurst Av. Hayes —3C 8
Doghurst Dri. W Dray —3C 8
Doghurst La. Coul —7D 82
Dogkennel Green. —3L 117
Dogkennel Grn. Ran C —3L 117
Dolby Rd. SW6 —5L 13
Dolby Ter. Charl —4K 161
Dollary Pde. King T —2A 42
(off Kingston Rd.)
Dolleyshill Cvn. Pk. Norm —8K 91
Dollis Clo. M'bowr —4G 182
Dollis Dri. Farnh —9J 109
Dolly's Hill. —2L 109
Dolman Rd. W4 —1C 12
Dolphin Clo. Hasl —2C 188
Dolphin Clo. Surb —4K 41
Dolphin Ct. Brack —3A 32
Dolphin Ct. Stai —4J 21
Dolphin Ct. N. Stai —4J 21
Dolphin Est. Sun —9F 22
Dolphin Ho. SW18 —7N 13
Dolphin Rd. Sun —9F 22
Dolphin Rd. N. Sun —9F 22
Dolphin Rd. S. Sun —9F 22
Dolphin Rd. W. Sun —9F 22
Dolphin Sq. W4 —3D 12
Dolphin St. King T —1L 41 (3K 203)
Doman Rd. Camb —2L 69
Dome Hill. Cat —5B 104
Dome Hill Peak. Cat —4B 104
Dome, The. Red —2D 122
Dome Way. Red —2D 122
Domewood. —5D 164
Dominica Ter. Deep —6H 71
(off Cyprus Rd.)
Dominion Rd. Croy —6C 46
Donald Rd. Croy —6K 45
Donald Woods Gdns. Surb —8A 42
Doncaster Wlk. Craw —5E 182
Doncastle Rd. Brack —2K 31
Doneraile St. SW6 —5J 13
Donkey La. Ab C —3L 137
Donkey La. Horl —3H 163
Donkey La. W Dray —1L 7
Donkey Town. —9A 52
Donlan Dri. Farn —4H 89
Donnafields. Bisl —3D 72
Donne Clo. Craw —1F 182
Donne Ct. SE24 —1N 29
Donne Gdns. Wok —2G 74
Donnelly Ct. SW6 —3K 13
(off Dawes Rd.)
Donne Pl. Mitc —3F 44
Donnington Clo. Camb —2N 69
Donnington Ct. Craw —6L 181
Donnington Rd. Wor Pk —8F 42
Donnybrook. Brack —6M 31
Donnybrook Rd. SW16 —8G 29
Donovan Clo. Eps —6C 60
Doods Pk. Rd. Reig —2A 122
Doods Pl. Reig —2B 122
Doods Rd. Reig —2A 122
Doods Way. Reig —2B 122
Doomsday Garden. H'ham —7N 197
Doomsday Green. —8N 197
Doone Clo. Tedd —7G 24
Doral Way. Cars —2D 62
Doran Ct. Red —3B 122
Doran Dri. Red —3B 122
Doran Gdns. Red —3B 122
Dora Rd. SW19 —6M 27
Dora's Green. —7B 108
Dora's Grn. La. Dipp —1A 128
Dora's Grn. La. Ews & Dipp —5C 108
Dora's Grn. Rd. Dipp —1A 128
Dorcas Ct. Camb —3N 69
Dorchester Ct. Reig —2B 122
Dorchester Ct. Stai —5J 21
Dorchester Ct. Wok —3C 74
Dorchester Dri. Felt —9F 8
Dorchester Gro. W4 —1D 12
Dorchester M. N Mald —3C 42
Dorchester M. Twic —9J 11
Dorchester Rd. Mord —6N 43
Dorchester Rd. Wey —9C 38
Dorchester Rd. Wor Pk —7H 43
Doreen Clo. Farn —7K 69
Dore Gdns. Mord —6N 43
Dorian Dri. Asc —9B 18
Doria Rd. SW6 —5L 13
Doric Dri. Tad —7L 81
Dorien Rd. SW20 —1J 43
Dorin Ct. Warl —7E 84
Dorincourt. Wok —2G 74
Doris Rd. Afrd —7E 22
Dorking. —4H 119 (2K 201)
Dorking & District Mus.
—5G 119 (2K 201)
Dorking Bus. Pk. Dork
—4F 118 (1J 201)
Dorking Clo. Wor Pk —8J 43
Dorking Football Club.
—4G 119 (1K 201)
Dorking Halls. —4H 119 (1M 201)
Dorking Rd. Bookh —4B 98
Dorking Rd. Chil —9G 114
Dorking Rd. Eps —3N 79 (8J 201)
Dorking Rd. Gom & Ab H —8E 116
Dorking Rd. Lea —9H 79
Dorking Rd. Tad —7D 100
Dorking Rd. Warn & K'fold —8G 178
Dorking Vs. Knap —4G 72
Dorlcote. Witl —5B 152
Dorlcote Rd. SW18 —1C 28
Dorling Dri. Eps —8E 60
Dorly Clo. Shep —4F 38
Dormans. Craw —4M 181
Dormans Av. D'land —9C 146
Dormans Clo. D'land —2C 166
Dormans Gdns. Dor P —4A 166
Dormans High St. D'land —2C 166
Dormansland. —1C 166
Dormans Park. —4A 166
Dormans Pk. Rd. Dor P —3A 166
Dormans Pk. Rd. E Grin —7N 165
Dormans Rd. D'land —9C 146
Dormans Sta. Rd. D'land —3B 166
Dormay St. SW18 —8N 13
Dormer Clo. Crowt —2F 48
Dormers Clo. G'ming —4G 133
Dorncliffe Rd. SW6 —5K 13
Dorney Gro. Wey —8C 38
Dorney Way. Houn —8M 9
Dornford Gdns. Coul —6N 83
Dornton Rd. SW12 —3F 28
Dornton Rd. S Croy —3A 64 (8F 200)
Dorothy Pettingell Ho. Sutt —9N 43
(off Angel Hill)
Dorrien Wlk. SW16 —3H 29
Dorrington Ct. SE25 —1B 46
Dorrit Cres. Guild —1H 113
Dorset Av. E Grin —7M 165
Dorset Ct. Camb —7D 50
Dorset Ct. Eps —8E 60
Dorset Dri. Wok —4D 74
Dorset Gdns. E Grin —7M 165
Dorset Gdns. Mitc —3K 45
Dorset Rd. SW19 —9M 27
Dorset Rd. Afrd —4M 21
Dorset Rd. Ash V —8F 90
Dorset Rd. Beck —2G 46
Dorset Rd. Mitc —1C 44
Dorset Rd. Sutt —6M 61
Dorset Rd. Wind —5F 4
Dorset Sq. Eps —6C 60
Dorset Va. Warf —7C 16
Dorset Way. Byfl —6M 55
Dorset Way. Twic —2D 24
Dorset Waye. Houn —3N 9
Dorsten Pl. Craw —6K 181
Dorsten Sq. Craw —6L 181
Dorton Vs. W Dray —3B 8
Dorton Way. Rip —8K 75
Douai Clo. Farn —1A 90
Douai Gro. Hamp —9C 24
Doughty Ho. SW10 —2N 13
(off Netherton Gro.)
Douglas Av. N Mald —3G 42
Douglas Clo. Guild —6N 93
Douglas Clo. Wall —3J 63
Douglas Ct. Big H —4G 86
Douglas Ct. Cat —9N 83
Douglas Ct. King T —7L 203
Douglas Dri. Croy —9K 47
Douglas Dri. G'ming —6J 133
Douglas Gro. Lwr Bo —6H 129
Douglas Ho. Reig —2M 121
Douglas Ho. Surb —7M 41
Douglas Houses. Bookh —2A 98
Douglas Johnstone Ho. SW6 —2L 13
(off Clem Attlee Ct.)
Douglas La. Wray —8B 6
Douglas Mans. Houn —6B 10
Douglas Pl. Farn —9M 69
Douglas Rd. Add —9K 37
Douglas Rd. Esh —8B 40
Douglas Rd. Houn —6B 10
Douglas Rd. King T —1A 42
Douglas Rd. Reig —2M 121
Douglas Rd. Stanw —9M 7
Douglas Rd. Surb —8M 41
Douglas Robinson Ct. SW16 —8J 29
(off Streatham High Rd.)
Douglas Sq. Mord —5M 43
Doultons, The. Stai —8J 21
Dounesforth Gdns. SW18 —2N 27
Dove Clo. Craw —1B 182
Dove Clo. S Croy —7G 64
Dove Clo. Wall —4K 63
Dove Cote Clo. Wey —9C 38
Dovecote Gdns. SW14 —6C 12
Dovedale Clo. Guild —9C 94
Dovedale Clo. Owl —5J 49
Dovedale Cres. Craw —5N 181
Dovedale Ri. Mitc —8D 28
Dovehouse Grn. Wey —9E 38
Dove M. SW5 —1N 13
Dover Ct. Cranl —7B 156
Dovercourt Av. T Hth —4L 45
Dovercourt La. Sutt —9A 44
Doverfield Rd. SW2 —1J 29
Doverfield Rd. Guild —9C 94
Dover Gdns. Cars —9D 44
Dover Ho. Rd. SW15 —7F 12
Dover Pk. Dri. SW15 —9G 12
Doversgreen. —7N 121
Dovers Grn. Rd. Reig —6N 121
Doversmead. Knap —3H 73
Dover Ter. Rich —5M 11
(off Sandycombe Rd.)
Doveton Rd. S Croy —2A 64
Dowdeswell Clo. SW15 —7D 12
Dowding Ct. Crowt —1H 49
Dowding Rd. Big H —2F 86
Dower Av. Wall —5F 62
Dower Pk. Wind —7B 4
Dower Wlk. Craw —4M 181
Dowes Ho. SW16 —4J 29
Dowlands La. Small & Copt —8A 144
Dowlans Clo. Bookh —5A 98
Dowlans Rd. Bookh —5B 98
Dowler Ct. King T —1L 203
Dowlesgreen. —1C 30
Dowman Clo. SW19 —9N 27
Downbury M. SW18 —8M 13
Downe. —7J 67
Downe Av. Cud —8M 67
Downe Clo. Horl —6C 142
Downer Mdw. G'ming —3H 133
Downe Rd. Cud —9L 67
Downe Rd. Kes —5G 66
Downe Rd. Mitc —1D 44
Downes Clo. Twic —9H 11
Downes Ho. Croy —7A 200
Downe Ter. Rich —9L 11
Downfield. Wor Pk —7E 42
Down Hall Rd. King T
—9K 25 (2J 203)
Down House Mus. —8J 67
Downhurst Rd. Ewh —4F 156
Downing Av. Guild —4J 113
Downing St. Farnh —1G 129
Downland Clo. Eps —5G 81
Downland Ct. Craw —5A 182
Downland Dri. Craw —5A 182
Downland Gdns. Eps —5G 81
Downland Pl. Craw —5A 182
Downlands Clo. Coul —1F 82
Downlands Rd. Purl —1J 83
Downland Way. Eps —5G 81
Down La. Comp —9E 112
Downmill Rd. Brack —1L 31
Down Park. —9D 164
Down Pl. W6 —1G 13
Down Rd. Guild —3D 114
Down Rd. Tedd —7H 25
Downs Av. Eps —1D 80
Downsbridge Rd. Beck —1N 47
Downs Ct. Red —9E 102
Downscourt Rd. Purl —8M 63
Downs Hill Rd. Eps —1D 80
Downshire Way. Brack —1M 31
(in two parts)
Downs Ho. Rd. Eps —5D 80
Downside. —5J 77
Downside. Brack —2M 31
Downside. Cher —7H 37
Downside. Eps —1D 80 (8M 201)
Downside. Hind —2B 170
Downside. Sun —9H 23
Downside. Twic —4F 24
Downside Bri. Rd. Cobh —1J 77
Downside Clo. SW19 —7A 28
Downside Comn. Rd. D'side —5J 77
Downside Ct. Mers —7G 102
Downside Ind. Est. Cher —7H 37
Downside Orchard. Wok —4C 74
Downside Rd. D'side —3J 77
Downside Rd. Guild —4D 114
Downside Rd. Sutt —3B 62
Downside Wlk. Bren —2K 11
(off Windmill Rd.)
Downs La. Lea —1H 99
Downs Link. Brmly —3B 134
Downs Link. Brmly & Sham G
—6C 134
Downs Link. Chil —8F 114
Downs Link. Cranl —4H 155
Downs Link. Rud —6B 176
Downs Link. Shalf —2A 134
Downs Link. Slin —8D 176
Downs Lodge Ct. Eps
—1D 80 (8N 201)
Downsman Ct. Craw —6B 182
Downs Residential Site, The. Cat
—5E 104
Downs Rd. Beck —1L 47
(in two parts)
Downs Rd. Coul —5G 83
Downs Rd. Eps —1D 80 (8N 201)
(Epsom)
Downs Rd. Eps —7A 80
(Langley Bottom)
Downs Rd. Mick —6J 99
Downs Rd. Purl —7M 63
Downs Rd. Sutt —6N 61
Downs Rd. T Hth —9N 29
Downs Side. Sutt —7L 61
Downs, The. SW20 —8J 27
Downs, The. Lea —3H 99
Down St. W Mol —4A 40
Downs Vw. Dork —3K 119
Downs Vw. Iswth —4F 10
Downs Vw. Tad —8G 80
Downsview Av. Wok —8B 74
Downsview Clo. D'side —6J 77
Downsview Ct. Guild —8M 93
Downsview Gdns. SE19 —8M 29

Downsview Gdns.—E. Park La.

Downsview Gdns. Dork —6H 119
Downsview Rd. SE19 —8N 29
Downs Vw. Rd. Bookh —5C 98
Downsview Rd. Head D —4H 169
Downsview Rd. H'ham —2A 198
Downs Way. Bookh —4C 98
Downs Way. Eps —3E 80
Downsway. Guild —3G 114
Downsway. Orp —2N 67
Downs Way. Oxt —5A 106
Downsway. S Croy —7B 64
Downs Way. Tad —8G 80
Downsway. Whyt —3C 84
Downs Way Clo. Tad —8F 80
Downsway, The. Sutt —5A 62
Downs Wood. Eps —4G 80
Downswood. Reig —9B 102
Downton Av. SW2 —3J 29
Downview Clo. Hind —3B 170
Down Yhonda. Elst —8G 131
Doyle Gdns. Yat —2B 68
Doyle Rd. SE25 —3D 46
D'Oyly Carte Island. Wey —7C 38
Draco Ga. SW15 —6H 13
Dragmire La. Mitc —2B 44
Dragon La. Wey —7B 56
Dragoon Ct. Alder —2K 109
Drake Av. Cat —9N 83
Drake Av. Myt —4E 90
Drake Av. Slou —1N 5
Drake Av. Stai —6H 21
Drake Clo. Brack —4N 31
Drake Clo. H'ham —2L 197
Drake Ct. Surb —8L 203
Drakefield Rd. SW17 —4E 28
Drake Rd. Chess —2N 59
Drake Rd. Craw —6C 182
Drake Rd. Croy —6K 45
Drake Rd. Horl —8C 142
Drake Rd. Mitc —5E 44
Drakes Clo. Cranl —7N 155
Drake's Clo. Esh —1A 58
Drakes Way. Wok —9N 73
Drakewood Rd. SW16 —8H 29
Draper Clo. Iswth —5D 10
Drax Av. SW20 —8F 26
Draycot Rd. Surb —7N 41
Draycott. Brack —4C 32
Dray Ct. Guild —4L 113
Dray Ct. Wor Pk —7E 42
Drayhorse Dri. Bag —5J 51
Draymans Way. Iswth —6F 10
Drayton Clo. Brack —1B 32
Drayton Clo. Fet —2E 98
Drayton Clo. Houn —8N 9
Drayton Gdns. SW10 —1N 13
Drayton Rd. Croy —8M 45 (2A 200)
Dresden Way. Wey —2D 56
Drew Ho. SW16 —4J 29
Drewitts Ct. W on T —7G 39
Drew Pl. Cat —1A 104
Drewstead Rd. SW16 —3H 29
Drift Bridge. (Junct.) —1H 81
Drift La. Stoke D —4N 77
Drift Rd. W Hor —2E 96
Drift Rd. Wink —1L 17
Drift, The. Brom —1H 66
Drift Way. Coln —4E 6
Driftway, The. Bans —2H 81
Driftway, The. Craw —2B 182
Driftway, The. Lea —1H 99
(in two parts)
Driftway, The. Mitc —9E 28
Driftwood Dri. Kenl —4M 83
Drill Hall Rd. Cher —6J 37
Drive Mans. SW6 —5K 13
(off Fulham Rd.)
Drive Mead. Coul —1J 83
Drive Rd. Coul —7H 83
Drivers Mead. Ling —8M 145
Drive Spur. Tad —8N 81
Drive, The. SW6 —5K 13
Drive, The. SW16 —2K 45
Drive, The. SW20 —8H 27
Drive, The. Afrd —8E 22
Drive, The. Bans —4K 81
Drive, The. Beck —1K 47
Drive, The. Cobh —1M 77
Drive, The. Copt —7N 163
Drive, The. Coul —1J 83
Drive, The. Cranl —8N 155
Drive, The. Dat —4L 5
Drive, The. Eps —3E 60
Drive, The. Esh —7C 40
Drive, The. Farnh —4G 129
Drive, The. Felt —1K 23
Drive, The. Fet —9E 78
Drive, The. G'ming —9H 133
Drive, The. Guild —3J 113
(Beech Gro.)
Drive, The. Guild —5J 113
(Farnham Rd.)
Drive, The. Guild —7L 113
(Sandy La.)
Drive, The. Horl —9F 142
Drive, The. Houn —5D 10
Drive, The. King T —8B 26
Drive, The. Lea —1L 99
Drive, The. Loxw —5F 192
Drive, The. Mord —4A 44
Drive, The. Pep H —7B 132
(in two parts)
Drive, The. Rusp —2D 180
Drive, The. Surb —6L 41
Drive, The. Sutt —8L 61
Drive, The. T Hth —3A 46
Drive, The. Vir W —4B 36
Drive, The. Wall —6G 62
Drive, The. W Wick —6N 47
Drive, The. Wok —7L 73
Drive, The. Won —5D 134
Drive, The. Wray —8N 5
Drodges Clo. Brmly —3B 134
Droitwich Clo. Brack —2B 32
Dromore Rd. SW15 —9K 13
Drove Rd. Alb —5N 115
Drove Rd. Guild —5H 115
(in two parts)
Drove Rd. W Hor & Ran C —4C 116
Drovers Ct. King T —3L 203
Drovers Lnd. Fleet —1D 88
Drovers Rd. S Croy
—2A 64 (8D 200)
Drovers Way. Ash G —3G 111
(in two parts)
Drovers Way. Brack —2D 32
Drovers Way. Farnh —6F 108
Druce Wood. Asc —9J 17
Druids Clo. Asht —7M 79
Druids Way. Brom —3N 47
Drumaline Ridge. Wor Pk —8D 42
Drummond Cen. Croy
—8N 45 (3B 200)
Drummond Clo. Brack —9D 16
Drummond Gdns. Eps —7B 60
Drummond Pl. Twic —1H 25
Drummond Rd. Croy
(in two parts) —8N 45 (3B 200)
Drummond Rd. Guild
—3N 113 (3C 202)
Drummond Rd. If'd —4K 181
Drungewick La. Loxw —9L 193
Drury Clo. M'bowr —5H 183
Drury Cres. Croy —8L 45
Dryad St. SW15 —6J 13
Dry Arch Rd. Asc —6C 34
Dryburgh Rd. SW15 —6G 13
Dryden. Brack —6M 31
Dryden Mans. W14 —2K 13
(off Queen's Club Gdns.)
Dryden Rd. SW19 —7A 28
Dryden Rd. Farn —8L 69
Drynham Pk. Wey —9F 38
Du Cane Ct. SW17 —2E 28
Ducavel Ho. SW2 —2K 29
Duchess Clo. Crowt —9G 30
Duchess Clo. Sutt —1A 62
Duchess of Kent Barracks. Alder
—1N 109
Ducklands. Bord —7A 168
Ducks Wlk. Twic —8J 11
Dudley Clo. Add —9L 37
Dudley Ct. C Crook —7B 88
Dudley Dri. Mord —7K 43
Dudley Gro. Eps —1B 80 (8H 201)
Dudley Rd. SW19 —7M 27
Dudley Rd. Afrd —6A 22
Dudley Rd. Felt —2D 22
Dudley Rd. King T
—2M 41 (5M 203)
Dudley Rd. Rich —5M 11
Dudley Rd. W on T —5N 39
Dudset La. Houn —4H 9
Duffield Rd. Tad —2G 100
Duffins Orchard. Ott —4E 54
Dugdale Ho. Egh —6E 20
(off Pooley Grn. Rd.)
Duke Clo. M'bowr —7G 182
Duke of Cambridge Clo. Twic
—9D 10
Duke of Cornwall Av. Camb —6B 50
Duke of Edinburgh Rd. Sutt —8B 44
Duke Rd. W4 —1C 12
Duke's Av. W4 —1C 12
Dukes Av. Houn —7M 9
Dukes Av. N Mald —2E 42
Dukes Av. Rich —5J 25
Dukes Clo. Afrd —5D 22
Dukes Clo. Cranl —8B 156
Dukes Clo. Farnh —6F 108
Dukes Clo. Hamp —6N 23
Dukes Ct. Wok —4B 74
Dukes Covert. Bag —1J 51
Duke's Dri. G'ming —4E 132
Dukes Ga. W4 —1B 12
Dukes Grn. Av. Felt —8H 9
Dukes Head Pas. Hamp —8C 24
Dukes Hill. Wold —7H 85
(in two parts)
Dukeshill Rd. Brack —9N 15
Dukes La. Asc —8D 18
Dukes Pk. Alder —7D 90
Duke's Ride. Crowt —3D 48
Dukes Ride. N Holm —8K 119
Duke's Rd. Newd —4A 160
(in two parts)
Dukes Rd. W on T —2L 57
Dukes Ter. Alder —1N 109
Duke St. Rich —7K 11
Duke St. Sutt —1B 62
Duke St. Wind —3F 4
Duke St. Wok —4B 74
Dukes Wlk. Farnh —6F 108
Duke's Warren, The & Mosses Wood. —6C 138
Dukes Wood. Crowt —2G 49
(in two parts)
Dulverton Rd. S Croy —6F 64
Dumas Clo. Yat —1B 68
Du Maurier Clo. C Crook —1A 108
Dumbarton Ct. SW2 —1J 29
Dumbarton Rd. SW2 —1J 29
Dumbleton Clo. King T —9A 26
Dumsey Eyot. Cher —6N 37
Dumville Dri. God —9E 104
Dunally Pk. Shep —6F 38
Dunbar Av. SW16 —1L 45
Dunbar Av. Beck —3H 47
Dunbar Ct. W on T —7K 39
Dunbar Rd. Frim —7D 70
Dunbar Rd. N Mald —3B 42
Dunbar St. SE27 —4N 29
Dunboe Pl. Shep —6D 38
Dunbridge Ho. SW15 —9E 12
(off Highcliffe Dri.)
Duncan Dri. Guild —2C 114
Duncan Dri. Wokgm —3C 30
Duncan Gdns. Stai —7J 21
Duncannon Cres. Wind —6A 4
Duncan Rd. Rich —7L 11
Duncan Rd. Tad —6K 81
Duncans Yd. W'ham —4M 107
Duncombe Rd. G'ming —9G 133
Duncroft. Stai —5G 20
Duncroft. Wind —6C 4
Duncroft Clo. Reig —3L 121
Duncton Clo. Craw —1N 181
Dundaff Clo. Camb —1E 70
Dundas Clo. Brack —3N 31
Dundas Gdns. W Mol —2B 40
Dundee Rd. SE25 —4E 46
Dundela Gdns. Wor Pk —1G 61
Dundonald Rd. SW19 —8K 27
Dundrey Cres. Red —7J 103
Dunedin Dri. Cat —3B 104
Dunelm Gro. SE27 —4N 29
Dunfee Way. W Byf —8N 55
Dunford Pl. Binf —8K 15
Dungarvan Av. SW15 —7F 12
Dungates La. Buck —2F 120
Dungells Farm Clo. Yat —2C 68
Dungells La. Yat —2B 68
Dunheved Clo. T Hth —5L 45
Dunheved Rd. N. T Hth —5L 45
Dunheved Rd. S. T Hth —5L 45
Dunheved Rd. W. T Hth —5L 45
Dunkeld Rd. SE25 —3A 46
Dunkirk St. SE27 —5N 29
Dunleary Clo. Houn —1N 23
Dunley Dri. New Ad —4L 65
Dunlin Clo. Red —8C 122
Dunlin Ri. Guild —1F 114
Dunmall Dri. Purl —1B 84
Dunmore. Guild —2G 113
Dunmore Rd. SW20 —9H 27
Dunmow Clo. Felt —4M 23
Dunmow Hill. Fleet —3B 88
Dunmow Ho. Byfl —9N 55
Dunnets. Knap —4H 73
Dunning's Rd. E Grin —3A 186
Dunnymans Rd. Bans —2L 81
Dunottar Clo. Red —5D 122
Dunraven Av. Red —1F 142
Dunsborough Park. —7L 75
Dunsbury Clo. Sutt —5N 61
Dunsdon Av. Guild —4L 113
Dunsfold. —4D 174
Dunsfold Aerodrome. Duns & G'ming —4F 174
Dunsfold Clo. Craw —4M 181
Dunsfold Comn. Duns —5B 174
Dunsfold Ri. Coul —9H 63
Dunsfold Rd. Alf —5E 174
Dunsfold Rd. Loxh & Cranl —1C 174
Dunsfold Rd. Plais —2N 191
Dunsfold Way. New Ad —5L 65
Dunsford Way. SW15 —9G 13
Dunsmore Gdns. Yat —1A 68
Dunsmore Rd. W on T —5J 39
Dunstable Rd. Rich —7L 11
Dunstable Rd. W Mol —3N 39
Dunstall Pk. Farn —7M 69
Dunstall Rd. SW20 —7G 27
Dunstall Way. W Mol —2B 40
Dunstan Rd. Coul —4H 83
Dunster Av. Mord —7J 43
Dunton Clo. Surb —7L 41
Duntshill Rd. SW18 —2N 27
Dunvegan Clo. W Mol —3B 40
Dunvegan Ho. Red —3D 122
Dupont Rd. SW20 —1J 43
Duppas Av. Croy —1M 63 (7A 200)
Duppas Clo. Shep —4E 38
Duppas Ct. Croy —5A 200
Duppas Hill La. Croy
—1M 63 (6A 200)
Duppas Hill Rd. Croy
—1L 63 (6A 200)
Duppas Hill Ter. Croy
—9M 45 (5A 200)
Duppas Rd. Croy —9L 45
Durand Clo. Cars —7D 44
Durban Rd. SE27 —5N 29
Durban Rd. Beck —1J 47
Durbin Rd. Chess —1L 59
Durfold Dri. Reig —3A 122
Durfold Hill. Warn —6H 179
Durfold Rd. H'ham —1K 197
Durfold Wood. Plais —2M 191
Durford Cres. SW15 —2G 26
Durham Av. Houn —1N 9
Durham Clo. SW20 —1G 43
Durham Clo. Craw —7C 182
(in two parts)
Durham Clo. Guild —1J 113
Durham Ct. Tedd —5E 24
Durham Rd. SW20 —9G 27
Durham Rd. Felt —1K 23
Durham Rd. Owl —5K 49
Durham Wharf. Bren —3J 11
Durkins Rd. E Grin —7N 165
(in two parts)
Durleston Pk. Dri. Bookh —3C 98
Durley Mead. Brack —4D 32
Durlston Rd. King T —7L 25
Durning Pl. Asc —2M 33
Durning Rd. SE19 —6N 29
Durnsford Av. SW19 —3M 27
Durnsford Av. Fleet —6B 88
Durnsford Rd. SW19 —3M 27
Durnsford Way. Cranl —8A 156
Durrant Way. Orp —2M 67
Durrell Rd. SW6 —4L 13
Durrell Way. Shep —5E 38
Durrington Av. SW20 —8H 27
Durrington Pk. Rd. SW20 —9H 27
Dutch Barn Clo. Stanw —9M 7
Dutchells Copse. H'ham —2L 197
Dutch Elm Av. Wind —3J 5
Dutch Gdns. King T —7A 26
Dutch Yd. SW18 —8M 13
Duval Pl. Bag —4J 51
Duxberry Av. Felt —4K 23
Duxhurst La. Reig —8N 141
Dwelly La. Eden —6D 126
Dye Ho. Rd. Thur —6E 150
Dyer Ho. Hamp —9B 24
Dyer Rd. Wokgm —1D 30
Dyers Almshouses. Craw —2B 182
Dyers Fld. Small —8M 143
Dyers La. SW15 —7G 13
Dykes Path. Wok —2E 74
Dymchurch Clo. Orp —1N 67
Dymes Path. SW19 —3J 27
Dymock St. SW6 —6N 13
Dynevor Pl. Guild —8F 92
Dynevor Rd. Rich —8L 11
Dysart Av. King T —6J 25
Dyson Clo. Wind —6E 4
Dyson Ct. Dork —5G 119 (3K 201)
Dyson Wlk. Craw —8N 181

Eady Clo. H'ham —6M 197
Eagle Clo. Crowt —9F 30
Eagle Clo. Wall —3J 63
Eagle Hill. SE19 —7N 29
Eaglehurst Cotts. Binf —6H 15
Eagle Rd. Guild —3N 113 (3D 202)
Eagles Dri. Tats —5F 86
(in two parts)
Eagles Nest. Sand —6F 48
Eagle Trad. Est. Mitc —5D 44
Ealing Pk. Gdns. W5 —1J 11
Ealing Rd. Bren —1K 11
Ealing Rd. Trad. Est. Bren —1K 11
Eardley Cres. SW5 —1M 13
Eardley Rd. SW16 —6G 29
Earldom Rd. SW15 —7H 13
Earle Cft. Warf —8A 16
Earle Gdns. King T —8L 25
Earles Mdw. H'ham —2A 198
Earleswood. Cobh —8M 57
Earleydene. Asc —7M 33
Earl Rd. SW14 —7B 12
Earlsbourne. C Crook —9C 88
Earlsbrook Rd. Red —5D 122
Earl's Court. —1M 13
Earl's Court Exhibition Building. —1M 13
Earls Ct. Gdns. SW5 —1N 13
Earl's Ct. Rd. W8 & SW5 —1M 13
Earl's Ct. Sq. SW5 —1N 13
Earlsfield. —2A 28
Earlsfield Rd. SW18 —2A 28
Earls Gro. Camb —9C 50
Earlsthorpe M. SW12 —1E 28
Earlswood. —5D 122
Earlswood. Brack —6N 31
Earlswood Av. T Hth —4L 45
Earlswood Clo. H'ham —4M 197
Earlswood Ct. Red —5D 122
Earlswood Rd. Red —4D 122
Early Commons. Craw —2D 182
(in two parts)
Easby Cres. Mord —5N 43
Eashing. —7C 132
Eashing Bridge. —8B 132
Eashing La. Milf & G'ming —9C 132
Easington Pl. Guild —4B 114
East Av. Farnh —6J 109
East Av. Wall —2K 63
East Av. W Vill —6G 56
Eastbank Rd. Hamp H —6C 24
East Bedfont. —1F 22
Eastbourne Gdns. SW14 —6B 12
Eastbourne Rd. SW17 —7E 28
Eastbourne Rd. W4 —2B 12
Eastbourne Rd. Bren —1J 11
Eastbourne Rd. Felb —4J 165
Eastbourne Rd. Felt —3L 23
Eastbourne Rd. God —1F 124
Eastbourne Rd. Newc & Ling —9H 145
Eastbourne Rd. S God & Blind H —9G 125
Eastbrook Clo. Wok —3C 74
Eastbury Ct. Brack —9L 15
Eastbury Gro. W4 —1D 12
Eastbury La. Comp —9D 112
Eastbury Rd. King T —8L 25 (1K 203)
Eastchurch Rd. H'row A —5F 8
East Clandon. —9M 95
Eastcote Av. W Mol —4N 39
Eastcote Ho. Eps —6D 60
East Ct. E Grin —8B 166
East Cres. Wind —4C 4
Eastcroft Ct. Guild —4C 114
Eastcroft M. H'ham —7F 196
Eastcroft Rd. Eps —4D 60
Eastdean Av. Eps —9A 60
East Dri. Cars —5C 62
East Dri. Vir W —6K 35
Eastern Av. Cher —2J 37
Eastern Industrial Area, Bracknell. —1B 32
Eastern La. Crowt —3L 49
Eastern Perimeter Rd. H'row A —5G 8
Eastern Rd. Alder —2B 110
Eastern Rd. Brack —1B 32
Eastern Vw. Big H —4E 86
Easter Way. S God —6H 125
East Ewell. —6H 61
Eastfield Rd. Red —4G 122
Eastfields. Witl —5C 152
Eastfields Rd. Mitc —1E 44
E. Flexford La. Wanb —5C 112
East Gdns. SW17 —7C 28
East Gdns. Wok —4E 74
Eastgate. Bans —1L 81
Eastgate Gdns. Guild —4A 114 (4E 202)
East Grn. B'water —2H 69
East Grinstead. —1B 186
E. Grinstead Rd. Ling —8N 145
East Grinstead Town Mus. —8B 166
Easthampstead. —4N 31
Easthampstead Mobile Home Pk. Wokgm —8H 31
Easthampstead Rd. Brack —1M 31
Easthampstead Rd. Wokgm —2B 30
Eastheath. —5A 30
Eastheath Av. Wokgm —4A 30
Eastheath Gdns. Wokgm —5A 30
East Hill. SW18 —8N 13
East Hill. Big H —5D 86
East Hill. Dor P —4A 166
East Hill. Oxt —7A 106
East Hill. S Croy —6B 64
East Hill. Wok —3E 74
E. Hill Ct. Oxt —8A 106
E. Hill La. Copt —4A 164
E. Hill Rd. Oxt —7A 106
East Horsley. —7G 96
Eastlands Clo. Oxt —5N 105
Eastlands Way. Oxt —5N 105
East La. King T —2K 41 (5J 203)
East La. W Hor —4D 96
Eastleigh Clo. Sutt —4N 61
Eastleigh Rd. H'row A —6G 8
Eastleigh Wlk. SW15 —1F 26
Eastleigh Way. Felt —2H 23
Eastly End. —2F 36
East Mall. Stai —5H 21
(off Elmsleigh Shop. Cen.)
Eastman Ho. SW4 —1G 29
Eastmead. Farn —1N 89
Eastmead. Wok —4L 73
East Meads. Guild —4J 113
Eastmearn Rd. SE27 —3N 29
East M. H'ham —6J 197
East Molesey. —3D 40
Eastmont Rd. Esh —8E 40
Eastney Rd. Croy —7M 45 (1A 200)
Eastnor Clo. Reig —5L 121
Eastnor Pl. Reig —5M 121
Eastnor Rd. Reig —6M 121
East Pk. Craw —4B 182
E. Park La. Newc —2F 164

East Pl.—Elm Pk.

East Pl. SE27 —5N 29
East Ramp. H'row A —4C 8
East Ring. Tong —5E 110
East Rd. SW19 —7A 28
East Rd. Felt —1E 22
East Rd. King T —9L 25 (1L 203)
East Rd. Reig —2L 121
East Rd. Wey —4E 56
East Shalford. —9C 114
E. Shalford La. Guild —8A 114
East Sheen. —7B 12
E. Sheen Av. SW14 —8C 12
E. Station Rd. Alder —3N 109
E. Stratton Clo. Brack —4D 32
East St. Bookh —3B 98
East St. Bren —3J 11
East St. Cher —6J 37
East St. Eps —9D 60 (6M 201)
East St. Farnh —9H 109
East St. H'ham —7J 197
East St. Rusp —2C 180
East St. Turn H —5D 184
East Surrey Mus. —2D 104
E. View Cotts. Cranl —7L 155
E. View La. Cranl —7L 155
East Wlk. Reig —3N 121
East Way. Croy —8H 47
Eastway. Eps —8B 60
East Way. Guild —3J 113
Eastway. Gat A —3F 162
Eastway. Mord —4J 43
Eastway. Wall —1G 62
Eastway E. Gat A —3F 162
(off Eastway)
E. Whipley La. Sham G —3H 155
Eastwick Dri. Bookh —1A 98
Eastwick Pk. Av. Bookh —2B 98
Eastwick Rd. Bookh —3B 98
Eastwick Rd. W on T —3J 57
Eastwood. Craw —3D 182
Eastwood Lodge. Brmly —4B 134
Eastwood Rd. Brmly —4B 134
Eastwood St. SW16 —7G 28
Eastworth. —7K 37
Eastworth Rd. Cher —7J 37
Eaton Ct. Guild —1C 114
Eaton Dri. King T —8N 25
Eaton Ho. Guild —5B 114
(off St Lukes Sq.)
Eaton Pk. Cobh —1M 77
Eaton Pk. Rd. Cobh —1M 77
Eaton Rd. Camb —2N 69
Eaton Rd. Houn —7D 10
Eaton Rd. Sutt —3A 62
Eatonville Rd. SW17 —3D 28
Eatonville Vs. SW17 —3D 28
Ebbage Ct. Wok —5A 74
Ebbas Way. Eps —2A 80
Ebbisham Clo. Dork
—5G 118 (3J 201)
Ebbisham La. Tad —8E 80
(in two parts)
Ebbisham Rd. Eps —1A 80
Ebbisham Rd. Wor Pk —8H 43
Ebenezer Wlk. SW16 —9G 28
Ebner St. SW18 —8N 13
Ebor Cotts. TW10 —4D 26
Ebury Clo. Kes —1G 67
Ebury M. SE27 —4M 29
Ecclesbourne Rd. T Hth —4N 45
Eccleshill. N Holm —9J 119
Echelforde Dri. Afrd —5B 22
Echo Barn La. Wrec —6D 128
Echo Pit Rd. Guild —7A 114 (8F 202)
Ecob Clo. Guild —8J 93
Ecton Rd. Add —1K 55
Eddeys Clo. Head D —3G 169
Eddeys La. Head D —3G 168
Eddington Hill. Craw —8N 181
Eddington Rd. Brack —5K 31
Eddiscombe Rd. SW6 —5L 13
Eddy Rd. Alder —3A 110
Eddystone. Cars —7B 62
Eddystone Ct. Churt —9L 149
Eddystone Wlk. Stai —1N 21
Ede Clo. Houn —6N 9
Edenbridge. —2L 147
Edenbridge Trad. Cen. Eden —3M 147
Eden Brook. Ling —7A 146
Eden Clo. New H —6K 55
Eden Clo. Slou —1C 6
Edencourt Rd. SW16 —7F 28
Edencroft. Brmly —4B 134
Edenfield Gdns. Wor Pk —9E 42
Eden Gro. Rd. Byfl —9N 55
Edenhurst Av. SW6 —6L 13
Eden M. SW17 —4A 28
Eden Park. —4K 47
Eden Pk. Av. Beck —3H 47
(in two parts)
Eden Rd. SE27 —5M 29
Eden Rd. Beck —3H 47
Eden Rd. Craw —5L 181
Eden Rd. Croy —1A 64 (6D 200)
Edenside Rd. Bookh —2N 97
Edensor Gdns. W4 —3D 12
Edensor Rd. W4 —3D 12
Eden St. King T —1K 41 (4J 203)
Eden Va. E Grin —7N 165
(in two parts)
Edenvale Clo. Mitc —8E 28
Edenvale Rd. Mitc —8E 28
Edenvale St. SW6 —5N 13
Eden Wlk. King T —1L 41 (4K 203)
Eden Way. Beck —4J 47
Eden Way. Warl —5H 85
Ederline Av. SW16 —2K 45
Edes Fld. Reig —5K 121
Edgar Clo. Worth —3J 183
Edgar Ct. N Mald —1D 42
Edgarley Ter. SW6 —4K 13
Edgar Rd. Houn —1N 23
Edgar Rd. S Croy —5A 64
Edgar Rd. Tats —8F 86
Edgbarrow Ct. Crowt —4F 48
Edgbarrow Ri. Sand —5F 48
Edgcumbe Pk. Dri. Crowt —2F 48
Edgeborough Ct. Guild —4B 114
Edge Clo. Wey —4B 56
Edgecoombe. S Croy —4F 64
Edgecoombe Clo. King T —8C 26
Edgedale Clo. Crowt —3G 49
Edgefield Clo. Cranl —6L 155
Edgefield Clo. Red —8E 122
Edge Hill. SW19 —8J 27
Edge Hill. Guild —4B 114
Edge Hill Ct. SW19 —8J 27
Edgehill Ct. W on T —7K 39
Edgehill Rd. Mitc —9F 28
Edgehill Rd. Purl —6L 63
Edgeley. Bookh —2M 97
Edgeley Cvn. Pk. Alb —3N 135
Edgell Clo. Vir W —2B 36
Edgell Rd. Stai —6H 21
Edgel St. SW18 —7N 13
Edgemoor Rd. Frim —3G 70
Edgepoint Clo. SE27 —6M 29
Edgewood Clo. Crowt —9F 30
Edgewood Grn. Croy —7G 47
Edgeworth Clo. Whyt —5D 84
Edgington Rd. SW16 —7H 29
Edinburgh Clo. Ash V —8E 90
Edinburgh Ct. SW20 —4J 43
Edinburgh Ct. Alder —2L 109
(off Queen Elizabeth Dri.)
Edinburgh Ct. King T —5K 203
Edinburgh Dri. Stai —7M 21
Edinburgh Gdns. Wind —5G 5
Edinburgh Rd. Sutt —8A 44
Edinburgh Way. E Grin —2B 186
Edison Pl. Craw —4D 182
Edith Gdns. Surb —6A 42
Edith Gro. SW10 —2N 13
Edith Ho. W6 —1H 13
(off Queen Caroline St.)
Edith Rd. SE25 —4A 46
Edith Rd. SW19 —7N 27
Edith Rd. W14 —1K 13
Edith Row. SW6 —4N 13
Edith Summerskill Ho. SW6 —3L 13
(off Clem Attlee Est.)
Edith Ter. SW10 —3N 13
Edith Vs. W14 —1L 13
Edmonds Ct. Brack —9A 16
Edmund Rd. Mitc —2C 44
Edna Rd. SW20 —1J 43
Edney Clo. C Crook —7C 88
Edrich Rd. Broadf —8M 181
Edridge Rd. Croy —9N 45 (5C 200)
Edward Av. Camb —1M 69
Edward Av. Mord —4B 44
Edward Clo. Hamp H —6C 24
Edward Ct. Stai —7L 21
Edward Ct. Wokgm —3A 30
Edward Rd. Big H —5G 87
Edward Rd. Coul —2H 83
Edward Rd. Croy —6B 46
Edward Rd. Farnh —4H 129
Edward Rd. Felt —8E 8
Edward Rd. Hamp H —6C 24
Edward Rd. W'sham —3A 52
Edwards Clo. Wor Pk —8J 43
Edwards Ct. S Croy —7E 200
Edward II Av. Byfl —1A 76
Edward St. Alder —2L 109
Edward Way. Afrd —3A 22
Edwin Clo. W Hor —3E 96
Edwin Pl. Croy —1E 200
Edwin Rd. Twic —2E 24
(in two parts)
Edwin Rd. W Hor —3D 96
Edwinstray Ho. Felt —3A 24
Eelmoor Plain Rd. Alder —9J 89
Eelmoor Rd. Alder —8J 89
Eelmoor Rd. Farn —3L 89
Effie Pl. SW6 —3M 13
Effie Rd. SW6 —3M 13
Effingham. —5L 97
Effingham Clo. Sutt —4N 61
Effingham Common. —2H 97
Effingham Comn. Rd. Eff —1H 97
Effingham Ct. Wok —6A 74
(off Constitution Hill)
Effingham Hill. —1L 117
Effingham Junction. —1H 97
Effingham La. Copt —5B 164
Effingham Lodge. King T
—3K 41 (8J 203)
Effingham Pl. Eff —5L 97
Effingham Rd. Burs & Copt —4N 163
Effingham Rd. Croy —6K 45
Effingham Rd. Reig —4N 121
Effingham Rd. Surb —6H 41
Effort St. SW17 —6C 28
Effra Rd. SW19 —7N 27
Egbury Ho. SW15 —9E 12
(off Tangley Gro.)
Egerton Ct. Guild —3H 113
Egerton Pl. Wey —3D 56
Egerton Rd. SE25 —2B 46
Egerton Rd. Camb —9L 49
Egerton Rd. Guild —3H 113
Egerton Rd. N Mald —3E 42
Egerton Rd. Twic —1E 24
Egerton Rd. Wey —3D 56
Egerton Way. Hayes —3C 8
Eggars Ct. Alder —3N 109
Eggar's Hill. Alder —4M 109
Eggleton Clo. C Crook —8A 88
Egham. —6C 20
Egham Bus. Village. Egh —9E 20
Egham By-Pass. Egh —6B 20
Egham Clo. SW19 —3K 27
Egham Clo. Sutt —8K 43
Egham Cres. Sutt —9K 43
Egham Hill. Egh —7N 19
Egham Hythe. —6F 20
Egham Mus. —6C 20
Egham Roundabout. Stai —6G 20
Egham Wick. —8K 19
Eglantine Rd. SW18 —8N 13
Egleston Rd. Mord —5N 43
Egley Dri. Wok —9N 73
Egley Rd. Wok —9N 73
(in two parts)
Eglinton Rd. Tilf —4N 149
Eglise Rd. Warl —4H 85
Egliston M. SW15 —6H 13
Egliston Rd. SW15 —6H 13
Egmont Av. Surb —7M 41
Egmont Pk. Rd. Tad —3F 100
Egmont Rd. N Mald —3E 42
Egmont Rd. Surb —7M 41
Egmont Rd. Sutt —4A 62
Egmont Rd. W on T —6J 39
Egmont Way. Tad —6K 81
Egremont Rd. SE27 —4L 29
Eight Acres. Hind —2A 170
Eighteenth Rd. Mitc —3J 45
Eileen Rd. SE25 —4A 46
Eileen Wilkinson Ho. SW6 —2L 13
(off Clem Attlee Ct.)
Eindhoven Clo. Cars —7E 44
Eland Pl. Croy —9M 45 (4A 200)
Eland Rd. Alder —3B 110
Eland Rd. Croy —9M 45 (4A 200)
Elberon Av. Croy —5G 45
Elbe St. SW6 —5N 13
Elborough Rd. SE25 —4D 46
Elborough St. SW18 —2M 27
Elbow Mdw. Coln —4H 7
Elcho Rd. Brkwd —6N 71
Elderberry Gro. SE27 —5N 29
Elderberry Rd. Lind —5B 168
Elder Clo. Guild —9C 94
Elderfield Pl. SW17 —5F 28
Elder Gdns. SE27 —6N 29
Eldergrove. Farn —4C 90
Elder Oak Clo. SE20 —1E 46
Elder Oak Ct. SE20 —1E 46
(off Anerley Ct.)
Elder Rd. SE27 —5N 29
Elder Rd. Bisl —2D 72
Eldersley Clo. Red —1D 122
Elderslie Clo. Beck —4K 47
Eldertree Pl. Mitc —9G 28
Eldertree Way. Mitc —9G 28
Elder Way. N Holm —9J 119
Elderwood Pl. SE27 —6N 29
Eldon Av. Croy —8F 46
Eldon Av. Houn —3A 10
Eldon Dri. Lwr Bo —6J 129
Eldon Pk. SE25 —3E 46
Eldon Rd. Cat —8A 84
Eldrick Ct. Felt —2E 22
Eldridge Clo. Felt —2H 23
Eleanora Ter. Sutt —2A 62
(off Lind Rd.)
Eleanor Av. Eps —6C 60
Eleanor Clo. Pass —9C 168
Eleanor Ct. Guild —5N 113 (6D 202)
Eleanor Gro. SW13 —6D 12
Eleanor Ho. W6 —1H 13
(off Queen Caroline St.)
Electric Pde. Surb —5K 41
Electric Theatre, The.
—4M 113 (5B 202)
Elfin Gro. Tedd —6F 24
Elgal Clo. Orp —2K 67
Elgar Av. SW16 —2J 45
Elgar Av. Crowt —9G 30
Elgar Av. Surb —7N 41
Elgar Way. H'ham —4A 198
Elger Way. Copt —6L 163
Elgin Av. Afrd —7D 22
Elgin Clo. H'ham —5M 197
Elgin Ct. S Croy —7B 200
Elgin Cres. Cat —9D 84
Elgin Cres. H'row A —5F 8
Elgin Gdns. Guild —2C 114
Elgin Pl. Wey —3D 56
Elgin Rd. Croy —8C 46
Elgin Rd. Sutt —9A 44
Elgin Rd. Wall —3G 62
Elgin Rd. Wey —2B 56
Elgin Way. Frim —6D 70
Eliot Clo. Camb —8F 50
Eliot Dri. Hasl —2C 188
Eliot Gdns. SW15 —7F 12
Elis David Almshouses. Croy
—9M 45 (5A 200)
Elizabethan Clo. Stanw —1M 21
Elizabethan Way. Craw —4G 183
Elizabethan Way. Stanw —1M 21
Elizabeth Av. Bag —5K 51
Elizabeth Av. Stai —7L 21
Elizabeth Barnes Ct. SW6 —5N 13
Elizabeth Clo. Brack —3A 32
Elizabeth Clo. Sutt —1L 61
Elizabeth Cotts. Kew —4M 11
Elizabeth Ct. Alder —2L 109
(off Queen Elizabeth Dri.)
Elizabeth Ct. G'ming —4H 133
Elizabeth Ct. Horl —8E 142
Elizabeth Ct. Tedd —6E 24
Elizabeth Ct. Whyt —5C 84
Elizabeth Ct. Wokgm —2A 30
Elizabeth Cres. E Grin —7B 166
Elizabeth Dri. C Crook —8B 88
Elizabeth Fry Ho. Hayes —1G 8
Elizabeth Fry Ho. Ott —3F 54
(off Vernon Clo.)
Elizabeth Gdns. Asc —4M 33
Elizabeth Gdns. Sun —2K 39
Elizabeth Ho. W6 —1H 13
(off Queen Caroline St.)
Elizabeth Rd. G'ming —4H 133
Elizabeth Rd. Wokgm —2C 30
Elizabeth Way. SE19 —8N 29
Elizabeth Way. Felt —5K 23
Elkins Gdns. Guild —9C 94
Elkins Gro. Farnh —1E 128
Ellaline Rd. W6 —2J 13
Elland Rd. W on T —8L 39
Ellenborough Clo. Brack —9B 16
Ellenborough Pl. SW15 —7F 12
Ellenbridge Way. S Croy —5B 64
Ellen Dri. Fleet —1D 88
Ellen's Green. —5H 177
Elleray Ct. Ash V —8E 90
Elleray Rd. Tedd —7F 24
Ellerby St. SW6 —4J 13
Ellerdine Rd. Houn —7C 10
Ellerker Gdns. Rich —9L 11
Ellerman Av. Twic —2N 23
Ellerton Rd. SW13 —4F 12
Ellerton Rd. SW18 —2B 28
Ellerton Rd. SW20 —8F 26
Ellerton Rd. Surb —8M 41
Ellery Clo. Cranl —9N 155
Ellery Rd. SE19 —8N 29
Elles Av. Guild —3E 114
Elles Clo. Farn —2N 89
Ellesfield Av. Brack —3K 31
Ellesmere Av. Beck —1L 47
Ellesmere Ct. W4 —1C 12
Ellesmere Dri. S Croy —1E 84
Ellesmere Pl. W on T —2F 56
Ellesmere Rd. W4 —2B 12
Ellesmere Rd. Twic —9J 11
Ellesmere Rd. Wey —4F 56
Elles Rd. Farn —3K 89
Elleswood Ct. Surb —6K 41
Ellice Rd. Oxt —7B 106
Ellie M. Afrd —3N 21
Ellingham. Wok —6A 74
Ellingham Rd. Chess —3K 59
Ellington Rd. Felt —5G 22
Ellington Rd. Houn —5B 10
Ellington Way. Eps —4G 81
Elliot Clo. M'bowr —4G 182
Elliott Gdns. Shep —3B 38
Elliott Pk. Ind. Est. Alder —2C 110
Elliott Ri. Asc —1H 33
Elliott Rd. W4 —1D 12
Elliott Rd. T Hth —3M 45
Ellis Av. Onsl —5J 113
Ellis Clo. Coul —7K 83
Ellis Farm Clo. Wok —9N 73
Ellisfield Dri. SW15 —1F 26
Ellison Clo. Wind —6C 4
Ellison Rd. SW13 —5E 12
Ellison Rd. SW16 —8H 29
Ellison Way. Tong —5D 110
Ellison Way. Wokgm —2A 30
Ellis Rd. Coul —7K 83
Ellis Rd. Crowt —1F 48
Ellis Rd. Mitc —5D 44
Ellman Rd. Craw —5L 181
Ellora Rd. SW16 —6H 29
Ellson Clo. M'bowr —5G 182
Ellwood Pl. Craw —3L 181
Elm Av. Afrd —3N 21
Elm Bank. Yat —8B 48
Elmbank Av. Eng G —7L 19
Elmbank Av. Guild —4K 113
Elm Bank Gdns. SW13 —5D 12
Elmbourne Rd. SW17 —4E 28
Elmbridge Av. Surb —4A 42
Elmbridge Cotts. Cranl —7J 155
Elm Bri. Est. Wok —6B 74
Elmbridge La. Old Wok & Wok
—6B 74
Elmbridge Mus. —1B 56
Elmbridge Rd. Cranl —8G 154
Elmbridge Village. Cranl —8H 155
(off Essex Dri.)
Elmbrook Clo. Sun —9J 23
Elmbrook Rd. Sutt —1L 61
Elm Clo. SW20 —3H 43
Elm Clo. Bord —6A 168
Elm Clo. Cars —7D 44
Elm Clo. Lea —9H 79
Elm Clo. Rip —2J 95
Elm Clo. S Croy —3B 64
Elm Clo. Stanw —2M 21
Elm Clo. Surb —6B 42
Elm Clo. Tad —8B 100
Elm Clo. Twic —3B 24
Elm Clo. Warl —4G 84
Elm Clo. Wok —2N 73
Elm Corner. —6B 76
Elm Cotts. Eden —8K 127
Elm Cotts. Mitc —1D 44
Elm Ct. Knap —4G 73
Elm Ct. Sand —5K 49
Elm Ct. W Mol —3B 40
Elmcourt Rd. SE27 —3M 29
Elm Cres. Farnh —5J 109
Elm Cres. King T —9L 25 (2L 203)
Elmcroft. Bookh —2A 98
Elm Cft. Dat —4M 5
Elmcroft Clo. Chess —9L 41
Elmcroft Clo. Felt —9G 9
Elmcroft Clo. Frim G —7D 70
Elmcroft Dri. Afrd —6B 22
Elmcroft Dri. Chess —9L 41
Elmdene. Surb —7B 42
Elmdene Clo. Beck —5J 47
Elmdon Rd. Houn —5L 9
Elmdon Rd. H'row A —6G 8
Elm Dri. Chob —6J 53
Elm Dri. E Grin —9C 166
Elm Dri. Lea —1H 99
Elm Dri. Sun —1K 39
Elm Dri. Wink —3M 17
Elmer Cotts. Fet —1G 98
Elmer Gdns. Iswth —6D 10
Elmer M. Fet —9G 78
Elmers Dri. Tedd —7H 25
Elmers End. —3H 47
Elmers End Rd. SE20 —1F 46
Elmerside Rd. Beck —3H 47
Elmers Rd. SE25 —6D 46
Elmers Rd. Ockl —6C 158
Elmfield. Bookh —1A 98
Elmfield Av. Mitc —9E 28
Elmfield Av. Tedd —6F 24
Elm Fld. Cotts. Wood S —2D 112
Elmfield Ct. Lind —4A 168
(off Liphook Rd.)
Elmfield Ho. Guild —1E 114
Elmfield Rd. SW17 —3E 28
Elmfield Way. S Croy —5C 64
Elm Gdns. Clay —3F 58
Elm Gdns. Eps —6H 81
Elm Gdns. Mitc —3H 45
Elmgate Av. Felt —4J 23
Elm Gro. SW19 —8K 27
Elm Gro. Bisl —3D 72
Elm Gro. Cat —9B 84
Elm Gro. Eps —1B 80
Elm Gro. Farnh —5H 109
Elm Gro. H'ham —7L 197
Elm Gro. King T —9L 25 (2L 203)
Elm Gro. Sutt —1N 61
Elmgrove Clo. Wok —6G 73
Elm Gro. Pde. Wall —9E 44
Elm Gro. Rd. SW13 —4F 12
Elm Gro. Rd. Cobh —3L 77
Elmgrove Rd. Croy —6E 46
Elmgrove Rd. Farn —1N 89
Elmgrove Rd. Wey —1B 56
Elm Hill. —9K 91
Elm Hill. Norm —1J 111
Elm Ho. King T —1N 203
Elmhurst Av. Mitc —8F 28
Elmhurst Ct. Croy —1A 64 (7D 200)
Elmhurst Ct. Guild —4B 114
Elmhurst Dri. Dork —7H 119
Elmhurst La. Slin —9J 195
Elmhurst Lodge. Sutt —4A 62
Elm La. Ock —6B 76
Elm La. Tong —4D 110
Elm Lodge. SW6 —4H 13
Elm M. Gray —6A 170
Elmore Rd. Coul —8D 82
Elm Pk. SW2 —1K 29
Elm Pk. Cranl —7J 155
Elm Pk. S'dale —7B 34

228 A-Z Surrey

Elm Pk. Gdns. S Croy —6F 64
Elm Pk. Rd. SE25 —2C 46
Elm Pl. Alder —4A 110
Elm Rd. SW14 —6B 12
Elm Rd. Beck —1J 47
Elm Rd. Chess —1L 59
Elm Rd. Clay —3F 58
Elm Rd. Eps —3E 60
Elm Rd. Farnh —5J 109
Elm Rd. Felt —2F 22
Elm Rd. G'ming —3J 133
Elm Rd. Hors —2B 74
Elm Rd. King T —9M 25 (2M 203)
Elm Rd. Lea —9H 79
Elm Rd. N Mald —1C 42
Elm Rd. Purl —9M 63
Elm Rd. Red —3C 122
Elm Rd. T Hth —3A 46
Elm Rd. Wall —7E 44
Elm Rd. Warl —4G 84
Elm Rd. W'ham —3N 107
Elm Rd. Wind —6E 4
Elm Rd. Wok —5N 73
Elm Rd. W. Sutt —6L 43
Elms Cres. SW4 —1G 29
Elmshaw Rd. SW15 —8F 12
Elmshorn. Eps —3H 81
Elmside. Guild —4K 113
Elmside. Mill —1C 152
Elmside. New Ad —3L 65
Elmsleigh Ct. Sutt —9N 43
Elmsleigh Ho. Twic —3D 24
(off Staines Rd.)
Elmsleigh Rd. Farn —1L 89
Elmsleigh Rd. Stai —6H 21
Elmsleigh Rd. Twic —3D 24
Elmsleigh Shop. Cen. Stai —5H 21
Elmslie Clo. Eps —1B 80
Elms Rd. Alder —3M 109
Elms Rd. Fleet —4D 88
Elms Rd. Wokgm —3A 30
Elmstead Clo. Eps —2D 60
Elmstead Gdns. Wor Pk —9F 42
Elmstead Rd. W Byf —9J 55
Elms, The. SW13 —6E 12
Elms, The. B'water —2K 69
Elms, The. Clay —4F 58
Elms, The. Croy —7N 45
(off Tavistock Rd.)
Elms, The. Tong —4D 110
Elms, The. Warf P —7F 16
Elmstone Rd. SW6 —4M 13
Elmsway. Afrd —6B 22
Elmswood. Bookh —2N 97
Elmsworth Av. Houn —5B 10
Elm Tree Av. Esh —6D 40
Elm Tree Clo. Afrd —6C 22
Elmtree Clo. Byfl —9N 55
Elm Tree Clo. Cher —8G 37
Elm Tree Clo. Horl —7F 142
Elmtree Rd. Tedd —5E 24
Elm Vw. As —1F 110
Elm Vw. Ct. S'hall —1A 10
Elm Vw. Ho. Hayes —1E 8
Elm Wlk. SW20 —3H 43
Elm Wlk. Orp —1H 67
Elm Way. Eps —2C 60
Elm Way. Wor Pk —9H 43
Elmwood Av. Felt —3H 23
Elmwood Clo. Asht —4K 79
Elmwood Clo. Eps —4F 60
Elmwood Clo. Wall —8F 44
Elmwood Ct. Asht —4K 79
Elmwood Dri. Eps —3F 60
Elmwood Rd. W4 —2B 12
Elmwood Rd. Croy —6M 45
Elmwood Rd. Mitc —2D 44
Elmwood Rd. Red —8E 102
Elmwood Rd. Wok —6G 73
Elmworth Gro. SE21 —3N 29
Elphinstone Clo. Brkwd —8C 72
Elphinstone Ct. SW16 —7J 29
Elsa Ct. Beck —1J 47
Elsdon Rd. Wok —5K 73
Elsenham St. SW18 —2L 27
Elsenwood Cres. Camb —8E 50
Elsenwood Dri. Camb —8E 50
Elsinore Av. Stai —1N 21
Elsinore Ho. W6 —1H 13
(off Fulham Pal. Rd.)
Elsinore Way. Rich —6A 12
Elsley Clo. Frim G —8D 70
Elsrick Av. Mord —4M 43
Elstan Way. Croy —6H 47
Elstead. —7H 131
Elstead Ct. Sutt —7K 43
Elstead Ho. SW2 —1K 29
(off Redlands Way)
Elstead Pk. Flst —9F 130
Elstead Rd. Seale —7C 110
Elstead Rd. Shack —5N 131
Elsted Clo. Craw —1N 181
Elston Pl. Alder —4A 110
Elston Rd. Alder —4A 110
Elswick St. SW6 —5N 13
Elsworth Clo. Felt —2F 22
Elsworthy. Th Dit —5E 40
Elthiron Rd. SW6 —4M 13
Elthorne Ct. Felt —2K 23
Elton Clo. King T —8J 25
Elton Rd. King T —9M 25 (1N 203)
Elton Rd. Purl —8G 62
Eltringham St. SW18 —7N 13
Elveden Clo. Wok —4K 75
Elvedon Rd. Cobh —7J 57
Elvetham Clo. Fleet —2B 88
Elvetham Pl. Fleet —2A 88
Elvetham Rd. Fleet —2A 88
Elwell Clo. Egh —7C 20
Elwill Way. Beck —3M 47
Ely Clo. Craw —7C 182
Ely Clo. Frim —7E 70
Ely Clo. N Mald —1E 42
Ely Pl. Guild —1J 113
Ely Rd. Croy —4A 46
Ely Rd. Houn —6K 9
Ely Rd. H'row A —5G 8
Elysium Pl. SW6 —5L 13
(off Elysium St.)
Elysium St. SW6 —5L 13
Elystan Clo. Wall —4G 62
Emanuel Dri. Hamp —6N 23
Embankment. SW15 —5J 13
Embankment, The. Twic —2G 25
Embankment, The. Wray —1M 19
Embassy Ct. Wall —3F 62
Ember Cen. W on T —8M 39
Ember Clo. Add —2M 55
Embercourt Rd. Th Dit —5F 40
Ember Farm Av. E Mol —5D 40
Ember Farm Way. E Mol —5D 40
Ember Gdns. Th Dit —6E 40
Ember La. Esh —6D 40
Emberwood. Craw —1A 182
Embleton Rd. Head D —3G 168
Embleton Wlk. Hamp —6N 23
Emden St. SW6 —4N 13
Emerald Ct. Coul —2H 83
Emerson Ct. Crowt —2G 49
Emerton Rd. Fet —8C 78
Emery Down Clo. Brack —2E 32
Emily Davison Dri. Eps —5G 80
Emley Rd. Add —9J 37
Emlyn La. Lea —9G 79
Emlyn Rd. Horl —7C 142
Emlyn Rd. Red —5E 122
Emmanuel Clo. Guild —9K 93
Emmanuel Rd. SW12 —2G 28
Emmets Nest. Binf —7H 15
Emmets Pk. Binf —7H 15
Emmetts Clo. Wok —4N 73
Emms Pas. King T —1K 41 (4J 203)
Empire Vs. Red —4E 142
Empress Av. Farn —9N 69
Empress Pl. SW6 —1M 13
Emsworth Clo. M'bowr —6G 183
Emsworth Ct. SW16 —4J 29
Emsworth St. SW2 —3K 29
Ena Rd. SW16 —2J 45
Enborne Gdns. Brack —8B 16
Endale Clo. Cars —8D 44
Endeavour Way. SW19 —5N 27
Endeavour Way. Croy —6J 45
Endlesham Rd. SW12 —1E 28
Endsleigh Clo. S Croy —6F 64
Endsleigh Gdns. Surb —5J 41
Endsleigh Gdns. W on T —2K 57
Endsleigh Rd. Red —7G 102
Ends Pl. Warn —9C 178
End Way. Surb —6N 41
Endymion Rd. SW2 —1K 29
Enfield Rd. Ash V —8F 90
Enfield Rd. Bren —1K 11
Enfield Rd. Craw —7N 181
Enfield Rd. H'row A —5F 8
Enfield Wlk. Bren —1K 11
Engadine Clo. Croy —9C 46
Engadine St. SW18 —2L 27
Engalee. E Grin —8M 165
England Way. N Mald —3A 42
Englefield. H'ham —6F 196
Englefield Clo. Croy —5N 45
Englefield Clo. Eng G —7M 19
Englefield Green. —6M 19
Englefield Rd. Knap —4F 72
Engleheart Dri. Felt —9G 9
Englehurst. Eng G —7M 19
Englemere Pk. Asc —3H 33
Englemere Pk. Oxs —9B 58
Englemere Rd. Brack —8L 15
Englesfield. Camb —1G 71
Englewood Rd. SW12 —1G 28
Engliff La. Wok —3J 75
English Gdns. Wray —7N 5
Enmore Av. SE25 —4D 46
Enmore Gdns. SW14 —8C 12
Enmore Rd. SE25 —4D 46
Enmore Rd. SW15 —7H 13
Ennerdale. Brack —3M 31
Ennerdale Clo. Craw —5N 181
Ennerdale Clo. Felt —2G 22
Ennerdale Clo. Sutt —1L 61
Ennerdale Gro. Farnh —6F 108
Ennerdale Rd. Rich —5M 11
Ennismore Av. W4 —1E 12
Ennismore Av. Guild —3B 114
Ennismore Gdns. Th Dit —5E 40
Ennor Ct. Sutt —1H 61
Ensign Clo. Purl —8L 63
Ensign Clo. Stanw —2M 21
Ensign Way. Stanw —2M 21
Enterdent Cotts. God —2G 124
Enterdent Rd. God —3F 124
Enterdent, The. God —2G 125
Enterprise Clo. Croy —7L 45
Enterprise Ct. Craw —8B 162
Enterprise Est. Guild —8A 94
Enterprise Ho. H'ham —7H 197
Enterprise Ind. Est. Ash V —6D 90
Enterprise Way. SW18 —7M 13
Enterprise Way. Eden —9K 127
Enterprise Way. Tedd —7F 24
Enton Green. —4E 152
Enton La. Ent —7D 152
Envis Way. Guild —8F 92
Eothen Clo. Cat —2D 104
Epirus M. SW6 —3M 13
Epirus Rd. SW6 —3L 13
Epping Wlk. Craw —5D 182
Epping Way. Brack —3D 32
Epple Rd. SW6 —4L 13
Epsom. —9C 60 (6L 201)
Epsom Bus. Pk. Eps —7D 60
Epsom Clo. Camb —7A 50
Epsom Downs. —6D 80
Epsom Downs Metro Cen. Tad —7G 81
Epsom Downs Racecourse. —5D 80
Epsom Gap. Lea —2H 79
Epsom La. N. Eps —5G 80
Epsom La. S. Tad —8H 81
Epsom Pl. Cranl —7A 156
Epsom Playhouse. —7K 201
Epsom Rd. Asht —5M 79
Epsom Rd. Craw —5E 182
Epsom Rd. Croy —1L 63
Epsom Rd. E Clan & W Hor —9N 95
Epsom Rd. Eps —7E 60
Epsom Rd. Guild —4A 114 (5E 202)
Epsom Rd. Lea —8H 79
Epsom Rd. Sutt —6L 43
Epsom Sq. H'row A —5G 8
Epworth Rd. Iswth —3H 11
Eresby Dri. Beck —7K 47
Erfstadt Ct. Wokgm —3B 30
Erica Clo. W End —9B 52
Erica Ct. Wok —5N 73
Erica Dri. Wokgm —3C 30
Erica Gdns. Croy —9L 47
Erica Way. Copt —7L 163
Erica Way. H'ham —3K 197
Ericcson Clo. SW18 —8M 13
Eridge Clo. Craw —3G 182
Eriswell Cres. W on T —3F 56
Eriswell Rd. W on T —1G 57
Erkenwald Clo. Cher —6G 37
Ermine Clo. Houn —5K 9
Ermyn Clo. Lea —8K 79
Ermyn Cotts. Horne —5D 144
Ermyn Way. Lea —8K 79
Erncroft Way. Twic —9F 10
Ernest Av. SE27 —5M 29
Ernest Clo. Beck —4K 47
Ernest Clo. Lwr Bo —5G 129
Ernest Cotts. Eps —4E 60
Ernest Gdns. W4 —2A 12
Ernest Gro. Beck —4J 47
Ernest Rd. King T —1A 42
Ernest Sq. King T —1A 42
Ernle Rd. SW20 —8G 27
Ernshaw Pl. SW15 —8K 13
Erpingham Rd. SW15 —6H 13
Erridge Rd. SW19 —1M 43
Errington Dri. Wind —4D 4
Errol Gdns. N Mald —3F 42
Erskine Clo. Craw —7K 181
Erskine Clo. Sutt —9C 44
Erskine Rd. Sutt —1B 62
Esam Way. SW16 —6L 29
Escombe Dri. Guild —7L 93
Escot Rd. Sun —8G 22
Escott Pl. Ott —3E 54
Esher. —1B 58
Esher Av. Sutt —9J 43
Esher Av. W on T —6H 39
Esher By-Pass. Clay & Chess —5H 59
Esher By-Pass. Cobh —9G 57
Esher By-Pass. Esh —7A 58
Esher Clo. Esh —2B 58
Esher Common. (Junct.) —5C 58
Esher Cres. H'row A —5G 8
Esher Gdns. SW19 —3J 27
Esher Grn. Esh —1B 58
Esher Green Dri. Esh —9B 40
Esher M. Mitc —2E 44
Esher Pk. Av. Esh —1B 58
Esher Pl. Av. Esh —1A 58
Esher Rd. Camb —6F 50
Esher Rd. E Mol —5D 40
Esher Rd. W on T —2L 57
Eskdale Ct. Ash V —8D 90
(off Lakeside Clo.)
Eskdale Gdns. Purl —1A 84
Eskdale Way. Camb —2G 71
Esmond St. SW15 —7K 13
Esparto St. SW18 —1N 27
Essame Clo. Wokgm —2C 30
Essendene Clo. Cat —1B 104
Essendene Rd. Cat —1B 104
Essenden Rd. S Croy —4B 64
Essex Av. Iswth —6E 10
Essex Clo. Add —1L 55
Essex Clo. Frim —7E 70
Essex Clo. Mord —6J 43
Essex Ct. SW13 —5E 12
Essex Dri. Cranl —8H 155
Essex Pl. W4 —1B 12
(in two parts)
Essex Pl. Sq. W4 —1C 12
Essex Ri. Warf —8D 16
Essex Rd. W4 —1C 12
(in two parts)
Estate Cotts. Mick —5K 99
Estcots Dri. E Grin —9B 166
Estcourt Rd. SE25 —5E 46
Estcourt Rd. SW6 —3L 13
Estella Av. N Mald —3G 43
Estoria Clo. SW2 —1L 29
Estreham Rd. SW16 —7H 29
Estridge Clo. Houn —7A 10
Eswyn Rd. SW17 —5D 28
Eternit Wlk. SW6 —4H 13
Ethel Bailey Clo. Eps —8N 59
Ethelbert Rd. SW20 —9J 27
Ethelbert St. SW12 —2F 28
Ethel Rd. Afrd —6N 21
Etherley Hill. Ockl —3A 158
Etherstone Grn. SW16 —5L 29
Etherstone Rd. SW16 —5L 29
Eton. —2G 4
Eton Av. Houn —2N 9
Eton Av. N Mald —4C 42
Eton Clo. SW18 —1N 27
Eton Clo. Dat —2K 5
Eton Ct. Eton —3G 4
Eton Ct. Stai —6H 21
Eton Pl. Farnh —5G 108
Eton Rd. Dat —1J 5
Eton Rd. Hayes —3G 8
Eton Sq. Eton —3G 4
Eton St. Rich —8L 11
Eton Wick. —1C 4
Eton Wick Rd. Eton W & Eton —1D 4
Etwell Pl. Surb —5M 41
Eureka Rd. King T —1N 41 (4N 203)
Europa Pk. Rd. Guild —2M 113 (1A 202)
Eustace Cres. Wokgm —9C 14
Eustace Rd. SW6 —3M 13
Eustace Rd. Guild —1F 114
Euston Rd. Croy —7L 45
Evans Clo. M'bowr —4H 183
Evans Gro. Felt —3A 24
Evans Ho. Felt —3A 24
Evedon. Brack —6N 31
Eveline Rd. Mitc —9D 28
Evelyn Av. Alder —4N 109
Evelyn Av. T'sey —2E 106
Evelyn Clo. Felb —6H 165
Evelyn Clo. Twic —1B 24
Evelyn Clo. Wok —7N 73
Evelyn Cotts. God —6H 125
Evelyn Cotts. Ab C —3L 137
Evelyn Cres. Sun —9G 22
Evelyn Gdns. God —8F 104
Evelyn Gdns. Rich —7L 11
Evelyn Mans. W14 —2K 13
(off Queen's Club Gdns.)
Evelyn Rd. Ham —4J 25
Evelyn Rd. SW19 —6N 27
Evelyn Rd. Rich —6L 11
Evelyn Ter. Rich —6L 11
Evelyn Wlk. Craw —6C 182
Evelyn Way. Eps —7N 59
Evelyn Way. Stoke D —3N 77
Evelyn Way. Sun —9G 22
Evelyn Way. Wall —1H 63
Evelyn Woods Rd. Alder —6A 90
Evendon's Clo. Wokgm —5A 30
Evendon's La. Wokgm —5A 30
Evenlode Way. Sand —7H 49
Evenwood Clo. SW15 —8K 13
Everard La. Cat —9E 84
Everatt Clo. SW18 —9L 13
Everdon Rd. SW13 —2F 12
Everest Ct. Wok —3H 73
Everest Rd. Camb —7B 50
Everest Rd. Crowt —1G 49
Everest Rd. Stanw —1M 21
Everglade. Big H —5F 86
Evergreen Ct. Stanw —1M 21
Evergreen Oak Av. Wind —6K 5
Evergreen Rd. Frim —4D 70
Evergreen Way. Stanw —1M 21
Everington St. W6 —2J 13
(in two parts)
Everlands Clo. Wok —5A 74
Eve Rd. Iswth —7G 11
Eve Rd. Wok —2D 74
Eversfield Rd. H'ham —7L 197
Eversfield Rd. Reig —3N 121
Eversfield Rd. Rich —5M 11
Eversley Cres. Iswth —4D 10
Eversley Pk. SW19 —7G 26
Eversley Rd. SE19 —8N 29
Eversley Rd. Surb —3M 41 (8M 203)
Eversley Rd. Yat —8A 48
Eversley Way. Croy —1K 65
Eversley Way. Egh & Thor —1E 36
Everton Rd. Croy —7D 46
Evesham Clo. Reig —2L 121
Evesham Clo. Sutt —4M 61
Evesham Ct. Rich —9M 11
Evesham Grn. Mord —5N 43
Evesham Rd. Mord —5N 43
Evesham Rd. Reig —2L 121
Evesham Rd. N. Reig —2L 121
Evesham Ter. Surb —5K 41
Evesham Wlk. Owl —6J 49
Ewald Rd. SW6 —5L 13
Ewelands. Horl —7G 142
Ewell. —6E 60
Ewell By-Pass. Eps —4F 60
Ewell Ct. Av. Eps & Ewe —2D 60
Ewell Downs Rd. Eps —7F 60
Ewell Ho. Gro. Eps & Ewe —6E 60
Ewell Pk. Gdns. Eps —4F 60
Ewell Pk. Way. Ewe —3F 60
Ewell Rd. Dit H & Surb —6H 41
Ewell Rd. Surb —5L 41
Ewell Rd. Sutt —4J 61
Ewen Cres. SW2 —1L 29
Ewhurst. —5F 156
Ewhurst Av. S Croy —5C 64
Ewhurst Clo. Craw —3A 182
Ewhurst Clo. Sutt —5H 61
Ewhurst Ct. Mitc —2B 44
Ewhurst Green. —6F 156
Ewhurst Rd. Cranl —7N 155
Ewhurst Rd. Craw —3N 181
Ewhurst Rd. Peasl & Ewh —5E 136
Ewhurst Towermill. —9C 136
Ewins Clo. As —2E 110
Ewood La. Newd —5M 139
(in two parts)
Ewshot. —4C 108
Ewshot Hill Cross. Ews —5B 108
Ewshot La. C Crook & Ews —1A 108
Excalibur Clo. If'd —4K 181
Excelsior Clo. King T —1N 41 (4N 203)
Exchange Rd. Asc —4N 33
Exchange Rd. Craw —3C 182
Exeforde Av. Afrd —5B 22
Exeter Clo. Craw —7C 182
Exeter Ct. Surb —8K 203
Exeter Gdns. Yat —8A 48
Exeter Ho. Felt —3N 23
(off Watermill Way)
Exeter M. SW6 —3M 13
Exeter Pl. Guild —1J 113
Exeter Rd. As —1E 110
Exeter Rd. Croy —6B 46
Exeter Rd. Felt —4N 23
Exeter Rd. H'row A —6F 8
Exeter Way. H'row A —5F 8
Explorer Av. Stai —2N 21
Eyebright Clo. Croy —7G 47
Eyhurst Clo. Kgswd —1L 101
Eyhurst Pk. Tad —1A 102
Eyhurst Spur. Tad —2L 101
Eyles Clo. H'ham —4H 197
Eylewood Rd. SE27 —6N 29
Eyot Gdns. W6 —1E 12
Eyot Grn. W4 —1E 12
Eyston Dri. Wey —6D 56

Fabian Rd. SW6 —3L 13
Facade, The. Reig —2M 121
Factory La. Croy —7L 45 (2A 200)
Factory Sq. SW16 —7J 29
(off Streatham High Rd.)
Fagg's Rd. Felt —7G 8
Fairacre. N Mald —2D 42
Fairacres. SW15 —7E 12
Fairacres. Cobh —8L 57
Fair Acres. Croy —5J 65
Fairacres. Howl —7E 128
Fairacres. Tad —8H 81
Fairacres Ind. Est. Wind —5A 4
Fairbairn Clo. Purl —9L 63
Fairborne Way. Guild —9K 93
Fairbourne. Cobh —9L 57
Fairbourne Clo. Wok —5K 73
Fairbourne La. Cat —9N 83
Fairbriar Ct. Eps —7M 201
Fairburn Ct. SW15 —8K 13
Fairburn Ho. W14 —1L 13
(off Ivatt Pl.)
Fairchildes Av. New Ad —8N 65
Fairchildes Rd. Warl —1N 85
Faircroft Ct. Tedd —7G 25
Faircross. Brack —2N 31
Fairdale Gdns. SW15 —7G 13
Fairdene Rd. Coul —5H 83
Fairfax. Brack —9M 15
Fairfax Av. Eps & Ewe —5G 60
Fairfax Av. Red —2C 122

Fairfax Clo. W on T —7J 39
Fairfax Ho. King T —5M 203
Fairfax Ind. Est. Alder —2C 110
Fairfax M. SW15 —7H 13
Fairfax M. Farn —3B 90
Fairfax Rd. Farn —7N 69
Fairfax Rd. Tedd —7G 25
Fairfax Rd. Wok —7D 74
Fairfield. —8H 79
Fairfield App. Wray —9N 5
Fairfield Av. Dat —3M 5
Fairfield Av. Horl —9E 142
Fairfield Av. Stai —5H 21
Fairfield Av. Twic —2B 24
Fairfield Clo. Dat —3N 5
Fairfield Clo. Dork —3H 119
Fairfield Clo. Ewe —2D 60
Fairfield Clo. Guild —2K 113
Fairfield Clo. Mitc —8C 28
Fairfield Cotts. Bookh —3B 98
Fairfield Ct. Lea —8H 79
(off Linden Rd.)
Fairfield Dri. SW18 —8N 13
Fairfield Dri. Dork —3H 119
Fairfield Dri. Frim —3C 70
Fairfield E. King T —1L 41 (3L 203)
Fairfield Halls & Ashcroft Theatre. —9A 46 (4D 200)
Fairfield Ind. Est. King T —2M 41 (6N 203)
Fairfield La. W End —8D 52
Fairfield Lodge. Guild —2K 113
Fairfield N. King T —1L 41 (3L 203)
Fairfield Pk. Cobh —1L 77
Fairfield Path. Croy —9A 46 (4E 200)
Fairfield Pl. King T —2L 41 (5L 203)
Fairfield Ri. Guild —2J 113
Fairfield Rd. Beck —1K 47
Fairfield Rd. Croy —9A 46 (4E 200)
Fairfield Rd. E Grin —1B 186
Fairfield Rd. King T —1L 41 (4L 203)
Fairfield Rd. Lea —8H 79
Fairfield Rd. Wray —9N 5
Fairfields. Cher —7J 37
Fairfield S. King T —1L 41 (4L 203)
Fairfields Rd. Houn —6C 10
Fairfield St. SW18 —8N 13
Fairfield, The. Farnh —1H 129
(in two parts)
Fairfield Wlk. Lea —8H 79
(off Fairfield Rd.)
Fairfield Way. Coul —1H 83
Fairfield Way. Eps —2D 60
Fairfield W. King T —1L 41 (4L 203)
Fairford Av. Croy —4G 47
Fairford Clo. Croy —4H 47
Fairford Clo. Reig —1A 122
Fairford Clo. W Byf —1H 75
Fairford Ct. Sutt —4N 61
Fairford Gdns. Wor Pk —8E 42
Fairgreen Rd. T Hth —4M 45
Fairhaven. Egh —6B 20
Fairhaven Av. Croy —5G 46
Fairhaven Ct. Egh —6B 20
Fairhaven Ct. S Croy —8C 200
Fairhaven Rd. Red —8E 102
Fairholme. Felt —1E 22
Fairholme Cres. Asht —4J 79
Fairholme Gdns. Farnh —2H 129
Fairholme Rd. W14 —1K 13
Fairholme Rd. Afrd —6N 21
Fairholme Rd. Croy —6L 45
Fairholme Rd. Sutt —3L 61
Fairland Clo. Fleet —5C 88
Fairlands. —8F 92
Fairlands Av. Guild —8F 92
Fairlands Av. Sutt —8M 43
Fairlands Av. T Hth —3K 45
Fairlands Ct. Guild —8F 92
Fairlands Rd. Guild —7F 92
Fair La. Coul —3A 102
Fairlawn. Bookh —2N 97
Fairlawn. Wey —2F 56
Fair Lawn Clo. Clay —3F 58
Fairlawn Clo. Felt —5N 23
Fairlawn Clo. King T —7B 26
Fairlawn Cres. E Grin —8L 165
Fairlawn Dri. E Grin —8L 165
Fairlawn Dri. Red —5C 122
Fairlawn Gro. Bans —9B 62
Fairlawn Pk. Wind —7B 4
Fairlawn Pk. Wok —1A 74
Fairlawn Rd. SW19 —8L 27
Fairlawn Rd. Sutt —7A 62
(in three parts)
Fairlawns. Add —2K 55
Fairlawns. Guild —3E 114
Fairlawns. Horl —9F 142
Fairlawns. Sun —2G 39
Fairlawns. Twic —9J 11
Fairlawns. Wall —2F 62
Fairlawns. Wdhm —7H 55
Fairlawns Clo. Stai —7K 21
Fairlight Av. Wind —5G 4
Fairlight Clo. Wor Pk —1H 61
Fairlight Rd. SW17 —5B 28
Fairline Ct. Beck —1M 47
Fairlop Wlk. Cranl —8H 155
Fairmead. Surb —7A 42
Fairmead. Wok —5M 73
Fairmead Clo. Coll T —8K 49
Fairmead Clo. Houn —3L 9
Fairmead Clo. N Mald —2C 42
Fairmead Ct. Rich —5A 12
Fairmead Rd. Croy —6K 45
Fairmead Rd. Eden —7L 127
Fairmeads. Cobh —9N 57
Fairmile. —8M 57
Fairmile. Fleet —7A 88
Fairmile Av. SW16 —6H 29
Fairmile Av. Cobh —9M 57
Fairmile Ct. Cobh —8M 57
Fairmile Ho. Tedd —5G 25
Fairmile La. Cobh —8L 57
Fairmile Pk. Copse. Cobh —9N 57
Fairmile Pk. Rd. Cobh —9N 57
Fairoak Clo. Kenl —2M 83
Fairoak Clo. Oxs —8D 58
Fairoak La. Oxs & Chess —8C 58
Fairoaks Airport. Chob —6A 54
Fairoaks Cvn. Pk. Guild —7D 92
Fairoaks Ct. Add —2K 55
(off Lane Clo.)
Fairs Rd. Lea —6G 79
Fairstone Ct. Horl —7F 142
Fair St. Houn —6C 10
Fairview. Eps —7H 61
Fair Vw. H'ham —5G 197
Fairview Av. Wok —5A 74
Fairview Clo. Wok —5B 74
Fairview Ct. Afrd —6B 22
Fairview Ct. Stai —7J 21
Fairview Dri. Orp —1M 67
Fairview Dri. Shep —4A 38
Fairview Gdns. Farnh —6J 109
Fairview Ho. SW2 —1K 29
Fairview Ind. Est. Oxt —2C 126
Fairview Pl. SW2 —1K 29
Fairview Rd. SW16 —9K 29
Fairview Rd. As —1F 110
Fairview Rd. Eps —7E 60
Fairview Rd. Head D —4G 169
Fairview Rd. Sutt —2B 62
Fairview Rd. Wokgm —3B 30
Fairview Ter. Head —3F 168
Fairwater Dri. New H —5M 55
Fairwater Ho. Tedd —5G 25
Fairway. SW20 —2H 43
Fairway. Cars —7A 62
Fairway. Cher —7K 37
Fairway. Copt —8M 163
Fairway. Guild —2F 114
Fairway. If'd —4J 181
Fairway. Vir W —5M 35
Fairway Clo. Copt —8L 163
Fairway Clo. Croy —4H 47
Fairway Clo. Eps —1B 60
Fairway Clo. Houn —8K 9
Fairway Clo. Wok —6L 73
Fairway Gdns. Beck —5N 47
Fairway Heights. Camb —9F 50
Fairways. Afrd —7C 22
Fairways. Hind —3N 169
Fairways. Iswth —4E 10
Fairways. Kenl —4N 83
Fairways. Tedd —8K 25
Fairways, The. Red —6B 122
Fairway, The. Camb —3E 70
Fairway, The. Farn —4F 88
Fairway, The. Farnh —5J 109
Fairway, The. G'ming —9J 133
Fairway, The. Lea —5G 79
Fairway, The. N Mald —9C 26
Fairway, The. W Mol —2B 40
Fairway, The. Wey —7B 56
Fairway, The. Worp —2F 92
Fairwell La. W Hor —6C 96
Faithfull Clo. Warf —7N 15
Fakenham Way. Owl —6J 49
Falaise. Egh —6A 20
Falaise Clo. Alder —2N 109
Falcon Clo. W4 —2B 12
Falcon Clo. Craw —1B 182
Falcon Clo. Light —7K 51
Falcon Ct. Frim —5B 70
Falcon Ct. Wok —9E 54
Falcon Dri. Stanw —9M 7
Falconhurst. Oxs —2D 78
Falcon Rd. Guild —4N 113 (4D 202)
(in two parts)
Falcon Rd. Hamp —8N 23
Falconry Ct. King T —5L 203
Falcons Clo. Big H —4F 86
Falcon Way. Felt —8J 9
Falcon Way. Sun —1F 38
Falcon Way. Yat —9A 48
Falconwood. E Hor —2G 96
Falconwood. Egh —6A 20
Falcon Wood. Lea —7F 78
Falconwood Rd. Croy —5J 65
Falcourt Clo. Sutt —2N 61
Falkland Ct. Farn —5C 90
Falkland Gdns. Dork —6G 119
Falkland Gro. Dork —6G 118
Falkland Ho. W14 —1L 13
(off Edith Vs.)
Falkland Pk. Av. SE25 —2B 46
Falkland Rd. Dork —6G 119 (4K 201)
Falklands Dri. H'ham —4A 198
Falkner Ct. Farnh —1H 129
Falkner Rd. Farnh —1G 128
Falkners Clo. Fleet —1D 88
Fallow Deer Clo. H'ham —5A 198
Fallowfield. Fleet —1D 88
Fallowfield. Yat —8A 48
Fallowfield Way. Horl —7F 142
Fallsbrook Rd. SW16 —7F 28
Falmer Clo. Craw —5B 182
Falmouth Clo. Camb —2E 70
Falmouth Rd. W on T —1K 57
Falstaff M. Hamp H —6D 24
Falstone. Wok —5L 73
Famet Av. Purl —9N 63
Famet Clo. Purl —9N 63
Famet Gdns. Kenl —9N 63
Famet Wlk. Purl —9N 63
Fanes Clo. Brack —9L 15
Fane St. W14 —2L 13
Fangrove Pk. Lyne —7C 36
Fanshawe Rd. Rich —5J 25
Fantail, The. (Junct.) —1H 67
Fanthorpe St. SW15 —6H 13
Faraday Av. E Grin —3B 186
Faraday Cen., The. Craw —9D 162
Faraday Ct. Craw —8C 162
Faraday Mans. W14 —2K 13
(off Queen's Club Gdns.)
Faraday Rd. SW19 —7M 27
Faraday Rd. Craw —8D 162
Faraday Rd. Farn —8A 70
Faraday Rd. W Mol —3A 40
Faraday Way. Croy —7K 45
Farcrosse Clo. Sand —7H 49
Farebrothers. Warn —9F 178
Fareham Dri. Yat —8A 48
Fareham Rd. Felt —1K 23
Farewell Pl. Mitc —9C 28
Farhalls Cres. H'ham —3M 197
Faringdon Clo. Sand —6H 49
Faringdon Dri. Brack —4B 32
Farington Acres. Wey —9E 38
Faris Barn Dri. Wdhm —8H 55
Faris La. Wdhm —7H 55
Farleigh. —1J 85
Farleigh Common. —1H 85
Farleigh Ct. Guild —3H 113
Farleigh Ct. S Croy —2N 63 (8B 200)
Farleigh Ct. Rd. Warl —1J 85
Farleigh Dean Cres. Croy —7L 65
Farleigh Rd. New H —7J 55
Farleigh Rd. Warl —5G 85
Farleton Clo. Wey —3E 56
Farley Copse. Brack —9K 15
Farley Ct. Farn —3B 90
Farleycroft. W'ham —4L 107
Farley Green. —3M 135
Farley Heath. —4L 135
Farley Heath Rd. Alb —7J 135
Farley La. W'ham —4K 107
Farley Nursery. W'ham —5L 107
Farley Pk. Oxt —8N 105
Farley Pl. SE25 —3D 46
Farley Rd. S Croy —4D 64
Farleys Clo. W Hor —4D 96
Farley Wood. —1J 31
Farlington Pl. SW15 —1G 26
Farlow Rd. SW15 —6J 13
Farlton Rd. SW18 —2N 27
Farm Av. SW16 —5J 29
Farm Av. H'ham —5H 197
Farm Clo. SW6 —3M 13
Farm Clo. Asc —4N 33
Farm Clo. Brack —9K 15
Farm Clo. Byfl —8A 56
Farm Clo. Coul —7D 82
Farm Clo. Craw —2E 182
Farm Clo. Crowt —9H 31
Farm Clo. E Grin —1D 186
Farm Clo. E Hor —6G 96
Farm Clo. Fet —2D 98
Farm Clo. Guild —9N 93
Farm Clo. Loxw —5J 193
Farm Clo. Lyne —5C 36
Farm Clo. Shep —6B 38
Farm Clo. Stai —6G 20
Farm Clo. Sutt —4B 62
Farm Clo. Wall —6G 63
Farm Clo. Warn —1F 196
Farm Clo. W Wick —1B 66
Farm Clo. Worp —7F 92
Farm Clo. Yat —1C 68
Farm Cotts. Wokgm —9A 14
Farm Ct. Frim —4D 70
Farmdale Rd. Cars —4C 62
Farm Dri. Croy —8J 47
Farm Dri. Fleet —1C 88
Farm Dri. Old Win —9L 5
Farm Dri. Purl —8H 63
Farmers Rd. Stai —6G 20
Farmet Ct. E Grin —7M 165
(off Halsford La.)
Farmfield Cotts. Horl —3N 161
Farmfield Dri. Charl —2N 161
Farm Fields. S Croy —7B 64
Farm Ho. Clo. Wok —2F 74
Farmhouse Rd. SW16 —8G 29
Farmington Av. Sutt —9B 44
Farm La. SW6 —2M 13
Farm La. Add —4J 55
Farm La. Asht —3N 79
Farm La. Croy —8J 47
Farm La. E Hor —6G 96
Farm La. Purl —6G 63
Farm La. Send —2E 94
Farm La. Trad. Est. SW6 —2M 13
Farmleigh Clo. Craw —1G 182
Farmleigh Gro. W on T —2G 56
Farm M. Mitc —1F 44
Farm Rd. Alder —1C 110
Farm Rd. Esh —7B 40
Farm Rd. Frim —4C 70
Farm Rd. Houn —2M 23
Farm Rd. Mord —4N 43
Farm Rd. Stai —7K 21
Farm Rd. Sutt —4B 62
Farm Rd. Warl —6H 85
Farm Rd. Wok —7D 74
Farmstead. Eps —5N 59
Farmstead Dri. Eden —9L 127
Farmview. Cobh —3L 77
Farm Vw. Lwr K —5L 101
Farm Vw. Yat —1C 68
Farm Wlk. Ash G —4G 111
Farm Wlk. Guild —5J 113
Farm Wlk. Horl —8D 142
Farm Way. Stai —9H 7
Farm Way. Wor Pk —9H 43
Farm Yd. Wind —3G 5
Farnan Rd. SW16 —6J 29
Farnborough. —2N 89
(Aldershot)
Farnborough. —2L 67
(Orpington)
Farnborough Aerospace Pk. Farn —5L 89
Farnborough Airfield. —5K 89
Farnborough Airfield. Farn —5K 89
Farnborough Av. S Croy —5G 65
Farnborough Bus. Cen. Farn —3L 89
Farnborough Comn. Orp —1H 67
Farnborough Cres. S Croy —5H 65
Farnborough Ga. Retail Pk. Farn —7A 70
Farnborough Green. —8A 70
Farnborough Hill. Orp —2M 67
Farnborough Park. —2A 90
Farnborough Rd. Alder & Farnh —4J 109
Farnborough Rd. Farn —5N 89
Farnborough Street. —1B 90
Farnborough St. Farn —8B 70
Farnborough Way. Orp —2L 67
Farncombe. —4H 133
Farncombe Hill. G'ming —4G 132
(in two parts)
Farncombe St. G'ming —4H 133
Farnell M. SW5 —1N 13
Farnell M. Wey —9C 38
Farnell Rd. Iswth —6D 10
Farnell Rd. Stai —4J 21
Farney Fld. Peasl —2E 136
Farnham. —1H 129
Farnham Bus. Cen. Farnh —9H 109
Farnham Bus. Pk. Farnh —2G 128
Farnham By-Pass. Farnh —3E 128
Farnham Castle. —9G 109
Farnham Clo. Brack —1B 32
Farnham Clo. Craw —9A 182
Farnham Ct. Sutt —3K 61
Farnham Gdns. SW20 —1G 42
Farnham La. Hasl —9E 170
Farnham Maltings. —1H 129
Farnham Mus. —1G 128
Farnham Pk. Clo. Farnh —6G 108
Farnham Pk. Dri. Farnh —6G 109
Farnham Retail Pk. Farnh —9K 109
Farnham Rd. Elst —6E 130
Farnham Rd. Ews & C Crook —3A 108
Farnham Rd. Fleet —4E 88
Farnham Rd. Guild —6G 112 (6A 202)
Farnham Rd. Holt P —1A 148
Farnham Trad. Est. Farnh —8L 109
Farnhurst La. Alf —4H 175
Farningham. Brack —5C 32
Farningham Ct. SW16 —8H 29
Farningham Cres. Cat —1D 104
Farningham Rd. Cat —1D 104
Farnley. Wok —4J 73
Farnley Rd. SE25 —3A 46
Farquhar Rd. SW19 —4M 27
Farquharson Rd. Croy —7N 45
Farrell Clo. Camb —3A 70
Farrer Ct. Twic —1K 25
Farrer's Pl. Croy —1G 64
Farrier Clo. Sun —2H 39
Farriers Clo. Eps —8D 60
Farriers Rd. Eps —8D 60
Farriers, The. Brmly —6C 134
Farrier Wlk. SW10 —2N 13
Farthing Barn La. Orp —5J 67
Farthing Fields. Head —4D 168
Farthingham La. Ewh —4F 156
Farthings. Knap —3H 73
Farthings Hill. H'ham —5F 196
Farthings, The. King T —9N 25
Farthing Street. —5H 67
Farthing St. Orp —4H 67
Farthings Wlk. H'ham —5F 196
Fassett Rd. King T —3L 41 (7K 203)
Fauconberg Ct. W4 —2B 12
(off Fauconberg Rd.)
Fauconberg Rd. W4 —2B 12
Faulkner Clo. Craw —9N 181
Faulkner Pl. Bag —3J 51
Faulkners Rd. W on T —2K 57
Favart Rd. SW6 —4M 13
Faversham Rd. Beck —1J 47
Faversham Rd. Mord —5N 43
Faversham Rd. Owl —6J 49
Fawcett Clo. SW16 —6L 29
Fawcett Rd. Croy —9N 45 (5A 200)
Fawcett Rd. Wind —4E 4
Fawcett St. SW10 —2N 13
Fawcus Clo. Clay —3E 58
Fawe Pk. Rd. SW15 —7L 13
Fawler Mead. Brack —3D 32
Fawley Clo. Cranl —8A 156
Fawns Mnr. Clo. Felt —2D 22
Fawns Mnr. Rd. Felt —2E 22
Fawsley Clo. Coln —3G 6
Fay Cotts. Fay —5D 180
Faygate. —8E 180
Faygate Bus. Cen. Fay —8E 180
Faygate La. Rusp & Fay —2D 180
Faygate La. S God —9H 125
Faygate Rd. SW2 —3K 29
Fayland Av. SW16 —6G 28
Fay Rd. H'ham —3J 197
Fearn Clo. E Hor —7F 96
Fearnley Cres. Hamp —6M 23
Featherbed La. Croy & Warl —4J 65
Feathers La. Wray —3C 20
Featherstone. Blind H —2G 145
Fee Farm Rd. Clay —4F 58
Felbridge. —6K 165
Felbridge Av. Craw —2H 183
Felbridge Cen., The. E Grin —7K 165
Felbridge Clo. SW16 —5L 29
Felbridge Clo. E Grin —7M 165
Felbridge Clo. Frim —4D 70
Felbridge Clo. Sutt —5N 61
Felbridge Ct. Felb —6K 165
Felbridge Ct. Felt —2J 23
(off High St.)
Felbridge Ct. Hayes —2E 8
Felbridge Rd. Felb —7G 164
Felcot Rd. Felb —7F 164
Felcott Clo. W on T —9K 39
Felcott Rd. W on T —9K 39
Felcourt. —2M 165
Felcourt La. Felc —2L 165
Felcourt Rd. Felc & Ling —3M 165
Felday. —6J 137
Felday Glade. Holm M —6J 137
Felday Houses. Holm M —4J 137
Felday Rd. Ab H —9G 116
Feldemore. —5K 137
Feldemore Cotts. Holm M —5K 137
Felden St. SW6 —4L 13
Feld, The. Felb —7K 165
Felgate M. W6 —1G 12
Felix Dri. W Cla —6J 95
Felix La. Shep —5F 38
Felix Rd. W on T —5H 39
Felland Way. Reig —7B 122
Fellbrook. Rich —4H 25
Fellcott Way. H'ham —7F 196
Fellmongers Yd. Croy —4B 200
Fellowes Rd. Cars —9C 44
Fellow Grn. W End —9C 52
Fellow Grn. Rd. W End —9C 52
Fellows Rd. Farn —4B 90
Fell Rd. Croy —9N 45 (4C 200)
(in two parts)
Felmingham Rd. SE20 —1F 46
Felsberg Rd. SW2 —1J 29
Felsham Rd. SW15 —6H 13
Felstead Rd. Eps —7C 60
Feltham. —3H 23
Feltham Av. E Mol —3E 40
Felthambrook Ind. Est. Felt —4J 23
Felthambrook Way. Felt —4J 23
Feltham Bus. Complex. Felt —3J 23
Felthamhill. —6G 23
Feltham Hill Rd. Afrd —6B 22
Felthamhill Rd. Felt —5H 23
Feltham Rd. Afrd —5B 22
Feltham Rd. Mitc —1D 44
Feltham Rd. Red —8D 122
Feltham Wlk. Red —8D 122
Felwater Ct. E Grin —7K 165
Fenby Clo. H'ham —4A 198
Fenchurch Rd. M'bowr —5F 182
Fencote. Brack —5B 32
Fendall Rd. Eps —2B 60
Fender Ho. H'ham —6H 197
Fenelon Pl. W14 —1L 13
Fengates Rd. Red —3C 122

Fenhurst Clo.—Folly La. S.

Fenhurst Clo. H'ham —7F 196
Fennel Clo. Croy —7G 47
Fennel Clo. Farn —1G 89
Fennel Clo. Guild —9D 94
Fennel Cres. Craw —7N 181
Fennells Mead. Eps —5E 60
Fenn Ho. Iswth —4H 11
Fennscombe Ct. W End —9B 52
Fenns La. W End —9B 52
Fenns Way. Wok —2A 74
Fenn's Yd. Farnh —1G 128
Fenton Av. Stai —7L 21
Fenton Clo. Red —3E 122
Fenton Ho. Houn —2A 10
Fenton Rd. Red —3E 122
Fentum Rd. Guild —1K 113
Fenwick Clo. Wok —5L 73
Fenwick Pl. S Croy —4M 63
Ferbies. Fleet —7B 88
Ferguson Av. Surb —4M 41 (8N 203)
Ferguson Clo. Brom —2N 47
Fermandy La. Craw D —9D 164
Fermor Dri. Alder —1L 109
Fern Av. Mitc —3H 45
Fernbank Av. W on T —6M 39
Fernbank Cres. Asc —9H 17
Fernbank M. SW12 —1F 28
Fernbank Pl. Asc —9G 17
Fernbank Rd. Add —2J 55
Fernbank Rd. Asc —2G 33
Fernbrae Clo. Rowl —8G 128
Fern Clo. Crowt —9G 30
Fern Clo. Warl —5H 85
Fern Cotts. Ab H —8F 116
Fern Ct. As —3D 110
Ferndale. Guild —1H 113
Ferndale Av. Cher —9G 36
Ferndale Av. Houn —6M 9
Ferndale Rd. SE25 —4E 46
Ferndale Rd. Afrd —6M 21
Ferndale Rd. Bans —3L 81
Ferndale Rd. C Crook —9A 88
Ferndale Rd. Wok —3B 74
Ferndale Way. Orp —2M 67
Fernden Heights. Hasl —6F 188
Fernden La. Hasl —5F 188
Fernden Ri. G'ming —4H 133
Ferndown. Craw —8H 163
Ferndown. Horl —6E 142
Ferndown Clo. Guild —4C 114
Ferndown Clo. Sutt —3B 62
Ferndown Ct. Guild —2M 113 (1B 202)
Ferndown Gdns. Cobh —9K 57
Ferndown Gdns. Farn —1K 89
Fern Dri. C Crook —7A 88
Fernery, The. Stai —6G 21
Ferney Ct. Byfl —8M 55
Ferney Meade Way. Iswth —5G 11
Ferney Rd. Byfl —8M 55
Fern Gro. Felt —1J 23
Fernham Rd. T Hth —2N 45
Fernhill. —3J 103
Fern Hill. Oxs —1D 78
Fernhill Clo. B'water —5L 69
Fernhill Clo. Brack —8L 15
Fernhill Clo. Craw D —9E 164
Fernhill Clo. Farnh —6G 109
Fernhill Clo. Wok —7M 73
Fernhill Dri. Farnh —6G 109
Fernhill Gdns. King T —6K 25
Fernhill La. B'water —5K 69
Fernhill La. Farnh —6G 109
Fernhill La. Wok —7M 73
(in two parts)
Fernhill Pk. Wok —7M 73
Fern Hill Pl. Orp —2L 67
Fernhill Rd. B'water & Farn —4K 69
Fernhill Rd. Horl —3H 163
Fernhill Wlk. B'water —5L 69
Fernhurst. —9F 188
Fernhurst Clo. Craw —1N 181
Fernhurst Rd. SW6 —4K 13
Fernhurst Rd. Afrd —5D 22
Fernhurst Rd. Croy —6E 46
Ferniehurst. Camb —2D 70
Fernihough Clo. Wey —6B 56
Fernlands Clo. Cher —9G 37
Fern La. Houn —1N 9
Fernlea. Bookh —2B 98
Fernlea Rd. SW12 —2F 28
Fernlea Rd. Mitc —1E 44
Fernleigh Clo. Croy —1L 63
Fernleigh Clo. W on T —9J 39
Fernleigh Ri. Deep —7G 71
Fernley Ho. G'ming —3H 133
Fern Rd. G'ming —5J 133
Ferns Clo. S Croy —6E 64
Fernshaw Clo. SW10 —2N 13
Fernshaw Rd. SW10 —2N 13
Fernside Av. Felt —5J 23
Fernside Rd. SW12 —2D 28
Ferns Mead. Farnh —2F 128
Ferns, The. Farnh —5H 109
Fernthorpe Rd. SW16 —7G 28
Fern Towers. Cat —3D 104
Fern Wlk. Afrd —6M 21
Fern Way. H'ham —3K 197
Fernwood. Croy —5H 65
Fernwood Av. SW16 —5H 29
Feroners Clo. Craw —5E 182
Feroners Ct. Craw —5E 182
(off Feroners Clo.)
Ferrard Clo. Asc —9H 17
Ferraro Clo. Houn —2A 10
Ferrers Av. Wall —1H 63
Ferrers Rd. SW16 —6H 29
Ferrier Ind. Est. SW18 —7N 13
(off Ferrier St.)
Ferrier St. SW18 —7N 13
Ferriers Way. Eps —5H 81
Ferring Clo. Craw —2N 181
Ferris Av. Croy —9J 47
Ferry Av. Stai —8G 21
Ferry La. SW13 —2E 12
Ferry La. Bren —2L 11
Ferry La. Cher —4J 37
(in two parts)
Ferry La. Guild —7M 113
Ferry La. Rich —2M 11
Ferry La. Shep —7B 38
Ferry La. Wray —3D 20
Ferrymoor. Rich —4H 25
Ferry Quays. Bren —3K 11
(in two parts)
Ferry Rd. SW13 —3F 12
Ferry Rd. Tedd —6H 25
Ferry Rd. Th Dit —5H 41
Ferry Rd. Twic —2H 25
Ferry Rd. W Mol —2A 40
Ferry Sq. Bren —3L 11
Ferry Sq. Shep —6C 38
Festing Rd. SW15 —6J 13
Festival Ct. M'bowr —5G 183
Festival Wlk. Cars —2D 62
Fetcham. —1D 98
Fetcham Comn. La. Fet —9D 78
Fetcham Downs. —4D 98
Fetcham Pk. Dri. Fet —1E 98
Fettes Rd. Cranl —7B 156
Fickleshole. —1N 85
Fiddicroft Av. Bans —1N 81
Fiddlers Copse. Fern —9E 188
Field Clo. Chess —2J 59
Field Clo. Guild —1F 114
Field Clo. Hayes —3D 8
Field Clo. Houn —4J 9
Field Clo. S Croy —1E 84
Field Clo. W Mol —4B 40
Fieldcommon. —6N 39
Fieldcommon La. W on T —7M 39
Field Ct. SW19 —4M 27
Field Ct. Oxt —5A 100
Field Dri. Eden —9M 127
Field End. Coul —1H 83
Field End. Farnh —8L 109
Fieldend. H'ham —3A 198
Field End. Twic —5F 24
Field End. W End —9C 52
Fieldend Rd. SW16 —9G 29
Fielden Pl. Brack —1B 32
Fielders Grn. Guild —3C 114
Fieldfare Av. Yat —9A 48
Fieldgate La. Mitc —1C 44
Field Ho. Clo. Asc —7L 33
Fieldhouse Rd. SW12 —2G 29
Fieldhouse Vs. Bans —2C 82
Fieldhurst. Slou —1B 6
Fieldhurst Clo. Add —2K 55
Fielding Av. Twic —4C 24
Fielding Gdns. Crowt —3G 48
Fielding Ho. W4 —2D 12
(off Devonshire Rd.)
Fielding M. SW13 —2G 12
(off Jenner Pl.)
Fielding Rd. Coll T —9K 49
Fieldings, The. Bans —4L 81
Fieldings, The. Horl —7F 142
Fieldings, The. Wok —3J 73
Field La. Bren —3J 11
Field La. Frim —5D 70
(in three parts)
Field La. G'ming —4J 133
Field La. Tedd —6G 24
Field Pk. Brack —9B 16
Field Path. Farn —5L 69
Field Place. —3D 196
Field Pl. G'ming —4H 133
Field Pl. N Mald —5E 42
Field Pl. Cotts. Broad H —3D 196
Field Rd. W6 —1K 13
Field Rd. Farn —5L 69
Field Rd. Felt —9J 9
Fieldsend Rd. Sutt —2K 61
Fieldside Clo. Orp —1L 67
Field Stores App. Alder —1A 110
Fieldview. SW18 —2B 28
Field Vw. Egh —6E 20
Field Vw. Felt —5E 22
Fieldview. Horl —7F 142
Fld. View Cotts. G'ming —7E 132
Field Wlk. Horl —9D 142
(off Ct. Lodge Rd.)
Field Wlk. Small —7N 143
Field Way. Alder —1C 110
Fieldway. Hasl —1G 189
Fieldway. New Ad —4L 65
Field Way. Rip —3H 95
Field Way. Tong —5D 110
Fifehead Clo. Afrd —7N 21
Fife Rd. SW14 —8B 12
Fife Rd. King T —1L 41 (3K 203)
(in two parts)
Fife Way. Bookh —3A 98
Fifield La. Fren —9H 129
Fifth Cross Rd. Twic —3D 24
Figges Rd. Mitc —8E 28
Filbert Cres. Craw —3M 181
Filby Rd. Chess —3M 59
Filey Clo. Big H —6D 86
Filey Clo. Craw —5L 181
Filey Clo. Sutt —4A 62
Filmer Gro. G'ming —6H 133
Filmer Rd. SW6 —4K 13
Filmer Rd. Wind —5A 4
Finborough Ho. SW10 —2N 13
(off Fawcett St.)
Finborough Rd. SW10 —1N 13
Finborough Rd. SW17 —7D 28
Finborough Theatre, The. —2N 13
(off Finborough Rd.)
Fincham End Dri. Crowt —3E 48
Finchampstead Ridges. —4A 48
Finchampstead Rd. Finch & Wokgm —8A 30
Finch Av. SE27 —5N 29
Finch Clo. Knap —4F 72
Finch Cres. Turn H —4F 184
Finchdean Ho. SW15 —1E 26
Finch Dri. Felt —1L 23
Finches Ri. Guild —1D 114
Finch Rd. Guild —3N 113 (3D 202)
Findhorn Clo. Coll T —8J 49
Findings, The. Farn —6K 69
Findlay Dri. Guild —8J 93
Findon Clo. SW18 —9M 13
Findon Ct. Add —2H 55
Findon Rd. Craw —1N 181
Findon Way. Broad H —5D 196
Finlay Gdns. Add —1L 55
Finlays Clo. Chess —2N 59
Finlay St. SW6 —4J 13
Finmere. Brack —6A 32
Finnart Clo. Wey —1D 56
Finnart Ho. Dri. Wey —1D 56
Finney Dri. W'sham —3A 52
Finney La. Iswth —4G 11
Finsbury Clo. Craw —7A 182
Finstock Grn. Brack —3D 32
Fintry Pl. Farn —7K 69
Fintry Wlk. Farn —7K 69
Fiona Clo. Bookh —2A 98
Fir Acre Rd. Ash V —7D 90
Firbank Dri. Wok —6L 73
Firbank La. Wok —6L 73
Firbank Pl. Eng G —7L 19
Firbank Way. E Grin —9N 165
Fir Clo. Fleet —5A 88
Fir Clo. W on T —6H 39
Fircroft. Fleet —4A 88
Fircroft Clo. Wok —5B 74
Fircroft Ct. Wok —5B 74
Fircroft Rd. SW17 —3D 28
Fircroft Rd. Chess —1M 59
Fircroft Way. Eden —9L 127
Fir Dene. Orp —1H 67
Firdene. Surb —7B 42
Fir Dri. B'water —3J 69
Fireball Hill. Asc —6A 34
Fire Bell La. Surb —5L 41
Firefly Clo. Wall —4J 63
Fire Sta. M. Beck —1K 47
Fire Sta. Rd. Alder —1N 109
Fire Thorn Clo. Fleet —6B 88
Firfield Rd. Add —1J 55
Firfield Rd. Farnh —4F 128
Firfields. Wey —3C 56
Firglen Dri. Yat —8C 48
Fir Grange Av. Wey —2C 56
Fir Gro. N Mald —5E 42
Firgrove. Wok —6L 73
Firgrove Ct. Farn —1N 89
Firgrove Ct. Farnh —2G 129
Firgrove Hill. Farnh —2H 129
Firgrove Pde. Farn —1N 89
Firgrove Rd. Evo & Yate —9A 48
Firgrove Rd. Farn —1N 89
Firlands. Brack —4A 32
Firlands. Horl —7F 142
Firlands. Wey —3F 56
Firlands Av. Camb —1B 70
Firle Clo. Craw —1C 182
Firle Ct. Eps —8E 60
Fir Rd. Felt —6L 23
Fir Rd. Sutt —7L 43
Firs Av. SW14 —7B 12
Firs Av. Brmly —5C 134
Firs Av. Wind —6C 4
Firsby Av. Croy —7G 47
Firs Clo. Clay —3E 58
Firs Clo. Dork —7G 119
Firs Clo. Farn —3A 90
Firs Clo. Mitc —9F 28
Firs Dene Clo. Ott —3F 54
Firs Dri. Houn —3J 9
Firs La. Sham G —7F 134
Firs Rd. Kenl —2M 83
First Av. SW14 —6D 12
First Av. Eps —5D 60
First Av. Tad —3K 101
(off Holly Lodge Mobile Home Pk.)
First Av. W on T —5J 39
First Av. W Mol —3N 39
First Clo. W Mol —2C 40
First Cross Rd. Twic —3E 24
Firs, The. Bisl —3D 72
Firs, The. Bookh —2C 98
Firs, The. Brack —4D 32
Firs, The. Byfl —8M 55
Firs, The. Cat —9A 84
Firs, The. Guild —7L 113
First Quarter Ind. Pk. Eps —7D 60
First Slip. Lea —5G 79
Firstway. SW20 —1H 43
Firsway. Guild —2J 113
Firswood Av. Eps —2D 60
Firth Gdns. SW6 —4K 13
Fir Tree All. Alder —2M 109
(off Victoria Rd.)
Fir Tree Av. Hasl —2B 188
Firtree Av. Mitc —1E 44
Firtree Clo. SW16 —6G 29
Fir Tree Clo. Asc —6L 33
Fir Tree Clo. Craw —9N 161
Fir Tree Clo. Eps —2H 81
Fir Tree Clo. Esh —2C 58
Firtree Clo. Ewe —1E 60
Fir Tree Clo. Lea —1J 99
Firtree Clo. Sand —6E 48
Firtree Gdns. Croy —1K 65
Fir Tree Gro. Cars —4D 62
Fir Tree Pl. Afrd —6D 22
Fir Tree Rd. Bans —1H 81
Fir Tree Rd. Eps —3G 80
Fir Tree Rd. Guild —9M 93
Fir Tree Rd. Houn —7M 9
Fir Tree Rd. Lea —1J 99
Fir Tree Wlk. Reig —3B 122
Fir Tree Way. Fleet —5C 88
Fir Wlk. Sutt —3J 61
Firway. Gray —4K 169
Firwood Clo. Wok —6H 73
Firwood Dri. Camb —1A 70
Firwood Rd. Vir W —5H 35
Fisher Clo. Craw —5C 182
Fisher Clo. Croy —7C 46
Fisher Clo. W on T —1J 57
Fisher Grn. Binf —7G 15
Fisher La. C'fold & Duns —1G 191
Fisherman Clo. Rich —5H 25
Fisherman's Pl. W4 —2E 12
Fishermen's Clo. Alder —8C 90
Fisher Rowe Clo. Brmly —5C 134
Fishers. Horl —7G 142
Fisher's Clo. SW16 —4H 29
Fishers Ct. H'ham —4J 197
Fishers Dene. Clay —4G 58
Fisher's La. W4 —1C 12
Fisherstreet. —5C 190
Fisher St. C'fold —4C 190
Fishers Wood. Asc —7F 34
Fishponds Clo. Wokgm —4A 30
Fishponds Rd. SW17 —5C 28
Fishponds Rd. Kes —2F 66
Fishponds Rd. Wokgm —4A 30
Fiske Ct. Yat —9D 48
Fitchet Clo. Craw —1N 181
Fitzalan Ho. Ewe —6E 60
Fitzalan Rd. Clay —4E 58
Fitzalan Rd. H'ham —4N 197
Fitzgeorge Av. W14 —1K 13
Fitzgeorge Av. N Mald —9C 26
Fitzgerald Av. SW14 —6D 12
Fitzgerald Rd. SW14 —6C 12
Fitzgerald Rd. Th Dit —5G 40
Fitzhugh Gro. SW18 —1B 28
Fitzjames Av. W14 —1K 13
Fitzjames Av. Croy —8D 46
Fitzjohn Clo. Guild —9E 94
Fitzrobert Pl. Egh —7C 20
Fitzroy Clo. Brack —5M 31
Fitzroy Ct. Croy —6A 46
Fitzroy Cres. W4 —3C 12
Fitzwilliam Av. Rich —5M 11
Fitzwilliam Ho. Rich —7K 11
Fitzwygram Clo. Hamp H —6C 24
Fiveacre Clo. T Hth —5L 45
Five Acres. Craw —1C 182
Five Acres Clo. Lind —4A 168
Five Elms Rd. Brom —1F 66
Five Oaks. Add —3H 55
Five Oaks Clo. Wok —6G 73
Five Oaks Rd. Slin —9J 195
Five Ways Bus. Cen. Felt —4J 23
Fiveways Corner. (Junct.) —1K 63
Flag Clo. Croy —7G 47
Flambard Way. G'ming —7G 133
Flamborough Clo. Big H —6D 86
Flamsteed Heights. Craw —8N 181
Flanchford Rd. Leigh —9E 120
Flanchford Rd. Reig —5H 121
Flanders Ct. Egh —6E 20
Flanders Cres. SW17 —8D 28
Flats, The. B'water —2G 69
Flaxley Rd. Mord —5N 43
Flaxman Ho. W4 —1D 12
(off Devonshire St.)
Flaxmore Pl. Beck —5N 47
Fleece Rd. Surb —7J 41
Fleet. —4A 88
Fleet Bus. Pk. C Crook —9C 88
Fleet Clo. W Mol —4N 39
Fleet La. W Mol —5N 39
Fleet Rd. Alder —6F 88
Fleet Rd. Fleet —5A 88
Fleet Rd. Fleet & Farn —2E 88
Fleetside. W Mol —4N 39
Fleetway. Egh —2E 36
Fleetwood Clo. Chess —4K 59
Fleetwood Clo. Croy —9C 46
Fleetwood Clo. Tad —7J 81
Fleetwood Ct. Stanw —9M 7
Fleetwood Ct. W Byf —9J 55
Fleetwood Rd. King T —2A 42
Fleetwood Sq. King T —2A 42
Fleming Cen., The. Craw —8C 162
Fleming Clo. Farn —8B 70
Fleming Ct. Croy —2L 63
Fleming Mead. Mitc —8C 28
Fleming Wlk. E Grin —3B 186
Fleming Way. Craw —8C 162
Fleming Way. Iswth —7F 10
Fleming Way Ind. Cen. Craw —7D 162
Flemish Fields. Cher —6J 37
Fletcher Clo. Craw —5C 182
Fletcher Clo. Ott —3G 54
Fletcher Gdns. Brack —9J 15
Fletcher Rd. Ott —3F 54
Fletchers Clo. H'ham —7L 197
Fleur Gates. SW19 —1J 27
Flexford. —3M 111
Flexford Grn. Brack —5K 31
Flexford Rd. Norm —4M 111
(in two parts)
Flexlands La. W End —6E 52
Flint Clo. Bans —1N 81
Flint Clo. Bookh —4C 98
Flint Clo. G Str —3N 67
Flint Clo. M'bowr —6F 182
Flint Clo. Red —2D 122
Flint Cotts. Lea —8H 79
(off Gravel Hill)
Flintgrove. Brack —9B 16
Flint Hill. Dork —7H 119
Flint Hill Clo. Dork —8H 119
Flintlock Clo. Stai —7J 7
Flitwick Grange. Milf —1C 152
Flock Mill Pl. SW18 —2N 27
Flood La. Twic —2G 25
Flora Gdns. Croy —7M 65
Floral Ct. Asht —5J 79
Floral Ho. Cher —7H 37
(off Fox La. S.)
Florence Av. Mord —4A 44
Florence Av. New H —7J 55
Florence Clo. W on T —6J 39
Florence Clo. Yat —9B 48
Florence Ct. SW19 —7K 27
Florence Ct. Knap —5F 72
Florence Gdns. W4 —2B 12
Florence Gdns. Stai —8K 21
Florence Ho. King T —1N 203
Florence Rd. Coll T —8J 49
Florence Rd. SW19 —7N 27
Florence Rd. Beck —1H 47
Florence Rd. Felt —2J 23
Florence Rd. Fleet —7B 88
Florence Rd. King T —8M 25 (1N 203)
Florence Rd. S Croy —5A 64
Florence Rd. W on T —6J 39
Florence Ter. SW15 —4D 26
Florence Way. SW12 —2D 28
Florence Way. Knap —5F 72
Florian Av. Sutt —1B 62
Florian Rd. SW15 —7K 13
Florida Ct. Stai —5J 21
Florida Rd. Shalf —9A 114
Florida Rd. T Hth —9M 29
Floss St. SW15 —5H 13
Flower Cres. Ott —3D 54
Flower La. God —8G 105
Flowersmead. SW17 —3E 28
Flower Wlk. Guild —6M 113 (8B 202)
Floyd's La. Wok —3J 75
Flyers Way, The. W'ham —4M 107
Foden Rd. Alder —3M 109
Folder's La. Brack —8A 16
Foley M. Clay —3E 58
Foley Rd. Big H —5F 86
Foley Rd. Clay —4E 58
Folkestone Ct. Slou —1C 6
Follett Clo. Old Win —9L 5
Folly Clo. Fleet —6B 88
Follyfield Rd. Bans —1M 81
Follyhatch La. As —1J 111
Folly Hill. Farnh —6F 108
Folly La. Holmw —4H 139
Folly La. N. Farnh —5G 108
Folly La. S. Farnh —6F 108

Fuchsia Pl.—Gilham La.

Fuchsia Pl. Brack —1B 32
Fuchsia Way. W End —9B 52
Fugelmere Rd. Fleet —3D 88
Fugelmere Wlk. Fleet —3D 88
Fulbourn. King T —4N 203
Fulbourne Clo. Red —1C 122
Fulbrook Av. New H —7J 55
Fulford Ho. Eps —4C 60
Fulford Rd. Cat —8A 84
Fulford Rd. Eps —4C 60
Fulfords Hill. Itch —9A 196
Fulfords Rd. Itch —9B 196
Fulham. —5K 13
Fulham Broadway. (Junct.) —3M 13
Fulham B'way. SW6 —3M 13
Fulham Clo. Craw —7N 181
Fulham Ct. SW6 —4M 13
Fulham F.C. —4J 13
Fulham High St. SW6 —5K 13
Fulham Pal. Rd. W6 & SW6 —1H 13
Fulham Pk. Gdns. SW6 —5L 13
Fulham Pk. Rd. SW6 —5L 13
Fulham Rd. SW6 —5K 13
Fulham Rd. SW10 & SW3 —3N 13
Fullbrook La. Elst —6G 130
Fullbrooks Av. Wor Pk —7E 42
Fullers Av. Surb —8M 41
Fullers Farm Rd. W Hor —2B 116
Fuller's Griffin Brewery & Vis. Cen. —2E 12
Fullers Hill. W'ham —4M 107
Fullers Rd. Rowl —7B 128
Fullers Va. Head —4E 168
Fullers Way N. Surb —5M 41
Fullers Way S. Chess —1L 59
Fuller's Wood. Croy —2K 65
Fullers Wood La. S Nut —4G 123
Fullerton Clo. Byfl —1A 76
Fullerton Ct. Tedd —7G 25
Fullerton Dri. Byfl —1N 75
Fullerton Rd. SW18 —8N 13
Fullerton Rd. Byfl —1N 75
Fullerton Rd. Cars —5C 62
Fullerton Rd. Croy —6C 46
Fullerton Way. Byfl —1N 75
Fuller Way. Hayes —1G 8
Fullmer Way. Wdhm —6H 55
Fulmar Clo. If'd —4J 181
Fulmar Ct. Surb —5M 41
Fulmar Dri. E Grin —7C 166
Fulmead St. SW6 —4N 13
Fulmer Clo. Hamp —6M 23
Fulstone Clo. Houn —7N 9
Fulvens. Peasl —2F 136
Fulwell. —5D 24
Fulwell Pk. Av. Twic —3D 24
Fulwell Rd. Tedd —5D 24
Fulwood Gdns. Twic —9F 10
Fulwood Wlk. SW19 —2K 27
Furlong Clo. Wall —7F 44
Furlong Rd. Westc —6C 118
Furlong Way. Gat A —2D 162
(off Gatwick Way)
Furlough, The. Wok —3C 74
Furmage St. SW18 —1N 27
Furnace Dri. Craw —5D 182
Furnace Farm Rd. Craw —5E 182
Furnace Green. —5E 182
Furnace Pde. Craw —5E 182
Furnace Pl. Craw —5E 182
Furnace Rd. Felb —7E 164
Furnace Wood. —6F 164
Furneaux Av. SE27 —6M 29
Furness. Wind —5A 4
Furness Pl. Wind —5A 4
Furness Rd. SW6 —5N 13
Furness Rd. Mord —5N 43
Furness Row. Wind —5A 4
Furness Sq. Wind —5A 4
Furness Wlk. Wind —5A 4
(off Furnace Sq.)
Furness Way. Wind —5A 4
Furniss Ct. Cranl —8H 155
Furnival Clo. Vir W —5N 35
Furrows Pl. Cat —1C 104
Furrows, The. W on T —8K 39
Furse Clo. Camb —2G 70
Furtherfield. Cranl —6N 155
Furtherfield Clo. Croy —5L 45
Further Vell-Mead. C Crook —9A 88
Furzebank. Asc —3A 34
Furze Clo. Ash V —5E 90
Furze Clo. Horl —8H 143
Furze Clo. Red —2D 122
Furzedown. —6F 28
Furzedown Clo. Egh —7A 20
Furzedown Dri. SW17 —6F 28
Furzedown Rd. SW17 —6F 28
Furzedown Rd. Sutt —7A 62
Furzefield. Craw —2N 181
Furze Fld. Oxs —9D 58
Furzefield Chase. Dor P —4A 166
Furzefield Cres. Reig —5A 122
Furzefield Rd. E Grin —9N 165
Furzefield Rd. H'ham —3A 198
Furzefield Rd. Reig —5A 122
Furze Gro. Tad —8L 81
Furze Hill. —8L 81
Furze Hill. Farnh —9B 110
Furze Hill. Kgswd —7L 81
Furze Hill. Purl —7J 63
Furze Hill. Red —2C 122
Furzehill Cotts. Pirb —9N 71
Furze Hill Cres. Crowt —3H 49
Furze Hill Rd. Head D —5G 168
(in two parts)
Furze La. E Grin —6L 165
Furze La. G'ming —3J 133
Furze La. Purl —7J 63
Furzemoors. Brack —4N 31
Furzen La. Rud & Oke H —6H 177
Furze Rd. Add —3H 55
Furze Rd. Rud —9E 176
Furze Rd. T Hth —2N 45
Furze Va. Rd. Head D —5G 169
Furze Vw. Slin —9J 195
Furzewood. Sun —9H 23
Fuzzens Wlk. Wind —5B 4
Fydler's Clo. Wink —7M 17
Fyfield Clo. B'water —1J 69
Fyfield Clo. Brom —3N 47

Gable Ct. Red —2E 122
(off St Anne's Mt.)
Gable End. Farn —1N 89
Gables. Gray —6B 170
Gables Av. Afrd —6A 22
Gables Clo. Ash V —8E 90
Gables Clo. Dat —2K 5
Gables Clo. Farn —1M 89
Gables Clo. Kingf —7B 74
(in two parts)
Gables Ct. Kingf —7B 74
Gables Rd. C Crook —9A 88
Gables, The. Bans —4L 81
Gables, The. Copt —7M 163
Gables, The. Horl —9E 142
Gables, The. H'ham —4K 197
Gables, The. Oxs —8C 58
Gables Way. Bans —4L 81
Gabriel Clo. Felt —5M 23
Gabriel Dri. Camb —2F 70
Gabriel Rd. M'bowr —7G 183
Gadbridge La. Ewh —6F 156
Gadbrook Rd. Bet —9B 120
Gadd Clo. Wokgm —1E 30
Gadesden Rd. Eps —3B 60
(in two parts)
Gaffney Clo. Alder —6B 90
Gage Clo. Craw D —9F 164
Gage Ridge. F Row —7G 187
Gaggle Wood. Man H —9B 198
Gainsborough. Brack —5A 32
Gainsborough Clo. Camb —9D 50
Gainsborough Clo. Esh —7E 40
Gainsborough Clo. Farn —3B 90
Gainsborough Ct. W4 —1A 12
(off Chaseley Dri.)
Gainsborough Ct. Fleet —4D 88
Gainsborough Ct. W on T —1H 57
Gainsborough Dri. Asc —2H 33
Gainsborough Dri. S Croy —9D 64
Gainsborough Gdns. Iswth —8D 10
Gainsborough Mans. W14 —2K 13
(off Queen's Club Gdns.)
Gainsborough Rd. Craw —7D 182
Gainsborough Rd. Eps —6B 60
Gainsborough Rd. N Mald —5C 42
Gainsborough Rd. Rich —5M 11
Gainsborough Ter. Sutt —4L 61
(off Belmont Ri.)
Gaist Av. Cat —9E 84
Galahad Rd. If'd —3K 181
Galata Rd. SW13 —3F 12
Galba Ct. Bren —3K 11
Gale Barracks. Alder —9N 89
(off Alison's Rd.)
Gale Clo. Hamp —7M 23
Gale Clo. Mitc —2B 44
Gale Cres. Bans —4M 81
Gale Dri. Light —6L 51
Galena Ho. W6 —1G 12
(off Galena Rd.)
Galena Rd. W6 —1G 13
Galen Clo. Eps —7N 59
Galesbury Rd. SW18 —9N 13 & 1A 28
Gales Clo. Guild —9F 94
Gales Dri. Craw —3D 182
Gales Pl. Craw —3E 182
Galgate Clo. SW19 —2J 27
Galleries, The. Alder —2M 109
(off High St.)
Gallery Ct. SW10 —2N 13
Gallery Rd. Brkwd —6A 72
Galleymead Rd. Coln —4H 7
Gallop, The. S Croy —4E 64
Gallop, The. Sutt —5B 62
Gallop, The. Wind —1F 18
Gallop, The. Yat —8C 48
Galloway Clo. Fleet —1D 88
Galloway Path. Croy —1A 64 (7D 200)
Gallwey Rd. Alder —1N 109
(in two parts)
Gally Hill Rd. C Crook —8A 88
Gallys Rd. Wind —5A 4
Galpin's Rd. T Hth —4J 45
Galsworthy Rd. Cher —6J 37
Galsworthy Rd. King T —8A 26
Galton Rd. Asc —5C 34
Galvani Way. Croy —7K 45
Galveston Rd. SW15 —8L 13
Galvins Clo. Guild —9K 93
Galway Rd. Yat —2B 68
Gambles La. Rip —2L 95
Gambole Rd. SW17 —5C 28
Gamlen Rd. SW15 —7J 13
Gander Grn. Cres. Hamp —9A 24
Gander Grn. La. Sutt —8K 43
Gangers Hill. God & Wold —6H 105
Ganghill. Guild —1C 114
Ganymede Ct. Craw —6K 181
Gapemouth Rd. Pirb —9H 71
Gap Rd. SW19 —6M 27
Garbetts Way. Tong —6D 110
Garbrand Wlk. Eps —3E 60
Garden Av. Mitc —8F 28
Garden Clo. SW15 —1H 27
Garden Clo. Add —1M 55
Garden Clo. Afrd —7D 22
Garden Clo. Bans —2M 81
Garden Clo. E Grin —2B 186
Garden Clo. Farn —2K 89
Garden Clo. Hamp —6N 23
Garden Clo. Lea —2J 99
Garden Clo. Sham G —7F 134
Garden Clo. Wall —2J 63
Garden Ct. Croy —8C 46
Garden Ct. Hamp —6N 23
Garden Ct. Rich —4M 11
Gardener Gro. Felt —3N 23
Gardeners Clo. Warn —9E 178
Gardeners Ct. H'ham —7K 197
Gardeners Green. —6D 30
Gardeners Grn. Rusp —3B 180
Gardener's Hill Rd. Wrec —6G 128
Gardeners Rd. Croy —7M 45 (1A 200)
Gardeners Rd. Wink R —7E 16
Gardener's Wlk. Bookh —4B 98
Gardenfields. Tad —8K 81
Garden Ho. La. E Grin —2B 186
Gardenia Dri. W End —9C 52
Garden La. SW2 —2K 29
Garden Pl. H'ham —4J 197
Garden Rd. SE20 —1F 46
Garden Rd. Rich —6N 11
Garden Rd. W on T —5J 39
Gardens, The. Beck —1M 47
Gardens, The. Cobh —6D 76
Gardens, The. Esh —1A 58
Gardens, The. Felt —8E 8
Gardens, The. Pirb —9C 72
Gardens, The. Tong —5D 110
Garden Wlk. Beck —1J 47
Garden Wlk. Coul —1E 102
Garden Wlk. Craw —3A 182
Garden Wlk. H'ham —4J 197
Garden Wood Rd. E Grin —9L 165
Gardiner Ct. S Croy —3N 63
Gardner Ho. Felt —3A 24
Gardner La. Craw D —1D 184
Gardner Rd. Guild —3N 113 (2C 202)
Garendon Gdns. Mord —6N 43
Garendon Rd. Mord —6N 43
Gareth Clo. Wor Pk —8J 43
Gareth Ct. SW16 —4H 29
Garfield Pl. Wind —5G 4
Garfield Rd. SW19 —6A 28
Garfield Rd. Add —2L 55
Garfield Rd. Camb —1A 70
Garfield Rd. Twic —2G 25
Garibaldi Rd. Red —4D 122
Garland Rd. E Grin —8N 165
Garlands Ct. Croy —6E 200
Garlands Rd. Lea —8H 79
Garlands Rd. Red —4D 122
Garland Way. Cat —9A 84
Garlichill Rd. Eps —4G 81
Garnet Fld. Yat —1A 68
Garnet Rd. T Hth —3N 45
Garrad's Rd. SW16 —4H 29
Garrard Rd. Bans —3M 81
Garratt Clo. Croy —1J 63
Garratt Ct. SW18 —1N 27
Garratt La. SW18 & SW17 —9N 13
Garratts La. Bans —3L 81
Garratt Ter. SW17 —5C 28
Garrett Clo. M'bowr —5G 183
Garrick Clo. Rich —8K 11
Garrick Clo. Stai —9J 21
Garrick Clo. W on T —1J 57
Garrick Cres. Croy —8B 46 (3F 200)
Garrick Gdns. W Mol —2A 40
Garrick Ho. W4 —2D 12
Garrick Ho. King T —8K 203
Garrick Rd. Rich —5N 11
Garricks Ho. King T —4J 203
Garrick Wlk. Craw —6C 182
Garrick Way. Frim G —7C 70
Garrison Clo. Houn —8N 9
Garrison La. Chess —4K 59
Garrones, The. Craw —2H 183
Garsdale Ter. W14 —1L 13
(off Aisgill Av.)
Garside Clo. Dork —7K 119
Garside Clo. Hamp —7D 24
Garson Clo. Esh —2N 57
Garson La. Wray —1N 19
Garson's La. Warf —2E 16
Garston Gdns. Kenl —2A 84
Garston La. Kenl —1A 84
Garstons, The. Bookh —3A 98
Garswood. Brack —5A 32
Garth Clo. W4 —1C 12
Garth Clo. Farnh —4F 128
Garth Clo. King T —6M 25
Garth Clo. Mord —9J 43
Garth Ct. W4 —1C 12
Garth Ct. Dork —7H 119
Garth Hunt Cotts. Brack —7N 15
Garth Rd. W4 —1C 12
Garth Rd. King T —6M 25
Garth Rd. Mord —5H 43
Garth Rd. Ind. Est. Mord —7J 43
Garthside. Ham —6L 25
Garth Sq. Brack —8N 15
Garth, The. As —3D 110
Garth, The. Cobh —9M 57
Garth, The. Farn —1B 90
Garth, The. Hamp —7B 24
Gartmoor Gdns. SW19 —2L 27
Garton Clo. If'd —4K 181
Garton Pl. SW18 —9N 13 & 1A 28
Gascoigne Rd. New Ad —8M 65
Gascoigne Rd. Wey —9C 38
Gasden Copse. Witl —5A 152
Gasden Dri. Witl —4A 152
Gasden La. Witl —4A 152
Gaskarth Rd. SW12 —1F 28
Gaskyns Clo. Rud —1E 194
Gassiot Rd. SW17 —5D 28
Gassiot Way. Sutt —9B 44
Gasson Wood Rd. Craw —5K 181
Gastein Rd. W6 —2J 13
Gaston Bell Clo. Rich —6M 11
Gaston Bri. Rd. Shep —5E 38
Gaston Rd. Mitc —2E 44
Gaston Way. Shep —4E 38
Gate Cen., The. Bren —3G 11
Gateford Dri. H'ham —2M 197
Gatehouse Clo. King T —8B 26
Gatehouse Clo. Wind —7E 4
Gates Clo. M'bowr —7G 182
Gatesden Clo. Fet —1C 98
Gatesden Rd. Fet —9C 78
Gates Grn. Rd. W Wick & Kes —1B 66
Gateside Rd. SW17 —4D 28
Gate St. Brmly —1C 154
(in two parts)
Gateway. Wey —9C 38
Gateways. Guild —3C 114
Gateways. Surb —8L 203
Gateways Ct. Wall —2F 62
Gateways, The. Rich —7K 11
(off Park La.)
Gateway, The. Wok —1D 74
Gatfield Gro. Felt —3A 24
Gatfield Ho. Felt —3N 23
Gatley Av. Eps —2A 60
Gatley Dri. Guild —9B 94
Gatton. —6D 102
Gatton Bottom. —4F 102
Gatton Bottom. Reig —8A 102
Gatton Clo. Reig —9A 102
Gatton Clo. Sutt —5N 61
Gatton Pk. Bus. Cen. Red —7F 102
Gatton Pk. Ct. Red —9D 102
Gatton Pk. Rd. Reig —1B 122
Gatton Rd. SW17 —5C 28
Gatton Rd. Reig —1A 122
Gatwick. —5K 131
Gatwick Airport Spectator Gallery. —3E 162
Gatwick Bus. Pk. Gat A —6F 162
Gatwick Ga. Low H —5C 162
Gatwick Ga. Ind. Est. Low H —5C 162
Gatwick International Distribution Cen. Craw —6F 162
Gatwick Metro Cen. Horl —8F 142
Gatwick Rd. SW18 —1L 27
Gatwick Rd. Craw —9F 162
Gatwick Way. Gat A —2D 162
Gatwick Zoo & Aviaries. —4H 161
Gauntlet Cres. Kenl —7A 84
Gauntlett Rd. Sutt —2B 62
Gavell Rd. Cobh —9H 57
Gaveston Clo. Byfl —9A 56
Gaveston Rd. Lea —7G 78
Gavina Clo. Mord —4C 44
Gayfere Rd. Eps —2F 60
Gayhouse La. Out —3A 144
Gayler Clo. Blet —2C 124
Gaynesford Rd. Cars —4D 62
Gay St. SW15 —6J 13
Gayton Clo. Asht —5L 79
Gayton Ct. Reig —2M 121
Gayville Rd. SW11 —1D 28
Gaywood Clo. SW2 —2K 29
Gaywood Rd. Asht —5M 79
Geary Clo. Small —1M 163
Geffers Ride. Asc —1J 33
Gemini Clo. Craw —5K 181
Genesis Bus. Cen. H'ham —5M 197
Genesis Bus. Pk. Wok —2E 74
Genesis Clo. Stanw —2A 22
Geneva Clo. Shep —1F 38
Geneva Rd. King T —3L 41 (8L 203)
Geneva Rd. T Hth —4N 45
Genoa Av. SW15 —8H 13
Genoa Rd. SE20 —1F 46
Gentles La. Pass & Head —8F 168
Genyn Rd. Guild —4L 113 (5A 202)
George Denyer Clo. Hasl —1G 189
George Eliot Clo. Witl —5C 152
George Gdns. Alder —5A 110
George Gro. Rd. SE20 —1D 46
Georgeham Rd. Owl —5J 49
George Horley Pl. Newd —1A 160
Georgelands. Rip —8K 75
George Lindgren Ho. SW6 —3L 13
(off Clem Attlee Ct.)
George Pinion Ct. H'ham —5H 197
George Rd. Fleet —4C 88
George Rd. G'ming —4H 133
George Rd. Guild —3N 113 (3C 202)
George Rd. King T —8A 26
(in two parts)
George Rd. Milf —9C 132
George Rd. N Mald —3E 42
George Sq. SW19 —2M 43
George's Rd. Tats —7F 86
George's Sq. SW6 —2L 13
(off N. End Rd.)
Georges Ter. Cat —9A 84
George St. Brkwd —8L 71
George St. Croy —8N 45 (3C 200)
George St. Houn —5N 9
George St. Rich —8K 11
George St. Stai —5H 21
George Wyver Clo. SW19 —1K 27
Georgian Clo. Camb —8C 50
Georgian Clo. Craw —4H 183
Georgian Clo. Stai —5K 21
Georgian Ct. SW16 —5J 29
Georgian Ct. Croy —1E 200
Georgia Rd. N Mald —3B 42
Georgia Rd. T Hth —9M 29
Georgina Ct. Fleet —4B 88
Gerald Ct. H'ham —6L 197
Geraldine Rd. SW18 —8N 13
Geraldine Rd. W4 —2N 11
Gerald's Gro. Bans —1J 81
Geranium Clo. Crowt —8G 30
Gerard Av. Houn —1A 24
Gerard Rd. SW13 —4E 12
Germander Dri. Bisl —2D 72
Gerrards Mead. Bans —3L 81
Gervis Ct. Iswth —3C 10
Ghyll Cres. H'ham —8M 197
Giant Arches Rd. SE24 —1N 29
Gibbet La. Camb —7E 50
Gibbins La. Warf —6B 16
(in two parts)
Gibbon Rd. King T —9L 25 (1L 203)
Gibbons Clo. M'bowr —6G 183
Gibbons Clo. Sand —8H 49
Gibbon Wlk. SW15 —7F 12
Gibb's Acre. Pirb —1C 92
Gibbs Av. SE19 —6N 29
Gibbs Brook La. Oxt —5N 125
Gibbs Clo. SE19 —7N 29
Gibbs Grn. W14 —1L 13
(in three parts)
Gibbs Sq. SE19 —6N 29
Gibbs Way. Yat —2A 68
Giblets La. H'ham —1M 197
Giblets Way. H'ham —1L 197
Gibraltar Barracks. B'water —4D 68
Gibraltar Cres. Eps —6D 60
Gibson Clo. Chess —2J 59
Gibson Clo. Iswth —6E 10
Gibson Ct. Esh —8F 40
Gibson Ct. Slou —1B 6
Gibson Ho. Sutt —1M 61
Gibson Pl. Stanw —9L 7
Gibson Rd. Sutt —2N 61
Gibsons Hill. SW16 —8L 29
Gidd Hill. Coul —3E 82
Giffard Dri. Farn —9L 69
Giffards Clo. E Grin —9B 166
Giffards Mdw. Farnh —2K 129
Giffard Way. Guild —9K 93
Giggshill. —6G 40
Giggshill Gdns. Th Dit —7G 40
Giggshill Rd. Th Dit —6G 40
Gilbert Clo. SW19 —8N 27
(off High Path)
Gilbert Rd. SW19 —8A 28
Gilbert Rd. Camb —5A 70
Gilbert St. Houn —6C 10
Gilbert Way. Croy —8K 45
Gilbey Rd. SW17 —5C 28
Gilders Rd. Chess —4M 59
Gilesmead. Eps —8M 201
Giles Travers Clo. Egh —2E 36
Gilham La. F Row —7G 187

Gorse La.—Green Man La.

Gorse La. *Wrec* —5G **128**
Gorse Path. *Wrec* —5F **128**
Gorse Pl. *Wink R* —7F **16**
Gorse Ri. *SW17* —6E **28**
Gorse Rd. *Croy* —1K **65**
Gorse Rd. *Frim* —4C **70**
Gorse Way. *Fleet* —6B **88**
Gorsewood Rd. *Wok* —6G **73**
Gorst Rd. *SW11* —1D **28**
Gort Clo. *Alder* —6C **90**
Gosberton Rd. *SW12* —2D **28**
Gosbury Hill. *Chess* —1L **59**
Gosden Clo. *Brmly* —3B **134**
Gosden Clo. *Craw* —4E **182**
Gosden Common. —3A 134
Gosden Comn. *Brmly* —4A **134**
Gosden Cotts. *Brmly* —4D **104**
Gosden Hill Rd. *Guild* —8E **94**
Gosden Rd. *W End* —9C **52**
Gosfield Rd. *Eps* —8C **60** (5K **201**)
Goslar Way. *Wind* —5E **4**
Gosnell Clo. *Frim* —3H **71**
Gospel Green. —5B 190
Gossops Dri. *Craw* —4L **181**
Gossops Green. —4L 181
Gossops Grn. La. *Craw* —4M **181**
Gossops Pde. *Craw* —4L **181**
Gostling Rd. *Twic* —2A **24**
Goston Gdns. *T Hth* —2L **45**
Gostrode La. *C'fold* —2D **190**
Goswell Hill. *Wind* —4G **4**
Goswell Rd. *Wind* —4G **4**
Gothic Ct. *Hayes* —2E **8**
Gothic Rd. *Twic* —3D **24**
Goudhurst Clo. *Worth* —3J **183**
Goudhurst Keep. *Worth* —3J **183**
Gough Ho. *King T* —3K **203**
Gough Rd. *Fleet* —3A **88**
Gough's Barn La. *Binf* —1M **15**
(in two parts)
Gough's La. *Brack* —9A **16**
Gough's Mdw. *Sand* —8G **48**
Gould Ct. *Guild* —1F **114**
Goulding Gdns. *T Hth* —1N **45**
Gould Rd. *Felt* —1F **22**
Gould Rd. *Twic* —2E **24**
Government Ho. Rd. *Alder* —5M **89**
Government Rd. *Alder* —9B **90**
Governor's Rd. *Coll T* —9L **49**
Govett Av. *Shep* —4D **38**
Govett Gro. *W'sham* —2A **52**
Gowan Av. *SW6* —4K **13**
Gower Pk. *Coll T* —8J **49**
Gower Rd. *Horl* —8C **142**
Gower Rd. *Iswth* —2F **10**
Gower Rd. *Wey* —3E **56**
Gower, The. *Egh* —2D **36**
Gowland Pl. *Beck* —1J **47**
Gowrie Pl. *Cat* —9N **83**
Graburn Way. *E Mol* —2D **40**
Grace Bennett Clo. *Farn* —7M **69**
Grace Ct. *Croy* —4A **200**
Gracedale Rd. *SW16* —6F **28**
Gracefield Gdns. *SW16* —4J **29**
Grace Reynolds Wlk. *Camb* —9A **50**
Grace Rd. *Broadf* —8M **181**
Grace Rd. *Croy* —5N **45**
Gracious Pond Rd. *Chob* —4K **53**
Graemesdyke Av. *SW14* —6A **12**
Graffham Clo. *Craw* —1N **181**
Grafham. —2E 154
Grafton Clo. *Houn* —2M **23**
Grafton Clo. *W Byf* —9H **55**
Grafton Clo. *Wor Pk* —9D **42**
Grafton Ct. *Felt* —2E **22**
Grafton Pk. Rd. *Wor Pk* —8D **42**
Grafton Rd. *Croy* —7L **45**
Grafton Rd. *N Mald* —2D **42**
Grafton Rd. *Wor Pk* —9C **42**
Grafton Way. *W Mol* —3N **39**
Graham Av. *Mitc* —9E **28**
Graham Clo. *Croy* —8K **47**
Graham Gdns. *Surb* —7L **41**
Graham Rd. *SW19* —8L **27**
Graham Rd. *Hamp* —5A **24**
Graham Rd. *Mitc* —9E **28**
Graham Rd. *Purl* —9L **63**
Graham Rd. *W'sham* —3N **51**
Grailands Clo. *Fern* —9G **188**
Grainger Rd. *Iswth* —5F **10**
Grampian Clo. *Hayes* —3E **8**
Grampian Rd. *Sand* —5E **48**
Grampian Way. *Slou* —1C **6**
Grampion Clo. *Sutt* —4A **62**
Granada St. *SW17* —6C **28**
Granard Av. *SW15* —8G **13**
Granard Rd. *SW12* —1D **28**
Granary Clo. *Horl* —6E **142**
Granary Way. *H'ham* —7F **106**
Grand Av. *Camb* —9A **50**
Grand Av. *Surb* —4A **42**
Grand Dri. *SW20* —1H **43**
Granden Rd. *SW16* —1J **45**
Grandfield Ct. *W4* —2C **12**
Grandis Cotts. *Rip* —9K **75**
Grandison Rd. *Wor Pk* —8H **43**
Grand Pde. SW14 —7B 12
(off Up. Richmond Rd. W.)
Grand Pde. *Craw* —3B **182**
Grand Pde. *Surb* —7N **41**
Grand Pde. M. *SW15* —8K **13**
Grandstand Rd. *Eps* —4E **80**
Grand Vw. Av. *Big H* —4E **86**
Grange Av. *SE25* —1B **46**
Grange Av. *Crowt* —1G **48**
Grange Av. *Twic* —3E **24**
Grangecliffe Gdns. *SE25* —1B **46**
Grange Clo. *Blet* —2A **124**
Grange Clo. *Camb* —7F **50**
Grange Clo. *Craw* —1E **182**
Grange Clo. *Eden* —2L **147**
Grange Clo. *G'ming* —6K **133**
Grange Clo. *Guild* —8L **93**
Grange Clo. *Houn* —2N **9**
Grange Clo. *Lea* —7K **79**
Grange Clo. *Mers* —6F **102**
Grange Clo. *W'ham* —4L **107**
Grange Clo. *W Mol* —3D **40**
Grange Clo. *Wray* —9A **6**
Grange Ct. *Egh* —6B **20**
Grange Ct. *Mers* —6F **102**
Grange Ct. *Shep* —3B **38**
Grange Ct. *S God* —7H **125**
Grange Ct. *Stai* —6J **21**
Grange Ct. *Sutt* —4N **61**
Grange Ct. *W on T* —8H **39**
Grange Cres. *Craw D* —2E **184**
Grange Dri. *Mers* —6F **102**
Grange Dri. *Wok* —2A **74**
Grange End. *Small* —8L **143**
Grange Est. *C Crook* —8A **88**
Grange Farm Rd. *As* —1E **110**
Grangefields Rd. *Guild* —6N **93**
Grange Gdns. *SE25* —1B **46**
Grange Gdns. *Bans* —9N **61**
Grange Hill. *SE25* —1B **46**
Grange Lodge. *SW19* —7J **27**
Grange Lodge. *Wind* —3A **4**
Grange Mans. *Eps* —4E **60**
Grange Mdw. *Bans* —9N **61**
Grange M. *Felt* —5H **23**
Grange Mt. *Lea* —7K **79**
Grange Pk. *Cranl* —7A **156**
Grange Pk. *Wok* —2A **74**
Grange Pk. Pl. *SW20* —8G **26**
Grange Pk. Rd. *T Hth* —3A **46**
Grange Pl. *Stai* —1L **37**
Grange Rd. *SW13* —4F **12**
Grange Rd. *W4* —1A **12**
Grange Rd. *As* —2F **110**
Grange Rd. *Brack* —9A **16**
Grange Rd. *Camb* —1C **70**
Grange Rd. *Cat* —3D **104**
Grange Rd. *Chess* —1L **59**
Grange Rd. *C Crook* —8A **88**
Grange Rd. *Craw D* —2D **184**
Grange Rd. *Egh* —6B **20**
(in two parts)
Grange Rd. *Farn* —7N **69**
Grange Rd. *Guild* —7L **93**
Grange Rd. *King T* —2L **41** (5K **203**)
Grange Rd. *Lea* —7K **79**
Grange Rd. *New H* —6J **55**
Grange Rd. *Pirb* —9N **71**
Grange Rd. *S Croy* —6N **63**
Grange Rd. *Sutt* —4M **61**
Grange Rd. *T Hth & SE25* —3A **46**
Grange Rd. *Tilf* —2N **149**
Grange Rd. *Tong* —6C **110**
Grange Rd. *W on T* —1M **57**
Grange Rd. *W Mol* —3B **40**
Grange Rd. *Wok* —1A **74**
Grange, The. *SW19* —7J **27**
Grange, The. *W4* —1A **12**
Grange, The. *W14* —1L **13**
Grange, The. *Chob* —6H **53**
Grange, The. *Croy* —8J **47**
Grange, The. *Fren* —3J **149**
Grange, The. *Horl* —5F **142**
Grange, The. *N Mald* —4E **42**
Grange, The. *Old Win* —8L **5**
Grange, The. Vir W —3A 36
(off Holloway Dri.)
Grange, The. *W on T* —8J **39**
Grange, The. *Wor Pk* —9C **42**
Grange Va. *Sutt* —4N **61**
Grangeway. *Small* —8L **143**
Grangewood Dri. *Sun* —8G **22**
Grangewood Ter. *SE25* —1A **46**
Gransden Clo. *Ewh* —5F **156**
Grantchester. King T —1N 41
(off St Peters Rd.)
Grant Clo. *Shep* —5C **38**
Grantham Clo. *Owl* —6K **49**
Grantham Rd. *W4* —3D **12**
Grantley Av. *Won* —5D **134**
Grantley Clo. *Shalf* —1A **134**
Grantley Ct. *Farnh* —5E **128**
Grantley Dri. *Fleet* —6A **88**
Grantley Gdns. *Guild* —2K **113**
Grantley Rd. *Guild* —2K **113**
Grantley Rd. *Houn* —5K **9**
Granton Rd. *SW16* —9G **29**
Grant Pl. *Croy* —7C **46**
Grant Rd. *Crowt* —4H **49**
Grant Rd. *Croy* —7C **46**
Grants La. *Oxt & Eden* —1E **126**
Grant Wlk. *Asc* —7B **34**
Grant Way. *Iswth* —2G **10**
Grantwood Clo. *Red* —8E **122**
Granville Av. *Felt* —3H **23**
Granville Av. *Houn* —8A **10**
Granville Clo. *Byfl* —9A **56**
Granville Clo. *Croy* —8B **46** (3F **200**)
Granville Clo. *Wey* —3D **56**
Granville Gdns. *SW16* —9K **29**
Granville Pl. *SW6* —3N **13**
Granville Rd. *SW18* —1L **27**
Granville Rd. *SW19* —8M **27**
Granville Rd. *Oxt* —7B **106**
Granville Rd. *W'ham* —4L **107**
Granville Rd. *Wey* —4D **56**
Granville Rd. *Wok* —7B **74**
Granwood Ct. *Iswth* —4E **10**
Grapsome Clo. *Chess* —4J **59**
Grasholm Way. *Slou* —1E **6**
Grasmere Av. *SW15* —5C **26**
Grasmere Av. *SW19* —2M **40**
Grasmere Av. *Houn* —9B **10**
Grasmere Clo. *Egh* —8D **20**
Grasmere Clo. *Felt* —2G **22**
Grasmere Clo. *Guild* —2D **114**
Grasmere Ct. *Sutt* —3A **62**
Grasmere Gdns. *H'ham* —2A **198**
Grasmere Rd. *SE25* —5E **46**
Grasmere Rd. *SW16* —6K **29**
Grasmere Rd. *Farn* —2K **89**
Grasmere Rd. *Farnh* —6F **108**
Grasmere Rd. *Light* —6M **51**
Grasmere Rd. *Purl* —7M **63**
Grasmere Way. *Byfl* —8A **56**
Grassfield Clo. *Coul* —6F **82**
Grasslands. *Small* —8L **143**
Grassmere. *Horl* —7G **142**
Grassmount. *Purl* —6G **63**
Grass Way. *Wall* —1G **62**
Gratton Dri. *Wind* —7B **4**
Grattons Dri. *Craw* —9G **162**
Grattons, The. *Slin* —5M **195**
Gravel Hill. *Croy* —3G **64**
Gravel Hill. *Lea* —8H **79**
Gravel Hill Rd. *B'ley*
(in two parts) —6A **120** & 7A **128**
Gravelly Hill. *Cat* —6C **104**
Gravel Pits Cotts. *Gom* —8D **116**
Gravel Pits La. *Gom* —8D **116**
Gravel Rd. *C Crook* —7C **88**
Gravel Rd. *Farn* —5B **90**
Gravel Rd. *Farnh* —5G **108**
Gravel Rd. *Twic* —2E **24**
Gravenel Gdns. SW17 —6C 28
(off Nutwell St.)
Graveney Rd. *SW17* —5C **28**
Graveney Rd. *M'bowr* —4G **182**
Gravetts La. *Guild* —8H **93**
Gravetye Clo. *Craw* —5E **182**
Gray Clo. *Add* —2K **55**
Grayham Cres. *N Mald* —3C **42**
Grayham Rd. *N Mald* —3C **42**
Graylands. *Wok* —3A **74**
Graylands Clo. *Wok* —3A **74**
Graylands Ct. *Guild* —4B **114**
Gray Pl. *Ott* —3F **54**
Grays Clo. *Hasl* —9J **171**
Grayscroft Rd. *SW16* —8H **29**
Grayshot Dri. *B'water* —1H **69**
Grayshott. —6A 170
Grayshott. *Gray* —6B **170**
Grayshott Laurels. *Lind* —4B **168**
Grayshott Rd. *Head D* —3G **169**
Grays La. *Afrd* —5C **22**
Gray's La. *Asht* —6M **79**
(in two parts)
Grays Rd. *G'ming* —4J **133**
Grays Rd. *W'ham* —8K **87**
Grayswood. —7K 171
Grays Wood. *Horl* —8G **143**
Grayswood Comn. *G'wood* —8K **171**
Grayswood Copse. *G'wood* —7K **171**
Grayswood Dri. *Myt* —4E **90**
Grayswood Gdns. *SW20* —1G **42**
Grayswood Rd. *Hasl & G'wood*
—1H **189**
Great Austins. *Farnh* —3J **129**
Gt. Austins Ho. *Farnh* —3J **129**
Great Benty. *W Dray* —1N **7**
Great Bookham. —4B 98
Great Bookham Common. —8N 77
Great Burgh. —4H 81
Gt. Chertsey Rd. *W4* —5B **12**
Gt. Chertsey Rd. *Felt* —4N **23**
Gt. Church La. *W6* —1J **13**
Great Cockcrow Railway. —7F 36
Great Ellshams. *Bans* —3M **81**
Great Enton. —6D 152
Greatfield Clo. *Farn* —6N **69**
Greatfield Rd. *Farn* —6M **69**
Greatford Dri. *Guild* —3F **114**
Gt. Gatton Clo. *Croy* —6H **47**
Gt. George St. *G'ming* —7H **133**
Gt. Goodwin Dri. *Guild* —1D **114**
Greatham Rd. *M'bowr* —6G **182**
Greatham Wlk. *SW15* —2F **26**
Greathed Manor. —1E 166
Great Hollands. —5L 31
Gt. Hollands Rd. *Brack* —5K **31**
Gt. Hollands Sq. *Brack* —5L **31**
Great Ho. Ct. *E Grin* —1B **186**
Greathurst End. *Bookh* —2N **97**
Greatlake Ct. Horl —7F 142
(off Tanyard Way)
Gt. Mead. *Eden* —9L **127**
Gt. Oaks Pk. *Guild* —7D **94**
Great Quarry. *Guild*
—6N **113** (8D **202**)
Gt. South W. Rd. *Bedf & Felt* —1D **22**
Great Tattenhams. *Eps* —5G **81**
Gt. West Rd. *W4 & W6* —1E **12**
Gt. West Rd. *Houn & Iswth* —5L **9**
Gt. West Rd. *Iswth & Bren* —3D **10**
Gt. West Trad. Est. *Bren* —2H **11**
Greatwood Clo. *Ott* —5E **54**
Gt. Woodcote Dri. *Purl* —6H **63**
Gt. Woodcote Pk. *Purl* —6H **63**
Greaves Pl. *SW17* —5C **28**
Grebe Ct. *Sutt* —2L **61**
Grebe Cres. *H'ham* —7N **197**
Grebe Ter. *King T* —2L **41** (5K **203**)
Grecian Cres. *SE19* —7M **29**
Green Acre. *Alder* —3L **109**
Green Acre. *Knap* —3H **73**
Greenacre. *Wind* —5B **4**
Greenacre Ct. *Eng G* —7M **19**
Greenacre Pl. *Hack* —8F **44**
Greenacres. *Bookh* —2B **98**
Greenacres. *Bord* —5A **168**
Greenacres. *Craw* —4E **182**
Green Acres. *Croy* —9C **46**
Greenacres. *H'ham* —4J **197**
Greenacres. *Oxt* —5A **106**
Green Acres. *Runf* —1A **130**
Greenacres Clo. *Orp* —1L **67**
Green Bank Cotts. *F Grn* —3M **157**
Greenbank Way. *Camb* —4B **70**
Greenbush La. *Cranl* —9A **156**
Green Bus. Cen., The. *Stai* —5E **20**
Green Clo. *Brom* —2N **47**
Green Clo. *Cars* —8D **44**
Green Clo. *Felt* —6M **23**
Greencourt Av. *Croy* —8E **46**
Greencourt Gdns. *Croy* —7E **46**
Greencroft. *Farn* —1N **89**
Greencroft. *Guild* —3D **114**
Green Cft. *Wokgm* —9D **14**
Greencroft Rd. *Houn* —4N **9**
Green Cross. —9M 149
Grn. Cross La. *Churt* —9M **149**
Green Curve. *Bans* —1L **81**
Green Dene. *E Hor* —4D **116**
Grn. Dragon La. *Bren* —1L **11**
Green Dri. *Rip* —1H **95**
Green Dri. *Slou* —1A **6**
(in two parts)
Green Dri. *Wokgm* —4D **30**
Greene Fielde End. *Stai* —8M **21**
Green End. *Chess* —1L **59**
Green End. *Yat* —8C **48**
Green Farm Clo. *Orp* —3N **67**
Green Farm Rd. *Bag* —4K **51**
Greenfield. *Eden* —2M **147**
Greenfield. *Farnh* —4F **128**
Greenfield Av. *Surb* —6A **42**
Greenfield Link. *Coul* —2J **83**
Greenfield Rd. *Farnh* —4E **128**
Greenfield Rd. *Slin* —5L **195**
Greenfields Clo. *Horl* —6C **142**
Greenfields Clo. *H'ham* —2N **197**
Greenfields Pl. *Bear G* —7K **139**
Greenfields Rd. *Horl* —6D **142**
Greenfields Rd. *H'ham* —3N **197**
Greenfields Way. *H'ham* —2N **197**
Greenfield Way. *Crowt* —9F **30**
Grn. Finch Clo. *Crowt* —1E **48**
Greenfinch Way. *H'ham* —1J **197**
Greenford Rd. *Sutt* —1N **61**
(in two parts)
Green Gdns. *Orp* —2L **67**
Green Glades. *C Crook* —8A **88**
Greenham Ho. *Houn* —6D **10**
Greenham Wlk. *Wok* —5M **73**
Greenham Wood. *Brack* —5A **32**
Greenhanger. *Churt* —1M **169**
Greenhaven. *Yat* —1A **68**
Greenhayes Av. *Bans* —1M **81**
Green Hayes Clo. *Reig* —3A **122**
Greenhayes Gdns. *Bans* —2M **81**
Green Hedge. *Twic* —8J **11**
Green Hedges Av. *E Grin* —8N **165**
Green Hedges Clo. *E Grin* —8N **165**
Greenheys Pl. *Wok* —5B **74**
Green Hill. *Orp* —8H **67**
Greenhill. *Sutt* —8A **44**
Greenhill Av. *Cat* —8E **84**
Greenhill Clo. *Camb* —9G **51**
Greenhill Clo. *Farnh* —4F **128**
Greenhill Clo. *G'ming* —8G **132**
Greenhill Gdns. *Guild* —1E **114**
Green Hill La. *Warl* —4H **85**
Green Hill Rd. *Camb* —9G **51**
Greenhill Rd. *Farnh* —4J **129**
Greenhills. *Farnh* —3K **129**
Greenhill Way. *Farnh* —5F **128**
Greenholme. *Camb* —1H **71**
Greenhow. *Brack* —2M **31**
Greenhurst La. *Oxt* —1B **126**
Greenhurst Rd. *SE27* —6L **29**
Greenlake Ter. *Stai* —8J **21**
Greenlands. *Ott* —9E **36**
Greenlands Rd. *Camb* —5N **69**
Greenlands Rd. *Stai* —5J **21**
Greenlands Rd. *Wey* —9C **38**
Green La. *SW16 & T Hth* —8K **29**
Green La. *Alf* —5H **175**
Green La. *Asc* —9B **18**
Green La. *Asht* —4J **79**
Green La. *Bad L* —6L **109**
Green La. *Bag* —5K **51**
Green La. *Bear G* —1H **159**
Green La. *B'water* —2K **69**
Green La. *Blet* —9B **104**
Green La. *Byfl* —8A **56**
Green La. *Cat* —9N **83**
Green La. *Cher & Add* —8G **36**
Green La. *Chess* —5K **59**
(in two parts)
Green La. *Chob* —6J **53**
Green La. *Churt* —1L **169**
Green La. *Cobh* —8M **57**
Green La. *Craw* —1C **182**
Green La. *Craw D* —6C **164**
Green La. *Crowt* —9F **32**
Green La. *Dat* —4L **5**
Green La. *Dock* —4D **148**
Green La. *Egh* —5D **20**
(in two parts)
Green La. *Farnh* —3F **128**
Green La. *Felt* —6M **23**
Green La. *Frog* —2G **69**
Green La. *G'ming* —2G **133**
Green La. *Guild* —3D **114**
Green La. *Hasl* —4F **188**
Green La. *H'ham* —5L **179**
Green La. *Houn* —6J **9**
Green La. *Lea* —8K **79**
(in two parts)
Green La. *Leigh* —3D **140**
Green La. *Ling* —8M **145**
Green La. *Lwr K & Coul* —4L **101**
Green La. *Milf* —2B **152**
Green La. *Mord* —6H **43**
(Battersea Cemetery)
Green La. *Mord* —5M **43**
(Morden)
Green La. *Newd* —2C **160**
(in two parts)
Green La. *N Mald* —4D **42**
Green La. *Ock* —2C **96**
Green La. *Ockl* —7M **157**
Green La. *Out* —1J **140**
Green La. *Purl* —7G **63**
Green La. *Red* —1C **122**
(Carlton Rd.)
Green La. *Red* —8E **122**
(Spencer's Way)
Green La. *Reig* —3L **121**
Green La. *Sand* —8H **49**
Green La. *Sham G* —5H **135**
Green La. *Shep* —5D **38**
Green La. *Ship B* —3K **163**
Green La. *Sun* —8G **22**
Green La. *Thorpe & Stai* —1E **36**
(in two parts)
Green La. *Tilf* —5B **130**
Green La. *W on T* —3J **57**
Green La. *Warl* —3H **85**
Green La. *W Cla* —5J **95**
Green La. *W Mol* —4B **40**
Green La. *Wind* —5D **4**
Green La. *Wok* —8L **73**
Green La. *Wokgm* —6F **14**
Green La. *Wood S* —1D **112**
Green La. *Wor Pk* —7F **42**
Green La. *Worth* —3H **183**
(in two parts)
Green La. *Yat* —9A **48**
Green La. Av. *W on T* —2K **57**
Green La. Cvn. Pk. *Red* —1J **143**
Green La. Clo. *Byfl* —8A **56**
Green La. Clo. *Camb* —8A **50**
Green La. Clo. *Cher* —8G **36**
Green La. Cotts. *Churt* —9L **149**
Green La. Cotts. *Farnh* —7L **109**
Green La. E. *Norm* —4K **111**
(in two parts)
Green La. Gdns. *T Hth* —1N **45**
Green Lanes. *Eps* —5D **60**
(in two parts)
Green La. W. *Ash G* —4J **111**
Green La. W. *W Hor* —3B **96**
Greenlaw Gdns. *N Mald* —6E **42**
Green Leaf Av. *Wall* —1H **63**
Greenleaf Clo. *SW2* —1L **29**
Greenleas. *Frim* —4C **70**
Green Leas. *King T* —5L **203**
Green Leas. *Sun* —7G **23**
Green Leas Clo. *Sun* —7G **23**
Greenleas Clo. *Yat* —8B **48**
Greenleaves Ct. *Afrd* —7C **22**
Green Leys. *C Crook* —9A **88**
Green Man La. *Felt* —7H **9**

Hackenden La.—Harrington Clo.

Hackenden La. E Grin —8A 166
(in two parts)
Hacketts La. Wok —1H 75
Hackhurst Downs. —6G 116
Hackhurst La. Ab H —8G 116
Haddenhurst Ct. Binf —7H 15
Haddon Clo. N Mald —4E 42
Haddon Clo. Wey —9F 38
Haddon Rd. Sutt —1N 61
Hadfield Rd. Stanw —9M 7
Hadleigh Clo. SW20 —1L 43
Hadleigh Dri. Sutt —5M 61
Hadleigh Gdns. Frim G —8C 70
Hadley Gdns. W4 —1C 12
Hadley Gdns. S'hall —1N 9
Hadley Pl. Wey —4D 56
Hadley Rd. Mitc —3H 45
Hadleys. Rowl —8D 128
Hadley Wood Ri. Kenl —2M 83
Hadmans Clo. H'ham —7J 197
Hadrian Clo. Stai —1N 21
Hadrian Clo. Wall —4J 63
Hadrian Ct. Sutt —4N 61
Hadrians. Farnh —8K 109
Hadrian Way. Stanw —1M 21
(in two parts)
Haggard Rd. Twic —1H 25
Hagley Rd. Fleet —4A 88
Haigh Cres. Red —5F 122
Haig La. C Crook —8C 88
Haig Pl. Mord —5M 43
Haig Rd. Alder —3A 110
Haig Rd. Big H —4G 86
Haig Rd. Camb —9L 49
Hailes Clo. SW19 —7A 28
Hailey Pl. Cranl —6A 156
Hailsham Av. SW2 —3K 29
Hailsham Clo. Owl —6J 49
Hailsham Clo. Surb —6K 41
Hailsham Rd. SW17 —7E 28
Haines Ct. Wey —2E 56
Haines Wlk. Mord —6N 43
Haining Clo. W4 —1N 11
Haining Gdns. Myt —2E 90
Hainthorpe Rd. SE27 —4M 29
Haldane Pl. SW18 —2N 27
Haldane Rd. SW6 —3L 13
Haldon Rd. SW18 —9L 13
Hale. —7J 109
Halebourne La. Chob & W End —4D 52
Hale Clo. Orp —1L 67
Hale End. Brack —3D 32
Hale Ends. Wok —8L 73
Hale Ho. Clo. Churt —9L 149
Hale Ho. La. Churt —9L 149
Hale Path. SE27 —5M 29
Hale Pit Rd. Bookh —4C 98
Hale Pl. Farnh —7K 109
Hale Reeds. Farnh —6J 109
Hale Rd. Farnh —7J 109
Hales Fld. Hasl —2G 189
Hales Oak. Bookh —4C 98
Halesowen Rd. Mord —6N 43
Hale St. Stai —5G 21
Hales Wood. Cobh —1J 77
Hale Way. Frim —6B 70
Halewood. Brack —5L 31
Half Acre. Bren —2K 11
Half Moon Cotts. Rip —8L 75
Half Moon Hill. Hasl —2G 189
Half Moon St. Bag —4J 51
Halford Rd. SW6 —2M 13
Halford Rd. Rich —8L 11
Halfpenny Clo. Chil —9F 114
Halfpenny La. Asc —6D 34
Halfpenny La. Guild —6E 114
Halfway Grn. W on T —9J 39
Halfway La. G'ming —7D 132
Haliburton Rd. Twic —8G 11
Halifax Clo. Craw —9J 163
Halifax Clo. Farn —2L 89
Halifax Clo. Tedd —7E 24
Halimote Rd. Alder —3M 109
Haling Down Pas. Purl —6M 63
(in two parts)
Haling Gro. S Croy —4N 63
Haling Pk. Gdns. Croy —3M 63
Haling Pk. Rd. S Croy —2M 63 (8A 200)
Haling Rd. S Croy —3A 64
Hallam Rd. SW13 —6G 13
Hallam Rd. G'ming —5J 133
Halland Clo. Craw —2E 182
Halland Ct. Eden —2L 147
Hallane Ho. SE27 —6N 29
Hallbrooke Gdns. Binf —8K 15
Hall Clo. Camb —9C 50
Hall Clo. G'ming —4H 133
Hall Ct. Dat —3L 5
Hall Ct. Tedd —6F 24
Hall Dene Clo. Guild —2F 114
Halley Clo. Craw —8N 181
Halley Dri. Asc —1H 33
Halley's App. Wok —4K 73
Halley's Ct. Wok —5K 73
Halley's Wlk. Add —4L 55
Hall Farm Cres. Yat —1C 68
Hall Farm Dri. Twic —1D 24
Hallgrove Bottom. Bag —2K 51
Hall Gro. Farm Ind. Est. Bag —2K 51
Hall Hill. Oxt —9N 105
Halliards, The. W on T —5H 39
Halliford Clo. Shep —3E 38
Halliford Rd. Shep & Sun —4F 38
Hallington Clo. Wok —4L 73
Hall La. Hayes —3E 8
Hall La. Yat —1B 68
Hallmark Clo. Coll T —7K 49
Hallmead Rd. Sutt —9N 43
Hallowell Av. Croy —1J 63
Hallowell Clo. Mitc —2E 44
Hallowfield Way. Mitc —2C 44
Hall Place. —1G 175
Hall Pl. Wok —3C 74
Hall Pl. Dri. Wey —2F 56
Hall Rd. Brmly —5B 134
Hall Rd. Iswth —8D 10
Hall Rd. Wall —6F 62
Halls Farm Clo. Knap —4G 73
Hallsland. Craw D —1F 184
Hallsland Way. Oxt —2B 126
Hall Way. Purl —9M 63
Halnaker Wlk. Craw —6L 181
Halsford Cft. E Grin —7L 165
Halsford Grn. E Grin —7L 165
Halsford La. E Grin —8L 165
Halsford Pk. Rd. E Grin —8M 165
Halstead Clo. Croy —9N 45 (4B 200)
Halters End. Gray —6M 169
Ham. —4J 25
Hamble Av. B'water —1J 69
Hamble Clo. Wok —4K 73
Hambleden Ct. Brack —3C 32
Hambledon. —9F 152
Hambledon Gdns. SE25 —2C 46
Hambledon Hill. Eps —3D 80
Hambledon Pk. Hamb —9E 152
Hambledon Pl. Bookh —1A 98
Hambledon Rd. SW18 —1L 27
Hambledon Rd. Busb & G'ming —9J 133
(in two parts)
Hambledon Rd. Cat —1A 104
Hambledon Rd. Hamb & Hydc —7G 153
Hambledon Va. Eps —3B 80
Hamblehyrst. Beck —1L 47
Hamble St. SW6 —6N 13
Hambleton Clo. Frim —3F 70
Hambleton Clo. Wor Pk —8H 43
Hambleton Ct. Craw —5A 182
Hambleton Hill. Craw —5A 182
Hamble Wlk. Wok —5K 73
Hambridge Way. SW2 —1L 29
Hambrook Rd. SE25 —2E 46
Hambro Rd. SW16 —7H 29
Ham Clo. Rich —4J 25
(in two parts)
Ham Comn. Rich —4K 25
Hamesmoor Rd. Myt —1C 90
Hamesmoor Way. Myt —1D 90
Ham Farm Rd. Rich —5K 25
Hamfield Clo. Oxt —5M 105
Ham Ga. Av. Rich —4K 25
Hamhaugh Island. Shep —8B 38
Ham House. —2J 25
Hamilton Av. Cobh —9H 57
Hamilton Av. Surb —8N 41
Hamilton Av. Sutt —8K 43
Hamilton Av. Wok —2G 75
Hamilton Clo. Bag —4J 51
Hamilton Clo. Bord —5A 168
Hamilton Clo. Cher —7H 37
Hamilton Clo. Eps —8B 60
Hamilton Clo. Felt —6G 22
Hamilton Clo. Guild —7K 93
Hamilton Clo. Purl —8M 63
Hamilton Ct. SW15 —6K 13
Hamilton Ct. Bookh —3B 98
Hamilton Ct. Croy —7D 46
Hamilton Cres. Houn —8B 10
Hamilton Dri. Asc —6B 34
Hamilton Dri. Guild —7K 93
Hamilton Gordon Ct. Guild —2M 113 (1B 202)
Hamilton Ho. W4 —2D 12
Hamilton M. SW18 —2M 27
Hamilton M. SW19 —8M 27
Hamilton Pde. Felt —5G 23
Hamilton Pl. Alder —3L 109
Hamilton Pl. Guild —7K 93
Hamilton Pl. Kgswd —9L 81
Hamilton Pl. Sun —8J 23
Hamilton Rd. SE27 —5N 29
Hamilton Rd. SW19 —8N 27
Hamilton Rd. Bren —2K 11
Hamilton Rd. C Crook —7C 88
Hamilton Rd. Felt —5G 22
Hamilton Rd. H'ham —5H 197
Hamilton Rd. T Hth —2A 46
Hamilton Rd. Twic —2E 24
Hamilton Rd. M. SW19 —8N 27
Hamilton Way. Wall —5H 63
Ham Island. —7N 5
Ham La. Elst —7H 131
Ham La. Eng G —5L 19
Ham La. Old Win —8M 5
(in two parts)
Hamlash La. Fren —1H 149
Hamlet Gdns. W6 —1F 12
Hamlet St. Warf —9C 16
Hamm Ct. Wey —8N 37
Hammer. —3B 188
Hammer Bottom. —2A 188
Hammerfield Dri. Ab H —1G 136
Hammer Hill. Hasl —4A 100
Hammer La. Bram C —9A 170
Hammer La. Churt & Gray —1K 169
Hammer La. Cranl —3M 175
Hammer La. Hasl —2A 188
Hammer Pond Cotts. Thur —4K 151
Hammerpond Rd. Colg —9E 198
Hammerpond Rd. H'ham & Man H —7M 197
Hammersley Rd. Alder —6N 89
Hammersmith. —1H 13
Hammersmith Bri. SW13 & W6 —2G 13
Hammersmith Bri. Rd. W6 —1H 13
Hammersmith B'way. W6 —1H 13
Hammersmith Flyover. (Junct.) —1H 13
Hammersmith Flyover. W6 —1H 13
Hammersmith Gro. W6 —1H 13
Hammersmith Ind. Est. W6 —2H 13
Hammersmith Rd. W6 & W14 —1J 13
Hammersmith Ter. W6 —1F 12
Hammer Va. Hasl —2A 188
Hammerwood. —7K 167
Hammerwood Copse. Hasl —3B 188
Hammerwood Park. —8L 167
Hammerwood Rd. Ash W —3F 186
Hammer Yd. Craw —4B 182
Hamm Moor La. Add —2N 55
Hammond Av. Mitc —1F 44
Hammond Clo. Hamp —9A 24
Hammond Clo. Wok —2M 73
Hammond Ct. Brack —9M 15
(off Crescent Rd.)
Hammond Rd. Craw —9N 181
Hammond Rd. Wok —2M 73
Hammond Way. Light —6M 51
Ham Moor. —1N 55
Hamond Clo. S Croy —5M 63
Hampden Av. Beck —1H 47
Hampden Clo. Craw —9J 163
Hampden Rd. Beck —1H 47
Hampden Rd. King T —2N 41
Hampers Ct. H'ham —6K 197
Hamper's La. H'ham —6N 197
Hampshire Clo. Alder —6B 110
Hampshire Ct. Add —2L 55
Hampshire Ri. Warf —7D 16
Hampshire Rd. Camb —7D 50
Hampstead La. Dork —6F 118
Hampstead Rd. Dork —6G 118
Hampstead Wlk. Craw —7A 182
Hampton. —9B 24
Hampton & Richmond Borough F.C. —9B 24
Hampton Clo. SW20 —8H 27
Hampton Clo. C Crook —9B 88
Hampton Court. —3E 40
Hampton Court. (Junct.) —2E 40
Hampton Ct. Av. E Mol —5D 40
Hampton Ct. Cres. E Mol —2D 40
Hampton Court Palace. —3F 40
Hampton Ct. Pde. E Mol —3E 40
Hampton Ct. Rd. Hamp —1C 40
Hampton Ct. Way. Th Dit & E Mol —8E 40
Hampton Farm Ind. Est. Felt —4M 23
Hampton Gro. Eps —7E 60
Hampton Hill. —6C 24
Hampton La. Felt —5M 23
Hampton Rd. Croy —5N 45
Hampton Rd. Farnh —6F 108
Hampton Rd. Red —8D 122
Hampton Rd. Tedd —6D 24
Hampton Rd. Twic —4D 24
Hampton Rd. Wor Pk —8F 42
Hampton Rd. E. Felt —5N 23
Hampton Rd. W. Felt —4M 23
Hampton Way. E Grin —2B 186
Hampton Wick. —9J 25 (1H 203)
Ham Ridings. Rich —6M 25
Hamsey Green. —3E 84
Hamsey Grn. Gdns. Warl —3E 84
Hamsey Way. S Croy —2E 84
Ham St. Rich —2H 25
Ham, The. Bren —3J 11
Ham Vw. Croy —5H 47
Hanah Ct. SW19 —8J 27
Hanbury Dri. Big H —9D 66
Hanbury Path. Wok —1F 74
Hanbury Rd. If'd —4K 181
Hanbury Way. Camb —3A 70
Hancock Rd. SE19 —7N 29
Hancocks Mt. Asc —5A 34
Hancombe Rd. Sand —6F 48
Handcroft Rd. Croy —6M 45 (1A 200)
Handcross. —8N 199
Handel Mans. SW13 —3H 13
Handford La. Yat —1C 68
Handinhand La. Tad —8B 100
Handley Page Rd. Wall —4K 63
Handside Clo. Wor Pk —7J 43
Handsworth Ho. Craw —4B 182
(off Brighton Rd.)
Hanford Clo. SW18 —2M 27
Hanford Row. SW19 —7H 27
Hangerfield Clo. Yat —1B 68
Hanger Hill. Wey —3C 56
Hanger, The. Head —2D 168
Hangrove Hill. Orp —9K 67
Hanley Clo. Wind —4A 4
Hannah Clo. Beck —2M 47
Hannah M. Wall —4G 63
Hannah Peschar Gallery Garden. —8A 158
Hannay Wlk. SW16 —3H 29
Hannell Rd. SW6 —3K 13
Hannen Rd. SE27 —4M 29
Hannibal Rd. Stanw —1M 21
Hannibal Way. Croy —2K 63
Hanover Av. Felt —2H 23
Hanover Clo. Craw —5D 182
(in two parts)
Hanover Clo. Eng G —7L 19
Hanover Clo. Frim —5C 70
Hanover Clo. Red —6G 102
Hanover Clo. Rich —3N 11
Hanover Clo. Sutt —1K 61
Hanover Clo. Wind —4C 4
Hanover Clo. Yat —8C 48
Hanover Ct. SW15 —7E 12
Hanover Ct. Dork —5F 118 (2H 201)
Hanover Ct. Guild —1N 113
Hanover Ct. H'ham —5M 197
Hanover Ct. Wok —6A 74
Hanover Dri. Fleet —1D 88
Hanover Gdns. Brack —6L 31
Hanover Gdns. Farn —8K 69
Hanover Rd. SW19 —8A 28
Hanover St. Croy —9M 45 (4A 200)
Hanover Ter. Iswth —4G 11
Hanover Wlk. Wey —9E 38
Hanover Way. Wind —5C 4
Hansler Gro. E Mol —3D 40
Hanson Clo. SW12 —1F 28
Hanson Clo. SW14 —6B 12
Hanson Clo. Camb —8F 50
Hanson Clo. Guild —9B 94
Hanworth. —6M 31 (Bracknell)
Hanworth. —6M 23 (Feltham)
Hanworth Clo. Brack —5A 32
Hanworth La. Cher —7H 37
Hanworth Rd. Brack —7M 31
Hanworth Rd. Felt —2J 23
Hanworth Rd. Hamp —5N 23
Hanworth Rd. Houn —2M 23
Hanworth Rd. Red —8D 122
Hanworth Rd. Sun —8H 23
(in two parts)
Hanworth Ter. Houn —7B 10
Hanworth Trad. Est. Cher —7H 37
Hanworth Trad. Est. Felt —4M 23
Harberson Rd. SW12 —2F 28
Harbledown Rd. SW6 —4M 13
Harbledown Rd. S Croy —7D 64
Harbord St. SW6 —4J 13
Harborough Rd. SW16 —5K 29
Harbour Av. SW10 —4N 13
Harbour Clo. Farn —6M 69
Harbourfield Rd. Bans —2N 81
Harbridge Av. SW15 —1E 26
Harbury Rd. Cars —5C 62
Harcourt Av. Wall —1F 62
Harcourt Clo. Egh —7E 20
Harcourt Clo. Iswth —6G 11
Harcourt Cotts. P'ham —8N 111
Harcourt Fld. Wall —1F 62
Harcourt Lodge. Wall —1F 62
Harcourt M. Wray —9A 6
Harcourt Rd. SW19 —8M 27
Harcourt Rd. Brack —5N 31
Harcourt Rd. Camb —1M 69
Harcourt Rd. T Hth —5K 45
Harcourt Rd. Wall —1F 62
Harcourt Rd. Wind —4B 4
Harcourt Ter. SW10 —1N 13
Harcourt Way. S God —6H 125
Hardcastle Clo. Croy —5D 46
Hardcourts Clo. W Wick —1L 65
Hardell Clo. Egh —6C 20
Hardel Ri. SW2 —2M 29
Hardel Wlk. SW2 —1L 29
Harden Farm Clo. Coul —8G 83
Hardham Clo. Craw —1M 181
Harding Clo. Croy —9C 46
Harding Rd. Eps —6D 80
Harding's Clo. King T —9M 25 (1M 203)
Hardings Rd. Dork —2A 140
Hardman Rd. King T —1L 41 (3L 203)
Hardwell Way. Brack —3C 32
Hardwick Clo. Oxs —2C 78
Hardwicke Av. Houn —4A 10
Hardwicke Rd. Reig —2M 121
Hardwicke Rd. Rich —5J 25
Hardwick La. Lyne —6E 36
Hardwick Rd. Red —5B 122
Hardwicks Way. SW18 —8M 13
Hardy Av. Yat —2B 68
Hardy Clo. Craw —2G 182
Hardy Clo. Horl —8C 142
Hardy Clo. H'ham —4H 197
Hardy Clo. N Holm —9H 119
Hardy Grn. Crowt —3G 48
Hardy Ho. SW4 —1G 29
Hardy Rd. SW19 —8N 27
Hardys Clo. E Mol —3E 40
Harebell Hill. Cobh —1L 77
Harecroft. Dork —8J 119
Harecroft. Fet —2B 98
Harefield. Esh —9E 40
Harefield Av. Sutt —5K 61
Harefield Rd. SW16 —8K 29
Hare Hill. Add —3G 55
Harehill Clo. Pyr —2J 75
Harelands Clo. Wok —4M 73
Harelands La. Wok —5M 73
(in two parts)
Hare La. Clay —2D 58
Hare La. Craw —9N 161
Hare La. G'ming —5J 133
Hare La. Ling —7F 144
Harendon. Tad —8H 81
Hares Bank. New Ad —6N 65
Harestone Dri. Cat —2C 104
Harestone Hill. Cat —4C 104
Harestone La. Cat —3B 104
(in two parts)
Harestone Valley Rd. Cat —4B 104
Hareward Rd. Guild —1E 114
Harewood Clo. Craw —9E 162
Harewood Clo. Reig —9A 102
Harewood Gdns. S Croy —2E 84
Harewood Rd. SW19 —7C 28
Harewood Rd. Iswth —3F 10
Harewood Rd. S Croy —3B 64
Harfield Rd. Sun —1L 39
Harkness Clo. Eps —3H 81
Harland Av. Croy —9C 46
Harland Clo. SW19 —2N 43
Harlands Gro. Orp —1K 67
Harlech Gdns. Houn —2K 9
Harlech Rd. B'water —2J 69
Harlequin Av. Bren —2G 11
Harlequin Cen. S'hall —1K 9
Harlequin Clo. Iswth —8E 10
Harlequin Rd. Tedd —8H 25
Harlequins R.U.F.C. —1E 24
Harlequin Theatre. —2D 122
Harley Gdns. Orp —1N 67
Harlington. —2E 8
Harlington Cen., The. Fleet —4A 88
(off Fleet Rd.)
Harlington Clo. Hayes —3D 8
Harlington Corner. (Junct.) —4E 8
Harlington Rd. E. Felt —1J 23
Harlington Rd. W. Felt —9J 9
Harlington Way. Fleet —4A 88
Harlow Ct. Reig —3B 122
(off Wray Comn. Rd.)
Harman Pl. Purl —7M 63
Harmans Dri. E Grin —9D 166
Harmans Mead. E Grin —9D 166
Harmanswater. —3C 32
Harman's Water Rd. Brack —4A 32
Harmar Clo. Wokgm —2D 30
Harmondsworth. —2M 7
Harmondsworth La. W Dray —2N 7
Harmondsworth Rd. W Dray —1N 7
Harmony Clo. Bew —5K 181
Harmony Clo. Wall —5H 63
Harms Gro. Guild —9E 94
Harold Rd. SE19 —8N 29
Harold Rd. Sutt —1B 62
Harold Rd. Worth —3J 183
Haroldslea. Horl —1H 163
(in two parts)
Haroldslea Clo. Horl —1G 163
Haroldslea Dri. Horl —1G 162
Harold Wilson Ho. SW6 —2L 13
(off Clem Attlee Ct.)
Harpenden Rd. SE27 —4M 29
Harper Dri. M'bowr —7G 182
Harper M. SW17 —4A 28
Harper's Rd. As —1G 111
Harpesford Av. Vir W —4L 35
Harps Oak La. Red —3D 102
Harpton Clo. Yat —8C 48
Harpton Pde. Yat —8C 48
Harpurs. Tad —9J 81
Harrier Clo. Cranl —6N 155
Harrier Ct. Craw —9H 163
(off Bristol Clo.)
Harrier Ct. Houn —6M 9
Harriet Gdns. Croy —8D 46
Harriet Ho. SW6 —3N 13
(off Wandon Rd.)
Harriet Tubman Clo. SW2 —1K 29
Harrington Clo. Croy —8J 45
Harrington Clo. Leigh —1F 140
Harrington Clo. Wind —7C 4

Headley Hill Rd. Head —4F 168
Headley La. Mick —7J 99
Headley La. Pass —8D 168
Headley Pk. Cotts. Head —9B 148
Headley Rd. Eps —5A 80
(in two parts)
Headley Rd. Gray —5K 169
Headley Rd. Lea & Eps —9J 79
Headley Rd. Lind —4B 168
Headon Ct. Farnh —2J 129
Headway Clo. Rich —5J 25
Headway, The. Eps —5E 60
Healy Dri. Orp —1N 67
Hearmon Clo. Yat —9D 48
Hearn. —1F 168
Hearne Rd. W4 —2N 11
Hearn Va. Head D —2F 168
Hearnville Rd. SW12 —2E 28
Hearn Wlk. Brack —9C 16
Hearsey Gdns. B'water —9G 49
(in two parts)
Heathacre. Coln —4G 6
Heatham Pk. Twic —1F 24
Heathbridge. Wey —4B 56
Heathbridge App. Wey —3B 56
Heath Bus. Cen. Houn —7C 10
Heath Bus. Cen. Salf —4F 142
Heath Clo. Bans —1N 81
Heath Clo. Broad H —5E 196
Heath Clo. Farnh —5H 109
Heath Clo. Hayes —3E 8
Heath Clo. Hind —2A 170
Heath Clo. Ott —2D 54
Heath Clo. Stanw —9L 7
Heath Clo. Vir W —3N 35
Heath Clo. Wokgm —4A 30
Heathcote. Tad —8J 81
Heathcote Clo. Ash V —1E 110
(off Church Path)
Heathcote Dri. E Grin —8L 165
Heathcote Rd. As —1F 110
Heathcote Rd. Camb —1B 70
Heathcote Rd. Eps —1C 80 (8L 201)
Heathcote Rd. Twic —9H 11
Heath Cotts. Hind —3A 170
Heath Cotts. Lwr Bo —8J 129
Heath Ct. Bag —4J 51
Heath Ct. Broad H —5F 196
Heath Ct. Croy —7D 200
Heath Ct. Houn —7N 9
Heathcroft Av. Sun —8G 22
Heathdale Av. Houn —6M 9
Heathdene. Tad —5K 81
Heathdene Rd. SW16 —8K 29
Heathdene Rd. Wall —4F 62
Heathdown Rd. Wok —2F 74
Heath Dri. SW20 —3H 43
Heath Dri. Brkwd —7D 72
Heath Dri. Send —9D 74
Heath Dri. Sutt —5A 62
Heath Dri. Tad —3F 100
Heath End. —5H 109
Heather Clo. Alder —3K 109
Heather Clo. Ash V —8F 90
Heather Clo. Copt —8M 163
Heather Clo. Farnh —5E 128
Heather Clo. Guild —2L 113
Heather Clo. Hamp —9N 23
Heather Clo. H'ham —3K 197
Heather Clo. Iswth —8D 10
Heather Clo. New H —6K 55
Heather Clo. Red —9F 102
Heather Clo. Tad —9K 81
Heather Clo. Wok —2M 73
Heather Cotts. Hind —1B 170
Heather Ct. Hind —5D 170
Heatherdale Clo. King T —7N 25
Heatherdale Rd. Camb —2A 70
Heatherdene. W Hor —3E 96
Heatherdene Av. Crowt —3D 48
Heatherdene Clo. Mitc —3B 44
Heather Dri. Asc —6E 34
Heather Dri. C Crook —8A 88
Heather Dri. Lind —4A 168
Heatherfields. New H —6K 55
Heather Gdns. Farn —3J 89
Heather Gdns. Sutt —3M 61
Heatherlands. Horl —7F 142
(in two parts)
Heatherlands. Sun —7H 23
Heatherley Clo. Camb —1N 69
Heatherley Rd. Camb —1N 69
Heather Mead. Frim —4D 70
Heather Mead Ct. Frim —4D 70
Heathermount. Brack —3C 32
Heathermount Dri. Crowt —1E 48
Heathermount Gdns. Crowt —1F 48
Heather Pl. Esh —1B 58
Heather Ridge Arc. Camb —2G 71
Heatherset Clo. Esh —2C 58
Heatherset Gdns. SW16 —8K 29
Heatherside. —2G 71
Heatherside Clo. Bookh —3N 97
Heatherside Dri. Vir W —5K 35
Heatherside Rd. Eps —4C 60
Heathersland. Dork —8J 119
Heathers, The. Stai —1A 22
Heathervale Cvn. Pk. New H —6L 55
Heathervale Rd. New H —6K 55
Heathervale Way. New H —6L 55
Heather Vw. Cotts. Fren —1H 149
Heather Wlk. Brkwd —8A 72
Heather Wlk. Craw —6N 181
Heather Wlk. Small —8N 143
Heather Wlk. Twic —1A 24
(off Stephenson Rd.)
Heather Wlk. W Vill —6F 56
Heather Way. Chob —4H 53
Heatherway. Crowt —2F 48
Heatherway. Felb —3J 165
Heather Way. Hind —5D 170
Heather Way. S Croy —5G 65
Heathfield. Cobh —1A 78
Heathfield. Craw —9H 163
(in two parts)
Heathfield Av. SW18 —1B 28
Heathfield Av. Asc —4B 34
Heathfield Clo. G'ming —9H 133
Heathfield Clo. Kes —2E 66
Heathfield Clo. Wok —6C 74
Heathfield Ct. W4 —1C 12
Heathfield Ct. Fleet —9A 88
Heathfield Dri. Mitc —9C 28
Heathfield Dri. Red —8C 122
Heathfield Gdns. W4 —1B 12
Heathfield Gdns. Croy
—1A 64 (6C 200)
Heathfield N. Twic —1E 24
Heathfield Rd. SW18 —1B 28
Heathfield Rd. Croy —1A 64 (6D 200)
Heathfield Rd. Kes —2E 66
Heathfield Rd. W on T —1M 57
Heathfield Rd. Wok —5C 74
Heathfields Ct. Houn —8M 9
Heathfield S. Twic —1F 24
Heathfield Sq. SW18 —1D 28
Heathfield Ter. W4 —1B 12
Heathfield Va. S Croy —5G 65
Heath Gdns. Twic —2F 24
Heath Gro. Sun —8G 23
Heath Hill. Dock —7D 148
Heath Hill. Dork —5H 119 (2M 201)
Heath Hill Rd. N. Crowt —2G 48
Heath Hill Rd. S. Crowt —2G 49
Heath Ho. Rd. Wok —9G 73
Heathhurst Rd. S Croy —5A 64
Heathlands. Brack —3M 31
Heathlands. Tad —9J 81
Heathlands Clo. Sun —1H 39
Heathlands Clo. Twic —3F 24
Heathlands Clo. Wok —1A 74
Heathlands Ct. Wokgm —8E 30
Heathlands Ct. Yat —2D 68
Heathlands Rd. Wokgm —5E 30
Heathland St. Alder —2M 109
Heathlands Way. Houn —8M 9
Heath La. Alb —1N 135
Heath La. Cron & Ews —6A 108
Heath La. Farnh —5H 109
Heath La. G'ming —9K 133
Heathmans Rd. SW6 —4L 13
Heath Mead. SW19 —4J 27
Heath Mill La. Worp —3E 92
(in two parts)
Heathmoors. Brack —4A 32
Heathpark Dri. W'sham —3B 52
Heath Pl. Bag —4J 51
Heath Ride. Finch & Crowt —1A 48
Heath Ridge Grn. Cobh —9A 58
Heath Ri. SW15 —9J 13
Heath Ri. Camb —1B 70
Heath Ri. Rip —1K 95
Heath Ri. Vir W —3N 35
Heath Ri. Westc —7C 118
Heath Rd. Bag —4J 51
Heath Rd. Cat —1A 104
Heath Rd. Hasl —3B 188
Heath Rd. Houn —7B 10
Heath Rd. Oxs —8C 58
Heath Rd. T Hth —2N 45
Heath Rd. Twic —2F 24
Heath Rd. Wey —1B 56
Heath Rd. Wok —2B 74
Heathrow. Gom —8D 116
Heathrow Airport. —6C 8
Heathrow Boulevd. W Dray —3A 8
(in two parts)
Heathrow Causeway Cen. Houn
—6H 9
Heathrow Clo. W Dray —4K 7
Heathrow International Trad. Est.
Houn —6J 9
Heathside. Esh —9E 40
Heathside. Houn —1N 23
Heathside. Wey —2C 56
Heathside Clo. Esh —9E 40
Heathside Ct. Tad —1H 101
Heathside Cres. Wok —4B 74
Heathside Gdns. Wok —4C 74
Heathside La. Hind —3B 170
Heathside Pk. Camb —8G 50
Heathside Pk. Rd. Wok —5B 74
Heathside Pl. Eps —5J 81
Heathside Rd. Wok —5B 74
Heath, The. —3C 56
Heath, The. Cat —2N 103
Heath, The. P'ham —8A 112
Heath Va. Bri. Rd. Ash V —7E 90
Heath Vw. E Hor —3G 97
Heathview Gdns. SW15 —1H 27
Heathview Rd. Milf —3B 152
Heathview Rd. T Hth —3L 45
Heathway. Asc —9J 17
Heathway. Camb —1B 70
Heathway. Cat —3N 103
Heathway. Croy —9J 47
Heathway. E Hor —2G 97
Heath Way. H'ham —3K 197
Heathway Clo. Camb —1B 70
Heathwood Clo. Yat —8C 48
Heathyfields Rd. Farnh —6E 108
Heaton Rd. Mitc —8F 28
Hebbecastle Down. Warf —7N 15
Hebdon Rd. SW17 —4C 28
Heber Mans. W14 —2K 13
(off Queen's Club Gdns.)
Heckfield Pl. SW6 —3M 13
Heddon Clo. Iswth —7G 10
Heddon Wlk. Farn —7M 69
Hedgecourt Pl. Felb —6H 165
Hedge Cft. Yat —9A 48
Hedgecroft Cotts. Rip —8K 75
Hedgehog La. Hasl —2F 188
Hedgerley Ct. Wok —4M 73
Hedger's Almshouses. Guild —2F 114
(off Wykeham Rd.)
Hedgeside. Craw —8A 182
Hedgeway. Guild —5K 113
Hedingham Clo. Horl —7G 142
Hedley Rd. Twic —1A 24
Heenan Clo. Frim G —7C 70
Heidegger Cres. SW13 —3G 13
Heighton Gdns. Croy
—2M 63 (8A 200)
Heights Clo. SW20 —8G 27
Heights Clo. Bans —3K 81
Heights, The. Wey —6B 56
Helby Rd. SW4 —1H 29
Helder St. S Croy —3A 64
Heldmann Clo. Iswth —7D 10
Helena Clo. Wall —4J 63
Helena Rd. Wind —5G 4
Helen Av. Felt —1J 23
Helen Clo. W Mol —3D 40
Helen Ct. Farn —1N 89
Helford Wlk. Wok —5K 73
Helgiford Gdns. Sun —8F 22
Helicon Ho. Craw —4A 182
Helix Bus. Pk. Camb —3N 69
Helix Rd. SW2 —1K 29
Helm Clo. Eps —8N 59
Helme Clo. SW19 —6L 27
Helmsdale. Brack —4B 32
Helmsdale. Wok —5L 73
Helmsdale Rd. SW16 —9H 29
Helston Clo. Frim —7E 70
Helston La. Wind —4E 4
Helvellyn Clo. Egh —8D 20
Hemingford Rd. Sutt —1H 61
Hemlock Clo. Kgswd —1K 101
Hemming Clo. Hamp —9A 24
Hemmyng Corner. Warf —7A 16
Hempshaw Av. Bans —3D 82
Hemsby Rd. Chess —3M 59
Hemsby Wlk. Craw —5F 182
Hemsley Ct. Guild —9K 93
Hemwood Rd. Wind —6A 4
Henbane Ct. Craw —7M 181
Henbit Clo. Tad —6G 81
Henchley Dene. Guild —9F 94
Henderson Av. Guild —8L 93
Henderson Rd. SW18 —1C 28
Henderson Rd. Big H —8E 66
Henderson Rd. Craw —8N 181
Henderson Rd. Croy —5A 46
Henderson Way. H'ham —8F 196
Hendham Rd. SW17 —3C 28
Hendon Gro. Eps —5N 59
Hendon Way. Stanw —9M 7
Hendrick Av. SW12 —1D 28
Heneage Cres. New Ad —6M 65
Henfield Rd. SW19 —9L 27
Henfold Cotts. Newd —9N 139
Henfold Dri. Bear G —8K 139
Henfold La. Holmw —4L 139
Henfold La. Newd —7M 139
Hengelo Gdns. Mitc —3B 44
Hengist Clo. H'ham —7G 197
Hengist Way. Brom —3N 47
Hengrove Cres. Afrd —4M 21
Henhurst Cross La. Cold —8G 138
Henhurst La. Cold —8G 138
Henley Av. Sutt —9K 43
Henley Bank. Guild —5K 113
Henley Clo. Farn —6K 69
Henley Clo. Iswth —4F 10
Henley Clo. M'bowr —6H 183
Henley Ct. Wok —7D 74
Henley Dri. Frim G —7C 70
Henley Dri. King T —8E 26
Henley Fort Bungalows. Guild
—6K 113
Henley Gdns. Yat —1C 68
Henley Ga. Norm & Pirb —5N 91
Henley Pk. Norm —7N 91
Henley Way. Felt —6L 23
Henlow Pl. Rich —3K 25
Henlys Roundabout. (Junct.) —5K 9
Hennessey Ct. Wok —9E 54
Henrietta Ho. W6 —1H 13
(off Queen Caroline St.)
Henry Doulton Dri. SW17 —5E 28
Henry Hatch Wlk. Sutt —4A 62
Henry Jackson Rd. SW15 —6J 13
Henry Macaulay Av. King T
—9K 25 (2J 203)
Henry Peters Dri. Tedd —6E 24
Henshaw Clo. Craw —5L 181
Henslow Way. Wok —1F 74
Henson Rd. Craw —2F 183
Hensworth Rd. Afrd —6M 21
Henty Clo. Craw —6K 181
Henty Wlk. SW15 —8G 12
Hepple Clo. Iswth —5H 11
Hepplestone Clo. SW15 —9G 13
Hepplewhite Clo. Craw —8N 181
Hepworth Cft. Coll T —9K 49
Hepworth Rd. SW16 —8J 29
Hepworth Way. W on T —7G 39
Heracles Clo. Wall —4J 63
Herald Ct. Alder —3N 109
Herald Gdns. Wall —8F 44
Herbert Clo. Brack —4N 31
Herbert Cres. Knap —5H 73
Herbert Gdns. W4 —2A 12
Herbert Morrison Ho. SW6 —2L 13
(off Clem Attlee Ct.)
Herbert Rd. SW19 —8L 27
(in two parts)
Herbert Rd. King T —2M 41 (6M 203)
Herbs End. Farn —9H 69
Hereford Clo. Craw —7C 182
Hereford Clo. Eps —9C 60 (7L 201)
Hereford Clo. Guild —1J 113
Hereford Clo. Stai —9K 21
Hereford Copse. Wok —6L 73
Hereford Ct. Sutt —4M 61
Hereford Gdns. Twic —2C 24
Hereford Ho. SW10 —3N 13
(off Fulham Rd.)
Hereford La. Farnh —6G 109
Hereford Mead. Fleet —1C 88
Hereford Rd. Felt —2K 23
Hereford Sq. SW7 —1N 13
Hereford Way. Chess —2J 59
Hereward Av. Purl —7L 63
Hereward Rd. SW17 —5D 28
Heriot Rd. Cher —6J 37
Heritage Hill. Kes —2F 66
Heritage Lawn. Horl —7G 142
Herlwyn Gdns. SW17 —5D 28
Herm Clo. Craw —7M 181
Herm Clo. Iswth —3C 10
Hermes Clo. Fleet —4D 88
Hermes Way. Wall —4H 63
Hermitage Bri. Cotts. Wok —6F 72
Hermitage Clo. Clay —3G 58
Hermitage Clo. Farn —4B 90
Hermitage Clo. Frim —5D 70
Hermitage Clo. Shep —3B 38
Hermitage Dri. Asc —1J 33
Hermitage Gdns. SE19 —8N 29
Hermitage Grn. SW16 —9J 29
Hermitage La. SE25 —5D 46
(in two parts)
Hermitage La. SW16 —8K 29
Hermitage La. E Grin —1B 186
Hermitage La. Wind —6D 4
Hermitage Pde. Asc —2M 33
Hermitage Path. SW16 —9J 29
Hermitage Rd. SE19 —8N 29
Hermitage Rd. E Grin —7N 165
Hermitage Rd. Kenl —2N 83
Hermitage Rd. Wok —6G 72
Hermitage, The. SW13 —4E 12
Hermitage, The. Felt —4G 23
Hermitage, The. King T
—3K 41 (7J 203)
Hermitage, The. Rich —8L 11
Hermitage, The. Warf —6B 16
Hermitage Woods Cres. Wok —6H 73
Hermitage Woods Est. Wok —6H 73
Hermits Rd. Craw —2D 182
Hermongers. —8H 177
Hermonger's La. Rud —7G 176
Hernbrook Dri. H'ham —8L 197
Herndon Clo. Egh —5C 20
Herndon Rd. SW18 —8N 13
Herne Rd. Surb —8K 41
Heron Clo. Asc —9H 17
Heron Clo. C Crook —7D 88
Heron Clo. Craw —1A 182
Heron Clo. Eden —9L 127
Heron Clo. Guild —9L 93
Heron Clo. Myt —1D 90
Heron Clo. Sutt —2L 61
Heron Ct. Dork —1K 201
Heron Ct. Eps —1F 80
Heron Ct. King T —2L 41 (6K 203)
Heron Dale. Add —2M 55
Herondale. Brack —6A 32
Herondale. Hasl —2C 188
Herondale. S Croy —5G 65
Herondale Av. SW18 —2B 28
Heronfield. Eng G —7M 19
Heron Pl. E Grin —1B 186
Heron Rd. Croy —8B 46
Heron Rd. Twic —7G 11
Heronry, The. W on T —3H 57
Heronsbrook. Asc —1B 34
Herons Clo. Copt —5D 164
Herons Ct. Light —7N 51
Herons Cft. Wey —3D 56
Heron Shaw. Cranl —9N 155
Herons Lea. Copt —5D 164
Heron's Pl. Iswth —6H 11
Heron Sq. Rich —8K 11
Herons Way. Brkwd —8A 72
Heron's Way. Wokgm —1D 30
Herons Wood Ct. Horl —7F 142
Herontye Dri. E Grin —1B 186
Heron Wlk. Wok —1E 74
Heron Way. H'ham —6N 197
Heron Wood Rd. Alder —4B 110
Herretts Gdns. Alder —3B 110
Herrett St. Alder —4B 110
Herrick Clo. Craw —1G 182
Herrick Clo. Frim —3G 70
Herrings La. Cher —5J 37
Herrings La. W'sham —2A 52
Herriot Ct. Yat —2B 68
Herschel Grange. Warf —6B 16
Herschel Wlk. Craw —8N 181
Hersham. —2L 57
Hersham By Pass. W on T —2J 57
Hersham Clo. SW15 —1F 26
Hersham Gdns. W on T —1J 57
Hersham Green. —2L 57
Hersham Grn. Shop. Cen. W on T
—2L 57
Hersham Pl. W on T —2L 57
Hersham Rd. W on T —7H 39
Hersham Trad. Est. W on T —8M 39
Hershell Ct. SW14 —7A 12
Hertford Av. SW14 —8C 12
Hertford Sq. Mitc —3J 45
Hertford Way. Mitc —3J 45
Hesiers Hill. Warl —4A 86
Hesiers Rd. Warl —3A 86
Hesketh Clo. Cranl —7N 155
Heslop Rd. SW12 —2D 28
Hesper M. SW5 —1N 13
Hessle Gro. Eps —7E 60
Hestercombe Av. SW6 —5K 13
Hesterman Way. Croy —7K 45
Hester Ter. Rich —6N 11
Heston. —3A 10
Heston Av. Houn —2M 9
Heston Cen., The. Houn —1K 9
Heston Grange. Houn —2N 9
Heston Grange La. Houn —2N 9
Heston Ind. Cen. Houn —2K 9
Heston Ind. Mall. Houn —3N 9
Heston Rd. Houn —3A 10
Heston Rd. Red —7D 122
Heston Wlk. Red —7D 122
Hetherington Rd. Shep —1D 38
Hethersett Clo. Reig —9A 102
Hever Rd. Eden —3M 147
Hevers Av. Horl —7D 142
Hevers Corner. Horl —7D 142
Hewers Way. Tad —7G 81
Hewitt Clo. Croy —9K 47
Hewitts Ind. Est. Cranl —7K 155
Hewlett Pl. Bag —4K 51
Hexham Clo. Owl —5J 49
Hexham Clo. Worth —3J 183
Hexham Gdns. Iswth —3G 11
Hexham Rd. SE27 —3N 29
Hexham Rd. Mord —7N 43
Hextalls La. Blet —6A 104
Heybridge Av. SW16 —8J 29
Heyford Av. SW20 —2L 43
Heyford Rd. Mitc —1C 44
Heymede. Lea —1J 99
Heythorpe Clo. Wok —4J 73
Heythorp St. SW18 —2L 27
Heywood Ct. G'ming —4F 132
Heywood Dri. Bag —5G 51
Hibbert's All. Wind —4G 4
Hibernia Gdns. Houn —7A 10
Hibernia Rd. Houn —7A 10
Hibiscus Gro. Bord —7A 168
Hickey's Almshouses. Rich —7M 11
Hickling Wlk. Craw —5F 182
Hickmans Clo. God —1F 124
Hicks La. B'water —1G 69
Hidcote Clo. Wok —3D 74
Hidcote Gdns. SW20 —2G 42
Higgins Wlk. Hamp —7M 23
(off Abbott Clo.)
Higgs La. Bag —4H 51
(in two parts)
Highacre. Dork —8H 119
Highams Hill. Craw —4L 181
Highams Hill. Warl —8C 66
Highams La. Chob —3D 52
High Barn Rd. Eff & Ran C —7L 97
Highbarrow Rd. Croy —7D 46
High Beech. Brack —3D 32

Hindell Clo.—Hope Way

Hindell Clo. *Farn* —6M 69
Hindhead. —5D 170
Hindhead Clo. *Craw* —5A 182
Hindhead Common. —4E 170
Hindhead Rd. *Hasl & Hind* —1C 188
Hindhead Way. *Wall* —2J 63
Hine Clo. *Coul* —9G 83
Hinkler Clo. *Wall* 4J 63
(in two parts)
Hinstock Clo. *Farn* —2M 89
Hinton Av. *Houn* —7L 9
Hinton Clo. *Crowt* —9G 31
Hinton Dri. *Crowt* —9G 31
Hinton Rd. *Hurst* —1A 14
Hinton Rd. *Wall* —3G 63
Hipley Ct. *Guild* —4C 114
Hipley St. *Wok* —7D 74
Hitchcock Clo. *Shep* —2A 38
Hitchings Way. *Reig* —7M 121
Hitherbury Clo. *Guild*
—6M 113 (8B 202)
Hitherfield Rd. *SW16* —3K 29
Hitherhooks Hill. *Binf* —9K 15
Hithermoor Rd. *Stal* —9H 7
Hitherwood. *Cranl* —8N 155
Hitherwood Clo. *Reig* 1B 122
H. Jones Cres. *Alder* —1A 110
Hoadlands Cotts. *Hand* —6N 199
Hoadly Rd. *SW16* —4H 29
Hobart Ct. *S Croy* —8E 200
Hobart Gdns. *T Hth* —2A 46
Hobart Pl. *Rich* —1M 25
Hobart Rd. *Wor Pk* —9G 42
Hobbes Wlk. *SW15* —8G 12
Hobbs Clo. *W Byf* —9K 55
Hobbs Ind. Est. *Newc* —2H 165
Hobbs Rd. *SE27* —5N 29
Hobbs Rd. *Broadf* —7M 181
Hobill Wlk. *Surb* —5M 41
Hocken Mead. *Craw* —1H 183
Hockering Est. *Wok* —5D 74
Hockering Gdns. *Wok* —5C 74
Hockering Rd. *Wok* —5C 74
Hockford Clo. *Pirb* —4F 92
Hodge La. *Wink* —6L 17
(in two parts)
Hodges Clo. *Bag* —6H 51
Hodgkin Clo. *M'bowr* —4G 182
Hodgson Gdns. *Guild* —9C 94
Hoe. —3F 136
Hoebrook Clo. *Wok* —8N 73
Hoe La. *Hasc* —6N 153
Hoe La. *Peasl & Ab H* —3F 136
Hoffman Clo. *Brack* —7B 16
Hogarth Av. *Afrd* —7D 22
Hogarth Bus. Cen. *W4* —2D 12
Hogarth Clo. *Coll T* —9K 49
Hogarth Clo. *Houn* —3M 9
Hogarth Cres. *SW19* —9B 28
Hogarth Cres. *Croy* —6N 45
Hogarth Gdns. *Houn* —3A 10
Hogarth La. *W4* —2D 12
Hogarth Pl. SW5 —1N 13
(off Hogarth Rd.)
Hogarth Rd. *SW5* —1N 13
Hogarth Rd. *Craw* —6D 182
Hogarth Roundabout. (Junct.)
—2E 12
Hogarth's House. —2D 12
(off Hogarth La.)
Hogarth Ter. *W4* —2D 12
Hogarth Way. *Hamp* —9C 24
Hogden Clo. *Tad* —3L 101
Hogdon La. *Ran C* —9M 97
(in four parts)
Hog Hatch. —6F 108
Hoghatch La. *Farnh* —6F 108
Hog's Back. *Guild* —6H 113 (8A 202)
Hog's Back. *P'ham* —7L 111
Hog's Back. *Seale* —8B 110
(in two parts)
Hog's Back Brewery. —7D 110
Hogscross La. *Coul* —1D 102
Hog's Hill. *Craw* —6B 182
Hogs Hill. *Fern* —9F 188
Hogshill La. *Cobh* —1J 77
(in three parts)
Hogsmill Ho. *King T* —5M 203
Hogsmill Wlk. *King T* —5K 203
Hogsmill Way. *Eps* —2B 60
Hogtrough La. *God* —5K 105
(in two parts)
Hogtrough La. *S Nut* —4G 123
Hogwood Rd. *Loxw* —5E 192
Holbeach M. *SW12* —2F 28
Holbeche Clo. *Yat* —1A 68
Holbeck. *Brack* —5L 31
Holbein Rd. *Craw* —6D 182
Holborn Way. *Mitc* —1D 44
Holbreck Pl. *Wok* —5B 74
Holbrook. —9L 179
Holbrook Clo. *Farnh* —4L 109
Holbrooke Pl. *Rich* —8K 11
Holbrook Mdw. *Egh* —7E 20
Holbrook School La. *H'ham* —1L 197
Holbrook Way. *Alder* —5N 109
Holcombe Clo. *W'ham* —4M 107
Holcombe St. *W6* —1G 13
Holcon Ct. *Red* —9E 102
Holcroft Ct. *E Grin* —6B 166
Holden Brook La. *Ockl* —7M 157
Holdernesse Clo. *Iswth* —4G 10
Holdernesse Rd. *SW17* —4D 28
Holderness Way. *SE27* —6M 29
Holder Rd. *Alder* —3C 110
Holder Rd. *M'bowr* —6F 182
Holdfast La. *Hasl* —9K 171
Hole Hill. —5B 118
Holehill La. *Westc* —4A 118
Hole La. *Eden* —5H 127
Holford Rd. *Guild* —3E 114
Holland. —2C 126
Holland Av. *SW20* —9E 26
Holland Av. *Sutt* —5M 61
Holland Clo. *Farnh* —3K 129
Holland Clo. *Red* —3D 122
Holland Ct. *Surb* —6K 41
Holland Cres. *Oxt* —2C 126
Holland Gdns. *Egh* —1H 37
Holland Gdns. *Fleet* —5B 88
Holland La. *Oxt* —2C 126
Holland Pines. *Brack* —6L 31
Holland Rd. *SE25* —4D 46
Holland Rd. *Oxt* —2C 126
Hollands Field. *Broad H* —4E 196
Hollands, The. *Felt* —5L 23
Hollands, The. *Wok* —5A 74
Hollands, The. *Wor Pk* —7E 42
Hollands Way. *E Grin* —6C 166
Hollands Way. *Warn* —9F 178
Hollerith Ri. *Brack* —5N 31
Holles Clo. *Hamp* —7A 24
Hollies Av. *W Byf* —9H 55
Hollies Clo. *SW16* —7L 29
Hollies Clo. *Twic* —3F 24
Hollies Ct. *Add* —2L 55
Hollies, The. Add —2L 55
(off Crockford Pk. Rd.)
Hollies, The. *B'water* —5M 69
Hollies Way. *SW12* —1E 28
Hollin Ct. *Craw* —9C 162
Hollingbourne Cres. *Craw* —9A 182
Hollingsworth Ct. *Surb* —6K 41
Hollingsworth Rd. *Croy* —3E 64
Hollington Cres. *N Mald* —5E 42
Hollingworth Clo. *W Mol* —3N 39
Hollingworth Way. *W'ham* —4M 107
Hollis Row. *Red* —5D 122
Hollis Wood Dri. *Wrec* —6D 128
Hollman Gdns. *SW16* —7M 29
Holloway Clo. *W Dray* —1N 7
Holloway Dri. *Vir W* —3A 36
Holloway Hill. —9H 133
Holloway Hill. *Cher* —9E 36
Holloway Hill. *G'ming* —7G 133
Holloway La. *W Dray* —2N 7
Holloway St. *Houn* —6B 10
Hollow Clo. *Guild* —4L 113
Hollow La. *D'land & E Grin* —1D 166
Hollow La. *Head* —3D 168
Hollow La. *Vir W* —2M 35
Hollow La. *Wott* —9L 117
Hollows, The. *Bren* —2M 11
Hollow, The. *Craw* —4L 181
Hollow, The. *Ews* —5A 108
Hollow, The. *Lwr E* —7C 132
Hollow Way. *Gray* —5A 170
Holly Acre. *Yat* —1C 68
Holly Av. *Frim* —3F 70
Holly Av. *New H* —6J 55
Holly Av. *W on T* —7L 39
Hollybank. *W End* —9C 52
Hollybank Clo. *Hamp* —6A 24
Holly Bank Rd. *W Byf* —1J 75
Holly Bank Rd. *Wok* —8L 73
Hollybrook Pk. *Bord* —6A 168
Hollybush Clo. *Craw* —2C 182
Hollybush Ind. Est. *Alder* —8C 90
Hollybush La. *Alder* —8C 90
Hollybush La. *Fren* —1H 149
Holly Bush La. *Hamp* —8N 23
Hollybush La. *Rip* —6M 75
Hollybush Ride. *Finch* —3B 48
(in two parts)
Hollybush Ride. *W'sham* —9K 33
Hollybush Rd. *Craw* —2C 182
Hollybush Rd. *King T* —6L 25
Holly Clo. *Alder* —2A 110
Holly Clo. *Beck* —3M 47
Holly Clo. *Craw* —1E 182
Holly Clo. *Eng G* —7L 19
Holly Clo. *Farn* —1M 89
Holly Clo. *Felt* —6M 23
Holly Clo. *Head* —4H 169
Holly Clo. *H'ham* —3A 198
Holly Clo. *Longc* —9K 35
Holly Clo. *Wall* —4F 62
Holly Clo. *Wok* —6L 73
Hollycombe. *Eng G* —5M 19
Holly Ct. Cher —7H 37
(off King St.)
Holly Ct. *Crowt* 3D 48
Holly Ct. *Sutt* —4M 61
Holly Cres. *Beck* —4J 47
Holly Cres. *Wind* —5A 4
Hollycroft Clo. *S Croy* —2B 64
Hollycroft Clo. *W Dray* —2B 8
Hollycroft Gdns. *W Dray* —2B 8
Hollydale Dri. *Brom* —1H 67
Holly Dri. *Old Win* —9H 5
Holly Farm Rd. *S'hall* —1M 9
Hollyfield Rd. *Surb* —6M 41
Hollyfields Clo. *Camb* —1N 69
Holly Grn. *Wey* —1F 56
Hollygrove Clo. *Houn* —7N 9
Holly Hedge Clo. *Frim* —4C 70
Hollyhedge Rd. *Cobh* —1J 77
Holly Hedge Rd. *Frim* —4C 70
Holly Hill Dri. *Bans* —4M 81
Hollyhock Dri. *Bisl* —2D 72
Hollyhook Clo. *Crowt* —1F 48
Holly Ho. *Brack* —5N 31
Holly Ho. *Bren* —2J 11
Holly La. *Bans* —3M 81
Holly La. *G'ming* —8F 132
Holly La. *Worp* —7F 92
Holly La. E. *Bans* —3N 81
Holly La. W. *Bans* —4M 81
Holly Lea. *Guild* —6N 93
Holly Lodge Mobile Home Pk. *Tad*
—4K 101
Hollymead. *Cars* —9D 44
Hollymead Rd. *Coul* —5E 82
Hollymeoak Rd. *Coul* —6F 82
Hollymoor La. *Eps* —6C 60
Hollyridge. *Hasl* —2F 188
Holly Rd. *W4* —1C 12
Holly Rd. *Alder* —3A 110
Holly Rd. *Farn* —1L 89
Holly Rd. *Hamp* —7C 24
Holly Rd. *Houn* —7B 10
Holly Rd. *Reig* —5N 121
Holly Rd. *Twic* —2F 24
Holly Spring Cotts. *Brack* —8B 16
Holly Spring La. *Brack* —9A 16
Holly Tree Clo. *SW19* —2J 27
Hollytree Gdns. *Frim* —6B 70
Holly Tree Rd. *Cat* —9B 84
Holly Wlk. *Wind* —5B 18
Hollywater. —8A 168
Hollywater Rd. *Bord* —8A 168
Hollywater Rd. *Pass* —9A 168
Holly Way. *B'water* —2J 69
Holly Way. *Mitc* —3H 45
Hollywood M. *SW10* —2N 13
Hollywood Rd. *SW10* —2N 13
Hollywoods. *Croy* —5J 65
Holman Clo. *Craw* —9N 181
Holman Ct. *Eps* —5F 60
Holman Hunt Ho. W6 —1K 13
(off Field Rd.)
Holman Rd. *Eps* —2B 60
Holmbank Dri. *Shep* —3F 38
Holmbrook Clo. *Farn* —1H 89
Holmbrook Gdns. *Farn* —1H 89
Holmbury Av. *Crowt* —9F 30
Holmbury Clo. *Craw* —5A 182
Holmbury Ct. *SW17* —4D 28
Holmbury Ct. *S Croy* —2B 64
Holmbury Dri. *N Holm* —8J 119
Holmbury Gro. *Croy* —4J 65
Holmbury Hill Rd. *Holm M* —9J 137
Holmbury Keep. Horl —7G 142
(off Langshott La.)
Holmbury La. *Holm M* —1L 157
Holmbury St Mary. —6K 137
Holmbush Clo. *H'ham* —2K 197
Holmbush Ct. *Fay* —8G 181
Holmbush Potteries Ind. Est. *Fay*
—8H 181
Holmbush Rd. *SW15* —9K 13
Holm Clo. *Wdhm* —8G 55
Holm Ct. *G'ming* —4G 132
Holmcroft. *Craw* —4C 182
Holmcroft. *Tad* —3G 101
Holmdene Clo. *Beck* —1M 47
Holmead Rd. *SW6* —3N 13
Holme Chase. *Wey* —3D 56
Holme Clo. *Crowt* —9F 30
Holme Green. —5E 30
Holmes Clo. *Asc* —5N 33
Holmes Clo. *Wok* —8B 74
Holmesdale Av. *SW14* —6A 12
Holmesdale Clo. *SE25* —2C 46
Holmesdale Clo. *Guild* —2D 114
Holmesdale Pk. *Nutf* —3K 123
Holmesdale Rd. *Croy & SE25* —4A 46
Holmesdale Rd. *N Holm* —9H 119
Holmesdale Rd. *Reig* —2M 121
Holmesdale Rd. *Rich* —4M 11
Holmesdale Rd. *S Nut* —5K 123
Holmesdale Rd. *Tedd* —8J 25
Holmesdale Ter. *N Holm* —9H 119
Holmesdale Vs. *Mid H* 2H 139
Holmes Rd. *SW19* —8A 28
Holmes Rd. *Twic* —3F 24
Holmethorpe. —9F 102
Holmethorpe Av. *Red* —9F 102
Holmethorpe Ind. Est. *Red* —9F 102
Holmewood Clo. *Wokgm* —6A 30
Holmewood Gdns. *SW2* —1K 29
Holmewood Rd. *SE25* —2B 46
Holmewood Rd. *SW2* —1J 29
Holming End. *H'ham* —3A 198
Holmlea Ct. *Croy* —6E 200
Holmlea Rd. *Dat* —4N 5
Holmlea Wlk. *Dat* —4M 5
Holmoak Clo. *SW15* —9L 13
Holmoaks Ho. *Beck* —1M 47
Holmside Rd. *SW12* —1E 28
Holmsley Clo. *N Mald* —5E 42
Holmsley Ho. SW15 —1E 26
(off Tangley Gro.)
Holm Ter. *Dork* —8H 119
Holmwood Av. *S Croy* —9C 64
Holmwood Clo. *Add* —2J 55
Holmwood Clo. *E Hor* —6F 96
Holmwood Clo. *Sutt* —5J 61
Holmwood Common. —3J 139
Holmwood Corner. —6K 139
Holmwood Gdns. *Wall* —3F 62
Holmwood Rd. *Chess* —2K 59
Holmwood Rd. *Sutt* —5H 61
Holmwood Vw. Rd. *Mid H* —2H 139
Holne Chase. *Mord* —5L 43
Holroyd Clo. *Clay* —5F 58
Holroyd Rd. *SW15* —7H 13
Holroyd Rd. *Clay* —5F 58
Holsart Clo. *Tad* —9G 81
Holstein Av. *Wey* —1B 56
Holst Mans. *SW13* —2H 13
Holsworthy Way. *Chess* —2J 59
Holt Clo. *Farn* —7A 70
Holt La. *Wokgm* —1A 30
Holton Heath. *Brack* —3D 32
Holt Pound. —7C 128
Holt Pound Cotts. *Rowl* —7B 128
Holt Pound La. *Holt P* —6B 128
Holt, The. *Mord* —3M 43
Holt, The. *Wall* —1G 62
Holtwood Rd. *Oxs* 9C 58
Holtye. —7N 167
Holtye Av. *E Grin* —7B 166
Holtye Common. —6N 167
Holtye Rd. *E Grin* —8B 166
Holtye Wlk. *Craw* —5E 182
Holwood Clo. *W on T* —8K 39
Holwood Pk. Av. *Orp* —1H 67
Holybourne Av. *SW15* —1F 26
Holyhead Ct. *King T* —8J 203
Holyoake Av. *Wok* —4M 73
Holyoake Cres. *Wok* —4M 73
Holyport Rd. *SW6* —3J 13
Holyrood. *L Kgin* 2C 188
Holyrood Pl. *Craw* —7N 181
Holywell Clo. *Farn* —7M 69
Holywell Clo. *Stai* —2N 21
Holywell Way. *Stai* —2N 21
Hombrook Dri. *Brack* —9K 15
Hombrook Ho. *Brack* 9K 16
Homebeech Ho. Wok —5A 74
(off Mt. Hermon Rd.)
Home Clo. *Cars* —8D 44
Home Clo. *Craw* —1G 183
Home Clo. *Fet* 8D 78
Home Clo. *Vir W* —5N 35
Home Ct. *Felt* —2H 23
Home Ct. *Surb* —4K 41 (8J 203)
Home Farm Clo. *Bet* —4D 120
Home Farm Clo. *Eps* —4J 81
Home Farm Clo. *Esh* —3B 58
Home Farm Clo. *Farn* —8B 70
Home Farm Clo. *Ott* —4C 54
Home Farm Clo. *Shep* —3F 38
Home Farm Clo. *Th Dit* —6F 40
Home Farm Cotts. *Pep H* —6N 131
Home Farm Gdns. *W on T* —8K 39
Home Farm Rd. *G'ming* —9H 133
Homefield. *Mord* —3M 43
Homefield. *Thur* —7G 150
Homefield Av. *W on T* —1L 57
Homefield Clo. *Horl* —7F 142
Homefield Clo. *Lea* —8J 79
Homefield Clo. *Wdhm* —8G 55
Homefield Ct. *SW16* —4J 29
Homefield Gdns. *Mitc* —1A 44
Homefield Gdns. *Tad* —7H 81
Homefield Pk. *Sutt* —3N 61
Homefield Rd. *SW19* —7J 27
Homefield Rd. *W4* —1E 12
Homefield Rd. *Coul & Cat* —6M 83
Homefield Rd. *W on T* —6M 39
Homefield Rd. *Warl* —6F 84
Homegreen Ho. *Hasl* —2E 188
Homeland Dri. *Sutt* —5N 61
Homelands. *Lea* —8J 79
Home Lea. *Orp* —2N 67
Homelea Clo. *Farn* —6N 69
Homeleigh Cres. *Ash V* —5E 90
Home Mdw. *Bans* —3M 81
Homemead Rd. *Croy* —5G 45
Home Pk. *Oxt* —9C 106
Home Pk. Clo. *Brmly* —5B 134
Home Pk. Ct. *King T* —8J 203
Homepark Ho. *Farnh* —1H 129
Home Pk. Pde. *King T* —3H 203
Home Pk. Rd. *SW19* —5L 27
Home Pk. Rd. *Yat* —9C 48
Home Pk. Ter. *King T* —3H 203
Home Pk. Wlk. *King T*
—3K 41 (8J 203)
Homer Rd. *Croy* —5G 47
Homersham Rd. *King T* —1N 41
Homers Rd. *Wind* —4A 4
Homesdale Rd. *Cat* —1A 104
Homestall. *Guild* —3G 113
Homestall Rd. *Ash W* —9C 166
Homestead. *Cranl* —6A 156
Homestead & Middle Vw. Mobile
Home Pk. *Norm* —9B 92
Homestead Gdns. *Clay* —2E 58
Homestead Rd. *SW6* —3L 13
Homestead Rd. *Cat* —1A 104
Homestead Rd. *Eden* —7K 127
Homestead Rd. *Stai* —7K 21
Homestead Way. *New Ad* —7M 65
Homestream Ho. *H'ham* —7H 197
Homethorne Ho. *Craw* 4A 180
Home Vs. *Alb* —3L 135
Homewater Ho. *Eps*
—9D 60 (6M 201)
Homewaters Av. *Sun* —9G 23
Homewood. *Cranl* —7B 156
Homewood Clo. *Hamp* —7N 23
Homewoods. *SW12* —1G 28
Homeworth Ho. Wok —5A 74
(off Mt. Hermon Rd.)
Hone Hill. *Sand* —7G 48
Hones Yd. Bus. Pk. *Farnh* —1J 129
Honeybrook Rd. *SW12* —1G 28
Honeycrock Ct. *Red* —1E 142
Honeycrock La. *Red* —1E 142
Honeydown Cotts. *N'chap* —8F 190
Honey Hill. *Wokgm* —6E 30
Honeyhill Rd. *Brack* 9M 15
Honey La. *Rowh & Oke H* —6M 177
Honeypot La. *Eden* —8F 126
Honeypots Rd. *Wok* —9N 73
Honeysuckle Bottom. *E Hor* —3F 116
Honeysuckle Clo. *Crowt* —9F 30
Honeysuckle Clo. *Horl* —7G 143
Honeysuckle Clo. *Yat* —9A 48
Honeysuckle Gdns. *Croy* —6G 46
Honeysuckle La. *Craw* —9A 162
Honeysuckle La. *Head D* —4G 168
Honeysuckle La. *N Holm* —8J 119
Honeysuckle Wlk. *H'ham* —3N 197
Honeywood Heritage Cen. —1D 62
Honeywood La. *Oke H* —4M 177
Honeywood Rd. *H'ham* —4N 197
Honeywood Rd. *Iswth* —7G 10
Honeywood Wlk. *Cars* —1D 62
Honister Gdns. *Fleet* —3D 88
Honister Heights. *Purl* —1A 84
Honister Wlk. *Camb* —2H 71
Honnor Gdns. *Iswth* 5D 10
Honnor Rd. *Stai* —8M 21
Hood Av. *SW14* —8B 12
Hood Clo. *Croy* 7M 45 (1A 200)
Hood Rd. *SW20* —8E 26
Hook. 2K 59
Hooke Rd. *E Hor* —3G 97
Hookfield. *Eps* 9B 60 (7H 201)
Hookfield M. *Eps* —9B 60 (6H 201)
Hook Heath. —8L 73
Hook Heath Av. *Wok* —6L 73
Hook Heath Gdns. *Wok* —8J 73
Hook Heath Rd. *Wok* —8H 73
Hook Hill. *S Croy* 6B 64
(in two parts)
Hook Hill La. *Wok* —8L 73
Hook Hill Pk. *Wok* —8L 73
Hook Ho. La. *Duns* —3M 173
Hookhouse Rd. *Duns* —1N 173
Hook Junction. (Junct.) —9K 41
Hook La. *Bisl* —9N 51
Hook La. *P'ham* —8N 111
Hook La. *Shere* —1B 136
Hookley Clo. *Elst* —8J 131
Hookley La. *Elst* —8J 131
Hook Mill La. *Light* —5A 52
Hook Ri. Bus. Cen. *Chess* —9N 41
Hook Ri. N. *Surb* —9L 41
Hook Ri. S. *Surb* —9L 41
Hook Ri. S. Ind. Pk. *Chess* —9M 41
Hook Rd. *Chess & Surb* —2K 59
Hook Rd. *Eps* —4B 60 (5L 201)
Hookstile La. *Farnh* —2H 129
Hookstone La. *W End* —7C 52
Hook St. *Alf* —8K 175
Hookwood. —9B 142
Hookwood Corner. *Oxt* —6D 106
Hookwood Park. —6D 106
Hookwood Pk. *Oxt* —6D 106
Hooley. —8F 82
Hooley La. *Red* —4D 122
Hope Av. *Brack* —6C 32
Hope Clo. *Bren* —1L 11
Hope Clo. *Sutt* —2A 62
Hope Cotts. *Brack* —2A 32
Hope Ct. *Craw* —8N 181
Hope Fountain. *Camb* —2E 70
Hope Grant's Rd. *Alder* —9M 89
(in two parts)
Hope Ho. *Croy* 6F 200
Hope La. *Farnh* —6G 108
Hopeman Clo. *Coll T* —7J 49
Hopes Clo. *Houn* —2A 10
Hope St. *Elst* —7H 131
Hope Way. *Alder* —1L 109

Hopfield. Hors —3A 74
Hopfield Av. Byfl —8N 55
Hop Garden. C Crook —9A 88
Hopgarden Clo. Eden —9M 127
Hophurst Clo. Craw D —1E 184
Hophurst Dri. Craw D —1E 184
Hophurst Hill. Craw D —8G 164
Hophurst La. Craw D —1E 184
Hopkins Ct. Craw —8N 181
Hopper Va. Brack —5M 31
Hoppety, The. Tad —9J 81
Hoppingwood Av. N Mald —2D 42
Hopton Ct. Guild —3H 113 (off Pk. Barn Dri.)
Hopton Gdns. N Mald —5F 42
Hopton Rd. SW16 —6J 29
Hopwood Clo. SW17 —4A 28
Horace Rd. King T —2M 41 (6M 203)
Horatio Av. Warf —9C 16
Horatio Ho. W6 —1J 13 (off Fulham Pal. Rd.)
Horatio Pl. SW19 —9M 27
Horatius Way. Croy —2K 63
Hordern Ho. H'ham —7G 196
Horder Rd. SW6 —4K 13
Horewood Rd. Brack —5N 31
Horizon Ho. Eps —9D 60 (6M 201)
Horley. —8F 142
Horley Lodge La. Red —3D 142
Horley Rd. Charl —4L 161
Horley Rd. Red —5D 122
Horley Row. Horl —7D 142
Hormer Clo. Owl —6J 49
Hornbeam Clo. Farn —9H 69
Hornbeam Clo. H'ham —7M 197
Hornbeam Clo. Owl —6J 49
Hornbeam Cres. Bren —3H 11
Hornbeam Rd. Guild —9M 93
Hornbeam Rd. Reig —6N 121
Hornbeam Ter. Cars —7C 44
Hornbeam Wlk. Rich —3M 25
Hornbeam Wlk. W Vill —6F 56
Hornbrook Copse. H'ham —8M 197
Hornbrook Hill. H'ham —8M 197
Hornby Av. Brack —6B 32
Hornchurch Clo. King T —5K 25
Hornchurch Hill. Whyt —5C 84
Horndean Clo. SW15 —2F 26
Horndean Clo. Craw —8H 163
Horndean Rd. Brack —5D 32
Horne. —6C 144
Horne Ct. Hill. Horne —4C 144
Horner La. Mitc —1B 44
Horne Rd. Shep —3B 38
Horne Way. SW15 —5H 13
Hornhatch. Chil —9D 114
Hornhatch Clo. Chil —9D 114 (in two parts)
Hornhatch La. Guild —9C 114
Horn Rd. Farn —9K 69
Horns Green. —4N 87
Hornshill La. Rud —2A 194
Horsa Clo. Wall —4J 63
Horse & Groom Cvn. Site. Brack —3A 32
Horseblock Hollow. Cranl —3B 156
Horsebrass Dri. Bag —5J 51
Horsecroft. Bans —4L 81
Horse Fair. King T —1K 41 (3H 203)
Horsegate Ride. Asc —5L 33 (Coronation Rd.)
Horsegate Ride. Asc —4F 32 (Swinley Rd.)
Horse Hill. Horl —6M 141
Horsell. —3M 73
Horsell Birch. Hors —2L 73 (in two parts)
Horsell Birch. Wok —2K 73 (in three parts)
Horsell Comn. Rd. Wok —1M 73
Horsell Ct. Cher —6K 37
Horsell Moor. Wok —4N 73
Horsell Pk. Wok —3N 73
Horsell Pk. Clo. Wok —3N 73
Horsell Ri. Wok —2N 73
Horsell Ri. Clo. Wok —2N 73
Horsell Va. Wok —3A 74
Horsell Way. Wok —3M 73
Horse Ride. Cars —6C 62
Horseshoe Bend. Gray —6M 169
Horseshoe Clo. Camb —7D 50
Horseshoe Clo. Craw —2H 183
Horseshoe Cres. Bord —6A 168
Horseshoe Cres. Camb —7D 50
Horse Shoe Grn. Sutt —8N 43
Horseshoe La. Ash V —6E 90
Horseshoe La. Cranl —6L 155
Horseshoe La. E. Guild —2D 114
Horseshoe La. W. Guild —2D 114
Horseshoe, The. Bans —2L 81
Horseshoe, The. Coul —9H 63
Horseshoe, The. G'ming —8F 132
Horsham. —6J 197
Horsham Arts Cen. —6K 197
Horsham Bus. Pk. K'fold —5J 179
Horsham Gates. H'ham —5L 197
Horsham Mus. —7J 197
Horsham Northern By-Pass. Warn —2H 197
Horsham Rd. Ab H & Holm M —2G 136
Horsham Rd. Alf —6J 175
Horsham Rd. Bear G —2K 159
Horsham Rd. Brmly & Cranl —1E 154
Horsham Rd. Brmly & Shalf —2N 133
Horsham Rd. Capel —2J 179
Horsham Rd. Cowf —9H 195
Horsham Rd. Cranl & Rud —8N 155
Horsham Rd. Craw —7K 181
Horsham Rd. Dork —6G 119 (4K 201)
Horsham Rd. Ewh & Wal W —6F 156
Horsham Rd. Felt —9D 8
Horsham Rd. F Grn —5M 157
Horsham Rd. Hand —9K 199
Horsham Rd. Holmw & Bear G —4J 139
Horsham Rd. N Holm & Mid H —9H 119
Horsham Rd. Owl —6J 49
Horsham Rd. Peas P —2M 199
Horsham Rd. Rusp —6N 179
Horsley Clo. Eps —9C 60 (6K 201)
Horsley Dri. King T —6K 25
Horsley Dri. New Ad —4M 65
Horsley Rd. Cobh & D'side —9H 77
Horsnape Gdns. Binf —7G 15
Horsneile La. Brack —8N 15
Hortensia Ho. SW10 —3N 13 (off Hortensia Rd.)
Hortensia Rd. SW10 —3N 13
Horticultural Pl. W4 —1C 12
Horton. —6C 6 (Colnbrook)
Horton. —7B 60 (Ewell)
Horton Country Pk. —4A 60
Horton Footpath. Eps —7B 60
Horton Gdns. Eps —7B 60
Horton Gdns. Hort —6B 6
Horton Hill. Eps —7B 60
Horton Ho. W6 —1K 13 (off Field Rd.)
Horton La. Eps —7N 59
Horton Pk. Children's Farm. —6N 59
Horton Pl. W'ham —4M 107
Horton Rd. Coln —6G 6
Horton Rd. Dat —3L 5
Horton Rd. Hort & Coln —5C 6
Horton Rd. Stai —7H 7
Hortons Way. W'ham —4M 107 (in two parts)
Horton Trad. Est. Hort —6D 6
Horton Way. Croy —4G 46
Horvath Clo. Wey —1E 56
Hosack Rd. SW17 —3E 28
Hosey Comn. La. W'ham —7N 107
Hosey Comn. Rd. Eden —2L 127
Hosey Hill. —6N 107
Hosey Hill. W'ham —5M 107
Hoskins Clo. Hayes —1G 8
Hoskins Pl. E Grin —6C 166
Hoskins Rd. Oxt —7A 106 (in two parts)
Hoskins Wlk. Oxt —7A 106 (off Station Rd. W.)
Hospital Bri. Rd. Twic —1B 24
Hospital Bridge Roundabout. (Junct.) —3B 24
Hospital Hill. Alder —1M 109
Hospital Rd. Alder —1M 109
Hospital Rd. Houn —6A 10
Hostel Rd. Farn —5N 89
Hotham Clo. W Mol —2A 40
Hotham Rd. SW15 —6H 13
Hotham Rd. SW19 —8A 28
Hotham Rd. M. SW19 —8A 28
Houblon Rd. Rich —8L 11
Houghton Clo. Hamp —7M 23
Houghton Rd. M'bowr —6G 182
Houlder Cres. Croy —3M 63
Houlton Ct. Bag —5J 51
Hound Ho. Rd. Shere —1B 136
Houndown La. Thur —6E 150
Hounslow. —6B 10
Hounslow Av. Houn —8B 10
Hounslow Bus. Pk. Houn —7B 10
Hounslow Cen. Houn —6B 10
Hounslow Gdns. Houn —8B 10
Hounslow Rd. Felt —2J 23
Hounslow Rd. Hanw —5L 23
Hounslow Rd. Twic —9B 10
Hounslow Urban Farm. —8H 9
Hounslow West. —5M 9
Household Cavalry Mus. —6F 4
Houseman Rd. Farn —8L 69
Ho. Plat Ct. C Crook —9A 88 (off Annettes Cft.)
Houston Pl. Esh —7D 40
Houston Way. Crowt —2C 48
Houstoun Ct. Houn —3N 9
Hove Gdns. Sutt —7N 43
Howard Av. Eps —6F 60
Howard Clo. Asht —5M 79
Howard Clo. Fleet —4D 88
Howard Clo. Hamp —8C 24
Howard Clo. Lea —1J 99
Howard Clo. Sun —7G 22
Howard Clo. Tad —3E 100
Howard Clo. W Hor —3E 96
Howard Cole Way. Alder —2K 109
Howard Ct. Reig —2A 122
Howard Dri. Farn —1G 89
Howard Gdns. Guild —2C 114
Howard M. Reig —1M 121
Howard Ridge. Burp —8C 94
Howard Rd. SE25 —4D 46
Howard Rd. Afrd —5M 21
Howard Rd. Bookh —5B 98
Howard Rd. Coul —2G 83
Howard Rd. Craw —7K 181
Howard Rd. Dork —5G 118 (2J 201)
Howard Rd. Eff J —1H 97
Howard Rd. H'ham —4N 197
Howard Rd. Iswth —6F 10
Howard Rd. N Mald —2D 42
Howard Rd. N Holm —9J 119
Howard Rd. Reig —4N 121
Howard Rd. Surb —5M 41
Howard Rd. Wokgm —3B 30
Howards Clo. Wok —7C 74
Howards Crest Clo. Beck —1M 47
Howards Ho. Reig —2N 121
Howard's La. SW15 —7G 13
Howards La. Add —3H 55
Howards Rd. Wok —7B 74
Howard St. Th Dit —6H 41
Howberry Rd. T Hth —9N 29
Howden Ho. Houn —1M 23
Howden Rd. SE25 —1C 46
Howe Dri. Cat —9A 84
Howe La. Binf —1K 15
Howell Clo. Warf —7A 16
Howell Hill Clo. Eps —7H 61
Howell Hill Gro. Eps —6H 61
Howes Gdns. C Crook —7A 88
Howe, The. Farn —4F 88
Howgate Rd. SW14 —6C 12
Howitts Clo. Esh —3A 58
Howland Ho. SW16 —4J 29
How La. Coul —4E 82
Howley Rd. Croy —9M 45 (4A 200)
Howorth Ct. Brack —3C 32
Howsman Rd. SW13 —2F 12
Howson Ter. Rich —9L 11
Hoylake Clo. If'd —4J 181
Hoylake Gdns. Mitc —2G 44
Hoyland Ho. Craw —3L 181
Hoyle Cotts. Bear G —1K 159
Hoyle Rd. SW17 —6C 28
Hubbard Dri. Chess —3K 59
Hubbard Rd. SE27 —5N 29
Hubberholme. Brack —2M 31
Hubert Clo. SW19 —9A 28 (off Nelson Gro. Rd.)
Huddington Glade. Yat —1A 68
Huddlestone Cres. Red —6H 103
Hudson Ct. Guild —3J 113
Hudson Rd. Craw —5C 182
Hudson Rd. Hayes —2E 8
Hudsons. Tad —8J 81
Huggins Pl. SW2 —2K 29
Hugh Dalton Av. SW6 —2L 13
Hughenden Rd. Wor Pk —6F 42
Hughes Rd. Afrd —7D 22
Hughes Rd. Wokgm —1C 30
Hughes Wlk. Croy —6N 45
Hugh Gaitskell Clo. SW6 —2L 13
Hugh Herland Ho. King T —2L 41 (6L 203)
Hugon Rd. SW6 —6N 13
Huguenot Pl. SW18 —8N 13
Hullbrook La. Sham G —7F 134
Hullmead. Sham G —7G 134
Hulton Clo. Lea —1J 99
Hulverston Clo. Sutt —6N 61
Humber Clo. Sand —7J 49
Humber Way. Sand —7J 49
Humber Way. Slou —1C 6
Humbolt Clo. Guild —3J 113
Humbolt Rd. W6 —2K 13
Hummer Rd. Egh —5C 20
Humphrey Clo. Fet —9C 78
Humphrey Pk. C Crook —1A 108 (in two parts)
Humphries Yd. Brack —3A 32
Hungerford Clo. Sand —7H 49
Hungerford Sq. Wey —1E 56
Hungry Hill La. Send —4L 95
Hunnels Clo. C Crook —1A 108
Hunstanton Clo. Coln —3E 6
Hunstanton Clo. If'd —4J 181
Hunston Rd. Mord —7N 43
Hunter Ct. Eps —6N 59
Hunter Ho. SW5 —1M 13 (off Old Brompton Rd.)
Hunter Ho. Craw —6B 182
Hunter Rd. SW20 —9H 27
Hunter Rd. Craw —6B 182
Hunter Rd. Farn —2L 89
Hunter Rd. Guild —4A 114 (5F 202)
Hunter Rd. T Hth —2A 46
Hunters Chase. S God —6J 125
Hunters Clo. SW12 —2E 28
Hunters Clo. Eps —9B 60 (6J 201)
Hunters Ct. Rich —8K 11
Huntersfield Clo. Reig —9N 101
Hunters Gro. Orp —1K 67
Hunters M. Wind —4F 4
Hunter's Rd. Chess —9L 41
Hunter's Way. Croy —1B 64
Hunting Clo. Esh —1A 58
Huntingdon Clo. Mitc —2J 45
Huntingdon Gdns. W4 —3B 12
Huntingdon Gdns. Wor Pk —9H 43
Huntingdon Rd. Red —3D 122
Huntingdon Rd. Wok —4J 73
Huntingfield. Croy —4J 65
Huntingfield Rd. SW15 —7F 12
Huntingfield Way. Egh —8F 20
Huntingford Clo. Hind —2A 170
Hunting Ga. Dri. Chess —4L 59
Hunting Ga. M. Sutt —9N 43
Hunting Ga. M. Twic —2E 24
Huntley Way. SW20 —1F 42
Huntly Rd. SE25 —3B 46
Hunts Clo. Guild —2G 112
Huntsgreen Ct. Brack —1A 32
Hunts Hill. —9M 91
Hunts Hill Rd. Norm —8L 91
Hunts La. Camb —3N 69
Huntsmans Clo. Felt —5J 23
Huntsmans Clo. Fet —2D 98
Huntsmans Clo. Warl —6F 84
Huntsmans Ct. Cat —8N 83 (off Coulsdon Rd.)
Huntsmans Mdw. Asc —9K 17
Huntsman's M. Myt —2D 90
Huntsmoor Rd. Eps —2C 60
Huntspill St. SW17 —4A 28
Hurland La. Head —5E 168
Hurlands Bus. Cen. Farnh —8L 109
Hurlands Clo. Farnh —8L 109
Hurlands La. Duns —7B 174
Hurlands Pl. Farnh —8L 109
Hurley Clo. W on T —8J 39
Hurley Ct. Brack —3C 32
Hurley Gdns. Guild —9C 94
Hurlford. Wok —4K 73
Hurlingham. —6N 13
Hurlingham Bus. Pk. SW6 —6M 13
Hurlingham Ct. SW6 —6L 13
Hurlingham Gdns. SW6 —6L 13
Hurlingham Retail Pk. SW6 —6N 13
Hurlingham Rd. SW6 —5L 13
Hurlingham Sq. SW6 —6M 13
Hurlstone Rd. SE25 —4B 46
Hurn Ct. Houn —5L 9
Hurn Ct. Rd. Houn —5L 9
Hurnford Clo. S Croy —6B 64
Huron Clo. G Str —3N 67
Huron Rd. SW17 —3E 28
Hurricane Rd. Wall —3K 63
Hurricane Way. Slou —1D 6
Hurst-an-Clays. E Grin —1A 186
Hurst Av. H'ham —5K 197
Hurstbourne. Clay —3F 58
Hurstbourne Ho. SW15 —9E 12 (off Tangley Gro.)
Hurst Clo. Brack —4M 31
Hurst Clo. Chess —2N 59
Hurst Clo. Craw —5L 181
Hurst Clo. H'ley —2B 100
Hurst Clo. Wok —7M 73
Hurst Ct. H'ham —5K 197
Hurstcourt Rd. Sutt —8N 43
Hurst Cft. Guild —6A 114 (8F 202)
Hurstdene Av. Stai —7K 21
Hurst Dri. Tad —4F 100
Hurst Farm Clo. Milf —9C 132
Hurst Farm Rd. E Grin —1N 185
Hurstfield Rd. W Mol —2A 40
Hurst Green. —1B 126
Hurst Grn. Clo. Oxt —1C 126
Hurst Grn. Rd. Oxt —1B 126
Hurst Gro. W on T —7G 38
Hurst Hill. Rusp —7N 179
Hurst Hill Cotts. Brmly —6C 134
Hurstlands. Oxt —1C 126
Hurst La. E Mol —3C 40
Hurst La. Egh —1C 36
Hurst La. H'ley —2B 100
Hurstleigh Clo. Red —1D 122
Hurstleigh Dri. Red —1D 122
Hurst Lodge. Wey —3E 56
Hurstmere Clo. Gray —6B 170
Hurst Park. —1C 40
Hurst Rd. Alder —9A 90 (in two parts)
Hurst Rd. Croy —2A 64 (8D 200)
Hurst Rd. Eps —7C 60
Hurst Rd. Farn —6N 69
Hurst Rd. H'ley —1C 100
Hurst Rd. Horl —7C 142
Hurst Rd. H'ham —4J 197
Hurst Rd. W on T & W Mol —4K 39
Hurstview Grange. S Croy —4M 63
Hurst Vw. Rd. S Croy —4B 64
Hurstway. Pyr —1G 75
Hurst Way. S Croy —3B 64
Hurstwood. Asc —5L 33
Hurtbank Cotts. Holm M —5K 137
Hurtmore. —4C 132
Hurtmore Bottom. —5C 132
Hurtmore Chase. Hurt —4E 132
Hurtmore Rd. Hurt —4C 132
Hurtwood La. Alb —5N 135
Hurtwood Rd. W on T —6N 39
Huson Rd. Warf —7A 16
Hussar Ct. Alder —2K 109
Hussars Clo. Houn —6M 9
Hutchingsons Rd. New Ad —7M 65
Hutchins Way. Horl —6D 142
Hutsons Clo. Wokgm —9C 14
Hutton Clo. W'sham —4A 52
Hutton Rd. Ash V —7E 90
Huxley Clo. G'ming —4G 132
Huxley Rd. Sur R —3G 113
Huxleys Experience. —9M 197
Hyacinth Clo. Hamp —7A 24
Hyacinth Rd. SW15 —2F 26
Hyde Clo. Afrd —7F 22
Hyde Dri. Craw —4K 181
Hyde Farm M. SW12 —2H 29
Hyde Heath Ct. Craw —1H 183
Hyde La. Churt & Thur —9B 150
Hyde La. Ock —7C 76
Hyde Rd. Rich —8M 11
Hyde Rd. S Croy —9B 64
Hydestile. —4G 153
Hydestile Cotts. Hamb —5G 152
Hyde Ter. Afrd —7F 22
Hydethorpe Rd. SW12 —2G 28
Hyde Wlk. Mord —6M 43
Hydon Heath. —5J 153
Hydon Heath. —6J 153
Hydons, The. Hyde —5H 153
Hylands Clo. Craw —4E 182
Hylands Clo. Eps —2B 80
Hylands M. Eps —2B 80
Hylands Rd. Eps —2B 80
Hylle Clo. Wind —4B 4
Hyndman Clo. Craw —9N 181
Hyperion Ct. Bew —5K 181
Hyperion Ho. SW2 —1K 29
Hyperion Pl. Eps —5C 60
Hyperion Wlk. Horl —1F 162
Hyrstdene. S Croy —1M 63 (7A 200)
Hythe Clo. Brack —4C 32
Hythe End. —3D 20
Hythe End Rd. Wray —3B 20
Hythe Fld. Av. Egh —7F 20
Hythe Pk. Rd. Egh —6E 20
Hythe Rd. Stai —6F 20
Hythe Rd. T Hth —1A 46
Hythe, The. Stai —6G 20

Iberian Av. Wall —1H 63
Iberian Way. Camb —9E 50
Ibis La. W4 —4B 12
Ibsley Gdns. SW15 —2F 26
Icehouse Wood. Oxt —9A 106
Icklesham Ho. Craw —6L 181 (off Salvington Rd.)
Icklingham Ga. Cobh —8K 57
Icklingham Rd. Cobh —8K 57
Idlecombe Rd. SW17 —7E 28
Idmiston Rd. SE27 —4N 29
Idmiston Rd. Wor Pk —6E 42
Idmiston Sq. Wor Pk —6E 42
Ifield. —2M 181
Ifield Av. Craw —9M 161
Ifield Clo. Red —5C 122
Ifield Dri. Craw —2L 181
Ifield Green. —1M 181
Ifield Grn. If'd —9M 161
Ifield Pk. Craw —3L 181
Ifield Rd. SW10 —2N 13
Ifield Rd. Charl —6K 161
Ifield Rd. Craw —2N 181
Ifield St. If'd —1L 181
Ifield Watermill. —4K 181
Ifieldwood. —9J 161
Ifield Wood. If'd —2H 181
Ifold. —6E 192
Ifold Bri. La. Loxw —4E 192
Ifoldhurst. Loxw —6E 192
Ifold Rd. Red —5E 122
Ikona Ct. Wey —2D 56
Ilex Clo. Eng G —8L 19
Ilex Clo. Sun —1K 39
Ilex Clo. Yat —9A 48
Ilex Ho. Add —6J 55
Ilex Way. SW16 —6L 29
Ilford Ct. Cranl —8H 155
Illingworth. Wind —6B 4
Illingworth Clo. Mitc —2B 44
Illingworth Gro. Brack —9D 16
Imadene Clo. Lind —5A 168
Imadene Cres. Lind —5A 168
Imber Clo. Esh —7D 40
Imber Ct. Trad. Est. E Mol —5D 40
Imber Cross. Th Dit —5F 40
Imber Gro. Esh —6D 40

Kelvedon Clo.—Kingsley Rd.

Kelvedon Clo. King T —7N 25
Kelvedon Rd. SW6 —3L 13
Kelvin Av. Lea —6F 78
Kelvin Av. Tedd —7E 24
Kelvinbrook. W Mol —2B 40
Kelvin Bus. Cen. Craw —9D 162
Kelvin Clo. Eps —3N 59
Kelvin Ct. Iswth —5E 10
Kelvin Dri. Twic —9H 11
Kelvin Gdns. Croy —6J 45
Kelvin Gro. Chess —9K 41
Kelvington Clo. Croy —6H 47
Kelvin La. Craw —8D 162
Kelvin Way. Craw —8D 162
Kemble Clo. Wey —1E 56
Kemble Cotts. Add —1J 55
Kemble Rd. Croy —9M 45
Kembleside Rd. Big H —5E 86
Kemerton Rd. Beck —1L 47
Kemerton Rd. Croy —6C 46
Kemishford. Wok —1K 93
Kemnal Pk. Hasl —1H 189
Kemp Ct. Bag —5K 51
Kemp Gdns. Croy —5N 45
Kempsford Gdns. SW5 —1M 13
Kempshott Rd. SW16 —8H 29
Kempshott Rd. H'ham —4H 197
Kempson Rd. SW6 —4M 13
Kempton Av. Sun —9J 23
Kempton Ct. Farn —3L 89
Kempton Ct. Sun —9J 23
Kempton Pk. Racecourse. —8K 23
Kempton Rd. Hamp —1N 39
(in three parts)
Kempton Wlk. Croy —5H 47
Kemsing Clo. T Hth —3N 45
Kemsley Rd. Tats —6F 86
Kendal Clo. Farn —1K 89
Kendal Clo. Felt —2G 22
Kendal Clo. Reig —2B 122
Kendale Clo. M'bowr —7G 183
Kendal Gdns. Sutt —8A 44
Kendal Gro. Camb —2H 71
Kendal Ho. SE20 —1D 46
(off Derwent Rd.)
Kendall Av. Beck —1H 47
Kendall Av. S Croy —5A 64
Kendall Av. S. S Croy —6N 63
Kendall Ct. SW19 —7B 28
Kendall Rd. Beck —1H 47
Kendall Rd. Iswth —5G 10
Kendal Pl. SW15 —8L 13
Kendor Av. Eps —7B 60
Kendra Hall Rd. S Croy —4M 63
Kendrey Gdns. Twic —1E 24
Kendrick Clo. Wokgm —3B 30
Keneally. Wind —5A 4
Kenilford Rd. SW12 —1F 28
Kenilworth Av. SW19 —6M 27
Kenilworth Av. Brack —9A 16
Kenilworth Av. Stoke D —1B 78
Kenilworth Clo. Bans —3N 81
Kenilworth Clo. Craw —7N 181
Kenilworth Cres. Fleet —3D 88
Kenilworth Dri. W on T —9L 39
Kenilworth Gdns. Stai —6L 21
Kenilworth Rd. Afrd —4M 21
Kenilworth Rd. Eps —2F 60
Kenilworth Rd. Farn —9H 69
Kenilworth Rd. Fleet —4C 88
Kenley. —1N 83
Kenley Clo. Cat —7A 84
(in two parts)
Kenley Ct. Kenl —2M 83
Kenley Gdns. T Hth —3M 45
Kenley La. Kenl —1N 83
Kenley Rd. SW19 —1M 43
Kenley Rd. Head D —4G 169
Kenley Rd. King T —1A 42
Kenley Rd. Twic —9H 11
Kenley Wlk. Sutt —1J 61
Kenlor Rd. SW17 —6B 28
Kenmara Clo. Craw —9E 162
Kenmara Ct. Craw —8E 162
Kenmare Dri. Mitc —8D 28
Kenmare Rd. T Hth —5L 45
Kenmore Clo. C Crook —8C 88
Kenmore Clo. Frim —6B 70
Kenmore Clo. Rich —3N 11
Kenmore Rd. Kenl —1M 83
Kennard Ct. F Row —6G 187
Kenneally Clo. Wind —5A 4
Kenneally Pl. Wind —5A 4
Kenneally Row. Wind —5A 4
(off Liddell Sq.)
Kenneally Wlk. Wind —5A 4
(off Guards Rd.)
Kennedy Av. E Grin —7N 165
Kennedy Clo. Mitc —9E 28
Kennedy Ct. Beck —5J 47
Kennedy Rd. H'ham —7K 197
Kennel Av. Asc —9K 17
Kennel Clo. Asc —7K 17
Kennel Clo. Fet —2C 98
Kennel Grn. Asc —9J 17
Kennel La. Brack —8N 15
Kennel La. Fet —9B 78
(in two parts)
Kennel La. Fren —9H 129
Kennel La. Hkwd —9B 142
Kennel La. W'sham —2N 51
Kennel Ride. Asc —9K 17
Kennels La. Farn —2G 88
Kennel Wood. Asc —9K 17
Kennel Wood Cres. New Ad —7N 65
Kennet Clo. As —3E 110
Kennet Clo. Craw —4L 181
Kennet Clo. Farn —8K 69
Kenneth Rd. Bans —2B 82
Kenneth Younger Ho. SW6 —2L 13
(off Clem Attlee Ct.)
Kennet Rd. Iswth —6F 10
Kennet Sq. SW19 —9B 28
Kennett Ct. W4 —3A 12
Kenny Dri. Cars —5E 62
Kenrick Sq. Blet —2B 124
Kensington Av. T Hth —9L 29
Kensington Gdns. King T
(in two parts) —2K 41 (6J 203)
Kensington Hall Gdns. W14 —1L 13
Kensington Mans. SW5 —1M 13
(off Trebovir Rd., in two parts)
Kensington Rd. Craw —7N 181
Kensington Ter. S Croy —4A 64
Kensington Village. W14 —1L 13
Kent Clo. Mitc —3J 45
Kent Clo. Orp —3N 67
Kent Clo. Stai —7M 21
Kent Dri. Tedd —6E 24
Kent Folly. Warf —7D 16
Kent Ga. Way. Croy —3J 65
Kent Hatch. —9K 107
Kent Hatch Rd. Oxt —7E 106
Kent Ho. W4 —1D 12
(off Devonshire St.)
Kentigern Dri. Crowt —2J 49
Kenton Av. Sun —1L 39
Kenton Clo. Brack —1B 32
Kenton Clo. Frim —4D 70
Kenton Ct. Twic —9K 11
Kentone Ct. SE25 —3E 46
Kentons La. Wind —5B 4
Kenton Way. Wok —4J 73
Kent Rd. E Mol —3C 40
Kent Rd. Fleet —4C 88
Kent Rd. King T —2K 41 (5J 203)
Kent Rd. Rich —3N 11
Kent Rd. W Wick —7L 47
Kent Rd. W'sham —2A 52
Kent Rd. Wok —3D 74
Kent's Pas. Hamp —9N 23
Kent Way. Surb —9L 41
Kentwode Grn. SW13 —3F 12
Kentwyns Dri. H'ham —8L 197
Kentwyns Ri. S Nut —4K 123
Kenward Ct. Str G —7B 120
Kenway Rd. SW5 —1N 13
Kenwith Av. Fleet —4D 88
Kenwood Clo. W Dray —2B 8
Kenwood Dri. Beck —2M 47
Kenwood Dri. W on T —3J 57
Kenwood Pk. Wey —3E 56
Kenwood Ridge. Kenl —4M 83
Kenworth Gro. Light —6L 51
Kenwyn Rd. SW20 —9H 27
Kenya Ct. Horl —7D 142
Kenya Ter. Deep —6J 71
Kenyngton Ct. Sun —6H 23
Kenyngton Dri. Sun —6H 23
Kenyon Mans. W14 —2K 13
(off Queen's Club Gdns.)
Kenyons. W Hor —6C 96
Kenyon St. SW6 —4J 13
Keogh Clo. Ash V —3F 90
Keple Pl. SW13 —2G 13
Keppel Rd. Dork —3H 119
Keppel Spur. Old Win —1L 19
Kepple Pl. Bag —4J 51
Kepple St. Wind —5G 5
Kerria Way. W End —9B 52
Kerrill Av. Coul —6L 83
Kerry Clo. Fleet —1C 88
Kerry Ter. Wok —3D 74
Kersey Dri. S Croy —8F 64
Kersfield Rd. SW15 —9J 13
Kershaw Clo. SW18 —1B 28
Kersland Cotts. G'ming —4C 132
Kerves La. H'ham —9K 197
Keston. —2E 66
Keston Av. Coul —6L 83
Keston Av. Kes —2E 66
Keston Av. New H —7J 55
Keston Ct. Surb —8M 203
Keston Gdns. Kes —1E 66
Keston Mark. —1G 67
Keston Mark. (Junct.) —1F 66
Keston Pk. Clo. Kes —1H 67
Keston Rd. T Hth —5L 45
Kestrel Av. Stai —4H 21
Kestrel Clo. Craw —1A 182
Kestrel Clo. Eden —9L 127
Kestrel Clo. Eps —7A 60
Kestrel Clo. Ews —5C 108
Kestrel Clo. Guild —1F 114
Kestrel Clo. H'ham —3L 197
Kestrel Clo. King T —5K 25
Kestrel Ct. S Croy —3N 63
Kestrel Wlk. Turn H —4F 184
Kestrel Way. New Ad —5N 65
Kestrel Way. Wok —2L 73
Keswick Av. SW15 —6D 26
Keswick Av. SW19 —1M 43
Keswick Av. Shep —2F 38
Keswick Clo. Camb —2H 71
Keswick Clo. If'd —5J 181
Keswick Clo. Sutt —1A 62
Keswick Dri. Light —7M 51
Keswick Rd. SW15 —8K 13
Keswick Rd. Bookh —3B 98
Keswick Rd. Egh —8D 20
Keswick Rd. Fet —2C 98
Keswick Rd. Twic —9C 10
Keswick Rd. W Wick —8N 47
Keswick Rd. Witl —4A 152
Ketcher Grn. Binf —5H 15
Kettering St. SW16 —7G 28
Kettlewell Clo. Wok —1N 73
Kettlewell Dri. Wok —1A 74
Kettlewell Hill. Wok —1A 74
Ketton Grn. Red —6H 103
Kevan Dri. Send —3G 95
Kevin Clo. Houn —5L 9
Kevins Dri. Yat —8D 48
Kevins Gro. Fleet —4C 88
Kew. —3N 11
Kew Bridge. (Junct.) —2N 11
Kew Bri. Bren —2M 11
Kew Bri. Arches. Rich —2N 11
Kew Bri. Ct. W4 —1N 11
Kew Bri. Distribution Cen. Bren —1M 11
Kew Bri. Rd. Bren —2M 11
Kew Bridge Steam Mus. —1M 11
Kew Cres. Sutt —9K 43
Kew Foot Rd. Rich —7L 11
Kew Gardens Plants & People Exhibition. —3M 11
Kew Gdns. Rd. Rich —3M 11
Kew Green. (Junct.) —3M 11
Kew Grn. Rich —2M 11
Kew Mdw. Path. Rich —4A 12
(in two parts)
Kew Palace. —2L 11
Kew Retail Pk. Rich —4A 12
Kew Rd. Rich —2N 11
Keymer Clo. Big H —3E 86
Keymer Rd. SW2 —3K 29
Keymer Rd. Craw —5A 182
Keynes Clo. C Crook —9C 88
Keynsham Rd. Mord —7N 43
Keynsham Wlk. Mord —7N 43
Keynsham Way. Owl —5J 49
Keys Ct. Croy —5D 200
Keysham Av. Houn —4H 9
Keywood Dri. Sun —7H 23
Khama Rd. SW17 —5C 28
Khartoum Rd. SW17 —5B 28
Khartoum Rd. Witl —4B 152
Kibble Grn. Brack —5A 32
Kidborough Down. Bookh —5A 98
Kidborough Rd. Craw —4L 181
Kidbrooke Park. —8F 186
Kidbrooke Pk. —8F 186
Kidbrooke Ri. F Row —7G 187
Kidderminster Pl. Croy —7M 45
Kidderminster Rd. Croy —7M 45
Kidmans Clo. H'ham —3M 197
Kidworth Clo. Horl —6D 142
Kielder Wlk. Camb —2G 71
Kier Pk. Asc —2N 33
Kilberry Clo. Iswth —4D 10
Kilburns Mill Clo. Wall —8F 44
Kilcorral Clo. Eps —1F 80
Kilkie St. SW6 —5N 13
Killarney Rd. SW18 —9N 13 & 1A 28
Killasser Ct. Tad —1H 101
Killester Gdns. Wor Pk —1G 61
Killick Ho. Sutt —1N 61
Killicks. Cranl —6A 156
Killieser Av. SW2 —3J 29
Killinghurst La. Hasl & C'fold —2N 189
Killinghurst Park. —1A 190
Killy Hill. Chob —4H 53
Kilmaine Rd. SW6 —3K 13
Kilmarnock Pk. Reig —2N 121
Kilmartin Av. SW16 —2L 45
Kilmartin Gdns. Frim —5D 70
Kilmington Clo. Brack —6C 32
Kilmington Rd. SW13 —2F 12
Kilmiston Av. Shep —5D 38
Kilmore Dri. Camb —2F 70
Kilmorey Gdns. Twic —8H 11
Kilmorey Rd. Twic —7H 11
Kilmuir Clo. Coll T —8J 49
Kiln Clo. Craw D —2E 184
Kiln Clo. Hayes —2E 8
Kiln Copse. Cranl —6N 155
Kiln Cotts. Newd —7C 140
Kilnfield Rd. Rud —9E 176
Kiln Fields. Hasl —9G 171
Kiln La. Asc —4D 34
Kiln La. Bisl —4E 72
Kiln La. Brack —1M 31
Kiln La. Brock —4A 120
Kiln La. Eps —7D 60
Kiln La. Horl —6E 142
Kiln La. Lwr Bo —5G 129
Kiln La. Rip —2J 95
Kiln La. Wink —7M 17
Kilnmead. Craw —2C 182
Kilnmead Clo. Craw —2C 182
Kiln Meadows. Guild —8F 92
Kiln M. SW17 —6B 28
Kiln Ride. Finch —8A 30
Kiln Ride Extension. Finch —1A 48
Kiln Rd. Craw D —2E 184
Kilnside. Clay —4G 58
Kiln Wlk. Red —8E 122
Kiln Way. Alder —5N 109
Kiln Way. Gray —4K 169
Kilnwood La. Fay —6E 180
Kilross Rd. Felt —2E 22
Kilrue La. W on T —1G 57
Kilrush Ter. Wok —3C 74
Kilsha Rd. W on T —5K 39
Kimbell Gdns. SW6 —4K 13
Kimber Clo. Wind —6D 4
Kimber Ct. Guild —1F 114
Kimberley. Brack —7A 32
Kimberley. C Crook —9C 88
Kimberley Clo. Horl —8C 142
Kimberley Clo. Slou —1B 6
Kimberley Pl. Purl —7L 63
Kimberley Ride. Cobh —9B 58
Kimberley Rd. Beck —1G 47
Kimberley Rd. Craw —2F 182
Kimberley Rd. Croy —5M 45
Kimberley Wlk. W on T —6J 39
Kimber Rd. SW18 —1M 27
Kimbers La. Farnh —9J 109
Kimble Rd. SW19 —7B 28
Kimmeridge. Brack —5C 32
Kimpton Ind. Est. Sutt —8L 43
Kimpton Rd. Sutt —8L 43
Kinburn Dri. Egh —6A 20
Kincha Lodge. King T —1M 203
Kindersley Clo. E Grin —7D 166
Kinfauns Rd. SW2 —3L 29
King Acre Ct. Stai —4G 20
King Charles Cres. Surb —6M 41
King Charles Ho. SW6 —3N 13
(off Wandon Rd.)
King Charles Rd. Surb —4M 41
King Charles Wlk. SW19 —2K 27
Kingcup Clo. Croy —6G 46
Kingcup Dri. Bisl —2D 72
King Edward Clo. C Hosp —9D 196
King Edward Ct. Wind —4G 4
King Edward Dri. Chess —9L 41
King Edward M. SW13 —4F 12
King Edward Rd. C Hosp —9D 196
King Edward's Clo. Asc —9J 17
King Edward VII Av. Wind —3H 5
King Edwards Gro. Tedd —7H 25
King Edwards Mans. SW6 —3M 13
(off Fulham Rd.)
King Edward's Ri. Asc —8J 17
King Edward's Rd. Asc —9J 17
Kingfield. —7C 74
Kingfield Clo. Wok —7B 74
Kingfield Dri. Wok —7B 74
Kingfield Gdns. Wok —7B 74
Kingfield Green. —7B 74
Kingfield Rd. Wok —7A 74
Kingfisher Clo. Bord —7A 168
Kingfisher Clo. C Crook —8B 88
Kingfisher Clo. Craw —8E 162
Kingfisher Clo. Farn —8H 69
Kingfisher Clo. W on T —2M 57
Kingfisher Ct. SW19 —3J 27
Kingfisher Ct. Dork —1K 201
Kingfisher Ct. Houn —8B 10
Kingfisher Ct. Wok —1E 74
Kingfisher Dri. Guild —1E 114
Kingfisher Dri. Red —9E 102
Kingfisher Dri. Rich —5H 25
Kingfisher Dri. Stai —5H 21
Kingfisher Dri. Yat —9A 48
Kingfisher Gdns. S Croy —7G 65
Kingfisher La. Turn H —4F 184
Kingfisher Ri. E Grin —1B 186
Kingfisher Wlk. As —1D 110
Kingfisher Way. Beck —4G 46
Kingfisher Way. H'ham —3J 197
King Gdns. Croy —2M 63 (8A 200)
King George Av. E Grin —7M 165
King George Av. W on T —7L 39
King George Clo. Sun —6F 22
King George's Dri. New H —6J 55
King George's Hill. —5N 137
King George VI Av. Big H —3F 86
King George VI Av. Mitc —3D 44
King George's Trad. Est. Chess —1N 59
Kingham Clo. SW18 —1A 28
King Henry M. Orp —2N 67
King Henry's Dri. New Ad —5L 65
King Henry's Reach. W6 —2H 13
King Henry's Rd. King T —2A 42
King John's Clo. Wray —9M 5
Kinglake Ct. Wok —5H 73
Kingpost Pde. Guild —9D 94
Kings Acre. S Nut —6K 123
Kings Arbour. S'hall —1M 9
King's Arms All. Bren —2K 11
Kings Arms Way. Cher —7H 37
Kings Av. SW12 & SW4 —2H 29
King's Av. Brkwd —6A 72
Kings Av. Byfl —8M 55
King's Av. Cars —4C 62
Kings Av. Houn —4B 10
Kings Av. N Mald —3D 42
Kings Av. Red —5C 122
King's Av. Sun —6G 23
Kings Av. Tong —4C 110
Kingsbridge Cotts. Wokgm —9C 30
Kingsbridge Rd. Mord —5J 43
Kingsbridge Rd. S'hall —1N 9
Kingsbridge Rd. W on T —6J 39
Kingsbrook. Lea —5G 79
Kingsbury Cres. Stai —5F 20
Kingsbury Dri. Old Win —1K 19
Kings Chase. E Mol —2C 40
Kingsclear Pk. Camb —2B 70
Kingsclere Clo. SW15 —1F 26
Kingscliffe Gdns. SW19 —2L 27
Kings Clo. Stai —8M 21
Kings Clo. Th Dit —5G 41
Kings Clo. W on T —7J 39
Kings Copse. E Grin —1B 186
Kingscote. —5J 185
Kingscote Hill. Craw —5N 181
Kingscote Rd. Croy —6E 46
Kingscote Rd. N Mald —2C 42
Kings Ct. W6 —1F 12
Kings Ct. Byfl —7M 55
King's Ct. H'ham —5L 197
King's Ct. Tad —9G 81
Kings Ct. Tong —4C 110
Kingscourt Rd. SW16 —4H 29
King's Cres. Camb —7A 50
Kingscroft. Fleet —5B 88
Kingscroft La. Warf —3D 16
Kingscroft Rd. Bans —2B 82
Kingscroft Rd. Lea —7H 79
Kings Cross La. S Nut —5H 123
Kingsdene. Tad —8G 80
Kingsdown Av. S Croy —6M 63
Kingsdowne Rd. Surb —6L 41
Kingsdown Rd. Eps —9F 60
Kingsdown Rd. Sutt —2K 61
Kings Dri. Surb —6N 41
Kings Dri. Tedd —6D 24
Kings Dri. Th Dit —6H 41
Kings Dri. W on T —5G 57
Kings Farm Av. Rich —7N 11
Kingsfield. Alb —4N 135
Kingsfield. Wind —4A 4
Kingsfold. —3H 179
Kingsfold Ct. K'fold —4H 179
Kingsford Av. Wall —4J 63
Kingsgate. Craw —3C 182
Kings Ga. G'ming —5J 133
(off King's Rd.)
Kingsgate Bus. Cen. King T —9L 25 (1K 203)
Kingsgate Rd. King T —9L 25 (2K 203)
Kingsgrove Ind. Est. Farn —2M 89
Kings Head La. Byfl —7M 55
Kingshill Av. Wor Pk —6F 42
Kings Keep. SW15 —8J 13
Kings Keep. Fleet —7B 88
Kings Keep. King T —3L 41 (8K 203)
King's Keep. Sand —6G 49
Kingsland. —2N 159
Kingsland. Newd —2N 159
Kingsland Ct. Craw —3E 182
Kings La. Eng G —6A 20
(Egham)
Kings La. Eng G —6K 19
(Englefield Green)
Kings La. Sutt —3B 62
Kings La. W'sham —2B 52
Kings La. Wrec —5E 128
Kingslawn Clo. SW15 —8G 13
Kingslea. H'ham —5L 197
Kingslea. Lea —7G 79
Kingsleigh Pl. Mitc —2D 44
Kingsley Av. Bans —2M 81
Kingsley Av. Camb —2A 70
Kingsley Av. Eng G —7L 19
Kingsley Av. Houn —5C 10
Kingsley Av. Sutt —1B 62
Kingsley Clo. Crowt —4G 49
Kingsley Clo. Horl —6D 142
Kingsley Ct. Sutt —4N 61
Kingsley Ct. Wor Pk —8E 42
(off Avenue, The)
Kingsley Dri. Wor Pk —8E 42
Kingsley Green. —6E 188
Kingsley Gro. Reig —6M 121
Kingsley Mans. W14 —2K 13
(off Greyhound Rd.)
Kingsley Rd. SW19 —6N 27
Kingsley Rd. Craw —6N 181
Kingsley Rd. Croy —7L 45
Kingsley Rd. Farn —8L 69

Leaveland Clo.—Links Way

Leaveland Clo. *Beck* —3K **47**
Leavesden Rd. *Wey* —2C **56**
Leaves Green. —7F 66
Leaves Grn. *Brack* —5B **32**
Leaves Grn. Cres. *Kes* —7E **66**
Leaves Grn. Rd. *Kes* —7F **66**
Lea Way. *Alder* —1D **110**
Leaway. *Bad L* —7M **109**
Leawood Rd. *Fleet* —6A **88**
Leazes Av. *Cat* —1L **103**
Leazes La. *Cat* —1L **103**
Lebanon Av. *Felt* —6L **23**
Lebanon Dri. *Cobh* —9A **58**
Lebanon Gdns. *SW18* —9M **13**
Lebanon Gdns. *Big H* —4F **86**
Lebanon Pk. *Twic* —1H **25**
Lebanon Rd. *SW18* —8M **13**
Lebanon Rd. *Croy* —7B **46**
Le Chateau. *Croy* —5E **200**
Lechford Rd. *Horl* —9E **142**
Leckford Rd. *SW18* —3A **28**
Leckhampton Pl. *SW2* —1L **29**
Leconfield Av. *SW13* —6E **12**
Ledbury Pl. *Croy* —1N **63** (7C **200**)
Ledbury Rd. *Croy* —1A **64** (8C **200**)
Ledbury Rd. *Reig* —3M **121**
Ledger Clo. *Guild* —1D **114**
Ledger Dri. *Add* —2H **55**
Ledgers La. *Warl* —4L **85**
Ledgers Rd. *Warl* —3K **85**
Lee Acre. *Dork* —7J **119**
Leechcroft Rd. *Wall* —9E **44**
Leech La. *Dork & H'ley* —4A **100**
Leechpool La. *H'ham* —4N **197**
Lee Ct. *Alder* —4A **110**
Leegate Clo. *Wok* —3L **73**
Lee Grn. La. *H'ley* —2A **100**
Leehurst. *Milf* —1B **152**
Lee Rd. *SW19* —9N **27**
Lee Rd. *Alder* —2K **109**
Leeside. *Rusp* —3B **180**
Leeson Gdns. *Eton W* —1B **4**
Leeson Ho. *Twic* —1H **25**
Lees, The. *Croy* —8J **47**
Lee St. *Horl* —8C **142**
Leeward Gdns. *SW19* —6K **27**
Leeways, The. *Sutt* —3K **61**
Leewood Way. *Eff* —5K **97**
Lefroy Pk. *Fleet* —4A **88**
Leger Clo. *C Crook* —8A **88**
Legge Cres. *Alder* —3K **109**
Leggyfield Ct. *H'ham* —3H **197**
Legion Ct. *Mord* —5M **43**
Legoland. —8A 4
Legrace Av. *Houn* —5L **9**
Legsheath La. *E Grin* —8M **185**
Leicester. *Brack* —6C **32**
Leicester Av. *Mitc* —3J **45**
Leicester Clo. *Wor Pk* —1H **61**
Leicester Ct. *Craw* —3H **183**
Leicester Ct. Twic —9K 11
(off Clevedon Rd.)
Leicester Rd. *Croy* —6B **46**
Leigh. —1F 140
Leigham Av. *SW16* —4J **29**
Leigham Clo. *SW16* —4K **29**
Leigham Ct. Rd. *SW16* —3J **29**
Leigham Dri. *Isw* —3E **10**
Leigham Hall Pde. SW16 —4J 29
(off Streatham High Rd.)
Leigham Va. *SW16 & SW2* —4K **29**
Leigh Clo. *Add* —4H **55**
Leigh Clo. *N Mald* —3B **42**
Leigh Clo. Ind. Est. *N Mald* —3C **42**
Leigh Corner. *Cobh* —2K **77**
Leigh Ct. Clo. *Cobh* —1K **77**
Leigh Cres. *New Ad* —4L **65**
Leigh Hill Rd. *Cobh* —2K **77**
Leighlands. *Craw* —1G **183**
Leigh La. *Farnh* —3K **129**
Leigh Orchard Clo. *SW16* —4K **29**
Leigh Pk. *Dat* —3L **5**
Leigh Pl. *Cobh* —2K **77**
Leigh Pl. Cotts. *Leigh* —9F **120**
Leigh Pl. La. *God* —1G **125**
Leigh Pl. Rd. *Leigh* —9F **120**
Leigh Rd. *Bet* —9B **120**
Leigh Rd. *Cobh* —1J **77**
Leigh Rd. *Houn* —7D **10**
Leigh Sq. *Wind* —5A **4**
Leighton Gdns. *Croy* —7M **45**
Leighton Gdns. *S Croy* —9E **64**
Leighton Mans. W14 —2K 13
(off Greyhound Rd.)
Leighton St. *Croy* —7M **45** (1A **200**)
Leighton Way. *Eps* —1C **80** (8L **201**)
Leinster Av. *SW14* —6B **12**
Leipzig Rd. *C Crook* —1C **108**
Leisure La. *W Byf* —8K **55**
Leisure West. *Felt* —3J **23**
Leith Clo. *Crowt* —9F **30**
Leithcote Gdns. *SW16* —5K **29**
Leithcote Path. *SW16* —4K **29**
Leith Dri. *Alder* —1L **109**
Leith Gro. *Bear G* —7K **139**
Leith Hill La. *Ab C* —4M **137**
Leith Hill Place. (East) —9B 138
Leith Hill Place. (West) —1N 157
Leith Hill Rd. *Holm M* —9A **138**
Leith Hill Tower. —8B 138
Leith Lea. *Bear G* —7K **139**
Leith Rd. *Bear G* —8J **139**
Leith Rd. *Eps* —8D **60**
Leith Towers. *Sutt* —4N **61**
Leith Va. Cotts. *Ockl* —7A **158**
Leith Vw. *N Holm* —9J **119**
Leith Vw. Cotts. *K'fold* —3H **179**
Leith Vw. Rd. *H'ham* —3N **197**
Lela Av. *Houn* —5K **9**
Le Marchant Rd. *Frim & Camb* —3D **70**
Le May Clo. *Horl* —7E **142**
Lemington Gro. *Brack* —5N **31**
Lemmington Way. *H'ham* —1M **197**
Lemon's Farm Rd. *Ab C* —5N **137**
Lemuel St. *SW18* —9N **13**
Lendore Rd. *Frim* —6B **70**
Lenelby Rd. *Surb* —7N **41**
Leney Clo. *Wokgm* —9C **14**
Len Freeman Pl. *SW6* —2L **13**
Lenham Rd. *Sutt* —1N **61**
Lenham Rd. *T Hth* —1A **46**
Lennard Rd. *Croy* —7N **45** (1B **200**)
Lennel Gdns. *C Crook* —7D **88**
Lennox Ct. Red —2E 122
(off St Anne's Ri.)
Lennox Gdns. *Croy* —1M **63** (7A **200**)
Lennox Ho. Twic —9K 11
(off Clevedon Rd.)
Lenten Clo. *Peasl* —2E **136**
Lenton Ri. *Rich* —6L **11**
Leo Ct. *Bren* —3K **11**
Leominster Rd. *Mord* —5A **44**
Leominster Wlk. *Mord* —5A **44**
Leonard Av. *Mord* —4A **44**
Leonard Clo. *Frim* —6B **70**
Leonard Rd. *SW16* —9G **28**
Leonardslee Ct. *Craw* —5F **182**
Leonard Way. *H'ham* —6M **197**
Leopold Av. *SW19* —6L **27**
Leopold Av. *Farn* —9N **69**
Leopold Rd. *SW19* —5L **27**
Leopold Rd. *Craw* —3A **182**
Leopold Ter. *SW19* —6L **27**
Le Personne Homes. Cat —9A 84
(off Banstead Rd.)
Le Personne Rd. *Cat* —9A **84**
Leppington. *Brack* —7N **31**
Leret Way. *Lea* —8H **79**
Lerry Clo. *W14* —2L **13**
Lesbourne Rd. *Reig* —4N **121**
Leslie Dunne Ho. *Wind* —5B **4**
Leslie Gdns. *Sutt* —3M **61**
Leslie Gro. *Croy* —7B **46** (1E **200**)
Leslie Gro. Pl. *Croy* —7B **46** (1F **200**)
Leslie Pk. Rd. *Croy* —7B **46** (1F **200**)
Leslie Rd. *Chob* —6H **53**
Leslie Rd. *Dork* —3K **119**
Lessingham Av. *SW17* —5D **28**
Lessness Rd. *Mord* —5A **44**
Lestock Way. *Fleet* —4D **88**
Letchworth Av. *Felt* —1G **22**
Letchworth Ct. *Bew* —6K **181**
Letchworth St. *SW17* —5D **28**
Letcombe Sq. *Brack* —3C **32**
Letterstone Rd. *SW6* —3L **13**
Lettice St. *SW6* —4L **13**
Levana Clo. *SW19* —2K **27**
Levehurst Ho. *SE27* —6N **29**
Leveret Clo. *New Ad* —7N **65**
Leveret La. *Craw* —1N **181**
Leverkusen Rd. *Brack* —2N **31**
Levern Dri. *Farnh* —6H **109**
Leverson St. *SW16* —7G **28**
Levett Rd. *Lea* —7H **79**
Levylsdene. *Guild* —3E **114**
Levylsdene Ct. *Guild* —3F **114**
Lewes Clo. *Craw* —3G **183**
Lewesdon Clo. *SW19* —2J **27**
Lewes Rd. *F Grn & F Row* —1B **186**
Lewes Rd. *F Row* —9G **186**
Lewin Rd. *SW14* —6C **12**
Lewin Rd. *SW16* —7H **29**
Lewins Rd. *Eps* —1A **80**
Lewis Clo. *Add* —1L **55**
Lewisham Clo. *Craw* —7A **182**
Lewisham Way. *Owl* —6J **49**
Lewis Ho. *Brack* —5N **31**
Lewis Rd. *Mitc* —1B **44**
(in two parts)
Lewis Rd. *Rich* —8K **11**
Lewis Rd. *Sutt* —1N **61**
Leworth Pl. *Wind* —4G **4**
Lexden Rd. *Mitc* —3H **45**
Lexington Ct. *Purl* —6N **63**
Lexton Gdns. *SW12* —2H **29**
Leyborne Pk. *Rich* —4N **11**
Leybourne Av. *Byfl* —9N **55**
Leybourne Clo. *Byfl* —9A **56**
Leybourne Clo. *Craw* —8A **182**
Leyburn Gdns. *Croy* —8B **46**
Leycester Clo. *W'sham* —1M **51**
Leyfield. *Wor Pk* —7D **42**
Leylands La. *Stai* —7H **7**
(in two parts)
Ley Rd. *Farn* —6M **69**
Leyside. *Crowt* —2F **48**
Leys Rd. *Oxs* —9D **58**
Leys, The. *W on T* —1N **57**
Leyton Rd. *SW19* —8A **28**
Lezayre Rd. *Orp* —3N **87**
Liberty Av. *SW19* —9A **28**
Liberty Hall Rd. *Add* —2J **55**
Liberty La. *Add* —2J **55**
Liberty M. *SW12* —1F **28**
Liberty Ri. *Add* —3J **55**
Library Way. *Twic* —1C **24**
Lichfield Ct. *Rich* —7L **11**
Lichfield Ct. *Surb* —8K **203**
Lichfield Gdns. *Rich* —7L **11**
Lichfield Rd. *Houn* —6K **9**
Lichfield Rd. *Rich* —4M **11**
Lichfields. *Brack* —1C **32**
Lichfield Ter. *Rich* —8L **11**
Lichfield Way. *S Croy* —6G **65**
Lickey Ho. W14 —2L 13
(off N. End Rd.)
Lickfolds Rd. *Rowl* —9D **128**
Liddell. *Wind* —6A **4**
Liddell Pl. *Wind* —5A **4**
Liddell Sq. *Wind* —5A **4**
Liddell Way. *Asc* —4K **33**
Liddell Way. *Wind* —6A **4**
Liddington Hall Dri. *Guild* —9H **93**
Liddington New Rd. *Guild* —9H **93**
Lidiard Rd. *SW18* —3A **28**
Lido Rd. *Guild* —2N **113** (1D **202**)
Lidsey Clo. *M'bowr* —5G **183**
Lidstone Clo. *Wok* —4L **73**
Lifetimes Mus. —9N 45 (4C 200)
(off High St.)
Liffords Pl. *SW13* —5E **12**
Lifford St. *SW15* —7J **13**
Lightermans Wlk. *SW18* —7M **13**
Lightwater. —6L 51
Lightwater By-Pass. *Light* —5L **51**
Lightwater Country Pk. & Vis. Cen. —6K 51
Lightwater Mdw. *Light* —7M **51**
Lightwater Rd. *Light* —7M **51**
Lightwood. *Brack* —5B **32**
Lilac Av. *Wok* —7N **73**
Lilac Clo. *Guild* —8M **93**
Lilac Ct. *Tedd* —5F **24**
Lilac Gdns. *Croy* —9K **47**
Lilian Rd. *SW16* —9G **28**
Lille Barracks. *Alder* —6B **90**
Lilleshall Rd. *Mord* —5D **44**
Lilley Ct. *Crowt* —3G **49**
Lilley Dri. *Kgswd* —9N **81**
Lillian Rd. *SW13* —2F **12**
Lillie Mans. W14 —2K 13
(off Lillie Rd.)
Lillie Rd. *SW6* —2J **13**
Lillie Rd. *Big H* —5F **86**
Lillie Yd. *SW6* —2M **13**
Lilliot's La. *Lea* —6G **79**
Lily Clo. *W14* —1J **13**
(in two parts)
Lily Ct. *Wokgm* —2A **30**
Lilyfields Chase. *Ewh* —6F **156**
Lily Hill Dri. *Brack* —1C **32**
Lily Hill Rd. *Brack* —1C **32**
Lilyville Rd. *SW6* —4L **13**
Lime Av. *Asc* —5F **32**
Lime Av. *Camb* —9F **50**
Lime Av. *H'ham* —4N **197**
Lime Av. *Wind* —4J **5**
(Windsor)
Lime Av. *Wind* —4C **18**
(Windsor Great Park)
Limebush Clo. *New H* —5L **55**
Lime Clo. *Cars* —8D **44**
Lime Clo. *Copt* —7M **163**
Lime Clo. *Craw* —9A **162**
Lime Clo. *Reig* —6N **121**
Lime Clo. *W Cla* —6K **95**
Lime Ct. *Mitc* —1D **44**
Lime Cres. *As* —2F **110**
Lime Cres. *Sun* —1K **39**
Limecroft. *Yat* —1B **68**
Limecroft Clo. *Eps* —4C **60**
Limecroft Rd. *Knap* —4E **72**
Lime Dri. *Fleet* —1D **88**
Lime Gro. *Add* —1J **55**
Lime Gro. *Guild* —8L **93**
Lime Gro. *N Mald* —2C **42**
Lime Gro. *Twic* —9F **10**
Lime Gro. *Warl* —5H **85**
Lime Gro. *W Cla* —6J **95**
Lime Gro. *Wok* —8A **74**
Lime Mdw. Av. *S Croy* —9D **64**
Limerick Clo. *SW12* —1G **28**
Limerick Clo. *Brack* —9M **15**
Lime Rd. *Rich* —7M **11**
Limes Av. *SW13* —5E **12**
Limes Av. *Cars* —7D **44**
Limes Av. *Croy* —9L **45**
Limes Av. *Horl* —9F **142**
Limes Clo. *Afrd* —6B **22**
Limes Fld. Rd. *SW14* —6D **12**
Limes Gdns. *SW18* —9M **13**
Limes M. *Egh* —6B **20**
Limes Pl. *Croy* —6A **46**
Limes Rd. *Beck* —1L **47**
Limes Rd. *Croy* —6A **46**
Limes Rd. *Egh* —6B **20**
Limes Rd. *Farn* —9H **69**
Limes Rd. *Wey* —1B **56**
Limes Row. *F'boro* —2K **67**
Limes, The. *SW18* —9M **13**
Limes, The. *E Mol* —3B **40**
Limes, The. *Eden* —2L **147**
Limes, The. *Felb* —5K **165**
Limes, The. *Hors* —2N **73**
Limes, The. *Lea* —1H **99**
Limes, The. *Wind* —4A **4**
Lime St. *Alder* —2L **109**
Lime Tree Av. *Esh* —7D **40**
Limetree Clo. *SW2* —2K **29**
Lime Tree Clo. *Bookh* —2A **98**
Lime Tree Ct. *Asht* —5L **79**
Lime Tree Ct. *S Croy* —3N **63**
Lime Tree Gro. *Croy* —9J **47**
Lime Tree Pl. *Mitc* —9F **29**
Lime Tree Rd. *Houn* —4B **10**
Limetree Wlk. *SW17* —6E **28**
Lime Tree Wlk. *Vir W* —3A **36**
Lime Tree Wlk. *W Wick* —1B **66**
Lime Wlk. *Brack* —3A **32**
Lime Wlk. *Shere* —8A **116**
Limeway Ter. *Dork* —3G **118**
Limewood Clo. *Beck* —4M **47**
Limewood Clo. *Wok* —7G **73**
Lime Works Rd. *Mers* —4G **102**
Limpsfield. —7D 106
Limpsfield Av. *SW19* —3J **27**
Limpsfield Av. *T Hth* —4K **45**
Limpsfield Chart. —8G 107
Limpsfield Chart. —9H 107
Limpsfield Common. —8D 106
Limpsfield Rd. *S Croy* —8D **64**
Linacre Ct. W6 —1J 13
(off Talgarth Rd.)
Linacre Dri. *Rud & Cranl* —7D **176**
Lince La. *Westc* —5D **118**
Linchfield Rd. *Dat* —4M **5**
Linchmere. —6A 188
Linchmere Pl. *Craw* —2M **181**
Linchmere Rd. *Hasl* —5A **188**
Lincoln Av. *SW19* —4J **27**
Lincoln Av. *Twic* —3C **24**
Lincoln Clo. *SE25* —5D **46**
Lincoln Clo. *Ash V* —8D **90**
Lincoln Clo. *Camb* —2F **70**
Lincoln Clo. *Craw* —6C **182**
Lincoln Clo. *Horl* —9E **142**
Lincoln Ct. *S Croy* —8C **200**
Lincoln Dri. *Wok* —2G **74**
Lincoln M. *SE21* —3N **29**
Lincoln Rd. *SE25* —2E **46**
Lincoln Rd. *Dork* —3J **119**
Lincoln Rd. *Felt* —4N **23**
Lincoln Rd. *Guild* —1J **113**
Lincoln Rd. *Mitc* —4J **45**
Lincoln Rd. *N Mald* —2B **42**
Lincoln Rd. *Wor Pk* —7G **42**
Lincolnshire Gdns. *Warf* —8C **16**
Lincolns Mead. *Ling* —8M **145**
Lincoln Wlk. *Eps* —6C **60**
(in two parts)
Lincoln Way. *Sun* —9F **22**
Lincombe Ct. *Add* —2K **55**
Lindale Clo. *Vir W* —3J **35**
Lindbergh Rd. *Wall* —4J **63**
Linden. *Brack* —4D **32**
Linden Av. *Coul* —3F **82**
Linden Av. *E Grin* —8M **165**
Linden Av. *Houn* —8B **10**
Linden Av. *T Hth* —3M **45**
Linden Clo. *Craw* —6E **182**
Linden Clo. *H'ham* —4L **197**
Linden Clo. *New H* —7J **55**
Linden Clo. *Tad* —7J **81**
Linden Clo. *Th Dit* —6F **40**
Linden Ct. *Camb* —8D **50**
Linden Ct. *Eng G* —7L **19**
Linden Ct. *Lea* —8H **79**
Linden Cres. *King T* —1M **41** (4N **203**)
Linden Dri. *Cat* —2N **103**
Linden Gdns. *W4* —1D **12**
Linden Gdns. *Lea* —8J **79**
Linden Gro. *N Mald* —2D **42**
Linden Gro. *Tedd* —6F **24**
Linden Gro. *W on T* —8G **39**
Linden Gro. *Warl* —5H **85**
Lindenhill Rd. *Brack* —9L **15**
Linden Ho. *Hamp* —7A **24**
Linden Ho. *Slou* —1D **6**
Linden Lea. *Dork* —7J **119**
Linden Leas. *W Wick* —8N **47**
Linden Pit Path. *Lea* —7J **79**
(Linden Gdns.)
Linden Pit Path. *Lea* —8H **79**
(Linden Rd.)
Linden Pl. *E Hor* —4F **96**
Linden Pl. *Eps* —8D **60** (5N **201**)
Linden Pl. *Mitc* —3C **44**
Linden Pl. *Stai* —5J **21**
Linden Rd. *Guild* —3N **113** (2C **202**)
Linden Rd. *Hamp* —8A **24**
Linden Rd. *Head D* —4G **169**
Linden Rd. *Lea* —8H **79**
Linden Rd. *Wey* —5D **56**
Lindens Clo. *Eff* —6M **97**
Lindens, The. *W4* —4B **12**
Lindens, The. *Copt* —7M **163**
Lindens, The. *Farnh* —2J **129**
Lindens, The. *New Ad* —3M **65**
Linden Way. *Purl* —6G **63**
Linden Way. *Rip* —3H **95**
Linden Way. *Shep* —4D **38**
Linden Way. *Wok* —8B **74**
Lindfield Gdns. *Guild* —2B **114**
Lindfield Rd. *Croy* —5C **46**
Lindford. —3A 168
Lindford Chase. *Lind* —4A **168**
Lindford Rd. *Bord* —3A **168**
Lindford Wey. *Lind* —4A **168**
Lindgren Wlk. *Craw* —8N **181**
Lindisfarne Rd. *SW20* —8F **26**
Lindley Ct. *King T* —9J **25**
Lindley Pl. *Kew* —4N **11**
Lindley Rd. *God* —8F **104**
Lindley Rd. *W on T* —9L **39**
Lindores Rd. *Cars* —6A **44**
Lind Rd. *Sutt* —2A **62**
Lindrop St. *SW6* —5N **13**
Lindsay Clo. *Chess* —4L **59**
Lindsay Clo. *Eps* —9B **60** (7H **201**)
Lindsay Clo. *Stanw* —8M **7**
Lindsay Ct. *Croy* —6D **200**
Lindsay Dri. *Shep* —5F **38**
Lindsay Rd. *Hamp H* —5B **24**
Lindsay Rd. *New H* —6J **55**
Lindsay Rd. *Wor Pk* —8G **43**
Lindsey Clo. *Mitc* —3J **45**
Lindsey Gdns. *Felt* —1E **22**
Lindum Clo. *Alder* —3M **109**
Lindum Dene. *Alder* —3M **109**
Lindum Rd. *Tedd* —8J **25**
Lindway. *SE27* —6M **29**
Linersh Dri. *Brmly* —5C **134**
Linersh Wood Clo. *Brmly* —6C **134**
Linersh Wood Rd. *Brmly* —5C **134**
Lines Rd. *Hurst* —5A **14**
Linfield Clo. *W on T* —2J **57**
Ling Cres. *Head D* —3G **169**
Ling Dri. *Light* —8K **51**
Lingfield. —7N 145
Lingfield Av. *King T* —3L **41** (8L **203**)
Lingfield Common. —6M 145
Lingfield Comn. Rd. *Ling* —6M **145**
Lingfield Dri. *Worth* —2J **183**
Lingfield Gdns. *Coul* —6M **83**
Lingfield Park Racecourse. —9A 146
Lingfield Rd. *SW19* —6J **27**
Lingfield Rd. *E Grin* —6N **165**
Lingfield Rd. *Eden* —3H **147**
Lingfield Rd. *Wor Pk* —9H **43**
Lingmala Gro. *C Crook* —8C **88**
Lings Coppice. *SE21* —3N **29**
Lingwell Rd. *SW17* —4C **28**
Lingwood. *Brack* —5A **32**
Lingwood Gdns. *Isw* —3E **10**
Link Av. *Wok* —2F **74**
Linkfield. *W Mol* —2B **40**
Linkfield Corner. *Red* —3B **122**
(Hatchlands Rd.)
Linkfield Corner. *Red* —3C **122**
(Linkfield St.)
Linkfield Gdns. *Red* —3C **122**
Linkfield La. *Red* —2C **122**
Linkfield Rd. *Isw* —5F **10**
Linkfield St. *Red* —3C **122**
Link La. *Wall* —3H **63**
Link Rd. *Add* —1N **55**
Link Rd. *Dat* —4M **5**
Link Rd. *Felt* —1G **23**
Link Rd. *Wall* —7E **44**
Links Av. *Mord* —3M **43**
(in two parts)
Links Brow. *Fet* —2E **98**
Links Clo. *Asht* —4J **79**
Links Clo. *Ewh* —4F **156**
Linkscroft Av. *Afrd* —7C **22**
Links Gdns. *SW16* —8L **29**
Links Grn. Way. *Cobh* —1A **78**
Linkside. —2N 169
Linkside. *N Mald* —1D **42**
Linkside E. *Hind* —2A **170**
Linkside N. *Hind* —2N **169**
Linkside S. *Hind* —3A **170**
Linkside W. *Hind* —2N **169**
Links Pl. *Asht* —4K **79**
Links Rd. *SW17* —7E **28**
Links Rd. *Afrd* —6N **21**
Links Rd. *Asht* —5J **79**
Links Rd. *Brmly* —4A **134**
Links Rd. *Eps* —9F **60**
Links Rd. *W Wick* —7M **47**
Links, The. *Asc* —1J **33**
Links, The. *W on T* —8H **39**
Links Vw. Av. *Brock* —3N **119**
Links Vw. Ct. *Hamp* —5D **24**
Links Vw. Rd. *Croy* —9K **47**
Links Vw. Rd. *Hamp H* —6C **24**
Links Way. *Beck* —5K **47**
Links Way. *Bookh* —6M **97**

Links Way—Longwood Dri.

Links Way. Farn —2H 89
Link, The. Craw —3B 182
(in two parts)
Link, The. Tedd —7F 24
Linkway. SW20 —3G 43
Linkway. Camb —2A 70
Linkway. Crowt —2E 48
Linkway. Fleet —7A 88
Linkway. Guild —2J 113
Linkway. Rich —3H 25
Link Way. Stai —7K 21
Linkway. Wok —4E 74
Linkway Pde. Fleet —7A 88
Linkway, The. Sutt —5A 62
Linley Ct. Sutt —1A 62
Linnell Clo. Craw —9N 181
Linnell Rd. Red —4E 122
Linnet Clo. S Croy —6G 65
Linnet Clo. Turn H —4F 184
Linnet Gro. Guild —1F 114
Linnet M. SW12 —1E 28
Linsford Bus. Pk. Myt —2C 90
Linsford La. Myt —2D 90
Linslade Clo. Houn —8M 9
Linstead Rd. Farn —6K 69
Linstead Way. SW18 —1K 27
Linsted La. Head —2C 168
Lintaine Clo. SW6 —2K 13
Linton Clo. Mitc —6D 44
Linton Glade. Croy —5H 65
(in two parts)
Linton Gro. SE27 —6M 29
Lintons La. Eps —8D 60
Lintott Ct. Stanw —9M 7
Lintott Gdns. H'ham —5L 197
Linver Rd. SW6 —5M 13
Lion & Lamb Way. Farnh —1G 128
Lion & Lamb Yd. Farnh —1G 129
Lion Av. Twic —2F 24
Lion Clo. Hasl —1D 188
Lion Clo. Shep —2N 37
Lionel Rd. N. Bren —1L 11
Lionel Rd. S. Bren —1M 11
Lion Ga. Gdns. Rich —6M 11
Liongate M. E Mol —2F 40
Lion Grn. Hasl —2D 188
Lion Grn. Rd. Coul —3H 83
Lion La. Gray & Hasl —8D 170
Lion La. Red —2D 122
Lion La. Turn H —5D 184
Lion Mead. Hasl —2D 188
Lion Pk. Av. Chess —1N 59
Lion Retail Pk. Wok —3D 74
Lion Rd. Croy —4N 45
Lion Rd. Twic —2F 24
Lion's La. Alf —3K 175
(in two parts)
Lion Way. Bren —3K 11
Lion Way. C Crook —8C 88
Lion Wharf Rd. Iswth —6H 11
Lipcombe Cotts. Alb —3L 135
Liphook Rd. Hasl —2C 188
Liphook Rd. Head & Pass —6D 168
Liphook Rd. Lind —4A 168
Liphook Rd. Pass & Hasl —4A 188
Liphook Rd. W'hill —9A 168
Lipscomb's Corner. —1M 179
Lipsham Clo. Bans —9B 62
Lisbon Av. Twic —3C 24
Liscombe. Brack —6N 31
Liscombe Ho. Brack —6N 31
Lisgar Ter. W14 —1L 13
Liskeard Dri. Farn —8M 69
Lisle Clo. SW17 —5F 28
Lismore. SW19 —6L 27
(off Woodside)
Lismore Clo. Iswth —5G 10
Lismore Cres. Craw —6N 181
Lismore Rd. S Croy —3B 64
Lismoyne Clo. Fleet —3A 88
Lissoms Rd. Coul —5E 82
Lister Av. E Grin —3A 186
Lister Clo. Mitc —9C 28
Listergate Ct. SW15 —7H 13
Lister Ho. Hayes —1F 8
Litchfield Av. Mord —6L 43
Litchfield Rd. Sutt —1A 62
Litchfield Way. Guild —5J 113
Lithgow's Rd. H'row A —7F 8
Little Acre. Beck —2K 47
Lit. Austins Rd. Farnh —3J 129
Little Benty. W Dray —1M 7
Lit. Birch Clo. New H —5M 55
Little Birkets. —1L 157
Lit. Boltons, The. SW5 & SW10 —1N 13
Little Bookham. —2N 97
Little Bookham Common. —9M 77
Lit. Bookham St. Bookh —1N 97
Little Borough. Brock —4N 119
Littlebrook Clo. Croy —5G 47
Lit. Browns La. Eden —8G 127
Little Buntings. Wind —6C 4
Little Collins. Out —4M 143
Littlecombe Clo. SW15 —9J 13
Lit. Common La. Blet —1M 123
Little Comptons. H'ham —6M 197
Little Copse. Fleet —6A 88
Little Copse. Yat —8C 48
Littlecote Clo. SW19 —1K 27
Little Ct. W Wick —8N 47
Little Crabtree. Craw —2A 182
Lit. Cranmore La. W Hor —6C 96
Little Cft. Yat —1C 68
Littlecroft Rd. Egh —6B 20
Littledale Clo. Brack —2C 32
Little Dimocks. SW12 —3F 28
Little Elms. Hayes —3E 8
Lit. Ferry Rd. Twic —2H 25
Littlefield Clo. As —3E 110
Littlefield Clo. Guild —8G 92
Littlefield Clo. King T —1L 41 (4L 203)
Littlefield Common. —7E 92
Littlefield Gdns. As —3E 110
Littlefield Ho. King T —4K 203
Littlefield Way. Guild —8F 92
Littleford La. B'hth —2G 134
Little Fryth. Finch —1B 48
Little Grebe. H'ham —3J 197
Little Grn. Rich —7K 11
Lit. Green La. Cher —9G 36
Lit. Green La. Farnh —4F 128
Lit. Green La. Farm Est. Cher —1F 54
Little Gro. Dork —7J 119
(off Stubs Hill)
Little Halliards. W on T —5H 39
Little Hatch. H'ham —3M 197
Little Haven. —3M 197
Lit. Haven La. H'ham —3M 197
Littleheath La. Cobh —1A 78
Lit. Heath Rd. Chob —5H 53
Littleheath Rd. S Croy —4E 64
Little Hide. Guild —1D 114
Lit. Holland Bungalows. Cat —1A 104
Little Kiln. G'ming —3H 133
Lit. King St. E Grin —9A 166
Little Kings Wood. —5E 116
Little London. —1A 136
Little London. Alb —1N 135
Little London. Witl —5B 152
Lit. London Hill. Warn —8G 179
Little Lullenden. Ling —6N 145
Lit. Manor Gdns. Cranl —8M 155
Little Mead. Cranl —8K 155
Littlemead. Esh —1D 58
Little Mead. Wok —3J 73
Lit. Mead Ind. Est. Cranl —7K 155
Little Moor. Sand —6H 49
Lit. Moreton Clo. W Byf —8K 55
Little Orchard. Wok —1C 74
Little Orchard. Wdhm —7J 55
Little Orchards. Eps —8M 201
Lit. Orchard Way. Shalf —1A 134
Little Paddock. Camb —7E 50
Lit. Park Dri. Felt —3M 23
Little Parrock. —8M 187
Little Platt. Guild —2G 112
Lit. Queen's Rd. Tedd —7F 24
Little Ringdale. Brack —3C 32
Lit. Roke Av. Kenl —1M 83
Lit. Roke Rd. Kenl —1N 83
Littlers Clo. SW19 —9A 28
Lit. St Leonard's. SW14 —6B 12
Little Sandhurst. —6F 48
Little St. Guild —8L 93
Lit. Sutton La. Slou —1E 6
Little Thatch. G'ming —5J 133
Lit. Thurbans Clo. Farnh —5F 128
Littleton. —8K 113
(Guildford)
Littleton. —2B 38
(Shepperton)
Littleton Common. —8D 22
Littleton La. Guild —8K 113
Littleton La. Reig —5J 121
Littleton La. Shep —6M 37
Littleton Rd. Afrd —8D 22
Littleton St. SW18 —3A 28
Lit. Tumners Ct. G'ming —4H 133
Little Vigo. Yat —2A 68
Lit. Warkworth Ho. Iswth —5H 11
Lit. Warren Clo. Guild —5D 114
Lit. Wellington St. Alder —2M 109
Littlewick. —3J 73
Littlewick Rd. Knap & Wok —3H 73
Littlewood. Cranl —7A 156
Little Woodcote. —7E 62
Lit. Woodcote Est. Cars —7E 62
Lit. Woodcote La. Cars —8F 62
Little Woodlands. Wind —6C 4
Lit. Wood St. King T —1K 41 (3J 203)
Littleworth Av. Esh —2D 58
Littleworth Comn. Rd. Esh —9D 40
Littleworth La. Esh —1D 58
Littleworth Pl. Esh —1D 58
Littleworth Rd. Esh —2D 58
Littleworth Rd. Seale —2C 130
Liverpool Rd. King T —8N 25
Liverpool Rd. T Hth —2N 45
Livesey Clo. King T —2M 41 (5M 203)
Livingstone Mans. W14 —2K 13
(off Queen's Club Gdns.)
Livingstone Rd. Cat —9A 84
Livingstone Rd. Craw —5C 182
Livingstone Rd. H'ham —7K 197
Livingstone Rd. Houn —7C 10
Livingstone Rd. T Hth —1N 45
Llanaway Clo. G'ming —5J 133
Llanaway Rd. G'ming —5J 133
Llangar Gro. Crowt —2F 48
Llanthony Rd. Mord —4B 44
Llanvair Clo. Asc —5L 33
Llanvair Dri. Asc —5K 33
Lloyd Av. SW16 —9J 29
Lloyd Av. Coul —1E 82
Lloyd Pk. Av. Croy —1C 64
Lloyd Rd. Wor Pk —9H 43
Lloyds Ct. Craw —9C 162
Lloyds Way. Beck —4H 47
Lobelia Rd. Bisl —2D 72
Lochaline St. W6 —2H 13
Lochinvar St. SW12 —1F 28
Lochinver. Brack —6N 31
Lock Clo. Wdhm —8G 55
Locke King Clo. Wey —4B 56
Locke King Rd. Wey —4B 56
Lockesley Sq. Surb —5K 41
Lockets Clo. Wind —4A 4
Locke Way. Wok —4B 74
Lockfield Dri. Knap —3H 73
Lockfield Dri. Wok —5J 73
Lockhart Rd. Cobh —9K 57
Lockhurst Hatch La. Alb —5N 135
Lockie Pl. SE25 —2D 46
Lock La. Wok —3K 75
Lockner Holt. —9H 115
Lock Path. Dor —2A 4
(in two parts)
Lock Rd. Alder —8B 90
Lock Rd. Guild —9N 93
Lock Rd. Rich —5J 25
Locksbottom. —1J 67
Locks La. Mitc —9D 28
Locksley Dri. Wok —4J 73
Locksmeade Rd. Rich —5J 25
Locks Mdw. D'land —1C 166
Locks Ride. Asc —9F 16
Lockswood. —5H 193
Lockswood. Brkwd —7E 72
Lockton Chase. Asc —2H 33
Lockwood Clo. Farn —6K 69
Lockwood Clo. H'ham —3N 197
Lockwood Ct. Craw —1D 182
Lockwood Path. Wok —9F 54
Lockwood Way. Chess —2N 59
Lockyer Ho. SW15 —6J 13
Locomotive Dri. Felt —2H 23
Loddon Clo. Camb —9E 50
Loddon Rd. Farn —8J 69
Loddon Way. As —3E 110
Loder Clo. Wok —9F 54
Lodge Av. SW14 —6D 12
Lodge Av. Croy —9L 45
Lodgebottom Rd. Mick —5N 99
Lodge Clo. Alder —4A 110
Lodge Clo. Craw —3A 182
Lodge Clo. E Grin —9M 165
Lodge Clo. Eng G —6N 19
Lodge Clo. Eps —6H 61
Lodge Clo. Fet —9D 78
Lodge Clo. Iswth —4H 11
Lodge Clo. N Holm —9J 119
Lodge Clo. Stoke D —3N 77
Lodge Clo. Wall —7E 44
Lodge Gdns. Beck —4J 47
Lodge Gro. Yat —9E 48
Lodge Hill. Purl —2L 83
Lodge Hill Clo. Lwr Bo —5J 129
Lodge Hill Rd. Lwr Bo —5J 129
Lodge La. Holmw —4L 139
Lodge La. New Ad —3K 65
Lodge La. Red —3C 142
Lodge La. W'ham —5L 107
Lodge Pl. Sutt —2N 61
Lodge Rd. Croy —5M 45
Lodge Rd. Fet —9C 78
Lodge Rd. Wall —2F 62
Lodge Wlk. Horl —8D 142
(off Thornton Pl.)
Lodge Way. Afrd —3N 21
Lodge Way. Shep —1D 38
Lodge Way. Wind —6B 4
Lodkin Hill. Hasc —4N 153
Lodsworth. Farn —2J 89
Loft Ho. Pl. Chess —3J 59
Logan Clo. Houn —6N 9
Logmore La. Westc & Dork —7B 118
Lois Dri. Shep —4C 38
Lollesworth La. W Hor —4D 96
(in two parts)
Loman Rd. Myt —1E 90
Lomas Clo. Croy —4M 65
Lombard Bus. Pk. Croy —6K 45
Lombard Rd. SW19 —1N 43
Lombard Roundabout. (Junct.) —6K 45
Lombard St. Shack —5K 131
Lombardy Clo. Wok —4J 73
Lomond Gdns. S Croy —4H 65
Loncin Mead Av. New H —5L 55
London Biggin Hill Airport. —1F 86
London Biggin Hill Civil Airport. —8F 66
London Butterfly House. —4H 11
London Fields Ho. Craw —8A 182
London-Gatwick Airport. —4D 162
London-Gatwick Airport. Gat A —4C 162
London Gatwick Airport, North Terminal. —2C 162
London Gatwick Airport, South Terminal. —3E 162
London Heathrow Airport. —6C 8
London Heathrow Airport. —6C 8
London-Heathrow Airport. H'row A —5N 7
London La. E Hor —9G 97
London La. Shere —7B 116
London Rd. SW16 —9K 29
London Rd. SW17 & Mitc —8D 28
London Rd. Asc & S'hill —2M 33
London Rd. Asc & Vir W —7B 34
London Rd. Bag & W'sham —2K 51
London Rd. B'water & Camb —2J 69
London Rd. Brack & Asc —1B 32
London Rd. Brack & Binf —1G 31
London Rd. Camb & Bags —9A 50
London Rd. Cat —1A 104
London Rd. Craw —2B 182
London Rd. Dat —3L 5
(in two parts)
London Rd. Dork —4H 119 (1M 201)
London Rd. E Grin —6K 165
London Rd. Eve & B'water —4A 68
London Rd. Ewe —5E 60
London Rd. F Row —5G 186
London Rd. Guild —4A 114 (4E 202)
(in two parts)
London Rd. Hind —5D 170
London Rd. H'ham —6J 197
London Rd. Houn —6C 10
London Rd. Iswth & Bren —5F 10
London Rd. Iswth & Twic —8G 10
London Rd. King T —1L 41 (3L 203)
(in two parts)
London Rd. Mitc & Wall —6E 44
London Rd. Mord —4M 43
London Rd. Red —2D 122
London Rd. Reig —3M 121
London Rd. Slou & Coln —1A 6
London Rd. Stai & Afrd —5J 21
London Rd. S'dale —3D 34
London Rd. T Hth & Croy —4L 45 (1A 200)
London Rd. Vir W & Eng G —1K 35
London Rd. W'ham —1L 107
London Rd. W'sham & Asc —9M 33
London Rd. Wokgm —2C 30
London Rd. N. Mers —4F 102
London Road Roundabout. (Junct.) —9G 10
London Rd. S. Mers —8E 102
London Scottish & Richmond R.U.F.C. —6K 11
London Sq. Guild —3A 114 (3F 202)
London Stile. W4 —1N 11
London St. Cher —6J 37
Loneacre. W'sham —3B 52
Lone Oak. Small —1M 163
Lonesome. —9G 28
Lonesome La. Reig —7N 121
Lonesome Way. SW16 —9F 28
Longacre. As —2E 110
Long Acre. Craw D —1D 184
Longacre Pl. Cars —3E 62
Long Beech Dri. Farn —2H 89
Longbourne Grn. G'ming —3H 133
Longbourne Way. Cher —5H 37
Longboyds. Cobh —2J 77
Long Bri. Farnh —1H 129
Longbridge Ga. Gat A —2C 162
(off Gatwick Way)
Longbridge Roundabout. Horl —9C 142
Longbridge Wlk. Horl —1D 162
Longbridge Way. Horl —1D 162
Longbridge Way. Gat A —1D 162
Longchamp Clo. Horl —8G 143
Long Clo. Craw —3H 183
Long Comn. Sham G —8E 134
Long Copse Clo. Bookh —1B 98
Longcroft Av. Bans —1A 82
Longcross. —9K 35
Long Cross Hill. Head —4D 168
Longcross Rd. Longc —9J 35
Longdene Rd. Hasl —2F 188
Long Ditton. —7J 41
Longdon Wood. Kes —1G 66
Longdown. Fleet —7A 88
Longdown Chase Cotts. Gray —6E 170
Longdown Clo. Lwr Bo —5H 129
Longdown La. N. Eps —1F 80
Longdown La. S. Eps —1F 80
Longdown Lodge. Sand —7G 48
Longdown Rd. Eps —1F 80
Longdown Rd. Guild —6D 114
Longdown Rd. Lwr Bo —6G 128
Longdown Rd. Sand —6F 48
Long Dyke. Guild —1D 114
Longfellow Clo. H'ham —1L 197
Longfellow Rd. Wor Pk —8F 42
Longfield Av. Wall —7E 44
Longfield Clo. Farn —6M 69
Longfield Cres. Tad —7H 81
Longfield Dri. SW14 —8A 12
Longfield Dri. Mitc —8C 28
Longfield Rd. As —2E 110
Longfield Rd. Dork —6F 118
Longfield Rd. H'ham —8G 196
Longfield St. SW18 —1M 27
Longford. —4K 7
Longford Av. Felt —9F 8
Longford Av. Stai —2N 21
Longford Cir. W Dray —4K 7
Longford Clo. Camb —2B 70
Longford Clo. Hamp H —5A 24
Longford Clo. Hanw —4M 23
Longford Ct. Eps —1B 60
Longford Gdns. Sutt —9A 44
Longford Ho. Hamp —5A 24
Longfordmoor. —4J 7
Longford Rd. Twic —2A 24
Longford Wlk. SW2 —1L 29
Longford Way. Stai —2N 21
Long Garden M. Farnh —1G 129
(off Long Garden Wlk.)
Long Garden Pl. Farnh —9G 109
Long Garden Wlk. E. Farnh —9G 109
Long Garden Wlk. W. Farnh —9G 108
Long Garden Way. Farnh —1G 128
Long Gore. G'ming —2H 133
Long Gro. Rd. Eps —6A 60
Longheath Gdns. Croy —4F 46
Long Hedges. Houn —5A 10
Long Hill. Seale —2C 130
Long Hill. Wold —8G 85
(in three parts)
Long Hill Rd. Asc —1E 32
Longhope Dri. Wrec —5F 128
Long Houses. Pirb —2A 92
Longhurst Rd. Craw —8M 181
Longhurst Rd. Croy —5E 46
Longhurst Rd. E Hor —7F 96
Longlands Av. Coul —1E 82
Longlands Way. Camb —1H 71
Long La. Croy —5E 46
Long La. Stai & Stanw —3A 22
Long La. Wokgm —7E 14
Longleat Sq. Farn —2C 90
Longleat Way. Felt —1E 22
Longley Rd. SW17 —7C 28
Longley Rd. Croy —6M 45
Longley Rd. Farnh —2J 129
Longley Trad. Est. Craw —4C 182
Long Lodge Dri. W on T —9K 39
Longmead. Fleet —7B 88
Longmead. Guild —3E 114
Longmead. Wind —4B 4
Longmead Bus. Cen. Eps —7C 60
Longmead Clo. Cat —9B 84
Longmead Ho. SE27 —6N 29
Longmeadow. Bookh —3N 97
Longmeadow. Frim —3D 70
Long Mdw. Clo. W Wick —6M 47
Long Mdw. Vs. Charl —5K 161
Longmead Rd. SW17 —6D 28
Longmead Rd. Eps —7C 60
Longmead Rd. Th Dit —6E 40
Longmere Gdns. Tad —6H 81
Longmere Rd. Craw —1B 182
Long Mickle. Sand —6F 48
Longmoors. Brack —9K 15
Longmore Rd. W on T —1M 57
Longpoles Rd. Cranl —8A 156
Long Reach. Ock & W Hor —1B 96
Longridge Gro. Wok —1H 75
Longridge Rd. SW5 —1M 13
Longridge Rd. Rich —9M 11
Long Rd., The. Rowl —8E 128
Longs Clo. Wok —3J 75
Longs Ct. Rich —7M 11
Longsdon Way. Cat —2D 104
Long Shaw. Lea —7G 78
Longshot Ind. Est. Brack —1K 31
Longshot La. Brack —2K 31
(in two parts)
Longshott Ct. SW5 —1M 13
(off W. Cromwell Rd.)
Longside Clo. Egh —9E 20
Longstaff Cres. SW18 —9M 13
Longstaff Rd. SW18 —9M 13
Longstone Rd. SW17 —6F 28
Long's Way. Wokgm —1D 30
Longthornton Rd. SW16 —1G 45
Long Wlk. SW13 —5D 12
Long Wlk. Crock H —9K 107
Long Wlk. E Clan —8N 95
Long Wlk. Eps —6H 81
Long Wlk. N Mald —2B 42
Long Wlk. W Byf —1L 75
Long Wlk., The. Wind —2G 19
Longwater Ho. King T —6J 203
Longwater Rd. Brack —5A 32
Long Ways. Stai —9G 21
Longwood Dri. SW15 —9F 12

Longwood Rd.—Maddox Pk.

Longwood Rd. *Kenl* —3A **84**
(in two parts)
Longwood Vw. *Craw* —6E **182**
Longyard Ho. *Horl* —6F **142**
Lonsdale Ct. *Surb* —6K **41**
Lonsdale Gdns. *SW16* —3K **45**
Lonsdale M. *Rich* —4N **11**
Lonsdale Rd. *SE25* —3E **46**
Lonsdale Rd. *SW13* —4E **12**
Lonsdale Rd. *Dork* —4H **119** (1M **201**)
Lonsdale Rd. *Wey* —4B **56**
Look Out Countryside & Heritage Cen., The. —7B 32
Loop Rd. *Eps* —3B **80**
Loop Rd. *Wok* —7B **74**
Loppets Rd. *Craw* —5D **182**
Lorac Ct. *Sutt* —4M **61**
Loraine Gdns. *Asht* —4L **79**
Loraine Ho. *Wall* —1F **62**
Loraine Rd. *W4* —2A **12**
Lord Chancellor Wlk. *King T* —9B **20**
Lordell Pl. *SW19* —7H **27**
Lord Knyvett Clo. *Stanw* —9M **7**
Lord Knyvetts Ct. *Stanw* —9M **7**
Lord Napier Pl. *W6* —1F **12**
Lord Roberts M. *SW6* —3N **13**
Lordsbury Fld. *Wall* —6G **62**
Lords Clo. *SE21* —3N **29**
Lords Clo. *Felt* —3M **23**
Lordsgrove Clo. *Tad* —7G **81**
Lordshill Common. —7E 134
Lords Hill Cotts. *Sham G* —7E **134**
Lordshill Rd. *Sham G* —6E **134**
Lords Wood Ho. *Coul* —9H **83**
Loretto Clo. *Cranl* —7A **156**
Lorian Dri. *Reig* —2A **122**
Loriners. *Craw* —6B **182**
Loriners Clo. *Cobh* —1H **77**
Loring Rd. *Iswth* —5F **10**
Loring Rd. *Wind* —4C **4**
Lorne Av. *Croy* —6G **47**
Lorne Gdns. *Croy* —6G **47**
Lorne Gdns. *Knap* —6G **72**
Lorne Rd. *Rich* —8M **11**
Lorne, The. *Bookh* —4A **98**
Lorraine Rd. *Camb* —7D **50**
Lory Ridge. *Bag* —3J **51**
Loseberry Rd. *Clay* —2D **58**
Loseley House. —9H 113
Loseley Park. —9J 113
Loseley Pk. Farm. —9J 113
Loseley Rd. *G'ming* —3H **133**
Losfield Rd. *Wind* —4B **4**
Lothian Rd. *Brkwd* —8L **71**
Lothian Wood. *Tad* —9G **80**
Lots Rd. *SW10* —3N **13**
Lotus Clo. *SE21* —4N **29**
Lotus Rd. *Big H* —5H **87**
Loubet St. *SW17* —7D **28**
Loudwater Clo. *Sun* —3H **39**
Loudwater Rd. *Sun* —3H **39**
Loughborough. *Brack* —5C **32**
Louisa Ct. *Twic* —3E **24**
Louise Margaret Rd. *Alder* —1A **110**
Louis Fields. *Guild* —8F **92**
Louisville Rd. *SW17* —4E **28**
Lovatt Ct. *SW12* —2F **28**
Lovat Wlk. *Houn* —3M **9**
Lovedean Ct. *Brack* —5C **32**
Lovejoy La. *Wind* —5A **4**
Lovekyn Clo. *King T* —1L **41** (3M **203**)
Lovelace Clo. *Eff J* —1H **97**
Lovelace Dri. *Wok* —3G **75**
Lovelace Gdns. *Surb* —6K **41**
Lovelace Gdns. *W on T* —2K **57**
Lovelace Rd. *SE21* —3N **29**
Lovelace Rd. *Brack* —3K **31**
Lovelace Rd. *Surb* —6J **41**
Lovelands La. *Chob* —9F **52**
Lovelands La. *Tad* —5N **101**
Love La. *God* —1F **124**
Love La. *SE25* —2E **46**
(in two parts)
Love La. *As* —2F **110**
Love La. *Mitc* —2C **44**
(in two parts)
Love La. *Mord* —6M **43**
Love La. *Ockl* —6C **158**
Love La. *Surb* —8J **41**
Love La. *Sutt* —3K **61**
Love La. *Tad* —4E **100**
Love La. *Yat* —9A **48**
Loveletts. *Craw* —4M **181**
Lovel La. *Wink* —5L **17**
Lovell Path. *If'd* —4K **181**
Lovell Rd. *Rich* —4J **25**
Lovells Clo. *Light* —6M **51**
Lovelock Clo. *Kenl* —4N **83**
Lovel Rd. *Wink* —5K **17**
Lovers La. *Fren* —3H **149**
Lovers La. *H'ham* —9J **197**
Lovett Dri. *Cars* —6A **44**
Lovett Rd. *Stai* —5D **20**
Lovibonds Av. *Orp* —1K **67**
Lowbury. *Brack* —3C **32**
Lowburys. *Dork* —8H **119**
Lowdell's Clo. *E Grin* —6M **165**
Lowdell's Dri. *E Grin* —6M **165**
Lowdell's La. *E Grin* —6L **165**
Lowe Clo. *Alder* —1L **109**
Lowe Clo. *Craw* —9N **181**
Lwr. Addiscombe Rd. *Croy* —7B **46** (1F **200**)
Lower Ashtead. —6K 79
Lwr. Barn Clo. *H'ham* —3M **197**
Lwr. Barn Rd. *Purl* —8N **63**
Lower Bourne. —4J 129
Lwr. Breache Rd. *Ewh* —6H **157**
Lwr. Bridge Rd. *Red* —3D **122**
Lwr. Broadmoor Rd. *Crowt* —3H **49**
Lower Canes. *Yat* —9A **48**
Lwr. Charles St. *Camb* —9A **50**
Lwr. Church La. *Farnh* —1G **129**
Lwr. Church Rd. *Sand* —6D **48**
Lwr. Church St. *Croy* —8M **45** (3A **200**)
Lwr. Common S. *SW15* —6G **13**
Lwr. Coombe St. *Croy* —1N **63** (6B **200**)
Lwr. Court Rd. *Eps* —7B **60**
Lower Dene. *E Grin* —9C **166**
Lwr. Downs Rd. *SW20* —9J **27**
Lwr. Drayton Pl. *Croy* —8M **45** (3A **200**)
Lower Dunnymans. *Bans* —1L **81**
Lower Eashing. —7C 132
Lwr. Eashing. *Lwr E* —7B **132**
Lwr. Edgeborough Rd. *Guild* —4B **114**
Lwr. Farm Rd. *Eff* —2J **97**
Lwr. Farnham Rd. *Alder* —5N **109**
Lower Feltham. —4G 23
Lower Forecourt. Gat A —3F 162
(off Ring Rd. S.)
Lwr. George St. *Rich* —8K **11**
Lower Green. —8B 40
Lwr. Green Rd. *Esh* —8B **40**
Lwr. Green W. *Mitc* —2C **44**
Lwr. Grove Rd. *Rich* —9M **11**
Lwr. Guildford Rd. *Knap* —4G **72**
Lower Halliford. —6E 38
Lwr. Ham La. *Elst* —7J **131**
Lwr. Hampton Rd. *Sun* —2K **39**
Lwr. Ham Rd. *King T* —9K **25** (1K **203**)
Lower Hanger. *Hasl* —2A **188**
Lwr. Hill Rd. *Eps* —8A **60**
Lowerhouse La. *Wal W* —7K **157**
Lwr. House Rd. *Brook* —9K **151**
Lower Kingswood. —5L 101
Lower Mall. *W6* —1G **12**
Lwr. Manor Rd. *G'ming* —5H **133**
Lwr. Manor Rd. *Milf* —1B **152**
Lwr. Marsh La. *King T* —3M **41** (7M **203**)
(in two parts)
Lower Mere. *E Grin* —1B **186**
Lower Mill. *Eps* —4E **60**
Lwr. Mill Fld. *Bag* —5H **51**
Lower Moor. *Yat* —1C **68**
Lwr. Morden La. *Mord* —5H **43**
Lwr. Mortlake Rd. *Rich* —7L **11**
Lwr. Moushill La. *Milf* —1A **152**
Lwr. Nelson St. *Alder* —2M **109**
Lwr. Newport Rd. *Alder* —4B **110**
Lower Northfield. *Bans* —1L **81**
Lower Nursery. *Asc* —4D **34**
Lwr. Park Rd. *Coul* —5C **82**
Lower Peryers. *E Hor* —6F **96**
Lwr. Pillory Downs. *Cars* —9F **62**
Lwr. Pyrford Rd. *Wok* —3K **75**
Lwr. Richmond Rd. *SW15* —6G **13**
Lwr. Richmond Rd. *Rich & SW14* —6N **11**
Lower Rd. *Bookh* —3A **98**
Lower Rd. *Eff* —5L **97**
Lower Rd. *F Row* —6H **187**
Lower Rd. *G'wood* —7K **171**
Lower Rd. *Kenl* —9M **63**
Lower Rd. *Red* —5B **122**
Lower Rd. *Sutt* —1A **62**
Lower Sandfields. *Send* —2F **94**
Lwr. Sandhurst Rd. *Finch & Sand* —5A **48**
Lwr. Sawley Wood. *Bans* —1L **81**
Lower Shott. *Bookh* —4A **98**
Lower South Park. —9D 124
Lwr. South Pk. *S God* —9D **124**
Lwr. South St. *G'ming* —7G **133**
Lwr. South Vw. *Farnh* —9H **109**
Lower Sq. *F Row* —6H **187**
Lower Sq. *Iswth* —6H **11**
Lower Sq., The. *Sutt* —2N **61**
Lower St. *Hasl* —2F **188**
Lower St. *Shere* —8B **116**
Lwr. Sunbury Rd. *Hamp* —1N **39**
Lwr. Tanbridge Way. *H'ham* —6H **197**
Lwr. Teddington Rd. *King T* —9K **25** (1H **203**)
Lwr. Village Rd. *Asc* —4M **33**
Lwr. Weybourne La. *Farnh & Bad L* —6L **109**
Lwr. Wokingham Rd. *Finch & Crowt* —1C **48**
Lwr. Wood Rd. *Clay* —3H **59**
Lowestoft Wlk. *Craw* —5F **182**
Loweswater Wlk. *Camb* —2H **71**
Lowfield Clo. *Light* —7L **51**
Lowfield Heath. —5C 162
Lowfield Heath Ind. Est. *Low H* —5C **162**
Lowfield Heath Postmill. —4H 161
Lowfield Heath Rd. *Charl* —4L **161**
Lowfield Rd. *Slin* —5L **195**
Lowfield Way. *Low H* —5C **162**
Lowicks Rd. *Tilf* —4N **149**
Lowlands Dri. *Stanw* —8M **7**
Lowlands Rd. *B'water* —2H **69**
Low La. *Bad L* —6N **109**
Lowndes Bldgs. *Farnh* —9G **108**
Lowry Clo. *Coll T* —9J **49**
Lowry Cres. *Mitc* —1C **44**
Lowther Rd. *SW13* —4E **12**
Lowther Rd. *King T* —9M **25** (1N **203**)
Lowthorpe. *Wok* —5K **73**
Loxford Ct. *Cranl* —8H **155**
Loxford Ho. *Eps* —8D **60** (5N **201**)
Loxford Rd. *Cat* —3C **104**
Loxford Way. *Cat* —3C **104**
Loxhill. —9A 154
Loxley Rd. *SW18* —2B **28**
Loxley Rd. *Hamp* —5N **23**
Loxwood. —4H 193
Loxwood Av. *C Crook* —6A **88**
Loxwood Clo. *Felt* —2E **22**
Loxwood Farm Pl. *Loxw* —4H **193**
Loxwood Rd. *Alf* —9H **175**
Loxwood Rd. *Plais* —6B **192**
Loxwood Rd. *Rud* —4N **193**
Loxwood Wlk. *Craw* —1L **181**
(in two parts)
Lucan Dri. *Stai* —8M **21**
Lucas Clo. *E Grin* —9C **166**
Lucas Clo. *Yat* —1C **68**
Lucas Dri. *Yat* —1C **68**
Lucas Fld. *Hasl* —2C **188**
Lucas Grn. Rd. *W End* —2A **72**
Lucas Rd. *Warn* —9E **178**
Lucerne Clo. *Wok* —6A **74**
Lucerne Dri. *M'bowr* —6H **183**
Lucerne Rd. *T Hth* —4M **45**
Lucie Av. *Afrd* —7C **22**
Lucien Rd. *SW17* —6E **28**
Lucien Rd. *SW19* —3N **27**
Lucilina Dri. *Eden* —3L **147**
Luckley Path. *Wokgm* —2B **30**
(in two parts)
Luckley Rd. *Wokgm* —5A **30**
Luckley Wood. *Wokgm* —5A **30**
Luddington Av. *Vir W* —1B **36**
Ludford Clo. *Croy* —9M **45** (6A **200**)
Ludgrove. *Wokgm* —5C **30**
Ludlow. *Brack* —6N **31**
Ludlow Clo. *Frim* —7E **70**
Ludlow Rd. *Felt* —5H **23**
Ludlow Rd. *Guild* —4L **113**
Ludovick Wlk. *SW15* —7D **12**
Ludshott Common. —6J 169
Ludshott Gro. *Head D* —4G **169**
Luff Clo. *Wind* —6B **4**
Luffs Mdw. *N'chap* —9D **190**
Luke Rd. *Alder* —4K **109**
Luke Rd. E. *Alder* —4K **109**
Lullarook Clo. *Big H* —3E **86**
Lullenden. —5H 167
Lulworth Av. *Houn* —4B **10**
Lulworth Clo. *Craw* —6M **181**
Lulworth Clo. *Farn* —7M **69**
Lulworth Cres. *Mitc* —1C **44**
Lumley Ct. *Horl* —7E **142**
Lumley Gdns. *Sutt* —2K **61**
Lumley Rd. *Horl* —7E **142**
Lumley Rd. *Sutt* —2K **61**
Lunar Clo. *Big H* —3F **86**
Luna Rd. *T Hth* —2N **45**
Lundy Clo. *Craw* —6A **182**
Lundy Dri. *Hayes* —1F **8**
Lunghurst Rd. *Wold* —7J **85**
Lupin Clo. *SW2* —3M **29**
Lupin Clo. *Bag* —6G **51**
Lupin Clo. *Croy* —7G **46**
Lupin Clo. *W Dray* —1M **7**
Lupin Ride. *Crowt* —8G **30**
Lurgan Av. *W6* —2J **13**
Luscombe Ct. *Brom* —1N **47**
Lushington Dri. *Cobh* —1J **77**
Lushington Ho. *W on T* —5K **39**
Lusted Hall La. *Tats* —7D **86**
Lusteds Clo. *Dork* —8J **119**
Lutea Ho. Sutt —4A 62
(off Walnut M.)
Luther Rd. *Tedd* —6F **24**
Lutterworth Clo. *Brack* —8A **16**
Luttrell Av. *SW15* —8G **13**
Lutyens Clo. *Craw* —5K **181**
Luxford Clo. *H'ham* —3M **197**
Luxford's La. *E Grin* —4D **186**
Luxted. —1J 87
Luxted Rd. *Dow* —8J **67**
Lyall Pl. *Farnh* —5G **108**
Lychett Minster Clo. *Brack* —3D **32**
Lych Ga. Clo. *Sand* —7E **48**
Lych Ga. Ct. *Eden* —2L **147**
Lych Way. *Wok* —3N **73**
Lyconby Gdns. *Croy* —6H **47**
Lydbury. *Brack* —2D **32**
Lydden Gro. *SW18* —1N **27**
Lydden Rd. *SW18* —1N **27**
Lydele Clo. *Wok* —2B **74**
Lydens La. *Hever* —6N **147**
Lydford Clo. *Farn* —7M **69**
Lydford Clo. *Frim* —7E **70**
Lydhurst Av. *SW2* —3K **29**
Lydney. *Brack* —6N **31**
Lydney Clo. *SW19* —3K **27**
Lydon Ho. *Craw* —9B **162**
Lye Copse Av. *Farn* —6N **69**
Lyefield La. *F Grn* —4K **157**
Lyell Pl. E. *Wind* —6A **4**
Lyell Pl. W. *Wind* —6A **4**
Lyell Rd. *Wind* —6A **4**
Lyell Wlk. E. *Wind* —6A **4**
Lyell Wlk. W. *Wind* —6A **4**
Lye, The. *Tad* —9H **81**
Lyfield. *Oxs* —1B **78**
Lyford Rd. *SW18* —1B **28**
Lygon Ho. SW6 —4K 13
(off Fulham Pal. Rd.)
Lyham Clo. *SW2* —1J **29**
Lyle Clo. *Mitc* —6E **44**
Lymbourne Clo. *Sutt* —6M **61**
Lymden Gdns. *Reig* —4N **121**
Lyme Regis Rd. *Bans* —4L **81**
Lymescote Gdns. *Sutt* —8M **43**
Lyminge Gdns. *SW18* —2C **28**
Lymington Av. *Yat* —1A **68**
Lymington Clo. *SW16* —1H **45**
Lymington Ct. *Sutt* —9N **43**
Lymington Gdns. *Eps* —2E **60**
Lynchborough Rd. *Pass* —9C **168**
Lynchen Clo. *Houn* —4J **9**
Lynchford La. *Farn* —5C **90**
Lynchford Rd. *Ash V* —5D **90**
Lynchford Rd. *Farn* —6N **89**
(in two parts)
Lynch Rd. *Farnh* —1J **129**
Lyncroft Gdns. *Eps* —5F **60**
Lyncroft Gdns. *Houn* —8C **10**
Lyndale. *Th Dit* —6E **40**
Lyndale Ct. *Red* —9E **102**
Lyndale Ct. *W Byf* —9J **55**
Lyndale Dri. *Fleet* —4E **88**
Lyndale Rd. *Red* —9D **102**
Lynde Ho. *W on T* —5K **39**
Lynden Hyrst. *Croy* —8C **46**
Lyndford Ter. *Fleet* —6A **88**
Lyndhurst Av. *SW16* —1H **45**
Lyndhurst Av. *Alder* —6A **110**
Lyndhurst Av. *B'water* —9H **49**
Lyndhurst Av. *Sun* —2H **39**
Lyndhurst Av. *Surb* —7A **42**
Lyndhurst Av. *Twic* —2N **23**
Lyndhurst Clo. *Brack* —2E **32**
Lyndhurst Clo. *Craw* —4B **182**
Lyndhurst Clo. *Croy* —9C **46**
Lyndhurst Clo. *Orp* —1K **67**
Lyndhurst Clo. *Wok* —2N **73**
Lyndhurst Ct. Sutt —4M 61
(off Grange Rd.)
Lyndhurst Dri. *N Mald* —6D **42**
Lyndhurst Farm Clo. *Felb* —6G **165**
Lyndhurst Rd. *Asc* —3L **33**
Lyndhurst Rd. *Coul* —3E **82**
Lyndhurst Rd. *Reig* —6M **121**
Lyndhurst Rd. *T Hth* —3L **45**
Lyndhurst Vs. *Red* —9D **102**
Lyndhurst Way. *Cher* —9G **36**
Lyndhurst Way. *Sutt* —5M **61**
Lyndon Av. *Wall* —9E **44**
Lyndsey Clo. *Farn* —1G **88**
Lyndum Pl. *Lind* —4A **168**
Lyndwood Dri. *Old Win* —9K **5**
Lyne. —5C 36
Lyne Clo. *Vir W* —5B **36**
Lyne Crossing Rd. *Lyne* —5C **36**
Lynegrove Av. *Afrd* —6D **22**
Lyneham Rd. *Crowt* —2G **48**
Lyne La. *Vir W* —5C **36**
(in two parts)
Lyne Rd. *Vir W* —5N **35**
Lynford Ct. *Croy* —7F **200**
Lynmead Clo. *Eden* —8K **127**
Lynmouth Av. *Mord* —5J **43**
Lynmouth Gdns. *Houn* —3L **9**
Lynn Clo. *Afrd* —6E **22**
Lynn Ct. *Whyt* —5C **84**
Lynne Clo. *Orp* —3N **67**
Lynne Clo. *S Croy* —7F **64**
Lynne Ct. *S Croy* —7F **200**
Lynne Wlk. *Esh* —2C **58**
Lynn Rd. *SW12* —1F **28**
Lynn Wlk. *Reig* —6N **121**
Lynn Way. *Farn* —7L **69**
Lynscott Way. *S Croy* —5M **63**
Lynstead Ct. *Beck* —1H **47**
Lynton Clo. *Chess* —1L **59**
Lynton Clo. *E Grin* —8C **166**
Lynton Clo. *Farnh* —4F **128**
Lynton Clo. *Iswth* —7F **10**
Lynton Pk. Av. *E Grin* —8B **166**
Lynton Rd. *Croy* —5L **45**
Lynton Rd. *N Mald* —4C **42**
Lynwick St. *Rud* —1C **194**
Lynwood. *Guild* —4L **113**
Lynwood Av. *Coul* —2F **82**
Lynwood Av. *Egh* —7A **20**
Lynwood Av. *Eps* —1E **80**
Lynwood Chase. *Brack* —8A **16**
Lynwood Clo. *Lind* —4B **168**
Lynwood Clo. *Wok* —9F **54**
Lynwood Ct. *Eps* —9E **60**
Lynwood Ct. *H'ham* —5J **197**
Lynwood Ct. *King T* —1A **42**
Lynwood Cres. *Asc* —5B **34**
Lynwood Dri. *Myt* —2E **90**
Lynwood Dri. *Wor Pk* —8F **42**
Lynwood Gdns. *Croy* —1K **63**
Lynwood Rd. *SW17* —4D **28**
Lynwood Rd. *Eps* —1E **80**
Lynwood Rd. *Red* —1E **122**
Lynwood Rd. *Th Dit* —8F **40**
Lynx Hill. *E Hor* —6G **96**
Lyon Clo. *M'bowr* —7G **183**
Lyon Ct. *H'ham* —6L **197**
Lyon Oaks. *Warf* —7N **15**
Lyon Rd. *SW19* —9A **28**
Lyon Rd. *Crowt* —1H **49**
Lyon Rd. *W on T* —8M **39**
Lyons Clo. *Slin* —5L **195**
Lyons Ct. *Dork* —5H **119** (2L **201**)
Lyonsdene. *Tad* —5L **101**
Lyons Dri. *Guild* —7K **93**
Lyons Rd. *Slin* —5L **195**
Lyon Way. *Frim* —5A **70**
Lyon Way Ind. Est. *Frim* —5A **70**
Lyric Clo. *M'bowr* —5H **183**
Lyric Rd. *SW13* —4E **12**
Lyric Theatre. —1H 13
Lysander Gdns. *Surb* —5M **41**
Lysander Rd. *Croy* —3K **63**
Lysias Rd. *SW12* —1F **28**
Lysia St. *SW6* —3J **13**
Lysons Av. *Ash V* —5D **90**
Lyson's Rd. *Alder* —3M **109**
Lysons Wlk. *SW15* —7F **12**
Lyster M. *Cobh* —9K **57**
Lytchgate Clo. *S Croy* —4B **64**
Lytcott Dri. *W Mol* —2N **39**
Lytham. *Brack* —5K **31**
Lytham Ct. *S'hill* —4N **33**
Lythe Hill. —2L 189
Lythe Hill Pk. *Hasl* —3J **189**
Lytton Dri. *Craw* —2H **183**
Lytton Gdns. *Wall* —1H **63**
Lytton Gro. *SW15* —8J **13**
Lytton Pk. *Cobh* —8N **57**
Lytton Rd. *Wok* —3D **74**
Lyveden Rd. *SW17* —7D **28**
Lywood Clo. *Tad* —9H **81**

M

Mabbotts. *Tad* —8J **81**
Mabel St. *Wok* —5N **73**
Maberley Rd. *Beck* —2G **46**
Mablethorpe Rd. *SW6* —3K **13**
Macadam Av. *Crowt* —9H **31**
McAlmont Ridge. *G'ming* —4G **132**
Macaulay Av. *Esh* —8F **40**
Macaulay Rd. *Cat* —9B **84**
Macbeth Ct. *Warf* —9C **16**
Macbeth St. *W6* —1G **13**
McCarthy Rd. *Felt* —6L **23**
Macclesfield Rd. *SE25* —4E **46**
MacDonald Rd. *Farnh* —5G **109**
Macdonald Rd. *Light* —8K **51**
McDonalds Almshouses. *Farnh* —2F **128**
McDonough Clo. *Chess* —1L **59**
Mace La. *Cud* —9M **67**
Macfarlane La. *Iswth* —2F **10**
McGrigor Barracks. *Alder* —1N **109**
McIndoe Rd. *E Grin* —7N **165**
McIntosh Clo. *Wall* —4J **63**
McIver Clo. *Felb* —6J **165**
McKay Clo. *Alder* —1A **110**
McKay Rd. *SW20* —8G **27**
McKay Trad. Est. *Coln* —5G **7**
Mackenzie Rd. *Beck* —1F **46**
McKenzie Way. *Eps* —5N **59**
McKernan Ct. *Sand* —7E **48**
Mackie Rd. *SW2* —1L **29**
Mackies Hill. *Peasl* —4E **136**
Mackrells. *Red* —6A **122**
Maclaren M. *SW15* —7H **13**
Macleod Rd. *H'ham* —7L **197**
MacNaghten Woods. *Camb* —9C **50**
McNaughton Clo. *Farn* —2H **89**
Macphail Clo. *Wokgm* —9D **14**
McRae La. *Mitc* —6D **44**
Macrae Rd. *Yat* —9B **48**
Madan Rd. *W'ham* —3M **107**
Madans Wlk. *Eps* —2C **80** (8L **201**)
(in two parts)
Maddison Clo. *Tedd* —7F **24**
Maddox La. *Bookh* —9M **77**
(in two parts)
Maddox Pk. *Bookh* —1M **97**

Madehurst Ct.—Margaret Ingram Clo.

Madehurst Ct. *Craw* —6L **181**
Madeira Av. *H'ham* —6J **197**
Madeira Clo. *W Byf* —9J **55**
Madeira Cres. *W Byf* —9H **55**
Madeira Rd. *SW16* —6J **29**
Madeira Rd. *Mitc* —3D **44**
Madeira Rd. *W Byf* —9H **55**
Madeira Wlk. *Reig* —2B **122**
Madeira Wlk. *Wind* —4G **5**
Madeley Rd. *C Crook* —7C **88**
Madgehole La. *Sham G* —7J **135**
Madingley. *Brack* —7N **31**
Madox Brown End. *Coll T* —8K **49**
Madrid Rd. *SW13* —4F **12**
Madrid Rd. *Guild* —4L **113**
Maesmaur Rd. *Tats* —8F **86**
Mafeking Av. *Bren* —2L **11**
Mafeking Rd. *Wray* —3D **20**
Magazine Pl. *Lea* —9H **79**
Magazine Rd. *Cat* —9M **83**
Magdala Rd. *Iswth* —6G **11**
Magdala Rd. *S Croy* —4A **64**
Magdalen Clo. *Byfl* —1N **75**
Magdalen Cres. *Byfl* —1N **75**
Magdalene Clo. *Craw* —9G **162**
Magdalene Rd. *Owl* —5L **49**
Magdalene Rd. *Shep* —3A **38**
Magdalen Rd. *SW18* —2A **28**
Magellan Ter. *Craw* —8E **162**
Magna Carta La. *Wray* —2N **19**
Magna Carta Monument. —3N 19
Magna Rd. *Eng G* —7L **19**
Magnolia Clo. *King T* —7A **26**
Magnolia Clo. *Owl* —6J **49**
Magnolia Ct. *Horl* —8E **142**
Magnolia Ct. *Rich* —4A **12**
Magnolia Ct. Sutt —4M 61
(off Grange Rd.)
Magnolia Ct. *Wall* —2F **62**
Magnolia Dri. *Big H* —3F **86**
Magnolia Pl. *Guild* —9M **93**
Magnolia Rd. *W4* —2A **12**
Magnolia St. *W Dray* —1M **7**
Magnolia Way. *Eps* —2B **60**
Magnolia Way. *Fleet* —6B **88**
Magnolia Way. *N Holm* —8K **119**
Magpie Clo. *Bord* —7A **168**
Magpie Clo. *Coul* —5G **83**
Magpie Clo. *Ews* —4C **108**
Magpie Grn. *Eden* —9L **127**
Magpie Wlk. *Craw* —1D **182**
Maguire Dri. *Frim* —3G **71**
Maguire Dri. *Rich* —5J **25**
Mahonia Clo. *W End* —9C **52**
Maida Rd. *Alder* —9N **89**
Maidenbower. —5G **183**
Maidenbower Dri. *M'bowr* —5G **182**
Maidenbower La. *M'bowr* —5F **182**
(in two parts)
Maidenbower Pl. *M'bowr* —5G **183**
Maidenbower Sq. *M'bowr* —5G **183**
Maidenhead Rd. *Warf* —3N **15**
Maidenhead Rd. *Wind* —3A **4**
Maidenhead Rd. *Wokgm* —6C **14**
Maiden La. *Craw* —1A **182**
Maiden's Green. —3F **16**
Maiden's Grn. *Wink* —3F **16**
Maidenshaw Rd. *Eps*
—8C **60** (5K **201**)
Maids of Honour Row. *Rich* —8K **11**
Main Dri. *Brack* —8D **16**
Mainprize Rd. *Brack* —9C **16**
Main Rd. *Big H & Kes* —9E **66**
Main Rd. *Crock H & Eden* —6K **127**
Main Rd. *K'ley* —9A **148**
Main Rd. *Wind* —3A **4**
Mainstone Clo. *Deep* —7G **71**
Mainstone Cres. *Brkwd* —8A **72**
Mainstone Rd. *Bisl* —3C **72**
Main St. *Add* —9N **37**
Main St. *Felt* —6L **23**
Main St. *Yat* —8C **48**
Maisie Webster Clo. *Stanw* —1L **21**
Maisonettes, The. *Sutt* —2L **61**
Maitland Clo. *Houn* —6N **9**
Maitland Clo. *W on T* —8M **39**
Maitland Clo. *W Byf* —9J **55**
Maitland Rd. *Farn* —5N **89**
Maitlands Clo. *Tong* —6C **110**
Maize Cft. *Horl* —7G **142**
Maize La. *Warf* —7B **16**
Majestic Way. *Mitc* —1D **44**
Majors Farm Rd. *Dat* —3M **5**
Major's Hill. *Worth* —4N **183**
Makepiece Rd. *Brack* —8N **15**
Malacca Farm. *W Cla* —5K **95**
Malan Clo. *Big H* —4G **87**
Malbrook Rd. *SW15* —7G **13**
Malcolm Dri. *Surb* —7K **41**
Malcolm Gdns. *Hkwd* —1B **162**
Malcolm Gavin Clo. *SW17* —3C **28**
Malcolm Rd. *SE25* —5D **46**
Malcolm Rd. *SW19* —7K **27**
Malcolm Rd. *Coul* —2H **83**
Malden Av. *SE25* —3E **46**
Malden Ct. *N Mald* —2G **42**
Malden Green. —7F **42**
Malden Grn. Av. *Wor Pk* —7E **42**
Malden Hill. *N Mald* —2E **42**
Malden Hill Gdns. *N Mald* —2E **42**
Malden Junction. (Junct.) —4D **42**
Malden Pk. *N Mald* —5E **42**
Malden Rd. *N Mald* —4D **42**
Malden Rd. *Sutt* —1H **61**
Malden Rushett. —7J **59**
Malden Way. *N Mald* —5C **42**
Maldon Ct. *Wall* —2G **62**
Maldon Rd. *Wall* —2F **62**
Malet Clo. *Egh* —7F **20**
Maley Av. *SE27* —3M **29**
Malham Clo. *M'bowr* —6G **183**
Malham Fell. *Brack* —3M **31**
Mallard Clo. *As* —1D **110**
Mallard Clo. *Hasl* —2C **188**
Mallard Clo. *Horl* —6E **142**
Mallard Clo. *H'ham* —3J **197**
Mallard Clo. *Red* —9E **102**
Mallard Clo. *Twic* —1A **24**
Mallard Ct. *Dork* —1K **201**
Mallard Pl. *E Grin* —1B **186**
Mallard Pl. *Twic* —4G **24**
Mallard Rd. *S Croy* —6G **65**
Mallards Reach. *Wey* —8E **38**
Mallards, The. *Frim* —4D **70**
Mallards, The. *Stai* —1K **37**
Mallards Way. *Light* —7L **51**
Mallard Wlk. *Beck* —4G **47**
Mallard Way. *Eden* —9L **127**
Mallard Way. *Wall* —5G **63**
Mallard Way. *Yat* —9A **48**
Malling Clo. *Croy* —5F **46**
Malling Gdns. *Mord* —5A **44**
Mallinson Rd. *Croy* —9H **45**
Mallow Clo. *Croy* —7G **46**
Mallow Clo. *H'ham* —2L **197**
Mallow Clo. *Lind* —4B **168**
Mallow Clo. *Tad* —7G **81**
Mallow Cres. *Guild* —9D **94**
Mallowdale Rd. *Brack* —6C **32**
Mall Rd. *W6* —1G **13**
Mall, The. *SW14* —8B **12**
Mall, The. *Bren* —2K **11**
Mall, The. *Croy* —8N **45** (2B **200**)
Mall, The. *Surb* —4K **41**
Mall, The. *W on T* —2L **57**
Malmains Clo. *Beck* —3N **47**
Malmains Way. *Beck* —3M **47**
Malmesbury Rd. *Mord* —6A **44**
Malmstone Av. *Red* —6G **103**
Malta Barracks. *Alder* —8L **89**
Malta Rd. *Deep* —6J **71**
Maltby Rd. *Chess* —3N **59**
Malt Hill. *Egh* —6A **20**
Malt Hill. *Warf* —5C **16**
Malthouse Clo. *C Crook* —8A **88**
Malt Ho. Clo. *Old Win* —1L **19**
Malthouse Ct. *W End* —8C **52**
Malthouse Dri. *W4* —2E **12**
Malthouse Dri. *Felt* —6L **23**
Malthouse La. *Hamb* —9F **152**
Malthouse La. *W End* —1E **92**
(Chapel La., in two parts)
Malthouse La. *W End* —9C **52**
(Commonfields)
Malthouse Mead. *Witl* —5C **152**
Malthouse Pas. SW13 —5E 12
(off Maltings Clo.)
Malthouse Rd. *Craw* —5B **182**
Malthouses, The. *Cranl* —7N **155**
Malt Ho., The. *Tilf* —8A **130**
Maltings. *W4* —1N **11**
Maltings Clo. *SW13* —5E **12**
Maltings Lodge. W4 —2D 12
(off Corney Reach Way)
Maltings Pl. *SW6* —4N **13**
Maltings, The. *Byfl* —9A **56**
Maltings, The. *Oxt* —9B **106**
Maltings, The. *Stai* —5G **20**
Malting Way. *Iswth* —6F **10**
Malus Clo. *Add* —4H **55**
Malus Dri. *Add* —4H **55**
Malva Clo. *SW18* —8N **13**
Malvern Clo. *SE20* —1D **46**
Malvern Clo. *Mitc* —2G **44**
Malvern Clo. *Ott* —3E **54**
Malvern Clo. *Surb* —7L **41**
Malvern Ct. *Eps* —1C **80** (8L **201**)
Malvern Ct. *Slou* —2C **6**
Malvern Ct. *Sutt* —4M **61**
Malvern Dri. *Felt* —6L **23**
Malvern Rd. *Craw* —4A **182**
Malvern Rd. *Farn* —7J **69**
Malvern Rd. *Hamp* —8A **24**
Malvern Rd. *Hayes* —3F **8**
Malvern Rd. *Surb* —8L **41**
Malvern Rd. *T Hth* —3L **45**
Malwood Rd. *SW12* —1F **28**
Malyons, The. *Shep* —5E **38**
Manatee Pl. *Wall* —9H **45**
Manawey Bus. Units. *Alder* —3C **110**
Manbre Rd. *W6* —2H **13**
Manchester Rd. *T Hth* —2N **45**
Mandeville Clo. *SW19* —8K **27**
Mandeville Clo. *Guild* —9K **93**
Mandeville Ct. *Egh* —5C **20**
Mandeville Dri. *Surb* —7K **41**
Mandeville Rd. *Iswth* —5G **10**
Mandeville Rd. *Shep* —4B **38**
Mandora Rd. *Alder* —9N **89**
Mandrake Rd. *SW17* —4D **28**
Manfield Pk. *Cranl* —5K **155**
Manfield Rd. *As* —2E **110**
Manfred Rd. *SW15* —8L **13**
Mangles Ct. *Guild* —4M **113** (4B **202**)
Mangles Rd. *Guild* —1N **113**
Manitoba Gdns. *G Str* —3N **67**
Manley Bri. Rd. *Rowl* —6D **128**
Mannamead. *Eps* —6D **80**
Mannamead Clo. *Eps* —6D **80**
Mann Clo. *Craw* —9N **181**
Mann Clo. *Croy* —9N **45** (4B **200**)
Manning Clo. *E Grin* —7N **165**
Manning Pl. *Rich* —9M **11**
Mannings Clo. *Craw* —9H **163**
Mannings Heath. —9C **198**
Mannings Hill. *Cranl* —4M **155**
Manningtree Clo. *SW19* —2K **27**
Mann's Clo. *Iswth* —8F **10**
Manny Shinwell Ho. SW6 —2L 13
(off Clem Attlee Ct.)
Manoel Rd. *Twic* —3C **24**
Manor Av. *Cat* —2B **104**
Manor Av. *Houn* —6L **9**
Manor Chase. *Wey* —2C **56**
Manor Circus. (Junct.) —6M **11**
Manor Clo. *Brack* —8M **15**
Manor Clo. *E Hor* —6F **96**
Manor Clo. *Hasl* —2C **188**
Manor Clo. *Horl* —8D **142**
Manor Clo. *Tong* —5D **110**
Manor Clo. *Warl* —4H **85**
Manor Clo. *Wok* —4H **75**
Manor Clo. *Wor Pk* —7D **42**
Manor Ct. *SW6* —4N **13**
Manor Ct. *SW16* —4J **29**
Manor Ct. *W3* —1N **11**
Manor Ct. *C Crook* —9B **88**
Manor Ct. *Craw* —9D **162**
Manor Ct. *H'ham* —3N **197**
Manor Ct. *King T* —9N **25**
Manor Ct. *Twic* —3C **24**
Manor Ct. *W Mol* —3A **40**
Manor Ct. *W Wick* —7L **47**
Manor Ct. *Wey* —1C **56**
Manor Cres. *Brkwd* —7A **72**
Manor Cres. *Byfl* —9A **56**
Manor Cres. *Eps* —8N **59**
Manor Cres. *Guild* —1L **113**
Manor Cres. *Hasl* —2C **188**
Manor Cres. *Surb* —5N **41**
Manorcrofts Rd. *Egh* —7C **20**
Manordene Clo. *Th Dit* —7G **40**
Manor Dri. *Eps* —3D **60**
Manor Dri. *Esh* —8F **40**
Manor Dri. *Felt* —6L **23**
Manor Dri. *Horl* —8D **142**
Manor Dri. *New H* —6J **55**
Manor Dri. *Sun* —1H **39**
Manor Dri. *Surb* —5M **41**
Manor Dri. N. *N Mald & Wor Pk*
—6C **42**
Manor Dri., The. *Wor Pk* —7D **42**
Manor Farm. *Wanb* —6N **111**
Manor Farm Av. *Shep* —5C **38**
Mnr. Farm Bus. Cen. *Tong* —7D **110**
Mnr. Farm Clo. *As* —3D **110**
Mnr. Farm Clo. *Wind* —6C **4**
Mnr. Farm Clo. *Wor Pk* —7D **42**
Mnr. Farm Cotts. *Wanb* —6N **111**
Mnr. Farm Ct. *Egh* —6C **20**
Manor Farm Estate. —1M **19**
Mnr. Farm La. *Egh* —6C **20**
Mnr. Farm Rd. *SW16* —1L **45**
Manor Fields. *SW15* —9J **13**
Manorfields. *Craw* —7J **181**
Manor Fields. *H'ham* —4N **197**
Manor Fields. *Milf* —9B **132**
Manor Fields. *Seale* —7F **110**
Manor Gdns. *SW20* —1L **43**
Manor Gdns. *W4* —1D **12**
Manor Gdns. *Chil* —9E **114**
Manor Gdns. *Eff* —6L **97**
Manor Gdns. *G'ming* —4H **133**
Manor Gdns. *Guild* —1L **113**
Manor Gdns. *Hamp* —8B **24**
Manor Gdns. *Lwr Bo* —6J **129**
Manor Gdns. *Rich* —7M **11**
Manor Gdns. *S Croy* —3C **64**
Manor Gdns. *Sun* —9H **23**
Manorgate Rd. *King T* —9N **25**
Manor Grn. *Milf* —1B **152**
Mnr. Green Rd. *Eps* —9A **60**
Manor Gro. *Beck* —1L **47**
Manor Gro. *Rich* —7N **11**
Manor Hill. *Bans* —2D **82**
Manor Ho. Ct. *Eps* —9B **60** (7J **201**)
Manor Ho. Ct. *Shep* —6C **38**
Manor Ho. Dri. *Asc* —8L **17**
Manor Ho. Flats. *Tong* —6C **110**
Manor Ho. Gdns. *Eden* —2L **147**
Manorhouse La. *Bookh* —4M **97**
Manor Ho. La. *Dat* —3L **5**
Manor Ho., The. *Kgswd* —1A **102**
Manor Ho. Way. *Iswth* —6H **11**
Manor La. *Felt* —3H **23**
Manor La. *Hayes* —2E **8**
Manor La. *H'ham* —8A **198**
Manor La. *Sham G* —8G **134**
Manor La. *Sun* —1H **39**
Manor La. *Sutt* —2A **62**
Manor La. *Tad* —7M **101**
Manor Lea. *Hasl* —2C **188**
Manor Lea Clo. *Milf* —9B **132**
Manor Lea Rd. *Milf* —9B **132**
Manor Leaze. *Egh* —6D **20**
Manor Lodge. *Guild* —1L **113**
Manor Pk. *Rich* —7M **11**
Mnr. Park Clo. *W Wick* —7L **47**
Manor Pk. Dri. *Yat* —1C **68**
Manor Pk. Ind. Est. *Alder* —3A **110**
Mnr. Park Rd. *Sutt* —2A **62**
Mnr. Park Rd. *W Wick* —7L **47**
Manor Pl. *Bookh* —4A **98**
Manor Pl. *Felt* —2H **23**
Manor Pl. *Mitc* —2G **45**
Manor Pl. *Stai* —6K **21**
Manor Pl. *Sutt* —1N **61**
Manor Pl. *W on T* —6G **39**
Manor Rd. *SE25* —3D **46**
Manor Rd. *SW20* —1L **43**
Manor Rd. *Alder* —4L **109**
Manor Rd. *Afrd* —6A **22**
Manor Rd. *Beck* —1L **47**
Manor Rd. *E Grin* —8M **165**
Manor Rd. *E Mol* —3D **40**
Manor Rd. *Eden* —2K **147**
Manor Rd. *Farn* —1B **90**
Manor Rd. *Farnh* —8K **109**
Manor Rd. *Guild* —1L **113**
Manor Rd. *H'ham* —3N **197**
Manor Rd. *Mitc* —3G **44**
Manor Rd. *Red* —7G **102**
Manor Rd. *Reig* —1L **121**
Manor Rd. *Rich* —7N **11**
Manor Rd. *Rip* —1H **95**
Manor Rd. *Shur R* —1F **14**
Manor Rd. *Sutt* —4L **61**
Manor Rd. *Tats* —7G **86**
Manor Rd. *Tedd* —6G **25**
(in two parts)
Manor Rd. *Tong & Ash* —5D **110**
Manor Rd. *Twic* —3C **24**
Manor Rd. *Wall* —1F **62**
Manor Rd. *W on T* —6G **39**
Manor Rd. *W Wick* —8L **47**
Manor Rd. *Wind* —5B **4**
Manor Rd. *Wok* —3M **73**
Manor Rd. *Wokgm* —6A **30**
Manor Rd. N. *Esh* —9F **40**
Manor Rd. N. *Wall* —1F **62**
Manor Rd. S. *Esh* —1E **58**
Manor Royal. *Craw* —9C **162**
Mnr. Royal Ind. Est. *Craw* —8C **162**
Manor Ter. *G'ming* —5J **133**
Manor, The. *Milf* —1C **152**
Manor Va. *Bren* —1J **11**
Manor Wlk. *Alder* —3N **109**
(in two parts)
Manor Wlk. Horl —8D 142
(off Manor Dri.)
Manor Wlk. *Wey* —2C **56**
Manor Way. *Bag* —5J **51**
Manor Way. *Bans* —3D **82**
Manor Way. *Beck* —1K **47**
Manor Way. *Egh* —7B **20**
Manor Way. *Guild* —6H **113**
Manor Way. *Mitc* —2G **44**
Manor Way. *Old Wok* —8D **74**
Manor Way. *Oxs* —2C **78**
Manor Way. *Purl* —8J **63**
Manor Way. *S Croy* —3B **64**
Manor Way. *Wor Pk* —7D **42**
Manor Way, The. *Wall* —1F **62**
Mnr. Wood Rd. *Purl* —9J **63**
Mansard Beeches. *SW17* —6E **28**
Manse Clo. *Hayes* —2E **8**
Mansel Clo. *Guild* —7L **93**
Mansell Clo. *Wind* —4B **4**
Mansell Way. *Cat* —9A **84**
Mansel Rd. *SW19* —7K **27**
Mansfield Clo. *Asc* —9H **17**
Mansfield Cres. *Brack* —5N **31**
Mansfield Dri. *Red* —6H **103**
Mansfield Pl. *Asc* —1H **33**
Mansfield Pl. *S Croy* —3A **64**
Mansfield Rd. *Chess* —2J **59**
Mansfield Rd. *S Croy* —3A **64**
Manship Rd. *Mitc* —8E **28**
Mansions, The. *SW5* —1N **13**
Manston Av. *S'hall* —1A **10**
Manston Clo. *SE20* —1F **46**
Manston Dri. *Brack* —5A **32**
Manston Gro. *King T* —6K **25**
Manston Rd. *Guild* —8C **94**
Mantilla Rd. *SW17* —5E **28**
Mantlet Clo. *SW16* —8G **29**
Manville Gdns. *SW17* —4F **28**
Manville Rd. *SW17* —3E **28**
Manygate La. *Shep* —6D **38**
Manygate Mobile Home Est. Shep
(off Mitre Clo.) —5E **38**
Manygates. *SW12* —3F **28**
Maori Rd. *Guild* —3B **114**
Maple Clo. *Ash V* —6D **90**
Maple Clo. *B'water* —1H **69**
Maple Clo. *Craw* —9A **162**
Maple Clo. *Hamp* —7M **23**
Maple Clo. *H'ham* —3N **197**
Maple Clo. *Mitc* —9F **28**
Maple Clo. *Sand* —6E **48**
Maple Clo. *Whyt* —4C **84**
Maple Ct. *Brack* —3D **32**
Maple Ct. *Croy* —6C **200**
Maple Ct. *Croy* —6B **200**
Maple Ct. *Eng G* —7L **19**
Maple Ct. *Hors* —3M **73**
Maple Ct. *N Mald* —2C **42**
Mapledale Av. *Croy* —8D **46**
Mapledrakes Clo. *Ewh* —5F **156**
Mapledrakes Rd. *Ewh* —5F **156**
Maple Dri. *Crowt* —9H **31**
Maple Dri. *E Grin* —9C **166**
Maple Dri. *Light* —7K **51**
Maple Dri. *Red* —9D **122**
Maple Gdns. *Stai* —3N **21**
Maple Gdns. *Yat* —1C **68**
Maplegreen. *Craw* —4A **182**
Maple Gro. *Bren* —3H **11**
Maple Gro. *Guild* —1N **113**
Maple Gro. *Wok* —8A **74**
Maple Gro. Bus. Cen. *Houn* —7K **9**
Maplehatch Clo. *G'ming* —9H **133**
Maple Ho. *King T* —8K **203**
Maplehurst. *Brom* —1N **47**
Maplehurst. *Lea* —1D **98**
Maplehurst Clo. *King T*
—3L **41** (8K **203**)
Maple Ind. Est. *Felt* —4H **23**
Maple Leaf Clo. *Big H* —3F **86**
Maple Leaf Clo. *Farn* —2L **89**
Mapleleaf Clo. *S Croy* —7F **64**
Maple Lodge. *Hasl* —4J **189**
Maple M. *SW16* —6K **29**
Maple Pl. *Bans* —1J **81**
Maple Rd. *SE20* —1E **46**
Maple Rd. *Asht* —6K **79**
Maple Rd. *Red* —7D **122**
Maple Rd. *Rip* —2J **95**
Maple Rd. *Surb* —5K **41** (8K **203**)
Maple Rd. *Whyt* —4C **84**
Maplestead Rd. *SW2* —1K **29**
Maples, The. *Bans* —1N **81**
Maples, The. *Clay* —4G **59**
Maples, The. *Ott* —3D **54**
Maples, The. *Tedd* —8J **25**
Maplethorpe Rd. *T Hth* —3L **45**
Mapleton Cres. *SW18* —9N **13**
Mapleton Rd. *SW18* —9M **13**
(in two parts)
Mapleton Rd. *W'ham* —8N **107**
Maple Wlk. *Alder* —4B **110**
Maple Wlk. *Sutt* —6N **61**
Maple Way. *Coul* —8F **82**
Maple Way. *Felt* —4H **23**
Maple Way. *Head D* —3G **169**
Marbeck Clo. *Wind* —4A **4**
Marble Hill Clo. *Twic* —1H **25**
Marble Hill Gdns. *Twic* —1H **25**
Marble Hill House. —1J 25
Marbles Way. *Tad* —6J **81**
Marbull Way. *Warf* —7N **15**
Marchbank Rd. *W14* —2L **13**
March Ct. *SW15* —7G **12**
Marcheria Clo. *Brack* —5N **31**
Marches Rd. *Warn & K'fold*
—5D **178**
Marches, The. *K'fold* —4H **179**
Marchmont Rd. *Rich* —8M **11**
Marchmont Rd. *Wall* —4G **62**
March Rd. *Twic* —1G **24**
March Rd. *Wey* —2B **56**
Marchside Clo. *Houn* —4L **9**
Marcuse Rd. *Cat* —1A **104**
Marcus St. *SW18* —9N **13**
Marcus Ter. *SW18* —9N **13**
Mardale. *Camb* —2G **71**
Mardell Rd. *Croy* —4G **46**
Marden Cres. *Croy* —5K **45**
Marden Park. —1H **105**
Marden Rd. *Croy* —5K **45**
Mardens, The. *Craw* —2N **181**
Mare La. *Binf* —1K **15**
(in two parts)
Mare La. *Hasc* —6L **153**
Mareschal Rd. *Guild*
—5M **113** (7A **202**)
Mares Fld. *Croy* —9B **46**
Maresfield Ho. Guild —2F 114
(off Merrow St.)
Mareshall Av. *Warf* —7N **15**
Mare St. *Hasc* —6N **153**
Mareth Clo. *Alder* —2N **109**
Marfleet Clo. *Cars* —8C **44**
Margaret Clo. *Stai* —8M **21**
Margaret Herbison Ho. SW6 —2L 13
(off Clem Attlee Ct.)
Margaret Ho. W6 —1H 13
(off Queen Caroline St.)
Margaret Ingram Clo. SW6 —2L 13
(off Rylston Rd.)

Margaret Lockwood Clo.—Meadowside

Margaret Lockwood Clo. *King T* —3M **41** (7N **203**)
Margaret Rd. *Guild* —4M **113** (4B **202**)
Margaret Way. *Coul* —6M **83**
Margery. —7M 101
Margery Gro. *Tad* —7K **101**
Margery La. *Lwr K & Tad* —7L **101**
Margin Dri. *SW19* —6J **27**
Margravine Gdns. *W6* —1J **13**
Margravine Rd. *W6* —1J **13**
Marham Gdns. *SW18* —2C **28**
Marham Gdns. *Mord* —5A **44**
Marian Ct. *Sutt* —2N **61**
Marian Rd. *SW16* —9G **29**
Maria Theresa Clo. *N Mald* —4C **42**
Mariette Way. *Wall* —5J **63**
Marigold Clo. *Crowt* —9E **30**
Marigold Ct. *Guild* —9A **94**
Marigold Dri. *Bisl* —2D **72**
Marigold Way. *Croy* —7G **46**
Marina Av. *N Mald* —4G **42**
Marina Clo. *Cher* —7L **37**
Marina Way. *Tedd* —8K **25**
Marinefield Rd. *SW6* —5N **13**
Mariner Gdns. *Rich* —4J **25**
Mariners Dri. *Farn* —8A **70**
Mariners Dri. *Norm* —9M **91**
Marion Av. *Shep* —4C **38**
Marion Rd. *Craw* —5F **182**
Marion Rd. *T Hth* —4N **45**
Marius Pas. *SW17* —3E **28**
Marius Rd. *SW17* —3E **28**
Marjoram Clo. *Farn* —1G **89**
Marjoram Clo. *Guild* —8K **93**
Marke Clo. *Kes* —1G **66**
Markedge La. *Coul* —2C **102**
Markenfield Rd. *Guild* —3N **113** (3C **202**)
Markenhorn. *G'ming* —4G **132**
Market Cen., The. *S'hall* —1J **9**
Marketfield Rd. *Red* —3D **122**
Marketfield Way. *Red* —3D **122**
Market Pde. *Felt* —4M **23**
Market Pl. *Brack* —1N **31**
Market Pl. *Bren* —3J **11**
Market Pl. *Coln* —3E **6**
Market Pl. *King T* —1K **41** (3J **203**)
Market Pl. *Wokgm* —2B **30**
Market Rd. *Rich* —6N **11**
Market Sq. *H'ham* —7J **197**
Market Sq. *Stai* —6G **21**
Market Sq. *W'ham* —4M **107**
Market Sq. *Wok* —4A **74**
Market St. *Brack* —1N **31**
Market St. *Guild* —4N **113** (5C **202**)
Market St. *Wind* —4G **5**
Market Ter. Bren —2L 11
(off Albany Rd.)
Market, The. *Sutt* —7A **44**
Market Way. *W'ham* —4M **107**
Markfield. *Croy* —6J **65**
(in three parts)
Markfield Rd. *Cat* —4E **104**
Markham Ct. *Camb* —9B **50**
Markham M. *Wokgm* —2A **30**
Markham Rd. *Capel* —5J **159**
Markhole Clo. *Hamp* —8N **23**
Mark Oak La. *Fet* —9A **78**
Marksbury Av. *Rich* —6N **11**
Marks Rd. *Warl* —5H **85**
Marks Rd. *Wokgm* —9A **14**
Marks St. *Reig* —2N **121**
Markville Gdns. *Cat* —3D **104**
Mark Way. *G'ming* —3F **132**
Markway. *Sun* —1K **39**
Markwick La. *Loxh* —6L **153**
Marlborough Clo. *SW19* —7C **28**
Marlborough Clo. *Craw* —7A **182**
Marlborough Clo. *Fleet* —5E **88**
Marlborough Clo. *H'ham* —3K **197**
Marlborough Clo. *W on T* —9L **39**
Marlborough Ct. *Dork* —5H **119** (3L **201**)
Marlborough Ct. *S Croy* —7F **200**
Marlborough Ct. *Wall* —4C **62**
Marlborough Ct. W'ham —5L 107
(off Croydon Rd.)
Marlborough Ct. *Wokgm* —1C **30**
Marlborough Dri. *Wey* —9D **38**
Marlborough Gdns. *Surb* —6K **41**
Marlborough Hill. *Dork* —5H **119** (3L **201**)
Marlborough Park. —6B 90
Marlborough Ri. *Camb* —9C **50**
Marlborough Rd. *SW19* —7C **28**
Marlborough Rd. *W4* —1B **12**
Marlborough Rd. *Afrd* —6M **21**
Marlborough Rd. *Dork* —5H **119** (2L **201**)
Marlborough Rd. *Felt* —3L **23**
Marlborough Rd. *Hamp* —7A **24**
Marlborough Rd. *Iswth* —4H **11**
Marlborough Rd. *Rich* —9M **11**
Marlborough Rd. *Slou* —1N **5**
Marlborough Rd. *S Croy* —4N **63**
Marlborough Rd. *Sutt* —9M **43**
Marlborough Rd. *Wok* —3C **74**
Marlborough Vw. *Farn* —9H **69**
Marld, The. *Asht* —6M **79**
Marles La. *Bil* —7D **194**
(in two parts)
Marlet Corner. *Rud* —1E **194**
Marley Av. *Hasl* —5C **188**
Marley Clo. *Add* —3H **55**
Marley Combe Rd. *Hasl* —3D **188**
Marley Common & Wood. —5D 188
Marley Hanger. *Hasl* —5E **188**
Marley La. *Hasl* —3C **188**
Marley Ri. *Dork* —8G **119**
Marlhurst. *Eden* —8K **127**
Marlin Clo. *Sun* —7F **22**
Marlingdene Clo. *Hamp* —7A **24**
Marlings Clo. *Whyt* —4B **84**
Marlins Clo. *Sutt* —2A **62**
Marlow Clo. *SE20* —2E **46**
Marlow Ct. *Craw* —2B **182**
Marlow Cres. *Twic* —9F **10**
Marlow Dri. *Sutt* —8J **43**
Marlowe Ho. *King T* —8J **203**
Marlowe Sq. *Mitc* —3G **44**
Marlowe Way. *Croy* —8J **45**
Marlow Ho. *Surb* —8L **203**
Marlow Ho. *Tedd* —5G **25**
Marlow Rd. *SE20* —2E **46**
Marlpit Av. *Coul* —4J **83**
Marlpit Clo. *E Grin* —7A **166**
Marlpit Clo. *Eden* —8L **127**
Marlpit Hill. —8K 127
Marlpit La. *Coul* —3H **83**
Marl Rd. *SW18* —7N **13**
Marlyns Clo. *Guild* —9C **94**
Marlyns Dri. *Guild* —8C **94**
Marmot Rd. *Houn* —6L **9**
Marnell Way. *Houn* —6L **9**
Marneys Clo. *Eps* —2N **79**
Marnfield Cres. *SW2* —2L **29**
Marnham Pl. *Add* —1L **55**
Marqueen Towers. *SW16* —8J **29**
Marquis Ct. *King T* —8J **203**
Marrick Clo. *SW15* —7F **12**
Marriott Clo. *Felt* —9E **8**
Marriott Lodge Clo. *Add* —1L **55**
Marrowbrook Clo. *Farn* —2M **89**
Marrowbrook La. *Farn* —3L **89**
Marrowells. *Wey* —9G **38**
Marryat Pl. *SW19* —5K **27**
Marryat Rd. *SW19* —6J **27**
Marryat Sq. *SW6* —4K **13**
Marshall Clo. *SW18* —9N **13** & 1A **28**
Marshall Clo. *Farn* —7L **69**
Marshall Clo. *Frim* —4H **71**
Marshall Clo. *Houn* —8N **9**
Marshall Clo. *S Croy* —9D **64**
Marshall Pde. *Wok* —2H **75**
Marshall Pl. *New H* —5L **55**
Marshall Rd. *Coll T* —8J **49**
Marshall Rd. *G'ming* —6H **133**
Marshall Rd. *M'bowr* —5G **182**
Marshalls Clo. *Eps* —9B **60** (6J **201**)
Marshall's Rd. *Sutt* —1N **61**
Marsham Ho. *Brack* —8N **15**
Marsh Av. *Eps* —6D **60**
Marsh Av. *Mitc* —1D **44**
Marsh Clo. *Bord* —6A **168**
Marsh Ct. *Craw* —8N **181**
Marsh Farm Rd. *Twic* —2F **24**
Marshfield. *Dat* —4M **5**
Marsh Green. —6L 147
Marsh Grn. Rd. *M Grn* —8G **147**
Marshlands Cotts. *Newd* —7B **160**
Marsh La. *Add* —1K **55**
Marshwood Rd. *Light* —7A **52**
Marston. *Eps* —7B **60**
Marston Av. *Chess* —3L **59**
Marston Ct. *W on T* —7K **39**
Marston Dri. *Farn* —7N **69**
Marston Dri. *Warl* —5H **85**
Marston Rd. *Farnh* —1E **128**
Marston Rd. *Tedd* —6H **25**
Marston Rd. *Wok* —4L **73**
Marston Way. *SE19* —8M **29**
Marston Way. *Asc* —1J **33**
Martel Clo. *Camb* —8G **50**
Martell Rd. *SE21* —4N **29**
Martens Pl. *G'ming* —5H **133**
Martin Clo. *Craw* —1B **182**
Martin Clo. *S Croy* —7G **64**
Martin Clo. *Warl* —3E **84**
Martin Clo. *Wind* —4A **4**
Martin Ct. *S Croy* —8F **200**
Martin Cres. *Croy* —7L **45**
Martindale. *SW14* —8B **12**
Martindale Av. *Camb* —2G **71**
Martindale Clo. *Guild* —1F **114**
Martindale Rd. *SW12* —1F **28**
Martindale Rd. *Houn* —6M **9**
Martindale Rd. *Wok* —5K **73**
Martineau Clo. *Esh* —1D **58**
Martineau Dri. *Dork* —7H **119**
Martingale Clo. *Sun* —3H **39**
Martingale Ct. *Alder* —2K **109**
Martingales Clo. *Rich* —4K **25**
Martin Gro. *Mord* —2M **43**
Martin Rd. *Guild* —1K **113**
Martins Clo. *B'water* —2J **69**
Martins Clo. *Guild* —2E **114**
Martins Clo. *W Wick* —7N **47**
Martin's Dri. *Wokgm* —9A **14**
Martin's Heron. —2D 32
Martin's La. *Brack* —2C **32**
Martins Pk. Cvn. Pk. *Farn* —7J **69**
Martins, The. *Craw D* —1F **184**
Martins Wood. *Milf* —3B **152**
Martinsyde. *Wok* —4F **74**
Martin Way. *SW20 & Mord* —2K **43**
Martin Way. *Frim* —5C **70**
Martin Way. *Wok* —5K **73**
Martlets Clo. *H'ham* —3J **197**
Martlets, The. *Craw* —3C **182**
Marts, The. *Rud* —1E **194**
Martyns Pl. *E Grin* —1B **186**
Martyr Rd. *Guild* —4N **113** (5C **202**)
Martyrs Av. *Craw* —9A **162**
Martyr's Green. —7E 76
Martyr's La. *Wok* —8D **54**
Marvell Clo. *Craw* —1G **182**
Marville Rd. *SW6* —3L **13**
Marwell. *W'ham* —4K **107**
Mary Adelaide Clo. *SW15* —5D **26**
Mary Drew Almshouses. *Egh* —7N **19**
Mary Flux Ct. SW5 —1N 13
(off Bramham Gdns.)
Maryhill Clo. *Kenl* —4N **83**
Mary Ho. W6 —1H 13
(off Queen Caroline St.)
Maryland Rd. *T Hth* —9M **29**
Maryland Way. *Sun* —1H **39**
Mary Macarthur Ho. *W6* —2K **13**
Mary Mead. *Warf* —7B **16**
Mary Rd. *Guild* —4M **113** (4B **202**)
Mary Rose Clo. *Hamp* —9A **24**
Mary Smith Ct. SW5 —1M 13
(off Trebovir Rd.)
Mary's Ter. *Twic* —1G **24**
(in two parts)
Mary Va. *G'ming* —9G **133**
Marzena Ct. *Houn* —9C **10**
Masault Ct. Rich —7L 11
(off Kew Foot Rd.)
Mascotte Rd. *SW15* —7J **13**
Masefield Ct. *Surb* —8K **41**
Masefield Gdns. *Crowt* —4G **48**
Masefield Rd. *Craw* —6K **181**
Masefield Rd. *Hamp* —5N **23**
Masefield Way. *Stai* —2A **22**
Maskall Clo. *SW2* —2L **29**
Maskani Wlk. *SW16* —8G **29**
Maskell Rd. *SW17* —4A **28**
Maskell Way. *Farn* —2H **89**
Mason Clo. *E Grin* —8A **166**
Mason Clo. *Hamp* —9N **23**
Mason Clo. *Yat* —1D **68**
Masonettes. Eps —6C 60
(off Sefton Rd.)
Masonic Hall Rd. *Cher* —5H **37**
Mason Pl. *Sand* —7E **48**
Mason Rd. *Craw* —5C **182**
Mason Rd. *Farn* —8K **69**
Mason Rd. *Sutt* —2N **61**
Mason's Av. *Croy* —9N **45** (5C **200**)
Mason's Bri. Rd. *Red* —8F **122**
Masons Fld. *Man H* —9B **198**
Masons Paddock. *Dork* —3G **118**
Masons Pl. *Mitc* —9D **28**
Mason's Yd. *SW19* —6J **27**
Mason Way. *Alder* —5N **109**
Massetts Rd. *Horl* —9D **142**
Massingberd Way. *SW17* —5F **28**
Master Clo. *Oxt* —7A **106**
Maswell Park. —8C 10
Maswell Pk. Cres. *Houn* —8C **10**
Maswell Pk. Rd. *Houn* —8B **10**
Matcham Ct. Twic —9K 11
(off Clevedon Rd.)
Matham Rd. *E Mol* —4D **40**
Matheson Rd. *W14* —1L **13**
Mathew Ter. *Alder* —2A **110**
Mathias Clo. *Eps* —9B **60** (7J **201**)
Mathisen Way. *Coln* —4G **7**
Mathon Ct. *Guild* —3B **114**
Matilda Clo. *SE19* —8N **29**
Matlock Cres. *Sutt* —1K **61**
Matlock Gdns. *Sutt* —1K **61**
Matlock Pl. *Sutt* —1K **61**
Matlock Rd. *Cat* —8B **84**
Matlock Way. *N Mald* —9C **26**
Maton Ho. SW6 —3L 13
(off Estcourt Rd.)
Matthew Arnold Clo. *Cobh* —1H **77**
Matthew Arnold Clo. *Stai* —7L **21**
Matthew Ct. *Mitc* —4H **45**
Matthew Rd. *Alder* —4K **109**
Matthews Chase. *Binf* —8L **15**
Matthews Clo. *Farn* —5C **90**
Matthews Ct. *Asc* —3A **34**
Matthews Dri. *M'bowr* —7F **182**
Matthews Gdns. *New Ad* —7N **65**
Matthewsgreen. —9A 14
Matthewsgreen Rd. *Wokgm* —9A **14**
Matthews La. *Stai* —5H **21**
Matthews Rd. *Camb* —7A **50**
Matthews St. *Reig* —7M **121**
Matthews Way. *Fleet* —3A **88**
Matthey Pl. *Craw* —9H **163**
Maudsley Ho. *Bren* —1L **11**
Maultway Clo. *Camb* —7F **50**
Maultway Cres. *Camb* —7F **50**
Maultway N. *Camb* —6E **50**
(in two parts)
Maultway, The. *Camb* —7F **50**
Maunsell Pk. *Craw* —3F **182**
Maureen Ct. *Beck* —1F **46**
Maurice Av. *Cat* —9A **84**
Maurice Ct. *Bren* —3K **11**
Mavins Rd. *Farnh* —3J **129**
Mavis Av. *Eps* —2D **60**
Mavis Clo. *Eps* —2D **60**
Mawbey Rd. *Ott* —3F **54**
Mawson Clo. *SW20* —1K **43**
Mawson La. *W4* —2E **12**
Maxine Clo. *Sand* —6G **48**
Maxton Wlk. *Craw* —8N **181**
Maxwell Clo. *Croy* —7J **45**
Maxwell Dri. *W Byf* —7L **55**
Maxwell Rd. *SW6* —3N **13**
Maxwell Rd. *Atrd* —7D **22**
Maxwell Way. *Craw* —9E **162**
May Bate Av. *King T* —9K **25** (1J **203**)
Maybelle Clo. *Bear G* —8K **139**
Mayberry Pl. *Surb* —6M **41**
Maybourne Ri. *Wok* —2N **93**
Maybrick Clo. *Sand* —6E **48**
Maybury. —3E 74
Maybury Clo. *Frim* —6B **70**
Maybury Clo. *Tad* —6K **81**
Maybury Ct. *S Croy* —8A **200**
Maybury Est. *Wok* —3F **74**
Maybury Hill. *Wok* —3D **74**
Maybury Rd. *Wok* —4B **74**
Maybury St. *SW17* —6C **28**
May Clo. *Chess* —3M **59**
May Clo. *G'ming* —9E **132**
May Clo. *Head* —5D **168**
May Clo. *Owl* —7J **49**
May Cres. *As* —3C **110**
Maycross Av. *Mord* —3L **43**
Mayday Rd. *T Hth* —5M **45**
Maydwell Av. *Slin* —6J **195**
Mayell Clo. *Lea* —1J **99**
Mayes Clo. *M'bowr* —4G **182**
Mayes Clo. *Warl* —5G **85**
Mayes Green. —7M 157
Mayes La. *Warn* —7E **178**
Mayfair Av. *Twic* —1C **24**
Mayfair Av. *Wor Pk* —7F **42**
Mayfair Clo. *Surb* —7L **41**
Mayfield. *Craw* —3H **183**
Mayfield. *D'land* —1C **166**
Mayfield. *Lea* —8J **79**
Mayfield. *Rowl* —8E **128**
Mayfield Av. *W4* —1D **12**
Mayfield Av. *New H* —6K **55**
Mayfield Clo. *SE20* —1E **46**
Mayfield Clo. *Afrd* —7C **22**
Mayfield Clo. *Bad L* —6N **109**
Mayfield Clo. *New H* —6L **55**
Mayfield Clo. *Red* —9E **122**
Mayfield Clo. *Th Dit* —7H **41**
Mayfield Clo. *W on T* —1H **57**
Mayfield Ct. *Red* —8D **122**
Mayfield Cres. *T Hth* —3K **45**
Mayfield Gdns. *Stai* —7H **21**
Mayfield Gdns. *W on T* —1H **57**
Mayfield Grn. *Bookh* —5A **98**
Mayfield Rd. *SW19* —9L **27**
Mayfield Rd. *Camb* —5N **69**
Mayfield Rd. *Farn* —7L **69**
Mayfield Rd. *S Croy* —5A **64**
Mayfield Rd. *Sutt* —3B **62**
Mayfield Rd. *T Hth* —3K **45**
Mayfield Rd. *W on T* —1H **57**
Mayfield Rd. *Wey* —2A **56**
Mayflower Clo. *Craw* —4H **183**
Mayflower Dri. *Yat* —8A **48**
Mayford. —9M 73
Mayford Clo. *SW12* —1D **28**
Mayford Clo. *Beck* —2G **47**
Mayford Clo. *Wok* —9N **73**
Mayford Rd. *SW12* —1D **28**
Mayhurst Av. *Wok* —3E **74**
Mayhurst Clo. *Wok* —3E **74**
Mayhurst Cres. *Wok* —3E **74**
Maynard Clo. *SW6* —3N **13**
Maynard Clo. *Copt* —6N **163**
Maynard Ct. *Stai* —5J **21**
Maynooth Gdns. *Cars* —6D **44**
Mayo Rd. *Croy* —4A **46**
Mayo Rd. *W on T* —6H **39**
Maypole Rd. *Ash W* —3G **186**
Maypole Rd. *E Grin* —8N **165**
May Rd. *Twic* —2E **24**
Mayroyd Av. *Surb* —8N **41**
Mays Clo. *Wey* —6A **56**
Mays Cft. *Brack* —3M **31**
Maysfield Rd. *Send* —1F **94**
May's Green. —7F 76
Mays Gro. *Send* —1F **94**
Mays Hill Rd. *Brom* —1N **47**
Mays Rd. *Tedd* —6D **24**
May's Rd. *Wokgm* —2D **30**
May St. *W14* —1L **13**
Maytree Clo. *Guild* —8M **93**
Maytrees. *Knap* —4F **72**
Maytree Wlk. *SW2* —3L **29**
Maywater Clo. *S Croy* —7A **64**
Maywood Dri. *Camb* —8F **50**
Maze Rd. *Rich* —3N **11**
Meachen Ct. *Wokgm* —2B **30**
Mead Av. *Red* —2E **142**
Mead Clo. *Cranl* —8N **155**
Mead Clo. *Egh* —7D **20**
Mead Clo. *Red* —9E **102**
Mead Ct. *Egh* —7E **20**
Mead Ct. *Knap* —3H **73**
Mead Cres. *Bookh* —3A **98**
Mead Cres. *Sutt* —9C **44**
Meade Clo. *W4* —2N **11**
Meade Ct. *Bag* —4K **51**
Meade Ct. *Tad* —2F **100**
Mead End. *Asht* —4M **79**
Meades Clo. *D'land* —1D **166**
Meades, The. *D'land* —1C **166**
Meades, The. *Wey* —3D **56**
Meadfoot Rd. *SW16* —8G **28**
Meadhurst Pk. *Sun* —7F **22**
Meadhurst Rd. *Cher* —7K **37**
Meadlands Dri. *Rich* —3K **25**
Mead La. *Cher* —6K **37**
Mead La. *Farnh* —1G **128**
Mead La. Cvn. Pk. *Cher* —7L **37**
Meadow App. *Copt* —7L **163**
Meadow Av. *Croy* —5G **47**
Meadow Bank. *E Hor* —5G **96**
Meadow Bank. *Farnh* —1G **128**
Meadowbank. *Surb* —5M **41**
Meadowbank Clo. *SW6* —3H **13**
Meadowbank Gdns. *Houn* —4H **9**
Meadowbank Rd. *Light* —6N **51**
Meadow Brook. *Oxt* —8M **105**
Meadow Brook Clo. *Coln* —4H **7**
Meadowbrook Ct. *Iswth* —6E **10**
Meadow Brook Ind. Cen. *Craw* —9E **162**
Meadowbrook Rd. *Dork* —4G **119** (1K **201**)
Meadow Clo. *SW20* —3H **43**
Meadow Clo. *Ash V* —4D **90**
Meadow Clo. *B'water* —2J **69**
Meadow Clo. *Copt* —7L **163**
Meadow Clo. *Esh* —9F **40**
Meadow Clo. *G'ming* —4H **133**
Meadow Clo. *H'ham* —3N **197**
Meadow Clo. *Houn* —9A **10**
Meadow Clo. *Milf* —1D **152**
Meadow Clo. *Old Win* —9L **5**
Meadow Clo. *Purl* —9H **63**
Meadow Clo. *Rich* —2L **25**
Meadow Clo. *Sutt* —8A **44**
Meadow Clo. *W on T* —1N **57**
Meadow Cotts. *W End* —8C **52**
Meadow Ct. *Eps* —9B **60** (7J **201**)
Meadow Ct. *Farn* —1L **89**
Meadow Ct. *Fleet* —4A **88**
Meadow Ct. *Houn* —9B **10**
Meadow Ct. *Stai* —4G **20**
Meadowcroft. W4 —1N 11
(off Brooks Rd.)
Meadowcroft Clo. *Craw* —4L **181**
Meadowcroft Clo. *E Grin* —8M **165**
Meadow Cft. Clo. *Horl* —2G **162**
Meadow Dri. *Rip* —1H **95**
Mdw. Farm La. *H'ham* —1M **197**
Meadow Gdns. *Stai* —6F **20**
Meadow Ga. Asht —4L 79
(off Meadow Rd.)
Meadow Hill. *Coul* —1G **82**
Meadow Hill. *N Mald* —5D **42**
Meadow Ho. Guild —2F 114
(off Merrow St.)
Meadowlands. *Cobh* —9H **57**
Meadowlands. *Craw* —3A **102**
Meadowlands. *Oxt* —3C **126**
Meadowlands. *W Cla* —8K **95**
Meadowlands Cvn. Pk. *Add* —9N **37**
Meadow La. *Eden* —8K **127**
Meadow La. *Eton* —2E **4**
Meadow La. *Fet* —9C **78**
Meadow La. *Stai* —5H **21**
Meadowlea Clo. *Harm* —2M **7**
Meadow Pl. *W4* —3D **12**
Meadow Ri. *Coul* —9H **63**
Meadow Ri. *Knap* —4F **72**
Meadow Rd. *SW19* —8A **28**
Meadow Rd. *Atrd* —6E **22**
Meadow Rd. *Asht* —4L **79**
Meadow Rd. *Clay* —3E **58**
Meadow Rd. *Farn* —7N **69**
Meadow Rd. *Felt* —3M **23**
Meadow Rd. *Guild* —8C **94**
Meadow Rd. *Sutt* —1C **62**
Meadow Rd. *Vir W* —4H **35**
Meadow Rd. *Wokgm* —2A **30**
Meadows End. *Sun* —9H **23**
Meadowside. *Bookh* —1A **98**
Meadowside. *Horl* —7F **142**
Meadowside. *Stai* —6J **21**
Meadowside. *Twic* —1K **25**
Meadowside. *W on T* —8K **39**

Meadowside. (Mobile Homes Pk.)—Millfield Rd.

Meadowside. (Mobile Homes Pk.) *Ling* —5M **145**
Meadowside Rd. *Sutt* —5K **61**
Meadows Leigh Clo. *Wey* —9C **38**
*Meadows, The. As —2F **110***
(off Chester Rd.)
Meadows, The. *Camb* —1K **69**
Meadows, The. *Churt* —9L **149**
Meadows, The. *Guild* —6M **113** (8B **202**)
Meadows, The. *Warl* —4G **85**
Meadow Stile. *Croy* —9N **45** (5C **200**)
Meadowsweet Clo. *SW20* —3H **43**
Meadow, The. *Copt* —7L **163**
Meadow Va. *Hasl* —2E **188**
Meadow Vw. *Bord* —6A **168**
Meadow Vw. *Small* —8N **143**
Meadow Vw. *Stai* —8H **7**
Meadowview Rd. *Eps* —5D **60**
Meadow Vw. Rd. *T Hth* —4M **45**
Meadow Wlk. *Eps* —3D **60**
(in two parts)
Meadow Wlk. *Tad* —2G **100**
Meadow Wlk. *Wall* —9F **44**
Meadow Wlk. *Wokgm* —2A **30**
Meadow Way. *Add* —1K **55**
Meadow Way. *Alder* —1D **110**
Meadow Way. *B'water* —1H **69**
Meadow Way. *Bookh* —1B **98**
Meadow Way. *Brack* —8M **15**
Meadow Way. *Chess* —2L **59**
Meadow Way. *Old Win* —9L **5**
Meadow Way. *Orp* —1J **67**
Meadow Way. *Reig* —7N **121**
Meadow Way. *Rowl* —8E **128**
Meadow Way. *Tad* —4K **81**
Meadow Way. *W End* —8C **52**
Meadow Way. *W Hor* —3E **96**
Meadow Way. *Wokgm* —3A **30**
Meadway. *Houn* —2M **9**
Mead Path. *SW17* —5A **28**
Mead Pl. *Croy* —7N **45** (1A **200**)
Mead Rd. *Cat* —1C **104**
Mead Rd. *Cranl* —7N **155**
Mead Rd. *Craw* —2D **182**
Mead Rd. *Eden* —4M **147**
Mead Rd. *Hind* —5D **170**
Mead Rd. *Rich* —4J **25**
Mead Rd. *W on T* —1M **57**
Meadrow. *G'ming* —6J **133**
Meadrow Ct. *G'ming* —5K **133**
Meadside Clo. *Beck* —1H **47**
Meads Rd. *Guild* —3D **114**
Meads, The. *E Grin* —2A **186**
Meads, The. *Hasl* —2D **188**
Meads, The. *Mord* —4C **44**
Meads, The. *Sutt* —9K **43**
Mead, The. *Asht* —6L **79**
Mead, The. *Beck* —1M **47**
Mead, The. *Dork* —8J **119**
Mead, The. *Farn* —2N **89**
Mead, The. *Wall* —3H **63**
Mead, The. *W Wick* —7N **47**
Mead Vale. —5B 122
Meadvale. *H'ham* —6F **196**
Meadvale Rd. *Croy* —6C **46**
Mead Way. *SW20* —3H **43**
Meadway. *Afrd* —5B **22**
Meadway. *Beck* —1M **47**
Mead Way. *Coul* —5J **83**
Mead Way. *Croy* —8H **47**
Meadway. *Eff* —6M **97**
Meadway. *Eps* —8B **60** (5H **201**)
Meadway. *Esh* —5B **58**
Meadway. *Frim* —4D **70**
Mead Way. *Guild* —7E **94**
Meadway. *Hasl* —2D **188**
Meadway. *Oxs* —1E **78**
Meadway. *Stai* —8J **21**
Meadway. *Surb* —7B **42**
Meadway. *Twic* —2D **24**
Meadway. *Warl* —3F **84**
Meadway Clo. *Stai* —8H **21**
Meadway Ct. *Tedd* —6J **25**
Meadway Dri. *Add* —4L **55**
Meadway Dri. *Wok* —3M **73**
Meadway, The. *Horl* —8G **142**
Meare Clo. *Tad* —1H **101**
Meath Green. —6D 142
Meath Grn. Av. *Horl* —6D **142**
Meath Grn. La. *Horl* —3C **142**
Medawar Rd. *Sur R* —4G **113**
Medcroft Gdns. *SW14* —7B **12**
Mede Clo. *Wray* —2N **19**
Mede Ct. *Stai* —4G **20**
Mede Fld. *Fet* —2D **98**
Medfield St. *SW15* —1F **26**
Medhurst Clo. *Chob* —5J **53**
Medieval Undercroft.
(off Chapel St.) —5N 113 (6C 202)
Medina Av. *Esh* —9E **40**
Medina Sq. *Eps* —5N **59**
Medlake Rd. *Egh* —7E **20**
Medland Clo. *Wall* —7E **44**
Medlar Clo. *Craw* —9A **162**
Medlar Clo. *Guild* —1M **113**
Medlar Dri. *B'water* —3L **69**
*Medmenham. Cars —7B **62***
(off Pine Cres.)
Medonte Clo. *Fleet* —5C **88**
Medora Rd. *SW2* —1K **29**
Medway. *Turn H* —4D **184**
Medway Clo. *Croy* —5F **46**
Medway Clo. *F Row* —7J **187**
Medway Ct. *H'ham* —3A **198**
Medway Dri. *E Grin* —3N **185**
Medway Dri. *Farn* —8K **69**
Medway Dri. *F Row* —7J **187**
Medway Ho. *King T* —9K **25** (1J **203**)
Medway Rd. *Craw* —4L **181**
Medway Vw. *F Row* —7J **187**
Medwin Wlk. *H'ham* —6J **197**
Medwin Way. *H'ham* —6J **197**
Meek Rd. *SW10* —3N **13**
Melancholy Wlk. *Rich* —3J **25**
Melbourne Clo. *Wall* —2G **62**
*Melbourne Mans. W6 —2K **13***
(off Musard Rd.)
Melbourne Rd. *SW19* —9M **27**
Melbourne Rd. *Tedd* —7J **25**
Melbourne Rd. *Wall* —2F **62**
*Melbourne Ter. SW6 —3N **13***
(off Moore Pk. Rd.)
Melbourne Way. *H'ham* —3M **197**
Melbray M. *SW6* —5L **13**
Melbury Clo. *Cher* —6J **37**
Melbury Clo. *Clay* —3H **59**
Melbury Clo. *W Byf* —1J **75**
Melbury Gdns. *SW20* —9G **26**
Meldon Clo. *SW6* —4N **13**
Meldone Clo. *Surb* —6A **42**
Meldrum Clo. *Oxt* —1B **126**
Melford Clo. *Chess* —2M **59**
Melfort Av. *T Hth* —2M **45**
Melfort Rd. *T Hth* —2M **45**
Melina Ct. *SW15* —6F **12**
Melksham Clo. *H'ham* —7L **197**
Melksham Clo. *Owl* —6J **49**
Meller Clo. *Croy* —9J **45**
Mellersh Hill Rd. *Won* —4D **134**
Mellison Rd. *SW17* —6C **28**
Mellor Clo. *W on T* —6N **39**
*Mellor Wlk. Wind —4G **4***
(off Batchelors Acre)
Mellow Clo. *Bans* —1A **82**
Mellows Rd. *Wall* —2H **63**
Melody Rd. *SW18* —8N **13**
Melody Rd. *Big H* —5E **86**
Melrose. *Brack* —7N **31**
Melrose Av. *SW16* —2K **45**
Melrose Av. *SW19* —3L **27**
Melrose Av. *Farn* —9H **69**
Melrose Av. *Mitc* —8F **28**
Melrose Av. *Twic* —1B **24**
Melrose Cres. *Orp* —1M **67**
Melrose Gdns. *N Mald* —2C **42**
Melrose Gdns. *W on T* —2K **57**
Melrose Rd. *SW13* —5E **12**
Melrose Rd. *SW18* —9L **13**
Melrose Rd. *SW19* —1M **43**
Melrose Rd. *Big H* —3E **86**
Melrose Rd. *Coul* —2F **82**
Melrose Rd. *Wey* —2B **56**
*Melrose Tudor. Wall —2J **63***
(off Plough La.)
Melsa Rd. *Mord* —5A **44**
Melton Ct. *Sutt* —4A **62**
Melton Fields. *Eps* —5C **60**
Melton Pl. *Eps* —5C **60**
Melton Rd. *Red* —8G **102**
Melville Av. *SW20* —8F **26**
Melville Av. *Frim* —5D **70**
Melville Av. *S Croy* —2C **64**
Melville Ct. *Guild* —6M **113** (8B **202**)
Melville Rd. *SW13* —4F **12**
*Melville Ter. Farnh —1G **128***
(off Fox Yd.)
Melvin Rd. *SE20* —1F **46**
Melvinshaw. *Lea* —8J **79**
Membury Clo. *Frim* —7E **70**
Membury Wlk. *Brack* —3C **32**
Memorial Clo. *Houn* —2N **9**
Mendip Clo. *SW19* —3K **27**
Mendip Clo. *Hayes* —3E **8**
Mendip Clo. *Slou* —1C **6**
Mendip Clo. *Wor Pk* —7H **43**
Mendip Rd. *Brack* —4C **32**
Mendip Rd. *Farn* —7K **69**
Mendip Wlk. *Craw* —3N **181**
Mendora Rd. *SW6* —3K **13**
Menin Way. *Farnh* —2J **129**
Menlo Gdns. *SE19* —8N **29**
Meon Clo. *Farn* —8J **69**
Meon Clo. *Tad* —9G **80**
Meon Ct. *Iswth* —5E **10**
Meopham Rd. *Mitc* —9G **28**
Merantun Way. *SW19* —9N **27**
Mercer Clo. *M'bowr* —6G **182**
Mercer Clo. *Th Dit* —6G **40**
Mercer Rd. *Warn* —9J **179**
Mercia Wlk. *Wok* —4B **74**
Mercier Rd. *SW15* —8K **13**
Mercury Cen. *Felt* —8H **9**
Mercury Clo. *Bord* —6A **168**
Mercury Clo. *Craw* —6K **181**
*Mercury Ho. Bren —2J **11***
(off Glenhurst Rd.)
Mercury Rd. *Bren* —2J **11**
Merebank. *Bear G* —7K **139**
Merebank La. *Croy* —2K **63**
Mere Clo. *SW15* —1J **27**
Meredyth Rd. *SW13* —5F **12**
Mere End. *Croy* —6G **47**
Merefield Gdns. *Tad* —6J **81**
Mere Rd. *Shep* —5C **38**
Mere Rd. *Tad* —2G **101**
Mere Rd. *Wey* —9E **38**
Mereside Pl. *Vir W* —7K **35**
(Knowle Hill)
Mereside Pl. *Vir W* —4N **35**
(Virginia Water)
Merevale Cres. *Mord* —5A **44**
Mereway Rd. *Twic* —2D **24**
Mereworth Dri. *Craw* —1H **183**
Meridian Clo. *Bew* —6L **181**
Meridian Ct. *S'dale* —7M **33**
Meridian Gro. *Horl* —7G **143**
Meridian Way. *E Grin* —7B **166**
Merivale Rd. *SW15* —7K **13**
Merland Clo. *Tad* —7H **81**
Merland Grn. *Tad* —7H **81**
Merland Ri. *Eps* —6H **81**
Merle Common. —5D 126
Merle Comn. Rd. *Oxt* —4C **126**
Merle Way. *Fern* —9E **188**
Merlewood. *Brack* —4B **32**
Merlewood Clo. *Cat* —7A **84**
Merlin Cen. *Craw* —8A **162**
Merlin Clo. *Croy* —1B **64** (6F **200**)
Merlin Clo. *If'd* —3K **181**
Merlin Clo. *Mitc* —2C **44**
Merlin Clo. *Slou* —2D **6**
Merlin Clo. *Wall* —3K **63**
Merlin Clove. *Wink R* —7F **16**
Merlin Ct. *Frim* —5B **70**
Merlin Ct. *Wok* —1E **74**
Merling Clo. *Chess* —2J **59**
Merlin Gro. *Beck* —3J **47**
Merlins Clo. *Farnh* —2H **129**
Merlin Way. *E Grin* —7C **166**
Merlin Way. *Farn* —2J **89**
Merredene St. *SW2* —1K **29**
Merrilands Rd. *Wor Pk* —7H **43**
Merrilyn Clo. *Clay* —3G **58**
Merrington Rd. *SW6* —2M **13**
Merritt Gdns. *Chess* —3J **59**
Merrivale Gdns. *Wok* —4M **73**
Merron Clo. *Yat* —1B **68**
Merrow. —2D 114
Merrow Bus. Cen. *Guild* —9F **94**
Merrow Chase. *Guild* —3E **114**
Merrow Comn. Rd. *Guild* —9E **94**
Merrow Copse. *Guild* —2D **114**
Merrow Ct. *Guild* —3F **114**
Merrow Ct. *Mitc* —1B **44**
Merrow Cft. *Guild* —2E **114**
Merrow Downs. —4F 114
Merrow La. *Guild* —7E **94**
Merrow Pl. *Guild* —1F **114**
Merrow Rd. *Sutt* —5J **61**
Merrow St. *Guild* —1F **114**
Merrow Way. *Guild* —2F **114**
Merrow Way. *New Ad* —3M **65**
Merrow Woods. *Guild* —1D **114**
Merryacres. *Witl* —4B **152**
Merryfield Dri. *H'ham* —5G **197**
Merryhill Rd. *Brack* —8M **15**
Merryhills Clo. *Big H* —3F **86**
Merryhills La. *Loxw* —3J **193**
Merrylands. *Cher* —9G **37**
Merrylands Rd. *Bookh* —1N **97**
Merryman Dri. *Crowt* —1E **48**
Merrymeet. *Bans* —1D **82**
Merryweather Ct. *N Mald* —4D **42**
Merrywood Gro. *Tad* —8K **101**
Merrywood Pk. *Camb* —2D **70**
Merrywood Pk. *Reig* —1N **121**
Merrywood Pk. Cvn. Site. *Tad* —8A **100**
Merryworth Clo. *As* —3D **110**
Mersey Ct. *King T* —9K **25** (1J **203**)
Mersham Rd. *T Hth* —2A **46**
Merstham. —6G 102
Merstham Rd. *Mers* —7L **103**
Merthyr Ter. *SW13* —2G **13**
Merton. —8A 28
Merton Av. *W4* —1E **12**
Merton Clo. *Owl* —5L **49**
Merton Gdns. *Tad* —6J **81**
Merton Hall Gdns. *SW20* —9K **27**
Merton Hall Rd. *SW19* —8K **27**
Merton High St. *SW19* —8N **27**
Merton Ind. Pk. *SW19* —9N **27**
Merton Mans. *SW20* —1J **43**
Merton Park. —1M 43
Merton Pk. Pde. *SW19* —9L **27**
*Merton Pl. SW19 —9A **28***
(off Nelson Gro. Rd.)
Merton Rd. *SE25* —4D **46**
Merton Rd. *SW18* —9M **13**
Merton Rd. *SW19* —8N **27**
Merton Rd. *Craw* —9N **181**
Merton Wlk. *Lea* —5G **79**
Merton Way. *Lea* —6G **79**
Merton Way. *W Mol* —3B **40**
Mervyn Rd. *Shep* —6D **38**
Merwin Way. *Wind* —5A **4**
Metana Ho. *Craw* —7E **162**
Metcalf Rd. *Afrd* —6C **22**
Metcalf Wlk. *Felt* —5M **23**
Metcalf Way. *Craw* —8B **162**
Meteor Way. *Wall* —4J **63**
Metro Ind. Cen. *Iswth* —5E **10**
Meudon Av. *Farn* —2N **89**
Mews Ct. *E Grin* —3B **186**
Mews End. *Big H* —5F **86**
Mews, The. *Charl* —3K **161**
Mews, The. *Duns* —4B **174**
Mews, The. *Guild* —4M **113** (4A **202**)
Mews, The. *Reig* —2N **121**
Mews, The. *Twic* —9H **11**
Mexfield Rd. *SW15* —8L **13**
Meyrick Clo. *Knap* —3H **73**
Michael Cres. *Horl* —1E **162**
Michael Fields. *F Row* —7G **186**
Michaelmas Clo. *SW20* —2H **43**
Michaelmas Clo. *Yat* —2C **68**
Michael Rd. *SE25* —2B **46**
Michael Rd. *SW6* —4N **13**
*Michael Stewart Ho. SW6 —2L **13***
(off Clem Attlee Ct.)
Micheldever Way. *Brack* —5D **32**
Michelet Clo. *Light* —6M **51**
Michelham Gdns. *Tad* —7H **81**
Michelham Gdns. *Twic* —4F **24**
Michell Clo. *H'ham* —6G **197**
Michelsdale Dri. *Rich* —7L **11**
Michel's Row. *Rich* —7L **11**
Mickleham. —6J 99
Mickleham By-Pass. *Mick* —6H **99**
Mickleham Downs. —4K 99
Mickleham Downs. —5K 99
Mickleham Dri. *Mick* —4J **99**
Mickleham Gdns. *Sutt* —3K **61**
Mickleham Way. *New Ad* —4N **65**
Mickle Hill. *Sand* —6F **48**
Micklethwaite Rd. *SW6* —2M **13**
Mick Mill's Race. *H'ham* —7E **198**
Midas Metropolitan Ind. Est. *Mord* —6H **43**
Middle Av. *Farnh* —3J **129**
Middle Bourne. —4H 129
Middle Bourne La. *Lwr Bo* —5G **129**
Middle Church La. *Farnh* —1G **129**
Middle Clo. *Camb* —9F **50**
Middle Clo. *Coul* —7L **83**
Middle Clo. *Eps* —8D **60**
Middle Farm Clo. *Eff* —5L **97**
Middle Farm Pl. *Eff* —5K **97**
Middlefield. *Farnh* —4F **128**
(in two parts)
Middlefield. *Horl* —7G **143**
Middlefield Clo. *Farnh* —3F **128**
Middlefields. *Croy* —5H **65**
Middle Gordon Rd. *Camb* —1A **70**
Middle Grn. *Brock* —5A **120**
Middle Grn. *Stai* —8M **21**
Middle Grn. Clo. *Surb* —5M **41**
Middle Hill. *Alder* —1M **109**
Middle Hill. *Eng G* —5M **19**
Middle La. *Eps* —8D **60**
Middle La. *Tedd* —7F **24**
Middlemarch. *Witl* —5B **152**
Middlemead Clo. *Bookh* —3A **98**
Middlemead Rd. *Bookh* —3N **97**
Middle Mill Hall. *King T* —2M **41** (6L **203**)
Middlemoor Rd. *Frim* —5C **70**
Middle Old Pk. *Farnh* —8E **108**
Middle Rd. *SW16* —1H **45**
Middle Rd. *Lea* —8H **79**
Middle Row. *E Grin* —1B **186**
Middlesex Ct. *W4* —1E **12**
*Middlesex Ct. Add —2L **55***
(off Marnham Pl.)
Middlesex Rd. *Mitc* —4J **45**
Middle St. *Brock & Str G* —4A **120**
Middle St. *Croy* —8N **45** (3C **200**)
(in two parts)
Middle St. *H'ham* —6J **197**
Middle St. *Shere* —8B **116**
Middleton Gdns. *Farn* —8K **69**
Middleton Rd. *Camb* —9C **50**
Middleton Rd. *D'side* —6J **77**
Middleton Rd. *Eps* —6C **60**
Middleton Rd. *H'ham* —6G **197**
Middleton Rd. *Mord* —5N **43**
Middleton Rd. *N Mald* —2B **42**
Middleton Way. *If'd* —4K **181**
Middle Wlk. *Wok* —4A **74**
Middle Way. *SW16* —1H **45**
Midgarth Clo. *Oxs* —1C **78**
Midgeley Rd. *Craw* —1D **182**
Midholm Rd. *Croy* —9H **47**
Mid Holmwood. —2H 139
Mid Holmwood La. *Mid H* —2H **139**
Midhope Clo. *Wok* —6A **74**
Midhope Gdns. *Wok* —6A **74**
Midhope Rd. *Wok* —6A **74**
Midhurst Av. *Croy* —6L **45**
Midhurst Clo. *Craw* —2M **181**
Midhurst Rd. *Hasl* —4E **188**
Midleton Clo. *Milf* —9C **132**
Midleton Ind. Est. *Guild* —3L **113**
Midleton Ind. Est. Rd. *Guild* —2L **113**
Midleton Rd. *Guild* —2L **113**
Midmoor Rd. *SW12* —2G **29**
Midmoor Rd. *SW19* —9J **27**
Mid St. *S Nut* —6K **123**
Midsummer Av. *Houn* —7N **9**
Midsummer Wlk. *Wok* —3N **73**
Midway. *Sutt* —6L **43**
Midway. *W on T* —8J **39**
Midway Av. *Cher* —2J **37**
Midway Av. *Egh* —2D **36**
Midway Clo. *Stai* —4K **21**
Miena Way. *Asht* —4K **79**
Mike Hawthorn Dri. *Farnh* —9H **109**
Milbanke Ct. *Brack* —1L **31**
Milbanke Way. *Brack* —1L **31**
Milborne Rd. *M'bowr* —7G **182**
Milbourne La. *Esh* —3C **58**
Milbrook. *Esh* —3C **58**
Milburn Wlk. *Eps* —2D **80**
Milbury Grn. *Warl* —5N **85**
Milcombe Clo. *Wok* —5M **73**
Milden Clo. *Frim G* —8E **70**
Milden Gdns. *Frim G* —8D **70**
Mile Path. *Wok* —8J **73**
(in two parts)
Mile Rd. *Wall* —7F **44**
Miles Ct. *Croy* —3A **200**
Miles La. *Cobh* —9M **57**
Miles La. *Tand* —5J **125**
Miles Pl. *Light* —8K **51**
Miles Pl. *Surb* —3M **41** (8M **203**)
Miles Rd. *As* —1F **110**
Miles Rd. *Eps* —8C **60**
Miles Rd. *Mitc* —2C **44**
Miles's Hill. *Holm M* —8K **137**
Milestone Clo. *Rip* —9J **75**
Milestone Clo. *Sutt* —4B **62**
Milestone Green. (Junct.) —7C **12**
Milestone Ho. *King T* —6J **203**
Milford. —1C 152
Milford By-Pass Rd. *Milf* —2A **152**
Milford Gdns. *Croy* —4F **46**
Milford Gro. *Sutt* —1A **62**
Milford Heath Rd. *Milf* —2B **152**
Milford Lodge. *Milf* —2C **152**
Milford M. *SW16* —4K **29**
Milford Rd. *Elst* —7H **131**
Milkhouse Ga. *Guild* —5N **113** (6D **202**)
Milking La. *Kes* —7F **66**
(in two parts)
Millais. *H'ham* —5N **197**
Millais Clo. *Craw* —7L **181**
Millais Ct. *H'ham* —4N **197**
Millais Rd. *N Mald* —6D **42**
Millais Way. *Eps* —1B **60**
Millan Clo. *New H* —6K **55**
Millbank, The. *Craw* —3L **181**
Millbay La. *H'ham* —7H **197**
Mill Bottom. —4K 139
Millbourne Rd. *Felt* —5M **23**
Millbridge. —9J 129
Mill Bri. Rd. *Yat* —7A **48**
Millbrook. *Guild* —5N **113** (6B **202**)
Millbrook. *Wey* —1F **56**
Millbrook Way. *Coln* —5G **7**
Mill Chase Rd. *Bord* —5A **168**
Mill Clo. *Bag* —4H **51**
Mill Clo. *Bookh* —2A **98**
Mill Clo. *Cars* —8E **44**
Mill Clo. *E Grin* —2A **186**
Mill Clo. *Hasl* —2C **188**
Mill Clo. *Horl* —7C **142**
Mill Copse Rd. *Hasl* —4F **188**
Mill Corner. *Fleet* —1D **88**
Mill Cotts. *E Grin* —2A **186**
Mill Cotts. *Rud* —3E **194**
Mill Ct. *Red* —9G **103**
Millennium Cotts. *Alb* —8L **115**
*Millennium Ho. Bew —6L **181***
(off Meridian Clo.)
Millennium Ho. *Farnh* —2F **128**
Miller Clo. *Mitc* —6D **44**
Miller Rd. *SW19* —7B **28**
Miller Rd. *Croy* —7K **45**
Miller Rd. *Guild* —9E **94**
Millers Clo. *Stai* —6K **21**
Millers Copse. *Eps* —6C **80**
Millers Copse. *Out* —4M **143**
Miller's Ct. *W4* —1E **12**
Millers Ct. *Egh* —7F **20**
Millers Ga. *H'ham* —3K **197**
Miller's La. *Old Win* —9J **5**
Miller's La. *Out* —4M **143**
Mill Farm Av. *Sun* —8F **22**
Mill Farm Bus. Pk. *Houn* —1M **23**
Mill Farm Cres. *Houn* —2M **23**
Mill Farm Rd. *H'ham* —4N **197**
Millfield. —7M 177
Mill Fld. *Bag* —4H **51**
Millfield. *King T* —2M **41** (5M **203**)
Millfield. *Sun* —9E **22**
Millfield La. *Tad* —3L **101**
Millfield Rd. *Houn* —2M **23**

Millford. *Wok* —4L **73**
Millgate Ct. *Farnh* —9J **109**
Mill Grn. *Binf* —8K **15**
Mill Grn. *Mitc* —6E **44**
Mill Grn. Bus. Pk. *Mitc* —6E **44**
Mill Grn. Rd. *Mitc* —6E **44**
Millhedge Clo. *Cobh* —3M **77**
Mill Hill. *SW13* —5F **12**
Mill Hill. *Brock* —4B **120**
Mill Hill. *Eden* —3L **147**
Mill Hill La. *Brock* —3A **120**
Mill Hill Rd. *SW13* —5F **12**
Millholme Wlk. *Camb* —2G **71**
Mill Ho. La. *Egh & Cher* —3D **36**
Millhouse Pl. *SE27* —5M **29**
Millins Clo. *Owl* —6K **49**
Mill La. *Asc* —1C **34**
Mill La. *Brack* —3L **31**
Mill La. *Brmly* —5B **134**
Mill La. *Byfl* —9A **56**
Mill La. *Cars* —1D **62**
Mill La. *C'fold* —7D **172**
Mill La. *Chil* —8H **115**
Mill La. *Copt* —7B **164**
Mill La. *Cron* —3G **148**
Mill La. *Croy* —9K **45**
Mill La. *Dork* —4H **119** (1L **201**)
Mill La. *Duns* —4A **174**
Mill La. *Egh* —3E **36**
Mill La. *Eps* —5E **60**
Mill La. *Felb* —5H **165**
Mill La. *Fet* —9G **78**
Mill La. *F Grn* —3L **157**
Mill La. *G'ming* —7G **132**
Mill La. *Guild* —5N **113** (6C **202**)
Mill La. *Hasl* —4G **188**
Mill La. *Hkwd* —8B **142**
Mill La. *Hort* —6D **6**
Mill La. *If'd* —1M **181**
Mill La. *Itch* —8B **196**
Mill La. *Limp C* —9H **107**
Mill La. *Lind* —5B **168**
Mill La. *Ling* —1B **166**
Mill La. *Newd* —7C **140** (in two parts)
Mill La. *Orp* —6J **67**
Mill La. *Oxt* —1B **126**
Mill La. *P'mrsh* —2M **133**
Mill La. *Pirb* —2A **92**
Mill La. *Red* —9G **103**
Mill La. *Rip* —0M **75**
Mill La. *W'ham* —5L **107**
Mill La. *Wind* —3D **4**
Mill La. *Witl* —5C **152**
Mill La. *Yat & Sand* —7C **48**
Millmead. *Byfl* —0A **50**
Millmead. *Esh* —8A **40**
Millmead. *Guild* —5M **113** (6B **202**)
Mill Mead. *Stai* —5H **21**
Millmead Ct. *Guild* —5M **113** (7B **202**)
Millmead Ter. *Guild* —5M **113** (7B **202**)
Millmere. *Yat* —8C **48**
Mill Pl. *Dat* —5N **5**
Mill Pl. *King T* —2M **41** (5L **203**)
Mill Pl. Cvn. Pk. *Dat* —5N **5**
Mill Plat. *Iswth* —5G **10** (in two parts)
Mill Plat Av. *Iswth* —5G **10**
Millpond Ct. *Add* —2N **55**
Mill Pond Rd. *W'sham* —1M **51**
Mill Ride. *Asc* —9G **17**
Mill Rd. *SW19* —8A **28**
Mill Rd. *Cobh* —2K **77**
Mill Rd. *Craw* —2F **182**
Mill Rd. *Eps* —8E **60** (5N **201**)
Mill Rd. *Esh* —8A **40**
Mill Rd. *Holmw* —4J **139**
Mill Rd. *P'mrsh* —2M **133**
Mill Rd. *Tad* —1J **101**
Mill Rd. *Twic* —3C **24**
Mill Shaw. *Oxt* —1B **126**
Millshot Clo. *SW6* —4H **13**
Millside. *Cars* —8D **44**
Millside Ct. *Bookh* —3A **98**
Millside Pl. *Iswth* —5H **11**
Mills Rd. *W on T* —2K **57**
Mills Row. *W4* —1C **12**
Mills Spur. *Old Win* —1L **19**
Millstead Clo. *Tad* —9G **81**
Mill Stream. *Farnh* —6K **109**
Millstream, The. *Hasl* —3C **188**
Mill St. *Coln* —3F **6**
Mill St. *King T* —2L **41** (5L **203**)
Mill St. *Red* —4C **122**
Mill St. *W'ham* —5M **107**
Millthorpe Rd. *H'ham* —4M **197**
Mill Vw. Clo. *Ewe* —4E **60**
Mill Vw. Clo. *Reig* —1B **122**
Mill Vw. Gdns. *Croy* —9G **46**
Mill Way. *Dork* —2M **99**
Mill Way. *E Grin* —2A **186**
Mill Way. *Felt* —8J **9**
Mill Way. *Reig* —3B **122**
Millwood. *Turn H* —4H **185**
Millwood Rd. *Houn* —8C **10**
Millman Clo. *Brack* —1E **32**
Milne Clo. *Craw* —6K **181**
Milne Pk. E. *New Ad* —7N **65**
Milne Pk. W. *New Ad* —7N **65**
Milner App. *Cat* —8D **84**
Milner Clo. *Cat* —9C **84**
Milner Dri. *Cobh* —8N **57**
Milner Dri. *Twic* —1D **24**
Milner Pl. *Cars* —1E **62**
Milner Rd. *SW19* —9N **27**
Milner Rd. *Cat* —9D **84**
Milner Rd. *King T* —2K **41** (6J **203**)
Milner Rd. *Mord* —4B **44**
Milner Rd. *T Hth* —2A **46**
Milnthorpe Rd. *W4* —2C **12**
Millwood Rd. *H'ham* —6J **107**
Milton Av. *Croy* —6A **46**
Milton Av. *Sutt* —9B **44**
Milton Av. *Westc* —6D **118**
Milton Clo. *Brack* —5N **31**
Milton Clo. *Hort* —6C **6**
Milton Clo. *Sutt* —9B **44**
Milton Ct. *SW18* —8M **13**
Milton Ct. *Dork* —5E **118**
Milton Ct. *Twic* —4E **24**
Milton Ct. *Wokgm* —1A **30**
Miltoncourt La. *Dork* —5E **118** (2H **201**)
Milton Cres. *E Grin* —1M **185**
Milton Dri. *Shep* —3N **37**
Milton Dri. *Wokgm* —1A **30**
Milton Gdns. *Eps* —1D **80** (8M **201**)
Milton Gdns. *Stai* —8A **22**
Milton Gdns. *Wokgm* —2A **30**
Milton Grange. *Ash V* —8E **90**
Milton Ho. *Sutt* —9M **43**
Milton Lodge. *Twic* —1F **24**
Milton Mans. W14 —2K 13 (off Queen's Club Gdns.)
Milton Mt. *Craw* —9H **163**
Milton Mt. Av. *Craw* —1G **183**
Milton Rd. *SW14* —6C **12**
Milton Rd. *SW19* —7A **28**
Milton Rd. *Add* —3J **55**
Milton Rd. *Cat* —8A **84**
Milton Rd. *Craw* —2G **182**
Milton Rd. *Croy* —7A **46**
Milton Rd. *Egh* —6B **20**
Milton Rd. *Hamp* —8A **24**
Milton Rd. *H'ham* —5J **197**
Milton Rd. *Mitc* —8E **28**
Milton Rd. *Sutt* —9M **43**
Milton Rd. *Wall* —3G **63**
Milton Rd. *W on T* —9L **39**
Milton Rd. *Wokgm* —9A **14**
Miltons Cres. *G'ming* —9E **132**
Milton St. *Westc* —6D **118**
Miltons Yd. Witl —6C 152 (off Petworth Rd.)
Milton Way. *Fet* —3C **98**
Milton Way. *W Dray* —1A **0**
Milward Gdns. *Binf* —1H **31**
Mimbridge. —9K 53
Mimosa Clo. *Lind* —4B **168**
Mimosa St. *SW6* —4L **13**
Mina Rd. *SW19* —9M **27**
Minchin Clo. *Lea* —9G **79**
Minchin Grn. *Binf* —6H **15**
Mincing La. *Chob* —4J **53**
Mindelheim Av. *E Grin* —8D **166**
Minden Rd. *Sutt* —8L **43**
Minehead Rd. *SW16* —6K **29**
Minehurst Rd. *Myt* —1D **90**
Minerva Clo. *Stai* —8J **7**
Minerva Rd. *King T* —1M **41** (3M **203**)
Minimax Clo. *Felt* —9H **9**
Mink Ct. *Houn* —5K **9**
Minley. —4C 68
Minley Clo. *Farn* —1K **89**
Minley Ct. *Reig* —2M **121**
Minley Gro. *Fleet* —2C **88**
Minley La. *B'water* —4C **68**
Minley Link Rd. *Farn* —1G **88**
Minley Rd. *B'water & Farn* —6E **68** (in two parts)
Minley Rd. *Fleet & B'water* —7B **68**
Minniedale. *Surb* —4M **41** (8N **203**)
Minorca Av. *Deep* —4J **71**
Minorca Rd. *Deep* —5J **71**
Minorca Rd. *Wey* —1B **56**
Minoru Pl. *Binf* —6J **15**
Minstead Clo. *Brack* —2D **32**
Minstead Dri. *Yat* —1B **68**
Minstead Gdns. *SW15* —1E **26**
Minstead Way. *N Mald* —5D **42**
Minster Av. *Sutt* —8M **43**
Minster Ct. *Camb* —2L **69**
Minster Dri. *Croy* —1B **64**
Minster Gdns. *W Mol* —3N **39**
Minsterley Av. *Shep* —3F **38**
Minster Rd. *G'ming* —9H **133**
Minstrel Gdns. *Surb* —3M **41** (8N **203**)
Mint Gdns. *Dork* —4G **119** (1K **201**)
Mint La. *Lwr K* —7M **101**
Mint Rd. *Bans* —3A **82**
Mint Rd. *Wall* —1F **62**
Mint St. *G'ming* —7G **132**
Mint, The. *G'ming* —7G **132**
Mint Wlk. *Croy* —9N **45** (4C **200**)
Mint Wlk. *Knap* —4H **73**
Mint Wlk. *Warl* —4G **85**
Mirabel Rd. *SW6* —3L **13**
Miranda Wlk. *Bew* —5K **181**
Misbrooks Grn. Rd. *Bear G & Capel* —1L **159**
Missenden Clo. *Felt* —2G **23**
Missenden Gdns. *Mord* —5A **44**
Mission Sq. *Bren* —2L **11**
Mistletoe Clo. *Croy* —7G **46**
Mistletoe Rd. *Yat* —2C **68**
Misty's Fld. *W on T* —7K **39**
Mitcham. —2D 44
Mitcham Garden Village. *Mitc* —4E **44**
Mitcham Ind. Est. *Mitc* —9F **28**
Mitcham La. *SW16* —7G **28**
Mitcham Pk. *Mitc* —3C **44**
Mitcham Rd. *SW17* —6D **28**
Mitcham Rd. *Camb* —0E **60**
Mitcham Rd. *Croy* —5J **45** (1A **200**)
Mitchell Gdns. *Slin* —5M **195**
Mitchell Pk. Farm Cotts. *N'chap* —8G **190**
Mitchell Rd. *Orp* —1N **67**
Mitchells Clo. *Shalf* —9A **114**
Mitchells Rd. *Craw* —3D **182**
Mitchells Row. *Shalf* —1A **134**
Mitchener's La. *Blet* —3A **124**
Mitchley Av. *Purl & S Croy* —9N **63**
Mitchley Gro. *S Croy* —9D **64**
Mitchley Hill. *S Croy* —9C **64**
Mitchley Vw. *S Croy* —9D **64**
Mitford Clo. *Chess* —3J **59**
Mitford Wlk. *Craw* —6M **181**
Mitre Clo. *Shep* —5E **38**
Mitre Clo. *Sutt* —4A **62**
Mitre Clo. *Warf* —7N **15**
Mixbury Gro. *Wey* —3E **56**
Mixnams La. *Cher* —2J **37**
Mizen Clo. *Cobh* —1L **77**
Mizen Way. *Cobh* —2K **77**
Moat Ct. *Asht* —4L **79**
Moated Farm Dri. *Add* —4L **55**
Moat Rd. *E Grin* —8A **166**
Moat Side. *Felt* —5K **23**
Moats La. *S Nut* —1J **143**
Moat, The. *N Mald* —9D **26**
Moat Wlk. *Craw* —2G **183**
Moberley Rd. *SW4* —1H **29**
Modder Pl. *SW15* —7J **13**
Model Cotts. *SW14* —7B **12**
Model Cotts. *Pirb* —8A **72**
Moffat Ct. *SW19* —6M **27**
Moffat Rd. *SW17* —5D **28**
Moffat Rd. *T Hth* —1N **45**
Moffats Clo. *Sand* —7F **48**
Mogador. —6K 101
Mogador Rd. *Lwr K* —6K **101**
Mogden La. *Iswth* —8F **10**
Moir Clo. *S Croy* —5D **64**
Mole Abbey Gdns. *W Mol* —2B **40**
Mole Bus. Pk. *Lea* —8F **78**
Mole Clo. *Craw* —1N **181**
Mole Clo. *Farn* —8J **69**
Mole Ct. *Eps* —1B **60**
Molember Ct. *E Mol* —3E **40**
Molember Rd. *E Mol* —4E **40**
Mole Rd. *Fet* —8D **78**
Mole Rd. *W on T* —2L **57**
Moles Clo. *Wokgm* —3C **30**
Molesey Av. *W Mol* —4N **39**
Molesey Clo. *W on T* —1M **57**
Molesey Dri. *Sutt* —8K **43**
Molesey Pk. Av. *W Mol* —4B **40**
Molesey Pk. Clo. *E Mol* —4C **40**
Molesey Pk. Rd. *W Mol* —4B **40**
Molesey Rd. *W on T* —2L **57**
Molesford Rd. *SW6* —4M **13**
Molesham Clo. *W Mol* —2B **40**
Molesham Way. *W Mol* —2B **40**
Moles Hill. *Oxs* —7D **58**
Moles Mead. *Eden* —1L **147**
Mole St. *Ockl* —3A **158**
Molesworth Rd. *Cobh* —9H **57**
Mole Valley Pl. *Asht* —6K **79**
Molins Ct. Craw —6M 181 (off Brideoake Clo.)
Mollison Dri. *Wall* —4H **63**
Molloy Ct. *Wok* —3C **74**
Molly Huggins Clo. *SW12* —1G **28**
Molly Millars Bri. *Wokgm* —4A **30**
Molly Millars Clo. *Wokgm* —4A **30**
Molly Millars La. *Wokgm* —3A **30**
Molyneux Dri. *SW17* —5F **28**
Molyneux Rd. *G'ming* —4J **133**
Molyneux Rd. *Wey* —2B **56**
Molyneux Rd. *W'sham* —3A **52**
Monahan Av. *Purl* —8K **63**
Monarch Clo. *Craw* —6M **181**
Monarch Clo. *Felt* —1F **22**
Monarch Clo. *W Wick* —1D **66**
Monarch M. *SW16* —6L **29**
Monarch Pde. *Mitc* —1D **44**
Monaveen Gdns. *W Mol* —2B **40**
Moncks Row. SW15 —9L 13 (off W. Hill Rd.)
Mondial Way. *Hayes* —3D **8**
Money Av. *Cat* —9B **84**
Money Rd. *Cat* —9A **84**
Mongers La. *Eps* —6E **60** (in two parts)
Mongomery Ct. *W4* —3B **12**
Monkleigh Rd. *Mord* —2K **43**
Monks All. *Binf* —6G **14**
Monks Av. *W Mol* —4N **39**
Monks Clo. *Asc* —5M **33**
Monks Clo. *Farn* —1A **90**
Monks Ct. *Reig* —3N **121**
Monks Cres. *Add* —2K **55**
Monks Cres. *W on T* —7J **39**
Monksdene Gdns. *Sutt* —9N **43**
Monks Dri. *Asc* —5M **33**
Monksfield. *Craw* —3D **182**
Monks Grn. *Fet* —8C **78**
Monks Gro. *Comp* —8B **112**
Monkshanger. *Farnh* —1K **129**
Monks Hood Clo. *Wokgm* —1D **30**
Monks La. *Eden* —6F **126**
Monks La. *Oke H* —4N **177**
Monks Orchard. —6H 47
Monks Orchard Rd. *Beck* —7K **47**
Monks Path. *Farn* —9B **70**
Monks Pl. *Cat* —9F **84**
Monks Rd. *Bans* —4M **81**
Monks Rd. *Vir W* —3N **35**
Monks Rd. *Wind* —5A **4**
Monks Wlk. *Asc* —5M **33**
Monk's Wlk. *Egh & Cher* —2F **36**
Monk's Wlk. *Farnh* —4L **129**
Monk's Wlk. *Reig* —3N **121**
Monks Way. *Beck* —5K **47**
Monks Way. *Stai* —8M **21**
Monks Way. *W Dray* —2N **7**
Monks Well. *Farnh* —2N **129**
Monkswell La. *Coul* —2N **101**
Monkton La. *Farnh* —7K **109**
Monkton Pk. *Farnh* —8L **109**
Monmouth Av. *King T* —8J **25**
Monmouth Clo. *Mitc* —3J **45**
Monmouth Gro. *W5* —1L **11**
Mono La. *Felt* —3J **23**
Monro Dri. *Guild* —9K **93**
Monroe Dri. *SW14* —8A **12**
Monro Pl. *Eps* —5N **59**
Mons Barracks. *Alder* —8A **90**
Mons Clo. *Alder* —8C **90**
Monsell Gdns. *Stai* —6G **21**
Monson Rd. *Red* —9D **102**
Mons Wlk. *Egh* —6F **20**
Montacute Clo. *Farn* —1B **90**
Montacute Rd. *Mord* —5B **44**
Montacute Rd. *New Ad* —5M **65**
Montague Av. *S Croy* —8B **64**
Montague Clo. *Camb* —1N **69**
Montague Clo. *Light* —6L **51**
Montague Clo. *W on T* —6J **39**
Montague Clo. *Wokgm* —9D **14**
Montague Dri. *Cat* —9N **83**
Montague Rd. *SW19* —8N **27**
Montague Rd. *Croy* —7M **45** (1A **200**)
Montague Rd. *Houn* —6B **10**
Montague Rd. *Rich* —9L **11**
Montagu Gdns. *Wall* —1G **62**
Montagu Rd. *Dat* —4L **5**
Montana Clo. *S Croy* —6A **64**
Montana Gdns. *Sutt* —2A **62**
Montana Rd. *SW17* —4E **28**
Montana Rd. *SW20* —9H **27**
Monteagle La. *Yat* —1A **68**
Montem Rd. *N Mald* —3D **42**
Montford Rd. *Sun* —3H **39**
Montfort Pl. *SW19* —2J **27**
Montfort Ri. *Red* —2D **142**
Montgomerie Dri. *Guild* —7K **93**
Montgomery Av. *Esh* —8F **40**
Montgomery Clo. *Mitc* —3J **45**
Montgomery Clo. *Sand* —7G **49**
Montgomery Ct. *S Croy* —8F **200**
Montgomery of Alamein Ct. *Brack* —9B **16**
Montgomery Path. *Farn* —2L **89**
Montgomery Rd. *Farn* —2L **89**
Montgomery Rd. *Wok* —5A **74**
Montholme Rd. *SW11* —1D **28**
Montolieu Gdns. *SW15* —8G **13**
Montpelier Ct. *Wind* —5F **4**
Montpelier Rd. *Purl* —6M **63**
Montpelier Rd. *Sutt* —1A **62**
Montpelier Row. *Twic* —1J **25**
Montreal Ct. *Alder* —3L **109**
Montrell Rd. *SW2* —2J **29**
Montreux Ct. *Craw* —3N **181**
Montrose Av. *Dat* —3M **5**
Montrose Av. *Twic* —1B **24**
Montrose Clo. *Afrd* —7D **22**
Montrose Clo. *Fleet* —5C **88**
Montrose Clo. *Frim* —4C **70**
Montrose Gdns. *Mitc* —1D **44**
Montrose Gdns. *Oxs* —8D **58**
Montrose Gdns. *Sutt* —8N **43**
Montrose Rd. *Felt* —9E **8**
Montrose Wlk. *Wey* —9C **38**
Montrose Way. *Dat* —4N **5**
Montrouge Cres. *Eps* —3H **81**
Montserrat Rd. *SW15* —7K **13**
Monument Bri. Ind. Est. E. *Wok* —2D **74**
Monument Bri. Ind. Est. W. *Wok* —2C **74**
Monument Grn. *Wey* —9C **38**
Monument Hill. *Wey* —1C **56**
Monument Rd. *Wey* —1C **56**
Monument Rd. *Wok* —1C **74**
Monument Way E. *Wok* —2D **74**
Monument Way W. *Wok* —2C **74**
Moon Hall Rd. *Ewh* —1D **156**
Moons Hill. *Fren* —9G **129**
Moon's La. *D'land* —3F **166**
Moons La. *H'ham* —7L **197**
Moor Clo. *Owl* —6K **49**
Moorcroft Clo. *Craw* —2N **181**
Moorcroft Rd. *SW16* —4J **29**
Moordale Av. *Brack* —9K **15**
Moore Clo. *SW14* —6B **12**
Moore Clo. *Add* —2K **55**
Moore Clo. *C Crook* —8D **88**
Moore Clo. *Mitc* —1F **44**
Moore Clo. *Tong* —4D **110**
Moore Clo. *Wall* —4J **63**
Moore Ct. *H'ham* —7G **196**
Moore Gro. Cres. *Egh* —7B **20**
Moore Pk. Ct. SW6 —3N 13 (off Fulham Rd.)
Moore Pk. Rd. *SW6* —3M **13**
Moore Rd. *SE19* —7N **29**
Moore Rd. *Brkwd* —8M **71**
Moore Rd. *C Crook* —8B **88**
Moores Grn. *Wokgm* —9D **14**
Moores La. *Eton W* —1C **4**
Moore's Rd. *Dork* —4H **119** (1M **201**)
Moore Way. *Sutt* —5M **61**
Moorfield. *Hasl* —3D **188**
Moorfield Cen., The. *Sly I* —8N **93**
Moorfield Rd. *Chess* —2L **59**
Moorfield Rd. *Guild & Sly I* —8N **93**
Moorfields Clo. *Stai* —9G **21**
Moorhayes Dri. *Stai* —2L **37**
Moorhead Rd. *H'ham* —3A **198**
Moorholme. *Wok* —6A **74**
Moorhouse. —5H 107
Moorhouse Bank. —6J 107
Moorhouse Rd. *Oxt & W'ham* —9H **107**
Moorhurst La. *Holmw* —7G **138**
Moorings, The. *Bookh* —3A **98**
Moorings, The. *Felb* —7K **165**
Moorings, The. *Hind* —6C **170**
Moor Junction. (Junct.) —3K **7**
Moorland Clo. *Twic* —1A **24**
Moorland Rd. *M'bowr* —6G **183**
Moorland Rd. *W Dray* —2L **7**
Moorlands Clo. *Fleet* —5C **88**
Moorlands Clo. *Hind* —5C **170**
Moorlands Pl. *Camb* —1M **69**
Moorlands Rd. *Camb* —2M **69**
Moorlands, The. *Wok* —8B **74**
Moor La. *Brack* —2H **31**
Moor La. *Chess* —1L **59**
Moor La. *D'land & M Grn* —9D **146**
Moor La. *Stai* —2F **20**
Moor La. *W Dray* —2L **7**
Moor La. *Wok* —9A **74**
Moormead Dri. *Eps* —2D **60**
Moor Mead Rd. *Twic* —9G **11**
Moormede Cres. *Stai* —5H **21**
Moor Pk. Horl —9F 142 (off Aurum Clo.)
Moor Pk. Cres. *If'd* —4J **181**
Moor Pk. Gdns. *King T* —8D **26**
Moor Pk. Ho. Brack —5K 31 (off St Andrews)
Moor Pk. La. *Farnh* —9K **109** (in two parts)
Moor Pk. Way. *Farnh* —1L **129**
Moor Pl. *E Grin* —8N **165**
Moor Pl. *W'sham* —2M **51**
Moor Rd. *Farn* —6M **69**
Moor Rd. *Frim* —6D **70**
Moor Rd. *Hasl* —3A **188**
Moorside Clo. *Farn* —5M **69**
Moors La. *Elst* —8G **130**
Moorsom Way. *Coul* —4H **83**
Moors, The. *Tong* —5C **110**
Moor, The. —3F 20
Moray Av. *Coll T* —7J **49** (in two parts)
Moray Ct. *S Croy* —8B **200**
Morcote Clo. *Shalf* —1A **134**
Mordaunt Dri. *Wel C* —4G **48**
Morden. —2N 43
Morden Clo. *Brack* —3D **32**
Morden Clo. *Tad* —7J **81**
Morden Ct. *Mord* —3N **43**
Morden Ct. Pde. *Mord* —3N **43**
Morden Gdns. *Mitc* —3B **44**
Morden Hall Rd. *Mord* —2N **43**
Morden Park. —5K 43
Morden Rd. *SW19* —9N **27**
Morden Rd. *Mord & Mitc* —3A **44**
Morden Way. *Sutt* —6M **43**
More Circ. *G'ming* —4H **133**

More Clo.—Neville Rd.

More Clo. W14 —1J 13
More Clo. Purl —7L 63
Morecombe Clo. Craw —5L 181
Morecoombe Clo. King T —8A 26
Moreland Av. Coln —3E 6
Moreland Clo. Coln —3E 6
More La. Esh —9B 40
Morella Clo. Vir W —3N 35
Morella Rd. SW12 —1D 28
More Rd. G'ming —4H 133
Moresby Av. Surb —6A 42
Moretaine Rd. Afrd —4M 21
Moreton Almshouses. W'ham —4M 107
Moreton Av. Iswth —4E 10
Moreton Clo. C Crook —9A 88
Moreton Clo. Churt —9K 149
Moreton Rd. S Croy —2A 64 (8E 200)
Moreton Rd. Wor Pk —8F 42
Morgan Ct. Afrd —6C 22
Morgan Rd. Tedd —7E 24
Morgan's Green. —7C 194
Morgan Wlk. Beck —3L 47
Morie St. SW18 —8N 13
Moring Rd. SW17 —5E 28
Morland Av. Croy —7B 46
Morland Clo. Hamp —6N 23
Morland Clo. Mitc —2C 44
Morland Rd. Alder —5N 109
Morland Rd. Croy —7B 46
Morland Rd. Sutt —2A 62
Morland's Rd. Alder —8B 90
Morley Clo. Yat —1A 68
Morley Ct. Fet —8D 78
Morley Rd. Farnh —2H 129
Morley Rd. S Croy —6C 64
Morley Rd. Sutt —7L 43
Morley Rd. Twic —9K 11
Morningside Rd. Wor Pk —8G 43
Mornington Av. W14 —1L 13
Mornington Clo. Big H —4F 86
Mornington Cres. Houn —4J 9
Mornington Rd. Afrd —6D 22
Mornington Wlk. Rich —5J 25
Morrell Av. H'ham —3M 197
Morris Clo. Croy —4H 47
Morris Gdns. SW18 —1M 27
Morrish Rd. SW2 —1J 29
Morrison Ct. Craw —8N 181
Morris Rd. Farn —5B 90
Morris Rd. Iswth —6F 10
Morris Rd. S Nut —5J 123
Morston Clo. Tad —7G 81
Morten Clo. SW4 —1H 29
Morth Gdns. H'ham —7J 197
Mortimer Clo. SW16 —3H 29
Mortimer Cres. Wor Pk —9C 42
Mortimer Ho. W14 —1K 13 (off N. End Rd.)
Mortimer Rd. Big H —8E 66
Mortimer Rd. Capel —4K 159
Mortimer Rd. Mitc —9D 28
Mortlake. —6C 12
Mortlake Clo. Croy —9J 45
Mortlake Crematorium. Rich —5B 12
Mortlake Dri. Mitc —9C 28
Mortlake High St. SW14 —6C 12
Mortlake Rd. Rich —3N 11
Mortlake Ter. Rich —3N 11 (off Mortlake Rd.)
Morton. Tad —8J 81
Morton Clo. Craw —9N 181
Morton Clo. Frim —7D 70
Morton Clo. Wall —4K 63
Morton Clo. Wok —2M 73
Morton Gdns. Wall —2G 62
Morton M. SW5 —1N 13
Morton Rd. E Grin —2A 186
Morton Rd. Mord —4B 44
Morton Rd. Wok —2M 73
Morval Clo. Farn —1K 89
Morven Rd. SW17 —4D 28
Moselle Clo. Farn —9J 69
Moselle Rd. Big H —5G 87
Mosford Clo. Horl —6D 142
Mospey Cres. Eps —2E 80
Moss End. —3N 15
Mosses Wood. —9D 138
Mossfield. Cobh —9H 57
Moss Gdns. Felt —3H 23
Moss Gdns. S Croy —4G 64
Moss La. G'ming —7G 133
Mosslea Rd. Whyt —3C 84
Mossville Gdns. Mord —2L 43
Moston Clo. Hayes —1G 8
Mostyn Ho. Brack —8N 15 (off Merryhill Rd.)
Mostyn Rd. SW19 —9L 27
Mostyn Ter. Red —4E 122
Moth Clo. Wall —4J 63
Motspur Park. —5F 42
Motspur Pk. N Mald —5E 42
Motts Hill La. Tad —1F 100
Mouchotte Clo. Big H —8D 66
Moulsham Copse La. Yat —8A 48
Moulsham Grn. Yat —8A 48
Moulsham La. Yat —8A 48
Moulton Av. Houn —5M 9
Mt. Angelus Rd. SW15 —1E 26
Mt. Ararat Rd. Rich —8L 11
Mount Arlington. Brom —1N 47 (off Park Hill Rd.)
Mount Av. Cat —2N 103
Mountbatten Clo. Craw —7A 182
Mountbatten Ct. Alder —2M 109 (off Birchett Rd.)
Mountbatten Gdns. Beck —3H 47
Mountbatten M. SW18 —1A 28
Mountbatten Ri. Sand —6E 48
Mountbatten Sq. Wind —4F 4
Mount Clo. Cars —5E 62
Mount Clo. Craw —2H 183
Mount Clo. Ewh —5F 156
Mount Clo. Fet —1E 98
Mount Clo. Kenl —3A 84
Mount Clo. Wok —8M 73
Mount Clo., The. Vir W —5N 35
Mountcombe Clo. Surb —6L 41
Mount Cotts. If'd —2H 181
Mount Ct. SW15 —6K 13
Mount Ct. Guild —5M 113 (6B 202)
Mount Ct. W Wick —8N 47
Mount Dri., The. Reig —1B 122
Mountearl Gdns. SW16 —4K 29
Mt. Ephraim La. SW16 —4H 29
Mt. Ephraim Rd. SW16 —4H 29
Mt. Felix. W on T —7G 38
Mount Hermon. —6N 73
Mt. Hermon Clo. Wok —6N 73
Mt. Hermon Rd. Wok —6N 73
Mount La. Brack —2A 32
Mount La. Turn H —5D 184
Mount Lee. Egh —6B 20
Mount M. Hamp —9B 24
Mt. Nod Rd. SW16 —4K 29
Mount Pk. Cars —4E 62
Mt. Park Av. S Croy —5M 63
Mount Pl. Guild —5M 113 (6B 202)
Mount Pleasant. SE27 —5N 29
Mount Pleasant. Big H —4F 86
Mount Pleasant. Brack —2A 32 (in two parts)
Mount Pleasant. Eff —6M 97
Mount Pleasant. Eps —6E 60
Mount Pleasant. Farnh —2F 128
Mount Pleasant. Guild —5M 113 (7B 202)
Mount Pleasant. Sand —6F 48
Mount Pleasant. W Hor —7C 96
Mount Pleasant. Wey —9B 38
Mount Pleasant. Wokgm —2A 30
Mt. Pleasant Clo. Light —6L 51
Mt. Pleasant Rd. Alder —2A 110
Mt. Pleasant Rd. Cat —1D 104
Mt. Pleasant Rd. Lind —4L 168
Mt. Pleasant Rd. Ling —7M 145
Mt. Pleasant Rd. N Mald —2B 42
Mount Ri. Red —5B 122
Mount Rd. SW19 —3M 27
Mount Rd. Chess —2M 59
Mount Rd. Chob —8L 53
Mount Rd. Cranl —8N 155
Mount Rd. Felt —4M 23
Mount Rd. Mitc —1B 44
Mount Rd. N Mald —2C 42
Mount Rd. Wok —8L 73
Mountsfield Clo. Stai —9J 7
Mounts Hill. Wink —3N 17
Mountside. Guild —5L 113 (7A 202)
Mt. Side Pl. Wok —5B 74
Mount St. Dork —5G 118 (2J 201)
Mount, The. Coul —2E 82
Mount, The. Cranl —8N 155
Mount, The. Craw —1G 180
Mount, The. Eps —6E 60
Mount, The. Esh —3A 58
Mount, The. Ewh —4F 156
Mount, The. Fet —1E 98
Mount, The. Fleet —3B 88
Mount, The. G'wood —7K 171
Mount, The. Guild —5M 113 (8A 202)
Mount, The. Head —3F 168
Mount, The. Knap —6F 72
Mount, The. N Mald —2E 42
Mount, The. S Croy —8C 200
Mount, The. Tad —4L 101
Mount, The. Vir W —5N 35
Mount, The. Warl —6D 84
Mount, The. Wey —8F 38
Mount, The. Wok —5N 73 (off Elm Rd.)
Mount, The. Wok —6K 73 (off St John's Hill Rd.)
Mount, The. Wor Pk —1G 61
Mount Vw. Alder —3M 109
Mount Vw. S'hall —1L 9
Mountview Clo. Red —5C 122
Mountview Dri. Red —5C 122
Mount Vw. Rd. Clay —4H 59
Mount Vs. SE27 —4M 29
Mount Way. Cars —5E 62
Mount Wood. W Mol —2B 40
Mountwood Clo. S Croy —6E 64
Moushill La. Milf —2B 152
Mowat Ct. Wor Pk —8E 42 (off Avenue, The)
Mowatt Rd. Gray —7B 170
Mowbray Av. Byfl —9N 55
Mowbray Cres. Egh —6C 20
Mowbray Dri. Craw —5L 181
Mowbray Gdns. Dork —3H 119
Mowbray Rd. Rich —4J 25
Mower Clo. Wokgm —1E 30
Mower Pl. Cranl —6N 155
Mowshurst. —8M 127
Moylan Rd. W6 —2K 13
Moyne Ct. Wok —5J 73
Moyne Rd. Craw —7A 182
Moys Clo. Croy —5J 45
Moyser Rd. SW16 —6F 28
Muchelney Rd. Mord —5A 44
Muckhatch La. Egh —2D 36
Muggeridge Clo. S Croy —2A 64 (8E 200)
Muggeridges Hill. Rusp —1L 179
Mugswell. —3N 101
Muirdown Av. SW14 —7C 12
Muir Dri. SW18 —1C 28
Muirfield Clo. If'd —4J 181
Muirfield Ho. Brack —5K 31 (off St Andrews)
Muirfield Rd. Wok —5K 73
Mulberries, The. Farnh —8L 109
Mulberry Av. Stai —2N 21
Mulberry Av. Wind —6J 5
Mulberry Bus. Pk. Wokgm —4A 30
Mulberry Clo. SW16 —5G 28
Mulberry Clo. Ash V —9E 90
Mulberry Clo. Crowt —3H 49
Mulberry Clo. H'ham —3J 197
Mulberry Clo. Owl —7J 49
Mulberry Clo. Wey —9C 38
Mulberry Clo. Wok —1A 74
Mulberry Ct. Brack —4C 32
Mulberry Ct. Guild —1F 114
Mulberry Ct. Surb —6K 41
Mulberry Ct. Twic —4F 24
Mulberry Ct. Wokgm —2B 30
Mulberry Cres. Bren —3H 11
Mulberry Dri. Slou —1A 6
Mulberry Ho. Brack —8N 15
Mulberry Ho. Short —1N 47
Mulberry La. Croy —7C 46
Mulberry M. Wall —3G 62
Mulberry Pl. W6 —1F 12
Mulberry Rd. Craw —9N 161
Mulberry Trees. Shep —6E 38
Mulgrave Ct. Sutt —3N 61 (off Mulgrave Rd.)
Mulgrave Rd. SW6 —2L 13
Mulgrave Rd. Croy —9A 46 (5D 200)
Mulgrave Rd. Frim —4D 70
Mulgrave Rd. Sutt —4L 61
Mulgrave Way. Knap —5H 73
Mulholland Clo. Mitc —1F 44
Mullards Clo. Mitc —7D 44
Mullein Wlk. Craw —7M 181
Mullens Rd. Egh —6D 20
Muller Rd. SW4 —1H 29
Mullins Path. SW14 —6C 12
Mulroy Dri. Camb —9E 50
Multon Rd. SW18 —1B 28
Muncaster Clo. Afrd —5B 22
Muncaster Rd. Afrd —6C 22
Munday Ct. Binf —8K 15
Munday's Boro. P'ham —8L 111
Munday's Boro Rd. P'ham —8L 111
Munden St. W14 —1K 13
Mund St. W14 —1L 13
Mundy Ct. Eton —2G 4
Munnings Dri. Coll T —9J 49
Munnings Gdns. Iswth —8D 10
Munslow Gdns. Sutt —1B 62
Munstead Heath Rd. G'ming & Brmly —1K 153
Munstead Pk. G'ming —8M 133
Munstead Vw. Guild —7L 113
Munstead Vw. Rd. Brmly —6N 133
Munster Av. Houn —8M 9
Munster Ct. SW6 —5L 13
Munster Ct. Tedd —7J 25
Munster M. SW6 —3K 13
Munster Rd. SW6 —3K 13
Munster Rd. Tedd —7H 25
Murdoch Clo. Stai —6J 21
Murdoch Rd. Wokgm —3B 30
Murfett Clo. SW19 —3K 27
Murray Av. Houn —8B 10
Murray Ct. Asc —5N 33
Murray Ct. Craw —8M 181
Murray Ct. H'ham —4A 198
Murray Ct. Twic —3D 24
Murray Grn. Wok —1E 74
Murray Ho. Ott —3E 54
Murray Rd. SW19 —7J 27
Murray Rd. W5 —1J 11
Murray Rd. Farn —2L 89
Murray Rd. Ott —3E 54
Murray Rd. Rich —3H 25
Murray Rd. Wokgm —2A 30
Murray's La. W Byf —1M 75
Murray Ter. W5 —1K 11
Murrellhill La. Binf —8H 15
Murrell Rd. As —1E 110
Murrells La. Camb —3N 69
Murrell's Wlk. Bookh —1A 98
Murreys Ct. Asht —5K 79
Murreys, The. Asht —5J 79
Murtmead La. P'ham —9L 111
Musard Rd. W6 —2K 13
Muscal. W6 —2K 13 (off Field Rd.)
Muschamp Rd. Cars —8C 44
Museum Hill. Hasl —2H 189
Mus. of Eton Life. —2G 4
Mus. of Fulham Palace. —5K 13
Mus. of Richmond. —8K 11 (off Whittaker Av.)
Mus. of Rugby, The. —9E 10
Musgrave Av. E Grin —2A 186
Musgrave Cres. SW6 —3M 13
Musgrave Rd. Iswth —4F 10
Mushroom Castle. Wink R —7F 16
Musquash Way. Houn —5K 9
Mustard Mill Rd. Stai —5H 21
Mustow Pl. SW6 —5L 13
Mutton Hill. Brack —9H 15
Mutton Hill. D'land —3C 166
Mutton Oaks. Binf —1J 31
Muybridge Rd. N Mald —1B 42
Myers Way. Frim —4H 71
Mylne Clo. W6 —1F 12
Mylne Sq. Wokgm —2C 30
Mylor Clo. Wok —1A 74
Mynn's Clo. Eps —1A 80
Mynthurst. —4G 141
Mynthurst. Leigh —4G 141
Myrke. —1J 5
Myrke, The. Dat —1J 5
Myrna Clo. SW19 —8C 28
Myrtle Av. Felt —8F 8
Myrtle Clo. Coln —4G 6
Myrtle Clo. Light —7M 51
Myrtle Dri. B'water —1J 69
Myrtle Gro. N Mald —1B 42
Myrtle Rd. Croy —9K 47
Myrtle Rd. Dork —4G 119 (1K 201)
Myrtle Rd. Hamp H —7C 24
Myrtle Rd. Houn —5C 10
Myrtle Rd. Sutt —2A 62
Mytchett. —1D 90
Mytchett Farm Cvn. Pk. Myt —3D 90
Mytchett Heath. Myt —3E 90
Mytchett Lake Rd. Myt —4E 90
Mytchett Pl. Rd. Myt & Ash V —2E 90
Mytchett Rd. Myt —1D 90
Myton Rd. SE21 —4N 29

Naafi Roundabout. Alder —2N 109
Nadine Ct. Wall —5G 62
Nailsworth Cres. Red —7H 103
Nairn Clo. Frim —4C 70
Nalderswood. —4H 141
Naldrett Clo. H'ham —4M 197
Naldretts La. Rud —3E 194
Nallhead Rd. Felt —6K 23
Namba Roy Clo. SW16 —5K 29
Namton Dri. T Hth —3K 45
Napier Av. SW6 —6L 13
Napier Clo. Alder —6C 90
Napier Clo. Crowt —2H 49
Napier Ct. SW6 —6L 13 (off Ranelagh Gdns.)
Napier Ct. Cat —9B 84
Napier Dri. Camb —8E 50
Napier Gdns. Guild —2D 114
Napier La. Ash V —9E 90
Napier Rd. SE25 —3E 46
Napier Rd. Afrd —8E 22
Napier Rd. Crowt —3H 49
Napier Rd. Iswth —7G 10
Napier Rd. H'row A —4M 7
Napier Rd. S Croy —4A 64
Napier Wlk. Afrd —8E 22
Napier Way. Craw —9E 162
Napoleon Av. Farn —8N 69
Napoleon Rd. Twic —1H 25
Napper Clo. Asc —1G 33
Napper Pl. Cranl —9N 155
Nappers Wood. Fern —9E 188
Narborough St. SW6 —5N 13
Narrow La. Warl —6E 84
Naseby. Brack —7N 31
Naseby Clo. Iswth —4E 10
Naseby Ct. W on T —8K 39
Nash. —3C 66
Nash Clo. Farn —1L 89
Nash Clo. Sutt —9B 44
Nash Dri. Red —1D 122
Nash Gdns. Asc —1J 33
Nash Gdns. Red —1D 122
Nashlands Cotts. Hand —6N 199
Nash La. Kes —4C 66
Nash Pk. Binf —7G 15
Nash Rd. Craw —6C 182
Nash Rd. Slou —1B 6
Nassau Rd. SW13 —4E 12
Nasturtium Dri. Bisl —2D 72
Natalie Clo. Felt —1E 22
Natalie M. Twic —4D 24
Natal Rd. SW16 —7H 29
Natal Rd. T Hth —2A 46
Neale Clo. E Grin —7L 165
Neale Ho. E Grin —8A 166
Neath Gdns. Mord —5A 44
Neb La. Oxt —9M 105
Needham Clo. Wind —4B 4
Needles Bank. God —9E 104 (in two parts)
Needles Clo. H'ham —7H 197
Neil Clo. Afrd —6D 22
Neil Wates Cres. SW2 —2L 29
Nella Rd. W6 —2J 13
Nell Ball. Plais —6A 192
Nell Gwynne Av. Shep —5E 38
Nell Gwynne Clo. Asc —3A 34
Nell Gwynne Clo. Eps —7N 59
Nello James Gdns. SE27 —5N 29
Nelson Clo. Alder —3A 110
Nelson Clo. Big H —4G 86
Nelson Clo. Brack —9C 16
Nelson Clo. Croy —7M 45 (1A 200)
Nelson Clo. Farnh —4J 109
Nelson Clo. Felt —2G 23
Nelson Clo. M'bowr —4G 183
Nelson Clo. W on T —7J 39
Nelson Ct. Cher —7J 37
Nelson Gdns. Guild —2C 114
Nelson Gdns. Houn —9A 10
Nelson Gro. Rd. SW19 —9A 28
Nelson Ind. Est. SW19 —9N 27
Nelson Rd. SW19 —8N 27
Nelson Rd. Afrd —6N 21
Nelson Rd. Cat —1A 104
Nelson Rd. Farnh —4J 109
Nelson Rd. H'ham —5H 197
Nelson Rd. Houn —9A 10
Nelson Rd. H'row A —4A 8
Nelson Rd. N Mald —4C 42
Nelson Rd. Wind —6C 4
Nelson Rd. M. SW19 —8N 27
Nelson's La. Hurst —4A 14
Nelson St. Alder —2M 109
Nelson Wlk. Eps —5N 59
Nelson Way. Camb —2L 69
Nene Gdns. Felt —3N 23
Nene Rd. H'row A —4C 8
Nene Rd. Roundabout. H'row A —4C 8
Nepean St. SW15 —9F 12
Neptune Clo. Bew —5K 181
Neptune Rd. Bord —7A 168
Neptune Rd. H'row A —4E 8
Nero Ct. Bren —3K 11
Nesbit Ct. Craw —6K 181
Netheravon Rd. W4 —1E 12
Netheravon Rd. S. W4 —1E 12
Netherby Pk. Wey —2F 56
Nethercote Av. Wok —4J 73
Netherfield Rd. SW17 —4E 28
Netherlands, The. Coul —6G 83
Netherleigh Pk. S Nut —6J 123
Nether Mt. Guild —5L 113
Nethern Ct. Rd. Wold —1K 105
Netherne Dri. Coul —8F 82
Netherne La. Coul —1G 102 (in two parts)
Netherne-on-the-Hill. —9G 83
Netherton. Brack —3M 31
Netherton Gro. SW10 —2N 13
Netherton Rd. Twic —8G 11
Nether Vell-Mead. C Crook —9A 88
Netherwood. Craw —5N 181
Netley Clo. Cheam —2J 61
Netley Clo. Craw —9A 182
Netley Clo. Gom —7D 116
Netley Clo. New Ad —4M 65
Netley Dri. W on T —6N 39
Netley Gdns. Mord —6A 44
Netley Pk. —6D 116
Netley Rd. Bren —2L 11
Netley Rd. Mord —6A 44
Netley St. Farn —5N 89
Nettlecombe. Brack —5B 32
Nettlecombe Clo. Sutt —5N 61
Nettlefold Pl. SE27 —4M 29
Nettles Ter. Guild —3N 113 (3C 202)
Nettleton Rd. H'row A —4C 8
Nettlewood Rd. SW16 —8H 29
Neuman Cres. Brack —5M 31
Nevada Clo. Farn —2J 89
Nevada Clo. N Mald —3B 42
Nevelle Clo. Binf —9J 15
Nevern Mans. SW5 —1M 13 (off Warwick Rd.)
Nevern Pl. SW5 —1M 13
Nevern Rd. SW5 —1M 13
Nevern Sq. SW5 —1M 13
Nevile Clo. Craw —6M 181
Neville Av. N Mald —9C 26
Neville Clo. Bans —1N 81
Neville Clo. Esh —3N 57
Neville Clo. Houn —5B 10
Neville Duke Rd. Farn —6L 69
Neville Gill Clo. SW18 —9M 13
Neville Ho. Yd. King T —1L 41 (3K 203)
Neville Rd. Croy —6A 46
Neville Rd. King T —1N 41

254 A-Z Surrey

Neville Rd.—Northfield Ct.

Neville Rd. Rich —4J 25
Neville Wlk. Cars —6C 44
Nevis Rd. SW17 —3F 28
New Addington. —6M 65
Newall Rd. H'row A —4D 8
Newark Clo. Guild —7D 94
Newark Clo. Rip —8J 75
Newark Cotts. Rip —8J 75
Newark Ct. W on T —7K 39
Newark La. Wok —8H 75
Newark Rd. Craw —1D 182
Newark Rd. S Croy —3A 64
Newark Rd. W'sham —1M 51
New Ashgate Gallery. —1G 129
New Barn Clo. Wall —3K 63
New Barn La. Newd —9B 140
New Barn La. Ockl —7A 158
Newbarn La. W'ham —5L 87
New Barn La. Whyt —3B 84
New Barns Av. Mitc —3H 45
(in two parts)
New Battlebridge La. Red —8F 102
Newberry Cres. Wind —5A 4
New Berry La. W on T —2L 57
Newbolt Av. Sutt —2H 61
Newborough Grn. N Mald —3C 42
Newbridge Clo. Broad H —5C 196
New Bridge Cotts. Cranl —7K 155
(off Elmbridge Rd.)
Newbridge Ct. Cranl —7K 155
New B'way. Hamp H —6D 24
Newbury Gdns. Eps —1E 60
Newbury Rd. Craw —3H 183
Newbury Rd. H'row A —4A 8
New Causeway. Reig —6N 121
Newchapel. —1H 165
Newchapel Rd. Ling —1J 165
New Chapel Sq. Felt —2J 23
New Clo. SW19 —2A 44
New Clo. Felt —6M 23
New Colebrooke Ct. Cars —4E 62
(off Stanley Rd.)
Newcombe Gdns. SW16 —5J 29
Newcome Pl. Alder —5B 110
Newcome Rd. Farnh —6K 109
New Coppice. Wok —6H 73
New Cotts. Pirb —9A 72
New Cotts. Turn H —5D 184
New Ct. Add —9L 37
New Cross Rd. Guild —1K 113
New Dawn Clo. Farn —2J 89
Newdigate. —1A 160
Newdigate Rd. Bear G —9K 139
Newdigate Rd. Leigh —1D 140
Newdigate Rd. Rusp —1B 180
Newell Green. —6B 10
Newell Grn. Warf —6A 16
New England Hill. W End —8A 52
Newenham Rd. Bookh —4A 98
New Farthingdale. D'land —2C 166
Newfield Av. Farn —8K 69
Newfield Clo. Hamp —9A 24
Newfield Rd. Ash V —7E 90
New Forest Ride. Brack —6C 32
Newfoundland Rd. Deep —6H 71
Newgate. Croy —7N 45
Newgate Clo. Felt —3M 23
Newhache. D'land —1C 166
Newhall Gdns. W on T —8K 39
Newhaven Cres. Afrd —6E 22
Newhaven Rd. SE25 —4A 46
New Haw. —4L 55
New Haw Rd. Add —2L 55
New Heston Rd. Houn —3N 9
New Horizons Ct. Bren —2J 11
Newhouse Bus. Cen. Fay —1B 198
Newhouse Clo. N Mald —6D 42
Newhouse Cotts. Newd —6B 160
New Ho. Farm La. Wood S —2F 112
New Ho. La. Red —2H 143
Newhouse Wlk. Mord —6A 44
Newhurst Gdns. Warf —6B 16
New Inn La. Guild —8D 94
New Kelvin Av. Tedd —7E 24
New Kings Rd. SW6 —5L 13
Newlands. Fleet —7B 88
Newlands Av. Th Dit —7E 40
Newlands Av. Wok —8B 74
Newlands Clo. Horl —6D 142
Newlands Clo. S'hall —1M 9
Newlands Clo. W on T —1M 57
Newlands Clo. Yat —1C 68
Newlands Corner. —5J 115
Newlands Corner Countryside Cen. —5J 115
Newlands Ct. Add —2K 55
(off Addlestone Pk.)
Newlands Ct. Cat —8N 83
(off Coulsdon Rd.)
Newlands Cres. E Grin —8N 165
Newlands Cres. Guild —5B 114
Newlands Dri. Ash V —9F 90
Newlands Dri. Coln —6G 7
Newlands Est. Witl —5C 152
Newlands Pk. Copt —7B 164
Newlands Pl. F Row —6H 187
Newlands Rd. SW16 —1J 45
Newlands Rd. Camb —5N 69
Newlands Rd. Craw —4A 182
Newlands Rd. H'ham —4J 197
Newlands, The. Wall —4G 63
Newlands Way. Chess —2J 59
Newlands Wood. Croy —5J 65
New La. Wok —9A 74
New Lodge Dri. Oxt —6B 106
New Malden. —3D 42
Newman Clo. M'bowr —5G 182
Newman Rd. Croy —7K 45
Newman Rd. Ind. Est. Croy —6K 45
Newmans Ct. Farnh —5F 108
Newmans La. Surb —5K 41
Newmans Pl. Asc —6E 34
Newmarket Rd. Craw —6E 182
New Mdw. Asc —9H 17
New Mile Rd. Asc —1M 33
New Mill Cotts. Hasl —2B 188
Newminster Rd. Mord —5A 44
New Moorhead Dri. H'ham —2B 198
Newnes Path. SW15 —7G 12
Newnet Clo. Cars —7D 44
Newnham Clo. T Hth —1N 45
New N. Rd. Reig —6L 121
New Pde. Afrd —5A 22
New Pk. Pde. SW2 —1J 29
(off New Pk. Rd.)
New Pk. Rd. SW2 —2H 29
New Pk. Rd. Afrd —6D 22
New Pk. Rd. Cranl —7N 155
New Pl. Croy —3K 65
New Pl. Gdns. Ling —7A 146
New Pond Rd. Comp & G'ming —1G 132
New Poplars Ct. As —3E 110
Newport Dri. Warf —7N 15
Newport Rd. SW13 —4F 12
Newport Rd. Alder —3A 110
Newport Rd. H'row A —4B 8
New Rd. Alb —8M 115
New Rd. Asc —8J 17
New Rd. Bag & W'sham —4K 51
New Rd. Bedf —9E 8
New Rd. B'water —2K 69
New Rd. Brack —1B 32
New Rd. Bren —2K 11
New Rd. Chil —1D 134
New Rd. C Crook —7C 88
New Rd. Crowt —2H 49
New Rd. Dat —4N 5
New Rd. Dork —6K 119
New Rd. E Clan —9N 95
New Rd. Esh —9C 40
New Rd. Felt —2J 23
New Rd. F Grn —4M 157
New Rd. Gom —0D 116
New Rd. Hanw —6M 23
New Rd. Hasl —3D 188
New Rd. Hayes —3D 8
New Rd. Houn —7B 10
New Rd. Hyde —4H 153
New Rd. King T —8N 25
New Rd. Limp —8D 106
New Rd. Milf —1B 152
New Rd. Mitc —7D 44
New Rd. Oxs —7F 58
New Rd. Rich —5J 25
New Rd. Sand —7F 48
New Rd. Shep —2B 38
New Rd. Small —8M 143
New Rd. Stai —6E 20
New Rd. Tad —1H 101
New Rd. Tand —5K 125
New Rd. Tong —6D 110
New Rd. W Mol —3A 40
New Rd. Wey —2D 56
New Rd. Won —3D 134
New Rd. Wmly —1C 172
New Rd. Hill. Kes —5G 67
Newry Rd. Twic —8G 11
Newsham Rd. Wok —4J 73
New Sq. Felt —2D 22
Newstead Clo. G'ming —5G 132
Newstead Ri. Cat —4E 104
Newstead Wlk. Cars —6A 44
Newstead Way. SW19 —5J 27
New St. Craw —2E 182
New St. H'ham —7K 197
New St. Stai —5J 21
New St. W'ham —5L 107
Newton Av. E Grin —3B 186
Newton Ct. Old Win —9K 5
Newton La. Old Win —9L 5
Newton Mans. W14 —2K 13
(off Queen's Club Gdns.)
Newton Rd. SW19 —8K 27
Newton Rd. Craw —8D 162
Newton Rd. Farn —0D 70
Newton Rd. Iswth —5F 10
Newton Rd. H'row A —4N 7
Newton Rd. Purl —8G 63
Newtonside Orchard. Old Win —9K 5
Newton's Yd. SW18 —8M 13
Newton Way. Tong —5C 110
Newton Wood Rd. Asht —3M 79
New Town. —7K 197
New Town. Copt —7M 163
Newtown Rd. Sand —7G 48
New Way. G'ming —7E 132
New Wickham La. Egh —8C 20
New Windsor. —6G 4
New Wokingham Rd. Wokgm & C'then —9F 30
New Zealand Av. W on T —7G 38
Nexus Pk. Ash V —5D 90
Nicholas Ct. W4 —2D 12
(off Corney Reach Way)
Nicholas Gdns. Wok —3G 75
Nicholas Rd. Croy —1J 63
Nicholes Rd. Houn —7A 10
Nicholls. Wind —6A 4
Nicholls Wlk. Wind —6A 4
Nichols Clo. Chess —3J 59
Nicholsfield. Loxw —4H 193
Nicholson M. Egh —6C 20
(off Nicholson Wlk.)
Nicholson M. King T —3L 41 (7L 203)
Nicholson Rd. Croy —7C 46
Nicholson Wlk. Egh —6C 20
Nicola Clo. S Croy —3N 63
Nicol Clo. Twic —9H 11
Nicosia Rd. SW18 —1C 28
Nicotiana Ct. C Crook —9A 88
(off Annettes Cft.)
Nigel Fisher Way. Chess —4J 59
Nigel Playfair Av. W6 —1G 12
Nightingale Av. W Hor —2E 96
Nightingale Clo. W4 —2B 12
Nightingale Clo. Big H —2E 86
Nightingale Clo. Cars —8E 44
Nightingale Clo. Cobh —7L 57
Nightingale Clo. Craw —1A 182
Nightingale Clo. E Grin —2N 185
Nightingale Clo. Eps —0N 59
Nightingale Clo. Farn —8H 69
Nightingale Ct. SW6 —4N 13
(off Maltings Pl.)
Nightingale Ct. Red —2E 122
(off St Anne's Mt.)
Nightingale Ct. Short —1N 47
Nightingale Ct. Wok —5H 73
Nightingale Cres. Brack —4A 32
Nightingale Cres. W Hor —3D 96
Nightingale Dri. Eps —3A 60
Nightingale Dri. Myt —2E 90
Nightingale Gdns. Sand —7G 49
Nightingale Ho. Eps —8D 60 (5M 201)
Nightingale Ho. Ott —3F 54
Nightingale Ind. Est. H'ham —5K 197
Nightingale La. SW12 & SW4 —1D 28
Nightingale La. Rich —1L 25
Nightingale La. Turn H —4F 184
Nightingale M. King T —5J 203
Nightingale Rd. As —1G 111
Nightingale Rd. Bord —7A 168
Nightingale Rd. Cars —9D 44
Nightingale Rd. E Hor —3G 96
Nightingale Rd. Esh —2N 57
Nightingale Rd. G'ming —6H 133
Nightingale Rd. Guild —3N 113 (2D 202)
Nightingale Rd. Hamp —6A 24
Nightingale Rd. H'ham —5K 197
Nightingale Rd. S Croy —7G 64
Nightingale Rd. W on T —6K 39
Nightingale Rd. W Mol —4B 40
Nightingales. Cranl —9N 155
Nightingales Clo. H'ham —6M 197
Nightingale Shott. Egh —7B 20
Nightingale Sq. SW12 —1E 28
Nightingales, The. Stai —1A 22
Nightingale Wlk. Wind —6F 4
Nightingale Way. Blet —3B 124
Nightjar Clo. Ews —4C 108
Nikols Wlk. SW18 —7N 13
Nimbus Rd. Eps —6C 60
Nimrod Ct. Craw —9H 163
(off Wakehams Grn. Dri.)
Nimrod Rd. SW16 —7F 28
Nineacres Way. Coul —3J 83
Nine Elms Clo. Felt —2G 23
Ninehams Clo. Cat —7A 84
Ninehams Gdns. Cat —7A 84
Ninehams Rd. Cat —8A 84
Ninehams Rd. Tats —8E 86
Nine Mile Ride. Asc —6J 33
Nine Mile Ride. Crowt & Brack (in two parts) —7L 31
Nine Mile Ride. Wok —1A 48
Nineteenth Rd. Mitc —3J 45
Ninfield Ct. Craw —7L 181
Ninhams Wood. Orp —1J 67
Niton Rd. Rich —6N 11
Niton St. SW6 —3J 13
Niven Clo. M'bowr —4H 183
Niven Ct. S'hill —3A 34
Noahs Ct. Turn H —5D 184
Nobel Dri. Hayes —4E 8
Noble Corner. Houn —4A 10
Noble Ct. Mitc —1B 44
Nobles Way. Egh —7A 20
Noel Ct. Houn —6N 9
Noke Dri. Red —2E 122
Nonsuch Ct. Av. Eps —6G 60
Nonsuch Pl. Sutt —4J 61
Nonsuch Trad. Est. Eps —7D 60
Nonsuch Wlk. Sutt —6H 61
(in two parts)
Nook, The. Sand —7F 48
Noons Corner Rd. Ab C —3N 137
Norbiton. —1N 41
Norbiton Av. King T —9N 25
Norbiton Comn. Rd. King T —2A 42
Norbiton Hall. King T —1M 41 (3N 203)
Norbury. —1K 45
Norbury Av. SW16 —9K 29
Norbury Av. Houn —7D 10
Norbury Clo. SW16 —9L 29
Norbury Ct. Rd. SW16 —2J 45
Norbury Cres. SW16 —9K 29
Norbury Cross. SW16 —2J 45
Norbury Hill. SW16 —8L 29
Norbury Park. —4H 99
Norbury Pk. —5F 98
Norbury Ri. SW16 —2J 45
Norbury Rd. Reig —3L 121
Norbury Rd. T Hth —1N 45
Norbury Trad. Est. SW16 —1K 45
Norbury Way. Bookh —3C 98
Norcutt Rd. Twic —2E 24
Norfolk Av. S Croy —6C 64
Norfolk Chase. Warf —8D 16
Norfolk Clo. Craw —7K 181
Norfolk Clo. Horl —9E 142
Norfolk Clo. Twic —9H 11
Norfolk Ct. H'ham —3A 198
Norfolk Ct. N Holm —9K 119
Norfolk Farm Clo. Wok —3F 74
Norfolk Farm Rd. Wok —2F 74
Norfolk Gdns. Houn —8N 9
Norfolk Ho. Rd. SW16 —4H 29
Norfolk La. Mid H —2H 139
Norfolk Rd. SW19 —8C 28
Norfolk Rd. Clay —2E 58
Norfolk Rd. Dork —5G 119 (3K 201)
Norfolk Rd. Felt —2K 23
Norfolk Rd. Holmw —5J 139
Norfolk Rd. H'ham —6K 197
Norfolk Rd. T Hth —2N 45
Norfolk Ter. W6 —1K 13
Norfolk Ter. H'ham —6K 197
Norgrove St. SW12 —1E 28
Norheads La. Warl —8C 86
(in two parts)
Norhyrst Av. SE25 —2C 46
Nork. —2J 81
Nork Gdns. Bans —1K 81
Nork Ri. Bans —3J 81
Nork Way. Bans —3H 81
Norlands La. Egh —2G 36
Norley La. Sham G —8D 134
Norley Va. SW15 —2F 26
Norman Av. Eps —8F 60
Norman Av. Felt —3M 23
Norman Av. S Croy —6N 63
Norman Av. Twic —1J 25
Normanby Clo. SW15 —8L 13
Norman Clo. Bord —6A 168
Norman Clo. Tad —6G 81
Norman Colyer Ct. Eps —6C 60
Norman Ct. Eden —1K 147
Norman Ct. Farnh —2H 129
Norman Cres. Houn —3L 9
Normand Gdns. W14 —2K 13
(off Greyhound Rd.)
Normand M. W14 —2K 13
Normand Rd. W14 —2L 13
Normandy. —9M 91
Normandy. H'ham —7J 197
Normandy Barracks. Alder —9M 89
Normandy Clo. Deep —6J 71
Normandy Clo. E Grin —1B 186
Normandy Clo. M'bowr —5F 182
Normandy Common. —9L 91
Normandy Gdns. H'ham —7J 197
Normandy Wlk. Egh —6E 20
Norman Hay Ind. Est. W Dray —3A 8
Norman Ho. Felt —3N 23
(off Watermill Way)
Normanhurst. Afrd —6B 22
Normanhurst Clo. Craw —3D 182
Normanhurst Dri. Twic —8G 11
Normanhurst Rd. SW2 —3K 29
Normanhurst Rd. W on T —8L 39
Norman Keep. Warf —9D 16
Norman Rd. SW19 —8A 28
Norman Rd. Afrd —7E 22
Norman Rd. Sutt —2M 61
Norman Rd. T Hth —4M 45
Normansfield Av. Tedd —8J 25
Normans Gdns. E Grin —9A 166
Normans La. Eden —4G 147
Norman's Rd. Small —8N 143
Normanton Av. SW19 —3M 27
Normanton Rd. S Croy —2B 64 (8F 200)
Normington Clo. SW16 —6L 29
Norney. —5B 132
Norney. Shack —5B 132
Norrels Dri. E Hor —4G 96
(in two parts)
Norrels Ride. E Hor —3G 97
Norreys Av. Wokgm —2C 30
Norris Hill Rd. Fleet —5D 88
Norris Rd. Stai —5H 21
Norroy Rd. SW15 —7J 13
Norstead Pl. SW15 —3F 26
North Acre. Bans —3L 81
Northampton Clo. Brack —2B 32
Northampton Rd. Croy —8D 46
Northanger Rd. SW16 —7J 29
North Ascot. —9H 17
North Ash. H'ham —4J 197
North Av. Cars —4E 62
North Av. Farnh —5J 109
North Av. Rich —4N 11
North Av. W Vill —5F 56
Northborough Rd. SW16 —2H 45
Northbourne. G'ming —3J 133
N. Breache Rd. Ewh —4H 157
North Bridge. —3F 172
Northbrook Copse. Brack —5D 32
Northbrook Rd. Alder —4N 109
Northbrook Rd. Croy —4A 46
North Camp. —6A 90
N. Camp Sta. Roundabout. Farn —5C 90
Northchapel. —9D 190
North Cheam. —9J 43
Northcliffe Clo. Wor Pk —9D 42
North Clo. Alder —3C 110
North Clo. Craw —2D 182
North Clo. Farn —6M 69
North Clo. Felt —9E 8
North Clo. Mord —3K 43
North Clo. N Holm —9J 119
North Clo. Wind —4C 4
North Comn. Wey —1D 56
Northcote. Add —1M 55
Northcote. Oxs —1C 78
Northcote Av. Iswth —8G 10
Northcote Av. Surb —6A 42
Northcote Clo. W Hor —3D 96
Northcote Cres. W Hor —3D 96
Northcote La. Sham G —5F 134
Northcote Rd. Ash V —6D 90
Northcote Rd. Croy —5A 46
Northcote Rd. Farn —8L 69
Northcote Rd. N Mald —2B 42
Northcote Rd. Twic —8G 11
Northcote Rd. W Hor —3D 96
Northcott. Brack —7M 31
North Ct. G'ming —4E 132
Northcroft Clo. Eng G —6L 19
Northcroft Gdns. Eng G —6L 19
Northcroft Rd. Eng G —6L 19
Northcroft Rd. Eps —4D 60
Northcroft Vs. Eng G —6L 19
Northdale Ct. SE25 —2C 46
North Dene. Houn —4B 10
North Down. S Croy —7B 64
Northdown Clo. H'ham —4M 197
Northdown La. Guild —6A 114 (8F 202)
Northdown Rd. Sutt —6M 61
Northdown Rd. Wold —2K 105
Northdowns. Cranl —9N 155
N. Downs Cres. New Ad —5L 65
(in two parts)
N. Downs Rd. New Ad —6L 65
Northdown Ter. E Grin —7N 165
North Dri. SW16 —5G 28
North Dri. Beck —3L 47
North Dri. Brkwd —8N 71
North Dri. Houn —5C 10
North Dri. Orp —1N 67
North Dri. Vir W —5H 35
North East Surrey Crematorium. Mord —5H 43
North End. —7L 165
North End. Croy —8N 45 (2B 200)
North End. E Grin —7L 165
N. End Cres. W14 —1L 13
N. End Ho. W14 —1K 13
N. End La. Asc —6E 34
N. End La. Orp —7J 67
N. End Pde. W14 —1K 13
(off N. End Rd.)
N. End Rd. W14 & SW6 —1K 13
Northernhay Wlk. Mord —3K 43
Northern Perimeter Rd. H'row A —4C 8
Northern Perimeter Rd. W. H'row A —4N 7
Northey Av. Sutt —6J 61
N. Eyot Gdns. W6 —1E 12
N. Farm Rd. Farn —6L 69
North Farnborough. —1N 89
North Feltham. —9J 9
N. Feltham Trad. Est. Felt —8J 9
Northfield. Light —7M 51
Northfield. Shalf —2A 134
Northfield. Witl —6C 152
Northfield Clo. Alder —3B 110
Northfield Clo. C Crook —7D 88
Northfield Ct. Stai —9K 21

A-Z Surrey 255

Northfield Cres.—Oaksway

Northfield Cres. Sutt —1K 61
Northfield Pl. Wey —4C 56
Northfield Rd. C Crook —7C 88
Northfield Rd. Cobh —9H 57
Northfield Rd. Eton W —1C 4
Northfield Rd. Houn —2L 9
Northfield Rd. Stai —9K 21
Northfields. SW18 —7M 13
Northfields. Asht —5L 79
(in two parts)
Northfields. Eps —7D 60
Northfields Prospect Bus. Cen. SW18 —7M 13
North Fryerne. Yat —7C 48
North Gdns. SW19 —8B 28
Northgate. —2C 182
Northgate Av. Craw —3C 182
Northgate Dri. Camb —8E 50
Northgate Pl. Craw —2C 182
Northgate Rd. Craw —3B 182
N. Gate Rd. Farn —3A 90
North Grn. Brack —9B 16
North Gro. Cher —5H 37
N. Hatton Rd. H'row A —4E 8
N. Heath Clo. H'ham —3K 197
N. Heath Est. H'ham —2K 197
N. Heath La. H'ham —4K 197
N. Holmes Clo. H'ham —3A 198
North Holmwood. —9H 119
N. Hyde La. S'hall & Houn —1L 9
Northington Clo. Brack —5D 32
Northlands Av. Orp —1N 67
Northlands Bungalows. Newd —2A 160
Northlands Cotts. Warn —5D 178
Northlands Rd. H'ham —1L 197
Northlands Rd. Warn —6D 178
North La. Alder —1B 110
North La. Tedd —7F 24
N. Lodge Clo. SW15 —8J 13
N. Lodge Dri. Asc —1G 33
North Looe. —9H 61
North Mall. Fleet —4A 88
North Mall. Stai —5H 21
(off Elmsleigh Shop. Cen.)
North Mead. Craw —1C 182
Northmead. Farn —1N 89
North Mead. Red —9D 102
North Moors. Sly I —8A 94
North Munstead. —2L 153
N. Munstead La. G'ming —1K 153
Northolt Rd. H'row A —4M 7
North Pde. Chess —2M 59
North Pde. H'ham —4J 197
N. Park La. God —9D 104
North Pl. SW18 —8M 13
North Pl. Mitc —8D 28
North Pl. Tedd —7F 24
N. Pole La. Kes —3B 66
North Rd. SW19 —7A 28
North Rd. Alder —6B 90
(in two parts)
North Rd. Asc —9F 16
North Rd. Ash V —9D 90
North Rd. Bren —2L 11
North Rd. Craw —1E 182
North Rd. Felt —9E 8
North Rd. Guild —9L 93
North Rd. Reig —6L 121
North Rd. Rich —6N 11
North Rd. Surb —5K 41
North Rd. W on T —2K 57
North Rd. W Wick —7L 47
North Rd. Wok —3C 74
Northrop Rd. H'row A —4F 8
North Sheen. —6N 11
North Side. Tong —5D 110
Northspur Rd. Sutt —9M 43
N. Station App. S Nut —5K 123
Northstead Rd. SW2 —3L 29
North St. Cars —9D 44
North St. Dork —5G 119 (2K 201)
North St. Egh —6B 20
North St. G'ming —4H 133
North St. Guild —4N 113 (5C 202)
North St. H'ham —6K 197
North St. Iswth —6G 10
North St. Lea —8G 79
North St. Red —2D 122
North St. Turn H —5D 184
North St. Wink —5K 17
North Ter. Wind —3G 5
North Town. —2B 110
Northtown Trad. Est. Alder —2C 110
Northumberland Av. Iswth —4F 10
Northumberland Clo. Stanw —9N 7
Northumberland Clo. Warf —8D 16
Northumberland Cres. Felt —9F 8
Northumberland Gdns. Iswth —3G 11
Northumberland Gdns. Mitc —4H 45
Northumberland Pl. Rich —8K 11
Northumberland Row. Twic —2E 24
N. Verbena Gdns. W6 —1F 12
North Vw. SW19 —6H 27
North Vw. Brack —2H 31
N. View Cres. Eps —4G 81
North Wlk. New Ad —3L 65
(in two parts)
Northway. G'ming —4E 132
Northway. Guild —1K 113
Northway. Gat A —2D 162
(off Gatwick Way)
Northway. Mord —2K 43
Northway. Wall —1G 63
Northway Rd. Croy —5C 46
Northweald La. King T —6K 25
N. Weylands Ind. Est. W on T —8M 39
Northwood Av. Knap —5G 72
Northwood Av. Purl —8L 63
N. Wood Ct. SE25 —2D 46
Northwood Pk. Craw —8E 162
Northwood Rd. Cars —3E 62
Northwood Rd. H'row A —4M 7
Northwood Rd. T Hth —1M 45
N. Worple Way. SW14 —6C 12
Norton Av. Surb —6A 42
Norton Clo. Worp —5G 93
Norton Gdns. SW16 —1J 45
Norton La. D'side —6G 77
Norton Pk. Asc —4N 33
Norton Rd. Camb —2G 71
Norton Rd. Wokgm —3B 30
Norwich Av. Camb —3C 70
Norwich Rd. Craw —5E 182
Norwich Rd. T Hth —2N 45
Norwood Clo. Eff —6M 97
Norwood Clo. S'hall —1A 10
Norwood Clo. Twic —3D 24
Norwood Farm La. Cobh —7H 57
Norwood Grn. Rd. S'hall —1A 10
Norwood High St. SE27 —4M 29
Norwood Hill. —7J 141
Norwood Hill. Horl —9H 141
Norwood Hill Rd. Charl —8K 141
Norwood New Town. —7N 29
Norwood Pk. Rd. SE27 —6N 29
Norwood Rd. SE24 —2M 29
Norwood Rd. SE27 —3M 29
Norwood Rd. Eff —6M 97
Norwood Rd. S'hall —1N 9
Norwood Ter. S'hall —1B 10
Notley End. Eng G —8M 19
Notson Rd. SE25 —3E 46
Nottingham Clo. Wok —5J 73
Nottingham Ct. Wok —5J 73
(off Nottingham Clo.)
Nottingham Rd. SW17 —2D 28
Nottingham Rd. Iswth —5F 10
Nottingham Rd. S Croy —1N 63 (7B 200)
Nova M. Sutt —7K 43
Nova Rd. Croy —7M 45
Novello St. SW6 —4M 13
Nowell Rd. SW13 —2F 12
Nower Rd. Dork —5G 118 (3J 201)
Nower, The. Knock —6N 87
Nowhurst Bus. Pk. Broad H —2A 196
Nowhurst La. Broad H —3A 196
Noyna Rd. SW17 —4D 28
Nuffield Ct. Houn —3N 9
Nuffield Dri. Owl —6L 49
Nugee Ct. Crowt —2G 49
Nugent Clo. Duns —3B 174
Nugent Rd. SE25 —2C 46
Nugent Rd. Sur R —3G 112
Numa Ct. Bren —3K 11
Nunappleton Way. Oxt —1C 126
Nuneaton. Brack —5C 32
Nunns Fld. Capel —5J 159
Nuns Wlk. Dork —8B 98
Nuns Wlk. Vir W —4N 35
Nuptown. —2D 16
Nuptown La. Warf —2D 16
Nursery Av. Croy —8G 46
Nursery Clo. SW15 —7J 13
Nursery Clo. Capel —4J 159
Nursery Clo. Croy —8G 46
Nursery Clo. Eps —6D 60
Nursery Clo. Felt —1J 23
(in two parts)
Nursery Clo. Fleet —5E 88
Nursery Clo. Frim G —7D 70
Nursery Clo. Tad —3G 100
Nursery Clo. Wok —3M 73
Nursery Clo. Wdhm —6H 55
Nursery Gdns. Chil —9D 114
Nursery Gdns. Hamp —5N 23
Nursery Gdns. Houn —8N 9
Nursery Gdns. Stai —7K 21
Nursery Gdns. Sun —1G 39
Nursery Hill. Sham G —6F 134
Nurserylands. Craw —3M 181
Nursery La. Asc —9J 17
Nursery La. Hkwd —9B 142
Nursery Rd. SW19 —1N 43
(Merton)
Nursery Rd. SW19 —8K 27
(Wimbledon)
Nursery Rd. G'ming —4J 133
Nursery Rd. Knap —4G 73
Nursery Rd. Sun —1F 38
Nursery Rd. Sutt —1A 62
Nursery Rd. Tad —3F 100
Nursery Rd. T Hth —3A 46
Nursery Way. Oxt —7A 106
Nursery Way. Wray —9N 5
Nutbourne. Farnh —5K 109
Nutbourne Cotts. Hamb —2H 173
Nutcombe. —7C 170
Nutcombe Down. —6C 170
Nutcombe La. Dork —5F 118 (2H 201)
Nutcombe La. Hind —9C 170
Nutcroft Gro. Fet —8E 78
Nutfield. —2K 123
Nutfield Clo. Cars —9C 44
Nutfield Ct. Nutf —1K 123
Nutfield Marsh Rd. Nutf —9H 103
Nutfield Park. —6L 123
Nutfield Rd. Coul —3E 82
Nutfield Rd. Mers —7G 102
Nutfield Rd. Red & Nutf —3F 122
Nutfield Rd. T Hth —3M 45
Nuthatch Clo. Ews —5C 108
Nuthatch Clo. Stai —2A 22
Nuthatch Gdns. Reig —7A 122
Nuthatch Way. H'ham —1K 197
Nuthatch Way. Turn H —4F 184
Nuthurst. Brack —4C 32
Nuthurst Av. SW2 —3K 29
Nuthurst Av. Cranl —7N 155
Nuthurst Clo. Craw —2M 181
Nutley. Brack —7M 31
Nutley Clo. Yat —1C 68
Nutley Ct. Reig —3L 121
(off Nutley La.)
Nutley Gro. Reig —3M 121
Nutley La. Reig —2L 121
Nutmeg Ct. Farn —9H 69
Nutshell La. Farnh —6H 109
Nutty La. Shep —2D 38
Nutwell St. SW17 —6C 28
Nutwood. G'ming —5G 133
(off Frith Hill Rd.)
Nutwood Av. Brock —4B 120
Nutwood Clo. Brock —4B 120
Nye Bevan Ho. SW6 —3L 13
(off St Thomas's Way)
Nyefield Pk. Tad —4F 100
Nylands Av. Rich —4N 11
Nymans Clo. H'ham —1N 197
Nymans Ct. Craw —6F 182
Nymans Gdns. SW20 —2G 42

Oakapple Clo. Craw —8N 181
Oakapple Clo. S Croy —1E 84
Oak Av. Croy —7K 47
Oak Av. Egh —8E 20
Oak Av. Hamp —6M 23
Oak Av. Houn —3L 9
Oak Av. Owl —6J 49
Oakbank. Fet —1C 98
Oak Bank. New Ad —3M 65
Oakbank. Wok —6A 74
Oakbank Av. W on T —6N 39
Oakbury Rd. SW6 —5N 13
Oak Clo. C'fold —5D 172
Oak Clo. Copt —7L 163
Oak Clo. G'ming —3H 133
Oak Clo. Sutt —8A 44
Oak Clo. Tad —8A 100
Oakcombe Clo. N Mald —9D 26
Oak Corner. Bear G —7J 139
Oak Cottage Clo. Wood S —2F 112
Oak Cotts. Hand —5N 199
Oak Cotts. Hasl —2C 188
(in two parts)
Oak Ct. Craw —8B 162
Oak Ct. Farn —4C 90
Oak Ct. Farnh —2G 129
Oak Cft. E Grin —1C 186
Oakcroft Bus. Cen. Chess —1M 59
Oakcroft Clo. W Byf —1H 75
Oakcroft Rd. Chess —1M 59
Oakcroft Rd. W Byf —1H 75
Oakcroft Vs. Chess —1M 59
Oakdale. Brack —5B 32
Oakdale La. Crock H —2L 127
Oakdale Rd. SW16 —6J 29
Oakdale Rd. Eps —5C 60
Oakdale Rd. Wey —9B 38
Oakdale Way. Mitc —6E 44
Oak Dell. Craw —2G 183
Oakdene. Asc —5C 34
Oakdene. Chob —6J 53
Oakdene. Tad —7K 81
Oakdene Av. Th Dit —7G 40
Oakdene Clo. Bookh —5C 98
Oakdene Clo. Brock —5B 120
Oakdene Ct. W on T —9J 39
Oakdene Dri. Surb —6B 42
Oakdene M. Sutt —7L 43
Oakdene Pde. Cobh —1J 77
Oakdene Rd. Bookh —2N 97
Oakdene Rd. Brock —5A 120
Oakdene Rd. Cobh —1J 77
Oakdene Rd. G'ming —8G 133
Oakdene Rd. P'mrsh —2M 133
Oakdene Rd. Red —3D 122
Oak Dri. Tad —8A 100
Oake Ct. SW15 —8K 13
Oaken Coppice. Asht —6N 79
Oaken Copse. C Crook —9C 88
Oaken Copse Cres. Farn —7N 69
Oak End. Bear G —8J 139
Oaken Dri. Clay —3F 58
Oak End Way. Wdhm —8G 55
Oakengates. Brack —7M 31
Oaken La. Clay —1E 58
Oakenshaw Clo. Surb —6L 41
Oakey Dri. Wokgm —3A 30
Oak Farm Clo. B'water —1H 69
Oakfield. Plais —6A 192
Oakfield. Wok —4H 73
Oakfield Clo. N Mald —4E 42
Oakfield Clo. Wey —1D 56
Oakfield Cotts. Hasl —7M 189
Oakfield Ct. Horl —8E 142
(off Consort Way)
Oakfield Dri. Reig —1M 121
Oakfield Gdns. Beck —4L 47
Oakfield Gdns. Cars —7C 44
Oakfield Glade. Wey —1D 56
Oakfield La. Kes —1E 66
Oakfield Rd. SW19 —4J 27
Oakfield Rd. Afrd —6C 22
Oakfield Rd. Asht —4K 79
Oakfield Rd. B'water —2K 69
Oakfield Rd. Cobh —1J 77
Oakfield Rd. Croy —7N 45 (1B 200)
Oakfield Rd. Eden —7K 127
Oakfields. Camb —1N 69
Oakfields. Guild —1H 113
Oakfields. Wal W —1L 177
Oakfields. W on T —7H 39
Oakfields. W Byf —1K 75
Oakfields. Worth —1H 183
Oakfield St. SW10 —2N 13
Oakfield Way. E Grin —7B 166
Oak Gdns. Croy —8K 47
Oak Glade. Eps —8N 59
Oak Grange Rd. W Cla —7K 95
Oak Grove. —9K 49
Oak Gro. Cranl —9A 156
Oak Gro. Loxw —4J 193
Oak Gro. Sun —8J 23
Oak Gro. W Wick —7M 47
Oak Gro. Cres. Coll T —9K 49
Oak Gro. Rd. SE20 —1F 46
Oakhall Dri. Sun —6G 22
Oakhaven. Craw —5B 182
Oakhill. —7M 197
Oak Hill. Burp —7E 94
Oakhill. Clay —3G 58
Oak Hill. Eps —3C 80
Oakhill. Surb —6L 41
Oak Hill. Wood S —1E 112
Oakhill Clo. Asht —5J 79
Oakhill Cotts. Oke H —1N 177
Oakhill Ct. SW20 —8J 27
Oakhill Cres. Surb —6L 41
Oakhill Dri. Surb —6L 41
Oakhill Gdns. Wey —8F 38
Oakhill Gro. Surb —5L 41
Oakhill Path. Surb —5L 41
Oakhill Pl. SW15 —8M 13
Oakhill Rd. SW15 —8L 13
Oakhill Rd. SW16 —9J 29
Oakhill Rd. Add —3H 55
Oakhill Rd. Asht —5J 79
Oakhill Rd. Beck —1M 47
Oakhill Rd. Head D —4G 169
Oakhill Rd. H'ham —6L 197
Oakhill Rd. Reig —4N 121
Oakhill Rd. Surb —5L 41
Oakhill Rd. Sutt —9N 43
Oakhurst. Chob —5H 53
Oakhurst. Gray —6B 170
Oakhurst Clo. Tedd —6E 24
Oakhurst Gdns. E Grin —8M 165
Oakhurst La. Loxw —2G 193
Oakhurst Ri. Cars —6C 62
Oakhurst Rd. Eps —3B 60
Oakington Av. Hayes —1E 8
Oakington Dri. Sun —1K 39
Oakland Av. Farnh —5K 109
Oakland Ct. Add —9K 37
Oaklands. Cranl —9M 155
Oaklands. Fet —2D 98
Oaklands. Hasl —1G 188
Oaklands. Horl —8G 143
Oaklands. H'ham —6L 197
Oaklands. Kenl —1N 83
Oaklands. S God —7H 125
Oaklands. Yat —9C 48
Oaklands Av. Esh —7D 40
Oaklands Av. Iswth —2F 10
Oaklands Av. T Hth —3L 45
Oaklands Av. W Wick —9L 47
Oaklands Bus. Cen. Wokgm —5A 30
Oaklands Clo. Asc —8K 17
Oaklands Clo. Chess —1J 59
Oaklands Clo. H'ham —8L 197
Oaklands Clo. Shalf —2A 134
Oaklands Dri. Asc —8K 17
Oaklands Dri. Red —5F 122
Oaklands Dri. Twic —1C 24
Oaklands Dri. Wokgm —3A 30
Oaklands Est. SW4 —1G 29
Oaklands Gdns. Kenl —1N 83
Oaklands La. Big H —9D 66
Oaklands La. Crowt —1F 48
(in two parts)
Oaklands Pk. Wokgm —4A 30
Oaklands Rd. SW14 —6C 12
Oaklands Way. Tad —9H 81
Oaklands Way. Wall —4H 63
Oakland Way. Eps —3D 60
Oak La. Broad H —5E 196
Oak La. Eng G —4M 19
Oak La. Iswth —7E 10
Oak La. Twic —1G 25
Oak La. Wind —4D 4
Oak La. Wok —3D 74
Oaklawn Rd. Lea —5E 78
Oaklea. Ash V —8E 90
Oak Leaf Clo. Eps —8B 60 (5H 201)
Oak Leaf Clo. Guild —2G 113
Oak Leaf Ct. Asc —9H 17
Oaklea Pas. King T —2K 41 (5J 203)
Oakleigh. God —8F 104
Oakleigh Av. Surb —7N 41
Oakleigh Flats. Eps —1D 80 (8M 201)
Oakleigh Gdns. Orp —1N 67
Oakleigh Rd. H'ham —4M 197
Oakleigh Way. Mitc —9F 28
Oakleigh Way. Surb —7N 41
Oakley Av. Croy —1K 63
Oakley Clo. Add —1M 55
Oakley Clo. E Grin —2D 186
Oakley Clo. Iswth —4D 10
Oakley Ct. Red —2E 122
(off St Anne's Ri.)
Oakley Dell. Guild —1E 114
Oakley Dri. Brom —1G 66
Oakley Dri. Fleet —5B 88
Oakley Gdns. Bans —2N 81
Oakley Ho. G'ming —3H 133
Oakley M. Wind —5B 4
Oakley Rd. SE25 —4E 46
Oakley Rd. Brom —1G 66
Oakley Rd. Camb —2N 69
Oakley Rd. Warl —5D 84
Oakley Wlk. W6 —2J 13
Oak Lodge. Crowt —2H 49
Oak Lodge. Hasl —4J 189
Oak Lodge Clo. W on T —2K 57
Oaklodge Dri. Red —2E 142
Oak Lodge Dri. W Wick —6L 47
Oak Lodge La. W'ham —3M 107
Oak Mead. G'ming —3G 133
Oakmead Grn. Eps —2B 80
Oakmead Pl. Mitc —9C 28
Oakmead Rd. SW12 —2E 28
Oakmead Rd. Croy —5H 45
Oakmede Pl. Binf —7H 15
Oak Pk. W Byf —9G 55
Oak Pk. Gdns. SW19 —2J 27
Oak Pl. SW18 —8N 13
Oak Ridge. Dork —8H 119
Oakridge. W End —9C 52
Oak Rd. Cat —9B 84
Oak Rd. Cobh —2L 77
Oak Rd. Craw —4A 182
Oak Rd. Farn —2A 90
Oak Rd. Lea —5G 79
Oak Rd. N Mald —1C 42
Oak Rd. Reig —2N 121
Oak Rd. W'ham —3M 107
Oak Row. SW16 —1G 45
Oaks Av. Felt —3M 23
Oaks Av. Wor Pk —9G 43
Oaks Cvn. Pk., The. Chess —9J 41
Oaks Clo. H'ham —2A 198
Oaks Clo. Lea —8G 79
Oakshade Rd. Oxs —1C 78
Oakshaw. Oxt —5N 105
Oakshaw Rd. SW18 —1N 27
Oaks Ho. Cvn. Pk., The. Bear G —1K 159
Oakside Ct. Horl —7G 143
Oakside La. Horl —7G 143
Oaks La. Croy —9F 46
(in two parts)
Oaks La. Mid H —3H 139
Oaks Rd. Croy —2E 64
Oaks Rd. Kenl —1M 83
Oaks Rd. Reig —2B 122
Oaks Rd. Stanw —9M 7
Oaks Rd. Wok —4A 74
Oaks Sq., The. Eps —6L 201
Oaks, The. Brack —1B 32
Oaks, The. C'fold —5E 172
Oaks, The. Dork —8H 119
Oaks, The. E Grin —1C 186
Oaks, The. Eps —1D 80
Oaks, The. Farn —2J 89
Oaks, The. Mord —3K 43
Oaks, The. Stai —5H 21
Oaks, The. Tad —1H 101
(off Tadworth St.)
Oaks, The. W Byf —1J 75
Oaks, The. Yat —1C 68
Oaks Track. Cars —7D 62
Oaks Way. Cars —4D 62
Oaks Way. Eps —6G 80
Oaks Way. Kenl —1N 83
Oaksway. Surb —7K 41

Oak Tree Clo. ...Hor —2E 96
Oak Tree Clo. A...—8R 76
Oak Tree Clo. ...k & W Hor —7N 75
Oak Tree Clo. ...or —4F 96
Oak Tree C...94
Oak Tree C...
Oak Tree ...29
Oak Tree ...109
Oak Tre...
Oak T...4F 156
Oa...
Oa...
Oa...

...l...
(off H...
...almers...
Palmers Ho...
Palmerston Clo...
Palmerston Clo. ...
Palmerston Ct. Surt...
Palmerston Gro. SW19...
Palmerston Mans. W14 —
(off Queen's Club Gdns.)
Palmerston Rd. SW14 —7B 12
Palmerston Rd. SW19 —8M 27
Palmerston Rd. Cars —1D 62
Palmerston Rd. Croy —4A 46
Palmerston Rd. Houn —4C 10
Palmerston Rd. Orp —1L 67
Palmerston Rd. Sutt —2A 62
Palmerston Rd. Twic —9E 10
Palm Gro. Guild —7M 93
Pampisford Rd. Purl —7L 63
Pams Way. Eps —2C 60
Pankhurst Clo. Iswth —6F 10
Pankhurst Ct. Craw —8N 181
Pankhurst Dri. Brack —4B 32
Pankhurst Rd. W on T —6K 39
Panmuir Rd. SW20 —9G 27
Pannell Clo. E Grin —1N 185
Pannells. Lwr Bo —6J 129
Pannells Clo. Cher —7H 37
Pannells Ct. Guild
—4N 113 (5D 202)
Pan's Gdns. Camb —2D 70
Pantile Rd. Wey —1E 56
Pantiles Clo. Wok —5L 73
Papercourt La. Rip —9H 75
Paper M. Dork —4H 119 (1M 201)
Papermill Clo. Cars —1E 62
Papworth Way. SW2 —1L 29
Parade Ct. E Hor —4F 96
Parade M. SE27 —3M 29
Parade Rd. Deep —6H 71
Parade, The. Ash V —9E 90
Parade, The. Cars —2D 62
(off Doynon Rd.)
Parade, The. Clay —3E 58
Parade, The. Craw —2C 182
Parade, The. Croy —5J 45
Parade, The. E Grin —7L 165
Parade, The. Eps —9C 60 (7L 201)
(in two parts)
Parade, The. Frim —6B 70
Parade, The. Hamp —6D 24
Parade, The. H'ham —5G 197
(off Caterways)
Parade, The. King T —3L 203
Parade, The. Lea —7G 79
(off Kingston Rd.)
Parade, The. Red —4E 122
Parade, The. Stai —6F 20
Parade, The. Sun —8G 23
Parade, The. Sutt —9L 43
Parade, The. Tad —6K 81
Parade, The. Vir W —5N 35
Parade, The. W'ind —4A 4
Parade, The. Wor Pk —1E 60
Parade, The. Yat —9D 48
Paradise Rd. Rich —8K 11
Paragon Cotts. E Clan —9M 95
Paragon Gro. Surb —5M 41
Paragon Pl. Surb —5M 41
Paragon Technology Cen. Wdhm
—7C 54

Parbury Ri. Chess —3L 59
Parchmore Rd. T Hth —1M 45
Parchmore Way. T Hth —1M 45
Pares Clo. Wok —3N 73
Parfitts Clo. Farnh —1F 128
Parfour Dri. Kenl —3N 83
Parfrey St. W6 —2H 13
Parham Rd. Craw —2L 181
Parish Clo. As —3F 110
Parish Clo. Farnh —6F 108
Parish Ct. Surb —4L 41
Parish Ho. Craw —4B 182
Parish La. Peas P
—1N 199 & 9F 182
Parish Rd. Farn —5A 90
Park Av. SW14 —7C 12
Park Av. Camb —2A 70
Park Av. Cars —3E 62
Park Av. Oat —2R 104
Park Av. Eden —1K 147
Park Av. Egh —7E 20
Park Av. Houn —9B 10
Park Av. Mitc —8F 28
Park Av. Pep H —6N 131
Park Av. Red —2D 142

Old Farm Dri. Brack —8A 16
Old Farm Ho. Dri. Oxs —2D 78
Old Farm Pas. Hamp —9C 24
Old Farm Pl. Ash V —9D 90
Old Farm Rd. Guild —9N 93
Old Farm Rd. Hamp —7N 23
(in two parts)
Old Farnham La. Farnh —3H 129
(GU9)
Old Farnham La. Farnh —2A 128
(GU10)
Old Ferry Dri. Wray —9M 5
Oldfield Clo. Horl —1D 162
Oldfield Ct. Surb —8M 203
Oldfield Gdns. Asht —6K 79
Oldfield Ho. W4 —1D 12
(off Devonshire Rd.)
Oldfield Rd. SW19 —7K 27
Oldfield Rd. Hamp —9N 23
Oldfield Rd. Horl —1D 162
Oldfields Rd. Sutt —9L 43
Oldfields Trad. Est. Sutt —9M 43
Oldfieldwood. Wok —4D 74
...orge Ct. Tad —9B 114
...ne Cres. Shep —5C 38
...ne End. Sand —8G 49
...o. Cat —8M 83
...m Rd. Lwr Bo —5J 129
...ern —9F 188
...Camb —8A 50
...d Rd. Broad H —4D 196
...d Rd. Frim G & Pirb
—9F 70
...La. W'ham —5L 87
...re Rd. Hasl —3G 189
...y Farnh —5H 109
—3M 67
...7N 73
...Wok —7N 73
...H'ham —9L 179
...orth —3K 183
...Rd. Bear G —6J 139
...Rd. Craw —5N 181
...o. SW17 —2D 28
...W19 —6K 27
...os —6E 60
...Twic —9J 11
...Isl —1D 72
...V'sham —4M 51
...am —6J 197
—GH 11
...urt —8L 149
...ck —3D 120
...yt —7L 149
...Rural Life Cen.
—8L 129
... Wor Pk —8D 42
...rack —9B 16
...M 109

...C 110

...F 148
...bh —4C 76
...106

...86
...h —9H 77
...ning —8E 132
—9K 63
—9H 11
...Hor —4H 97
...s —6F 80

...ck —5J 99
...42
...Pk —9C 42
—4N 73
—1M 181
—1M 181
—9C 10
...p —2B 38
...E 114
—1N 13
...9B 162
—9F 94
...102
—3J 197
...188
...6
—9A 48
...2H 189
—6C 22
...82
...M 59
...56
...39
—3J 183
...—4F 128
—1M 163

...1
...45 (4A 200)
...113
...8
...1

Old Pk. Av. SW12 —1E 28
Old Pk. Clo. Farnh —1E 108
Old Pk. La. Farnh —5E 108
(Odiham Rd.)
Old Pk. La. Farnh —7F 108
(Up. Old Pk. La.)
Old Pk. M. Houn —3N 9
Old Parvis Rd. W Byf —8L 55
Old Pasture Rd. Frim —4D 70
Old Pharmacy Ct. Crowt —3G 49
Old Pond Clo. Camb —5A 70
Old Portsmouth Rd. Camb —1E 70
Old Portsmouth Rd. G'ming
—3L 133
Old Portsmouth Rd. Thur —6H 151
Old Post Cotts. Broad H —5D 196
Old Pottery Clo. Reig —5N 121
Old Pound Clo. Iswth —5G 10
Old Pound Cotts. If'd —2J 181
Old Priory La. Warf —7B 16
Old Pump Ho. Clo. Fleet —3D 88
Old Quarry, The. Hasl —4D 188
Old Rectory Clo. Brmly —6B 134
Old Rectory Clo. Tad —2F 100
Old Rectory Dri. As —2F 110
Old Rectory Gdns. Farn —1B 90
Old Rectory Gdns. G'ming —9J 133
Old Rectory La. E Hor —4F 96
Old Redstone Dri. Red —4E 122
Old Reigate Rd. Bet —3A 120
Old Reigate Rd. Dork —3L 119
Oldridge Rd. SW12 —1E 28
Old Rd. Add —4H 55
Old Rd. Buck —3B 120
Old Rd. E Grin —9B 166
Old Row Ct. Wokgm —2B 30
Old St Mary's. W Hor —7C 96
Old Sawmill La. Crowt —1H 49
Old School Clo. SW19 —1M 43
Old School Clo. As —1E 110
(in two parts)
Old School Clo. Beck —1G 47
Old School Clo. Fleet —4B 88
Old School Ct. Wray —1A 20
Old School Ho. Eden —2L 147
Old School La. Brock —6A 120
Old School La. Yat —9R 48
Old School M. Wey —1E 56
Old School Pl. Ling —7N 145
Old School Pl. Wok —8A 74
Old Schools La. Eps —5E 60
Old School Sq. Th Dit —5F 40
Old School Ter. Fleet —4B 88
(off Old School Clo.)
Old Slade La. Iver —1H 7
Old Sta. App. Lea —8G 78
Old Sta. Clo. Craw D —2E 104
Old Sta. Gdns. Tedd —7G 24
(off Victoria Rd.)
Old Sta. Way. G'ming —6H 133
Oldstead. Brack —4B 32
Old Surrey Hall. —6G 166
Old Swan Yd. Cars —1D 62
Old Thorn. —6F 172
Old Tilburstow Rd. God —3F 124
Old Town. Croy —9M 45 (4A 200)
Old Tye Av. Big H —3G 87
Old Welmore. Yat —1D 68
Old Westhall Clo. Warl —6F 84
Old Wickhurst La. Broad H —7D 196
Old Windsor. —8K 5
Old Windsor Lock. Old Win —8M 5
Old Woking. —8D 74
Old Wokingham Rd. Wokgm &
Crowt —6G 31
Old Woking Rd. W Byf —9H 55
Old Woking Rd. Wok —6D 74
Oldwood Chase. Farn —2G 89
Old York Rd. SW18 —8N 13
Oleander Clo. Crowt —9F 30
Oleander Clo. Orp —2M 67
Oliver Av. SE25 —2C 46
Oliver Clo. W4 —2A 12
Oliver Clo. Add —1K 55
Oliver Gro. SE25 —3C 46
Olive Rd. SW19 —8A 28
Oliver Rd. Asc —1L 33
Oliver Rd. H'ham —7G 197
Oliver Rd. N Mald —1B 42
Oliver Rd. Sutt —1B 62
Olivette St. SW15 —6J 13
Olivia Ct. Wokgm —2A 30
Olivier Rd. M'bowr —4H 183
Ollerton. Brack —7M 31
Olley Clo. Wall —4J 63
Olveston Wlk. Cars —5B 44
O'Mahoney Ct. SW17 —4A 28
Omega Rd. Wok —3C 74
Omega Way. Egh —9E 20
Omnibus Building. Reig —4N 121
One Tree Hill Rd. Guild —4D 114
Ongar Clo. Add —3H 55
Ongar Hill. Add —3J 55
Ongar Pde. Add —3J 55
Ongar Pl. Add —3J 55
Ongar Rd. SW6 —2M 13
Ongar Rd. Add —2J 55
Onslow Av. Rich —8L 11

Onslow Av. Sutt —6L 61
Onslow Clo. Th Dit —7F 40
Onslow Clo. Wok —4C 74
Onslow Cres. Wok —4C 74
Onslow Dri. Asc —8L 17
Onslow Gdns. S Croy —8D 64
Onslow Gdns. Th Dit —7E 40
Onslow Gdns. Wall —3G 62
Onslow Ho. King T —1M 203
Onslow M. Cher —5H 37
Onslow Rd. Asc —6E 34
Onslow Rd. Croy —6K 45
Onslow Rd. Guild —3N 113 (3D 202)
Onslow Rd. N Mald —3F 42
Onslow Rd. Rich —8L 11
Onslow Rd. W on T —1G 57
Onslow St. Guild —4M 113 (5B 202)
Onslow Village. —5J 113
Onslow Way. Th Dit —7E 40
Onslow Way. Wok —2H 75
Ontario Clo. Small —9L 143
Openfields. Head —1D 168
Openview. SW18 —2A 28
Ophelia Ho. W6 —1J 13
(off Fulham Pal. Rd.)
Opladen Way. Brack —4A 32
Opossum Way. Houn —6K 9
Opus Pk. Sly I —8N 93
Oracle Cen. Brack —1A 32
Orange Ct. La. Orp —5J 67
Orangery, The. Rich —3J 25
Orbain Rd. SW6 —3K 13
Orchard Av. Afrd —7D 22
Orchard Av. Croy —8H 47
Orchard Av. Fell —8E 8
Orchard Av. Houn —3M 9
Orchard Av. Mitc —7E 44
Orchard Av. N Mald —1D 42
Orchard Av. Th Dit —7G 41
Orchard Av. Wind —4D 4
Orchard Av. Wdhm —7H 55
Orchard Bus. Cen. Red —3E 142
Orchard Clo. SW20 —3H 43
Orchard Clo. Afrd —7D 22
Orchard Clo. Ash V —8E 90
Orchard Clo. Bad L —6N 109
Orchard Clo. Bans —1N 81
Orchard Clo. B'water —5L G9
Orchard Clo. E Hor —2G 97
Orchard Clo. Eden —1K 147
Orchard Clo. Egh —6D 20
Orchard Clo. Fist —7H 131
Orchard Clo. Fet —9D 78
Orchard Clo. Guild —3D 114
Orchard Clo. Hasl —3D 188
Orchard Clo. Horl —7D 142
Orchard Clo. Lea —6F 78
Orchard Clo. Norm —3M 111
Orchard Clo. Th Dit —7H 41
Orchard Clo. W on T —6J 39
Orchard Clo. W End —9A 52
Orchard Clo. W Ewe —3A 60
Orchard Clo. Wok —3D 74
Orchard Clo. Wokgm —2C 30
Orchard Cotts. Charl —3L 161
Orchard Cotts. Chil —9G 114
Orchard Cotts. King T
—9M 25 (2N 203)
Orchard Ct. Brack —1A 32
Orchard Ct. Iswth —3D 10
Orchard Ct. Ling —8N 145
Orchard Ct. Twic —3D 24
Orchard Ct. Wall —2F 62
Orchard Ct. W Dray —3L 7
Orchard Ct. Wor Pk —7F 42
Orchard Dene. W Byf —9J 55
(off Madeira Rd.)
Orchard Dri. Asht —7K 79
Orchard Dri. Eden —1K 147
Orchard Dri. Shep —2F 38
Orchard Dri. Wok —2A 74
Orchard End. Cat —9B 84
Orchard End. Fet —2C 98
Orchard End. Rowl —8E 128
Orchard End. Wey —8F 38
Orchard Fld. Rd. G'ming —4J 133
Orchard Fields. Fleet —4A 88
Orchard Gdns. Alder —4A 110
Orchard Gdns. Chess —1L 59
Orchard Gdns. Cranl —8A 156
Orchard Gdns. Eff —6M 97
Orchard Gdns. Eps —1B 80
Orchard Gdns. Sutt —2M 61
Orchard Ga. Esh —7D 40
Orchard Ga. Sand —7G 49
Orchard Gro. Croy —6H 47
Orchard Hill. Cars —2D 62
Orchard Hill. Rud —1D 194
Orchard Hill. W'sham —4A 52
Orchard Ho. SW6 —3K 13
(off Varna Rd.)
Orchard Ho. Guild —2F 114
(off Morrow St.)
Orchard Ho. Tong —5D 110
Orchard La. SW20 —9G 27
Orchard La. E Mol —5D 40
Orchard Lea Clo. Wok —2G 75
Orchard Leigh. Lea —9H 79

Orchard Mains—Park Av.

Orchard Mains. Wok —6M 73
Orchard Mobile Home Pk. Tad —8A 100
Orchard Pk. Cvn. Site. Out —3K 143
Orchard Pl. Kes —5E 66
Orchard Pl. Wokgm —2B 30
Orchard Ri. Croy —7H 47
Orchard Ri. King T —9B 26
Orchard Ri. Rich —7A 12
Orchard Rd. Bad L —6M 109
Orchard Rd. Bren —2J 11
Orchard Rd. Chess —1L 59
Orchard Rd. Dork —6H 119
Orchard Rd. F'boro —2K 67
Orchard Rd. Farn —1M 89
Orchard Rd. Guild —8D 94
Orchard Rd. Hamp —8N 23
Orchard Rd. H'ham —7L 197
Orchard Rd. Houn —8N 9
Orchard Rd. King T —1L 41 (4K 203)
Orchard Rd. Mitc —7E 44
Orchard Rd. Old Win —9L 5
Orchard Rd. Onsl —5J 113
Orchard Rd. Reig —3N 121
Orchard Rd. Rich —6N 11
Orchard Rd. Shalf —9A 114
Orchard Rd. Shere —8B 116
Orchard Rd. Small —8N 143
Orchard Rd. S Croy —1E 84
Orchard Rd. Sun —8J 23
Orchard Rd. Sutt —2M 61
Orchard Rd. Twic —8G 11
Orchards Clo. W Byf —1J 75
Orchard Sq. W14 —1L 13
Orchards, The. H'ham —3M 197
Orchards, The. If'd —4J 181
Orchard St. Craw —3B 182
Orchard, The. Bans —2M 81
Orchard, The. Broad H —5D 196
Orchard, The. Eps —4E 60 (Meadow Wlk.)
Orchard, The. Eps —6E 60 (Tayles Hill)
Orchard, The. Horl —8E 142
Orchard, The. H'ham —4A 198
Orchard, The. Houn —5C 10
Orchard, The. Light —7L 51
Orchard, The. N Holm —9J 119
Orchard, The. Vir W —4A 36
Orchard, The. Wey —1C 56
Orchard, The. Wok —9A 74
Orchard Way. Add —2K 55
Orchard Way. Alder —4A 110
Orchard Way. Afrd —3A 22
Orchard Way. Camb —4N 69
Orchard Way. Croy —7H 47
Orchard Way. Dork —6H 119
Orchard Way. E Grin —1N 185
Orchard Way. Esh —3C 58
Orchard Way. Norm —3M 111
Orchard Way. Oxt —2C 126
Orchard Way. Reig —6N 121
Orchard Way. Send —3E 94
Orchard Way. Sutt —1B 62
Orchard Way. Tad —4L 101
Orchid Ct. Egh —5D 20
Orchid Dri. Bisl —2D 72
Orchid Mead. Bans —1N 81
Orde Clo. Craw —9H 163
Ordnance Clo. Felt —3H 23
Ordnance Rd. Alder —2N 109
Ordnance Roundabout. Alder —2N 109
Oregano Way. Guild —7K 93
Oregon Clo. N Mald —3B 42
Orestan La. Eff —5J 97
Orewell Gdns. Reig —5N 121
Orford Ct. SE27 —3M 29
Orford Gdns. Twic —3F 24
Organ Crossroads. (Junct.) —4F 60
Oriel Clo. Craw —9G 162
Oriel Clo. Mitc —3H 45
Oriel Ct. Croy —7A 46 (1D 200)
Oriel Dri. SW13 —2H 13
Oriel Hill. Camb —2B 70
Oriental Clo. Wok —4B 74
Oriental Rd. Asc —3A 34
Oriental Rd. Wok —4B 74
Orion. Brack —7M 31
Orion Cen., The. Croy —8J 45
Orion Ct. Bew —5J 181
Orlando Gdns. Eps —6C 60
Orleans Clo. Esh —8D 40
Orleans Ct. Twic —1H 25
Orleans House Gallery. —2H 25
Orleans Rd. Twic —1H 25
Orltons La. Rusp —8E 160
Ormathwaites Corner. Warf —8C 16
Ormeley Rd. SW12 —2F 28
Orme Rd. King T —1A 42
Ormerod Gdns. Mitc —1E 44
Ormesby Wlk. Craw —5F 182
Ormond Av. Hamp —9B 24
Ormond Av. Rich —8K 11
Ormond Cres. Hamp —9B 24
Ormond Dri. Hamp —8B 24
Ormonde Av. Eps —6C 60
Ormonde Ct. SW15 —7H 13
Ormonde Rd. SW14 —6B 12
Ormonde Rd. G'ming —5H 133
Ormonde Rd. Wok —3M 73
Ormonde Rd. Wokgm —3A 30
Ormond Rd. Rich —8K 11
Ormsby. Sutt —4N 61
Ormside Way. Red —8F 102
Orpin Rd. Red —8F 102
Orpwood Clo. Hamp —7N 23
Orwell Clo. Farn —8K 69
Orwell Clo. Wind —6G 4
Osborne Av. Stai —2A 22
Osborne Clo. Beck —3H 47
Osborne Clo. Felt —6L 23
Osborne Clo. Frim —6D 70
Osborne Ct. Craw —7N 181
Osborne Ct. Farn —5A 90
Osborne Ct. Wind —5F 4
Osborne Dri. Fleet —6C 88
Osborne Dri. Light —7L 51
Osborne Gdns. T Hth —1N 45
Osborne La. Warf —6A 16
Osborne M. Wind —5F 4
Osborne Pl. Sutt —2B 62
Osborne Rd. Egh —7B 20
Osborne Rd. Farn —4A 90
Osborne Rd. Houn —6N 9
Osborne Rd. King T —8L 25
Osborne Rd. Red —9E 102
Osborne Rd. T Hth —1N 45
Osborne Rd. W on T —7H 39
Osborne Rd. Wind —5F 4
Osborne Rd. Wokgm —2B 30
Osborne Ter. SW17 —6D 28 (off Church La.)
Osborn Rd. Farnh —8J 109
Osbourne Ho. Twic —3C 24
Osgood Av. Orp —2N 67
Osgood Gdns. Orp —2N 67
Osier Ct. Bren —2L 11 (off Ealing Rd.)
Osier M. W4 —2D 12
Osier Pl. Egh —7E 20
Osiers Ct. King T —2J 203
Osiers Rd. SW18 —7M 13
Osier Way. Bans —1K 81
Osier Way. Mitc —4D 44
Osman's Clo. Brack —8F 16
Osmond Gdns. Wall —2G 62
Osmunda Bank. Dor P —4A 166
Osmund Clo. Worth —3J 183
Osnaburgh Hill. Camb —1N 69
Osney Clo. Craw —4A 182
Osney Wlk. Cars —5B 44
Osprey Clo. Fet —9C 78
Osprey Clo. Sutt —2L 61
Osprey Gdns. S Croy —6H 65
Ostade Rd. SW2 —1K 29
Osterley. —3D 10
Osterley Av. Iswth —3D 10
Osterley Clo. Wokgm —3E 30
Osterley Ct. Iswth —4D 10
Osterley Cres. Iswth —4E 10
Osterley Gdns. T Hth —1N 45
Osterley La. S'hall —1A 10 (in two parts)
Osterley Lodge. Iswth —3E 10 (off Church Rd.)
Osterley Pk. House. —2C 10
Osterley Rd. Iswth —3E 10
Oswald Clo. Fet —9C 78
Oswald Clo. Warf —8C 16
Oswald Rd. Fet —9C 78
Osward. Croy —5J 65 (in four parts)
Osward Rd. SW17 —3D 28
Otford Clo. Craw —9A 182
Othello Gro. Warf —9C 16
Otho Ct. Bren —3K 11
Otterbourne Rd. Croy —8N 45 (2B 200)
Otterburn Gdns. Iswth —3G 10
Otterburn St. SW17 —7D 28
Otter Clo. Crowt —9F 30
Otter Clo. Ott —3D 54
Otterden Clo. Orp —1N 67
Ottermead La. Ott —3E 54
Otter Mdw. Lea —6F 78
Ottershaw. —3E 54
Ottershaw Pk. Ott —4C 54 (in two parts)
Ottway's Av. Asht —6K 79
Ottways La. Asht —7K 79
Otway Clo. Craw —5L 181
Oulton Wlk. Craw —5F 182
Ouseley Rd. SW12 —2D 28
Ouseley Rd. Old Win —1M 19
Ousley Rd. Wray —1M 19
Outdowns. Eff —8J 97 (in two parts)
Outram Pl. Wey —2D 56
Outram Rd. Croy —8C 46
Outwood. —3N 143
Outwood Common. —3A 144
Outwood Ho. SW2 —1K 29 (off Deepdene Gdns.)
Outwood La. Blet & Out —2A 124
Outwood La. Kgswd & Coul —9N 81
Outwood Postmill. —3A 144
Oval Ho. Croy —1F 200
Oval Rd. Croy —8A 46 (2E 200)
Oval, The. Bans —1M 81
Oval, The. G'ming —4J 133
Oval, The. Guild —4K 113
Oval, The. Wood S —2E 112
Overbrook. G'ming —6K 133
Overbrook. W Hor —7C 96
Overbury Av. Beck —2L 47
Overbury Cres. New Ad —6M 65
Overdale. Asht —2L 79
Overdale. Blet —2N 123
Overdale. Dork —4J 119
Overdale Av. N Mald —1B 42
Overdale Ri. Frim —3C 70
Overdene Dri. Craw —3M 181
Overford Clo. Cranl —8M 155
Overford Dri. Cranl —8N 155
Overhill. Warl —6F 84
Overhill Rd. Purl —6L 63
Overhill Way. Beck —4N 47
Overlord Clo. Camb —7A 50
Overstand Clo. Beck —4K 47
Overstone Gdns. Croy —6J 47
Overthorpe Clo. Knap —4H 73
Overton Clo. Alder —6A 110
Overton Clo. Iswth —4F 10
Overton Ct. Sutt —4M 61
Overton Ho. SW15 —1E 26 (off Tangley Gro.)
Overton Rd. Sutt —3M 61
Overton Shaw. E Grin —6A 166
Overton's Yd. Croy —9N 45 (4B 200)
Oveton Way. Bookh —4A 98
Ovington Ct. Wok —3J 73
Owen Clo. Croy —5A 46
Owen Ho. Twic —1H 25
Owen Mans. W14 —2K 13 (off Queen's Club Gdns.)
Owen Pl. Lea —9H 79
Owen Rd. G'ming —5J 133
Owen Rd. W'sham —2A 52
Owers Clo. H'ham —6L 197
Owlbeech Ct. H'ham —4A 198
Owlbeech Pl. H'ham —4A 198
Owlbeech Way. H'ham —4A 198
Owl Clo. S Croy —6G 65
Owletts. Craw —2H 183
Owlscastle Clo. H'ham —3K 197
Owlsmoor. —6K 49
Owlsmoor Rd. Owl —7J 49 (in two parts)
Ownstead Gdns. S Croy —7C 64
Ownsted Hill. New Ad —6M 65
Oxberry Av. SW6 —5K 13
Oxdowne Clo. Stoke D —1B 78
Oxenden Ct. Tong —4C 110
Oxenden Rd. Tong —4C 110
Oxenhope. Brack —3M 31
Oxfield. Eden —9M 127
Oxford Av. SW20 —1K 43
Oxford Av. Hayes —3G 8
Oxford Av. Houn —1A 10
Oxford Clo. Afrd —8D 22
Oxford Clo. Mitc —2G 44
Oxford Ct. W4 —1A 12
Oxford Ct. Felt —5L 23
Oxford Cres. N Mald —5C 42
Oxford Gdns. W4 —1N 11
Oxford Rd. SE19 —7N 29
Oxford Rd. SW15 —7K 13
Oxford Rd. Cars —3C 62
Oxford Rd. Craw —7C 182
Oxford Rd. Farn —4A 90
Oxford Rd. Guild —5N 113 (6D 202)
Oxford Rd. H'ham —6K 197
Oxford Rd. Owl —5K 49
Oxford Rd. Red —2C 122
Oxford Rd. Tedd —6D 24
Oxford Rd. Wall —2G 62
Oxford Rd. Wokgm —2A 30
Oxford Rd. E. Wind —4F 4
Oxford Rd. N. W4 —1A 12
Oxford Rd. S. W4 —1N 11
Oxford Ter. Guild —5N 113 (6D 202)
Oxford Way. Felt —5L 23
Ox La. Eps —5F 60
Oxleigh Clo. N Mald —4D 42
Oxlip Clo. Croy —7G 46
Oxshott. —9D 58
Oxshott Ri. Cobh —9L 57
Oxshott Rd. Lea —3E 78
Oxshott Way. Cobh —2M 77
Oxted. —7A 106
Oxted Clo. Mitc —2B 44
Oxted Grn. Milf —3B 152
Oxted Rd. God —8F 104
Oxtoby Way. SW16 —9H 29
Oyster Hill. —2B 100
Oyster La. Byfl —6M 55

Pachesham Dri. Lea —3F 78
Pachesham Park. —3F 78
Pachesham Pk. Lea —3G 78
Pacific Clo. Felt —2G 23
Packer Clo. E Grin —7C 166
Packway. Farnh —4K 129
Padbrook. Oxt —7C 106 (in two parts)
Padbrook Clo. Oxt —7C 106
Padbury Clo. Felt —2E 22
Paddock Cvn. Site, The. Vir W —5A 36
Paddock Clo. Bear G —7K 139
Paddock Clo. Camb —9E 50
Paddock Clo. F'boro —1K 67
Paddock Clo. Hamb —9F 152
Paddock Clo. Ling —8M 145
Paddock Clo. Oxt —9B 106
Paddock Clo. Wor Pk —7D 42
Paddock Gdns. E Grin —2A 186
Paddock Gro. Bear G —7K 139
Paddock Ho. Guild —2F 114 (off Merrow St.)
Paddockhurst Rd. Craw —4M 181
Paddockhurst Rd. Turn H —9K 183
Paddocks Clo. Asht —5L 79
Paddocks Clo. Cobh —1K 77
Paddocks Mead. Wok —3H 73
Paddocks Rd. Guild —8C 94
Paddocks, The. Bookh —4B 98
Paddocks, The. Croy —3K 65
Paddocks, The. New H —6K 55
Paddocks, The. Norm —3N 111
Paddocks, The. Wey —9F 38
Paddocks Way. Asht —5L 79
Paddocks Way. Cher —7K 37
Paddock, The. Brack —2A 32
Paddock, The. Cranl —7M 155
Paddock, The. Craw —2H 183
Paddock, The. Crowt —1F 48
Paddock, The. Dat —4L 5
Paddock, The. Ewh —6F 156
Paddock, The. G'ming —8J 133
Paddock, The. Gray —5M 169
Paddock, The. Guild —2F 114
Paddock, The. Hasl —9E 170
Paddock, The. Head —4D 168
Paddock, The. Light —7M 51
Paddock, The. Westc —6B 118
Paddock, The. W'ham —4L 107
Paddock, The. Wink —2M 17
Paddock Wlk. Warl —6E 84
Paddock Way. Eps —7H 61
Paddock Way. G'wood —7L 171
Paddock Way. Oxt —9B 106
Paddock Way. Wok —1D 74
Padstow Wlk. Craw —5K 181
Padstow Wlk. Felt —2G 22
Padwick Rd. H'ham —6N 197
Pageant Wlk. Croy —9B 46 (4F 200)
Page Clo. Hamp —7M 23
Page Ct. H'ham —7K 197
Page Cres. Croy —2M 63
Page Cft. Add —8K 37
Pagehurst Rd. Croy —6E 46
Page Rd. Felt —9E 8
Page's Cft. Wokgm —3C 30
Pages Yd. W4 —2E 12
Paget Av. Sutt —9B 44
Paget Clo. Camb —8F 50
Paget Clo. Hamp —5D 24
Paget Clo. H'ham —8L 197
Paget La. Iswth —6D 10
Paget Pl. King T —7B 26
Paget Pl. Th Dit —7F 40
Pagewood. —3J 161
Pagewood Clo. M'bowr —5H 183
Pagoda Av. Rich —6M 11
Paice Grn. Wokgm —1C 30
Pain's Clo. Mitc —1F 44
Pains Hill. —9E 106
Painshill. (Junct.) —9G 56
Pains Hill. Oxt —1E 126
Paisley Rd. Cars —7B 44
Pakenham Clo. SW12 —2E 28
Pakenham Dri. Alder —1L 109
Pakenham Rd. Brack —6B 32
Palace Dri. Wey —9C 38
Palace Grn. Croy —4J 65
Palace Mans. King T —8J 203
Palace M. SW6 —3M 13
Palace Rd. SW2 —2K 29
Palace Rd. E Mol —2D 40
Palace Rd. King T —3K 41 (8J 20
Palace Rd. W'ham —8J 87
Palace Vw. Croy —1J 65
Palace Way. Wey —9C 38
Palestine Gro. SW19 —9B 28
Palestra Ho. Craw —3A 182
Palewell Comn. Dri. SW14 —8C 1
Palewell Pk. SW14 —8C 12
Palgrave Ho. Twic —1C 24
Pallant Way. Orp —1J 67
Pallingham Dri. M'bowr —6G 18
Palliser Ct. W14 —1K 13
Palliser Rd. W14 —1K 13
Palmer Av. Sutt —1H 61
Palmer Clo. Horl —6D 142
Palmer Clo. Houn —4A 10
Palmer Clo. Red —4E 122
Palmer Clo. W Wick —9N 47

Park Av.—Peddlars Gro.

Park Av. Shep —2F 38
Park Av. Stai —7H 21
Park Av. W Wick —8M 47
Park Av. Wokgm —3A 30
(in two parts)
Park Av. Wray —8N 5
Park Av. E. Eps —3F 60
Park Av. M. Mitc —8F 28
Park Av. W. Eps —3F 60
Park Barn. —2H 113
Pk. Barn Dri. Guild —1H 113
Pk. Barn E. Guild —2J 113
Park Chase. G'ming —9H 133
Park Chase. Guild —3A 114 (3E 202)
Park Clo. W4 —2C 12
Park Clo. Cars —3D 62
Park Clo. Esh —3A 58
Park Clo. Fet —2D 98
Park Clo. G'wood —8K 171
Park Clo. Hamp —9C 24
Park Clo. Holt P —9A 128
Park Clo. Houn —8C 10
Park Clo. King T —9N 25 (1N 203)
Park Clo. New H —6K 55
Park Clo. Str G —8A 120
Park Clo. W on T —8G 38
Park Clo. Wind —5G 5
Park Copse. Dork —5K 119
Park Corner. Wind —6B 4
Pk. Corner Dri. E Hor —6F 96
Park Cotts. F Grn —2L 157
Park Ct. Farnh —9J 109
Park Ct. Hamp W —9J 25
Park Ct. N Mald —3C 42
Park Ct. S Croy —8B 200
Park Ct. Wok —5B 74
Park Cres. Asc —4C 34
Park Cres. F Row —7J 187
Park Cres. Twic —2D 24
Parkdale Cres. Wor Pk —9C 42
Park Dri. SW14 —8C 12
Park Dri. Asc —5C 34
Park Dri. Asht —5N 79
Park Dri. Brmly —5B 134
Park Dri. Cranl —6A 156
Park Dri. Wey —2C 56
Park Dri. Wok —5B 74
Parker Clo. Craw —4H 183
Parke Rd. SW13 —4F 12
Parke Rd. Sun —3H 39
Parker Rd. Croy —1N 63 (6C 200)
Parker's Clo. Asht —6L 79
Parkers Ct. Dag —4J 51
Parker's Hill. Asht —6L 79
Parker's La. Asht —6L 79
Parkers La. Maid G —4F 16
Pk. Farm Clo. H'ham —1K 197
Pk. Farm Ind. Est. Camb —5A 70
Pk. Farm Rd. H'ham —1K 197
Pk. Farm Rd. King T —8L 25
Parkfield. G'ming —9H 133
Parkfield. H'ham —5J 197
Parkfield. Iswth —4E 10
Parkfield Av. SW14 —7D 12
Parkfield Av. Felt —4H 23
Parkfield Clo. Craw —4L 181
Parkfield Cres. Felt —4H 23
Parkfield Pde. Felt —4H 23
Parkfield Rd. Felt —4H 23
Parkfields. SW15 —7H 13
Parkfields. Croy —7J 47
Parkfields. Oxs —7D 58
Parkfields. Yat —1C 68
Parkfields Av. SW20 —9G 26
Parkfields Clo. Cars —1E 62
Parkfields Rd. King T —6M 25
Park Gdns. King T —6M 25
Parkgate. —7C 140
Pk. Gate Clo. King T —7A 26
Pk. Gate Cotts. Cranl —7K 155
Pk. Gate Ct. Hamp H —7C 24
Pk. Gate Ct. Wok —5A 74
Parkgate Gdns. SW14 —8C 12
Parkgate Rd. Newd —9A 140
Parkgate Rd. Reig —4N 121
Parkgate Rd. Wall —2E 62
Park Grn. Bookh —2A 98
Pk. Hall Rd. SE21 —4N 29
Pk. Hall Rd. Reig —1M 121
Pk. Hall Trad. Est. SE21 —4N 29
Parkham Ct. Brom —1N 47
Park Hill. Cars —3C 62
Park Hill. C Crook —8A 88
Park Hill. Rich —9M 11
Parkhill Clo. B'water —2J 69
Pk. Hill Clo. Cars —2C 62
Pk. Hill Ct. SW17 —4D 28
Pk. Hill M. S Croy —8E 200
Pk. Hill Ri. Croy —8B 46
Parkhill Rd. B'water —2J 69
Pk. Hill Rd. Brom —1N 47
Pk. Hill Rd. Croy —8B 46 (3F 200) & (6F 200)
Parkhill Rd. Eps —7E 60
Pk. Hill Rd. Wall —4F 62
Park Horsley. E Hor —7H 97
Park Ho. Dri. Reig —5L 121
Park House Gardens. —6K 197 (off North St.)
Park Ho. Gdns. Twic —8J 11
Parkhurst. Eps —6B 60
Parkhurst Fields. Churt —9L 149
Parkhurst Gro. Horl —7D 142
Parkhurst Rd. Guild —2K 113
Parkhurst Rd. Horl —7C 142
Parkhurst Rd. Sutt —1B 62
Parkland Av. Slou —1N 5
Parkland Dri. Brack —9C 16
Parkland Gdns. SW19 —2J 27
Parkland Gro. Afrd —5B 22
Parkland Gro. Farnh —4L 109
Parkland Rd. Afrd —5B 22
Parklands. Add —2L 55
Parklands. Bookh —1A 98
Parklands. N Holm —9H 119
Parklands. Oxt —9A 106
Parklands. Red —1F 122
Parklands. Surb —4M 41
Parklands Clo. SW14 —8B 12
Parklands Clo. Cher —9E 36
Parklands Cotts. Shere —1A 136
Parklands Ct. Houn —5L 9
Parklands Gro. Iswth —4F 10
Parklands Pde. Houn —5L 9
Parklands Pl. Guild —3D 114
Parklands Rd. SW16 —6F 28
Parklands Way. Wor Pk —8D 42
Park La. Asht —5M 79
Park La. Ash W —3F 186
Park La. Binf —9K 15
Park La. Brook —2J 171
Park La. Camb —1A 70
Park La. Cars —1E 62
Park La. Churt —9G 149
Park La. Coul —8H 83
Park La. Cran —3H 9
Park La. Croy —9A 46 (3D 200)
Park La. Guild —9F 94
Park La. Hort —6C 6
Park La. Ockl —4F 158
Park La. Reig —5K 121
Park La. Rich —7K 11
Park La. Sutt —3K 61
Park La. Tedd —7F 24
Park La. Wink —2M 17
Park La. E. Reig —6L 121
Park La. Mans. Croy —5D 200
Park Langley. —3M 47
Parklawn Av. Eps —9A 60
Pk. Lawn Av. Horl —6D 142
Pk. Lawn Rd. Wey —1D 56
Parkleigh Rd. SW19 —1N 43
Park Ley Rd. Wold —7G 85
Parkleys. Rich —5K 25
Parkleys Pde. Rich —5K 25 (off Parkleys)
Park Mnr. Sutt —4A 62 (off Christchurch Pk.)
Parkmead. SW15 —9G 12
Parkmead. Cranl —6A 156
Park M. SE24 —1N 29
Park M. Stai —1A 22
Parkpale La. Bet —8N 119
Park Pl. C Crook —8A 88
Park Pl. Dork —7G 118
Park Pl. Hamp H —7C 24
Park Pl. H'ham —7J 197
Park Pl. Wok —5B 74 (off Hill Vw. Rd.)
Park Ride. Wind —1A 18
Park Ri. H'ham —4H 197
Park Ri. Lea —8H 79
Park Ri. Clo. Lea —8H 79
Park Rd. SE25 —3B 46
Park Rd. SW19 —7B 28
Park Rd. W4 —3B 12
Park Rd. Alb —9N 115
Park Rd. Alder —4N 109
Park Rd. Afrd —6C 22
Park Rd. Asht —5L 79
Park Rd. Bans —2N 81
Park Rd. Brack —1B 32
Park Rd. Camb —3N 69
Park Rd. Cat —1B 104
Park Rd. Cheam —3K 61
Park Rd. Crow —9A 126
Park Rd. Dor P —4A 166
Park Rd. E Grin —9N 165
Park Rd. E Mol —3C 40
Park Rd. Egh —5C 20
Park Rd. Esh —1B 58
Park Rd. Farn —4C 90
Park Rd. Farnh —8J 109
Park Rd. Fay —8E 180
Park Rd. Felt —5L 23
Park Rd. F Row —7H 187
Park Rd. G'ming —9H 133
Park Rd. Guild —3N 113 (3C 202)
Park Rd. Hack —8F 44
Park Rd. Hamp H —5B 24
Park Rd. Hamp W —9J 25
Park Rd. Hand —9N 199
Park Rd. Hasl —2G 188
Park Rd. Houn —8B 10
Park Rd. Iswth —4H 11
Park Rd. Kenl —2N 83
Park Rd. King T —6M 25 (1N 203)
Park Rd. N Mald —3C 42
Park Rd. Oxt —6B 106
Park Rd. Red —1D 122
Park Rd. Rich —9M 11
Park Rd. Sand —8H 49
Park Rd. Shep —7B 38
Park Rd. Slin —5L 195
Park Rd. Small —1N 163
Park Rd. Stanw —9K 7
Park Rd. Sun —8J 23
Park Rd. Surb —5M 41
Park Rd. Tedd —7F 24
Park Rd. Twic —9J 11
Park Rd. Wall —2F 62
Park Rd. Warl —1A 86
Park Rd. Wok —4B 74
(in two parts)
Park Rd. Wokgm —2A 30
Park Rd. Ho. King T —8N 25 (1N 203)
Park Rd. N. W4 —1C 12
Park Rd. Roundabout. Farn —5C 90
Park Row. Farnh —9G 109
Parkshot. Rich —7K 11
Parkside. SW19 —4J 27
Parkside. Craw —3C 182
Parkside. E Grin —9M 165
Parkside. Farnh —6H 109
Parkside. Hamp H —6D 24
Parkside. New H —7K 55
Parkside. Sutt —3K 61
Parkside Av. SW19 —6J 27
Parkside Clo. E Hor —3G 96
Parkside Cotts. W Cla —1J 115
Parkside Ct. Wey —1B 56
Parkside Cres. Surb —5B 42
Parkside Gdns. SW19 —5J 27
Parkside Gdns. Coul —4F 82
Parkside M. H'ham —6K 197
Parkside Pl. E Hor —3G 96
Parkside Rd. Asc —5D 34
Parkside Rd. Houn —8B 10
Park Sq. Esh —1B 58
Park Sq. Wink —2M 17
Parkstead Rd. SW15 —8F 12
Parkstone Dri. Camb —2A 70
Park Street. —5K 195
Park St. Bag —4J 51
Park St. Camb —9A 50
Park St. Coln —4F 6
Park St. Croy —9N 45 (3C 200)
Park St. Guild —5M 113 (6B 202)
Park St. H'ham —6K 197
Park St. Slin —5K 195
Park St. Tedd —7E 24
Park St. Wind —4G 5
Parkstreet La. Slin —5J 195
Park Ter. Cars —9C 44
Park Ter. Wor Pk —7F 42
Park Ter. Courtyard. H'ham —7K 197 (off Park Ter. W.)
Park Ter. E. H'ham —7K 197
Pk. Terrace W. H'ham —7K 197
Park, The. Bookh —1A 98
Park, The. Cars —2D 62
Park, The. Dork —7G 118
Park, The. Eng G —8M 19
Parkthorne Rd. SW12 —1H 29
Park Vw. Add —2L 55
Park Vw. Bag —4H 51
Park Vw. Bookh —3A 98
Park Vw. Craw —4A 182
Park Vw. Horl —8E 142
Park Vw. N Mald —2E 42
Pk. View Clo. Eden —1K 147
Parkview Ct. SW6 —5K 13
Parkview Ct. SW18 —8M 13
Pk. View Ct. Wok —6B 74
Pk. View Rd. Croy —7D 46
Pk. View Rd. Red —1E 142
Pk. View Rd. Wold —9H 85
Parkview Va. Guild —9E 94
Park Vs. B'water —1L 69
Parkville Rd. SW6 —3L 13
Park Wlk. Asht —6M 79
Parkway. SW20 —3J 43
Park Way. Bookh —1A 98
Parkway. Camb —3A 70
Park Way. Craw —2F 182
Parkway. Crowt —2F 48
Parkway. Dork —4G 119 (1K 201)
Park Way. Felt —1J 23
Parkway. Guild —2A 114 (1D 202)
Parkway. Horl —8E 142
Park Way. H'ham —6J 197
Parkway. New Ad —5L 65
Park Way. W Mol —2B 40
Park Way. Wey —9H 38
Parkway, The. Houn —5J 9
Parkway, The. Houn & S'hall —1H 9
Parkway Trad. Est. Houn —2K 9
Parkwood Av. Esh —7C 40
Pk. Wood Clo. Bans —2J 81
Parkwood Gro. Sun —2H 39
Parkwood Rd. SW19 —6L 27
Pk. Wood Rd. Bans —2J 81
Parkwood Rd. Iswth —4F 10
Parkwood Rd. Nutf —2J 123
Parkwood Rd. Tats —8G 87
Pk. Wood Vw. Bans —3H 81
Park Works Rd. Nutf —2K 123
Parley Dri. Wok —4M 73
Parliamentary Rd. Brkwd —8L 71
Parliament M. SW14 —5B 12
Parnell Clo. M'bowr —5H 183
Parnell Gdns. Wey —7B 56
Parnham Av. Light —7A 52
Parr Av. Eps —5G 61
Parr Clo. Lea —7F 78
Parr Ct. Felt —5K 23
Parrington Ho. SW4 —1H 29
Parris Cft. Dork —8J 119
Parrock La. Cole H —8M 187
Parrs Clo. S Croy —5A 64
Parrs Pl. Hamp —8A 24
Parry Clo. Eps —4G 60
Parry Clo. H'ham —4B 198
Parry Dri. Wey —6B 56
Parry Rd. SE25 —2B 46
Parsley Gdns. Croy —7G 46
Parsonage Bus. Pk. H'ham —4L 197
Parsonage Clo. Warl —3J 85
Parsonage Clo. Westc —7C 118
Parsonage La. Westc —6C 118
Parsonage La. Wind —4D 4
Parsonage Rd. Cranl —7M 155
Parsonage Rd. Eng G —6N 19
Parsonage Rd. H'ham —4K 197
Parsonage Sq. Dork —2K 201
Parsonage Way. Frim —5C 70
Parsonage Way. H'ham —4L 197
Parsons Barracks. Alder —2A 110 (off Ordnance Rd.)
Parsons Clo. C Crook —8A 88
Parsons Clo. Hasl —9G 171
Parsons Clo. Horl —7C 142
Parsons Cotts. As —1G 111
Parsons Fld. Sand —7G 49
Parsonsfield Clo. Bans —2J 81
Parsonsfield Rd. Bans —3J 81
Parsons Green. —4M 13
Parson's Grn. SW6 —4M 13
Parsons Grn. Guild —1N 113
Parsons Grn. Hasl —9G 171
Parsons Grn. Ct. Guild —9N 93
Parson's Grn. La. SW6 —4M 13
Parsons La. Hind —3A 170
Parson's Mead. Croy —7M 45 (1A 200)
Parsons Mead. E Mol —2C 40
Parson's Ride. Brack —6D 32
Parson's Wlk. H'ham —8F 196
Parthenia Rd. SW6 —4M 13
Parthia Clo. Tad —6G 81
Parthings La. H'ham —9E 196
Partridge Av. Yat —9A 48
Partridge Clo. Ews —4C 108
Partridge Clo. Frim —5C 70
Partridge Knoll. Purl —8M 63
Partridge La. Newd —7C 140
Partridge La. Rusp —8C 160
Partridge Mead. Bans —2H 81
Partridge Pl. Turn H —3F 184
Partridge Rd. Hamp —7N 23
Partridge Way. Guild —1F 114
Parvis Rd. W Byf & Byfl —9K 55
Paschal Rd. Camb —7D 50
Passage, The. Rich —8L 11
Passfield. —8D 168
Passfield Common. —9B 168
Passfield Enterprise Cen. Pass —9C 168
Passfield Mill Bus. Pk. Pass —8C 168
Passfield Rd. Pass —9D 168
Passfields. W14 —1L 13 (off Star St.)
Passingham Ho. Houn —2A 10
Pastens Rd. Oxt —9F 106
Paston Clo. Wall —9G 44
Pasture, The. Craw —3G 182
Pasture Wood Rd. Holm M —6K 137
Patching Clo. Craw —2L 181
Patchings. H'ham —5M 197
Paterson Rd. Afrd —6M 21
Pates Mnr. Dri. Felt —1E 22
Pathfield. C'fold —5E 172
Pathfield Clo. C'fold —5E 172
Pathfield Clo. Rud —1E 194
Pathfield Rd. SW16 —7H 29
Pathfield Rd. Rud —1E 194
Pathfields. Shere —9B 116
Pathfields Clo. Hasl —1G 189
Pathfinders, The. Farn —2H 89
Path Link. Craw —2C 182
Path, The. SW19 —9N 27
Pathway, The. Binf —6H 15
Pathway, The. Send —3H 95
Patmore La. W on T —3G 56
Patricia Gdns. Sutt —7M 61
Patrick Gdns. Warf —8C 16
Patrington Clo. Craw —6M 181
Patten All. Rich —8K 11
Patten Ash Dri. Wokgm —1D 30
Patten Av. Yat —1B 68
Patten Rd. SW18 —1C 28
Patterdale Clo. Craw —5N 181
Patterson Clo. Frim —3G 71
Paul Clo. Alder —4K 109
Paul Ct. Egh —6F 20
Paul Gdns. Croy —8C 46
Pauline Cres. Twic —2C 24
Pauls Mead. Ling —6A 146
Paul's Pl. Asht —6A 80
Paved Ct. Rich —8K 11
Pavement Sq. Croy —7D 46
Pavement, The. Craw —3C 182
Pavement, The. Iswth —6G 11 (off South St.)
Pavilion Gdns. Stai —8K 21
(in two parts)
Pavilion La. Alder —1K 109
Pavilion Rd. Alder —3K 109
Pavilions End, The. Camb —3B 70
Pavilion, The. Reig —1C 122
Pavilion Way. E Grin —1A 186
Pavillion, The. Kgswd —1A 102
Paviours. Farnh —9G 109
Pawley Clo. Tong —5D 110
Pawsons Rd. Croy —5N 45
Pax Clo. Bew —5K 181
Paxton Clo. Rich —5M 11
Paxton Clo. W on T —6K 39
Paxton Gdns. Wok —8G 54
(in two parts)
Paxton Rd. W4 —2D 12
Payley Dri. Wokgm —9D 14
Payne Clo. Craw —1H 183
Paynesfield Av. SW14 —6C 12
Paynesfield Rd. Tats —8E 86
(in two parts)
Paynes Green. —1D 178
Paynes Wlk. W6 —2K 13
Peabody Clo. Croy —7F 46
Peabody Est. SE24 —1M 29
Peabody Est. SW6 —2L 13 (off Lillie Rd.)
Peabody Est. W6 —1H 13
Peabody Hill. SE21 —2M 29
Peabody Rd. Farn —4B 90
Peace Clo. SE25 —3B 46
Peacemaker Clo. Bew —5K 181
Peaches Clo. Sutt —4K 61
Peach St. Wokgm —2B 30
Peach Tree Clo. Farn —7M 69
Peacock Av. Felt —2E 22
Peacock Cotts. Brack —3H 31
Peacock Gdns. S Croy —6H 65
Peacock La. Wokgm —4G 31
Peacocks Shop. Cen., The. Wok —4A 74
Peacock Wlk. Craw —6M 181
Peacock Wlk. Dork —6G 119 (4K 201)
Peaked Hill. —1A 110
Peakfield. Fren —3H 149
Peak Rd. Guild —9K 93
Peaks Hill. Purl —6H 63
Peaks Hill Ri. Purl —6J 63
Peall Rd. Croy —5K 45
Peall Rd. Ind. Est. Croy —5K 45
Pearce Clo. Mitc —1E 44
Pearce Rd. W Mol —2B 40
Pearl Ct. Wok —3H 73
Pearmain Clo. Shep —4C 38
Pears Av. Shep —2F 38
Pearscroft Ct. SW6 —4N 13
Pearscroft Rd. SW6 —4N 13
Pearson Rd. Craw —3F 182
Pears Rd. Houn —6C 10
Peartree Av. SW17 —4A 28
Pear Tree Av. Fleet —3A 88
Pear Tree Clo. Add —2J 55
Pear Tree Clo. Chess —2N 59
Pear Tree Clo. Lind —5A 168
Peartree Clo. Mitc —1C 44
Peartree Clo. S Croy —1E 84
Pear Tree Ct. Camb —7F 50
Peartree Grn. Duns —2N 173
Pear Tree Hill. Salf —3E 142
Pear Tree La. Rowl —8E 128
Pear Tree Rd. Add —2J 55
Pear Tree Rd. Afrd —6D 22
Pear Tree Rd. Lind —5A 168
Peary Clo. H'ham —2K 197
Peascod St. Wind —4F 4
Pease Pottage. —1M 199
Pease Pottage Hill. Craw —8A 182
Peaslake. —5E 136
Peaslake La. Peasl —5E 136
Peasmarsh. —2M 133
Peat Comn. Elst —9G 131
Peat Cotts. Elst —9G 131
Peatmoor Clo. Fleet —3A 88
Peatmore Av. Wok —3J 75
Peatmore Clo. Wok —3J 75
Peatmore Dri. Brkwd —8N 71
Pebble Clo. Tad —6D 100
Pebble Hill Rd. Bet —7D 100
Pebble La. Lea —2M 99
Pebworth Ct. Red —1E 122
Peddlars Gro. Yat —9D 48

Pipers Cft. C Crook —9B **88**
Pipers End. Slin —5M **195**
Piper's End. Vir W —2N **35**
Piper's Gdns. Croy —6H **47**
Pipers La. N'chap —8D **190**
Pipers Patch. Farn —1N **89**
Pipewell Rd. Cars —5C **44**
Pippbrook. —4J 119 (1M 201)
Pippbrook Gdns. Dork —4H **119**
Pippin Clo. Croy —7J **47**
Pippins Ct. Afrd —7C **22**
Pipson La. Yat —1C **68**
Pipsons Clo. Yat —9C **48**
Piquet Rd. SE20 —1F **46**
Pirbright. —1C 92
Pirbright Camp. —8M 71
Pirbright Cres. New Ad —3M **65**
Pirbright Grn. Pirb —1C **92**
Pirbright Rd. SW18 —2L **27**
Pirbright Rd. Farn —2A **90**
Pirbright Rd. Norm —1J **111**
Pirbright Ter. Pirb —1C **92**
Piries Pl. H'ham —6J **197**
(off East St.)
Pisley Rd. Ockl —6N **157**
Pitcairn Rd. Mitc —8D **28**
Pitchfont La. Oxt —2B **106**
(in two parts)
Pitch Hill. —1D 156
Pitch Place. —7E 150
(Godalming)
Pitch Place. —7K 93
(Guildford)
Pitch Pl. Binf —6J **15**
Pit Farm Rd. Guild —3C **114**
Pitfold Av. Hasl —2B **188**
Pitfold Clo. Hasl —2C **188**
Pitlake. Croy —8M **45** (2A **200**)
Pitland Street. —6K 137
Pitland St. Holm M —6K **137**
Pit La. Eden —8L **127**
Pitson Clo. Add —1M **55**
Pitt Cres. SW19 —5N **27**
Pitt Pl. Eps —1D **80** (8N **201**)
Pitt Rd. Eps —1D **80** (8N **201**)
Pitt Rd. Orp —1L **67**
Pitt Rd. T Hth —4N **45**
Pitts Clo. Binf —7J **15**
Pitts Rd. Alder —9N **89**
Pittville Gdns. SE25 —2D **46**
Pitt Way. Farn —9L **69**
Pitwood Grn. Tad —7H **81**
Pitwood Pk. Ind. Est. Tad —7G **81**
Pixham. —3K 119
Pixham End. Dork —2J **119**
Pixham La. Dork —2J **119**
Pixholme Gro. Dork —3J **119**
Pixton Hill. —5K 187
Pixton Way. Croy —5H **65**
Place Ct. Alder —5A **110**
Place Farm Rd. Blet —8A **104**
Placehouse La. Coul —6K **83**
Plain Ride. Wind —2N **17**
Plaistow. —6B 192
Plaistow Rd. C'fold —3G **190**
Plaistow Rd. Duns —1M **191**
Plaistow Rd. Kird —8D **192**
Plaistow Rd. Loxw —5D **192**
Plaistow St. Ling —7N **145**
Plane Ho. Short —1N **47**
Planes, The. Cher —6L **37**
Plane Tree Cres. Felt —4J **23**
Plantagenet Clo. Wor Pk —1C **60**
Plantagenet Pk. Warf —9D **16**
Plantain Cres. Craw —7M **181**
Plantation La. Warl —6H **85**
Plantation Row. Camb —1N **69**
Plantation Wharf. SW11 —6N **13**
Plas Newydd. Dor P —4B **166**
Plateau, The. Warf P —8E **16**
Plat, The. Eden —2M **147**
Plat, The. H'ham —5C **197**
Platt Mdw. Guild —9F **94**
Platt, The. SW15 —6J **13**
Platt, The. D'land —1C **166**
Platt, The. Hand —8N 199
(off Windmill Platt)
Plaws Hill. Peasl —5E **136**
Playden Ct. Craw —6L **181**
Playfair Mans. W14 —2K 13
(off Queen's Club Gdns.)
Playfair St. W6 —1H **13**
Playground Clo. Beck —1G **47**
Pleasance Rd. SW15 —8G **12**
Pleasance, The. SW15 —7G **12**
Pleasant Gro. Croy —9J **47**
Pleasant Pl. W on T —3K **57**
Pleasant Vw. Pl. Orp —2K **67**
Pleasure Pit Rd. Asht —5A **80**
Plesman Way. Wall —5J **63**
Plevna Rd. Hamp —9B **24**
Plough Clo. If'd —1L **181**
Plough Ind. Est. Lea —7G **79**
Ploughlands. Brack —9L **15**
Plough La. SW19 & SW17 —6N **27**
Plough La. D'side —4H **77**
Plough La. Ewh —6G **156**
Plough La. H'ham —3L **197**
Plough La. Purl —5J **63**
Plough La. Tedd —6G **24**
Plough La. Wall —1J **63**
Plough La. Wokgm —1E **30**
Plough La. Clo. Wall —2J **63**
Ploughmans End. Iswth —8D **10**
Plough Rd. D'land —9C **146**
Plough Rd. Eps —5C **60**
Plough Rd. Small —8M **143**
Plough Rd. Yat —8D **48**
Plough Wlk. Eden —9L **127**
Plover Clo. Craw —1A **182**
Plover Clo. Eden —9L **127**
Plover Clo. Stai —4H **21**
Plovers Ri. Bkwd —7D **72**
Plovers Rd. H'ham —5M **197**
Plum Clo. Felt —2H **23**
Plum Gth. Bren —1K **11**
Plummer La. Mitc —1D **44**
Plummer Rd. SW4 —1H **29**
Plumpton Way. Cars —9C **44**
Plumtree Clo. Wall —4H **63**
Plymouth Ct. Surb —8L **203**
Pocket Clo. Binf —1J **31**
Pockford Rd. C'fold —5F **172**
Pococks La. Eton —1H **5**
Podmore Rd. SW18 —7N **13**
Poels Ct. E Grin —8A **166**
Pointers Cotts. Rich —3J **25**
Pointers Green. —5H 77
Pointers Hill. Westc —7C **118**
Pointers Rd. Cobh —3D **76**
Pointers, The. Asht —7L **79**
Point Pleasant. SW18 —7M **13**
Polden Clo. Farn —7K **69**
Polecat. —8D 170
Polecat Copse. —9D 170
Polecat Hill. Hind —8D **170**
Polehamptons, The. Hamp —8C **24**
Polesden Gdns. SW20 —1G **42**
Polesden Lacey. —8C 98
Polesden Lacey. —8B 98
Polesden La. Rip —1H **95**
Polesden Rd. Bookh —7B **98**
Polesden Vw. Bookh —5D **98**
Poles La. Low H —6A **182**
Polesteeple Hill. Big H —4F **86**
Police Sta. Rd. W on T —3K **57**
Polkerris Way. C Crook —9C **88**
Pollard Clo. Old Win —8L **5**
Pollard Gro. Camb —2G **71**
Pollard Rd. Mord —4B **44**
Pollard Rd. Wok —3D **74**
Pollardrow Av. Brack —9L **15**
(in two parts)
Pollards. Craw —4M **181**
Pollards Cres. SW16 —2J **45**
Pollards Dri. H'ham —5L **197**
Pollards Hill E. SW16 —2K **45**
Pollards Hill N. SW16 —2J **45**
Pollards Hill S. SW16 —2J **45**
Pollards Hill W. SW16 —2K **45**
Pollards Oak Cres. Oxt —1C **126**
Pollards Oak Rd. Oxt —1C **126**
Pollards Wood Hill. Oxt —8D **106**
Pollards Wood Rd. SW16 —2J **45**
Pollards Wood Rd. Oxt —9D **106**
Pollocks Path. Gray —7B **170**
Polmear Clo. C Crook —9C **88**
Polsted La. Comp —1E **132**
Poltimore Rd. Guild —5K **113**
Polworth Rd. SW16 —6J **29**
Polyanthus Way. Crowt —8G **30**
Polygon Bus. Cen. Coln —5H **7**
Pond Clo. Loxw —4H **193**
Pond Clo. W on T —3G **57**
(in two parts)
Pond Copse La. Loxw —3H **193**
Pond Cottage La. Beck —7K **47**
Pond Cft. Yat —9D **48**
Pond Farm Clo. Tad —2G **100**
Pondfield Ho. SE27 —6N **29**
Pondfield La. Plais —4D **192**
Pondfield Rd. G'ming —4J **133**
Pondfield Rd. Kenl —3M **83**
(in two parts)
Pondfield Rd. Rud —9E **176**
Pond Head La. Ockl —6L **157**
Pond Hill Gdns. Sutt —3K **61**
Pond La. Churt —6H **149**
Pond La. Peasl —4D **136**
Pond Mdw. Guild —3H **113**
Pond Moor Rd. Brack —4N **31**
Pond Piece. Oxs —9B **58**
Pond Pl. Asht —4L **79**
Pond Rd. Egh —7E **20**
Pond Rd. Head D —5F **168**
Pond Rd. Wok —7K **73**
Pondside Clo. Hayes —2E **8**
Ponds La. Alb & Shere —2N **135**
(in three parts)
Ponds, The. Wey —3E **56**
Pondtail. —5M 167
(Edenbridge)
Pondtail. —5D 88
(Fleet)
Pondtail Clo. Fleet —6D **88**
Pondtail Clo. H'ham —2K **197**
Pondtail Copse. H'ham —2K **197**
Pondtail Dri. H'ham —1K **197**
Pondtail Gdns. Fleet —5D **88**
Pondtail Rd. Fleet —5D **88**
Pondtail Rd. H'ham —3J **197**
Pond Vw. Clo. Fleet —3C **88**
Pond Way. E Grin —9D **166**
Pond Way. Tedd —7J **25**
Pond Wood Rd. Craw —1E **182**
Ponsonby Rd. SW15 —1G **26**
Pony Chase. Cobh —9N **57**
Pook Hill. C'fold —5B **172**
Pool Clo. W Mol —4N **39**
Poole Ct. Houn —5M **9**
Poole Ct. Rd. Houn —5M **9**
Pool End. —4B 38
Pool End Clo. Shep —4B **38**
Poole Rd. Eps —3C **60**
Poole Rd. Wok —5A **74**
Pooles Cotts. Rich —3K **25**
Pooles La. SW10 —3N **13**
Pooley Av. Egh —6D **20**
Pooley Green. —6E 20
Pooley Grn. Clo. Egh —6E **20**
Pooley Grn. Rd. Egh —6D **20**
Poolmans Rd. Wind —6A **4**
Pool Rd. Alder —5A **110**
Pool Rd. W Mol —4N **39**
Pootings. —4M 127
Pootings Rd. Crock H & Four E —3M **127**
Pope Clo. SW19 —7B **28**
Pope Clo. Felt —2G **22**
Popes Av. Twic —3E **24**
Popes Clo. Coln —3D **6**
Popes Ct. Twic —3E **24**
Popes Gro. Croy —9J **47**
Popes Gro. Twic —3E **24**
Popes La. Oxt —3A **126**
Popes Mead. Hasl —1G **189**
Popeswood. —9J 15
Popeswood Rd. Binf —8J **15**
Popham Clo. Brack —4D **32**
Popham Clo. Hanw —4N **23**
Popham Gdns. Rich —6N **11**
Popinjays Row. Cheam —3J 61
(off Netley Clo.)
Poplar Av. Lea —9H **79**
Poplar Av. Mitc —9D **28**
Poplar Av. W'sham —1L **51**
Poplar Clo. Brack —2B **32**
Poplar Clo. Coln —4G **7**
Poplar Clo. Craw —9A **162**
Poplar Clo. Farn —9H **69**
Poplar Clo. Myt —2E **90**
Poplar Cotts. Guild —9H **93**
Poplar Ct. SW19 —6M **27**
Poplar Ct. Frim G —8D 70
(off Beech Rd.)
Poplar Ct. Twic —9J **11**
Poplar Cres. Eps —3B **60**
Poplar Dri. Bans —1J **81**
Poplar Farm Clo. Eps —3B **60**
Poplar Gdns. N Mald —1C **42**
Poplar Gro. N Mald —1C **42**
Poplar Gro. Wok —6A **74**
Poplar Ho. Langl —1B **6**
Poplar La. F Row —8G **187**
Poplar Rd. SW19 —1M **43**
Poplar Rd. Afrd —6D **22**
Poplar Rd. Lea —9H **79**
Poplar Rd. Shalf —1A **134**
Poplar Rd. Sutt —7L **43**
Poplar Rd. S. SW19 —2M **43**
Poplars, The. Asc —4L **33**
Poplars, The. H'ham —5L **197**
Poplar Vs. Frim G —8D 70
(off Beech Rd.)
Poplar Wlk. Cat —1B **104**
Poplar Wlk. Croy —8N **45** (1B **200**)
Poplar Wlk. Farnh —5J **109**
Poplar Way. Felt —4H **23**
Poppy Clo. Wall —7E **44**
Poppyhills Rd. Camb —7D **50**
Poppy La. Croy —6F **46**
Poppy Pl. Wokgm —2A **30**
Porchester. Asc —3L **33**
Porchester Rd. King T —1A **42**
Porchfield Clo. Sutt —6N **61**
Porridge Pot All. Guild —5N **113** (7B **202**)
Portal Clo. SE27 —4L **29**
Portesbery Hill Dri. Camb —9C **50**
Portesbery Rd. Camb —9B **50**
Portia Gro. Warf —9C **16**
Portinscale Rd. SW15 —8K **13**
Portland Av. N Mald —6E **42**
Portland Bus. Cen. Dat —4L 5
(off Manor Ho. La.)
Portland Cres. Felt —5E **22**
Portland Dri. C Crook —9A **88**
Portland Dri. Red —7H **103**
Portland Ho. Red —7G **103**
Portland Pl. SE25 —3D 46
(off Portland Rd.)
Portland Pl. Eps —8D **60**
Portland Rd. SE25 —3D **46**
Portland Rd. Afrd —4N **21**
Portland Rd. Dork —4G **119** (1K **201**)
Portland Rd. E Grin —1A **186**
Portland Rd. King T —2L **41** (6L **203**)
Portland Rd. Mitc —1C **44**
Portland Ter. Rich —7K **11**
Portley La. Cat —8B **84**
Portley Wood Rd. Whyt —7C **84**
Portman Av. SW14 —6C **12**
Portman Clo. Brack —9M **15**
Portman Rd. King T —1M **41** (4N **203**)
Portmore Pk. Rd. Wey —1A **56**
(in two parts)
Portmore Quays. Wey —1A **56**
Portmore Way. Wey —9B **38**
Portnall Dri. Vir W —5G **35**
Portnall Ri. Vir W —4J **35**
Portnall Rd. Vir W —4J **35**
Portnalls Clo. Coul —3F **82**
Portnalls Ri. Coul —3F **82**
Portnalls Rd. Coul —5F **82**
Portsmouth Av. Th Dit —6G **40**
Portsmouth Rd. SW15 —1G **27**
Portsmouth Rd. Cobh & Esh —9G **57**
Portsmouth Rd. Esh & Th Dit
(High St.) —1C **58**
Portsmouth Rd. Esh —3A **58**
(Stony Hill)
Portsmouth Rd. Frim & Cam —5B **70**
Portsmouth Rd. Guild —7M **113** (8B **202**)
Portsmouth Rd. Hind & Thur —5E **170**
Portsmouth Rd. Lip & Hind —9M **169** & 1A **188**
Portsmouth Rd. Milf & G'ming —1D **152**
Portsmouth Rd. Rip & Send —3H **95**
(Clandon Rd.)
Portsmouth Rd. Rip & Cobh —8M **75**
(High St.)
Portsmouth Rd. Th Dit & King T —6G **41** (8H **203**)
Portswood Pl. SW15 —9E **12**
Portugal Gdns. Twic —3C **24**
Portugal Rd. Wok —3B **74**
Port Way. Bisl —3D **72**
Portway. Eps —5F **60**
Portway Cres. Eps —5F **60**
Postford Farm Cotts. Alb —1J **135**
Postford Mill Cotts. Chil —7H **115**
Post Horn Clo. F Row —8K **187**
Post Horn La. F Row —8J **187**
Post Ho. La. Bookh —3A **98**
Post La. Twic —2D **24**
Postmill Clo. Croy —9F **46**
Post Office All. Hamp —1B **40**
Post Office Row. Oxt —9G **107**
Potbury Clo. Wink —7M **17**
Pot Common. —8G 131
Potley Hill Rd. Yat —9E **48**
Potter Clo. Mitc —1F **44**
Potteries La. Myt —2D **90**
Potteries, The. Farn —8J **69**
Potteries, The. Ott —3G **54**
Potterne Clo. SW19 —1J **27**
Potters Clo. Croy —7H **47**
Potters Clo. Milf —9C **132**
Potters Cres. As —1F **110**
Potter's Cft. H'ham —6L **197**
Pottersfield. Craw —2B **182**
Potters Ga. Farnh —1F **128**
Potters Gro. N Mald —3B **42**
Potter's Hill. Hamb —5F **152**
Potters Ind. Pk. C Crook —8D **88**
Potter's La. SW16 —7H **29**
Potters La. Send —1D **94**
Potters Pl. H'ham —6J **197**
Potters Rd. SW6 —5N **13**
Potters Way. Reig —7A **122**
Pottery Ct. Wrec —5E **128**
Pottery La. Wrec —5E **128**
Pottery Rd. Bren —2L **11**
Poulcott. Wray —9A **6**
Poulett Gdns. Twic —2G **24**
Poulters Wood. Kes —2F **66**
Poulton Av. Sutt —9B **44**
Pound Clo. G'ming —7H **133**
Pound Clo. Head —4E **168**
Pound Clo. Loxw —3H **193**
Pound Clo. Surb —7J **41**
Pound Ct. Asht —5M **79**
Pound Ct. Wood S —2E **112**
Pound Cres. Fet —8D **78**
Pound Farm La. Ash G —2H **111**
Pound Fld. Guild —2N **113** (2C **202**)
Poundfield Ct. Wok —8E **74**
Poundfield Gdns. Wok —7E **74**
(in two parts)
Poundfield Rd. Wok —7E **74**
Pound Hill. —3G 183
Pound Hill. Wood S —2E **112**
Pound Hill Pde. Craw —2G **183**
Pound Hill Pl. Craw —3G **183**
Pound La. Eps —8B **60** (5H **201**)
Pound La. G'ming —7H **133**
(in two parts)
Pound La. Hurst —4A **14**
Pound La. W'sham —3N **51**
Pound La. Wood S —2E **112**
Pound Pl. Shalf —9B **114**
Pound Pl. Clo. Shalf —9B **114**
Pound Rd. Alder —3A **110**
Pound Rd. Bans —4L **81**
Pound Rd. Cher —6K **37**
Pound St. Cars —2D **62**
Povey Cross. —1B 162
Povey Cross Rd. Horl —1B **162**
Powderham Ct. Knap —5G **72**
Powder Mill La. Twic —1N **23**
Powell Clo. Chess —2K **59**
Powell Clo. Guild —5J **113**
Powell Clo. Horl —7C **142**
Powell Clo. Wall —4J **63**
Powell Ct. S Croy —7A **200**
Powells Clo. Dork —8J **119**
Powell's Wlk. W4 —2D **12**
Power Rd. W4 —1N **11**
Powers Ct. Twic —1K **25**
Pownall Gdns. Houn —7B **10**
Pownall Rd. Houn —7B **10**
Poyle. —4G 7
Poyle Cvn. Pk. Coln —6G **6**
Poyle Clo. Coln —5G **6**
Poyle Gdns. Brack —9B **16**
Poyle Ho. Guild —2F 114
(off Merrow St.)
Poyle Ind. Est. Coln —6H **7**
Poyle Rd. Coln —6G **6**
Poyle Rd. Guild —5A **114** (7E **202**)
Poyle Rd. Tong —6D **110**
Poyle Technical Cen. Coln —5G **7**
Poyle Ter. Guild —5N **113** (6D **202**)
Poyle Trad. Est. Coln —6G **7**
Poynders Ct. SW4 —1G **28**
Poynders Gdns. SW4 —1G **29**
Poynders Rd. SW4 —1G **28**
Poynes Rd. Horl —6C **142**
Poynings Rd. If'd —4J **181**
Prairie Clo. Add —9K **37**
Prairie Rd. Add —9K **37**
Pratts La. W on T —1L **57**
Pratts Pas. King T —1L **41** (4K **203**)
Prebend Mans. W4 —1E 12
(off Chiswick High Rd.)
Precincts, The. Mord —5M **43**
Precinct, The. Cranl —6N **155**
Precinct, The. Egh —6C **20**
Precinct, The. W Mol —2B **40**
Premier Pde. Horl —8F 142
(off High St.)
Premier Pl. SW15 —7K **13**
Prentice Clo. Farn —6N **69**
Prentice Ct. SW19 —6L **27**
Prentis Rd. SW16 —5H **29**
Presburg Rd. N Mald —4D **42**
Presbury Ct. Wok —5K **73**
Prescott. Brack —6L **31**
Prescott Clo. SW16 —8J **29**
Prescott Rd. Coln —5G **6**
Presentation M. SW2 —3K **29**
Preshaw Cres. Mitc —2C **44**
Prestbury Cres. Bans —3D **82**
Preston Clo. Twic —4E **24**
Preston Ct. W on T —7K **39**
Preston Dri. Eps —3D **60**
Preston Gro. Asht —4J **79**
Preston La. Tad —8G **81**
Preston Pl. Rich —8L **11**
Preston Rd. SE19 —7M **29**
Preston Rd. SW20 —8E **26**
Preston Rd. Shep —4B **38**
Prestwick Clo. If'd —4J **181**
Prestwick Clo. S'hall —1M **9**
Prestwick La. G'wood —7L **171**
Prestwood Clo. Craw —9N **161**
Prestwood Gdns. Croy —6N **45**
Prestwood La. If'd —9H **161**
Prestwood La. Rusp —9F **160**
Pretoria Rd. SW16 —7F **28**
Pretoria Rd. Cher —7H **37**
Pretty La. Coul —8G **82**
Prey Heath Clo. Wok —2M **93**
Prey Heath Rd. Wok —2L **93**
Preymead Ind. Est. Bad L —5N **109**
Price Clo. SW17 —4D **28**
Price Gdns. Warf —7N **15**
Price Rd. Croy —2M **63** (8A **200**)
Prices La. Reig —6M **121**
Price Way. Hamp —7M **23**
Priddy's Yd. Croy —8N **45** (3B **200**)
Prides Crossing. Asc —8L **17**
Pridham Rd. T Hth —3A **46**
Priest Av. Wokgm —3E **30**
Priestcroft Clo. Craw —3M **181**
Priest Hill. Egh & Old Win —4M **19**
Priest Hill. Oxt —7D **106**
Priest La. W End —9N **51**
(in two parts)
Priestley Gdns. Wok —7C **74**
Priestley Rd. Mitc —1E **44**
Priestley Rd. Sur R —3G **112**
Priestley Way. Craw —8E **162**
Priest's Bri. SW14 & SW15 —6D **12**
Priestwood. —9M 15

Redhouse Rd.—Riverdale Rd.

Redhouse Rd. Croy —5H 45
Redhouse Rd. Tats —7E 86
Redkiln Clo. H'ham —5M 197
Redkiln Way. H'ham —4M 197
Redlake La. Wokgm —6E 30
Redland Gdns. W Mol —3N 39
Redlands. —5G 139
(Beare Green)
Redlands. —5A 108
(Hog Hatch)
Redlands. Coul —3J 83
Redlands. Tedd —7G 25
Redlands Cotts. Mid H —2H 139
Redlands La. Cron & Ews —5A 108
Redlands La. Mid H —2G 139
Redlands, The. Beck —1L 47
Redlands Way. SW2 —1K 29
Red La. Clay —3G 58
Red La. Dork —1L 139
Red La. Head —2G 168
Red La. Oxt —3D 126
Redleaves Av. Afrd —7C 22
Redlees Clo. Iswth —7G 10
Redlin Ct. Red —1D 122
Red Lion Bus. Pk. Surb —9M 41
Red Lion La. Chob —5H 53
Red Lion La. Farnh —2G 129
Red Lion Rd. Chob —5H 53
Red Lion Rd. Surb —8M 41
Red Lion Sq. SW18 —8M 13
Red Lion St. Rich —8K 11
Red Lodge. W Wick —7M 47
Red Lodge Rd. W Wick —7M 47
Redmayne Clo. Camb —2G 71
Red River Ct. H'ham —3H 197
Red Rd. Light —9H 51
Red Rd. Tad —1A 120
Red Rose. Binf —6H 15
Red Rover. (Junct.) —7E 12
Redruth Ho. Sutt —4N 61
Redshank Ct. If'd —4J 181
(off Stoneycroft Wlk.)
Redstart Clo. New Ad —6N 65
Redstone Hill. Red —2E 122
Redstone Hollow. Red —4E 122
Redstone Mnr. Red —3E 122
Redstone Pk. Red —3E 122
Redstone Rd. Red —4E 122
Redvers Buller Rd. Alder —6A 90
Redvers Rd. Brack —4N 31
Redvers Rd. Warl —5G 84
Redway Dri. Twic —1C 24
Redwing Av. G'ming —2G 133
Redwing Clo. H'ham —5M 197
Redwing Clo. S Croy —7G 64
Redwing Gdns. W Byf —8K 55
Redwing Ri. Guild —1F 114
Redwing Rd. Wall —3K 63
Redwood. Egh —1G 37
Redwood Clo. Craw —1C 182
Redwood Clo. Kenl —1N 83
Redwood Ct. Surb —6K 41
Redwood Dri. Asc —5E 34
Redwood Dri. Camb —2H 71
Redwood Est. Houn —2J 9
Redwood Gro. Chil —9E 114
Redwood Mnr. Hasl —1G 188
Redwood Mt. Reig —9M 101
Redwoods. SW15 —2F 26
Redwoods. Add —3J 55
Redwoods, The. Wind —6G 4
Redwoods Way. C Crook —8C 88
Redwood Wlk. Surb —7K 41
Reed Av. Orp —1N 67
Reed Clo. Alder —7B 90
Reed Dri. Red —6E 122
Reedham Dri. Purl —9K 63
Reedham Pk. Av. Purl —3L 83
Reedings. If'd —5J 181
Reed Pl. W Byf —9G 54
Reedsfield Clo. Afrd —5C 22
Reedsfield Rd. Afrd —5C 22
Reed's Hill. Brack —4N 31
Reeds Rd., The. Fren & Tilf —1J 149
Reeds, The. —8L 129
Rees Gdns. Croy —5C 46
Reeve Ct. Guild —8K 93
Reeve Rd. Reig —7A 122
Reeves Corner. Croy —8M 45 (3A 200)
Reeves Path. Hayes —1G 8
Reeves Rd. Alder —3A 110
Reeves Way. Wokgm —4A 30
Regal Cres. Wall —9F 44
Regal Dri. E Grin —1B 186
Regalfield Clo. Guild —8J 93
Regal Pl. SW6 —3N 13
(off Maxwell Rd.)
Regan Clo. Guild —7L 93
Regatta Ho. Tedd —5G 25
Regatta Point. Bren —2M 11
Regency Clo. Hamp —6N 23
Regency Ct. Add —9M 37
(off Albert Rd.)
Regency Ct. Sutt —1N 61
Regency Ct. Tedd —7H 25
Regency Dri. W Byf —9H 55
Regency Gdns. W on T —7K 39
Regency M. Iswth —8E 10
Regency Wlk. Croy —5H 47
Regency Wlk. Rich —8L 11
(off Grosvenor Av.)
Regent Clo. Fleet —5B 88
Regent Clo. Houn —4J 9
Regent Clo. New H —5M 55
Regent Clo. Red —7G 102
Regent Ct. Bag —5K 51
Regent Ct. Guild —1L 113
Regent Cres. Red —1D 122
Regent Ho. Eps —7D 60
Regent Ho. Red —2D 122
Regent Pk. Lea —5G 78
Regent Pl. SW19 —6A 28
Regent Pl. Croy —7C 46
Regent Rd. Surb —4M 41
Regents Clo. Craw —7A 182
Regents Clo. S Croy —3B 64
Regents Clo. Whyt —5B 84
Regents Ct. King T —2K 203
Regents Dri. Kes —2F 66
Regents M. Horl —8E 142
Regents Pl. Sand —7H 49
Regent St. W4 —1N 11
Regent St. Fleet —5B 88
Regents Wlk. Asc —5N 33
Regent Way. Frim —5D 70
Regimental Mus. of The Royal Logistic Corps. Mus. —8H 71
(off Princess Royal Barracks)
Regiment Clo. Farn —2H 89
Regina Rd. SE25 —2D 46
Regina Rd. S'hall —1M 9
Reid Av. Cat —8A 84
Reid Clo. Coul —3F 82
Reidonhill Cotts. Knap —5E 72
Reigate. —3M 121
Reigate Av. Sutt —7M 43
Reigate Bus. M. Reig —2L 121
Reigate Clo. Craw —9H 163
Reigate Heath. —3J 121
Reigate Heath Postmill. —3H 121
Reigate Hill. Reig —8A 102
Reigate Hill Clo. Reig —9M 101
Reigate Hill Interchange. (Junct.) —7N 101
Reigate Mus., The. —3N 121
Reigate Priory Mus. —3M 121
Reigate Rd. Brock —2N 119
Reigate Rd. Dork —4J 119 (1M 201)
Reigate Rd. Eps —6E 60
Reigate Rd. Lea —9J 79
Reigate Rd. Reig & Horl —1N 141
Reigate Rd. Reig & Red —3N 121
Reigate Towermill. —1B 122
Reigate Way. Wall —2J 63
Reindorp Clo. Guild —4K 113
Relko Ct. Eps —7C 60
Relko Gdns. Sutt —2B 62
Rembrandt Ct. Eps —3E 60
Rembrandt Way. W on T —8J 39
Renaissance Ho. Eps —6N 201
Rendle Clo. Croy —4C 46
Renfree Way. Shep —6B 38
Renfrew Ct. Houn —5M 9
Renfrew Rd. Houn —5L 9
Renfrew Rd. King T —8A 26
Renmans, The. Asht —3M 79
Renmuir St. SW17 —7D 28
Rennels Way. Iswth —5E 10
Rennie Clo. Afrd —4M 21
Rennie Ter. Red —4E 122
Renown Clo. Croy —7M 45 (1A 200)
Renton Clo. SW2 —1K 29
Replingham Rd. SW18 —2L 27
Reporton Rd. SW6 —3K 13
Repton Av. Hayes —1E 8
Repton Clo. Cars —2C 62
Reservoir Clo. T Hth —3A 46
Restavon Cvn. Site. Berr G —3K 87
Restmor Way. Wall —8E 44
Restormel Clo. Houn —8A 10
Restwell Av. Cranl —4K 155
Retreat Rd. Rich —8K 11
Retreat, The. SW14 —6D 12
Retreat, The. Cranl —6L 155
Retreat, The. Egh —6N 19
Retreat, The. Fleet —7A 88
Retreat, The. Surb —5M 41
Retreat, The. T Hth —3A 46
Retreat, The. Wor Pk —8G 43
Reubens Ct. W4 —1A 12
(off Chaseley Dri.)
Revell Clo. Fet —9B 78
Revell Dri. Fet —9B 78
Revell Rd. King T —1A 42
Revell Rd. Sutt —3L 61
Revelstoke Av. Farn —9N 69
Revelstoke Rd. SW18 —3L 27
Revesby Clo. W End —9A 52
Revesby Rd. Cars —5B 44
Rewell St. SW6 —3N 13
Rewley Rd. Cars —5B 44
Rex Av. Afrd —7B 22
Rex Ct. Hasl —2D 188
Reynard Clo. H'ham —3A 198
Reynard Mills Trad. Est. Bren —1J 11
Reynolds Av. Chess —4L 59
Reynolds Clo. SW19 —9B 28
Reynolds Clo. Cars —7D 44
Reynolds Grn. Coll T —9J 49
Reynolds Pl. Craw —2A 182
Reynolds Pl. Rich —9M 11
Reynolds Rd. Craw —2A 182
Reynolds Rd. N Mald —6C 42
Reynolds Way. Croy —1B 64
Rheingold Way. Wall —5J 63
Rhine Banks. Farn —9J 69
Rhine Barracks. Alder —1M 109
Rhodes Clo. Egh —6D 20
Rhodes Ct. Egh —6E 20
(off Pooley Grn. Clo.)
Rhodesia Ter. Deep —6H 71
Rhodesmoor Ho. Ct. Mord —5M 43
Rhodes Way. Craw —6D 182
Rhododendron Clo. Asc —8J 17
Rhododendron Ride. Egh —7J 19
Rhododendron Rd. Frim —5E 70
Rhododendron Wlk. Asc —8J 17
Rhodrons Av. Chess —2L 59
Rialto Rd. Mitc —1E 44
Ribble Pl. Farn —8K 69
Ribblesdale. Dork —7H 119
Ribblesdale Rd. SW16 —7F 28
Ricardo Ct. Brmly —6B 134
Ricardo Rd. Old Win —9L 5
Ricards Rd. SW19 —6L 27
Ricebridge La. Reig —6G 120
Rices Corner. Won —2C 134
Rices Hill. E Grin —9B 166
Richard Burbidge Mans. SW13
(off Brasenose Dri.) —2H 13
Richard Clo. Fleet —6A 88
Richards Clo. Ash V —8E 90
Richards Clo. Hayes —2E 8
Richards Fld. Eps —5C 60
Richard Sharples Ct. Sutt —4A 62
Richardson Ct. Craw —8N 181
Richards Rd. Stoke D —1B 78
Richbell Clo. Asht —5K 79
Richborough Ct. Craw —3A 182
Richens Clo. Houn —5D 10
Richland Av. Coul —1E 82
Richlands Av. Eps —1F 60
Rich La. SW5 —1N 13
Richmond. —8K 11
Richmond Av. SW20 —9K 27
Richmond Av. Felt —9F 8
Richmond Bri. Twic —9K 11
Richmond Circus. (Junct.) —7L 11
Richmond Clo. Big H —6D 86
Richmond Clo. Eps —1D 80 (8M 201)
Richmond Clo. Farn —2J 89
Richmond Clo. Fet —2C 98
Richmond Clo. Fleet —7A 88
Richmond Clo. Frim —5D 70
Richmond Ct. Craw —4C 182
Richmond Ct. Mitc —2B 44
Richmond Cres. Stai —6H 21
Richmond Dri. Shep —5E 38
Richmond Grn. Croy —9J 45
Richmond Gro. Surb —5M 41
Richmond Hill. Rich —9L 11
Richmond Hill Ct. Rich —9L 11
Richmond Ho. Sand —8K 49
Richmond Mans. Twic —9K 11
Richmond M. Tedd —6F 24
Richmond Pde. Twic —9J 11
(off Richmond Rd.)
Richmond Pk. —2A 26
Richmond Pk. Rd. SW14 —8B 12
Richmond Pk. Rd. King T —9L 25 (1K 203)
Richmond Rd. Coll T —7K 49
Richmond Rd. SW20 —9G 26
Richmond Rd. Coul —2F 82
Richmond Rd. Croy —9J 45
Richmond Rd. G'ming —5G 133
Richmond Rd. H'ham —4J 197
Richmond Rd. Iswth —6G 11
Richmond Rd. King T —5K 25 (1K 203)
Richmond Rd. Stai —6H 21
Richmond Rd. T Hth —2M 45
Richmond Rd. Twic —1H 25
Richmond Way. E Grin —1B 186
Richmond Way. Fet —1B 98
(in two parts)
Richmondwood. Asc —7E 34
Rickard Clo. SW2 —2L 29
Rickards Clo. Surb —8L 41
Ricketts Hill Rd. Tats —5F 86
Rickett St. SW6 —2M 13
Rickfield. Craw —4M 181
Rickford. Worp —4G 92
Rickford Hill. Worp —4G 93
Rickman Clo. Brack —5A 32
Rickman Ct. Add —9K 37
Rickman Cres. Add —9K 37
Rickman Hill. Coul —5F 82
Rickman Hill Rd. Coul —5F 82
Rickmans Green. —7H 163
Rickman's La. Plais —6B 192
Ricksons La. W Hor —5C 96
Rickwood. Horl —7F 142
Rickyard. Guild —3L 113
Riddings, The. Cat —3C 104
Riddlesdown. —9N 63
Riddlesdown Av. Purl —7N 63
Riddlesdown Rd. Purl —6N 63
(in two parts)
Ride La. Alb —4M 135
(in two parts)
Riders Way. God —9F 104
Ride, The. Bren —1H 11
Ride, The. Loxw —5D 192
Ride Way. Ews —9C 136
Rideway Clo. Camb —2N 69
Ridgebridge Hill. —1H 155
Ridge Clo. Str G —7A 120
Ridge Clo. Wok —8L 73
Ridge Ct. Warl —5D 84
Ridge Ct. Wind —6F 4
Ridgegate Clo. Reig —1B 122
Ridge Green. —6J 123
Ridge Grn. S Nut —6J 123
Ridge Grn. Clo. S Nut —6J 123
Ridgehurst Dri. H'ham —7F 196
Ridgelands. Fet —2D 98
Ridge Langley. S Croy —6D 64
Ridgemead Rd. Eng G —4K 19
Ridgemoor Clo. Hind —4C 170
Ridgemount. Guild —4L 113
Ridgemount. Wey —8F 38
Ridgemount Av. Coul —4F 82
Ridgemount Av. Croy —7G 47
Ridgemount Est. Deep —7G 70
Ridge Mt. Rd. Asc —8D 34
Ridgemount Way. Red —5B 122
Ridge Pk. Purl —6H 63
Ridge Rd. Mitc —8F 28
Ridge Rd. Sutt —7K 43
Ridgeside. Craw —3D 182
Ridges, The. —3A 48
Ridges, The. Guild —8M 113
Ridges Yd. Croy —9M 45 (4A 200)
Ridge, The. Coul —1J 83
Ridge, The. Eps —5B 80
Ridge, The. Fet —2D 98
Ridge, The. Purl —6G 63
Ridge, The. Rud —9E 176
Ridge, The. S'dale —6D 34
Ridge, The. Surb —4N 41
Ridge, The. Twic —1D 24
Ridge, The. Wok —4D 74
Ridge, The. Wold —4K 105
Ridgeway. E Grin —2A 186
Ridge Way. Eden —8L 127
Ridgeway. Eps —8B 60
Ridge Way. Felt —4M 23
Ridgeway. Hors —2N 73
Ridgeway. Rich —9L 11
Ridgeway. Vir W —4A 36
Ridgeway Clo. Cranl —7B 156
Ridgeway Clo. Dork —7G 118
Ridgeway Clo. Light —7L 51
Ridgeway Clo. Oxs —1C 78
Ridgeway Clo. Wok —2N 73
Ridgeway Ct. Red —4D 122
Ridgeway Cres. Orp —1N 67
Ridgeway Dri. Dork —8G 119
Ridgeway Gdns. Wok —2N 73
Ridgeway Ho. Horl —1E 162
(off Crescent, The)
Ridgeway Pde. C Crook —8B 88
Ridgeway Rd. Dork —7G 118
Ridgeway Rd. Iswth —3E 10
Ridgeway Rd. Red —3D 122
Ridgeway Rd. N. Iswth —3E 10
Ridgeway, The. Brack —2A 32
Ridgeway, The. Brkwd —7C 72
Ridgeway, The. Cranl —7A 156
Ridgeway, The. Croy —9K 45
Ridgeway, The. Fet —2E 98
Ridgeway, The. Guild —4C 114
Ridgeway, The. Horl —1E 162
Ridgeway, The. H'ham —4H 197
Ridgeway, The. Light —6M 51
Ridgeway, The. Oxs —1C 78
Ridge Way, The. S Croy —5B 64
Ridgeway, The. W on T —7G 38
Ridgewood Dri. Frim —3H 71
Ridgley Rd. C'fold —5D 172
Ridgmount Rd. SW18 —8N 13
Ridgway. —2J 75
Ridgway. SW19 —8H 27
Ridgway. Pyr —2J 75
Ridgway Ct. SW19 —7J 27
Ridgway Gdns. SW19 —8J 27
Ridgway Hill Rd. Farnh —3H 129
Ridgway Pde. Farnh —4H 129
(off Ridgway Rd.)
Ridgway Pl. SW19 —7K 27
Ridgway Rd. Farnh —4H 129
Ridgway Rd. Pyr —2H 75
Ridgway, The. Sutt —4B 62
Riding Ct. Rd. Dat —3M 5
Riding Hill. S Croy —9D 64
Ridings La. Ock —1C 96
Ridings, The. Add —3G 55
Ridings, The. Asht —4K 79
Ridings, The. Big H —4G 86
Ridings, The. Cobh —8A 58
Ridings, The. E Hor —3F 96
Ridings, The. Eps —2D 80
Ridings, The. Ewe —5E 60
Ridings, The. Frim —3F 70
Ridings, The. Reig —1B 122
Ridings, The. Rip —1J 95
Ridings, The. Sun —9H 23
Ridings, The. Surb —4N 41
Ridings, The. Tad —7L 81
Ridings, The. Worth —2H 183
Riding, The. Cranl —6N 155
Riding, The. Wok —1D 74
Ridlands Gro. Oxt —8G 106
Ridlands La. Oxt —8F 106
Ridlands Ri. Oxt —8G 106
Ridley Clo. Fleet —6A 88
Ridley Ct. SW16 —7J 29
Ridley Ct. Craw —9H 163
Ridley Rd. SW19 —8N 27
Ridley Rd. Warl —5F 84
Ridsdale Rd. Wok —4L 73
Riesco Dri. Croy —3F 64
Rifle Butts All. Eps —1E 80
Rifle Way. Farn —2H 89
Rigault Rd. SW6 —5K 13
Rigby Clo. Croy —9L 45
Riggindale Rd. SW16 —6H 29
Rillside. Craw —6E 182
Rill Wlk. E Grin —9D 166
Rimbault Clo. Alder —6B 90
Rimmer Clo. Craw —9N 181
Rinaldo Rd. SW12 —1F 28
Ringford Rd. SW18 —8L 13
Ringley Av. Horl —8E 142
Ringley Oak. H'ham —4M 197
Ringley Pk. Av. Reig —4B 122
Ringley Pk. Rd. Reig —3A 122
Ringley Rd. H'ham —4L 197
Ringmead. Brack —4K 31
Ringmer Av. SW6 —4K 13
Ringmore Dri. Guild —9E 94
Ringmore Rd. W on T —9K 39
Ring Rd. N. Gat A —2F 162
Ring Rd. S. Gat A —3G 162
Ringstead Rd. Sutt —1B 62
Ring, The. Brack —1A 32
Ringway. S'hall —1L 9
Ringwood. Brack —6L 31
Ringwood Av. Croy —6J 45
Ringwood Av. Red —9D 102
Ringwood Clo. Asc —3M 33
Ringwood Clo. Craw —5C 182
Ringwood Gdns. SW15 —2F 26
Ringwood Lodge. Red —9E 102
Ringwood Rd. B'water —9H 49
Ringwood Rd. Farn —7A 70
Ringwood Way. Hamp H —5A 24
Ripley. —8L 75
Ripley Av. Egh —7A 20
Ripley By-Pass. Rip —1L 95
Ripley Clo. New Ad —3M 65
Ripley Ct. Mitc —1B 44
Ripley Gdns. SW14 —6C 12
Ripley Gdns. Sutt —1A 62
Ripley La. Rip & W Hor —1N 95
Ripley Rd. Hamp —8A 24
Ripley Rd. Send & E Clan —4L 95
Ripley Springs. —7A 20
Ripley Way. Eps —7N 59
Ripon Clo. Camb —3H 71
Ripon Clo. Guild —1J 113
Ripon Gdns. Chess —2K 59
Ripplesmere. Brack —3B 32
Ripplesmore Clo. Sand —7G 48
Ripston Rd. Afrd —6E 22
Risborough Dri. Wor Pk —6F 42
Rise Rd. Asc —4B 34
Rise, The. Craw —3G 183
Rise, The. Crowt —2E 48
Rise, The. E Grin —1B 186
Rise, The. E Hor —4F 96
Rise, The. Eps —6E 60
Rise, The. S Croy —5F 64
Rise, The. S'dale —5B 34
Rise, The. Tad —7H 81
Rise, The. Wokgm —1A 30
Ritchie Clo. M'bowr —7G 182
Ritchie Rd. Croy —5E 46
Ritherdon Rd. SW17 —3E 28
River Ash Estate. —6G 39
River Av. Th Dit —6G 41
River Bank. E Mol —2E 40
Riverbank. Stai —7H 21
River Bank. Th Dit —4F 40
Riverbank. Westc —5B 118
Riverbank, The. Wind —3E 4
Riverbank Way. Bren —2J 11
River Ct. Surb —8H 203
River Ct. Wok —1E 74
River Crane Way. Felt —3N 23
(off Watermill Way)
Riverdale. Wrec —4D 128
Riverdale Dri. SW18 —2N 27
Riverdale Dri. Wok —8B 74
Riverdale Gdns. Twic —9J 11
Riverdale Rd. Felt —5M 23
Riverdale Rd. Twic —9J 11

Riverdene Ind. Est.—Rosewood Gro.

Riverdene Ind. Est. *W on T* —2L **57**
Riverfield Rd. *Stai* —7H **21**
River Gdns. *Cars* —8E **44**
River Gdns. *Felt* —8J **9**
River Gdns. Bus. Cen. *Felt* —8J **9**
River Gro. Pk. *Beck* —1J **47**
Riverhead Dri. *Sutt* —6N **61**
River Hill. *Cobh* —2J **77**
Riverhill. *Wor Pk* —8C **42**
Riverholme Dri. *Eps* —5C **60**
River Island Clo. *Fet* —8D **78**
River La. *Farnh* —4D **128**
River La. *Fet* —8D **78**
(in two parts)
River La. *Rich* —1K **25**
River La. *Stoke D* —3M **77**
Rivermead. *Byfl* —9A **56**
Rivermead. *E Mol* —2C **40**
River Mead. *H'ham* —7H **107**
River Mead. *If'd* —9M **161**
Rivermead. *King T* —4K **41** (8J **203**)
Rivermead Clo. *Add* —4L **55**
Rivermead Clo. *Tedd* —6H **25**
Rivermead Ct. *SW6* —6L **13**
Rivermead Rd. *Camb* —4N **69**
River Meads Av. *Twic* —4A **24**
Rivermede. *Bord* —5A **168**
River Mole Bus. Pk. *Esh* —8A **40**
River Mt. *W on T* —6G **38**
Rivermount Gdns. *Guild* —6M **113**
Rivernook Clo. *W on T* —4K **39**
River Pk. Av. *Stai* —5F **20**
River Reach. *Tedd* —6J **25**
River Rd. *Stai* —9H **21**
River Rd. *Wind* —3A **4**
River Rd. *Yat* —7A **48**
River Row. *Farnh* —4E **128**
River Row Cotts. *Farnh* —3E **128**
Rivers Clo. *Farn* —4C **90**
Riversdale Rd. *Th Dit* —4G **40**
Riversdell Clo. *Cher* —6H **37**
Rivers Ho. W4 —1N 11
(off Chiswick High Rd.)
Riverside. *Cher* —9J **37**
Riverside. *Dork* —3K **119**
Riverside. *Eden* —2L **147**
Riverside. *Egh* —4C **20**
Riverside. *F Row* —6G **187**
Riverside. *Guild* —1N **113**
Riverside. *Horl* —1E **162**
Riverside. *H'ham* —6G **196**
Riverside. *Rich* —8K **11**
Riverside. *Shep* —6F **38**
Riverside. *Stai* —9H **21**
(Laleham Rd.)
Riverside. *Stai* —6H **21**
(Temple Gdns.)
Riverside. *Sun* —1L **39**
Riverside. *Twic* —2H **25**
Riverside. *Wray* —1M **19**
Riverside Av. *E Mol* —4D **40**
Riverside Av. *Light* —7N **51**
Riverside Bus. Cen. *SW18* —2N **27**
Riverside Bus. Cen. *Guild*
—3M **113** (3A **202**)
Riverside Bus. Pk. *Farnh* —9J **109**
Riverside Clo. *Brkwd* —7C **72**
Riverside Clo. *Farn* —9L **69**
Riverside Clo. *King T*
—6K **41** (7J **203**)
Riverside Clo. *Stai* —9H **21**
Riverside Clo. *Wall* —9F **44**
Riverside Ct. *Dork* —3K **119**
Riverside Ct. *Eden* —2M **147**
Riverside Ct. *Farnh* —9H **109**
Riverside Ct. *Felt* —1F **22**
Riverside Ct. *Fet* —9G **78**
Riverside Ct. Isw'th —5F 10
(off Woodlands Rd.)
Riverside Dri. *W4* —3C **12**
Riverside Dri. *Brmly* —4C **134**
Riverside Dri. *Esh* —1A **58**
Riverside Dri. *Mitc* —4C **44**
Riverside Dri. *Rich* —4H **25**
Riverside Dri. *Stai* —6G **21**
(Chertsey La.)
Riverside Dri. *Stai* —8H **21**
(Wheatsheaf La.)
Riverside Gdns. *W6* —1G **13**
Riverside Gdns. *Old Wok* —8D **74**
Riverside Ind. Pk. *Farnh* —9J **109**
Riverside M. *Croy* —9J **45**
Riverside Pk. *Add* —2N **55**
Riverside Pk. *Camb* —3M **69**
Riverside Pk. *Coln* —5G **6**
Riverside Pk. *Farnh* —9J **109**
Riverside Pl. *Stanw* —9M **7**
Riverside Rd. *SW17* —5N **27**
Riverside Rd. *Stai* —8H **21**
Riverside Rd. *Stanw* —8M **7**
(in two parts)
Riverside Rd. *W on T* —1M **57**
Riverside, The. *E Mol* —2D **40**
Riverside Wlk. *SW6* —6K **13**
Riverside Wlk. W4 —2E 12
(off Chiswick Wharf)
Riverside Wlk. *G'ming* —6G **133**
Riverside Wlk. *Isw'th* —6E **10**
Riverside Wlk. *King T*
—2K **41** (3H **203**)
Riverside Wlk. *W Wick* —7L **47**
Riverside Wlk. Wind —3G 5
(off Thames Side)
Riverside Way. *Camb* —3M **69**
Riverstone Ct. *King T*
—9M **25** (2M **203**)
River St. *Wind* —3G **4**
River Ter. *W6* —1H **13**
River Vw. *Add* —2L **55**
Riverview. *Guild* —3M **113** (2A **202**)
Riverview Gdns. *SW13* —2G **13**
Riverview Gdns. *Cobh* —9G **57**
River Vw. Gdns. *Twic* —3F **24**
Riverview Gro. *W4* —2A **12**
Riverview Rd. *W4* —3A **12**
Riverview Rd. *Eps* —1B **60**
River Wlk. *W6* —3H **13**
River Wlk. *W on T* —5H **39**
River Way. *Eps* —2C **60**
Riverway. *Stai* —9K **21**
River Way. *Twic* —3B **24**
Riverway Est. *P'mrsh* —3L **133**
Riverwood Ct. *Guild* —1M **113**
Rives Av. *Yat* —1A **68**
Rivett Drake Rd. *Guild* —8K **93**
Rivey Clo. *W Byf* —1H **75**
Road Ho. Est. *Old Wok* —8C **74**
Roakes Av. *Add* —8K **37**
Roasthill La. *Eton W* —2A **4**
Robert Clo. *W on T* —2J **57**
Robert Gentry Ho. *W14* —1K **13**
Robert Owen Ho. *SW6* —4J **13**
Robertsbridge Rd. *Cars* —7A **44**
Roberts Clo. *Stanw* —9L **7**
Roberts Clo. *Sutt* —4J **61**
Robertson Ct. *Wok* —5H **73**
Robertson Way. *As* —3D **110**
Roberts Rd. *Alder* —3A **110**
Roberts Rd. *Camb* —9M **49**
Robert St. *Croy* —9N **45** (4C **200**)
Roberts Way. *Eng G* —8M **19**
Robert Way. *H'ham* —1M **197**
Robert Way. *Myt* —2D **90**
Robin Clo. *Add* —2M **55**
Robin Clo. *Ash V* —7E **90**
Robin Clo. *Craw* —1A **182**
Robin Clo. *E Grin* —8B **166**
Robin Clo. *Hamp* —6M **23**
Robin Gdns. *Red* —1E **122**
Robin Gro. *Bren* —2J **11**
Robin Hill. *G'ming* —4G **133**
Robin Hill Dri. *Camb* —3E **70**
Robin Hood. (Junct.) —4D **26**
Robin Hood Clo. *Farn* —7M **69**
Robinhood Clo. *Mitc* —2G **45**
Robin Hood Clo. *Wok* —5J **73**
Robin Hood Cres. *Knap* —4H **73**
Robin Hood La. *SW15* —4D **26**
Robinhood La. *Mitc* —2G **45**
Robin Hood La. *Sutt* —2M **61**
Robin Hood La. *Sut G* —2B **94**
Robin Hood La. *Warn* —3E **196**
Robin Hood Rd. *SW19 & SW15*
—6F **26**
Robin Hood Rd. *Knap & Wok*
(in two parts) —4G **73**
Robin Hood Way. *SW15 & SW20*
—4D **26**
Robin Hood Works. Knap —4H 73
(off Robin Hood Rd.)
Robin La. *Sand* —7G **49**
Robin Row. *Turn H* —4F **184**
Robin's Bow. *Camb* —2N **69**
Robin's Ct. *Beck* —1N **47**
Robins Ct. *S Croy* —7F **200**
Robins Dale. *Knap* —4F **72**
Robins Gro. *W Wick* —1C **66**
Robins Gro. Cres. *Yat* —9A **48**
Robinson Rd. *SW17 & SW19*
—7C **28**
Robinson Rd. *Craw* —4B **182**
Robinson Way. *Bord* —7A **168**
Robinsway. *W on T* —1K **57**
Robinswood Ct. *H'ham* —4M **197**
Robin Way. *Guild* —8L **93**
Robin Way. *Stai* —4H **21**
Robin Willis Way. *Old Win* —9K **5**
Robinwood Pl. *SW15* —5C **26**
Robson Rd. *SE27* —4M **29**
Roby Dri. *Brack* —6B **32**
Robyns Way. *Eden* —3M **147**
Roche Rd. *SW16* —9K **29**
Rochester Av. *Felt* —3G **23**
Rochester Clo. *SW16* —8J **29**
Rochester Gdns. *Cat* —9B **84**
Rochester Gdns. *Croy* —9B **46**
Rochester Gro. *Fleet* —5A **88**
Rochester Pde. *Felt* —3H **23**
Rochester Rd. *Cars* —1D **62**
Rochester Rd. *Stai* —7F **20**
Rochester Wlk. *Reig* —8M **121**
Roche Wlk. *Cars* —5D **44**
Rochford Way. *Croy* —5J **45**
Rock Av. *SW14* —6C **12**
Rock Clo. *Mitc* —1D **44**
Rockdale Dri. *Gray* —6B **170**
Rockery, The. *Farn* —2J **89**
Rockfield Clo. *Oxt* —9B **106**
Rockfield Rd. *Oxt* —7B **106**
Rockfield Way. *Coll T* —7J **49**
Rock Gdns. *Alder* —3L **109**
Rockhampton Clo. *SE27* —5L **29**
Rockhampton Rd. *SE27* —5L **29**
Rockhampton Rd. *S Croy* —3B **64**
Rock Hill. *Hamb* —8G **152**
Rockingham Clo. *SW15* —7E **12**
Rockland Rd. *SW15* —7K **13**
Rock La. *Wrec* —6F **128**
Rockshaw Rd. *Red* —5G **102**
Rocks La. *SW13* —4F **12**
Rocks, The. *Ash W* —3E **186**
Rockwood Park. —4M 185
Rocky La. *Reig* —6D **102**
Rocque Ho. SW6 —3L 13
(off Estcourt Rd.)
Rodale Mans. *SW18* —9N **13**
Rodborough Hill Cotts. *Milf* —3N **151**
Roden Gdns. *Croy* —5B **46**
Rodenhurst Rd. *SW4* —1G **29**
Rodgate La. *Hasl* —3A **190**
Rodgers Ho. SW4 —1H 29
(off Clapham Pk. Est.)
Roding Clo. *Cranl* —8H **155**
Rodmel Ct. *Farn* —4C **90**
Rodmill La. *SW2* —1J **29**
Rodney Clo. *Croy* —7M **45** (1A **200**)
Rodney Clo. *N Mald* —4D **42**
Rodney Clo. *W on T* —7K **39**
Rodney Gdns. *W Wick* —1C **66**
Rodney Grn. *W on T* —8K **39**
Rodney Pl. *SW19* —9A **28**
Rodney Rd. *Mitc* —2C **44**
Rodney Rd. *N Mald* —4D **42**
Rodney Rd. *Twic* —9A **10**
Rodney Rd. *W on T* —8K **39**
Rodney Way. *Coln* —4G **7**
Rodney Way. *Guild* —2C **114**
Rodona Rd. *Wey* —7E **56**
Rodsall La. *P'ham* —3K **131**
Rodway Rd. *SW15* —1F **26**
Rodwell Ct. *Add* —1L **55**
Roebuck Clo. *Asht* —7L **79**
Roebuck Clo. *Felt* —5J **23**
Roebuck Clo. *H'ham* —4A **198**
Roebuck Clo. *Reig* —3M **121**
Roebuck Est. *Binf* —8H **15**
Roebuck Rd. *Chess* —2N **59**
Roedean Cres. *SW15* —9D **12**
Roedeer Copse. *Hasl* —2C **188**
Roehampton. —1F 26
Roehampton Clo. *SW15* —7F **12**
Roehampton Ga. *SW15* —9D **12**
Roehampton High St. *SW15* —1F **26**
Roehampton Lane. (Junct.) —2G **27**
Roehampton La. *SW15* —7F **12**
Roehampton Va. *SW15* —4E **26**
Roffe's La. *Cat* —2A **104**
Roffey. —4N 197
Roffey Clo. *Horl* —8D **142**
Roffey Clo. *Purl* —3M **83**
Roffey Park. —2F 198
Roffey's Clo. *Copt* —6L **163**
Roffords. *Wok* —4L **73**
Roffye Ct. *H'ham* —4N **197**
Rogers Clo. *Cat* —9E **84**
Rogers Clo. *Coul* —5M **83**
Roger Simmons Ct. *Bookh* —2N **97**
Rogers La. *Warl* —5J **85**
Rogers Mead. *God* —1E **124**
Rogers Rd. *SW17* —5B **28**
Rokeby Clo. *Brack* —9B **16**
Rokeby Ct. *Wok* —4J **73**
Rokeby Pl. *SW20* —8G **27**
Roke Clo. *Kenl* —1N **83**
Roke Clo. *Witl* —5B **152**
Roke La. *Witl* —6N **151**
Roke Lodge Rd. *Kenl* —9M **63**
Roke Rd. *Kenl* —2N **83**
Rokers La. *Shack* —4A **132**
(in two parts)
Rokes Pl. *Yat* —9A **48**
Roland Way. *Wor Pk* —8E **42**
Rolinsden Way. *Kes* —2F **66**
Rollesby Rd. *Chess* —3N **59**
Rolleston Rd. *S Croy* —4A **64**
Rollit Cres. *Houn* —8A **10**
Rolston Ho. *Hasl* —2D **188**
Romana Ct. *Stai* —5J **21**
Romanby Ct. *Red* —4D **122**
Roman Clo. *Felt* —8K **9**
Romanfield Rd. *SW2* —1K **29**
Romanhurst Av. *Brom* —3N **47**
Romanhurst Gdns. *Brom* —3N **47**
Roman Ind. Est. *Croy* —6B **46**
Roman Ride. *Crowt* —2C **48**
Roman Rd. *Dork* —7G **119**
Roman Rd. *M Grn* —5M **147**
Romans Bus. Pk. *Farnh* —9J **109**
Romans Way. *Wok* —2J **75**
Roman Way. *Cars* —5D **62**
Roman Way. *Croy* —8M **45** (2A **200**)
Roman Way. *Farnh* —8K **109**
Roman Way. *Warf* —9D **16**
Romany Gdns. *Sutt* —6M **43**
Romany Rd. *Knap* —2F **72**
Romany, The. *Farn* —4F **88**
Roma Read Clo. *SW15* —1G **26**
Romayne Clo. *Farn* —9M **69**
Romberg Rd. *SW17* —4E **28**
Romeo Hill. *Warf* —9D **16**
Romeyn Rd. *SW16* —4K **29**
Romily Ct. *SW6* —5K **13**
Romley Ct. *Farnh* —2J **129**
Rommany Rd. *SE27* —5N **29**
(in two parts)
Romney Clo. *Afrd* —6D **22**
Romney Clo. *Chess* —1L **59**
Romney Ho. *Brack* —3C **32**
Romney Lock Rd. *Wind* —3G **5**
Romney Rd. *N Mald* —5C **42**
Romola Rd. *SE24* —2M **29**
Romsey Clo. *Alder* —6A **110**
Romsey Clo. *B'water* —9H **49**
Romsey Clo. *Orp* —1K **67**
Romulus Ct. *Bren* —3K **11**
Rona Clo. *Craw* —6N **181**
Ronald Clo. *Beck* —3J **47**
Ronelean Rd. *Surb* —8M **41**
Ronneby Clo. *Wey* —9F **38**
Roof of the World Cvn. Pk. *Tad*
—9A **100**
Rookeries Clo. *Felt* —4J **23**
Rookery Clo. *Fet* —2E **98**
Rookery Dri. *Westc* —7A **118**
Rookery Hill. *Asht* —5N **79**
Rookery Hill. *Out* —4L **143**
Rookery La. *Small* —6L **143**
Rookery Rd. *Orp* —6H **67**
Rookery Rd. *Stai* —6K **21**
Rookery, The. *Westc* —7A **118**
Rookery Way. *Lwr K* —5L **101**
Rook La. *Cat* —3K **103**
Rookley Clo. *Sutt* —5N **61**
Rooks Hill. *Brmly* —9D **134**
Rooksmead Rd. *Sun* —1H **39**
Rooks Nest. —8H 105
Rookstone Rd. *SW17* —6D **28**
Rookswood. *Brack* —8N **15**
Rook Way. *H'ham* —2M **197**
Rookwood Av. *N Mald* —3F **42**
Rookwood Av. *Owl* —5K **49**
Rookwood Av. *Wall* —1H **63**
Rookwood Clo. *Red* —7F **102**
Rookwood Ct. *Guild*
—6M **113** (8A **202**)
Rookwood Pk. *H'ham* —5F **196**
Roosthole Hill. *Man H* —8C **198**
Roothill La. *Bet* —1N **139**
Ropeland Way. *H'ham* —1L **197**
Ropers Wlk. *SW2* —1L **29**
Roper Way. *Mitc* —1E **44**
Rope Wlk. *Sun* —2K **39**
Rorkes Drift. *Myt* —1D **90**
Rosa Av. *Afrd* —5B **22**
Rosalind Franklin Clo. *Guild* —4H **113**
Rosaline Rd. *SW6* —3K **13**
Rosaline Ter. SW6 —3K 13
(off Rosaline Rd.)
Rosamund Clo. *S Croy*
—1A **64** (7E **200**)
Rosamund Rd. *Craw* —5F **182**
Rosamun St. *S'hall* —1M **9**
Rosary Clo. *Houn* —5M **9**
Rosary Gdns. *SW7* —1N **13**
Rosary Gdns. *Afrd* —5C **22**
Rosary Gdns. *Yat* —9C **48**
Rosaville Rd. *SW6* —3L **13**
Roseacre. *Oxt* —3C **126**
Roseacre Clo. *Shep* —4B **38**
Roseacre Gdns. *Chil* —9H **115**
Rose & Crown Pas. *Isw'th* —4G **10**
Rose Av. *Mitc* —9D **28**
Rose Av. *Mord* —4A **44**
Rosebank. *SW6* —3H **13**
Rosebank. *Eps* —1B **80** (8J **201**)
Rosebank Clo. *Tedd* —7G **25**
Rose Bank Cotts. *Wok* —9A **74**
Rosebay. *Wokgm* —9D **14**
Roseberry Av. *T Hth* —1N **45**
Roseberry Gdns. *Orp* —1N **67**
Rosebery Av. *Eps* —1D **80** (8N **201**)
Rosebery Av. *N Mald* —1E **42**
Rosebery Clo. *Mord* —5J **43**
Rosebery Cres. *Wok* —7B **74**
Rosebery Gdns. *Sutt* —1N **61**
Rosebery Rd. *SW2* —1J **29**
Rosebery Rd. *Eps* —6C **80**
Rosebery Rd. *Houn* —8C **10**
Rosebery Rd. *King T* —1A **42**
Rosebery Rd. *Sutt* —3L **61**
Rosebery Sq. *King T* —1A **42**
Rosebine Av. *Twic* —1D **24**
Rosebriars Clo. *Wok* —3J **75**
Rosebriars. *Cat* —7B **84**
Rosebriars. *Esh* —2C **58**
(in two parts)
Rosebury Dri. *Bisl* —2D **72**
Rosebury Rd. *SW6* —5N **13**
Rosebushes. *Eps* —3G **81**
Rose Cotts. *Fay* —9H **181**
Rose Cotts. *F Row* —6G **187**
Rose Cotts. *Kes* —7E **66**
Rose Cotts. *Wmly* —8D **152**
Rose Ct. *Wokgm* —2B **30**
Rosecourt Rd. *Croy* —5K **45**
Rosecroft Clo. *Big H* —5H **87**
Rosecroft Gdns. *Twic* —2D **24**
Rosedale. *Alder* —2A **110**
Rosedale. *Asht* —5J **79**
Rosedale. *Binf* —6H **15**
Rosedale. *Cat* —1B **104**
Rosedale Clo. *Craw* —5M **181**
Rosedale Gdns. *Brack* —4M **31**
Rosedale Pl. *Croy* —6G **47**
Rosedale Rd. *Eps* —2F **60**
Rosedale Rd. *Rich* —6L **11**
Rosedene Av. *SW16* —4K **29**
Rosedene Av. *Croy* —6J **45**
Rosedene Av. *Mord* —4M **43**
Rosedene Gdns. *Fleet* —3A **88**
Rosedene La. *Coll T* —9J **49**
Rosedew Rd. *W6* —2J **13**
Rose End. *Wor Pk* —7J **43**
Rosefield Clo. *Cars* —2C **62**
Rosefield Gdns. *Ott* —3F **54**
Rosefield Rd. *Stai* —5J **21**
Rose Gdns. *Farn* —2K **89**
Rose Gdns. *Felt* —3H **23**
Rose Gdns. *Stanw* —1M **21**
Rose Gdns. *Wokgm* —2B **30**
Roseheath Rd. *Houn* —8N **9**
Rose Hill. —5G 119 (3L 201)
(Dorking)
Rosehill. —7A 44
(Sutton)
Rose Hill. *Binf* —6H **15**
Rosehill. *Clay* —3G **58**
Rose Hill. *Dork* —5G **119** (3K **201**)
Rosehill. *Hamp* —9A **24**
Rosehill. *Sutt* —9N **43**
Rose Hill Arch M. *Dork* —2L **201**
Rosehill Av. *Sutt* —7A **44**
Rosehill Av. *Wok* —3M **73**
Rosehill Ct. Mord —6A 44
(off St Helier Av.)
Rosehill Ct. Pde. Mord —6A 44
(off St Helier Av.)
Rosehill Farm Mdw. *Bans* —2N **81**
Rosehill Gdns. *Sutt* —8N **43**
Rosehill Pk. W. *Sutt* —7A **44**
Rosehill Rd. *SW18* —9N **13**
Rosehill Rd. *Big H* —4E **86**
Rose Hill Roundabout. (Junct.)
—6A **44**
Rose La. *Rip* —8L **75**
Roseleigh Clo. *Twic* —9K **11**
Rosemary Av. *Ash V* —5E **90**
Rosemary Av. *Houn* —5L **9**
Rosemary Av. *W Mol* —2A **40**
Rosemary Clo. *Croy* —5J **45**
Rosemary Clo. *Farn* —9J **69**
Rosemary Clo. *Oxt* —2C **126**
Rosemary Ct. *Hasl* —1G **188**
Rosemary Ct. *Horl* —7C **142**
Rosemary Cres. *Guild* —8J **93**
Rosemary Gdns. *SW14* —6B **12**
Rosemary Gdns. *B'water* —1H **69**
Rosemary Gdns. *Chess* —1L **59**
Rosemary La. *SW14* —6B **12**
Rosemary La. *Alf* —9E **174**
Rosemary La. *B'water* —9H **49**
Rosemary La. *Charl* —3K **161**
(in two parts)
Rosemary La. *Egh* —8D **36**
Rosemary La. *Horl* —9F **142**
Rosemary La. *Rowl* —7D **128**
Rosemary Rd. *SW17* —4A **28**
Rosemead. *Cher* —6K **37**
Rosemead Av. *Felt* —3G **22**
Rosemead Av. *Mitc* —2G **45**
Rosemead Clo. *Red* —5B **122**
Rosemont Rd. *N Mald* —2B **42**
Rosemont Rd. *Rich* —8L **11**
Rosemount Av. *W Byf* —9J **55**
Rosendale Rd. *SE24 & SE21* —1N **29**
Roseneath Dri. *C'fold* —5E **172**
Roseneath Rd. *SW11* —1E **28**
Rose Pk. Cvn. Site. *Ott* —5G **54**
Rosery, The. *Croy* —5G **46**
Rosery, The. *Egh* —1G **36**
Roses Cotts. *Dork* —5G **119** (2K **201**)
Roses La. *Wind* —5A **4**
Rose St. *Wokgm* —2B **30**
Rosethorn Clo. *SW12* —1H **29**
Rosetrees. *Guild* —4C **114**
Rose Vw. *Add* —2L **55**
Roseville Av. *Houn* —8A **10**
Roseville Rd. *Hayes* —1H **9**
Rosevine Rd. *SW20* —9H **27**
Rose Wlk. *Craw* —5N **181**
Rose Wlk. *Fleet* —3A **88**
Rose Wlk. *Purl* —7H **63**
Rose Wlk. *Surb* —4A **42**
Rose Wlk. *W Wick* —8M **47**
Rosewarne Clo. *Wok* —5K **73**
Rosewood. *Sutt* —6A **62**
Rosewood. *Th Dit* —8G **40**
Rosewood. *Wok* —6C **74**
Rosewood Dri. *Shep* —4A **38**
Rosewood Gro. *Sutt* —8A **44**

Ryefield Rd.—St Marys Mill

Ryefield Rd. *SE19* —7N **29**
Rye Gro. *Cranl* —7J **155**
Rye Gro. *Light* —4C **52**
Ryehurst La. *Binf* —5K **15**
Ryeland Clo. *Fleet* —1D **88**
Ryelands. *Craw* —4M **181**
Ryelands. *Horl* —7G **142**
Ryelands Clo. *Cat* —8B **84**
Ryelands Ct. *Lea* —6G **79**
Ryelands Pl. *Wey* —9F **38**
Ryelaw Rd. *C Crook* —8B **88**
Ryemead La. *Wink* —4G **17**
Ryersh La. *Capel* —3H **159**
Rye Wlk. *SW15* —8J **13**
Ryfold Rd. *SW19* —4M **27**
Ryland Clo. *Felt* —5G **23**
Rylandes Rd. *S Croy* —5E **64**
Ryle Rd. *Farnh* —3G **128**
Rylston Rd. *SW6* —2L **13**
Rymer Rd. *Croy* —6B **46**
Rysted La. *W'ham* —4L **107**
Ryst Wood Rd. *F Row* —7K **187**
Rythe Ct. *Th Dit* —6G **41**
Rythe Rd. *Clay* —2D **58**
Rythe, The. *Esh* —6B **58**

Sabah Ct. *Afrd* —5B **22**
Sable Clo. *Houn* —6K **9**
Sabre Ct. *Alder* —2K **109**
Sachel Ct. Dri. *Alf* —7H **175**
Sachel Ct. M. *Alf* —7G **174**
Sachel Ct. Rd. *Alf* —6F **174**
Sachel Hill La. *Alf* —7F **174**
Sackville Clo. *E Grin* —7M **165**
Sackville College. —9C **166**
Sackville Cotts. *Blet* —2A **124**
Sackville Ct. *E Grin* —1B **186**
Sackville Gdns. *E Grin* —7M **165**
(in two parts)
Sackville Ho. *SW16* —4J **29**
Sackville La. *E Grin* —7L **165**
Sackville Rd. *Sutt* —4M **61**
Saddleback Rd. *Camb* —7C **50**
Saddleback Way. *Fleet* —1C **88**
Saddlebrook Pk. *Sun* —8F **22**
Saddler Corner. *Sand* —8G **49**
Saddler Row. *Craw* —6B **182**
Saddlers Clo. *Guild* —2F **114**
Saddlers M. *King T* —9J **25**
Saddlers Scarp. *Gray* —6M **169**
Saddlers Way. *Eps* —6C **80**
Saddlewood. *Camb* —2A **70**
Sadler Clo. *Mitc* —1D **44**
Sadlers Ride. *W Mol* —1C **40**
Sadlers Way. *Hasl* —1H **189**
Saffron Clo. *Craw* —6M **181**
Saffron Clo. *Croy* —5J **45**
Saffron Clo. *Dat* —4L **5**
Saffron Ct. *Farn* —1H **89**
Saffron Ct. *Felt* —1D **22**
Saffron Platt. *Guild* —8K **93**
Saffron Rd. *Brack* —3N **31**
Saffron Way. *Surb* —7K **41**
Sage Wlk. *Warf* —8B **16**
Sailmakers Ct. *SW6* —5N **13**
Sailors La. *Thur* —8D **150**
Saintoin Rd. *SW17* —3E **28**
St Agatha's Dri. *King T* —7M **25**
St Agatha's Gro. *Cars* —7D **44**
St Agnes Rd. *E Grin* —8A **166**
St Albans Av. *Felt* —6L **23**
St Albans Av. *Wey* —9B **38**
St Alban's Clo. *Wind* —4G **5**
St Albans Clo. *Wood S* —2E **112**
St Alban's Gdns. *Tedd* —6G **25**
St Alban's Gro. *Cars* —6C **44**
St Alban's Rd. *King T* —7L **25**
St Alban's Rd. *Reig* —1M **121**
St Alban's Rd. *Sutt* —1L **61**
St Albans Roundabout. *Farn* —5A **90**
St Alban's St. *Wind* —4G **5**
St Albans Ter. *W6* —2K **13**
St Andrews. *Brack* —5K **31**
St Andrews. *Cranl* —6K **155**
St Andrews. Horl —9F 142
(off Aurum Clo.)
St Andrew's Av. *Wind* —5C **4**
St Andrew's Clo. *Crowt* —1E **48**
St Andrew's Clo. *Iswth* —4E **10**
St Andrew's Clo. *Old Win* —9K **5**
St Andrews Clo. *Reig* —4N **121**
St Andrews Clo. *Shep* —3E **38**
St Andrews Clo. *Wok* —4M **73**
St Andrew's Clo. *Wray* —9A **6**
St Andrew's Ct. *SW18* —3A **28**
St Andrews Ct. *Sutt* —9C **44**
St Andrew's Cres. *Wind* —5C **4**
St Andrews Gdns. *Cobh* —9K **57**
St Andrew's Ga. *Wok* —5B **74**
St Andrews Mans. W14 —2K 13
(off St Andrews Rd.)
St Andrews M. *SW12* —2H **29**
St Andrew's Rd. *W14* —2K **13**
St Andrew's Rd. *Cars* —9C **44**
St Andrew's Rd. *Coul* —3E **82**
St Andrew's Rd. *Croy* —1N **63** (6B **200**)
St Andrews Rd. *If'd* —4J **181**
St Andrew's Rd. *Surb* —5K **41**
St Andrew's Sq. *Surb* —5K **41**
St Andrew's Wlk. *Cobh* —2J **77**
St Andrew's Way. *Frim* —7D **70**
St Andrews Way. *Oxt* —9G **107**
St Anne's Av. *Stanw* —1M **21**
St Annes Boulevd. *Red* —1F **122**
St Anne's Ct. *W Wick* —1A **66**
St Anne's Dri. *Red* —2E **122**
St Annes Dri. *Wokgm* —2F **30**
St Annes Dri. N. *Red* —1E **122**
St Annes Glade. *Bag* —4H **51**
St Anne's Mt. *Red* —2E **122**
St Anne's Ri. *Red* —2E **122**
St Annes Rd. *Craw* —9G **163**
St Anne's Rd. *G'ming* —6K **133**
St Ann's Clo. *Cher* —5H **37**
St Ann's Ct. *Vir W* —4B **36**
St Ann's Cres. *SW18* —9N **13**
St Ann's Hill. *SW18* —8N **13**
St Anns Hill Rd. *Cher* —5E **36**
St Ann's Pk. Rd. *SW18* —9N **13** & 1A **28**
St Ann's Pas. *SW13* —6D **12**
St Ann's Rd. *SW13* —5E **12**
St Ann's Rd. *Cher* —5G **36**
(in two parts)
St Anns Way. *Berr G* —3K **87**
St Ann's Way. *S Croy* —3M **63**
St Anthony's Clo. *SW17* —3C **28**
St Anthonys Clo. *Brack* —9M **15**
St Anthony's Way. *Felt* —7G **9**
St Arvan's Clo. *Croy* —9B **46**
St Aubin Clo. *Craw* —7L **181**
St Aubyns. *Dork* —7G **119**
St Aubyn's Av. *SW19* —6L **27**
St Aubyn's Av. *Houn* —8A **10**
St Augustine's Av. *S Croy* —3N **63**
St Augustine's Clo. *Alder* —3B **110**
St Austins. *Gray* —6B **170**
St Barnabas Clo. *Beck* —1M **47**
St Barnabas Ct. *Craw* —2G **182**
St Barnabas Gdns. *W Mol* —4A **40**
St Barnabas Rd. *Mitc* —8E **28**
St Barnabas Rd. *Sutt* —2B **62**
St Bartholomews Ct. *Guild* —5B **114**
St Benedict's Clo. *SW17* —6E **28**
St Benedicts Clo. *Alder* —3M **109**
St Benet's Clo. *SW17* —3C **28**
St Benet's Gro. *Cars* —6A **44**
St Bernards. *Croy* —9B **46** (5F **200**)
St Bernard's Clo. *SE27* —5N **29**
St Brelades Clo. *Dork* —7G **119**
St Brelades Rd. *Craw* —7L **181**
St Catherines. *Wey* —9C **38**
St Catherines. *Wok* —6M **73**
St Catherines Clo. *Chess* —3K **59**
St Catherine's Clo. *SW17* —3C **28**
St Catherine's Ct. *Brmly* —4B **134**
St Catherines Ct. *Felt* —2H **23**
St Catherines Ct. *Stai* —5J **21**
St Catherine's Cross. *Blet* —3B **124**
St Catherine's Dri. *Guild* —7L **113**
St Catherine's Hill. *Guild* —7M **113**
St Catherines Pk. *Guild* —5B **114**
St Catherines Rd. *Craw* —9G **163**
St Catherines Rd. *Frim* —5D **70**
(in two parts)
St Cecilia's Clo. *Sutt* —7K **43**
St Chads Clo. *Surb* —6J **41**
St Charles Pl. *Wey* —2B **56**
St Christopher's. *Ling* —7N **145**
St Christophers Clo. *Alder* —2B **110**
St Christopher's Clo. *Hasl* —2E **188**
St Christopher's Clo. *H'ham* —4J **197**
St Christopher's Clo. *Iswth* —4E **10**
St Christophers Gdns. *Asc* —9H **17**
St Christopher's Gdns. *T Hth* —2L **45**
St Christopher's Grn. *Hasl* —2E **188**
St Christopher's M. *Wall* —2G **62**
St Christopher's Pl. *Farn* —2L **89**
St Christopher's Rd. *Farn* —2M **89**
St Christopher's Rd. *Hasl* —2E **188**
St Clair Clo. *Oxt* —8M **105**
St Clair Clo. *Reig* —3A **122**
St Clair Dri. *Wor Pk* —9G **42**
St Claire Cotts. *D'land* —1D **166**
St Clair's Rd. *Croy* —8B **46** (3F **200**)
St Clare Bus. Pk. *Hamp* —7C **24**
St Clement Rd. *Craw* —7L **181**
St Clements Ct. *Farn* —7N **69**
St Clements Mans. SW6 —2J 13
(off Lillie Rd.)
St Cloud Rd. *SE27* —5N **29**
St Crispins Way. *Ott* —5E **54**
St Cross Rd. *Farnh* —9H **109**
St Cross Rd. *Frim G* —7E **70**
St Cuthberts Clo. *Eng G* —7N **19**
St Cyprian's St. *SW17* —5D **28**
St David's. *Coul* —4K **83**
St David's Clo. *Farn* —6L **69**
St David's Clo. *Farnh* —5K **109**
St David's Clo. *Reig* —2A **122**
St David's Clo. *W Wick* —6L **47**
St David's Dri. *Eng G* —8M **19**
St Denis Rd. *SE27* —5N **29**
St Denys Clo. *Knap* —6F **73**
St Dionis Rd. *SW6* —5L **13**
St Dunstan's. (Junct.) —3L **61**
St Dunstan's Clo. *Hayes* —1G **9**
St Dunstan's Hill. *Sutt* —2K **61**
St Dunstan's La. *Beck* —5M **47**
St Dunstan's Rd. *SE25* —3C **46**
St Dunstan's Rd. *W6* —1J **13**
St Dunstan's Rd. *Felt* —4G **23**
St Dunstan's Rd. *Houn* —5J **9**
(in two parts)
St Edith Clo. *Eps* —1B **80** (8J **201**)
St Edmund Clo. *Craw* —9B **162**
St Edmund's Clo. *SW17* —3C **28**
St Edmund's La. *Twic* —1B **24**
St Edmunds Sq. *SW13* —2H **13**
St Edmund's Steps. *G'ming* —7G **133**
St Edward's Clo. *E Grin* —9M **165**
St Edward's Clo. *New Ad* —7N **65**
St Elizabeth Dri. *Eps* —1B **80** (8J **201**)
St Faith's Rd. *SE21* —2M **29**
St Francis Gdns. *Copt* —6N **163**
St Francis Wlk. *Bew* —5K **181**
St George's Av. *Wey* —3C **56**
St Georges Bus. Pk. *Wey* —5B **56**
St George's Clo. *Bad L* —7N **109**
St Georges Clo. *Horl* —8F **142**
St George's Clo. *Wey* —2D **56**
St Georges Clo. *Wind* —4B **4**
St George's Ct. *SW15* —7L **13**
St Georges Ct. *Add* —1L **55**
St George's Ct. *Craw* —2B **182**
St Georges Ct. *E Grin* —7M **165**
St Georges Ct. *Owl* —5K **49**
St George's Gdns. *Eps* —1E **80**
St Georges Gdns. *H'ham* —4L **197**
St George's Gdns. *Surb* —8A **42**
St George's Gro. *SW17* —4B **28**
St George's Hill. —6D **56**
St George's Hill. *Red* —2H **143**
St George's Ind. Est. *Camb* —3N **69**
St George's Ind. Est. *King T* —6K **25**
St George's La. *Asc* —2M **33**
(in two parts)
St George's M. Farnh —9G 109
(off Bear La.)
St George's Pl. *Twic* —2G **25**
St George's Rd. *SW19* —8L **27**
(in two parts)
St George's Rd. *Add* —1L **55**
St George's Rd. *Alder* —3N **109**
St Georges Rd. *Bad L* —6N **109**
(in two parts)
St George's Rd. *Beck* —1L **47**
St George's Rd. *Camb* —9B **50**
St George's Rd. *Farnh* —2J **129**
St George's Rd. *Felt* —5L **23**
St George's Rd. *King T* —8N **25** (1N **203**)
St George's Rd. *Mitc* —2F **44**
St George's Rd. *Red* —2H **143**
St Georges Rd. *Rich* —6M **11**
St George's Rd. *Twic* —8H **11**
St George's Rd. *Wall* —2F **62**
St George's Rd. *Wey* —3F **56**
St George's Rd. E. *Alder* —3N **109**
St George's Sq. *N Mald* —2D **42**
St George's Wlk. *Croy* —9N **45** (3C **200**)
St George's Yd. Farnh —1G 129
(off Castle St.)
St Giles Clo. *Orp* —2M **67**
St Gothard Rd. *SE27* —5N **29**
(in two parts)
St Helens. *Th Dit* —6F **40**
St Helen's Cres. *SW16* —9K **29**
St Helens Cres. *Sand* —7G **48**
St Helens Rd. *SW16* —9K **29**
St Helier. —6C **44**
St Helier Av. *Mord* —6A **44**
St Helier Clo. *Craw* —7M **181**
St Helier Clo. *Wokgm* —5A **30**
St Helier's Av. *Houn* —8A **10**
St Hilda's Av. *Afrd* —6N **21**
St Hilda's Clo. *SW17* —3C **28**
St Hilda's Clo. *Craw* —8G **163**
St Hilda's Clo. *Horl* —8F **142**
St Hilda's Clo. *Knap* —4G **73**
St Hilda's Rd. *SW13* —2G **12**
Saint Hill. —5M **185**
Saint Hill Grn. *E Grin* —5N **185**
Saint Hill Rd. *E Grin* —3L **185**
St Hughes Clo. *SW17* —3C **28**
St Hughs Clo. *Craw* —9G **163**
St Ives. *Craw* —2G **182**
St James Av. *Eps* —7E **60**
St James Av. *Farnh* —8J **109**
St James Av. *Sutt* —2M **61**
St James Clo. *Eps* —1D **80** (8M **201**)
St James Clo. *N Mald* —4E **42**
St James Clo. *Wok* —5K **73**
St James Ct. *Asht* —4K **79**
St James Ct. *Farnh* —9H **109**
St James M. *Wey* —1C **56**
St James Rd. *Cars* —9C **44**
St James Rd. *E Grin* —9N **165**
St James Rd. *Fleet* —5A **88**
St James Rd. *Mitc* —8E **28**
St James Rd. *Purl* —9M **63**
St James' Rd. *Surb* —5K **41**
St James Rd. *Sutt* —2M **61**
St James's Av. *Beck* —2H **47**
St James's Av. *Hamp H* —6C **24**
St James's Clo. *SW17* —3D **28**
St James's Cotts. *Rich* —8K **11**
St James's Ct. *King T* —2L **41** (6K **203**)
St James's Dri. *SW17 & SW12* —2D **28**
St James's Pk. *Croy* —6N **45**
St James's Pl. *Cranl* —7L **155**
St James's Rd. *Croy* —6M **45**
St James's Rd. *Hamp H* —6B **24**
St James's Rd. *King T* —1K **41** (4J **203**)
St James St. *W6* —1H **13**
St James Ter. *SW12* —2E **28**
St James' Ter. *Farnh* —9H **109**
St James Wlk. *Craw* —8A **182**
St Joan Clo. *Craw* —9D **162**
St John Clo. *H'ham* —7L **197**
St John's. —5C **122**
(Redhill)
St Johns. —6K **73**
(Woking)
St John's. *N Holm* —9J **119**
St John's. *Red* —5C **122**
St John's Av. *SW15* —8J **13**
St John's Av. *Eps* —8F **60**
St John's Av. *Lea* —8H **79**
St Johns Chu. Rd. *Wott* —8N **117**
St John's Clo. *SW6* —3M **13**
St John's Clo. *E Grin* —8A **166**
St John's Clo. *Guild* —4K **113**
St John's Clo. *Lea* —8J **79**
St John's Ct. *Brkwd* —7C **72**
St John's Ct. *Egh* —6C **20**
St John's Ct. *Farn* —9J **69**
St John's Ct. *Iswth* —5F **10**
St John's Ct. *King T* —7L **203**
St Johns Ct. *S God* —7J **125**
St John's Ct. Westc —6C 118
(off St John's Rd.)
St Johns Ct. *Wok* —6K **73**
St John's Cres. *Broad H* —5E **196**
St Johns Dri. *SW18* —2N **27**
St John's Dri. *W on T* —7K **39**
St John's Dri. *Wind* —5D **4**
St John's Gro. *SW13* —5E **12**
St Johns Gro. *Farnh* —3G **129**
St John's Gro. *Rich* —7L **11**
St John's Hill. *Coul* —4L **83**
(in two parts)
St John's Hill. *Purl* —3L **83**
St John's Hill Rd. *Wok* —6K **73**
St John's Lye. *Wok* —6J **73**
(in three parts)
St John's Mdw. *Blind H* —3G **145**
St John's M. *Wok* —6K **73**
St Johns Pas. *SW19* —7K **27**
St Johns Ri. *Berr G* —3K **87**
St John's Ri. *Wok* —5L **73**
St John's Rd. *SW19* —8K **27**
St John's Rd. *Asc* —8K **17**
St John's Rd. *Cars* —9C **44**
St John's Rd. *Craw* —3A **182**
St John's Rd. *Croy* —9M **45** (4A **200**)
St John's Rd. *E Grin* —8A **166**
St John's Rd. *E Mol* —3D **40**
St John's Rd. *Farn* —1J **89**
St John's Rd. *Farnh* —3G **129**
St John's Rd. *Felt* —5M **23**
St John's Rd. *Guild* —4J **113**
St John's Rd. *Hamp W* —1J **41**
St John's Rd. *Iswth* —5F **10**
St John's Rd. *Lea* —8J **79**
St John's Rd. *N Mald* —2B **42**
St John's Rd. *Red* —5D **122**
St John's Rd. *Rich* —7L **11**
St John's Rd. *Sand* —8G **49**
St John's Rd. *Sutt* —9N **43**
St John's Rd. *Westc* —6C **118**
St John's Rd. *Wind* —5D **4**
St John's Rd. *Wok* —6J **73**
St Johns St. *Crowt* —2G **49**
St Johns St. *G'ming* —5J **133**
St John's Ter. SW15 —4D 26
(off Kingston Va.)
St John's Ter. Rd. *Red* —5D **122**
St John's Way. *Cher* —7J **37**
St Joseph's Rd. *Alder* —3M **109**
St Jude's Clo. *Eng G* —6M **19**
St Judes Rd. *Eng G* —5M **19**
St Julian's Clo. *SW16* —5L **29**
St Julian's Farm Rd. *SE27* —5L **29**
St Katherines Rd. *Cat* —3D **104**
St Lawrence Bus. Cen. *Felt* —3J **23**
St Lawrence Ct. *Chob* —7H **53**
St Lawrence Ho. Chob —7H 53
(off Bagshot Rd.)
St Lawrence's Way. *Reig* —3M **121**
St Lawrence Way. *Cat* —1N **103**
St Leonard's Av. *Wind* —5F **4**
St Leonards Ct. *SW14* —6B **12**
St Leonard's Dri. *Craw* —5E **182**
St Leonards Forest. —4C **198**
St Leonard's Gdns. *Houn* —4M **9**
St Leonard's Hill. *Wind* —7A **4**
St Leonard's Park. —5A **198**
St Leonards Pk. *E Grin* —9N **165**
St Leonard's Ri. *Orp* —1N **67**
St Leonard's Rd. *SW14* —6A **12**
St Leonard's Rd. *Clay* —3F **58**
St Leonard's Rd. *Croy* —9M **45**
St Leonard's Rd. *Eps* —6H **81**
St Leonard's Rd. *H'ham* —8L **197**
St Leonard's Rd. *Surb* —4K **41**
St Leonard's Rd. *Th Dit* —5G **40**
St Leonard's Rd. *Wind* —6D **4**
(Imperial Rd.)
St Leonard's Rd. *Wind* —9A **4**
(Queen Adelaide's Ride)
St Leonards Sq. *Surb* —4K **41**
St Leonard's Wlk. *SW16* —8K **29**
St Louis Rd. *SE27* —5N **29**
St Luke's Clo. *SE25* —5F **46**
St Lukes Ct. *Wok* —1E **74**
St Luke's Pas. *King T* —9M **25** (1M **203**)
St Luke's Rd. *Old Win* —9K **5**
St Luke's Rd. *Whyt* —5C **84**
St Lukes Sq. *Guild* —4B **114**
St Margaret Dri. *Eps* —1B **80** (8J **201**)
St Margarets. —9H **11**
St Margaret's. *Guild* —3B **114**
St Margaret's Av. *Afrd* —6C **22**
St Margarets Av. *Berr G* —3K **87**
St Margaret's Av. *Dor P* —4A **166**
St Margaret's Av. *Sutt* —9K **43**
St Margarets Bus. Cen. *Twic* —9H **11**
St Margarets Cotts. *Fern* —9F **188**
St Margarets Ct. *SW15* —7G **12**
St Margaret's Cres. *SW15* —8G **13**
St Margaret's Dri. *Twic* —8H **11**
St Margaret's Gro. *Twic* —9G **11**
St Margaret's Rd. *Coul* —8F **82**
St Margaret's Rd. *E Grin* —7B **166**
St Margarets Rd. *Iswth & Twic* —7H **11**
St Margarets Roundabout. (Junct.) —9H **11**
St Marks Clo. *SW6* —4M **13**
St Mark's Clo. *Farn* —4A **90**
St Mark's Gro. *SW10* —3N **13**
St Mark's Hill. *Surb* —5L **41**
St Mark's La. *H'ham* —2L **197**
St Mark's Pl. *SW19* —7L **27**
St Mark's Pl. *Farnh* —6G **109**
St Marks Pl. *Wind* —5F **4**
St Mark's Rd. *SE25* —3D **46**
St Mark's Rd. *Binf* —8H **15**
St Mark's Rd. *Eps* —5H **81**
St Marks Rd. *Mitc* —1D **44**
St Mark's Rd. *Tedd* —8H **25**
St Marks Rd. *Wind* —5F **4**
St Martha's Av. *Wok* —8B **74**
St Marthas Ct. *Chil* —9D **114**
St Martin Clo. *Hand* —9N **199**
St Martin's Av. *Eps* —1D **80** (8M **201**)
St Martins Clo. *E Hor* —7F **96**
St Martins Clo. *Eps* —9D **60** (7N **201**)
St Martin's Ct. *Afrd* —6L **21**
St Martin's Ct. *E Hor* —7F **96**
St Martins Dri. *W on T* —9K **39**
St Martins Est. *SW2* —2L **29**
St Martins La. *Beck* —4L **47**
St Martins M. *Dork* —5G **119** (2K **201**)
St Martins M. *Pyr* —3J **75**
St Martin's Wlk. *Dork* —4H **119** (1L **201**)
St Martins Way. *SW17* —4A **28**
St Mary Av. *Wall* —9E **44**
St Marys. *Wey* —9E **38**
St Mary's Av. *Brom* —2N **47**
St Mary's Av. *Stanw* —1M **21**
St Mary's Av. *Tedd* —7F **24**
St Mary's Av. Central. *S'hall* —1B **10**
St Mary's Av. S. *S'hall* —1B **10**
St Mary's Clo. *Chess* —4M **59**
St Mary's Clo. *Eps* —4E **60**
St Mary's Clo. *Fet* —1D **98**
St Mary's Clo. *Oxt* —7A **106**
St Mary's Clo. *Sand* —7H **49**
St Mary's Clo. *Stanw* —1M **21**
St Mary's Clo. *Sun* —3H **39**
St Mary's Ct. *Wall* —1G **62**
St Mary's Ct. *W'ham* —4M **107**
St Mary's Cres. *Iswth* —3D **10**
St Mary's Cres. *Stanw* —1M **21**
St Mary's Dri. *Craw* —1F **182**
St Mary's Dri. *Felt* —1D **22**
St Marys Garden. *Worp* —5H **93**
St Mary's Gdns. *Bag* —4J **51**
St Mary's Gdns. *H'ham* —7J **197**
St Mary's Grn. *Big H* —5E **86**
St Mary's Gro. *SW13* —6G **12**
St Mary's Gro. *W4* —2A **12**
St Mary's Gro. *Big H* —5E **86**
St Mary's Gro. *Rich* —7M **11**
St Mary's Hill. *Asc* —5N **33**
St Mary's La. *Wink* —4H **17**
St Marys M. *Rich* —3J **25**
St Marys Mill. *C'fold* —6E **172**

St Mary's Mt.—School All.

St Mary's Mt. *Cat* —2C **104**
St Marys Pl. *Farnh* —9H **109**
St Mary's Rd. *SE25* —2B **46**
St Mary's Rd. *SW19* —6K **27**
St Mary's Rd. *Asc* —6M **33**
St Mary's Rd. *Ash V* —8E **90**
St Mary's Rd. *Camb* —9A **50**
St Mary's Rd. *Dit H* —6J **41**
St Mary's Rd. *E Mol* —4D **40**
St Mary's Rd. *Lea* —9H **79**
St Mary's Rd. *Reig* —4N **121**
St Mary's Rd. *S Croy* —6A **64**
St Mary's Rd. *Surb* —5K **41**
St Mary's Rd. *Wey* —1E **56**
St Mary's Rd. *Wok* —4M **73**
St Mary's Rd. *Wor Pk* —8D **42**
St Mary's Wlk. *Blet* —2A **124**
St Mary's Wlk. *H'ham* —7J **197**
St Mary's Way. *Guild* —1H **113**
St Matthew's Av. *Surb* —7L **41**
St Matthew's Rd. *Red* —2D **122**
St Maur Rd. *SW6* —4L **13**
St Michael's Av. *Guild* —7F **92**
St Michaels Clo. *Fleet* —5C **88**
St Michael's Clo. *W on T* —8K **39**
St Michael's Clo. *Wor Pk* —8E **42**
St Michaels Cotts. *Wokgm* —8H **31**
St Michael's Ct. Wey —2D 56
(off Princes Rd.)
St Michael's Rd. *Alder* —3N **109**
St Michael's Rd. *Afrd* —6B **22**
St Michael's Rd. *Camb* —1N **69**
St Michael's Rd. *Cat* —9A **84**
St Michael's Rd. *Croy* —7N **45** (1C **200**)
St Michaels Rd. *E Grin* —8A **166**
St Michael's Rd. *Farn* —8N **69**
St Michael's Rd. *Sand* —7E **48**
St Michael's Rd. *Wall* —3G **62**
St Michael's Rd. *Wok* —1F **74**
St Mildred's Rd. *Guild* —2B **114**
St Monica's Rd. *Kgswd* —8L **81**
St Nazaire Clo. *Egh* —6E **20**
St Nicholas Av. *Bookh* —3B **98**
St Nicholas Cen. *Sutt* —2N **61**
St Nicholas Clo. *Fleet* —4A **88**
St Nicholas Ct. *Craw* —2G **182**
St Nicholas Ct. *King T* —8K **203**
St Nicholas Cres. *Pyr* —3J **75**
St Nicholas Dri. *Shep* —6B **38**
St Nicholas Glebe. *SW17* —6E **28**
St Nicholas Hill. *Lea* —9H **79**
St Nicholas Rd. *Sutt* —2N **61**
St Nicholas Rd. *Th Dit* —5F **40**
St Nicholas Way. *Sutt* —1N **61**
St Nicolas Av. *Cranl* —7N **155**
St Nicolas Clo. *Cranl* —7N **155**
St Normans Way. *Eps* —6F **60**
St Olaf's Rd. *SW6* —3K **13**
St Olaves Clo. *Stai* —8H **21**
St Olaves Wlk. *SW16* —1G **45**
St Omer Barracks. *Alder* —8B **90**
St Omer Ridge. *Guild* —4C **114**
St Omer Rd. *Guild* —4C **114**
St Oswald's Rd. *SW16* —9M **29**
St Paul's Clo. *Add* —2J **55**
St Paul's Clo. *Afrd* —6D **22**
St Paul's Clo. *Cars* —7C **44**
St Paul's Clo. *Chess* —1K **59**
St Paul's Clo. *Hayes* —1E **8**
St Paul's Clo. *Houn* —5M **9**
St Pauls Clo. *Tong* —5D **110**
St Paul's Ct. *Houn* —6M **9**
St Paul's Ga. *Wokgm* —1A **30**
St Paul's Rd. *Bren* —2K **11**
St Paul's Rd. *Rich* —6M **11**
St Paul's Rd. *Stai* —6F **20**
St Paul's Rd. *T Hth* —2N **45**
St Paul's Rd. *Wok* —4C **74**
St Paul's Rd. E. *Dork* —5H **119** (3M **201**)
St Paul's Rd. W. *Dork* —6G **119** (4K **201**)
St Paul's Studios. W6 —1K 13
(off Talgarth Rd.)
St Paul's Wlk. *King T* —8N **25**
St Peters Av. *Berr G* —3K **87**
St Peter's Clo. *SW17* —3C **28**
St Peter's Clo. *Old Win* —8K **5**
St Peter's Clo. *Stai* —7H **21**
St Peter's Clo. *Wok* —7E **74**
St Peters Ct. *W Mol* —3A **40**
St Peter's Gdns. *SE27* —4L **29**
St Peters Gdns. *Wrec* —5E **128**
St Peter's Gdns. *Yat* —9C **48**
St Peter's Gro. *W6* —1F **12**
St Peters Mead. *As* —2F **110**
St Peters Pk. *Alder* —4K **109**
St Peters Rd. *W6* —1F **12**
St Peter's Rd. *Craw* —3A **182**
St Peter's Rd. *Croy* —1A **64** (6D **200**)
St Peter's Rd. *King T* —1N **41**
St Peters Rd. *Old Win* —8K **5**
St Peters Rd. *Twic* —8H **11**
St Peter's Rd. *W Mol* —3A **40**
St Peter's Rd. *Wok* —8D **74**
St Peter's Sq. *W6* —1E **12**
St Peter's St. *S Croy* —2A **64** (8E **200**)
St Peter's Ter. *SW6* —3L **13**
St Peter's Vs. *W6* —1F **12**
St Peter's Way. *Cher* —1F **54**
St Peter's Way. *Frim* —7D **70**
St Peter's Way. *Hayes* —1E **8**
St Peter's Wharf. *W4* —1F **12**
St Philip's Av. *Wor Pk* —8G **42**
St Philip's Ga. *Wor Pk* —8H **43**
St Philips Rd. *Surb* —5K **41**
St Phillips Ct. *Fleet* —4B **88**
St Pier's La. *Ling* —8B **146**
St Pinnock Av. *Stai* —9J **21**
St Richard's M. Craw —3D 182
(off Broomdashers Rd.)
St Sampson Rd. *Craw* —7L **181**
St Saviour's College. *SE27* —5N **29**
St Saviours Pl. *Guild* —3M **113** (3B **202**)
St Saviour's Rd. *Croy* —5M **45**
Saints Clo. *SE27* —5M **29**
St Sebastian's Clo. *Wokgm* —9D **30**
St Simon's Av. *SW15* —8H **13**
St Stephen Clo. *Craw* —9B **162**
St Stephen's Av. *Asht* —3L **79**
St Stephens Clo. *Hasl* —2D **188**
St Stephen's Cres. *T Hth* —2L **45**
St Stephen's Gdns. *SW15* —8L **13**
St Stephen's Gdns. *Twic* —9J **11**
St Stephen's Pas. *Twic* —9J **11**
St Stephen's Rd. *Houn* —9A **10**
St Stevens Clo. *Hasl* —1G **188**
St Swithun's Clo. *E Grin* —9B **166**
St Theresa Clo. *Eps* —1B **80** (8J **201**)
St Theresa's Rd. *Felt* —7G **9**
St Thomas Clo. *Surb* —7M **41**
St Thomas Clo. *Wok* —4M **73**
St Thomas Dri. *E Clan* —9N **95**
St Thomas Rd. *W4* —2B **12**
St Thomas's M. *Guild* —5B **114**
St Thomas's Way. *SW6* —3L **13**
St Thomas Wlk. *Coln* —3F **6**
St Vincent Clo. *SE27* —6M **29**
St Vincent Clo. *Craw* —4H **183**
St Vincent Rd. *Twic* —9C **10**
St Vincent Rd. *W on T* —9J **39**
St Winifreds. *Kenl* —2N **83**
St Winifred's Rd. *Big H* —5H **87**
St Winifred's Rd. *Tedd* —7H **25**
Salamanca. *Crowt* —2D **48**
Salamanca Pk. *Alder* —1L **109**
Salamander Clo. *King T* —6J **25**
Salamander Quay. *King T* —9K **25** (2H **203**)
Salbrook Rd. *Red* —2E **142**
Salcombe Dri. *Mord* —7J **43**
Salcombe Rd. *Afrd* —4N **21**
Salcot Cres. *New Ad* —6M **65**
Salcott Rd. *Croy* —9J **45**
Sale Garden Cotts. *Wokgm* —3B **30**
Salehurst Rd. *Worth* —3J **183**
Salem Pl. *Croy* —9N **45** (5B **200**)
Salerno Clo. *Alder* —1M **109**
Sales Ct. *Alder* —3L **109**
Salesian Gdns. *Cher* —7J **37**
Salesian Vw. *Farn* —5C **90**
Salford Rd. *SW2* —2H **29**
Salfords. —2E 142
Salfords Ind. Est. *Red* —3F **142**
Salfords Way. *Red* —2E **142**
Salisbury Av. *Sutt* —3L **61**
Salisbury Clo. *Wokgm* —6A **30**
Salisbury Clo. *Wor Pk* —9E **42**
Salisbury Ct. *Cars* —2D **62**
Salisbury Gdns. *SW19* —8K **27**
Salisbury Gro. *Myt* —1D **90**
Salisbury M. *SW6* —3L **13**
Salisbury Pas. SW6 —3L 13
(off Dawes Rd.)
Salisbury Pavement. SW6 —3L 13
(off Dawes Rd.)
Salisbury Pl. *W Byf* —7L **55**
Salisbury Rd. *God* —9F **104**
Salisbury Rd. *SE25* —5D **46**
Salisbury Rd. *SW19* —8K **27**
Salisbury Rd. *As* —1E **110**
Salisbury Rd. *Bans* —1N **81**
Salisbury Rd. *B'water* —1H **69**
Salisbury Rd. *Cars* —3D **62**
Salisbury Rd. *Craw* —7C **182**
(in two parts)
Salisbury Rd. *Farn* —1A **90**
Salisbury Rd. *Felt* —2K **23**
Salisbury Rd. *H'ham* —8G **196**
Salisbury Rd. *Houn* —6K **9**
Salisbury Rd. *H'row A* —8D **8**
Salisbury Rd. *N Mald* —2C **42**
Salisbury Rd. *Rich* —7L **11**
Salisbury Rd. *Wok* —6A **74**
Salisbury Rd. *Wor Pk* —1C **60**
Salisbury Ter. *Myt* —2E **90**
Salix Clo. *Sun* —8J **23**
Salliesfield. *Twic* —9D **10**
Salmons La. *Whyt* —7B **84**
Salmons La. W. *Cat* —7B **84**
Salmons Rd. *Chess* —3L **59**
Salmons Rd. *Eff* —7J **97**
Salomons Memorial. —1K 119
Saltash Clo. *Sutt* —1L **61**
Saltbox Hill. *Big H* —9D **66**
Salt Box Rd. *Guild* —7J **93**
Saltdean Clo. *Craw* —6B **182**
Salterford Rd. *SW17* —7E **28**
Salterns Rd. *M'bowr* —6G **182**
Salter's Hill. *SE19* —6N **29**
Saltire Gdns. *Brack* —9M **15**
Salt La. *Hyde* —4G **153**
Saltram Rd. *Farn* —3C **90**
Salvador. *SW17* —6D **28**
Salvation Pl. *Lea* —2G **98**
Salvia Ct. *Bisl* —3D **72**
Salvington Rd. *Craw* —6L **181**
Salvin Rd. *SW15* —6J **13**
Salwey Clo. *Brack* —5N **31**
Samaritan Clo. *Bew* —5K **181**
Samarkand Clo. *Camb* —2F **70**
Samels Ct. *W6* —1F **12**
Samian Pl. *Binf* —8K **15**
Samos Rd. *SE20* —1E **46**
Samphire Clo. *Craw* —6M **181**
Sampleoak La. *Chil* —9G **114**
Sampson Pk. *Binf* —9J **15**
Sampson's Almshouses. *Farnh* —2E **128**
Sampsons Ct. *Shep* —4D **38**
Samuel Gray Gdns. *King T* —9K **25** (1J **203**)
Samuel Johnson Clo. *SW16* —5K **29**
Samuel Lewis Trust Dwellings.
(off Vanston Pl.) SW6 —3M 13
Samuel Lewis Trust Dwellings.
(off Lisgar Ter.) W14 —1L 13
Samuel Richardson Ho. W14 —1L 13
(off N. End Cres.)
San Carlos App. *Alder* —2A **110**
Sanctuary Rd. *H'row A* —9B **8**
Sanctuary, The. *Mord* —5M **43**
Sandal Rd. *N Mald* —4C **42**
Sandalwood. *Guild* —4L **113**
Sandalwood Av. *Cher* —9G **36**
Sandalwood Rd. *Felt* —4J **23**
Sandbanks. *Felt* —2F **22**
Sandbourne Av. *SW19* —1N **43**
Sandcross La. *Reig* —6L **121**
Sandell's Av. *Afrd* —5D **22**
Sandeman Way. *H'ham* —8L **197**
Sanders Clo. *Hamp H* —6C **24**
Sandersfield Gdns. *Bans* —2M **81**
Sandersfield Rd. *Bans* —2N **81**
Sanderstead. —8D 64
Sanderstead Clo. *SW12* —1G **29**
Sanderstead Ct. Av. *S Croy* —9D **64**
Sanderstead Hill. *S Croy* —7B **64**
Sanderstead Rd. *S Croy* —4A **64**
Sandes Pl. *Lea* —5G **79**
Sandfield Gdns. *T Hth* —2M **45**
Sandfield Rd. *T Hth* —2M **45**
Sandfields. *Send* —2F **94**
Sandfield Ter. *Guild* —4N **113** (4C **202**)
Sandford Ct. *Alder* —3L **109**
Sandford Down. *Brack* —4D **32**
Sandford Rd. *Alder* —3L **109**
Sandford Rd. *Farnh* —5G **109**
Sandford St. *SW6* —3N **13**
Sandgate La. *SW18* —2C **28**
Sandhawes Hill. *E Grin* —6C **166**
Sandheath Rd. *Hind* —2A **170**
Sand Hill. *Farn* —7N **69**
Sand Hill Ct. *Farn* —7N **69**
Sandhill La. *Craw D* —2E **184**
Sandhills. —9A 152
Sandhills. *Wall* —1H **63**
Sandhills. *Wmly* —9A **152**
(in two parts)
Sandhills Ct. *Vir W* —4A **36**
Sandhills La. *Vir W* —4A **36**
Sandhills Mdw. *Shep* —6D **38**
Sandhills Rd. *Reig* —4M **121**
Sandhurst. —8G 49
Sandhurst Av. *Surb* —6A **42**
Sandhurst Clo. *S Croy* —5B **64**
Sandhurst La. *B'water* —9G **48**
Sandhurst Rd. *Crowt* —4G **49**
Sandhurst Rd. *Finch* —8A **30**
Sandhurst Rd. *Yat* —8E **48**
Sandhurst Way. *S Croy* —4B **64**
Sandiford Rd. *Sutt* —8L **43**
Sandilands. *Croy* —8D **46**
Sandilands Rd. *SW6* —4N **13**
Sandlands Gro. *Tad* —1F **100**
Sandlands Rd. *Tad* —1F **100**
Sandon Clo. *Esh* —6D **40**
Sandown Av. *Esh* —2C **58**
Sandown Clo. *B'water* —1J **69**
Sandown Clo. *Houn* —4H **9**
Sandown Ct. *Craw* —3H **183**
Sandown Ct. Red —2C 122
(off Station Rd.)
Sandown Ct. *Sutt* —4N **61**
Sandown Cres. *Alder* —5N **109**
Sandown Dri. *Cars* —5E **62**
Sandown Dri. *Frim* —4B **70**
Sandown Ga. *Esh* —9D **40**
Sandown Lodge. *Eps* —1C **80**
Sandown Pk. Racecourse. —9C 40
Sandown Rd. *SE25* —4E **46**
Sandown Rd. *Coul* —3E **82**
Sandown Rd. *Esh* —1C **58**
Sandpiper Clo. *If'd* —5J **181**
Sandpiper Rd. *S Croy* —7G **64**
Sandpiper Rd. *Sutt* —2L **61**
Sandpit Cotts. *Pirb* —9B **72**
Sandpit Hall Rd. *Chob* —8K **53**
Sandpit Heath. *Guild* —8G **92**
Sandpit La. *Knap* —1E **72**
(in two parts)
Sandpit Rd. *Red* —4C **122**
Sandpit Site. *Wey* —6B **56**
Sandpits Rd. *Croy* —1G **64**
Sandpits Rd. *Rich* —3K **25**
Sandra Clo. *Houn* —8B **10**
Sandringham Av. *SW20* —9K **27**
Sandringham Clo. *SW19* —2J **27**
Sandringham Clo. *E Grin* —1C **186**
Sandringham Clo. *Wok* —3J **75**
Sandringham Ct. *Sutt* —5M **61**
Sandringham Dri. *Afrd* —5M **21**
Sandringham Gdns. *Houn* —4H **9**
Sandringham Pk. *Cobh* —8A **58**
Sandringham Rd. *Craw* —7N **181**
Sandringham Rd. *H'row A* —8N **7**
Sandringham Rd. *T Hth* —4N **45**
Sandringham Rd. *Wor Pk* —9F **42**
Sandringham Way. *Frim* —6D **70**
Sandrock. *Hasl* —2G **188**
Sandrock Cotts. *N'chap* —8D **100**
Sandrock Hill Rd. *Wrec* —5E **128**
Sandrock Pl. *Croy* —1G **64**
Sandrock Rd. *Westc* —7B **118**
Sandroyd Way. *Cobh* —9A **58**
Sands Clo. *Seale* —1B **130**
Sands End. —4N 13
Sand's End La. *SW6* —4N **13**
Sands Rd. *Farnh & Seale* —9A **110**
Sands, The. —2C 130
Sandy Bury. *Orp* —1M **67**
Sandy Clo. *Wok* —4E **74**
Sandycombe Rd. *Felt* —2H **23**
Sandycombe Rd. *Rich* —6M **11**
Sandycoombe Rd. *Twic* —9J **11**
Sandy Cft. *Eps* —6H **61**
Sandy Cross. —8C 110
Sandy Dri. *Cobh* —7A **58**
Sandy Dri. *Felt* —2F **22**
Sandy Hill Rd. *Farnh* —5F **108**
Sandy Hill Rd. *Wall* —5G **62**
Sandy Holt. *Cobh* —9N **57**
Sandy La. *Alb* —1L **135**
Sandy La. *Asc* —4D **34**
Sandy La. *Bet* —4D **120**
Sandy La. *Blet* —1M **123**
Sandy La. *Brack* —8A **16**
Sandy La. *Camb* —9C **50**
Sandy La. *Chav D* —9F **16**
Sandy La. *Chob* —5H **53**
Sandy La. *C Crook* —9B **88**
Sandy La. *Cobh & Oxs* —8N **57**
Sandy La. *Comp* —8G **112**
Sandy La. *Craw D* —1C **184**
Sandy La. *E Grin* —9A **166**
Sandy La. *Farn* —8H **69**
Sandy La. *G'ming* —5G **133**
Sandy La. *G'wood* —8J **171**
Sandy La. *Guild* —8K **113**
Sandy La. *Hasl* —1A **188**
Sandy La. *Hind* —8D **170**
Sandy La. *Kgswd* —2L **101**
(in two parts)
Sandy La. *Limp* —5D **106**
Sandy La. *Milf* —2B **152**
Sandy La. *Mitc* —9E **28**
(in two parts)
Sandy La. *Norm* —9B **92**
Sandy La. *Oxt* —7M **105**
Sandy La. *Pyr* —4J **75**
(in two parts)
Sandy La. *Reig* —4G **120**
Sandy La. *Rich* —3J **25**
Sandy La. *Sand* —6E **48**
Sandy La. *Send* —1E **94**
Sandy La. *Shere* —8B **116**
Sandy La. *S Nut & Nutf* —4H **123**
Sandy La. *Sutt* —4K **61**
Sandy La. *Tedd* —8G **24**
Sandy La. *Tilf* —4M **149**
Sandy La. *Vir W* —3A **36**
(in three parts)
Sandy La. *W on T* —5J **39**
Sandy La. *W'ham* —3M **107**
Sandy La. *Wok* —4D **74**
Sandy La. N. *Wall* —2H **63**
Sandy La. S. *Wall* —5G **62**
Sandy Mead. *Eps* —6N **59**
Sandy Ride. *S'hill* —3B **34**
Sandy Rd. *Add* —3J **55**
Sandy Way. *Cobh* —8A **58**
Sandy Way. *Croy* —9J **47**
Sandy Way. *W on T* —7G **38**
Sandy Way. *Wok* —4E **74**
San Feliu Ct. *E Grin* —8D **166**
Sanger Av. *Chess* —2L **59**
Sanger Dri. *Send* —1E **94**
Sangers Dri. *Horl* —8D **142**
Sangers Wlk. *Horl* —8D **142**
Sangley Rd. *SE25* —3B **46**
Sankey La. *Fleet* —1E **88**
Santina Clo. *Farnh* —4J **109**
Santos Rd. *SW18* —8M **13**
Sanway. —1N 75
Sanway Clo. *Byfl* —1N **75**
Sanway Rd. *Byfl* —1N **75**
Saphora Clo. *Orp* —2M **67**
Sapphire Cen., The. *Wokgm* —4A **30**
Sappho Ct. *Wok* —3H **73**
Sapte Clo. *Cranl* —7B **156**
Saracen Clo. *Croy* —5A **46**
Sarah Way. *Farn* —1N **89**
Sarel Way. *Horl* —6F **142**
Sargent Clo. *Craw* —7D **182**
Sarjant Path. SW19 —3J 27
(off Blincoe Clo.)
Sark Clo. *Craw* —7M **181**
Sark Clo. *Houn* —3A **10**
Sarsby Dri. *Stai* —3C **20**
Sarsen Av. *Houn* —5A **10**
Sarsfeld Rd. *SW12* —3D **28**
Sarum. *Brack* —7K **31**
Sarum Cres. *Wokgm* —1C **30**
Sarum Grn. *Wey* —9F **38**
Satellite Bus. Village. *Craw* —8C **162**
Satis Ct. *Eps* —7E **60**
Saturn Clo. *Bew* —5K **181**
Saturn Cft. *Wink R* —7F **16**
Saunders Clo. *Craw* —3F **182**
Saunders Copse. *Wok* —9L **73**
Saunders La. *Wok* —9H **73**
Saunton Av. *Hayes* —3G **8**
Saunton Gdns. *Farn* —8M **69**
Savernake Wlk. *Craw* —6D **182**
Savernake Way. *Brack* —5C **32**
Savery Dri. *Surb* —6J **41**
Savile Clo. *N Mald* —4D **42**
Savile Clo. *Th Dit* —7F **40**
Savile Gdns. *Croy* —8C **46**
Saville Cres. *Afrd* —7E **22**
Saville Gdns. *Camb* —1F **70**
Saville Rd. *Twic* —2F **24**
Savill Gdns. *SW20* —2F **42**
Savill Gardens, The. —7H 19
Savill Ho. *SW4* —1H **29**
Savin Lodge. Sutt —4A 62
(off Walnut M.)
Savona Clo. *SW19* —8J **27**
Savory Wlk. *Binf* —7G **15**
Savoy Av. *Hayes* —1F **8**
Savoy Gro. *B'water* —3J **69**
Sawkins Clo. *SW19* —3K **27**
Sawpit La. *E Clan* —9N **95**
Sawtry Clo. *Cars* —6C **44**
Sawyers Clo. *Wind* —3B **4**
Sawyer's Hill. *Rich* —1M **25**
Saxby Rd. *SW2* —1J **29**
Saxby's La. *Ling* —7N **145**
Saxley. *Horl* —7G **142**
Saxon Av. *Felt* —3M **23**
Saxonbury Av. *Sun* —2J **39**
Saxonbury Clo. *Mitc* —2B **44**
Saxonbury Gdns. *Surb* —7J **41**
Saxon Bus. Cen. *SW19* —1A **44**
Saxon Clo. *Surb* —5K **41**
Saxon Cres. *H'ham* —4H **197**
Saxon Cft. *Farnh* —2H **129**
Saxon Dri. *Warf* —9D **16**
Saxonfield Clo. *SW2* —2K **29**
Saxon Ho. *Felt* —3N **23**
Saxon Lodge. *Croy* —1C **200**
Saxon Rd. *SE25* —4A **46**
Saxon Rd. *Afrd* —7E **22**
Saxon Rd. *W on T* —9L **39**
Saxon Rd. *Worth* —4J **183**
Saxons. *Tad* —8J **81**
Saxon Way. *Old Win* —9L **5**
Saxon Way. *Reig* —2L **121**
Saxon Way. *W Dray* —2L **7**
Saxon Way Ind. Est. *W Dray* —2L **7**
Saxony Way. *Yat* —2B **68**
Sayers Clo. *Fet* —1C **98**
Sayers Clo. *Frim G* —7C **70**
Sayers Clo. *H'ham* —6L **197**
Sayers, The. *E Grin* —9M **165**
Sayer's Wlk. *Rich* —1M **25**
Sayes Ct. *Add* —2L **55**
Sayes Ct. Farm Dri. *Add* —2K **55**
Scallows Clo. *Craw* —2E **182**
Scallows Rd. *Craw* —2E **182**
Scampton Rd. *H'row A* —9A **8**
Scania Wlk. *Wink R* —7F **16**
Scarborough Clo. *Big H* —5E **86**
Scarborough Clo. *Sutt* —7L **61**
Scarborough Rd. *H'row A* —9D **8**
Scarbrook Rd. *Croy* —9N **45** (5B **200**)
Scarlet Oaks. *Camb* —3C **70**
Scarlett Clo. *Wok* —5J **73**
Scarlette Mnr. Way. *SW2* —1L **29**
Scarlett's Rd. *Alder* —1M **109**
Scarth Rd. *SW13* —6E **12**
Scawen Clo. *Cars* —1E **62**
Scholars Rd. *SW12* —2G **28**
Scholars Wlk. *Guild* —4L **113**
School All. *Twic* —2G **25**

School Allotment Ride—Sherborne Clo.

School Allotment Ride. *Wind* —1M **17**
School Clo. *Bisl* —2C **72**
School Clo. *Guild* —9N **93**
School Clo. *H'ham* —2N **197**
School Cotts. *Asc* —9H **17**
School Cotts. *Wok* —9M **73**
School Fld. *Eden* —1L **147**
School Hill. *Crowt* —3J **49**
School Hill. *Red* —6G **102**
School Hill. *Sand* —6F **48**
School Hill. *Seale* —8F **110**
School Hill. *Warn* —9F **178**
School Hill. *Wrec* —4E **128**
School Ho. La. *Tedd* —8H **25**
School La. *Add* —2J **55**
School La. *Asc* —9H **17**
School La. *Ash W* —3F **186**
School La. *Bag* —6H **51**
(in two parts)
School La. *Cat* —4C **104**
School La. *C'fold* —5E **172**
School La. *E Clan* —9N **95**
School La. *Egh* —6C **20**
School La. *Ews* —4C **108**
School La. *Fet* —9D **78**
School La. *F Row* —7H **187**
School La. *King T* —9J **25**
School La. *Lwr Bo* —5J **129**
School La. *Mick* —5J **99**
School La. *Norm* —9K **91**
School La. *Ock* —9C **76**
School La. *Pirb* —9B **72**
School La. *P'ham* —8N **111**
School La. *Shack* —5B **132**
School La. *Shep* —5C **38**
School La. *Surb* —7N **41**
School La. *Tad* —3F **100**
School La. *Westc* —6D **118**
School La. *W Hor* —7C **96**
School La. *W'sham* —2A **52**
School La. *Worp* —6H **93**
School La. *Yat* —9A **48**
School Pas. *King T* —1M **41** (4N **203**)
School Rd. *Asc* —4A **34**
School Rd. *Afrd* —7C **22**
School Rd. *E Mol* —3D **40**
School Rd. *Gray* —6N **169**
School Rd. *Hamp H* —7C **24**
School Rd. *Hasl* —3D **188**
School Rd. *Houn* —6C **10**
School Rd. *King T* —9J **25**
School Rd. *Rowl* —8D **128**
School Rd. *W on T* —2G **57**
School Rd. *W Dray* —2M **7**
School Rd. *W'sham* —1L **51**
School Rd. *Wokgm* —2C **30**
School Rd. Av. *Hamp H* —7C **24**
School Road Junction. (Junct.) —7C **22**
School Wlk. *Horl* —8C **142**
School Wlk. *Sun* —3G **38**
Schroder Ct. *Eng G* —6L **19**
Schroders Av. *Red* —1F **122**
Schubert Rd. *SW15* —8L **13**
Scillonian Rd. *Guild* —4K **113**
Scilly Isles. (Junct.) —8E **40**
Scizdons Climb. *G'ming* —7J **133**
Scoles Cres. *SW2* —2L **29**
Scope Way. *King T* —3L **41** (7L **203**)
Scory Clo. *Craw* —6M **181**
Scotia Rd. *SW2* —1L **29**
Scotland Bri. *New H* —7J **55**
Scotland Bri. Rd. *New H* —7J **55**
Scotland Clo. *Ash V* —8E **90**
Scotland Farm Rd. *Ash V* —8E **90**
Scotland Hill. *Sand* —6F **48**
Scotland La. *Hasl* —3F **188**
Scotlands Clo. *Hasl* —3F **188**
Scotney Clo. *Orp* —1J **67**
Scots Clo. *Stai* —2M **21**
Scotsdale Clo. *Sutt* —4K **61**
Scotshall La. *Warl* —2M **85**
Scott Clo. *SW16* —9K **29**
Scott Clo. *Eps* —2B **60**
Scott Clo. *Guild* —1K **113**
Scott Clo. *W Dray* —1A **8**
Scott Farm Clo. *Th Dit* —7H **41**
Scott Gdns. *Houn* —3L **9**
Scott Rd. *Craw* —6D **182**
Scotts Av. *Brom* —1N **47**
Scotts Av. *Sun* —8F **22**
Scott's Ct. *Farn* —7N **69**
Scotts Dri. *Hamp* —8B **24**
Scotts Farm Rd. *Eps* —3B **60**
Scott's Gro. Clo. *Chob* —9G **52**
Scott's Gro. Rd. *Chob* —9E **52**
Scott's Hill. *Out* —5A **144**
Scott's La. *Brom* —2N **47**
Scotts La. *W on T* —1L **57**
Scotts Way. *Sun* —8F **22**
Scott Ter. *Brack* —9C **16**
Scott Trimmer Way. *Houn* —5M **9**
Scrutton Clo. *SW12* —1H **29**
Scutley La. *Light* —5B **52**
Scylla Cres. *H'row A* —1C **22**
Scylla Pl. *St J* —6K **73**
Scylla Rd. *H'row A* —9C **8**
Seabrook Dri. *W Wick* —8N **47**
Seaford Ct. *Wokgm* —2C **30**
Seaford Rd. *Craw* —8M **181**
Seaford Rd. *H'row A* —8M **7**
Seaford Rd. *Wokgm* —2C **30**
Seaforth Av. *N Mald* —4G **42**
Seaforth Gdns. *Eps* —1E **60**
Seagrave Lodge. SW6 —2M **13**
(off Seagrave Rd.)
Seagrave Rd. *SW6* —2M **13**
Sealand Rd. *H'row A* —9D **8**
Seale. —8F **110**
Seale Hill. *Reig* —5M **121**
Seale La. *Seale* —8B **110**
Seale La. *Seale & P'ham* —8J **111**
Seale Rd. *Seale & Elst* —3F **130**
Searchwood Rd. *Warl* —5E **84**
Searle Rd. *Farnh* —3H **129**
Searle's Vw. *H'ham* —3L **197**
Seaton Clo. *SW15* —2G **27**
Seaton Clo. *Twic* —9D **10**
Seaton Dri. *Afrd* —3N **21**
Seaton Rd. *Camb* —1N **69**
Seaton Rd. *Mitc* —1C **44**
Seaton Rd. *Twic* —9C **10**
Sebastopol La. *Wmly* —9A **152**
Sebastopol Rd. *Alder* —2N **109**
Secombe Centre. —2N **61**
Second Av. *SW14* —6D **12**
Second Av. *W on T* —5J **39**
Second Clo. *W Mol* —3C **40**
Second Cross Rd. *Twic* —3E **24**
Seddon Ct. *Craw* —8N **181**
Seddon Hill. *Warf* —7N **15**
Seddon Rd. *Mord* —4B **44**
Sedgefield Clo. *Worth* —2J **183**
Sedgemoor. *Farn* —7N **69**
Sedgewick Clo. *Craw* —3G **182**
Sedgwick La. *H'ham* —9M **197**
Sedleigh Rd. *SW18* —9L **13**
Sedlescombe Rd. *SW6* —2M **13**
Seebys Oak. *Coll T* —9J **49**
Seely Rd. *SW17* —7E **28**
Seething Wells. —5J **41**
Seething Wells La. *Surb* —5J **41**
Sefton Clo. *W End* —9C **52**
Sefton Ct. *Houn* —4B **10**
Sefton Rd. *Croy* —7D **46**
Sefton Rd. *Eps* —6C **60**
Sefton St. *SW15* —6H **13**
Sefton Vs. *N Holm* —9H **119**
Segrave Clo. *Wey* —4D **56**
Segsbury Gro. *Brack* —3C **32**
Sekhon Ter. *Felt* —4A **24**
Selborne Av. *Alder* —5N **109**
Selborne Clo. *B'water* —9H **49**
Selborne Gdns. *Farnh* —4F **128**
Selborne Rd. *Croy* —9B **46**
Selborne Rd. *N Mald* —1D **42**
Selbourne Av. *New H* —5K **55**
Selbourne Av. *Surb* —8M **41**
Selbourne Clo. *Craw* —8H **163**
Selbourne Clo. *New H* —5K **55**
Selbourne Rd. *Guild* —9C **94**
Selbourne Sq. *God* —8F **104**
Selby Clo. *Chess* —4L **59**
Selby Grn. *Cars* —6C **44**
Selby Rd. *SE20* —1D **46**
Selby Rd. *Afrd* —7D **22**
Selby Rd. *Cars* —6C **44**
Selbys. *Ling* —6A **146**
Selby Wlk. *Wok* —5L **73**
Selcroft Rd. *Purl* —8M **63**
Selham Clo. *Craw* —2M **181**
Selhurst. —5A **46**
Selhurst Clo. *SW19* —2J **27**
Selhurst Clo. *Wok* —2B **74**
Selhurst Common. —3C **154**
Selhurst New Rd. *SE25* —5B **46**
Selhurst Pl. *SE25* —5B **46**
Selhurst Rd. *SE25* —5B **46**
Selkirk Rd. *SW17* —5C **28**
Selkirk Rd. *Twic* —3C **24**
Sellar's Hill. *G'ming* —4G **132**
Sellincourt Rd. *SW17* —6C **28**
Sells, The. *Guild* —5B **114**
Selsdon. —6F **64**
Selsdon Av. *S Croy* —3A **64**
Selsdon Clo. *Surb* —4L **41**
Selsdon Cres. *S Croy* —6F **64**
Selsdon Pk. Rd. *S Croy & Croy* —5G **65**
Selsdon Rd. *SE27* —4L **29**
Selsdon Rd. *New H* —7J **55**
Selsdon Rd. *S Croy* —2A **64** (8D **200**)
Selsey Ct. *Craw* —7M **181**
Selsey Rd. *Craw* —7M **181**
Selsfield Common. —8E **184**
Selsfield Rd. *Turn H & E Grin* —6D **184**
Seltops Clo. *Cranl* —8A **156**
Selwood Clo. *Stanw* —9L **7**
Selwood Gdns. *Stanw* —9L **7**
Selwood Rd. *Chess* —1K **59**
Selwood Rd. *Croy* —8E **46**
Selwood Rd. *Sutt* —7L **43**
Selwood Rd. *Wok* —7D **74**
Selwyn Av. *Rich* —6L **11**
Selwyn Clo. *Craw* —9G **163**
Selwyn Clo. *Houn* —7M **9**
Selwyn Clo. *Wind* —5A **4**
Selwyn Dri. *Yat* —9A **48**
Selwyn Rd. *N Mald* —4C **42**
Semaphore Rd. *Guild* —5A **114** (7E **202**)
Semley Rd. *SW16* —1J **45**
Semper Clo. *Knap* —4H **73**
Sen Clo. *Brack* —7A **16**
Send. —2F **94**
Send Barns La. *Send* —2F **94**
Send Clo. *Send* —1E **94**
Send Hill. *Send* —3E **94**
Send Marsh. —1H **95**
Send Marsh Grn. *Rip* —1H **95**
Send Marsh Rd. *Send & Rip* —2F **94**
Send Pde. Clo. *Send* —1E **94**
Send Rd. *Send* —1D **94**
Seneca Rd. *T Hth* —3N **45**
Senga Rd. *Wall* —7E **44**
Senhouse Rd. *Sutt* —9J **43**
Sepen Meade. *C Crook* —9A **88**
Sequoia Pk. *Craw* —5B **182**
Sergeant Ind. Est. *SW18* —9N **13**
Sergeants Pl. *Cat* —9N **83**
Serpentine Grn. *Red* —7H **103**
Serrin Way. *H'ham* —3L **197**
Servite Ho. Wor Pk —8E **42**
(off Avenue, The)
Servius Ct. *Bren* —3K **11**
Setley Way. *Brack* —2D **32**
Setter Combe. *Wart* —7B **16**
Settrington Rd. *SW6* —5N **13**
Sett, The. *Yat* —1A **68**
Seven Acres. *Cars* —8C **44**
Seven Arches App. *Wey* —4A **56**
Seven Hills Clo. *W on T* —5F **56**
Seven Hills Rd. *W on T* —5F **56**
Seven Hills Rd. S. *Cobh* —9F **56**
Sevenoaks Clo. *Sutt* —6M **61**
Sevenoaks Rd. *Orp* —2N **67**
Sevenoaks Rd. *Prat B* —4N **67**
Severells Copse. —4N **137**
Severn Clo. *Sand* —7H **49**
Severn Ct. *King T* —9K **25** (1J **203**)
Severn Cres. *Slou* —1D **6**
Severn Dri. *Esh* —8G **41**
Severn Dri. *W on T* —8L **39**
Severn Rd. *Farn* —9K **69**
Severn Rd. *M'bowr* —4G **182**
Seward Rd. *Beck* —1G **47**
Sewell Av. *Wokgm* —9A **14**
Sewer's Farm Rd. *Ab C* —5N **137**
Sewill Clo. *Charl* —3L **161**
Seymour Av. *Cat* —1N **103**
Seymour Av. *Eps* —5G **61**
Seymour Av. *Mord* —6J **43**
Seymour Clo. *E Mol* —4C **40**
Seymour Ct. *Cobh* —9G **57**
Seymour Ct. *Crowt* —3D **48**
Seymour Ct. *Fleet* —3B **88**
Seymour Dri. *Camb* —7F **50**
Seymour Gdns. *Felt* —5K **23**
Seymour Gdns. *Surb* —4M **41**
Seymour Gdns. *Twic* —1H **25**
Seymour Ho. Sutt —3N **61**
(off Mulgrave Rd.)
Seymour M. *Ewe* —6F **60**
Seymour Pl. *SE25* —3E **46**
Seymour Rd. *SW18* —1L **27**
Seymour Rd. *SW19* —4J **27**
Seymour Rd. *Cars* —2E **62**
Seymour Rd. *Craw* —7M **181**
Seymour Rd. *E Mol* —4C **40**
Seymour Rd. *G'ming* —8E **132**
Seymour Rd. *Hamp H* —6C **24**
Seymour Rd. *Head D* —5H **169**
Seymour Rd. *King T* —9K **25** (2H **203**)
Seymour Rd. *Mitc* —6E **44**
Seymour Ter. *SE20* —1E **46**
Seymour Vs. *SE20* —1E **46**
Seymour Wlk. *SW10* —2N **13**
Seymour Way. *Sun* —8G **22**
Shackleford. —4A **132**
Shackleford Rd. *Elst & Shack* —7L **131**
Shackleford Rd. *Shack* —4A **132**
Shackleford Rd. *Wok* —7C **74**
Shacklegate La. *Tedd* —5E **24**
Shackleton Clo. *Ash V* —8D **90**
Shackleton Rd. *Craw* —6C **182**
Shackleton Wlk. Guild —3H **113**
(off Chapelhouse Clo.)
Shackstead La. *G'ming* —8F **132**
Shadbolt Clo. *Wor Pk* —8E **42**
Shadyhanger. *G'ming* —5H **133**
Shady Nook. *Farnh* —6G **108**
Shaef Way. *Tedd* —8G **25**
Shaftesbury Av. *Felt* —9H **9**
Shaftesbury Clo. *Brack* —4B **32**
Shaftesbury Ct. SW6 —4N **13**
(off Maltings Pl.)
Shaftesbury Ct. *SW16* —4H **29**
Shaftesbury Ct. *Farn* —5A **90**
Shaftesbury Ct. *Wokgm* —1C **30**
Shaftesbury Cres. *Stai* —8M **21**
Shaftesbury Ho. *Coul* —9H **83**
Shaftesbury Mt. *B'water* —4J **69**
Shaftesbury Pl. W14 —1L **13**
(off Warwick Rd.)
Shaftesbury Rd. *Bookh* —1J **47**
Shaftesbury Rd. *Bisl* —3C **72**
Shaftesbury Rd. *Cars* —6B **44**
Shaftesbury Rd. *M'bowr* —5H **183**
Shaftesbury Rd. *Rich* —6L **11**
Shaftesbury Rd. *Wok* —4D **74**
Shaftesbury Way. *Twic* —4D **24**
Shakespeare Av. *Felt* —9H **9**
Shakespeare Gdns. *Farn* —9J **69**
Shakespeare Rd. *Add* —1M **55**
Shakespeare Way. *Felt* —5K **23**
Shakespeare Way. *Warf* —8C **16**
Shalbourne Ri. *Camb* —1B **70**
Shalden Ho. *SW15* —9E **12**
Shalden Rd. *Alder* —4B **110**
Shaldon Dri. *Mord* —4K **43**
Shaldon Way. *W on T* —9K **39**
Shale Grn. *Red* —7H **103**
Shalesbrook La. *F Row* —8H **187**
(in two parts)
Shalford. —9A **114**
Shalford Clo. *Orp* —1L **67**
Shalford Mill. —8A **114**
Shalford Rd. *Guild & Shalf* —6N **113** (8D **202**)
Shalstone Rd. *SW14* —6A **12**
Shalston Vs. *Surb* —5M **41**
Shambles, The. *Guild* —5N **113** (6C **202**)
Shamley Green. —7G **134**
Shamrock Clo. *Fet* —8D **78**
Shamrock Clo. *Frim* —6B **70**
Shamrock Cotts. *Guild* —6L **93**
Shamrock Rd. *Croy* —5K **45**
Shandys Clo. *H'ham* —7G **196**
Shanklin Ct. *Alder* —3A **110**
Shannon Clo. *S'hall* —1L **9**
Shannon Corner. (Junct.) —3F **42**
Shannon Corner Retail Pk. *N Mald* —3F **42**
Shannon Ct. *Croy* —1C **200**
Shanti Ct. *SW18* —2M **27**
Shap Cres. *Cars* —7D **44**
Sharland Clo. *T Hth* —5L **45**
Sharnbrook Ho. *W14* —2M **13**
Sharon Clo. *Bookh* —2A **98**
Sharon Clo. *Craw* —6E **182**
Sharon Clo. *Eps* —9B **60** (6J **201**)
Sharon Clo. *Surb* —7J **41**
Sharon Ct. *S Croy* —8C **200**
Sharon Rd. *W4* —1C **12**
Sharp Ho. *Twic* —9K **11**
Sharpthorne Clo. *If'd* —3L **181**
Shaw Clo. *Eps* —7C **60**
Shaw Clo. *Ott* —3E **54**
Shaw Clo. *S Croy* —8C **64**
Shaw Ct. *Old Win* —8K **5**
Shaw Cres. *S Croy* —8C **64**
Shaw Dri. *W on T* —6K **39**
Shaw Farm. —7H **5**
Shawfield Cotts. *As* —2D **110**
Shawfield La. *As* —2D **110**
Shawfield Rd. *As* —3D **110**
Shawford Ct. *SW15* —1F **26**
Shawford Rd. *Eps* —3C **60**
Shawley Cres. *Eps* —5H **81**
Shawley Way. *Eps* —5G **81**
Shaw Pk. *Crowt* —4G **48**
Shaw Rd. *Tats* —7E **86**
Shaws Cotts. Guild —7J **93**
(off Worplesdon Rd.)
Shaws Path. Hamp W —9J **25**
(off High St.)
Shaws Rd. *Craw* —2D **182**
Shaw Way. *Wall* —4J **63**
Shaxton Cres. *New Ad* —5M **65**
Shearing Dri. *Cars* —6A **44**
Shears Ct. *Sun* —8F **22**
Shears, The. (Junct.) —8F **22**
Shearwater Ct. If'd —4J **181**
(off Stoneycroft Wlk.)
Shearwater Rd. *Sutt* —2L **61**
Sheath's La. *Oxs* —9B **58**
Sheen Comn. Dri. *Rich* —7N **11**
Sheen Ct. *Rich* —7N **11**
Sheen Ct. Rd. *Rich* —7N **11**
Sheendale Rd. *Rich* —7M **11**
Sheen Ga. Gdns. *SW14* —7B **12**
Sheengate Mans. *SW14* —7C **12**
Sheen La. *SW14* —8B **12**
Sheen Pk. *Rich* —7L **11**
Sheen Rd. *Rich* —8L **11**
Sheen Way. *Wall* —2K **63**
Sheen Wood. *SW14* —8B **12**
Sheepbarn La. *Warl* —8B **66**
Sheepcote Clo. *Houn* —3H **9**
Sheepcote Rd. *Eton W* —1D **4**
Sheepcote Rd. *Wind* —5B **4**
Sheepfold Rd. *Guild* —9J **93**
Sheep Green. —3C **158**
Sheephatch La. *Tilf* —6N **129**
Sheep Ho. *Farnh* —3H **129**
Sheephouse Grn. *Wott* —9N **117**
Sheephouse La. *Ab C* —7N **137**
Sheephouse La. *Wott & Ab C* —8N **117**
Sheephouse Way. *N Mald* —7C **42**
Sheeplands Av. *Guild* —1E **114**
Sheep Wlk. *Eps* —8C **80**
Sheep Wlk. *Reig* —9L **101**
Sheep Wlk. *Shep* —4B **38**
Sheepwalk La. *E Hor & Ran C* —3G **116**
Sheep Wlk. M. *SW19* —7J **27**
Sheep Wlk., The. *Shep* —6A **38**
Sheep Wlk., The. *Wok* —5F **74**
Sheerwater. —1F **74**
Sheerwater Av. *Wdhm* —8G **55**
Sheerwater Rd. *Wok* —8G **54**
Sheet's Heath La. *Brkwd* —6D **72**
Sheet St. *Wind* —5G **5**
Sheet St. Rd. *Wind* —5A **18**
Sheffield Clo. *Craw* —6F **182**
Sheffield Clo. *Farn* —1L **89**
Sheffield Rd. *H'row A* —9D **8**
Sheffield Way. *H'row A* —8E **8**
Shefford Cres. *Wokgm* —9C **14**
Shelburne Dri. *Houn* —9A **10**
Sheldon Clo. *Craw* —4H **183**
Sheldon Clo. *Reig* —4N **121**
Sheldon Ct. *Guild* —4B **114**
Sheldon St. *Croy* —9N **45** (5B **200**)
Sheldrick Clo. *SW19* —1B **44**
Shelley Av. *Brack* —1C **32**
Shelley Clo. *Bans* —2J **81**
Shelley Clo. *Coul* —4K **83**
Shelley Clo. *Craw* —1G **182**
Shelley Clo. *Fleet* —5B **88**
Shelley Clo. *Slou* —1C **6**
Shelley Ct. *Camb* —1A **70**
Shelley Cres. *Houn* —4L **9**
Shelley Dri. *Broad H* —5C **196**
Shelley Ri. *Farn* —8L **69**
Shelley Rd. *E Grin* —9M **165**
Shelley Rd. *H'ham* —5H **197**
Shelleys Ct. *H'ham* —4N **197**
Shelley Wlk. *Yat* —1A **68**
Shelley Way. *SW19* —7B **28**
Shellfield Clo. *Stai* —8J **7**
Shellwood Cross. —4D **140**
Shellwood Dri. *N Holm* —9J **119**
Shellwood Rd. *Leigh* —1B **140**
Shelson Av. *Felt* —4G **22**
Shelton Av. *Warl* —4F **84**
Shelton Clo. *Guild* —7K **93**
Shelton Clo. *Warl* —4F **84**
Shelton Rd. *SW19* —9M **27**
Shelvers Grn. *Tad* —8H **81**
Shelvers Hill. *Tad* —8G **81**
Shelvers Spur. *Tad* —8H **81**
Shelvers Way. *Tad* —8H **81**
Shenfield Clo. *Coul* —6G **82**
Shenley Rd. *Houn* —4M **9**
Shenstone Clo. *Finch* —8A **30**
Shenstone Pk. *S'hill* —3B **34**
Shepherd & Flock Roundabout. *Farnh* —9K **109**
Shepherd Clo. *Craw* —6C **182**
Shepherd's Bush Rd. *W6* —1H **13**
Shepherds Chase. *Bag* —5J **51**
Shepherds Clo. *Shep* —5C **38**
Shepherds Ct. *Farnh* —3H **129**
Shepherdsgrove La. *Hamm* —5H **167**
Shepherds Hill. *Brack* —9A **16**
Shepherd's Hill. *Cole H* —8M **187**
Shepherd's Hill. *Guild* —1K **113**
Shepherd's Hill. *Hasl* —2G **188**
Shepherd's Hill. *Red* —4G **102**
Shepherd's Hill Bungalows. Hasl
(off Shepherd's Hill) —2G **189**
Shepherds La. *Brack* —8M **15**
Shepherd's La. *Guild* —9J **93**
Shepherds La. *W'sham* —2C **52**
Shepherds Wlk. *Eps* —8A **80**
Shepherds Wlk. *Farn* —7K **69**
Shepherds Way. *Crowt* —3D **48**
Shepherd's Way. *Guild* —7A **114**
(in two parts)
Shepherds Way. *H'ham* —3N **197**
Shepherds Way. *S Croy* —4G **64**
Shepherds Way. *Tilf* —7A **130**
Shepiston La. *Hayes* —1C **8**
Shepley Clo. *Cars* —9E **44**
Shepley Dri. *Asc* —5F **34**
Shepley End. *Asc* —4F **34**
Sheppard Clo. *King T* —3L **41** (8L **203**)
Sheppard Ho. *SW2* —2L **29**
Shepperton. —5D **38**
Shepperton Bus. Pk. *Shep* —4D **38**
Shepperton Ct. *Shep* —5C **38**
Shepperton Ct. Dri. *Shep* —4C **38**
Shepperton Film Studios. —2A **38**
Shepperton Green. —3B **38**
Shepperton Rd. *Lale & Shep* —2L **37**
Sheppey Clo. *Craw* —6N **181**
Sheraton Clo. *B'water* —2K **69**
Sheraton Dri. *Eps* —9B **60** (6J **201**)
Sheraton Wlk. *Craw* —8N **181**
Sherborne Clo. *Coln* —4G **7**
Sherborne Clo. *Eps* —4H **81**

Somerset Gdns.—Springfield Rd.

Somerset Gdns. *Tedd* —6E **24**
Somerset Gro. *Warf* —8D **16**
Somerset Ho. *Red* —2D **122**
Somerset Lodge. *Bren* —2K **11**
Somerset Rd. *SW19* —4J **27**
Somerset Rd. *Bren* —2J **11**
Somerset Rd. *Farn* —4A **90**
Somerset Rd. *King T* —1M **41** (4N **203**)
Somerset Rd. *Red* —5B **122**
Somerset Rd. *Tedd* —6E **24**
Somerset Waye. *Houn* —2M **9**
Somers Pl. *SW2* —1K **29**
Somers Pl. *Reig* —2M **121**
Somers Rd. *SW2* —1K **29**
Somers Rd. *Reig* —2L **121**
Somerswey. *Shalf* —2A **134**
Somerton Av. *Rich* —6A **12**
Somerton Clo. *Purl* —2L **83**
Somertons Clo. *Guild* —9K **93**
Somerville Av. *SW13* —2G **13**
Somerville Ct. Red —*2C* **122**
(off Oxford Rd.)
Somerville Cres. *Yat* —9D **48**
Somerville Dri. *Craw* —9G **163**
Somerville Rd. *Cobh* —1A **78**
Somerville Rd. *Eton* —1F **4**
Sondes Farm. *Dork* —5F **118** (3H **201**)
Sondes Pl. Dri. *Dork* —5F **118**
Sonia Gdns. *Houn* —3A **10**
Sonnet Wlk. *Big H* —5D **86**
Sonninge Clo. *Coll T* —7J **49**
Sonning Gdns. *Hamp* —7M **23**
Sonning Rd. *SE25* —5D **46**
Sontan Ct. *Twic* —2D **24**
Soper Dri. *Cat* —1A **104**
Sophia Ho. W6 —*1H* **13**
(off Queen Caroline St.)
Sopwith Av. *Chess* —2L **59**
Sopwith Clo. *Big H* —3F **86**
Sopwith Clo. *King T* —6M **25**
Sopwith Dri. *Wey* —7N **55**
Sopwith Rd. *Houn* —3K **9**
Sopwith Way. *King T* —9L **25** (2K **203**)
Sorbie Clo. *Wey* —3E **56**
Sorrel Bank. *Croy* —6H **65**
Sorrel Clo. *Craw* —7M **181**
Sorrel Clo. *Farn* —9H **69**
Sorrel Clo. *Wokgm* —9D **14**
Sorrel Dri. *Light* —8K **51**
Sorrell Clo. *Eden* —9L **127**
Sorrell Rd. *H'ham* —3L **197**
Sorrento Rd. *Sutt* —9M **43**
Sotheron Rd. *SW6* —3N **13**
S. Albert Rd. *Reig* —2L **121**
Southall La. *Houn & S'hall* —2J **9**
Southam Ho. Add —*2K* **55**
(off Addlestone Pk.)
Southampton Clo. *B'water* —9H **49**
Southampton Gdns. *Mitc* —4J **45**
Southampton Rd. *H'row A* —9N **7**
Southampton St. *Farn* —5N **89**
Southampton Way. *H'row A* —9N **7**
South Ascot. —5L 33
S. Atlantic Dri. *Alder* —1A **110**
South Av. *Cars* —4E **62**
South Av. *Egh* —7E **20**
South Av. *Farnh* —6J **109**
South Av. *Rich* —5N **11**
South Av. *Wey* —6B **56**
South Av. *W Vill* —6F **56**
South Bank. *Surb* —5L **41**
Southbank. *Th Dit* —6H **41**
South Bank. *W'ham* —4M **107**
S. Bank Ter. *Surb* —5L **41**
South Beddington. —3H 63
S. Black Lion La. *W6* —1F **12**
S. Bolton Gdns. *SW5* —1N **13**
S. Border, The. *Purl* —7H **63**
Southborough. —7L 41
Southborough Clo. *Surb* —7K **41**
Southborough Rd. *Surb* —7L **41**
Southbridge Pl. *Croy* —1N **63** (6B **200**)
Southbridge Rd. *Croy* —1N **63** (6B **200**)
Southbrook. *Craw* —8A **182**
Southbrook Rd. *SW16* —9J **29**
Southby Dri. *Fleet* —4C **88**
South Camp. —9A 90
S. Circular Rd. *SW15* —7F **12**
South Clo. *Craw* —2D **182**
South Clo. *Mord* —5M **43**
South Clo. *Twic* —4A **24**
South Clo. *Wok* —3M **73**
South Clo. *Wokgm* —2D **30**
(Peach St.)
South Clo. *Wokgm* —4C **30**
(South Dri.)
South Clo. Grn. *Red* —7E **102**
Southcote. *Wok* —2N **73**
Southcote Av. *Felt* —3G **23**
Southcote Av. *Surb* —6A **42**
Southcote Dri. *Camb* —1E **70**
Southcote Rd. *SE25* —4E **46**
Southcote Rd. *Red* —8G **102**
Southcote Rd. *S Croy* —6B **64**
South Cft. *Eng G* —6L **19**
Southcroft Av. *W Wick* —8M **47**
Southcroft Rd. *SW17 & SW16* —7F **28**
South Croydon. —2A 64
Southdean Gdns. *SW19* —3L **27**
Southdown Clo. *H'ham* —3N **197**
Southdown Dri. *SW20* —8J **27**
Southdown Rd. *SW20* —9J **27**
Southdown Rd. *Cars* —5E **62**
Southdown Rd. *W on T* —1M **57**
Southdown Rd. *Wold* —9J **85**
South Dri. *Bans* —9C **62**
South Dri. *Brkwd* —8N **71**
South Dri. *Coul* —2H **83**
South Dri. *Dork* —5J **119** (2N **201**)
South Dri. *Orp* —2N **67**
South Dri. *Cutt* —6K **61**
South Dri. *Vir W* —7K **35**
South Dri. *Wokgm* —3B **30**
S. Ealing Rd. *W5* —1K **11**
S. Eden Pk. Rd. *Beck* —5L **47**
South End. *Bookh* —4B **98**
South End. *Croy* —1N **63** (6C **200**)
Southerland Clo. *Wey* —1D **56**
Southern Av. *SE25* —2C **46**
Southern Av. *Felt* —2H **23**
Southern Av. *Red* —1E **142**
Southern Bungalows. *Chil* —1D **134**
Southern Cotts. *Stai* —8J **7**
Southern Industrial Area, Bracknell. —2K 31
Southern Perimeter Rd. *H'row A* —8K **7**
(in two parts)
Southern Rd. *Camb* —9A **50**
Southerns La. *Coul* —3A **102**
Southern Way. *Farn* —2J **89**
Southern Way. *Farnh* —2H **129**
Southey Ct. *Bookh* —2B **98**
Southey Rd. *SW19* —8M **27**
S. Farm La. *Bag* —5L **51**
South Farnborough. —5B 90
Southfield Gdns. *Twic* —5F **24**
Southfield Pl. *Wey* —4C **56**
Southfields. —1M 27
Southfields. *E Mol* —5E **40**
Southfields Av. *Afrd* —7C **22**
Southfields Ct. *Sutt* —8M **43**
Southfields M. *SW18* —9M **13**
Southfields Pas. *SW18* —9M **13**
Southfields Rd. *SW18* —9M **13**
Southfields Rd. *Wold* —9L **85**
Southfleet Rd. *Orp* —1N **67**
South Gdns. *SW19* —8B **28**
Southgate. —5B 182
Southgate Av. *Craw* —6B **182**
Southgate Av. *Felt* —5F **22**
Southgate Dri. *Craw* —5B **182**
Southgate Pde. *Craw* —5B **182**
Southgate Rd. *Craw* —5B **182**
South Godstone. —7H 125
South Gro. *Cher* —5H **37**
South Gro. *Fleet* —1D **88**
South Gro. *H'ham* —7K **197**
South Hill. *G'ming* —7H **133**
South Hill. *Guild* —5N **113** (6D **202**)
S. Hill Rd. *Brack* —5M **31**
S. Hill Rd. *Brom* —2N **47**
S. Holmes Rd. *H'ham* —4A **198**
South Holmwood. —5J 139
South Kensington. —1N 13
Southlands. *E Grin* —2A **186**
Southlands Av. *Horl* —7D **142**
Southlands Av. *Orp* —1M **67**
Southlands Clo. *As* —3E **110**
Southlands Clo. *Coul* —4K **83**
Southlands Clo. *Wokgm* —3C **30**
Southlands Dri. *SW19* —3J **27**
Southlands La. *Tand & Oxt* —3L **125**
Southlands Rd. *As* —3E **110**
Southlands Rd. *Wokgm* —4C **30**
Southland Way. *Houn* —8D **10**
South La. *As* —3F **110**
South La. *King T* —2K **41** (5J **203**)
(in two parts)
South La. *N Mald* —3C **42**
South La. W. *N Mald* —3C **42**
Southlea. —5L 5
Southlea Rd. *Dat & Old Win* —4L **5**
South Lodge. *Twic* —9C **10**
S. Lodge Av. *Mitc* —3J **45**
S. Lodge Rd. *W on T* —5H **57**
South London Crematorium. *Mitc* —1G **44**
Southly Clo. *Sutt* —9M **43**
S. Lynn Cres. *Brack* —4N **31**
South Mall. *Fleet* —4A **88**
South Mall. Stai —*5H* **21**
(off Elmsleigh Shop. Cen.)
South Mead. *Eps* —4E **60**
South Mead. *Red* —9D **102**
South Mdw. *Crowt* —4J **49**
South Mdw. La. *Eton* —2F **4**
Southmead Rd. *SW19* —2K **27**
Southmead Rd. *Alder* —4N **109**
South Merstham. —7H 103
Southmont Rd. *Esh* —8E **40**
South Munstead. —4M 153
S. Munstead La. *G'ming* —3L **153**
South Norwood. —3C 46
South Norwood Country Pk. —3F 46
S. Norwood Hill. *SE25* —1B **46**
South Nutfield. —5K 123
S. Oak Rd. *SW16* —5K **29**
South Pde. *Horl* —7D **142**
South Pde. *Red* —6G **102**
South Pde. *Wall* —3G **62**
South Park. —6D 124
(Godstone)
South Park. —6M 121
(Reigate)
S. Park Gro. *N Mald* —3B **42**
S. Park Hill Rd. *S Croy* —2A **64** (8E **200**)
S. Park La. *Blet* —5D **124**
S. Park M. *SW6* —6N **13**
S. Park Rd. *SW19* —7M **27**
South Path. *Wind* —4F **4**
S. Pier Rd. *Gat A* —3F **162**
South Pl. *Surb* —6M **41**
South Ridge. *Wey* —6C **56**
Southridge Pl. *SW20* —8J **27**
South Ri. *Cars* —5C **62**
South Rd. *SW19* —7A **28**
South Rd. *Ash V* —9E **90**
South Rd. *Bisl* —3C **72**
South Rd. *Crowt* —4K **49**
South Rd. *Eng G* —7M **19**
South Rd. *Felt* —6L **23**
South Rd. *Guild* —1L **113**
South Rd. *Hamp* —7M **23**
South Rd. *Reig* —4N **121**
South Rd. *St G* —5C **56**
South Rd. *Twic* —4D **24**
South Rd. *Wey* —2D **56**
South Rd. *Wok* —2M **73**
South Rd. *Wokgm* —6J **31**
Southsea Rd. *King T* —3L **41** (7K **203**)
South Side. *Cher* —2J **37**
South Side. *Tong* —5D **110**
Southside Comn. *SW19* —7H **27**
Southside House. —7H 27
S. Station App. *S Nut* —5J **123**
South Street. —6J 87
South St. *Dork* —6G **119** (4K **201**)
South St. *Eps* —9C **60** (7K **201**)
South St. *Farn* —4C **90**
South St. *Farnh* —1H **129**
South St. *G'ming* —7G **133**
(in two parts)
South St. *H'ham* —7J **197**
South St. *Isleth* —6G **10**
South St. *Stai* —6H **21**
South Ter. *Dork* —6H **119** (4L **201**)
South Ter. *Surb* —5L **41**
South Vw. *Brack* —2J **31**
South Vw. *Eps* —6N **59**
South Vw. *Eton W* —1E **4**
Southview. *Fren* —1J **149**
Southview Clo. *SW17* —6E **28**
Southview Clo. *Copt* —7B **164**
S. View Ct. *SE19* —8N **29**
S. View Ct. *Wok* —5A **74**
Southview Gdns. *Wall* —4G **63**
S. View Rd. *Asht* —6K **79**
Southview Rd. *Head D* —4G **168**
Southview Rd. *Warl* —6D **84**
(in three parts)
Southview Rd. *Wold* —2L **105**
Southviews. *S Croy* —6G **65**
Southville Clo. *Eps* —5C **60**
Southville Clo. *Felt* —2F **22**
Southville Cres. *Felt* —2F **22**
Southville Rd. *Felt* —2F **22**
Southville Rd. *Th Dit* —6G **41**
South Wlk. *Alder* —2B **110**
South Wlk. *Reig* —3N **121**
South Wlk. *W Wick* —9N **47**
Southwark Clo. *Craw* —7N **181**
Southwark Clo. *Yat* —9B **48**
Southwater Clo. *If'd* —3M **181**
Southway. *SW20* —4H **43**
Southway. *Camb* —2N **69**
South Way. *Cars* —6B **62**
South Way. *Croy* —9H **47**
Southway. *Guild* —3H **113**
Southway. *Wall* —1G **63**
Southway Ct. *Guild* —3H **113**
Southwell Cotts. *Charl* —3K **161**
Southwell Pk. Rd. *Camb* —1N **69**
Southwell Rd. *Croy* —5L **45**
S. Western Rd. *Twic* —9G **11**
South West Middlesex Crematorium. *Felt* —2M **23**
Southwick. *Bag* —6J **51**
Southwick Clo. *E Grin* —8N **165**
Southwick Ct. *Brack* —5C **32**
South Wimbledon. —7N 27
Southwold. *Brack* —7K **31**
Southwood. —2J 89
Southwood. *Wokgm* —4C **30**
Southwood Av. *Coul* —2G **83**
Southwood Av. *King T* —9B **26**
Southwood Av. *Knap* —5G **73**
Southwood Av. *Ott* —4E **54**
Southwood Bus. Cen. *Farn* —1J **89**
Southwood Chase. *Cranl* —9A **156**
Southwood Clo. *Wor Pk* —7J **43**
Southwood Cres. *Swd B* —1J **89**
Southwood Dri. *Surb* —6B **42**
Southwood Gdns. *Esh* —9G **40**
Southwood La. *Farn* —2J **89**
Southwood La. *Fleet* —2E **88**
Southwood Rd. *Farn* —2J **89**
Southwood Village Cen. *Farn* —2J **89**
S. Worple Av. *SW14* —6D **12**
S. Worple Way. *SW14* —6C **12**
Sovereign Clo. *Purl* —6K **63**
Sovereign Ct. *Asc* —6E **34**
Sovereign Ct. *Houn* —6A **10**
Sovereign Ct. *W Mol* —3N **39**
Sovereign Dri. *Camb* —8F **50**
Soyer Ct. *Wok* —5H **73**
Space Waye. *Felt* —9H **9**
Spa Clo. *SE25* —1B **46**
Spa Ct. *SW16* —5K **29**
Spa Dri. *Eps* —1N **79**
Spa Hill. *SE19* —9N **29**
Spalding Rd. *SW17* —6F **28**
Sparks Clo. *Hamp* —7M **23**
Sparrow Clo. *Hamp* —7M **23**
Sparrow Farm Dri. *Felt* —1K **23**
Sparrow Farm Rd. *Eps* —1F **60**
Sparrowhawk Clo. *Ews* —5C **108**
Sparrow Row. —3E 52
Sparrow Row. *Chob* —3E **52**
Sparrows Mead. *Red* —9E **102**
Sparvell Rd. *Knap* —6E **72**
Sparvell Way. *Camb* —9A **50**
Spats La. *Head D* —1D **168**
Speakers Ct. *Croy* —7A **46**
Spear M. *SW5* —1M **13**
Speart La. *Houn* —3M **9**
Speedbird Way. *Harm* —3K **7**
Speedwell Clo. *Eden* —9M **127**
Speedwell Clo. *Guild* —9E **94**
Speedwell Way. *H'ham* —3L **197**
Speer Rd. *Th Dit* —5F **40**
Speirs Clo. *N Mald* —5E **42**
Speke Rd. *T Hth* —1A **46**
Spelthorne Gro. *Sun* —8G **22**
Spelthorne La. *Afrd* —9D **22**
Spelthorne Mus. —6G 21
Spence Av. *Byfl* —1N **75**
Spencer Clo. *C Crook* —8D **88**
Spencer Clo. *Eps* —6D **80**
Spencer Clo. *Frim G* —8C **70**
Spencer Clo. *Wok* —9E **54**
Spencer Ct. *Lea* —1J **99**
Spencer Ct. *Orp* —2L **67**
Spencer Gdns. *SW14* —8B **12**
Spencer Gdns. *Eng G* —6N **19**
Spencer Hill Rd. *SW19* —8K **27**
Spencer Mans. W14 —*2K* **13**
(off Queen's Club Gdns.)
Spencer M. W6 —*2K* **13**
(off Queen's Club Gdns.)
Spencer Pk. *E Mol* —4C **40**
Spencer Pl. *Croy* —6A **46**
Spencer Rd. *SW19* —7K **27**
Spencer Rd. *SW20* —9G **27**
Spencer Rd. *W4* —3B **12**
Spencer Rd. *Brack* —9L **15**
Spencer Rd. *Cat* —8A **84**
Spencer Rd. *Cobh* —2J **77**
Spencer Rd. *E Mol* —3C **40**
Spencer Rd. *Iswth* —4C **10**
Spencer Rd. *Mitc* —2E **44**
Spencer Rd. *Mit J* —6E **44**
Spencer Rd. *S Croy* —2B **64**
Spencer Rd. *Twic* —4E **24**
Spencers La. *Horl* —1L **161**
Spencers Pl. *H'ham* —4H **197**
Spencers Rd. *Craw* —4A **182**
(in two parts)
Spencer's Rd. *H'ham* —5H **197**
Spencer's Way. *Red* —8E **122**
Spencer Wlk. *SW15* —7J **13**
Spenser Av. *Wey* —5B **56**
Spenser M. *SE21* —3N **29**
Spiceall. *Comp* —1E **132**
Spicer Clo. *W on T* —5K **39**
Spicers Fld. *Oxs* —9D **58**
Spice's Yd. *Croy* —1N **63** (6C **200**)
Spiers Way. *Horl* —1F **162**
Spindle Way. *Craw* —4D **182**
Spindlewood Gdns. *Croy* —1B **64** (6F **200**)
Spindlewoods. *Tad* —9G **81**
Spinis. *Brack* —7K **31**
Spinnaker Ct. *Hamp W* —2H **203**
Spinners Grn. *Brack* —4N **31**
Spinners Wlk. *Wind* —4F **4**
Spinney Clo. *Beck* —3L **47**
Spinney Clo. *Cobh* —7A **58**
Spinney Clo. *Craw D* —1F **184**
Spinney Clo. *H'ham* —2A **198**
Spinney Clo. *N Mald* —4D **42**
Spinney Clo. *Wor Pk* —8E **42**
Spinney Cft. *Oxs* —2D **78**
Spinney Dri. *Felt* —1D **22**
Spinney Hill. *Add* —2G **55**
Spinney La. *Wink* —2M **17**
Spinney Oak. *Ott* —3F **54**
Spinney, The. *SW13* —3G **12**
Spinney, The. *SW16* —4G **29**
Spinney, The. *Asc* —4B **34**
Spinney, The. *Bookh* —2B **98**
Spinney, The. *Camb* —9G **51**
Spinney, The. *Craw* —5N **181**
Spinney, The. *Eps* —9D **60** (7M **201**)
(Epsom)
Spinney, The. *Eps* —6G **81**
(Tattenham Corner)
Spinney, The. *Gray* —5M **169**
Spinney, The. *Hasl* —9G **171**
Spinney, The. *Horl* —6E **142**
Spinney, The. *Oxs* —8C **58**
Spinney, The. *Purl* —7M **63**
Spinney, The. *Send* —5L **95**
Spinney, The. *Shot* —3B **188**
Spinney, The. *Sun* —9H **23**
Spinney, The. *Sutt* —1H **61**
Spinney, The. *Yat* —8B **48**
Spinney Way. *Cud* —7M **67**
Spinning Wlk., The. *Shere* —8B **116**
Spinningwheel La. *Binf* —1H **15**
(in two parts)
Spital. —6E 4
Spital Heath. *Dork* —4J **119**
Spitals Cross. —9L 127
Spitals Cross Estate. —9M 127
Spitfire Est., The. *Houn* —1K **9**
Spitfire Rd. *H'row A* —9D **8**
Spitfire Rd. *Wall* —4K **63**
Spitfire Way. *Houn* —1K **9**
Splash, The. *Warf* —7N **15**
Spode La. *Cowd* —1N **167**
Spoil La. *Tong* —5D **110**
Spokane Clo. *Alder* —4L **109**
Spook Hill. *N Holm* —1H **139**
Spooner Ho. *Houn* —2A **10**
Spooners Rd. *H'ham* —4N **197**
Spooner Wlk. *Wall* —2J **63**
Spout Hill. *Croy* —2K **65**
Spout La. *Crock H* —3L **127**
Spout La. *Stai* —7J **7**
Spout La. N. *Stai* —7K **7**
Spratts All. *Ott* —3G **54**
Spratts La. *Ott* —3G **54**
Spray La. *Twic* —9E **10**
Spread Eagle Wlk. *Eps* —9C **60** (6L **201**)
Spreakley. —2G 149
Spreighton Rd. *W Mol* —3B **40**
Spring Av. *Egh* —7A **20**
Springbok Cotts. *Alf* —7F **174**
Springbok Est. *Alf* —7F **174**
(in two parts)
Spring Bottom La. *Blet* —5L **103**
Spring Clo. *G'ming* —3H **133**
Spring Clo. La. *Sutt* —3K **61**
Spring Copse. *Copt* —7N **163**
Spring Copse. *E Grin* —7B **166**
Spring Copse Bus. Pk. *Slin* —5K **195**
Springcopse Rd. *Reig* —5A **122**
Spring Corner. *Felt* —4H **23**
Spring Cotts. *Holmw* —6J **139**
Spring Cotts. *Surb* —4K **41**
Spring Ct. *Eps* —5E **60**
Spring Ct. *Guild* —8L **93**
Springcross Av. *B'water* —3J **69**
Springfarm Rd. *Hasl* —3C **188**
Springfield. *E Grin* —6N **165**
Springfield. *Elst* —7H **131**
Springfield. *Light* —7A **52**
Springfield. *Oxt* —8N **105**
Springfield Av. *SW20* —2L **43**
Springfield Av. *Hamp* —7B **24**
Springfield Clo. *Knap* —5H **73**
Springfield Clo. *Wind* —5E **4**
Springfield Ct. *Craw* —4B **182**
Springfield Ct. *H'ham* —6J **197**
Springfield Ct. *King T* —6K **203**
Springfield Ct. *Wall* —2F **62**
Springfield Cres. *H'ham* —6H **197**
Springfield Dri. *Lea* —6E **78**
Springfield Gdns. *W Wick* —8L **47**
Springfield Gro. *Sun* —9G **23**
Springfield La. *Colg* —5F **198**
Springfield La. *Fleet* —4A **88**
Springfield La. *Wey* —1C **56**
Springfield Meadows. *Wey* —1C **56**
Springfield Pk. *H'ham* —5J **197**
Springfield Pk. Rd. *H'ham* —6H **197**
Springfield Pl. *N Mald* —3B **42**
Springfield Rd. *SW19* —6L **27**
Springfield Rd. *Afrd* —6A **22**
Springfield Rd. *Ash V* —8E **90**
Springfield Rd. *Binf* —1H **31**
Springfield Rd. *Camb* —1E **70**
Springfield Rd. *Craw* —4A **182**
Springfield Rd. *Eden* —2K **147**
Springfield Rd. *Eps* —6H **61**
Springfield Rd. *Guild* —4A **114** (4E **202**)
Springfield Rd. *H'ham* —6H **197**
(in two parts)
Springfield Rd. *King T* —2L **41** (6L **203**)

Summerleigh—Tankerville Rd.

Summerleigh. Wey —3E 56
(off Gower Rd.)
Summerley St. SW18 —3N 27
Summerly Av. Reig —2M 121
Summer Rd. E Mol & Th Dit —4E 40
Summersbury Dri. Shalf —2A 134
Summersbury Hall. Shalf —2A 134
Summersby Clo. G'ming —4J 133
Summers Clo. Sutt —4M 61
Summers Clo. Wey —7B 56
Summers La. Hurt —3D 132
Summer's Rd. G'ming —4J 133
Summerstown. —4A 28
Summerstown. SW17 —4A 28
Summersvere Clo. Craw —9E 162
Summerswood Clo. Kenl —3A 84
Summer Trees. Sun —9J 23
Summerville Gdns. Sutt —3L 61
Summerwood Rd. Iswth —8F 10
Summit Av. Farn —1G 88
Summit Bus. Pk. Sun —8H 23
Summit Pl. Wey —4B 56
Sumner Clo. Fet —2D 98
Sumner Clo. Orp —1L 67
Sumner Ct. Farnh —9H 109
Sumner Gdns. Croy —7L 45
Sumner Pl. Add —2J 55
Sumner Rd. Croy —7L 45
Sumner Rd. Farnh —9H 109
Sumner Rd. S. Croy —7L 45
Sun All. Rich —7L 11
Sun Brow. Hasl —3D 188
Sunbury. —2K 39
Sunbury Av. SW14 —7C 12
Sunbury Av. Pas. SW14 —7D 12
Sunbury Common. —8G 23
Sunbury Ct. Eton —2G 4
Sunbury Ct. Island. Sun —2L 39
Sunbury Ct. M. Sun —1L 39
Sunbury Ct. Rd. Sun —1K 39
Sunbury Cres. Felt —5G 23
Sunbury Cross. (Junct.) —8H 23
Sunbury Cross Shop. Cen. Sun —8G 23
Sunbury La. W on T —5H 39
Sunburylock Ait. W on T —3J 39
Sunbury Pk. Walled Garden. —2J 39
Sunbury Rd. Eton —2G 4
Sunbury Rd. Felt —4G 23
Sunbury Rd. Sutt —9J 43
Sunbury Way. Hanw —6K 23
Sun Clo. Eton —2G 4
Sundale Av. S Croy —6F 64
Sunderland Ct. Stanw —9N 7
Sunderland Rd. H'row A —9N 7
Sundew Clo. Craw —7M 181
Sundew Clo. Light —7A 52
Sundew Clo. Wokgm —1D 30
Sundial Av. SE25 —2C 46
Sundials Cvn. Site. Hkwd —9B 142
Sundon Cres. Vir W —4L 35
Sundown Av. S Croy —7C 64
Sundown Rd. Afrd —6D 22
Sundridge Pl. Croy —7D 46
Sundridge Rd. Croy —6C 46
Sundridge Rd. Wok —6C 74
Sun Hill. Wok —8K 73
Sun Inn Rd. Duns —4B 174
Sunken Rd. Croy —2F 64
Sunkist Way. Wall —5J 63
Sunlight Clo. SW19 —7A 28
Sunmead Clo. Fet —9F 78
Sunmead Rd. Sun —2H 39
Sunna Gdns. Sun —1J 39
Sunniholme Ct. S Croy —8B 200
Sunning Av. Asc —6B 34
Sunningdale. —4D 34
Sunningdale Av. Felt —3M 23
Sunningdale Clo. Surb —8L 41
Sunningdale Ct. Craw —5B 182
Sunningdale Ct. Iswth —9D 10
(off Whitton Dene)
Sunningdale Golf Course. —8E 34
Sunningdale Rd. Sutt —9L 43
Sunninghill. —4A 34
Sunninghill Clo. Asc —3A 34
Sunninghill Ct. Asc —3A 34
Sunninghill Park. —8A 18
Sunninghill Rd. Asc —4A 34
Sunninghill Rd. W'sham —9L 33
Sunninghill Rd. Wink & Asc —6A 18
Sunningvale Av. Big H —2E 86
Sunningvale Clo. Big H —2F 86
Sunny Av. Craw D —1D 184
Sunny Bank. SE25 —2D 46
Sunnybank. Asc —3L 33
Sunnybank. Eps —3B 80
Sunnybank. Warl —4H 85
Sunnybank Rd. Farn —8J 69
(in two parts)
Sunnybank Vs. Blet —1C 124
Sunnycroft Rd. SE25 —2D 46
Sunnycroft Rd. Houn —5B 10
Sunnydell La. Wrec —5F 128
(in two parts)
Sunnydene Rd. Purl —9M 63
Sunny Down. Witl —5B 152
Sunny Hill. Witl —5B 152
Sunnyhill Clo. Craw D —1D 184
Sunnyhill Rd. SW16 —5J 29
Sunny Hill Rd. Alder —2J 109
Sunnyhurst Clo. Sutt —9M 43
Sunnymead. Craw —3B 182
Sunnymead. Craw D —1E 184
(in two parts)
Sunnymead Av. Mitc —2H 45
Sunnymead Rd. SW15 —8G 12
Sunnymeads. —7A 6
Sunnymede Av. Cars —7B 62
Sunnymede Av. Eps —5D 60
Sunny Nook Gdns. S Croy —3A 64
Sunny Ri. Cat —2A 104
Sunnyside. —2A 186
Sunnyside. SW19 —7K 27
Sunnyside. Eden —9K 127
Sunnyside. Fleet —3A 88
Sunny Side. Knap —6E 72
Sunnyside. W on T —4K 39
Sunnyside Cotts. Holm M —6K 137
Sunnyside Pas. SW19 —7K 27
Sunnyside Rd. Head D —5H 169
Sunnyside Rd. Tedd —5D 24
Sunny Vw. Clo. Alder —3A 110
Sunoak Rd. H'ham —6B 198
Sun Pas. Wind —4G 4
Sunray Av. Surb —8A 42
Sun Ray Est. Sand —7F 48
Sunrise Clo. Felt —4N 23
Sun Rd. W14 —1L 13
Sunset Gdns. SE25 —1C 46
Sunshine Way. Mitc —1D 44
Sunstone Gro. Red —7H 103
Sunvale Av. Hasl —2B 188
Sunvale Clo. Hasl —2B 188
Superior Dri. G Str —3N 67
Surbiton. —5K 41
Surbiton Ct. Surb —5J 41
Surbiton Cres. King T —3L 41 (8K 203)
Surbiton Hall Clo. King T —3L 41 (8K 203)
Surbiton Hill Pk. Surb —4M 41
Surbiton Hill Rd. Surb —3L 41 (8K 203)
Surbiton Pde. Surb —5L 41
Surbiton Rd. Camb —6E 50
Surbiton Rd. King T —3K 41 (7J 203)
Surly Hall Wlk. Wind —4C 4
Surrenden Ri. Craw —9A 182
Surrey Av. Camb —2M 69
Surrey Ct. Guild —3L 113
Surrey Ct. Warf —8D 16
Surrey Cres. W4 —1N 11
Surrey Gdns. Eff J —9H 77
Surrey Gro. Sutt —9B 44
Surrey Heath Mus. —9B 50
Surrey Hills Av. Tad —8B 100
Surrey Hills Residential Pk. Tad —8B 100
Surrey Research Pk., The. Sur R —3G 112
Surrey Rd. W Wick —7L 47
Surrey St. Croy —8N 45 (3B 200)
Surrey Technology Cen. Guild —4G 113
Surrey Towers. Add —2L 55
(off Garfield Rd.)
Surridge Ct. Bag —5J 51
Surridge Gdns. SE19 —7N 29
Sussex Av. Iswth —6E 10
Sussex Clo. Knap —5F 72
Sussex Clo. N Mald —3D 42
Sussex Clo. Reig —4B 122
Sussex Clo. Twic —9H 11
Sussex Ct. Add —2L 55
Sussex Ct. Knap —4F 72
Sussex Gdns. Chess —3K 59
Sussex Gdns. Fleet —1C 88
Sussex Lodge. H'ham —4J 197
Sussex Mnr. Bus. Pk. Craw —8E 162
Sussex Pl. W6 —1H 13
Sussex Pl. Knap —5F 72
Sussex Pl. N Mald —3D 42
Sussex Rd. Cars —4D 62
Sussex Rd. Knap —5F 72
Sussex Rd. Mitc —4J 45
Sussex Rd. N Mald —3D 42
Sussex Rd. S Croy —3A 64
Sussex Rd. W Wick —7L 47
Sutherland Av. Big H —4F 86
Sutherland Av. Jac —6A 94
Sutherland Av. Sun —1G 39
Sutherland Chase. Asc —9J 17
Sutherland Dri. SW19 —9B 28
Sutherland Dri. Burp —9B 94
Sutherland Gdns. SW14 —6D 12
Sutherland Gdns. Sun —1G 39
Sutherland Gdns. Wor Pk —7G 42
Sutherland Gro. SW18 —9K 13
Sutherland Gro. Tedd —6E 24
Sutherland Rd. W4 —2D 12
Sutherland Rd. Croy —6L 45
Sutton. —2N 61
(Cheam)
Sutton. —1E 6
(Colnbrook)
Sutton Abinger. —3H 137
Sutton Arc. Sutt —2N 61
Sutton Av. Wok —6H 73
Sutton Comn. Rd. Sutt —6L 43
Sutton Ct. W4 —2B 12
Sutton Ct. Sutt —3A 62
Sutton Ct. Rd. W4 —3B 12
Sutton Ct. Rd. Sutt —3A 62
Sutton Dene. Houn —4B 10
Sutton Gdns. SE25 —4C 46
Sutton Gdns. Red —7H 103
Sutton Green. —4B 94
Sutton Grn. Rd. Sut G —4A 94
Sutton Gro. Sutt —1B 62
Sutton Hall Rd. Houn —3A 10
Sutton La. Ab H & Ab C —3J 137
Sutton La. Houn —6N 9
Sutton La. Slou —2D 6
Sutton La. Sutt & Bans —7N 61
Sutton La. N. W4 —1B 12
Sutton La. S. W4 —2B 12
Sutton Park. —5B 94
Sutton Pk. Rd. Sutt —3N 61
Sutton Pl. Ab H —3G 136
Sutton Pl. Slou —2D 6
Sutton Rd. Camb —6E 50
Sutton Rd. Houn —4A 10
Sutton Sq. Houn —4N 9
Sutton United F.C. —1M 61
Sutton Way. Houn —4N 9
Swabey Rd. Slou —1C 6
Swaby Rd. SW18 —2A 28
Swaffield Rd. SW18 —1N 27
Swail Ho. Eps —7L 201
Swain Clo. SW16 —7F 28
Swain Rd. T Hth —4N 45
Swains Rd. SW17 —8D 28
Swaledale. Brack —4M 31
Swaledale Clo. Craw —6A 182
Swaledale Gdns. Fleet —1C 88
Swale Rd. Farn —8K 69
Swallow Clo. Milf —3B 152
Swallow Clo. Stai —5H 21
Swallow Clo. Yat —9A 48
Swallowdale. S Croy —5G 65
Swallow Fld. D'land —1C 166
Swallowfield. Eng G —7L 19
Swallowfields. Horl —8F 142
(off Rosemary La.)
Swallow Gdns. SW16 —6H 29
Swallow La. Mid H —2H 139
Swallow Pk. Cvn. Site. Surb —9M 41
Swallow Ri. Knap —4F 72
Swallow Rd. Craw —1A 182
Swallow St. Turn H —4F 184
Swallowtail Rd. H'ham —2L 197
Swanage Rd. SW18 —1A 28
Swan Barn Rd. Hasl —2H 189
Swan Cen., The. SW17 —4N 27
Swan Cen., The. Lea —8H 79
Swan Clo. Croy —6B 46
Swan Clo. Felt —5M 23
Swancote Grn. Brack —4N 31
Swan Ct. SW6 —3M 13
(off Fulham Rd.)
Swan Ct. Guild —1N 113
Swan Ct. Iswth —6H 11
(off Swan St.)
Swan Ct. Lea —9H 79
Swandon Way. SW18 —8N 13
Swan La. Charl —3L 161
Swan La. Eden —8L 127
Swan La. Guild —4N 113 (5C 202)
Swan La. Sand —8G 48
Swan M. SW6 —4L 13
Swan Mill Gdns. Dork —3J 119
Swann Ct. Iswth —6G 11
(off South St.)
Swanns Mdw. Bookh —4A 98
Swann Way. Broad H —5E 196
Swan Pl. SW13 —5E 12
Swan Ridge. Eden —8M 127
Swan Rd. Felt —6M 23
Swanscombe Rd. W4 —1D 12
Swansea Rd. Felt —9D 8
Swans Ghyll. F Row —6G 187
Swan Sq. H'ham —6J 197
Swan St. Iswth —6H 11
Swansway, The. Wey —9B 38
Swan Ter. Wind —3E 4
Swan, The. (Junct.) —8M 47
Swanton Gdns. SW19 —2J 27
Swan Wlk. H'ham —6J 197
Swan Wlk. Shep —6F 38
Swanwick Clo. SW15 —1E 26
Swanworth La. Mick —6G 99
Swathling Ho. SW15 —9E 12
(off Tunworth Cres.)
Swaynesland Rd. Eden —3H 127
Swayne's La. Guild —3G 114
Sweeps Ditch Clo. Stai —9J 21
Sweeps La. Egh —6B 20
Sweetbriar. Crowt —9F 30
Sweet Briar La. Eps —1C 80 (8K 201)
Sweet La. Peasl —3F 136
Sweetwater Clo. Sham G —7F 134
Sweetwater La. Sham G —7F 134
Sweetwater La. Wmly —7D 152
Sweetwell Rd. Brack —1K 31
Swievelands Rd. Big H —6D 86
Swift Ct. Sutt —4N 61
Swift La. Bag —4K 51
Swift La. Craw —1A 182
Swift Rd. Farnh —5H 109
Swift Rd. Felt —4M 23
Swift's Clo. Farnh —2N 129
Swift St. SW6 —4L 13
Swinburne Cres. Croy —5F 46
Swinburne Rd. SW15 —7F 12
Swindon Rd. H'ham —4H 197
Swindon Rd. H'row A —8D 8
Swinfield Clo. Felt —4M 23
Swingate Rd. Farnh —3J 129
Swinley Rd. Asc —2G 32
Swinley Rd. Bag —1H 51
Swires Shaw. Kes —1F 66
Swiss Clo. Wrec —7F 128
Swissland Hill. Dor P —4N 165
Switchback La. Rowl —7E 128
(in three parts)
Swithin Chase. Warf —8C 16
Swyncombe Av. W5 —1H 11
Sybil Thorndike Casson Ho. SW5
(off Old Brompton Rd.) —1M 13
Sycamore Av. H'ham —2B 198
Sycamore Clo. Cars —1D 62
Sycamore Clo. Craw —9A 162
Sycamore Clo. Felt —4H 23
Sycamore Clo. Fet —1F 98
Sycamore Clo. Frim —5C 70
Sycamore Clo. Sand —7G 48
Sycamore Cotts. Camb —3N 69
(off Frimley Rd.)
Sycamore Ct. G'ming —3J 133
Sycamore Ct. Houn —7M 9
Sycamore Ct. N Mald —2D 42
Sycamore Ct. Wind —6F 4
Sycamore Cres. C Crook —7A 88
Sycamore Dri. Ash V —6E 90
Sycamore Dri. E Grin —9C 166
Sycamore Dri. Frim —4C 70
Sycamore Dri. Wrec —5F 128
Sycamore Gdns. Mitc —1B 44
Sycamore Gro. N Mald —2C 42
Sycamore Ho. Short —1N 47
Sycamore Ri. Bans —1J 81
Sycamore Ri. Brack —2B 32
Sycamore Rd. SW19 —7H 27
Sycamore Rd. Farn —3A 90
(in two parts)
Sycamore Rd. Guild —3N 113 (2C 202)
Sycamores, The. B'water —1G 68
Sycamores, The. Farn —2B 90
Sycamore Wlk. Eng G —7L 19
Sycamore Wlk. Reig —6A 122
Sycamore Way. Tedd —7J 25
Sycamore Way. T Hth —4L 45
Sydcote. SE21 —2N 29
Sydenham Ct. Croy —1D 200
Sydenham Pl. SE27 —4M 29
Sydenham Rd. Croy —7N 45 (2C 200)
Sydenham Rd. Guild —5N 113 (6D 202)
Sydney Av. Purl —8K 63
Sydney Clo. Crowt —9H 31
Sydney Cres. Afrd —7C 22
Sydney Pl. Guild —4B 114
Sydney Rd. SW20 —1J 43
Sydney Rd. Felt —2H 23
Sydney Rd. Guild —4B 114
Sydney Rd. Rich —7L 11
Sydney Rd. Sutt —1M 61
Sydney Rd. Tedd —6F 24
Sykes Dri. Stai —6K 21
Sylvan Clo. Oxt —7D 106
Sylvan Clo. S Croy —6E 64
Sylvan Clo. Wok —4D 74
Sylvan Est. SE19 —1C 46
Sylvan Gdns. Surb —6K 41
Sylvan Ridge. Sand —6F 48
Sylvan Rd. SE19 —1C 46
Sylvan Rd. Craw —5E 182
Sylvanus. Brack —6L 31
Sylvan Way. C Crook —8A 88
Sylvan Way. Red —4E 122
(in two parts)
Sylvan Way. W Wick —1A 66
Sylvaways Clo. Cranl —7B 156
Sylverdale Rd. Croy —9M 45 (4A 200)
Sylverdale Rd. Purl —9M 63
Sylverns Ct. Warf —8B 16
Sylvestrus Clo. King T —9N 25
Symondson M. Binf —5H 15
Syon Ga. Way. Bren —3G 11
Syon House & Pk. —4J 11
Syon La. Iswth —2F 10
Syon Pk. Gdns. Iswth —3F 10
Syon Pl. Farn —1B 90
Sythwood. Wok —3L 73
Szabo Cres. Norm —3M 111

Tabarin Way. Eps —3H 81
Tabor Ct. Sutt —3K 61
Tabor Gdns. Sutt —3L 61
Tabor Gro. SW19 —8K 27
Tachbrook Rd. Felt —1G 23
Tadlow. King T —5N 203
Tadmor Clo. Sun —3G 39
Tadorne Rd. Tad —8H 81
Tadpole La. Ews —3C 108
Tadworth. —9H 81
Tadworth Av. N Mald —3E 42
Tadworth Clo. Tad —9J 81
Tadworth Ct. Tad —8J 81
Tadworth Park. —8J 81
Tadworth St. Tad —1H 101
Taffy's Row. Mitc —2C 44
Tailworth St. Houn —5C 10
Tait Rd. Croy —6B 46
Talavera Pk. Alder —1M 109
Talbot Clo. Myt —1E 90
Talbot Clo. Reig —4N 121
Talbot La. H'ham —7J 197
Talbot Pl. Bag —3J 51
Talbot Pl. Dat —4M 5
Talbot Rd. Afrd —6N 21
Talbot Rd. Cars —2E 62
Talbot Rd. Farnh —3G 128
Talbot Rd. Iswth —7G 11
Talbot Rd. Ling —8N 145
Talbot Rd. T Hth —3A 46
Talbot Rd. Twic —2E 24
Talcott Path. SW2 —2L 29
Taleworth Clo. Asht —7K 79
Taleworth Pk. Asht —7K 79
Taleworth Rd. Asht —6K 79
Talgarth Dri. Farn —3B 90
Talgarth Mans. W14 —1K 13
(off Talgarth Rd.)
Talgarth Rd. W6 & W14 —1J 13
Talina Cen. SW6 —4N 13
Talisman Clo. Crowt —2C 48
Talisman Way. Eps —3H 81
Tallis Clo. Craw —6L 181
Tall Pines. Eps —7E 60
Tall Trees. SW16 —2K 45
Tall Trees. Coln —4F 6
Tall Trees. E Grin —1B 186
Tally Rd. Oxt —9G 107
Talma Gdns. Twic —9E 10
Talman Clo. If'd —4K 181
Tamar Clo. M'bowr —4G 182
Tamarind Clo. Guild —7K 93
Tamarind Ct. Egh —6B 20
Tamarisk Ri. Wokgm —1B 30
Tamar Way. Slou —1D 6
Tamerton Sq. Wok —6A 74
Tamesis Gdns. Wor Pk —8D 42
Tamian Ind. Est. Houn —7K 9
Tamian Way. Houn —7K 9
Tamworth. Brack —6B 32
Tamworth Dri. Fleet —1C 88
Tamworth La. Mitc —1F 44
Tamworth Pk. Mitc —2F 44
Tamworth Pl. Croy —8N 45 (3B 200)
Tamworth Rd. Croy —8M 45 (3A 200)
Tamworth St. SW6 —2M 13
Tamworth Vs. Mitc —3F 44
Tanbridge Pk. H'ham —7G 197
Tanbridge Pl. H'ham —7H 197
Tanbridge Retail Pk. H'ham —7H 197
Tandem Cen. Retail Pk. SW19 —9B 28
Tandem Way. SW19 —9B 28
Tandridge. —2K 125
Tandridge Ct. Cat —9D 84
Tandridge Gdns. S Croy —9C 64
Tandridge Hill La. God —6J 105
Tandridge La. Tand & Oxt —1K 125
Tandridge Rd. Warl —6G 84
Tanfield Ct. H'ham —6H 197
Tanfield Rd. Croy —1N 63 (6B 200)
Tangier Ct. Alder —2L 109
Tangier Ct. Eton —2G 5
Tangier La. Eton —2G 4
Tangier Rd. Guild —4C 114
Tangier Rd. Rich —7N 11
Tangier Way. Tad —4K 81
Tangier Wood. Tad —5K 81
Tangle Oak. Felb —6H 165
Tanglewood. Finch —9A 30
Tanglewood Clo. Croy —9F 46
Tanglewood Clo. Longc —9L 35
Tanglewood Clo. Wok —3F 74
Tanglewood Ride. W End —8A 52
Tanglewood Way. Felt —4J 23
Tangley Dri. Wokgm —4A 30
Tangley Gro. SW15 —9E 12
Tangley La. Guild —8J 93
Tangley Pk. Rd. Hamp —6N 23
Tanglyn Av. Shep —4C 38
Tangmere Gro. King T —6K 25
Tangmere Rd. Craw —3L 181
Tanhouse La. Wokgm —3A 30
Tanhouse Rd. Oxt —1N 125
Tanhurst Ho. SW2 —1K 29
(off Redlands Way)
Tanhurst La. Holm M —2M 157
Tankerton Rd. Surb —8M 41
Tankerton Ter. Croy —5K 45
Tankerville Rd. SW16 —8H 29

274 A-Z Surrey

Tank Rd.—Tideswell Rd.

Tank Rd. *Sand* —1L **69**
Tanners Clo. *W on T* —5J **39**
Tanners Ct. *Brock* —4A **120**
Tanners Dean. *Lea* —9J **79**
Tannersfield. *Shalf* —2A **134**
Tanner's Hill. *Brock* —5A **120**
Tanners La. *Hasl* —1G **188**
Tanners Mead. *Eden* —2L **147**
Tanners Mdw. *Brock* —7A **120**
Tanners Yd. *Bag* —4H **51**
Tannery Clo. *Beck* —4G **46**
Tannery Clo. *Slin* —5L **195**
Tannery La. *Brmly* —3B **134**
Tannery La. *Send* —1F **94**
Tannery, The. *Red* —3D **122**
Tansy Clo. *Guild* —1E **114**
Tantallon Rd. *SW12* —2E **28**
Tanyard Av. *E Grin* —1C **186**
Tanyard Clo. *H'ham* —7L **197**
Tanyard Clo. *M'bowr* —6G **182**
Tanyard Way. *Horl* —6F **142**
Tapestry Clo. *Sutt* —4N **61**
Taplow Ct. *Mitc* —3C **44**
Tapners Rd. *Bet* —8E **120**
Tara Ct. *Beck* —1L **47**
Tarbat Ct. *Coll T* —7J **49**
Target Clo. *Felt* —9F **8**
Target Hill. *Warf* —8B **16**
Tarham Clo. *Horl* —6C **142**
Tarmac Way. *W Dray* —3K **7**
Tarnbrook Way. *Brack* —6C **32**
Tarn Clo. *Farn* —3K **89**
Tarn Rd. *Hind* —6B **170**
Tarragon Clo. *Brack* —8B **16**
Tarragon Clo. *Farn* —1H **89**
Tarragon Ct. *Guild* —8K **93**
Tarragon Dri. *Guild* —7K **93**
Tarrant Grn. *Warf* —8A **16**
Tarrington Clo. *SW16* —4H **29**
Tartar Hill. *Cobh* —9K **57**
Tartar Rd. *Cobh* —9K **57**
Tasker Clo. *Hayes* —3D **8**
Tasman Ct. *Sun* —8F **22**
Tasso Rd. *W6* —2K **13**
*Tasso Yd. W6 —2K **13***
(off Tasso Rd.)
*Tatchbury Ho. SW15 —9E **12***
(off Tunworth Cres.)
Tate Clo. *Lea* —1J **99**
Tate Rd. *Sutt* —2M **61**
Tate's Way. *Rud* —1E **194**
Tatham Ct. *Craw* —8N **181**
Tatsfield. —8E 86
Tatsfield Green. —8G 86
Tatsfield La. *Tats* —8H **87**
Tattenham Corner. —5G 80
Tattenham Corner Rd. *Eps* —4E **80**
Tattenham Cres. *Eps* —6F **80**
Tattenham Gro. *Eps* —5G **80**
Tattenham Way. *Tad* —5J **81**
Tattersall Clo. *Wokgm* —3D **30**
Taunton Av. *SW20* —1G **42**
Taunton Av. *Cat* —1C **104**
Taunton Clo. *Craw* —2H **183**
Taunton Clo. *Sutt* —7M **43**
Taunton La. *Coul* —6L **83**
Tavern Clo. *Cars* —6C **44**
Tavistock Clo. *Stai* —8M **21**
*Tavistock Ct. Croy —7A **46***
(off Tavistock Rd.)
Tavistock Cres. *Mitc* —3J **45**
Tavistock Gdns. *Farn* —7N **69**
Tavistock Ga. *Croy* —7A **46** (1D **200**)
Tavistock Gro. *Croy* —6A **46**
Tavistock Rd. *Cars* —7B **44**
Tavistock Rd. *Croy* —7A **46** (1D **200**)
Tavistock Rd. *Fleet* —5A **88**
Tavistock Wlk. *Cars* —7B **44**
Tawfield. *Brack* —6K **31**
Tawny Clo. *Felt* —4H **23**
Tawny Cft. *Sand* —7K **49**
Tayben Av. *Twic* —9E **10**
Tay Clo. *Farn* —8K **69**
Tayles Hill Dri. *Eps* —6E **60**
Taylor Av. *Rich* —5A **12**
Taylor Clo. *Eps* —7N **59**
Taylor Clo. *Hamp H* —6C **24**
Taylor Clo. *Houn* —4C **10**
Taylor Clo. *Orp* —1N **67**
*Taylor Ct. SE20 —1F **46***
(off Elmers End Rd.)
Taylor Rd. *Asht* —4K **79**
Taylor Rd. *Mitc* —8C **28**
Taylor Rd. *Wall* —2F **62**
Taylor's Bushes Ride. *Wink* —3N **17**
Taylors Clo. *Lind* —4A **168**
Taylors Ct. *Felt* —3H **23**
Taylors Cres. *Cranl* —7A **156**
Taylors La. *Lind* —4A **168**
Taylor Wlk. *Craw* —3A **182**
Taymans Track. *Hand* —8L **199**
Taynton Dri. *Red* —8H **103**
Teal Clo. *H'ham* —3J **197**
Teal Clo. *S Croy* —7G **64**
Teal Ct. *Dork* —1K **201**
Tealing Dri. *Eps* —1C **60**
Teal Pl. *Sutt* —2L **61**
Teasel Clo. *Craw* —6N **181**
Teasel Clo. *Croy* —7G **46**
Teazlewood Pk. *Lea* —4G **78**
Tebbit Clo. *Brack* —1B **32**
Teck Clo. *Iswth* —5G **11**
Tedder Clo. *Chess* —2J **59**
Tedder Rd. *S Croy* —4F **64**
Teddington. —6G 24
*Teddington Bus. Pk. Todd —7F **24***
(off Station Rd.)
Teddington Clo. *Eps* —6C **60**
Teddington Pk. *Tedd* —6F **24**
Teddington Pk. Rd. *Tedd* —5F **24**
Tedham La. *God* —3E **144**
Tees Clo. *Farn* —8K **69**
Teesdale. *Craw* —6A **182**
Teesdale Av. *Iswth* —4G **11**
Teesdale Gdns. *SE25* —1B **46**
Teesdale Gdns. *Iswth* —4G **11**
Teevan Clo. *Croy* —6D **46**
Teevan Rd. *Croy* —7D **46**
Tegg's La. *Wok* —3H **75**
Tekels Av. *Camb* —1B **70**
Tekels Pk. *Camb* —1C **70**
Tekels Way. *Camb* —3C **70**
Telconia Clo. *Head D* —5H **169**
Telegraph La. *Clay* —2F **60**
Telegraph Pas. *SW2* —1J **29**
Telegraph Rd. *SW15* —1G **27**
Telegraph Track. *Cars* —7E **62**
Telephone Pl. *SW6* —2L **13**
Telferscot Rd. *SW12* —2H **29**
Telford Av. *SW2* —2H **29**
Telford Av. *Crowt* —9H **31**
Telford Ct. *Guild* —3B **114**
Telford Dri. *W on T* —6K **39**
Telford Pl. *Craw* —4C **182**
Telford Rd. *Twic* —1A **24**
Telham Ct. *Craw* —9L **181**
Tellisford. *Esh* —1B **58**
Temperley Rd. *SW12* —1E **28**
Tempest Rd. *Egh* —7E **20**
Templar Clo. *Sand* —7F **48**
Templar Ct. *Eden* —9L **127**
Templar Pl. *Hamp* —8A **24**
Temple Av. *Croy* —8J **47**
Temple Bar Rd. *Wok* —6J **73**
Temple Clo. *Craw* —4H **183**
Temple Clo. *Eps* —8C **60** (5K **201**)
Templecombe M. *Wok* —3D **74**
Templecombe Way. *Mord* —4K **43**
Temple Ct. *Eps* —8C **60**
Templecroft. *Afrd* —7E **22**
Templedene Av. *Stai* —8K **21**
Temple Fld. Clo. *Add* —3K **55**
Temple Gdns. *Stai* —9H **21**
Temple La. *Capel* —4L **159**
Templeman Clo. *Purl* —3L **83**
Templemere. *Wey* —9F **38**
Temple Rd. *Big H* —4F **86**
Temple Rd. *Croy* —1A **64** (6D **200**)
Temple Rd. *Eps* —8C **60** (5K **201**)
Temple Rd. *Houn* —7B **10**
Temple Rd. *Rich* —5M **11**
Temple Rd. *Wind* —5F **4**
Temple's Clo. *Farnh* —2A **130**
Temple Sheen. *SW14* —7B **12**
Temple Sheen Rd. *SW14* —7A **12**
Templeton Clo. *SE19* —1A **46**
Templeton Pl. *SW5* —1M **13**
Temple Way. *Brack* —9K **15**
Temple Way. *Sutt* —9B **44**
Temple Wood Dri. *Red* —9D **102**
Ten Acre. *Wok* —5K **73**
Ten Acre La. *Egh* —1E **36**
Ten Acres. *Fet* —2D **98**
Ten Acres Clo. *Fet* —2D **98**
Ten Acre Wlk. *Rowl* —7E **128**
(in two parts)
Tenbury Ct. *SW12* —2H **29**
Tenby Dri. *Asc* —4A **34**
Tenby Rd. *Frim* —6E **70**
Tenchley's La. *Oxt* —9F **106**
(in two parts)
Tenham Av. *SW2* —2H **29**
Tenniel Clo. *Guild* —1L **113**
Tennis Ct. La. *E Mol* —2F **40**
Tennison Clo. *Coul* —7M **83**
Tennison Rd. *SE25* —3C **46**
Tennyson Av. *N Mald* —4G **43**
Tennyson Av. *Twic* —2F **24**
Tennyson Clo. *Craw* —1F **182**
Tennyson Clo. *Felt* —9G **9**
Tennyson Clo. *H'ham* —2L **197**
*Tennyson Ct. SW6 —4N **13***
(off Maltings Pl.)
*Tennyson Mans. W14 —2L **13***
(off Queen's Club Gdns.)
Tennyson Ri. *E Grin* —9M **165**
Tennyson Rd. *SW19* —7A **28**
Tennyson Rd. *Add* —1N **55**
Tennyson Rd. *Afrd* —6N **21**
Tennyson Rd. *Houn* —5C **10**
Tennyson's La. *Hasl* —3H **189**
Tentelow La. *S'hall* —1A **10**
Tenterden Gdns. *Croy* —6D **46**
Tenterden Rd. *Croy* —6D **46**
Teresa Va. *Warf* —7C **16**
Tern Rd. *If'd* —4J **181**
Terrace Gdns. *SW13* —5E **12**
Terrace Hill. *Croy* —5A **200**
Terrace La. *Rich* —9L **11**
Terrace Rd. *W on T* —6H **39**
Terrace Rd. N. *Binf* —6H **15**
Terrace Rd. S. *Binf* —7H **15**
Terrace, The. *SW13* —5D **12**
Terrace, The. *Add* —2N **55**
Terrace, The. *Asc* —4A **34**
Terrace, The. *Camb* —1L **69**
Terrace, The. *Crowt* —2J **49**
Terrace, The. *Dork* —6J **119**
Terrace, The. *Farn* —2C **90**
Terrace, The. *Old Wok* —7C **74**
(in two parts)
Terrace, The. *Wokgm* —2A **30**
Terra Cotta Ct. *Wrec* —5E **128**
Terra Cotta Rd. *S God* —7F **124**
Terrapin Rd. *SW17* —4F **28**
Terry Rd. *Craw* —8N **181**
Tersha St. *Rich* —7M **11**
Tesimond Dri. *Yat* —1A **68**
Testard Rd. *Guild* —5M **113** (6A **202**)
Tester's Clo. *Oxt* —9D **106**
Testwood Rd. *Wind* —4A **4**
Tetcott Rd. *SW10* —2N **13**
(in two parts)
Teviot Clo. *Guild* —9K **93**
Tewkesbury Clo. *Byfl* —7M **55**
Tewkesbury Rd. *Cars* —7B **44**
Textile Est. *Yat* —8C **48**
Teynham Ct. *Beck* —2L **47**
Thackeray Clo. *SW19* —8J **27**
Thackeray Clo. *Iswth* —5G **11**
Thackeray Lodge. *Felt* —9E **8**
Thames Av. *Cher* —2J **37**
Thames Av. *Wind* —3G **4**
Thames Bank. *SW14* —5B **12**
Thames Clo. *Cher* —6K **37**
Thames Clo. *Farn* —8K **69**
Thames Clo. *Hamp* —1B **40**
Thames Cres. *W4* —3D **12**
Thames Ditton. —5G 40
Thames Ditton Miniature Railway. —7G 41
Thames Eyot. *Twic* —2G **24**
Thamesfield Ct. *Shep* —6D **38**
Thamesfield M. *Shep* —6D **38**
Thames Ga. *Stai* —1K **37**
Thamesgate Clo. *Rich* —5H **25**
Thames Ho. *King T* —7J **203**
Thameside. *Tedd* —8K **25**
Thameside. *W Mol* —2B **40**
Thameside Cen. *Bren* —2M **11**
Thames Lock. *Sun* —2K **39**
Thames Lock. *Wey* —8B **38**
Thames Mead. *W on T* —6H **39**
Thames Mead. *Wind* —4B **4**
Thames Mdw. *Shep* —7C **38**
Thames Mdw. *W Mol* —1A **40**
Thames Pl. *SW15* —6J **13**
(in two parts)
Thamespoint. *Tedd* —8K **25**
Thames Rd. *W4* —2N **11**
Thames Rd. *Wind* —3A **4**
Thames Side. *King T* —9K **25** (2J **203**)
Thames Side. *Stai* —1K **37**
Thames Side. *Th Dit* —5H **41**
Thames Side. *Wind* —3G **5**
Thames St. *Hamp* —9B **24**
Thames St. *King T* —1K **41** (3J **203**)
(in two parts)
Thames St. *Stai* —6H **21**
Thames St. *Sun* —3J **39**
Thames St. *W on T* —6G **39**
Thames St. *Wey* —8C **38**
Thames St. *Wind* —4G **4**
Thames Va. Clo. *Houn* —6A **10**
Thamesview Houses. *W on T* —5H **39**
Thames Village. *W4* —4D **12**
Thanescroft Gdns. *Croy* —9D **46**
Thanet Dri. *Kes* —1F **66**
Thanet Ho. *Croy* —6C **200**
Thanet Pl. *Croy* —1N **63** (6C **200**)
Tharp Rd. *Wall* —2H **63**
Thatcher Clo. *Craw* —6B **182**
Thatchers Clo. *Horl* —6F **142**
Thatchers Clo. *H'ham* —4L **197**
Thatchers La. *Worp* —5G **93**
Thatchers Way. *Iswth* —8D **10**
Thaxted Pl. *SW20* —8J **27**
Thaxton Rd. *W14* —2L **13**
Thayers Farm Rd. *Beck* —1H **47**
Theal Clo. *Coll T* —7J **49**
Theatre Ct. *Eps* —9C **60** (7K **201**)
Theatre Royal. —3G 5
Thelma Gro. *Tedd* —7G **24**
Thelton Av. *Broad H* —5D **196**
Theobald Rd. *Croy* —8M **45** (2A **200**)
Theobalds Way. *Frim* —3G **71**
Thepps Clo. *S Nut* —6K **123**
Therapia La. *Croy* —6H **45**
(in two parts)
Theresa Rd. *W6* —1F **12**
Theresa's Wlk. *S Croy* —5A **64**
Thetford Rd. *Afrd* —5N **21**
Thetford Rd. *N Mald* —5C **42**
Thetford Wlk. *Craw* —7K **181**
Thetis Ter. *Rich* —2N **11**
Theydon Clo. *Craw* —5E **182**
Thibet Rd. *Sand* —7H **49**
Thicket Cres. *Sutt* —1A **62**
Thicket Rd. *Sutt* —1A **62**
Thickthorne La. *Stai* —8L **21**
Third Clo. *W Mol* —3C **40**
Third Cross Rd. *Twic* —3D **24**
Thirlmere Clo. *Egh* —8D **20**
Thirlmere Clo. *Farn* —1K **89**
Thirlmere Cres. *C Crook* —8A **88**
Thirlmere Rd. *SW16* —5H **29**
Thirlmere Rd. *If'd* —5J **181**
Thirlmere Wlk. *Camb* —2H **71**
Thirsk Ct. *Alder* —2B **110**
Thirsk Rd. *SE25* —3A **46**
Thirsk Rd. *Mitc* —8E **28**
Thistlecroft Rd. *W on T* —1K **57**
Thistledene. *Th Dit* —5E **40**
Thistledene. *W Byf* —9H **55**
Thistledown Va. *Loxw* —4F **192**
Thistle Gro. *SW10* —1N **13**
Thistle Way. *Small* —8N **143**
Thistlewood Cres. *New Ad* —8N **65**
Thistleworth Clo. *Iswth* —3D **10**
*Thistleworth Marina. Iswth —7H **11***
(off Railshead Rd.)
Thistley La. *Cranl* —6N **155**
Thomas Av. *Cat* —8N **83**
Thomas Dri. *Warf* —8C **16**
Thomas Ho. *Sutt* —4N **61**
*Thomas Moore Ho. Reig —3A **122***
(off Reigate Rd.)
Thomas Turner Path. *Croy* —3C **200**
Thomas Wall Clo. *Sutt* —2N **61**
Thompson Av. *Rich* —6N **11**
Thompson Clo. *Slou* —1B **6**
Thompson's Clo. *Pirb* —1A **92**
Thompson's La. *Chob* —5G **53**
Thomson Ct. *Craw* —8N **181**
Thomson Cres. *Croy* —7L **45**
Thorburn Chase. *Coll T* —9K **49**
Thorburn Way. *SW19* —9B **28**
Thorkhill Gdns. *Th Dit* —7G **41**
Thorkhill Rd. *Th Dit* —7G **41**
Thorley Clo. *W Byf* —1J **75**
Thorley Gdns. *Wok* —2J **75**
Thornash Clo. *Wok* —2M **73**
Thornash Rd. *Wok* —2M **73**
Thornash Way. *Wok* —2M **73**
Thorn Bank. *Guild* —5K **113**
Thornbank Clo. *Stai* —8J **7**
Thornbury Av. *Iswth* —3D **10**
Thornbury Clo. *Crowt* —2G **48**
Thornbury Ct. *Iswth* —3E **10**
Thornbury Ct. *S Croy* —8E **200**
Thornbury Rd. *SW2* —1J **29**
Thornbury Rd. *Iswth* —3D **10**
Thorncliffe Rd. *SW4* —1J **29**
Thorncliffe Rd. *S'hall* —1N **9**
Thorn Clo. *Wrec* —7E **128**
Thorncombe Street. —1N 153
Thorncombe St. *Brmly* —1N **153**
Thorncroft. *Eng G* —8M **19**
Thorncroft Clo. *Coul* —6L **83**
Thorncroft Dri. *Lea* —1H **99**
Thorncroft Rd. *Sutt* —2N **61**
Thorndean St. *SW18* —3A **28**
Thorndike Clo. *SW10* —3N **13**
Thorndon Gdns. *Eps* —2D **60**
Thorndown La. *W'sham* —4A **52**
Thorndyke Clo. *Craw* —4H **183**
Thorne Clo. *Afrd* —8D **22**
Thorne Clo. *Crowt* —9F **30**
Thorne Ho. *Clay* —4H **59**
Thorneloe Gdns. *Croy* —2L **63**
Thorne Pas. *SW13* —5D **12**
Thornes Clo. *Beck* —2M **47**
Thorne St. *SW13* —6D **12**
Thorneycroft Clo. *W on T* —5K **39**
Thorney Hedge Rd. *W4* —1A **12**
Thornfield Grn. *B'water* —3L **69**
Thornfield Rd. *Bans* —4M **81**
Thornhill. *Brack* —3C **32**
Thornhill. *Craw* —5N **181**
Thornhill Av. *Surb* —8L **41**
*Thornhill Ho. W4 —1D **12***
(off Wood St.)
Thornhill Rd. *Alder* —9B **90**
Thornhill Rd. *Croy* —6N **45**
Thornhill Rd. *Surb* —8L **41**
Thornhill Way. *Shep* —4B **38**
Thornlaw Rd. *SE27* —5L **29**
Thornleas Pl. *E Hor* —4F **96**
Thorn Rd. *Wrec* —6F **128**
Thornsett Pl. *SE20* —1E **46**
Thornsett Rd. *SE20* —1E **46**
Thornsett Rd. *SW18* —2N **27**
*Thornsett Ter. SE20 —1E **46***
(off Croydon Rd.)
Thornton Av. *SW2* —2H **29**
Thornton Av. *W4* —1D **12**
Thornton Av. *Croy* —5K **45**
Thornton Clo. *Guild* —9K **93**
Thornton Clo. *Horl* —8C **142**
Thornton Cres. *Coul* —6L **83**
Thornton Dene. *Beck* —1K **47**
Thornton Gdns. *SW12* —2H **29**
Thornton Heath. —3N 45
Thornton Heath Pond. (Junct.) —4L **45**
Thornton Hill. *SW19* —8K **27**
Thornton Pl. *Horl* —8C **142**
Thornton Rd. *SW12* —1H **29**
Thornton Rd. *SW14* —7C **12**
Thornton Rd. *SW19* —7J **27**
Thornton Rd. *Cars* —7B **44**
Thornton Rd. *Croy & T Hth* —6K **45**
Thornton Rd. E. *SW19* —7J **27**
Thornton Row. *T Hth* —4L **45**
Thornton Wlk. *Horl* —8C **142**
Thornville Gro. *Mitc* —1B **44**
*Thornycroft Ho. W4 —1D **12***
(off Fraser St.)
Thornyhurst Rd. *Myt* —1E **90**
Thorold Clo. *S Croy* —6G **65**
Thorold Rd. *Farnh* —9H **109**
Thoroughfare, The. *Tad* —2F **100**
Thorp Clo. *Binf* —6H **15**
Thorpe. —2D 36
Thorpe By-Pass. *Egh* —1D **36**
Thorpe Clo. *New Ad* —7M **65**
Thorpe Clo. *Wokgm* —5A **30**
Thorpe Green. —3C 36
Thorpe Lea. —7E 20
Thorpe Lea Rd. *Egh* —7D **20**
Thorpe Pk. —3F 36
Thorpe Rd. *Cher* —4F **36**
Thorpe Rd. *King T* —8L **25**
Thorpe Rd. *Stai* —7F **20**
Thorpe's Clo. *Guild* —9K **93**
Thorpeside Clo. *Stai* —1G **37**
Thorsden Clo. *Wok* —6A **74**
Thorsden Ct. *Wok* —5A **74**
Thrale Rd. *SW16* —5G **28**
Three Acres. *H'ham* —7G **197**
Three Arch Bus. Pk. *Red* —7E **122**
Three Arches Pk. *Red* —7D **122**
Three Arch Rd. *Red* —7D **122**
Three Bridges. —2E 182
Three Bridges Rd. *Craw* —3D **182**
Three Gates. *Guild* —2E **114**
Three Gates La. *Hasl* —1H **189**
Three Mile Rd. *Holm M* —9H **137**
Three Pears Rd. *Guild* —3G **114**
Threestile Rd. *Warn* —8F **178**
Three Stiles Rd. *Farnh* —9E **108**
Threshers Corner. *Fleet* —1D **88**
Threshfield. *Brack* —4M **31**
Thrift La. *Knock* —4N **87**
Thrift Va. *Guild* —9F **94**
Thrigby Rd. *Chess* —3M **59**
Throgmorton Rd. *Yat* —1A **68**
Throwley Rd. *Sutt* —2N **61**
Throwley Way. *Sutt* —1N **61**
Thrupp Clo. *Mitc* —1F **44**
*Thrupp Ho. Guild —2F **114***
(off Merrow St.)
Thrupp's Av. *W on T* —2L **57**
Thrupp's La. *W on T* —2L **57**
Thundery Hill. *Seale* —8D **110**
Thurbans Rd. *Farnh* —4F **128**
Thurbarns Hill. *Bear G* —1L **159**
Thurlby Rd. *SE27* —5L **29**
Thurleigh Av. *SW12* —1E **28**
Thurleigh Rd. *SW12* —1D **28**
Thurleston Av. *Mord* —4K **43**
Thurlestone Clo. *Shep* —5D **38**
*Thurlestone Pde. Shep —5D **38***
(off High St.)
Thurlestone Rd. *SE27* —4L **29**
Thurlow Hill. *SE21* —2N **29**
Thurlow Ho. *SW16* —4J **29**
Thurlow Pk. Rd. *SE21* —3M **29**
Thurlow Wlk. *Cranl* —9N **155**
Thurlton Ct. *Wok* —3A **74**
Thurnby Ct. *Twic* —4E **24**
Thurne Way. *Rud* —1E **194**
Thurnham Way. *Tad* —7J **81**
Thursby Rd. *Wok* —5K **73**
Thursley. —6G 150
Thursley Cres. *New Ad* —4M **65**
Thursley Gdns. *SW19* —3J **27**
*Thursley Ho. SW2 —1K **29***
(off Holmewood Gdns.)
Thursley Rd. *Churt & Thur* —7A **150**
Thursley Rd. *Elst* —4F **150**
Thurso St. *SW17* —5B **28**
Thurstan Rd. *SW20* —8G **26**
Thurston Ho. *Fleet* —4A **88**
Thyer Clo. *Orp* —1L **67**
Thyme Ct. *Farn* —9H **69**
Thyme Ct. *Guild* —9D **94**
Tibbet's Clo. *SW19* —2J **27**
Tibbet's Corner. (Junct.) —1J **27**
Tibbet's Ride. *SW15* —1J **27**
Tichborne Clo. *B'water* —1J **69**
Tichborne Clo. *Frim* —3D **70**
Tichborne Pl. *Alder* —4B **110**
Tichmarsh. *Eps* —6B **60**
Tickleback Row. —3N 15
Tickleback Row. *Warf* —3N **15**
Tickners Heath. —6F 174
Tidenham Gdns. *Croy* —9B **46**
Tideswell Rd. *SW15* —7H **13**

Troon Clo. If'd —4J 101
Troon Ct. S'hill —4N 33
Trotsford Mdw. B'water —2H 69
Trotsworth Av. Vir W —3A 36
Trotsworth Ct. Vir W —3N 35
Trotters La. Chob —8L 53
Trotter Way. Eps —8A 60
Trotton Clo. M'bowr —6G 182
Trotts La. W'ham —5L 107
Trotwood Clo. Owl —5K 49
Troutbeck Wlk. Camb —3H 71
Trout Rd. Hasl —2C 188
Trouville Rd. SW4 —1G 28
Trowers Way. Red —9F 102
Trowlock Av. Tedd —7J 25
Trowlock Way. Tedd —7K 25
Troy Clo. Tad —7G 81
Troy La. Eden —9M 127
Troy Town. —7H 127
Truggers. Hand —8N 199
Trumble Gdns. T Hth —3M 45
Trumbull Rd. Brack —8M 15
Trumpets Hill Rd. Reig —4G 120
Trumps Green. —5N 35
Trumpsgreen Av. Vir W —5N 35
Trumps Grn. Clo. Vir W —4A 36
Trumpsgreen Rd. Vir W —7M 35
Trumps Mill La. Vir W —5B 36
Trundle Mead. H'ham —3J 197
Trunk Rd. Farn —1H 89
Trunley Heath Rd. Brmly —4M 133
Truslove Rd. SE27 —6L 29
Truss Hill Rd. Asc —4N 33
Trust Wlk. SE21 —2M 29
Trystings Clo. Clay —3G 59
Tubbenden Dri. Orp —1M 67
Tubbenden La. Orp —1M 67
Tubbenden La. S. Orp —2M 67
Tucker Rd. Ott —3F 54
Tuckers Corner. Cranl —7K 155
Tuckers Dri. Cranl —7K 155
Tuckey Gro. Rip —1H 95
Tucklow Wlk. SW15 —1E 26
Tudor Av. Hamp —8A 24
Tudor Av. Wor Pk —9G 42
Tudor Circ. G'ming —4H 133
Tudor Clo. SW2 —1K 29
Tudor Clo. Afrd —5N 21
Tudor Clo. Bans —2K 81
Tudor Clo. Bookh —2N 97
(in two parts)
Tudor Clo. Chess —2L 59
Tudor Clo. Cobh —9N 57
Tudor Clo. Coul —5L 83
Tudor Clo. E Grin —1B 186
Tudor Clo. Eps —6E 60
Tudor Clo. Gray —7B 170
Tudor Clo. Hamp —6C 24
Tudor Clo. M'bowr —4H 183
Tudor Clo. Small —8M 143
Tudor Clo. S Croy —2E 84
Tudor Clo. Sutt —2J 61
Tudor Clo. Wall —4G 63
Tudor Clo. Wok —4C 74
Tudor Clo. Wokgm —3E 30
Tudor Ct. As —3D 110
Tudor Ct. Big H —5G 86
Tudor Ct. Felt —5K 23
Tudor Ct. Red —2E 122
(off St Anne's Ri.)
Tudor Ct. Stanw —9N 7
Tudor Ct. Tedd —7F 24
Tudor Dri. King T —6K 25
Tudor Dri. Mord —5J 43
Tudor Dri. W on T —7L 39
Tudor Dri. Yat —2C 68
Tudor Gdns. SW13 —6D 12
Tudor Gdns. Twic —2F 24
Tudor Gdns. W Wick —9M 47
Tudor Ho. Brack —4N 31
Tudor La. Old Win —1M 19
Tudor Lodge Mans. Kgswd —8L 81
Tudor Pl. Mitc —8C 28
Tudor Rd. SE25 —4E 46
Tudor Rd. Afrd —7E 22
Tudor Rd. Beck —2M 47
Tudor Rd. G'ming —4H 133
Tudor Rd. Hamp —8A 24
Tudor Rd. Houn —7D 10
Tudor Rd. King T —8N 25
Tudors, The. Reig —9A 102
Tudor Wlk. Lea —7F 78
Tudor Wlk. Wey —9C 38
Tudor Way. C Crook —9B 88
Tudor Way. Wind —4B 4
Tuesley. —1F 152
Tuesley Corner. G'ming —8G 132
Tuesley La. G'ming —8G 133
Tufton Gdns. W Mol —1B 40
Tugela Rd. Croy —5A 46
Tuggles Plat. Warn —1E 196
Tugmutton Clo. Orp —1K 67
Tulip Clo. Croy —7G 46
Tulip Clo. Hamp —7N 23
Tulip Ct. H'ham —4J 197
Tulip Tree Ct. Belm —7M 61
Tullett Rd. M'bowr —7F 182
Tulls La. Stand —7C 168
Tull St. Mitc —6D 44
Tulse Clo. Beck —2M 47
Tulse Hill. —2M 29
Tulse Hill. SW2 —1L 29
Tulse Hill Est. SW2 —1L 29
Tulse Ho. SW2 —1L 29
Tulsemere Rd. SE27 —3N 29
Tulyar Clo. Tad —7G 81
Tumber St. H'ley —3B 100
Tumblewood Rd. Bans —3K 81
Tumbling Bay. W on T —5H 39
Tummons Gdns. SE25 —1B 46
Tunbridge La. Bram —8F 168
Tunley Rd. SW17 —2E 28
Tunnel Link Rd. H'row A —8B 8
Tunnel Rd. Reig —3M 121
Tunnel Rd. E. H'row A —4C 8
Tunnel Rd. W. H'row A —4B 8
Tunnmeade. If'd —4K 181
Tunsgate. Guild —5N 113 (6D 202)
Tunsgate Sq. Guild —6C 202
Tunstall Clo. Orp —1N 67
Tunstall Rd. Croy —7B 46
Tunstall Wlk. Bren —2L 11
Tunworth Cres. SW15 —9E 12
Tuppers Ct. Alb —8L 115
Tupwood La. Cat —3D 104
Tupwood Scrubbs Rd. Cat —6D 104
Turf Hill Rd. Camb —7D 50
Turfhouse La. Chob —5H 53
Turing Dri. Brack —5M 31
Turle Rd. SW16 —1J 45
Turnberry. Brack —5K 31
Turner Av. Mitc —9D 28
Turner Av. Twic —4C 24
Turner Clo. Guild —9B 94
Turner Ct. E Grin —7C 166
Turner Ho. Dear G —7J 139
Turner Ho. Twic —9K 11
(off Clevedon Rd.)
Turner Pl. Coll T —9J 49
Turner Rd. Big H —8E 66
Turner Rd. N Mald —6C 42
Turners Clo. Stai —6K 21
Turners Hill. —5D 184
Turners Hill Pk. Turn H —4G 184
Turners Hill Rd. Copt & Craw D —7B 164
Turners Hill Rd. Craw & Worth —3H 183
Turners Hill Rd. E Grin —4J 185
Turners Hill Rd. Turn H —5A 184
Turners La. W on T —9J 57
Turners Mead. C'fold —6F 172
Turners Mdw. Way. Beck —1J 47
Turner's Way. Croy —8L 45
Turner Wlk. Craw —6D 182
Turneville Rd. W14 —2L 13
Turney Rd. SE21 —1N 29
Turnham Clo. Guild —7M 113
Turnham Green. —1D 12
Turnham Grn. Ter. W4 —1D 12
Turnham Grn. Ter. M. W4 —1D 12
Turnoak Av. Wok —7A 74
Turnoak La. Wok —7A 74
Turnoak Pk. Wind —7B 4
Turnpike La. Sutt —2A 62
Turnpike Link. Croy —8B 46 (3F 200)
Turnpike Pl. Craw —1B 182
Turnpike Rd. Brack —1J 31
Turnpike Way. Iswth —4G 10
Turnstone Clo. S Croy —6H 65
Turnstone End. Yat —9A 48
Turnville Clo. Light —6L 51
Turpin Rd. Felt —9G 9
Turpins Ri. W'sham —1M 51
Turpin Way. Wall —4F 62
Turtledove Av. Turn H —4F 184
Tuscam Way. Camb —2L 69
Tuscany Gdns. Craw —9C 162
Tuscany Way. Yat —2B 68
Tushmore Av. Craw —9C 162
Tushmore Ct. Craw —1C 182
Tushmore Cres. Craw —9C 162
Tushmore La. Craw —1C 182
Tushmore Roundabout. Craw —1B 182
Tussock Clo. Craw —5M 181
Tuxford Clo. M'bowr —5G 182
Tweed Clo. Farn —8K 69
Tweeddale Rd. Cars —7B 44
Tweed La. If'd —9L 161
Tweed La. Str G —7N 119
(in two parts)
Tweed Rd. Slou —2D 6
Tweedsmuir Clo. Farn —2J 89
Twelve Acre Clo. Bookh —2N 97
Twelve Acre Cres. Farn —9J 69
Tweseldown Rd. C Crook —9C 88
Twickenham. —2G 25
Twickenham Clo. Croy —9K 45
Twickenham Rd. Felt —4N 23
Twickenham Rd. Iswth —8G 10
Twickenham Rd. Rich —7J 11
Twickenham Rd. Tedd —5G 24
(in two parts)
Twickenham Rugby Union Football Ground. —9E 10
Twickenham Trad. Est. Twic —9F 10
Twilley St. SW18 —1N 27
Twin Bridges Bus. Pk. S Croy —3A 64
Twining Av. Twic —4C 24
Twinoaks. Cobh —9A 58
Twisell Thorne. C Crook —9A 88
Twitten La. Felb —6H 165
Twitten, The. Craw —3A 182
Two Rivers Retail Pk. Stai —5G 21
Two Ways. Loxw —4J 193
Twycross Rd. G'ming —4G 132
Twycross Rd. Wokgm —1D 30
Twyford La. Wrec —5G 128
Twyford Rd. Binf —1H 15
Twyford Rd. Cars —7D 44
Twyford Rd. Wokgm —9A 14
Twyhurst Ct. E Grin —7N 165
Twyne Clo. Craw —5L 181
Twyner Clo. Horl —7H 143
Twynersh Av. Cher —5H 37
Twynham Rd. Camb —1A 70
Tybenham Rd. SW19 —2M 43
Tychbourne Dri. Guild —9E 94
Tydcombe Rd. Warl —6F 84
Tye La. H'ley —6D 100
Tye La. Orp —2L 67
Tylden Way. H'ham —2M 197
Tylecroft Rd. SW16 —1J 45
Tylehost. Guild —8K 93
Tyle Pl. Old Win —8K 5
Tyler Gdns. Add —1L 55
Tyler Rd. Craw —6B 182
Tylers Clo. God —8E 104
Tylers Ct. Cranl —7M 155
(off Rowland Rd.)
Tylor's Green. —8F 104
Tylers Path. Cars —1D 62
Tymperley Ct. H'ham —5L 197
(off King's Rd.)
Tynamara. King T —7J 203
Tynan Clo. Felt —2H 23
Tyndalls. Hind —5D 170
Tyndalls Wood. —6D 170
Tyne Clo. Craw —4G 183
Tyne Clo. Farn —8K 69
Tynedale Rd. Str G —7A 120
Tyne Ho. King T —9K 25 (1J 203)
Tynemouth Rd. Mitc —8E 28
Tynemouth St. SW6 —5N 13
Tynley Gro. Guild —6N 93
Tyrawley Rd. SW6 —4N 13
Tyrell Ct. Cars —1D 62
Tyrell Gdns. Wind —6C 4
Tyrell's Wood. —2N 99
Tyrrell Sq. Mitc —9C 28
Tyrwhitt Av. Guild —8L 93
Tythebarn Clo. Guild —7D 94
Tytherton. Brack —1A 32
Tyting Cotts. Guild —6E 114

Uckfield Gro. Mitc —8E 28
Udney Pk. Rd. Tedd —7G 25
Uffington Dri. Brack —3C 32
Uffington Rd. SE27 —5L 29
Ujima Ct. SW16 —5J 29
Ullathorne Rd. SW16 —5G 28
Ullswater. Brack —6K 31
Ullswater Av. Farn —2K 89
Ullswater Clo. SW15 —5C 26
Ullswater Clo. Farnh —6F 108
Ullswater Clo. Light —6M 51
Ullswater Ct. Ash V —8D 90
(off Lakeside Clo.)
Ullswater Cres. SW15 —5C 26
Ullswater Cres. Coul —3H 83
Ullswater Rd. SE27 —3M 29
Ullswater Rd. SW13 —3F 12
Ullswater Rd. Light —6M 51
Ulstan Clo. Wold —1K 105
Ulva Rd. SW15 —8J 13
Ulverstone Rd. SE27 —3M 29
Ulwin Av. Byfl —9N 55
Umbria St. SW15 —9F 12
Underhill Clo. G'ming —8H 133
Underhill La. Lwr Bo —4G 129
Underhill Pk. Rd. Reig —9M 101
Underhill Rd. Newd —1A 160
Underwood. Brack —5K 31
Underwood. New Ad —2M 65
Underwood Av. As —3C 110
Underwood Clo. Craw D —1E 184
Underwood Ct. Binf —7H 15
Underwood Ct. Cat —3B 104
Underwood Rd. Cat —4B 104
Underwood Rd. Hasl —1D 188
Undine St. SW17 —6D 28
Unicorn Ind. Est. Hasl —1F 188
Union Clo. Owl —5K 49
Union Ct. Rich —8L 11
Union Rd. Croy —6N 45
Union Rd. Deep —8H 71
Union Rd. Farnh —1H 129
Union St. Alder —2M 109
Union St. Brkwd —8L 71
Union St. Farn —1M 89
Union St. King T —1K 41 (3J 203)
Union Ter. Alder —2M 109
Unitair Cen. Felt —9D 8
Unity Clo. SE19 —6N 29
Unity Clo. New Ad —5L 65
University of Surrey Gallery. —3K 113
University Rd. SW19 —7B 28
Unstead La. Brmly —4M 133
Unstead Wood. P'mrsh —2M 133
Unwin Av. Felt —8E 8
Unwin Mans. W14 —2L 13
(off Queen's Club Gdns.)
Unwin Rd. Iswth —6E 10
Upavon Gdns. Brack —4D 32
Upcerne Rd. SW10 —3N 13
Upcroft. Wind —6E 4
Updown Hill. W'sham —3A 52
Upfield. Croy —9E 46
Upfield. Horl —9E 142
Upfield Clo. Horl —1F 162
Upfold Clo. Cranl —4K 155
Upfold La. Cranl —5K 155
Upfolds Grn. Guild —8E 94
Upgrove Mnr. Way. SE24 —1L 29
Upham Pk. Rd. W4 —1D 12
Upland Rd. Camb —8B 50
Upland Rd. S Croy —2A 64
Upland Rd. Sutt —4B 62
Upland Rd. Wold —7K 85
(in two parts)
Uplands. Asht —7K 79
Uplands. Beck —1K 47
Uplands Clo. SW14 —8A 12
Uplands Clo. Hasl —9H 171
Uplands Clo. Sand —7G 48
Uplands Dri. Oxs —1D 78
Uplands Rd. Farnh —2K 129
Uplands Rd. Kenl —3N 83
Upland Way. Eps —5H 81
Uppark Gdns. H'ham —2M 197
Up. Bourne La. Wrec —6F 128
Up. Bourne Va. Wrec —6F 128
Up. Bridge Rd. Red —3C 122
Up. Brighton Rd. Surb —5K 41
Up. Broadmoor Rd. Crowt —2H 49
Upper Butts. Bren —2J 11
Up. Charles St. Camb —9A 50
Up. Chobham Rd. Camb —3F 70
Up. Church La. Farnh —1G 129
Upper Clo. F Row —7H 187
Up. College Ride. Camb —7C 50
Up. Court Rd. Eps —7B 60
Up. Court Rd. Wold —1K 105
Upper Dri. Big H —5E 86
Upper Dunnymans. Bans —1L 81
Upper Eashing. —7D 132
Up. Edgeborough Rd. Guild —4D 114
Upper Elmers End. —4J 47
Up. Elmers End Rd. Beck —3H 47
Up. Elms Rd. Alder —3M 109
Up. Fairfield Rd. Lea —8H 79
Up. Farm Rd. W Mol —3N 39
Upper Forecourt. Gat A —3F 162
(off Ring Rd. S.)
Upper Gatton. —5B 102
Up. Gordon Rd. Camb —1B 70
Up. Green E. Mitc —2D 44
Up. Green W. Mitc —1D 44
(in two parts)
Up. Grotto Rd. Twic —3F 24
Upper Gro. SE25 —3B 46
Up. Guildown Rd. Guild —6L 113 (8A 202)
Upper Hale. —6H 109
Up. Hale Rd. Farnh —5F 108
Upper Halliford. —3F 38
Up. Halliford By-Pass. Shep —4F 38
Up. Halliford Grn. Shep —3F 38
Up. Halliford Rd. Shep —2F 38
Up. Ham Rd. Rich —5K 25
Upper Harestone. Cat —5D 104
Up. High St. Eps —9D 60 (6M 201)
Up. House La. Sham G —2H 155
Upper Ifold. —1B 192
Upper Kiln. Dork —7J 119
(off Stubs Hill)
Upper Mall. W6 —1F 12
(in two parts)
Up. Manor Rd. G'ming —4H 133
Up. Manor Rd. Milf —1B 152
Upper Mount. G'wood —8K 171
Up. Mulgrave Rd. Sutt —4K 61
Upper Norwood. —1B 46
Upper Nursery. Asc —4D 34
Up. Old Pk. La. Farnh —7E 108
Up. Palace Rd. E Mol —2C 40
Up. Park Rd. Camb —1B 70
Up. Park Rd. King T —7N 25
Upper Parrock. —7N 187
Upper Path. Dork —7H 119
Up. Pillory Down. Cars —9E 62
Upper Pines. Bans —4D 82
Up. Pinewood Rd. As —1H 111
Up. Queen St. G'ming —7H 133
Up. Richmond Rd. SW15 —7E 12
Up. Richmond Rd. W. Rich & SW14 —7N 11
Upper Rd. Wall —2H 63
Up. Rose Hill. Dork —6H 119 (4L 201)
Up. St Michael's Rd. Alder —4N 109
Up. Sawley Wood. Bans —1L 81
Up. Selsdon Rd. S Croy —4C 64
Upper Shirley. —1G 64
Up. Shirley Rd. Croy —8F 46
Up. South Vw. Farnh —9H 109
Upper Springfield. Elst —8J 131
Upper Sq. F Row —6H 187
Upper Sq. Iswth —6G 11
Upper Stanford. Pirb —3C 92
Up. Star Post Ride. Crowt —9N 31
Upper St. Fleet —4A 88
Upper St. Shere —7A 116
Up. Sunbury Rd. Hamp —9M 23
Up. Sutton La. Houn —3A 10
Up. Teddington Rd. King T —8J 25
Upperton Rd. Guild —4M 113 (6A 202)
Upper Tooting. —4D 28
Up. Tooting Pk. SW17 —3D 28
Up. Tooting Rd. SW17 —5D 28
Up. Tulse Hill. SW2 —1K 29
Up. Union St. Alder —2M 109
Up. Union Ter. Alder —2M 109
Upper Vann. —9J 153
Up. Vann La. Hamb —9K 153
Up. Vernon Rd. Sutt —2B 62
Up. Verran Rd. Camb —3B 70
Up. Village Rd. Asc —4N 33
Upper Wlk. Vir W —3A 36
Upper Way. Farnh —4F 128
Up. West St. Reig —3L 121
Up. Weybourne La. Farnh —4J 109
Up. Woodcote Village. Purl —8H 63
Upshire Gdns. Brack —3D 32
Upshott La. Wok —4H 75
Upton. Wok —4L 73
Upton Clo. Farn —2B 90
Upton Dene. Sutt —4N 61
Upton Rd. Houn —6A 10
Upton Rd. T Hth —1A 46
Upwood Rd. SW16 —9J 29
Urmston Dri. SW19 —2K 27
Usherwood Clo. Tad —9A 100
Uvedale Clo. New Ad —7N 65
Uvedale Cres. New Ad —7N 66
Uvedale Rd. Oxt —8B 106
Uverdale Rd. SW10 —3N 13
Uxbridge Ct. King T —8J 203
Uxbridge Rd. Felt —3K 23
Uxbridge Rd. Hamp H —5A 24
Uxbridge Rd. King T —3K 41 (8H 203)

Vachery La. Cranl —2N 175
Vaillant Rd. Wey —1D 56
Vale Border. S Croy —7G 65
Vale Clo. Coul —1J 83
Vale Clo. Lwr Bo —7H 129
Vale Clo. Orp —1J 67
Vale Clo. Twic —4G 24
Vale Clo. Wey —9E 38
Vale Clo. Wok —3A 74
Vale Cotts. SW15 —4D 26
Vale Ct. Ash V —6E 90
Vale Ct. Wey —9E 38
Vale Cres. SW15 —5D 26
Vale Cft. Clay —5F 58
Vale Dri. H'ham —6H 197
Vale Farm Rd. Wok —4A 74
Valentines. Plais —3N 191
Valentines Lea. N'chap —8D 190
Valentyne Clo. New Ad —7A 66
Vale Pde. SW15 —4D 26
Valerie Ct. Sutt —4N 61
Vale Rd. Ash V —6E 90
Vale Rd. Camb —2M 69
Vale Rd. Clay —5E 58
Vale Rd. Eps —1E 60
Vale Rd. Mitc —2H 45
Vale Rd. Sutt —1N 61
Vale Rd. Wey —9E 38
Vale Rd. Wind —3C 4
Vale Rd. Wor Pk —9E 42
Vale Rd. N. Surb —8L 41
Vale Rd. S. Surb —8L 41
Valery Pl. Hamp —8A 24
Vale St. SE27 —4N 29
Vale, The. Coul —1H 83
Vale, The. Croy —8G 47
Vale, The. Felt —9J 9
Vale, The. Houn —2M 9
Vale, The. Sun —7H 23
Vale Wood Dri. Lwr Bo —7J 129
Vale Wood La. Gray —5A 170
Valewood Rd. Hasl —4G 188
Valley Ct. Cat —9D 84
Valley Cres. Wokgm —9A 14
Valley End. —3D 52
Valley End Rd. Chob —3D 52
Valleyfield Rd. SW16 —6K 29
Valley Gardens, The. —1H 35
Valley Gdns. SW19 —8B 28
Valley La. Lwr Bo —5H 129
Valley M. Twic —3F 24

Valley Rd.—Wall Hill

Valley Rd. SW16 —6K 29
Valley Rd. Frim —6E 70
Valley Rd. Kenl —2A 84
Valley, The. Guild —7M 113
Valley Vw. Big H —5E 86
Valley Vw. G'ming —7G 132
Valley Vw. Sand —8F 48
Valley Vw. Gdns. Kenl —2B 84
Valley Wlk. Croy —8F 46
Vallis Way. Chess —1K 59
Valnay St. SW17 —6D 28
Valonia Gdns. SW18 —9L 13
Valroy Clo. Camb —9B 50
Vanbrugh Clo. Craw —6K 181
Vanbrugh Dri. W on T —6K 39
Van Common. —9E 188
Vancouver Clo. Eps —7B 60
Vancouver Ct. Small —8L 143
Vancouver Dri. Craw —9B 162
Vancouver Rd. Rich —5J 25
Vanderbilt Rd. SW18 —2N 27
Van Dyck Av. N Mald —6C 42
Vandyke. Brack —5K 31
Vandyke Clo. SW15 —1J 27
Vandyke Clo. Red —9D 102
Van Gogh Clo. Iswth —6G 10
Vanguard Clo. Croy —7M 45 (1A 200)
Vanguard Way. H'row A —5F 8
Vanguard Way. Wall —4J 63
Vann Bri. Clo. Fern —9E 188
Vanneck Sq. SW15 —8F 12
Vanners. Craw —2C 182
Vanners Pde. Byfl —9N 55
Vann Farm Rd. Ockl —6E 158
Vann Lake. Ockl —6F 158
Vann Lake Rd. Capel & Ockl —7F 158
Vann La. Hamb —9G 152
Vann Rd. Fern —9E 188
Vansittart Est. Wind —3F 4
Vansittart Rd. Wind —4E 4
Vanston Pl. SW6 —3M 13
Vantage W. W3 —1M 11
Vant Rd. SW17 —6D 28
Vapery La. Pirb —8A 72
Varley Way. Mitc —1B 44
Varna Rd. SW6 —3K 13
Varna Rd. Hamp —9B 24
Varney Clo. Farn —9K 69
Varsity Dri. Twic —8E 10
Varsity Row. SW14 —5B 12
Vaughan Almshouses. Afrd —6C 22
(off Feltham Hill Rd.)
Vaughan Clo. Hamp —7M 23
Vaughan Gdns. Eton W —1C 4
Vaughan Ho. SW4 —1G 29
Vaughan Rd. Th Dit —6H 41
Vaughan Way. Dork
—5G 118 (2J 201)
Vaux Cres. W on T —3J 57
Vauxhall Gdns. S Croy —3N 63
Veals Mead. Mitc —9C 28
Vectis Gdns. SW17 —7F 28
Vectis Rd. SW17 —7F 28
Vector Point. Craw —8D 162
Vegal Cres. Eng G —6L 19
Vellum Dri. Cars —9E 44
Velmead Clo. Fleet —6C 88
Velmead Rd. Fleet —6B 88
Vencourt Pl. W6 —1F 12
Ventnor Rd. Sutt —4N 61
Ventnor Ter. Alder —3A 110
Venton Clo. Wok —4L 73
Vera Rd. SW6 —4K 13
Verbania Way. E Grin —9D 166
Verbena Clo. W Dray —1M 7
Verbena Gdns. W6 —1F 12
Verdayne Av. Croy —7G 47
Verdayne Gdns. Warl —3F 84
Verdun Rd. SW13 —2F 12
Vereker Dri. Sun —2H 39
Vereker Rd. W14 —1K 13
Verge Wlk. Alder —5M 109
Vermont Rd. SW18 —9N 13
Vermont Rd. Sutt —9N 43
Verner Clo. Head —5D 168
Verne, The. C Crook —8B 88
Vernon Av. SW20 —1J 43
Vernon Clo. Eps —3B 60
Vernon Clo. H'ham —4N 197
Vernon Clo. Ott —3F 54
Vernon Ct. Farnh —1F 128
Vernon Dri. Asc —1H 33
Vernon Dri. Cat —9N 83
Vernon M. W14 —1K 13
(off Vernon St.)
Vernon Rd. SW14 —6C 12
Vernon Rd. Felt —3G 22
Vernon Rd. Sutt —2A 62
Vernon St. W14 —1K 13
Vernon Wlk. Tad —7J 81
Vernon Way. Guild —2J 113
Verona Dri. Surb —8L 41
Veronica Gdns. SW16 —9G 28
Veronica Rd. SW17 —3F 28
Verralls. Wok —4D 74
(in two parts)
Verran Rd. SW12 —1F 28
Verran Rd. Camb —3B 70
Verulam Av. Purl —8G 63
Veryan. Wok —4K 73
Vesey Clo. Farn —9M 69
Vevers Rd. Reig —6A 122
Vibart Gdns. SW2 —1K 29
Vibia Clo. Stanw —1M 21
Viburnum Ct. W End —9B 52
Vicarage Av. Egh —6D 20
Vicarage Clo. Bookh —3A 98
Vicarage Clo. Farnh —4J 129
Vicarage Clo. Ling —7N 145
Vicarage Clo. Tad —2K 101
Vicarage Clo. Wor Pk —7D 42
Vicarage Ct. Beck —2H 47
Vicarage Ct. Egh —7D 20
Vicarage Ct. Felt —1D 22
Vicarage Cres. Egh —6D 20
Vicarage Dri. SW14 —8C 12
Vicarage Dri. Beck —1K 47
Vicarage Farm Ct. Houn —3N 9
Vicarage Farm Rd. Houn —5M 9
Vicarage Fields. W on T —5K 39
Vicarage Gdns. SW14 —8B 12
Vicarage Gdns. Asc —4L 33
Vicarage Gdns. C Crook —9A 88
Vicarage Gdns. Gray —6A 170
Vicarage Gdns. Mitc —2C 44
Vicarage Ga. Guild —5K 113
Vicarage Hill. Farnh & Lwr Bo
—4J 129
Vicarage Hill. Loxw —5J 193
Vicarage Hill. W'ham —4M 107
Vicarage Ho. King T —3N 203
Vicarage La. Capel —4K 159
Vicarage La. Crowt & Bag —2E 50
Vicarage La. Eps —5F 60
(in two parts)
Vicarage La. Farnh —1G 129
(Downing St.)
Vicarage La. Farnh —5H 109
(Heath La.)
Vicarage La. Farnh —4J 129
(Vicarage Hill)
Vicarage La. Hasl —2D 188
Vicarage La. Horl —7D 142
Vicarage La. Lea —9H 79
Vicarage La. Send —4E 94
Vicarage La. Stai —2L 37
Vicarage La. Wray —2A 20
Vicarage La. Yat —8B 48
Vicarage Rd. SW14 —8B 12
Vicarage Rd. Bag —3G 50
Vicarage Rd. B'water —2K 69
Vicarage Rd. Chob —7G 53
Vicarage Rd. Craw D —2D 184
Vicarage Rd. Croy —9L 45
Vicarage Rd. Egh —6C 20
Vicarage Rd. Hamp W —9J 25
Vicarage Rd. King T —1K 41 (3J 203)
Vicarage Rd. Ling —7N 145
Vicarage Rd. Stai —4G 20
Vicarage Rd. Sun —6G 23
Vicarage Rd. Sutt —1N 61
Vicarage Rd. Tedd —6G 24
Vicarage Rd. Twic —3E 24
(Green, The)
Vicarage Rd. Twic —9C 10
(Kneller Rd.)
Vicarage Rd. Wok —8B 74
Vicarage Rd. Yat —8A 48
Vicarage Wlk. E Grin —9B 166
Vicarage Wlk. G'ming —6G 132
(off Borough Rd.)
Vicarage Wlk. W on T —6H 39
Vicarage Way. Coln —3E 6
Viceroy Ct. Croy —7A 46 (1D 200)
Vickers Clo. Wall —4K 63
Vickers Dri. N. Bro P —6N 55
Vickers Dri. S. Wey —7N 55
Vickers Rd. Ash V —8D 90
Vickers Way. Houn —8M 9
Victor Ct. Craw —9H 163
Victoria Almshouses. Red —9E 102
Victoria Almshouses. Reig —3A 122
Victoria Av. Camb —1M 69
Victoria Av. Houn —8A 10
Victoria Av. S Croy —6N 63
Victoria Av. Surb —5K 41
Victoria Av. Wall —9E 44
Victoria Av. W Mol —2B 40
Victoria Clo. Eden —3L 147
Victoria Clo. Horl —8E 142
Victoria Clo. W Mol —2A 40
Victoria Clo. Wey —9E 38
Victoria Cotts. Rich —4M 11
Victoria Ct. Bag —6J 51
Victoria Ct. Fleet —4A 88
Victoria Ct. H'ham —6K 197
Victoria Ct. Red —6E 122
Victoria Ct. Shalf —9A 114
(off Station Row)
Victoria Cres. SW19 —8L 27
Victoria Dri. SW19 —1J 27
Victoria Dri. B'water —2H 69
Victoria Gdns. Big H —2E 86
Victoria Gdns. Fleet —4A 88
Victoria Gdns. Houn —4M 9
Victoria Hill Rd. Fleet —4A 88
Victoria La. Hayes —1D 8
Victoria M. SW18 —2A 28
Victoria Pde. Rich —4N 11
(off Sandycombe Rd.)
Victoria Pl. Eps —8D 60 (5N 201)
Victoria Pl. Esh —1B 58
Victoria Pl. Rich —8K 11
Victoria Rd. SW14 —6C 12
Victoria Rd. Add —1M 55
Victoria Rd. Alder —2M 109
Victoria Rd. Asc —4L 33
Victoria Rd. Coul —2H 83
Victoria Rd. Cranl —7M 155
Victoria Rd. Craw —3A 182
Victoria Rd. Eden —3L 147
Victoria Rd. Eton W —1B 4
Victoria Rd. Farn —1M 89
Victoria Rd. Farnh —1H 129
Victoria Rd. Felt —2J 23
Victoria Rd. Fleet —4A 88
Victoria Rd. G'ming —7H 133
Victoria Rd. Guild —3A 114 (3E 202)
Victoria Rd. Horl —8E 142
Victoria Rd. King T —1M 41 (4M 203)
Victoria Rd. Knap —4G 72
Victoria Rd. Mitc —8C 28
Victoria Rd. Owl —6K 49
Victoria Rd. Red —4E 122
Victoria Rd. Stai —4G 20
Victoria Rd. Surb —5K 41
Victoria Rd. Sutt —2B 62
Victoria Rd. Tedd —7G 24
Victoria Rd. Twic —1H 25
Victoria Rd. Wey —9E 38
Victoria Rd. Wok —4A 74
Victoria Sq. Horl —8E 142
(off Consort Way)
Victoria St. Eng G —7M 19
Victoria St. H'ham —6K 197
Victoria St. Wind —4G 4
Victoria Ter. Deep —5H 71
Victoria Ter. Dork —5G 119 (3K 201)
Victoria Vs. Rich —6M 11
Victoria Way. E Grin —2B 186
Victoria Way. Wey —9E 38
Victoria Way. Wok —4A 74
Victor Rd. Tedd —5E 24
Victor Rd. Wind —6F 4
Victors Dri. Hamp —7M 23
Victory Av. Mord —4A 44
Victory Bus. Cen. Iswth —7F 10
Victory Cotts. Eff —6M 97
Victory Pk. Rd. Add —9L 37
Victory Rd. SW19 —8A 28
Victory Rd. Cher —7J 37
Victory Rd. H'ham —5H 197
Victory Rd. M. SW19 —8A 28
Victory Way. Houn —1K 9
Vidler Clo. Chess —3J 59
View Clo. Big H —3E 86
Viewfield Rd. SW18 —9L 13
Viewlands Av. W'ham —7N 87
View Ter. D'land —2C 166
Viggory La. Wok —2M 73
Vigo La. Yat —1B 68
Viking. Brack —4K 31
Viking Ct. SW6 —2M 13
(off Halford Rd.)
Village Clo. Wey —9E 38
Village Gdns. Eps —6E 60
Village Grn. Av. Big H —4G 87
Village Grn. Way. Big H —4G 87
Village Rd. Egh —2E 36
Village Row. Sutt —4M 61
Village St. Newd —1A 160
Village, The. —4D 18
Village, The. Ewh —4E 156
Village Way. Afrd —5A 22
Village Way. Beck —1K 47
Village Way. Cranl —7M 155
Village Way. S Croy —9D 64
Village Way. Yat —8C 48
Villas, The. Blind H —3H 145
Villiers Av. Surb —4M 41 (8M 203)
Villiers Av. Twic —2N 23
Villiers Clo. Surb —3M 41 (8N 203)
Villiers Gro. Sutt —5J 61
Villiers Mead. Wokgm —2A 30
Villiers Path. Surb —4L 41
Villiers Rd. Beck —1G 47
Villiers Rd. Iswth —5E 10
Villiers Rd. King T —3M 41 (7M 203)
Villiers, The. Wey —3E 56
Vinall Gdns. Broad H —4D 196
Vincam Clo. Twic —1A 24
Vincennes Est. SE27 —5N 29
Vincent Av. Cars —7B 62
Vincent Av. Surb —8B 42
Vincent Clo. Cher —6G 37
Vincent Clo. Coul —7D 82
Vincent Clo. Esh —9B 40
Vincent Clo. Fet —1B 98
Vincent Clo. H'ham —6M 197
Vincent Clo. W Dray —2B 8
Vincent Dri. Dork —6G 118 (4J 201)
Vincent Dri. Shep —2F 38
Vincent Grn. Coul —7D 82
Vincent La. Dork —5G 118 (2J 201)
Vincent Ri. Brack —2C 32
Vincent Rd. Cher —6G 37
Vincent Rd. Coul —3G 82
Vincent Rd. Croy —6B 46
Vincent Rd. Dork —5G 118 (3J 201)
Vincent Rd. Houn —5L 9
Vincent Rd. Iswth —4D 10
Vincent Rd. King T —2N 41
Vincent Rd. Stoke D —3M 77
Vincent Row. Hamp H —7C 24
Vincent Sq. Big H —9E 66
Vincent Wlk. Dork —5G 118 (2K 201)
Vincent Works. Dork —3J 201
Vine Clo. Alder —7M 89
Vine Clo. Holmw —4J 139
Vine Clo. Stai —8J 7
Vine Clo. Surb —5M 41
Vine Clo. Sutt —9A 44
Vine Clo. W Dray —1B 8
Vine Clo. Worp —4G 93
Vine Clo. Wrec —7F 128
Vine Cotts. Cranl —7K 155
Vine Cotts. N'chap —8D 190
Vine Farm Cotts. Worp —5G 93
Vine Ho. Clo. Myt —2E 90
Vine La. Wrec —6F 128
Vine Pl. Houn —7B 10
Viner Clo. W on T —5K 39
Vineries Clo. W Dray —2B 8
Vine Rd. SW13 —6E 12
Vine Rd. E Mol —3C 40
Vine Rd. Orp —3N 67
Vine Sq. W14 —1L 13
(off Star Rd.)
Vine St. Alder —3M 109
Vine Way. Wrec —6F 128
Vineyard Clo. King T
—2M 41 (5M 203)
Vineyard Hill Rd. SW19 —5L 27
Vineyard Pas. Rich —8L 11
Vineyard Path. SW14 —6C 12
Vineyard Rd. Felt —4H 23
Vineyard Row. Hamp W —9J 25
Vineyards, The. Felt —4H 23
(off High St.)
Vineyards, The. Sun —2H 39
Vineyard, The. Rich —8L 11
Viney Bank. Croy —5J 65
Viola Av. Felt —9K 9
Viola Av. Stai —2M 21
Viola Cft. Warf —9D 16
Violet Clo. Wall —6M 97
Violet Gdns. Croy —2M 63
Violet La. Croy —3M 63 (8A 200)
Virginia Av. Vir W —4M 35
Virginia Beeches. Vir W —2M 35
Virginia Clo. Asht —5K 79
Virginia Clo. N Mald —3B 42
Virginia Clo. Stai —2L 37
Virginia Clo. Wey —3D 56
Virginia Dri. Vir W —4M 35
Virginia Gdns. Farn —3A 90
Virginia Pk. Vir W —3A 36
Virginia Pl. Cobh —1H 77
Virginia Rd. T Hth —9M 29
Virginia Wlk. SW2 —1K 29
Virginia Water. —4A 36
Virginia Water. —2H 35
Viscount Clo. Ash V —8D 90
Viscount Gdns. W Byf —8N 55
Viscount Ind. Est. Coln —6G 6
Viscount Rd. Stanw —2N 21
Viscount Way. H'row A —7F 8
Vivian Clo. C Crook —7C 88
Vivien Clo. Chess —4L 59
Vivienne Clo. Craw —9B 162
Vivienne Clo. Twic —9K 11
Voewood Clo. N Mald —5E 42
Vogan Clo. Reig —6N 121
Volta Way. Croy —7K 45
Voss Ct. SW16 —7J 29
Vowels La. E Grin —8F 184
Vulcan Clo. Craw —7A 182
Vulcan Clo. Sand —8F 48
Vulcan Clo. Wall —4K 63
(off Handley Page Rd.)
Vulcan Ct. Sand —8F 48
Vulcan Way. New Ad —6A 66
Vulcan Way. Sand —8F 48

Wadbrook St. King T
—1K 41 (4J 203)
Waddington Av. Coul —7L 83
Waddington Clo. Coul —6M 83
Waddington Clo. Craw —6M 181
Waddington Way. SE19 —8N 29
Waddon. —9L 45
Waddon Clo. Croy —9L 45
Waddon Ct. Rd. Croy —9L 45
Waddon Marsh Way. Croy —7K 45
Waddon New Rd. Croy
—9M 45 (4A 200)
Waddon Pk. Av. Croy —1L 63
Waddon Rd. Croy —9L 45 (4A 200)
Waddon Way. Croy —3L 63
Wades La. Tedd —6G 24
Wadham. Owl —6L 49
Wadham Clo. Craw —9G 162
Wadham Clo. Shep —6D 38
Wadham Rd. SW15 —7K 13
Wadhurst Clo. SE20 —1E 46
Wadlands Brook Rd. E Grin —5N 165
Wagbullock Ri. Brack —5A 32
Wagg Clo. E Grin —9C 166
Waggon Clo. Guild —2H 113
Waggoners Hollow. Bag —5J 51
Waggoners Roundabout. (Junct.)
—4J 9
Waggoners Way. Gray —6M 169
Waggoners Wells. —8L 169
Waggoners Wells Rd. Gray —6M 169
Wagon Yd. Farnh —1G 129
Wagtail Clo. H'ham —1K 197
Wagtail Gdns. S Croy —6H 65
Wagtail Wlk. Beck —4M 47
Waight's Ct. King T —9L 25 (1L 203)
Wain End. H'ham —3K 197
Wainford Clo. SW19 —1J 27
Wainhouse Clo. Eden —9M 127
Wainscot. Asc —5C 34
Wainwright Clo. Wokgm —2F 30
Wainwright Gro. Iswth —7D 10
Wainwrights. Craw —6B 182
Wake Ct. Guild —9L 93
Wakefield Clo. Byfl —8N 55
Wakefield Rd. Rich —8K 11
Wakefords Copse. C Crook —1C 108
Wakefords Pk. C Crook —1C 108
(in three parts)
Wakehams Grn. Dri. Craw —9H 163
Wakehurst Dri. Craw —6B 182
Wakehurst M. H'ham —7F 196
Wakehurst Path. Wok —1E 74
Wakely Clo. Big H —5E 86
Walburton Rd. Purl —9G 63
Walbury. Brack —3C 32
Waldby Ct. Craw —6M 181
Waldeck Gro. SE27 —4M 29
Waldeck Rd. SW14 —6B 12
Waldeck Rd. W4 —2N 11
Waldeck Ter. SW14 —6B 12
(off Waldeck Rd.)
Waldegrave Av. Tedd —6F 24
Waldegrave Gdns. Twic —3F 24
Waldegrave Pk. Twic —5F 24
Waldegrave Rd. Tedd —5F 24
Waldegrove. Croy —9C 46
Waldemar Av. SW6 —4K 13
Waldemar Rd. SW19 —6M 27
Walden Cotts. Norm —1L 111
Walden Gdns. T Hth —2K 45
Waldens Pk. Rd. Wok —3M 73
Waldens Rd. Wok —4N 73
Waldo Pl. Mitc —8C 28
Waldorf Clo. S Croy —5M 63
Waldorf Heights. B'water —3J 69
Waldron Gdns. Brom —2N 47
Waldron Hill. Brack —9D 16
Waldronhyrst. S Croy
—1M 63 (7A 200)
Waldron Rd. SW18 —4A 28
Waldron's Path. S Croy
—1N 63 (7B 200)
Waldrons, The. Croy
—1M 63 (7A 200)
Waldrons, The. Oxt —9B 106
Waldy Ri. Cranl —6N 155
Wales Av. Cars —2C 62
Walesbeech. Craw —4E 182
Waleton Acres. Wall —3G 63
Waleys La. Ockl —9E 158
Walford Rd. N Holm —9H 119
Walham Green. —4N 13
Walham Grn. Ct. SW6 —3N 13
(off Waterford Rd.)
Walham Gro. SW6 —3M 13
Walham Ri. SW19 —7K 27
Walham Yd. SW6 —3M 13
Walker Clo. Felt —1G 22
Walker Clo. Hamp —7N 23
Walker Rd. M'bowr —5F 182
Walkerscroft Mead. SE21 —2N 29
Walkers Pl. SW15 —7K 13
Walker's Ridge. Camb —2C 70
Walkfield Dri. Eps —4G 81
Walking Bottom. Peasl —5D 136
Walk, The. Eton W —1D 4
Walk, The. Sun —8G 22
Walk, The. Tand —2K 125
Wallace Clo. Guild —9F 92
Wallace Clo. Shep —3E 38
Wallace Cres. Cars —2D 62
Wallace Fields. Eps —9F 60
Wallace Sq. Coul —9H 83
Wallace Wlk. Add —1L 55
Wallace Way. Alder —1L 109
Wallage La. Rowf —3N 183
Wallbrook Bus. Cen. Houn —6J 9
Wallcroft Clo. Binf —8K 15
Walldown Rd. W'hill —8A 168
Walled Garden, The. Bet —4C 120
Walled Garden, The. Loxw —1H 193
Walled Garden, The. Tad —9J 81
Waller La. Cat —1C 104
Wall Hill. —5G 186

Wall Hill Rd.—Watts Lea

Wall Hill Rd. Ash W & F Row —4F 186
Wallingford Clo. Brack —3C 32
Wallington. —3G 62
Wallington Corner. Wall —1F 62
(off Manor Rd. N.)
Wallington Ct. Wall —3F 62
(off Stanley Pk. Rd.)
Wallington Green. (Junct.) —1F 62
Wallington Rd. Camb —6E 60
Wallington Sq. Wall —3F 62
Wallis Ct. Craw —8D 162
Wallis M. Lea —9G 78
Wallis's Cotts. SW2 —1J 29
Wallis Way. H'ham —4N 197
Walliswood. —9L 157
Walliswood Grn. Rd. Wal W —1L 177
Wallner Way. Wokgm —3D 30
Wallorton Gdns. SW14 —7C 12
Walls Ct. Frim —6C 70
Walmer Clo. Crowt —2H 49
Walmer Clo. F'boro —1M 67
Walmer Clo. Frim —7E 70
Walmer Ct. Surb —8L 203
Walnut Clo. Alder —4M 109
Walnut Clo. Cars —2D 62
Walnut Clo. Eps —2E 80
Walnut Clo. Yat —2C 68
Walnut Dri. Kgswd —2K 101
Walnut Fields. Eps —5E 60
Walnut Gro. Bans —1J 81
Walnut La. Craw —9N 161
Walnut M. Sutt —4A 62
Walnuts, The. H'ham —4J 197
Walnut Tree Av. Mitc —2C 44
Walnut Tree Clo. SW13 —4E 12
Walnut Tree Clo. Bans —8K 61
Walnut Tree Clo. Guild —3M 113 (2A 202)
Walnut Tree Clo. Shep —2D 38
Walnut Tree Cotts. SW19 —6K 27
Walnut Tree Gdns. G'ming —4H 133
Walnut Tree Ho. SW10 —2N 13
(off Tregunter Rd.)
Walnut Tree La. Byfl —8M 55
Walnut Tree Pk. Guild —3M 113 (2A 202)
Walnut Tree Rd. Bren —2L 11
Walnut Tree Rd. Houn —2N 9
Walnut Tree Rd. Shep —1D 38
Walpole Av. Coul —6D 82
Walpole Av. Rich —5M 11
Walpole Ct. Twic —3E 24
Walpole Cres. Tedd —6F 24
Walpole Gdns. W4 —1B 12
Walpole Gdns. Twic —3E 24
Walpole M. SW19 —7B 28
Walpole Pk. Wey —4D 56
Walpole Pl. Tedd —6F 24
Walpole Rd. SW19 —7B 28
Walpole Rd. Croy —8A 46 (2D 200)
Walpole Rd. Old Win —1L 19
Walpole Rd. Surb —6L 41
Walpole Rd. Tedd —6F 24
Walpole Rd. Twic —3E 24
Walsham Rd. Felt —1J 23
Walsh Av. Warf —8C 16
Walsh Cres. New Ad —8A 66
Walsingham Gdns. Eps —1D 60
Walsingham Lodge. SW13 —4F 12
Walsingham Mans. SW6 —3N 13
(off Fulham Rd.)
Walsingham Rd. Mitc —4D 44
Walsingham Rd. New Ad —6M 65
Walstead Ho. Craw —4B 182
Walters Mead. Asht —4L 79
Walters Rd. SE25 —3B 46
Walter St. King T —9L 25 (2K 203)
Waltham Av. Guild —8L 93
Waltham Clo. Owl —6J 49
Waltham Rd. Cars —8D 44
Waltham Rd. Cat —9E 84
Walton & Hersham F.C. —8H 39
Walton Av. N Mald —3E 42
Walton Av. Sutt —9L 43
Walton Bri. Shep —6F 38
Walton Bri. Rd. Shep —6F 38
Walton Clo. Fleet —5A 88
Walton Ct. S Croy —8C 200
Walton Ct. Wok —2C 74
Walton Dri. Asc —9K 17
Walton Dri. H'ham —4A 198
Walton Gdns. Felt —5G 22
Walton Grn. New Ad —5L 65
Walton Heath. —5E 100
Walton Heath. Craw —1H 183
Walton Heath Golf Course. —5J 101
Walton La. Shep —6E 38
Walton La. Wey —8C 38
Walton-on-Thames. —7H 39
Walton on the Hill. —2F 100
Walton Pk. W on T —8L 39
Walton Pk. La. W on T —8L 39
Walton Rd. Eps —8B 80
(Epsom)
Walton Rd. Eps —4E 80
(Epsom Downs, in two parts)
Walton Rd. W on T —4K 39
Walton Rd. W Mol & E Mol —3N 39
Walton Rd. Wok —3B 74
Walton St. Tad —2F 100
Walton Ter. Wok —2D 74
Walton Way. Mitc —3G 44
Wanborough. —6N 111
Wanborough Common. —9C 112
Wanborough Dri. SW15 —2G 26
Wanborough Hill. Wanb —6N 111
Wanborough La. Cranl —6B 156
Wandle Bank. SW19 —8B 28
Wandle Bank. Croy —9J 45
Wandle Clo. As —3E 110
Wandle Clo. M'bowr —4G 182
Wandle Ct. Croy —9J 45
Wandle Ct. Eps —1B 60
Wandle Ct. Gdns. Croy —9J 45
Wandle Pk. Trad. Est., The. Croy —8M 45
Wandle Rd. SW17 —3C 28
Wandle Rd. Bedd —9J 45
Wandle Rd. Croy —9N 45 (5C 200)
Wandle Rd. Mord —3A 44
Wandle Rd. Wall —9F 44
Wandle Side. Croy —9K 45
Wandle Side. Wall —9F 44
Wandle Way. SW18 —2N 27
Wandle Way. Mitc —4D 44
Wandon Rd. SW6 —3N 13
(in two parts)
Wandsworth. —8N 13
Wandsworth Bri. SW6 & SW18 —6N 13
Wandsworth Bri. Rd. SW6 —4N 13
Wandsworth Common. —2D 28
Wandsworth Gyratory. (Junct.) —8N 13
Wandsworth High St. SW18 —8M 13
Wandsworth Plain. SW18 —8N 13
Wandsworth Shop. Cen. SW18 —9N 13
Wanmer Ct. Reig —2M 121
(off Birkheads Rd.)
Wansdown Pl. SW6 —3N 13
Wansdyke Clo. Frim —6D 70
Wansford Grn. Wok —4J 73
Wanstraw Gro. Brack —6C 32
Wantage Clo. Brack —4C 32
Wantage Clo. M'bowr —6G 182
Wantage Rd. Coll T —7J 49
Waplings, The. Tad —2G 100
Wapses Lodge. Wold —7E 84
Wapses Roundabout. (Junct.) —7D 84
Wapshott Rd. Stai —7G 20
Warbank Clo. New Ad —6A 66
Warbank Cres. New Ad —6A 66
Warbank La. King T —8E 26
Warbler's Grn. Cobh —1N 77
Warbleton Ho. Craw —6L 181
(off Salvington Rd.)
Warboys App. King T —7A 26
Warboys Rd. King T —7A 26
Warburton Clo. E Grin —9C 166
Warburton Rd. Twic —2B 24
Warbury La. Knap —2C 72
War Coppice Rd. Cat —5A 104
Ward Clo. S Croy —3B 64
Ward Clo. Wokgm —9C 14
Wardens Fld. Clo. G Str —3N 67
Ward La. Warl —3F 84
Wardle Clo. Bag —4J 51
Wardley St. SW18 —1N 27
Wardo Av. SW6 —4K 13
Ward Rd. SW19 —9A 20
Wardrobe, The. Rich —8K 11
(off Old Pal. Yd.)
Ward Royal. Wind —4F 4
Ward's Pl. Egh —7E 20
Wards Stone Pk. Brack —6C 32
Ward St. Guild —4N 113 (5D 202)
Ware Ct. Sutt —1L 61
Wareham Clo. Houn —7B 10
Wareham Rd. Brack —3D 32
Warehouse Theatre. —3E 200
Warenne Rd. Fet —9C 78
Warfield. —4C 16
Warfield Park. —8D 16
Warfield Rd. Brack —7A 16
Warfield Rd. Felt —1F 22
Warfield Rd. Hamp —9B 24
Warfield St. Warf —6A 16
Wargrove Dri. Coll T —7J 49
Warham Rd. S Croy —2M 63 (8A 200)
Waring St. SE27 —5N 29
Warkworth Gdns. Iswth —3G 10
Warlingham. —5G 84
Warlingham Rd. T Hth —3M 45
Warltersville Way. Horl —1G 162
Warminster Gdns. SE25 —1D 46
Warminster Rd. SE25 —1C 46
Warminster Sq. SE25 —1D 46
Warminster Way. Mitc —9F 28
Warner Av. Sutt —8K 43
Warner Clo. Hamp —6N 23
Warner Clo. Hayes —3E 8
Warner Clo. M'bowr —7G 182
Warner Ct. Coll T —8K 49
Warner Pde. Hayes —3E 8
Warners La. Alb —1N 135
Warners La. King T —5K 25
Warnford Ho. SW15 —9D 12
(off Tunworth Cres.)
Warnham. —9F 178
Warnham Ct. Warn —1F 196
Warnham Ct. M. Warn —1F 196
Warnham Ct. Rd. Cars —4D 62
Warnham Ho. SW2 —1K 29
(off Up. Tulse Hill)
Warnham Mnr. Warn —1C 196
Warnham Rd. Broad H —4D 196
Warnham Rd. Craw —5E 182
Warnham Rd. H'ham —3H 197
Warramill Rd. G'ming —6K 133
Warren Av. Orp —2N 67
Warren Av. Rich —7A 12
Warren Av. S Croy —4G 64
Warren Av. Sutt —6L 61
Warren Clo. SE21 —1N 29
Warren Clo. Esh —1B 58
Warren Clo. Felb —7H 165
Warren Clo. Fleet —6C 88
Warren Clo. Sand —7F 48
Warren Corner. —5B 108
Warren Corner. Ews —5B 108
Warren Cotts. Hand —8N 199
Warren Ct. Croy —7B 46
Warren Ct. Wey —2B 56
Warren Cutting. King T —8C 26
Warren Down. Brack —9K 15
Warren Dri. Craw —2M 181
Warren Dri. Kgswd —9L 81
Warren Dri. N. Surb —7A 42
Warren Dri. S. Surb —7B 42
Warrenore La. Wey —4E 50
Warren Footpath. Twic —2J 25
Warren Hill. Eps —3C 80
Warren Home Farm. Wok —6K 75
Warren Ho. Rd. Wokgm —7C 14
Warrenhyrst. Guild —4C 114
Warren La. Alb —8L 115
Warren La. Oxs —7C 58
Warren La. Oxt —3C 126
Warren La. Wok —5J 75
Warren Lodge Dri. Kgswd —2K 101
Warren Mead. Bans —2H 81
Warrenne Heights. Red —5D 122
Warrenne Rd. Brock —5B 120
Warrenne Way. Reig —3M 121
Warren Pk. King T —7B 26
Warren Pk. Tad —9B 100
Warren Pk. Thur —5K 151
Warren Pk. Warl —5G 84
Warren Pk. Rd. Sutt —3B 62
Warren Ri. Frim —4C 70
Warren Ri. N Mald —9C 26
Warren Rd. SW19 —7C 28
Warren Rd. Afrd —8F 22
Warren Rd. Bans —1H 81
Warren Rd. Croy —7B 46
Warren Rd. G'ming —4H 133
Warren Rd. Guild —4B 114
Warren Rd. King T —7B 26
Warren Rd. New H —6J 55
Warren Rd. Orp & Chels —2N 67
Warren Rd. Purl —8M 63
Warren Rd. Reig —2N 121
Warren Rd. Twic —9C 10
Warren Row. Asc —1H 33
Warren, The. —3D 32
(Bracknell)
Warren, The. —1C 156
(Ewhurst)
Warren, The. Alder —3L 109
Warren, The. Asht —6L 79
Warren, The. Brack —3E 32
Warren, The. Cars —5B 62
Warren, The. E Hor —8G 96
Warren, The. Farnh —4K 109
Warren, The. Houn —3N 9
Warren, The. Kgswd —1K 101
Warren, The. Oxs —8C 58
Warren, The. Wor Pk —1C 60
Warren Way. Wey —2D 56
Warrington Clo. Bew —7K 181
Warrington Ct. Croy —5A 200
Warrington M. Alder —4K 109
Warrington Rd. Croy —9M 45 (6A 200)
Warrington Rd. Rich —8K 11
Warrington Spur. Old Win —9L 5
Warsop Trad. Est. Eden —3M 147
Warwick. W14 —1L 13
(off Kensington Village)
Warwick. Brack —5C 32
Warwick Av. Egh —9E 20
Warwick Av. Stai —7L 21
Warwick Clo. Alder —4A 110
Warwick Clo. Camb —3F 70
Warwick Clo. Hamp —8C 24
Warwick Clo. Holmw —4H 139
Warwick Ct. Brom —1N 47
Warwick Deeping. Ott —2E 54
Warwick Dri. SW15 —6G 12
Warwick Gdns. Asht —4J 79
Warwick Gdns. Th Dit —4F 40
Warwick Gdns. T Hth —2L 45
Warwick Gro. Surb —6M 41
Warwick Ho. King T —1L 203
Warwick La. Wok —6K 73
Warwick Lodge. Twic —4B 24
Warwick Pl. Th Dit —5G 40
Warwick Quadrant. Red —2E 122
(off London Rd.)
Warwick Rd. SE20 —2E 46
Warwick Rd. W14 & SW5 —1L 13
Warwick Rd. Afrd —6N 21
Warwick Rd. Ash V —5E 90
Warwick Rd. Coul —1G 83
Warwick Rd. Holmw —5J 139
Warwick Rd. Houn —6J 9
Warwick Rd. King T —9J 25
Warwick Rd. N Mald —2B 42
Warwick Rd. Red —2D 122
Warwick Rd. Sutt —1A 62
Warwick Rd. Th Dit —4F 40
Warwick Rd. T Hth —2L 45
Warwick Rd. Twic —2E 24
Warwicks Bench. Guild —5N 113 (7D 202)
Warwick's Bench La. Guild —6B 114
Warwick's Bench Rd. Guild —6A 114 (8E 202)
Warwick Vs. Egh —9E 20
Warwick Wold. —7L 103
Warwick Wold Rd. Red —7L 103
Wasdale Clo. Owl —5J 49
Washford Clo. Bord —5A 168
Washford La. Lind —4A 168
Washington Clo. Reig —1M 121
Washington Dri. Wind —6B 4
Washington Rd. SW13 —3F 12
Washington Rd. Bew —6K 181
Washington Rd. King T —1N 41 (4N 203)
Washington Rd. Wor Pk —8G 42
Washpond La. Warl —5M 85
Wasp Green. —3N 143
Wasp Grn. La. Out —3N 143
Wassand Clo. Craw —3E 182
Watchetts Dri. Camb —4A 70
Watchetts Lake Clo. Camb —3B 70
Watchetts Rd. Camb —2N 69
Watchfield Ct. W4 —1B 12
Watchmoor Pk. Camb —3M 69
Watchmoor Point. Camb —2M 69
Watchmoor Rd. Camb —3M 69
Watchmoor Trade Cen. Camb —2M 69
Watcombe Cotts. Rich —2N 11
Watcombe Pl. SE25 —4E 46
Watcombe Rd. SE25 —4E 46
Watercress Way. Wok —4L 73
Waterden Clo. Guild —4B 114
Waterden Rd. Guild —4A 114 (4F 202)
Waterer Gdns. Tad —5J 81
Waterer Ri. Wall —3H 63
Waterers Ri. Knap —4G 72
Waterfall Clo. Vir W —2K 35
Waterfall Cotts. SW19 —7B 28
Waterfall Rd. SW19 —7B 28
Waterfall Ter. SW17 —7C 28
Waterfield. Tad —7G 81
(in two parts)
Waterfield Clo. H'ham —5L 197
Waterfield Dri. Tad —6G 81
Waterfield Dri. Warl —6F 84
Waterfield Gdns. SE25 —3A 46
Waterfield Gdns. Bew —5K 181
Waterfield Grn. Tad —7G 81
Waterfields. Lea —6H 79
Waterford Clo. Cobh —7M 57
Waterford Rd. SW6 —3N 13
(in two parts)
Waterford Way. Wokgm —2B 30
Waterfront Bus. Pk. Fleet —2C 88
Watergardens, The. King T —7B 26
Waterham Rd. Brack —5N 31
Waterhouse Clo. W6 —1J 13
Waterhouse La. Blet —1C 124
Waterhouse La. Kenl —6N 83
Waterhouse La. Kgswd —8K 81
Waterhouse Mead. Coll T —8J 49
Waterlakes. Eden —3L 147
Waterlands La. Rowh —9M 177
Water La. Ab H —3J 137
Water La. Alb —6K 115
Water La. Bisl —6B 72
Water La. Blet —8M 103
Water La. Bookh —3L 97
(in two parts)
Water La. Chob —5E 52
Water La. Cobh —2M 77
Water La. Eden —4F 146
Water La. Ent —7D 152
Water La. Farn —7M 69
Water La. Farnh —8K 109
Water La. King T —9K 25 (2J 203)
Water La. Rich —8K 11
Water La. S God —7G 124
Water La. T'sey —4C 106
Water La. Twic —2G 25
Water La. W'ham —5M 107
Water Lea. Craw —4E 182
Waterloo Clo. Camb —8F 50
Waterloo Clo. Felt —2G 23
Waterloo Clo. Wokgm —3D 30
Waterloo Cres. Wokgm —3D 30
Waterloo Park. —1N 109
Waterloo Pl. Cars —9D 44
(off Wrythe La.)
Waterloo Pl. Crowt —3G 49
Waterloo Pl. Kew —2N 11
Waterloo Pl. Rich —7L 11
Waterloo Rd. Alder —3A 110
Waterloo Rd. Crowt —3F 48
Waterloo Rd. Eps —8C 60 (5L 201)
Waterloo Rd. Sutt —2B 62
Waterloo Rd. Wokgm —3D 30
Waterlow Rd. Reig —4A 122
Waterman Clo. Bord —7A 168
Watermans Bus. Pk. Stai —5F 20
Watermans Clo. King T —8L 25
Watermans Ct. Bren —2K 11
(off High St.)
Waterman St. SW15 —6J 13
Watermead. Felt —2F 22
Watermead. Tad —8G 81
Watermead. Wok —3J 73
Watermead La. Cars —6D 44
Watermeadow La. SW6 —5N 13
Watermill Clo. Rich —4J 25
Water Mill Ho. Felt —3A 24
Watermill Way. SW19 —9B 28
Watermill Way. Felt —3N 23
Waterperry La. Chob —6J 53
Water Rede. C Crook —1A 108
Waters Dri. Stai —4H 21
Waters Edge. SW6 —4H 13
Watersedge. Eps —1B 60
Waterside. —4A 146
Waterside. Beck —1J 47
Waterside. E Grin —9D 166
Waterside. Horl —6E 142
Waterside. Tad —7G 81
Waterside. W Dray —3L 7
Waterside Bus. Cen. Iswth —7H 11
Waterside Clo. Bew —5K 181
Waterside Clo. Bord —5A 168
Waterside Clo. G'ming —6K 133
Waterside Clo. Surb —8L 41
Waterside Ct. Fleet —2C 88
Waterside Dri. W on T —4H 39
Waterside La. G'ming —8F 132
Waterside M. Fleet —2C 88
Waterside M. Guild —1M 113
Waterside Pk. Ind. Est. Brack —1K 31
(Cookham Rd.)
Waterside Pk. Ind. Est. Brack —9L 15
(Western Rd.)
Waterside Rd. Guild —9N 93
Waterside Trad. Est. Add —1N 55
Waterside Way. SW17 —5A 28
Waterside Way. Wok —5L 73
Waterslade. Red —3C 122
Watersmeet Clo. Guild —7C 94
Waters Pl. SW15 —5H 13
Watersplash Clo. King T —2L 41 (5K 203)
Watersplash La. Asc —9A 18
Watersplash La. Hayes —1H 9
(in two parts)
Watersplash La. Warf —7N 15
Watersplash Rd. Shep —4B 38
Waters Rd. King T —1A 42
Waters Sq. King T —2A 42
Water Tower Hill. Croy —1A 64 (6E 200)
Water Vw. Horl —8H 143
Waterway Rd. Lea —9G 78
Waterworks Cotts. F Row —6H 187
Waterworks Dri. F Row —5H 187
Waterworks Yd. Croy —9N 45 (4B 200)
Watery La. SW20 —1L 43
Watery La. Chob —6G 52
Watery La. C Crook —1A 108
Watery La. Hayes —1F 8
Watery La. Lyne —6F 36
Wates Way. Mitc —5D 44
Watford Clo. Guild —3B 114
Wathen Rd. Dork —4H 119 (1M 201)
Watlings Clo. Croy —5H 47
Watney Cotts. SW14 —6B 12
Watney Rd. SW14 —6B 12
Watney's Rd. Mitc —4H 45
Watson Av. Sutt —8K 43
Watson Clo. SW19 —7C 28
Watson Clo. M'bowr —5G 182
Watson Ho. Reig —2M 121
Watson Rd. Westc —6C 118
Wattendon Rd. Kenl —3M 83
Wattlehurst Farm. —2H 179
Watts Clo. Tad —9J 81
Watts Farm Pde. Chob —6J 53
(off Barnmead)
Watts Gallery, The. —8E 112
Watt's La. Tad —9J 81
Watts La. Tedd —6G 24
Watts Lea. Hors —2K 73

W. Kensington Ct.—Wickham Rd.

W. Kensington Ct. W14 —1L 13
(off Edith Vs.)
W. Kensington Mans. W14 —1L 13
(off Beaumont Cres.)
Westland Clo. *Stanw* —9N **7**
Westland Ct. *Farn* —1J **89**
Westlands. *H'ham* —5L **197**
Westlands Ct. *Eps* —2B **80**
Westlands Ter. *SW12* —1G **28**
Westlands Way. *Oxt* —5N **105**
West La. *Ab H* —8L **117**
West La. *E Grin* —1N **185**
Westleas. *Horl* —6C **142**
Westlees Clo. *N Holm* —8K **119**
West Leigh. *E Grin* —2A **186**
Westleigh Av. *SW15* —8G **13**
Westleigh Av. *Coul* —3E **82**
Westleigh Ct. *S Croy* —7F **200**
Westley Mill. *Binf* —1K **15**
Westmacott Dri. *Felt* —2G **22**
Westmead. *SW15* —9G **12**
West Mead. *Eps* —3D **60**
Westmead. *Farn* —2N **89**
Westmead. Farnh —1G 128
(off Hart, The)
Westmead. *Wind* —6E **4**
Westmead. *Wok* —4L **73**
Westmead Corner. *Cars* —1C **62**
Westmead Dri. *Red* —2E **142**
Westmead Rd. *Sutt* —1B **62**
West Meads. *Guild* —4J **113**
Westminster Av. *T Hth* —1M **45**
Westminster Clo. *Felt* —2H **23**
Westminster Clo. *Fleet* —3B **88**
Westminster Clo. *Tedd* —6G **24**
Westminster Ct. *Guild*
—4A **114** (5E **202**)
Westminster Ct. *Wok* —8D **74**
Westminster Rd. *M'bowr* —4G **182**
Westminster Rd. *Sutt* —8B **44**
West Molesey. —3A 40
Westmont Rd. *Esh* —8E **40**
Westmore Grn. *Tats* —7E **86**
Westmoreland Dri. *Sutt* —4N **61**
Westmoreland Rd. *SW13* —4E **12**
Westmoreland Rd. *Brom* —4N **47**
Westmore Rd. *Tats* —8E **86**
Westmorland Clo. *Eps* —6D **60**
Westmorland Clo. *Twic* —9H **11**
Westmorland Ct. *Surb* —6K **41**
Westmorland Dri. *Camb* —3F **70**
Westmorland Dri. *Warf* —7D **16**
Westmorland Sq. Mitc —4J 45
(off Westmorland Way)
Westmorland Way. *Mitc* —3H **45**
West Mt. *Guild* —5M **113** (7A **202**)
(in two parts)
West Norwood. —4M 29
West Norwood Crematorium.
SE27 —4N **29**
Weston Av. *Add* —1K **55**
Weston Av. *Th Dit* —6E **40**
Weston Av. *W Mol* —2M **39**
Weston Clo. *Coul* —7K **83**
Weston Clo. *G'ming* —5H **133**
Weston Ct. *G'ming* —5H **133**
Weston Ct. *King T* —6K **203**
Weston Dri. *Cat* —8N **83**
Weston Farm Cotts. *Alb* —8K **115**
Westonfields. *Alb* —8L **115**
Weston Gdns. *Iswth* —4E **10**
Weston Gdns. *Wok* —3G **75**
Weston Green. —7E 40
Weston Grn. *Th Dit* —8E **40**
(in two parts)
Weston Grn. Rd. *Esh* —7D **40**
(in two parts)
Weston Gro. *Bag* —5K **51**
Weston Lea. *W Hor* —3E **96**
Weston Pk. *King T* —1L **41** (3K **203**)
Weston Pk. *Th Dit* —7E **40**
Weston Pk. Clo. *Th Dit* —7E **40**
Weston Rd. *Eps* —7D **60**
Weston Rd. *Guild* —2K **113**
(in two parts)
Weston Rd. *Th Dit* —7E **40**
Westons Clo. *H'ham* —1K **197**
Weston Way. *Wok* —3G **75**
Weston Yd. *Alb* —8L **115**
Westover Clo. *Sutt* —5N **61**
Westover Rd. *SW18* —1A **28**
Westover Rd. *Fleet* —4C **88**
West Pal. Gdns. *Wey* —9C **38**
West Pde. *H'ham* —4J **197**
West Pk. Av. *Rich* —4N **11**
W. Park Clo. *Houn* —2N **9**
W. Park Rd. *Copt & Newc* —6C **164**
W. Park Rd. *Eps* —8M **59**
W. Park Rd. *Hand* —9N **199**
W. Park Rd. *Rich* —4N **11**
West Pl. *SW19* —6H **27**
West Ramp. *H'row A* —4B **8**
West Ridge. *Seale* —7C **110**
West Ring. *Tong* —5D **110**
West Rd. *Camb* —1B **70**
West Rd. *Chess* —8J **59**
West Rd. *Farn* —7N **69**
West Rd. *Felt* —9E **8**
West Rd. *Guild* —4A **114** (4F **202**)
West Rd. *King T* —9B **26**
West Rd. *Reig* —4N **121**
West Rd. *Wey* —5C **56**
West Rd. *Wokgm* —6H **31**
Westrow. *SW15* —9H **13**
W. Sheen Va. *Rich* —7M **11**
W. Side Comn. *SW19* —6H **27**
Westside Ct. *W End* —9B **52**
Westside Ho. *Red* —1F **142**
West St. *Bren* —2J **11**
West St. *Cars* —9D **44**
West St. *Craw* —4B **182**
West St. *Croy* —1N **63** (6C **200**)
West St. *Dork* —5G **119** (2K **201**)
West St. *D'land* —1C **166**
West St. *E Grin* —1A **186**
West St. *Eps* —9B **60** (7J **201**)
West St. *Ewe* —6D **60**
West St. *Farnh* —2E **128**
West St. *Hasl* —1G **189**
West St. *H'ham* —6J **197**
West St. *Reig* —3K **121**
West St. *Sutt* —2N **61**
West St. *Wok* —4B **74**
West St. La. *Cars* —1D **62**
(in two parts)
W. Street Pl. *Croy* —6C **200**
W. Temple Sheen. *SW14* —8A **12**
West Vw. *Felt* —1D **22**
W. View Av. *Whyt* —5C **84**
Westview Clo. *Red* —5C **122**
W. View Cotts. *Newd* —2A **160**
W. View Gdns. *E Grin* —1A **186**
W. View Rd. *Head D* —5H **169**
W. View Rd. *Warl* —6E **84**
Westville Rd. *Th Dit* —7G **41**
Westward Ho. *Guild* —1B **114**
Westwates Clo. *Brack* —9B **16**
Westway. *SW20* —2G **40**
West Way. *Cars* —6B **62**
Westway. *Cat* —9A **84**
Westway. *Copt* —7K **163**
West Way. *Craw* —2E **182**
West Way. *Croy* —8H **47**
Westway. *Guild* —1J **113**
West Way. *Houn* —4N **9**
Westway. *Gat A* —3F **162**
West Way. *Shep* —5E **38**
West Way. *Slin* —5L **195**
West Way. *W Wick* —5N **47**
Westway. *Wmly* —1C **172**
Westway Clo. *SW20* —2G **43**
W. Way Gdns. *Croy* —8G **47**
Westway Gdns. *Red* —9E **102**
Westways. *Eden* —1L **147**
Westways. *Eps* —1E **60**
Westways. *W'ham* —4L **107**
Westwell M. *SW16* —7J **29**
Westwell Rd. *SW16* —7J **29**
Westwell Rd. App. *SW16* —7J **29**
Westwick. *King T* —4N **203**
Westwick Gdns. *Houn* —5J **9**
West Wickham. —7M 47
Westwood Av. *SE19* —9N **29**
Westwood Av. *Wdhm* —8H **55**
Westwood Clo. *Esh* —9D **40**
Westwood Ct. *Guild* —2J **113**
Westwood Gdns. *SW13* —6E **12**
Westwood La. *Norm & Wanb*
—1L **111**
Westwood Rd. *SW13* —6E **12**
Westwood Rd. *Coul* —5H **83**
Westwood Rd. *W'sham* —8B **34**
Wetherby Gdns. *SW5* —1N **13**
Wetherby Gdns. *Farn* —5A **90**
Wetherby Mans. SW5 —1N 13
(off Earl's Ct. Sq.)
Wetherby M. *SW5* —1N **13**
Wetherby Pl. *SW7* —1N **13**
Wetherby Way. *Chess* —4L **59**
Wetlands Cen., The. —4G 13
Wettern Clo. *S Croy* —6B **64**
Wetton Pl. *Egh* —6B **20**
Wexfenne Gdns. *Wok* —3K **75**
Wexford Rd. *SW12* —1D **28**
Wey Av. *Cher* —2J **37**
Weybank. *Wis* —3N **75**
Weybank Clo. *Farnh* —1H **129**
Weybarton. *Byfl* —9A **56**
Weybourne. —6K 109
Weybourne Pl. *S Croy* —6A **64**
Weybourne Rd. *Farnh & Alder*
—7K **109**
Weybourne St. *SW18* —3A **28**
Weybridge. —1B 56
Weybridge Bus. Pk. *Add* —1N **55**
Weybridge Mead. *Yat* —8D **48**
Weybridge Pk. *Wey* —2B **56**
Weybridge Rd. *Add* —1N **55**
Weybridge Rd. *T Hth* —3L **45**
Weybridge Trad. Est. *Add* —1M **55**
Weybrook Dri. *Guild* —7D **94**
Wey Clo. *As* —3E **110**
Wey Clo. *Camb* —1N **69**
Wey Clo. *W Byf* —9K **55**
Weycombe Rd. *Hasl* —1G **189**
Wey Ct. *Eps* —1B **60**
Wey Ct. *G'ming* —5K **133**
Wey Ct. *Guild* —4M **113** (4B **202**)
Wey Ct. *New H* —5M **55**
Wey Ct. Clo. *G'ming* —5J **133**
Weycrofts. *Brack* —8L **15**
Weydon Farm La. *Farnh* —3G **128**
Weydon Hill Clo. *Farnh* —3G **129**
Weydon Hill Rd. *Farnh* —3G **129**
Weydon La. *Farnh* —4E **128**
Weydon Mill La. *Farnh* —2G **128**
Weydown Clo. *SW19* —2K **27**
Weydown Clo. *Guild* —7K **93**
Weydown Cotts. *Hasl* —8G **170**
Weydown Ind. Est. *Hasl* —2F **188**
(in two parts)
Weydown La. *Guild* —7K **93**
Weydown Rd. *Hasl* —2F **188**
Wey Hill. *Hasl* —2F **188**
Weylands Clo. *W on T* —7N **39**
Weylands Pk. *Wey* —3E **56**
Weylea Av. *Guild* —9C **94**
Wey Mnr. Rd. *New H* —5M **55**
Weymead Clo. *Cher* —7L **37**
Wey Meadows. *Add* —2N **55**
Weymede. *Byfl* —8A **56**
Weymouth Ct. *Sutt* —4M **61**
Wey Retail Pk. *Byfl* —8N **55**
Wey Rd. *G'ming* —6K **133**
Wey Rd. *Wey* —9A **38**
Weyside. *Farnh* —1H **129**
Weyside Clo. *Byfl* —8A **56**
Weyside Gdns. *Guild* —1M **113**
Weyside Pk. *G'ming* —6K **133**
Weyside Rd. *Guild* —1L **113**
Weysprings. *Hasl* —1D **188**
Weystone Rd. *Add* —1A **56**
Weyvern Pk. *P'mrsh* —2L **133**
Weyvern Pl. *P'mrsh* —2L **133**
Weyview Clo. *Guild* —1M **113**
Wey Vw. Ct. *Guild*
—4M **113** (4A **202**)
Weywood Clo. *Farnh* —5L **109**
Weywood La. *Farnh* —5K **109**
Whaley Rd. *Wokgm* —9C **14**
Wharfedale Gdns. *T Hth* —3K **45**
Wharfedale St. *SW10* —1N **13**
Wharfenden Way. *Frim G* —8D **70**
Wharf La. *Send* —5M **75**
(Mill La.)
Wharf La. *Send* —1E **94**
(Send Rd.)
Wharf La. *Twic* —2G **24**
Wharf Rd. *Ash V* —9F **90**
Wharf Rd. *Frim G* —8D **70**
Wharf Rd. *Guild* —3M **113** (3B **202**)
Wharf Rd. *Wray* —1M **19**
Wharf St. *G'ming* —7H **133**
Wharf, The. *G'ming* —6H **133**
Wharf Way. *Frim G* —8E **70**
Wharncliffe Gdns. *SE25* —1D **46**
Wharncliffe Rd. *SE25* —1B **46**
Whateley Rd. *Guild* —8L **93**
Whatley Av. *SW20* —2J **43**
Whatley Grn. *Brack* —5N **31**
Whatmore Clo. *Stai* —9J **7**
Wheatash Rd. *Add* —8K **37**
Wheatbutts, The. *Eton W* —1C **4**
Wheatfield Way. *Horl* —6F **142**
Wheatfield Way. *King T*
—1L **41** (5K **203**)
Wheathill Rd. *SE20* —2E **46**
Wheat Knoll. *Kenl* —3N **83**
Wheatlands. *Houn* —2A **10**
Wheatlands Rd. *SW17* —4E **28**
Wheatley. *Brack* —4K **31**
Wheatley Ho. SW15 —1F 26
(off Ellisfield Dri.)
Wheatley Rd. *Alder* —1L **109**
Wheatley Rd. *Iswth* —6F **10**
Wheatsheaf Clo. *H'ham* —3L **197**
Wheatsheaf Clo. *Ott* —3F **54**
Wheatsheaf Clo. *Wok* —3A **74**
Wheatsheaf La. *SW6* —3H **13**
Wheatsheaf La. *Stai* —8H **21**
Wheatsheaf Ter. *SW6* —3L **13**
Wheatstone Clo. *Craw* —7F **162**
Wheatstone Clo. *Mitc* —9C **28**
Wheeler Av. *Oxt* —7N **105**
Wheeler La. *Witl* —4B **152**
Wheeler Rd. *M'bowr* —5F **182**
Wheelers La. *Brock* —5A **120**
Wheelers La. *Eps* —1A **80** (8H **201**)
Wheelers La. *Small* —9L **143**
Wheelerstreet. —4C 152
Wheelerstreet. *Witl* —4C **152**
Wheelers Way. *Felb* —7H **165**
Wheelwrights La. *Gray* —5M **169**
Wheelwrights Pl. *Coln* —3E **6**
Whelan Way. *Wall* —9H **45**
Wherwell Rd. *Guild*
—5M **113** (6A **202**)
Whetstone Rd. *Farn* —1H **89**
Whimbrel Clo. *S Croy* —7A **64**
Whinfell Clo. *SW16* —6H **29**
Whin Holt. *Fleet* —7B **88**
Whins Clo. *Camb* —2N **69**
Whins Dri. *Camb* —2N **69**
Whipley Clo. *Guild* —7D **94**
Whistler Clo. *Craw* —6D **182**
Whistler Gro. *Coll T* —7J **49**
Whistley Clo. *Brack* —2C **32**
Whitby Clo. *Big H* —6D **86**
Whitby Clo. *Farn* —4C **90**
Whitby Gdns. *Sutt* —8B **44**
Whitby Rd. *Sutt* —8B **44**
Whitchurch Clo. *Alder* —6B **110**
White Acres Rd. *Myt* —1D **90**
Whitebeam Dri. *Reig* —6N **121**
Whitebeam Gdns. *Farn* —2H **89**
White Beam Way. *Tad* —8F **80**
White Beech La. *C'fold* —4K **173**
Whiteberry Rd. *Ab C* —3D **138**
Whitebines. *Farnh* —1J **129**
White Bri. Av. *Mitc* —2B **44**
Whitebridge Clo. *Felt* —9G **9**
White Bushes. —8E 122
Whitebushes. *Red* —8F **122**
White City. *Crowt* —2J **49**
(in two parts)
White Cottage Clo. *Farnh* —6J **109**
Whitecroft. *Horl* —7F **142**
Whitecroft Clo. *Beck* —3N **47**
Whitecroft Way. *Beck* —4M **47**
White Down La. *Ran C* —4K **117**
Whitefield Av. *Purl* —3L **83**
Whitefield Clo. *SW18* —9K **13**
White Ga. *Wok* —7B **74**
Whitegates. *Whyt* —6D **84**
Whitegate Way. *Tad* —7G **81**
Whitehall. —3K 61
Whitehall Cres. *Chess* —2K **59**
Whitehall Dri. *If'd* —3K **181**
Whitehall Farm La. *Vir W* —1A **36**
(in two parts)
Whitehall Gdns. *W4* —2A **12**
Whitehall La. *Egh* —8B **20**
Whitehall La. *S Pk* —7L **121**
Whitehall La. *Wray* —9C **6**
Whitehall Pde. E Grin —9A 166
(off London Rd.)
Whitehall Pk. Rd. *W4* —2A **12**
Whitehall Pl. *Wall* —1F **62**
Whitehall Rd. *T Hth* —4L **45**
White Hart Clo. *Hayes* —2E **8**
White Hart Ct. *H'ham* —4J **197**
White Hart Ct. *Rip* —8L **75**
White Hart Ind. Est. *B'water* —2K **69**
White Hart La. *SW13* —6D **12**
White Hart La. *Wood S* —2D **112**
White Hart Meadows. *Rip* —8L **75**
White Hart Row. *Cher* —6J **37**
Whitehead Clo. *SW18* —1A **28**
White Hermitage. *Old Win* —8M **5**
White Heron M. *Tedd* —7F **24**
White Hill. *Chip* —1C **102**
White Hill. *S Croy* —6A **64**
White Hill. *W'sham* —1M **51**
Whitehill Clo. *Camb* —8B **50**
Whitehill La. *Blet* —6A **104**
Whitehill La. *Cobh* —1D **96**
Whitehill Pk. *W'hill* —9A **168**
Whitehill Pl. *Vir W* —4A **36**
Whitehill Rd. *Stand* —8A **168**
White Horse Dri. *Eps*
—1B **80** (8H **201**)
Whitehorse La. *SE25* —3A **46**
White Horse La. *Rip* —8L **75**
Whitehorse Rd. *Croy & T Hth* —6N **45**
Whitehorse Rd. *H'ham* —2A **198**
White Horse Rd. *Wind* —6A **4**
White Ho. SW4 —1H 29
(off Clapham Pk. Est.)
White House. *Alfd* —1L **55**
White Ho. Dri. *Guild* —3D **114**
White Ho. Gdns. *Yat* —8B **48**
White Ho. La. *Guild* —7N **93**
(in two parts)
White Ho. Wlk. *Farnh* —5J **109**
Whiteknights. *Cars* —7B **62**
White Knights Rd. *Wey* —4D **56**
White Knobs Way. *Cat* —3D **104**
Whitelands Dri. *Asc* —9H **17**
White La. *Ash G & Tong* —3G **110**
White La. *Guild* —5E **114**
White La. *Tats & T'sey* —1D **106**
Whiteley. *Wind* —3B **4**
Whiteley's Cotts. *W14* —1L **13**
Whiteley's Way. *Hanw* —4A **24**
Whiteley Village. —5F 56
White Lilies Island. *Wind* —3D **4**
White Lion Ct. *Iswth* —6H **11**
White Lion Wlk. *Guild*
—4N **113** (5C **202**)
White Lion Way. *Yat* —8C **48**
White Lodge. *SE19* —8M **29**
White Lodge Clo. *Sutt* —4A **62**
Whitelodge Gdns. *Red* —2E **142**
Whitely Hill. —8K 183
Whitely Hill. *Turn H* —8K **183**
Whitemore Rd. *Guild* —8N **93**
White Oak Dri. *Beck* —1M **47**
Whiteoaks. *Bans* —9N **61**
White Post. —3C 124
Whitepost Hill. *Red* —3C **122**
(in two parts)
White Post La. *Wrec* —7F **128**
White Rd. *Coll T* —9L **49**
White Rd. *Brock* —2N **119**
(in two parts)
White Rose La. *Lwr Bo* —4G **129**
White Rose La. *Wok* —5B **74**
Whites La. *Dat* —2L **5**
Whites La. *Pirb* —2D **92**
(in two parts)
Whites Rd. *Farn* —4C **90**
Whitestile Rd. *Bren* —1J **11**
Whiteswan M. *W4* —1D **12**
Whitethorn Av. *Coul* —2E **82**
Whitethorn Clo. *As* —3F **110**
Whitethorn Cotts. *Cranl* —5K **155**
Whitethorn Gdns. *Croy* —8E **46**
Whitewalls. Craw —9L 181
(off Rusper Rd.)
White Way. *Bookh* —4B **98**
Whiteways Ct. *Stai* —8K **21**
Whitewood. —5D 144
Whitewood Cotts. *Tats* —7E **86**
Whitewood La. *S God* —5D **144**
Whitfield Clo. *Guild* —9K **93**
Whitfield Clo. *Hasl* —8G **171**
Whitfield Rd. *Hasl* —9G **171**
Whitford Gdns. *Mitc* —2D **44**
Whitgift Av. *S Croy* —2M **63** (8A **200**)
Whitgift Cen. *Croy* —8N **45** (2C **200**)
Whitgift Ct. *S Croy* —8C **200**
Whitgift Sq. *Croy* —8N **45** (3C **200**)
Whitgift St. *Croy* —9N **45** (5B **200**)
Whitgift Wlk. *Craw* —6B **182**
Whither Dale. *Horl* —7C **142**
Whitland Rd. *Cars* —7B **44**
Whitlet Clo. *Farnh* —2G **128**
Whitley Clo. *Stanw* —9N **7**
Whitley Rd. *Yat* —2C **68**
Whitlock Dri. *SW19* —1K **27**
Whitmead Clo. *S Croy* —3B **64**
Whitmead La. *Tilf* —6C **130**
Whitmoor La. *Guild* —4N **93**
Whitmoor Rd. *Bag* —4K **51**
Whitmoor Va. *Gray* —2K **169**
Whitmoor Va. Rd. *Gray* —2L **169**
Whitmore Clo. *Owl* —7J **49**
Whitmore Grn. *Farnh* —6K **109**
Whitmore La. *Asc* —4D **34**
Whitmore Rd. *Beck* —2J **47**
Whitmores Clo. *Eps* —2B **80**
Whitmore Way. *Horl* —7C **142**
Whitnell Way. *SW15* —8H **13**
Whitstable Clo. *Beck* —1J **47**
Whitstable Pl. *Croy* —1N **63** (7C **200**)
Whittaker Av. *Rich* —8K **11**
Whittaker Ct. *Asht* —4K **79**
Whittaker Pl. Rich —8K 11
(off Whittaker Av.)
Whittaker Rd. *Sutt* —9L **43**
Whittingham Ct. *W4* —3D **12**
Whittingstall Rd. *SW6* —4L **13**
Whittington Rd. *Craw* —6B **182**
Whittlebury Clo. *Cars* —4D **62**
Whittle Clo. *Ash V* —8D **90**
Whittle Clo. *Sand* —6F **48**
Whittle Cres. *Farn* —7L **69**
Whittle Rd. *Houn* —3K **9**
Whittle Way. *Craw* —6E **162**
Whitton. —1C 24
Whitton Dene. *Houn* —8C **10**
Whitton Mnr. Rd. *Iswth* —9C **10**
Whitton Rd. *Brack* —2D **32**
Whitton Rd. *Houn* —7B **10**
Whitton Rd. *Twic* —9E **10**
Whitton Road Roundabout. (Junct.)
—9F **10**
Whitton Waye. *Houn* —9A **10**
Whitworth Rd. *SE25* —2B **46**
Whitworth Rd. *Craw* —8B **162**
Whopshott Av. *Wok* —3M **73**
Whopshott Clo. *Wok* —3M **73**
Whopshott Dri. *Wok* —3M **73**
Whynstones Rd. *Asc* —5L **33**
Whyteacre. *Whyt* —7E **84**
Whyte Av. *Alder* —4B **110**
Whytebeam Vw. *Whyt* —5C **84**
Whytecliffe Rd. N. *Purl* —7M **63**
Whytecliffe Rd. S. *Purl* —7L **63**
Whytecroft. *Houn* —3L **9**
Whyteleafe. —5C 84
Whyteleafe Bus. Village. *Whyt*
—4C **84**
Whyteleafe Hill. *Whyt* —7B **84**
(in two parts)
Whyteleafe Rd. *Cat* —7B **84**
Wicket Hill. *Wrec* —5F **128**
Wickets, The. *Afrd* —5N **21**
Wicket, The. *Croy* —2K **65**
Wickham Av. *Croy* —8H **47**
Wickham Av. *Sutt* —2H **61**
Wickham Chase. *W Wick* —7N **47**
Wickham Clo. *Bag* —1J **51**
Wickham Clo. *C Crook* —7A **88**
Wickham Clo. *Horl* —7D **142**
Wickham Clo. *N Mald* —4E **42**
Wickham Ct. *C Crook* —7A **88**
Wickham Ct. *Surb* —8M **203**
Wickham Ct. Rd. *W Wick* —8M **47**
Wickham Cres. *W Wick* —8M **47**
Wickham La. *Egh* —8C **20**
Wickham Pl. *C Crook* —7A **88**
Wickham Rd. *Beck* —1L **47**
Wickham Rd. *Camb* —7C **50**
Wickham Rd. *C Crook* —7A **88**